CW01501482

NS

Greek Poetry

From Homer to Seferis

GREEK POETRY

From Homer to Seferis

by

C. A. TRYPANIS

FABER AND FABER

London & Boston

First published in 1981
by Faber and Faber Limited
3 Queen Square London WC1N 3AU
Phototypeset by
Western Printing Services Limited, Bristol
Printed in Great Britain by
Redwood Burn Limited
Trowbridge, Wiltshire

© *C. A. Trypanis 1981*

British Library Cataloguing in Publication Data

Trypanis, Constantine Athanasius
Greek poetry
1. Greek poetry – History and criticism
2. Byzantine poetry – History and criticism
3. Greek poetry, Modern – History and criticism
881'.009   PA3092
ISBN 0-571-08346-3

To

JEANNE TSATSOS

poet and friend

Contents

PART TWO: THE HELLENISTIC AGE

SECTION I: THE ALEXANDRIAN AGE
(323–146 B.C.)

SECTION II: THE GRECO-ROMAN WORLD: THE TRANSITION TO CLASSICISM (146 B.C.–A.D. 100)

Contents

PART THREE: THE BYZANTINE WORLD

SECTION I: FROM HERACLIUS TO THE RESTORATION OF THE IMAGES (641–843)

SECTION II: FROM THE RESTORATION OF THE IMAGES TO THE FOURTH CRUSADE (843–1204)

Preface

Since my early schooldays I have been drawn to Greek poetry, and when I reached the age of twenty I became deeply interested in its history as well, in that long, uninterrupted course it has followed from Homer to the present day. Since then I have not only read avidly all the ancient, medieval and modern Greek poets I could lay my hands on, as well as numerous books about them, but I have also kept copious notes and starred the poems and the passages that I considered outstanding. The outcome of this practice, which in the course of time has become increasingly disciplined, is the present volume, a book more of love than of scholarship.

This study, which covers roughly three thousand years of poetry, begins with the Homeric epics and ends with Seferis. No living poets are included, for they are too close to us for their work to be properly assessed as yet. A brief historical survey introduces each section, to serve as a framework within which the poets should be seen. This is especially necessary for the years between the death of Alexander the Great (323 B.C.) and the liberation of Greece from the Turks (A.D. 1829), because even the average educated person knows relatively little about them.

As would be expected, the debt I owe to a very large number of scholars and critics is incalculable. It is impossible to quote them all by name or to express my gratitude and my thanks to each one of them separately. All I can do is to stress that should this survey of Greek poetry have any virtue, it is due to them and not to me. The mistakes and the omissions are, of course, my own.

It remains for me to thank the Chairman and the Directors of Faber and Faber Ltd, as well as the Director and the Academic Board of the University of Chicago Press, for undertaking the publication of so unremunerative a book, and their staff for the care they have expended on its production.

Athens, March 1979

Part One

ANCIENT GREECE

SECTION I

From the Mycenaean World to the Persian Wars (c. 2000–490 B.C.)

Introduction

The successive waves of Greeks who, in the course of the second millennium B.C. invaded the southern Balkan peninsula[1] from the north, found there an old civilization, which seems already to have been considerably developed. In later centuries the Greeks referred to these pre-Hellenic peoples as *Pelasgoi*, *Cares* and *Leleges*; and modern scholarship accepts the existence of an older 'Aegean' stratum of population with which the Indo-European Greeks were fused.

Some few centuries later the Greek invaders came under the influence of Minoan Crete. The result was the creation of one of the most brilliant periods of civilization in the whole history of Greece: the great days of Mycenaean art and architecture, of commercial expansion and political organization (c. 1700–1120 B.C.). The most important Mycenaean centres were the fortified cities of the Argolid, the western Peloponnese and the Boeotian plain.

As reflected in the Homeric epics, Mycenaean Greece seems to have consisted of a number of more or less independent states, each centred on a great palace—Sparta, Mycenae, Pylos, Thebes and others—all of which owed allegiance to the kingdom of Agamemnon at Mycenae, 'rich in gold'. To this no doubt idealized poetic picture the decipherment in 1952 of the Pylos tablets—written in Linear B, the Mycenaean script—has added a more realistic dimension. From them (and it must be stressed that they are only partial evidence) may be traced the existence of an autocratic government, operating through numerous officials, whose task it was to measure, count, record and distribute the vast royal possessions; a state in which slavery was widespread, labour specialized and land tenure organized in a very complicated manner.

The great period of the Mycenaean Greeks lay between the years 1700 and 1120 B.C., during which they not only conquered the Cretan empire (c. 1400 B.C.) but also captured and destroyed 'windy' Troy (c. 1200 B.C.). To that period have been traced the origins of, among other things, Greek mythology in its main lines and the Greek epic tradition.

But substantial new folk migrations, again from the north, brought
Mycenaean power to an end. Whether it is to the Dorians (who intro-
duced the use of iron into Greek lands) or to the other northern barbarians
in whose train the Dorians followed, that responsibility for the catastrophe
should be assigned, in about 1120 B.C. the Mycenaeans disappear from
view; and for the next three and a half centuries, until the founding of the
Olympic Games in 776 B.C., the darkness is almost unbroken.[2]

The invasions which overthrew Mycenaean power were on a much
larger scale than those of about 2000–1700 B.C., and in many parts of the
mainland they resulted in a complete change of population and acute
cultural decline. In some places the invaders expelled the previous inhabi-
tants; in others they held them in serfdom; in others they merged with
them. Attica and Arcadia alone preserved their independence, and to
them fled refugees from other Mycenaean centres.

The peoples who were displaced from Thessaly and areas south of
Thessaly, speakers of the Aeolic dialect, moved overseas to occupy Lesbos
and the north-western parts of Asia Minor. Others, ousted from the
Peloponnese and led by refugees under Athenian protection, occupied the
islands of the central Aegean and the central parts of western Asia Minor.
Their speech, together with that of the Athenians, made up the Ionic
group of dialects. Finally, those Dorians who pressed on after the almost
complete capture of the Peloponnese went on to occupy Melos, part of
Crete, the southern Sporades and the southern part of western Asia
Minor. The islands and mainland of the north-west of Greece were
overrun by the rearguard of the Dorian invaders. Thus the map of Greece
was largely fixed by 900 B.C.—a map entirely different from that of the
Mycenaean period. The newcomers, together with the peoples of My-
cenaean origin, were destined to produce a second age of great, but very
different, achievement.

The dark years following the arrival of the Dorians were marked, from
800 onwards, by recovery from invasion and by the beginnings of the city-
state, the *polis*, which was an indispensable first step towards political
revival and a movement away from the earlier unit of organization, the
village.

The first movements towards a cultural revival were made in Ionia in
the east, where the epic reached its apogee and where the Greeks were
inspired by their contacts with the Phoenicians and Lydians to new
achievements in seafaring and art; above all, it was in Ionia that the Greek
alphabet made its first appearance.

An important effect of the political and cultural revival was to provide
the impetus for a new colonial movement. During the period 750–550
B.C., as seafaring gained in importance, commercial states such as Mile-
tus, Paros, Chalcis, Megara and Corinth took the lead in the planting of
hundreds of small *poleis* along the shores of the northern Aegean, the Black

Sea, the north-western mainland, Italy, Sicily, southern France, Spain and Cyrenaica.

An important beneficiary of the expansion of trade which followed the colonial movement was Aegina, whose wealth made her the first state of the western Aegean to adopt, soon after 650 B.C., the Lydian invention of coinage. As trade and the use of money revolutionized the Greek economy, we see the gradual decline of aristocratic ideals and a great widening of horizons, as well as the awakening of the individual consciousness, which expressed itself in lyric poetry.

Athens, which escaped the Dorian invasions, also benefited from the new economic expansion. There, however, wealth and privilege were still the prerogatives of the leaders of groups united by the blood tie—clans, phratries and tribes. The unrest to which this situation led was briefly halted in 594 by Solon, the founder of the progressive Athenian state. But Solon's purposes were thwarted by prolonged faction. It was left to Pisistratus, an enlightened party leader, partially to fulfil them when he seized power and ruled as tyrant (564–527 B.C.). Many wealthy Greek states had already experienced the benefits of rule by capable tyrants; the legacy which such men left, however, was one of political animosity.

It should also be noted that at this period relations between states were eased by the influence of the religious centres and festivals of Delphi, Olympia, Dodona, Delos, Nemea and Isthmia, and by the common bond of aristocratic oligarchy which, in the archaic period at least, had in a sense united the Greek cities.

In about 550 B.C. Sparta was the first to initiate a system of lasting alliances, for war often broke out between rival cities. However, Ionian Athens, herself a member of the alliance, resented its dominance by Dorian Sparta and broke away. After the break Cleisthenes united the relatively large Athenian state by his democratic reforms.

The expansion of Greece and the maturing of her city-states had taken place at a time when her neighbours were backward or unaggressive. But the sudden rise of Persia was to change the situation, as we shall see later.

CHAPTER 1

Epic Poetry

THE ORIGINS OF THE GREEK POETIC TRADITION

Greek poetry constitutes the longest uninterrupted tradition of the Western world. For us, as for the Classical Greeks, it begins with the *Iliad* and the *Odyssey*, two poems on the grand scale which, for splendour and sustained beauty, have not been equalled in all the Greek poetry that has followed them. Traditionally, they have been attributed to Homer; and it is with them that our study will begin, for nothing is known of the work of rtain legendary figures like Orpheus, Linus or Musaeus, to whom were ascribed in antiquity the beginnings of poetry.

The Homeric poems, however, are not the beginning, but rather the outcome, of a long oral tradition, which for hundreds of years was developed by gifted singers until the *Iliad* and the *Odyssey* acquired, in the eighth and seventh centuries B.C., the monumental form which they have retained to the present day.

This does not mean that writing was unknown in the days of those early oral singers; in fact, we know that a Mycenaean script existed, no matter how laborious or imprecise its nature may have been. But as research into the oral poetry of other peoples has shown — that of the southern Slavs, the Indians, the Russians and the Scandinavians — professional or semi-professional singers compose and transmit poetry without the help of writing, which, strange as it may appear, seriously interferes with their craft. By contrast, what aids the memory of the oral singer is the accompaniment of his recitation by music.

In the Homeric epics themselves we find evidence pointing to the existence of a pre-Homeric poetry, which was partly epic in nature and partly lyrical. As examples of the latter, we hear of wedding songs (XVIII, 493) and laments (XXIV, 721f.) and, on feast days, of songs which accompanied the dance of the young (XVIII, 603f.; 8, 262f.).[1] Moreover, hymns were chanted at the festivals of the gods (I, 473; 22, 329); and working songs existed, like the *Linos* for the vintage (XVIII, 570) or those with which women accompanied their weaving (5, 61; 10, 221). In one instance we even hear of a magic song which had the power to staunch the flow of blood (19, 457).

Side by side with these kinds of lyrical poetry, we also hear of heroic lays—the *klea andron*—sung either by the warriors themselves (IX, 186) or by professional singers like Demodocus and Phemius at the palaces of Alcinous and Odysseus (8, 261, 471; 13, 28). Moreover, older examples of such lays could also be used in admonishing younger men (IX, 528); and there were other entertaining, mythical narratives some of which described the deeds of the gods (I, 472f.; 8, 44, 266f.).

It is unfortunately impossible to define with any accuracy how far back this Greek poetic tradition goes. The Mycenaean objects, geography, mythology and customs found in the *Iliad* and the *Odyssey*, as well as certain Mycenaean linguistic elements present in the poems, show that in all probability Greek epic poetry might be traced at least as far back as Mycenaean times. For even if, as has been suggested,[2] all the Mycenaean elements found in the epics could have been absorbed in early post-Mycenaean times, it is nevertheless unlikely that the idea of narrative poetry and, more particularly, that the hexameter itself were invented at that later period. But how far back we can trace it remains uncertain; and just as uncertain remains the question of the date at which musical accompaniment was replaced by straightforward recitation; for the hexameter, as we know it today, is a purely recitative verse.

The Greek conception of a heroic age of the 'distant past', as portrayed in the *Iliad* and *Odyssey*, was most probably fashioned on the mainland after the Mycenaean collapse. But its survival is due largely to the Ionians, who, knowing that their original home lay across the sea, preserved the memory of a glorious past, when the Achaeans ruled the lands around the Aegean. For the Greek tradition of epic poetry, which had originated in Mycenaean Greece, was brought by Greek immigrants across the Aegean to their new homes on the western coast of Asia Minor. There the Ionian Greeks developed it further and brought it to its culmination in the eighth century, when the *Iliad*, as we know it, was composed. It is interesting to note that by the seventh century, when the *Odyssey* had achieved its monumental form, we find the singer occupying a place of honour in the poem.[3]

But when Demodocus in the *Odyssey* is complimented by Odysseus for singing *kata kosmon* ('in the right order') the story of the wooden horse or when he takes the story of Achilles and Odysseus from an *oime*,[4] or song sequence, it is not clear whether he was using a fixed text or improvising from memory. On the other hand, it is very hard to believe that Achilles improvised the *klea andron* which Demodocus sang in his hut (IX, 189–9). In both cases it is evident that behind the pre-Homeric bards there existed a corpus of sagas, and that amateur singers who are said to have sung them sang to the accompaniment of the lyre.

THE HOMERIC EPICS

The poet Homer

The ancients attributed both the *Iliad* and the *Odyssey* to Homer, whom they considered the greatest of poets; only a small group of Alexandrian scholars, the *Chorizontes*, opposed this view, maintaining that the two epics were not by the same hand. At the same time, the ancients knew nothing definite about the life and person of Homer; even his name was strange to them, and they suggested several fantastic derivations to explain it.[5]

Among the mass of spurious information which has come down to us, perhaps the only persuasive items are that Homer was an Ionian Greek, particularly associated with Smyrna and Chios. On the island of Chios a rhapsodic guild, the *Homeridae*, even claimed 'at one time' to be of his family; though later they did not claim to be more than rhapsodes who sang and preserved the Homeric poems.

The ancient world did not attribute to Homer only the *Iliad* and the *Odyssey*. Other narrative hexameter poems, such as the *Thebais*, the *Cypria*, the *Hymn to Apollo* and even the humorous *Margites* and *Batrachomyomachia* were also ascribed to him, though less persistently. This, however, is not entirely surprising: lesser and later works are often attributed to a great name, and Homer was for the Greeks 'the poet' *par excellence*.

The fact that the information which has come down to us from antiquity is so vague supports the view that the life of Homer should be placed before the seventh century B.C.; for in that century as the use of the Greek alphabet spread, a flood of literary and historical records begins to flow. Moreover, Callinus, who in that century makes the first mention of Homer,[6] provides a *terminus ante quem* for the poet's life which is supported by contemporary allusions, imitations and graphic representations. These seem to presuppose an *Iliad*, though it is not necessarily the *Iliad* we have today. However, it is impossible to determine how much further back than the seventh century Homer might be placed.

The dispute about the person of Homer and his authorship of the *Iliad* and the *Odyssey* is known as the 'Homeric Question'. It started in antiquity and flared up again in the modern world, from the eighteenth century onwards, challenging the unity of the poems and extending into other related areas. There is no doubt that the long controversy promoted

Homeric studies and helped our understanding of the poems; but it can now be left to students of the history of scholarship, for decisive proof has at last been given that both the *Iliad* and the *Odyssey* belong to the realm of *oral* poetry and are subject to the rules peculiar to that art. This has given the matter a completely new complexion.

This new direction in Homeric studies is due chiefly to the work of an American scholar, Milman Parry, who unfortunately died young and was unable to develop his pioneering work. He showed that the peculiar technique of the Homeric epics, with their recurrent epithets, formulaic phrases and descriptions of situations and scenes, is in reality a means of protecting the singer from a breakdown in improvisation. Thus, for example, it was shown that for each of thirty-seven leading characters in the two poems a stock descriptive phrase exists of exactly the same length, extending from the caesura to the end of the line, and that for each character, according to a principle which has been named 'epic economy', normally only one such phrase exists.[7]

At the same time a negative check was provided by the fact that no such system of metrically identical epithets is to be found in authors of comparable works (for example, Apollonius Rhodius) known to have committed their work directly to writing. Positive confirmation, on the other hand, has been found in the study of comparable phenomena in the surviving oral traditions of the Soviet Union, Cyprus, Crete, Ireland and Yugoslavia.

That the Homeric poems were oral compositions is, of course, no new claim. It had already been put forward by Robert Wood in 1767 and was developed later by F. August Wolf. But in the light of Milman Parry's work it is no longer possible to deny the assertion.

The *Iliad* and the *Odyssey*

Both the Homeric epics have, in their present form, a carefully conceived design and a clear basic structure. Thus the essential plot of the *Iliad*, a poem of 15,537 lines, can be outlined as follows.

During the siege of Troy Achilles withdraws from the fighting because he is insulted by King Agamemnon, the leader of the Achaean army. His withdrawal leads to set-backs for the Achaeans, who send an embassy to persuade him to rejoin them. The embassy fails to move Achilles, and the peril of the Acheans becomes acute. At that point Achilles allows his dearest friend, Patroclus, to go to their aid. Clad in Achilles' armour, Patroclus drives the Trojans back from the Greek camp but is killed by Hector under the walls of Troy. To avenge the death of his friend, Achilles resolves to take part in the fighting himself, drives the Trojans into their city and, in grand single-handed combat, kills Hector, who alone remains outside the walls to face him. Finally, Achilles, after maltreating the body of Hector, returns it for burial to his old father, Priam, who has come to the Achaean camp with royal gifts for its ransom.

Around this central theme a number of episodes cluster, which both develop and obscure it. Indeed, a closer examination of the text reveals much that is troubling and often baffling, for it soon becomes evident that the story develops not in a natural, flowing manner but with pauses and interruptions, and there are many disproportionately developed episodes which would appear originally to have been intended for separate recitation. At the same time, much of the material we meet, though of a general epic nature, is not directly connected with the overall plot of the poem, and this immediately casts doubts on its unity both of structure and of authorship.

It is all too clear, for example, that the contents of Books II to X have little to do with the 'Design of Zeus', which in Book I is stated to be the subject of the whole epic. Indeed, they often contradict it. Moreover, it is possible to trace alternative versions of the same episodes, arising from conflation, such as the *Diapeira* (Agamemnon's testing of the morale of his companions) of Book II or the embassy of Book IX; and there are as well many repetitions and contradictions in the narrative.

No doubt many of these difficulties are due to the nature of oral poetry, which adapts and revises epic material for centuries before reaching the stage at which it is finally committed to writing. In poetry of this kind literary analysis is of little help, especially in the task of distinguishing the individual voices of poets who have contributed to so complex a structure. But it can be helpful in tracing the broad development whereby the monumental epics reached their present form.

It becomes evident, for example, that the rhapsodies we find in the *Iliad* are of three kinds: those which are isolated and self-contained (in fact, they are models of composition), such as Books I, XVI and XXII; those which form relatively independent groups, closely interconnected through their subject-matter, such as Books XX and XXI, and Books XIII, XIV and XV; and, finally, those whose only purpose is to join together longer or shorter parts of the poem—for example, Book VIII or parts of Books II and VII.[8]

Helped by these and other such guide-lines—for instance, the relevance to the main plot of the only four battle scenes which are described in the whole of the *Iliad*—one can trace a process of gradual accretion, having at its heart a relatively short poem on the wrath of Achilles, an *Ur-Ilias*, and developing with the passage of time into the great, monumental composition which we know today. The successive stages of this development are, of course, obscure, and the important last transition from a large to a monumental poem is particularly strange and baffling. Moreover, the question of the size of the *Ur-Ilias* is bitterly controversial;

indeed, it should be mentioned that many distinguished scholars do not believe that it ever existed.

However that may be, the structure of our *Iliad* cannot be understood without an examination of the basic epic motifs which go to make it up. A canvas so large and complex naturally involves the use of a great number of epic motifs; but the main framework of the poem is formed by the interlocking of no more than four traditional themes: the wrath, the close friendship,[9] the single combat and the old father motifs. In all these Achilles is the hero and must therefore comply with the traditional demands of each one of them: implacable wrath *vis-à-vis* him who offers insult, self-sacrifice in avenging his friend, victory over his opponent and respect for the old father.

It is the interconnection of the first two themes, wrath and close friendship, which lends such tragic depth to the *Iliad* and at the same time constitutes its true originality. For by presenting the wrath of Achilles as the instrument of the destruction of Patroclus, his dearest friend, the poet made the suffering of his hero more cruel and his fury for vengeance more fierce. The old father motif, to be sure, acts as a check upon that fury and introduces a nobler touch to Achilles' character—it has been called the beginning of the humane tradition of the West—but even so, the great epic dies away amid the hero's inconsolable grief and the dark fore-knowledge of his own doom.

On the other hand, the combat between Achilles and Hector is the culmination of the vengeance theme, as well as the crowning point of the whole epic, as Virgil well understood when he took it as a model for the combat between Aeneas and Turnus in the *Aeneid*. It should also be added that single-handed combats occupy an important place in the epic tradition, because they reflect the highest ideals of epic poetry—they demonstrate the *aristeia*, the excellence, the prowess of the hero—and, by stressing the role of the individual, enhance the human interest and increase the power of the poetry.

The question has been raised of whether the *Iliad*'s story is original or at least partly modelled on 'older' epics like the *Wrath of Meleager* or the *Aethiopis*. In the latter Achilles is presented in battle with the Aethiopian prince Memnon. But in view of the nature of oral poetry and the great antiquity of the story motifs in question, such inquiries can hardly be productive, for it is impossible to tell which tradition may have influenced which, and at what stage of their long history this may have happened. Each in turn may have served as a pattern for the other as the oral tradition developed.

In contrast to the *Iliad*, which has no villains, the *Odyssey* is a story of adventure which has both heroes and villains. Its theme, the return of the wandering husband to his faithful wife, is an ancient and widespread one. In being drawn into the orbit of the Trojan saga, it was developed into an epic of rich complexity, which incorporated many other stories of equal antiquity. Its ingenious plot has been called 'the despair of all its imitators'. In outline it is as follows.

On his way back to Ithaca from Troy, Odysseus is detained on the island of the sea nymph Calypso, while a group of insolent men have taken possession of his palace, representing themselves as suitors of his wife, Penelope. On the advice of Athene, Telemachus, Odysseus' son, visits Nestor at Pylos and Menelaos at Sparta, in search of news about his father. There he learns that Odysseus is still alive.

Hermes, as messenger of the Olympian gods, induces Calypso to allow Odysseus to leave for Ithaca. On his way, the latter is shipwrecked and takes refuge on the island of the Phaeacians, where Nausicaa, the king's daughter, finds him and leads him to her father's palace. There, in the course of a banquet, Odysseus reveals his name and relates his various adventures since leaving Troy.

The Phaeacians send Odysseus back to Ithaca, where he is received by the swineherd Eumaeus, recognized by his son and then, disguised as a beggar, goes to his palace. After various scenes depicting the insolence of the suitors, Penelope, inspired by Athene, proposes a contest, promising to marry the man strong enough to string Odysseus' bow. This feat is achieved by Odysseus alone; and, helped by Eumaeus, the cowherd Philetius and his own son, he succeeds in killing all the suitors and in punishing by death the unfaithful among his housemaids. He is finally recognized by Penelope, but immediately prepares for battle against supporters of the suitors whom he has just killed. Athene, however, intervenes and establishes peace on Ithaca.

The *Odyssey*, then, consists of two strands of narrative, which are first developed separately and then united into a single thread. Having first described the journey of Telemachus after he receives news of his father (Books 1–4), the narrative starts afresh and describes the wanderings and adventures of Odysseus (Books 5–12). When both these narrative strands have run their course and Odysseus has returned to Ithaca, the first thread is picked up again and united with the second so as to present Odysseus and Telemachus in action together against the suitors of Penelope, whom they kill as a necessary preliminary to the reunion of husband and wife (Books 13–24).

As was the case with the *Iliad*, a closer examination of the text of the *Odyssey* reveals a number of inconsistencies and harsh transitions which, again, usually arise from the conflation of variant accounts of certain scenes and episodes. There are also some later expansions of the text, the work of rhapsodists: the clearest example is the end of the *Odyssey*, the so-called 'Continuation' (23, 296, to the end of 24), which appears to be the beginning of the cyclic epic *Telegonia*.[10] Alexandrian scholarship pointed out that the true end of the *Odyssey* occurs at 23, 296, and this view has been fully confirmed by modern arguments based on an analysis of language and versification.

It has been hotly argued that Books 1 to 4 formed no part of the original *Odyssey* of Homer but were probably an independent poem about the journey of Telemachus, which was added only later to the *Odyssey*. Such cannot have been the case, for the interlocking of Odysseus' wanderings with Telemachus' journey in Books 14 to 15 is so skilfully done, and the stories of Odysseus and Telemachus so fully and organically blended in the third part of the *Odyssey* (Books 13 to 24), that, as we have them today, they could have been shaped only by a single poet, albeit with much help from older traditional songs and themes.

And, certainly, these traditional songs and themes have left many traces in the *Odyssey*, as can be seen clearly in two longer stories, the Cyclops and the Descent into the Underworld. More particularly, some of Odysseus' adventures are undoubtedly based on older stories about the voyage of the Argonauts. It seems that the latter formed a nucleus around which the later adventures of Odysseus developed. Perhaps, indeed, the only significant original contribution of the assembler of the monumental poem is the Phaeacian episode.

It need hardly be added here that the whole geography of the *Odyssey* is purely 'poetic', and that all attempts to trace Odysseus' wanderings on a map were, as early as the Hellenistic period, rightly and ironically dismissed by Eratosthenes. Yet this idle pursuit has been renewed with vigour in modern times, such is the fascination the *Odyssey* exercises over its readers.

The *Odyssey*, some imperfections notwithstanding, is a magnificent accomplishment and includes some of the most striking descriptive poetry ever written, such as the landing of Odysseus at Scheria, his meeting with Nausicaa and his final arrival at Ithaca. Moreover, it has touches of tenderness, fancy, irony and lyricism superior to their equivalents in the *Iliad*. Nevertheless, the *Odyssey* fails to achieve the monumental effect of the earlier poem, nor can the two be compared in vitality and tension.

Other obvious differences also exist between the *Iliad* and the *Odyssey*, which go far beyond the different levels of poetic intensity of the two that Pseudo-Longinus so strikingly expresses. Believing that Homer was the author of both the epics, he writes: 'In the *Odyssey* one could compare Homer with the setting sun, who retains his size without his vigour.'[11]

There are, for example, significant differences in vocabulary between the two poems, for the *Odyssey*'s departures from the vocabulary of the *Iliad* exceed the degree of variation which could be attributed to the dissimilarity of the subject-matter of the two poems. There are differences in matters of morality and in the treatment of the gods; in the *Odyssey*, unlike the *Iliad*, the gods are concerned with the worth of human actions, and the human actors are readier to be restrained by moral scruples. In the social organization of the two poems as well there are differences; and the 'Mycenaean' content in the *Odyssey* is much more restricted than in the *Iliad*, which is another indication of a later date of composition. There are, too, mythological novelties in the *Odyssey* which have no part in the *Iliad*; nor should we ignore the great advance in structural technique which the former has made over the latter. There is little in the *Odyssey* that could be regarded as a separate episode, independent of the story as a whole (how loosely knit the structure of the *Iliad* is by comparison); and the flash-back technique which it uses is an innovation, at least as far as Western literature is concerned. The accumulation of such differences adds weight to the arguments against the common authorship of the two monumental epics.

It is, strictly speaking, impossible to date poems which belong to an oral tradition stretching over centuries. Nevertheless, a rough date can be assigned to the moment when the monumental compositions had reached the form we know. In this difficult task we are guided first by phenomena in the poems which can be dated by archeological and linguistic criteria and, second, by the datable external effects of the poems themselves.

As regards the archeological criteria, it can be safely said that there is nothing in the epics that can be dated later than 700 B.C. The only exception, a mention in the *Iliad* of the Attic custom of bringing home for burial the ashes of warriors who had fallen abroad (VII, 334f.), is clearly an interpolation. At the same time, there are certain elements, like the reference to the Phoenicians, the pairs of casting-spears and, possibly, the appearance of temples as roofed, independent buildings, which suggest a date around 900 as a *terminus post quem*.

Linguistic criteria, it must be admitted, are of little help in dating the epics beyond placing them earlier than Hesiod (c. 700 B.C.) and the oldest of the Homeric Hymns (c. 650 B.C.). Nor does the presence of more recent elements in the mixed language of the Homeric epics rule out a ninth- or eighth-century date.

On the other hand, as regards the external datable effects of the poems, we find a number of quotations from and references to them in seventh-century elegiac, iambic and lyric poets. To them may be added the couplet found on an Ischian jug (not later than 700 B.C.) which refers to the cup of Nestor (XI, 632). But the earliest figure scenes indisputably derived from the epics are to be found on vases after that date. It has also been suggested that the new hero cults which spread over the Greek mainland from the eighth century onwards may have been a result of the wide currency which the Homeric poems enjoyed in Greek lands during the eighth and seventh centuries. Finally, it should not be overlooked that by the middle of the seventh century Greek personal poetry first emerged, in the form of elegiac, iambic and lyric verse. The days of the older, impersonal singers, like those who shaped the *Iliad* and the *Odyssey*, were already over.

Such evidence as we have, therefore, points to the eighth and the beginning of the seventh centuries as the period in which the *Iliad* and the *Odyssey* were completed. Some facts favour the eighth century in the case of the *Iliad*, notably the appearance on vases, from that time onwards, of representations of the Trojan cycle, the rise of the hero cults and references to hoplites, a form of soldiery unknown before about 750 B.C. Thus, the eighth century may be taken as the probable date at which the monumental *Iliad* reached its present form; and as stylistic similarities do not allow for a separation of more than two or three generations between the two epics, the end of the eighth or the beginning of the seventh would accordingly be the probable date in the case of the *Odyssey*.

It also appears very likely that both the poems were committed to writing at the time of their monumental composition or very soon after. For had they continued to be transmitted orally for several generations, a much greater influence of later ideas and language would have been discernible, no matter how well the great prestige of the epics had preserved their textual integrity. Moreover, had they first been committed to writing in the sixth century, as is implied by the tradition attributing an Athenian recension under Solon or Pisistratus, the intervention of literary techniques of composition would certainly have reduced the ease and simplicity with which the old formulae were used.

The sixth-century redaction of the Homeric poems which, tradition tells us, was made to ensure the recitation of the poems 'in their proper order' at the festival of the Panathenaea, was therefore probably not the first written text of Homer. Nevertheless, there is evidence that such a redaction was made: for not only did the Athenians in the fourth century attempt to resolve, by reference to Homer (no other text was available), a dispute with Megara over the island of Salamis, but also the language of the epics has a number of Attic elements and (in the manuscripts) spellings. An Athenian recension is undoubtedly among the ancestors of the present manuscript tradition of the two epics.

Apparently the sixth-century Athenian text of Homer, no doubt as a result of the later political and cultural ascendancy of Athens, became the authoritative version of the poems; and it was a descendant or descendants of that text which was used by the Alexandrian scholars of the third century B.C. Several scholars—in particular Zenodotus, Aristophanes of Byzantium and Aristarchus—worked on the text until the edition of Aristarchus (c. 180 B.C.) became the standard text for all succeeding ages. Numerous fragments of Homeric papyri from the first century onwards show us that our Homer is the Homer of Aristarchus and that the poems have suffered no alteration of any importance since his time.

But for what audience, the question remains, were monumental poems of such length composed? At least three days of solid recitation are necessary for a performance of the *Iliad* or the *Odyssey*, and at a large religious festival or in a market-place it would have been impossible to secure the same audience day after day; nor could weddings, small fairs or funerals accommodate a poem on such a scale. Another factor which tells against any full performance in instalments is the very structure of the epics, which does not fall into suitable episodes of roughly similar length. On the contrary, the *Iliad* in particular contains, as we have seen, long sections whose only function is to link other self-contained episodes. Such long, uninteresting passages would embarrass any serial performance, even one given before a captive audience at the court of a king, a tyrant or a nobleman.

It appears that we are faced with an unparalleled phenomenon in the literature of the world: two very long, narrative poems, carefully put together with no audience in mind—in fact, composed in the full realization that the recitation of them only could be in detached sections.

This difficult problem raises another: who were the composers of the epics, and what was their purpose? Two main possibilities come to mind—for the claims of a sixth-century Athenian commission have already been dismissed.

In the first place, we could suppose that in the course of the seventh century some Ionian guild of poets, such as the *Homeridae* of Chios, put together as much of the Trojan material as it had at its disposal and constructed out of it first the 'loosely knit' *Iliad* and then, some hundred years later, the 'closely knit' *Odyssey*. As a basis for their work the poets may well have used well-constructed shorter poems—an *Ur-Ilias* and an *Ur-Odyssey*—whose general outline can perhaps even now be roughly discerned in the greater structure to which they contributed. These monumental compilations would not have been designed for recitation in their entirety. Rather, they would have been intended as compendiums of epic poetry, from which rhapsodes could choose and recite parts as occasion offered.

The crucial objection to this view is the fact that there is no obvious motive for such collective effort on the part of a rhapsodic guild. As far as we know, it is quite unparalleled in eighth- or seventh-century Greece.

The second possibility—and this seems to be much more likely—is to consider each of the monumental epics as the work of a single poet. The great new departure would, of course, be the creation of the first poet, the monumental *Iliad*, for it would have been through his example that the composition of the *Odyssey* was undertaken.

The gifted oral poet who composed the *Iliad*—and he could have been called Homer, though we have no other proof than the poem's attribution in antiquity[12]—probably used part of his own Trojan repertoire in this ambitious undertaking, combining it with other, older material available to him. Such a leap from the relatively large to the colossal, it has been rightly argued,[13] is more appropriate to the ambition, ability and reputation of an individual than to the collective effort of a school. As examples of a parallel phenomenon at a similar date have been adduced the great Geometric *amphora* and *krater*, each of which is just over 2 metres high and towers above all its predecessors.

No doubt in competition with the monumental *Iliad*, a few generations later another gifted oral poet put together the monumental *Odyssey*. And at that point, as far as we know, such monumental compositions ceased to be made, for the other epics of the Theban and Trojan cycles were much shorter and much less ambitious.

What must be excluded absolutely is the suggestion that the *Iliad* and the *Odyssey* are mere agglomerations of Trojan epic material. The clear underlying structure which unites each, and their frequent cross-references and transitional passages, place such a view completely out of court.

The Homeric narrative

The Homeric epics are composed in dactylic hexameters. About the origins of the metre nothing can be said with certainty, although it has been suggested that they were not Mycenaean but Minoan and Hittite, a proposition which cannot be proved. What is certain is that the original hexameter was not spoken but sung, probably to some primitive chant rather than to a recognizable tune, and was accompanied by a stringed instrument. Greek heroic poetry used the single line as its unit of composition and was always sung or recited by a single bard.

The hexameter verse is a powerful instrument of narrative and an excellent means of maintaining the movement and music of language. The skill with which the Greek oral poets combined the elaborate technique of the hexameter with the demands of straightforward narrative is particularly noteworthy.

In the language of the epics a predominantly Ionic dialect is amalgamated with Arcado-Cypriot, Aeolic and even Attic forms. But its essential artificiality goes even beyond this mixture of dialects, extending to the creation, usually by analogy, of new forms, inflexions and compounds and to the almost arbitrary lengthening of certain syllables as a means of meeting metrical difficulties.

Although various hypotheses have been put forward to explain the dialectal mixture of the epic language, none has been universally accepted. But one conclusion seems inescapable: dialectal mixture must have been a characteristic of the language in which the epics were actually composed; for, as we have seen, the *Iliad* and the *Odyssey* are the culmination of a continuous tradition of oral poetry, and their linguistic components are of origins diverse in both locality and date. How strange to reflect that poetry of such stature was composed in an artificial, 'literary' language, which was never actually spoken in any part of Greece but which was still widely being admired and copied over a millennium and a half later.

We have already seen how the Homeric narrative is largely determined by the techniques of oral poetry, which in its turn depends to a large extent on the structure of the dactylic hexameter. In order to create a language which fitted the needs of versification and which would provide safe-guards against a metrical break-down during recitation, the poets in-vented and relied on a variety of formulae.

Some of these stock expressions are very short, but the most usual ones, those which cover the most common human ideas and situations, gener-ally fill the space between the bucolic diaeresis or one of the three Homeric caesurae and the end of the line. Others fill the space between the beginning of the verse and the caesura; while yet others occupy whole verses or series of verses. For one should consider as formulae certain descriptive passages, such as the preparation of a meal or a sacrifice, the reception given to a stranger or setting sail, many of which cover several lines and are repeated in similar situations. Moreover, as has been pointed out, the Greek epic is formulaic not only in its language but also in its themes, whether major themes, on which the structure of a whole epic depends, or minor ones, which are woven into various parts of the narra-tive.

One of the most striking formulaic usages is the stock epithet, the regular employment of an ornamental epithet with the same fixed noun. This should be singled out for consideration because it became one of the common characteristics of the epic style. Stock expressions of this kind exist for gods, heroes, things, places, situations, actions. They describe things not as they were on a particular occasion, but as they essentially and immutably are. About half the adjectives in the *Iliad* and the *Odyssey* are of this nature.[14] Our first reaction is to be struck by their beauty. They flow unceasingly through the changing moods of the poem, unobtrusively blending with it yet, by their indifference to the story, giving a permanent, unchanging sense of strength and beauty. But it is clear that they are often used for mere convenience's sake, and their fixed use ultimately weakens the initial descriptive value of the epithet. The result is that ornamental epithets are often out of keeping with particular contexts in which they are used. The sky may be called 'starry' in the daytime; ships are called 'swift' even when they are moored. On the other hand, these fixed epithets add a certain dignity to the things described, a ceremonial touch which is well in keeping with the elevated tone of the epic.

The formulaic technique is also responsible for the retention in the epics of archaic words beyond the period when their meaning was understood, so that they became merely a decorative element of the epic diction, whose artistic effect depended on a vague connotation and a beautiful sound — *in carmine gemae*, 'jewels within the poem', as Martial described such words. The total effect of this formulaic technique of composition is undeniably vivid. We soon realize that each formulaic phrase is chosen by the epic poet with as much care as literary poets give to a choice of single words, a circumstance which is as surprising to us as the discovery that the entire Homeric diction is an artificial, 'literary' language.

But perhaps the most extraordinary result of the formulaic technique is the cultural amalgam to which it gave rise in the Homeric epics. For there is irrefutable evidence in both the *Iliad* and the *Odyssey* of cultural elements originating from periods more than half a millennium apart. There is much in the poems that refers back to the Mycenaean age: the body-shield, the cup of Nestor, the silver-studded swords, the boar's-tusk helmet and the *zoma* of *Odyssey*, 14, 482, to say nothing of the overall political organization of the *Iliad* or the geography of the 'Catalogue of Ships' from the same poem. Side by side we find elements no less conspicuous which reflect the Geometric and Orientalizing periods: the pairs of casting-spears, the leather shields with bronze faces and no blazons, the iron axes, knives and arrowheads, the references to the Phoenicians as traders, the hoplite armament, the lamp of Athene and the brooch of Odysseus.[15] But that is not all: there are also some few passages which look to the fifth century, the most important of them being, as we saw, in the *Iliad*, VII, 334ff. These last examples, however, can safely be regarded as interpolations which entered the poems after they had been committed to writing.

Such elements, originating in widely different ages, found their way into the poems because of the conservatism inherent in a formulaic, oral technique. The old and the new exist side by side, and become inextricably blended, so that literary analysis can do no more than disentangle the strange mixture a little. Nor can historically identifiable elements be used to date the parts of the poem in which they are found. The epic narrative has been rightly compared with a dough in which several ingredients have been kneaded together. There can be no division into older and newer parts, even if some of the ingredients can be isolated and separately dated.

This cultural amalgam is responsible for one of the strangest phenomena of the epics, the *composite description*. Metrical formulae, which were traditionally associated with certain nouns, continued in use even after a cultural change had made them no longer strictly applicable. The result was often that a single description might combine characteristics really belonging to different epochs and juxtapose descriptions which could never have coexisted in the real world.

The Homeric poems speak, for example, of a helmet essentially non-metallic, surmounted with a horse-hair crest and reinforced with various attachments whose original function was already obscure long before the monumental compositions were completed. A later period then applied to this helmet a number of colourful and elaborate elements belonging to a time when helmets were of a different kind. The result is a helmet which never existed.

Many such confused and confusing composite descriptions exist, of shields, chariots, battles and palaces. But even when impossible elements are introduced—a spear, stuck fast in a warrior's breast, quivers to his heartbeat (XIII, 442–4); horses are said (a thing unknown in nature) to trample the bodies of the dead (XX, 498f.)—still the poetic illusion remains intact.

But only relatively few descriptions in the two epics are of the composite variety. In the remainder one is astonished by the continually varied presentation of similar episodes, especially in scenes of killing and wounding, and even more by the clarity of the images presented. In a few sweeping strokes a person, an object or a situation is conjured up before our eyes, for no Greek poetry is more evocative than that of the Homeric epics or produces a greater effect seemingly with so little effort. One is constantly amazed at the ability of those poets to observe significant detail and to break a thing down into its component parts so as to make its real meaning clear to all.

The approach in the description of persons, objects and places is rather different. In the case of its heroes, the epic avoids giving any detailed description of their physical appearance. Our picture of them is always built up indirectly through their actions, their words, the stock epithet or an appropriate simile. We are made to feel that a man who acts or talks in such and such a manner must have an appearance to match. Achilles, for example, or Diomedes cannot be conceived as small, delicate men; and when the poet speaks of ξανθός Menelaus ('fair-haired' Menelaus) we immediately credit him also with blue eyes and a light complexion. Again, to quote only one such example, when in *Iliad*, XVII, 132f. Ajax, shielding the body of Patroclus, is compared with a lion, a picture of the powerful, scowling hero leaps to the eye.[16]

In this manner the epic poet makes his audience (or reader) share in the creative experience: each is left to conjure up his own ideal picture of the various heroes instead of being compelled to accept the poet's.

In the few cases in which a characteristic detail is given of a hero's physical appearance, it is because that detail is pertinent to an action or event and not in order to describe the man. Thus we are told that Hector has long, dark hair only because it is dragged in the dust behind Achilles' chariot (XXII, 401f.), and that Achilles has auburn hair only because he cuts off an 'auburn lock' to offer to the dead Patroclus (XXIII, 141f.).

The one mortal whose picture is drawn in any detail is Thersites, a low figure of fun (II, 216f.) whose ugliness the poet takes delight in emphasizing

for comic effect. This is fully in keeping with the Greek approach of the
Classical period, which held that the portrayal of beauty should be
idealized, while ugliness should be presented realistically.

The epic poets also avoid direct description of the inanimate objects
and works of art which often enter the narrative. Palaces, garments,
furniture, ornaments and metalwork are held up for admiration not as
artefacts whose beauty merits detailed description, but as products of
'Phoenician art' or as works of Hephaestus or Athene. There are, of
course, some notable exceptions to this practice, such as the descriptions
of the cup of Nestor, the baldric of Heracles, the boar's-tusk helmet of
Odysseus, the breastplate of Agamemnon and, above all, the shield of
Achilles, which is the first *ecphrasis* (description of a work of art in verse) in
Greek literature. But in each of these cases the very elaboration empha-
sizes how exceptional the description is. Of other objects, when a detailed
description might have been expected—the sceptre of Agamemnon, the
Pelian ashen spear of Achilles or the bow of Odysseus—we are often given
no description at all, but rather their history and the names of notable
persons with whom they have been associated.

Similarly, little attempt is made to describe the physical setting of the
various episodes, and the scenes of frequently recurring actions are never
portrayed. Strange surroundings, on the other hand, naturally excite the
poet's imagination; so, for example, we are told much more about the land
of the Cyclopes than about the camp of the Greeks or the plain before
Troy, where all the fighting of the *Iliad* takes place. Of interest in this
context are certain idyllic landscapes which we meet in the *Odyssey*, such
as the cave of Calypso (5, 63–74), the garden of Alcinous (7, 112–32) or
the harbour of Phorcys (13, 96–112). These strike a new note in the epic
context and are the forerunners of a trend in Greek poetry which reached
its apogee in the post-Classical world in the idylls of Theocritus.

The epic employs three narrative modes; first, an objective narrative
mode, in which the poet himself is absent and the story proceeds as if it
were unfolding on its own; second, a subjective narrative mode, in which
the poet interferes directly in order to interpret or clarify certain aspects of
the action; and third, a dramatic mode, in which the heroes themselves
develop the plot or reveal their own personalities through direct speech.
Of the three, the last is used much more than the other two and is even
more common in the *Odyssey* than in the *Iliad*.[17]

The objective narrative mode is direct and simple, a circumstance due,
no doubt, to the regard which oral poetry must have to its listeners. The
vitality and constant progress of the narrative is such that the numerous
slight inconsistencies which we discern in a careful reading of the text go
quite unnoticed at first hearing.

It is important to bear in mind that Greek epic, like Greek tragedy,
dealt with stories whose outcome was already known to the audience, and

that therefore the kind of interest which it tried to create was different from that excited by modern narrative poetry or modern fiction. What chiefly mattered was how the poet would present and elaborate his theme. Everybody knew that Odysseus returned and was reunited with Penelope: the real objects of suspense are the means by which he escapes from his various dangers and the accomplishment of his plan by disguise and ruse. Similarly, in the *Iliad* the audience knew in nearly every encounter who would be killed and who would survive. What really mattered was the heroic approach to the inevitable event.

The poet's concern for his audience also led him to repeat incidents, motifs, patterns, formulae and epithets. Although, as we have seen, much of the reason for this lies in the formulaic technique of oral poetry, whose object was to protect the poet from a metrical break-down, another motive also existed—the poet's desire to assist the listener's memory and to relieve him of undue mental effort. For the same reason we often find the poet foretelling the outcome of an action and always introducing by name all newcomers to the story and relating them to other known characters.

But this strange partnership between poet and audience is perhaps nowhere more clearly evident than when the poet omits the motivation for an act, leaving it to the listener to supply it for himself. This happens at a number of impressive moments, of which the most important example is in Book XVI. No real reason is given there why Achilles should allow Patroclus to come to the help of the Greeks while refusing to aid them himself.[18] Here, as in all other such instances, the characters in the poems are expected to know things of which, according to the strict development of the plot, they should be ignorant, but since the poet has told the audience of them, the discrepancy is not immediately apparent. It has been truly said that only the poet's relationship with his reader is real and permanent. His relationship with his characters is purely imaginative and transitory.

The subjective narrative mode, in which the poet intervenes in his own person, is used mainly to introduce explanations which cannot be made in the objective mode. An oral poet must anticipate such questions as will rise in the mind of his audience and must furnish the details along with the facts. On the whole, such interventions are short; occasionally, in the course of one of them the poet will address the Muse or one of his characters by name. Among other things, they also give the listener time to grasp the significance of an important moment in the story by suggesting the crisis or by hinting at the sequel, for example XV, 60if.; XVII, 278f.; 22, 32f.

The last of the three, the dramatic narrative mode, is used widely and successfully. Through direct speeches the characters come to life, and their inner world is brought to light. Because of his use of dialogue, Homer has been called 'the first tragedian'. His influence upon Attic drama was, of course, enormous.

The Homeric speeches fall into two groups, the public and the private. The first category presents the words of the chiefs as they discuss or explain their opinions in council, address the assembly or bring messages as official ambassadors; to the latter belong the speeches in which the heroes privately discuss, exhort, provoke and abuse each other. The speakers in each case express their sentiments spontaneously, without rhetoric. Theirs is a primitive kind of eloquence, in which the whole personality of the speaker pours out forcefully with his words; and it is that which sways the hearer, not the arguments put forward, which are few and never discussed. The epic heroes simply make their statement and demand to be believed without more ado. They rarely develop or analyse what they have to say. In style the speeches are less elaborate than are the narrative parts of the epic, and one of their features is to present at their conclusion a number of *gnomae*. This gnomic element is one of the more striking characteristics of the Homeric epics. With arresting directness, the wisdom of generations is given in a few words and with an elevated moral tone. Perhaps their greatest asset is their terseness, which keeps the didactic element of the poems from being tedious.

The Homeric speeches serve not only to present the characters as living personalities but also, by repeating what has already been said, to refresh the memory of the hearer and to emphasize what is significant. Moreover, they often foretell what is to happen and so prepare the audience for it. Again, if in a moment fraught with emotion there is no opportunity for dialogue, the monologue is used, and the characters 'think aloud'. Some of the monologues are among the most moving parts of the poems—for example, that of Hector before his meeting with Achilles, in which the subtle interplay between thought and feeling is admirably traced (**XXII**, 99ff.).

Within the framework of these three narrative modes the epic developed a number of styles with which to differentiate and enliven the narrative. Both the *Iliad* and the *Odyssey* are marked by a smooth, periodic style, which is, however, less vivid in the latter. Side by side with this, in many places we find a markedly succinct style, which can occasionally give the impression of confusion, so compact does the expression become.[19] As opposed to these two styles, on certain formal and dramatic occasions the language becomes stately and sonorous to match the events, so that one can fairly speak of a heightened, majestic style which clearly differs from the simple flow of the narrative. Familiar examples of this are Zeus' oath to Thetis (**I**, 528–30) and the description of Athene in **V**, 733–47. The stateliness of the language is achieved through the use of long, sonorous words and of hyperbole which sometimes verges on the absurd. The majestic style, which on the whole is not found in the *Odyssey*, is rare also in the *Iliad* and is often absent from passages in which it would heighten the drama.

Akin to the majestic style, and equally absent from the *Odyssey* in its more extreme form, is a decorated, lyrical style, which is employed particularly in the descriptions of gods. It is limited largely to the long episode known as Hera's Beguilement of Zeus, which occupies a large part of Books XIII to XV of the *Iliad*. But other good examples of the style are found also in XIII, 18f. and XIV, 347–51.

Throughout the *Iliad* and the *Odyssey* there are, of course, numerous lyrical passages which, extending to no more than an epithet or a single phrase, hardly amount to a proper style. For the same reason, the occasional use of stress and variation which we meet briefly and sporadically in the poems and which depend on little more than a careful arrangement of words and phrases cannot be called a 'rhetorical' style.[20]

By all these means the Homeric epics achieve both a unity and a diversity of style most desirable in poems of their monumental size. Of the two, the *Odyssey* has a markedly narrower stylistic range, and its excesses are almost entirely confined to large-scale expansions, such as the 'Continuation' (23, 296, to the end of 24).

Another chief characteristic of the epic manner is the brilliant use of so-called Homeric similes. They are among the most striking elements of epic technique. Of them 182 fully developed examples occur in the *Iliad*, compared with only thirty-nine in the *Odyssey*. Through these extended similes everyday life enters the epic, bringing an earthy element to the elevated, heroic world. They speak of things the audience knows at first hand, which appeal directly to the senses; through their imagery we see, hear, touch, smell and taste. They also serve to place the events of the battlefield in a wider temporal context. Life is felt by the listener to be rolling onwards independently of the war, and this helps to give reality to the conflict and to deepen its impact.

In the Homeric similes not only are the theme, the place and the time given, but often also circumstantial details quite irrelevant to the point of comparison. An example is seen in VIII, 559f., where the watchfires of the Trojans are likened to the stars about the moon on a clear, still night. The poet adds that 'all the stars are seen to gladden the shepherd's heart.' It is this human focus to a universalized comparison which is appealing and which raises so many of these similes to the level of great poetry.

The Homeric similes speak of the changing seasons, the clearness of starry nights, the full moon, the evening star, violent storms, mountain streams, forest fires, smoke rising from a burning city, the eternal changes of the sea. Just as powerful are the scenes drawn from wild life—lions, boars or swooping hawks, the wounded fawn at the mercy of a hound—and there are also many scenes from everyday life: men reaping barley, a woman shooing the flies away from her child, boys beating an ass, a potter shaping a pot on the wheel.

Each of these similes—and we have mentioned only a small selection

—has its own poetry; and those drawn from humble daily life suggest that the heroic world is not everything, that there are times when it can best be seen at its true worth by comparison with something more simple and homely, even undignified. But, however humble the points of comparison, none is incompatible with epic dignity (*semnotes*). A simile can often bring to the audience's mind a great phenomenon outside its experience by reference to a smaller thing which it has seen. In *Iliad*, XXI, 362f., for example, the seething water of the river Xanthus is compared with that of a boiling cauldron.

Detailed examination has shown that more recent linguistic elements tend to be found in the fully developed similes,[21] which suggests that the latter must belong to a more recent stage of the epic tradition.[22]

In contrast to the simile, metaphor plays a small role in the Homeric poems and is usually not put to striking use. This is no bad thing, for a laboured use of metaphor can reduce the grand manner to mere artificiality and bombast. The Homeric poems are protected from such a fate by the fact that traditional formulaic poetry has a way of draining metaphors of their meaning; in the process they become mere 'epic' words and phrases, used as simple equivalents for others with no metaphorical content. The phrase ἔπεα πτερόεντα ('winged words'), for example, occurs 123 times in the two epics. Its frequent use is clearly due to the fact that it is metrically helpful, rather than to the original force of the metaphor.

There are not many metaphors in Homer which extend beyond one word: κάρηνα, 'heads', for the peaks of mountains; ἔθεεν, 'it ran', for the passage of a ship; ῥοδοδάκτυλος Ἠώς, 'rosy-fingered dawn'; χαλκοχίτωνες Ἀχαιοί, 'bronze-shirted Achaeans'; and so forth. Few indeed are the longer real metaphors which are meant to be felt as such, as in *Iliad*, I, 249. Aristotle had the highest praise for such Homeric metaphors which, as he said, move 'from the living to the lifeless'. (*Rhetoric*, 1411, B 31). An example is seen in *Iliad*, XI, 574, where the spears 'stood in the ground yearning to sate themselves in flesh'.

The world of men and the world of the gods

The Homeric epics move on two planes, that of the mortals and that of the gods, and those two worlds are very different. While happiness, laughter and immortality prevail in the world of the gods, strife and death are the lot of mortals.

The *Iliad* and the *Odyssey* depict a world of men which is far richer and more magnificent than the real surroundings in which the later stages of the epic tradition developed—an idealized, heroic world, not unlike that which appears in the epic traditions of other peoples at other times. At war the

Homeric men take delight in their bronze armour, which is often studded with gold or silver, or inlaid with enamel; they are proud of their horses; when sacrificing or feasting they slay whole hecatombs of oxen and pigs; and they observe a strict decorum in their dealings with one another. In times of peace their palaces and gardens, their clothes and furnishings take on an exceptional splendour. But though the epic brings its figures into a human orbit (and it is the humanization of the epic world which is perhaps the greatest Homeric achievement), they still retain a lofty, heroic distinction.

This world of men, which in some respects differs from the *Iliad* to the *Odyssey*, is one more of those composite pictures fashioned by the processes of the epic tradition. It consists of elements which belong to different, often widely separated, historical ages, ranging from the Mycenaean to the Orientalizing periods—a feature due, as we have seen, to the formulaic oral technique.

In Homeric society the laws of battle are brutal, and captives are enslaved unless a large ransom is paid for them. It is possible, especially on the Trojan side, to trace some Oriental practices. Priam, for example, has several wives. Hecuba, of course, holds the place of honour, but Laothoe is also of some standing, for her father had 'given her many gifts' at her marriage.

One of the most attractive features of this society is its respect for the laws of hospitality. Its ties are so strong that even warriors on the battlefield cease fighting if they discover that their opponent is their *xenos*, as can be seen from the episode of Glaucus and Diomedes in *Iliad*, VI, 119f.

In the *Odyssey* we learn more about epic society in peacetime. In Ithaca we come across a kind of local feudal system. Penelope's suitors are rich land-owners who lead a life of pleasure but who also organize ambushes to destroy their enemies or to acquire wealth. They have their own ships and their own dependants. On the Island of the Phaeacians, on the other hand, life is somewhat different. There a sort of patriarchal rule exists. King Alcinous convenes meetings of the princes of the Phaeacians and provides lavish hospitality. But the way of life is otherwise simple. Nausicaa, the king's daughter, drives her companions to the river to wash the family's linen, and the queen herself supervises the servants of the palace. Another interesting insight is provided by the *Odyssey*'s view of the singer's status as honourable, which points to a development in the bard's profession since the time of the *Iliad*.

The womenfolk of the epic heroes are seen as grand and beautiful; they wear sumptuous dresses and are adorned with much jewellery—a kind of diadem (ἄμπυξ) around their heads and bands around their temples (ἀναδέσμη)—and they wear veils, another Oriental trait. Inheritors of Cretan culture, these Achaean ladies had developed a taste for refined luxury which was designed to enhance their beauty. For in the epics the real *arete* of a woman is in her dignity and her personal appearance, though she also enjoys an elevated social status as mistress of her household, and sober morality and domestic prudence are honoured. As is seen in the famous *Teichoscopia* in *Iliad*, III, 146f., it was for her beauty that Helen was honoured in Troy, despite the calamities she had brought to the Trojans.

In turning to the portrayal in the epics of the characters of their heroes, we are struck by the great variety we find, ranging from the most savage violence to the deepest humanity and tenderness. Certain scenes depict, and delight in depicting, primitive emotions or crude natures ruled by the instincts. These men fight for plunder: the purpose of their raiding is to seize cattle, horses or women; and it is from an unequal distribution of that booty that their quarrels arise. Angry insults come swiftly to their mouths, and they feel little compassion for a defeated enemy. Not only did Achilles mutilate the corpse of Hector and drag it behind his chariot; the other Achaean warriors, too, approached to insult it.

Yet along with these savage scenes we also come across others marked by extreme delicacy of feeling and deep humanity. Nothing in the epics surpasses the effect of Priam's speech when he comes to Achilles' hut to ransom the body of his dead son; Achilles' answer is hardly less moving when compassion fills his heart for the old man weeping at his feet and for the whole of humanity suffering under the indifferent eyes of the gods that are secure from pain. Marital and paternal tenderness too are revealed with great sensitivity in the famous farewell scene between Hector and Andromache on the walls of Troy (VI, 369ff.).

Women's psychology is depicted with particular adroitness in the epics. A remarkable example is Nausicaa, the young princess whose tact and modesty are equalled only by her courage and kindness when confronted by the unkempt figure of the shipwrecked Odysseus. She is the forerunner of these courageous yet maidenly figures which Attic tragedians were later to present so strikingly. In such portraits the epic displays an astonishing awareness of what in modern terms could be called a complex psychology.

Such subtlety is also at work in the characters of the three main heroes of the epics, Achilles, Odysseus and Hector, the representatives of three different types of heroic excellence. But we cannot properly understand them unless we first consider the epic notion of *arete*—prowess in battle, courage in the face of adversity—which is the central element in the personality of all the main Homeric heroes.

In the epic the brave man is the nobleman, the man of rank, and battle and victory are the highest distinction, the real meaning of his life. Thus great strength of sinew and spirit are the essence of epic *arete*: valour (which, it should be remembered, is quite without those moral connotations which the literature of the Middle Ages saw in fighting). The famous line: αἰὲν ἀριστεύειν καὶ ὑπείροχον ἔμμεναι ἄλλων (VI, 208) 'to be always the winner and above all others' summarizes with clarity that notion of early Greek *arete*.

Closely connected with this is the idea of honour, the honour shown by his equals to the bearer of *arete*. Not to be paid his due of honour was the greatest blow which could be dealt to the nobleman of epic. The greater the hero, the stronger his desire for honour, since honour followed achievement and therefore proved, both to society and to the man himself, what he was really worth. Praise and censure (ἔπαινος and ψόγος) were the sources of honour and disgrace respectively; and it was only in the form of posthumous fame, expressed in an ideal picture of his deeds, that the epic fighter could achieve some measure of immortality.

It is in this light that we must see Achilles. His wrath arises from the lack of honour shown him. His crushing anger and his refusal to help the Achaeans—insult for insult, retribution in kind—do nothing to diminish his heroic stature but are rather expressions of it. His is no modern, self-centred thirst for glory, nor is his behaviour without a sense of proportion or patriotism. But there is more than that to the Achilles seen in our *Iliad*, for as the epic tradition developed, the older one-dimensional figure was overlaid with a more rounded heroic type. The clearest indication of this is perhaps Book IX—in its present form a 'later' book—in which the heroic ideal is not confined to the man of action but includes the 'speaker of words'. There this new intellectual element is actually equated with the traditional value of prowess in battle: μύθων τε ῥητῆρ' ἔμεναι πρηκτῆρά τε ἔργων (IX, 443) ('to be a speaker of words and doer of deeds') is now the ideal; and this presupposes both the tradition of open debate, as seen in the epics, and the full development of the city-state, in which speech is as significant a weapon for winning wars as the spear and the sword.

But even the Achilles of Book IX remains fundamentally unrelenting, because behind him stands the implacable figure of the primitive Achilles. He refuses all the royal gifts and asks to be requited in kind for the bitter humiliation he has suffered. For the original heroes of epic amends could not be made otherwise than in kind, humiliation for humiliation. It was the attitude of Ajax, whom dishonour drove mad and who even in Hades remained unrelenting and shunned Odysseus, dwarfing the shadows of the dead (11, 543f.).

If Achilles finally relents and joins the battle, it is the death of Patroclus which induces him to do so, not the gifts of the Achaeans—which, incidentally, he also accepts. Thus the original 'wrath-motif', with its emphasis on Achilles' selfish anger, gives way, as we have seen, to the 'close friendship motif' and the burning desire of Achilles to avenge his friend. For Patroclus he is prepared to sacrifice both his honour and his life, the two most important attributes of the epic code. This in turn gives way to a nobler feeling of compassion, when the 'old father motif' of Book

XXIV compels the hero to cast aside every other emotion in favour of respect and compassion for Priam. It is through these three successive motifs that Achilles' personality is revealed. But it would be too much to say that his character in the process 'develops'. He is just as fierce and primitive as he was in Book I when, in the final stages of the epic, he loses his temper with Priam and threatens to treat him as peremptorily as he has treated Hector. As the *Iliad* progresses, Achilles is shown to be capable of sacrifice and compassion; but behind him ever looms the fierce, self-regarding primitive hero, without whom the *Iliad* would never have achieved such power or such dark depths.

But no epic hero can be truly great unless he defeats a great opponent. In the latter role is cast Hector, a man whose nature is totally different from that of Achilles. Both are, of course, great and brave warriors; but Hector embodies much more than Trojan courage—he stands for the very existence of Troy. He is a representative of that new ideal of personal heroism which, closely linking a man's duty with his city and his family, provides another reflection of the rise, in the post-Mycenaean Greek world, of the city-state and the place in the life of man which the family unit had come to occupy.

For in Hector, side by side with the great warrior (who retains some very primitive traits, as was the case with Achilles), there coexists a very human figure, movingly revealed when he bids farewell to his wife and plays with his baby son, or in his consideration for his mother and Helen. Everything is done to make Hector engaging. His role as the doomed father, son and lover of his country has a sombre appeal; but above all he is the champion of Troy, and in his death is involved the fall of the whole city. We know that when he is gone the city is doomed, and this it is that makes the *Iliad* a true epic of Troy rather than an *Achilleis* or a song about the exploits of several heroes.

There is a sense in which the *Odyssey* is a stage of the epic on its road to becoming the novel. The very first line of the poem stresses the dominant trait of the character of Odysseus, the central figure: versatility. 'Tell me, Muse, of the "man of many resources" . . . ' (ἄνδρα . . . πολύτροπον). Prudence is perhaps his chief virtue, though he is certainly also brave and strong, and in him the warrior of Troy lives on. How else could he have killed his wife's suitors on Ithaca or defeated the young athletes at the Phaeacian games? But these manifestations of prowess capture the imagination less than his magnificent resourcefulness. He is a man who uses his wits to get him out of tight corners, who knows how to dissemble and to wait for the right moment.

Moreover, he is the master of calculated and persuasive words. When he leaves Calypso he knows how to disarm her with compliments, and when he appears before the startled Nausicaa, 'terrifying and all crusted with dry salt', he knows how to flatter her. Through ingenuity he triumphs over the brute force of the Cyclops. His shrewdness never deserts him, and his invention is boundless. He is one of those representative figures in which a whole race can be recognized: Themistocles, Alcibiades, Theramenes—even Juvenal's Graeculus, Michael Psellus or the great Eleutherios Venizelos.

Yet somehow for us—though certainly not for antiquity—his stature is diminished by the fact that Athene accompanies him at almost every step, either in her own divine form or in that of a mortal. Her intervention reduces the tension of the tale. To us the hero's actions are much more exciting during the sea adventures, when Athene is absent from his side.

But the Homeric narrative does not concentrate exclusively on the great leading figures of Achilles, Hector, Ajax, Diomedes, Odysseus and Penelope. It shows an interest, equal in quality if not in quantity, in many characters unimportant to the plot, such as Axylus and Dresus, Theano and Ikmalion; nor are the humblest creatures on earth ever despised for their lack of heroic glamour. The epic creates a microcosm of the world in which its heroes lived, and although it was tied to the past by the story it told and by the conservative tendencies of the formulaic technique, it still succeeded in fusing the past with the present so as to produce a harmonious whole, which included almost every aspect of life. Its men and women form a richly varied gallery of human types, which are presented for their human appeal almost without comment or criticism. For centuries they served as educational examples for the Greeks, who looked to the lives and achievements of the Homeric heroes for guidance.

It is hard to assess the epic notion of the human soul. Among other difficulties, the language of Homer knows no word corresponding to our own 'soul'. The Homeric *psyche* is in meaning closer to the 'breath soul' or 'shadow soul' which, leaving the body at death, passes to the shadowy realm of Hades, where it endures an afterlife of misery. In the living man *psyche* is the foundation of all thoughts and desires, but we know virtually nothing of its nature or of the manner in which it is supposed to operate.

If we turn to the human personality, we find that in the epics man's will and divine purpose are closely bound together, for human actions and divine commands appear as two concepts essentially complementary yet capable of coming into conflict. This is another of those points in which a difference can be traced between the *Iliad* and the *Odyssey*, for in the latter much more emphasis is laid on a man's making his own decisions and taking responsibility for them. This was to become one of the mainsprings of Attic tragedy, a form which, to a large extent, had its roots in the Homeric epics.

If we now turn to the world of the gods, we shall observe that the treatment of the Homeric gods is a strange mixture of crude superstition and sophisticated satire, which we can only explain as the product of a long religious tradition. The earliest elements in the *Iliad* obviously date from a period when the Olympian pantheon was regarded with real awe; but later additions reflect a time when religious feeling in the Ionian world had waned. These detailed and, to our eyes, strange scenes depicting the Olympians were an important ingredient of the epic technique. Through them the poet was able to give shape to his vast and varied material, for they both motivated and developed the main heroic narrative.

The gods in Homer are conceived as living on the top of Mount Olympus, from where they descend at their pleasure, either in their own divine shapes (which are anthropomorphic) or in the form of human beings. Like mortals, they have their rivalries and violent passions, and they may even be harmed by men: for example, Aphrodite in *Iliad*, V, is wounded by Diomedes. Alone among the gods Zeus stands above all this. He never descends to earth and never takes part in the battles of men or gods. He convenes the assemblies of the gods, arbitrates in their quarrels and imposes on them his all-powerful will.[23]

Above and beyond the Olympian gods there exists an obscure, indistinct power before which even Zeus himself is impotent. It is Fate or Destiny. The 'father of men and gods' sighs in *Iliad*, XXII, when he is compelled to abandon Hector, the warrior who has sacrificed to him so many oxen. The god consults the decree of Destiny, represented in the concrete form of a balance: 'and Hector's death-day was heavier and dragged down towards death, and Phoebus Apollo forsook him' (XXII, 212f.).

The epic pantheon unites gods of diverse origin. Together with Father Zeus, the Indo-European sky god, we find Athene and Hera, who were originally Mycenaean palace goddesses, and also Asiatic gods like Ares, Aphrodite, Hephaestus and Apollo; at the same time, such things as winds, rivers, Eos, Erinys and Eileithyia are also worshipped as gods and goddesses.

This picture of Zeus ruling over a body of subordinate gods seems to reflect the political organization of the Mycenaean world when the king of Mycenae was overlord of the 'whole of Greece'. Like Agamemnon, Zeus has full power by right of inheritance, and the other gods appear as his retainers, whom he summons to council, just as Agamemnon summons his own chiefs. The epic thus gives us not only a heroic but also a divine mythology, which deals with the relation of god to god, an aspect of the lore of the gods which is not essentially religious.

The Homeric gods, unlike the mortals of the poems, are happy. It is only against this background of divine felicity that the misery and suffering of the world of men can be measured. The joy of the gods is seen from the start of the *Iliad* but is particularly conspicuous in the latter half. The long episode called the Beguilement of Zeus by Hera, covering most of Books XIII to XV, is perhaps the best example of it. In particular, the passage which describes Poseidon driving across the sea in his full splendour (XIII, 17ff.) provides a memorable picture of that superhuman elation which serves in the poems to heighten the endless strife, suffering and death which are the lot of mankind.

The influence of this divine happiness touches even the material things connected with the world of the gods. In essence, of course, they resemble the material things which mortals use—they could hardly avoid doing so—but over all of them there lingers a glow of Olympian beatitude.

Side by side with such respectful treatment, however, the gods in the last and most developed stages of the epic are shown as figures of fun. The most famous passage in this connection is the scene from *Iliad*, I, which rings with the laughter of the gods. Throughout the poem this comedy of the gods continues, culminating in the Battle of the Gods of Book XX, in which all the gods, immune from physical pain, set about each other with a will. Yet this irreverence is never present in any scene describing contact between gods and men; and the tenderness of many lines in the burlesque scenes shows us that they are intended as comedy rather than farce.

It is against the background of the life of the gods that the tragic theme of the *Iliad* is developed. As the atmosphere of the story becomes more loaded with pain and suffering, the scenes representing the gods grow more fantastic and broadly comic. It may be said, with truth, that it is owing to its treatment of the gods that the *Iliad* does not remain simply a great tragedy but in a remarkable way reveals as profound a sense of comedy as of tragedy.

In the *Odyssey* the gods have a much smaller role. There too they play their part in furthering the action, but, with the exception of Athene, they are less closely connected with it. The idea of a council in heaven at the beginning of Books 1 and 5—the only such scenes in the poem—is clearly borrowed from the *Iliad*. But there is a striking contrast between the tumultuous Olympian disputes in the *Iliad* and the majestic council of superhuman beings in the *Odyssey*. The Zeus who presides over the latter council does not assert his supremacy by means of threats or physical violence. The personification of a cosmic moral order, he begins his speech about the fate of Odysseus with a general discussion of the problem of human suffering and the certain connection between destiny and human error. In the *Odyssey* it is stressed that the gods are not the cause of the evil that befalls man, that they honour justice and punish the wicked. In fact, the entire poem seeks constantly to justify the ways of god to man, for the whole story of Odysseus' sufferings and of the *hubris* of the suitors, the cause of their downfall, is informed by a moral and religious ideal.

The two worlds, divine and mortal, in which the Homeric narrative moves give it a strange double aspect. Every event is seen from two points of view, for each happens both on earth and in heaven. The effect of this is to reveal the limitations and short-sightedness of all human actions, for they depend, whether or not their agents know the fact, on the inscrutable decrees of superhuman forces.

At the same time, because the epic holds the gods to be implicated in every human circumstance, it is compelled to fit them into the general world scheme so as to define their eternal significance. This it does by measuring all human actions by moral and religious standards. The Greek epic thus possesses a far richer and more objective view of life than is found, for example, in any of the epics of the Middle Ages. It not only expresses the anthropocentric tendency of all later Greek thought; it also contains the germ of all subsequent Greek philosophy.

It must also be remembered that the Homeric conception of a world of the gods standing above and controlling the world of men was passed on to Virgil, Tasso and Milton—to mention only three authors of great literary epics—and to most of the epic parodies up to Voltaire's *Pucelle*.

The poetic excellence of the Homeric poems

The Homeric epics run counter to all that literary critics usually consider essential for the creation of great poetry. The language they employ was never a living idiom but an artificial poetic diction; the unit of composition was not the living word but a series of much used, stilted formulae; neither epic is the work of a single mind—rather, each is a product of the work of many poets belonging to widely different ages. Moreover, both poems contain composite descriptions of things that have never existed as described; in both, variants of scenes and episodes have been confusingly conflated; and their overall structure is clearly 'episodic'.

Yet the effect created by both the *Iliad* and the *Odyssey* is overwhelming. On what does it depend? In art generally, and in poetry particularly, the answers to such questions, if there are any at all, are difficult and many-sided. Nevertheless, some answers may be suggested.

The principal source of the epics' grandeur is the nobility and depth of the emotions described in them. They range from the wild indignation of the insulted warrior to the tragic despair of the young wife bidding farewell to her soldier husband; from the deep love of the old father for his dead son to the delicate shyness of the young affianced princess or the exhilarating reunion of husband and wife after long years of separation and suffering.

Much of the power of the emotions portrayed is due to the fact that in the epics life is always depicted against the sombre background of death. This endows it with a unique distinction. All that a man loves and loses is seen as if through the twilight of death and in a spirit of heroic regret which becomes an integral part of the epic mood, for the tragedy of one man's fate invariably broadens out to give us a deeper understanding of the tragic predicament of all humanity. But at the same time human tenderness is never allowed to degenerate into sentimentality. It is always presented in association with the highest and most manly aspirations, so that the fury of battle and the dearest memories of life are inextricably fused.

In this connection too we must not allow the courtesies of Glaucus and Diomedes or the civilized hospitality of Nestor to disguise from us the essential primitiveness and savagery of the heroic world. Hector is not always the devoted husband of *Iliad*, VI, nor the kind brother-in-law of Helen. At *Iliad*, XVII, 125f., for example, he starts to drag off the body of Patroclus so as to cut off the head and throw it to the dogs of Troy; and at XVIII, 176f., we learn that he wants to stick the head on a stake. Telemachus too, in a gruesome manner, elaborates his father's order to cut the throats of the guilty maidservants (*Odyssey*, 22, 443ff.; 462ff.). These crudities, in spite of their horror, give power and passion to the poems and provide an important reminder that the characters of their actors should not be sentimentalized.

Second, there is the dramatic manner in which the poet handles his material. At crucial points in the poems distinct characters—Agamemnon, Achilles, Odysseus, Hector—are brought to vivid, dramatic life; and their attitudes, as they speak and act in conflict with each other, provide the real force of the poems. Moreover, such scenes are of manageable length, and though some are naturally more highly charged than others, they display, on the whole, a striking economy of treatment. In both the epics few are the incidental themes which imply merely an ornamental view of poetry or a failure to understand the interrelation of parts in a dramatic structure.

Third, there is the sense of wonder with which the poet approaches his heroic world of the past, in which humanity is depicted in ideal terms. The warriors are taller, stronger and braver 'than men are today'; the women are 'white-armed', 'fair-ankled' and 'beautifully girdled'; the armour, the chariots, the buildings, the furniture, the clothes, the vessels are all conceived as exquisite; gold, silver, ivory, wool, linen and cedarwood abound. And the close contact between men and gods—gods who constantly interfere in the lives of the mortals—invests with something of a heavenly splendour that epic world from which the vulgar and the low are so markedly absent.

Thus the Homeric poems evoke in the mind of the hearer (or reader) the delight of the ideal, while at the same time carefully avoiding any intrusion of 'impossible' elements which would fragment the ideal picture. For that reason, when the Homeric epics exaggerate—something which all epic narratives have a tendency to do—the overstatements are never monstrous, fanciful or grotesque. They are always tempered by an awareness of human limitations and weaknesses. Even in the *Odyssey*, much of the material of which is taken from folk tales and sailors' yarns, the supernatural element is tempered and humanized and thus lifted into the realm of true poetry. The illusion of reality is never shattered. We always feel that we are in a real and not a fairy-tale world, and the feeling is enhanced by the fact that Homeric heroes never command magic powers. The supernatural is always presented as a function of the world of the gods, in which it can more readily be accepted. The humanization of saga and folk tale is, as has already been mentioned, among the greatest achievements of the Greek epic.

A fourth cause is to be found in the heroic view of life, tragic but inspiring, which may be described as hopelessness out of which grows not hope but glory. This is the spirit which permeates the magnificent reply of Hector to the appeal of Andromache in VI, 441–65, where we see a man facing doom with equanimity, contemplating certain death which, according to his code, he must meet and through which he must bear witness to the value of human life—the hero cheating death of its victory by making it the servant of a man's glory.

This tragic view of life is heightened by the epic device of casting the shadow of a coming tragedy across the scene of every triumph. Even when Achilles, at the very peak of his heroic achievement, finally slays Hector the words of the dying hero cast the shadow of death over the triumphant victor: 'Have a care, for I may be made into the gods' curse upon you, on that day when, for all your valour, Paris and Phoebus Apollo destroy you at the Scaean Gates' (XXII, 358f.).

By these means the impotence of mortal man is underlined; but at the same time the epics emphasize the splendour of the heroic code of conduct, which can snatch glory from human weakness in that inevitable confrontation of man with Fate (*Μοῖρα*).

Finally, there are the dignity and grandeur of the hexameter's majestic beat, and the wealth, brilliance and solemnity of the epic diction. For in the Homeric epics truly 'the manner fits the matter'. The form is worthy of and appropriate for the material it clothes.

The influence of the Homeric epics

The influence of the Homeric epics on subsequent Greek literature can hardly be exaggerated. In fact, standing as they do at the very threshold of Greek history, they were to become the teachers of the whole Western world.

The epic, elegiac, iambic and lyric poets who followed drew freely on Homer, as did the early epigrammatists and composers of oracles. Extracts of Homer were learned by heart at school (indeed, we know of instances when both epics were memorized in their entirety by certain scholars), and when the city-states began to take an interest in the education of their citizens, the Homeric epics were included in city festivals, especially those of Athens and Syracuse. The influence of Homer on the development of Attic tragedy is acknowledged by Aeschylus himself, when he remarks that his plays are 'slices' from Homer's banquets; and when we recall that history and the philosophical treatise, the two types of prose literature which had the greatest educational influence, were created out of a conflict between new ideas and the old assumptions of epic poetry, we can certainly endorse Plato's view[24] that Homer was the educator of Greece.

But that influence was not felt in literature and education alone. It was also paramount in art, in vase painting, mural painting and sculpture; for by the fifth century the Olympian gods had assumed a form which owed more to Homer than to the pantheon as we know it from earlier times.

Aristotle's great admiration for Homer was passed on by him to his pupil, Alexander, whose successors, the Hellenistic kings, fostered Homeric scholarship. For it was the scholars of Alexandria, with contributions from the antiquarian historians of Pergamum, who gave to the world the final text of Homer and a great deal of information about it. Above all, Homer became the standard textbook of the Hellenistic world, as is proved by the large numbers of extant Homeric papyri.

The Hellenistic poets both stood in awe of the Homeric epics and drew on them in their own strange way. And as we move on to the last decades of the ancient world, we find that it is again to Homer that the waning Hellenic spirit turned. But Quintus Smyrnaeus was a wooden and inferior imitator, and Nonnus, full of Oriental exuberance, was quite alien to the great model he set out to supersede.

The Byzantine Greeks rejected as false and ungodly the moral and religious teachings of the Homeric epics, but they fully accepted their aesthetic merits. Their admiration as we shall see, bore strange fruit in the *Homerokentra*, centos constructed from Homeric lines and half-lines, such as the verses of the Empress Eudocia; and it is remarkable that famous Byzantine scholars like Photius and Eustathius could be bishops of the Orthodox Church and at the same time great admirers and students of Homer.

In fact, throughout the life of the Byzantine Empire, Homer was used as a textbook in school, where it was taught side by side with the Scriptures. This custom persisted in the church schools of the East even after the fall of Constantinople in 1453, right up to the liberation of Greece in the nineteenth century. At that time Homer was included in the curriculum of the schools of the new Greek kingdom, so that it is true to say that not a single generation of Greeks has been educated, from the sixth century B.C. to the present day, without having been introduced to Homer, and that this constitutes the longest uninterrupted educational tradition in the Western world.

To turn from this tradition and to trace the influence on Western Europe of the Homeric poems in all their manifestations would be to spin out an interminable list of great names. Of these undoubtedly the most important is that of Virgil, whose *Aeneid* was, until the French Revolution, considered in the West to be the masterpiece of epic poetry. Homer's influence on Latin poetry had begun to assert itself, of course, before Virgil's time, with Livius Andronicus' translation of the *Odyssey* and with the poetry of Ennius, and it continued to do so for centuries. But it was in the footsteps of Virgil particularly that there followed the long line of literary works from Valerius Flaccus to Claudian, and then from Claudian to Ariosto, all of which owe a debt, although usually an indirect one, to the Homeric poems. Among them Dante's *Divina Commedia* occupies a very special place.

With the Quattrocènto and the Renaissance, Homer again became a chief object of enthusiasm; yet direct imitations are not found in Italian poetry. In France it was the Pléiade, with Pierre Ronsard, that developed the special feeling for Homer which in the eighteenth century spread to England and thence to Germany. The names of Milton, Pope, Lessing and Goethe suffice to illustrate the significance of the English and German contributions to the European tradition of literary epic. In the revival of Homeric studies in Germany at the turn of the eighteenth century Homer came to be considered the expression of absolute beauty, outside time and place. Oddly enough, the Romantic movement, in spite of the great admiration it felt for Homer, was not influenced by his poetry, probably because of its 'impersonal' nature. But it is true to say that from the beginning of the nineteenth century to the present day Homer has been universally considered the founder and father-figure of the whole Classical tradition.

HESIOD

Hesiod (c. 680 B.C.) was honoured by the Greeks as an epic poet second only to Homer. His father was an emigrant from Aeolian Cyme, who had established himself at Ascra in the Boeotian highlands—a place which was, as the poet tells us, 'bad in winter, stuffy in summer, good at no time of the year'.[25] Yet it was nearby, in the foothills of Mount Helicon, that the young Hesiod had the mystical experience, described in the *prooemium* (prelude) to his *Theogony*,[26] which turned him into a poet. As he was tending his sheep, he saw the Muses dancing round the violet-dark spring and the altar of Zeus, and then he heard their shrill laughter and their passionate voices singing at the summit of the mountain as they disappeared into a thick cloud. It was they who summoned him to proclaim in verse 'What will be and what has been'.

Thus Hesiod had a double calling, that of poet and that of seer, combined, for the first time in Greek poetry, as far as we know, in the same person. Hesiod is the first poet in Greek to address his own community in his own person, with the assurance of superior insight and without basing his claims to leadership on noble birth, public office or prowess in battle. The obvious comparison with the prophets of Israel has often been made.

The poetry of Hesiod clearly owes much to the Homeric style and diction—the techniques of oral poetry still prevailed—but it is very probable that he wrote his poems down or dictated them;[27] in which case the *Theogony* would be the first Greek poem known to us which does not, strictly speaking, belong to the world of oral poetry. At the same time—and this too is an important landmark—Hesiod abandoned the self-suppression of the Ionic bards and came forward in his own person, giving the reader some biographical data in both of his extant poems and even, in the *prooemium* to the *Theogony*, naming himself in what constitutes the first *sphragis* in Greek poetry.[28] This new personal element opened the way which Archilochus and, after him, other iambic, elegiac and lyric poets were to follow.

Two principal works of Hesiod survive to this day. the *Theogony*,[29] or book of the Generation of the Gods; and the *Works and Days*. Of a third, the *Catalogue of Women*, which was ascribed to him in antiquity, we have only fragments.

The *Theogony* is a work of wide scope, describing the origin, genealogies and functions of the gods (including such non-Olympian divinities as Earth, Sea and Sky) and the events which led up to the kingship of Zeus. Although Hesiod's *Theogony* is the only representative of its type to survive, it was, as we shall see, by no means unique. In the archaic period the genre was cultivated as actively as was the heroic.

The structure of the *Theogony*[30] is based on the 'succession myth', which relates how the rule of the world passed from one to another of three divinities: Uranus, Kronos and Zeus. The whole work is prefaced by a hymn to the Muses (1–104).

The transference of power from one of these divinities to another is violent. Kronos castrates his father Uranus and thus wins the kingdom, then he devours his own children; but the new-born Zeus is saved by his mother and concealed on Crete. There the future ruler of the world grows up until, in battle with the Titans, he wins the throne and keeps it ever after. The poem is remarkable for the moral progression in terms of which it presents the coming of Zeus, whose victory over Kronos and the Titans is seen as a victory for law, order and justice.

In his conception of a just Zeus Hesiod goes far beyond the theology of the *Odyssey*; in fact, it is with the *Theogony* that the line of development starts which leads to Solon and culminates in the lofty Aeschylean conception of Zeus. Although Hesiod attributed noble qualities to the ruler of the universe, however, he did not regard the world as a happy place to live in, and both of his extant poems are marked by a deep pessimism.

Hesiod's 'succession myth' has striking parallels in Akkadian and Hittite texts and seems to have come from the Near East, so a connection with Oriental mythology may well be assumed. The myth may have been transmitted from the East during the Minoan–Mycenaean period, when Greece was open to Oriental influences, or it may have been handed down to Hesiod as part of a traditional epic theogony—for, as we know, continuous poetic development existed from the Bronze Age to historical times. Whichever is the case, it is clear that a considerable span of time must be assumed, since all the foreign elements in Hesiod's mythology have been fully assimilated.

If the 'succession myth' is the backbone of the *Theogony*, the genealogies are its flesh and blood. In Hesiod's scheme the first powers to be born were Chaos, Earth and Eros (116–22). From Chaos and Earth, in two separate lines, some 300 gods descended (for Hesiod the word 'god' embraces beings of very diverse kinds, among them gods of cult and of mythology; elements of the visible world, such as Uranus, Aether and rivers; things which we should call abstractions, such as Death, Sleep, Deceit, Strife and Power; as well as other beings not known to us in myth or cult—for example, Meliae, Thaumas, Keto, Astraeus and others.)

To work into a system the formerly fluid legends of the gods and their offspring was no easy affair. The genealogical relationships of the gods of mythology and cult must have been a matter of traditional knowledge to the poet, but in other cases he probably had to improvise; his inventions are often conditioned by association rather than by logical development.

At the same time it is noteworthy that in Hesiod's explanation of the world moral forces take their place beside the natural forces of the earth and air. The poet is not content merely to show the relationships of the traditional divinities but aspires to unite all religious elements—cult, myth and psychological experience—into a history of the origins of the world and the beginnings of human life. In doing this he not only gives new interpretations to old deities, but he also introduces fresh personifications to satisfy the urge towards abstract thinking which was then gaining strength in the Greek world. For it is also interesting to observe that the elements of the visible world (Uranus, Ge and the rest) were thought of as having simultaneously anthropomorphic shapes and their own physical forms of sky, earth and so on—a conceptual fluidity characteristic of archaic Greece. In the realm of humbler mythology, with its numerous rivers and river gods, woods and wood nymphs, that habit of thought lasted for a very long time and gave rise to many light-hearted inventions in Hellenistic poetry

As we have seen, Hesiod brings Eros into his scheme of things. The predominant place the god occupies in the *Theogony* as a cosmic force which creates love has been attributed to the cult of Eros in Thespiae, by which a Boeotian poet could well have been influenced. However that may be, the Hesiodic idea of Eros and his description[31] had a stimulating effect on later poetry and philosophy: Archilochus, Sappho and Plato are but a few of those who owe a debt to Hesiod.

Another section of the *Theogony* which was to have a bearing on the development of Greek poetry is the entertaining passage dealing with the myth of Prometheus. This aetiological excursus influenced all subsequent Greek poetry of the genre. First, it explains why the parts of sacrificed animals which are reserved for the gods should consist of the bones wrapped in fat. Then we learn how men came to have fire. Finally, Hesiod gives the reasons why women were created, and why they are so designed that man's life is as insupportable without them as with them. Hesiod was as sternly critical of women in his *Works and Days*. In fact, he is the first misogynist in Greek poetry, anticipating in this respect Semonides and many other later poets. In Hesiod, however, the attack has not advanced beyond the general—it is womankind as a whole that is condemned. It is not until Archilochus that we find satire attacking a specific woman.

Finally, in the *prooemium* of the *Theogony* two further interesting elements make their first appearance in Greek poetry. The first is the distinction drawn between the arts and the lower sphere of day-to-day necessities: the Muses are not friendly to the shepherds, calling them idle wretches, no more than bellies. The second element is the beginnings of the literary polemic. The Muses, speaking of their own activities, say that their language is often falsehood, bearing merely the appearance of truth, but they claim that they can also speak the truth if they are so inclined. It seems that in Hesiod's view there were two kinds of poetry, the truthful and the misleading: he himself feels called upon to enshrine the truth in his verses. This is a prefiguring of the way that early philosophers took the poets to task for untruthfulness and thus establishes a tradition which was to flourish in Classical, Hellenistic, Byzantine and even modern Greek poetry.

The *Theogony* ends with the marriages of Zeus and the other Olympians and a list of the goddesses who lay with mortal men. This last section, which leads on to the *Catalogue of Women or Ehoiai* ('Hοῖαι),[32] is post-Hesiodic, though opinions differ as to where the authentic part ends.

The *Works and Days* is more celebrated than the *Theogony*, which ante-dates it.[33] It is addressed to Hesiod's brother Perses, against whom he had a grievance. It appears that on their father's death there was a dispute between the two brothers over the inheritance, and that the lawsuit (through the injustice and corruption of the judges, as Hesiod believed) went in favour of Perses. The work is lacking in design and abounds in entertaining irrelevancies; but what becomes evident on examination is that the poem begins with the concrete fact of the lawsuit with the brother—which lends a dramatic quality to the first part of the poem— then broadens out into a discussion of the powers to which human life is subject, in the process leading the reader from the particular to the general.

Thus, despite its starting-point, the poem ultimately offers advice about living a life of honest toil. Hesiod speaks out against dishonesty and idleness, using in turn myths, such as the Prometheus myth and the story of Pandora (42–105) or the story of the Five Ages of the World (106– 201); parable (202–12); allegory (286–92); proverbial maxims; direct exhortation; and threats of divine anger.

Besides moral advice, much practical instruction is given on agriculture, seafaring and social and religious conduct. The final section, the *Days*, consists of an almanac of the days in the month which are favourable or unfavourable for different operations. It is regarded by many as a later addition.

In the *Works and Days* there is sharp conflict between a pessimistic view of life, in which toil and hardship are seen as the lot of man, and a religious belief in absolute moral values. In his desire to teach his brother the truth Hesiod speaks, characteristically, through a myth concerning the two kinds of strife (*eris*) which exist in the world. One is evil and is sent by the gods to plague mankind, while the other, 'emulation', is good and leads to honourable competition. Perses, Hesiod says, should abandon his destructive opposition to his brother and, directed by the force of emulation, gain his livelihood by honest toil, for that is what justice demands (11– 41).

Thus work and justice, the two subjects of the poem, are stated, and the bond uniting the two is made clear. For, in Hesiod's view, man's instinct for *eris* must be satisfied, whether for good or for ill. If directed towards work, it is beneficial, acting as an incentive to achievement; but if it turns towards rivalry, it proves destructive. Thus the only way to achieve justice is through work, a maxim in which the poem's whole moral is expressed. (Indeed, in the poem work is actually equated with justice.) From this premise the poem launches into a description of the life and work of the peasant and, finally, of the peasant calendar.

That toil and hardship is the gods' portion for man is explained by two other myths which follow and which partly complement each other. The first is that of Prometheus. The poet takes up the story, which he has already told in the *Theogony*, of the theft of fire by Prometheus and its punishment by Zeus, who sends woman into the world. Despite the warning of his brother, Prometheus, Epimetheus receives the captivating stranger. But she, in opening the lid of a box (*pithos*) which she has brought with her, causes every evil known to man to fly out and infest the world. Hope alone is trapped in the box when Pandora replaces the lid.

The miseries of the world are then illustrated by a second myth, that of the 'ages of the world' (106–201), according to which the earth has been inhabited by five succeeding ages: the Golden, the Silver, the Bronze, the Age of Heroes and that of Iron. To the steady decline from the Golden Age to that of Iron, Hesiod's own, there is acknowledged to be only one exception: the Heroic Age.

Hesiod's view is that those who abandon themselves to excess perish miserably, while those who practise justice are honoured by the gods. It is now up to the present age, that of the Iron generation, to decide its own fate. It should bear in mind that justice preserves society, while excess destroys it.

The myth of the 'ages of the world' is followed first by an admonition to the kings, Hesiod's unjust judges, and to the poet's brother Perses, and second by the fable of the hawk and the nightingale—the first fable in Greek poetry—which is introduced to demonstrate the horrors of the concept 'might is right'. The miseries of the Age of Iron in which the poet lives are depicted in detail; it is a world in which hardships, sickness and moral depravity prevail. The fate of the present generation will be sealed when *Aidos* (Shame) and *Nemesis* (Righteous Anger) leave the world. Hesiod's pessimism is no resigned scepticism. Zeus, in his view, has provided a means whereby mankind can avoid this disastrous battle of each against each: the indestructible saving power of *Dike* (Justice), a concept which was to become one of the basic themes of Greek thought and literature. In fact, by connecting Zeus with *Dike*, Hesiod takes a great step forward in the history of religion.[34]

From lines 383ff. start the enumeration and description of the work of the fields, and the structure of the poem becomes much simpler. Advice on agriculture, as we have seen, is followed by advice on navigation, and the poem gradually ebbs amid a final series of unassimilated pieces of advice. Among these, some of the superstitious maxims and the final section concerning fortunate and unfortunate days cannot be genuinely the work of Hesiod.

The *Works and Days* is by no means a course of systematic instruction in husbandry; rather, it is a mixture of practical advice and hints culled from general experience. The harsher side of peasant life is not disguised, and for this very reason it is the first poem in European literature in which true value is assigned to the toil that wins our bread. The poet believes that heroism is shown not only in the field of battle, but also in the endless, quiet struggle of the farmer against the stubborn earth and the elements. The slow, changeless wisdom of the countryman and his relentless daily toil are here presented for the first time as *arete*. In the process—and this, too, is a landmark in European literature—Hesiod becomes the first Western poet to write of nature for its own sake.

Of Hesiod's poetry we may say that it teaches in the real sense of the word, not simply in that broad sense in which all great poets teach, even without intending to do so. His object is to impress on men's memories certain things which it is good for them to know: moral and religious truths, practical advice on agriculture, housekeeping, navigation, astronomy and divination. That is why he is rightly considered the father of didactic poetry and thus the founder of a school whose influence on Greek poetry can be traced without interruption to our own era.

In order to achieve its aims, successful didactic poetry sets out to please as well as to teach, on the ground that pleasure is the best aid to memory. But in this latter respect Hesiod's poetry falls far short of the Homeric epics. There may be more reflection in Hesiod, but there is certainly less imagination. He never indulges in the beautiful for its own (or the reader's) sake but contents himself with seeing that everything is clear and useful, directing the reader towards the right and the seemly. He is a teacher before he is an artist; he does not know how to tell a story, nor how to develop it, nor how to bring it to life by introducing vivid figures; and there are no tragic destinies in his poetry. It contains, of course, some fine passages, such as his magnificent description of winter[35] or that of Zeus attacking the Titans.[36] But despite these beauties it has been truly said that one must forget Homer in order to enjoy Hesiod, who lives always in the harsh present and on the whole ignores the grandeur of the heroic past.[37] Quintilian was perfectly right when he said that Hesiod *raro adsurgit* —least of all in the long, boring catalogues of gods and their offspring which take up so much of the *Theogony*. Indeed, this style of narration by catalogue came to be called by the Alexandrians the *Hesiodios Tropos*.[38] While it is true that the word-music and the mythological and other associations of such catalogues of names may have a certain charm of their own, in the long run they become tedious.

Hesiod has been called a visionary and a prophet, but this is a misrepresentation. He does not quote oracles or the sayings of the gods, nor does he have any real contact with the supernatural, except in his first meeting with the Muses, an experience which cannot, however, be called truly mystical. Moreover, he does not advance a new moral code or introduce new gods. He merely repeats with conviction what was in his own day already old and known to thousands. He cannot even be called a preacher in any real sense.

Nevertheless, his influence on Classical Greek thought and literature was very great; in the Hellenistic world it was he and not Homer who was considered the founder of what came to be known as the 'School of Callimachus', and his influence on the Virgil of the *Georgics* was also far-reaching. In fact, Hesiod's stature and influence are sufficient to justify the comparison between him and Homer which antiquity repeatedly made and which gave rise to the story of a competition between the two fathers of the epic.[39]

Hesiod's literary posterity is more varied than that of Homer and includes more obscure poets. The genealogical *epos*, which he pioneered, has two lines of development, of which the first lived on, as we shall see, in the regional traditions of various parts of Greece. We hear of the Naupactian, the Samian and the Phocaean Verses; but either they are transmitted without the author's name, or they are given to poets of local fame, the regional equivalents of the Boeotian Hesiod: 'Carcinus' of Naupactus, 'Eumelus' of Corinth and 'Asius' of Samos. The other line of development grew out of the *Ehoiai* poetry. As this genre developed in the hands of Mimnermus, Antimachus and Hermesianax, it took on the colour of romantic or erotic elegy, often taking the form of lists of lovers of past ages, sometimes even with the names of their children.

The didactic element in Hesiod also gave rise to more than one line of development. Out of it grew, on the one hand, the moralizing or gnomic epics of Phocylides, the proverbs of the Seven Wise Men, the Elegies of Solon and Theognis; and its influence can be detected even on the iambics of Archilochus, Semonides of Amorgos, and Hipponax. On the other hand, it gave rise to the poetry of science and learning. Hesiod himself was credited with an *Astronomy* and a *Tour of the Earth*. In general, however, epics with such subjects cannot be traced to individual authors before the fourth century B.C. and did not achieve real popularity until the Hellenistic period. But from early times the main stream of didactic epic became religious. 'Hesiod' fell under the spell of 'Orpheus'.

In addition to the genuinely Hesiodic works discussed above, the prestige of the poet's name attracted to itself several poems which were certainly not by him. The *Shield of Heracles*, a short, second-rate epic of 480 lines, owing something to Homer's account of the *Shield of Achilles*, is a case in point. Heracles' fight with Cycnus forms the subject-matter of what is, by any standard, a quite disproportionate work: the full Homeric apparatus, including divine interventions, taunting speeches and long similes, is lavished on an encounter in which but two blows are struck. However, the poem is interesting as the only surviving specimen of a type which must once have been common—the short heroic lay. The *Catalogue of Women*, or *Ehoiai*, which was a continuation of the *Theogony* in five books, containing heroic genealogies and many narrative annotations, is another such instance. Numerous citations and extensive papyrus fragments survive, but although the ancient world considered it genuinely Hesiodic and it offered material for tragedy, it does not antedate the sixth century.

Several other narrative and didactic poems, now lost, were also attributed to Hesiod, all wrongly, among them two concerned with episodes in the story of Heracles.[40]

THE HOMERIC HYMNS

Like doctors, seers and artisans, the rhapsodes of the archaic period were originally itinerant; and it is through these wandering bards—the *Homeridae*—that knowledge of Homer was spread throughout the Greek lands. As a factor in the unification of Greek literature, this was of enormous significance.

A further activity of the *Homeridae* was the production of what we know as the Homeric Hymns.[41] It was a custom in early antiquity to introduce an epic recitation at feasts and public holidays with the invocation of a god, particularly the god at whose festival the rhapsode was performing. Depending on his talent, the bard might, before going on to the *Iliad*, the *Odyssey* or any other long epic composition, offer his audience and the local god a new poem of merit; or he might content himself with a few formal, pious verses of no great importance.

Both these varieties are given the name of *prooemion*. Examples of both kinds found their way into a collection of thirty-three hymns preserved more or less complete in a number of manuscripts. Most of the poems probably belong to the seventh century B.C., but only six are of real importance. They are dedicated to the gods Apollo, Demeter, Hermes, Aphrodite, Dionysus and Pan.

The *Hymn to Apollo*, as transmitted, consists of what are really two hymns, one to the Delian (III, 1–178), and the other to the Delphic Apollo (III, 179–end), which have been joined together. The *Hymn to Apollo of Delos* is perhaps the earliest of all the so-called Homeric Hymns. Its date cannot be exactly determined, but most scholars would place it in the seventh century. Its subject is the birth of Apollo (a rather unusual version);[42] and it also contains some biographical details about its author, for at the end we learn that he is a blind man dwelling in 'craggy Chios'. This seems to be the source (or one of the sources) of the later idea that Homer was a blind Chian bard.[43]

The *Hymn to Apollo of Delphi* is a later composition, wrongly transmitted as a continuation of the previous Hymn. It is much poorer poetry but is important for the large number of mythological and geographical references it contains. It tells of Apollo's choice of a site for his temple. Fixing on Delphi, he kills its resident dragon, punishes Telphusa, a nymph of the spring, and transports a ship-load of Cretans to be priests at his shrine.

The *Hymn to Demeter* (II) is one of the best such poems to have survived. It is a short epic in itself, written by a man of wide range and singular talent, which in 495 lines tells of Demeter's sorrows and of how, in her quest for the abducted Persephone, she comes to Eleusis, where, after reclaiming her daughter, she founds the celebrated Mysteries. A seventh-century date for the Hymn is probable, since it makes no mention of Athens, which annexed Eleusis in 610 B.C. The presumption is that the latter was still independent when the Hymn was written.

The *Hymn to Hermes* (IV) is a delightful piece of poetry which takes us into a world of gay adventure, quite unconcerned with moral questions. The poet laughs with and at his god in telling how Hermes invented the lyre on the day he was born and tricked Apollo by stealing his cattle, and how the divine brothers were reconciled. The poem cannot be fixed earlier than the seventh century for, among other things, the language departs considerably from Homeric usage. In particular the *digamma* is much neglected.

The *Hymn to Aphrodite* (V) reflects discredit on the goddess, for it tells how Zeus, to punish her for the havoc she has caused among the gods, makes her fall in love with a mortal, Anchises. After obtaining her desire in the guise of a mortal, she reveals herself as a goddess—Anchises is struck blind in the process—and foretells the birth of Aeneas. Although no exact date can be given for him, the writer, whoever he may have been, was a good poet and a fairly early one.

Dionysus is also the subject of a Hymn (VII) of unknown date and authorship,[44] of which we can only say that it is not very late. It tells in fifty-nine lines how the god is captured by Tyrrhenian pirates but turns into a lion and pursues his captors into the sea. The *Hymn to Pan* (XIX) is even shorter and probably much later,[45] for Pan was scarcely known outside his native Arcadia until after the sixth century B.C. The legend of Pan's birth and his presentation on Olympus by his father Hermes, is told here not directly by the poet, but as though from the mouth of Pan's company, the mountain nymphs.

The remaining twenty-seven Homeric Hymns celebrate various gods and demigods, among them Helios and Selene, and are of little significance (if any) as poetry.[46]

EPIC POETRY OTHER THAN THE HOMERIC AND THE HESIODIC

In the archaic Greek world a large body of epic verse circulated in addition to the Homeric and Hesiodic poems. Only a few fragments of this verse have survived, and a few names of poems and poets, which add little to our knowledge and appreciation of Greek poetry. There is, however, little doubt that this verse influenced representational art of the sixth and fifth centuries, as well as lyrical poetry and drama.

The disseminators of this material, the rhapsodes, were originally itinerant. Gradually, however, they settled into local guilds, to which

city-states gave certain rights, so that they sometimes enjoyed a very long
local life. Thus in Chios, as we have seen, we find the *Homeridae*, and in
Colophon (one of the cities, incidentally, which laid claim to Homer) the
epic tradition continued, apparently without interruption, down to Anti-
machus and Nicander in Hellenistic times.

In archaic times epic production flourished in mainland Greece, for on
the old Greek soil and the major islands numerous stories similar to those
which had existed in Ionia circulated, awaiting their poets; and the
aristocracy of the mainland and the islands were eager for their own
achievements and those of their forefathers and the founders of their cities
to be celebrated in verse.

Such material as has survived from those older and apparently lesser
epics may be conveniently classified as follows.[47]

Theogonies, theomachies and astronomical poems

The early Greeks, like other peoples, attempted to explain the origin of the
world in terms of the mating and the offspring of primeval divinities. But
the various divine genealogies and the many lost theogonical poems in
which they did this seem often to give different accounts from those in
Hesiod and Homer. Thus Herodotus' statement that these two poets gave
the Greeks their gods is only partly true.

Of the lost theogonies and theomachies, one, the *Titanomachia*, deserves
mention, if only for one beautiful fragment which has survived.[48] The
greater part of the poem, however, remains a matter for speculation, and
its authorship is a problem equally obscure. It has been attributed to
Eumelus of Corinth (eighth century B.C.), to Arctinus of Miletus (prob-
ably also eighth century) or 'to anyone else who rejoices in being called
author', as Athenaeus puts it.[49]

In conjunction with poetry of this kind there existed a body of hex-
ameter verse on the constellations, their identification and their myth-
ology. This, too, is now lost.

The Trojan epic cycle

The term epic cycle is used to describe a collection of early Greek epics
arranged in an artificial series so as to form a narrative extending from the
beginning of the world to the end of the Heroic Age. Apart from the *Iliad*
and the *Odyssey*, we possess only scanty fragments of the poems involved,
and our knowledge even of which poems were included in the total series is
incomplete. We are best informed about those that dealt with the Trojan

War and related events, including what is called the Trojan Cycle, which seems to have been compiled not later than the fourth century B.C.

There were six such works, besides the Homeric poems, that were attributed to different poets of the seventh and sixth centuries. These were entitled the *Cypria*, the *Aethiopis*, the *Mikra Ilias*, the *Iliou Persis*, the *Nostoi* and the *Telegonia*. The material of these non-Homeric epics was not, however, as in the case of the *Iliad* and the *Odyssey*, assimilated into the structure of the individual poem. Belonging at least partly to the oral tradition, the lays and groups of lays were left for each reciter to modify and select from as he chose. So it comes about that to many of these poems are attached the names of more than one poet—many of which probably belonged to real rhapsodes. It is not known at what date these epics assumed their final shape.

Our knowledge of the epics rejected from the Homeric corpus comes almost entirely from the ancient handbooks of mythology which, having extracted from the epics their legendary and historical content, reassembled them in groups of cycles. Our main authority is Proclus,[50] and it is in him that we find a summary of the Trojan Cycle. But from quotations in earlier writers it can be seen that the individual poems covered much more ground than is allowed for in his brief account.

These cyclic poems (the term is conventionally taken to exclude the *Iliad* and the *Odyssey*) were sometimes loosely attributed to Homer,[51] but Herodotus refutes the idea in the case of the *Cypria*[52] and queries it in the case of the *Epigonoi*;[53] and later writers generally use the names of obscurer poets or the expression ὁ (τὰ Κύπια, etc.) ποιήσας.

Like the *Iliad* and the *Odyssey*, the six lost epics of the Trojan Cycle drew on traditional tales, many of them very old. The first part of the Cycle consisted of the *Cypria*,[54] allegedly by Stasinus of Cyprus (or, according to others, by Hegesias of Cyprian Salamis), and is said to have comprised eleven books, which formed a long preface to the *Iliad*. It dealt with all the events preceding the Trojan War—the wedding of Peleus and Thetis, the judgement of Paris and the abduction of Helen—and all the earlier part of the war until the point where the *Iliad* begins. The *Cypria* were read and valued throughout Classical antiquity: Herodotus, Euripides, Plato and Aristotle were familiar with them, and the tragedians drew much material from them.

After the *Cypria* the tale was taken up by the *Iliad*, which was followed in its turn by the *Aethiopis*. This consisted of five books and was ascribed to Arctinus of Miletus (c. 700 B.C.). It chiefly concerned the death of the Amazon Penthesilea at the hand of Achilles; the death of Thersites; the arrival of Memnon, son of Eos, to aid the Trojans, bringing weapons made by Hephaestus; the defeat of Memnon by Achilles; as well as the latter's own death and burial.

There followed the *Mikra Ilias*, a poem in four books attributed to

Lesches of Mytilene (or Pyrrha), Thestorides of Phocaea, Cynaethon, and Diodorus of Erythrae. It included the death of Ajax as well as the fetching of Philoctetes and Neoptolemus to the Greek camp, the episode of the Trojan Horse, the part played by Sinon, and the Greek entry into Troy. Presumably, the poem acquired the name, Ἰλιάς independently of our *Iliad*, and was then called 'little' (μικρά) in order to distinguish between the two.

The fourth of the cyclic epics was the *Iliou Persis*, or the *Sack of Troy*, a work also attributed to Arctinus or to Lesches (c. 700 B.C.), his contemporary and, by general consent, a superior poet. It consisted of two books and included the episodes of the Wooden Horse and of Laocoon and the two snakes, the sack of Troy and the departure of the Greeks. In this version, it is interesting to note, Aeneas and his followers left the city before the sack, and not afterwards, as Virgil tells the tale. The title *Iliou Persis* was shared by a poem by Stesichorus.

Fifth came the *Nostoi*, or the *Return of the Heroes*, reportedly in five books and ascribed to the Troizenian poet Agias (or Hegias), who is quite unknown to us, or to Eumelus. The poem told of the return from Troy of various Greek heroes and ended with the murder of Agamemnon, the revenge of Orestes and Menelaus' homecoming. The *Odyssey* itself is aware of an Ἀχαιῶν νόστοι (1, 326; 10, 15); and Stesichorus also wrote a *Nostoi*.

The cycle was completed by the *Telegonia*, which consisted of two books and was attributed to Eugammon of Cyrene (c. 566 B.C.). The subject-matter combined tradition with invention. It gave an account of Odysseus' wanderings in Thesprotia; of a second marriage of the hero and a victorious campaign against the Bryges; of the wanderings of Odysseus to placate Poseidon; of the search for his father by Telegonus, Odysseus' son by Circe; of Telegonus' landing in Ithaca, his plunder and the ensuing fight in which he kills Odysseus — the tragic father-and-son theme. At the end Circe, having conferred immortality on the survivors, marries Telemachus, while Telegonus takes Penelope to wife.[55]

The cyclic epics, more interesting for their content than for their poetry, were important sources of material for Attic tragedy and hence not unfamiliar in fifth-century Athens; however, they passed gradually into oblivion. They were, of course, quoted in scholia by Alexandrian scholars, some of whom (Zenodotus, for example) tried to reconcile Homer with the cyclic poets and to explain Homer through them. On the other hand, the school of Aristarchus underlined the difference between them and dismissed with contempt the works of these Homeric *epigonoi*.[56]

The erudite Hellenistic and Roman poets also continued to draw on the cyclic epics; but the general public, and even the specialists, simply used prose summaries of them. Thus they survived, though discredited, until the Classicizing Period (A.D. 100–330), when Peisander of

Laranda reassembled nearly all of the cyclical material and much more besides in his gigantic epic *Heroic Theogamies*.[57] In the process, he caused their final disappearance.[58]

The Theban epics

Besides the Hesiodic *Catalogue of Women*,[59] which presented systematically the legends concerning Cadmus, his descendants and his successors at Thebes, there were three other great epic poems devoted to Thebes and her blood-stained history—the *Oedipodeia*, the *Thebais* and the *Epigonoi*. These are usually known as the Theban Cycle which was treated by ancient grammarians as an introduction to the Trojan Cycle.

The *Oedipodeia*, a work of 6600 lines, was ascribed to Cynaethon, a Lacedaemonian poet whom Eustathius[60] placed before the middle of the eighth century B.C., certainly too early a date. The poem dealt with the defeat of the Sphinx and Oedipus' marriage with Jocasta. Moreover, we know that in the *Oedipodeia* the curse of Jocasta, who took her own life, pursued Oedipus till he fell in battle against the Minyae—a different version of the myth from the familiar Sophoclean one.

Next came the *Thebais*, in 700 lines, which Callinus, as early as the seventh century B.C., ascribed to Homer and which Pausanias valued next only to the *Iliad* and the *Odyssey*. The subject-matter included the repeated curse called down on his sons by Oedipus and fulfilled by their killing each other, as well as the repulse of the expedition of the Seven against Thebes. Echoes found in later poetry suggest that the siege was described in the poem in great detail.

Of equal length to the preceding poem, the *Epigonoi* (the 'lay of those who come after') was likewise ascribed to Homer by Herodotus,[61] though not without doubts. Whereas in the *Thebais* the men of Tydeus' generation failed to conquer Thebes, the *Epigonoi* tells how the next generation succeeded in this venture.

The Theban epics provided much material for the mythological warfare which was sometimes waged between Greek city-states. The Attic tragedians also drew on them extensively.

Loosely connected with the Theban epics were two mantic poems, the *Alcmaeonis* and the *Melampodeia*. The first dealt with the story of Alcmaeon, son of the seer Amphiaraus, a Theban counterpart of Orestes, and the second—which was also attributed to Hesiod—with Melampus, the prophet who used the voices of birds and reptiles for divining.

Argive, Corinthian, Naupactian, Samian, Cretan and Attic epics

For their stories about Argos, Tiryns, Mycenae and their heroic past later writers on the Argolid drew on a now-lost epic, the *Phoronis*, named after the mythical King Phoroneus, whom it held up as the first man and ancestor of the human race.

We know little of the *Phoronis*, and even less about another Argive epic, the *Danais*. Of the dates of both these obscure poems all that can be said with certainty is that they were earlier than the prose writer Acusilaus (c. 450 B.C.), who made use of them, along with the great mass of genealogical poetry ascribed to Hesiod.[62]

The tale of the Argonauts and their bold voyage over dangerous, unknown waters (echoes of it are found in the *Odyssey*) would naturally have spread during the early stages of Greek colonial expansion in the eighth century B.C. The story seems to have found special favour in Corinth, and it was the Corinthian Eumelus, the son of Amphilytus and a member of the great family of the Bacchiadae (c. 730 B.C.), who linked an epic local Corinthian cult with the story of Jason. We know little of Eumelus except that he was also, as we have seen, credited with the *Titanomachia*. Another work ascribed to him, the *Corinthiaca*, was probably not connected with the Argonaut story, and he is less assuredly associated with the surviving fragments of a poem on Dionysus called the *Europia*.

The shadowy figure of Eumelus hangs over all subsequent Corinthian poetry. No other Corinthian poet is named in the archaic period; and although he gave his city a glorious (and largely fictitious) history, he was also probably the reason why her local epic tradition became prematurely fossilized.[63]

More than a century after Eumelus the story of the Argonauts was again made the subject of a poem by Epimenides, the religious teacher and wonder-worker of Crete (c. 500 or 600 B.C.). The titles of his works— *Theogony, Cretica*—reveal his interest in local history and the theogonical tradition, but he is also named as author of a poem about the building of the Argo and the journey of Jason to the Colchians, which is said to have been 5000 lines long. There exist some fragments which evidently come from it.[64]

By contrast with Eumelus, Asius of Samos can be dated from reasonably substantial evidence. The son of Amphiptolemus (early sixth century),[65] he set out to provide his native island with a mythological prehistory which would rival that of Crete. He seems to have been a patriot, a tendentious mythologist and genealogist, and a satirist who shows something of the light-hearted, critical spirit of his time.

As far as we can see, Attica contributed little to epic poetry.[66] The epics mentioned on Athenian subjects, notably the Theseus legends, emerge late by comparison with the poetry of Boeotia, the Argolid and Corinth; and they were overtaken from about 500 B.C. by tragedy, the new — and to the Athenians more stimulating — poetic expression of heroic ideas.

Theseus, for Athenian reasons, vied in popularity with Heracles as a mythical figure. But specific literary evidence for Athenian Theseus epics is scanty, and the names of their composers were lost early. Plutarch mentions 'the author of the *Theseus*',[67] a poem which may well have been composed late in the sixth century. The *Minyas*—its title is unexplained —is also said to have contained events from Theseus' life, and it is known that the same work was the source of Polygnotus' celebrated painting of Hades at Delphi.[68]

Epics about Heracles

The end of the traditional epics came as the idea of literary property gathered strength. A rhapsode like Cynaethus would manipulate the Homeric passages he recited without wishing to publish the results as his own work. Onomacritus would attribute to Orpheus his laborious theology without intending dissimulation. But by the sixth and fifth centuries Homer, Hesiod and 'Orpheus' had made room for a new breed of poets who stood on their own feet and spoke in their own person.

The first such man of whom we hear is Pisander of Camirus in Rhodes (c. 650 B.C.), who wrote an epic called the *Heracleia*. It dealt with the tale of Heracles, a story which can be traced back to very early times—in Homer it is already well developed—and probably goes back to the Mycenaean age. In his treatment of the story Pisander seems to have been chiefly concerned with those labours which the hero performed for Eurystheus, and there is reason for supposing that he was the first to limit the number of Heracles' labours to twelve.[69] We do not know how long the *Heracleia* was, nor indeed anything more about it save that its author was highly regarded on Rhodes, as is also evident from Theocritus' epigrams.

Poets less enterprising than Pisander limited themselves to individual episodes from the life of Heracles. Such a man was Creophylos of Samos, whose epic on the sack of Oechalia was even thought good enough to be attributed to Homer.[70] Others believed Creophylos to have received the poem from Homer when being entertained as his guest, while others called him a Chian and Homer's son-in-law. Creophylos seems, in fact, to have been one of the first bards to be numbered among the *Homeridae* without also being called a descendant of Homer. His date is unknown, but the link with Homer would imply a period nearer 700 than 600 B.C.

As we have seen, there were three more poems concerned with episodes in the story of Heracles which were spuriously ascribed to Hesiod. These are the *Wedding of Keyx* and the *Aegimius*, which related how the Dorians of

Doris were aided by Heracles in a war with the Lapiths, and the pseudo-Hesiodic *Shield of Heracles*, discussed above. Such poems cannot have been on a very large scale.

When Panyassis, son of Polyarchus of Halicarnassus, who fell in battle against the tyrant Lygdamis in 460 B.C., set out to give expression to the Heracles legends in their fullest form, he returned to a continuous treatment in the manner of Pisander. His *Heracleias* was in fourteen books and a total of 9000 verses. Ancient critics praised the poem's structure and placed the author, together with Homer, Hesiod, Antimachus and Pisander, in the canon of the five great epic poets. Such literary remains as have reached us show a poet who, while accepting and using the traditional tales, delights in moralizing and in the unusual. We know almost nothing, on the other hand, of the same poet's *Ionica*, a poem in 7000 verses dealing with the foundation of the Ionian colonies.

To round off the picture of the epic prior to the Alexandrian period, mention should be made of Choerilus of Samos, of the late fifth century, whose *Persica* is one of the earliest important historical epics in the modern sense.[71] In more than one book it told of the Persian Wars and contained a catalogue of the tribes which crossed the Hellespont with Xerxes. Surviving fragments attest to the skill and originality of Choerilus, who was also probably the author of the *Samiaca*, a poem about the foundation and history of Samos. Lysander, the Spartan general and statesman, while in Samos cultivated the poet in the hope of epic immortality, and Archelaus invited him to the Macedonian court, where he died in 395 B.C.

Epic parodies and related trifles

As the epic tradition grew old, it produced a few trifles, including parodies. In antiquity the most famous of these was the *Margites*, a work frequently (though wrongly) ascribed to Homer. Its hero, a renowned idiot, was unable to count above five; he would not lie with his bride for fear she would give a bad report of him to her mother; and when he had grown up he still did not know whether it was his father or his mother who gave him birth. He was a man who 'knew many works, but knew them all ill'.[72]

The asymmetrical arrangement of hexameters and trimeters which is found in the *Margites* is not unique in early Greek poetry, as the *Silloi* of Xenophanes show. In fact, a trimeter followed by two hexameters appears in one of the most ancient Greek inscriptions, written retrograde on the 'Cup of Nestor' from Pithekoussai.[73] Thus, while we cannot claim the *Margites* for Homer, it may well have been composed by an early Ionian epic poet in a moment of playful relaxation.

A less celebrated work was the *Cercopes*, a tale of certain mischievous people so named, who were turned into monkeys. Only one true epic parody survives, the *Batrachomyomachia* or *Battle of the Frogs and Mice*. It is rather poor fun, in which the heroic frogs are hard-pressed by the mice until Zeus sends an army of crabs which routs the mice and ends the battle.[74] It belongs to the late sixth or early fifth century[75] but contains many later interpolations.

Both the *Batrachomyomachia* and the *Margites*, in addition to their Homeric ascription, were also associated by some with the name of Pigres (c. 500 B.C.), a Carian said to have been the brother of Queen Artemisia who fought at Salamis. He is also credited with the production of an *Iliad* converted into elegiacs!

Religious, philosophical and scientific epic poetry

Early Greek literature, as preserved, is entirely secular. The literature of religion, which treated of the gods as gods, is lost. But religious writings existed in early times and in large quantities, as can be seen from hints in several authors.

Most of the old religious poems seem to have been ascribed to the mythical singers Orpheus and Musaeus in just the same way as heroic verse was attributed to Homer and didactic poems to Hesiod. But of the nature of that early religious poetry we know little prior to the religious revival of the sixth century, which is associated with the name of Ono-macritus, who influenced the religious policy of Pisistratus and Hipparchus and engaged in editing or forging the ancient Orphic poems and the oracles of Musaeus. He is never quoted as an independent author, however.

Some few fragments are preserved which are thought to have come from the Orphic works, but the majority of the poems mentioned as Orphic are clearly of false attribution. The dates and personalities of the alleged authors are unknown to us. The most important Orphic poem we know of was the *Rhapsodic Theogony* in twenty-four books, from which Neo-Platonic writers, and especially Proclus, quote various passages. Its age is a matter of dispute. It is most probably a compilation and not much older than the authors who quote it, but it may incorporate some earlier elements, for from the sixth and fifth centuries B.C. various theogonies and cosmogonies circulated under the name of Orpheus.[76]

The epic hexameter was also used by the Greeks when they wished to treat in verse philosophical or scientific subjects, for to them it was the proper measure for narrative poetry. Such was the practice adopted by three leading early philosophers associated with Italy and Sicily: Xenophanes, Parmenides and Empedocles.

Xenophanes of Colophon (c. 510 B.C.) wrote epic verses mainly on the

founding of Colophon and the colonization of Elea, which are the oldest
known epics of contemporary history. The extant fragments of Xenophanes,
however, all come from either his satires (*Silloi*) or from elegiac occasional
poems. He became the poet of the intellectual enlightenment in Magna
Graecia, criticizing Homer and Hesiod for their treatment of the gods and
denying that the gods resembled men. In his elegies he turned his criti-
cism on society, condemning the accepted views of *arete* and claiming that
its aims were of less social value than his own intellectual achievements.
For his views he claimed probability and propriety, not truth. He ex-
ercised a lasting influence on ancient religious thought.

In the history of poetry Xenophanes is significant not only for his
innovation in the field of the 'contemporary' epic, but also for the new and
individual literary form he devised, the *Silloi*. These poems in hexameters,
with the occasional iambic line, were directed against false or obsolete
values. To a large extent they foreshadowed Hellenistic popular philo-
sophy and Roman satire, and they were imitated in the third century B.C.
by Timon of Phlius.[77] The surviving fragments of Xenophanes, although
clear and sober, do not provide evidence of any great poetic genius.

Parmenides of Elea (c. 490 B.C.) is said to have given laws to his city. His
didactic poem, which survives in large fragments, is in prosaic but vigor-
ous hexameters, taking its place in the didactic tradition which goes back
to Hesiod. In it we find the earliest separation of philosophy from science
and the earliest discussion of philosophical method: Parmenides broke
new ground in not being content with mere assertion unsupported by
proofs of his doctrines.

Of the three philosopher-poets, Empedocles, son of Meton of Acragas
(c. 493–433 B.C.), was the only true poet. His philosophy was to him more
than knowledge, for he was a versatile man, combining the roles of
philosopher, scientist, poet, orator and statesman with those of mysta-
gogue, miracle-worker, healer and claimant of divine honours. It is not
surprising that he acquired legendary fame.

His two hexameter poems totalled 5000 verses. The first, *Περὶ Φύσεως*
(*On Nature*) was in two books, in which he expounded a cosmology in the
archaic fashion. His views accorded with the Orphic and Pythagorean
teachings of immortality and metamorphosis which were so widely cur-
rent in Magna Graecia at the time. The second, *Καθαρμοί* (the *Purifica-
tions*), dealt with the destiny of the human soul. About 350 verses of the
first and 100 of the second are extant. It is very probable that his poems
inspired Lucretius in his attempt to win the world over to Epicureanism
through the medium of verse.

The kind of didactic and proverbial style that we meet in Hesiod was
continued and developed by Phocylides (c 544–541), the elegiac and
hexameter poet of Miletus. His work is gnomic in character: he often
begins his lines with the formula *καὶ τόδε Φωκυλίδου* ('And this is by

Phocylides'). He wrote of traditional matters, such as husbandry, the evils of women, the Mean and so on. Some time in the first century A.D. a gnomic poem in 230 hexameters was circulated under his name, which, however, shows a knowledge of the Old Testament.[78]

This first period of Greek hexameter poetry can be traced, as we have seen, from the eighth century to the Persian Wars. In quality it ranges from the noble to the insignificant. Apart from the two Homeric epics, Hesiod and the Homeric Hymns, few fragments have survived, sufficient only to give us a very limited notion of a vast body of verse which long ago vanished from sight for ever. It was composed in traditional but constantly developing epic language, and much of it must have belonged to the oral tradition or must at least have been transmitted orally even in places where writing was well-known. It clearly shows how early and how widespread was the Greeks' love of poetry.

But although we cannot hope for a clearer picture of these lost epics and the manner of their composition, we may reflect that in their capacity as mythological handbooks they supplied material for the lyric poets and the Attic tragedians, and for numerous painters, vase painters and sculptors of the sixth and fifth centuries.

CHAPTER 2

Lyric Poetry

At the time that the post-Homeric rhapsodes were composing in the epic hexameter, there appear in Ionia two other poetic forms, the iambic and the elegiac. When we first meet them, early in the seventh century, they have reached such an advanced state of development that we must assume them to have been in use for a long time, a conclusion which is confirmed by their names, iambus and elegy, whose uncertain etymology also points to their great age.

Iambic and elegiac verse is often called lyric poetry, but the use of the word 'lyric' to indicate all poetry that is not epic or dramatic is modern and inaccurate. The word implies that the poetry was sung to the accompaniment, if not of the lyre itself, then of some other musical instrument. But epic poetry, too, was originally sung, as we have seen; while, on the other hand, the lyric elegy and iambus very soon began to drop their musical accompaniment. All Greek poetry, in fact, originated in some combination of words with music; and the various genres of poetry thereafter followed one of two lines of development. Either they gradually shed their music as the words gained the ascendancy, or they fell more completely under the sway of the music as the poets aimed at the expression of less specific thoughts.

What form the music of the ancient Greeks took is a question both obscure and controversial. But it can be stated that just as there was heroic legend, so too there existed song in most parts of the Greek world before our earliest records. The style seems to have varied from place to place, and music was later classified on a geographical basis: there emerged the 'Phrygian mode', the 'Ionian', the 'Dorian', the 'hypo-Dorian', the 'hyper-Phrygian', the 'Lesbian' and so on. The terminology must remain a puzzle to us, both because it is so crude and because it implies a knowledge of the styles themselves which we cannot recapture.

No doubt the genres of personal poetry and choral song which we begin to hear about from the seventh century onwards had a traditional origin. Indeed, we have already seen how Homer seems to show knowledge of the monody in his mention of the Linus song, sung by a boy (XVIII, 570). He also speaks of several kinds of choral song, notably the dirge (XVIII, 50–1, 314–16; XXIV, 746–7), the paean (I, 472–4), the *hymenaeus* (XVIII, 493), the *hyporchema*, or song accompanied by mimetic dancing (8, 256–65) and the maiden song (XVI, 182–3). All five kinds are found in the poems of, for example, Pindar. In fact, love songs, hymns to the gods, war chants, laments, even satire have existed in illiterate societies at many times and in many parts of the world. What happened in the post-Homeric world was that they began to be written down, as the great epics had already been written down. The first personal poems we know to have been so immortalized were those of Archilochus.

This transition from an 'oral' to a literate society gave rise to some important new features in Greek literature. First, side by side with the professional rhapsodes, amateurs began composing poetry, and this introduced a new immediacy and intimacy to Greek verse. Second, as has already been mentioned, a change in the attitude of poets to the work of their predecessors emerged. In the absence of literacy there was no literary property. A poet or rhapsodist was not able, and did not seek, to prevent others from repeating or reconstructing his verses once he had delivered his recitation. Naturally, in an 'oral' society, as was that of the Mycenaean and post-Mycenaean world, formulaic phrases and whole passages became traditional or proverbial and were preserved in men's memories; and this traditional material was freely used in the composition of new poems.[1]

Such old habits of composition did not die immediately with the introduction of writing. The scanty remains of early Greek personal poetry provide such examples of poets quoting, paraphrasing or adapting older work. It was, in fact, a compliment to a predecessor, and the practice continued even with the Attic tragedians.[2]

Nevertheless, the spread of literacy marks the beginning of a new awareness of literary property and the feeling that the poet is proud to be an individual. In Hesiod's *sphragis* to the *prooemium* of his *Theogony* we have already seen an example of this tendency.[3] Some of the proverbial philosophers and gnomic poets are so anxious to preserve their claims to their work that they introduce into a couplet or a line their own names — 'thus said Phocylides' or 'proverb of Hipparchus' — in order to identify the work as their own. Another aspect of the new ideas about literary property is seen in the mention of one poet by another. The first literary reference to a source in extant Greek literature is made by Semonides of Amorgos, quoting Homer, though Solon of Athens before him names his older contemporary, Mimnermus, in order to correct him.

The third new feature of Greek literature was that the introduction of writing established a body of 'classics'. Once a particular kind of poetry had been admirably composed and preserved in written form, younger poets became reluctant to try their hand at it again. The existence of classics in a genre to some extent inhibited further work along the same lines. The original spirits continually moved on to develop new branches of literature, until the time came when they realized that there was 'nothing new under the sun'.

This tendency, together with the swift development of Greek social, economic and political life, was responsible for the way in which Greek poetry evolved. The various successive genres of poetry and prose were swiftly and systematically raised to classical perfection: but the result in each case was that a period of comparative sterility followed, as though Greek literature were a field that had been over-cultivated.

If we now turn to metrics, it should be stated that the basis of ancient Greek prosody was *quantitative* rhythm—the difference between long and short syllables—rather than *dynamic* rhythm, which depends on set numbers of syllables and set stress accents within a line. As already mentioned, as far as we know the oldest metre in Greek poetry was the hexameter, the metre of Homeric poetry. In Homer we find it already fully developed, and Hesiod uses it without further changes for all his poems, varied though they are in subject-matter. The pentameter, which first occurs in the elegiac couplets of Callinus, and the trimeter, which probably makes its first appearance in the *Margites*, are certainly both older than Archilochus (c. 650 B.C.); but as early as c. 600 B.C. the poetry of Archilochus, Alcman, Sappho and Alcaeus already reveals a greater wealth of rhythms and types of line and simple strophe than the whole of subsequent Greek poetry was to contribute, and in Stesichorus' work we can trace the main features of Pindar's triadic structure.

In the sixth century Anacreon added further rhythmical elements to Greek verse, and the technique of the complicated strophe reached its fullest development in the hands of Simonides, who was active between 530 and 468 B.C. Not only in this respect, but in rhythmic technique also, neither his nephew Bacchylides nor Pindar seems to have advanced beyond him in any important respect. At about the same time Corinna produced a few further rhythmical innovations. This great variety of rhythms, with the addition of the anapaest (of Dorian origin) and of the dochmiac (whose origin is unknown) was later used by the Attic dramatists to differentiate the various styles they developed.

As even this brief sketch shows, the metrical diversity and inventiveness of this period were particularly notable and have not been equalled in the subsequent history of Greek poetry, except perhaps for that of early Byzantine religious poetry (fourth to seventh centuries A.D.), which employed dynamic rhythms of an almost equal complexity. At the same time it should be stressed that we do not know how or exactly when the various metrical structures of early Greek poetry came into being, for they appear fully developed from the moment we first meet them. Another point worth mentioning is that in early Greek verse rhythm seems to have been independent of a poem's character. Archilochus, the Lesbian poets and later Pindar and Bacchylides use a similar metre in poems of entirely different character and a variety of different metres in poems of similar character. Nor is the internal structure of the line varied metrically so as to correspond with different moods in the same poem.

On the other hand, we should remember that the metres of certain great poems came to be seen as essential features of the genres with which they were associated. Thus an epic could only be written in hexameters, and an epigram, as a rule, would be cast in elegiac couplets. In this way a rhythm could acquire a character of its own, not as a result of its beat, but by virtue of its purely literary associations. The same is true of certain dialectal usages connected with particular literary genres: the flavour of Ionic had connotations of epic, Doric of choral poetry, and Aeolic of erotic verse. Such means of giving verse a special character were further developed by the Attic dramatists, as we shall presently see.

IAMBIC POETRY

The origins of iambic poetry are to be found in the early fertility cults, a widespread feature of which was coarse, often violently obscene invective. This literary 'ugliness', corresponding to a deliberate 'ugliness' in some religious art, was supposed to have an apotropaic function; its purpose was to ward off evil. Such ritual obscenity came to be so closely associated with the iambus that 'to speak in iambs' ($i\alpha\mu\beta i\zeta\varepsilon\iota\nu$) came to mean the same as 'to abuse' or 'to revile'.[4] Of course, those early iambic invectives and crude, ribald jokes are a far cry from the highly cultivated iambic verses we know from seventh-century Greek literature.

In the seventh century a great iambic and elegiac poet appeared whom the Greeks considered almost as great as Homer, Archilochus of Paros.[5] Of his poetry only a few brief fragments have survived, but they are enough to reveal a highly unconventional and powerful personality.

Archilochus' father was a leading man in Paros, but his mother was a slave. Financial difficulties drove him to leave his native island and to lead the life of a mercenary soldier, fighting in Thasos and Euboea, unhappy in love, quarrelling with his friends and hounded by his enemies. He met his death in battle, and legend says that his slayer, Callondas, nicknamed 'Crow', was expelled from Apollo's temple at Delphi in punishment for his deed.

Archilochus' elegies centre on his war experiences. His approach to war is realistic, fully anti-heroic and anti-Homeric, as can be seen from the celebrated fragment in which he expresses no sense of shame for abandoning his shield in battle and getting away with his life.[6] It is in similar bold opposition to the heroic ethos that Archilochus speaks when he declares that no one enjoys honour after death, for favour attaches itself only to the living,[7] as well as when he distinguishes the inner from the outer man, ridiculing the officer who is proud of his appearance but praising the short, bandy-legged general who is truly brave. If one bears in mind the authority of Homer and his heroic view in seventh-century Greece — indeed, in the whole of antiquity — one is struck by the powerful independence of Archilochus' spirit. It has been pointed out that his attitude is rooted in the great age of colonization, which challenged the status and ideals of the aristocracy; for overseas expansion had opened the eyes of many Greeks to the possibilities of other social systems. But Archilochus' unashamed frankness in rejecting the heroic ethos horrified posterity.

A man of such forceful and independent character was certain to make bitter enemies. The most famous of his quarrels was with his fellow citizen Lycambes, whose daughter, Neoboule, the poet had wished to marry. When Lycambes withdrew his consent Archilochus attacked his former love and all her family with lampoons of such violence that it is said that all the members of the family committed suicide.[8] Thus in Archilochus we see the first shift of Greek poetry from Hesiod's comprehensive attack on womankind to the satire of individual women, an important further move towards the new individualism. In 1974 an important new fragment of Archilochus was published in which the poet maintains he seduced not only Neoboule but her younger sister too.[9] It was to counter this accusation that Dioscorides wrote his own epigram.[10]

The poet's quarrel with Lycambes and his family is the most famous example of his powers of invective, but quarrels and abuse, as Pindar tells us, were the rule in his life.[11] He was known to the Greeks as 'the Scorpion', and in modern times he has been called the first known 'poet of hate'. But not all his poetry was innovatory and bitter. He wrote of other things, such as wine and love, which have been the subjects of lyric poetry at all periods. In these too he showed his unconventional attitude.

In Archilochus we find for the first time a motif which was to dominate all subsequent Greek poetry — the idea that love is not a blessing but a passion, which seizes men like a damaging disease. It crawls into the heart, blinds the eyes and takes away the understanding;[12] it pierces to the very marrow;[13] and it weakens the limbs.[14] This view of love originally owed something to Hesiod,[15] but it was through Archilochus in particular that it passed to later poets, from Sappho and Theocritus down to the modern Greek folk songs and modern Greek poetry.

In Archilochus we also find the first occurrence of the word 'dithyramb', which defies accurate explanation and is probably not Greek. He tells us[16] that when under the influence of wine he sings and leads others in singing the dithyramb. From the inscriptional life of Archilochus it is also clear that he tried to introduce a fertility cult of Dionysus into Paros but was opposed.[17]

If Archilochus rejected the heroic approach to life of the epics, he was still close enough to the heroic world to feel that his own honour and emotions were all-important and to believe that no redress could compensate for their neglect. But the general character of his poetry is as unlike the epic as possible; for he abandoned Homeric dignity and decency and avoided the use of the epic hexameter. Even his hymns to gods were composed not in dactylic hexameters but in iambic metres. One of them became very famous indeed, for it established itself as the song of victory used by the victors at Olympia.[18]

Archilochus experimented with different rhythms, building up his stanzas from iambic, trochaic and dactylic elements rather than taking over the metres of traditional song. He has been called the father of iambic poetry, and his paternity may perhaps also extend to the elegiac, which does not mean that he was the inventor of both, but that he was responsible for turning them into excellent vehicles for poetic expression. He was as unconventional in style and diction as in subject-matter and metrics. His style is not ornate; it has few adjectives, and his similes are short. There is poignancy and liveliness in his writing, and he makes frequent use of apostrophe. In his language he drew on the vernacular, a further important contribution to the development of Greek poetic diction. Except in his elegiacs, in which the traditional language of the epic is chiefly used, he employs a vivid contemporary speech, rich in metaphors and colloquialisms.[19] In this respect his lead was followed by the Greek monodists who, in the main, kept to vernacular speech. His greatest legacy to Greek poetry is the change of emphasis from the heroic and impersonal to the contemporary and personal, without which lyrical poetry could never have developed. For this reason he is much more than the creator of lyrical satire and the first realist in Western poetry; he is the ultimate parent of all personal literature in Western lands.

Archilochus' fearless originality so greatly impressed Classical and post-Classical antiquity that not only was he included by the Alexandrians in the canon of iambic poets, but in the course of the first century B.C. an elaborately inscribed monument was erected in his honour on Paros. Even prior to this he had been commemorated on his native island by an inscription of the third century B.C., which gives extracts of his poetry, together with a pious biography.

A younger contemporary of Archilochus was the iambic poet Semonides of Amorgos. He was born on Samos but, by founding a colony on Amorgos, associated his name with the latter island. He wrote both iambic and elegiac poetry, whose dominant note is pessimism.

In his long *Iambus on Women*—the second part of which is an example of

archaic ring composition—he delights in denigrating the sex, thus follow-
ing an anti-feminist tradition which, as far as we can ascertain, goes back
to Hesiod but is clearly much older. Behind these attacks no doubt lies the
sexual antagonism which is an element of universal and age-old folk lore
and which must have played its part in folk festivals. Semonides describes
nine evil types of woman, seven of which are compared with animals—
the swine, the fox, the dog, the ass, the weasel, the horse and the ape. At
the end he acknowledges the existence of one good type, sprung, he says,
from the bee.

Semonides has also been credited with a piece of elegiac verse on the
shortness of life, which quotes the beautiful line from the *Iliad* (VI, 146) in
which the poet notes that men are as transitory as the leaves of the trees,
but which ends somewhat lamely with an appeal to men to enjoy life. He is
also said to have written a history of Samos in two books of elegiacs. If this
information is to be trusted, the work is the first known topographical
history written in elegiacs rather than the traditional hexameters.

Judged by his extant fragments, Semonides has plenty of humour and
some gift for satire; but another man much more significant in the tradi-
tion of iambic poetry is Hipponax of Ephesus (c. 540 B.C.). Banished
from his native city, he moved to Clazomenae. The fact that he was exiled
by a tyrant and the association of his name with horses have led some
scholars to believe that he came from an aristocratic family. He was soon
reduced to utter poverty, however, and lived miserably as an exile,
complaining that *Plutus* (wealth) was blind,[20] a subject later to be made
into a comedy by Aristophanes. In another fragment[21] he prays to Hermes
for a coat and boots, for he is bitterly cold and frost-bitten. Of his
invectives, the most famous are his attacks on the sculptors Bupalus and
Athenis, who are said to have made a statue that caricatured him and
whom—so the story goes—he drove to suicide. He also attacked the
painter Mimnes.[22]

Polemon credited Hipponax with the invention of parody (*Ath.*, 698 b),
and indeed fragments[23] reveal that there once existed a mock-heroic
hexameter poem by him on the adventures of the glutton Eurymedon-
tiadeus. Another aspect of his output appears in a large papyrus fragment
which shows how startlingly uninhibited he could be over erotic matters.
It recalls the experiences of Encolpius in Petronius (c. 138)—who indeed
may well have used Hipponax as his model.

Hipponax invented a new iambic metre, the *scazon* or *choliambus*, in
which the iambic trimeter ends with a spondee; in this metre he wrote
most of his poems, but he also used the epodic form—that is, a regular
iambic trimeter followed by an iambic dimeter. The invention of choli-
ambics was also attributed to Ananius, a sixth-century writer, who wrote
a poem listing foods according to the season of the year—the first gastro-
nomical poem. Hipponax's style is terse and vivid, and, like Archilochus,

he drew part of his vocabulary from contemporary speech. Indeed, at times he goes so far as to introduce foreign words from Lydian and Phrygian. He is essentially a realistic poet, interested in the events of the moment rather than in general questions or speculation. In this respect he is the forerunner of the Sicilian and the Alexandrian mime. His greatest virtue was his wit, which seems to have carried him through all his troubles.

Hellenistic readers found his witty verses to their taste. Callimachus, in his *Iambi* (No. 1) invoked Hipponax's ghost and said that all writers of iambics turn to Ephesus for inspiration. There is no doubt that the writings of Hipponax secured a long and influential career for the choliambic metre, if not for much else.

ELEGIAC POETRY

By alternating the dactylic hexameter with the pentameter, something quite new was given to poetry. The unit of composition was no longer the paragraph but the couplet, a change which allowed the poet to express himself on a scale smaller than that of the unrestricted periods of the old epic style. As it first appears in the seventh century, the elegiac couplet lies half-way between the free epic style and lyric monody. Its origin lay in songs accompanied by the flute; and as that instrument itself chiefly accompanied marching and feasting, the first elegiacs are military and amorous. They retain epic language and rhythm, but the poet is at liberty to talk of himself when he chooses. The metre was to have a long and honourable career in Greek literature, enduring down to the fall of Byzantium and even beyond.

One of the earliest examples of the military elegiac is a poem by Callinus of Ephesus (c. 670 B.C.) in which he urges his countrymen to take arms against an enemy (which modern scholars believe to have been the Cimmerians). Callinus was presumably a member of the military aristocracy, and for all his elegiac metre, his approach is rooted in the epic world of Homer which Archilochus rejected so totally. The appeal is to the sense of honour. Since a man must die when he must, why should he not die gloriously in battle instead of remaining at home, obscure and unmourned? The epic echo can also be traced in the verbal form of his poetry.

The Spartan Tyrtaeus (c. 650 B.C.) — the story that he was an Athenian schoolmaster is clearly untrue — used the same metre for his patriotic exhortations to his countrymen in their war against the Messenians. He is said to have led the Spartans and to have helped to take Messene.[24]

His poems, collected in five books in Alexandria, contained war songs, exhortations in elegiac verse and a poem called Πολιτεία for the Lacedaemonians. He is no great stylist but has a vivid imagination and a real feeling for the horrors and the glories of war. His simple verse has sincerity and a persuasive power that comes from a direct appeal to pride and courage. Its debt to the heroic epic, both in its spirit and in its language, is manifest.

Mimnermus of Colophon (c. 630 B.C.) developed the other aspect of the elegy, its amatory character. He is the first hedonist in Western literature, and his influence descends not only to all subsequent Greek love poetry, but also to Propertius, Tibullus and Ovid and, through them, to all later Western poets of love.

Mimnermus was haunted by the brevity of youth, which passes 'like the dream of a moment', and by the horror of old age, which is 'worse than death'.[25] All that matters, he unashamedly proclaims, is pleasure and especially love: 'What would life be, what pleasure, without golden Aphrodite?' But he somehow tempers his hedonism with a respect for truth and for warlike qualities.[26]

Mimnermus also naturally borrowed from Homer, but not to excess, and the unheroic sweetness of his cadences lends an attraction to his melancholy mood. One of the two books of his collected poems was called after a flute player named Nanno, with whom he was in love. It seems to have been a collection of poems on very different themes, including mythology[27] and history.[28] He seems also to have written a *Smyrneis*, a historical poem on Smyrna, which may have been included in the *Nanno*.

Until the sixth century B.C. the new Greek intellectual life flourished in the east and west but Attica remained silent. Gradually, however, the expression of all Greek thought and art converged on Athens, as the Classical age of Greece emerged. The precursor of the age, and the first Attic poet, is Solon, c. 639–559, son of Execestides, the Athenian statesman.

Solon was of noble descent, but his means were moderate—indeed, it has been suggested that he was a merchant. His life (he was chief *archon* in 594–3) was lived at a time of bitter social strife, as a result of which he was given full powers by the Athenians to make peace between aristocracy and people. His acts included the abolition of debts and the reform of, among other things, coinage. He also changed many aspects of the constitution of Athens. In later ages he was considered one of the seven sages, and we hear of long travels undertaken by him after he had finished his legislative work. He died in Cyprus and his bones, we are told, were scattered on the island of Salamis.

The Athenians trusted Solon chiefly because of his actions during the struggle with Megara over the possession of Salamis. Wishing to urge the Athenians to war, he decided to make public his warlike elegy, later called the *Salamis*, under cover of feigned madness because of an Athenian prohibition of such propaganda.

His medium of poetic expression was iambic, elegiac and trochaic verse, in which he wrote political poems that were circulated, just as the speeches and pamphlets of his successors two centuries later were circulated. He was the first to use elegiac poetry for expressing political thought. One fragment[29] presents the philosophy which guided him and shows that his views on life were those of conventional, aristocratic morality—prosperity and a good reputation, happiness for his friends and misery for his enemies.

But Solon asks only for such prosperity as the gods allow, for ill luck follows wealth acquired by treachery or violence. *Hubris*, he maintains, leads a man beyond the bounds of moderation, until *Dike* (the personified power of Justice) finds him out and punishes him through *Ate* (blindness visited by the gods on men, yet arising from the guilty hearts of men themselves). For Solon, as for Hesiod, the true guardian of the moral law is Zeus, and his elegy speaks in a really inspired manner of the vengeance of Zeus and of divine retribution falling upon sinful man with the sweeping power of a sudden gale. It combines insight into the limitations of human action and of 'empty' human hopes with a deep belief in the moral government of the universe. Its ultimate message is that wisdom lies in moderation and the Golden Mean.

This belief in the interaction of *Hubris, Dike* and *Ate*, which implies a confidence in the moral order of the world, contrasts strongly with Solon's grief at the unhappy lot of man. Such a collision of values characterized the intellectual climate which was to produce Attic tragedy. In this respect Solon, in so many ways the heir of Hesiod, is also the ancestor of Aeschylus and thus the bond between the two.

In another famous elegy, the *Eunomia* (Good Order),[30] Solon gives us a glimpse of his political thought. He applies to the life of the community a morality which he considers valid for the individual and shows that greed and injustice destroy political life and lead to a universal malaise in which peace and freedom are lost. In yet another of his poems we see that, unlike Archilochus, he believes that after death there is life—in the memory of one's friends; and, as we have seen, he corrects Mimnermus, who had maintained that life was not worth living after the age of sixty. Solon believes that a man should live to eighty as long as he continues to learn as he grows old.

It is sad to reflect that all Solon's wisdom and all his great efforts did not ultimately prevent Pisistratus from establishing himself as a tyrant in Athens. By attempting to satisfy all parties, Solon had inevitably satisfied none. As for his poetry, although it has immense historical interest, one must admit that on the whole it does not avoid a certain hardness and the dullness of the practical man.

Theognis of Megara (c. 540 B.C.) is one of the most notable of early elegiac poets. Born probably at the beginning of the sixth century, he lived at a time when his city was torn by violent struggle between nobles and democrats, but details and chronology are obscure. In that struggle Theognis was on the side of the nobles, who longed for the happy days when Megara was governed by its aristocracy. He felt utter contempt for democracy and the 'new men' which it produced. The poet seems to have travelled widely, for he mentions visits to Euboea, Sparta and Sicily, but he stresses that 'nothing is dearer than one's native land'. We do not know when or where he died.

Attached to Theognis' name is a collection of some 1400 elegiac verses, which present many difficult problems. The whole collection is probably an anthology, drawn from different poets of between about 700 and 460 B.C. Certainly, the first book contains a few couplets by known authors, including Mimnermus (ll. 795–6, 1020–2), Tyrtaeus (ll. 935–8, 1003–6), Solon (ll. 227–32, 315–18, 585–90, 1253–4) and Euenus (ll. 465–96); elsewhere there are repetitions which look like variations on the same theme.

The poems, usually known as the *Theognidea*, are mostly concerned with the *symposium*—the men's drinking party—and partly reflect the drinker's code of behaviour, according to which moderation should be observed. It is here that the maxim *in vino veritas* makes its first appearance: ἀνδρὸς δ' οἶνος ἔδειξε νόον (l. 500). In fact, the keynote of the whole collection seems to be the pursuit of moderation, an ideal which foreshadows the theory of Aristotle that every virtue is a mean between two vices.

One of the main preoccupations of the *Theognidea* is the political situation within the state (only a small group of couplets reveals concern about the growing threat of Persia), that threatened nobility, whose heart was in horses, dogs and boys (ll. 1255f.).

Money, they observe, now compels good families to make unworthy matches for the sake of sordid gain, whereas in horses, sheep and asses proper breeding is observed! Here again we clearly see the aristocratic conviction that inherited ability is absolute, depending on the blood. We shall find it again and again in Greek poetry, in various contexts.

There are genuinely touching lines among the *Theognidea*: the poet hears a bird's cry announcing spring, and his heart flutters because other men own his fields; or he mourns the worthlessness of life in superb verses which are to find their echo in Bacchylides and Sophocles. However, the best and most famous poem in the collection is Theognis' own promise of immortality to Cyrnus—because the lips of men will sing his name in Theognis' poetry for ever—a motif which, from Sappho[31] onwards, has often been repeated in Western literature. But the poet concludes with a pathetic couplet, complaining that Cyrnus mocks and tricks him—a surprising ending which, as has been pointed out, recalls some of Shakespeare's sonnets.

The *Theognidea* also contain a large gnomic element, which is also found in the poetry of Theognis himself. For genuine work by Theognis appears in the collection, in spite of its contradictions of tone and content and its chronological difficulties. The starting-point for determining this is the so-called 'seal' (ll. 19–23),[32] in which the poet names both himself and his favourite boy, Cyrnus. Thus we may claim for Theognis most verses mentioning the boy, bearing in mind, of course, that the identification is not indisputable evidence of authenticity.

The genuine poems of Theognis probably formed a nucleus around which gradually gathered verses composed by others for similar functions until the collection took its present form. The poems are thus elegies on divers occasions, and they may have formed a song-book to be used at *symposia*. Theognis' own poetry has many gnomic observations on wealth and poverty, the evils of life, the caprice of fortune, the deceitfulness of friends and such topics, and also claims justice as chief of the virtues ($\dot{\varepsilon}\nu$ $\delta\dot{\varepsilon}$ $\delta\iota\kappa\alpha\iota\sigma\sigma\acute{\upsilon}\nu\eta$ $\sigma\upsilon\lambda\lambda\acute{\eta}\beta\delta\eta\nu$ $\pi\tilde{\alpha}\sigma'$ $\dot{\alpha}\varrho\varepsilon\tau\acute{\eta}$ $\dot{\varepsilon}\sigma\tau\iota\nu$: l. 147) and the just man as the virtuous man.

The second book of *Theognidea* is a collection of elegiac poems dealing with the love of boys;[33] among them there is at least one piece by Theognis himself. This book illustrates a side of Greek life which is difficult for modern people to understand. The poems were intended to be sung at *symposia*, and we have a red-figure bowl from Tanagra of the fifth century, on which a man reclining at dinner is represented as singing the song that we find in the *Theognidea*.[34]

All these songs of the *Theognidea* are free from the superficial indecencies which mar later collections (such as Straton's *Mousa Paidike*) and are expressed in strikingly moderate terms.

EPIGRAM AND *SCOLION*

Two other poetic forms, the epigram and the *scolion*, are closely related to the elegy, the first in form and the second in content.

Epigramma means 'inscription'; since inscriptions in verse were more memorable than those in prose, the term came to denote exclusively poetic inscriptions. Greek poetic epigrams were composed continuously for more than two thousand years. The long history of the genre is usually divided into five stages—the Archaic, the Classical, the Hellenistic, the Greco-Roman and the Byzantine—of which only the first concerns us here.

The two earliest extant inscriptions in verse are both of the eighth century. The first is the few lines we saw written on a bowl from Ischia, known as 'Nestor's Goblet', and consists of an iambic trimeter with an irregular opening and two hexameters.[35] The second is an imperfect sentence on a Dipylon jug,[36] which it promises as a prize to the best dancer. The latter is also, as it happens, the earliest monument to the Attic dialect.

From then on, short-verse epigrams were inscribed on tombs, votive offerings and even road signs.[37] At first they were cast in dactylic hexameters, in which, as might be expected, the influence of the epic is evident. Later the elegiac couplet began to be used, and eventually predominated, no doubt as a result of its compact shape, sententious tone and the melancholy associations which made it particularly suitable for epitaphs. Iambic and trochaic epigrams are also found in this period, but they are much less common.

The archaic epigrams are all anonymous. Typically, they are a brief address in which the tomb (occasionally, the dead man) or the votive offering speaks to the passer-by, giving him the relevant details with strict restraint of emotion. It is this admirable control and purpose which made the epigram an art form whose austere reserve and simplicity reached, by the sixth and fifth centuries, a perfection never to be equalled. The best-known examples from this latter period are the epitaphs on the soldiers who fell in the Persian Wars. Perhaps the most striking is that inscribed on the burial place of the Lacedaemonian dead at Thermopylae: 'Stranger, tell the Lacedaemonians that we lie here, obedient to their commands.'

The most versatile poet of the age, Simonides of Ceos, was an expert at composing epitaphs and dedications, and in later times almost all the well-known epigrams of this period passed as his. Simonides was, of course, not alone in having striking epigrams wrongly attributed to him. The process began with Homer, who was credited with several epigrams, some of which are excellent, and it continued unabated for so long that very many attributions must be viewed with scepticism.

In the course of the fifth century, as we shall see, the old restraint of feeling gave way to the expression of personal emotions, and a set of motifs evolved which were used over and over again. The influence of Attic tragedy began to be felt, especially in the sepulchral epigrams.

The *scolion*, the second of the two genres related to the elegy, is specifically attached to the drinking party. Ancient sources speak of it as a form of song which did not proceed from drinker to drinker in regular sequence but was taken up at will by the best singers. From the irregular course which it took around the company came its name, *scolion*, meaning 'crooked', 'zig-zag'. In the beginning such songs were presumably improvised, a practice which can be paralleled today in modern Greek folk song. But soon distinguished poets like Simonides came to compose examples of the genre, which would have been committed to writing at an early stage. Such outstanding examples were combined with snatches of anonymous popular songs, taken from their context, and the two kinds were circulated together in anthologies.

There survive several scattered examples of such Attic drinking songs, but we possess a short and particularly noteworthy collection of twenty-five songs, preserved in Athenaeus.[38] Most of them are of four lines, composed in simple lyric metres. In them the aristocratic revellers sing, between drinks, of their joys and cares and of the code by which they live. One song adjures the company to have dealings only with the virtuous, while another, anticipating Euripides, advocates looking into a man's heart before making a friend of him. The best poetry comes in two poems, of two stanzas each, wishing that their writers might be a lyre in the hands of the boys at the Dionysia or a golden ornament worn by a beautiful and virtuous woman. The political element too is strong; no fewer than four songs (10–13) praise Harmodius and Aristogiton as the founders of Athenian freedom.

There are many indications that this little collection in Athenaeus should be dated to the late sixth or early fifth century, and in it there shines some of that unique quality which was to mark Attic literature of the Classical period.

A *scolion* of Hybrias from Crete, which celebrates his weapons,[39] is a very different matter. Though later in date than the previous examples it deserves mention here as an indication of the form such drinking songs must have taken among the serious-minded early Dorians.

MONODY (*CITHAROEDIA*)

The art of music was advanced in the Aegean world long before the Homeric epics reached their final form, but its development in the Greek world took an important new turn in the eighth century, when more richly toned instruments were introduced from Phrygia and Lydia. The flute acquired a new importance as rival to the lyre—a rivalry which is reflected in the myth of a contest between Apollo the harpist and the Phrygian flute player, Marsias.

The lyric poets were not only poets but also musicians, and they generally composed their own melodies as well as their words; for Greek lyric poetry was always composed to be sung and was invariably accompanied by music. This music has not survived, so we cannot appreciate the full effect of these works; but it is true to say that the music was strictly subordinate to the words.

The name Terpander is an important one, although his songs have not been preserved, and it is doubtful not only whether the fragments attributed to him are genuine, but also whether he is rightly credited with the invention of the seven-stringed lyre.[40] Two facts, however, we do know about him. He founded a school of lyric poetry on his native Lesbos; and he was so famous as a *citharoedos*, or solo singer accompanying himself on the lyre, that he was invited to Sparta so that he might calm the passions of civil strife with his music.

He is said to have composed *nomes* (in which he set his own or Homer's words to music), *prooemia* (preludes, which were probably similar in nature to the Homeric Hymns) and *scolia*. It is probably his example that served to regularize some of the metres used by the Lesbian singers two generations later. Certainly, they looked back to him as a master of the lyrical art.

Sappho and Alcaeus—their names are household words—were contemporaries and were probably exiled at the same time, though one was driven to the east and the other to the west. It is even said, but the story must be doubted, that Alcaeus made proposals of love to Sappho, which she rejected. The poetry of both may perhaps have its origins in folk songs, but it is neither choral nor popular in character. There is, in truth, little in common between the two poets beyond the employment of certain common metres and of the Lesbian dialect, which between them they fashioned into a fine literary medium. Yet despite their differences, they together established a tradition of erotic poetry which persisted until the end of the ancient world.

Politics, war, his own exile, sea voyages and drinking were the chief themes of Alcaeus, whereas Sappho confined her songs to a relatively narrow round of feminine interests. But she was the more accomplished poet—an opinion held also by ancient critics. Plato himself is said to have written the couplet in which she is called the 'tenth Muse'.

Alcaeus

Alcaeus was born in about 620 B.C. of an aristocratic family in Mytilene on Lesbos. His life mirrors the disturbed age in which he lived. When he was still a boy his two brothers overthrew the tyrant Melanchros, who was succeeded in turn by Myrsilus and Pittacus. The poet's early years seem to have been spent in combating all three, as a result of which he was exiled to Pyrrha. He also took part in the war of the Lesbians against the Athenians for the possession of Sigeum, and like Archilochus, told in a poem how he lost his shield, which the Athenians hung triumphantly in a temple. During his years of exile he probably enlisted as a mercenary and visited Lydia and Egypt.[41] He seems also to have been in Thrace.

Apparently reconciled with Pittacus, he later returned to Lesbos, but the date of his death is unknown.

Alcaeus was extrovert and aggressive, better at hating than loving; he lived and drank hard. Of his political poems—probably all written during his exile—the most famous is one which compared his city under the rule of the tyrants to a storm-tossed ship, and which, if it did not originate the phrase the 'ship of state', may well have helped to make it the commonplace it is today.[42]

His life in exile was not pleasant, as surviving fragments of his poems show.[43] There are, however, certain beautiful lines which speak of moments unmarred by bitterness and despair, while others give a striking indication of the vigour of Alcaeus' political feelings.[44] In his political verses Alcaeus paints a vivid picture of himself as an adventurer, fighting in the streets of Mytilene or in the fields of exile, rousing his cowed and sullen companions to renewed efforts or wandering embittered through the world, singing of wine and war and of the men whom he hated and of those he loved. But of his later life, after his return from exile, we know very little, save for one passage from a drinking song[45] where he talks of pouring myrrh over his head and his 'grey-haired chest'—which suggests that he must have reached an advanced age.

As well as political poems, Alcaeus cultivated other types of poetry, including hymns to gods, some mythological verse and erotic poetry. His hymns to the gods—to Apollo, Hermes (to which Horace[46] is indebted), Hephaestus, the Dioscuri and Eros—are not cult hymns. Like the Homeric hymns, they chiefly sing of the attributes and adventures of divine personages. They are literary exercises intended for entertainment rather than for devotional purposes, and they have many strange features. Side by side with these hymns proper we find fragments containing references to mythical figures. They probably come from short lyrical poems on mythological subjects, for Alcaeus, like Sappho, apparently took stock epic themes and arranged them for performance among his circle.

Perhaps above all Alcaeus was a poet of wine and love. Among his drinking poems there is nothing as formal as the Attic *scolion*; any occasion is fit for drinking, but, as has been shown, the description in some at least is not original. The model for one,[47] for example, is to be found in Hesiod,[48] so once again we observe the force of tradition in an art which did not always aim at unqualified originality.

Of Alcaeus' amatory poems little is preserved, but from Horace we know the name of his favourite boy: Lycus of the black eyes and black hair (*Lycum nigris oculis nigroque/crine decorum*). Contemporary women seldom appear in his surviving poetry and the well-known line, 'Pure Sappho of the dark tresses and the honey-sweet smile' is certainly not by him. There is, however, one remarkably amatory fragment which deserves mention. A woman tells of her misfortune, probably the result of a disastrous love affair. There is no indication who she is, or indeed whether she is a real or a mythological figure, for from the first line only the heroine speaks. Of this genre, the dramatic monologue, lyric poetry provides very few surviving examples before the Alexandrian age: this, indeed, seems to be the first. Horace was influenced by it in one of his odes,[49] which, however, also contains elements drawn from the poetry of Sappho.

As a metrician Alcaeus, though less speculative than Sappho, is imaginative and bold. He uses stanzas of two or four lines in a wide variety of metres, including the Greater and Lesser Asclepiads, the Sapphic and his own Alcaic stanzas,[50] as well as a number of other strophes of his own invention.

His style is simple, making use, as we have already seen, of vernacular Aeolic, with occasional Homeric elements. The sentences are short, and he does not burden them with many adjectives or figures of speech: at most from time to time he employs an elaborate allegory.[51] There is also an almost total lack of the gnomic element. As Dionysius of Halicarnassus observed,[52] if we were to remove the metre from Alcaeus' poetry it would sometimes be as if we were reading a political speech. In the hymns, however, the language is more elevated, and in the fragments treating of mythological subjects the debt to the epic manner is understandably obvious. His success arises from the immediacy with which he conveys impressions of the world about him. Dionysius was right when he gave as the characteristics of Alcaeus' poetry, brevity, sweetness and force.

In the Alexandrian period Aristophanes of Byzantium and Aristarchus edited his poems in at least ten books, which were probably arranged according to subject. His reputation and influence in that period were extensive, and he was included in the Alexandrian canon of the nine great lyric poets.

Sappho

Sappho was born at Eresus on Lesbos in about 612 B.C. She came from an aristocratic family, married young and had a daughter, Cleis, to whom she was devoted. Like Alcaeus, she was involved in the political troubles of her native island and, when banished from it, took refuge in Sicily. Of her husband we know nothing save his name, Cercylas. She was presumably a widow when she returned from exile and set up in Mytilene an establishment for training the daughters of well-to-do families in music and dance. From her verse it is clear that other such 'finishing schools' existed at the time on Lesbos. The familiar story of Sappho's love for Phaon and her suicide by leaping from the Leucadian cliff is clearly a later fabrication, probably arising from the misunderstanding by later readers of a poem of hers on Phaon, who was worshipped on Lesbos as a god.

Sappho's is a woman's world. Her school was her life, and the principal themes of her poetry, as far as they are known, are the ephemeral pleasures and pains of that leisurely, graceful society. There are hardly any political or domestic allusions in it and only a few to persons and events in her own family. Similarly, there is no evidence of the existence of any sort of ceremonial poetry, apart from epithalamia. Some few of her poems[53] seem to have been modelled on folk songs. But these few exceptions apart, all her poems must have been composed for informal recitation by the poet herself to her circle of companions.

In her verse Sappho reveals her feelings freely: her love for a favourite; her grief at parting, when girls she had loved would leave to be married; her nostalgia in recalling the simple pleasures they had shared; her jealousy for such rivals as Gorgo, Mica or Andromeda.[54] It is the combination of strong feelings with exquisite delicacy of expression that gives her poetry its unique quality, a quality which captivated antiquity. She never makes the mistake of directing her verse at the intellect, for she knows that real poetry does not demand immediate thought but, rather, feeling and an instinctive response. She therefore writes so as to make her hearers feel first and only then think along the lines she chooses.

Her subjects are usually personal, and her treatment of them contains little narrative, but they all have directness and power. Horace, who had read all Sappho's poetry, described her as *querentem/Sappho puellis de popu-laribus*. That was the dominant note of her most beautiful songs, for her affections were clearly intense and jealous, and her sensitive nature probably made her difficult to live with. The simile in one fragment[55] about the friend who outshines the women of Sardis as the moon outshines the stars is followed by a passage whose influence on later poetry was immense. There the description of a moonlit night is not an extended simile of the sort familiar from Homer but something new: a magnificent description of the very night on which Sappho and Atthis send their thoughts across the sea.

In the modern world Sappho's stature as a lyric poet of the highest order is based mainly on two poems. The first is her only surviving complete ode,[56] in which she invokes Aphrodite, imploring her not to break Sappho's heart with pain and sorrow but to help her as she has done once before. The second is the celebrated poem in which she describes her sensations on seeing and hearing the girl she loves.[57]

Pseudo-Longinus, who quotes the poem,[58] considered it a love poem, and as such it was regarded throughout antiquity. Catullus translated (or, rather, paraphrased) it, and elements from it were often used by Greek and Roman poets to describe the pathology of love. And it is largely on the evidence of this ode that most modern writers have accepted the scurrilities which the Athenian comic poets heaped on Sappho's name. But whatever the intimacies of her life may have been, it is clear that in her own day on Lesbos her reputation was unblemished.[59]

It might be worth adding that Maximus of Tyre (c. A.D. 125–85) compared the lovely girls who were Sappho's friends and pupils with the handsome young men who were Socrates' disciples in Athens, and her rivals, Gorgo and Andromeda, to his opponents Prodicus, Gorgias and Protagoras.[60] However, the fact remains that it is only the physical beauty of her companions that Sappho praises; there is never a word about any spiritual, moral or intellectual qualities they may have.[61]

Of the poems addressed by Sappho to members of her family, the most famous is that on the journey home from Egypt of her brother Charaxus, in which she also prays that the *hetaera* Doricha, with whom he has had a costly love affair, may never again bother him. But new discoveries have revealed fragments showing how tender were the poet's relations with her daughter.

It was natural that the services of such a gifted poet should have been called upon by her fellow citizens for the composition of wedding songs, and, in fact, some of the most beautiful fragments of her poetry come from such epithalamia. Side by side with these, the few humorous fragments of her poetry which survive also all come from such wedding songs, of which genre they formed a traditionally ribald, playful part. It must be confessed, however, that her humour in such places is heavy and flat. And it may be added that one of the most famous—and exquisite—of her traditional ascriptions:[62]

> The moon is gone
> and the Pleiades set
> midnight is here;
> time passes on,
> yet alone I lie.

is now thought not to have been written by her, and that Attic forms found in one fragment,[63] a narrative poem on the wedding of Hector and Andromache, have raised some doubts about its authenticity.

Sappho's language is simple. She uses the vernacular of Lesbos, and her every verse is direct and unaffected. Homeric elements are few except in the dactylic verses and almost never occur as mere ornaments of style. Among her metrical innovations is included the Sapphic stanza, consisting of three Sapphic eleven-syllable lines, and one Adoneus,[64] which was later to be used with such effect by Horace. Hers also is a poem[65] that marks the first explicit appearance in Western literature of the idea that song confers immortality.

In the whole history of Greece no other woman poet achieved Sappho's fame or exerted her influence on the development of lyrical poetry. Fifth-century vases testify to her popularity in Athens, as does the portrait of her which was set up on the Athenian Acropolis; the Syracusans also erected a statue of her in their town hall. She was greatly admired by the Alexandrians, who collected her work into nine books, arranged according to metre, and included her in their canon of lyric poets. She was read in schools up to the fourth century A.D., as Themistius tells us. The source of her unique success is perhaps best summed up by Pseudo-Longinus as 'the skill with which she selects and binds together the most striking and vehement circumstances of passion'.[66]

Anacreon of Teos

No less famous than Sappho and Alcaeus of Lesbos was the Ionian Anacreon of Teos (c. 563–478 B.C.), the son of Scythinus. His poems, however, belong to a totally different world, for the sixth century was a time of expansion and change. Economic prosperity and contact with foreign cultures had led to the rise of a more pleasure-loving society, to which the age of the tyrannies brought a reasonable degree of political calm. These new social and political conditions made it possible for the poet to travel in search of patrons, and this had a profound influence on his work, since now it fell to the poet's lot to comply with his patron's individual whims of taste rather than with the traditions of a fixed society.

Thus Anacreon did not confine himself to writing for a circle in his native land but looked for patrons abroad. The Persian danger had in any case induced him early in life (c. 545) to leave Teos and to join in the foundation of the colony of Abdera in Thrace. He found his first patron in Polycrates, the Tyrant of Samos, whose son he was employed to instruct in music; on Polycrates' death (c. 522) he went to Athens, to the court of Hipparchus, on whose downfall he found refuge with the art-loving rulers of Thessaly. Later in life he returned to Athens, where after his death he was honoured by a statue on the Acropolis.

In the world of Anacreon's patrons the time for singing was over the wine, so most of his songs were of wine and love, suited to convivial gatherings. He took little interest in politics or war, and, as he himself tells us, he too threw away his shield in battle, as had become fashionable for soldier-poets since Archilochus.[67] He may also have written odes for sacred festivals;[68] and the Alexandrians certainly knew of iambic and elegiac poetry by him, which is now lost.

Anacreon did not take life too seriously, and he enjoyed his drinking, but he was also careful to comply with the standard of behaviour in the aristrocratic *symposia* which he was now attending and which were very different from the rowdy drinking bouts of an Alcaeus.[69]

Anacreon certainly knew the delight and the intensity of love, but, unlike Sappho, he never seems to have experienced its darker side. His passions were neither lasting nor deep. In contrast to the experience of

Alcaeus, women played a considerable part in the life and writing of Anacreon. They were, it is true, mostly flute girls or the kind of slave girl who attended banquets. But handsome boys, flute players like Bathyllus of Samos or aristocratic youths like Critias in Athens, uncle of the famous Athenian statesman of the same name, were also among his favourites. Not surprisingly, the hedonistic Anacreon hated old age and the prospect of death and, unlike Solon, found in learning no consolation for growing old. Nevertheless, he is said to have lived to the age of eighty-five.

Anacreon uses an Ionic vernacular with very few traces of Homeric or Aeolic language. He is a master of words, employing many striking new epithets. No less remarkable are his original and individual images. His picture of Eros setting to work on his victim like a blacksmith was to enjoy a long and varied life, eventually re-entering the Greek tradition in the sixteenth-century verse romance *Erotokritos* by way of the emblem books (*emblemata amatoria*) of Western Europe.[70]

His metres are usually simple. He favours a stanza made up of glyconics, with pherecrateans for *clausulae*; and he often used a minor Ionic verse, with anaclasis, called after him the anacreontic.[71] He is remarkable for his combination of fancy and wit, which prevents him from taking life too seriously. On the whole, his poetry is characterized by a gentle resignation, though he can also be sharp and cruel, as in his poem on Artemon.[72] His works were edited in antiquity by Aristarchus and made up six books of *Mele* (Μέλη), *Iamboi* (Ἴαμβοι) and *Elegeia* (Ἐλεγεῖα); and he was included in the Alexandrian canon of lyric poets.

Anacreon's Hellenistic and Byzantine imitators left a large number of poems whose form and content were modelled on his and were known as the *Anacreontea*.[73] In them charm often gave way to artificiality and insipidity, but nonetheless they had a huge influence on the poets of the seventeenth and eighteenth centuries in France, England and Germany. These countless imitations also had the effect of presenting Anacreon to posterity as a bibulous old lecher, an impression which is not confirmed by the surviving genuine fragments. There is nothing degraded or degenerate in his poetry.

Corinna, Telesilla, Praxilla

Quite separate from the main stream of lyric development was the poetry written in different parts of Greece by women for women, the most important of whom were Corinna, Telesilla, and perhaps Praxilla. All wrote a special kind of traditional verse which told local myths in simple language.

Corinna, the lyricist of Tanagra, was thought in antiquity to be an older contemporary of Pindar, whom she was said to have defeated in several poetry competitions. Another tradition makes her the pupil of the lyrical poetess Myrtis, who came from Anthedon on the north coast of Boeotia. Substantial papyrus remains of two of Corinna's poems[74] have been found which enable us to form a clearer picture of her poetry than was hitherto possible. In the first she describes a contest in song between the mountain gods, Cithaeron and Helicon, which is decided by the gods at the Muses' invitation. Cithaeron is proclaimed the winner amid an angry shower of rocks from Helicon, a bad loser. In the second the seer Acraephen foretells the destiny of the daughters of Asopus, who will be found worthy of the love of great gods and from whom will descend great princely houses.

All else that we know of Corinna's poetry is connected with Boeotian myths—some purely local, others more widely known—with such titles as *Boeotus, Seven Against Thebes, Euonymie, Iolaus* and *Cataplous* (the *Return of Orion*). In another of her works, whose title we know to have been *Ϝεροῖα*,[75] a word of uncertain meaning, she proudly speaks of her poems and their success. The view held before the discovery of this papyrus that the title was *Γεροῖα* (*Geroia: Old Wives' Tales*) is no longer tenable.

Corinna's language does not perfectly reflect her native Boeotian, for it contains elements drawn from the common stock of Greek poetic diction. Nevertheless, a Boeotian colouring is evident.[76] Her verse forms, such as minor Ionics and choriambic dimeters, are simple.

She enjoyed some celebrity in the ancient world. She was added as a tenth poet to the Alexandrian canon of the nine lyric poets; Ovid named after her the central figure of his love elegies; and Pausanias saw in Tanagra the monument set up in her honour.[77] Nevertheless, there is no reference to her before the first century B.C. Furthermore, the text of her poems as transmitted is in the reformed Boeotian spelling of the third century B.C., a fact which has led certain scholars to believe that she herself lived in that century. As Page puts it: *Manet res in ambiguo.* However, if (as seems more probable) she wrote earlier, her works must at some time have been transliterated from the original script.

Telesilla came from Argos and lived in the fifth century B.C. She was famous for arming the women of Argos after their city's defeat by Cleomenes.[78] The Telesilleion metre, also known as the acephalous glyconic,[79] was named after her by the Alexandrians. Like Corinna, she seems to have addressed her poems to a mainly female audience.[80] Nine fragments of her work survive, all of which seem to come from hymns to Apollo and Artemis in particular, but an Epidaurian hymn to the mother of the gods, sometimes ascribed to her because of the Telesilleion metre in which it is written, seems to be a later imitation.

Praxilla of Sicyon deserves mention here, although she lived later, in the middle of the fifth century (c. 451 B.C.). She wrote dithyrambs, drinking songs and hymns, including one to Adonis, of which a line became proverbial for its silliness.[81] Adonis is there made to say that when he died high in the list of things he missed were 'the beautiful cucumbers, apples and pears'. In spite of this lapse, her memory was held in honour, for in the fourth century her fellow citizen Lysippus cast a statue of her in bronze.

It will be noticed that it was in Lesbos, Boeotia and the Peloponnese that women were able to win a lasting reputation for poetry, certainly not in Athens.

CHORAL LYRIC POETRY

Lyric poetry, in the sense of song accompanied by a musical instrument, existed from a very early period in Greece, in both the monodic and the choral form. Homer, as we have already seen, betrays a knowledge of several kinds of the latter: the dirge, the paean, the *hymenaeus*, the *hyporchema* and the maiden song. In all of them the procedure seems to have been the same, although the occasion for each was different. There was a choir and a choir leader, and each song was accompanied by music and dancing. These characteristics survived for centuries, and the different types of song known to Homer were standard parts of Greek life long after his day.

Another early type of choral song was the *prosodion*, or processional song. Homer makes no mention of it, but we know it was already in existence in the middle of the eighth century, when Eumelus of Corinth wrote one such for the Messenian choir which was sent to Delos (Paus., 4, 33.2).[82] The dithyramb is also, as its unexplained name would suggest, of great antiquity, though the Greeks maintained that it was invented at Corinth in the age of Periander by the Lesbian harpist Arion. That this is no more than a legend is attested by the fact that the dithyramb, as we saw, is mentioned by Archilochus long before the days of Periander.

Whatever the origins of choral lyric, the genre has an important place in the history of Greek poetry, and indeed of Greek cultural life generally, by forming the link between epic and tragedy, the two major literary forms of the ancient world. Lyric spoke with many voices, ranging from the Boeotian Pindar's old-fashioned, aristocratic austerity to the forward-looking versatility of the Ionian Simonides.

The first hint of organized choral poetry among the Greeks is found in Sparta, to which the musician Thaletas of Gortyn in Crete was summoned in the middle of the seventh century to write songs exhorting the Spartan citizens to be law-abiding. He is also said to have written paeans,[83] of which nothing is known.

Alcman

Alcman is one of the few choral poets of the seventh century of whom any fragments survive. He was probably a Lydian from Sardis who, like Thaletas, came to Sparta while she was still open to foreign influence. Some have said that he was a Laconian from Messoa, but support for his Sardian origin has been found in a fragment of his own,[84] in which he may be addressing himself. It has also been claimed that he was a slave who was granted his liberty because of his poetic skill.

From what we can gather, Alcman's poetry is mainly concerned with Spartan feasts and festivals. His lyrical poems were later collected in six books, but his language did not interest the Atticists, and his work was left to perish.

His output seems to have been mainly choral and to have been sung by choirs of maidens. Of one of his maiden songs more than half survives,[85] but its brilliant images and melodic beauty are unfortunately accompanied by several insoluble problems of interpretation. In it, all the traditional features of the ode are observed: first, the myth (in this case, that of the sons of Hippocoön, slain by Heracles); second, the maxims; and finally, the address to personalities. The poem has been variously ascribed to festivals of Artemis, the Dioscuri, Dionysus and Helen; and it seems to have been sung at night in some sort of competition with another choir. The section dealing with personalities, into which Alcman passes very abruptly, is of special interest. Its remarks are addressed directly to the girl singers and to the onlookers.

The many unsolved problems of this poem do not stop us from enjoying its freshness and unconventional quality. Not the least of its virtues is the swift movement of the metre, with recurring strophes of fourteen lines in a mainly trochaic and dactylic rhythm.

Alcman also wrote on cosmology,[86] and some of his fragments come from hymns to the Dioscuri, Hera, Athena, Apollo and Aphrodite, while one seems to describe a nocturnal festival of Dionysus.[87] He also wrote in hexameters what may have been preludes to recitations of Homer. He writes with unaffected charm about simple matters, and there are occasional fairy-tale touches, as when he speaks about the ways of the birds, or how the partridges taught him to sing.[88]

The *Suda* credits him with the invention of love poems, but his fragments give no evidence of this beyond the tender emotions which he describes between the different members of the choir. Again, the beautiful fragment in which he describes the stillness of the night[89] should not be seen as pure nature poetry in the style of modern descriptive lyrics. Like Sappho,[90] Theocritus,[91] Apollonius Rhodius[92] and Virgil,[93] he is probably marking the contrast between the peace of nature and the unrest of a human heart. His metres are varied and usually simple, though some fragments exist in which he shows an advanced technique.

Stesichorus of Himera

The first important literary figure of the world of the western Greeks was Stesichorus of Himera (c. 630–553). He seems to have taken part in politics and was exiled as a result of his attempt to prevent Phalaris from installing himself as tyrant of Acragas. It is said that he lived to extreme old age.

His significance must be judged today mainly from what the ancient Greeks said of him, since the scanty surviving fragments of his work give little idea of his art. But enough remains of his poetry for us to see that he was the precursor of Pindar and Simonides.

Stesichorus wrote lyrics in an artificial epic dialect marked with a slight tinge of Dorian. What gives him a special place in the history of Greek poetry is that, abandoning the old connections of the choral ode with ritual, he turned it into a form of lyrical narrative. This had the effect of drawing his poetry close to the epic, from which he borrowed many of his subjects. As Quintilian succinctly puts it, 'in his lyrics he sustains the heavy weight of the epic'.[94]

A new fragment[95] has confirmed what the *Suda* had previously maintained, namely, that it was Stesichorus who replaced Alcman's single strophe with the triple division of the epodic scheme. This enlargement of the choral framework suited his epic subjects, which called for a more massive structure; and this lead of Stesichorus' was followed by Pindar.

Thus Stesichorus is of key importance in that stage of Greek poetry which stands between epic and tragedy, especially as regards the transmission of myth. For it was he who started, or at least promoted, the literary career of such famous themes as the murder of Agamemnon or the Egyptian Helen. This close connection with the epic is also responsible for the objective quality of Stesichorus' choral poetry, in contrast with the pronounced subjective character of Alcman's poetry.

Two poems connected with the Trojan Cycle, a *Helen* and a *Palinodia*, gave rise to a legend about Stesichorus. In the first poem he is said to have included everything found in the myth cycle which was unfavourable to Helen. For this reason the gods blinded him, but, prompted by Helen herself, he wrote the second, the *Palinodia*, retracting what he had said in the first, and thus regained his sight.

Stesichorus did not draw his inspiration only from the subjects of the great epics or from the myths surrounding Heracles, whose cult was important in the West. He also used the popular legends of his country and developed their erotic themes, thus breaking new ground. His lyric treatment of popular love stories, as in his *Calyca* or his *Rhadina*, carried the germ of the romance, later to be developed in prose by the Greek novel writers; and his lyric pastoral, *Daphnis*, was the earliest example of bucolic poetry.

Surviving fragments show that he used a kind of dactylo-epitrite metre. His works were later collected in twenty-six books and exerted great influence, starting with the visual arts of the archaic period[96] and ending with the Alexandrians, in whose canon of lyric poets he was also included.

Another new fragment[97] has proved to contain the famous simile known from the *Iliad* (VIII, 306–8), in which a dying warrior, bending his head, is likened to a broken poppy. The theme passed to Virgil, from Virgil to Ariosto, and from Ariosto it found its way into the *Erotokritos* of Kornaros, the sixteenth-century Cretan verse romance, and thus returned to the mainstream of the Greek poetic tradition, a unique phenomenon in the history of poetry.

Ibycus of Rhegium

The poetry of another Greek from southern Italy, Ibycus of Rhegium (c. 560 B.C.), also reflects the changing conditions through which poets were living. His life seems to fall into two periods. In the first, during which he was still living in his native Rhegium, he wrote choral lyrics in the epic style, probably under the influence of Stesichorus. Among the stories he used were the legend of the Argonauts and tales from the Trojan Cycle. During the second period he worked at the court of Polycrates in Samos, where he composed love poetry which, to judge from its fragments, was as passionate as anything of Sappho's. Ibycus had to write for his living, and a recent fragment from Egypt gives a glimpse of him as a courtier of the tyrant, Polycrates, and of his son. This is pure court poetry, designed to please and to amuse.

To the ancients[98] he was the most passionate of all Greek poets and more susceptible than Anacreon or Alcaeus to the charms of beautiful youths. His style is rich and brilliant, but its heavy luxuriance contrasts strongly with the immediacy of Sappho.

He too was included in the canon of the nine lyrical poets by the Alexandrians, who collected his works into seven books. They seem largely to have consisted of choral poems, of which some were *encomia* and personal love songs, written in a wide variety of metres. His most important innovation seems to have been the use of choral lyric to express erotic passion.

Simonides of Ceos

If Stesichorus extended the scope of the choral hymn from gods to heroes, and if Ibycus used it to express personal emotions, a third poet, Simonides, succeeded in making it encompass the achievements of contemporary men.

The son of Leoprepes, he was born in Iulis on Ceos (c. 558–468 B.C.), some six years after Anacreon and forty years before Pindar, and grew up in a society which disapproved of all luxury. This upbringing is reflected in his poems, whose striking simplicity gives them a special place in the history of choral lyric. An Ionian by birth and temperament, he chose the Doric choral form for his lyrics, which were therefore composed in an artificial epic language with a Dorian tinge, similar to that of Stesichorus.

Simonides led an itinerant life which took him—he had a reputation for stinginess—to the tables of the great. From Hipparchus in Athens[99] he moved to the Scopads in Thessaly, then back to Athens again during the Persian Wars, where he is reputed to have belonged to the circle of Themistocles. His wanderings took him finally to the court of Hiero in Syracuse. He died in Sicily at the age of ninety and was buried at Acragas.

He wrote various kinds of poetry—hymns, *scolia* and *encomia*, dirges, epinician odes, elegies and inscriptional epigrams for dedications; but his reputation was first won by his songs in honour of the victors at the Pan-Hellenic Games. Victors in great athletic contests had undoubtedly been widely acclaimed long before Simonides, and certainly songs must have been improvised to celebrate their homecoming. But before Simonides we never hear on such occasions of a song composed by a great poet and sung by a chorus. We must therefore assume that it was he who opened up this new field for choral lyric.

By bringing athletic events into the sphere of high art, this development led to a connection between sport and art in the Greek world unparalleled before or since Pindar's death. Simonides' treatment of such contests does not, however, dwell on the technical details of sport. What is stressed is the world of the spirit. This is related to traditional myths, and finally the whole event is assessed and reconciled with the basic problems of human existence. That is the reason for the many maxims of general validity which are to be found in the epinician ode. All these elements are, however, strung together according to loose mental associations rather than any strict scheme of articulation.

The genre can, of course, best be studied in relation to the work of Pindar, for the fragments of Simonides' victory odes are not extensive. Yet, scanty though they may be, they still contain elements quite at variance with the ponderous seriousness of Pindar. One such example is the praise of a mortal and his favourable comparison with the sons of gods,[100] an idea which would have seemed blasphemous to earlier generations and is quite foreign to the piety of Pindar.

It is probable that Simonides was a pioneer in other kinds of choral lyric. Before his day laments for the dead and consolation in bereavement were expressed in elegiacs, as can be seen in the poetry of Archilochus and Mimnermus. But in the choral *threnos* of Simonides they found a new form. This is a development parallel to that whereby Ibycus brought into the scope of the choral ode such themes of the Lesbian monody as love.

Simonides may have been the first to make the *threnos*, or dirge, an accepted form of lyric poetry, but he did not sacrifice a sense of proportion and a purity of style when dealing with topics which were traditional to the epitaph. Only small fragments of his *threnoi* have survived, but the strange circumstances that gave rise to one of them became famous in antiquity. Just before the palace roof at Crannon fell, killing most of Scopas' guests, it is said that Simonides was called out of the hall by two unknown young men. The story was that they were the Dioscuri in disguise. Simonides later gave them their reward by celebrating them at great length in an ode. The *threnos* in question is also remarkable for introducing a simile which, in its humbleness, reveals one more facet of Simonides' artistic versatility. Human fortunes, he says, change 'as swiftly as a fly darts from one spot to another'. The dirge was the genre in which Horace says that Simonides excelled; and Catullus too speaks of Simonidean 'tears', as if his mastery of the artistic lament were proverbial.

The theme that all earthly things are transitory, often found in Greek poetry, is presented very forcefully by Simonides,[101] when he speaks of deadly Charybdis as being the end of all things in the world: courage, virtue and riches come to her in the end. Even posthumous fame sinks into the grave.[102] However, in celebrating the memory of those who fell at Thermopylae, he is capable of turning the lament into a song of praise by boldly uniting *threnos* with encomium, and all complaint at the transitoriness of life is suppressed. Only the highest praise is expressed, as is proper in an encomium.

This poem illustrates Simonides' participation through his poetry in the Greeks' great struggle for freedom, another respect in which he stands in direct contrast to Pindar, whose native city of Thebes had sided with the enemy during the Persian Wars. The defeat of the Persians brought Simonides great fame, for he wrote poems not only on the fallen at Thermopylae, but also on the fighters of Artemisium and Salamis, as well as a magnificent series of epigrams for the tombs of the heroic dead.

We have seen how from early times metrical inscriptions had been carved on the tombs of both men and women. But as taken over by Simonides, the form was transformed into something that was truly magnificent. In two to four lines he would immortalize the men of his time, using exactly the right words of praise. The story goes that Aeschylus himself wrote an epigram for the dead of Marathon, but it was judged inferior to that of Simonides, since it lacked 'tenderness and sympathy'—an admirable description of the qualities of Simonides at his best. We should remember, however, that the authenticity of these epigrams is often very doubtful. They were probably not collected until the fourth century and, in their inscribed form, would not have carried their author's name.[103]

Those qualities of tenderness and sympathy are also superbly expressed in Simonides' celebrated 'Danae fragment', a survival from which poem we do not know.[104] These deservedly famous lines illustrate the fact that Simonides' pathos embraced themes wider than that of death alone. His own saying that 'painting is silent poetry; poetry is spoken painting'[105] is borne out in his poetry. In the opinion of Dionysius of Halicarnassus, Simonides' art excelled even that of Pindar in the expression of sorrow through the use not of grandiose words, but of words that go straight to the heart.[106]

Simonides also composed drinking songs, for he had to sing at the tables of his hosts. Plato quotes one of them,[107] in which the poet seeks to substitute as the proper test of the good man a clear conscience in place of the traditional standard of all-round excellence. In another fragment of a drinking song[108] we meet for the first time the three types of life—money-loving, pleasure-loving and honour-loving—which were later to become so important to Greek ethical doctrines.

Simonides boasts towards the end of his activities in Athens that he has gained sixty-five victories with a male chorus:[109] that is to say, that he had successfully competed that number of times with dithyrambs in the Dionysia. He was honoured in antiquity not only as a poet but also as a sage, and many apophthegms are attributed to him. His powers of memory were also renowned, and he is said to have devised a system of memory training.

In his poetry Simonides gave perhaps the clearest expression to certain sides of the Ionian character—particularly in the prominence he accords to the human element. At the same time the Doric contribution to the choral ode is seen at its peak in his verse, whose harmonious fusion of Doric and Ionic elements has been compared with that of the Parthenon.

Pindar

Pindar (518–438 B.C.), the second of Boeotia's great poets, was born at Cynoscephalae, near Thebes, into a family that claimed connection with the ancient Dorian aristocracy. As a boy he was sent to Athens to study music and poetry under Apollodorus and Agathocles, and it was no doubt there that he became versed in the art of the choral ode, which had entered a vigorous period of development after being made an official part of the festival of the Great Dionysia in 508. It has been assumed that in Athens Pindar moved in aristocratic circles, which may account for his connection with the Alcmaeonidae, the only Athenians he ever celebrates in his extant verse.[110]

During the second Persian War (480–79) Pindar's connection with the pro-Persian nobility in Thebes can hardly be doubted.[111] In the years following the Greek victory his political mistakes were a heavy burden to him, but by the time of his visit to Sicily (476–74) his position had been re-established. Theron of Acragas and Hiero of Syracuse welcomed him to their courts, and he celebrated some of their greatest victories at the Pan-Hellenic Games. His Sicilian years may be said to have seen his fullest artistic development.

After the poet's return to Greece his prestige in Sicily seems to have declined, for Hiero's victory in the chariot race at Olympia in 468 was commemorated by Bacchylides. Elsewhere in Greece, however, Pindar enjoyed a great and growing reputation. He was a guest of the great families of Rhodes, Tenedos, Abdera, Sparta, Corinth, Argos and Aegina and even of Alexander of Macedon,[112] but he devoted his greatest efforts above all to Arcesilas IV, king of Cyrene, for whom he wrote one of his masterpieces,[113] an ode of almost epic scale.

Though Pindar's origins and temperament were completely alien to the new Athenian democratic ideas, in 474 he wrote the celebrated dithyramb in praise of Athens, from which come the lines: 'O glorious Athens— shining, violet-crowned, worthy of song, bulwark of Greece, city of the gods'.[114] For this he is said to have been honoured by the Athenians but fined at Thebes. It is possible that he defended himself against the Theban charges in *Pyth.* IX. Later, however, when Athens conquered his beloved Aegina and then Boeotia, he characterized the 'violet-crowned' city in very different terms, as the arrogant Bellerophon, the murderous Aegisthus or the giant Porphyrion. But in his latest extant poem,[115] though he recognizes the desire of Aegina to be free of Athens, he sets the passing issues of politics in the wider context of human destiny. It is in the concluding lines of that song that we find the famous pessimistic words: 'What is man? The dream of a shadow, no more.' However that may be, by far the most striking Pindaric dithyrambic fragment we have is that found at Oxyrhynchus,[116] which was written for Thebes and was entitled *Heracles* or *Cerberos*.

When Pindar died at Argos in c. 438, not long before the outbreak of the Peloponnesian War, he had lived through one of the most eventful periods of Greek history. As he grew old, having tasted both glory and reproach and having grown wealthy through the generosity of his patrons, he saw the aristocratic society he had loved and all it had stood for crumbling away under the impact of Athenian imperialism and rationalism.

We can follow Pindar's development through a period of roughly fifty years, for the first of his surviving poems[117] was composed in 498, when he was about twenty, while the latest was written in 446. But a comparison of the four books of his epinician odes and the few fragments of other poems known to us with the seventeen books of his poetry that existed in Alexandrian times shows us how little we really know of his work. The lost works contained an impressive variety of poetry: hymns to gods, paeans, dithyrambs, *prosodia* (processional songs), *partheneia* (maiden songs), *hyporchemata* (songs accompanied by dancing), dirges and encomia.

The epinicians have, by accident, survived almost complete. Despite their peculiar character, they are probably typical of Pindar's work as a whole, for the new fragments of other poems that have been retrieved are little different from them in style and thought. Each of the four books deals with one of the great Pan-Hellenic Games: the Olympic, the Pythian, the Nemean and the Isthmian. Some of the odes were composed to be recited at the scene of the festival,[118] whereas others were sung when the victor returned to his home city. The ode would also be repeated on successive anniversaries at banquets, festivals or processions in honour of the victory. One at least[119] was chanted by the poet himself as a monody in the halls of the victor's palace.

The subject-matter of these odes consists of a great deal more than simple athletic success. In fact, the details of the actual Games do not seem to have interested Pindar. For him, victory in the Games raised questions of religious and metaphysical importance; it illustrated glory as proceeding from the gods and success as something won by the proper use of natural gifts and strenuous effort. He knows that nobody can avoid death. But life has moments of divine illumination—among which are the victories of the athletes. By celebrating those victories the poet can help to retain the memory of such achievements, which is the only immortality men can hope for. The Homeric character of this view is clear to see.

The structure of the epinician ode is formal and governed by strict rules. In its simpler form[120] it consists of a series of strophes or stanzas, each of which is metrically identical. More often, however, Pindar uses a more complex system involving a series of triads, each of which consists of strophe, antistrophe and epode.[121] No two poems of Pindar are metrically the same.[122] He uses three main classes of metre: the Dorian or dactylo-epitrite; the Aeolian, which is built up from such elements as the glyconic and the choriambic dimeter; and the paeonic.[123] Such rhythms no doubt depended to a large extent on the music which accompanied them and which is now lost.[124]

The metrical formality of the Pindaric odes is not matched by any corresponding formality of content, although each epinician ode contains four traditional elements: praise of the gods; statements about the victor's person and family; a myth illustrating the occasion; and grave general truths, presented in the form of maxims.

The lack of any evident pattern, of a 'unity', in Pindar's odes, has been a matter for much discussion among scholars. Such unity as can be traced resides only in the addition of 'athletic success' to the battery of ethical values to which the old aristocratic order had held. These values colour Pindar's attitude towards the gods, the heroic myths, human conduct and the position of the poet in society.[125] He seems to have considered such values eternal and immutable. He believed in the innate and inherited qualities of a man (the $\varphi\upsilon\acute{a}$)[126] and held that training can only develop such qualities, never impart them.[127] Therefore a man who merely *acquires* ability (as distinct from displaying innate ability conferred by blood) 'never walks with a sure foot'.[128] These views are fully illustrated in his use of the myths of the heroes, whose blood, he maintained, still ran in the veins of the noble families to which the noble victors belonged.

In Pindar the status of the poet and of poetic achievement is significant. The poet is placed next to the triumphant athlete but is no less meritorious than he. Like the *arete* of the Olympic victor, the art of the poet cannot be learned: it is essentially 'wisdom' and skill. Pindar frequently uses the word $\sigma o\varphi\acute{\iota}a$ when speaking about the poetic gift. Finally, and perhaps most significantly, his verse elevates athletic achievement to the realm of immortality. 'Noble deeds must perish if no one speaks of them', he tells us in one of his fragments.[129] But the celebration of athletic victory, like the victory itself, comes from the gods[130]—an essentially religious outlook.

Pindar has a lively awareness of a divine principle which he conceives as permeating the universe, but he is neither superstitious nor credulous. In his pantheon Zeus has pride of place, closely followed by the Delphic Apollo, the protector of aristocratic values. The poet's close connection with the sanctuary at Delphi was legendary in antiquity. During his life he enjoyed special privileges at Delphi, and after his death he was honoured there. We are told that his iron chair was preserved at the temple, and that before closing the temple gates the priest would cry: 'Let Pindar the poet enter the banquet of the gods!'

Pindar's use of myth is bold and allusive. He chooses freely from mythology but stresses only what is useful for his purpose. (In *Pyth.* IV, for example, the story of Jason and the Argonauts is told with masterly conciseness.) The real beauty of the myths in Pindar arises from his power of giving vivid, disjointed pictures; and the force with which he portrays such moments in myth is unique. Such an unforgettable moment is conveyed in the picture of Pelops, approaching the 'grey sea' in the dark of night and calling on Poseidon to help him with Hippodameia.[131]

Next to his use of the myths, we are struck by Pindar's proverbial wisdom; for his maxims often achieve great beauty and insight, closely connected with what he conceives as the poet's calling. The language in which all this is expressed, however, is one of elaborate artificiality.

Pindar's mixture of dialects, his many echoes of Homer, his massive sentence structure weighed down with rugged ornament, his emphasis on the noun, which reduces the verb to a mere prop in the sentence, his rejection of antithesis and of the usual Greek particles all combine to make him a poet who is very hard to read. An even greater difficulty is posed by his abruptness of manner. At the same time it must be admitted that he says a great deal in a small space, and this lends poetical power and weight to his undeniably majestic verse. We are dazzled by his virtuosity as he leads us through a series of different effects—narrative, personal, didactic—with breath-taking shifts from mood to mood.

To some extent, our knowledge of Pindar has been helped by papyrus discoveries, the larger fragments among which have given us some idea of his other works. It is our knowledge of the paeans and the *partheneia* that has been most greatly advanced. By contrast, the remains of the *prosodia* are very scanty, and we can determine very little about his *hyporchemata*. There is also much uncertainty as to which fragments should be considered to come from *scolia* and which from encomia. A beautiful fragment celebrating Pindar's favourite young athlete, Theoxenous, probably belongs to the latter class.

Pindar was acclaimed throughout antiquity as the greatest of lyric poets—'by far the chief of all the lyricists', as Quintilian says. He was called the 'Theban Eagle', and his poetry was compared with the thunderous flow of a river.[132] Indeed, to this day the Western world looks on his creations with awe. They may be alien to the concept of Greek 'Classicism', as it has come to be interpreted in the West since the Renaissance, but it is worth pointing out that Pindaric poetry was out of touch with the poetic fashions of its own day. Like most other forms of Greek literature, the lyric had been moving away from obscure force in the direction of lucidity—and in the writings of Simonides and Bacchylides it had already passed from one to the other. But Pindar set himself so firmly against this stream that we could find no greater contrast to the free expression of personal feeling of Ionian and Aeolian poetry, from Archilochus to Sappho, than Pindar's subordination of his verse to a religious and aristocratic ideal.

Pindar's idea of an aristocracy of race is the same as that expressed in plastic form in the Greek sculptures of the late Archaic and early Classical periods. The perfect harmony of body and soul which those sculptured athletes represented lives and speaks to us again in Pindar's poetry, telling of a unique moment when the Greek world saw the height of divinity in the human body and soul. And the resemblance goes even deeper. The statues show the same attitude as that of Pindar's poetry to the victorious athletes whom they depict: they do not record the individual features but rather the ideal male body, trained for victory. Pindar too writes about the victor not primarily as an individual but rather as the representative of an abstraction: the highest *arete*. As soon as the Greeks began to feel that the spirit was independent of the body or even hostile to it, that athletic–spiritual ideal became degraded. It lost its important position in life and survived merely as sport.

Pindar's poetry, which looked facts in the face and did not minimize evils — care, disease, old age and death — could never, by the very nature of its subjects, become universal poetry, as Homer's had done. In fact, one wonders if his poems can ever have been readily understood when sung. In *Nem.* V the poet tells us how his sweet song will 'sail off from Aegina in the big ships and the little fishing boats' as they return from the festival. Yet one cannot easily imagine a Dorian fisherman who could seize at one hearing a song of such complexity.

Bacchylides

In leaving Pindar we turn our backs on the aristocratic world, which from now on sinks ever deeper into silence. With Simonides' nephew Bacchylides (c. 470 B.C.?) we 're-enter the clamorous stream of history'.

Bacchylides was no more than a name to us until 1896, when a lucky papyrus find restored a considerable part of his work — the remains of fifteen epinician odes and six dithyrambs (which, however, have no connection with Dionysus, as one would have expected, and hardly mention his name). But we know that he also wrote hymns, paeans, processional songs, maiden songs, *hyporchemata* and encomia. He seems to have followed the fortunes of his uncle and to have been employed by the same patrons, for he too was a guest of Hiero. In Sicily he appears to have incurred the dislike of Pindar, who is thought to have made disparaging remarks about him.[133] He is also said to have been exiled to the Peloponnese. The date of his death is unknown.

His odes were written for festive occasions, and their structure recalls Pindar's epinician odes. But in style and spirit they belong to a totally different world. Bacchylides is a true Ionian: his style is limpid and gay and quite free of any didactic elements. He has a real gift for narrative and a fine command of epithets. Some of his stories, like the one about the rescue of Croesus of Lydia,[134] have a wonderful immediacy.

For his Athenian audience Bacchylides composed two striking poems about their national hero, Theseus.[135] One of them[136] is significant in the history of Greek poetry, for it is the only known example in a dithyramb of a dialogue between the chorus and their leader. The latter speaks the thoughts of Aegeus while his son is making his way to Athens, slaying monsters and robbers. It is not clear, however, whether this poem is a survival of an older form of dithyramb or has been influenced by the technique of early Attic drama.[137] Whichever is the case, Bacchylides points to a new age in which the main honours were to fall to drama; for after him and Pindar the golden age of the choral lyric came to an end. It fell from popularity, and its traditions were partly absorbed in the lyrical sections of the drama and partly debased into the new forms of dithyramb.[138]

It is true that the various types of older choral poetry persisted into the fifth century and even later: Euripides wrote an epinician for Alcibiades and Sophocles a paean for Asclepius. But as the Greek aristocracies fell into decay and tragedy gained in importance, the best poets seldom wrote choral hymns. Furthermore, the occasions which called for such hymns were no longer as important in the new world, in which the internal dissensions of Hellas began to have their effect on the old national festivals. The only popular choral poetry of the later fifth and fourth centuries was, as we shall see, the dithyramb, which underwent considerable changes, becoming looser in form, more concerned with music than with words and more artificial in language (Attic comedy later satirized this moribund phase of lyric poetry).

By the time of the Persian Wars. the great ages of both epic and lyric had passed away. As we have seen, the most important poetic activity had taken place mainly in the Greek world beyond the Aegean Sea—that is, in the Ionian and Aeolic areas—although Boeotia, represented by Hesiod and Pindar, and the western Greeks, with figures like Stesichorus and Ibycus, had their part to play as well. Nonetheless, by the end of this period the centre of interest had moved to Attica, and thereafter Athens dominated the cultural and political picture until the rise of the Macedonians and the conquest of the East by Alexander.

SECTION II

From the Persian Wars to the Death of Alexander (490–323 B.C.)

Introduction

The expansion of Greece and the maturing of the city-states had taken place at a time when neighbouring peoples were either undeveloped or quiescent. But the situation was changed by the sudden rise of Persia in the middle of the sixth century and by the conquest by that powerful empire of the Greek colonies on the western coast of Asia Minor.

The presence of the Persians in the Aegean world did not prevent the Greeks from warring among themselves, but they were also capable of joint action. When in 449 B.C. the Ionians revolted against their Persian masters, Athens and Eretria came to their support. But the revolt was finally crushed in the sea battle at Lade (a small island off Miletus, now joined to the mainland) and in retaliation for the intervention a Persian expeditionary force was sent against Greece proper. It started by destroying Eretria but was finally defeated by an alliance of Athens and Plataea at the famous battle of Marathon (490), a victory which was to influence the course of European history.

Nine years later Xerxes, with a huge army and a large fleet, invaded the Greek mainland from the north, but he was also defeated, at Salamis in 480 and at Plataea in 479. In the west also the Greeks of Sicily ensured their independence by decisively defeating the Carthaginians in 480, a victory which took place on the very same day as the battle of Salamis.

Greek self-confidence and pride were enormously strengthened by these victories over the Persians and Carthaginians. The result was a new Pan-Hellenic feeling which recognized the common bonds uniting Greeks while contrasting the Greek and 'barbarian' (or non-Greek) ways of life. The new feeling found expression in the worship of the Olympian gods, who transcended the lesser, merely local divinities, and in the great Pan-Hellenic festivals of Delphi, Olympia, Nemea and the Isthmus. But, soon after the Persian Wars, the power of traditional religion began to recede in Greece, giving way before rationalism, individualism and humanism. The new movements resulted in unparalleled intellectual and artistic achievements but also diminished creative political power.

In the aftermath of victory over the Persians, Sparta lost her leadership in the Greek world and was replaced by Athens. The Athenians, planning to carry the war into the Persian camp, organized their supporters into the so-called Delian League, which was in all except name an Athenian alliance. Under the leadership of Cimon, the League expelled the Persians from the Aegean world, and Greek maritime trade was safeguarded.

But in 462–1 an advanced democracy was established in Athens under the leadership of Ephialtes and Pericles, whose foreign policy was aggressive towards both Persia and Sparta and involved the exploitation of the League members. By energetic and courageous action Athens won a favourable peace with Persia and reached stalemate with Sparta. She also succeeded in converting her alliance into an empire, an achievement which was recognized at the start of the Thirty Years' Peace in 445.

The Peace, which divided the Greek states into two armed camps, produced a cessation of hostilities for only fourteen years: but they were the most splendid years of Athenian history. Athens was the acknowledged ruler of a Greek empire, the leading sea power in the Mediterranean and the centre of the artistic and intellectual life of the Hellenic world. The period is sometimes called the 'Age of Pericles'; it was Pericles who set the stamp of his personality on the policy and culture of the city and adorned it with the magnificent public buildings which still excite men's admiration today.

But in spite of the peace, Pericles was determined to eliminate Spartan power, and Sparta took up the challenge. The result was the long and disastrous Peloponnesian War (431–404), which ended in the complete defeat of Athens and the end of her empire. The Periclean dream was shattered for ever. But Sparta's victory was limited, for Persian influence on Greek affairs was again becoming strong. Sparta tried to unite the Greek states against the renewed Persian threat, but when Thebes and Athens rose against her she disgracefully traded the liberty of the Ionian Greeks in return for Persian help nearer home, and she also imposed her will on the Greek mainland cities by authoritarian means. Thebes and Athens once more rose against her, and Thebes, led by Epaminondas, decisively defeated the Spartan army at Leuctra (371), while the Athenians swept the seas clear of the Spartan navy.

Once in the position of power, however, Thebes and Athens soon quarrelled with one another and pursued separate imperialist policies which came to grief in the Social War (357–355) and the Sacred War (365–346). Meanwhile in Sicily the ruthless tyrant Dionysius of Syracuse had imposed unity after 405, had defeated Carthage again and had allied himself with Sparta. But his son, who succeeded him, was expelled by the Syracusans, who then suffered a period of anarchy.

This century of ceaseless political turmoil was also a time of great intellectual and artistic activity, during which Greek society was fast moving towards a common Hellenic outlook which transcended the boundaries of city-state nationalism. In one respect the city states failed totally: they were unable to unite the Greek world under a common leadership. This task was to be achieved finally by the Macedonians. Having shown its solidarity and military power over Thebes and Athens at the battle of Chaeroneia (338), the Macedonian state was in a position to persuade the Greeks to enter into a federal union with guarantees of autonomy and, finally, to ally themselves with the Macedonians in a joint war against Persia. The military genius of Philip II and of his son Alexander the Great raised Macedonia into a world power which came to adopt Greek culture wholesale.

Alexander succeeded to the throne after the murder of his father in 336 and at once devoted himself to the project of invading Asia. After conquering western and south-western Asia Minor, he defeated the Persian army at Issus (333) and spent the next year in occupying Phoenicia, Palestine and Egypt. In 331 he met and defeated at the battle of Gaugamela the Persian king Darius III, conquered the Persian capitals of Babylon, Susa, Persepolis and Ecbatana, where the vast treasures of the empire were stored, and assumed the title of *Basileus* ('Great King'). All further resistance he treated as rebellion; even so, the conquest of Bactria and Sogdiana took him three years of hard fighting.

The Indian expedition of 327–325 extended the eastern boundaries of Alexander's empire to the Hyphasis and the lower Indus. But having overrun the Punjab, Alexander was forced to turn back because his army refused to follow him further. After an arduous return journey to Persia the great conqueror died, a mere thirty-three years of age, of a fever in Babylon

Meanwhile, in Greece itself many city-states had resisted the Macedonians before the death of Alexander and continued to do so afterwards. But a war in 323–322 conducted by the Athenians and the Aetolian League ended in the defeat of the Athenians and the suicide of Demosthenes, the orator and leader of the anti-Macedonian faction. Thereafter the fortunes of the Greek states depended entirely on the strength of the kingdom of Macedonia. Such subsequent events and the results of Alexander's spectacular conquests will be discussed in Part Two, for they did not make themselves felt until the reign of his successors.

The period under consideration in this section produced some of the greatest achievements in poetry, philosophy, history, oratory, architecture and sculpture in the history of the world. The centre for all this intellectual and artistic activity was the city of Athens, where foreigners were welcome and freedom of thought and speech were possible.

The dramatic changes which the fifth century brought to the intellectual life of Greece were due to a great extent to the Sophistic movement, whose intellectual antecedents reached a long way back. The Sophists, after whom the movement is named, were itinerant teachers, who went from city to city giving instruction for a fee. The subjects they taught varied somewhat in content but were always associated with the art of succeeding in life. (Their nearest modern parallel is to be found in the many institutions which advertise their skill in training people for success in business or in life in general.) The Sophists flocked to Athens from all parts of Greece and had an influence at once enlightening and disruptive, which both enlarged and changed the Greek view of life. They shook belief in the old religious, moral, political and social systems, and eventually brought about the dissolution of the city-state. The proud fifth-century confidence in the democracy of the city-state thus became clouded with doubt and gave place to that disillusionment which can be seen in Plato. Demosthenes' appeals to the spirit, which would have inspired the age of Pericles, failed to awaken any enduring response in the perplexed fourth century.

In the field of poetry, and particularly in the dithyramb and the drama, the influence of the Sophists was paramount. It was through them that drama moved from the 'older' tragedy of Aeschylus and Sophocles to the 'modern' tragedy of Euripides and Agathon; from the political Old, to the social Middle Comedy; and from the older, disciplined dithyramb to the loose and turbulent works of Philoxenus and Timotheus. Moreover, by the fourth century poetry had lost its traditional and unique position as the teacher of the nation. Its place had been usurped by prose, which now reached full maturity. The great age of poetry was past, together with belief in the myths which had fed that poetry.

From inscriptions we know that the old festivals, with their poetic competitions, continued for centuries. But the quality of the works produced in that connection constantly declined, so that even in antiquity little was considered worth preserving. In fact, from the middle of the fourth century all the cultural tendencies had started to move towards the pattern typical of the Hellenistic age, which is discussed in Part Two. In many respects, trends which we consider Hellenistic were already asserting themselves even before the establishment of the kingdoms of Alexander's successors.

CHAPTER 3

Tragedy

During the archaic period there was on the mainland nothing comparable with the lively poetic and artistic activity we have followed in the eastern and western extremities of the Greek world. However, developments were taking place which would lead in the Peloponnese to the perfection of the dithyramb and, in Attica, of the dramatic form, one of the greatest achievements of all Greek literature. It is appropriate, therefore, to preface our discussion of Greek tragedy with a brief survey of the dithyramb.

DITHYRAMB AND TRAGEDY

The word dithyramb, of unknown (probably non-Greek) etymology, first appears in Archilochus.[1] He calls it the song of Dionysus which, when under the influence of wine, he sings and leads others to sing. The practice must, of course, have been much older than Archilochus. Such early, gay, unruly dithyrambs—songs of revelry, accompanied by dance—are said to have been given disciplined form by Arion of Methymna in Corinth, in about 600 B.C., during the rule of the tyrant Periander; for it was then that the dithyramb was first sung by a regular chorus and first treated of definitive subjects.[2] From Corinth the dithyramb was brought to Athens by Lasus of Hermione[3] (born c. 548–545), the great musical innovator[4] who lived at the court of Hipparchus; and from 509–508 it became a subject for competition at the reorganized Athenian festival of the Great Dionysia.

It has been argued, and probably rightly, that in the seventh and sixth centuries rulers like Periander in Corinth, Cleisthenes in Sicyon and Pisistratus in Athens attempted to use for political ends the hitherto rustic, popular cult of Dionysus, with its primitive, dithyrambic songs, seeing in it a force which could unite the warring political parties. The argument runs that they set out to establish a new state religion of Dionysus, which would ennoble the riotous festivities of the country folk.[5] And indeed it is likely that it was in this spirit that Pisistratus established in Athens the festivals of the City (or Great) Dionysia, which were later still further ennobled by the introduction of a more developed form of dithyramb—to say nothing of the drama—which would in some sense vie with the grand Homeric recitations of the Panathenaea.

Dithyrambs were performed at the City Dionysia on the day before that on which tragedies were presented. Five of the ten Athenian tribes provided one chorus each of men and the other choruses of boys. They were called 'cyclic choruses' because the fifty performers, who did not wear masks, danced in a circle around the altar or the flute player (for the accompaniment was the flute). Victory in the competition was shared—as in the case of tragedy—by the poet and the *choregos*, who bore the cost of the performance, and the victorious tribe was permitted as reward to set up its prize, a tripod, in public.[6]

The first victor of such a dithyrambic contest is said to have been Hypodicus of Chalcis in 509–508 B.C.[7] From then till about 470 B.C. the competition attracted poets of great eminence, such as Simonides, who, as already noted, won fifty-six prizes,[8] Pindar,[9] Bacchylides[10] and, even later, men like Ion of Chios.[11] The dithyrambs they composed, like other choral odes, were in regular strophe and antistrophe.

Of almost all the choral poetry that was presented year by year at the Dionysia, the Panathenaea and other festivals, only a few fragments survive. The exceptions, which alone give us some idea of the classical dithyramb, are the six examples by Bacchylides. To judge from them, there was, as we have seen, no close connection between their subject-matter and Dionysus, nor any special Dionysiac spirit in these early dithyrambs. It may well be that pre-Attic, Dorian dithyrambic tradition, influenced by the hero cults, was responsible for the broadening of the genre at Athens to embrace mythological figures unconnected with Dionysus.

Though the dithyramb was performed mainly in Athens, it branched out from an early age to other parts of the Greek world, notably Delphi because of the association of Dionysus with Apollo there. But the contrast between the paean—the lyric poem in honour of Apollo—and the dithyramb remained strong and significant.

About the second great period in the history of the dithyramb, which is connected with the names of Melanippides, Phrynis, Cinesias, Philoxenus and Timotheus, we shall speak later.[12]

THE SATYR PLAY AND THE ORIGINS OF TRAGEDY

Any attempt to trace the origins of tragedy further back than the fifth century B.C. is unfortunately full of uncertainties.[13] Ever since the Alexandrian period this has been one of the most obscure and most hotly disputed of literary questions, and it is far from certain that even Aristotle had reliable evidence at his disposal for any period earlier than the late sixth century.

Modern scholars with an ethnological background have brought to the study of the origins of tragedy a good deal of anthropological material that is valuable indeed but relates chiefly to the substructure of drama generally and thus does not concern us here. Such questions as the use of masks to effect that 'transformation' which is the first requirement for any dramatic performance, or the idea of 'possession', through which a man imitating daemonic powers is considered to carry those powers in his own body, have been illuminated by reference to material drawn from cultures of all times and places, including the fertility festivals of the early Greek farmers. But they should be kept distinct from the present study, which is concerned with the line of development in the Hellenic world that caused Attic tragedy to become an art form.

Aristotle's testimony on the matter is sadly inconsistent. In one place[14] he gives the dithyramb and in another[15] the primitive 'satyr drama' (a crude precursor of the satyr play) as the starting-point of tragedy. These two pieces of information cannot easily be reconciled, in spite of many brave efforts; for there is no clear evidence that the dithyramb was ever danced in satyr costume, nor is there a trace of any dramatic element in the dithyramb before Bacchylides, well into the fifth century. Moreover, the dithyramb, as we have seen, was performed by a chorus standing in a circle, while that of the drama formed a rectangle. It is possible that Aristotle's remarks were merely based on the inference that cruder and more primitive choral performances must of necessity have preceded the nobler form of tragedy. In just the same way, in another place[16] he wrongly 'derives' the more evolved from the more primitive forms of Greek verse so as to present a smooth, parallel ascent of the graver varieties into tragedies and the lighter kinds into comedy.

Since Aristotle's account of the origins of the tragic chorus is so confused and confusing, we are compelled to turn to the few other available sources on the subject, although they are obscure, mostly late and of doubtful reliability. The oldest of them is Herodotus,[17] who records that at Sicyon the τραγικοὶ χοροί which had commemorated the hero Adrastus were transferred by the tyrant Cleisthenes to the worship of Dionysus. But since it is quite unclear what he means by τραγικοὶ χοροί, the passage is hardly illuminating. A very much later notice from the *Suda* (tenth century A.D.)[18] ascribes to Arion of Methymna (c. 600 B.C.)—who is important, as we have seen, in the development of the dithyramb—the invention of the τραγικὸς τρόπος. The term probably means the style of diction or the mode in music which afterwards belonged to tragedy. Moreover, we have a statement by Johannes Diaconus (thirteenth century A.D.?), *On Hermogenes*,[19] which purports to come from Solon's elegies and says that the same Arion composed the first δρᾶμα τῆς τραγῳδίας, which can only mean that he presented the first tragic drama. And finally, another notice from the *Suda*[20] speaks of one Epigenes of Sicyon (a shadowy figure) as the 'first tragic poet', who was reproached for introducing into the worship of Dionysus themes which had nothing to do with the god.

All this information is so very patchy and unsatisfactory that there is little to be gained from a discussion of the many conflicting interpretations arising from these passages. One point emerges, however. There plainly existed before the days of Thespis—with whom, as we shall see, Attic tragedy truly begins—some kind of Doric choral performances with a 'tragic' colour, which may well have been transferred to Attica, together with the dithyramb, and which surely lies behind the claims of the Dorians to have 'invented' tragedy.[21] Moreover, the evidence of dialect points to a connection between the Dorian peoples and early 'tragic' lyrics. Doric influence is very evident in the choral songs of Attic tragedy, and a very considerable number of Doric words and forms also penetrated the basically Ionian–Attic language of the iambic spoken parts.

But precise details are wanting; and we encounter fresh difficulties when we look into the meaning of the word τραγῳδία itself. Its most probable interpretation—though not a certain one by any means—is 'the song of the goats' (τράγων ᾠδή), a song of men disguised as he-goats. This interpretation has led to a profitless search for evidence of goat satyrs in the Peloponnese. The true satyr, or Silenus, the follower of Dionysus, is always depicted with a horse's tail and a horse's ears.[22] Satyrs with goats' tails and ears are not found before the Hellenistic period and betray the influence of the Pan-type.

Alexandrian scholars did not accept this interpretation of the word 'tragedy', preferring to understand it as meaning 'song at the sacrifice of goats', or 'song sung in competition for the prize of a goat'. The latter is echoed in Horace's *Ars Poetica*.[23] With the bias of city-dwellers everywhere in favour of all that is rustic and primitive, the Alexandrians saw the origins of tragedy in the unsophisticated folk customs of Attic villagers—a view which cannot be lightly disregarded. For in the villages of Attica, as in other parts of the Greek world, rustic celebrations in honour of Dionysus seem to have been accompanied by primitive, non-choral, dramatic performances, mummery similar to that found at the festivals of vegetation gods in other parts of the world. Such village plays might well have been combined later with 'tragic' choruses.[24] In this connection it is worth recalling that Aristotle, when speaking of the origins of tragedy,[25] refers to improvisation.

But nothing we have said so far really accounts for the existence of the spoken parts of tragedy—the dialogues and monologues—without which drama cannot exist. The theory has been put forward that tragic dialogue grew out of the choral ode, by way of a dialogue that was originally sung. But this seems highly unlikely when we consider the very marked difference in language and style between the choral and the spoken parts of tragedy. More probable is the view that the spoken parts were a later, independent addition to the chorus. This is supported by the testimony of Themistius,[26] who presents it as an opinion of Aristotle that in an early stage of tragedy all that existed was a sung chorus, and that prologue and speech ($\acute{\varrho}\tilde{\eta}\sigma\iota\varsigma$) were added later by Thespis.[27] And indeed it is very likely that as the primitive, improvised chorus song developed into a more complex, artistic poem, it should have embraced themes which the audience could not easily follow without prior explanation in the form of a prologue. Similarly, a series of choral odes belonging to the same sequence might be made more readily comprehensible by the interpolation of narrated 'speeches'. The next step in such a development would be to make chorus leader and narrator address each other[28] and thus to create 'dialogue' as it must have existed in the work of Thespis, the first known tragedian.

Whatever its origins, tragedy, like the satyr play and comedy, was closely connected with the cult of Dionysus, and for many centuries the principal occasions for tragic performances remained the god's festivals in Attica. The very costume of the actors had direct links with Dionysus—the sleeved *chiton* and the *cothurni*, originally soft, high-fastening shoes such as those that the god is represented as wearing.

Yet, strangely enough, the subject-matter of tragedy was never generally Dionysiac, a state of affairs which reminds us of the dithyramb. 'Nothing to do with Dionysus' ($o\dot{v}\delta\grave{\epsilon}v\ \pi\varrho\grave{o}\varsigma\ \tau\grave{o}v\ \Delta\iota\acute{o}vv\sigma ov$) was a proverbial phrase in the ancient world and shows, by the various ways in which it was explained, that this question had also troubled the ancients. It is true that from time to time Greek plays dealt with the birth of the god or with attempts to oppose him (for example, *Lycurgus* or *Pentheus*), but there is no evidence of a time in the development of tragedy when the content of plays was essentially Dionysiac. Nor do we have any clear evidence of a transition from a Dionysiac to a non-Dionysiac character in fully developed tragedy. We have already seen[29] that Herodotus makes somewhat obscure mention of $\tau\varrho\alpha\gamma\iota\varkappa o\grave{\iota}\ \chi o\varrho o\acute{\iota}$ ('tragic choruses'). However the words should be interpreted, it remains true that in their context they firmly link songs of a hero cult with the worship of Dionysus. And it may well be that the status of the heroes as the normal subjects for tragedy arises from the widespread popularity in the late Archaic period of the hero cults and the profound influence they had on both myth and tragedy. The same cause might explain, at least partly, the important part played in Greek tragedy by lamentation (*threnos*), for the songs of the hero cult were usually laments for the hero's death.

Thus, by whatever path, after its career in epic and choral lyric the heroic myth entered a new phase of development in tragedy, in which poets made it a vehicle for ethical and religous problems.[30]

The history of the genre of tragedy as we know it begins with Thespis.[31] A native of the Attic deme of Icaria, where the cult of Dionysus flourished, he was the prize winner at the first contest for tragedy at the Dionysia in Athens, in one of the years between 535–533 B.C. However, his first use of a speaking actor must have been made some time before.[32] In the *Suda* he is said also to have invented the mask, which is improbable; it is likely that he merely made improvements to an existing mask. The *Suda* also gives a few titles of plays by him, including a *Pentheus*, but such plays as were already being circulated under his name in the fourth century were undoubtedly forgeries. We also hear, on late authority,[33] that he took his plays about to various parts of Attica on wagons.[34] Thus it seems probable that Thespis, presumably at some Dionysiac festival in his native Icaria, was the first man to stand up amid the wild chorus of singing and dancing beast-men—the 'goats', *sileni* and satyrs—and explain what the song was about by means of speeches addressed to the chorus and answered by it. Originally, he may have represented Dionysus himself or Silenus, who reared the young god and was his oldest servant.

The iambic trimeter, spoken verse without musical accompaniment, may also have owed its first employment in tragedy to Thespis. Certainly Aristotle tells us that the oldest kind of spoken verse (as opposed to sung choruses) was the trochaic tetrameter, which we know to have been accompanied by the αὐλός (flute). Whoever was responsible for this metrical innovation, it remains true that from the time of the introduction of the iambic trimeter we have two distinct types of tragic diction: that of the chorus, formal and archaic, with a Doric linguistic colouring, and that of the actor, the diction of the spoken word, which is basically Ionic–Attic in dialect. (However, it is the rich non-Attic vocabulary that often confers a certain strangeness on the language in which the characters speak. Words, song and dance, the three basic elements which tragedy retained as long as it was a living art-form, are thus seen to have been established from the very beginning, and it may well be that Thespis was the man responsible. If that is the case, he is the ultimate progenitor of the whole genre of tragedy which has been so admired over the centuries and which has had such a great influence over the development of Western theatre.

Even so, the original plays must have been short, noisy and wild. Only later, as Aristotle tells us, did tragedy achieve dignity. When the change took place we do not know, but if tragedy kept pace with the development of the other great art-forms of Athens, it was most probably at the turn of the sixth to the fifth century. This change of tone must have been accompanied by a change of scale, as a consequence of which the play came to be divided into scenes. Between scenes the actors would leave the stage while the chorus sang a *stasimon*, or 'song for chorus on stage', as opposed to the songs for its entrance and exit.

It appears probable that at the beginning a number of short plays with common content or story were performed together, a practice which would account for the existence of the trilogy and tetralogy with which we are familiar from later writers. But as tragedy achieved dignity and embraced the 'higher' myths, the playful and ribald element which had run through all sorts of play came to be relegated to the satyr play,[35] the last of a tetralogy to be presented. In it old Silenus, in company with the younger satyrs, lived on as a monument to the rude, primitive origins of tragedy. With the passage of time this play too was 'ennobled', until at the beginning of the fifth century Pratinas of Phlius, in the Argolid, gave shape to the originally formless satyr play and turned it into a real drama, in which plot, dance, song and words all played their parts, as in tragedy, but in which the original animal element (in the chorus at least) was never suppressed.

It is difficult to speak with any claim to exactness or certainty about the subsequent history of this kind of play, for only one complete example has survived (Euripides' *Cyclops*) and that from the fifth century. Some fragments of such plays do exist, however, a few of them quite long, and they permit us to draw some general observations.[36] For instance, it is clear that the satyr play occupied a position mid-way between tragedy and comedy, a genre which was very popular in antiquity. Pratinas composed no fewer than thirty-two successful satyr plays, and his son, Aristias, who followed in his father's footsteps, was considered the best writer of such plays after Aeschylus.[37]

By Aeschylus' time the satyr play had established its independence from the rest of the tetralogy; when connected to the subject-matter of the other plays, it constituted a travesty of the myth. That Sophocles also made his satyr plays independent of the rest of the tetralogy is not surprising in view of his abandonment of the connected trilogy. Several of Sophocles' satyr plays are known by title, and from some important surviving fragments we may detect the results of that refinement of the genre which we are told he brought about.[38] Euripides occasionally substituted for a satyr play a tragedy with a happy ending (such as the *Alcestis*), but this practice did not become general. Of the other tragedians, the most famous for his satyr plays, after Aeschylus and Aristias, was Achaeus of Eretria, who was good enough to be compared with the great Attic master, but was considered inferior to him.[39]

In the course of the fourth century the satyr play declined. From 342 onwards, as inscriptional evidence shows,[40] only one satyr play was performed at every dramatic festival, and it served as a prelude to all the tragedies in the competition. Later in the fourth century we lose all track of the genre, but, as we shall see, it survived to be given a new lease of life in the Alexandrian period, both in a 'pure' form and mixed with elements of comedy; and in the early Roman Empire too satyr plays were composed in Greek, presumably with some kind of chorus.[41] However, this kind of play did not pass on to the Roman stage.[42]

Satyric drama is the only form of Greek poetry which mixes slap-stick and the heroic, the former, generally speaking, provided by Silenus and his sons, the satyrs or *sileni* (although their place is occasionally taken by other rustic characters); the heroic element is provided by figures from the world of epic who were included in these plays. From the time of Pratinas onwards the *sileni* always have a distinctive costume: loincloths of goat skin (more rarely linen drawers), shaggy beards, horses' ears, phalli and sometimes horses' tails and legs.[43] Their character, as depicted in the satyr play, is that of comical drunkards and cowards, whose leaping, cavorting dance was suited to their half-animal nature.[44] The *Silenus par excellence* is the old Papposilenus, a being with many weaknesses but also with a sharp intellect.[45]

In satyr plays a division into semi-choruses was probably not uncommon, to judge once again by the *Cyclops* and the *Ichneutae*. In both of them there are also passages of non-antistrophic choral lyrics, satyric drama being perhaps, in this as in other respects, less formal than tragedy. Furthermore, the element of the fantastic which is seen in the satyrs and Silenus naturally ran through the whole of a satyr play, affecting all the other characters who appeared on stage, as well as their speeches.

Central characters of satyr plays were well-known heroes of epic and tragedy—even heroes of tragedies in the same tetralogy. But when they stepped on to the satyric stage, their dignity disappeared. Nevertheless, the costume of heroes in satyr plays was identical with that in tragedy.

Satyr plays were usually shorter than tragedies—sometimes no more than half their length. Their structure, as far as we can judge from the evidence at our disposal, was very similar to that of tragedy in both overall plan and separate parts. But, as we might expect, the satyr play greatly curtailed the lyrical and dramatic element.

The satyr play as a literary genre did not develop independently of tragedy. In fact, all the changes which the later form of drama underwent, such as reversals of fortune or the introduction of the *deus ex machina*, seem to have passed directly into the satyr play. The one rule was that a satyr play should have a happy ending.

From the little evidence available to us we can see that the setting and scenery of satyr plays were rustic[46] and that some of their most beloved themes seem to have had their origin in popular folk motifs: the monster (Syleus, Sciron, Polyphemus) which enslaves the woodland spirits (satyrs); the freeing of the latter by the hero (Heracles, Theseus, Odysseus); the pure maiden assaulted by lusty youths (Amymone, Iris, Helen, Pandora); the crafty, sly man (Sisyphus or Autolycus); and the 'great eater' (Heracles).

The language and metres of the satyr plays were, as far as we can judge, not very different from those of tragedy. The obscenities inherent in the genre and the satyric subject-matter were naturally expressed in words and phrases whose vulgarity was incompatible with tragic dignity, but even so the satyrs retained a semblance of propriety in their speeches.

Such was the satyr play which, during the great classical centuries, amused the Athenian audiences and provided an antidote to the sombre mood which tragedy created. Judged by modern standards, it appears to be an unsatisfactory, hybrid genre, which must have suffered from embracing so many incongruous elements. Its most striking feature— and one of the essentials of the genre—is that tragic characters were made to look ridiculous by the disruptive antics of a satyr chorus. Such elements ended by becoming fixed and thus boringly repetitive. They allowed little rejuvenation of the form, and, as they did not contain any of the true qualities of great literature, ultimately killed the satyr play.

THE PERFORMANCE OF TRAGIC DRAMA

The principal occasions on which tragedy was performed

Although both tragedy and dithyramb were intimately connected with the cult of Dionysus, the former, unlike the latter, was never an act of worship in which the chorus represented the Athenian people paying honour to the god. On the contrary, the tragic chorus always retained its own identity *vis-à-vis* the play, and the dialogue of tragedy made very little direct reference to Dionysus, instead choosing freely from the whole range of mythology. Still, the principal occasions of tragic drama in Attica were the festivals of Dionysus—above all the Great or City Dionysia. In this festival, instituted by Pisistratus in honour of Dionysus Eleuthereus and open to the whole Hellenic world, tragedy was presented from the eleventh to the thirteenth of the month *Elaphebolion* (March–April).[47] The festival took the form of a contest with prizes, and great pains were taken to ensure a fair verdict. The victorious poet was crowned with a wreath of ivy, and an honorarium was paid by the state to each contestant poet.

Throughout the fifth century and probably also, apart from a few exceptional years, through the earlier part of the fourth century B.C. three poets each year entered the competition for the prize in tragedy. Each of them presented four plays, of which the fourth was normally a satyr play. However, at some date before 341 B.C. it became the custom for a single satyr play to be presented at the beginning of the programme, and each tragic poet thereafter presented at most three plays. In the afternoons of the days of tragic performance comedies were presented.

The choice of the poets who were allowed to compete at the Great Dionysia rested with the relevant *archon* — the *archon* eponymous — who also appointed a *choregos*. The latter was a wealthy citizen who undertook to bear the heavy expenses of training and dressing a tragic or comic chorus and of paying the singers and probably the flute players as well. In the last decades of the fourth century the functions of the *choregos* were taken over by the *agonothetai*, citizens elected annually and provided with state funds to perform these same functions. From 386 B.C. the festival of the Great Dionysia was extended to allow the performance of one 'old' tragedy and one 'old' comedy in addition to the year's new dramas. And from that time it was decreed, in honour of Aeschylus, that whoever wished to revive one of his plays might do so. The dramatic competitions at the Dionysia continued down to the first century B.C., but under what regulations we cannot any longer say.

The Athenians also held the festival of the Lenaea in honour of the pan-Ionic Dionysus, to which only Athenians and metics were admitted. It took place in the month *Gamelion* (January–February) and was basically a festival of comedy. However, from about 432 onwards tragedy was also admitted, in the form of two tragedies without satyr play as opposed to the full tetralogy of the City Dionysia. In addition to these great festivals, many dramatic performances were also given at the rather less important festivals held at the Piraeus and at Salamis, as well as at the Rural Dionysia, where, no doubt, they helped to familiarize the inhabitants of Attica with the great tragedies.[48]

The actors, the chorus and their costumes

The actors, all male, were originally the choice of the poets; later they were chosen by the state. The first such 'speaker' was introduced by Thespis, and after him Aeschylus is said to have added the second and Sophocles the third actor. Greek tragedy never employed more than three actors, but their numbers could be supplemented by mute figures or characters who spoke so little that they could be left out of the reckoning. Another such device was the practice of dividing one role between two or three actors, which was only made possible by the use of the mask. In classical tragedy the importance of the protagonist was paramount. He alone is said to 'act the play', and only he could win the prize for acting (which was not necessarily awarded to the protagonist of the winning plays).

Greek actors used three kinds of delivery: unaccompanied speech, speech accompanied by music (a kind of recitative), and straightforward song. The first was normally employed in the parts of the play, whether in dialogue or monologue, which were written in iambic trimeters, the metre considered nearest akin to prose speech; the second was used for the delivery of tetrameters, and of iambics inserted in the midst of lyric systems; and the third for lyrics.

We have every reason for thinking that Athenian audiences attached great importance to the actor's voice. Among other things, their large, open theatres called for practised voice production rather than violent effort. The beauty of the actor's tone and his adaptability to the personality and mood of the character represented were also important criteria.

Thespis' introduction of the actor in about 535–533 B.C. resulted in a shift of dramatic emphasis from the musical–lyrical[49] to the spoken parts, so that dialogue eventually took place more naturally between actor and actor than between chorus and actor. But this does not mean, as was once thought, that a smooth line of development led from the domination of primitive drama by the chorus to the ancillary role it later played, which is familiar to us from the tragedies of Sophocles and Euripides. Indeed, Aeschylus' *Suppliants*, an example which we would otherwise assume from its dominant chorus to have belonged to that primitive stage, is now known to have had its first production as late as 463 B.C.[50] It is true that the choral element in Sophocles and Euripides rarely makes up more than a quarter of the whole play, often very much less, and that the relation of the chorus to the action is more or less consistent. Nevertheless, in the case of the later Euripides the range of variation is considerable. Furthermore, the line of development is confused by the practice, said by Aristotle to have begun with Agathon, of writing choral interludes (*embolima*) which could be transferred from one play to another and which seem to have been common in the mid-fourth century.

The number of participants in the tragic chorus appears to have been twelve in the plays of Aeschylus and fifteen in those of Sophocles and Euripides. The argument that their number was originally fifty, equal to the fifty singers of dithyramb (and to the fifty Danaids) is quite untenable. In certain tragedies the employment of a second chorus in at least one scene of the play is beyond doubt. Examples are Aeschylus' *Suppliants* and *Eumenides*, Sophocles' *King Oedipus* and Euripides' *Suppliants*, *Phaethon* and *Alexander*.

The formation of the tragic chorus was rectangular, unlike the circular chorus of dithyramb. It consisted of five files ($\zeta\upsilon\gamma\acute{\alpha}$) and three ranks ($\sigma\tauο\tilde{\iota}\chiο\iota$). Depending on the nature of the play, its entrance might be in single file or in some less orderly fashion. About the movements and attitudes of the chorus during the non-choral parts of the play there is little information. The *parodos*—the entrance of the chorus—and the *stasima*— choral odes sung during the action of the play when the chorus had reached its *stasis* or normal position—were as a rule sung by the whole chorus in unison; but there were exceptional scenes in which division into semi-choruses was made, and there was a form of lyric dialogue between the chorus and a principal actor, the *kommos*, which often took the place of a *stasimon*.

Little is known of the dancing of the chorus, although we know that gestures (χειρονομίαι) played an important part in what must have been a predominantly expressive or mimetic performance. But that the dancing was probably quite elaborate we may deduce from the information that Phrynichus and Aeschylus both invented a great number of dances (σχήματα ὀρχήσεως). And of the music that accompanied these 'religious' dances we know practically nothing, save that the instruments employed were the αὐλός, a double-reeded instrument like an oboe, and the lyre.

The costumes of actors and chorus are likewise in dispute,[51] although we have a certain amount of rather indecisive pictorial evidence from terracottas, vase paintings and occasional sculptures. The actors, we know, were masked and wore the same costumes for both tragedy and satyr plays; but in the latter the chorus was dressed differently so as to represent the half-animal satyrs and old Silenus, with a horse's tail and ears and a long phallus. The masks were naturalistic—our evidence starts with an *oenochoe* of about 470 B.C. from the *agora* of Athens—and were made out of plain linen, wood or cork until the last decades of the fourth century. At that time the ὄγκος was introduced, the very high forehead so characteristic of later tragic masks, which should probably be connected with the introduction at about that time of the raised stage. The mask, whose origin was probably religious, varied according to age, character and sex.

The actors' dress also varied but included the *chiton* with fitted sleeves and ornamented fabrics. The chorus in tragedy was not always clad uniformly and often wore costume indicative of foreign nationality or individual character. In late antiquity actors were padded to make them appear grander on stage. Footwear, when worn (for vase paintings often show bare-footed actors and chorus), was originally soft and came some way up the leg, in the form either of highly decorated boots or of soft-cuffed boots. The *cothurni*, a pair of raised and platform-soled boots, first appear in the middle of the second century B.C. and became the character-istic footwear of tragedy for Pollux, Lucian and the Latin authors. There is also evidence of the existence on the Greek stage of 'properties'—that is, items appropriate to certain characters, such as Hephaestus and

Dionysus, and carried by the actors representing those characters in order to identify the parts they played [52]

THE GREAT TRAGEDIANS

Aeschylus

The son of Euphorion of Eleusis, Aeschylus was born in 525/4 B.C. into a well-to-do family of landowners. As a young man he saw the end of tyranny in Athens, and the remainder of his life was spent under the developing Athenian democracy. He took part in the Persian Wars and fought at Marathon—where his brother Cynegeirus was killed—and probably also at Salamis. It is much less certain whether he took part in the sea battle at Artemisium or the battle of Plataea. On the evidence of Aristophanes' *Frogs* (ll. 885–7), many have believed that he was an initiate of the Eleusinian Mysteries, but other sources[53] seem to refute the idea. He was, however, a man of intense religious and patriotic convictions, firmly believing in the supremacy of justice and in his own conception of divine government. In the Greek victory against the Persians he saw the workings of divine justice in the historical process so clearly that any attempt to distinguish between Aeschylus the religious thinker and Aeschylus the poet (attempts have often been made) must destroy that very unity through which alone his work can be understood. Aeschylus' first efforts at tragedy were probably made early in the fifth century. His first drama victory was in 484,[54] but the earliest of his extant plays, the *Persians*, dates from 472. His poetic gifts were shared by his family. Both his sons, Euaion and Euphorion, wrote tragedies: indeed, the latter defeated Sophocles and Euripides in 431. His nephew, Philocles, also a tragedian, was victorious in the competition with no less a play than *King Oedipus*!

The poet paid two visits to Sicily. During the first he composed, in 470, the play *Aetnae* (or *Aetnaeae*) in honour of the foundation of the new city of Aetna by the tyrant Hiero, at whose court the poet was staying. The second visit followed the production of the *Oresteia* (458), and it ended with the poet's death at Gela in 456. Ancient writers imagined various causes for this second visit, ranging from the poet's pain at his defeat at the Dionysia by Sophocles in 468, or by Simonides in the composition of an epitaph on the heroes of Marathon, to the poor reception accorded the *Oresteia* on its first appearance. (None of these suggestions needs be taken seriously.) His tomb at Gela bore an epitaph, attributed to him, though probably wrongly, in which his military achievements were recorded but his poetic career passed over in silence. The tomb itself became a place of pilgrimage for lovers of tragedy, while in Athens, as we have seen, his memory was honoured by a unique decree which allowed anyone who so wished to enter the dramatic contest with one of Aeschylus' plays. But, as has several times been remarked, perhaps the finest memorial to Aeschylus' greatness is the fine portrait of him painted by Aristophanes in *The Frogs*. Once the grotesque and fanciful elements are removed, it gives a far more accurate picture of the tragedian than do any of the anecdotes concerning him which circulated in late antiquity.

Ancient estimates of the total number of Aeschylus' plays and poetic victories are very suspect. That contained in the Medicean Manuscript includes seventy-two titles but omits ten plays which are elsewhere ascribed to him, probably correctly. There appears to be some truth in the statement that many of his victories were gained by revivals of his plays after his death. However, the surviving plays of Aeschylus are but seven in number. They form a school selection of the Antonine period, made according to the aesthetic and moral criteria of that much later age. Of this selection the first to be written, as we have seen, is the *Persians*. Produced in 472, it was a 'single' play, unrelated in subject-matter to its companions in performance, the lost *Phineus* and *Glaucus*. (The satyr play which was performed at the same time was the *Prometheus*, also lost.) The subject of the *Persians* was historical and contemporary, the defeat of the Persians in the second Persian War. The scene is laid at the Persian capital of Susa, where in the very opening words of the chorus (the Elders of the Royal Council) a note of melancholy and despondency is evident. This atmosphere intensifies in the following Atossa scene, containing the account of her ominous dream; in the messenger's speech, which describes, in terms more graphic than in any other extant account, the battle of Salamis; and in the appearance of Darius' ghost. It reaches its climax in the closing scene, which brings on stage the wounded and bedraggled Xerxes; and the play closes amid long-drawn Oriental lamentation.

The stately tone of the *Persians* demonstrates a peculiarly Aeschylean technique, later perfected in the *Agamemnon*: the play begins with shadows, which gradually darken under an increasingly threatening sky. Narrow national patriotism or national hatred is strikingly absent from the play. The victory of the Greeks is seen as the victory of God's justice. The Persians are punished for their divine, not human, transgression. According to the dictates of a concept basic to Aeschylean tragedy, their *hubris* is punished with *Ate*, destruction. For *Ate* is the doom visited by the gods upon man; seen from the human point of view, it is blindness, which flatters man, encouraging him to transgress the bounds of moderation, and sets him on the path to his own destruction. The order of the world is disturbed by man's immoderate actions, and finally he falls, the victim of his own blindness. Thus has the Persian empire exceeded its αἴσιμον ('allotted measure'), and the *hubris* of Xerxes finds visible form when he dares to reverse the natural order of things—by turning sea into land (by bridging the Hellespont) and land into sea (by cutting the Athos canal)— and when he fails to respect the shrines of the (Greek) gods. His punishment is Salamis and Plataea.

The idea that Zeus punishes overweening ambition was not new. We find it in Solon, and it was a common notion among Aeschylus' contemporaries. What does seem to be new is the notion that when a man is inflamed with ambition Zeus goads him on (l. 742)—an idea that is expounded fully in the *Oresteia*.[55]

In the *Persians* the messenger's speeches are particularly magnificent. They are quite without that exaggeration which ruins so many speeches of patriotic triumph. Their presentation, however, is archaic, recalling the old epic catalogue poems. The names of strange countries, cities and men are strung together until the sheer enumeration gives a sense of power and size.

The play must have been a remarkable spectacle in peformance. The rich, oriental appearance of the actors and chorus, with their colourful garments and decorations, and the long lamentations at the end, with the music that accompanied them, must have given a strange, outlandish tone to the play. But throughout the tragedy the heroic temper is maintained, and Aeschylus succeeds in making great poetry out of the simple old religious notion that the gods overthrow the arrogant.

The second oldest of the extant Aeschylean plays is the *Seven Against Thebes*, the only survivor of a connected trilogy produced in 467. It contains little action but consists of a series of magnificent tableaux, whose stiff beauty has been compared with that of archaic sculpture and vase painting. In this trilogy the poet abandoned contemporary history and turned for his subject to the Theban epic cycle. We have seen how in the sixth and fifth centuries the Theban cycle was considered Homeric, so there is a real sense in which the *Seven Against Thebes* could have been considered, in Aeschylus' own phrase, a 'slice from Homer's banquets'. But it is a magnificent slice.

The trilogy had a thematic unity, as can be seen from the titles of the other, lost plays: the *Laius* and the *Oedipus*. Even the satyr play was related, as we can tell from its title, the *Sphinx*. The central subject was the curse laid upon the royal house of Thebes as a result of sin, and its inexorable punishment. Thrice the Delphic god warned Laius not to beget a son, but he disregarded the warning and thus committed a sin which recurred in three successive generations. For Aeschylus a family curse was a self-perpetuating sin carried in the blood. In the *Seven Against Thebes* we find this theme treated for the first time in a trilogy, for a smaller vehicle would not have been adequate to demonstrate the workings of Fate over many years.

In the exchanges between Eteocles and the chorus of Theban women—

the form of dialogue which is the original kernel of drama: the individual face to face with the chorus—we see him battling to save man's dignity and honour in a way which reminds us of Hector in his scene with Andromache in *Iliad*, VI. Seen in such a context, his eventual fall gives Eteocles a new dimension of tragic nobility whose influence was to be felt throughout Western drama.

The middle part of the play is also of special interest. It consists of a dialogue, more than 300 lines long, between Eteocles and the messenger, which includes seven pairs of speeches describing the champions who are ready to attack the seven gates of Thebes and the separate instructions given for meeting each of them. The judgement of antiquity that the play was 'full of Ares'[56] seems, on the basis of this passage, to be well-founded. But this is no conventional 'war poetry', for it touches also on very many other sides of life. One such example, and an unforgettable one, is the picture of the women of Thebes at the city's altars, begging the gods for help and listening to the sounds of the battle outside the walls.

At the seventh gate, in spite of the advice and the prayers of the women of Thebes, Eteocles insists on meeting his brother and his death, king against king, brother against brother, enemy against enemy. It is his own decision, taken freely. The battle will be engaged in order to protect his city's freedom, as is one of the ruler's basic duties; but it will also involve fratricide, one of the gravest sins for all men. Two conflicting duties are presented, which ensures that the man will sin whichever way he chooses. The dilemma, which arises out of the curse upon his house, is basic to the Aeschylean concept of tragedy. It is revealed for the first time here but is seen in full force in the *Oresteia*.

In Aeschylus' view, once a man accepts the need for action, he is seen as surrendering his will to it; he rushes into it (ll. 688f.).[57] The problems of fate, responsibility and action are, of course, much more complex and profound in Aeschylus than in Homer, but they are rooted in precisely the same notion that human motivation and divine will are inseparably intertwined. Perhaps the greatest tragedy for Aeschylean man is to feel, as Eteocles does, that he is abandoned by the gods.

In the *Seven Against Thebes* the long opening scenes which set the tone of the tragedy stand in sharp contrast to the swiftly moving final scenes in which it reaches its goal. A short messenger speech tells of the two brothers' deaths and leads into a final lamentation, reminiscent of the end of the *Persians*. However, the end of the *Seven Against Thebes*, as we have it, is probably the work of later adapters, for it is inconceivable that Aeschylus would have closed his trilogy with the opening of a further conflict, that of Antigone and Creon. On the other hand, we know that Aeschylus' plays were often produced after his death, and it seems probable that for some later production the end of his *Seven Against Thebes* was expanded and modified by elements drawn from Sophocles' *Antigone*.

The *Suppliants* was the first play of the Danaid trilogy, to which the *Egyptians* and the *Daughters of Danaus*, both lost, were the sequels. Formerly, in view of certain archaic features, it was commonly regarded as Aeschylus' earliest extant play, but from a fragmentary *Hypothesis* published in 1952[58] it appears that the Danaid trilogy was produced in competition with a work of Sophocles, and there is an indication (the *archon*'s name, Archemenides) that 463 may be the date of that competition.

In this play the most important role is that of the chorus, the daughters of Danaus, who flee with their father from Egypt to escape an incestuous marriage with the sons of Aegyptus, their kinsman. Reaching Argos, the home of their ancestors, they seek asylum there. The play examines the relationship of man and woman, and such plot as it contains tells of the efforts of the Danaids to secure protection, and of the appearance of a herald to announce the arrival of their rejected suitors from Egypt. The dominant role of the chorus, a purely archaic feature, is clearly a consequence of the fact that the *Suppliants* is the first play of the trilogy and that its majestic choral odes are intended to set the scene for all three tragedies. Though the daughters of Danaus were fifty in number, and fifty is the number given by Pollux for the oldest choruses (4, 110), we should reckon the play's chorus to number no more than the twelve which was standard in all the other plays of Aeschylus, for Aeschylus never adopted even Sophocles' relatively small increase of the chorus from twelve to fifteen.

The action of the play is slow, and the individuality of the characters is muffled by the grand and stately words which all alike use; moreover, there is a definite stiffness in the interchange of speeches. Even so, the tragedy has true dramatic tension. When the Suppliants pray to Zeus for deliverance or shrink in horror before the menacing herald the play's lack of action is compensated for by passion, tenderness and majestic spectacle, the last particularly evident in the splendid garments and adornments of the chorus, whose oriental magnificence reminds us of the *Persians*.

In the Danaid trilogy we have another presentation of Aeschylus' view of the tragic situation—the conflict of duties and the necessity for choice. In the *Suppliants* this is seen both in the Danaids themselves and in Pelasgus, the Argive king whose protection they have sought. The Danaids flee Egypt to escape the dilemma of having to commit either incest or murder. Finally, all but one of them, Hypermnestra, choose murder. The king of Argos, on the other hand, is faced by a conflict of duties: should he receive the Danaids and thus bring war upon his people, or reject their plea for protection and thus offend Zeus, the protector of suppliants? We do not know how Aeschylus resolved the moral dilemma of the Danaids. It is possible that the majority, who chose murder, were in the end purified of their guilt. Hypermnestra, however (who chose marriage because of her desire for children), was, as we know, brought to trial, at which she was probably acquitted by the intervention of Aphrodite and lived to found a line of Argive kings. Aeschylean trilogies seem often to have led up to a grand dilemma, which was resolved in the third play by a court judgement.

King Pelasgus, for his part, is driven to the decision of protecting the Danaids, but only after they have threatened to hang themselves on the images of the gods and thus pollute the city. His decision is afterwards ratified by a decree of the citizens of Argos — a good example of the way in which the Attic tragedians interpreted the Heroic Age by the standards and the practices of the city-state. It is quite possible, however, that Pelasgus paid for this decision with his life in the lost second play, and thus achieved the stature of the true tragic hero.[59] But the trilogy as a whole, full though it may have been of wrongs and suffering, ended by reconciling the conflicting elements of the divine order of the universe as Aeschylus saw it.

About the date of the first production of the *Prometheus Bound* we have no reliable information. In it Aeschylus leaves the world of men for that of the gods. The scene is set 'at the world's end', where, at the command of Zeus and as a punishment for stealing fire from heaven to help mankind, the Titan Prometheus is being nailed to a rock by Hephaestus and his attendants *Kratos* (Force) and *Bia* (Violence). In the dialogue, there is a sharp contrast between the compassion felt by Hephaestus and the ferocity of the daemon *Kratos*. But Prometheus remains silent until they have left and then, in his desolation, bursts out in the famous monologue:

> O divine air, and swift-winged winds, springs of the rivers, and numberless laughing flashes of the sea's waves, earth, mother of all, and the all-seeing circle of the sun, I call upon you: see what I, a god, suffer from the gods. . . .

The disgraced and deserted Prometheus is then visited by the chorus of Oceanids, by Ocean himself and by the wandering Io, who takes pity on him and from whose offspring Heracles will be born to end his sufferings. To them he foretells the future, explains how much he has done for man and complains of the way Zeus has treated him. He is confident that in the end Zeus will be humbled, for he knows a secret which controls the fate of the gods. And this secret he tells as Io departs: the king of gods will contract a marriage with Thetis, which will lead to his own destruction, for from that union will be born a powerful son who will do to Zeus what he did to his own father Cronus. Zeus sends Hermes to wrest the secret from Prometheus, but the prisoner refuses to disclose it, and, together with the chorus of Oceanids, who refuse to abandon him, he is hurled down to Tartarus in a mighty storm and earthquake. The end of the play reaches truly titanic dimensions.

The *Prometheus Bound* is one of the greatest and most inspired works of man. It is set in a transcendental world where issues are larger and clearer than those on earth. Prometheus personifies the spirit which is ready, with unyielding pride, to suffer punishment for the good it has done. His speeches are proud pieces of self-justification, in which he shows how his triumphant adversary, Zeus, is full of the ingratitude and abuse of power typical of all young tyrants.

Our sympathy and even our ethical judgements are, throughout this play, ranged chiefly on the side of Prometheus and against Zeus, a strange example of moral persuasion to come from a religious man like Aeschylus. We do not know the content of the play that followed. It is conceivable that in the lost *Prometheus Delivered* Aeschylus provided a conclusion foreshadowing the fall of Zeus, but it seems far more likely that he sketched a reconciliation between a Prometheus grown humbler through suffering and a Zeus grown more mellow through centuries of rule. The conflict was probably presented as one between the betterment of humanity and the necessity for order—that is, between two right causes.

Research has revealed numerous features which occur in this play alone among all the plays attributed to Aeschylus. In language and thought, in the treatment of themes and in the management of the chorus, the *Prometheus Bound* clearly stands apart from all the other Aeschylean plays we know. Our greatest difficulty, of course, is that of reconciling Zeus as represented in this play—the young tyrant of Olympus, ruling by sheer force and inflicting wanton suffering like Io's—with the just ruler of the universe as depicted in the other Aeschylean plays, in particular in the *Agamemnon*. One wonders, indeed, if such a reconciliation is possible. If it was achieved here, it must have been in the lost third play of the trilogy. The *Oresteia*, as we shall see, shows the civilized world to be the harmonization of originally opposed forces; and there is reason to believe that the Promethean trilogy ended in a similar reconciliation of the Olympians and the defiant Titan.

Out of these difficulties has arisen the view that either the play is not by Aeschylus, or, as it stands, it has been extensively rewritten.[60] But in spite of its novel and surprising elements, the most obvious among which is the relative simplicity of the language, there is an undeniable grandeur of conception in the play, as well as much else that is characteristic of Aeschylus. Nor are 'archaic' elements absent, such as a delight in the presentation of strange, distant lands which is occasioned by the description of Io's wanderings and which brings to mind the spectacular exoticism of the *Persians* and the *Suppliants*. The prevailing modern view is that the piece is genuine,[61] and that even if parts of it were later retouched, as was the end of the *Seven Against Thebes*, still the basic character of the play was not altered. As the other two plays are completely unknown to us, we cannot even know if the *Prometheus Bound* was the second play of the trilogy following the *Prometheus Pyrphoros* (the *Firebringer*). That it was certainly not the third is evident from our knowledge of the existence of the *Prometheus Delivered*. The great effect which this trilogy must have had on Athenians may be guessed from the fact that, as far as we know, no other tragedian was ever again to handle the myth of Prometheus.

In 458 Aeschylus produced his last and greatest work, the *Oresteia*. It is the only complete example of a tragic trilogy which has come down to us, and even so its satyr play, the *Proteus*, has been lost. The three plays are the *Agamemnon*, the *Libation Bearers* and the *Eumenides*. Time and again it has been called one of the greatest triumphs of the human spirit, and certainly it shows us Aeschylus still at his greatest at sixty-seven and still learning from his younger contemporaries. For though many archaic features are retained in the *Oresteia*, the extra actor and the painted scenery which had been introduced by Sophocles were both employed at its first production.

The story once again concerns inherited guilt: the curse of the house of Atreus. The story already had a long history, but there are innovations in Aeschylus' treatment of it, the most important probably being the dominant part played by Clytaemnestra in Agamemnon's murder[62] and the way the story is concluded in the *Eumenides*.

All three plays begin with prologues which set their tone. The *Agamemnon* opens with the watchman waiting on the palace roof for the beacon that will announce the fall of Troy. When, after ten years of waiting, he sees the flare his joy is soon lost in the recollection of the terrible secret which hangs over the house: the guilty love of Clytaemnestra for Aegisthus.

In less than forty verses Aeschylus creates the atmosphere of the drama—suspicion and impending doom—which permeates the great choruses that follow and which the magnificent insolence of Clytaemnestra may mitigate but cannot repeal. Agamemnon arrives and is persuaded by his wife's words to walk on a purple carpet and thus to depart from the moderation which ought to be shown by a conqueror.

Before the catastrophe a magnificent scene is introduced which broadens the play's scope. Clytaemnestra lures Cassandra, a second prey, into the palace. However, before entering into the accursed house of her own free will she is inspired by the god Apollo, who has already decreed that she will prophesy the truth in vain. In a vivid blend of visionary song and intelligible speech she depicts the history of the house of Atreus and sees before her inspired gaze a troop of Furies revelling and singing like wild drunkards in the palace from which they cannot be driven away.

Agamemnon's death cry is soon heard from inside the palace; the central door of the stage opens and Clytaemnestra is revealed, axe in hand, standing over the bodies of her two victims. There follows a long dispute between queen and chorus, during which the former tries to justify her actions. But it becomes clear that she, too, is now trapped in the curse of the house — a chain of sin and expiation which will extend into the future. She would gladly appease the ancestral daemon with sacrifices, in order to call a halt; but at this point Aegisthus appears, and, despite the angry protestations of the chorus, the two enter the palace, where they will now reign unchallenged.

In true Aeschylean fashion the long introductory parts of the play, especially the choral odes which follow the prologue and the anapaestic *parodos* of the chorus of Argive elders, are an introduction not only to the *Agamemnon*, but to the trilogy as a whole. A dark foreboding underlies the superficial rejoicing, and, as the play progresses, the clouds continue to darken, until the murder of Agamemnon is almost a relief from the unremitting tension. The long *parodos* speaks of the sailing of the Greek fleet and of the fearful choice which Agamemnon had to make — whether to sacrifice his child or to prevent his army from setting sail. Thus, once again, we see an Aeschylean hero under the yoke of *ananke* (necessity) and forced to choose between two unendurable alternatives. His duty to the army prevails, and he sacrifices his own child, thus allowing the Greek ships to set sail. But he has kindled in his wife's heart that hatred which can only be quenched by his own murder. However, Clytaemnestra's action is not motivated by hatred alone. Her own strong passion, which has driven her into the arms of Aegisthus, provides her with a double reason for killing her husband. And all this, as becomes clear, is but a part of a wider web.

In few passages does Aeschylus express his religious views as clearly as in the choric part of the *parodos* in the *Agamemnon*, where the figure of Zeus is represented as the personification and the guarantee of a universal and intelligible world order. The same passages contain the two basic principles which, for Aeschylus, lie behind human suffering. The first is human responsibility for action — δράσαντι παθεῖν ('the evil-doer must suffer'); and the second is the ultimate plan of Zeus: πάθει μάθος ('knowledge is born of suffering'). Such is the god of Aeschylus, and such the hard way by which he leads man to recognize reality.

In the *Agamemnon* Aeschylus also uses an effective dramatic device which he later repeats in the *Libation Bearers*. He brings into the atmosphere of tension and anxiety a normal, ordinary person who is free of the fears and agony of the participants of the drama. A joyful herald is introduced to announce the landing of the king, who contrasts the happiness and safety of the present moment with the hardships of the long campaign at Troy. In the *Libation Bearers* it is Orestes' old nurse who plays the equivalent part.

That play, the second of the trilogy, is similar in structure to the *Agamemnon*. Once again, a man's crime involves him in the fatal web of the house of Atreus and forces him to acknowledge that he is a link in the chain of guilt. As in the *Agamemnon*, so here too there are four scenes leading up to the confrontation of the main agents of the drama. At first we have a rather unsophisticated recognition scene between Electra and her brother Orestes, who has lived in exile since childhood. This is followed by a long, antiphonal 'duet', in which they call on their father's ghost to help them in their revenge. The scene has great poetic power and is not entirely irrelevant to the dramatic point, for it is only through such supernatural intervention that Orestes can bring himself to the point of killing his mother. The catastrophe, as in all of Aeschylus' plays, comes quickly. Orestes first kills Aegisthus; then, after exchanging with his mother a few deeply painful words, he kills her too, as she repeatedly cries out: 'My child . . . my child!'

After his crime Orestes, like his mother before him, seeks to justify himself. He calls on Helios to be his witness and has the net in which the unarmed Agamemnon was butchered brought out of the palace. But gradually horror overcomes him, and he begins to see the approaching Furies. Finally, in a scene of unmatched tragic grandeur, he rushes in madness off the stage in a desperate effort to reach Delphi, where he may seek to be purified.

Once again in Orestes we find that double motivation, divine decree and human will, which is one of the mainsprings of Aeschylus' drama (as, indeed, it is of the work of Homer). But once Apollo has ordered Orestes to kill his own mother, he recedes into the background: Orestes acts on his own volition. When he confronts his mother he again loses the power to act; but Pylades, his great friend, reminds him, significantly enough, of the Delphic god's will, and the deed is done.

The *Libation Bearers* ends in a scene of stormy passion, which stands in direct contrast with the opening scene of the *Eumenides*, the last play of the trilogy. There complete peace reigns as morning breaks over the Delphic sanctuary. The play must decide if Orestes has made the right choice in his tragic dilemma: whether to kill his mother and thus avenge his father's death, or to allow her to live because she is his mother. Can an end at last be made to this cry of blood for blood?

The answer appears to be more religious than ethical. When the priestess finishes her initial prayer the great doors of the temple are thrown open and Orestes is revealed, exhausted and asleep beside the *omphalos*, the sacred Centre of the Earth. But around him lie the fierce figures of the Furies, who have also fallen asleep, tired out by their chase. Yet Apollo has promised to support Orestes. Hermes, then, will guide him to Athens, where he will find judges to decide his case. Here Aeschylus handles the traditional material with some freedom, as though Apollo's usual powers of purification were not sufficient for the case. The Furies follow Orestes to Athens—which involves a change of scene—and try to bind him with their incantation and their dance: so terrifying was their appearance on the Attic stage, we are told, that women in the audience fainted. At this point Athene herself appears and sets up a court of justice, the Areopagus, in which may be tried cases involving the taking of human life.

In court Apollo speaks for Orestes; the Furies, through their leader, present their own case. This is a double confrontation. Not only Orestes, but also Apollo and Athene, representing the 'younger', Olympian gods, are facing an older generation of traditional deities, the *Erinyes*. In the younger age of the world the father is supreme, whereas in the old world order it is the mother who is all-important. The child stands between them. Aeschylus shows exceptional poetic power in presenting these two basic and opposing forces which were embedded in the religion of Athens. The play also alludes to recent history, as concerned the reforms of the Areopagus. For that aristocratic assembly of the city had been stripped, four years before the performance of the *Oresteia*, of all its old political powers, being left only the right to try cases of homicide and to supervise ceremonies. There can be no doubt that Aeschylus set great store by the state's new role as arbiter in cases involving the shedding of blood. Older Attic custom and law had held the family to be the bearer of that right and duty.

When the jurors cast their votes (Athene's is cast in favour of Orestes) they are equally divided; but an equal division means acquittal. In this verdict is a clear indication that the conflict of the *Oresteia*, which extends into the world of the gods, cannot be resolved by man. Only divine mercy can shatter the chain of sin and punishment and free Orestes.

The *Oresteia* concludes with the reconciliation of both mortals and gods. The ancient goddesses of revenge, though raging and threatening, are finally won over by Athene. Under the name of the *Eumenides*—'the wise and holy'— they will be honoured with a shrine in Athens and will give their blessing to the land of Attica. The old goddesses of revenge are thus turned into beneficial, vegetation goddesses. The final scene, the culmination of the whole trilogy, consists of a grand festive procession, which escorts the ancient divinities to their new seat of worship; and so, as the escorting chorus says: 'all-seeing Zeus and Fate together have come to their goal'. It has been observed that this great festival of reconciliation recalls at every point the *Panathenaea*, the festival of united Athens.[63]

The *Oresteia* is Aeschylus' greatest dramatic achievement, for in it he passed beyond the lyrical or recitative limitations of his other plays. Violent action is presented on the stage, and the language employed matches it in vigour; for the style has become more flexible and better equipped to suit the needs of the dramatic situation without, however, ceasing to be both powerful and elevated. There is a similar development in character drawing. The agents of the drama, and above all Clytaemnestra, are much more individualized than were the earlier types of heroic grandeur; and humbler characters, such as the watchman, or Orestes' nurse, are perfectly conceived.

In the judgement of antiquity, Aeschylus was the best writer of satyr plays,[64] and this estimate of the quality of his work in the field has been confirmed by more recent papyrus finds. We possess a reasonably large fragment of the *Net-Fishers* (Διχτυουλχοί), which came at the end of a trilogy on Perseus. The monstrously heavy catch made by these fishers was the chest containing Danae and Perseus. Though there is a big gap between the two larger fragments of the play which have survived, it is still possible to trace the development of the story in comic scenes between Danae and the lecherous Silenus. The play was more than 800 lines long, so we may deduce that satyr plays were not necessarily concise. Of the *Spectators at the Festival* (Θεωροί or *Visitors to the Isthmia* ἢ Ἰσθμιασταί) only fragments have survived, from which it appears that the plot concerned the intention of the satyrs to take part in the Isthmian Games, no doubt with disastrous results.

Since 1932 there have been several papyrus finds, including fragments of the lost *Niobe* and *Myrmidons*, which give an idea of the many excellent verses lost to posterity as a result of the disappearance of such plays. The complete catalogue is far too long to list here, but because of their Dionysiac subject-matter, mention should be made of the trilogy *Lycurgeia*, consisting of the *Edoni*, *Bassarae* and *Neanisci*, together with the satyr play *Lycurgus*; and of the tragedies *Bacchae*, *Semele*, *Pentheus*, *Xantriae* and the satyr play *Nurses of Dionysus* (Διονύσου Τροφοί).

When we first meet Aeschylus he is already past fifty. His early work is, therefore, a closed book to us. But there are good reasons for believing that he was truly the creator of tragedy as we know it. He it was who took the great step of adding the second actor, thus diminishing the chorus's role and making true dialogue the dominant element.[65] It is also likely that he was the creator of tragic dialogue in the forms which later become usual. Indeed, the chorus song, with speeches inserted here and there, is a far cry from the excellent trilogy structure of the *Oresteia*. It may well be that the trilogy made up of thematically linked plays is also an Aeschylean innovation;[66] and he is also thought to have contributed greatly to the advancement of the satyr play. Moreover, it was probably Aeschylus who organized the external presentation of the drama, with rich costumes and solemn dances, on the lines which were to become traditional.[67]

Unquestionably, the most striking feature of Aeschylus' poetry is its grandeur, which makes it more suitable for depicting the violent passions of pride and hatred than the tenderer emotions of the heart. The grand issues which he works out in his characters' lives are matched by the stature of those characters and the sonority of the language they speak. He is not afraid of compound words, each of which encompasses a whole picture in itself; of epithets strung endlessly together and passing rapidly from one image to another; and of metaphors which are drawn widely from both human life and the natural world. For Aristophanes he was 'the centaur of speech', and for Quintilian 'elevated and majestic, often to excess'.[68] More than a hundred words that never occur in any other Greek author are to be found in the scant seven tragedies and the few fragments which have survived of all his output.

The nobility and profundity of Aeschylus' thought is perhaps best expressed in his choruses, which are more developed in his tragedies than in those of his successors. Though all are strongly 'Aeschylean', each has a distinct character, and in most plays the chorus serves as a foil for the character of the leading personage. Aeschylus' choruses are never mere interludes in the action; they have a highly complex structure and an excellent capacity for suiting the rhythm to the ideas expressed. Many have recurring refrains.

The characters appearing in the Aeschylean plays are outsize, powerful and sustained by great passions; but they are essentially types, undifferentiated by the minute drawing of detail. We find no studies of character in Aeschylus. The great passions that inspire his characters leave little room for the contradictory emotions and thoughts which build the complex psychology of later tragedy and modern drama. Even Clytaemnestra in the *Agamemnon*, the most complex Aeschylean character, has a very simple woman's duplicity and little besides. The interest of a modern audience is mainly centred on the development and the quality of passion, whereas Aeschylus and his public were chiefly preoccupied with its effects. Nevertheless, the majority of Aeschylean heroes are more than mere puppets in the hands of destiny; they have a life of their own. Even secondary figures, such as Hephaestus and Kratos in the *Prometheus Bound*, have distinct, if monolithic, personalities. At the same time, there is a certain stiffness in their dialogues and little adaptation of style to speaker.

The grandeur of style and character in Aeschylus was accompanied, as we have seen, by visual grandeur and ceremony (Prometheus nailed to his solitary rock, or the Egyptian and oriental costumes in the *Suppliants* and the *Persians*), which are of a piece with the author's delight in the geography of strange lands. But the plots of the plays are usually of the kind described by Aristotle as 'simple' or 'straightforward' ($\dot{\alpha}\pi\lambda\tilde{\eta}$); that is, they are not complicated by reversals of fortune or by recognition scenes of the type which so often mark his successors' plays. Instead, they move relentlessly forward as the divine plan works itself out.

Aeschylus' inspiration was primarily religious and patriotic. He took contemporary ideas about inherited evil, of the curse upon a house and the dangers of great prosperity, but purified them so as to make them teach the lesson of the ultimate justice of a Providence in whose designs the rival actions of men and of supernatural powers were finally reconciled and combating wills made to work together. Such a scheme of ordered government and good will towards men is what 'Zeus' meant to him. In it there is room for both Apollo and the Eumenides; but it demands that every form of *hubris* must be pruned of its excess. Even Zeus himself, in the boldest of Aeschylus' conceptions, must grow in wisdom, and learn the spirit of good government. Justice, however long delayed, will always prevail when a man calls down a curse on his house by his own wrong-doing. And the cruellest suffering is seen in the end as only a step in the great and beneficent design of divine will.

In this way Aeschylus, with his own lofty notion of the divine, cast a new light on the old Homeric gods and myths, as well as on the history of his own day. His tragedies have been rightly called a great hymn in celebration of Zeus and *Dike*, for they are full of the same trust in the gods which was such a feature of Hesiod and Solon. The old aristocratic ideals of nobility, wealth and fame look paltry beside the grand Aeschylean conception of a divine principle which is not only the judge but also the educator of mankind.

If Aeschylus' religious views were in harmony with those of his public, the same may be said of his attitude to national pride—a Hellenic and, in particular, an Athenian pride. This is, of course, most pronounced in the *Persians*, where he puts eulogies of his country even into the mouth of her defeated enemy. Such a feeling was perhaps natural for a soldier who fought at Marathon and Salamis. But his whole dramatic output reflects and expresses the same spirit, both national and religious, of that heroic age; in consequence, its influence on the Athenians was enormous.

Sophocles

Sophocles, the son of Sophilus, a wealthy manufacturer, was born in about 496 B.C. at Colonus. His accomplishment in music and dancing attracted attention early in his life, and he is said to have led the paean of victory after the battle of Salamis. His master in music, we know, was Lamprus, one of the great teachers of the old school. Sophocles first embarked on the career of an actor; as such, it is said, he enchanted his audiences in the roles of Nausicaa and Thamyras. But he soon gave up his acting because of the weakness of his voice. His first victory as a tragedian was won in 468, when he defeated Aeschylus.

He took an honourable share in the duties of citizenship—by contrast, as we shall see, with Euripides. In 443/2 he acted as *Hellenotamias*, or imperial treasurer, and he was general at least twice; once in 440, as a colleague of Pericles, when the Samian revolt was crushed, and later as a colleague of Nicias. He was also appointed *proboulos* (Πρόβουλος) after the Sicilian disaster, in order to deal with the crisis.

He seems to have accepted the religion of his day without misgivings, for he was a priest of the healing deity usually called *Amynus* (the exact form of the name is doubtful). He also turned his house into a place of worship for Asclepius, until the temple built for that god was ready for use, and composed a paean in his honour. In recognition of his religious services he was honoured after his death as a hero with the title Δεξίων. He took a deep interest in literary questions of a more theoretical kind, for he wrote a prose work, *On the Chorus*, and founded a literary club, the Θίασος of the Muses. Soon after he died in 406 Aristophanes praised his gentle temperament[69] and called him 'happy and dexterous'.

Sophocles is said to have composed 123 plays, with which he won twenty-four victories. Eighteen of these were probably first prizes and the remainder second prizes. He won no third prize. Today, apart from several fragments, we possess only seven plays of his, which have survived as a result of being made into a school collection by an otherwise unknown grammarian, Sallustius.

The poet himself, so Plutarch tells us,[70] distinguished three styles of his own work. The first was the 'lofty' style of Aeschylus (ὄγκος); the second was his own 'pungent and artificial' style (πικρὸν καὶ κατάτεχνον); the third was the 'best kind of style, most suited to the expression of character' (ἠθικώτατον καὶ βέλτιστον). His extant plays all seem to belong to the third period, as the earliest of them was written some twenty-five years after his first appearance. Some critics have professed to find elements of the second period in the *Ajax* and the *Antigone* and of the first in certain of the fragments.

The *Ajax* is probably the oldest of the extant Sophoclean plays, as both its structure and other linguistic and stylistic elements tend to show. It was probably written in the fifties of the fifth century, and in it Sophocles' artistic development is already in full flower. The play deals with the destiny of Ajax, a single man, rather than with the destiny of a whole house. As a lone tragedy it is fully rounded and finished and stands independent of its lost companion plays. For Sophocles' tragedies, unlike those of Aeschylus, were on the whole not thematically linked.[71] We do not, indeed, know what other plays were presented with the *Ajax*, or for that matter with any other Sophoclean play, but that hardly affects our appreciation of the dramas.

The hero of the play is Ajax, the great warrior, whose honour has been injured beyond restitution. A noble but harsh man, he cannot endure dishonour and forms an evil plan of revenge — to kill the Achaean leaders because, by awarding the arms of Achilles to Odysseus, his greatest enemy, they have slighted him and treated him unfairly. He is made into a laughing-stock and his plan into a grotesque mockery by the goddess Athene, who strikes him with madness, so that he mistakes flocks of Greek sheep for his enemies and slaughters them.

The chorus of his men, sailors of Salamis, his slave–concubine Tecmessa and his little son represent in the play the bonds which attach him to life. When his madness is past (which is the point at which the play begins) he realizes that all honour is lost and he abandons them all, withdrawing into heroic isolation. In a scene of great power he escapes from his friends with a speech in warm praise of life and makes for a lonely spot where he may be free to take his own life; for 'to live in honour or to die in honour' befits the noble spirit (l. 497). His tragedy is the realization that there is no place in this world for a character such as his.

Ajax's men are jubilant at his apparent change of heart. But soon we hear him bid farewell to the sunlight and take his own life with Hector's sword, the dreadful gift of his former enemy. (This last scene of violent action clearly cannot have been visible to the audience.) The ode of jubilation sung by the chorus just before the catastrophe illustrates a typical Sophoclean technique, which we find again in the *Antigone* and the *Oedipus Tyrannus*. It was called in antiquity by a technical term, παρέκτασις, the 'stretching' or 'intensification' of the tragedy.[72]

The second half of the play is taken up with a long dispute between the leaders of the Greeks over the disposal of Ajax's body, at the end of which his enemy, Odysseus, secures burial for him. Sophocles is superior to his age in his depiction of Odysseus, for he accords him great humanity. Odysseus does not triumph over his fallen enemy; rather, through his insight into the dark lot of man, he becomes here the very type of the spectator in Sophoclean drama.

In the *Ajax* Athene, who appears on the stage, is presented as a cruel and dangerous deity who destroys those unwilling to submit to the gods' dark decrees. She speaks of the *hubris* of Ajax: but it does not appear that this is his main fault or the true reason for his downfall. What is responsible, rather, is his own outsize, heroic character, which he shares with all other Sophoclean heroes and which cannot be fitted into the world as we know it. Friedrich Welcker said long ago. 'Ajax fulfils his dramatic role more through what he is than through what he has done.'[73]

In antiquity the structure of the *Ajax* was considered defective, and modern critics find fault with it for having a second and scarcely shorter half following the hero's death. But this judgement is undiscerning. Quite as important as the hero's life in the ancient world was the fate of his body after death, and that is the question debated in the second part of the play. The 'diptych' form of the *Ajax* was also employed by Sophocles in his *Antigone* and *Women of Trachis*.

As far as we know, Sophocles was the first tragedian to present woman on the stage as a noble being, capable of shaping her own destiny. The play in which he did so was the *Antigone*, in the fifth century perhaps the most famous of all Sophocles' dramas. Produced in 441, it treated of Creon's denial of the rites of burial to Antigone's brother, the traitor Polyneices, and of the heroine's disobedience of the king's orders, her symbolic burial of the corpse and her subsequent death.

Antigone is driven to her actions by a deep moral sense, which is rooted in the old religious duties of blood and the clan, those 'unwritten and unrelaxing laws' (l. 454) which she invokes as the reason for her defiance. She was 'born not to hate, but to love' (l. 523), as she tells us, and it is from love and reverence that her act of disobedience springs.

Sophocles makes Creon's son fall in love with the heroine—and so deeply in love that after her death he takes his own life. But there is not a single scene in the play in which the two appear alone together, and Antigone never even mentions her betrothed (l. 572 is correctly attributed by ancient tradition to Ismene). Haemon's love for the heroine is introduced into the tragedy in order to strengthen and harden his father's decision and thus to drive him deeper into the *hubris* whose punishment will be his catastrophe. It is not intended as a sub-plot or parallel issue.

Neither the pleading of Antigone's sister Ismene, whose timidity underlines the heroine's resolution, nor the warning of the chorus of Theban elders succeeds in changing Antigone's mind. Nobly, she waves them both aside, for her values belong to a different world, a world as eternal as death; she feels that she no longer belongs to the world of the living (ll. 559–60).

It has often been pointed out that once Antigone has thrown a light coating of dust on her brother's corpse, thus 'burying' him in the eyes of the gods, there is no reason why she should return again to be caught attempting to repeat the symbolic burial. But this should not be seen as an inconsistency or a dramatic fault. The repetition clearly serves to stress her rebellion against Creon and to show the heroine triumphant for a moment before her final downfall. It is a subtle use of the Sophoclean technique of παρέκτασις which we saw in the *Ajax*. Similarly, the servile, almost humorous figure of the guard who brings her as a culprit before Creon should not be seen as an instance of mere comic relief or realism. His presence constitutes an intentional antithesis of mood, calculated to heighten the tragic situation.

As she leaves the stage to meet her death, Antigone bewails her fate in a lamentation full of self-pity. This seems strange to a modern audience, for it stands in sharp contrast to her whole character and her actions as revealed elsewhere in the play. But that would not have been the reaction of Sophocles' audience. In antiquity life was considered to have supreme value, and it was unthinkable that anybody, even the bravest hero, should leave it without bitter grief. Indeed, the ancient notion of the heroic presupposes a deep love of life. We should remember the story of Aristodemus, who, finding himself despised for being the only Spartan to survive the battle of Thermopylae, attempted to wipe out his shame by fighting bravely, and dying, at Plataea. He was not buried in the heroes' tomb on the battlefield because 'he wanted to die'.[74] The romantic death-wish was completely unknown in antiquity.

If there is any place in the play where an inconsistency of character does emerge, it is in the moment after the scene in which Creon's blindness, pride and folly suddenly collapse, as the king determines to save Antigone and salvage what can be salvaged. But inconsistency or no inconsistency, Creon's change of heart comes too late to alter the course of events. Driven on by his blind *hubris* and by the suspicious fears of a tyrant who never feels secure and who harshly punishes any disobedience, he has already wandered into sin, from which there is no redemption. Antigone, already in the hollow 'tomb' in which she has been buried alive, takes her own life and brings about her opponent's complete downfall. Haemon, Creon's only surviving son, and Eurydice, his wife, both commit suicide, and Creon is left, lonely and childless, to repent and to suffer, a broken man who has seen the truth too late.

The *Antigone* has rightly been called a play of two characters, for it contains two tragedies, that of the pious and heroic Antigone, which ends in glory through death, and that of the hubristic and harsh Creon, which ends in a life of misery. The 'diptych' form which we saw in the *Ajax* is again employed here, for the play continues long after Antigone's exit from the stage. As in the *Ajax*, the latter part of the drama is full of the conflict that rages over the refusal of a burial; and the poet's voice is raised against the vindictive will of authority which is not aware of its own limits.

Hegel's celebrated interpretation of the *Antigone*,[75] which saw Creon and Antigone as representing state and family battling for their own rights, is clearly untenable. The problem here is one of not equal but opposed rights. If there is a clash of two rights in the *Antigone*, then they are far from equal in Sophocles' eyes. The right of the state demands obedience from the citizen. The right of the gods demands obedience from the state. Antigone may have been disobedient to her king, but the king's disobedience to the gods of the dead was, to Sophocles, incomparably more serious. At one level the play manifestly discusses the validity of the state's claim to ultimate authority, a question which Sophocles answers in the negative. But it goes beyond that to touch on the basic problem of human *hubris* and its inevitable punishment.

The famous chorus (ll. 332ff.) praising the achievements of man, who sets no limits to his ambitions and his lust for power, is of great significance. It must be interpreted against the background of Athenian imperialism, of the anti-traditional ideas of the Sophists and of the historical period in which Sophocles lived, which were ready to break all bounds. In the context of the play its function is to illustrate the nature of Creon, who has transgressed the Mean and who does not respect the laws of the dead and the right of the gods. The clarity of its thought and the noble unity of its strophic structure lift this *stasimon* far above anything similar in the work of Aeschylus,[76] which seems loose, even flabby, by comparison with

Sophocles' serenity and balance. But there is much else in the play that is poetically fine, not least the famous chorus song on love (ll. 781ff.).

The character of a different woman, whose destiny decides her husband's fate is presented in the *Women of Trachis*. This play probably (though indications are very uncertain) belongs to the thirties of the fifth century. It is the only surviving Sophoclean tragedy named after its chorus and is no doubt so named because of its 'diptych' form, which gives equal weight to the fortune of two characters. The first part deals with the fate of Deianeira, and the second with the death of Heracles which arises from it.

Over the plot of the play hangs an oracle which determines its development and which is fulfilled by the death of Heracles. This is therefore a tragedy in which human guilt and human responsibility have little real place. The interest of the play resides in the agents' emotions and reactions to this inescapable framework.

Deianeira, Heracles' wife, no longer young, suffers from the absence of her husband and from torments of jealousy of young Iole, whom Heracles has sent to live alongside her as his concubine. She determines to send her husband, as a charm to win back his love, a shirt bathed in the poisoned blood of the centaur Nessus. She has been told by the dying centaur that his blood can recapture the love of her husband, but does not know that it may be fatal. On receiving the *chiton*, his wife's thanksgiving gift for his safe return, Heracles wears it and dies in excruciating agony.

In the first part of the play Deianeira's emotional state is portrayed with tenderness, insight and subtlety. Her first long speech sets out in advance what the audience needs to know in a manner reminiscent, as we shall see, of the Euripidean prologue. Indeed, the erotic motivation of her actions, and such elements as her farewell to her marriage bed and Heracles' final monody, have been attributed by many critics to the influence of Euripides. Though such influence is by no means impossible, the whole religious tone of the *Women of Trachis* and Deianeira's quiet devotion belong to a world entirely different from that of Euripides' passionate women and radical attacks on the gods.

The only possible expiation for Deianeira's unwitting deed is, of course, her death; and she leaves the stage to take her life in a dramatically effective silent exit that reminds us of Eurydice's in the *Antigone*. Deianeira's tragedy is followed in the second half of the play by that of Heracles, in which the great conqueror of cities is presented to the audience writhing in pain in a scene which, as far as we know, was the first occasion in Greek drama on which physical as well as spiritual agonies were shown on stage. Realizing that the old prophecies are being fulfilled, Heracles orders his son to prepare his funeral pyre on Mount Oeta and instructs him to marry Iole. Then the cortège carries the hero away and leaves the stage empty.

In the *Women of Trachis* the separate sequences in which the two destinies are worked out both show how a man's every step to avoid his fate brings him nearer to it. But the play ends on a note of questioning, almost of complaint. The apotheosis of Heracles is, rather unsatisfactorily, presented as a recompense for Deianeira's terrible mistake and for his own many labours and sufferings, 'not one of which', in the final words of Hyllus, 'is not Zeus'. This is a measure of Sophocles' deep piety and a sign that he ultimately accepts the divine will; but what lingers in the mind of the modern reader is the sense of outrage at the gods' injustice which is expressed by Hyllus, in an outcry like nothing else in Sophocles: 'see how little compassion the gods have shown . . . they who are called our fathers . . . what is here now is shameful for the gods' (ll. 1264ff.). At all events, regardless of divine justice or injustice, in this play Sophocles again shows how man in the grip of inescapable disaster finds his noblest self.

Nevertheless, the *Women of Trachis* is the feeblest of all the Sophoclean tragedies. Though the character drawing, especially that of Deianeira, is fine, the plot is loose, and the chorus songs are rather short and not very original.

King Oedipus is Sophocles' masterpiece. In it his art reached its fulfilment and its peak, and in tragic effect it is surpassed by no other Greek drama: indeed, Aristotle considered it the perfect tragedy. The same subject had earlier been treated by Aeschylus, but without doubt Sophocles handled it differently and more effectively.

Written soon after 430 but before 425, when Aristophanes parodied a part of it in his *Acharnians*,[77] *King Oedipus* reflects something of the horror which was felt while the plague devastated Athens. It deals with the story of a great man who is hunted and finally trapped by Fate. For Oedipus, who has heard of a prophecy that he will kill his father and marry his mother, has taken every step to avoid such monstrous calamities, only to find, years later that he has unwittingly done exactly what the oracle foretold. On learning the truth he blinds himself: Jocasta, his wife and mother, has already taken her own life.

The play's compactness and economy of construction is unique in Greek tragedy. All decisive action has taken place before the play begins (for which reason it has been called an analytic tragedy), and so the whole play centres on the dominating figure of Oedipus, a man whose own forceful character drives him deeper and deeper into disaster. At once culprit and detective, he pursues inquiry after inquiry until the full, dreadful truth is uncovered. Even apparent moments of hope in this relentless quest are pregnant with doom.

In its quest the quick brain of Oedipus often outruns itself and jumps to false conclusions. He is suspicious of Tiresias, the blind man who can see the truth; he suspects the loyal Creon of plotting against him; and he even attributes to his wife and mother a pride she does not possess. But in the end he goes boldly to meet his fate and grapples with it in a burning passion of truth and a readiness to suffer which make him one of the greatest figures of the tragic stage.

The other agents of the play are fit companions for Oedipus and serve to reveal various facets of his character. In particular, Jocasta, a woman ready to give ground and to compromise, 'to take life as it comes' (l. 979), provides an admirable foil to the hero's uncompromising nature. But the character of Oedipus towers above all, the self-confident man who has great faith in his own intellect yet is impotent before the gods' dark power, which inexorably follows its own course for all that the wit and will of man can accomplish.

We cannot help wondering what kind of gods are these who can punish so cruelly a man in no way guilty. For Oedipus' killing, in self-defence, of a stranger whom he could not know to be his father was not a sin in the eyes of the ancient world; and when he marries Jocasta there is no way for him to guess that she is his mother. All attempts by modern critics to find a fault in the hero which would totally, or even partially, justify his downfall have proved fruitless. The *Oedipus* is clearly not a drama of sin and atonement. It cannot even be seen as a drama of destiny, for, in a sense, the hero's own will and choice are the instruments of his catastrophe. The message that emerges is purely religious: divine government is inaccessible to mortal understanding and often fulfils itself in an appalling manner, while always remaining justified in the eyes of the gods and deserving of human reverence. Sophocles does not endeavour to explain the gods' dark designs, but, just as in the *Antigone*, he completely rejects the new iconoclasm of the Sophists, a challenge to everything traditionally held sacred. Instead he presents, in all its problematic grandeur, a divine morality which is incalculable and teaches that man's happiness lies in submission to the gods. For in acting heroically man opposes heaven and brings about his own destruction.

The recognition scene (ll. 1110–85) in *King Oedipus* is the finest passage in the play—indeed, possibly the finest scene in Greek tragedy, for nothing elsewhere matches the effect of Jocasta's final realization that she is married to her own son and her cry, as she retreats into the palace: 'Alas, alas! Wretched man, that is all I can call you; nothing after this.' But there is much else in the play that is fine, especially the lyrical parts, which are among the best that Sophocles ever composed and which are magnificently varied in mood and content. But above all we are struck again and again by the way in which the agents of the play speak words with a dreadful double meaning, of which they, at the time, are unaware. It is as though they are unwitting mouthpieces, compelled by divine power to speak words of tragic irony.

Oedipus emerges, blinded, at the end of the play, to sing, like Antigone, his own lament. Again, as with Antigone's parting song, modern audiences find in the fallen hero's words an unheroic self-pity that is alien to his character as so far revealed. It has been claimed that the *King Oedipus* would be a greater play if Sophocles had ended it with line 1306. But such a thing would have been unthinkable. Greek drama never finishes at its climax, with the catastrophe. An anticlimax always follows, which is designed to allow time for moral reflection and a purging (catharsis) of the pity and fear provoked by the play. Moreover, to be deprived of the sunlight by going blind was, for the Greeks, almost equivalent to death; this, together with the fact that Oedipus knows that he is an accursed man and that nobody will dare to be polluted by mentioning his name after his death, drives him to sing his own 'lament', as though he were already dead.

King Oedipus expresses the concept of the tragic with greater purity than any other play in European literature. Its grief and horror notwithstanding, it gives one a strange sense of elevation and an impression of balance, no doubt products of the poet's care never to obscure his belief in a grand cosmic order, eternally valid in spite of all change and all individual suffering. This belief sustains the play and lifts the audience above any feeling of ultimate despair, nihilism or chaos.

A similar sureness of structure is to be seen in the *Electra*, which was probably first produced around 420 B.C. The heroine of this play is a very different person from her namesake in Aeschylus' *Libation Bearers*. There, though she supports Orestes in avenging their father's death, she plays a role secondary to his. In the Sophoclean play, on the other hand, she is the major figure and the mainspring of all action. Like Antigone, she personifies the strong, almost masculine, will-power of certain women as she casts aside the warnings of her sister Chrysothemis, a figure as timid as Ismene in the *Antigone*, and successfully unmasks the hypocrisy of Clytaemnestra's arguments in a magnificent long *agon*. If her brother had not arrived on the scene, indeed, she would herself have dealt her mother's death-blow, but Orestes, who has been thought dead, does appear and performs his cruel duty. As his mother shrieks off-stage, he replies: 'It is done.' At that moment Electra utters the terrible cry: 'If you can, strike again.' Her words should not be interpreted as a condonation by Sophocles of the matricide, which, on the contrary, it was no part of his purpose to make a central issue of the play.[78]

We do not know whether the *Electra* was one of a trilogy, nor indeed do we need to know, as far as our appreciation of it is concerned. Sophocles' intention was to fill with violent passions and emotions all his characters, even Orestes' old tutor, who had earlier related the magnificent (and false) story of Orestes' participation in and death at the Pythian Games. But what the poet was interested in portraying above all were the heights and depths of Electra's emotions, which have a strange, tragic lyricism of their own. Sophocles found the very core of his tragedy in Electra's sorrow and loneliness, in her brooding over past injuries, in her hopes for her brother's return and, especially, in her lamentation over his supposed ashes, a scene of deep and intimate tenderness. The poet is much less interested in the ethical significance of the story than in what the characters think and feel. The lyrical parts, with the exception of the *parodos*, are quite short.

In the *Electra* the old, ritual tragedy has plainly undergone secularization, but of a kind different from that of Euripides. There has been no modification to the profoundly religious world-view of Sophocles, but a marked change of emphasis has brought the human beings into the centre of the action while causing the gods, who remain the rulers of man, to withdraw from the foreground. There are no oracles or seers to act as mouthpieces of the gods or to affect the action significantly, and the part played by Apollo as inciter to revenge is marginal.

The two late plays of Sophocles which are known to us, the *Philoctetes* and the *Oedipus at Colonus*, are not merely relics of a great man's art; they show the master at his most mature and, in many ways, at his best.

The *Philoctetes* was produced in 409. It tells, in a secularizing manner reminiscent of the *Electra*, of a short but vivid incident in the Trojan War, which both Aeschylus and Euripides treated earlier. In Sophocles' version Philoctetes, the leader of seven ships from Methone, is abandoned on the island of Lemnos by the Greeks on their way to Troy because of a festering wound in his leg. He keeps with him the bow and arrows which Heracles has given him and without which Troy cannot be captured. When the Greeks discover this fact they send Odysseus and Neoptolemus, Achilles' honest son, to bring him to Troy. But Philoctetes, embittered by privations and his long solitude, withstands their entreaties and machinations until Heracles appears as a *deus ex machina* and persuades him to take the journey to Troy as 'great Destiny' ordains.

Sophocles was departing from tradition in placing Philoctetes alone on an otherwise uninhabited island. The hero's bitter suffering heightens the tragic situation and provides a motive for his stubborn resistance to the entreaties of his former comrades, whom he now considers his enemies. The introduction into the story of Neoptolemus was also an original stroke on Sophocles' part. The straightforward, noble nature of Achilles' son will not allow him to lie. He thus makes an excellent foil for the cunning opportunism of his adviser, Odysseus, a man prepared to use any means to achieve his ends, and Sophocles makes the most of this contrast of character. Neoptolemus, finally persuaded by Odysseus that Philoctetes must be won over by a false story, finds himself, when facing his intended dupe, unable to carry out the plan. His φύσις, his true nature, gets the better of him and the truth emerges, creating a confrontation tragic both for Philoctetes, who has from the outset trusted and believed the 'son of noble Achilles', and for Neoptolemus, who learns to despise himself for the part he has been about to play: 'Everything becomes hateful when a man abandons his own nature and acts at variance with it' (ll. 902f.).

But, as in all Sophoclean plays, behind this variety of human types and their reactions stands the impersonal power of Destiny (*Moira*), indifferent alike to the cunning of Odysseus, the suffering of young Neoptolemus and the bitter complaints of Philoctetes. And it is to this great power of Destiny, here speaking through the lips of Heracles, that the hero finally bows, agreeing to leave for Troy. Heracles' injunction to revere the gods is no doubt the voice of Sophocles himself, for he kept to the end of his life the same pious convictions to be found in his earlier plays.

Philoctetes' last farewell to the land, the caves, the nymphs, the rocks and the springs that have witnessed his long exile, is beautiful poetry, and there is much fine psychological insight in the depiction, in simple and flowing language, of the play's conflict between honour and pragmatism. But at the same time one gets the impression that Sophocles must have been carried beyond this theme to have resorted to the Euripidean device of the *deus ex machina* in order to achieve a happy ending, in which angry words, injury and conflicting passions and motives can be resolved in a divine calm. Moreover, the songs sung by the chorus of Greek sailors are, surprisingly for Sophocles, short and unimportant in this play and there are no messenger speeches.

There can be little doubt that the *Philoctetes* reflects the contemporary clash in Athens between the old, aristrocratic notion of ἀρετή, of those inherited qualities which Pindar believed in, and the new Sophistic view that intellect and education were the greatest things in human life. Sophocles is clearly on the side of the old, aristocratic views, and the whole message of the *Philoctetes* might perhaps be summed up in the French proverb *Bon sang ne peut mentir*.

The *Oedipus at Colonus*, Sophocles' last play, which was composed when the poet was over eighty and produced after his death in 406 B.C., shows no signs of flagging inspiration. Sophocles had already dealt with the myth of Oedipus in his *King Oedipus*, in which he presents a hero suddenly destroyed by the gods at the peak of his power and glory. That mythical figure seems to have haunted the poet until his last years, when he turned to it again, in order to demonstrate the opposite of his previous teaching: that the gods can choose the most miserable and accursed of mortals and raise him to become a symbol of happiness and power just as inexplicably as they earlier cast him down.

The tragedy takes its story from a local Attic tradition that the body of Oedipus rested in Colonus, Sophocles' native deme, and that its presence would protect Athens for ever. As the play opens, the blind Oedipus, an exiled beggar, is led by his daughter, Antigone, to the grove of the

Eumenides at Colonus, where he knows he will at last find an end to both his sufferings and his long, eventful life. There he faces a number of adversities, which are presented in vigorous scenes: with mistrust and horror the local inhabitants try by force to throw the accursed man out of Attica; Creon, in response to a prophecy, tries by force to bring him back near to Thebes and seizes his daughters as hostages, thus 'blinding' him a second time; and finally Polyneices, his own ungrateful son, seeks help against his brother Eteocles. However, with the help of Theseus, the humane king of Athens, he manages to resist all these assaults and to have his daughters returned to him.

Then, in a scene of inscrutable, mystical grandeur, the thunder of Zeus is heard and a voice from heaven calling to Oedipus. The blind man, leading the sighted, moves calmly away to his mysterious end, which is witnessed by none save Theseus. The messenger's speech in which these events are described would be remarkable in any literature. There are, too, matchless specimens of tender and tragic lyricism in two of the play's chorus songs, the one a celebrated paean of praise to Colonus, where the nightingale sings and narcissus and crocus bloom, where Dionysus walks with the nymphs and the Muses accompany Aphrodite; and the other a reflection on old age. In the latter we are saddened to find that even a great and happy poet like Sophocles[79] can come to a grim, final conclusion about life: 'the best is never to be born' (l. 1225). Not even submission to the divine will, which Sophocles preached all his life, was able to bring him final *eudaemonia*. Nevertheless, the play as a whole has been rightly called the poet's 'swan-song to the beauty and greatness of Athens'.[80]

It is a mistake, though one often seen in print, to imagine that Oedipus in this play is transmuted into a divine figure because his suffering has 'purified' him of his sins. This is an essentially Christian interpretation of the play and alien to the whole spirit of the ancient world. The message of the play is indeed religious, but not moral in any narrow sense. The poet's intention is clearly to illustrate once again, and from a different angle, the inexplicable and unpredictable workings of the gods, so dark and awe-inspiring in the eyes of man. Above all, he teaches that one must never lose hope, that the darkest hour is before the dawn.

Even if changes were made to the play after the poet's death, there is no reason to believe that the middle section, with all its vigorous action, is the work, wholly or in part, of another hand. Nevertheless, the structure of the play is loose, and the fact remains that this is the only extant play of Sophocles which needs four, not three, actors for its performance.

Large fragments of a Sophoclean satyr play, the *Ichneutae*, have been retrieved from papyri. It belongs to the poet's early period, as can be seen from certain elements of style, and it tells in humorous strain the tale of the theft of Apollo's cattle by his brother Hermes — a tale, as we have seen, known also from the Homeric Hymn to Hermes. In Sophocles' version the satyrs follow Apollo like hounds, tracking down the thief. They find the stolen animals in a deep cave, where they are tricked, but also enchanted, by the sound of the lyre, newly invented by Hermes. Father Silenus, as always, is closely associated with the satyrs, and the setting of the play is the Arcadian mountains. An Arcadian nymph, Cylene by name, also appears, to the delight of the cavorting and leaping satyrs. The play ends with the reconciliation of the two brothers. It was apparently the convention that the satyrs should be the slaves of different masters in different satyr plays and that they should be released at the end of the play. Whose slaves they were in the *Ichneutae* we cannot tell.

Of the vast number of other Sophoclean plays—he is credited with 123—only a few fragments have survived; some, found on papyri, are from the *Eurypylus* and some probably from the *Scyrii*, and we also have scraps from the satyr play *Inachus*. Perhaps the most influential and celebrated of the lost plays was the tragedy *Tereus*, which told the story of Procne: to punish Tereus, her husband, for having violated her sister Philomela, Procne kills her son Itys. It is thought that Euripides was influenced by this play when he wrote the *Medea*.

Sophocles is credited by Aristotle[81] with having made three changes to the form of tragedy: the introduction of a third actor, the first use of painted scenery (σκηνογραφία) and the enlargement of the chorus from twelve to fifteen persons. At the same time he abandoned the massive framework of the connected trilogy, which Aeschylus had regularly used, and chose to compose three single, unrelated plays, each centred on one principal hero.[82] This has rightly been seen as something more than a mere technical difference, for it demonstrates a fundamental change in method and outlook from that of his great predecessor.[83]

The human agents of Sophocles' drama generally share the action with the gods. The poet's religious conceptions are thus of paramount importance to an understanding of his plays and call for a few words of explanation. For Aeschylus, a pious Athenian who had fought at Marathon and Salamis, the gods worked through the suffering of mankind to bring about the final triumph of order, justice and reconciliation, whose working out could only be shown over a long period of years. Sophocles, on the other hand, whose years of maturity were lived in an Athens where the Sophists were challenging all the traditional views,[84] did not believe that the passage of time proved the gods' beneficent intentions. In his plays the designs of the gods are remote and enigmatic, often being expressed in dark prophecies, in encouragement that seems to fail or in answers to prayers that bring about the opposite of what is prayed for. He makes it abundantly clear that life is unpredictable and cruel, and that neither the practice of virtue, nor the most powerful human intellect can guide man through its baffling perplexities. In his eyes life is based on an order which is governed by universal laws ultimately incomprehensible to man. When the balance of that order is disturbed it reasserts itself with a vengeance through the action of *Dike*.[85] Moreover, the transgressor will be punished by the inexorable gods, even if his disturbance of this universal order has been prompted by pure and innocent motives. For Sophocles' conception of the natural order seems to embrace the divine laws, which in their turn express themselves in natural sanctions.[86]

This uncertainty concerning the prevailing universal laws and the unpredictability of life that results from it has the effect of focusing dramatic concern on the inevitability of suffering, as seen from the position of the individual sufferer. The emphasis thus moves from the universal to the particular, from Destiny to the character of the hero, a shift which is related to Sophocles' abandonment of the Aeschylean connected trilogy. There is no doubt that the poet's chief interest and his greatest glory lie in his portrayal of noble characters. All Sophoclean heroes are violent, outsize figures ($\delta\varepsilon\iota\nu o\iota$, $\pi\varepsilon\rho\iota\sigma\sigma o\iota$), led by their own natures to disturb the natural order and balance of things and thus, necessarily, to bring about their own downfall. They are destined to suffer, and in their acceptance of this suffering lies their own peculiar form of nobility.

This strange fusion of character and destiny is one of the greatest triumphs of Sophocles' theatre. The poet succeeds in drawing a deep, tragic lyricism from his characters' agony, as in a series of sharply contrasted scenes, each more powerful than the last, he uncovers the true nature of a heroic 'soul' ($\psi v\chi\eta$). How deeply concerned Sophocles was with the drawing of character can also be seen by the way he introduces into his plays, usually at an early stage, scenes which serve that end but have no bearing on the development of the plot.[87]

In all the extant plays of Sophocles save the *Women of Trachis* the situations in which the characters are placed are basically the same, in spite of their human and dramatic variety. The hero is faced with the possibility of a compromise which his violent, heroic nature cannot accept. He is warned, advised and begged by his friends, threatened and abused by his enemies, urged on or checked by oracles and presentiments, but nothing will shake his iron resolution. It is not without reason that critics have discerned behind the Sophoclean conception of the hero the grand, unrelenting figure of the Homeric Achilles.

Perhaps no other ancient or modern dramatist has shown the whole range of human emotions so powerfully on the stage: grief, weariness, impatience, anger, scorn, unrestrained joy, pitiless hatred and utter despair. As well as experiencing the deepest spiritual anguish, Sophocles' characters suffer intense physical pain on stage (Sophocles was the first dramatist to require this). We have seen how Heracles writhes in distress when he dons the shirt of Nessus; how Philoctetes suffers intolerably from the festering wound in his leg; and, most striking of all, how Oedipus, when he emerges from the palace where he has put out his eyes, is caught in the claws of excruciating physical and psychological pain.

Sophocles was also, as we have seen, the first dramatist to present women as worthy representatives of humanity. In this too he must be seen as a great innovator, especially when we consider the position that women occupied in the Athenian society of his day.[88] And it is not only his grand, tragic heroines like Antigone, Electra, Tecmessa, Deianeira and Jocasta who are presented with admiration and understanding; the same may be said of secondary figures such as Ismene in the *Antigone* or Ismene and Antigone in the *Oedipus at Colonus*.

The question of whether Sophoclean characters are more than mere types who, in Wilhelm von Humboldt's words, 'despise and avoid everything too individual', has been much discussed.[89] Undoubtedly in them, as in all fifth-century art, there is an idealizing tendency towards the impersonal and the general; but the individual qualities which go to make up a real, living personality are never completely missing. Antigone is no mere type of the heroic maiden, any more than Oedipus (in *King Oedipus*) is merely typical of the too-confident ruler. They are both of them also individual, tangible human beings, who can easily be imagined in situations other than those of the plays in which they appear. They have none of the stiffness of certain Aeschylean characters, nor that lack of balance and consequence which are to be seen in so many Euripidean men and women. Sophocles' clear-cut, simple character drawing arises out of his concentration on the perfect clarity of the 'inner law' of a personality: Aristotle's $\varkappa \alpha \theta \delta \lambda o \upsilon$. Everything inessential is put aside.

The secondary figures of the Sophoclean plays, on the other hand, are closer to types than to characters. The chief function of each of them is to reveal one of the many facets of the hero's greatness of soul. But even they are never mere symbols, and in some cases, as, for example, the guard in *Antigone*, or the Corinthian messenger in *King Oedipus*, even a few humorous touches are permitted, which help to illustrate the non-heroic nature. However, the demands of tragic dignity ($\sigma \varepsilon \mu \nu \delta \tau \eta \varsigma$) never sanctioned too crude a realism.

From Aristotle to the present day critics have maintained that Sophocles presented men and women in his plays as better than they really are. This judgement is based not on an assessment of the virtues of individual tragic heroes but rather on the fact that they have no real vices; that their nature is free of anything base or contemptible. It is this that gives the impression of an implausibly noble humanity, victorious over suffering and death.

Sophocles' interest in character drawing and his success at it have rightly been connected with the central significance which fifth-century Attic culture placed on the $\psi \upsilon \chi \dot{\eta}$, or soul. It was a period when the soul was recognized as the centre of man's life on which all human actions depended — a view which reaches its fullest expression in the teachings of Socrates. As the body had a *cosmos*, a principle of order which the sculptor could express plastically, so the soul had an obvious harmony. The heroic soul, then, must have an extraordinary rhythm and structure, and it was this that Sophocles set out to explore in his portrayal of tragic heroes and heroines.

His interest in individual character also lies behind the second of his important innovations, the introduction of a third actor. This increase in the number of the cast enabled him to develop his plots more swiftly, and, more to Sophocles' point, to delineate his characters more sharply, a task for which the cut-and-thrust of dialogue is incalculably more effective than are the grand utterances of lyrical choruses, such as those that Aeschylus had used. Sophocles thus introduced 'triangular' scenes — that is, scenes between three persons, all involved in the same action but with contrasting hopes and fears. Indeed, there is a sense in which Sophocles introduced a fourth actor, for by increasing the numbers of the chorus he was able to detach its leader and to include him occasionally in the dialogue. In exploiting these developments Sophocles seems to have been alone, for neither Aeschylus nor Euripides shows much interest in dialogue between more than two persons.

Sophocles' delineation of character is matched by a great flexibility of style. He has at his command the whole range of dramatic speech, from the dignified and weighty to the extremely swift, light and even casual. His rhetoric, where he is rhetorical, is superb; no less effective is his utter simplicity in simple passages.

As we have seen, the structure of his tragedies takes two principal forms. In one, the 'diptych' form, the play falls into two parts. The first part concerns the fate of the hero or heroine; in the second an issue arising out of the first is alike brought to its conclusion. In the other type a single plot covers the whole play. There is nothing episodic or irrelevant in the structure of Sophocles' plays. Each stage of the action is derived from what has gone before according to the laws of strictest necessity or probability. Allusions to contemporary events are almost entirely avoided, even though many of the issues discussed must necessarily have had a special meaning for a fifth-century Athenian audience.

Sophocles was a master in expressing himself through sharp contrasts. We can see this clearly in his juxtaposition of contrasting characters, scenes and speeches, but it is in the speeches that antithesis is most strikingly employed, speech and counter-speech being a characteristic of Sophoclean drama.

Sophocles' manner of beginning and ending his plays deserves comment. In all his tragedies save the *Women of Trachis* the prologue — that part of the play which precedes the entrance of the chorus — is in dialogue and is organically connected with the remainder of the play, presenting in a few vivid lines the whole dramatic situation. Craftsmanship as careful is to be seen in the *lysis*, the unravelling of the plot. Save in the *Philoctetes*, which has recourse to the Euripidean *deus ex machina*, the unfolding of Sophocles' plots always develops from an inner necessity, which in turn arises out of the nature of the characters portrayed. There is nothing forced, external or unnatural about them.

But, as we have seen, Sophocles prolongs his plays beyond the moment of the actual catastrophe, preferring an anticlimactic ending for reasons partly connected with the place and significance of lamentation in the ancient world and partly arising from Greek tragedy's character as a moral study of an action and its consequences. The necessary dispassionate reflection and calm evaluation of events would be impossible if the play were to end with the catastrophe; in the relative calm of the anticlimax the true nature of the tragic reversal of fate can be more clearly grasped and the relative measures of human and divine responsibility better assessed.

This does not mean that the Sophoclean tragedy sets out to give a concise answer to a clear question. On the contrary, the problems are complex; and though the poet may often allow his sympathies to show, he never attempts to argue, to justify or even fully to explain the events he puts on stage. He is simply concerned to portray life and to stress how unpredictable human destiny is, that destiny which, through no fault of his own, can crush Oedipus at the height of his glory and then lift him again from the depths of misery to become a symbol of power and happiness.

The lyrical parts of Sophocles' tragedies — chorus songs, duets between protagonist and chorus, monodies sung from the stage — are, by comparison with those of Aeschylus, fairly short.[90] Permeated with a softer light, they are without the ominous, distant mystery of the older poet's work. Sophocles never uses them to develop the plot or simply to express his own views. Though their mood and tone vary according to the events taking place on stage, reason is always in full control of the poet's vivid emotions and brilliant imagination. Nevertheless, the frequent changes of rhythm within the Sophoclean stanza — more frequent and more strongly marked than in Euripides or even Aeschylus — suggest that the movements of his choric dance must have been striking and dramatic. By comparison with Aeschylus, Sophocles' choric diction might seem uncomplicated and his rhythms, for all their variety, very simple, even when he is expressing profound views of human destiny, the gods or the great laws of life.

But there are moments when Sophocles gives full rein to his imagination, and sudden, wild outbursts of joy flood the verse in the exultant chorus song which precedes the final catastrophe. Pathos and terror can be seen, for example, in some of the duets between protagonist and chorus.[91] On the other hand, Sophocles' monodies (a form he rarely employs) are marked by a restraint very different from the capricious fancies of Euripides.

Sophocles' stature as dramatist and lyric poet, as seen in the dialogue and lyrical parts of his tragedies, is matched by his mastery of the narrative verse of his messenger speeches,[92] in which, in order to bring before the audience the horror and wonder of the acts committed off-stage, what is called for is less a dramatic than a descriptive, epic technique. For such acts were considered incompatible with the dignity of tragedy and could only be reported, never acted before the audience.[93] Few narrative descriptions of this kind are more vivid or more moving than the Paedagogus' account of the Pythian Games in the *Electra*, or that of Oedipus' awe-inspiring end in the *Oedipus at Colonus*.

There are three further dramatic devices in which Sophocles particularly excels. The first is his use of tragic irony, which is to be seen both in individual speeches and in whole scenes of his plays. This is most effectively and most markedly used in *King Oedipus*. The second is his use of tragic silence. Far more effective than any words at a moment of high tragedy is a silent exit, such as that of Eurydice in the *Antigone*, when she overhears the news of her son's death, or that of the two shepherds in *King Oedipus*. After the full horror of Oedipus' identity has been revealed, they walk some thirty metres to a sad, silent exit. The third device is very similar to this: the silent comment, in which the spectacle on the stage speaks for itself more effectively than might any spoken words. Examples are the appearance on the stage at the end of *King Oedipus* of the hero's two young daughters, who do not speak a word when they are brought out to embrace their father, who is also their brother; or the urn scene in the *Electra*. Sophocles was well aware of the importance of spectacle in tragedy, as we may tell from his introduction of painted scenery to the Attic stage. It is, however, a view which Aristotle, in his *Poetics*, does not seem to share.[94]

Sophocles has been accused, with reason, of including in his plays a number of impossible and improbable circumstances. Why, for instance, is Antigone not killed at once, instead of being buried alive in a cave? Why do the gods wait so many years after Oedipus has become king before sending the pestilence to Thebes, and why do they allow him to father so many children by his incestuous union with his mother? Could Jocasta really know so little about her second husband's past—not even who his parents were—after so many years of marriage? Why does nobody suspect the truth when the pin that pierced Oedipus' ankles is mentioned?

But all these criticisms and other similar ones disappear when we see the plays performed. Sophocles' skill entraps us in the story and fills us with suspense as the swiftly moving plot unfolds in one compelling scene after another. So sure and firm is his hand in creating his desired illusion that we are led to the climax of his plays without having the time or the desire to reflect on any improbabilities in his plots. Looking at life with an unwavering eye but without cynicism or despair, Sophocles is unsurpassed at the creation of that illusion from which the audience cannot break away, one of the hallmarks of a great playwright in any age.

Euripides

Euripides, son of Mnesarchus or Mnesarchides, was born in about 480 B.C. in Salamis, where he spent much of his life on his family estate. The few biographical details which have reached us are drawn from scurrilous anecdotes, in which conservative Attic comedy mercilessly ridiculed this great innovative poet. What does seem certain is that he came from a middle-class, land-owning family of Phlya, a deme in the centre of Attica. His mother, Clito, was probably of high birth,[95] though in comedy she may have been presented as a greengrocer.[96] He seems to have been married twice (the names of his wives are given as Melito and Choerine) and many malicious stories circulated about his married life. He had three sons, the youngest of whom was the playwright of the same name who, after his father's death, produced the *Bacchae, Iphigeneia in Aulis* and *Alcmaeon in Corinth*, winning first prize.[97]

Euripides is represented in ancient anecdote as morose and withdrawn from human society; visitors down to Pliny's day were shown a cave in Salamis where he is said to have composed his tragedies, and he certainly avoided public office. Nevertheless, in his time he went on an embassy to Syracuse,[98] and he was the author of an elegy or epitaph on the Athenians who fell in the attack on that city[99] and possibly also of the epinician ode which celebrated Alcibiades' Olympian victory in 416 or 420, so he cannot have been quite lost to a sense of public duty. Shortly after 408 he left Athens for Magnesia in Thessaly, later moving to Macedonia, where he spent the last two years of his life as a guest of King Archelaus. In those unfamiliar surroundings he continued to compose tragedies, among them the *Bacchae*, the greatest of his surviving plays. It is said that his death occurred when he was torn to pieces by Molossian hounds, but this is hardly credible. He was buried in Pella (or Arethusa) in Macedonia, but he also had a cenotaph in Athens. According to tradition, when the news of Euripides' death reached Athens early in 406 Sophocles dressed his chorus in mourning at the *proagon* to the tragic performances in honour of his great rival.

Euripides has been called 'the poet of the Sophistic movement', a title which is only partly accurate. No doubt the teachings of the Sophists and of other enlightened men of his age influenced him, for he knew Anaxagoras, Prodicus and Protagoras and many of the other leading personalities of his time. It is even said to have been at Euripides' house that Protagoras first read his sceptical work on the gods. But the poet was never a pupil, in the strict sense, of any one of these thinkers, nor did he ever become a mere propagandist of their ideas. Their interests and their problems were largely his own, but he always retained his independence of thought and even occasionally criticized them.[100] Another tradition makes him one of the first Athenians to possess a private library, a rare thing in the fifth century.

The affinity of his views with those of the Sophists seems to have set public opinion against him, and certainly Attic comedy and the conservatives dealt severely with him. Aristophanes alone devoted the greater part of three of his extant comedies to attacking Euripides, and it is also reported that an indictment for impiety was brought against him by Cleon. We need not consider seriously the malicious accusations which claimed that others—slaves, indeed—wrote part of his tragedies for him; but it is true that Ctesiphon helped him in composing music for his plays. Like Sophocles, he seems to have moved away from the Aeschylean connected trilogy, although there appears sometimes to have been a connection of subject between his three tragedies (as, for example, in 415 between the *Alexander, Palamedes* and *Troades*, and in 410 between the *Oenomaus, Chrysippus* and *Phoenissae*).

Euripides first appeared in a a tragic contest in 455, when he won third prize. It was not until fourteen years later that he won first prize, and, although allowed by the city of Athens to submit twenty-two tetralogies in competition, he won only three more first prizes in his whole lifetime. It is our good fortune that beside the enlarged 'school edition' of his plays, we have also a part of a 'complete edition', so that we possess in all eighteen out of the eighty-eight plays he is thought to have composed. Of these surviving works one is a satyr play, the *Cyclops*.

In the personality of Euripides is expressed the dawning of a new age in which intellectuals and artists withdrew into isolation, no longer being or wishing to be the 'mouthpieces' of the city, but choosing to be individuals in the fullest sense of the word. As we shall see, this withdrawal of the genius from the multitude was to have momentous consequences for the history of Greek poetry in the Alexandrian era.

THE STUDY OF FEMALE CHARACTER

We know little about Euripides' early development, as his oldest surviving play, the *Alcestis* was performed in 438, a full seventeen years after his first dramatic competition. However, a few fragments survive from his *Daughters of Pelias*, one of the earliest plays he presented at Athens. Even in that can be traced many elements of the poet's style as we know it from his later tragedies. He makes use of the prologue; the diction is flowing; the verse faultless; and, above all, his interest in the psychology of passionate women must have appeared in the scenes in which he introduces Medea on to the stage. The fragments also bear witness to a thirst for sensation in the poet which seems to have found little sympathy among the judges, for the play was awarded a third prize. The Athenian audience was not yet ready for the new approach to religion and the novel handling of the myths to which, even thus early in his career, Euripides seems to have been committed.[101]

His deep interest in female psychology reappears in the *Alcestis*. This was the fourth play of a tetralogy, being preceded by a *Cressae*, an *Alcmaeon in Psophis* and a *Telephus*. It thus forms a substitute (an expedient which the unconventional Euripides adopted on other occasions too) for the traditional satyr play, which probably accounts for its happy ending. For all that, however, the *Alcestis* was clearly not conceived as light-hearted entertainment. The lamentations of Admetus and the fine speeches of the last scene undoubtedly belong to the serious tragic tradition and have no connection with the easy ribaldry of the satyr play.

The play deals with the legend of Admetus, king of Pherae, whose young wife Alcestis offers to die in his place and who is delivered by Heracles from *Thanatos* (Death) and restored to her husband and children.

In this play, the earliest to have survived complete, we can see two basic elements of Euripidean tragedy as a whole. The first is the view that man, and not the gods, is at the centre of the picture. This is the fundamental difference between Euripides and his two great predecessors, whose work was rooted in the traditional religious spirit of Attic tragedy and was deeply concerned with the religious education of its audience. The second element is the new type of heroic woman whom Euripides depicts in Alcestis. Her heroism does not derive from moral principles or traditional religious practices, but appears as a spontaneous outgrowth from her natural kindness and pride. It is the kind of heroism which we shall meet again in figures like Polyxena in the *Hecuba*, Macaria in the *Children of Heracles* and Iphigeneia in *Iphigeneia in Aulis*. They may be less elevated than Sophocles' Antigone, but for that very reason they are the more human and the more moving.

Euripides has been called the discoverer of psychology in drama. He is, however, less concerned with individual character drawing in the modern sense than with the generalized human reactions of love, hatred, joy and sorrow. In revealing certain sides of human passion and emotion he is certainly a master, but he often fails to consider the whole personality of his characters. He seems to concentrate rather on those facets of human nature which meet the demands of an individual scene in a play, even if they may be at odds with the total psychology of his heroes' characters. Thus the scenes in which Alcestis is seen as coldly reasoning or even calculating are completely out of keeping with her otherwise warm, emotional personality, and Admetus' calm acceptance of her noble offer to die is quite at variance with the strength of his later feelings and the pathos of his lamentation for her.

Two further elements characteristic of Euripidean drama emerge from the *Alcestis*. On the one hand, in the dispute between Admetus and his father, where argument is carefully matched with counter-argument, we see once more, just as in the case of Sophocles, the διϭϭοὶ λόγοι of the Sophists given dramatic form in a rhetorical contest reminiscent of the Athenian law courts. On the other hand, the appearance on stage of *Thanatos* provides us with our earliest surviving example of the use of the supernatural and the fantastic for theatrical effect. Such devices were to be used again in the magic cloak and the chariot of Helios in the *Medea*, in the figure of Lyssa in the *Heracles*, in Helen's phantom in the *Helen* and in the fire which emerges from the tomb of Semele in the *Bacchae*.

One of the plays of the *Alcestis* tetralogy was the *Telephus*. It has not survived, but we know something about it because of the outcry it provoked when first produced. For it presented King Telephus in beggar's clothes as he stealthily entered the Greek camp at Argos in order to find a cure for the wound that Achilles had dealt him. Such a costume for a king was felt to be contrary to the dignity of tragedy, and Euripides was held to be debasing the tragic stage. This is only one example among many others of the realism through which this great innovator tried to move away from the strict conventions of ancient theatre and to come closer to a theatre of illusion.

Euripides, as we have seen, was fascinated by the passions of women. This was particularly the case when those passions were morbid. In a whole series of violent plays such women occupy the centre of the stage: figures like Pasiphae, Canace, Sthenoboea, Melanippe, Antiope, Medea, Phaedra, Hecuba and Electra. But his interest in morbid or licentious female psychology is not rooted in a belief in the depravity of women, for bad men and good women are not rare in his work; it springs rather from his obsession with the springs of passion or, as in the incestuous plot of the *Aeolus*, with problems of ethics. The many quotable generalizations about female wickedness which are to be found in his tragedies should be seen as part of the rhetorical technique of putting statements about particular cases in general form.

A violent and passionate woman is the heroine of what is undoubtedly one of Euripides' masterpieces, the *Medea*. It was presented in 431, together with the lost *Philoctetes*, *Dictys* and *Theristae*, and it won a third prize. The theme of the play is the struggle between a mother's love for her children and an insulted wife's desire for revenge on her husband. Medea, abandoned by Jason, conceives a plan by which, with her own hands, she first kills Jason's new Corinthian bride and then her own children. The plot is well constructed, for the heroine reasons her way step by step towards her revenge, which makes the final catastrophe seem inevitable. The alternation of passion and reason in her breast is presented with real mastery. Furthermore, in the case of Medea (whose nature has less of the human in it) such an alternation is more acceptable than it seems in the case of Alcestis.

In Euripides' eyes Medea's inner world is a battleground of instinct against instinct. This is revealed in three magnificent speeches (ll.364ff., 1021ff. and 1236ff.), which are in reality monologues, even if the ever-present chorus is their supposed audience. Finally, in the third monologue, passion ($\theta\upsilon\mu\acute{o}\varsigma$) joins the interior battle and carries the day: 'I grasp the evil I will do, but my passion is stronger than my reason' (ll. 1078–9).

The *Medea* is a good illustration of how boldly Euripides could treat the myths he used in his plays. Medea, the murderer of her own children, is entirely his own creation, not to be traced in the original story. At the same time he made the myth a vehicle for problems quite alien to it: Medea becomes in his hands the heroine of what could be called a domestic drama, in which the violent passions of the wife and the boundless egotism of the husband are the mainsprings of an inevitable catastrophe.

As presented by Euripides, both husband and wife, though still representing two sets of values and two codes of heroic conduct that clash, are essentially bourgeois characters. Jason is no longer the great mythical figure but a cold, calculating opportunist; and Medea, though still a violent 'barbarian' woman, is the insulted wife—indeed, the avenger of womanhood against abuse by self-centred man, as is made explicit in the chorus's line (419f.): 'Honour comes to woman . . .'

Thus the relation of the sexes, which had for centuries been a taboo topic, was brought into the open by Euripides and made the subject of a great tragedy. In doing this he was both the inventor of domestic drama and the introducer to the stage of what we should call bourgeois realism.

Even at his best, Euripides is never as strict in devising the structure of his plays as is Sophocles. Motifs and scenes are frequently introduced which neither promote the action nor help in the delineation of character. One such scene in the *Medea* is that in which, after the heroine is banished from Corinth, King Aegeus is brought in to assure her of Athenian hospitality (Euripides as proudly and as irrelevantly alludes to the humanity of his native city in his 'political' plays, the *Children of Heracles* and the *Suppliant Women*). This scene is followed by the magnificent chorus song about Athens (ll. 824ff.), in which the poet sings of the air and light of Attica, her springs and flowers and the 'most sweet union' of art (the Muses) and love (the *Erotes*) which takes place in that blessed land. He tells us, in exquisitely lyrical terms, many of the same things about Athens as Pericles described in his famous funeral oration.[102]

The end of the *Medea* is very strange. In leaving the world borne on the magic chariot of her grandfather, Helios, the heroine at once abandons the sphere of human suffering and thus forfeits at a stroke all our sympathy for her suffering and guilt. There is also an aetiological element in the ending of this as of so many other Euripidean tragedies: here it is seen in Medea's explanation of the *aetion* (cause) of the cult of her children which was observed at Corinth. Nevertheless, imperfections notwithstanding, *Medea* had a great influence on the literature of the Western world, as the names of Ennius, Seneca, Corneille and Grillparzer show.

Euripides has been accused, not without reason, of delighting in the depiction of delirious and demented characters. The love he shows on stage is nearly always culpable and often incestuous. But the agents (or victims) of these passions are not really perverse so much as weak and ardent, dominated by irresistible forces. Within them a dark and desperate struggle is being waged, a battle not so much of instinct against reason as of instinct against instinct, as in the *Medea*.

This battle is admirably depicted in the *Hippolytus* (*Stephanephorus*), which won a first prize at its first production in 428. It was the second play which Euripides had written on the subject: the first, the lost *Hippolytus Calyptomenos*, had been a failure. Together with the *Medea* and the *Bacchae*, the surviving *Hippolytus* is considered, rightly, one of Euripides' masterpieces. Its theme is the overbearing passion which Phaedra, wife of Theseus, has conceived for her stepson Hippolytus. At first she struggles to repress her feelings. But her old nurse, without her knowledge, makes the fact known to Hippolytus, who is deeply shocked and angered. On hearing of this the queen hangs herself, but leaves a letter for Theseus in which she accuses Hippolytus of a guilty passion for her. In dismay and anger Theseus banishes Hippolytus from Troezen, the scene of the drama, and causes his death with the aid of Poseidon, only to realize too late that his son is not guilty.

Poetry that explored such pathological emotions could have been written only after the first half of the fifth century B.C., when the Greeks were ready to accept that such 'demonic' passions and obsessions were part of human nature. But even at that period the Athenians demanded a certain restraint on the part of the afflicted person. The first Euripidean *Hippolytus* failed, we are told, because of the way in which Phaedra offered her love directly to her stepson—a deed which caused him, in his revulsion, to cover his head; as a consequence, the epithet καλυπτόμενος was added to the play's title. It is worth noting that both Seneca and Racine, inspired by the Euripidean model, preferred to use this version of the story in their plays on the same subject.

As in the *Medea*, so here the tragic conflict has its origins in the passions—vast and elemental but still human—of its chief agents. Even the two goddesses Aphrodite and Artemis, who control the play, are seen more as symbols of emotions at war in the human breast than as the Olympian deities of tradition. The two protagonists, Hippolytus and Phaedra, are opposed in a polarity which is characteristic of Euripides' art. The virginal Hippolytus is a devotee of Artemis, the goddess of hunting and riding, those 'pure' pleasures in which he takes delight and pride. This pride, which leads him to spurn to the point of *hubris* the goddess of love, he even displays in his confrontation with his father, when he chooses to be exiled rather than to betray Phaedra's secret, which has been disclosed to him under oath. Phaedra, on the other hand, is all emotion and passion; hers is a nature which (adapting the myth to his own purposes) the poet sees as inherited (ll. 337f.). Hippolytus' proud purity and his involvement with the goddess Artemis no doubt exceed the proper human measure (l. 19) and prepare the way for his downfall. But this downfall does not come about until he meets Phaedra's completely opposed nature. This is a tragic situation new to Attic tragedy—that of two emotionally opposed characters who meet disaster through their confrontation.

Like other Euripidean plays, the *Hippolytus* contains many general philosophical speculations as well as many rhetorical elements, but it stands far above all the poet's other tragedies in point of freshness and sustained lyricism. The tender charm of the beginning, when Hippolytus is crowning the statue of Artemis, and the sad beauty of the final scene, in which he bids farewell to the goddess he has loved and worshipped but has never seen, are among the best in Greek tragedy.

The *Hippolytus* has been seen as a polemic against Socrates' doctrine that virtue depends on knowledge. Phaedra's words make it abundantly clear that understanding and passion, the two guiding forces in life, are often in complete opposition to each other, a point which the poet had already stressed in the *Medea*,[103] a play which had as great an influence on world literature as the *Hippolytus*.

This group of plays, centred on the fate of noble women, is completed by two further extant tragedies of Euripides, the *Hecuba* and the *Andromache*, both of which deal with the fate of women of the Trojan royal house taken prisoner by the Greeks.

The *Hecuba*, probably produced in 425, was much admired and was read for centuries afterwards. It falls into two parts: in the first Hecuba's daughter, Polyxena, is sacrificed on the tomb of Achilles; in the second Polymestor, a Thracian prince who, through cupidity, has killed Polydorus, Hecuba's youngest son, is drawn into an ambush and blinded. The play is marked by a lack of unity, a failing which it shares with many other Euripidean plays. It is only the figure of the old queen and the various manifestations of her wild hatred and great suffering which draw together the otherwise independent parts of the play.

In this play Euripides shows how extreme suffering distorts the character, how a great and noble woman can degenerate into a repulsive and bestial hag. He puts to the test, and finds wanting, the old, aristocratic views about the immutable firmness of a noble 'soul'—views which Sophocles, as we have seen, upholds in his *Philoctetes*. Once again, as in the *Alcestis*, the combination in one person of passionate emotion and dispassionate reasoning is very unconvincing. More striking is Euripides' technique of causing the horror to deepen from scene to scene by using a wonderfully calculated gradation of effects.

The part played by the chorus of captive Trojan women is quite minor, being reduced to little more than the singing of short passages between the main dramatic episodes. This points the way in which Euripidean tragedy was to develop. The actors with their 'songs from the stage' took over much more of the choral lyrical parts than was the case in older tragedy. This tendency later led to the development of a variety of drama which has been called 'grand opera' tragedy,[104] examples of which were Euripides' *Heracles* and *Trojan Women*.

The *Andromache* was probably presented in 429, a little earlier than the *Hecuba*. Not one of the poet's better plays, it tells of the fate of Andromache, Hector's wife, after the fall of Troy. Its main interest consists in the new notion of the hero which it presents, here seen as a person whose only role is to suffer passively an anguish which has little to do with his character or his actions. Euripides was later to develop further this type of tragic hero, as we shall presently see—the greatest example is Heracles in the play of the same name. We are thus, in the *Andromache*, at the beginning of a process whereby the tragic hero becomes the tragic martyr.

As a study of female psychology Euripides' *Electra*, which is among the last of his Athenian plays, produced in 417, might have earned a place here. However, it belongs more properly to another group (the last to be developed by the poet in his Athenian years), the realistic tragedies. It will thus be discussed later.

Euripides' interest in the fate of noble women was also evident in the lost play *Melanippe the Wise*, a tragedy produced before 411. The heroine was the granddaughter of the wise centaur Chiron, here presented, apparently, as a woman Sophist who, in a speech famous in antiquity, declared that no wonders exist in nature—a view that had already been propounded by Anaxagoras. We know that in this play she was successful in saving the lives of her two illegitimate children, whose father was Poseidon, but the details of the action are otherwise obscure. Ennius is known to have drawn on Euripides for his own play *Melanippa*.

THE 'POLITICAL PLAYS'

The political events of the last third of the fifth century B.C. left a clear mark on certain of Euripides' plays, often called his 'political plays'. From the patriotic exaltation of the *Medea* (ll. 824–65), we gradually come to a growing bitterness against the Spartans (*Andromache*, ll. 445ff.) and to bold attacks on the immorality of power politics in the *Bellerophon*,[105] and in the *Troades* which, as we shall see, was composed with reference to either the Athenian capture of Melos or the Sicilian expedition. The effects of the Peloponnesian War may be observed in other plays, from the war-weariness of *Helen* (ll. 1151–64) to the continuous undertone of hostility towards all demagogues and all the shames and deceptions of politics in the *Hecuba* (ll. 254f.), the *Suppliant Women* (ll. 726f.), the *Orestes* (ll. 885–952) and the *Iphigeneia in Aulis* (ll. 337f.). The other, more positive side of the coin, the poet's ideal of patriotism, is best seen in his two surviving 'political plays', the *Children of Heracles* and the *Suppliant Women*, both of which deal with the problem of the suppliant. Nevertheless, even in these plays the poet's chief interest remains the general human situation rather than the narrow presentation of Athenian patriotism.

The *Children of Heracles* (*Heraclidae*) which, with its 1055 lines, is the shortest of all the Euripidean plays, might be called a gem of concentrated presentation—although in its present form it is perhaps mutilated. It can be dated to roughly the beginning of the Peloponnesian War in 430. It deals, from a particular angle, with the theme of supplication and examines the conflict of might and right and the political aspects of gratitude; these are all set in the context of the myth of Demophon, king of Athens, who receives and protects in Attica the children of Heracles, who, under the care of Iolaus, their father's old friend, have fled from the tyrant Eurystheus of Corinth.

In his unbounded devotion old Iolaus is prepared to offer his life for his wards, when his hopes are dashed by an oracle demanding the sacrifice of a young life in return for the salvation of the Heraclidae. Overhearing the oracle's demands, Macaria, one of Heracles' daughters, offers her own life as a sacrifice for those of her brothers and sisters. With exemplary heroism she goes to her death by her own choice.

Praying to be given back his youth, old Iolaus arms himself to meet the tyrant Eurystheus. The scene in which the tottering old man puts on his weapons contains elements of the grotesque and comic, but in the context of the play as a whole serves as yet another demonstration of his remarkable devotion to his charges. For Iolaus has spent a lifetime trying to follow the rule of *nomos* (the law of the gods), and in the course of the play he is led through tribulation and unsparing effort to a final vindication of his code. Whatever the odds, he will not fail the last test. Such is his moral stature, and such his battle through trial, failure, privation and ridicule, that the gods must finally intervene: a miracle must happen. In the very heat of the battle he utters a vow (l. 851), which is answered by heaven. Miraculously rejuvenated, he captures Eurystheus with his own hands— a turn of events which, as reported in the messenger speech, the faithful may accept literally but which will be interpreted symbolically by the enlightened.[106] That interpretation, the message of the play, suggests that the man who asks the gods for help must be ready to do himself all that he asks of his helpers, if not more. To sit by the altar and pray is not enough. Hyllus, the eldest of Heracles' children, is faced with this same supreme challenge, and he too shuns the safety of the altar, preferring, as worthy partner of Iolaus and Macaria, to go defiantly to battle.

Such are the suppliants for whose sake Demophon faces war with Argos. Their opponents, Copreus and Eurystheus, whose sole object is κέρδος (self-interest), are also portrayed with vigour. The one is an advocate of violence, who will crack when faced by superior power. The other seeks security above all—it is fear that has turned him into a tyrant. He takes the prudent course and is lost.

The end of the play is marred by a spectacle of brutal cruelty, when Alcmene, Heracles' mother, in a paroxysm of hatred, demands the death of Eurystheus in spite of Athenian pleas for indulgence towards the captive. Burial is, however, promised to the body of the tyrant, who, before dying, announces that his tomb will safeguard the land of Attica.

The chorus songs of the *Children of Heracles*, like the whole play, are concise and vigorous. The Athenians no doubt felt flattered when they heard the sentiments which this play voices about Athens, for in a sense it presents an idealization of the city. But the final spectacle of inhuman slaughter and moral failure—a failure on the part not only of the foreigner Alcmene but also of the chorus which represents Athens—must have given food for thought to the more enlightened spectators. For the question of the fate of prisoners of war was of vital relevance in the second half of the fifth century in Greece.

The *Suppliant Women*, probably produced in 424, deals more fully with the same theme of supplication. It tells how Adrastus, king of Argos, accompanied by a chorus of suppliant women, seeks the aid of Theseus and the city of Athens in recovering the bodies of the Argive leaders, killed in the war of the Seven Against Thebes and denied burial by the Thebans.

The play is not an allegory on current affairs, for its theme is general rather than particular. But at the same time it is a political play, informed by contemporary ideas and practices. It works through the exposition of an argument which centres on the fearful question of 'life in a godless world'[107] and ends by revealing the foundations of appropriate and successful political action.

The progress of this argument, from the first posing of the problem to its final solution, is the very stuff of drama. The speakers, Theseus, Aethra, Adrastus and the Theban herald, each offer their individual contributions—bravery, compassion, humbled pride and bold loquacity—and so enliven the didactic monotony. But it is arguments, and not characters, that matter. At the same time the human reality is represented by the chorus of bereaved mothers, whose sorrow and lamentations underlie and colour the cut and thrust of argument.

In the second part, when the action has reached its goal and the bodies have been given for burial, the sorrow continues unrestrained, lifting the drama into the sphere of tragedy. In the two *commoe* the poet takes us back into an Aeschylean world, a world which is made more palpable by touches of Aeschylean diction. Another influence must have been the Athenian practice of public burial for those killed in battle and the 'funeral oration' which was delivered on such occasions, some of whose typical motifs are used here. In fact, many of the political ideas and ideals woven into this drama frequently make their appearance in public speeches of the fifth and fourth centuries, for they were dear to the Athenians.

What emerges as the central message of this play is that the guarantors of man's welfare are freedom and *nomos*. The ancient *nomos* that demanded respect for the suppliant and for the dead enemy can only be reinforced by the new views of Euripides' own day, for this *nomos* is seen as an element of that universal law to which human life must submit if it is to prosper.

One of the most notable things about the *Suppliant Women* is that it has no hero, for the Argive king is hardly a tragic figure, even if his *hubris* and his failure of judgement are the cause of the disaster. For once, then, Euripides has fashioned a rational world, held together by wholesome laws, in compliance with which lies man's security. The play greatly impressed the poet's countrymen and was called by an ancient critic an 'encomium of Athens'.

DRAMA WITH A FAIRY-TALE SETTING

There is one variety of Euripidean tragedy which is unfortunately not represented by a single extant play. That is the genre of the 'fairy-tale tragedies', so called because of their fantastic element and remoteness from ordinary life. Euripides appears to have experimented with this form on the way to evolving the tragicomedy, of which we shall speak later.

We know of three such 'fairy-tale' tragedies, the first of which to be produced was the *Bellerophon*, some time before 425. In this play the hero after whom it is named rides the winged horse Pegasus up into the sky in order to confirm that no gods live there. For, he argues, if they existed, they would never allow the impious to prosper and the pious to suffer, and: 'If gods do what is evil, they are not gods!' For this audacity Bellerophon (who is in part symbolic of the poet himself) is struck by Zeus' thunderbolt.

The play cannot have been a sheer work of fantasy, for a fragment[108] survives which attacks the naked immorality of power politics. It also contained a powerful religious and moral message, some indication of whose effectiveness is given by the fact that Aristophanes parodied it in his *Peace*.

The second such play was the *Phaethon*, produced in about 420,[109] whose hero was also struck by the thunderbolt of Zeus, on this occasion for his audacity in driving the chariot of his father, the Sun. Among the fragments which have survived from the play we are fortunate in having an exquisite chorus song, which opens with a description of nature's awakening at the first touch of dawn.

But the third such play, the *Andromeda*, produced in 412, was the most successful and is the most famous example of the Euripidean 'fairy-tale' genre with which the poet had been experimenting since at least the days of the *Bellerophon*. It was greatly admired, acted and read in the centuries that followed.

In the opening scene the heroine, Andromeda, chained to a cliff and watching the first glimmer of dawn, waited for her lover Perseus to rescue her from the sea monster that menaced her. The few small fragments that have come down to us—the appeal of the chorus to the echo of the cliffs, the words of Andromeda to her lover and deliverer—help us to catch a glimpse of the romantic beauty of the play as a whole, which seems to have been suffused throughout with an aura of superhuman mystery, of monsters and magic.

We have, in an anecdote related by Lucian,[110] an indication of the popularity of the *Andromeda* in antiquity. Apparently, the people of Abdera fell victim to a tragedy fever on first hearing the play, during which they went about declaiming iambics, 'especially singing the solos from the *Andromeda* and going through the speech of Perseus one after the other until the city was full of tragedians struck by fever recurring every seven days, pale and haggard, and crying out: "O Love, high monarch over gods and men" and so on'. This highly successful play seems to have been the only unclouded love story that Euripides wrote.

TRAGICOMEDY

Perhaps the most remarkable experiment that Euripides embarked upon, and certainly the one which had the greatest influence on the further development of Western theatre, was his tragicomedy—or, as others call it, romantic tragedy, romantic melodrama, romantic comedy, *drame romanesque* or *Intrigenstücke*, to list only a few of the names given at various times to the genre.

We have three surviving examples by which we can judge this type of Euripidean drama: the *Iphigeneia in Tauris*, the *Helen* and the *Ion*, all presented around 412. But we know that Euripides composed many other plays of the same nature, none of which has survived. The form is clearly a kind of domestic comedy,[111] which results from the poet's taking a potentially tragic situation and eliminating from it the ἀνήϰεστον, the 'incurable', the 'fatal'. In suppressing the irrevocable action which in tragedy permits no escape from the consequences, he was creating a new dramatic form. His efforts were thus expended in a virtuoso exercise in the creation of suspense, which is finally resolved in a happy escape from catastrophe. The mechanism of such escape is in that ἄγνοια (mistaken or unknown identity) and ἀναγνώρισις (recognition) which had led to such suffering in Sophocles' *King Oedipus* but which are here pressed into the service of a happy ending.

But this new dramatic form is still expressed in, and even to some extent hampered by, the tragic form. There is still a chorus, and there is still the myth as subject-matter. However, the heroic aspects of the myth are played down—very much so in the *Helen*—or replaced by a strange exoticism;[112] while the chorus is no longer able to illuminate in its song the deeper meaning of the action, for there is no such profundity in these plays of adventure. Instead it reverted to singing with lyric elegance of matters unrelated to the plot, a move which was to culminate, as we shall see, in the ἐμβόλιμα of Agathon, which were no more than choral interludes.

The type of drama that Euripides was pioneering here was to become the prevailing fashion in the next century—the domestic comedy of manners and situation, of family misunderstandings, of lost ones reclaimed by their families, the comedy of misapprehension, recognition and restoration which was developed by Menander and Philemon and was to form the main tradition of modern European comedy from Shakespeare to Oscar Wilde. Some of the ingredients of the domestic comedy have, it is true, been attributed to the influence of the fifth-century satyr play, but as so little of that genre has survived, the claim is very hard to substantiate.[113]

Like the *Andromeda*, the *Iphigeneia in Tauris*, probably produced before 412, also has an exotic and fairy-tale setting. Artemis has rescued Iphigeneia from being sacrificed at Aulis and has made her a priestess of her own in the strange land of the Taurians, a barbarous northern people who worship the goddess with human sacrifice. Iphigeneia's brother, Orestes, arrives in this distant land at the bidding of Apollo, having been charged to bring the image of the goddess to Greece, for that will relieve him from the madness which is a curse visited on him for the murder of his mother. He is caught in the attempt and condemned to be sacrificed to the goddess, but just in time Iphigeneia recognizes him. Through her clever help he is saved, and the image is brought back to Greece. Even the barbarian King Thoas is appeased for the outrage, for in the end Athene appears as a *dea ex machina*: the stolen image will be set up in Attica, and Iphigeneia will be its priestess there. The play thus ends with an aetiological explanation for the origins of the Attic cult of Artemis in Halae and Brauron.

Interesting and entertaining though the play may be, it is held together only by the mechanisms of intrigue and recognition, and it lacks the deep humanity of Goethe's play of the same name, which it inspired. The plot contains a theme which was a favourite with Euripides: a hostile fate threatens to make two closely related people into each other's murderers. This device notably increases the suspense before resolving it in the recognition. Though the characters lack the grand, heroic attitudes of Sophocles' figures, they still win our sympathy through moving gestures of generosity, as when Iphigeneia wants to bring about her brother's rescue even at the cost of her own safety, but Orestes for his part will only hear of a joint rescue or a joint death.

The *Helen*, performed with the *Andromeda* in 412, is the strangest of the Euripidean tragicomedies and must have struck the Athenians as a very revolutionary play when first produced. In this version of the myth Helen never actually reaches Troy but spends the years of the Trojan War in Egypt, from which she is eventually rescued by Menelaus. This sequence of events was not invented by Euripides, for Stesichorus had already used it in his famous *Palinode*, and, with a few extra episodes, we also find it in Herodotus.[114] Euripides' major and most surprising innovation lies in his characterization of Helen as a faithful, grieving wife, rivalling Penelope in honesty. This interpretation stands in direct contrast to the traditional view of Helen and, indeed, to the bitter treatment of Helen by Euripides himself in the *Trojan Women* (ll. 766–73). We can readily see why Aristophanes should call her 'the new Helen'.[115]

The atmosphere of the play is one of whimsical fantasy, not unlike that of Shakespeare's *Tempest* or Mozart's *Magic Flute*, with both of which it has been rightly compared. However, the differing effects the poet achieves in the various scenes, arresting though they may be when seen separately, ultimately destroy the unity of the play, mainly because appearance and reality are too frequently interchanged (see, for example, ll. 575, 577, 586), a favourite trick of the Sophists. However, the recognition scene is an excellent example of the tragicomic use of irony. In the end it is Helen who triumphs over the blustering Egyptian king and her own stupid, conceited husband, showing that good sense and sweetness of disposition can succeed where power fails. The delightful songs and graceful comic elements are certainly entertaining but prevent the play from evoking any tragic emotions whatsoever. And such is, of course, Euripides' intention: the play is a light-hearted, not a tragic, entertainment.

In the *Ion*, which is the latest of the extant Euripidean tragicomedies, dating from after 412, we find many of the elements which later became typical of New Comedy. The abandoned child which is later found and recognized by its mother (a motif which we know Euripides used repeatedly in his lost tragedies) and the virtuous but wronged heroine became so popular and were considered so effective that the Hellenistic theatre thrived upon them ever after.

The play tells of Creousa, the daughter of King Erechtheus of Athens, who has by Apollo a son, Ion, whom she abandons and whom the god causes to be brought to Delphi. Many years later his mother and her husband, Xanthus, find him there employed as a temple servant. Xanthus, believing Ion to be an illegitimate son of his own, adopts him, upon which Creousa, who is not yet aware of Ion's identity, becomes wild with jealousy and tries to kill him. But the murder plot fails, and the child is recognized by his mother when the priestess of Apollo shows her the clothes and ornaments with which he was abandoned. At the end Athene appears and tells Creousa and her son all that has happened; she foretells that Ion is destined to be the ancestor of the Ionians (yet another aetiological conclusion to a Euripidean play).

As with the *Iphigeneia in Tauris*, it is intrigue and recognition that hold together a play which contains hardly any tragic feeling. For it is *Tyche* (Chance) that ultimately brings about the solution. To the gods proper the poet is markedly hostile in this play, and Apollo in particular is shown in a bad light. He is presented as a shameful culprit who does not even dare to face the mortals he has duped lest he should hear the accusations which he richly deserves. The god of Delphi is shown to be less powerful even than *Tyche*, who is not the great power of Destiny but rather the personification of hazard, with all its capricious whims. It is possible that Euripides felt at liberty to assail Apollo thus because that god was so markedly a partisan of the enemy Dorians.

THE 'GRAND OPERA' PLAYS

In the course of the fifth century the art of music developed rapidly. The old principle of one note to one syllable was abandoned, as was the whole strophic system to some extent. The consequence was that greater skill was required in performance, and there was new scope for professional virtuosity.[116]

What was seen by the orthodox as a corruption of the musical art set in when a new school of poets,[117] and above all Timotheus, introduced (first of all to dithyramb and *nomos*) music of a much more elaborate and florid type and abandoned strophic responsion, as indeed Melanippides had already done. Such poets preferred long and complex stanzas in which metre—and, presumably, also music—constantly shifted. The style was introduced into tragedy by Euripides and Agathon, who are mocked by Aristophanes for their innovations,[118] their notes running hither and thither and their setting of a single syllable to several notes.[119] Such developments naturally robbed the words of much of their precision in utterance, and it is possible that the obscurity of the words of the tragic chorus which resulted from this may be one of the reasons for its rapid decline in the fourth century. And it is true that in many of Euripides' later odes we find a structureless flow of words with excited repetitions in which the music was clearly more important than the words. This new, emotional music was particularly suited to monodies—solo performances which were sometimes ornamental[120] but which sometimes took the place of an iambic speech at a dramatic climax.[121] The extreme case in an extant Euripidean play is the use of a monody in place of a messenger speech.[122]

But quite apart from such special cases, the new music seems truly to have taken over certain later Euripidean tragedies. Thus whole tragedies came to be directed more and more away from the straightforward play and towards grand opera,[123] in which music carried the weight and the words, even in long scenes, became secondary. In the extant plays such a tendency is first seen in the *Heracles*, produced in 417, and later, in a much more developed form, in the *Trojan Women*.

The *Heracles* includes a great hymn on the labours of Heracles (ll. 348ff.)—a traditional cult form—and a song on youth (ll. 637ff.) in celebration of the hero's vigour. But it also contains an emotionally charged song with a loose, non-strophic structure (ll. 1016ff.) which forms, indeed, a whole scene accompanied by music. This new departure was to change the very nature of Attic tragedy.

The *Heracles* falls into three parts. In the first Heracles arrives just in time to save his family from the villain Lycus; in the second the envious and vengeful Hera sends her agents, Lyssa ('Furious Madness') and Iris, to drive the hero mad, so that he will slaughter his own beloved wife and children; and in the third Theseus saves Heracles from despair at the realization of what he has done and helps him to accept the gods' afflictions as only a truly heroic nature can.

The play thus does not deal with a hero's active struggle with his destiny. The tragic effect is sought rather in passive suffering—almost martyrdom—and in acceptance of the pain which the gods have sent, in this case the fierce onslaught of Lyssa. It is not surprising, therefore, that in this tragedy more than in any other Euripides' outcry against the gods is so outspoken. In the first part of the play the suffering of Heracles' family provokes the famous cry: 'You are a god full of madness, or an unjust god!', and in the second part Hera seems like a monstrous evil-doer as she sends Lyssa to the noblest of men to force him to kill his wife and children whom he has just saved from Lycus. The abrupt swing from happiness to the depths of misery is more terrifying in the *Heracles* than in any other Euripidean play. But even at the lowest pitch of despair, as in the *Alcestis* and the *Hippolytus*, a glimmer of light softens the darkness of suffering and death: it is friendship, the last support in life for man, the heroic sufferer.

This friendship is displayed in Theseus who, in gratitude for Heracles' action in saving him from Hades, comes to the hero's aid and helps him to rise from his despair and to abandon the idea of taking his own life. He must live like a noble man, for 'he suffers what the gods sends his way, and refuses nothing' (l. 1227).

In this play we see the introduction of a motif which was to become important in Greek tragedy: the shedding of a hero's first tear. Just before Heracles is persuaded by Theseus to face his calamity he sheds the first tear of his life and feels a relief never known before.

The *Trojan Women* was produced in 415, during the first year of the Sicilian expedition, together with the lost plays, *Alexander, Palamedes* and *Sisiphus*. It came at the end of this trilogy of Trojan plays, each of which, however, was fully independent of its fellows. In antiquity it was reckoned to be one of the playwright's masterpieces.[124] As has already been mentioned, the employment in it of the 'new music' makes it, *mutatis mutandis*, closer in spirit to a grand opera than to a straightforward play. The subject is the fate of the Trojan prisoners after the fall of Troy, and during its action Hecuba, Cassandra, Andromache, Polyxena, the child Astyanax and the whole chorus of Trojan women parade before our eyes; the fate of each is worked out in individual scenes. Some of them are very powerful, among them that which presents Cassandra with her wandering mind, dancing and holding what she believes to be a torch lit for her wedding but is in reality a torch symbolizing the fall and the burning of Troy. And the scene of the parting between Andromache and her child is among the most heart-rending in any tragic literature. By contrast with these noble and blameless women, Helen, the cause of all the suffering, is represented in all her beauty and with much rhetoric. Soon she will again be enjoying the luxury of her 'golden mirror', while all these innocent women will be dragged to slavery and death.

The play as a whole has been summed up as a bitter outcry against the course of history, which knows no justice and from which we cannot escape. But even more than this, it is, on another level, a picture of the private face of a great conquest, an event which in anticipation seems joyous but whose reality is great misery. For Athene's favourites, the Greeks, have gone too far. They have committed *hubris* by insulting the altars of the gods and by defiling virgins in holy shrines. The goddess herself has turned against them, so that their great fleet, as it sails away, will be shattered by the storms, and the hungry Aegean rocks will be glutted with wrecked ships and dying men. On the other hand, the captive women, who have been cheated of everything—even death— find, as they start for the ships and their new lives of slavery, that there is something in life which neither slavery nor death can touch.

It has rightly been said that behind the action of this play lies a reference to the treatment of the Melians by the Athenians; nor can one fail to remember that it was through the great Sicilian expedition that Athens was brought to her doom.

But, side by side with such experimental plays, Euripides continued to write others traditional in form. To roughly the same period as the *Trojan Women* belong two other famous plays of his, both lost, in which philosophical themes were explored. In the first, *Antiope* (presented in about 412–408), the twin brothers Zethus and Amphion were made to represent respectively the man of action and the man of art and contemplation. In a great rhetorical battle each defends his own ideal in life, the βίος πρακτικός versus the βίος θεωρητικός, the practical against the theoretical life, a subject much discussed at the period. From the second such play, the *Chrysippus* (presented c. 410?), there survives a chorus song which the atomist philosophers quoted in defence of their views.

THE FULLY REALISTIC TRAGEDIES

As if Euripides had not tried his hand at a wide enough variety of tragic forms, he embarked, in his last Athenian years, on a new experiment in realistic tragedy (which was not really the happiest of his new departures).

The first fully fledged example of the new manner which has survived is the *Electra*, probably produced in 417. In a sense it is but one more in the poet's series of studies in warped female psychology, for the heroine is presented as a brooding creature of mingled heroism and demoralization, whose hate and love are both unsatisfied. The play's psychological realism and domestic character have stripped from the old myth all its heroic grandeur. In a new twist to the story Electra is married, though in name only, to a peasant farmer (who is, incidentally, the one decent person in the play). For the characters are otherwise poor beings in the claws of passion, a prey to their own doubts and regrets and moving from ruthlessness to remorse. Orestes, swept away by his sister's stronger will, succumbs to melancholia and delusions. The matricide is shown to be loathsome, and the god who ordained it (if any did), a power of darkness. The two killers are greeted with no approbation by the chorus: indeed, the only word of comfort is spoken by the Dioscuri, who appear in the end and lead events into their traditional course: Electra will marry Pylades, and Orestes will find redemption before the Areopagus. Yet even they pronounce the deed of vengeance to be evil. Critics disregarding its psychological realism and its new moral atmosphere[125] have called the *Electra* 'the meanest of Greek tragedies', 'the very worst of all Euripides' plays'.

The *Phoenician Women*, first performed some time between 412 and 408, also belongs to this group. It is the longest Greek play in existence and contains, in its present form, various spurious additions. The theme of the play is the Theban saga and the final battle of Polyneices and Eteocles, which is developed in a series of great set-piece pictures. Among these is a *teichoscopia*, in which Antigone watches the enemy from the walls of the city (an adaptation in drama of the famous epic device; cf. *Iliad*, III), and an *agon* between Eteocles and Polyneices, in which the former, with his boundless lust for power, is depicted according to the Sophistic notion of the true 'son of nature'.

The end of the play, in which Antigone refuses to accept the order denying burial to her brother, poses many questions of consequence and authenticity, which may be ultimately insoluble. Nevertheless, the play was widely read and even in Byzantine times retained its place in school curricula, together with the *Hecuba* and the *Orestes*. Other Theban plays composed by Euripides were an *Antigone* and an *Oedipus*, both now lost, which we know to have differed in treatment from their Sophoclean equivalents.

The *Orestes*, produced in 408, is the last surviving play of those the poet wrote before leaving Athens for Macedonia. Its lively plot and repeated reversals of fortune ensured it a great success in the theatre, but ancient critics maintained that it nevertheless contained only bad characters, with the single exception of Pylades.

The play opens in Argos with an impressive scene in which Electra nurses her brother, who has been mad and on the verge of death ever since murdering his mother. Tyndareos, Clytaemnestra's father, appears, demanding the punishment of his daughter's murderers and succeeds in rousing the city of Argos against the matricides. Menelaus, returned from Troy with Helen, refuses to intervene on behalf of Orestes and Electra and departs for Sparta. Left to his own devices, Orestes conducts his own defence before the Argive popular assembly but is unsuccessful: both he and his sister are convicted and instructed to take their own lives. Before doing so, however, they decide first to avenge themselves on Menelaus' daughter Hermione, their original intended victim, Helen, having escaped by divine intervention.

The final scene is full of confusion. In order to help his daughter, Menelaus intervenes on behalf of Orestes and Electra, but then, unexpectedly, the crazed Orestes orders the burning of the palace of the Atridae. At that point Apollo appears as a *deus ex machina*, with Helen seated beside him, and establishes order: Orestes will go to Athens, where he will be acquitted of guilt for his mother's murder and will later marry Hermione, while Electra will marry Pylades.

Of special interest is the scene in which a Phrygian slave relates Helen's miraculous escape in a strange, baroque style of description anticipating that of Timotheus in his *Persians*. The scene, which was accompanied by that 'new music' of which we have already spoken, is yet another indication of the delight which Euripides in his later years took in the exotic. However, not this scene alone but the whole play, and especially the final moments, show how in his last Athenian period the poet was increasingly striving after powerful theatrical effects. Unfortunately, such shock tactics—here as often elsewhere—disastrously devalued the quality of his work.

THE MACEDONIAN PLAYS

Euripides' inexhaustible creativity and inspiration continued even after he had settled in Macedonia, for it was there that he wrote his greatest masterpiece, the *Bacchae*, as well as the *Iphigeneia in Aulis*, the *Alcmaeon in Corinth* and probably also a trilogy which included the *Archelaus*, a play in honour of the Macedonian royal house.

The *Bacchae* retells a Theban legend, according to which King Pentheus resisted, to his own ruin, the coming of the cult of Dionysus. A mysterious young stranger, Dionysus in disguise, is brought to Thebes, where he is imprisoned in the palace stables. He easily escapes from his imprisonment, whereat the palace crashes to the ground and fire is seen to leap from the tomb of Semele. King Pentheus, pursuing the escaped stranger, catches up with him and is persuaded by him to spy on the Bacchic revels of the Theban women (among them his mother, Agave) on the mountain. However, he is caught by the women and torn to pieces. In her Bacchic frenzy Agave carries her own son's head on stage, thinking that it is the head of a dead lion.[12b] When, gradually, she comes to her senses and begins to lament her son, Dionysus appears; apparently (for a great part of his speech is lost), he foretells the future destinies of the house of Cadmus and justifies his cult and his own vengeance upon those who do not believe in him.

The play represents neither an attempt to convert the audience to the cult of Dionysus nor a realist's protest against that cult. Rather, it tries to explore and explain the nature of Dionysiac 'possession'. Euripides' interest in ecstatic mysticism is manifest in several of his later plays. It was probably first encouraged by the appearance in Athens, in the second half of the fifth century, of foreign orgiastic religions, like those of the Thracian Bendis or the Phrygian Sabazius; and it is likely that his stay in Macedonia, which had its own local Dionysiac cults, fed this interest.

The *Bacchae* shows how the Dionysiac cult could contain, and provide a relatively harmless outlet for, attacks of spontaneous mass hysteria, such as those which may well have been the origin of the ritual Greek *oribasia*. What the *parodos* of the play depicts is hysteria subjected to the service of religion, while the savage events of Mount Cythaeron represent hysteria in the raw, that dangerous, uncontained Bacchism which descends as a punishment upon the too-respectable and sweeps them away against their will. For the cult of Dionysus, like all other great dancing cults, such as those of the Asiatic Cybele or the Cretan Rhea, could either cause madness, or, in a homoeopathic dose, cure it; and Dionysus is seen as both the cause of madness (*Βάκχος: Bacchus*) and the liberator from madness (*Λύσιος: Lysius*). This double function must be kept in mind if we are to understand the play.[127]

The *Bacchae* contains many religious manifestations which look back to a primitive state of society: the ecstatic carriage of the head, the hysterical invulnerability (l. 761), the snake handling (ll. 1017f.), the raid on the Theban villages and the *sparagmos*, first on the Theban cattle and then on Pentheus. Such things no doubt belonged to a stage in the Dionysiac cult which fifth-century Athens had long outgrown, but their memory was probably preserved in ritual and legend, and it is quite possible that Euripides may have seen some of them practised in Macedonia in his own day.

Another aspect of the play that can give rise to misunderstanding today is the scene between Cadmus and Tiresias in which two honourable old men—the founder of Thebes and an honoured seer—are half-comically shown trying to find logical arguments in defence of the new god before proceeding, barbarically bedecked, to honour him in the wilds. The poet's intention here was probably to show that the Dionysiac frenzy, whether engendered or natural, was not limited to the young (cf. ll. 206f.) or to those of a lower station. There is no bitter irony running through the play or through this scene in particular, as has been suggested. Its strange admixture of exaltation and repulsion grows out of the feeling, shared by all practitioners of such rites, that they are at once holy and horrible; and it is this violent conflict of emotional attitudes, which lies at the root of all such religions, that the play seeks to explore.

It is then quite possible that this many-faceted poet, who was known as a rationalist and unbeliever, returned at the end of his life to the irrational and to a deeper understanding of religious feeling, which were quite the opposite of his earlier views. For this play does not try to resolve the Dionysiac enigma, as Aeschylus is thought to have done in his lost *Lycurgeia*, but gives simultaneous expression to both the rational and the irrational side of man, and we hear their voices with equal wonder and fascination.

The poet's treatment of the Dionysiac cult in this play may also be connected with his move away from Athens. In his later plays he praises more than once the unspoiled countryman who is neither rich nor poor and who works with his own hands;[128] and in the *Bacchae* we have not only several attacks (not all of them relevant to the plot) on those whom the world calls wise, but also a wonderful chorus about a fawn escaped from the hunters, which rejoices in the green and lonely places where no pursuing voice is heard and 'the little things of the woodland' live unseen (ll. 866f.). That is the poetic expression of the same feeling which seems to have driven Euripides away from Athens to live, and eventually to die, in distant, 'unspoiled' Macedonia.[129]

The structure of the *Bacchae* is extraordinary. The choruses are beautiful, connected organically with the action, and their length, as compared with that of the spoken parts, has been increased. On the other hand, the *stichomythiae* are vivid and disciplined. All these features are in marked contrast to the sort of tragedy Euripides had been writing before he left Athens.

Many scholars, critics and poets—among them Goethe and Schiller—have believed that the *Iphigeneia in Aulis* is one of Euripides' finest works. And indeed the play is full of psychological and emotional movement and of dramatic changes stemming from the plot. Scholars have even gone so far as to suggest that Euripides, who died leaving the play unfinished, was experimenting in it with a new kind of drama wherein the agents respond in an extremely 'modern' way.

The play begins[130] with Agamemnon bidding Clytaemnestra to bring their daughter Iphigeneia to Aulis, allegedly to marry her to Achilles but actually to sacrifice her to Artemis so that the Greek fleet can sail for Troy. But when the girl arrives at Aulis Agamemnon's distress is such that even Menelaus, who has been instrumental in having her brought there, suggests abandoning the whole expedition. Agamemnon, however, fearing his own army, is prepared to proceed with the sacrifice when Achilles, who knows nothing of any marriage plans and who is indignant that his name has been misused, intervenes to save her. She, however, though earlier terrified of death, bravely volunteers to be sacrificed as a patriotic duty. Our text, which is not complete, ends with a messenger bringing the news of the sacrifice, during which Artemis saves Iphigeneia and substitutes a goat on the altar.

The shifting psychology of both Agamemnon and Iphigeneia are striking. Agamemnon at first plans to kill his daughter, then bitterly repents and finally agrees to proceed with the planned sacrifice. Iphigeneia, on the other hand, when first she learns what is in store for her, is terrified of death and begs to be spared, but then, for no apparent good reason, she voluntarily and bravely offers herself for sacrifice.

Euripides often used the motif of the voluntary heroic sacrifice. Among examples we have already seen are those of Alcestis in the *Alcestis*, Macaria in the *Children of Heracles* and Polyxena in the *Hecuba*, and a similar sacrifice is made by Menestheus in the *Phoenician Women*. But in the *Iphigeneia in Aulis* the poet develops this motif fully so as to make it derive from the very plot of the play.

Iphigeneia's *volte-face* was condemned by Aristotle,[131] but Euripides had for years been interested in just such reversals of character, as can be seen from his Admetus in the *Alcestis* or his Heracles in the play of the same name. Indeed, as has been pointed out, there is a sense in which such a development, however crude, can be seen as a step towards modern psychological drama.

The *Iphigeneia in Aulis*, together with the *Bacchae* and the *Alcmaeon in Corinth*, were presented in Athens by the poet's son after his father's death in 406 and won a first prize. The *Iphigeneia in Aulis* probably had many revivals in later years, for there are indications of much reworking in our present text, especially in the hopeless transmission of the ending.

One other tragedy, the *Rhesus*, has also passed under the name of Euripides. Since, however, it is clearly not from his pen,[132] it will be discussed below.[133]

THE SATYR PLAYS

Of the Euripidean satyr plays the only one to have survived is the *Cyclops*, of unknown but probably late date. The subject is a parody of the Homeric Odysseus adventure; in Euripides' version of events the satyrs are slaves of the giant, and he is blinded not so that Odysseus and his companions may escape, but in revenge for the death of their comrades. Crude humour is drawn from the satyrs' proverbial cowardice and cunning and from the presentation of their leader Silenus as the drunken giant's cup-bearer and the grotesque object of his amorous designs. The figure of the Cyclops himself is a caricature of the materialistic approach to life adopted by those followers of 'natural justice' who had been the subject of such vigorous discussion among the Sophists.

On the whole, the crude humour of the *Cyclops* does not compare well with the playful lightness which marks the extant fragments of the other two great tragedians' satyr plays.

EURIPIDEAN INNOVATION: THE CONTENT OF TRAGEDY

In view of the essentially religious character of Attic tragedy, the boldest of Euripides' departures may well be considered to be his criticism of the gods. His object was not to preach atheism but rather to stress the need for the purification of divine morality;[134] for in all his plays, the power of the gods remains an important element.

It is not easy to determine what Euripides really thought about the gods, for his plays express the most contradictory views about them. Side by side with vigorous attacks on them, such as we find in the *Heracles* (ll. 1341f.) or in the *Bellerophon*,[135] are passages in which we are told that they must be trusted, that they help the good (*Electra*, ll. 1350ff.; *Iphigeneia in Aulis*, ll. 1189f.), that they punish the evil-doer (*Hippolytus*, ll. 1340f.; *Heracles*, ll. 901f.) and that they approve of the pious (*Hippolytus*, ll. 1339f.; *Electra*, ll. 1350f.). Of his plays the *Children of Heracles* and the *Suppliant Women* are particularly 'pious'. Yet the Euripidean gods are plainly not to be taken by men as moral examples. Only one Olympian escapes all censure: Athene, patron of the city of Athens.

The deities directly active in the Euripidean plays are the Olympian gods, of whom Zeus and Hera work only behind the scenes. But side by side with them exist some lesser personified powers, the *Daemones* or *Daemonia* (which are sometimes equated with the gods and sometimes distinguished from them),[136] as well as the figures of *Moira*, *Tyche* and *Potmos*, which occasionally also take the place of the gods. In fact, all that comes to man from a divine source is seen by Euripides as Ἀνάγκη (Necessity), before which the wise bow and which only the unwise resist.[137] In some few particularly interesting passages even Zeus himself is seen either as an indeterminate being (Ζεύς, ὅστις ὁ Ζεύς, *Heracles*, l. 1263)[138] or as a natural element ruling the world (*Trojan Women*, ll. 885f.), a point of view that betrays the influence of the natural philosophers.

Euripides was certainly no atheist, nor did he set out to found a new religion of his own in which the gods were 'moral'. Nevertheless, as a keen observer of the baffling inconsequence of life, he saw in the gods of traditional myth an unpredictability and self-righteousness for which he criticized them sharply. In doing so he shook the traditional religious foundation of tragedy, through which Aeschylus and Sophocles had seriously undertaken to give the Athenian citizens an education in religion. By his pioneer work in religion Euripides changed the whole character of the ancient theatre and opened the way to its secularization. He made possible the birth of New Comedy, which in its turn founded the long line which stretches through Roman and Renaissance drama to the secular theatre of our own day.

Euripides' attitude to realism was another bold innovation. He was the first dramatic poet to think that poetry should depict reality as he saw it. It is this above all that lies behind his move—as far as the strict conventions of Attic tragedy would permit him—from the prevailing 'theatre of convention' towards that 'theatre of illusion', which is predominant in the modern world. We have already seen how in the *Telephus* he brought on stage a king dressed in rags, which outraged an audience accustomed to grave tragic decorum.

In the same way Euripides refashioned mythology to fit the facts of real life as he saw them. He never went so far as to abandon mythology altogether and to construct imaginary plots of his own, as Agathon later did; but he gave the myths an unusual twist in order to make them suitable vehicles for expressing the realities of life. In this way bourgeois reality entered the myths and, through them, the Attic stage. Thus in his *Medea* he introduced into the old myth two contemporary problems of which there had been no trace in its traditional form: bourgeois marriage, and the repressive treatment of women in Athenian society. In the *Electra* he introduced the bourgeois *mésalliance*, for the heroine, in defiance of the traditional myth, is married to a simple farmer. Finally, in the *Orestes* the original force of the myth, (that is, the archaic duty of a family to exact blood for blood) is transformed into a sort of dispute at law, complete with the bourgeois legal terminology of Euripides' own day. In fact, the hotly disputed social and philosophical questions which he introduced into his plays were endless, all of them equally extraneous to the original myths which he was treating.

Yet Euripides possessed a rare capacity to fuse the heroic with the familiar. The strong maternal love of his Hecuba, Jocasta and Andromache, for example, resembles that of all mothers, but that does not make their feelings in any way commonplace.

In his later years, as we have seen, the poet subjected the myths to treatment even bolder than he had meted out to Medea, Electra and Orestes, for he made them the vehicles for pure entertainment in his plays of intrigue, which are free of any moral problem. It is hardly surprising that such a shrewd, pragmatic, middle-class, rationalist and even openly sentimental treatment of the myths, and the realistic staging which the dramatist introduced, should have offended fifth-century Athenian audiences; the approach was quite alien to the heroic tone to which they were accustomed. Yet it was Euripides' triumph to have made great poetry even out of this apparent devaluation.

The old tone of tragedy was as drastically modified by Euripides' introduction of those persuasive refinements of public speaking to which the Greeks gave the name rhetoric. Euripides' use of rhetoric in his plays is most clearly seen in the *agon*, a favourite device for discussing opposed points of view. There are many such set 'debates' in his tragedies, all of them made up of pairs of long speeches constructed on the pattern of rhetorical plea and counter-plea which so delighted the Athenians in the law courts as they closely followed argument for argument.

In his *agons* many antithetical views are discussed: *physis* against *nomos*, and βίος θεωρητικός against βίος πρακτικός. But perhaps the most significant of all such oppositions is that between objective and subjective guilt; Euripides challenges the old notion according to which a man who strays into guilt, wittingly or unwittingly, must of necessity be punished.[139] Set against this, his heroes' passionate self-vindication is also an outcry against the terrible injustice of man's fate.

A result of the rhetorical, analytical habits of speech of Euripides' characters is that they give an overwhelming impression of intellectualism and seem to indulge in constant analysis. They reflect everything that excited Euripides' age: the taste for and analysis of brilliant new ideas, the delicate distinctions, the constant use of antithesis, the paradoxical arguments. Euripides' references, in the surviving fragments, to philosophical, physical and cosmological speculation indicate a keen interest in such subjects.

It is therefore not surprising that the defenders of modernism — that is, of rhetorical as opposed to traditional thinking — should have rallied to

Euripides, and that conservatives, seeing this as intellectual and moral anarchy,[140] should have attacked with violence both poet and plays. And from one angle at least they were right, for it was this very 'rhetorical' rationalism that not only dealt the death-blow to Attic tragedy, but also greatly damaged the political power of the Athenian state.

The encroachment of rhetoric on tragedy also had an effect on Euripides' character drawing and partly accounts for the fact that he does not depict 'whole' men and women. For each character makes the best of his own case and in so doing fails to reveal the full and often antiphatical inward process of the spirit.

In the hands of Euripides tragedy was further modified, as we have seen, by new musical developments, including the detachment of the chorus songs from the structure of the plot, so that they become mere lyrical entr'actes, and the rise in importance of the actors' songs from the stage, to the accompaniment of the 'new music'. Other such developments included a tendency to compose choruses so that they would sound fascinating and seductive even without their music and to repeat the same words and sounds in the lyrics. The effect of all such changes was to accentuate the ornamental aspect of the lyric and to produce a tone of light sonority, variety and fluidity which was capable of depicting changing moods. A graceful entertainment was now the object of tragedy — in marked contrast to that of older, more serious tragedy, with its religious and moral mission.

The classic example of this is, of course, the *Helen*, in which the old poetic motifs have been given a completely new twist of feeling: indeed, the many surprises and changes of the plot often bring the tragedy perilously close to comedy. The same tendency can be seen in the *Orestes*, in which the death agony of the Phrygian slave is so far removed from the tragic as to be a caricature. And in the *Iphigeneia in Aulis*, when Clytaemnestra greets the unwitting Achilles as her future son-in-law, we are, if not close to comedy, then very far from the grand, tragic tone. The fluid, lyrical spirit which fills such plays and which is so different from the strict formalism of older tragedy also anticipates the coming Alexandrian era and the appearance of New Comedy.

This tone of graceful entertainment owes much to the poet's diction. He writes in a clear, natural language which, on the whole, approaches the speech of the ordinary life of his day. It is less synthetic in character than that of Sophocles and has nothing of the sonorous grandeur of Aeschylus, but it is incisive and agile and remarkably precise. The difference between the language of Euripides and that of his great predecessors becomes more pronounced in his later plays, in which the rhythm of the iambics grows more irregular; resolved feet come to be used more and more, sometimes two or more to one line; and line division between speakers becomes much freer. On occasion, however, Euripides uses a highly ornamented language; in his messenger speeches, in particular, he achieves extraordinary vividness. Another sign of Euripides' impatience with tragic metre is the way that, in the *Heracles* and probably all subsequent plays except the *Electra*, he tends to use trochaic tetrameters in preference to iambics for the more animated passages. All this, which was to have such an effect on the poetry of the Alexandrian period, was symptomatic of the great movement which fifth-century Athens was making towards subjectivism. But to Euripides' contemporaries it was merely another manifestation of a general decay in the standards of tragedy and of a piece with the revolution which rhetoric, realism and rationalism were bringing to the genre.

The lyrical impulse in the nature of Euripides is in some ways as powerful as his dramatic gifts. Unlike his two predecessors, he is not primarily moved by grandeur or perfect beauty; his imagination is captivated, rather, by smiling scenes, varied sensations and the grace of natural objects. He likes to depict in his chorus songs above all the amiable aspects of nature: meadows full of flowers, flowing streams, fountains and forests, flocks of sheep, the calm sea, the wind in the rigging of ships, the bright sky, the hills made gay by playful divinities. His frequent, sombre, restless thoughts he expresses mainly in dialogues and monologues: his imagination in its natural surge, as we see it in his lyrics, is not in the least morose. Most important of all, his lyrical vision is clear. His images are not confused, and if his colours, shapes and sounds do not achieve Sophoclean harmony, neither do they pile up on one another, as in the sonorous grandeur of Aeschylus' choruses.

One thing that is certainly missing from Euripides is the majesty or 'moral lyricism' of his two predecessors. His choruses contain no great ideas; even in the *Anage* chorus of the *Alcestis* there is nothing profound. What they do offer is fine and sensitive observation expressed in graceful images. This simplicity of the poet's thought in choric passages is also reflected in the metres he uses. For they are neither as complex nor as arresting as those of his predecessors, though their tempo is often remarkable.

EURIPIDES' INFLUENCE ON THE FORM OF TRAGIC DRAMA

Euripides' innovations, as we have seen, extend to the very form of tragedy itself. He it was who introduced the prologue, a long narrative speech in which a god or mortal recapitulates the story so far and even indicates what is to follow. In an age which knew neither playbills nor theatre programmes, the usefulness of this device was recognized by other tragedians, who took it over from Euripides.

Euripides also introduced innovations into the end of the play, chief among which was the *deus* (or *dea*) *ex machina*, a supernatural figure who appeared, spectacularly suspended above the stage, in order to impose a resolution on plots which Euripides had allowed to get out of hand, to bring back to the sphere of familiar myth stories which he had altered for his own dramaturgical reasons or sometimes to announce the destinies of the characters. Such a device is, no doubt, external to the plot and seems abrupt to us, but it was very successful with Attic audiences, as we can tell from the fact that even Sophocles, the great constructor of plots, was moved to use it in his *Philoctetes*.

But perhaps the most far-reaching of these formal changes was Euripides' use of his chorus in the *Trojan Women* and subsequent plays. We have already seen the effect of the development of the art of music in fifth-century Athens and of Euripides' introduction into his tragedies of the fashionable 'new music' and new musical instruments.[141] Thus while in the earliest of his extant plays the chorus songs are still composed very much in the Sophoclean manner and form integral parts of the play, with the passage of time his choruses become increasingly independent of the action, eventually dwindling into mere entr'actes. At the same time, the old division into strophes is abandoned — a feature which can be seen as early as the *Heracles* — and a looser, more sprawling structure becomes common.

This new emphasis on the musical element is also to be seen in the songs sung from the stage by the actors, the ἀπὸ σκηνῆς μέλη. In them too, as we have noted, the 'new music' was employed, a music designed to delight rather than to elevate the hearer and which seems to have been played on instruments other than the traditional *cithara* and *aulos*. As mentioned above, the extreme case of this tendency is the use of a monody in place of a messenger speech in the *Orestes* (ll. 1369–502).

Euripides marks a most important turning-point in the history of Greek poetry. He can rightly be regarded as the last of the great classical, and the first of the great Hellenistic poets,[142] for after his death poetry continued to develop along the lines which he had laid down. If his contemporaries reacted against his attitudes and against the examination of the many religious, social and philosophical questions which his plays touch upon, if they considered him an enemy of womankind for presenting so many monstrous and disturbed women on the stage, nevertheless in later ages his fame and popularity grew ever greater, so that in time he came to be rated far above Sophocles (a ranking that was not revised until the Classicizing reaction of the first century B.C.). Although he himself won only three first prizes in Athens during his lifetime, it was for the revival and presentation of Euripidean plays above all that so many of the great theatres of the Hellenistic world were built. It is to him that we owe the introduction of love and intrigue into the New Comedy — an event which was to have such repercussions that to this day a play is hardly conceivable without the love element. From him too the Alexandrian poets inherited their interest in all kinds of love, normal and abnormal, just as it was from him that they took the basis of their poetic language, a diction closer to the spoken idiom than is that of any other Attic poet.

When Aristotle says that Euripides was 'the most tragic of the tragedians',[143] he means that it was he who had the greatest effect upon his audiences. Euripides may have put on the tragic stage wicked, vicious figures such as Jason, Menelaus (in the *Andromache*) and Orestes, and he may have seen and despised the evils of his own society—the ignorant idleness of Athenian women, sheltered from the world, and the bad influence on the life of the city of certain professions, including those of athletes, seers and orators. But above and beyond all that stands his great compassion for suffering humanity which amply compensates for his many shortcomings as a dramatist. With Goethe we may say that he who would criticize Euripides should do so on his knees.[144]

THE LESSER TRAGEDIANS

The works of Aeschylus, Sophocles and Euripides, however important, give only a partial picture of Greek tragedy. As we can see from Aristotle's *Poetics* and from the lists of victors and plays performed at the Great Dionysia and the Lenaea,[145] the great three had not only successors but also important contemporaries, who often won the first prize in competition with them. So the superiority of the three major tragedians, which we assume, was not as uncontested in antiquity as we might think. A history of Greek poetry must seek as far as possible to redress this injustice. But unfortunately for this purpose, those many other ancient tragedians have left practically no remains, and we can glean only scanty and uncertain information about their plays beyond the certain fact that they must have been very numerous. Even Plato, we are told, as a young man experimented with the genre but soon gave it up.[146]

Interestingly enough, there seems to be some evidence that the ability to compose tragedies ran in families. Aristias and Polyphrasmon, the sons of the tragedians Pratinas and Phrynichus, were also tragic poets. The two sons of Aeschylus, Euphorion and Euaion, as well as his nephew Philocles and his two sons Morsimus and Melanthius, all composed tragedies; and the third and fourth generations of the same family still boasted dramatic poets. Sophocles' sons, too, Iophon and Ariston, inherited their father's abilities—in fact, the former is said to have composed no fewer than fifty tragedies and was considered by Aristophanes, after the death of his father and Euripides, to be the leading Athenian tragedian. Iophon's sons were also playwrights, and later still, in the Alexandrian period, a distant descendant of the great Sophocles, a man of the same name, is said to have composed tragedies.

In this respect the family of Euripides was less fertile, for it produced only two members, the poet's son and nephew, who had claims to the dramatic art. And another example of the inherited skill in drama is to be seen in the playwright Carcinus, a butt of Aristophanes' satire, whose three sons were all dramatic poets.

Not all the tragedians who competed in Attica's festivals were Athenians by birth. We have already come across Pratinas, from Phlious in the Peloponnese, but there were others: Acestor was a Mysian; Dionysius, tyrant of Syracuse, was a Sicilian and Theodectes of Phaselis was a Lycian. And such men could be of great importance to the dramatic art. Ion of Chios and Achaeus of Eretria both won a place in the Alexandrian canon of tragedians, while Aristarchus, a citizen of Tegea, is said to have influenced the technical structure of tragedy, and Neophron, a Sicyonian, composed a *Medea* which Euripides was not ashamed to imitate.

That such a great variety of men should have come from all parts of the Greek world to compete at Athens is an indication of how great the attraction of that city was and how important a victory at the Athenian dramatic festivals was considered throughout Greece. Of all these men, both Athenians and others, the majority were no doubt imitators; few would have had any original talent. Aeschylus, Sophocles and Euripides must at all times have been the great figures of the tragic stage; but even so we can find here and there the names of men who seem to have contributed something new, even if the true nature and value of that contribution may now be lost to us.

Pratinas (c. 500 B.C.) is reported to have composed fifty plays, of which thirty-two were satyric. The titles of some of them have survived: *Dysmaenae* (which in Sparta meant 'Bacchantes'), the *Caryatids* and the *Wrestlers*. A fragment of one of them,[147] significantly enough, attacks the growing predominance of the music over the words of the dithyramb. His son, Aristias, is also said to have been a distinguished poet of satyr plays, for which he won two prizes, the second of them in 467 B.C.[148] He is also said to have performed some of his father's plays after the latter's death — the *Perseus*, the *Tantalus* and the satyr play the *Wrestlers*.

We possess a mutilated inscription giving a list of the victors of the Great Dionysia,[149] from which we can see that Aeschylus was preceded in the competitions by no less than ten victorious tragedians. Two of these, Choerilus and Phrynichus, call for special mention.

Choerilus (c. 523 B.C.) is a somewhat shadowy figure, of whom we know little more than that he was an Athenian who competed with Aeschylus and Pratinas and that he is said to have won thirteen victories. He is also credited with making innovations in the tragic mask and costume. Only one of his plays, the *Alope*, is known by name. Nevertheless, his existing fragments bear witness to a considerable boldness of metaphor.[150]

Of Phrynichus (c. 510 B.C.), a more important figure, we know more.

The son of Polyphrasmon, he is credited with a dramatic victory in 511.[151] The titles of his mythological plays, among which were the *Pleuroniae* (from the story of Meleager and Oeneus), the *Aegyptii*, the *Danaides*, the *Antaeus*, the *Alcestis* (a satyr play?) and the *Actaeon*, show that he employed many of the themes used in later tragedy. But much more important is the fact that Phrynichus also used contemporary history as a subject for his plays, a precedent which was to be followed by Aeschylus in his *Persians* and, much later, by the Alexandrians. Examples of this sort from Phrynichus' work are the *Phoenissae*, a play dealing with the Persian Wars, with the scene laid in Persia, and the *Capture of Miletus* (at the hands of the Persians in 494 B.C.). For the latter, we are told, he was fined by the Athenians, on the grounds that he had reminded them of their friends' misfortunes.[152] In 476 no less a man than Themistocles was Phrynichus' *choregos* at the Great Dionysia.

Phrynichus was remembered for the beauty of his lyrics and for the great variety of dance forms which he invented. He is also said to have been the first to employ a female mask, which suggests that he was the first to introduce female characters into tragedy. The few fragments of his works which survive suggest that, like Choerilus, he employed metaphor freely.[153]

Through the plays of Phrynichus and Pratinas tragedy absorbed more lyrical, Ionian elements and assimilated them with the harsher, Dorian traits of the primitive tradition to produce a fusion of strength with grace which is typical of all the best art of classical Greece, in whatever form. The ground was thus prepared for the coming of Aeschylus.

Of Aristarchus of Tegea (c. 455 B.C.) we learn that he was the man who fixed the 'normal' length of tragedy — whatever that word implies;[154] he composed seventy plays, won two victories and his tragedy *Achilles* was later adapted into Latin by Ennius.[155] Of Neophron of Sicyon, whose date is a matter of dispute, we are told that he wrote 120 tragedies and that he was the first to introduce to the stage '*paedagogoi* and the torture of slaves'.[156] But of all the lesser tragedians of the fifth and fourth centuries it was Ion of Chios, Achaeus of Eretria and Agathon the Athenian who were most significant.

Ion of Chios was probably born in about 490, and he seems to have been equally at home on his native island and in Athens. He was on friendly terms with Cimon, and anecdotes tell of his meeting with Aeschylus at the Isthmian Games, with Sophocles at Chios and possibly with Socrates. A true Ionian, he was fond of wine and other pleasures. He died before 421.

Ion first appeared as a tragic poet at about 450, and we know that he was later defeated by Euripides, when the latter produced the *Hippolytus*; but he also won the first prize at the Great Dionysia for both tragedy and dithyramb, and upon that occasion made a present of Chian wine to every Athenian citizen![157] The number of his plays is variously given as twelve, thirty or forty.[158] The known titles include plays from the Trojan cycle (*Agamemnon*, *Laertes*, *Teucer*, and *Phrouroi*, the last of which dealt with Odysseus' entrance as a spy into Troy); and from the Heraclean cycle (*Alcmene*, *Eurytidae* and the satyric *Omphale*). We also hear of other titles, *Argivi*, *Phoenix* and a play called *Mega Drama* (*The Great Tragedy*), a title without parallel in Greek tragedy. Although Alexandrian critics admitted him to their canon of tragedians, his few surviving fragments are insignificant in quality and do nothing to explain his description in Pseudo-Longinus's treatise *On the Sublime*[159] as a faultless and perfectly finished writer in the 'smooth style', but without the force and fire of Pindar and Sophocles.

In addition to tragedies, this versatile poet composed elegiac poems, epigrams, encomia, paeans, hymns, *scolia*, possibly a comedy, at least one cosmological work in prose, a history of the foundation of Chios and memoirs.

Achaeus of Eretria (b. 484–481 B.C.) is reputed to have written forty-four (or thirty, or twenty-four plays), the first produced in about 447, and to have won one victory. Of his nineteen known titles more than half are probably satyr plays (for example, *Athla*, *Aethon*, *Alcmaeon*, *Kyknos*, *Omphale*), a genre in which he was considered second only to Aeschylus.[160] He too was admitted to the Alexandrian canon, although, in the opinion of Athenaeus,[161] he is lucid in style, but with a tendency to become obscure and enigmatic. One imagines that he was probably a good representative of the second rank of poets of the mid-fifth century, who were gifted but not particularly original: as Aristotle tells us,[162] monotony was one of the main reasons for the decline of tragedy.

The days of the Peloponnesian War (431–404) were significant for the history of Greek tragedy. The evidence at our disposal is scanty, but it is clear that the art of tragedy was passing through a crisis and that a need was felt for change and rejuvenation. As we have seen, the works of Euripides give proof of a restless experimentation, and the shock tactics which he used were adopted and developed by some of his younger contemporaries.

The leader of this younger group was the Athenian Agathon (c. 447–c. 402 B.C.), son of Teisamenus, an urbane young man, remarkable for his personal beauty; the celebration of his first dramatic victory is the setting of Plato's *Symposium*. Aristophanes in his *Thesmophoriazusae* mocks Agathon for his effeminacy, but he was without doubt the most distinguished tragic poet of the ancient world after the three great masters. He won his first victory at the Lenaea in 416, when he was probably under thirty years of age. About 407 he went to the court of King Archelaus in Macedonia and shortly afterwards died there. He belonged to the circle of the Sophists: Protagoras, Prodicus, Hippias. Indeed, his speech in the *Symposium* is an excellent parody of the manner of the Sophist Gorgias and some surviving quotations from his tragedies are in a pointed, epigrammatic style, which clearly betrays the Sophistic influence.

His most radical innovation was made in his Ἀνθεύς (not Ἄνθος), a tragedy in which, for the first time, both characters and plot were taken from the poet's own invention rather than from mythology or history. The precise quality of this play cannot now be estimated, since nothing survives. It has, however, been argued[163] that the surviving fragments of Alexander Aetolus' elegy *Apollo* represent an imitation of Agathon's lost play and that traces of the plot may be also found in Parthenius.[164]

This new development of Agathon's was a huge step forward in the history of Western theatre and was to lead directly to the New Comedy. There was henceforth no need for the agents of a play to be heroes and kings of legend or history; in working such a transformation Agathon could almost be said to be the creator of true bourgeois tragedy,[165] following the lead of Euripides. But if that is so, it must be admitted that Agathon's experiment of free invention does not seem to have been taken up by tragedians: rather, it was the comedians who were to make it their own.[166]

His second innovation was to turn the choral odes into mere interludes (*embolima*), without reference to the plot of the play. They could therefore be transferred without inconvenience from one tragedy to another. This not only changed the whole character of the ode itself, but also isolated the episodes of the play from one another, so that the future division of plays into acts must certainly have been facilitated by Agathon's innovation, in which, again, he was following the lead of Euripides. However, Aristotle's criticisms that Agathon failed through trying to crowd too many incidents into a single plot or to squeeze too long a story into a single play—one example being the entire sack of Troy—suggest that the poet also experimented with a form of tragedy closer to epic than to drama.

Finally, there were his musical innovations. He seems to have been the first to use in tragedy the chromatic scale and various florid musical figures. And we are told[167] that he was the first to introduce the 'hypophrygian' and 'hypo-dorian' modes. We are reminded of Euripides' use of the 'new music'.

All this shows Agathon as a modernizer unfettered by tradition. Yet, unfortunately, less than fifty lines have survived from all his works,[168] and they are mostly short, sententious fragments. Only six of his plays are known to us by title: *Aerope*, *Alcmaeon*, *Antheus*, *Mysoi*, *Telephus* and *Thyestes*.

As we have seen, Agathon was but one, albeit the centre, of a group of younger tragedians, all more or less imitators of Euripides—and, no doubt, exaggerators of his faults—and all under the influence of the Sophists: subtle, refined and loquacious but incapable of anything truly great. That, at least, is how Aristophanes depicts them in his *Frogs* (ll. 78–91).

Only a few of these men call for mention here, the first of whom is Critias the 'Handsome' (c. 460–403 B.C.), a figure of doubtful reputation in Athenian politics and one of the Thirty Tyrants. He was born of an aristocratic family, to which Plato's mother also belonged, and was an early associate of Socrates and of the Sophists. After a stormy political career, he was killed fighting against Thrasybulus in 403. His reputation as a violent and unscrupulous man persisted after his death, but nevertheless Plato honoured his memory in his *Dialogues*.

Critias wrote elegiac poems[169] and tragedies. In later antiquity it was doubtful whether certain plays were the work of Critias or of Euripides.[170] From his satyrical play *Sisyphus* there has survived a long fragment attacking the gods: religion is presented as the invention of a sly pedagogue. We know also of a *Pirithous* (it is described by Johannes Diaconus in *On Hermogenes*), and there are some papyrus fragments which are probably by him.

But apparently, side by side with this sententious, philosophical tragedy, there developed a different kind of drama, much more obscure, which seems to have depended for much of its effect on spectacle and clever staging.[171] The best representatives of this latter sort are probably Carcinus (c. 380–376 B.C.) and his three sons Xenocles, Xenotimus and Xenarchus. Carcinus[172] is said to have written 160 plays, and to have won eleven victories.[173] His successes started during the Peloponnesian War and continued well into the fourth century. Aristotle in his *Poetics* and his *Rhetoric* frequently cites Carcinus as a poet of fame and reputation, an estimate of his standing which would seem to be corroborated by the visit he made to Dionysius the Younger in Sicily. But if we are to judge by the proverbial phrase Καρκίνου ποιήματα, which came to be applied to obscure verse, we may assume that his poetry was not easy to follow.

Of Carcinus' three sons, the most famous was Xenocles. We know that he was popular in his day, for he was attacked by Aristophanes,[174] who uses epithets for him (μηχανοδίφης, δωδεκαμήχανος) which indicate a fondness for strange mechanical devices on stage. It can therefore be assumed that spectacle was of special significance to his tragedies.[175] In 415 he defeated at the Great Dionysia no less a contestant than Euripides with his *Lycaon* and *Athamas* (the latter was satyric).

The general picture of tragedy in the fourth century is of an exhausted genre. That above all is the reason for the many revivals in that century of old 'classical' plays, and it accounts for the fact that new works, when they did appear, were immediately abandoned and forgotten. Again and again the same myths were rehandled, and character drawing declined;[176] while, on the other hand, the essentially religious character of tragedy prevented the introduction of really radical changes which alone might have revivified the genre. It is on the whole elegance, and not power or originality, that characterized the new plays, and in the rhetorical speeches, with their conventional descriptions and reasoning, everything is done, as it were, by prescription.[177] Originality and reality, true observation of life passed from tragedy to New Comedy, to the plays of Menander and Philemon.

Of the few names worth mentioning, the most important are associated with the rhetorical school and the teachings of Isocrates (436–338 B.C.): twin influences which have justifiably been called the 'nursery' from which tragedy emerged in the fourth century. The first in importance is that of Aphareus (c. 350 B.C.), a pupil of Isocrates, who is said to have composed thirty-five tragedies and who appears in the *Didascaliae* of 341 as third with his *Peliades, Orestes* and *Auge*. Next are Astydamas the Older and Astydamas the Younger, father and son, who both belong to the fourth century and whom our sources seem often to confuse so that we cannot always be sure which poet is referred to in any one case. One of the two, probably the younger, was a pupil of Isocrates and won his first victory in 372. As the elder poet produced his first play in 398 and is said to have lived to the age of sixty, the inscriptions[178] which record Dionysiac victories by 'Astydamas' in 341 with *Achilles, Athamas* and *Antigone*, and in 340 with the *Parthenopaeus* and *Lycaon*, must refer to the son. The Athenians were so delighted with the *Parthenopaeus* that they honoured its poet by placing in the theatre a statue, a fragment of whose base still survives. But he was not allowed to inscribe on it the conceited verses which made his name a byword for vanity. He was evidently famous in his day.[179] Of the work of father and son together less than twenty lines have survived.

Another name which deserves mention is that of Theodectes of Phaselis (c. 375–334 B.C.), who came from Lycia to study in Athens under Plato, Isocrates and Aristotle and there won fame as an orator and a composer of popular riddles in verse. As a tragic poet he composed fifty plays, and in thirteen competitions won eight victories, of which seven were at the Great Dionysia. His monument at Phaselis was honoured by Alexander the Great, his fellow student under Aristotle.

His plays included a *Lynceus*, whose *peripeteia* Aristotle praised, a *Mausolus* in honour of the late king of Caria and a *Philoctetes*, in which the hand (and not, as in Sophocles, the foot) of the hero was bitten by a snake. Theodectes' fragments consist mainly of rather commonplace, if well-expressed, reflections and suggest that the poet was in the Euripidean tradition.[180]

There remains Chaeremon. Of his life we know nothing save that he lived in the middle of the fourth century. He was the author of a *Centaur*, which Aristotle called 'a rhapsody in which all metres were mixed'. (The term 'rhapsody' may imply some affinity with epic poetry, but Athenaeus calls the work a drama.) According to Aristotle,[181] Chaeremon's plays were better suited to reading than to acting; and indeed we can tell that he had in mind a reading audience, for a surviving fragment from his *Cheiron* (?) bears the acrostic *XAIPHMΩN*, thought to be the earliest surviving example of this device in tragedy.[182] By Aristotle he is also said to have indulged in far-fetched metaphors; and from Athenaeus[183] we learn of his special fondness for flowers, a taste which is given expression in several of his fragments. Finally, in the *Suda*, where he is wrongly called a comic poet, we are told that he also wrote satyr plays, whose titles are given us: Ἀχιλλεὺς Θερσιτοκτόνος and Ὀδυσσεὺς τραυματίας.[184]

The decline of tragedy in the fourth century, together with our limited knowledge of the genre at that period, prevents us from attributing to any of the known tragedians the play *Rhesus*, which has been handed down to us under the name of Euripides.[185] Arguments for its date are not conclusive,[186] but on balance it seems to belong to the early fourth century. All attempts to identify its author have failed.[187] It is a dramatization of the tenth book of the *Iliad*, the *Doloneia*, that episode of the Trojan War in which Odysseus and Diomedes kill first the Trojan counter-spy Dolon and then the Thracian king Rhesus, who has boastfully arrived to support the Trojans. To this basic framework the anapaestic opening of the play and the dawn song of the guards (ll. 527f.) add a charming lyrical note, while the balancing narratives of Rhesus in glory and in death contribute a vividness which is in the best tradition of messenger speeches. The structure of the play is clear, for the Dolon theme and the Rhesus theme are well blended through the persons of Odysseus and Diomedes; and it ends well enough, with a lament for Rhesus. But it fails to establish any living characters: none of the agents, except the Muse, awakes our sympathy. And the style uneasily combines archaic, pseudo-Aeschylean elements with certain Euripidean tricks of style. For example, the play's two divine interventions, one by Athene and the other by Terpsichore, are incongruous. Moreover, through various insinuations and accusations several secondary conflicts are kindled which die out too quickly and somehow blur the central effect. As a result, the play as a whole never achieves a real dramatic or tragic impact, nor are there any great thoughts or great moments to make up the lack. However, the play's use of chorus and spectacle gives evidence of an experimentation which may well reflect the desperate efforts of the fourth century to breathe new life into the dying form of tragedy.[188]

The state of tragedy in the fourth century shows that after the ordeal of the Peloponnesian War and the disastrous effect on society of the Sophistic movement, when Athens had lost the power to create great drama, the art of the producer and the actor began to overshadow that of the dramatist. We can tell how important the element of spectacle was in fourth-century tragedy from the evidence of paintings on contemporary Attic vases. In them actors and chorus are dressed in the richest of clothing, an exaggeration of the clothes worn by the rich men of the day. Fabrics were covered with elaborate patterns; actors wore ornamented boots; and the men's masks had long, flowing hair.[189]

There was a feeling that it was impossible to emulate the great tragedies of the past—a feeling which lies behind the practice, beginning in 386, of reviving an old 'classic' tragedy (a παλαιά) before the production of the new plays at the City Dionysia. Nevertheless, tragedy became immensely popular in the fourth century and spread beyond Athens and the local Attic theatres to Greek cities everywhere. One indication of this spread is provided by the many southern Italian vase paintings of tragic scenes. Tragic poets too, when they had made their name at Athens, grew rich by touring other Greek cities.[190] When Plato attacked the tragedy of the fifth century he was not talking about something past and gone, but about a force still vital and influential. But the great age of poetry in Greece undoubtedly ended with the fifth century. Thereafter, prose was the medium of serious thought.

CHAPTER 4

Comedy

OLD COMEDY

The origins and form of Old Comedy

Comedy is the last of the great species of poetry Greece gave to the world. In fifth-century Athens it was a high-spirited combination of literary parody, obscene buffoonery, unrestrained personal attacks, scintillating wit and magnificent lyrical poetry. The comic poets were exclusively authors of comedy, and none of the great tragedians ever tried his hand at it.[1]

The origins of this literary genre are obscure, and seem, as in the case of tragedy, to be connected with the cult of Dionysus, though with another aspect of that inspiring god. For it was Dionysus as the god of fertility, unbridled laughter and obscene fun that excited the comic poets. The word κωμῳδία (comedy) derives from the word κωμῳδοί,[2] the *comos* singers, men who revelled and sang enthusiastically, a great variety of whom we know from vase paintings and literary sources. These comic, or pre-dramatic, choruses, which existed in many parts of the Greek world, we see pretending to be satyrs, birds, fish, knights, giants on stilts, fat men, ugly women and so on, some of them probably representing fertility spirits.[3]

Aristotle, whose theory of the origin of comedy is the oldest and best-known, believes that it began with the ἐξάρχοντες (leaders) of phallic songs, many of which were still performed in his own day. His view is supported by Semus of Delos (c. 200 B.C.), who speaks about phallus bearers (φαλλοφόροι) who honoured Dionysus (perhaps in the theatre at Sicyon)[4] and mocked members of the audience. This clearly reminds us of the *parabasis* of Attic comedy, which is the true kernel of Old Comedy. Somewhat similar performances are also reported from other parts of the Greek world,[5] and epigraphical evidence[6] of the fourth century B.C. further supports Aristotle, for a humorous adult male chorus is presented as an archaic feature of the City Dionysia at Athens.[7]

The *comos*, however, whether phallic or not, cannot explain a great part of Old Comedy, such as the prologue, the *agon* (the set debate) and the dramatic scenes, on which the disguise has no bearing. For the origins of these many scholars have turned to Dorian sources, citing literary (and, more especially, archaeological) evidence, vase paintings and other monuments on which early Corinthian and Laconian performers are depicted.[8] The literary evidence includes Aristotle's *Poetics*, where mention is made of a tradition according to which comedy originated among Dorian peoples[9] in Megara in Greece proper and in Megara Hyblaea in Sicily.[10] But there is nothing certain to support the view of a Doric ancestry of Attic comedy, though at Megara there may have been some kind of comedy contemporary with the earlier Attic comic poets.[11]

An Attic *comos* entertainment in epirrhematic form (which, as we have seen, epigraphical evidence tells us was also an archaic feature of the City Dionysia) is most probably what stands behind Attic comedy.[12] The existence of early comic performances without masks or prologue and with only a few actors is also attested by Aristotle,[13] but the question of when the *comos* first acquired a dramatic character in Attica is at present not answerable. However that may be, it was only after scenes in iambic trimeters were added to the *comos* that pre-dramatic epirrhematic performances were converted into literary comedy, just as the addition of prologue and speeches to the dithyramb transformed it into tragedy. We have only to look at that crucial step in the history of tragedy half a century earlier to recognize the source of this innovation in comedy.[14] It should also be noted that the Ionic iambic metres, used in the iambic scenes of comedy, also speak for an Attic origin.

Finally, it should be added that the Parian Marble gives the name of Susarion as the originator of comedy in the Attic deme of Icaria, but a later tradition makes him a Megarian. He is probably a fictitious person,[15] a view supported by the fact that we hear nothing more about Attic comedy until seventy-five years later, when Chionides appears on the scene, most probably in 486 B.C.

What ultimately emerges from the long and laborious work of so many scholars on the origins of comedy is that whereas unrestrained vilification and the crudest sexual humour were practised at the festivals of many parts of Greece, it was only in Attica that a permanent literary form was given to those unruly improvisations, and it is to Attica that we must turn if we wish to learn about comedy.

Old Comedy — which is best defined for all practical purposes as the comedies produced in Athens during the fifth century B.C. — begins in 488/7 or 487/6, when the *archon* granted a chorus to the comic poet Chionides.[16] From then onwards the provision of comedies at the City

Dionysia each year was made the responsibility of the relevant magistrate. In the Dionysus festival of the Lenaea, held in the month Elaphebolion (March–April), comedies were included much later, shortly before 440 B.C. It must, of course, be added that Aristotle states[17] that before the state formally sanctioned comedy, comic performances were given by volunteers.

During the Peloponnesian War three comedies were performed annually at the City Dionysia and three at the Lenaea; before and after the war, five were performed. Comedies were also performed in the fourth century at the Rural Dionysia in various demes,[18] but we do not know how old this practice was.

The ground form of Old Comedy seems to have fallen into two parts, divided by the *parabasis*, in which the whole chorus came forward and addressed the audience directly. The first part opened with a prologue explaining the situation and ended with an *agon*, a debate between two parties. The animated entry of the chorus was not formal, as in tragedy, but was stormy and undisciplined, accompanied by an exchange of song and dialogue between actors and chorus. The second part of the play was made up of a series of farcical scenes—the so-called 'iambic scenes'— which were loosely connected and illustrated with examples and, usually in a disorderly manner, the circumstances of the first part. The end, the *exodos*, was a formless *comos*, or revel, after which the performers left the stage, exultant.[19]

The chorus, which consisted of twenty-four members[20] and gave its name to many plays, was of paramount significance in Old Comedy till the end of the fifth century, after which the *parabasis* and the epirrhematic structure[21] generally disappear. In their place the chorus simply sang interludes to break up the dialogue into scenes, a practice which appears in Aristophanes' *Ecclesiazusae* and *Plutus*.

As opposed to the formal and dignified chorus of tragedy, the chorus of Old Comedy was disorderly and rowdy in its entry, and many were the moments of undisciplined animation and improvisation throughout the play. Moreover, it was often hostile to the hero of the play, and it applauded and supported him only after being won over. It has been suggested that this sequence of hostility–contest–reconciliation between chorus and hero was a comic element dating from pre-literary times.

Old Comedy reached its highest flights of fantasy in the chorus, presenting it as birds, frogs, clouds, wasps and so on, a transformation particularly effective at its entry. In the course of the play the chorus often assumed a more meaningful role, which was out of keeping with its appearance but which had a peculiar comic effect of its own. When the chorus took part in the dialogue—normally speaking in iambic trimeters or, rarely, in trochaic tetrameters—the leader spoke for the whole, as he (or the leaders of the two semi-choruses in turn) did in recitative in the *parabasis*.

The agents of the plays in Old Comedy, though resembling the chorus in a way, were less fantastic. Those grotesque figures partook of human reality, but they had no noble feelings and no conscience. All that was serious and profound was on the whole excluded. Normal and perverted sex and excretion were humorously exploited, and the language used on those occasions was unbridled and vulgar, deriving partly, it is thought, from age-old agricultural rites.

The actors wore tights with an artificially exaggerated belly and phallus and the short *chiton*. These were so dominant that we are justified in speaking of them as the normal costume of Old Comedy, which enjoyed complete freedom in the production of masks, often grotesque, to suit its characters.[22] Most of the comedies of Aristophanes required four actors and, on occasion, supernumeraries for their performance.

If we now turn to the plot, we shall see that in Old Comedy it was as fanciful and absurd as the agents and the chorus, with a total indifference to time or changes of scenery. The vilification of prominent living men[23] and the frequent addresses to the audience made those plays very different indeed from comedy as we understand it. Religion and mythology were treated with great irreverence, some plays being burlesque versions of myths; gods, especially Dionysus, were presented as cowards, stupid and dishonest, though the true power of the gods was accepted and often upheld. The end of the plays had a festive, erotic character, often culminating in a marriage in recognition, so to speak, of the hero's triumph.[24] As has so aptly been said, the essential spirit of Old Comedy was a protest through humour and fantasy against all figures of power and influence— the gods, the politicians, the generals, the artists and the intellectuals.

The language of Old Comedy ranges from the most vulgar jargon to the elevated diction of tragedy, but basically it is simple, unpretentious Attic diction, 'the language of the market-place', enlivened, of course, in the hands of great poets. To this a number of new composite creations was added, which could provoke laughter, and words were borrowed from older iambic poets and popular songs.

To differentiate the separate parts of the plays a variety of rhythms was used: the comic iambic trimeter, the trochaic tetrameter *catelectic*, the anapaestic tetrameter *catalectic*, as well as iambic tetrameters and anapaestic dimeters in the spoken parts and great metrical freedom in the lyrics.[25] In these last the metres are on the whole similar to those used by other lyrical poets, but comedy is characterized by its systems (sequences of identical verses), which were generally used to address the audience directly. As in tragedy, speech was both unaccompanied and accompanied by an instrument and song.

The early comedians

In the fifth century we find two kinds of minor playful performance of an artistic nature taking place in Syracuse, the *dramata* of Epicharmus and the mimes of Sophron.[26] These were not comedies in the real sense of the word, as the *parabasis* (the chorus addressing itself directly to the audience), the true heart of Old Comedy, was absent.

Too little has survived to be able to know in any detail about the *dramata* of Epicharmus (early fifth century B.C.), who was probably a native of Syracuse, though other cities lay claim to him. The titles of his plays indicate that he was fond of mythological burlesques, in which Heracles and Odysseus were often the heroes. But *Logos* and *Logina* (Mr and Mrs Word) were also mythological characters, and other contrasting elements like land and sea, hope and wealth made their case in his plays in the form of an *agon*, one of the basic elements of Old Attic Comedy. The plurals of the titles of some of his plays (the *Persians*, the *Isthmians*, the *Sirens*) suggest a chorus, but this cannot be proved from the existing fragments, nor do we know the scale of his plays or the number of actors employed. Epicharmus uses a Sicilian Doric dialect, which is sophisticated and colourful, and a variety of spoken metres—trochaic, iambic and anapaestic—but no lyrics are found among the extant fragments. Philosophical and quasi-philosophical prose works were also attributed to him in antiquity.

Virtually nothing is known of the mimes of Xenarchus, the son of Epicharmus, and equally little about Deinolochus of Syracuse (or Acragas), described by the *Suda* as the son or pupil[27] of Epicharmus. A few scattered notices in Athenaeus and the *Suda* give us a little more information about Phormus a contemporary of Epicharmus, who also wrote mythological burlesques and whom they consider one of the inventors of comedy. Moreover, it is stated that he introduced a robe reaching to the actors' feet and that he decorated the stage with purple hangings. The only interest in this group of lesser writers lies in the evidence they afford of the existence of a small school of comic poets in Sicily in the early fifth century.

On the other hand, Sophron of Syracuse (c. 450 B.C.) gave literary form to the mimes, prose pieces which presented short scenes from daily life.[28] Keen observation and close fidelity to life in the manners and the language portrayed were Sophron's essential features; he used a Doric diction and wrote in a kind of rhythmic prose, disregarding in his improvisations artistic principles of structure.

The extant remains are very scanty—one important papyrus fragment and some 170 short citations—but we know that his work was divided into *Mimes of Men* (ἀνδρεῖοι) and *Mimes of Women* (γυναικεῖοι), and fragments indicate that the world of women was well represented.

Among the 'Mimes of Men' may be mentioned *The Tunny Fisher* and *The Fisherman and the Farmer*, and among the 'Mimes of Women', *The Needle-women*, *Women at Breakfast*, *The Sorceresses* and *The Mother-in-Law*. No less a man than Plato is said to have greatly admired Sophron's mimes,[29] which in the Alexandrian age influenced Theocritus and possibly Herodas.

Chionides, the first recorded victor at the City Dionysia,[30] can be considered the first true representative of Old Comedy. Any earlier names of comic poets such as Euetes, Myllus or Euxenides, are doubtful. In the Hellenistic age two plays, the *Heroes* and the *Beggars*, were ascribed to Chionides, but the authenticity of the latter was challenged. We also know the title of a third comedy, the *Persians* or *Assyrians*. The few surviving fragments ascribed to Chionides are of no importance.[31]

Magnes, according to Aristotle, is the second of the early Athenian comic poets. He won eleven victories at the City Dionysia, one of which was in 473/2 B.C. Eight titles of his plays have survived, which include *Frogs*, *Birds*, *Fig-Flies*, *Dionysus* and *Lydians*. According to Aristophanes (*Knights*, 518ff.) he fell out of favour in his old age. His surviving fragments are also insignificant.

The plays of Chionides and of Magnes apparently did not run to more than 300 verses,[32] most of which belonged to the chorus. If that is true, continuous plots could hardly have existed in their plays, which must have consisted of independent comic scenes.

The last comic poet we hear of before the great period of Attic comedy opened is Ecphantides. The first of the four victories he won at the City Dionysia must have been in 454 B.C. or shortly before. He is a shadowy figure, about whom we know very little, as only two titles of his plays (*Peirai?* and *Satyrs*) and five fragments have survived. It is said that his slave, Choirilus, helped him to compose his comedies, and that he looked down on Megarian comedy.[33]

The golden age of Old Comedy: Aristophanes and his predecessors and rivals

THE PREDECESSORS OF ARISTOPHANES

The great period of Old Comedy opens with Cratinus (c. 435 B.C.) who, with Aristophanes and Eupolis, was considered one of the greatest comic poets of antiquity. He was later included in the Alexandrian canon of the three most distinguished comic poets, which Horace cast in his well-known line:

Eupolis atque Cratinus Aristophanesque poetae.[34]

The poetic activities of Cratinus can be followed from the middle of the fifth century to about 423. He won six first prizes at the City Dionysia and three at the Lenaea. Twenty-eight titles of his plays have survived and over 460 fragments, so we can see that his subjects were as varied as those of Aristophanes, embracing politics, literary criticism, parodies of mythology and fairy-tale motifs. One of his favourite targets was Pericles, whom he attacked in his *Nemesis, Chirones* and the *Dionysalexandros*, the greater part of whose hypothesis has been preserved in a papyrus.[35] In it Dionysus, instead of Paris, is represented as judging the goddesses, and it is he who carries Helen off to Troy. There was a chorus of satyrs, which in the *parabasis* addressed the audience 'about the poets'.

The attacks of Cratinus were far more obscene than those of Aristophanes, and he is considered by some as having initiated the drama of political satire (but this is doubtful). Nor should the significance of political polemics be overrated, no matter how offensive, because as has appropriately been said, they are the jester's licence.

Cratinus also attacked the views of his age on religion and art. In his *Thracian Women* he attacked foreign cults like that of Bendis;[36] in his *Panoptae*, the Sophists; and in his *Archilochi* he presented a contest between great poets of the past, pointing the way to Aristophanes' *Frogs*.

The fairy-tale element on which Cratinus drew in some of his plays can be seen in the fragments of the *Ploutoi*,[37] and in his *Odysses* (᾿Οδυσσῆς), which was a parody of Odysseus' adventure with the Cyclops. The latter is of interest in the history of Greek poetry, for Platonius[38] (date uncertain) calls it an example of 'Middle Comedy ahead of its time', as it contained no ridicule of contemporary men.

Cratinus enjoyed great success with his last play, the *Wine Flask* (*Πυτίνη*), produced in 423, which was an answer to Aristophanes' attack on him in the *Knights*, in which he is represented as an old drunkard who has outlived his art. Cratinus presents himself as a man who has deserted his lawful wife Comedy in favour of his mistress Drink, and whose friends try to persuade him to reform. But he defends Dionysus, the god of wine and comedy, stating that 'He who drinks water begets nothing good' (οὐδὲν ἂν τέκοι χρηστόν).[39] With his *Wine Flask* he defeated Aristophanes, who competed at the same festival with no less a play than the *Clouds*.

The language and style of Cratinus are imaginative, closely knit and suggestive; Aristophanes was much impressed and influenced by him. In *Knights* (ll. 526ff.) he speaks of Cratinus' torrential fluency and vigour. (Platonius, however, for what he is worth, describes his work as comparatively graceless and inconsequential.)[40]

Finally, it should be added that, according to a statement of Tzetzes,[41] Cratinus limited the number of actors in comedy to three; until then the number had been unlimited.

After Cratinus we come to Crates, the comic poet who won three victories at the City Dionysia, the first almost certainly in 450 B.C. He started his career as an actor—he acted in the plays of Cratinus—and later turned to comic poetry, in which he was among the first, so Aristotle tells us, to give up personal invective (ἰαμβικὴ ἰδέα) and to construct plots of a 'general' nature (καθόλου).[42] Six titles of his plays survive; in one of his comedies, called *Animals*, the vegetarianism of Pythagoras is upheld. Aristophanes, who speaks of Crates with affection, also informs us that he often had to face the public's disapproval.

Pherecrates (c. 430 B.C.), who is close in spirit to Crates—he is even called his imitator—won his first victories at the City Dionysia and at the Lenaea between 440 and 430 B.C. He had the reputation in antiquity of a poet prolific in plots. Of his plays, nineteen titles (some probably spurious) and 250 fragments have survived. Among these a long fragment, probably belonging to the play *Chiron*,[43] presents Music as a woman complaining of the way in which contemporary musicians treat her. The titles of his plays—*Corianno*, *Petale* and *Thalatta*, all names of *hetaerae*—indicate that Pherecrates was a precursor of those plays of Middle and New Comedy in which *haeterae* were dominant. That he was inventive and imaginative can also be seen from plays like the *Savages* (Ἄγριοι), in which the fortunes of men who had left civilization to live among savages were depicted, or the *Miners* (Μεταλλῆς), in which the Underworld was presented as a land of unbelievable abundance,[44] or the *Deserters* in which the *parabasis* appears to have been uttered by a chorus of gods. His *Persians* was probably similar in theme to the *Miners*, and his Μυρμηκάνθρωποι spoke of Deucalion's Flood, and how Zeus re-populated the earth by turning ants into men. Pherecrates introduced *parabasis* and *agones* into his plays, and his language included vernacular elements. By the Atticist Phrynichus he is called Ἀττικώτατος ('most Attic').

The comic poets contemporary with Crates and Pherecrates do not seem to have shared their peaceful spirit, and this holds good also for their immediate successors. Thus Teclecledes (c. 440 B.C.), who won three victories at the City Dionysia, the first in about 445 B.C., and five at the Lenaea, attacked the politicians of his day,[45] and in his *Hesiodi* criticized the old poets; and Hermippus (c. 435 B.C.), who was a remarkably prolific author—he wrote forty plays and won at least one victory at the City Dionysia and four at the Lenaea, the first in about 430—is said to have brought an unsuccessful action against Aspasia for impiety and immorality.[46] He also was aggressive in his iambic poetry.[47] Ten titles and a hundred fragments of his plays have survived, in which we can see, among other things, Dionysus giving his opinion on different wines,[48] the imports to Athens from various Mediterranean countries,[49] Cleon's attack on Pericles in 431 or 430.[50] Several of Hermippus' titles indicate mythological burlesque.

Hermippus' brother Myrtilus, who also won a victory at the Lenaea, must have been another contemporary comic poet of some distinction.

This is more or less all of importance that we can gather—and it is regrettably little—about the predecessors of Aristophanes, to whom we must now turn as the only master of Old Comedy of whose work complete examples have survived.

ARISTOPHANES

Aristophanes (c. 450–c. 385 B.C.), the son of Philippus and a native of the deme of Cydathenaeum, is undoubtedly the greatest poet of Old Attic Comedy. He was born in the days of the Periclean peace and died shortly before 385, after the downfall of Athens. Very little is known about his life. From *Acharnians* (ll. 652ff.) it was once wrongly inferred that he was not Athenian but came from the island of Aegina, whereas Theagenes rightly explains[51] that he, or his father had merely bought some property there.[52] He had three sons, Ararus, Nicostratus and Philetaerus,[53] all of them comic poets, and at least once he served as a *prytanis*.[54] If he presented his first play in 427, he must have started composing comic poetry young, and he continued writing and developing his art till the end of his life. The last comedy he himself produced was performed in 388.[55]

Though a violent opposition to Cleon and the democratic party is evident in his plays, there are no grounds for assigning him to any political party, for political satire always strikes at the regime of the day. It is chiefly against the war, the Sophists and the deficiencies of Athenian democracy which undermined society that he so vigorously reacted.

Forty-four plays of Aristophanes were known to the Alexandrians, but four were of doubtful authenticity and were also attributed to Archippus. Aristophanes was, of course, included in the canon of the comedians of Old Comedy, and commentaries were written on his works. Today we possess only eleven of his plays; they have survived not because of their literary merits, but because the Atticists considered them an excellent source for their studies of old Attic Greek and antiquarians regarded them a mine of information about much that interested them.

The first play Aristophanes presented was the *Banqueters* (Δαιταλῆς), which won the second prize in 427. It contained arguments between a profligate son and his father and between the profligate and a virtuous young man.[56] It was the difference between the 'old' and the 'modern' education that interested Aristophanes; from early youth he seems to have been concerned with the Sophists and their views. The poet did not produce the play himself but entrusted the production to Callistratus; and he did the same with the *Acharnians*, the *Birds*, and *Lysistrata*. He entrusted the production of some more of his plays to others, so it seems that he was reluctant (or even unable) to produce them himself.[57]

The next year Aristophanes initiated his political attacks with the

Babylonians, by presenting the allied cities of Athens in the chorus labour-
ing at the handmill and wearing the masks of slaves. The play was
performed at the Dionysia in the presence of the representatives of the
allied cities and gave Cleon the occasion to launch a lawsuit against him.

Leaving aside plays of which we know the titles but hardly anything
more,[58] let us turn to the extant comedies, of which the *Acharnians* is the
oldest. It was produced at the Lenaea of 425 and won a first prize against
two formidable opponents, Cratinus and Eupolis. Its hero, Dicaiopolis,
disgusted at the way the war is being conducted by the Athenians, makes
a private peace treaty with the Spartans for himself and his household. He
is violently attacked for this by the chorus of charcoal burners from
Acharnae, the largest Attic deme. However, after visiting Euripides and
borrowing from him Telephus' beggar's rags and mask, he wins the
chorus over by delivering a speech proving that the Spartans are not
wholly to blame for the war, but that Pericles is also responsible. After this
the chorus approves of Dicaiopolis' further actions. A series of comic
scenes follows the *parabasis*, in which foreigners visit Dicaiopolis to trade
with him, as well as Athenians who wish to share in his good fortune and
finally a messenger who invites him to a feast.

Meanwhile Lamachus — the Athenian general, later killed during the
Sicilian expedition — who disapproves of the hero, has to leave to face an
enemy raiding party just as Dicaiopolis departs for the feast. They return
together. Dicaiopolis is grossly drunk and leaning on two flute girls with
whom he is flirting outrageously; Lamachus is carried on to the stage
groaning because he has been unheroically wounded jumping over a
ditch. The play ends with a rowdy uninhibited erotic *comos*.

The question remains open of whether this comedy is a free play of
fancy or had a political purpose directed against Cleon and Lamachus as
representing the war party. What is clear is that the poet delights in the
comic fantasy of a private peace between the sensible and hard-bitten
farmer and the Spartans — the truce takes the physical form of a wineskin
— and in deflating heroics.

For the first time in comedy we meet in the *Acharnians* a parody of
tragedy, both during Dicaiopolis' visit to Euripides and at the end of the
play when Lamachus with his hurt leg laments in paratragic style. As
tragedy, and in particular Euripides, is one of Aristophanes' favourite
targets, it is interesting to see how early in his career these attacks begin.

The *parabasis* of the chorus is fully developed,[59] containing essentially
two parts, one composed in lively anapaests intended for the marching
entry of the chorus, and another consisting of ritual song followed by lively
spoken passages. It is in the anapaests[60] that the poet expresses his
personal views and speaks of his dealings with Cleon, who persecuted him
unsuccessfully after the production of the *Babylonians* at the City Dionysia
of 426. They end with the *pnigos*,[61] the 'choking', so called because of the

breathless speed with which those verses were recited. The play, as we have seen, concludes with the erotic outburst of its *comos*. The erotic element plays a prominent part in the end of Aristophanes' comedies and often takes the form of a marriage.

Aristophanes, undaunted by Cleon's lawsuit, launched a violent attack against him in the *Knights* (Ἱππῆς), which brought him the first prize at the Lenaea of 424, one of the poet's greatest successes. Demos, the general public, is there represented as a wily and seemingly stupid old man, who in reality is much more shrewd than he appears to be. He has entrusted his household to a barbarian Paphlagonian slave, a true rascal, who makes life difficult for all, especially for his fellow slaves. Aristophanes, of course, presents Cleon under the cover of the Paphlagonian slave, because he was not a true-born Athenian, and the name Paphlagonian is also thought to be a pun on the verb παφλάζειν, to splutter. Two other slaves—who are supposed to be the generals Nicias and Demosthenes—conspire against him and, by stealing his oracle,[62] learn that an even more vile person will succeed him. This is the sausage seller, Agoracritus, who meets the Paphlagonian and surpasses him in shameless baseness, in eliciting votes and in crudely flattering Demos, who is secretly amused.

But Agoracritus turns out to be an able manager of Demos' affairs, for he rejuvenates him by boiling him[63] and presents him on the stage in the prime of life, dressed in the manner of the warriors of Marathon and Salamis and applauded by the chorus as king of the Hellenes.

Demos is upbraided for his former faults by his new adviser, who holds the traitors around him responsible. From now on he will behave better in every way. In spite of the serious note struck at this point, there is plenty of rollicking fun and obscenity on the part of the chorus, and the comedy ends with a dance of thirty girls representing the thirty years of the truce. The scholiast informs us that prostitutes were hired to perform that dance.

The play has been rightly characterized as a satire and not a farce. Its chief aim was to revile Cleon, of whom the poet deeply disapproved. Moreover, it was the first play Aristophanes staged in person, and we are told that no actor could be persuaded to play the role of Cleon. Even when the poet took the part himself, no mask maker would produce a mask that resembled that politician, such was the fear he inspired.

Of importance for the understanding of the play is the song scene between Demos and the chorus (ll. 1111ff.), where the old man makes it clear to the knights that he sees through the rascals who surround him and that at the right moment he will take back all they have stolen. This is similar to the startling change in old Demos at the end of the play, which many scholars consider defies all logic and psychology. But this is not surprising in the world of Old Comedy, where everything is acceptable, and logical and psychological consistency is certainly not demanded. This new image of the Demos was also necessary if the whole play were not to be taken as a direct attack on the audience, which ought to leave the theatre with the prospect of better times to come.

The structure of the play is also unusual, for the series of *agon* scenes, in which the competing parties surpass each other in vulgarity and abuse, continues even after the *parabasis*, although the normal place of the *agon* in Old Comedy is before it.

The appearance of the chorus has also been a matter of dispute among scholars. The most plausible view is that they were men with masks of horses, who carried others on their backs. Such representations are known from black-figure vases,[64] and this would be in keeping with the old tradition of animal choruses in comedy.

At the Dionysia of 423 Aristophanes produced the *Clouds*, of which we have only a revised version dating from the period 418–416. The revision was never completed and never performed.[65] The play ridiculed Socrates and brilliantly, if maliciously, attacked the Sophists; but it was a failure. Cratinus, as we have noted, won the first prize with his *Wine Flask*, and Ameipsias the second with the *Connus*, a play that also dealt with Socrates.

In the *Clouds* Phidippides, the son of an old peasant Strepsiades, who had married a woman socially superior to him, ruins his father with the fashionable extravagance of horse-racing. Strepsiades decides to send his son to Socrates to be taught the Sophistic rhetoric that will help him to rebut his creditors, but Phidippides refuses, and so the old peasant goes himself to learn the art of twisting the truth. However, because of his great stupidity, he only succeeds in becoming a laughing-stock at Socrates' *phrondisterion* ('college'), from which he is expelled. Phidippides is finally persuaded to go to the Socratic 'college', and for his instruction a dispute is staged between Just and Unjust Cause (Δίκαιος καὶ Ἄδικος Λόγος), which is the most brilliant *agon* in the whole of Aristophanes.

In it the immoral, pleasure-seeking representative of the modern age defeats the supporter of ancient piety and morality, and this has a great effect upon young Phidippides, who soon learns the ways of the school and, to the delight of his father, gets rid of two unpleasant creditors. But the young son does not limit himself to this success; he soon applies his new learning in attacking his father's old-fashioned tastes. At dinner, over a dispute about Euripides, he gives the old man a sound thrashing and then proceeds to justify his action. Strepsiades, infuriated, sets out with his slaves to burn down the *phrondisterion* of Socrates.

The comedy is named after its chorus of clouds, which lend themselves to a variety of purposes, for they not only serve as a vehicle of wonderful poetry—their first song is one of the most beautiful in all Greek literature —but also symbolize the new world of thought, the ungraspable relativity of the Sophists and the rejection of the gods based on natural phenomena.

One of the central questions posed by the *Clouds* is this: what did

Aristophanes really think about Socrates? Was he piling all the disagreeable qualities of the Sophists upon him simply for fun? Or is the answer, as has been suggested, that *proxime ad verum accessit.*[66] It appears probable that Aristophanes' representation contained elements of truth mixed with fantasy, which, with obvious comic purpose, were introduced as part of the poet's general attack on the new methods of education and thought that were undermining the sound, traditional views but with which Socrates had no connection. How dangerous and damaging that representation could be can be seen from Plato's *Apology,*[67] where he attributes to Old Comedy no small part in the misunderstanding and condemnation of Socrates.[68] (According to an anecdote, Socrates was in the audience when the *Clouds* was performed, and he got up to be seen, so that a comparison could be made between the image on the stage and the real man.)

In the next year, 422, Aristophanes won a second prize at the Lenaea with the *Wasps (Σφῆκες),*[69] in which he derided the eagerness of little old citizens to engage in jury service.[70] Many years later the play gave Racine the idea for his *Plaideurs.*

The conflict is once again between father and son but, by contrast with the *Clouds* (and the lost *Daitales*) it is the son who is troubled by the father's folly. The father, as his name Philocleon indicates, is a supporter of Cleon, the statesman Aristophanes so violently hated, whereas the son Bdelicleon ('he who abominates Cleon') is wholeheartedly against him. In his endeavour to cure his father of his enthusiasm for the law courts, Bdelicleon imprisons him in their house and prevents his release by his fellow jurors, the Wasps, who form the chorus—gnarled, reactionary old men dressed as wasps with long stings. Philocleon's attempts to break out are amusing; one imitates Odysseus' escape from the cave of the Cyclops.

A formal *agon* between father and son follows, in which Bdelicleon persuades his father that jurymen are the instruments of unreliable politicians who pocket most of the revenues. A private court is then instituted, in which a lawsuit conducted between two dogs is to be decided by Philocleon. The dog Labes ('Grab') of Aexonae is charged by a dog from Cydathenaeum with stealing Sicilian cheese—an allusion to Cleon, who in 425 had brought an action of embezzlement against General Laches of Aexonae. The verdict, as in the historical trial, was 'not guilty', but it is reached through a mistake of Philocleon, who is horrified and faints when he realizes what he has done. To cheer up his vulgar old father, Bdelicleon introduces him to more refined company, but he behaves disgustingly, quarrels and steals a pretty flute girl from the party in a typical coarse, erotic closing scene. Eventually, Philocleon returns, full of wine, dancing madly and challenging all those present to compete with him. This brings in the three dwarfish sons of Carcinus, and they all go dancing off the stage. The final *comos* in this play is particularly disorderly.

In this comedy all the characters are imaginary, the *parabasis* is strikingly delayed (ll. 1009ff.) and what follows is pure slap-stick comedy. On the whole, it is a good-humoured and amusing play but below the usual standard of Aristophanic verve and vigour.

At the Dionysia of 421 Aristophanes won another second prize with his *Peace (Εἰρήνη)*, which was performed a few months before the Peace of Nicias.[71] Though the play was clearly topical, it was Eupolis who won the first prize with his *Colaces*.[72]

In the *Peace* the vine grower Trygaeos (the name means 'vintager') breeds a huge dung-beetle, on which he rides up to heaven to ask Zeus what he has in mind for the Greeks, who are exhausted by the war. This is, of course, a parody of Euripides' famous play *Bellerophon*, in which the hero, riding Pegasus the winged horse, tries to reach heaven to find out if there are any gods there.[73] It is also a reference to a fable of Aesop, in which the dung-beetle once flew up to heaven.

Trygaeos, luckier than Bellerophon, reaches his goal and meets Hermes, who is persuaded to show him where Eirene (Peace) is buried. He notices, however, that all the other gods have moved away to a higher realm, far from the horrors of war and the complaints that are rising from earth. Polemos (War) reigns alone and unchecked in heaven; having buried Peace in a pit, he is preparing to pound up the cities of Greece in a gigantic mortar. Polemos appears in person on the stage, and while he is proceeding with his preparations Trygaeos listens, unnoticed—a scene foreshadowing the numerous eavesdropping scenes of later comedy. When Polemos leaves the stage to obtain a pestle Trygaeos calls on the Greeks (who appear as the chorus—farmers, merchants and workers from all over Greece), enlists the support of Hermes and leads a rescue party to free Eirene, who is pulled up by ropes from her pit.

At that moment two goddesses emerge, Opora, goddess of fruitfulness, and Theoria, a personification of joy at festivals, and they all return to earth, not on the dung-beetle but by a way that is shown to them by Hermes.[74]

After the *parabasis*, in which Aristophanes unashamedly blows his own trumpet, a sequence of loosely connected scenes follows, which take place on earth. Theoria is given over to the members of the Council, and Eirene receives her due offerings. The so-called second *parabasis*—which is in reality the second part of the *parabasis* proper—gives a peaceful picture of idyllic country life and can be seen as a precursor of pastoral poetry,[75] though a political undercurrent exists, as the peasants were the worst sufferers in the war and those who wished peace most.

More episodes follow showing the superiority of peaceful labour over the warmongers, for whom hard times are in store; and the play ends in a wedding procession and the happy union of Trygaeos and Opora.

Peace is one of the best comedies of Aristophanes, a brilliant political fantasia, also notable for the farcical treatment of the gods.

There was a second play by Aristophanes called *Peace*, which is now lost. The Alexandrians had no text of it, but the Pergamene Crates of Mallos (c. 160 B.C.) knew it, and a few fragments survive.[76] We cannot tell whether it was a revised version of our *Peace* or a totally different play.

After 421 there is an interval of seven years before we come to the *Birds*, the next surviving play by Aristophanes. We know, of course, the titles of a number of lost Aristophanic comedies, some taken from mythology, like *Daedalus*, the *Danaids*, or the *Women of Lemnos*, and others, like *Georgoi* and *Horai*, in which country life must have played some part, but we know nothing about their content and their dates. In 414, the year the *Birds* was performed at the Dionysia, Aristophanes also presented at the Lenaea the now lost *Amphiaraus*, a story of rejuvenation at the shrine of Amphiaraus at Thebes.

The *Birds* is Aristophanes' masterpiece. It was produced by Callistratus and, surprisingly, won second prize, the first having been awarded to Ameipsias with his *Revellers*. The general motif of the play is the perennial desire to escape from reality with all its troubles and take refuge in some imaginary land of happiness. It is also perhaps relevant to remember that when the *Birds* was being composed the Sicilian expedition was already launched, with all its hopes and its forebodings, although no reference to it can be found in the play. In the *Birds* two Athenian friends, Pisthetaerus ('True Friend') and Euelpides ('Good Hope'), leave their city because of its passion for litigation (it is the only reason they give for leaving) and, discovering the home of the hoopoe—which was once King Tereus, son-in-law of Pandion king of Athens—ask the bird if it knows of a city in which men can live quietly and happily. As none of the hoopoe's suggestions is satisfactory, Pisthetaerus comes to the conclusion that the birds must leave their vagrant ways and found a great new city in mid-air, from which they could starve the gods of the ascending fumes of sacrifice and thus force them to be more co-operative.

The chorus of birds is then summoned by a magnificent song from the hoopoe in which sounds of nature and words are exquisitely blended, one of the greatest lyrical achievements in the whole of Greek poetry. The *agon* is subsequently brought in by the chorus, which at first considers the two men enemies and the hoopoe a traitor but then, after a long speech by Pisthetaerus, accepts his plan for establishing a world kingdom of the birds, a dominion they once possessed before it was taken over by the gods. In the course of the *parabasis* which follows the two men are transformed into birds so as to be capable of offering further help if necessary, while the poet gives in its anapaestic part a theogony from a bird's eye point of view, probably freely adapted from the Orphic tradition.

After that the city of the birds is founded and named Nephelococcygia ('Cloud-Cuckoo-Town'), as a result of which Zeus is forced to come to terms with its inhabitants and sends to negotiate with them an embassy consisting of Poseidon (hardly an effective diplomat), Heracles, the crude glutton of comedy, and a barbarous Thracian, representing the foreign gods. The negotiations end with Zeus having to give up Basileia, the personification of his rule over the world, after which the marriage of Pisthetaerus and Basileia takes place. Once again, the play concludes with a *gamos*, but on a more solemn note than usual.

In giving the bare outline of the content of the play one is forced to omit all the delightful minor points and incidents in which this comedy excels. Such, for example, is the distinction between the characters of Pisthetaerus and Euelpides, the former being a man of sense and action, and the latter a buffoon or *bomolochos*; the fantastic, colourful composition of the chorus of birds; the appearance of a poet, a pedlar of oracles, the astronomer Meton, a seller of laws, an official from Athens—who are all sent on their way; the capture of Iris as she flies through the kingdom of the birds; the arrival of the dithyrambist Cinesias, who wants to be a nightingale, or of Prometheus, who appears under a parasol so as not to be seen by the gods. All these are presented in closely knit scenes and in a vivid diction that lends brightness to the topical jokes; and the play is set in a framework of exquisite lyrics, for the lyricism which pervades this whole play is unique, one of the great achievements in the history of poetry. The *Birds*, in which the free play of fantasy is more important than any political purpose, gives perennial delight and has been often imitated.

We do not know what Aristophanes wrote in the years between the presentation of the *Birds* and 411, when he brought out two plays, the *Thesmophoriazusae* and the *Lysistrata*, nor is it known at what festivals these comedies were performed.

The *Thesmophoriazusae* is a skilfully constructed farce, mostly literary in subject, which attacks Euripides and parodies scenes from his plays. In it the women of Athens, at the festival of the Thesmophoria (from which men were strictly excluded),[77] scheme how to avenge themselves on Euripides for presenting 'vicious' women on the stage. Euripides, aware of their plan, attempts through Mnesilochus—who was related to him by marriage—to persuade the poet Agathon, known for his beauty and his effeminate manners, to dress as a woman and go to the festival to defend him. But Agathon refuses, and so Mnesilochus dons a disguise and goes himself; his identity is soon suspected, however, when in a speech he states that in reality women are far worse than those Euripides presents in his tragedies. He is examined and, when his sex is discovered, takes refuge at an altar after he snatches the child of the principal speaker, a stratagem that Telephus had used in the Euripidean play of that name.[78] But the swaddling clothes of the 'child' he has snatched contain nothing but a wineskin, a further thrust at the Athenian women who in comedy were frequently accused of loving their wine too much.

As Mnesilochus is seated by the altar, closely guarded by a woman, the chorus in its *parabasis* engages in the praise of women and the disparagement of men, a revival within the framework of the play of the age-old battle of words between men and women which is thought to have been part of primitive fertility festivals. The *parabasis* is followed by a series of attempts by Euripides to rescue Mnesilochus, which are spirited parodies of scenes from Euripides' *Palamedes*, *Helen* and *Andromeda*. But the tragedian fails and finds himself taken into custody by one of the Scythians who served as policemen in Athens. Mnesilochus is not rescued until Euripides comes to terms with the women, promising a truce in the future, and the stupid Scythian guard goes off with a courtesan.

The play is clever and good-humoured—even Euripides comes off well—and is remarkable for the way in which it parodies contemporary tragedy not only in whole scenes but individual lines as well, which indicates that part at least of the Athenian audiences must have been well-versed in their tragedies.

Aristophanes wrote a second comedy with the title *Thesmophoriazusae*, which differed considerably from the play we have.

The *Lysistrata*, performed in 411, is one of the best comedies Aristophanes ever wrote. Its production he entrusted once again to Callistratus. The play's aim—the same as that of the *Acharnians* and *Peace*—was to end the war in a spirit of reconciliation and forgiveness. It is indeed surprising that in the middle of the city's struggle for survival a poet could openly declare that there was a good deal to be said for her enemy and that the best Athens could do was to come to terms with Sparta.

The plot is simple and outrageously funny, in spite of the serious undercurrent that runs through the play, for seriousness of purpose never seems to have checked Aristophanes' obscenity. The women of Greece, exhausted by the long war, conspire under the leadership of Lysistrata, a resolute Athenian matron, to force their menfolk to conclude peace by means of a 'sex strike'. Lysistrata and her accomplices capture the Acropolis, the storehouse of the state treasure with which the men are paying for the war. The chorus of old men which comes to storm the Acropolis and drive the women out is checked by the chorus of women;[79] this contest between the two choruses is followed by an *agon* between individuals, but there is no *parabasis* in this play. Whether that ancient kernel of Old Comedy was regarded as dispensable by 411 or was omitted in order not to interrupt the lively action of the play, we cannot tell; probably, as Lesky suggests,[80] both considerations were in the poet's mind.

The episodic sequences that follow are also less extended in the *Lysistrata* than in any other Aristophanic play. In these the women, captives of their own emotions, try to sneak away, whereas firm Myrhinne successfully resists her husband Cinesias, driving him to despair and distraction. The audience is then informed by a herald that the men of Sparta are no better off than those of Athens, for the Spartan women, with Lampito at their head, have been acting like the Athenians—and the result can be observed in the herald's own person! Finally, the Spartan ambassadors come to discuss terms of peace; Lysistrata appears, accompanied by the allegorical figure of Forgiveness—Aristophanes is fond of such allegorical figures at the ends of his plays—and addresses both parties with a solemn speech, one of the most noble in the whole of Aristophanes.

The comedy ends with a feast in honour of the ambassadors and songs in Attic and Laconian sung by guests and hosts alike. The end of the play is damaged, but not much seems to be missing. As in the *Acharnians* the Megarian and the Boeotian dialects play an important role in the comic effects, so in the *Lysistrata* the Laconian dialect is similarly used.

Aristophanes, though professing to ridicule the women in his *Lysistrata*, is in reality all along on their side. Nor are the jokes of the men at the women's expense refined or 'gallant', and each, as would be expected, is accused of every depravity. Aristophanes is thought to have made up for the lack of internal Athenian politics in this play by the most daring indecency, because politics were unsafe to air on the stage in 411, when the city was under an oligarchy. The *Lysistrata* has often been imitated, but unsuccessfully. In the modern world the incredibly uninhibited frankness with which sex is treated in Old Comedy is still hardly acceptable.

At about the same time as the *Lysistrata* Aristophanes wrote plays in which he attacked Alcibiades. His attitude does not seem to have been overtly hostile, as it had been towards Cleon; but in the play *Triphales* the love-life of that extraordinary man was treated in a highly Aristophanic manner, if we are to judge by the surviving fragments. It is thought that the *Triphales* dealt not only with Alcibiades' private but also with his public life. If that is so, it must be considered the last of the political plays of the fifth century. The Greek world never again enjoyed sufficient freedom of speech to attack its political leaders on the stage until the time of the twentieth-century Athenian Reviews (Ἐπιθεωρήσεις).

The death of Euripides gave Aristophanes the idea of dealing once again with a subject he had earlier treated in his *Gerytades*, the comparison between 'modern' and 'traditional' art. This he did in a masterly manner in the *Frogs*, with which he won the first prize at the Lenaea of 405. The plot runs thus. After the death of Euripides and Sophocles, Dionysus has no great tragedians left for his festivals, so decides to go down to Hades to bring Euripides back. Accompanied by his comic slave Xanthus, he first visits Heracles to get advice for his journey to the Underworld, and then sets out, disguised with club and lion skin, hoping to pass for the hero, who successfully entered Hades in the past to fetch Cerberus and got out alive again. When the two reach the river Styx Charon takes Dionysus over in his boat—which, however, Dionysus has to row himself—to a chorus of croaking frogs, which greatly trouble the god and give the play its name. On the other side of the 'water' he is reunited with Xanthias, who, being a slave, has not been ferried over in Charon's boat but has had to come on foot (that is, he has had to walk around the orchestra to the other side).

From there the two proceed on their journey (during which Dionysus displays enormous cowardice), till they meet the main chorus, composed of those initiated in the Eleusinian Mysteries, which directs them to Pluto's palace. This is the first appearance of the main chorus—that of the frogs is a subsidiary one—and their hymn of invocation to Iacchus is a masterpiece of Aristophanic poetry.

Dionysus then gets involved in various ridiculous incidents, a consequence partly of his cowardice and partly of the costume of Heracles he is wearing, for that hero is disliked in the Underworld because of his bullying manner, his dog snatching and his huge appetite. Finally, however, Dionysus is welcomed by Pluto.

The *parabasis*, an ardent appeal to the Athenians to grant pardon to political opponents and to cure the wounds of their city, is the last we have from an Aristophanic play and is not fully developed. It was considered so impressive, however, that a second performance of the *Frogs* was given in order to have it repeated—so the hypothesis tells us—but it is not known when that took place.

The audience is then informed by Aeacus and Xanthias, who have become friends, that Euripides is causing trouble in the Underworld by challenging the throne of tragedy, which is held and defended by Aeschylus. Dionysus is chosen as arbiter of the dispute between the two poets, and a long *agon* follows, a delightful farcical scene full of excellent literary criticism, in which the poets violently attack each other's style. In the end a pair of scales is consulted, and though three times the balance tilts in favour of Aeschylus, Dionysus is still reluctant to decide, so wise is the art of the one and so delightful that of the other. Finally, at Pluto's suggestion, the decision is based on a poet's usefulness to the community, so Dionysus brings Aeschylus back to earth with him as a guardian of men's morals.

The *Frogs*, a superb fantasy of literary criticism, shows Aristophanes at his best. There can be little doubt that he truly admired the moral stature of Aeschylus and disliked Euripides for his modernity, but he delivers some good points against both poets. Thus Euripides is rebuked for the structure of his prologues, his elaborate choric style and the lack of solemnity in his iambics, and Aeschylus for being bombastic and obscure. At the same time one senses that Aristophanes here, as in others of his plays, is well aware that when he is striking at Euripides he is attacking a great man. How could his parodies be worthy paratragedy if they were not ridiculing something of importance? One also wonders if the liberty the poet takes with Dionysus in this play is an indication that religious feeling was waning in 405, or if it is one more example of deep religious faith, which sometimes expresses itself in burlesque and even in abuse because it weighs too heavily upon society.[81]

With the *Frogs* the great days of Aristophanes and of Old Comedy came to an end. With the defeat of Athens at the hands of Sparta the conditions under which Old Comedy was possible no longer obtained. It was too expensive for an impoverished state, and its open and uninhibited criticism could not be tolerated by a defeated people whose confidence was shaken. Aristophanes survived well into the fourth century, but neither of the last two plays of his which we have, the *Ecclesiazusae* and *Plutus*, has the vigour or the brilliance of his earlier work.

The *Ecclesiazusae*, which was probably produced in 391, is the poorest of the poet's plays. It opens with the women of Athens plotting under their leader, Praxagora, to seize the state for themselves. They then fill a meeting of the Assembly, dressed in men's clothes, and pass a bill giving them totalitarian power. This having been achieved, they introduce a primitive communist state. Praxagora, to whose speech the women have listened, enthralled, before the *parodos* of the chorus (the chorus is formed by the women themselves), now once again outlines in a protracted *agon* the programme of the new regime for the benefit of her husband. This is followed by a series of grotesque scenes illustrating life in this new communist state, which concludes with an invitation to a communal feast, the chief dish of which has a name 168 letters long! Since there is no *parabasis* in which to place the appeal to the judges, it is relegated to the closing section of the play.

The *Ecclesiazusae* is a play lacking in vitality. It has almost no personal satire, no *parabasis* and a much curtailed part for the chorus. It is interesting that the plot bears a striking resemblance to the views on women set forth in Plato's *Republic*.[82] Though the two authors are, of course, independent of one another, the coincidence indicates that communism and the equality of the sexes were subjects which were much debated in the early fourth century.

The last play we have from Aristophanes is the *Plutus*. It was produced by the poet himself in 388 and won the second prize. It is also the second play he composed with the same name, the first having been presented, as we have seen, in 408. The *Plutus* deals with the old, bitter grievance that wealth is not justly distributed among men, but this theme is presented in a tame, almost fairy-tale manner, without much personal invective or obscenity and with a chorus whose role is severely curtailed. Its appearance is often indicated only by a marginal direction, *chorou* (meaning 'performance of the chorus'),[83] and there is no *parabasis*.

The whole plot is an allegory. The poor, honest, Chremylos visits Delphi to ask Apollo whether bringing his son up to be a rascal would not profit him more than rearing him as an honest man. Apollo bids him to take back home with him the first man he meets on leaving the temple. Chremylos obeys the god's command, and the stranger he meets turns out to be none other than Plutus, the god of wealth, represented as a blind wretch whose blindness is responsible for the sorry state of the world. Plutus is not easily persuaded to accept Chremylos' hospitality, but finally he gives in. In spite of the doubts of the neighbours and the protests of Penia (Poverty), who stands up for her rights in an *agon* with Chremylos — Poverty maintains that without her neither work, nor science, nor art, nor modesty, nor order would exist — Plutus is taken to the temple of Asclepius, where he miraculously recovers his eyesight.[84]

Plutus is now able to distinguish honest men from rogues, and the rest of the play is a series of episodes exemplifying the remarkable social consequences of this new skill of the god of wealth. Thus men grateful for their new opulence, frustrated sycophants, women whose lovers no longer need their money, Hermes seeking a new job because of the disorder in Olympus, the priest of Zeus Soter, who goes over to Plutus, all figure in these scenes. The *comos* at the end of the play is very subdued, a clear indication that the days of Old Comedy were over.

Besides the *Plutus* we also know of two late comedies by Aristophanes, the *Aioliscos*, a parody of tragedy with no choral songs, and the *Cocalus*, the last play the poet presented, from which Menander is said to have taken over two of his most important themes, seduction and recognition.[85] Both these plays were produced in 388 by the poet's son, Araros.

It is clear that in the late Aristophanes Old Comedy has lost many of its traditional features, the numerous jokes, the unbridled obscenity, the *parabasis* and the true significance of the chorus. Moreover, moral maxims begin to appear, and the slaves become more like the cunning stock figures of later comedy. This was noticed in antiquity, but the line of development that leads to New Comedy is not direct from Aristophanes or any other representative of Old Comedy. If we are to look for its real origins, we must turn to the late plays of Euripides.

Aristophanes is one of the greatest figures in the history of Greek poetry. His favourite media are satire, parody and exaggeration to the point of fantasy, combined with exquisite lyricism expressed in every vein, playful, dignified or superbly refined.[86] His favourite targets are men distinguished in politics, art and philosophy — like Cleon in the *Knights*, Euripides in the *Frogs* and Socrates in the *Clouds* — indeed, in all cultural expressions that a wider public could grasp. These were pilloried with a freedom that in our day would provide excellent cause for libel action. We should imagine the shortcomings of the public and private life of the President of the United States or the Prime Minister of Britain, or the relations of the countries of the Commonwealth with Britain, or the works of Ludwig Wittgenstein and T. S. Eliot (when they were still alive) burlesqued with unrestrained vigour on the stage of a modern theatre if we are to get some idea of what Aristophanes set out to do. No class, age or profession was spared, not even the gods and the heroes.

Amazing is Aristophanes' wealth of wit and comic imagination as he moves through so much diverse material, equally at home with the lowest vulgarity and obscenity—as in the *Lysistrata* or the *Ecclesiazusae*—and the most refined witticism—as in the *Clouds* and the *Frogs*; with fantastic ease he jumps from utter nonsense and slap-stick buffoonery to the greatest heights of delicate irony and earnest advice, without shattering the artistic illusion: a truly unique achievement.

Much of his criticism was, of course, pure fun and intended to raise a laugh. But personal dislike played a part in many of his attacks and there are also occasional touches of grim humour (for example, *Clouds*, ll. 439ff.). He produced works which were the mirror of his day but reflected the deeper meaning of life, for his purpose was as didactic as that of the great tragedians: to expose with genial ridicule, and with superb lyrical and satirical gifts, what was base, vulgar, dishonest, pretentious or subversive in the life of the city.

As already stated, we cannot assign any politics to Aristophanes, for it is the privilege of the satirist to attack all prominent men, no matter what their political beliefs. At the same time, it is clear that he looked back with admiration and affection to the 'old times' and to an idealized picture of the 'days of Marathon', as all conservatives did. He appears to have felt that tradition and conservatism were the only forces capable of counterbalancing the many disturbing innovations of his day. What is remarkable, and should be remembered, is that he survived not only the attacks of Cleon but also two oligarchic revolutions and two democratic restorations, and that in the face of his unbridled outspokenness.

A great part of Aristophanes' success is attributable to the language he uses, for he is a master of words. A great exponent of comic bathos, he uses sacred words at the most improper and unexpected moments; he lifts obscenity into the realm of great poetry through his language and his metres; he twists the meanings of adjectives and nouns; he plays on similarities in sound and meaning, particularly in proper names. Newly coined polysyllabic monstrosities, official language, slang, dialect, bits of old songs, tragic diction and, of course, the normal Attic vernacular are all found side by side in his dialogues, for he has a keen ear for the racy expression, the amusing, the incongruous and the pompous. His parodies of tragedy are magnificent, where lines and whole scenes are transformed into hilarious indecency or utter nonsense. In fact, Aristophanes imitates Euripides to such an extent that Cratinus invented the verb 'Euripid-Aristophanize' to describe the style of the two.

His speeches are admirably served by his comic trimeter and his trochaic, anapaestic and other recitative metres, which he uses freely and which add variety and vivacity to his verse. The finish of his lyrics is not perfect, and their rhythms are on the whole simple, but this is counter-balanced by his exquisite lightness of touch, his magnificent natural imagery and the admixture of sounds of nature with words which we find in them.

As has been repeatedly said, Aristophanes set out to amuse and to please, so his plays are full of incidents that happen as the audience would wish them to happen, and they all have a happy ending, an element required by the tradition of comedy and in particular that of the final *comos*. But his characters are not idealized fairy-tale figures; they are real men and women who behave like ordinary human beings. Impressive too is the place in life he gives to women and the common sense they display, which often puts men to shame. Aristophanes left no successors in his art, which ended with him, but he was carefully studied and much admired throughout antiquity.

ARISTOPHANES' CONTEMPORARIES AND RIVALS

In the age of Aristophanes there was much competition and a lively interest in comedy. Of the many comic poets of those days, the most distinguished were Eupolis, Phrynichus, Plato and Philonides, of whose works only titles and fragments have survived.

Eupolis (446–412 B.C.), the son of Sosipolis, was the foremost rival of Aristophanes and was considered one of the greatest poets of Old Comedy.[87] He presented his first play in 429[88] and won seven victories in his relatively short life, four at the Great Dionysia and three at the Lenaea. He died fighting 'in the Hellespont during the Peloponnesian War', and it is said that as a result of this, the Athenians passed a law exempting poets from military service.[89]

Fourteen titles and over 460 fragments of his plays have survived (fourteen were all that were known in antiquity, of which seven won prizes), including substantial papyrus fragments of Δῆμοι and, if the identification is correct, of Προσπάλτιοι.[90]

As one would have expected from a distinguished contemporary of Aristophanes, the plays of Eupolis dealt with the political, cultural and social problems of his day, but, by contrast with Aristophanes, whose writings are largely in favour of peace, Eupolis seems to have been a supporter of the war against Sparta. His *Slackers or Hermaphrodites* ('Αστράτευτοι ἢ 'Ανδρογύναι), as well as his *Taxiarchoi* (in which the veteran warrior Phormio was brought on to make a soldier even out of a cowardly Dionysus) showed concern for the armed forces of Athens.[91]

Eupolis' dislike of Cleon rivalled that of Aristophanes. In his *Golden Age* (Χρυσοῦν γένος) he poured bitter scorn on Athens for allowing a man like Cleon to rule. Nor was he more charitable to Hyperbolos, who succeeded Cleon, in his *Marikas* (*Catamite*), which was performed in 421. Aristophanes accused Eupolis of plagiarism in this play,[92] and he repeated that accusation in the *Anagyros*.[93] But Eupolis retorted in his *Baptae*, produced between 424 and 415, claiming that he had collaborated with Aristophanes in the *Knights*. A collaboration between the two young poets, who were originally friends, is very possible; but from 421 onwards that friendship clearly ceased. However that may be, themes which Aristophanes used in his *Babylonians* also appear in Eupolis' *Cities* (Πόλεις), which was produced in 420. This play was also concerned with the Athenian empire and the relation of Athens to her allies; it included personal references, in common with Aristophanes' *Clouds, Wasps* and *Peace*; and the members of the chorus, which represented different Greek cities, were individually characterized.

But the attacks of Eupolis were not only political. The cultural and social scene also excited him, and above all the circle of the Sophists and their activities. Thus he struck at Callias and his friends in his *Flatterers* (Κόλακες), which was performed in 421 at the City Dionysia and won the first prize, defeating Aristophanes' first *Peace*. The setting is the wealthy home of Callias—the very man whom we know from Plato's *Protagoras* and Xenophon's *Symposium*—whose table is besieged by droves of parasites. Among those derided are Protagoras and Alcibiades, who is accused of being a woman chaser, and Socrates also appears, not as a parasite but as a loquacious beggar who thinks out everything except the question of how to appease his hunger.[94] The sexual licence of the same circle was attacked a year later (420) in the play *Autolycus*, of which a revised version also appeared. The central figure was Autolycus, the athlete who won the *pancration* at the Panathenaea of 422, a favourite of Callias. In the *Baptae* too, which was presented roughly at the same time (c. 424–415), the licentious habits of Alcibiades were again assailed[95] in a setting that ridiculed the Thracian goddess Cotytto and her ceremonies of baptism. Out of this sprang a later anecdote, that in revenge Alcibiades threw Eupolis overboard and drowned him on their way to Sicily during the Sicilian expedition—baptism for baptism.[96] In his Φίλοι Aspasia figured, and in his play *Goats* (Αἶγες), which was named after its animal chorus, Eupolis indulged in a humorous criticism of 'modern' culture and, in particular, modern music.

The last and perhaps the most important of his plays was the *Demes* (Δῆμοι), probably produced in 412.[97] The failure of the Sicilian expedition and the lowering of Athenian morale that followed provoked fear that Athens may be sinking to utter destruction. So the poet returned to an idealized image of the past, of the Athens that defeated the Persians and established her great empire. To bring this before the eyes of his audience Eupolis summons from the kingdom of the dead four great leaders of the past, Solon, Miltiades, Aristides and Pericles, under the leadership of Myronides[98]—admittedly, a baffling choice—and sets them to judge the representatives of the modern age, whom they reprimand, convert or chastise. The chorus of the comedy consists of Attic demes, which also gave the play its name. It might be worth adding that from this play comes the famous description of the eloquence of Pericles, so often quoted.[99]

Eupolis was undoubtedly a keen observer and a passionate fighter. As a political champion and a social critic he was admirable, striking against all that was low and decadent. His style was characterized in antiquity as 'bitter and indecent'[100] and as 'inventive, powerful and attractive'.[101] However that may be, his extant fragments do not stand up well to comparison with the plays of Aristophanes. It is needless, of course, to add that the disappearance of the plays of such an outstanding personality is a great loss to literature.

Far inferior to Eupolis but still holding an honourable position among the comedians of his day is the Athenian Phrynichus (c. 425), who won two victories at the Lenaea and at least one at the City Dionysia. His first play was produced in 434 (or, according to one authority,[102] in 429). Eleven titles and 100 fragments of his plays have survived, but the genuineness of two, the *Connus* and the *Revellers*, has been challenged.

His comedy the *Solitary* (Μονότροπος) was produced in the same year as Aristophanes' *Birds* (414) and satirizes those wishing to escape from contemporary society; the subject of his *Muses* also brings to mind the *Frogs* of Aristophanes. It was produced in the same year as the *Frogs* (405) and contained a scene of competition between poets—probably Sophocles and Euripides—with the Muses, who formed the chorus, as judges. One fragment[103] from an unnamed play should also be mentioned; it refers humorously to the celebrated mutilation of the Herms on the eve of the Sicilian expedition. It is clear that Eupolis' interests were politics, poetry and music.

Plato, 'the comic poet' (c. 400?)—so called to distinguish him from the philosopher—was also Athenian and younger than both Eupolis and Phrynichus. He won his first victory at the City Dionysia after 414.[104] We have thirty titles and 270 fragments of his comedies, many of which were political; one at least, the *Envoys*, was produced in the fourth century. In fact, such was his bitterness and his directness that whole comedies of his were named after the politicians he viciously attacked, like *Hyperbolos*, *Pisander* or *Cleophon*. But Plato also dealt with more general political problems, as can be seen from his *Hellas* (otherwise known as the *Islands*).

Plato, following the tradition of his great predecessors, also ridiculed contemporary tragedians and musicians in his *Sophists*, and the decline of dancing (ὀρχηστική) in his Σκευαί; but at the same time, pointing in the direction of Middle Comedy, he cultivated the mythological burlesque, as titles like Νὺξ μακρά, Ζεὺς κακούμενος, *Adonis*, *Daedalus*, *Laius*—in which he parodied Euripides' *Chrysippus*—or *Phaon* indicate. (The *Phaon* was produced in 391 and dealt with the mythological phallic figure after which women ran.) And this was his greatest contribution to comedy, though some of his plays may well have also included political innuendo. Plato, whose language has many popular elements in it, is reputed to have been so poor that he sold his comedies to others to relieve his indigence.

Philonides started his career as a fuller, then became an actor and finally a comic poet. He also produced Aristophanes' *Wasps, Amphiaraus* and *Frogs*. For Aristophanes to have entrusted him with this he must have been a man of considerable talent. Though probably more a producer than a composer of comedies, he also distinguished himself in the field of original composition by winning a first prize at the Lenaea of 422 with his play Προαγών.[105] (In fact, his may well be the mutilated name given in an inscription[106] as the winner of the first prize at the City Dionysia in about 410.) Of his own plays only three titles survive.

Finally, before leaving Aristophanes' contemporaries mention should be made of Hegemon of Thasos, also known by the nickname Φακῆ ('lentil dish'), who first raised parody to the status of an independent literary genre, with a separate place of its own in competitions. (Hegemon is also reported to have composed a comedy named *Philine*.) Aristotle mentions him as ὁ τὰς παρῳδίας πρῶτος ποιήσας ('he who created parody'),[107] but Athenaeus[108] says more precisely that he was the first to enter τοὺς θυμελικοὺς ἀγῶνας (theatrical competitions) and to win contests for parody in Athens. A passage is also quoted by Athenaeus[109]— deriving from Polemon (c. 190 B.C.)—in which Hegemon's verses claim for his performances fifty *drachmae*, the second prize; and Polemon attests the victory of Hegemon at Athens with his *Gigantomachia* and other parodies.

Parody in Greek poetry, based on exaggeration and incongruity, is, of course, much older than Hegemon. One has only to remember the *Margites* and the *Batrachomyomachia*, Hipponax (who, according to Polemon[110] was the 'inventor' of the genre) and Epicharmus, to say nothing of Eupolis or its greatest master, Aristophanes. But here we have to reckon with a special kind of play and with special competitions[111] in which parody played the leading role; until the *citharoedes* later became the objects of parody, epic and tragedy were mainly their target.

That is practically all we can gather about Old Comedy, which for more than half a century so brilliantly expressed the Athenian satirical spirit and its wildest flights of fantasy.[112]

MIDDLE COMEDY

The form and content of Middle Comedy

The term Middle Comedy, which was coined in late Hellenistic days, may be conveniently employed to describe the period between the Old (political) Comedy of Aristophanes and the New Comedy of manners of Menander—the two peaks of ancient comedy (c. 404–c. 321 B.C.).[113] This was a period of transition and experimentation in which different types of play were composed, so that the exact flavour of Middle Comedy as a whole is difficult to grasp.

We know the names of fifty-one poets of that period,[114] and Athenaeus[115] assigns more than 800 comedies to the fifty-seven poets he knew, but not a single complete play has survived. The number of plays is so large that the poets of Middle Comedy must have plundered each other's works to produce such a corpus of work, and this supposition is supported by the many common titles and by some of the existing fragments. However that may be, the fragments and titles that have reached us are indeed informative, and it is probable that Plautus' *Persa* and possibly his *Poenulus Amphitruo* and *Menaechmi* are adaptations of Middle Comedy.[116]

The large number of comedies composed in the fourth century could not have been intended for Athenian productions only, and probably not even always for performance on the stage. This may account for a number of the changes we meet. These changes began early, for some are already evident in the last two surviving plays of Aristophanes, the *Ecclesiazusae* and the *Plutus*, which were forerunners, if not products, of Middle Comedy. In both the *parabasis* has disappeared, and the reduction of the lyrical element throws a new emphasis on the actors that leads to character comedy; and in the *Plutus* we have the first instance of a mythological comedy, for Plutus, the central figure, is drawn from mythology. Moreover, political criticism, though still evident, is clearly on the decline.

As already observed, it was the downfall of Athens in 404 B.C. that affected the comic stage so profoundly. Until then comedy had drawn much of its material from the political and cultural disputes that excited the city of Athens; but as the restoration did not bring back the old life, comedy turned to the mythological burlesque and to general social subjects. Thus in Middle Comedy we see that political satire on the whole recedes, though it does not disappear; literary parody loses its personal sting; and philosophy as an enterprise is no longer attacked. Only the personal absurdities of certain philosophers—usually Platonists and Pythagoreans—are ridiculed. Moreover, people in the fourth century are more reflective and have better manners, so that unbridled lust and obscenity are felt to be offensive. It is worth mentioning in this connection that the obscene costume of Old Comedy, with the grotesque padding and the phallus, was also probably given up in this period.[117]

When examining the titles and the fragments of Middle Comedy one cannot fail to be impressed by the variety of its subjects. However, in the earlier part of the period, mythological comedy seems to have played a dominant role, for something between half and a third of the dated plays have mythological titles. Later, between 350 and 320 B.C., the proportion falls to a tenth. Two types of such mythological comedy can be identified, though the distinction cannot always be rigidly maintained, as a great number of plays seem to overlap.

The first is pure mythological burlesque, a straight travesty of a myth, sometimes with political innuendo but often just for the fun of the travesty; for myths are no longer taken seriously and so the tragic stories are recast in the lowest contemporary terms. Eubulus' Dolon, for example, is so fat that he cannot tie his shoes up, and he has never had to wash up because he always licks the plates clean; Heracles, when asked to choose a book from Linus' library of 'classics', chooses Simos' cookery book;[118] Pelops complains of the poverty of Greek meals by comparison with the king of Persia's roast camel; a central place is accorded to the traditional comic figure of gluttonous Heracles; and so forth. The second is tragic parody, whose interest centres on the parody of tragic mythological treatments, especially those of Euripides. Such were, for example, Eubulus' *Auge* and *Ion*, or Anaxandrides' *Helen.*

But side by side with the mythological plays, others with fictitious plots based on ordinary life were also constructed,[119] following the lead given by Agathon in tragedy. Thus we find comedies whose titles are those of professions,[120] or of family relationships,[121] or of typical characters,[122] or of ethnic[123] or even simple events or things.[124] These groups recur in the works of all the poets of Middle Comedy, and among them were also riddles and plays of mistaken identity.

Middle Comedy seems to have been particularly interested in 'typical' people, stock figures mostly seen from the angle of their profession and in 'typical' situations. Nearly all the well-known stock figures of New Comedy—cooks, parasites, courtesans, pimps, soldiers, angry old men, young lovers, slaves—can be found in the fragments and the titles of Middle Comedy. Some of these go back to Old Comedy; the *miles gloriosus* goes back to Lamachus in Aristophanes' *Acharnians*, the cook and the slave to his *Plutus*, the courtesans to plays of Pherecrates, and Eupolis has a chorus of flatterers (Κόλακες) in a play of the same name. It is clear, however, that it was during the fourth century that the stock figures we find in later comedy were fashioned or established.

If we now turn to the structure of the plots, we shall observe the profound influence of the later Euripidean plays. Comedy, in its parodies of tragedy, proceeded to construct complete plots on the pattern of tragedy, and this lesson was transferred to comic plays dealing with everyday life, to plays in a non-mythological framework, thus turning tragedy into a comedy of manners. For Old Comedy had no properly constructed plots in the real sense of the word. The interest in ordinary life influenced the development of one particular type of comedy, dealing with a number of plausible, everyday incidents, such as love affairs or confidence tricks, and based on a group of stock characters—the play that leads to New Comedy and Menander. The similarity of such plots with tragedy was already recognized in antiquity in connection with New Comedy,[125] but plots of this pattern already existed in Middle Comedy, as, for example, in Alexis' Ἀγωνίς or Ἱππίσκος.

The influence of tragedy upon comedy should not be seen as depending on some external event like the 'tragic' legislation of Lycurgus (c. 390–325/4 B.C.?), who had taken measures to boost Athenian morale after Chaeronea. There is no particular moment in the fourth century when the development of comedy took a decisive turn away from the comic tradition towards the tragic,[126] as some scholars have maintained. After all, the comic application of rape and recognition had already been used by Aristophanes in his mythological burlesque *Cocalus*. So when the *Suda* says that Anaxandrides invented 'love affairs and rapes of maidens' in comedy it probably means that Anaxandrides was the first to use them as incidents of ordinary life in non-mythological plays.

One of the most characteristic elements in Middle Comedy is the decline of the chorus. This also must have come about gradually. Thus *agon* and *parabasis* appear only exceptionally, and even if we find a play named after its chorus in Eubulus' *Stephanopolides* (the *Garland Sellers*), which was produced in 345 B.C., and if instances can be found of a chorus still conversing with the actors[127] or singing especially composed lyrics,[128] the chorus is no longer organically connected with the plot. This must have become the normal practice before New Comedy set in. The choruses are simple, interpolated pieces, *embolima*.

The curtailing of the choral lyrics meant, of course, that in Middle Comedy metres became poorer and more monotonous. We find nothing like Aristophanes' polymetry, even if a certain variety can be found in the metres of the dialogue.[129] Like the metres, language too became poorer and much less vivid in Middle Comedy.

As already mentioned, the political references were greatly subdued, but they did not disappear. Aristotle, speaking about contemporary comedy[130]—that is, Middle Comedy—says that it replaced the αἰσχρολογία (abuse) of Old Comedy with ὑπόνοια (suggestion), the open attacks with covert ones. In general this is true, and it is repeated in late Hellenistic times;[131] but titles and fragments of Middle Comedy show that political plays existed—such, for example, was Eubulus' *Dionysius*, satirizing Dionysius of Syracuse, or Mnesimachus' *Philip*, which attacked Philip of Macedon—and that spiteful political abuse continued to be heard on the comic stage down to the last quarter of the fourth century.[132] So the decline in the political content of comedy was also gradual—a thing we do not gather from ancient theory—and the reason suggested for the change in antiquity, the temporary suppression of free speech in 404–403, cannot be accepted.[133]

Thus it is true to say that Middle Comedy is both backward- and forward-looking. It has taken much from Old Comedy and contains many elements that are usually associated with New Comedy. And this is important to bear in mind, for it proves that the literary comic tradition developed uninterruptedly from Old to New Comedy, even if in the course of this development it took over from tragedy and other sources a number of new elements.

Celebrated poets of Middle Comedy

It would be idle to enumerate the names of the vast number of poets of Middle Comedy we know,[134] as there is little we can say about them. We do know, however, that the five most prominent among them were Antiphanes, Anaxandrides, Eubulus, Alexis, and Timocles, to whom we must now turn.

Antiphanes (c. 408/5–c. 344 B.C.), who was one of the leading comic poets of the period, presented his first play between 386 and 383 and won thirteen victories, eight of which were at the Lenaea. The number of comedies atributed to him in antiquity was very large indeed, ranging from 260 to 365, so they could not all have been composed for Athenian performances. Of the 134 surviving titles of his plays, several suggest mythological burlesque and some, like his *Aiolos*, parodies of tragedy;[135] others were drawn from the plot of the play, while several refer to typical characters — for example, the *Superstitious Man* (*Oionistes*), the *Moralizing Man* (*Misoponeros*) — or to professions (*Agroikos, Butalion, Akestria*). Because of a gnomic strain that runs through his verse, Antiphanes found a place in Stobaeus' anthology, and there are many interesting citations from his work, for he dealt with problems of art, poetry and music, and he even seems to have been concerned with metaphysical problems.[136] But he is also quoted by Athenaeus for his references to food, a characteristic common of Middle Comedy. No less a man than Demetrius of Phalerum wrote a work on Antiphanes.

Anaxandrides (c. 400–c. 349) was probably of Rhodian birth and won the first prize ten times.[137] Forty-two titles and eighty fragments of his plays have reached us, of which fourteen are mythological, whereas others look back to Old Comedy (*Cities, Huntsmen* and so on), as do the political allusions in some of his fragments. But he also composed fictitious plots (*Madman, Samia*) and was, as we have seen, the first to use in comedy 'love affairs and rapes of maidens', according to the *Suda*.

The longer fragments show an elegant style and a moralizing tendency, which earned him, as it had earned Antiphanes, a place in anthologies. Fragment 34 (Kock) is of special interest, for it is an address to the audience in iambic tetrameters, which could be one of the few examples of a *parabasis* from this period. Anaxandrides was also known as a dithyrambic poet.

Eubulus (c. 376–372) is reputed to have composed 104 plays and to have won six victories at the Lenaea. Of some fifty-eight titles of his comedies that we know, about half indicate mythological burlesque; we have eleven titles identical with those of plays of Euripides and eight identical with those of other tragedians, so it is not surprising that in his fragments we meet with a parody of the tragic style. He also wrote a political play named *Dionysius*, in which he drew a character sketch of the tyrant of Syracuse, and several works that have the names of courtesans, foreshadowing the well-known practice of New Comedy. Other plays he named after professions: Σκυτεύς (the *Leather Cutter*), Πορνοβοσκός (the *Brothel Keeper*) and so on.

Of interest is the metrical variety found in his fragments, which is rare in Middle Comedy and which together with the political attacks and the title of his play Στεφανοπώλιδες (the *Garland Sellers*), named after the chorus, indicate that some of his comedies at least may have been cast in the style of traditional Old Comedy.

Eubulus was known and read in Rome.[138]

Alexis (c. 375–c. 275) is the most important of all the poets of Middle Comedy. He was born at Thurii, in the west, but apparently lived most of his life in Athens and composed no fewer than 245 plays. He is said to have been the teacher of Menander[139] (or, according to the *Suda*, his uncle), and Plutarch[140] records that he lived to be 105 years old! In the 350s he won his first Lenaean victory and in 347 a victory at the Great Dionysia, but no other information about his successes has reached us.

About 140 titles of his plays — of which fifteen are mythological — and 340 fragments survive, but it is impossible to estimate what part he played in the development of Greek comedy. The fragments display contemplation, elegance of language and wit, which justify his fame in antiquity,[141] for he was read and admired down to Roman times, and his plays were adapted by Roman comic poets.[142] Plautus' *Poenulus* may derive, at least in part, from Alexis' Καρχηδόνιος.[143]

It is interesting that he used both the older form of chorus, which was addressed by the actors — a kind of *parabasis* in Eupolidean metres[144] — and the newer form best-known from Menander.[145]

In his play *Agonis* (Ἀγωνίς) or *Hippiskos* (Ἱππίσκος) we have an early example of the type of plot which involves both a love affair and a confidence trick. We know that it was he who introduced the type and common name of the parasite into Attic comedy,[146] and the novelistic material he made use of (Aesop, Archilochus) is also of interest, as well as the parody of Plato in his *Phaedrus*. It is indeed a pity that so little is known about the life and works of so famous a comic poet.

Timocles (c. 330 B.C.), the last writer of Middle Comedy we shall deal with, came late in the period but promoted the personal lampoon with verve and originality, attacking, among others, the orators Demosthenes and Hyperides. He won the first prize at the Lenaea between 330 and 320, and his last datable fragment belongs to the days of Demetrius of Phalerum (317–307).

From the titles of his plays we can see that he cultivated the mythological burlesque (for example, *Κένταυρος*, *Ἥρωες*), as well as the comedy of manners (*Πολυπράγμων*, *Ἐπιχαιρέκακος*). The most original of his titles is undoubtedly *Orestautocleides* (*Ὀρεσταυτοκλείδης*)—Autocleides suffering the fate of Orestes, obsessed not by furies but by old prostitutes. (The point is lost, of course, if one is not aware tht Autocleides was a known homosexual of his day.)

We must now pass on to the other forms of fourth-century poetry and then come to New Comedy, a much more important and much more influential literary genre than Middle Comedy in the history of the Western theatre and one about which we are much better informed.

CHAPTER 5

Later Lyric, Elegiac and Epic Poetry

LYRIC POETRY

Different types of choral song, such as the encomium, the epinicean hymn and the paean survived into the middle of the fifth century and even later, since Euripides wrote an epinicean for Alcibiades and Sophocles a paean for Asclepius. But with the fall of the aristocracies and the rise of tragedy, the choral hymn seems to have declined. The only popular choral poetry of the later fifth and the fourth century was the dithyramb.

We have already spoken about the origins of the dithyramb[1] when discussing the origins of tragedy, and of its first great period when connected with the Dionysiac festivals of Athens. In those days the poetry was of the highest literary merit, and the music was subordinated to it.[2] But shortly before the middle of the fifth century the flute succeeded in gaining mastery over the words, which brings us to the second period of the history of the dithyramb, the one connected with the names of Melanippides, Phrynis, Cinesias, Philoxenus and Timotheus. This period extends to the middle of the fourth century, after which no names of distinguished poets are recorded, though those of famous flute players survive.[3]

This second period is characterized by a new and highly elaborate music, which prevailed to the detriment of the words, so that these became gradually more and more obsolete and unfashionable. Aristophanes may have condemned this new music and Pherecrates may have presented in his play *Cheiron* the personification of Music complaining to Justice about the treatment she has received at the hands of the new lyric poets,[4] but Euripides was clearly in sympathy with it, and in this he was followed by the majority of the young.

Among the earliest of this group of innovators was Diagoras of Melos (c. 490 B.C.), a famous free-thinker, who was exiled from Athens for ridiculing the Eleusinian Mysteries. Of his dithyrambs nothing has survived. But the notable change came with another native of Melos,

Melanippides, who was active from about 480 until about 436 B.C., when he went to Macedonia to the court of Perdiccas, where he died.

Melanippides' work is a landmark in the history of the dithyramb, for he altered its structure by introducing *anabolae* (ἀναβολαί), or lyrical solos, instead of the antistrophe of the older school. As all innovators, he was a controversial figure admired by many but also attacked as the first to 'corrupt' the art of music.[5] His scanty remains come from a *Danaids*, a *Marsyas* and a *Persephone*, but we cannot tell if these were dithyrambs or not. Meleager also included some of his poems in his *Garland*, which he calls hymns.[6]

The movement Melanippides began continued and the music became increasingly elaborate, as a result of which several kinds of lyric came to be abandoned towards the middle of the fourth century, such was the fashion for novelty.[7]

Next to Melanippides we hear of Cinesias[8] and Phrynis[9] as 'corrupters' of poetry and music, but little is known about them. Phrynis, who came from Mytilene, was attacked by Aristophanes,[10] and Plato[11] speaks of him as playing down to his audience. But the most famous and influential of the new school were Philoxenus and Timotheus.

Philoxenus of Cithera (436/5–380/79 B.C.), left his native island as a child, was enslaved by the Spartans and later attached himself to Melanippides, from whom he received his training as an artist. He spent some time at the court of Dionysius I at Syracuse, where the tyrant sent him to the quarries because he criticized his host's tragedies, according to one version of the story, or, according to another, because he engaged in an intrigue with one of his concubines. There he is said to have composed his most famous dithyramb, the *Cyclops*, in which the oafish Cyclops is presented in love with the nereid Galatea and sings a solo to her to the lyre. This work, of which only a few lines survive, was parodied by Aristophanes in *Plutus*,[12] and its influence can be traced down to the eleventh idyll of Theocritus. How greatly Philoxenus was admired can also be seen from Antiphanes' *Tritagonist*,[13] in which the central character says: 'Philoxenus is much the best of all poets. . . . He was a god among men and knew true music. . . .'

According to the *Suda*, Philoxenus wrote twenty-four dithyrambs and other sources refer to his *nomoi*. Other works of his were a *Hymenaios* which was performed at Ephesus, and a Γενεαλογία τῶν Αἰακιδῶν μελικῶς.[14] We are also told that he employed a well-known flute player, Antigenides, to accompany his works.

Timotheus (c. 450–c. 360 B.C.) was a native of Miletus and surpassed all his contemporaries in innovation. He made a boast of this achievement, for he tells us: 'I do not sing the old. My new is better . . . away with the old Muse'.[15] He is traditionally represented as the friend of Euripides, who is said to have encouraged him during his early failures, for at first

Timotheus was not popular in Athens. Timotheus is also said to have visited Macedonia, but this is not certain. Reports about his work are very confused, but it appears that he wrote mostly dithyrambs and *nomoi*.

In 1902 a fourth-century papyrus brought to light large portions of a *nome* of Timotheus called the *Persians*, to which Euripides, it is said, wrote the prologue.[16] This was produced in about 419–406 and is a description of the battle of Salamis, in which gross realism is combined with an absurd reproduction of the grand style. It is the only example of style of the 'later' dithyramb we have, for Timotheus was accused by his critics of composing *nomoi* in the literary style of dithyrambs.[17] In this the predominance of music over words was such that the words lost their power and often degenerated into elaborate periphrases. Moreover, most of the lyrics of Timotheus were *apolelymena*—that is, they were free of the strophe–antistrophe structure.

Among the known dithyrambs of Timotheus were *Ajax Mad*, *Elpenor*, *Nauplios*, in which he tried to depict a storm with the flute, *Birth Pangs of Semele*, in which the cries of the goddess were realistically rendered, and *Scylla*, criticized by Aristotle for the laments of Odysseus that it included. Much that we are told about Timotheus is also connected with the addition he made to the number of strings of the lyre. He is thought to have influenced Euripides, and he was greatly admired after his death; several revivals of his works are known.

The evidence we have at our disposal is not enough to estimate the value or the significance of this new development in poetry and music which continued into the fourth century in the hands of Polyidus and Telestes of Sicyon, the latter even being honoured with a statue in his native city. But after the fourth century the dithyramb seems to have lost its importance even in Athens, although before 300 B.C. the state itself took over the expenses of production. The epigraphical evidence proves the continuation of the dithyrambic competitions in various parts of the Greek world—in Delos, Miletus, Teos and Samos—during the Hellenistic age, while in Athens the custom continued well into the Empire.

To complete this general picture of the second period of the Greek dithyramb, one more name must be added—that of Licymnius of Chios, who, according to Aristotle,[18] composed in a style well-suited for reading, which is in keeping with what we have already seen in connection with fourth-century tragedy. Licymnius was also a rhetorician who wrote on language.[19]

The dithyramb, the paean and the *nome* were the only forms of lyric poetry which continued to be written down to the end of the fourth century. But the old divisions of form began to be confused. Not only did Timotheus compose a *nome*, the *Persians*, in the style of a dithyramb, but Aristonous, as we shall see presently, wrote a paean—a form of lyric poetry proper for Apollo—to Hestia, and Philodamus one to Dionysus;

and even Aristotle used the form of a paean in a poem composed in memory of his dead friend, Hermias, and addressed it to the abstract power Ἀρετά. This confusion persisted into the Hellenistic age and up to the end of the ancient world.

ELEGIAC AND EPIC POETRY

Symposia, which fifth-century Athens had inherited from the archaic period, continued to be held up to the end of the Classical era and were still the gatherings at which elegies and *scolia* were recited. In fact, much elegiac poetry seems to have been written in the fifth and even in the fourth century, and great poets like Sophocles, Euripides and Ion of Chios were among its contributors. The surviving fragments are few, however. Of these we must consider those which belong to the pen of two men who, though unequal in significance, are both well-known Athenian political figures.

The first is Dionysius Chalcus (c. 444 B.C.), so called after his introduction of bronze currency into Athens; he also took part in the colonization of Thurii. His elegies were sympotic—the surviving fragments speak of the pleasures of companionable drinking—and are noteworthy because Dionysius occasionally put the pentameter first in his elegiac couplets,[20] a sign that the old traditional forms were already losing their rigidity by the middle of the fifth century.

Of much greater significance are the elegies of Critias (460–404/3 B.C.) the handsome and notorious Athenian politician of aristocratic birth whom we have already met as a dramatist.[21] Critias has been called a 'modern post-Sophist Theognis', who expressed himself both in the form of the old aristocratic sympotic elegy and in the more modern forms of drama and prose. But the 'rowdy' modern dithyramb and the 'plebeian' iambics he never deigned to touch.

Of his elegies the first line survives of a book he dedicated to Plato's brothers Glaucus and Adeimantos, as well as fragments from an elegy on Alcibiades,[22] whose return to Athens he proposed in 411 or 407. Moreover he cast in elegiacs the Ἔμμετροι Πολιτεῖαι (*Political Constitutions*), a didactic work dealing with the constitutions of various Greek and foreign lands, which branched out to explore their culture and their politics; part of this work may well be the *Euremata*, another elegiac poem attributed to Critias, such is the similarity of their subject-matter.

The elegies of Critias are political elegies with a didactic Sophistic bent, and he is the last Athenian, as far as we can see, to have written such verse addressed to kindred political spirits; for this type of poetry came to an end with Alexander and the passing away of the old city-state. The didactic element of his verse, however, was taken over by the Alexandrian scholar-poets, and that is the reason why Critias is sometimes called their precursor.

Of Critias' poetry in hexameters we have a fairly large fragment, which contains an elegant tribute to Anacreon, a kind of *Makarismos*. It apparently comes from a longer didactic work dealing with the history of literature, one of the oldest of its kind.[23] No biographical details are given in it, only pithy characterizations.

Of his many and interesting prose writings, which were so close in spirit to his poetry, only some fragments survive.[24]

Better documented than the *scolion* or elegy is the epigram of the fifth and the fourth century. About the origins of the epigram and its great days between and after the Persian Wars—so intimately connected with Simonides—we have already spoken.[25] But even later we have a number of good sepulchral and dedicatory epigrams,[26] mostly anonymous, and a few by famous writers like Euripides[27] and Plato. Some of these are spuriously attributed to great names, mostly to Simonides. In the latter part of the fifth and in the fourth century the style of the epigram grew more elaborate, probably due to the influence of rhetoric, and its tone more emotional, perhaps under the influence of tragedy, but it continued to be serene and sincere.

Of the epigrams of the fourth century those attributed to Plato should be singled out. Not all of them are authentic, but the genuine ones have an intensity and an intimacy which are truly outstanding.[28]

To the same period also belongs—partly at least—the so-called *Peplus Arsitotelicus*. This is a mythological work of mixed content, alleged to be Aristotle's,[29] from which sixty-three fictitious epigrams have been preserved, mainly on the fallen in the Trojan War. They are of little literary value but point to the kind of fictitious epigram which subsequently flourished in the Hellenistic world.

Unfortunately, we are much less well-informed about the iambic verse of this period than about the elegiac. The only remains of independent iambic poems are a few tiny scraps, such as the fragments written by the comic poet Hermippus.[30]

Less overshadowed by tragedy was the epic in the fifth and the fourth centuries. About Choerilus of Samos and his *Persica*, which represents the end of epic poetry in the 'Homeric manner', we have already spoken.[31] Much more significant was his near-contemporary, Antimachus of Colophon, who followed a different line in his epic poetry and was greatly admired by many of the first generation of Alexandrian poets and critics.

Antimachus (c. 404 B.C.) was the first poet we know to combine the qualities of both scholar and poet. Unfortunately, very little information is available about his life. It is thought that he competed in a poetry competition at the Lysandreia in Samos before Lysander died (395 B.C.); and we are informed that he loved one Lyde[32]—probably his mistress—in whose memory he wrote a narrative elegy of that name to console himself for her loss. Finally, we hear that Plato sent Heracleides Ponticus[33] to Colophon to collect Antimachus' poems, from which it has been deduced that the poet probably died fairly early in the fourth century.

Five works attributed to Antimachus are known: *Thebais, Lyde, Deltoi, Artemis* and *Iachine*(?). The *Thebais*, an epic, deals with the first expedition against Thebes, but how far Antimachus made use of the old Theban epic cycle we cannot tell. He probably drew not only on the epic, but also on lyric and tragic versions of the story of Thebes. However that may be, he clearly set out to create a 'modern' epic, meant to be enjoyed side by side with the great Homeric epics, which he had carefully studied and of which he had also produced an edition. It was a learned absorption of Homeric devices he was after, and these he wished to re-establish and to promote in his own writings. And it is precisely in this that the great difference lies between him and his epic predecessors, who were mere imitators of Homer. Thus Antimachus initiated the second period of the Greek epic, which the Alexandrians further developed, for the great age of Attic literature produced no epic poetry of importance, and there is a large void between the *Persica* of Choerilus of Samos and the *Thebais* of Antimachus, which belongs to a different world.

Antimachus' second major poem is the elegy *Lyde*, an equally 'modern' work, which the poet wished to set beside the old Ionian erotic elegy of his fellow citizen Mimnermus. It included unhappy mythological love affairs in at least two books, but it was probably longer, in view of the poet's notorious diffuseness, confirmed by the surviving fragments on the voyage of the Argo. Demeter's wanderings, Bellerophon and Oedipus were other stories treated in that elegy. The *Lyde* may have contained a preface explaining the occasion of its composition, but there is no evidence that once the poet embarked on his mythological stories of unhappy love, he ever turned to lament his own loss.

For the literary historian the loss of the *Lyde* is one of the greatest that Greek literature has suffered. As a result of this we see Alexandrian poetry abruptly succeeding Classical poetry, for the link that joined them is lost.[34] Two of Antimachus' other works, the *Deltoi* and the *Artemis*,[35] are mere titles for us, and the authenticity of the third, the *Iachine*, is very doubtful. The significance of Antimachus for the history of Greek poetry is further proved by the bitter controversy which broke out over his work in the Alexandrian age. Callimachus condemned his prolixity and his stodginess;[36] Asclepiades and Posidippus, on the other hand, admired him greatly,[37] and we are told that he was 'on the lips of all men'.

The verse of Antimachus was poetry composed for the educated reader who was familiar with the Greek classics and could follow the poet's allusions in a diction enriched with glosses. Moreover, it seems that what mattered to him most was the inner world of the mythological heroes and its psychological analysis. Their achievements, their *res gestae*, came far behind. Naturally, love, the most powerful human emotion, was brought to the foreground, and in this he was clearly influenced by Euripides. At the same time, the verse of Antimachus was scholar's poetry, whose roots were in literature and not in life. Craftsmanship, the art of 'interpretation', variation and contamination were his major concerns, as well as the use of 'glosses', those *gemmae in carmine*, as Martial calls them. And this is confirmed by his scanty fragments, which contain a number of 'glosses', neologisms and obscure periphrases.

This 'new' poetry was not supposed to supersede or to drive out the great classics. It was intended to live beside them, offering novelty — in a sense supplementing them. A fusion of the two was, of course, impossible, within the boundaries of the Greek world. This became feasible only after Greek culture was transplanted to Rome and expressed in a foreign language which had no 'classical' literature of its own. So it is true to say that in the history of Greek literature Antimachus is a major landmark, for in his hands poetry severed its traditional classical bond with the city, with the whole community, and addressed itself to a closed circle of specialists. It was meant only for the educated few who could fully enjoy it, an approach that all learned Hellenistic poetry was later to embrace. Antimachus anticipates the scholar-poets of Alexandria by some hundred years. Moreover, he can justly be called the founder of narrative elegy, and in this he had many imitators.

Of course, a number of other epics were written in the fourth century, but names such as Dinarchus of Delos or Persinus of Ephesus tell us nothing. There were also hexameter poems on gastronomical lore, like Archestratus' *Hedypathea*,[38] or Matron's *Deipnon Attikon* (*Attic Meal*), or Philoxenus' *Deipnon*, which were not mere Homeric parodies but a challenge to use Homeric verse for various contemporary, mundane subjects.

But we can dispense with all this third-rate verse and turn, as we leave the Classical world, to the true and sad voice of a young girl, whose short *epyllion*[39] *The Distaff* — only 300 hexameter lines long — brought her recognition and fame in the Alexandrian era. This is Erinna, the poetess of the small island of Telos, near Rhodes, who probably lived at the end of the fourth century. She wrote *The Distaff* in local Doric (with a few Aeolisms) in memory of her friend Baucis, who died the day of her wedding.[40] Erinna herself died soon after, at the age of nineteen.

Remains of over fifty lines of this poem on a papyrus have been added to the few lines known from quotations; they show that in it Erinna recalled the childhood which she and Baucis had spent together and lamented her friend's death. The title of the poem probably refers to experiences of the two young girls before they parted. The delicacy and simplicity of the surviving fragments are indeed arresting.[41]

Erinna's *Distaff* has a special place in the history of Greek poetry, for it is the first example we meet of the *epyllion*, or short epic, which later became a popular poetic form from Theocritus to Ovid.[42] Its special interest lies in the absence of a mythological subject and in that strange combination of the unassuming, private, personal, autobiographical element and a diction with a Doric colour with the traditional, formal 'heroic' hexameter, a mixture whose 'novelty' commended the poems to the Alexandrians as much as its true lyrical merits. The *Distaff* can also be seen as a precursor of the 'lyrical epic', for it showed that the hexameter could assume new duties and still retain an easy flow. If the more complex lyrical metres proved beyond the capabilities of this and subsequent ages, the hexameter, employed for more than one purpose, came in to fill the gap.

Three epigrams by Erinna also survive, one dedicatory and two sepulchral, intended for Baucis' tomb. Furthermore, Pliny wrongly ascribes to her a poem[43] on the death of a cicada and a grasshopper, which is a work of Anyte of Tegea. But even if she did not initiate the epitaphs on dead animals, as was once thought—after all, these go back to the days of Simonides[44]—she appears to have been the first to compose a purely epideictic epigram on a work of art, although the name of the artist is not mentioned.[45]

The reputation of Erinna was such in the earlier Alexandrian age that she was called the 'female Homer'. She was compared with Sappho; her works were probably published by Asclepiades;[46] and her statue was set up in the Museum of Alexandria. From there it was later brought to Constantinople, where it perished in a fire.

In this highly unfruitful period in the history of ancient Greek poetry, extending from the end of the Peloponnesian War to the conquest of Asia,[47] the two notable exceptions that must be singled out are Antimachus of Colophon and Erinna of Telos.

Part Two

THE HELLENISTIC AGE

SECTION I

The Alexandrian Age (323–146 B.C.)

Introduction

At Alexander's death in June 323 B.C. Greece, united for the first time since Mycenaean days, extended her rule to the Indus in the east and from southern Russia to Egypt in the north and south. Only in the west was Greek influence contained by the power of Carthage and Rome.

But after Alexander's death his empire shrank and split, and Greece proper was no longer the only, or even the main, centre of influence and wealth. We need not go into the violent wars of Alexander's successors. It will suffice to say that with the battle of Ipsus (301 B.C.) the dream of Antigonus I to reassemble the whole of Alexander's conquests under his own rule was shattered, and that it was the battle of Corupedion (281 B.C.) that fixed the main political boundaries of the Hellenistic[1] world for the next hundred years.

From the ruins of Alexander's empire several states emerged. The Ptolemies ruled in Egypt; the Seleucids in Syria and, for a time, in Persia itself; various smaller states arose in Asia Minor. In northern Greece Macedonia remained a powerful kingdom but was not again to dominate the world; in the south the Greek city-states enjoyed varying degrees of freedom. However, Athenian hopes for political supremacy were soon shattered by Antipater, and from 317 to 307 Demetrius of Phalerum was the ruler of Athens under Macedonian protection. It is true that a shadow of her old democracy was established by Demetrius Poliorcetes, but, after a new and final resistance under Lachares, Macedonian rule was finally established there in 294 B.C.

In these years we meet with coalitions or 'leagues' among the Greek states, like the Aetolian and Achaean Confederacies, which were created in the hope of offering a united front against the interference of Macedonia; this, however, was seldom achieved, and the leagues even took to fighting one another. By the time the war of the Achaean Confederacy against the Aetolians came to an end (217 B.C.), events in the west were casting their shadow over Greece. For the last endeavour of the western Greeks to unite against Rome, which brought Pyrrhus, the king of Epirus, to Italy, had already failed in 275, and Rome was mistress of the whole of Italy and the sole rival of Carthage.

During the Second Punic War between Rome and Carthage, Philip V of Macedonia allied himself with Hannibal (215 B.C.); to counterbalance this the Romans sought the alliance of the Spartans and the Aetolians, acquiring thus a firm footing in Greece. Philip V was defeated at Cynoscephalae (197 B.C.), during the second of the three Macedonian Wars which followed, and his victor, the Roman consul Flamininus, declared Rome 'the protector of Greek freedom' at the Isthmian Games of 196 B.C.

Soon after, an important event in the east was the defeat of Antiochus III near Sipylus in 190 B.C., which enabled the small state of Pergamum to become a large power that ruled over all of Asia Minor. This, of course, was possible only because of Roman support.

The Third Macedonian War, which broke out not long after the proclamation of Greek 'freedom' by Flamininus, ended in the defeat of Philip's son, Perseus, at the battle of Pydna (168 B.C.) and the dissolution of the Macedonian empire. The Romans made Macedonia a Roman province in 148 B.C., suppressed the Achaean League in 146 B.C., and finally added Greece to their empire as a dependency of Macedonia that very year.

The year 146 B.C. is also a turning-point in the history of Greek letters. For it was then that Ptolemy VIII Physcon drove the scholars of the Museum out of Alexandria and a new period of ancient literature begins, that of the transition to Classicism.

Perhaps the most important cultural phenomenon of the Alexandrian era is that the city-state gave way to the notion of empire, a notion so severely attacked by classical theorists and tyranny-fearing democracies. The narrow limits of the classical *polis* were extended, and the *oecumene*, the inhabited world, was opened up for the Greeks to settle in and to spread their civilization.

The endeavour of Alexander to fuse Greek and Persian elements in a new cultural unit was abandoned by his successors, who, following in the footsteps of the old Macedonian kings—the tradition of Archelaus and Philip II—became the supporters and patrons of Hellenic art and culture.[2] The result of this was evident chiefly within the walls of the many newly founded large, Hellenistic cities;[3] for outside, the vast 'barbaric' populations—Egyptians, Persians, Syrians, Jews and so on—retained their own languages and cultures.

With the end of the independent city-state we also see the traditional religion of the Olympian gods deeply shaken among the Greeks. The scepticism and the doubt which, since the fifth century, had challenged all accepted religious, political and social views was now triumphant. Hellenistic man felt abandoned and alone, with royal patronage and protection as his one hope and the goddess *Tyche* (Fortuna) as the only deity in whom he came to believe.

These political and social changes had, naturally enough, a deep and lasting effect upon the Alexandrian men of letters. For, whereas Classical Greece recited, sang and discussed through the medium of the city-state, the Hellenistic men of culture withdrew from their fellow men and avoided the multitude. Poets, scholars and scientists worked as 'specialists' in their libraries and their studies, totally uninterested in public life, often feeling, in fact, a deep contempt for the *profanum vulgus*. Their works were directed at a limited public of appreciative connoisseurs; what they asked for was a powerful patron, peace and the opportunity to classify and study the new material the conquest of the East had revealed and the vast literary output of Classical Greece that was being amassed in the Hellenistic libraries and, like a *damnosa hereditas*, absorbed and oppressed their lives.

Athens, the capital of the Greek Classical world, was still a significant centre of learning and culture—after all, it was then that she gave the world New Comedy—and her major philosophical schools were in full action; but every day shrouded her deeper in the silence of a capital in decline, of a city in which the past was more significant than the present and contemplation more appropriate than action.

The real centre of the economic and the cultural life of the Greeks had shifted to Alexandria, the city founded by Alexander in 332/1 B.C. to be the capital of the universe, a role Fate denied her. However, under the Ptolemies Alexandria became the focus of economic, cultural and artistic excellence when she was chosen to be the capital of their new Egyptian kingdom. Ptolemy I, at the instigation of Demetrius of Phaleron, the peripatetic philosopher and statesman we have already met, who had taken refuge in Egypt, established in the grounds of his palace in Alexandria the Museum and the great Library, which became the true centre of learning and culture of the entire Hellenistic world.[4] This was organized on the pattern of an Athenian philosophical school and housed a band of scholars—all worshippers of the Muses—exempt from taxation and supported by a generous salary granted by the Ptolemies, who appointed a president, an Ἐπιστάτης or Ἱερεύς, as head of the institution. The office of the *Epistates* was an important one[5] (the holder was also responsible for the education of the Crown Prince), and men of great eminence held it.[6] The buildings, splendidly furnished, included a great library, a communal dining hall, an *exedra* (covered hall) for discussions and lectures, and a covered walk, a *peripatos*, with trees.

How strange state-supported scholars and poets appeared to the Greeks is evident from the spiteful lampoon by Timon of Phlius (c. 325 B.C.), which compares the Museum to a coop in which, instead of wild animals and exotic birds, for his pleasure the king feeds scholars and poets, who, by contrast with the animals, 'keep up their endless fights'.[7]

The reputation of the Museum suffered when, as already mentioned, political upheavals caused learned men, including the great Aristarchus, to flee from Alexandria in about 146 B.C.; thenceforth the city was rivalled by Pergamum and, to a lesser degree, by Athens, Antioch, Berytus and Rome.[8] Though this brought about the end of the great age of Alexandrian scholarship, the Museum survived, and Cleopatra, the last queen of the Ptolemies, is reputed to have taken part in its debates.[9] The *pax Romana* brought new prosperity to it, but it was later destroyed, probably by Zenobia, in 270 A.D. However, the Museum seems to have renewed its activities, for the *Suda* gives Theon, the father of the philosopher Hypatia (c. 400 A.D.), as its last member.[10]

The Ptolemies spared themselves no pains in concentrating in the libraries of Alexandria the vast literary inheritance of Classical Greece.[11] Thus the great Library of the Museum had amassed by the reign of Ptolemy II the huge number of 490,000 books—later the number rose to 700,000—and the daughter library of the Sarapeion, which was probably founded in the reign of Ptolemy III, had acquired 42,800.

Initially, the Ptolemies entrusted the arduous task of classifying this vast amount of literary material to three poets, because only poets could find their way about the mass of mythological and dialectal texts. Thus Zenodotus of Ephesus undertook to classify epic and lyric poetry, Alexander Aetolus tragic verse and Lycophron of Chalcis comic verse. To Callimachus later fell the hard task of preparing a catalogue of the books of the Alexandrian Library. This, known as the *Tables* (Πίνακες), filled 120 volumes and contained the name and biography of every author, a list of his works (even if not extant), the first line of every extant work and the number of verses if it were a poem. This huge enterprise—all books, from Homer to the last cookery book, were catalogued—was, of course, of unique significance in the history of Greek literature.[12]

The classification, copying and emendation of that formidable body of Classical authors not only gave birth to the new science of scholarship[13] but also influenced the course of Greek poetry. For the first Alexandrian scholars were, and considered themselves to be, primarily professional poets (literature had become a profession), and their acquaintance with that great corpus of literary material had a tremendous influence upon their art.[14] It proved an unsupportable burden—as 'classics' in any language often are—which suffocated nearly all attempts at creative originality.

At one level they were naturally spellbound by the linguistic wealth and the perfection of form Greek poetry displayed from Homer to Menander; but at another they realized that they were incapable of breaking free and creating new types of poetry, as the Ionians had created epic and the

Athenians drama. In their search for novelty the furthest they dared venture was to mix and mingle the old, clearly defined forms of poetry, which gave them the sense that they were creating and yet not shattering the spell of tradition. This resulted in poets trying their hand at a variety of poetric genres, a practice almost unknown in the Classical world,[15] and in the final disintegration of the traditional division of poetry into epic, lyric and dramatic.

The tradition of the scholar-poet, which, as we have seen, began with Antimachus of Colophon, was followed by his successors almost as a matter of course.[16] Though very little of their work survives, it appears that Philetas and Simmias and their contemporaries experimented in most of the poetical forms which the next generation of Alexandrians favoured —narrative elegy, *epyllion*, catalogue poetry, hymn, iambus, didactic poem, epigram and *paegnion*. To these, the poets of the golden age of Alexandrian poetry (c. 290–c. 240 B.C.), who continued to compose epics in the grand manner and to experiment with tragedy, added the pastoral.

In their search for novelty—the spirit of 'exploration' was characteristic of that period—the highbrow Alexandrian poets turned to scholarly and highly polished verse, which became the criterion of great art, and which for Callimachus and his followers was acceptable only if employed in poems of limited length; for them 'a long book is a great evil'. This attitude often led to an artificial and fastidious style, a delight in the use of archaic words, scholarly allusions, literary dialects and a number of intricate and varied metres known by the names of the poets who used them.[17]

It is indeed strange (and it appears incongruous) that so much of Alexandrian poetry should concentrate on the short, scholarly and highly finished poem, when in the years following the death of Alexander all other Greek art was striving to achieve superhuman effects in expressing the turbulent life of the post-Classical world; while town planners were planning their vast new cities and architects were building the majestic palaces and temples of the Hellenistic kings, while sculptors were fashioning their huge baroque marbles and bronzes and painters were at work on the gigantic pictures of Alexander's battles, the Alexandrian poets were chiselling their finely wrought verses, the *toreuton* and *kata technon* of their few lines. The delight in delicacy and brevity that permeated so much of highbrow Alexandrian poetry reached its culmination in the epigram and the *technopaegnion*, the figurative poems which portrayed on papyrus the shape of the subject they treated.

Moreover, as true religious feeling declined, the ancient gods and heroes became humanized, often reduced to mere aesthetic figures, and in poetry the traditional Pan-Hellenic myths were eschewed as having been used too often in the past and as therefore no longer exciting. Fresh, sensational episodes from mythology, and especially local myths with an aetiological content—those that gave a cause for the establishment of a cult or the foundation of a city—now became fashionable, for the object of poetry was no longer *prodesse* but *delectare*.

At the same time traditional patriotism gave way to court flattery—and often revolting court flattery, like the praises sung for the hair of Queen Stratonice, who was bald—and love, both ideal and sensual, came to assume a central position in all poetry, a development that was a Euripidean legacy and a product of the new realism and individualism which prevailed in the Hellenistic world. In fact, the portrayal of all kinds of love was astonishingly perceptive and detailed, ranging from the ideal passion of Medea for Jason in Apollonius' *Argonautica* to the seamy practices of Herodas and the homosexual love of the epigram. Later, in the days of Parthenius, this concern with love culminated in a morbid interest in unnatural passion and the realistic portrayal of erotic crime.[18] All this, together with the rest of Alexandrian pornographic literature, was transferred to Rome and continued there till the exile and death of Ovid.

Furthermore, big-city life, which was developing in the Hellenistic world, prompted a yearning for the tranquillity of country life and the lost peace of humanity, such as we find in the bucolic poets, the true precursors of the Roman *ruris amatores*.[19] This turn to the simple and the rustic brought into Alexandrian verse children, slaves,[20] animals and landscape,[21] subjects on the whole beyond the scope of Classical poetry.

But it should be stressed that in spite of their limitations and the fury of bigoted pedantry with which they waged war against their opponents, it was Callimachus and his followers who embarked on the one and only serious ancient endeavour to renew and revitalize the Greek poetic tradition, even if, as it appears, they finally did not win the day.[22] Throughout the Classical centuries no such attempt had ever been made. We cannot follow today the details of the celebrated literary battle among whose protagonists were Callimachus and his pupil Apollonius Rhodius. It is quite possible that personal and even political differences played their part in that embittered dispute which obliged Apollonius to withdraw to Rhodes.[23] In the initial stages at least the followers of both sides do not seem to have been sharply divided into those who condemned the long traditional poems and those who upheld them. For we see Asclepiades, a detractor of Callimachus, being praised by Theocritus[24] in the very work in which he also condemns the poets of long epic poems; and Posidippus, another of Callimachus' detractors, praising Mimnermus,[25] whom Callimachus, in his *Answer to the Telchines*,[26] considers a master of short, delicate verse. Moreover, Asclepiades commends Erinna in no uncertain terms for her brief and exquisite *epyllion*, *The Distaff*.[27]

In addition, it should be borne in mind that side by side with the scholarly, pedantic and aristocratic atmosphere of the Museum, the Library and the Court, which to a certain extent determined the statelier forms of Alexandrian poetry—the 'cyclic' poetry of the traditionalists and the new style championed by Callimachus—there existed the great and varied population of the capital of the Ptolemies (indeed, of every large Hellenistic city), for whose taste 'lower' literary forms were cultivated. Thus, recent discoveries of papyri have revealed the existence of a popular satiric and moralizing poetry which, in spirit at least, is quite alien to the products of the highbrow Alexandrians. Along with this we should take into account what may be called the popular, 'amusement' literature of the age, a mass of writing for which it is hard to find a comprehensive name, but which may be loosely designated 'the mime and its by-products',[28] whose farcical, humorous and frankly sensual character entertained the lower classes.

Strange as this may appear, the highbrow aristocratic and the low literary trends, no matter how firmly opposed, interacted and exercised an influence on each other; a continuous commerce of scholarly and realistic elements took place between them. In fact, the clearest connecting link between the two is to be found in such writers as Theocritus and Herodas, who handled the popular material according to the principles of Alexandrian art.

The example of the Ptolemies was followed by other Hellenistic kings, who fostered art and letters. In Pella, the Macedonian capital, Antigonus Gonatas gathered about him a circle of distinguished poets and philosophers; in Antioch Antiochus Soter built a great library which was to influence profoundly the later development of Greco–Syrian literature; and, most important of all, the Attalids in Pergamum attempted to establish a centre of learning supported by a library that would compete with the Alexandrian Museum.[29] And Alexandrian poetry not only flourished in these courts but spread along the shores of Asia Minor and some of the adjacent islands like Samos, Cos and Rhodes, penetrated into the Peloponnese and reached as far as southern Italy and Sicily.

What seems curious is that although Alexandrian poetry prospered in so many centres, and its poets were born in towns as far apart as Syracuse and Soloi or Tarentum and Naucratis, it has striking common features and a common literary atmosphere. This was due in the main to the important foundations of learning like the Museum of Alexandria and the Library of Pergamum,[30] to the expansion of the book trade and to the common curricula of the many schools of rhetoric and grammar that had spread across the Hellenistic world. But it was also the consequence of the great festivals organized by the Hellinistic kings[31] and the activity of the various professional troupes or guilds of poets, actors, singers, instrumentalists and trainers of choruses (the Σύνοδοι or Κοινὰ περὶ τὸν Διόνυσον) that were then established[32] on the pattern of the Athenian *synodos* of the third century, which, journeying from city to city, competed at the various σκηνικοί and θυμελικοὶ ἀγῶνες (competitions on the stage and in the orchestra). At the same time a great number of smaller shows (ἐπιδείξεις) were organized, in which poets and orators performed before large audiences. So there was no lack of opportunity for the new Alexandrian poetry to become known, and there was constant incentive for authors to compose new works.

It is true that the study of Alexandrian poetry is in a sense hampered by our ignorance of its true relationship to the literature of the fourth century B.C. For we know a great deal about Attic prose but very little about Attic (or indeed Greek) poetry of those years. Nevertheless, it was not till Atticism set in in the first century B.C. that the Greeks reacted against Alexandrianism and Alexandrian poetry for moral, aesthetic, anti-Eastern and pedagogical reasons. It was then that the Alexandrian poets, with very few exceptions, ceased to be copied and read and were consigned to an oblivion from which only very few things have been rescued.

But no matter how important for the history of Greek literature the poetry of the Alexandrian age may be or how interesting it is as verse, there can be little doubt that the conditions of those days tended to foster science rather than poetry. Hence the third and the second centuries B.C. were the great years of Greek natural science, medicine, mathematics and scholarship, and not of creative literature; and this to a certain extent accounts for the brevity of the golden age of Alexandrian poetry, which extended only from about 290 to 240 B.C. After that, with the exception of a few *epigonoi* (like Euphorion, Eratosthenes, Rhianus, Moschus, Bion and some epigrammatists), poetry seems to have been at a discount; and it was not till the age of Sulla, when Parthenius brought to Rome the Alexandrian theory of poetry, that Callimachus again became influential, though his teachings were then expressed in a new language and addressed to a different society, to a people gifted with qualities other than those of the Greeks.

CHAPTER 6

New Comedy

THE STRUCTURE AND PREOCCUPATIONS
OF NEW COMEDY

New Comedy made its appearance in the last quarter of the fourth century
B.C. and continued to flourish till the sixties of the third century, when
with the death of Philemon (264/3 B.C.), its true creative period came to an
end. It occupies a unique position in Hellenistic poetry, as it was born in
Athens, and Athens remained its centre throughout its life, in spite of the
fact that many of its poets were not Athenian and that the rest of Hellenis-
tic poetry strove to achieve independence from Attic poetry, which had
dominated the intellectual life of Greece for nearly two centuries.

Many were the influences that helped to create and develop New
Comedy, of which three should be singled out. First, the comic tradition,
whose roots lie with Old Comedy but which, as we saw, was greatly
transformed in the course of Middle Comedy. For it was then that the
chorus songs were suppressed and, with them, political and personal
satire; that the various recurring 'types'—men and women with a typical
significance in certain roles, evident from their names and their masks[1]—
were created; and that the comedy of manners, the realistic representa-
tion on the stage of daily life, took shape. The second influence was
tragedy, and in particular the plays of Euripides, with their love motifs,
intrigues, rapes, exposure of children and exciting recognitions, as well as
their prologues, their 'detached' chorus songs, their gnomes and, perhaps
above all, their simple and refined diction.[2] Third, Peripatetic ethics and
literary criticism were influential; for example, all that Aristotle says in his
Poetics about the types of recognition, the unity of action, the tokens or the
lysis and the *desis* of a play.

New Comedy is the domestic comedy of manners that presents
on the stage a certain social class, the *petite bourgeoisie*. Dionysiac and
supernatural elements are increasingly discarded. It is a comedy of

misunderstanding, recognition and redress, which has been rightly called the archetype and model of all modern comedy that descends through Plautus and Terence to the Renaissance, and from them to Shakespeare and Oscar Wilde.[3]

The society New Comedy presents on the stage is often disagreeable, for it is scandal that the poet relies on to liven up his plays now that political satire is no longer safe; only rarely does a stinging political remark make an appearance, giving a realistic touch to the plot. So we frequently see the rape of young girls, misunderstandings between husband and wife or between father and son, foreign officers and soldiers squandering their money in Athens, *hetaerae* and their entourage, pimps and parasites. There can be little doubt that this is not a true picture of contemporary Athenian society, for much of it, like frequent rapes, exposure of children and recognitions, is clearly due to the influence of tragedy and mythology, even if such happenings did occasionally occur. It has been rightly said that the roots of New Comedy are to be found in mythology rather than in domestic life.[4] The background of the human relations New Comedy presents consists on the whole of social problems and views which the Sophists had already examined, the very problems Euripides had presented in a mythical setting, such as the relationship of father and son, of master and slave, of rich and poor, of Greek and barbarian. Thus in a sense New Comedy, by making use of the material and plots of tragedy, became its moral and aesthetic critic.[5]

Of particular interest is the place of the gods in these plays. As with Old Comedy, the performances of New Comedy were also given at the festivals and in honour of Dionysus, but in them the power of the gods has greatly diminished. They appear like the powerless figures of Epicurean philosophy, and this explains the prominent place *Tyche* (Fortuna, the unforeseeable changes in life) has acquired in these plays. When religious reverence emerges it is not in deference to the traditional Olympian gods, but in honour of nature or the elements.[6]

Strange as it may seem, in New Comedy the plot as such is of little consequence to the poet, as can be seen from the frequent use of the same theme; there are several comedies with exactly the same plot.[7] In fact, so fixed was its technique and so abundant its composition, that the three greatest poets of New Comedy, alone, Menander, Philemon and Diphilus, are credited with some 300 plays. Originality was sought not in the plot but in accurate character drawing and mood; a deliberate effort was made to offer an artistic variation of the traditional matter employed. Against the background of the stock characters which New Comedy inherited from Middle Comedy and to which she no doubt added more—the Miser, the Flatterer, the Cunning Slave, the Cook, the Parasite, the Pimp, the *miles gloriosus*[8]—personal traits were stressed, which encouraged the substitution of the type for the individual and made it possible for New

Comedy to be enjoyed in any part of the Hellenistic world. An acquaintance with Athenian society, which Middle Comedy had presupposed, was no longer necessary.

Sharp observation of personal characteristics is, of course, required for this elevation of the individual hero from the 'type' in which he is rooted as the poet presents the trifling destinies, the loves and enmities that loom so large in the imagination of his characters. Therein also lies the fundamental difference between New Comedy and the *Characters* of Theophrastus, who converts the individual into a type. Moreover, in New Comedy it is this individuality in the character of man that is responsible for his destiny—his character is his *daemon*[9]—and it is also what distinguishes him from the animals.[10] So it is not surprising that very often it is the characters, rather than striking changes of fortune, that determine the course of the play. In fact, the word 'man' (ἄνθρωπος) acquires in New Comedy a deeper and greater significance,[11] so that the slave is regarded with broad sympathy and judged by the same criteria as the free man, and *philanthropia* (sympathy for one's fellow creatures) and friendship are greatly honoured. The main prerequisite for the plots of New Comedy is a happy ending. They strive to leave the audience with a sense that the standards of this world are sound, that once all is resolved, life is restored to peace—*tranquilla ultima*—everyone gets what he merits, and justice prevails.[12]

For New Comedy was seen primarily as an entertainment; in the late fourth century a weary city like Athens did not wish to be made to think or to be reminded of politics when it sought amusement. However, contemporary politics were not fully suppressed when they had a direct bearing on the fate of the individuals in the plays, as, for example, the tyrant Dionysius of Heraclia in Menander's *Fisherman*.

In New Comedy the division into five acts separated by a non-dramatic chorus seems to have become general. In exposition it made use of devices developed earlier in both comedy and tragedy, such as the prologue, which was also internally employed by Menander, and, of course, expository dialogue and monologue. The direct address to the audience, so important in Old Comedy, also lingers on. The change of setting from the fantasy of Old Comedy to the bourgeois reality of New Comedy resulted also in a change in the costumes of the actors, which became more like those of everyday life, and this realistic tendency was evident too in the masks, which were naturally influenced by New Comedy's stock characters.

The language of New Comedy was close to the spoken idiom of the time but always cultured and refined, carefully modulated to avoid shocking the audience. It is a forerunner of the *koine* of the Hellenistic period, which made the plays easily understood throughout the Greek-speaking world. The iambic trimeter was the basic metre employed, next to which the trochaic tetrameter comes in importance; but this metrical restraint did not impede colloquial liveliness.

It is true that in New Comedy we find nothing comparable with the lyricism of Old Comedy—it should be remembered that there are no chorus songs—or with its political fervour and verve, and that the mythological burlesque and melodrama, such as we met in Middle Comedy, did not disappear. But New Comedy expressed in a sober manner a riper wisdom and knowledge of life than either of its predecessors, and it is the universal validity of its ideas that enabled it to spread beyond Athens and to influence Western literature and thought so deeply. Not only were the plays acted for years throughout the Hellenistic world, but florilegia and collections of proverbs were drawn from them, and the Roman poets adapted them for the Roman stage, Plautus quite freely and Terence more faithfully.[13] Even Augustus on his deathbed is said to have quoted verses of Menander that summarized his whole life: 'As the play was a success, the applause gives us a friendly send-off'.[14]

It has been argued that in spite of its virtues, New Comedy ultimately portrays only a petty, narrow section of society and that the gigantic world-shattering events that took place in its day are not even suggested in its verses. This may be true, but the picture it gives of the society of that fascinating, if materialistic, age is not insignificant and certainly not tedious.

THE POETS OF NEW COMEDY

The representative triad of New Comedy canonized by ancient critics are Menander, Philemon and Diphilus. Of the other seventy or more playwrights only a few, notably Apollodorus of Carystus and Posidippus, are more than mere names to us.

Menander

Menander, the son of Diopeithes of Kephisia, a distinguished Attic citizen, was born in the year 342/1 B.C. and died, it is said, bathing in the sea in 293/2 B.C.[15] The distinguished comic poet Alexis was, as we have seen, his teacher in writing comedies (he is also said to have been Menander's uncle), and young Menander was for a time the pupil of the philosopher Theophrastus. He also served as an *ephebe* with Epicurus, but no trace of Epicurean philosophy can be found in the poet's works. Menander also had some association with Demetrius of Phalerum, which may have been a consequence of their Peripatetic interests. But the poet's relations with that fervent supporter of the anti-democratic regime of 317–307 nearly caused his ruin when Demetrius Poliorcetes captured Athens in 307 and set up a phantom of the old democracy. Menander declined the invitation of Ptolemy I to visit Egypt, and to the end of his life he was true to Athens as the metropolis of Hellenic culture. The amorous relationship which we are told he had with the courtesan Glycera is very doubtful indeed; the story was probably inspired by the name Glycera which he gave to more than one heroine in his plays.

Beginning in 321 with the *Orge*, Menander wrote more than 100 plays (105 or, according to some, 109), some of which must have been intended for country festivals, if not for foreign performances. Of these, nearly 100 titles have survived,[16] but in spite of that vast production, the poet was victorious only eight times. His fame was largely posthumous.[17] His comedies were still acted in Athens in the second century B.C., and scholars began producing commentaries on his works soon after his death. No less a man than Aristophanes of Byzantium considered Menander second only to Homer.[18] Menander was read and admired up to the end of the sixth century A.D. but not beyond it. The main reason for this is that the later schools of rhetoric and grammar did not consider Menander a model of pure Attic speech and therefore neglected him; in fact, the great Atticists, and in particular Phrynichus (he lived under Marcus Aurelius and Commodus), had waged war against him for using too many non-Attic words and forms in his plays. It is also probable that moral considerations had something to do with this neglect, for the 'concealed' treatment of love was considered more dangerous than the open obscenity of Aristophanes.

As a result, until recent times our knowledge of Menander was based only on the considerable number of quotations preserved by ancient authors—over 900, ranging from one word to sixteen lines—because of their grammatical interest or their sententious value, and on the Latin adaptations of some of his plays by Plautus and Terence. Mercifully, today, thanks to a number of papyrus finds, we are in a much more privileged position. We have one complete play, the *Dyskolos* (the *Curmudgeon*), and parts of five others large enough to permit direct literary judgements and conclusions. These are the *Epitrepontes* (the *Arbitrators*), the *Perikeiromene* (the *Cropped* or the *Shorn*, of which nearly half survives), the *Samia* (the *Woman of Samos*, which is practically complete),[19] the *Sikyonios* and the *Misoumenos*.[20] Moreover, there are smaller fragments, some of which are still significant, from the plays *Georgos*, *Heros*, *Theophoroumene*, *Kekryphalos*(?), *Kitharistes*, *Kolax*, *Koneiazomenai*, *Perinthia*, *Phasma* and *Dis Exapaton*.[21] In addition, we have fragments from two unidentified plays known as *Fabula Incerta* and *Comoedia Florentina* (which is thought to be the *Aspis*). These substantial finds of Menander's original text have made it easier for us to assess the way in which he was modified by his Latin adapters.[22] Thus Plautus' method, we now know, was free and easy, changing both the structure of the plays and the names of the agents,[23] and Terence, as we already knew, not only dispensed with the prologues but also 'contaminated' plays (that is, mixed scenes from different plays), a fact which he himself openly acknowledged (*Andr.*, 18).[24]

Of the plays we can reasonably reconstruct we shall briefly examine the *Dyskolos*, the *Samia*, the *Epitrepontes* and the *Perikeiromene*, which give us a fairly good idea of Menander's art as a playwright, for there can be little doubt that his plots and structure were repetitive to enable him to produce such a huge number of comedies in so relatively short a time.

The *Dyskolos*, the only play of Menander's which has survived complete, is an early play, so in it we do not see the poet at his best; it was produced and won the victory in 317. It is a character study and as such is closely related to Peripatetic ethics and the *Characters* of Theophrastus. In it we see the old farmer, Knemon, a confirmed misanthrope, living alone with his daughter and an old servant in the mountainous region of Phyle. Sostratos, a rich young Athenian, who has fallen in love with Knemon's daughter, tries hard to approach her father and succeeds only after the old man has accidentally fallen into a well and is saved by his stepson. This incident makes Knemon realize that he has been wrong to despise all men and to think that he can live without depending upon others. The ending is a happy one; Knemon agrees to the marriage of his daughter with Sostratos and adopts his stepson, who is to be married to Sostratos' sister. However, at the end of the play a burlesque scene is introduced unexpectedly, in which the former misanthrope is crudely ridiculed by two louts, a cook and a slave, who drag him along to join the wedding festivities with which the play concludes. This burlesque scene, quite out of place in a 'serious' play of conversion, is in iambic tetrameters and was accompanied by the flute. It is reminiscent of the closing *comos* scenes of Old Comedy; similar scenes were probably introduced by Menander at the end of the other plays, if we are to judge from Plautus' *Stichus* (an adaptation of Menander's first *Adelphoe*), in which the flute player is addressed.

The *Dyskolos* has a prologue in which Pan speaks, and no chorus songs organically connected with the plot. Between the acts, of which there are five, musical interludes or bands of revelling youths are introduced instead of chorus songs, a practice which we have already seen in Middle Comedy. Though no less than eighteen persons appear on the stage—of which at least eleven have speaking parts—this play could still be acted by only three actors and a number of mutes if necessary.

The other play of Menander's that has survived practically complete is the *Samia*,[25] which deals with a lover's intrigue and its consequences. It is a simple play, with no 'prehistory'—that is, the plot does not really start before the play begins—and only six characters, as opposed to the eighteen of the *Dyskolos*. Chrysis, a freeborn woman from Samos (the play is named *Samia* after her), is the concubine of an Athenian named Demeas, who has an adopted son, Moschion. Moschion is deeply in love with Plangon, the daughter of a neighbour, Nikeratos, who is a poor and superstitious man. When Plangon gives birth to a baby (whose father is Moschion) Chrysis, in order to help the young girl, undertakes to bring it up, pretending it is a foundling (in this part the papyrus is defective). But Demeas, returning from abroad with the intention of marrying Moschion to Plangon, accidentally finds out that his adopted son is the father of the baby and jumps to the conclusion that his concubine, Chrysis, is the mother. He drives her out of the house, and she takes refuge with Nikeratos, who somehow discovers the identity of the real mother of the child and is beside himself with rage. Finally, after various complications, all is settled and Moschion gets married to Plangon. The action in this play is fuelled by the irascibility and successive misunderstandings of the two fathers, Demeas and Nikeratos, encouraged by the fears, hesitation and eagerness of the other agents in the play. In fact, such is their irritability that Chrysis, the warm-hearted, friendly concubine, is not even allowed by either of the two old men to explain what the real situation is.

But the play in which we can see the art of Menander at its height is the *Epitrepontes*, which has survived reasonably complete and whose title is derived from one of its brilliant scenes. It is a play of the poet's full maturity in which the action, though it springs from improbable circumstances, is crisp and buoyant; character drawing is brilliant; speech is extremely decorous; and there are no burlesque scenes. It was probably produced after 304.[26] (Ancient literary criticism also observed a development in the art of the poet as he grew older.)[27]

In the *Epitrepontes* an Athenian, Charisios, has married Pamphile, the daughter of one Smikrines. Roughly five months after their marriage Charisios, who had been away from home, learns that his wife has given birth to a child and that she has abandoned it. In great distress—for he loves his wife—he ceases to live with her and tries vainly to find consolation with his friends and a girl harpist called Habrotonon, a good-natured person of loose morals.

Meanwhile, a countryman finds the abandoned child with some trinkets about it and gives it to another countryman to rear, though he wishes to retain the trinkets. To this the other objects. Smikrines, to whom the case is referred for arbitration—and from this the play takes its name—unaware that the child is his grandson, decides that the trinkets belong to the child and should be handed over with it. Then Charisios' slave, Onesimos, recognizes that one of the trinkets, a ring, belongs to his master; largely through the intervention of Habrotonon, it finally comes to light that the child is Pamphile's and that its father is Charisios, who raped her some time before their marriage, during a nocturnal festival, neither knowing who the other was in the dark. The play ends with a general reconciliation.

The premises on which the *Epitrepontes* is based are, of course, implausible, but the plot is well developed and the delineation of character excellent. The plot, with its striking changes of fortune, its prologue, its love motif, violation, exposure and recognition, is reminiscent of Euripides; but in the arbitration scene itself there is direct imitation of one of Sophocles' lost plays, the *Alope*, the legendary divine and royal personages having naturally been replaced by middle-class Athenians.

Finally, a few words must be added here about the *Perikeiromene* (the *Shorn*), a comedy of misunderstandings which was very famous in antiquity. In this play twins, Glycera and Moschion, have been separated since babyhood (the poet exploits the usual device of abandonment, discovery and adoption). Glycera, having been brought up by a poor woman, becomes the mistress of the sentimental and hot-tempered soldier Polemon who, returning from service in the army, imagines Moschion, a handsome young fool who believes that every woman is in love with him, to be her lover. In his rage Polemon cuts off Glycera's hair—a great insult in those days, and the act that gave the name to the play—and she takes refuge with Moschion's adopted mother, whose husband Pataekos, it emerges, is her real father. Finally, Glycera forgives Polemon and marries him with a sound dowry provided by her new-found father; Moschion also acquires a wife. In this play an abstraction, *Agnoia* (Ignorance or Misunderstanding) speaks the prologue, a practice which we also meet in others of Menander's plays, where *Methe* (Drunkenness) or *Orge* (Anger) perform that part. All these are Aristotelian forces which lead man to commit excusable crimes.

The preserved plays are only a small section of a very rich output and cannot therefore illustrate all the sides of Menander's art. They can, however, tell us a number of important things about it.[28] First, Menander appears a skilful maker of plots—even if he is repetitive and some are reworked versions of others—and a master of variety and surprise. Three actors and a number of mutes are all that are required for the production of his plays, for the chorus is completely separated from the action of the play; its song and dance is a mere entr'acte, indicated in our texts by a simple χοροῦ. In a few instances its appearance is announced as the entrance of a crowd of drunks.[29] In fact, in Menander's *Dyskolos* we find the last stage in the evolution of the Greek comic chorus, which later became a *comos*, a band of revellers who were not present in the course of the play but entered between the acts and at the end, having nothing to do with the plot.

Second, from the extant fragments it is evident that it is basically the characters and not the external events that determine the course of

Menander's plays. This is the keystone of his art and the greatest improvement he makes over Old Comedy, which attached no importance to the consistent development of character. In drawing his characters Menander enjoys casting conventional stock types of comedy in a new mould, even if the names used are as typical as the stock types themselves.[30] At the same time his characters, in whose delineation he makes much use of contrast, range through the whole of society; there are representatives of rich and poor, young and old, slave and freeman.

Menander attempts no profound psychological insight, and his characters are portrayed with mingled sympathy and irony, a superior but inoffensive wryness with which he observes mankind. But his world, with its love affairs, and its marriages, and its abandoned children, and its angry fathers, and its kind-hearted prostitutes, and its flatterers, and its cunning slaves, is a confined and limited world. It has no broader horizon. The great contemporary events — be they political, military, social, philosophical, literary or scientific — are passed over in silence. It is evident that he wrote to entertain a troubled age, which did not want to examine itself too closely. Moreover, he was not, and did not try to be, a hilariously funny writer. He rather wished to present ordinary bourgeois life operating under not too violent stress, and in this he was very successful. Though Menander's theatre is not committed to any special cause, as a man and as a writer he had his own ideals: the breaking down of social distinctions, the promotion of trust and understanding among all men and a belief in the divine — not the divinity of the gods of Olympus, but one which is found within man himself.[31] Of particular interest is the figure of *Tyche*, which dominates the superstitious world of Menander, a whimsical blind figure who should not be blamed for men's misfortunes yet still controls things (as in the *Commèdia Florentina*) and can lead men to happiness.[32]

For Menander, the cultured Greek was the pinnacle of humanity.[33] But he was also aware of a universal humanity that exceeded the limits of Hellenism, in which character alone, and not birth, was what mattered — a natural inclination for the good even 'the Aethiopian and the Scythian' could have.[34] This view was closely akin to one of his best-known phrases, *homo sum: humani nil a me alienum puto*,[35] but is best expressed in his famous line: ὡς χαρίεν ἄνθρωπος ἄν ἄνθρωπος ᾖ.[36] He quietly instructed his audiences that forbearance, understanding and magnanimity are the keys to happiness in life.

Menander had a great facility for writing; his diction is flowing, though it also contains a number of colloquialisms and simplifications (for example parataxis and asyndeta abound). These give life to the dialogue, for they are always in keeping with the status and mood of the speaker.[37] Occasionally, a tragic tone heightens the comic effect, but there are also actual references and allusions to tragedy.

Menander's poetry is rich in gnomes, succinctly and precisely expressed, which were later collected from his works and, with many spurious additions, included in various collections.[38] (His proverbs, which are often used with irony, show on the whole how to live without asking too much from life.) Nor should it go unmentioned that Menander's verse is masterly; his trimeters give the impression of colloquial speech, in which subtle variations of rhythm express the speaker's feelings or character. In his early plays at least he made use of the trochaic tetrameter, with its insistent rhythm, both for lively and for serious scenes.

Menander is one of the greatest figures in the entire history of poetry and one whose paramount influence on the Western theatre is felt to the present day.

Philemon

Ancient opinion ranked Philemon (c. 365–c. 264 B.C.), Damon's son, closest to Menander in New Comedy—*fortasse impar, certe aemulus*, as Apuleius puts it.[39] He came from Syracuse[40] or, according to Strabo, from Soloi of Cilicia[41] but was granted Athenian citizenship by 307/6 B.C.[42] It is probable that he was invited to visit the court of Ptolemy in Egypt and that he was shipwrecked off Cyrene on the way back. During his centagenarian life (we are told that he was in full command of his faculties to the end) he wrote ninety-seven comedies; sixty of their titles are known. He won his first victory at the Great Dionysia in 327 B.C. and at least three Lenaean victories later.

The only sources for comprehending his art are about 200 quotations from his works, Plautus' *Mercator*, *Trinummus* and probably the *Mostellaria*, for which Philemon had provided originals (the *Emporos*, *Thesauros* and possibly the *Phasma*) and a few papyrus fragments recovered in Egypt. Of these, however, none can be assigned to him with certainty.[43]

From the titles of his comedies we can see that mythological burlesque did not play a large part in Philemon's work—only two such titles can be ascertained, the *Myrmidons* and *Palamedes*—and that he also wrote plays whose central figures were known *hetaerae*, like *Neaira* or *Euripos*. Moreover, the recognition play is well represented, as his *Hypobolimaios* (modelled on Aristophanes' *Cocalus*), or the *Ring*, *Sard*, *Pterugion* and so on, show.

About the structure of his plays little can be gathered from extant evidence, but if Plautus' *Mercator* is any guide, Philemon's comedy concentrated on individual scenes and situations rather than on building a climax.[44] Furthermore, the only common element found in all three Roman imitations is a tendency towards surprise. Two more elements of his art can also be observed: first, the pronounced moralizing tendency, much of which is, of course, second-hand;[45] and second, the occasional shaping of scenes on certain patterns of tragedy.[46] From the extant fragments we can also gather that Philemon often worked out his similes at length, that he avoided obscene jokes and that occasionally contemporary references did appear.[47]

In short, Philemon's comedy was essentially a comedy of caricature that delighted in portraying the extravagant lover, the avaricious courtesan, the hungry parasite, the silly old dotard, the frightened slave, the boasting soldier. Most of this material had by his time become traditional, having already often been used in Middle Comedy, but its presentation was skilful and amusing.

And that is how antiquity regarded Philemon's work, if we are to trust Apuleius, who says that Philemon's plays contained much wit, plots neatly turned out, recognitions lucidly arranged, characters corresponding to reality, maxims agreeing with life and few seductions.[48] Philemon won many victories over Menander, though the verdict of the judges has been reversed by posterity.[49] However, his plays were revived after his death, and a statue was erected in his honour as late as the second century A.D.

Diphilus of Sinope

Diphilus of Sinope on the Black Sea was born about 360/50 B.C. He lived most of his life in Athens but died in Smyrna, probably at the beginning of the third century. He had, together with his father Dion and his brother Diodorus (who was also a writer of comedies), a tomb in Athens, of which we know the inscription.[50] The stories told about his connection with the *hetaera* Glycera are probably untrue.

Diphilus wrote about a hundred plays, winning three Lenaean victories. About sixty titles of these are known, mostly typical of New Comedy, in which the soldier, the parasite or the *hetaera* appears. Side by side with these we find titles which come from the sphere of mythology, such as the *Danaids* or *Peliads*, and others, like *Heracles*, *Theseus*, and *Hecate*, which acknowledge the identity of the speakers of the prologue, as is the case with Menander's *Heros*. Diphilus also wrote a comedy, *Sappho*—one of the six comedies we know from antiquity to have been written about her—in which, untroubled by chronology, he made Archilochus and Hipponax her lovers!

Though the extant fragments of Diphilus are few, we know something about his art from Latin adaptations. For Plautus recast the *Cleroumenos* in his *Casina*; a play of Diphilus with an unknown title (perhaps the *Pera?*) in his *Rudens*; and the *Schedia* in his *Vidularia*. It is also not impossible that the *Miles Gloriosus* was an adaptation of an original by Diphilus.[51] All four are recognition plays. Moreover, Terence informs us in his prologue to the *Adelphoe* (11) that Plautus also used Diphilus' *Synapothneskontes* in his *Commorientes*, but left a scene from the beginning of the play unused, which Terence inserted in his own comedy. He claims to have translated it word for word (ll. 155–96a). It is a rough comic scene, wittily constructed, in which a procurer abducts a girl and he himself is given a sound beating. Rough, noisy comedy is also found in the *Casina*, a play in which the father and son pursue the same girl, pretending to be her servants.

On the other hand, the *Rudens* is a play rightly admired. It does not have an original plot (the usual lovers, procurers and recognition scene are there), but the setting of the play, the strange African coast near Cyrene is extremely pleasing, as is the unmistakably Greek atmosphere—the atmosphere of the *Odyssey*, of the fisher idyll of Pseudo-Theocritus and of so many of the poems of the *Greek Anthology* that have clinging to their verses the murmur and odour of the sea. The fragments of the *Vidularia* show that it also dealt with material similar to that of the *Rudens*.

In general, we can say that Diphilus' comedy is rooted in Middle Comedy and derives from it its own delight in drinking, feasting and riddles. Spectacle and violent action play a large part in it; the dialogue is vivid and realistic, with sparing use of gnomes. From the Latin adaptations we also see that the speed of the action is of great importance to Diphilus. Of course, many of the stock characters of Middle Comedy appear in his plays, but we can also trace New Comedy themes, even if in his characterization he is inferior to Menander. It is worth bearing in mind that both Philemon and Diphilus were older than Menander, yet both were productive after his death.

Apollodorus of Carystus

This poet (c. 280 B.C.) has been confused with his older colleague and namesake, Apollodorus of Gela, who was a contemporary of Menander. This has caused a great deal of trouble in distinguishing which fragments and which titles of plays should be ascribed to each.[52] Moreover, Apollodorus of Carystus is sometimes referred to as Apollodorus 'the Athenian', which probably suggests that Athenian citizenship was granted to him, as we know it to have been granted to other poets.

Though Apollodorus of Carystus clearly obscured the memory of his earlier namesake, his own meagre fragments do not give us much to go on. He started to produce not long before 280 B.C., and he is said to have composed forty-seven dramas and to have won five victories.[53] His early play Ἑκυρά was the original of Terence's *Hecyra*, and his Ἐπιδικαζόμενος of Terence's *Phormio*.[54] These Latin adaptations indicate that Apollodorus was greatly influenced by Menander. He seems to have further developed Menander's stock characters, such as the parasite or the greedy *hetaera*, and may therefore perhaps be seen as representing a further stage in the evolution of naturalistic comedy.[55] Furthermore, one of his characteristics appears to have been a meticulously detailed approach to the organization of his plots.

Posidippus

Posidippus (c. 275 B.C.) from Kassandreia, a contemporary of Apollodorus of Carystus, was one of the few Hellenistic poets who was born in Macedonia. He won four victories at Athens from 289/8 B.C. onwards, and his success as a comic poet can also be seen from the fact that his works were performed even after his death; that he was imitated on the Roman stage;[56] and that a statue was erected in his honour, which is still extant, although the head has been reworked.[57] He also dedicated a monument in memory of his successes.[58] He is reputed to have composed thirty plays. Of these we have eighteen titles and forty-five fragments. He is alleged to have introduced slave cooks to the stage.[59]

Unfortunately, we can obtain no individual picture of the art, and hardly anything about the life, of the many other exponents of New Comedy. They remain for us mere shadows.

CHAPTER 7

Alexandrian Elegy

Alexandrian elegy has been called 'the glory of the Alexandrians',[1] but unfortunately only a few fragments have survived, so our knowledge of it is very incomplete. One of the major questions that arises is whether the Alexandrians composed elegies in which they expressed their own personal sentiments, their own amorous feelings, as they did in their short epigrams composed in elegiacs, or limited themselves to the narrative elegy which spoke of the sentiments of others, the love affairs of mythical or historical figures. The admiration which the Romans had for Philetas, Callimachus and Euphorion, as well as works like Philetas' *Bittis* or Hermesianax's *Leontion*, support the former view, but the surviving fragments show no trace of a subjective Hellenistic erotic elegy. They are all objective mythical narratives, without reference to the personal experiences of the poet.[2] However, it is not impossible that subjective Alexandrian love elegies did exist and that they later disappeared, condemned by the moralizing pedagogical views of the Atticists, who, as we know, were responsible for the suppression of entire literary genres like the Hellenistic *ethographia*.[3]

The surviving fragments indicate that, true to the spirit of its time, Alexandrian elegy chose rare or local myths for its subjects and favoured those with aetiological content. At the same time the erotic mythical element is stressed in a charming or tragic manner, and great erudition is displayed, mercifully with no didactic intent.

The structure of these poems is extremely loose; often one episode is strung next to another without any connecting link. The same loose structure is also found in the Alexandrian epic and *epyllion*, probably as a result of the influence of the Hesiodic catalogue poetry, which was greatly admired in those days. But, if the early Alexandrian elegists are loose in the structure of their works, they are strict in their metres. Their ear was sensitive to rhythm, and they honoured metrical perfection.

ALEXANDRIAN ELEGY BEFORE CALLIMACHUS

The founder of Alexandrian elegy—indeed, the founder of all highbrow Hellenistic poetry—was Philetas, son of Telephus, a native of Cos (c. 320 –c. 270 B.C.). In the history of Greek poetry Philetas occupies a significant position, for by following in the footsteps of Antimachus he firmly established the tradition of the scholar-poet in which nearly all the distinguished Alexandrians followed. The Callimachean school, the most characteristic and most influential school of poetry of the Alexandrian period, considered him a master of the short and fully finished poem in which it believed; and, as a teacher of Zenodotus, he is also seen as the founder of Alexandrian scholarship. In fact, Philetas' reputation was such that Ptolemy I invited him to undertake the education of his son, who later succeeded him as Ptolemy II Philadelphus. But Philetas did not stay in Alexandria. He returned to Cos, where he became the centre of a lively literary and scholarly circle, to which, among others, belonged Theocritus, Hermesianax and Zenodotus.[4] His grave seems to have been in his native island, where the Coans put up a statue in his honour.[5]

Philetas won lasting fame as an elegist and was included in the canon of the elegiac poets. Propertius and Ovid several times allude to him as their model, and the latter refers to one Battis or Bittis as having been sung by him. (This is also confirmed by Hermesianax, but we do not know if she was Philetas' wife or mistress, nor in what kind of verse he celebrated her charms or her loss.) Though it is unlikely that Philetas wrote subjective love elegies in the Roman manner, he could well have named a book of elegies after Bittis, following the example of Mimnermus' *Nanno* and Antimachus' *Lyde*.

Five titles of his works have survived: *Demeter, Hermes, Telephus, Epigrammata* and *Paegnia* (the last two may be alternative titles for one collection). Nevertheless, Philetas is not represented in the *Garland* of Meleager.[6]

The *Demeter* was a narrative elegy of which only twelve lines survive;[7] it recounted the goddess's wanderings and probably her visit to Cos and was admired by Callimachus. The *Hermes* was an *epyllion* in hexameters, which dealt, among other themes, with the love affair between Odysseus and the Aeolid Polymele. The emotions of Polymele formed the central subject, but Odysseus also told Aeolus of his wanderings, though not in the Homeric order. It has been unconvincingly argued that of this *epyllion* a short and disappointing fragment, fifty-four lines long, has been retrieved in papyrus.[8] About the *Telephus* all that can be said is that it included a reference to the marriage of Jason and Medea.[9]

Only a few isolated fragments of Philetas' poetry have come down to us, some of which show great delicacy; they are not enough, however, to make a judgement of his art possible. We must, therefore, rest with the admiration which great poets like Theocritus and Callimachus expressed for it and with the unequivocal approval of the Roman elegists. His influence as a teacher and pioneer is assured.

A pupil of Philetas was Hermesianax of Colophon, who was probably born in about 300 B.C. Nothing is known about his life.

His most famous work was the elegy *Leontion*, in three books.[10] It was named after the poet's mistress[11] and contained mythological and aetiological narratives, in which erudition alternated with the bucolic element, as the treatment of the Polyphemus–Galatea story suggests, as well as two other fragments dealing with bucolic love stories.[12] The second book of the *Leontion* contained the tale of Acreophon and Arsinoë, the rejected suitor and the unfeeling maiden who was punished by being turned into stone, and possibly the story of Leucippus' incest. But the longest fragment of the *Leontion* we possess comes from Book III and consists of a catalogue of fantastic love affairs. There Hermesianax, in the manner of contemporary Peripatetic biographers, speaks of the loves, unrequited or otherwise unlucky, of poets, starting with Orpheus and ending with Philetas, and of philosophers (Pythagoras, Socrates and Aristippus). It is thought that all these preposterous love stories, in which poets are presented as being in love with the heroines of their own works (for example, Homer with Penelope or Philoxenus with Galatea) or with the names of their own works (for example, Hesiod with *Ehoia*!) and philosophers with famous courtesans (for example, Socrates with Aspasia and Aristippus with Lais) served as an introduction to the narrative of the poet's own love for Leontion. However that may be, it is improbable that this was a subjective love elegy in the fashion of the Roman elegists.[13]

It is hardly credible that this type of narrative represents Alexandrian humour, as has been suggested.[14] Very rightly, it has been condemned by most modern critics as representing all the least admirable aspects of Alexandrian poetry—the fondness for 'glosses', the indulgence in unhappy love and in aetiology. Its only redeeming feature is perhaps the metrical dexterity it displays, though even there monotony sets in with the habit of ending the first half of a pentameter with an adjective and the second with the substantive which it qualifies.

We know one more title from the works of Hermesianax, the *Persica*, a poem which is thought to have contained the story of Nanis and Cyrus. Furthermore, a fragment cited from an elegy *On the Centaur Eurytion* has survived. To judge by what we have in our hands today, Hermesianax may easily be classed as the worst of the early Alexandrian poets.

An elegist greatly superior to Hermesianax is Phanocles. The place and date of his birth are unknown, but he probably also belongs to the first generation of Alexandrian poets.

Six fragments from his writings survive, which all seem to come from the same elegy, the Ἔρωτες ἢ Καλοί (*Loves* or *Beautiful Boys*). This was a catalogue poem, which dealt with the love affairs of gods like Dionysus or of heroes like Orpheus, Tantalus or Agamemnon with beautiful boys. It is possible that each episode began with a stereotype (Ἦ ὥς) in the Hesiodic manner.

The longest fragment of the Ἔρωτες describes the death of Orpheus and what followed immediately. It shows Phanocles to be an able narrative poet, whose language is simple and well-chosen and whose versification is careful, if a little monotonous; for, like Hermesianax, he tends always to place adjective and noun at the same points in his verses. In true Alexandrian manner, Phanocles is also interested in aetiology, and we even come across a rationalistic interpretation of myth in one of his fragments.[15]

Phanocles was read and admired till the end of antiquity and, with the exception of Callimachus, was very much more accomplished than his contemporary elegiac poets from whose works longer fragments have survived.

The fashion for elegies in catalogue form set by Antimachus and Philetas continued long after the days of Hermesianax and Phanocles, as can be seen from the writings of Sosicrates of Phanagoria (second century B.C.), who composed Ἠοίους (*Catalogues of Male Lovers*), or those of Nicaenetus of Abdera or Samos (early second century B.C.), who composed a Κατάλογος Γυναικῶν (*Catalogue of Women*).

Finally, we come to Alexander of Pleuron in Aetolia[16] (c. 280 B.C.), the son of Satyros, who made his name as a tragic poet and was included in the Pleiad of the Alexandrian tragedians.[17] In the eighties of the third century, as we have noted, he was entrusted by Ptolemy II Philadelphus with the preliminary sorting out (the *diorthosis*) of the tragedies collected for the Alexandrian Library. Later he appeared at the court of Antigonus Gonatas in Macedonia, where he also met Aratus, the poet of the *Phaenomena*.

Alexander, like most of his contemporaries, tried his hand at various kinds of poetry. Besides tragedies — of which only one title, the *Astragalistae* (the *Dice Players*), has survived — he also wrote elegies, *epyllia* like the *Halieus* (*Fisherman*) and the *Circa*, from each of which a fragment survives, epigrams, Ionic poems[18] in imitation of Sotades and the *Phaenomena*, possibly an astronomical poem. We also have from his pen a striking appreciation of Euripides in anapaestic tetrameters.[19]

Two titles and a few fragments of his elegies have reached us. The first is the *Apollo*, which was a collection of unhappy love stories in the form of a series of prophecies uttered by Apollo himself;[20] and the second was the *Muses*, which contained literary history. From the *Apollo* thirty-four lines survive,[21] dealing with the story of Antheus and Cleoboea. The language is burdened with erudition and the style extremely dry, barely brought to life by the short introductory monologue. Narratives in the form of prophecies have, of course, a long history in Greek literature, going back to no less a man than Aeschylus;[22] but this device became fashionable in the Alexandrian era,[23] and was later taken over by the Romans.

The elegies of Alexander, which at their best are second-rate poetry, bring us to the very heart of the Alexandrian elegy, to Callimachus, a key figure in the history of Greek poetry.

CALLIMACHUS THE CYRENIAN

Callimachus (c. 305–c. 240 B.C.), son of Battus, was born in Cyrene. Early in life he migrated to Alexandria and became a schoolmaster in its suburb Eleusis. Later he was given employment at the Alexandrian Library and, as we have seen, produced a monumental catalogue of its books in 120 volumes, which has been called the first scientific literary history. We now know that he never became *Prostates* (Director) of the Alexandrian Library.

Callimachus, like many early Alexandrian men of letters, was not only a poet but also a scholar. He is described as a pupil of Hermocrates of Iasos, and later he himself had a number of distinguished pupils, among whom were Apollonius Rhodius, Eratosthenes of Cyrene and Aristophanes of Byzantium. He is undoubtedly the most significant and the most fascinating among the Alexandrian scholar-poets.

The longest and most famous of Callimachus' poems was the *Aetia* (*Causes*), a narrative elegy of roughly 7000 lines in four books. It contained a series of aetiological legends connected with Greek history, customs and rites. The length of the *aetia* varied, and the poem was not an *aeisma dienekes*, with one single plot from beginning to end. The extant fragments indicate that in the first two books (about which we are, in general, less well-informed) Callimachus conversed with the Muses, but that in Books III and IV the various stories were not connected by a fictitious dialogue or in any other way.

Though a considerable number of fragments from the *Aetia* have been retrieved in papyri, it is impossible to reconstruct, even in outline, the course of the narrative.[24] We know, however, from an epigram of the Imperial age,[25] that the poet imagined himself carried in a dream from Libya to Mount Helicon, where the Muses instructed him in all manner of legendary lore. This makes Callimachus' *Aetia* the first known poem of the dream or vision genre, which holds such an important position in the literature of the Middle Ages.[26] At the same time the concentration and arrangement of religious and historical material into the form of *aetia*, and

the development itself of that literary genre, seem to have been Calli-
machus' creations.

In the *Aetia* Callimachus mingled with strictly aetiological stories, like
those of Acontius and Cydippe,[27] Acus,[28] or the Sicilian cities,[29] a number
of entertaining digressions about all kinds of *thaumasia*, strange and
wonderful things, which he had gleaned from obscure sources, from city
chroniclers, geographers and mythographers, and even from friends.[30]
This heterogeneous material,[31] whose origin was always mentioned — the
poet prided himself on the fact that he included only material whose
authenticity could be proved (*ouden amartyron aeido*) — was presented in a
lively and varied manner, so that the *Aetia* did not degenerate into a
tedious handbook of rare myths and traditions.

It appears that Callimachus published a second revised edition of the
Aetia, which was included in his collected works. As a general introduction
to these, and perhaps as a special introduction to the *Aetia*, he composed
the *Answer to the Telchines*, a polemical retort directed at his critics, in which
he expounded his final and most controversial views on poetry. For the
literary critics of Callimachus were many and persistent, including such
well-known names as Asclepiades and Posidippus, and these the poet
counter-attacked vigorously till the end of his life.

As the last *aetion* in the revised edition we find the *Plokamos*, the one
poem of Callimachus which can be definitely dated, for it deals with
events of 246/5 B.C., and which is also known from Catullus' adaptation.[32]
This was followed by the epilogue of the *Aetia*, in which, as in the initial
dream, reference is made to the poetry of Hesiod.

The quarrel between Callimachus and his pupil Apollonius (later
known as Apollonius Rhodius), an important episode in the bitter Alex-
andrian literary controversy between the writers of long, traditional epics
and those of short and very polished poems, is also connected with the
Aetia. For the freedom with which Apollonius refashioned in his own style
whole passages of Callimachean poetry, including passages of the *Aetia*,
suggests the conversion of a question of poetic theory into a personal feud.[33]
Callimachus was victorious and Apollonius retired, defeated, to Rhodes,[34]
but it appears that in the long run it was the long epic that won the day.[35]
However, tradition records a reconciliation between Callimachus and
Apollonius and claims that they were buried close to each other.[36]

It was during this dispute that Callimachus wrote the *Ibis*, a deliber-
ately obscure poem, in mockery of Apollonius — the ibis is an Egyptian
bird that revels in rubbish — which is now lost and which gave Ovid his
idea for a poem of the same name.[37]

In the final edition of Callimachus' works the *Aetia* were followed by the
Iambi, a book of iambic poems of approximately 1000 lines. The thirteen
poems included in this book are miscellaneous in content and character,
and the metres the poet employs predominantly are the *scazon* and the

iambic trimeter; but some pieces are in epodic form, and there are other experiments.

In iambs I–III and V Callimachus satirizes contemporary literary attitudes and morals. In IV and XIII he deals with his literary critics; VI describes, in astonishing detail, Phidias' statue of Zeus at Olympia for an intending tourist—it has been called a 'Baedeker in verse'; VII–XI are modelled more closely on the *Aetia*; XII celebrates the birth of a daughter to a friend Leon. A veritable *lanx satura*, the *Iambi* must have influenced Roman satire.

Several of the iambs seem to refer to Callimachus' earlier life in Alexandria, before he reached a commanding position. If that is so, then the first, which contains personification and parable (for he identifies himself with Hipponax), and certainly the last are later additions to the earlier occasional poems. At the end of the iambic poems we find a polemical epilogue corresponding to the prologue of the *Aetia*.

Very little has survived of Callimachus' lyrics, but enough to prove his skilful use of a variety of lyrical metres; his galliambics probably served as a model for Catullus and Varro. The most interesting fragments come from the *Ektheosis Arsinoës* (the *Deification of Arsinoë*), a poem in archebuleans, which dealt with the death—which, according to our calender, took place on 9 July 270 B.C.—and the deification of Arsinoë II, the wife of Ptolemy II Philadelphus. Callimachus maintained, as we know from the *Diegeseis*, that the queen was snatched away by the Dioscuri, and later also spoke about the altar and the holy enclosure which were established in her honour. The surviving fragments of the *Ektheosis Arsinoës* show the original and unconventional nature of the poem and Callimachus as a court poet at his best, for there is elegance, dignity and feeling in his poetry which outweigh the inevitable servile flattery.

As we have already seen, epic on the grand scale was avoided on principle by Callimachus. Instead, and in answer to his critics, he composed the *Hecale*, the most famous *epyllion*[38] in Greek literature and a kind of manifesto of Callimachus' views on poetry. The details of the narrative cannot be reconstructed, but we know that it described, in about 1000 perfectly finished hexameters, the victory of Theseus over the bull of Marathon. In true Alexandrian manner, the emphasis was laid not on the great heroic deed of Theseus but on the noble poverty of Hecale, the old woman who offers the hero hospitality in her humble hut when, on his way to Marathon, he is caught in a storm. The scene of the rustic meal in particular was greatly admired and copied.[39] The *Hecale*, which also contains a remarkable scene in which birds are the speakers, was one more aetiological poem explaining the name and cult of the Attic deme Hecale. For, as Theseus is returning victorious from Marathon to Athens, he finds that Hecale has died suddenly, and in her honour he establishes the *Hecalesia*, a yearly sacrifice to Zeus.[40]

A small number of fragments from the minor epic and elegiac poems of Callimachus have also survived. Of these the most interesting come from the *Sosibiou Nike* (the *Victory of Sosibius*), a poem celebrating the Isthmian victory of Sosibius, a minister of Ptolemy IV. It is a fascinating and characteristically Alexandrian effort to revive in elegiacs the Pindaric epinician ode, which naturally resulted in the lowering of the lyric tone.[41]

The only complete works of Callimachus which have come down to us—and the only ones transmitted in medieval manuscripts—are his hymns and his epigrams. The hymns, six in number, are addressed to Zeus (I), Apollo (II), Artemis (III), Delos (IV), Athene of Argos (V) and Demeter (VI); they cannot be dated precisely. With Callimachus the hymn passes from cult to literature,[42] for all his surviving hymns are literary pieces intended for reading or for recitation to a select audience, so it is not surprising that in some of them political propaganda appears (I, II and IV). Nonetheless, in several fine passages they convey a genuine sense of mystery and of the power of the divine.

Five of the Callimachean hymns are in hexameters and one (V) in elegiacs; variety in diction is also sought, for hymns I–IV are in the epic dialect, whereas V and VI are in Doric. But their greatest variety is in their style. Hymn I (*On Zeus*) reads at times like a humorous report on a learned controversy, whereas hymn III (*On Artemis*) approximates an *epyllion*, from which too the humorous element is not absent. Hymn IV (*On Delos*) is the longest of the six and blends the traditional with the topical as it strives to compete with the Homeric hymn to Delian Apollo. Court flattery has its place here again, taking the strange form of Apollo's speech *ex utero*, in which he dissuades wandering Leto from resting on Cos, for there a future god, Philadelphus, will be born. The god also prophesies the defeat of the Gauls at Delphi (279 B.C.), no doubt a *vaticinium post eventum*. But Callimachus' greatest originality is evident in hymns II (*On Apollo*), V (*On the Bath of Pallas*), and VI (*On Demeter*), where, through a combination of dramatic mime and lyric, the poet brings to life the spectacle itself and the emotions of the spectators. In hymn II the personality of the poet is to the fore throughout, stating that his poetry is spare, pure, undefiled and under Apollo's protection. In V, which contains some of Callimachus' finest verse, the poet identifies Athene with her image, so that the goddess's epiphany, and not the ceremonial ablution which gives the poem its name, is the real theme. In VI, which also contains some of the best Callimachean lines, the 'holy story' is presented in grotesquely gruesome terms; these, however, do not impair the epic element that runs through the poem.

In all six Callimachean hymns there are passages that reveal remarkable poetic intensity; it must be admitted, however, that the passages of great beauty are not sustained for long.

Of Callimachus' epigrams[43] some sixty survive, in which we can see much of the Alexandrian world passing before our eyes: its lovers, its soldiers, its carefree youths drinking at their *symposia*, its haughty queens, its old devoted nurses, its mourning parents and husbands. Callimachus displays variety not only in the subjects of his epigrams but also in their style. Perhaps more interesting than his dedications and epitaphs— though some of the latter are superb—are the occasional pieces prompted by the poet's own experiences and emotions, especially during his early manhood.

Of Callimachus' tragedies, comedies and satirical plays mentioned by the *Suda* nothing survives.[44]

Callimachus is a milestone in the history of Greek poetry, for, as already mentioned, his work represents the only serious attempt at the renewal of the Greek poetic tradition from the end of the Classical era to the early Christian centuries. Following in the footsteps of Ion of Chios, he became an exponent of *polyeidia*, variety in writing; for he tried his hand at many kinds of poetry, fused a number of formerly distinct poetic elements and rehandled much older material. The language of Callimachus is on the whole pure and his style concise. But he also employs many rare, colourful and conversational elements, even if the classical and especially the Homeric usages always shine through them.

In the sphere of metrics Callimachus is a master. The polish and finish of his verses are indeed impressive. Novelty and refinement he seeks in the stricter structure of the hexameter, which he achieves through caesurae and diaeresis, and in the use of lyrical as *kata stichon* metres. Nor should the casting of traditional hexameter hymns and epinician odes into elegiacs go unmentioned.

In his choice of subjects Callimachus followed the 'untrodden path', preferring the rarer versions of the Pan-Hellenic myths or obscure stories he found buried in local chronicles, and local historians. He did not even omit strange tales conveyed to him by word of mouth. The scholarly and antiquarian element which runs through much of his poetry, and which clearly adds a certain frigidity to his verse, is often relieved by personal, realistic and even humorous touches that do not allow his major works to degenerate into arid selections of obscure mythology and antiquarian quest; in fact, there are even passages of superb comic realism, as hymn VI shows.

But perhaps above all Callimachus prized the short and fully finished poem, in which every line was a masterpiece. According to his principles, a poetic theme could not be single and continuous unless it was short. But in his longer works, like the *Aetia* or the *Hecale*, the structure does not seem to have been carefully worked out, nor does it appear to be balanced. Traditional heroic scenes are dealt with too briefly, whereas ordinary day-to-day contents are unduly prolonged; moreover, there are many digressions, and independent scenes are often strung together with hardly any connecting links. However, the rapid changes of thought and subject, the asides, the allusions, the digressions, often humorous or sardonic, combine to bring before the reader the strange and complicated personality of the poet.

In Callimachus the gods are no longer taken seriously, even if in his hymns we find passages with a strange mystic feeling; however, nothing is ever said about them that is irreverent or in poor taste. On the other hand, the Ptolemies, whether deified or not, are treated with the utmost respect, and court flattery, though not of a distasteful nature, often appears in his poetry, a practice understandable in an age when all art was at the service of the king.

Callimachus is no original thinker—true philosophical thought is absent from his verse—nor is his strange sense of humour on the whole pleasing, for it is rarely witty, too often burlesque and occasionally even gruesome. But he is capable of true friendship; he shows sensitivity towards children (especially in his epitaphs) and to the beauty of boys and young men (all his erotic poetry is homosexual). But perhaps the trait of his character that emerges most clearly from his poetry is the capacity for violent rage and hatred, which is best seen in his celebrated answer to his critics, the *Telchines*, in the introduction to his collected works.

It has been said that in Callimachus geography and local mythology play the role that imagery, metaphor and simile play in the verse of other poets; that the world he portrays is intellectually restricted and does not reflect contemporary society or its politics. To a certain extent, these accusations by modern *Telchines* are just. Nonetheless, no matter what his defects, Callimachus is a major poet and one of great originality and extraordinary refinement. And that is why, before the reign of Philadelphus was a decade old, he had become a dominant figure in the Alexandrian literary world. Indeed, his fame and popularity spread so widely that in late antiquity it exceeded that of every other Hellenistic poet. This can be seen from the vast number of Callimachean papyri— even more than those of Euripides—and the many quotations found in grammarians, metricians, lexicographers and scholiasts. Only Homer is more frequently quoted. Callimachus impressed the Hellenistic world to the point of being included in the Alexandrian canon of elegiac poets, and later he was considered the father of the Roman innovators, the *poetae novi*. It is good that from an epigram composed by himself for his own tomb we can see how he would have wished posterity to remember him:

> This is the tomb of the son of Battus.
> He knew how to write great poetry
> And to be full of fun
> When wine was handed around.

Callimachus influenced his pupils greatly, and among them Philostephanus, who, following in his teacher's footsteps, wrote *paradoxa* in elegiacs.[45] Alongside him should be mentioned Archelaus of Chersonesus, who is the main surviving representative of the verse paradoxographers of the period.[46] He is said to have explained *paradoxa* to Ptolemy (probably Ptolemy I) in epigrams. Those that have survived are concerned with the creation of life from the decayed bodies of animals. Ptolemy himself wrote poetry in elegiacs, which is thought to have been in answer to Archelaus.[47] In addition, Callimachus' own nephew, Callimachus the Younger, deserves mention.

ALEXANDRIAN ELEGY AFTER CALLIMACHUS

The first bloom of Alexandrian elegy lasted roughly fifty years. After Callimachus the most noteworthy elegiac poet is Eratosthenes of Cyrene (c. 275–c. 194 B.C.), who succeeded Apollonius Rhodius as *Prostates*, Director of the Alexandrian Library.

Eratosthenes was a distinguished mathematician, astronomer, geographer, historian, critic, scholar and poet and was the first to call himself *philologos*. Among the Alexandrian specialists he was known as *beta*, which means 'next after the best specialist in each subject', and *pentathlos*, 'all-rounder', his best work being in geography. In fact, he was the first systematic geographer; his *Geographica*, in three books, sketched the history of the subject and dealt with physical, mathematical and ethnographical geography.

His most famous poem was the elegy *Erigone*, which, according to the author of *On the Sublime*,[48] was 'a short poem, blameless in every respect'. It treated of the story of Icarius and his daughter, in which the protagonists were metamorphosed into constellations—Icarius into the constellation of Boötes, his daughter into the Virgin, his faithful dog into Sirius and his wagon into the Wain. As recent research has shown,[49] this *epyllion* cast in elegiacs gave the *aetia* of the Attic Dionysus festivals and explained the origins of tragedy and comedy. The view that the *Erigone* was also influenced by the Osiris myth,[50] which has many elements in common with the story of Icarius, is not convincing.

Eratosthenes also wrote an *epyllion*, *Hermes*, in which he seems to have aimed at combining mythology with didactic poetry in a manner possibly consistent with his theory that 'poetry aims at delighting, not teaching the reader'. There the birth of the god was described, as well as the exploits of his youth and his ascent to the planets. Eratosthenes also composed a short epic, *Anterinys* or *Hesiod*, dealing with the death of Hesiod and the punishment of his murderers.

The few surviving fragments from the poems of Eratosthenes do not suffice to make a judgement of his art possible; they indicate, however, that an element of erudition must have been prevalent. Of his literary investigations, those in the field of Old Comedy were the most important.

The last elegiac poet of some distinction in the period under consideration was Nicander of Colophon (second century B.C.), known from his two surviving didactic poems.[51] His best-known elegiac work was entitled *Heterioumena* (*Metamorphoses*), of which nothing survives. (The work was used by Antoninus Liberalis and Ovid.)

So short-lived was the first florescence of Alexandrian elegy that we have to pass on to the next period (146 B.C.–A.D. 100) before we find another elegiac poet of note, Parthenius of Nicaea (first century B.C.), the last 'classic' poet of Hellenistic elegy, according to Pollianus, who was an epigrammatist of the Empire.[52]

CHAPTER 8

The Alexandrian Epic

THE *EPYLLION*

The grandeur of Attic tragedy had overshadowed the fifth- and fourth-century epic. Neither the *Heracleia* of Panyasis, nor the *Persica* of Choerilus of Samos, nor even the *Thebaid* of Antimachus of Colophon could hold their own against the literary trends of their day—and, of course, least of all the inferior poetry of Choerilus of Iasos, who was paid by Alexander the Great to celebrate as a 'new Homer' the 'new Achilles'. Nor were the mythological and genealogical works in the Hesiodic tradition—the late 'Catalogues of Heroines', which continued to be composed in the fifth century—any more impressive.[1] However, it has been convincingly argued[2] that in spite of the decline of the epic in the fifth and the fourth centuries, in the third the prevailing taste was still for long mythological epics with traditional themes, for encomia of tribes and cities and for long panegyrics on reigning monarchs, all of which are now lost, except for the *Argonautica* of Apollonius Rhodius and a few odd lines.[3]

Nevertheless, though no inspired poet appeared able to fashion Hellenistic history into a great epic, it is certain that the historical held much interest for the Alexandrians, and in their search for new poetic material they combined something of the old mythology with the history (or pseudo-history) of their own age. It is against this unscientific approach that Callimachus no doubt so rigorously reacted when he wrote his οὐδὲν ἀμάρτυρον ἀείδω. Moreover, he challenged equally the great heroic epic in the style of the cyclic poets, modernized in the spirit of Antimachus, maintaining that any such attempt would be rendered nugatory when compared with the *Iliad* and the *Odyssey*, as Theocritus so succinctly puts it (Idyll VII, 45ff.). Callimachus and his school revered Homer and Hesiod, and they were greatly, if indirectly, influenced by them; nearly all their contemporaries shared the same views. They felt deep contempt for the cyclic poems and the poetry of Antimachus. It was only later that Parthenius dared call the *Iliad* 'muck' and the *Odyssey* 'mud'.

The profound admiration of Callimachus and his Alexandrian followers for Homer, whom they considered incomparable and unapproachable, made them turn to other models, to the *epyllion*, the short, fully finished hexameter narrative (at which Erinna and Philetas had already tried their hands, the former in her much-praised *Distaff*, having dealt, it appears, with a more intimate theme than those of Philetas' *epyllia*). In this new kind of epic they believed that the length should be limited, that a perfect mastery of language and metre should be achieved and that the subject-matter should not be drawn from the widely known Pan-Hellenic myths, which had been dealt with innumerable times. At most, a few incidents from the life of an epic hero could be taken from the myths, which should be strung one after the other with weak connecting links (perhaps none at all), just as we saw in elegy, and in which the heroes of the past should be humanized and presented in an ordinary, 'unheroic' setting that would secure the response of the Alexandrian reader.[4] In style the *epyllion* varied. It was either entirely narrative or decorated with descriptive passages of a realistic nature; and realism led to the lightening of the epic style. The dramatic form was also frequently employed. One characteristic that distinguished the *epyllion* from all other types of poetry was the digression, a second story contained within the first and often quite unconnected with it in subject. (The digression apparently was often as important as the main subject.)

As a model of this new epic style, and as an answer to his critics, Callimachus composed the short epic *Hecale*, about which we have already spoken.[5] This was greatly admired by his contemporaries and his successors, who believed it to be a real masterpiece of language, technique and composition. Crinagoras, the epigrammatist in the Augustan period (to mention only one example), calls it 'a work delicately executed, for which the poet summoned all the Muses' power'.[6] The *Hecale* is unfortunately lost, except for some scanty fragments; but a few unmutilated examples of the Alexandrian *epyllion*, which deal with strictly defined and elaborately treated episodes from the heroic world, have mercifully survived. They give us some idea of that literary form which became a favourite among the Hellenistic poets, though it should be borne in mind that the Alexandrians never insisted upon rigid rules of composition to which the *epyllion* should conform. Each poet enjoyed complete liberty of action.

Although the battle between the followers of the long, traditional epic and the short, highly finished 'Callimachean' *epyllion* was protracted and bitter, and although Callimachus is said to have been victorious over Apollonius, it appears that the epic and not the *epyllion* won the day.[7] And this holds good not only for the Greek-speaking east but also for Rome. For the triumph was there speedy and complete after Virgil's *Aeneid*, which showed that long epics were both feasible and desirable. *Epyllia*, which from Catullus to Ovid had become fashionable, ceased to be composed. In fact, we have only one post-Virgilian *epyllion* (if the *Culex* is not to be considered such): the *Andromeda* at the end of the fourth book of Manilius' *Astronomica*.

Now that we know that Theocritus' *Heraclescus* is not a pure *epyllion* but a hymn, no matter how many elements of the *epyllion* it may have contained, we must turn to the only important surviving *epyllion* of the third century B.C., *Heracles the Lion Killer* which has been attributed to Theocritus. There can be little doubt, however, that it is not a genuine work of the great Syracusan poet. It consists of 281 hexameters and falls into three loosely connected parts dealing with the visit of Heracles to King Augeas, for whom he performed the well-known labour. The three sections of the poem are, in fact, so loosely related that the situation may be understood only by reference to their subtitles (of which we know only two, 'Heracles to the Peasant' and 'The Visitation'; the third subtitle is, unfortunately, missing) — a technique which has been compared to that of the modern cinema.

The first part, starting *ex abrupto*, consists of a dialogue of the hero with an old peasant, who describes Augeas' domains and offers to lead him to the king. Its charm resides mainly in the description of the rural surroundings (the reason, no doubt, why the whole poem was later attributed to Theocritus). The second section describes the vast herds of the king as they move to their stables at sunset and the victory of Heracles over a powerful bull that attacks him, attracted by the lion skin worn by the hero. The third shows Heracles on his way to the city in the company of Augeas' son Phyleus, during which the hero relates his victory over the Nemean lion, finally won by the strength of his hands and his club. This narrative also constitutes the usual 'digression' we find in the Alexandrian *epyllion*.

The loose structure of the poem is striking and characteristic, for it is neither unfinished nor mutilated. The unknown but able poet chose only certain scenes from a day in the life of Heracles and then referred indirectly to the famous events of the Heraclean saga. Thus the author demonstrated that a new and exciting poem could be made with material drawn even from the most generally familiar mythological cycles, provided the presentation was 'modern' and 'unheroic'. With this technique, however, plot and character drawing are completely suppressed.

And it is true that even in the circle of the well-known Pan-Hellenic myths material could be found for *epyllia*, as long as the treatment was 'modern' and the form 'refined'. This can also be seen from the surviving fragment of another anonymous *epyllion*, the *Diomedes*,[8] whose poet even ventured to borrow from the cyclic poem *Alcamaeonis*, in spite of the fact that the cyclic poets were 'proscribed and banished'. We can see that this fine *epyllion* dealt with the battles of Diomedes before the Trojan War, but the rustic hut of his faithful servant Pheidon occupies no little space in it, and there is some discussion about breeds of dogs. Once again, the chief interest appears to lie in the description of the surroundings and not in the heroic deeds of Diomedes.

A number of insignificant fragments from several other Alexandrian *epyllia* have survived in which other mythological figures appear,[9] but we cannot tell how they were treated.

Unfortunately, we possess nothing substantial of the older Alexandrian *epyllia* which dealt with erotic material; but from titles and surviving scraps it is clear that they concerned themselves with extraordinary love stories and that they indulged in detailed psychological description.[10]

After Callimachus the most celebrated and most prolific poet of *epyllia* was Euphorion of Chalcis 276/5 B.C.—but that date has been challenged as being too early). As a young man he had a lucrative liaison with the old widow of Alexander, ruler of Euboea and Corinth, and then spent some time studying philosophy in Athens, of which he also became a citizen. He was later appointed librarian by Antiochus the Great (223–187 B.C.) at Antioch on the Orontes and was buried there (or, according to another tradition, at Apamea). Archebulus of Thera is reputed to have been his teacher of poetry.

Euphorion wrote both verse and prose works.[11] In verse, apart from epigrams, some of which have survived,[12] his predilection seems to have been for *epyllia*—he wrote at least six—and composite catalogue epics on mythological subjects.

Of Euphorion's numerous poetic works, one, the *Chiliades*, attacked those who had defrauded him of money and guaranteed their eventual punishment by citing a list of prophecies to be fulfilled after long years. Similar in content was another poem, the *Curse* or the *Cup Thief*, in which he threatens with a catalogue of mythical punishments the thief who has stolen a cup from him.[13] There can be little doubt that the model for both these was the *Ibis* of Callimachus, whose style he slavishly imitated. We also hear of a poem by Euphorion called *Mopsopia*, an old name for Attica, or *Atakta* (*Miscellanea*), which consisted of a collection of Attic legends, and of a poetic epistle by the name of *Replies (Antigraphai) to Theodoridas*. The attribution to him of love elegies in the Roman fashion is based on a misunderstanding.

The poetry of Euphorion was proverbially obscure; this was due to the studied use of rare mythological references and affected language. He drew his subjects from the Trojan Cycle, from local legends of a gruesome nature or from aetiological and geographical topics. His vocabulary was basically Homeric—although he called Homer 'the untouchable'—but with a frequent use of 'glosses', words which had fallen into disuse, misunderstandings of Homeric words and ambiguous truncated words; nor were childish etymologies absent. His narrative technique consisted of undue amplification of detail and vain repetitions leading up to a summary treatment of the climax.[14] Moreover, his sentiment was mawkish.[15] The recent papyrus finds have not improved our estimate of Euphorion, who is shown to be a crude plagiarist of Callimachus and Apollonius Rhodius.[16] Nevertheless, Lycophron's *Alexandra* appears to be his debtor, and he exercised considerable influence upon later Greek poets like Nicander, Parthenius and Nonnus. His mannerisms were also imitated by the generation of Catullus in Rome—hence Cicero calls those poets *cantatores Euphorionis*[17]—and even Virgil was indebted to him for his subject-matter, as Servius indicates.

However, the mannerisms of Euphorion do not seem to have influenced all the later Alexandrians, as can be seen from the work of Moschus (c. 150 B.C.), the bucolic poet who was second in significance in the Hellenistic world.[18] He was Syracusan by birth but lived in Alexandria and is reputed to have been a pupil of Aristarchus.[19] His most important work is the *epyllion Europa*,[20] in which he gracefully and playfully describes the rape of Europa by Zeus. The poem is mutilated (166 hexameters have survived) and opens with a dream of Europa that is clearly influenced by the dream of Atossa in Aeschylus' *Persians*. The disproportionate space given to the description of Europa's flower basket is fully in the Alexandrian manner, for lengthy ecphrasis (description in verse of a work of art) of this kind—harking back to the description of Achilles' shield in the *Iliad*—was a usual feature of the Alexandrian *epyllion*. Typically Alexandrian too is the brilliant picture of Zeus, transformed into a bull, pursuing his bridal journey over the sea among Tritons blowing their shells and sea nymphs riding fantastic sea creatures. Nor is the hint of perversity in the tenderness of the maiden for the handsome bull less Hellenistic, nor are realistic plastic details such as Europa's grasping the bull's horn with one hand and lifting the fold of her garment with the other so that it will not be drenched by the waves. However, the end of their journey and the consummation of the nuptials are narrated briefly, and then the poem breaks off.

Moschus' *Europa* has little depth or originality, for there is no complexity of structure and no character drawing. It is a succession of pictures, not a single scene, with one digression, the description of Europa's basket. But its graceful—though occasionally too saccharine—verses are attractive and show that the *epyllion* survived as a living literary genre well into the second century B.C.; we also know that it was used by Ovid and that the rape of Europa, which became popular as a consequence of the popularity of Moschus' *epyllion*, influenced art down to the painting by Veronese in the Palace of the Doges in Venice.

Besides the *Europa*, three extracts of *bucolica* attributed to Moschus have been preserved by Stobaeus. The first draws the contrast between the delights of the countryman and the hard life of the fisherman, whereas the two others are erotic *paegnia* having little connection with bucolic verse.

The view has been put forward that the three pieces are not extracts of longer works but long, complete epigrams in hexameters. Similar in kind are two other poems of his which have survived, the *Runaway Love* in twenty-nine hexameters[21] and an epigram on Eros as ploughman.[22] In some sources Moschus is also credited, though clearly wrongly, with two more poems, the *Lament for Bion* and the *Megara*.[23]

Though we have no surviving examples, it appears that *epyllia* continued to be composed until the Augustan age. To some extent we can reconstruct what the genre must have been like in later Hellenistic times from the *Love Romances* of Parthenius,[24] the pseudo-Virgilian *Ciris* and Ovid's *Metamorphoses*. What emerges is *epyllia* in which unhappy love stories are prominent, sensational descriptions and scenes of horror abound and the study of morbid psychology is prevalent. We can gather that vice was usually punished and virtue rewarded, but the moral tone on the whole was low.[25]

THE LONG ALEXANDRIAN EPIC

Apollonius Rhodius

We must now return to the early third century to examine Apollonius Rhodius, the most important representative of the long epic in the Alexandrian world. He was born in Alexandria in about 295 B.C. or, less probably, in Naucratis, but he is generally called 'the Rhodian' because of his retirement to Rhodes.

Apollonius was not only a poet but also a distinguished scholar, who held the post of *Prostates* of the Alexandrian Library after Eratosthenes and was appointed tutor of Euergetes, later Ptolemy III. In his youth he was a pupil of Callimachus', as we have seen, and the quarrel between the two distinguished poets appears to have driven Apollonius into retirement on Rhodes.[26] However, as already noted, tradition claims that teacher and pupil were eventually reconciled and that they were buried close to one another.[27]

Apollonius was much more significant as a poet than as a scholar.[28] The titles of a number of his poems are known, treating mainly of legends connected with the founding (κτίσεις) of cities (of Alexandria, Naucratis, Caunus, Cnidus, Rhodes and possibly Lesbos),[29] of which only a few hexameters survive. We also know of a poem he composed in choliambics called *Canobus* and of epigrams, only one of which has survived, attacking

Callimachus.[30] His *magnum opus* was the *Argonautica*, the only great epic of the Hellenistic world which has come down to us in its entirety, but even that did not extend beyond 6000 lines. It is divided into four books (Apollonius is the first poet who divided his own work into books), the length of each being roughly that of a tragedy. Tradition speaks of two versions of this work, an early one, probably including only Books I and II, and a later, revised version, to which the last two books were added. This is also supported by the existence of three *prooemia*, a common one for Books I and II and separate ones for Books III and IV.

The *Argonautica* starts abruptly, no doubt because its readers would have been familiar with the beginning of the story and it would have wearied them to hear once again how Jason was bidden to bring back the Golden Fleece to Greece and how he enlisted his comrades. (Alexandrian poets avoided burdening their readers with detailed accounts of familiar matters.) Even the building of the *Argo* is dispatched in two lines. But when we reach the 'Catalogue of the Argonauts'—and a great epic poem was obliged to include a catalogue near the beginning, since the *Iliad* contained one—more than 200 lines are devoted to the enumeration of fifty-five heroes, in which scholarship and 'novelty' are displayed. For several older lists of the Argonauts existed from which an erudite poet could make up his own 'new' list. And that is what Apollonius did.

The character of Jason, which is quite weak, conventional and colourless—duty, and not the thirst for heroic adventure, is its hallmark—becomes evident from the beginning, in the parting scene with his mother. Lacking both energy and prudence, he is certainly no born leader, and this lack of a truly heroic central figure is one of the great weaknesses of the poem. It is circumstance, and not his personality, that makes Jason the leader.

When at last the *Argo* puts to sea, after the parting offering, some wrangling and a song by Orpheus, we come to a beautiful romantic description of the sea as the ship sails from Lemnos. This is a good example of the Alexandrian bent for describing landscape and seascape —most strikingly evident in the bucolic idylls and epigrams—which stands in direct contrast to Classical Greek poetry, which never portrays nature for nature's sake.[31] The geographical accuracy with which the first, uneventful part of the journey is described is also truly Alexandrian and reminds us that we have entered the great era of science.

The climax of the first book is the arrival of the Argonauts at Lemnos and their adventure with the women of the island, who have killed all the men of their homeland except for the old father of Queen Hypsipyle. During the Lemnian visit two characteristic Alexandrian elements become evident: first, the erotic motif and, second, the delight in ecphrasis. In the *Argonautica* it is a detailed description of Jason's cloak in which the poet indulges—a poor substitute for the description of the shield of

Achilles in the *Iliad* with which he tries, in Alexandrian terms, to compete.

The whole Lemnian episode is simply narrated. The dialogue is alive and free from rhetorical pathos, and the liaison between Jason and Hypsipyle is easily made and easily broken. There is no serious attempt on the part of the queen to keep her lover forever on Lemnos—which must be seen against the background of Calypso's or Circe's love for Odysseus—and there is not a word of sorrow or comfort on the part of the departing hero. This whole amatory episode, in which Jason comes off very badly, is played down so as not to overshadow the great love affair of Medea with Jason in Book III.

The adventures in the Hellespont and the Propontis which follow are hardly exciting, and the aetiological element is prominent. In fact, throughout his epic, whenever a stone, an altar or a historic ritual appears which is related to Jason or the Argonauts, Apollonius introduces it into his narrative—to its detriment—so great was the aetiological concern of the Alexandrians. Only the Hylas episode is of interest because it draws on Theocritus,[32] which it tries to refashion in lengthy, narrative style. (But the Theocritean version is by far the superior. It is also meant to explain why Heracles abandoned the expedition.)

At the opening of the second book Apollonius is again competing with, and drawing on, Theocritus when he describes the victory of Polydeuces over Amycus, the savage king of the Berbycians. (Theocritus' *Dioscuri*[33] is once again greatly superior.) Polydeuces' victory is followed by the story of King Phenius and the harpies, from whom the two sons of Boreas free the old seer. In return for this service he foretells the journey of the Argonauts to Colchis and gives them advice about how to pass the Clashing Rocks, the counterpart of the Scylla and Charybdis episode of the *Odyssey*. A description of the journey follows in which, with Athene's help, they succeed in rowing through the Cyanean rocks, which henceforth stand fixed; and then the poet drags heroes and readers along the southern coast of the Pontus 'through a real sea of tedium', as has been rightly said.

The Argonauts accomplish the last part of their voyage in the company of the four sons of Phrixus and Chalciope, whom they find shipwrecked on the island of Ares, and, sailing up the river Phasis, anchor near the city of Aea, where the *Argo* lies concealed in the rushes.

The *prooemium* which opens the third and best book of the *Argonautica*, by invoking Erato—the reference is to the etymology of the name—indicates that Eros (Love), will be the principal motif. No doubt here again (as in the figure of the old nurse, Polyxo, of Book I) the influence of Euripides is evident. For it was he who made love a basis for action in tragedy, and in his footsteps New Comedy had followed. But this is the first time that love is placed in the foreground of the action in a full-scale heroic epic,[34] and this is probably Apollonius' original contribution. For love dominates the whole second half of the *Argonautica*. All that Jason accomplishes is achieved through Medea's love, and whereas in Apollonius scenes involving the gods are few, one of over 150 lines is inserted in Book III, portraying the intervention of Aphrodite and Eros.

In true Alexandrian manner, Apollonius humanizes his gods. He presents them with a touch of amusing bourgeois philistinism—as, for example, in the charming scene when Hera and Athene beg Aphrodite to cause Medea to fall in love with Jason. This is an Aphrodite who makes her husband's bed and combs her own hair; and Eros is later portrayed as a disobedient child—a wilful child but one feared by the gods—completely free from the usual artificiality of allegorical figures, for the poet is a master in presenting the 'genre scenes' so characteristic of Alexandrian poetry.[35]

The negotiations of the Argonauts with King Aetes for acquiring the Golden Fleece fail, and so Jason is forced to undergo the test the king has set of ploughing a field with fire-belching bulls, sowing the teeth of a dragon and harvesting the crop. Jason is then advised to seek the help of Medea, who is an expert in magic.

The tracing of Medea's feelings which follows is superb; her inner conflict in the stillness of the night, her struggle between duty, modesty and love, which leads her to the verge of suicide until love and the love of life finally win the day and she decides to help Jason, are scenes of unique delicacy and psychological insight. Except for Sappho, no other Greek poet has so vividly portrayed the first awakening of love in a young woman's heart, nor followed so closely its development. In this lies the perennial charm of Book III of the *Argonautica*, as well as the enormous influence it has exercised upon the literature of the world. For without Apollonius' Jason and Medea, Virgil's Dido and Aeneas episode would not have existed, and on them depends a long line of lovers in the various literatures of the world. Equally well presented is Medea's meeting with Jason at the shrine of Hecate, where Jason, who at first sees her only as his saviour, is moved by Medea's surrender to love and finally asks her to come back to Colchis with him as his wife.

When, after this scene, Medea returns to the palace and crouches on a low stool, deep in thought, her role in Book III is over; the conflict in her heart, from the first awakening of love to her final surrender to Jason, has been portrayed with superb realistic fidelity, and all her traditional superhuman qualities have been suppressed. Now it is Jason who comes to the foreground and who, after making the preparations which will render him invulnerable, successfully performs the terrible task in the only truly heroic scenes of the epic. Here at last he is a hero of compelling force as he drags the fire-belching bulls to the yoke, sows the dragon's teeth, sets the earth-born warriors to fight one another and overcomes the survivors.

The fourth book is the longest in the poem and contains certain arresting scenes. The conquest of the Golden Fleece, the object of the long journey from Greece, is not yet achieved when Medea, full of guilt, leaves her home and flees to the Argonauts. But now she is no longer the pure, innocent maiden of Book III, so fully at the mercy of love. In Book IV, during the homeward journey, the Euripidean figure emerges, the passionate, wild, fearless sorceress who can also be cool, calculating and openly threatening. Her character contrasts sharply with that of Medea in Book III; and this lack of unity in the central heroine's character is one more of the great weaknesses of the *Argonautica*. Upon reaching the *Argo*, Medea displays no joy at Jason's success or at seeing her lover again. However, she lulls the fierce dragon to sleep, and at her bidding Jason snatches the shimmering fleece from the oak tree and carries it to the ship.

And so begins the homeward journey of the Argonauts, who are pursued by a great fleet which the king of the Colchians sends after them. Their return is by way of the Danube, the Po, the Rhône, North Africa and the Mediterranean Sea, a strange route which illustrates the geographical interests of the Alexandrians. This journey has been assigned by various authors to different sources, on which the scholia to the *Argonautica* (which probably derive ultimately from Theon) provide valuable information; and the many adventures of the Argonauts are overlaid with learned pedantry which has a grotesque effect on the narrative. For the Argonauts experience all the dangers and the marvellous adventures which Odysseus experiences in the *Odyssey*, recast, of course, in Alexandrian terms. (This recasting of famous old legends always held a special fascination for the Alexandrians.)

But there are some excellent passages. For example, characteristically Alexandrian and of great charm is the scene in which Thetis and the nereids help the *Argo* to pass through the Wandering Rocks, a baroque description on a level never reached again by Apollonius.

When at last the Argonauts reach Corcyra a strange marriage between Jason and Medea takes place in a cave as a result of Queen Arete's cunning intervention, and the Golden Fleece serves as their bridal couch. The marriage having been consummated, the pursuing Colchians, who also succeed in reaching Corcyra, are finally persuaded to leave. But the pure, young Medea of Book III has by now degenerated into the fearless sorceress of Book IV, who despises the man she once loved and who plans and perpetrates the murder of her pursuing brother.

The marriage of Jason and Medea does not bring about the end of the wanderings of the *Argo*, for the ship is driven by a storm to Africa, where she is hauled overland to the Tritonian Lake. Triton shows the Argonauts the passage back to the sea, and so the journey to Hellas continues. Several more adventures take place, and a series of minor aetiological legends carry the Argonauts to Aegina, where the poet suddenly takes his leave and considers his work finished.

The end of the *Argonautica* is both dull and ineffectual, for we are left in the dark about the fate of Medea, Jason and the Golden Fleece. The lack of structural unity is once again evident, as in so many other parts of that overburdened epic,[36] and this is one of the main reasons why the *Argonautica* fails to be a great poem. For Apollonius uses the methods of a chronicler, not those of an epic poet, and about three-quarters of the *Argonautica* is pure chronicle. Only when he loses himself in the romance of Medea in Book III does the story come alive. But, as has been said, the very success of the romance adds to the failure of the epic. Nor should the influence of the *epyllion* on Apollonius be underrated, as his love story, with its crime, the betrayal of the father and the magic practised by Medea, indicates.

Moreover, although the poet tries to renew the epic by introducing a love story and much erudite material, he offers his readers no new way of life and makes it abundantly clear that his attitude to the old heroic myths is one of coolly critical superiority. Without wholehearted, credulous admiration of the great past a 'heroic' epic can hardly be written. However, even if Apollonius fails as an epic poet because he tries to be both 'ancient' and 'modern', his psychological intensity is striking and a number of his similes are both new and arresting, like the beautiful one which compares Medea's palpitating heart with a cauldron flashing the dancing sunlight against a wall. Moreover, his descriptive powers are by no means negligible—his variety in portraying the appearance of morning and night is amazingly rich—and on occasion he even has the gift of suggesting atmosphere. The interest of Apollonius in geography has already been mentioned,[37] but what should be stressed here is the fine sense he has for the poetical value of strange and beautiful names.

The vocabulary of the *Argonautica* is taken mainly from Homer, but it also owes a debt to his immediate predecessors, like Aratus, Lycophron and Callimachus; Homeric and lexicographical studies seem to have played their part in enriching it. What is characteristic of Apollonius' style is that, in true Alexandrian manner, he is continually varying and interpreting the Homeric phrases. Not a single line of this could stand unaltered in Homer,[38] and he fully avoids the use of stock epithets and formulae. Perhaps his greatest achievement as a stylist is that he successfully adapts Homer's language to describe a new world of romantic sentiment. Metrically, his hexameter follows Homer rather than Callimachus.

Apollonius was much read and admired in late antiquity. The papyri show that he was highly esteemed in the Imperial period, and he is one of the few Alexandrian poets whose work has survived in medieval manuscripts. In the age of Caesar he was translated into Latin by Terentius

Varro Atacinus, and in the Flavian period Valerius Flaccus produced a free version of the *Argonautica*; of this we have the portion which was completed. Nor, of course, should his influence on Virgil, which we have already mentioned, be underrated.[39]

Encomiastic, legendary–historical and mythological epics

The older view that the short and fully finished epics of the Callimachean school virtually killed the traditional, long, mythological epic[40] has been rightly challenged.[41] What the evidence we can lay our hands on suggests is that Callimachean poetic theory became fashionable in the first half of the third century B.C., had a few followers in the second and later, in the days of Sulla, was revived by Parthenius and a group of poets and critics whose influence upon Roman poetry was considerable.

On the other hand, the followers of the traditional, long, 'Ionian' epic were many and they seem to have engaged in three kinds of epic poetry: the encomiastic epic, which dealt with contemporary history, the legendary–historical epic and the purely mythological epic. The large number of inscriptions set up in honour of various otherwise unknown epic poets who took part in artistic contests (Μουσικοὶ ἀγῶνες) of the Hellenistic world indicates that their work must have been well received. It need not surprise us that hardly anything of that vast epic output has survived, for all interest in the achievements of the Hellenistic kings disappeared after the Roman conquest of the Middle East, and Atticism, in conjunction with Classicism, dealt most Hellenistic writings a death-blow.

Encomiastic epics can be traced at least as far back as the close of the fifth century, when Lysander took Choerilus of Samos with him to compose verse panegyrics on his victories and Antimachus of Colophon unsuccessfully competed at the Lysandrea of Samos.[42] Furthermore, a recent papyrus find[43] has given us the mutilated remnants of an unknown and anonymous fourth-century epic on Philip II of Macedon, and, as we have already seen, Alexander the Great was accompanied on his campaigns by Choerilus of Iasos, whose task was to celebrate his triumphs in verse.[44]

It is therefore not surprising that the Hellenistic kings (who were worshipped as gods and for one of whom a famous hymn was composed even in 'democratic' Athens)[45] encouraged epic poets to celebrate their achievements, just as Alexander had done. The names of four such poets have survived: Simonides of Magnesia, who wrote in praise of Antiochus Soter (324–261 B.C.); Musaeus of Ephesus,[46] who celebrated the deeds of Eumenes I (d.241 B.C.) and of Attalus I (269–197 B.C.) of Pergamum; Leschides, who also celebrated the Attalids; and Theodorus, who wrote in honour of Cleopatra (69–30 B.C.). (The last of these, of course, belongs to the following period.) Four is admittedly a small number, but there can be little doubt that numerous other such poets were circulating in the Hellenistic courts, where flattery flourished, as we know from various other forms of Alexandrian poetry—elegy, hymn, lyric, idyll and epigram.

In the encomiastic epics historical and mythological material seems to have been combined, and the divine apparatus was also introduced (this is not surprising in works about kings and queens who were worshipped as gods). Direct contact with the divine did not appear strange or extraordinary;[47] naturally, the Homeric precedent was influential in this.

We are better informed about the legendary–historical epics, which concerned themselves with cities, lands and leagues of the Hellenistic world. And this genre was a natural development. For whereas the Hellenistic dynasties were soon forgotten after the Roman conquest of the East, the Greek cities continued to prosper, and local patriotism, as well as the widespread Hellenistic interest in *aetia* were instrumental in the survival of such poems. This type of epic should not be dissociated from the activities of the Peripatetic School, which was the leading school of philosophy in the Egyptian capital in the early Alexandrian age and which had distinguished itself by its researches not only into the psychology of love but also into local history and constitutions.[48] Thus Phaestos (of uncertain date), who was reputed to be a Callimachean, dealt with Sparta in his *Lacedaemonica*; Apollonius Rhodius, as we have seen, with Rhodes and Alexandria in his *Ktisis Rhodou* and *Ktisis Alexandrias*; and Rhianus with the Achaean League in his *Achaica* and with Sparta and Messenia in his *Messeniaca*. Information also exists about a number of other such poems. But this type of epic poetry too was doomed to disappear when Atticism prevailed. (It is interesting to see that foreign cities and peoples who were drawn into the orbit of Greek culture were later celebrated in similar epic verse, which also disappeared when Atticism became dominant.)[49]

About Rhianus' *Messeniaca* we can gather some further information from Pausanias,[50] who used that epic as one source for the Second Messenian War of about 650 B.C. Rhianus was born at Bene (less probably at Ceraea), on Crete, about 275 B.C. and began life as a slave and custodian of a wrestling school. Later—for his education was belated— he gained a reputation as a poet and Homeric scholar.[51]

The *Messeniaca* was divided into six books and seems to have been not a straightforward account of the Second Messenian War but a series of loosely knit heroic, romantic and often fantastic episodes in the life of the central hero, Aristomenes, a champion of Messenian liberty. Thus, in conjunction with the recounting of great heroic deeds, Aristomenes was presented as having been freed from captivity by a priestess of Demeter who had fallen in love with him; captured a second time, he was hurled by the Spartans into a deep pit, but was carried safely down on the wings of an eagle, later to be dragged by a jackal through a hole to freedom. On another occasion, when bound by Cretan archers and taken to a lonely farm, he was saved by a young girl who made his guards drunk; out of gratitude he gave her in marriage to his son, Gorgos. However, the defeat of the Messenians had to be reckoned with by the poet, and so Aristomenes, who through a Delphic prophecy had won a noble Rhodian as son-in-law, retired to Rhodes, where he died and was buried with high honours. If what we gather from Pausanias is correct, then love and robbery were two romantic motifs much used by Rhianus.

Most of the surviving titles of the other epics of Rhianus (*Thessalica, Achaica, Eliaca*) point to works with tribal themes; he also composed a *Heracleias* and epigrams,[52] many of which have a pederastic motif. The scanty remains of his work bear witness to lucid and simple language and little affectation or pedantry. It might also be worth mentioning that in enumerating the great works which were inspired by mythology or history Manilius[53] cites Rhianus, together with Homer, Antimachus and Apollonius Rhodius.

The evidence furnished by Pausanias about Rhianus' *Messeniaca* corroborates the view that fantastic and sensational material was fused with historical fact in the legendary–historical epics. (A somewhat similar admixture of mythical, pseudo-historical and true historical events can also be found in Ennius' *Annales*, of which more than 500 lines have come down to us; these were probably cast in the mould of the long legendary–historical Hellenistic epics.)

Many were the purely mythological epics that were composed in the Hellenistic world, but only their names and those of their authors survive, and the dates of most are a matter of dispute. As would be expected, the gods most frequently celebrated in these epics were the two most popular in the Hellenistic world, Heracles and Dionysus. Thus in addition to Rhianus' *Heracleias*, which was an epic in fourteen books, Theodorus[54] wrote twenty-two books on the battle of Heracles with the Giants, Diotimus of Adramyttion (third century B.C.?) composed the *Athla Heracleous* and Phaedimus of Amastris (second half of third century B.C.) a *Heracleis*; on Dionysus we know of the *Bacchica Epe* (Βαχχικὰ ῎Επη) of Theolytus of Methymna (early third century B.C.?) and the *Dionysias* of Neoptolemus of Parium (third century B.C.), the writer whose views on poetry Horace adopted in his *Ars Poetica*.[55] But various other traditional mythological subjects were repeatedly cast into epic form; it would be idle to enumerate all the titles and authors of such poems. It will suffice to mention that Menelaus of Aigai (date uncertain), who is also said to have been a Callimachean, Antagoras of Rhodes[56] (c. 300–260 B.C.), who was the most distinguished poet of the Older Academy in the days of Polemon, Crantor and Crates, and Demosthenes of Bithynia (third–second century B.C.) all wrote a *Thebaid*; that Musaeus of Ephesus (c. 170 B.C.)

composed a *Perseis* in ten books; and that both Cleon of Curion and Theolytus, who are otherwise unknown, wrote *Argonautica*. Practically nothing of all this vast epic output has survived, probably because the quality was low (which would explain the anger and bitterness of Callimachus). However that may be, the larger number of long mythological epics that were circulating in the Hellenistic world is surprising.

It has been suggested that the long Hellenistic epic came into its own in the last decades of the third century B.C., when the Seleucids gained political supremacy over the Ptolemies and Egypt lost her unchallenged cultural lead; for then cultural centres similar to the Alexandrian were established in Antioch and Pergamum, and many of the ablest men of letters were drawn to those cities. The turn to the long epic, as has been pointed out,[57] should perhaps not be dissociated from the appearance of the Asianic style in prose, poetry and art in general; even the 'new' Pergamene scholarship of Crates of Mallos, which abandoned the minute and pedantic Alexandrian scholarship and moved to a broad, philosophical interpretation of Homer, seems to be in keeping with that spirit. For it is true that the Asianic spirit and style, with its bent for the gigantic and the pathetic (one has only to remember the altar of Pergamum or the statues of Laocoön and of the dying Gaul) is of a kind with the length and pathos of the Hellenistic epic.

The grand Hellenistic epic whether encomiastic, legendary–historical or purely mythological, occupies an important place in the history of Greek poetry, even if only a few fragments of it have survived.[58] The Callimachean reaction to it—the Callimachean renaissance as it has been called—was, as we saw, but a short, transitory episode which blossomed in Alexandria in the first half of the third century B.C., petered out in the course of the second and enjoyed a revival in the first century B.C. which chiefly affected poetry.

THE DIDACTIC EPIC

Didactic poetry was greatly honoured by the Alexandrians, in spite of Aristotle's rejection. The great respect Hesiod enjoyed in the Hellenistic world and the reverence the scholar-poets felt for knowledge played no small part in this; they believed that it was proper and desirable to cast learned information into verse and thus make it more palatable and more accessible to wider circles; but the glosses they added to their poetry, which defeated the purpose of teaching useful information clearly and attractively, did not seem to bother them.

The Alexandrian didactic poets abandoned the lyrical–philosophical character of the older didactic epics—those of Xenophanes, Parmenides and Empedocles—and developed a pedagogical–scientific ideal which embraced the driest learned material. But even the best surviving examples (the *Phaenomena* of Aratus and the *Theriaca* and *Alexipharmaca* of Nicander) do not approach that ideal. They are simple compilations, full of manifest errors, which enjoyed an undeservedly long life in the ancient world because of their usefulness as school texts. In fact, their authors are no more than metaphrasts, who took a prose treatise and turned it into verse. Moreover, many of the later and lesser Alexandrian didactic poets abandoned the traditional dactylic hexameter and used other metres, most prominently the iambic trimeter.

A precursor to this new, 'scientific' Alexandrian epic can already be found in Classical times in the versified rhetoric of Euenus[59] and also possibly in Critias' *Emmetroi Politeiai* (῎Εμμετροι Πολιτεῖαι); nor should the *Erga* (῎Εργα) and the *Melissourglica* (Μελισσουργικά) of Menecrates of Ephesus[60] (born c. 340 B.C.), who was the teacher of Aratus, be overlooked.

The most important and the most successful Hellenistic didactic poet was Aratus. He was born in Soloi in Cilicia (c. 315–240/239 B.C.) and then studied in Athens, where he was taught Stoic philosophy by Zeno. In about 277 B.C. Antigonos Gonatas invited him to the Macedonian court, where he celebrated the king's marriage to Phila and, in a *Hymn to Pan*, his victory over the Celts (277 B.C.). It was at the king's request that he composed his major work, the *Phaenomena*, which was greeted with a flattering epigram by Callimachus.[61] Macedonia became his second home, and that is where he died, but he also visited Antiochus I in Syria. He is the only major Alexandrian poet who never visited Alexandria.

Aratus was not the first poet we know of to cast astronomical material in verse. We hear of one Cleostratus of Tenedos as his precursor, who met with little success. In his *Phaenomena* Aratus versified a prose treatise of Eudoxus of Cnidus (c. 390–337 B.C.) but frequently did not understand his source correctly because of his inadequate astronomical knowledge. His errors were widely criticized by his many ancient commentators, especially Hipparchus. However, the majesty of his subject, the splendour of the starry sky, clearly inspired him, for there is a certain feeling in his verse.

In the introduction Zeus is celebrated in the Stoic manner as the concrete expression of a world order. The poem then proceeds on a factual level as the poet refers to the poles, describes the northern and southern fixed stars, the circles of the celestial spheres and the rising and setting of the stars. The rest of the *Phaenomena* deals with weather signs, and here not Eudoxus but a Peripatetic source is probably followed.[62] The treatment is highly uneven; for example, the description of the fixed constellations takes up quite half the poem, whereas the planets are dispensed with in only a few verses.

Myths of the stars are only sparingly treated, and occasionally some Empedoclean philosophical ideas are worked into them. It is the Stoic creed, however, that permeates the whole poem. As would be expected in a 'scientific' work, the author's digressions constitute the best poetry, the longest being the description of the Golden Age (ll. 98–136) and of the storms at sea (ll. 408–435).

The style of Aratus is not exuberant, and his diction, drawn mostly from Homer, is relatively simple. But there are also a few glosses, some neologisms and some bad errors in the formation of epic words. The dactylic hexameter is fairly correct, but the refinements introduced by Callimachus are not observed.

The *Phaenomena*, because of its subject, does not make easy reading; yet, in spite of this, it was widely acclaimed in antiquity. The Romans adapted and translated the poem several times,[63] and it was even translated into Arabic. This was no doubt due to the great popularity the pseudo-science of astrology enjoyed in the late Hellenistic world.

Aratus also wrote many other poems, all of which are now lost, except for one epigram. Some have astrological or medical titles, but we also hear of *epikeedia*, elegies, hymns, *paegnia*, more epigrams and a collection of short poems with the title *Ta Kata Lepton* (whose meaning is uncertain), from which the *Catalepton* attributed to Virgil takes its name. Aratus also produced a critical edition of the *Odyssey*.

To the second century B.C. belongs Nicander of Colophon, the son of Anaxagoras, second in importance among the Alexandrian didactic poets, who was apparently a hereditary priest at Claros. Two of his poems have survived complete, the *Theriaca* and the *Alexipharmaca*, both written in hexameters.

The *Theriaca* deals with various snakes and other poisonous creatures and the best remedies for their bites, whereas the *Alexipharmaca* is an account of vegetable, mineral and animal poisons and their antidotes. The matter of both these incredibly arid poems is drawn from a prose treatise of Apollodorus the Iologos (early third century). But Nicander was neither a true scientist nor a real poet, in spite of the care he takes over his hexameters, which on the whole abide by the rules laid down by Callimachus. For he frequently introduces into his works popular superstitions and inaccurate descriptions, with few digressions and extremely rare similes. Moreover, he often disregards normal grammar and alters the meanings of words. In spite of all this, he was read and cited by many later writers, and even Virgil quarried his *Georgica*, a work on husbandry now lost, and probably also his *Melissourgica*, a work on apiculture, for his own *Georgics*.

The titles of many other of Nicander's works have survived; they indicate epics of the mythological and legendary–historical kind, elegies, versifications of scientific treatises and prose works of literary criticism.

Among them are the *Hetairioumena* (*Metamorphoses*), which was used by Antoninus Liberalis, and the *Ophiaca*, which dealt with legends connected with snakes.

The period under discussion was rich in didactic poets about whom little is known. They wrote on a variety of subjects, from diatribes of a moralizing nature to gastronomy, and in various metres (this was a departure which subsequent didactic poetry followed, for, abandoning the traditional dactylic hexameter, later didactic poets also employed a variety of metres, most prominently the iambic trimeter). Among the surviving names are Numenios of Heracleia, Philostephanus of Cyrene,[64] Neoptolemus of Parium (whose views on poetry were, as already noted, adopted by Horace), Gorgos of Notion, Amphiolos of Chios, Cleandros of Colophon, Eratoxenos of Athens and Archelaus of Chersonesus (in answer to whose work Ptolemy IV Philopator (244–205 B.C.) wrote Τὰ ἰδιοφυῆ in elegies).[65] Their home towns, so far apart, indicate that didactic poetry was widely acclaimed in the early Hellenistic centuries.[66]

CHAPTER 9

Alexandrian Drama

In the Hellenistic age drama, the most Attic of all poetic forms, followed the wide diffusion of Hellenism and became a popular kind of entertainment. Every city of any significance, old or new, acquired its theatre and established festivals within whose framework competitive dramatic performances took place. These were usually in honour of Dionysus, but drama also became part of other religious festivals, such as the Amphiaraia at Oropos, the Museia at Thespiae or the Soteria at Delphi. Nor were these theatrical contests limited to new plays. They also included revivals of old Classical plays—even of old satyr plays—which thus became known to a wider public throughout the Greek-speaking world.[1]

With the exception of New Comedy, which remained purely Attic, our knowledge of Alexandrian drama is very limited indeed. The poverty of our sources does not allow us to follow in any detail the development of that literary genre after the fourth century, when important changes and innovations were made in the theatre. It is true that most of these innovations were technical and external, but, in spite of that, they had a profound bearing upon the plays themselves.[2] Nor should we underrate the importance and influence of dramatic by-products (the various kinds of prose and musical mimes and pantomimes) which flourished in the Hellenistic world and outlived serious drama in the later Roman Empire.[3]

As in so much else, the Ptolemies aspired to take the lead in the field of drama. Thus Ptolemy II Phildelphus established lavish dramatic competitions in Alexandria and, in honour of Dionysus, had the Actors' Guild (οἱ περὶ τὸν Διόνυσον τεχνῖται) take part in the gigantic Alexandrian procession described by Callixenus.[4] Furthermore, he extended to members of all actors' guilds legal protection and exemption from certain taxes.[5] In the hope of establishing New Comedy in Alexandria, he also invited Menander and Philemon to visit Egypt, as we have seen, but in this his ambitions were thwarted.

TRAGEDY

Tradition and innovation

In spite of all the efforts of the Ptolemies, the established Attic dramatists, with Euripides as the most popular, remained the masters of the Alexandrian stage in the grand post-Classical theatres. But as well as revivals, a large number of new plays were also produced; it has been estimated that more than 400 were written,[6] and the names of more than sixty Hellenistic playwrights have come down to us.[7] The majority of these belong to the early third century B.C., and they come from all over the Greek world, so that one can justifiably speak of a revival of drama in that century. But the fashion then set survived until much later and was followed even by kings like Ptolemy Philopator (221–205/4 B.C.), who wrote plays, one of which was called *Adonis*. We also hear of one tragedian, Menelaus (mid-second century B.C.), who dramatized Cappadocian material at the court of King Ariarathes.

Drama, of course, continued to be produced and performed in Athens until at least the middle of the second century B.C., as indicated by the lists of victors of the Athenian dramatic competitions, the Great Dionysia and the Lenaea, which have been preserved in inscriptions.[8] We know nothing more than their names, however. If the thousands of dramatic verses which were then composed have practically all perished, this should not be put down solely to inferior poetic quality, as has often been maintained, but to the taste and demands of the Atticists, who were also responsible for the disappearance of so much other good Alexandrian verse.

Seven of the dramatists of the early Ptolemaic period were singled out as masters of the art and called the Pleiad. (It is in their memory that the French poets of the sixteenth century grouped around Ronsard called themselves '*La Pléiade*'.) But it is very hard to form an accurate picture of the Alexandrian Pleiad, for even the names of its members (and some are little more than that) are not always consistently cited. Five of these always occur: Alexander Aetolus, Lycophron of Chalcis, Philicus of Corcyra, Homeros of Byzantium (who was the son of the poetess Moiro or Myro) and Sositheus of Alexandria Troas. The remaining two places are filled variously by Sosiphanes of Syracuse, Dionysiades of Tarsus, Aeantiades and Euphronius.[9]

Of the products of these stars only a few titles and very few fragments indeed have survived. It is probable that they were imitated by the early Roman dramatists, but their works too have perished, so we are in the dark about the exact nature and the art of Hellenistic tragedy. The only sources of information now available are a number of inscriptions; the writing, often fragmentary, of some Alexandrian and post-Alexandrian scholars, commentators and lexicographers; Horace's *Ars Poetica*, which drew on Neoptolemus of Parium (third century B.C.);[10] certain works of art—sculptures, bronzes, terracottas, frescoes, mosaics and so on—representing dramatic scenes and characters with their masks; a number of inscriptions; and the remains of some Hellenistic theatres. To these should be added a fairly large part (269 lines) of the tragedy *Exagoge*, the work of Ezechiel, a writer of Jewish plays in Greek of the second century B.C.[11] For the only complete Alexandrian play which has come down to us, the *Alexandra* of Lycophron—if genuine[12]—is a strange work, totally out of the common run and therefore of little help; and such fragments of other Alexandrian tragedies as have survived are few and short.

Though the information that has been gleaned from these sources is scanty and much of it is technical and external, enough exists for us to establish that no important changes since the days of Sophocles and Euripides came about in the dramatic technique of the third century B.C. There were, however, certain other developments, of which the most significant should be noted.

First, the reduction of the role of the chorus, which is in keeping with the *proskenion*, the raised stage, that was introduced in the Greek theatres in the early third century.[13] This did not completely pre-empt intercommunication between the two levels of performance—the orchestra and the stage—but in practice it reduced the role of the chorus to that of human spectators, who stood in the orchestra watching and commenting on the deeds of the heroes.[14] Nor should it go unmentioned that the heroic status of these agents of tragedy had already been enhanced in the fourth century B.C. by the addition of the *onkos*, the tower of hair dressed over the forehead,[15] and was further stressed in the second century B.C. by the introduction of the thick-soled boot. The reduction of the role of the chorus began with Euripides, as we have seen, and it was Agathon who inaugurated the practice of inserting *embolima* between the episodes that were irrelevant to the plots[16] and could be transferred from play to play. In the third century, it has been assumed, the Alexandrian poets who adopted this practice had a suitable stock of songs about the gods, Fortuna, Love, *hubris* and so on, from which they could pick out the most appropriate for each tragic situation and insert it in their plays. But no matter how curtailed the role of the chorus may have been, choruses that were present during the episodes and were not strangers to the action continued to exist in the Alexandrian age. And this is attested by the titles of plays (like the *Men of Marathon* or the *Men of Pherae*, which were named after their choruses) that we know from inscriptional evidence, from Plutarch[17] and from other sources.[18] Nor could the frequent revivals of old plays be produced without choruses, and it is also significant that the chorus survived in Roman tragedy, whereas Roman comedy dropped it altogether.[19]

Second, the development of dramatic music. Though the origins can be traced to Euripides and Agathon,[20] its further evolution and its significance in the Alexandrian age is clear from surviving inscriptions which record performances of tragedies at various festivals of the Hellenistic world. For when the traditional lyric and musical elements of the chorus songs were reduced in conjunction with the suppression of the role of the chorus they were replaced by longer solos sung by the actors from the stage, who were accompanied by a tragic flute player (τραγικὸς αὐλητής), a new and indispensable member of the dramatic troupe.[21] Two possible examples of actors' solos of the first century B.C. or the first century A.D. have survived in an Oslo papyrus, accompanied by musical notation;[22] another papyrus[23] includes musical notation of the same date added to a monody which is earlier and possibly even Classical.[24] The second piece of the Oslo papyrus, an apostrophe to the island of Lemnos in iambic trimeters, is of special interest, for it shows that even pure dialogic metres could be set to music by a later interpreter and indicates the importance that non-choral music had in later tragedy.[25] Moreover, we know from a third-century epigram of Dioscorides[26] that a woman called Athenion sang the part of Cassandra in a play called the *Horse*, a Roman adaptation of which was probably Livius Andronicus' *Equus Trojanus*. There is no other evidence of a woman singing in a serious drama in the Hellenistic age.[27] So in the Hellenistic world we have new music composed for old tragic monodies, new tragic monodies and music for tragic iambic trimeters—therefore a new kind of 'singing tragedy'.[28] In New Comedy too such non-choral songs seem to have existed and were further developed in the period between Menander and Plautus.[29]

Third, greater emphasis was placed on characterization than on the plot, as we know from Aristotle's treatment of tragedy, and much care was bestowed upon the refinement and variation of the diction of the characters according to class, occupation, education and so on. This was no doubt due to the influence of rhetoric and to the developed sensitivity to diction of the Alexandrians.

Fourth, the Alexandrian playwrights turned to subjects which their Classical predecessors had not treated (a third of the titles we possess indicate the employment of new myths) and were also engaged in writing historical plays.[30] Such were the *Cassandreis*, the *Marathonioi* and perhaps the *Orphanos* of Lycophron, or the *Themistocles* and the *Men of Pherae* of Moschion (third century B.C.)[31] (It has also been thought that the title *Orphanos* may suggest a play with completely fictitious characters, following in the footsteps of Agathon.)

Fifth, a change of scene and scenery between the acts was favoured, and *periaktoi* (revolving prisms) were added to the stage machinery to make this easy.

Finally, it should be added that as far as we can gather, Alexandrian plays tended to be divided into five acts.

Though direct evidence is missing, it appears probable that Alexandrian tragedy was full of pathos (*hochpathetisch*),[32] which would be in keeping with the rest of Hellenistic art (with the exception of the Callimachean school of poetry) and with the popularity of Euripides, who was considered the 'most tragic' of the Classical tragedians and served as model for so many Alexandrians. Even the word *tragikos* acquires in this period its connotations of 'pathetic' (full of excessive suffering) and 'pompous'. And although, as already mentioned, the fragments of republican Roman tragedy do not suffice to permit us to draw any conclusions about Hellenistic plays, certain of Seneca's tragedies (like the *Medea* or the *Thyestes*, which are highly pathetic) are probably also influenced by Hellenistic models and can therefore provide us with some notion of their ethos.

At the same time, the information we have from antiquity clearly indicates that in the Alexandrian age the emotional scenes of many plays gave actors the opportunity to display their dramatic talent, often to over-play their parts and even to add lines of their own to the text;[33] the cheap success they secured by playing to the gallery prompted playwrights to write whole scenes with the actors and not the plot in mind, a development which, much to the detriment of tragedy, turned the Alexandrian stage from a theatre of the playwright to a theatre of the actor. It is probable that precisely because of this tragic excess, and not because of the inferior quality of their poetry, Hellenistic plays disappeared when Atticism prevailed, for they would naturally have been classed together with the exuberant Asianic prose and dubbed as aesthetically and morally unsuitable to be copied and read.

The tragedians of the Alexandrian era

Of the poets included in the Pleiad, three, Alexander Aetolus, Lycophron and Philicus, were considered particularly distinguished.

The little we know about the life and the works of Alexander Aetolus of Pleuron (c. 280 B.C.) has already been outlined in Chapter 7. Of his tragedies one title only, the *Astragalistae* (the *Dice Players*), has survived. The play dealt with the youth of Patroclus[34] but not a single fragment has reached us, so we are completely ignorant of the dramatic art of this important Alexandrian tragedian.

We are better informed about Lycophron of Chalcis (c. 320 B.C.), son of Socles, who was adopted by Lykos of Rhegium, the grammarian and tragic poet. As a young man Lycophron frequented the philosopher Menedemus at Eretria, and about 285–283 B.C. he came to Alexandria.

There Ptolemy II Philadelphus entrusted him with the preliminary classification of the comedies collected for the Alexandrian Library. According to Ovid (*Ibis*, 529ff.), he was killed by an arrow.

Tzetzes credits Lycophron with sixty-four (or forty-six) tragedies, and in the *Suda* we find the titles of twenty. The only surviving fragment of these comprises four lines and comes from the *Pelopidae*.[35] However, the *Suda* further assigns to him the *Alexandra*, 'the obscure poem'. This strange work has reached us complete and consists of a dramatic monologue, in 1474 tragic iambics, in which the slave set to watch Alexandra (Cassandra) reports her prophecies to Priam. The poetic device of the prophecy we have already observed when dealing with Alexandrian elegy (see Chapter 7). It was frequently used by the Alexandrians but never in a darker or stranger manner than in this unusual play.

The poem falls into three sections and has a prologue and two epilogues. The first section deals with the fall of Troy and the crime of Ajax, the second with the return of the Greeks and the third with the struggle between Asia and Europe. The central theme is the suffering of the Greeks in compensation for what the Trojans suffered (possibly suggested by the *Troades* of Euripides), but many of the concerns of the Trojan Cycle are also touched upon—in fact, the whole play could be described as an outsize messenger speech.

The passage in which Alexandra foretells Aeneas' arrival in Latium and the future glory of Rome (ll. 1226–80) and lines 1446–50, in which some see a reference to Pyrrhus and Rome's victory in the Tarentine War and others a reference to T. Quinctius Flamininus and his victory over Philip V at Cynoscephalae in 197 B.C., raised doubts, even in antiquity, as to the authenticity of the poem. Many scholars maintain that the author was a namesake, or even a descendant, of the Alexandrian tragedian. General grounds favour the later dating, after the battle of Cynoscephalae.[36]

The obscurity of the *Alexandra* is greater than that of any other Greek poem; deliberately confusing references to gods, heroes, animals and places, inconsistent myths and, above all, the language are responsible for this. A great number of *hapax eiremena*, glosses from epic and tragedy as well as vulgarisms and neologisms are employed, and the syntax indulges in an extravagant use of figures of speech and rhetoric. In metre, however, the author is strict; he allows few resolutions and observes the rules of the final cretic. It is indeed strange that a poem of this nature, which stands alone in the literature of the world and, strictly speaking, cannot be classed in any of the recognized branches of poetry, received approbation; Virgil and Ovid knew it, and in the first century A.D. Theon wrote a commentary on it.

To Lycophron are also attributed the play *Cassandreis*, connected with the founding of the city of Cassandreia in 316 B.C., most probably a historical play; the *Marathonioi* and the *Orphanos*,[37] possibly dealing with contemporary subjects; the satyr play *Menedemus*, in which he described the circle of Menedemus in Eretria; anagrams (for example, Πτολεμαῖος~'Απὸ Μέλιτος: 'Αϱσινόη~ Ἰον Ἡϱας); and a prose work on comedy, later attacked by various grammarians.

Philicus (not Philiscos) of Corcyra (c. 275/4 B.C.) was a priest of Dionysus at Alexandria and also possibly eponymous priest of Alexander.[38] At the famous procession of 275/4, which was held by Ptolemy II Philadelphus in Alexandria, he marched at the head of the *technitae*. The *Suda* attributes to him forty-two tragedies, but no certain title or fragment survives.

Philicus was not only a tragedian and a member of the Pleiad but also a lyric poet. He claimed to have invented the *metrum Philicium*, a catalectic choriambic hexameter.[39] Fragments from a *Hymn to Demeter*, retrieved in a papyrus[40] and cast in that metre, have been plausibly identified as coming from that poem. They are skilfully composed and display powers of realistic description. So far as we can see, the poem probably followed in outline the Homeric *Hymn to Demeter* and was not a cult poem but one intended for a learned audience. A sepulchral epigram on Philicus of the middle of the third century B.C. has also been retrieved from a papyrus.[41]

Two more members of the Pleiad should be noted: Sosiphanes, who is credited by the *Suda* with seventy-three tragedies and seven victories,[42] and Sositheus of Alexandria Troas, who, as we shall see, took a leading part in the effort to revive satyr plays in third-century Alexandria. He lived in Athens, Syracuse and Alexandria and is said to have written tragedies with distinction.

We also know of one royal tragedian, Ptolemy IV Philopator (c. 244–205 B.C.), who, as we saw, composed a tragedy called *Adonis*.[43] He was also a great admirer of Homer, to whose honour he dedicated a temple, the anonymous dedicatory poem of which survives.[44]

In 1950 E. Lobel published the remnants of a *Gyges* drama found in an Oxyrhynchus papyrus of the second or the beginning of the third century A.D.[45] Of the three surviving columns, the best-preserved contains sixteen trimeters from the queen's speech about the events of the previous night, in which she also informs us how she persuaded Candaules to leave the palace and that she invited Gyges to meet her. It is clear that the poet, who most probably belongs to the third century B.C.,[46] follows closely Herodotus' version of the story.[47] If the whole play was modelled on Herodotus — and this appears probable—then a change of scenery was necessary, which would be in keeping with the Hellenistic practice as we know it from Ezechiel's *Exagoge*.[48]

Attention should also be drawn to a fragment of a Hellenistic play published in 1968.[49] It consists of a dialogue between Priam, Cassandra, Deiphobus and a chorus in iambic verses. The subject is the combat between Hector and Achilles described in Book XXII of the *Iliad*, but it is less clear whether the dialogue contains a prophecy by Cassandra of the fight and Hector's death or is an eye-witness account. The former seems more likely. The identification of the play is uncertain, but language, metre and dramatic structure point to the Alexandrian period;[50] it has been suggested that it may have drawn on the *Hector* of Astydamas.

Finally, a few words should be added about the *Exagoge* of the Hellenized Jew Ezechiel (second century B.C.), mention of which has already been made. The 269 lines of this play on the Exodus which have been preserved (approximately a third of the work) include a long soliloquy by Moses recounting his career down to his flight to Midian; a dialogue in which Moses recounts a dream; a dialogue with God at the Burning of the Bush in which are given instructions concerning the wonders to be worked in Egypt and directions for the celebration of Passover; a messenger speech recounting the destruction of the Egyptians and the deliverance of the Hebrews; and an account of the springs of water, the palm trees and the appearance of a remarkable bird (apparently the phoenix) at Elim. On the whole, the poet follows the Bible closely, but we cannot say how the plot was constructed. It appears that the action fell into five episodes and that there were regular choral interludes. Apparently the unity of scene was not observed. The play was probably not intended to be performed.

Ezechiel, though not a Greek, is in the mainstream of the Hellenistic dramatic tradition. His language shows a knowledge of the three great Classical tragedians; his versification is sound and his imagery lively. His play, obviously intended for a Hellenized Jewish audience, may also have been enjoyed by others not of Jewish origin. Ezechiel apparently composed a number of such dramatizations, for both Eusebius and Clement speak of his tragedies in the plural.

THE SATYR PLAY

In the obscure and controversial field of Alexandrian drama one development emerges clearly—the effort to revive the almost defunct satyr play, which was once the necessary conclusion of every tragic trilogy. To achieve this, three new elements seem to have been added to the traditional 'mythological' satyr play: an idyllic bucolic atmosphere, the love motif so common in New Comedy, and attacks on living contemporary men, reminiscent of Old Comedy.

The evidence we have at our disposal is indeed restricted, but we can trace all three of these additions in the satyr plays of Sositheus of

Alexandria Troas, whom we have met as a member of the Pleiad. In his *Daphnis* or *Lityersis*, which dealt with the victory of Heracles over the cruel Phrygian king Lityersis,[51] the idyllic bucolic element was introduced as well as the love motif, for Daphnis finally won Thalia; and we are informed by Diogenes Laertius[52] that Sositheus attacked the philosopher Cleanthes when he was present at a performance (although in that instance it was the poet who was booed out of the theatre by the angry audience). However that may be, a laudatory epigram of Dioscorides[53] praises Sositheus for restoring to the satyr play its original 'coarseness and vitality'.[54]

Lycophron of Chalcis, as we have seen, also attacked Menedemus in a satyr play of that name,[55] in which he portrayed 'the high thinking and the low living' of that philosopher's circle at Eretria. In his pungency (*drymites*) Lycophron is thought to have followed Python of Byzantium or Catana, who was the author of a satyrical play called *Agen* (the meaning of the name remains unexplained), probably produced in the camp of Alexander on the Hydaspes (in the Punjab). Python's play attacked Harpalus, who had recently absconded with Alexander's treasure, and other contemporary persons, in the style of Old Comedy.[56]

But these efforts at renovation do not seem to have been truly successful, for as the extant fragments indicate, most satyr plays appear to have used mythological subjects in the traditional manner. The appearance of the names of poets of 'satyrs' (that is, satyr plays) found in catologues of winners from Teos, Magnesia, Samos, Delos and certain Boeotian cities[57] testifies to the revival of the satyr play in the Hellenistic world; in fact, satyric performances can be traced as late as the second century A.D., and some monuments showing stage *Papposelinoi* and satyrs can even be dated a century later.

COMEDY

For information about Hellenistic comedy the reader must turn to Chapter 6, on New Comedy. For although many of the comedies produced in those days in Athens were no doubt also presented in Alexandria[58] and a number of new 'Alexandrian' ones were composed,[59] Athens remained the real home of that literary genre. The majority of the surviving dramatic fragments of the Hellenistic age come from comedies, but they are unfortunately relatively few—only a few hundreds of lines—and their authors are unknown. Their language and their subjects are on the whole Attic, but here and there local Egyptian elements appear (references to Alexandrian names and events).

There is, however, one writer of comedies who was resident in Alexandria and produced his plays exclusively there. This was Machon of Sicyon — or, according to some, of Corinth — (c. 260–250 B.C.). From his epitaph by Dioscorides,[60] which was probably inscribed on his tomb,[61] we learn that he revived the invective of Attic comedy 'on the banks of the Nile'. His two surviving fragments belong not to the type of Old Comedy but to that of Middle or New Comedy (which, however, was not free of searing attacks). Machon also composed, in iambic verse, a collection of anecdotes — *chreiai*[62] (witty or clever sayings designed to be instructive) — which purported to record the words and deeds of notorious Athenian parasites, courtesans and so forth and from which 462 (mainly scurrilous) verses have been preserved. There is some humour in them but little variety, and their style is prosaic.

Phlyakes

Finally a word should be added here about the *phlyakes* (also called *hilotragodia* and, later, *fabulae Rhintonicae*), originally farces performed by *phlyakes* (jesters) in southern Italy and also perhaps — but there is no evidence to prove it — in Alexandria. This kind of play, which is related to Old Attic Comedy in both costume and obscene wit, was traditional in southern Italy, and vase paintings illustrate its early, and probably pre-literary, stage of development. Its origins may well be the same as those of Old Attic Comedy (that is, old Doric folk burlesques). But in the period under consideration it rose to become a poetic genre; and it was Rhinton of Tarentum (early third century) who turned it into 'literature'.

He was a potter's son contemporary with Ptolemy I; in an epitaph in his honour composed by Nossis of Locri he is called a Syracusan and is praised for the originality of his tragic *phlyakes*,[63] which indicates that the parody of heroes and of divine myths which Rhinton introduced for comic effect met with appreciation in the west. Nine titles are known of the thirty-eight pieces attributed to him, almost all burlesques of Euripides (*Heracles, Iphigeneia in Aulis, Medea, Orestes* and so on), but very few fragments have survived.[64] In a fragment from the *Orestes* a character points out that a curse just uttered will not scan as a tragic trimeter. His diction, which mixed 'Italian' with Doric elements, interested the later grammarians. (Perhaps Plautus' *Amphitryo* can give us an idea of the nature of Rhinton's plays.)

Other known authors of ludicrous scenes from mythology or daily life were Sciras of Tarentum (third century B.C.), from whose works one title only, *Meleagros*, survives and two verses parodying Euripides' *Hippolytus*,[65] and Sopater of Paphos (c. 330–c. 280 B.C.), who probably lived in Alexandria. Fourteen titles of his works have come down to us, of which

Bacchis, the *Suitors of Bacchis* and the *Marriage of Bacchis* (Βαχχίς, Βαχχίδος Μνηστῆρες and Βαχχίδος Γάμος) seem to form a triad. Some of the titles, such as *Orestes*, *Hippolytus* or *Nekyia*, indicate burlesques of tragedy or mythology. From his *Gauls* (Γαλάται) we have the longest extant phlyax fragment; it contains raillery against the Stoics and in spirit and language approaches Attic comedy.[66]

CHAPTER 10

The Literature of Popular Entertainment

THE MIME

According to the definition of an ancient grammarian, the mime is 'an imitation of life, embracing both what is proper and what is improper'; it is just this blend of the 'proper' and the 'improper' that seems to have given satisfaction to the masses in the Hellenistic age, whose inclination was for realism.[1]

In the period under consideration there were two kinds of mime, one spoken and one sung, the first a native of the Doric west, the second a product of the Ionian east. The spoken mime took two forms—the literary, which was intended to be read and not acted (such as the mimes of Theocritus and Herodas), and the popular, which was publicly acted and, strictly speaking, beyond the pale of literature. The spoken mime, which originated in Magna Graecia, is believed by certain scholars to have been a development of Dorian comedy imported from the Peloponnese,[2] for there is evidence that even there Dorian comedy concentrated on the realistic portrayal of life.[3] The sung mime, which was also publicly performed, was regarded as neither literature nor refined music.

Syracusan performers of mimes began to travel east as early as the fifth century B.C., but it was only at the beginning of the third that they, like all other travelling players, became a regular feature of the Greek world. In Xenophon's *Symposium*, which speaks of the mime of *Dionysus and Ariadne*, we have one of the few references to such performances before the Hellenistic Age.

The mime was originally, and remained, essentially a one-actor affair, but later the ἀρχιμῖμος, the original actor, took in complementary figures as the occasion demanded. Women, ἀρχιμῖμαι, appeared in mimes no less than men, and the importance of these 'actor-managers', both men and women, is well illustrated by their epitaphs. The popular spoken mime gradually pushed its way into the official programmes at games and other festivals (originally it was a mere side-show) and from about 270 B.C. onwards actors of spoken mimes (μιμολόγοι, βιολόγοι, ἠθολόγοι) appear with increasing frequency among other prize winners in inscriptions. However, in the Alexandrian age the great pretentious mimes we know from Caesar's days did not exist. The 'leap from the cabaret to the stage', as Körte so fittingly calls it,[4] had not yet been made. Later, of course, the Imperial mime controlled the theatre in both the east and the west and even survived the end of the ancient world in the wandering *jongleurs* of the Middle Ages.

On the whole, the mime, whether spoken or sung, had no claims to permanence. It was beyond the boundaries of literature and aimed at serving the needs of daily amusement. Occasionally, however, in the hands of gifted writers like Sophron and Herodas, it was lifted into the realm of literature and, in the hands of Theocritus, into the realm of great poetry. This transplantation naturally suppressed much of the mime's original crude realism, which was blended with many refined elements of the Greek literary tradition.

The literary spoken mime: Theocritus and Herodas

Sophron of Syracuse (c. 450 B.C.) is rightly considered the father of the literary mime. His mimes, which were greatly admired by Plato, were composed in a 'rhythmical prose'—whatever that may mean—and were divided according to their subject-matter into *Mimes of Men* (ἀνδρεῖοι) and *Mimes of Women* (γυναικεῖοι). Their essential feature was close fidelity to life, both in language and character delineation, and much of their freshness was due to their spirit of improvisation.[5] There was no fantastic element in them, no parody of mythology. In fact, in one respect Sophron stood nearer to the popular mime than did his imitators, as he wrote in 'prose'. For when Theocritus and Herodas composed their mimes in verse, they forfeited an important instrument of realism (Theocritus in a more pronounced manner than Herodas, for the hexameter, being more 'highbrow', is more prone to idealize than the *scazon*). The debt of Theocritus and Herodas to the urban mimes of Sophron is not easy to assess.[6] There are, of course, some striking verbal resemblances, but these two poets clearly did much more than modernize the earlier writer, for they were both men with great powers of observation and a keen interest in experimentation.

THEOCRITUS

Theocritus (c. 300–c. 260 B.C.) was a native of Syracuse but seems to have lived most of his life outside Sicily, perhaps first in southern Italy and then later in the east, in Cos and Alexandria. In his search for a powerful patron he turned first to the Sicilian Hiero (Idyll XVI); but when patronage was not granted he composed a panegyric for Ptolemy II Philadelphus (Idyll XVIII), from whom he received recognition. Some of his best poems, like Idylls II and VII, refer to Cos, where he probably spent some time in the circle of poets and friends who had gathered round Philetas.

In the battle between the advocates of the short and highly finished poem and those who were true to the long, traditional epic Theocritus seems to have been on the side of the former,[7] even though he praises Asclepiades, who, we now know, was one of Callimachus' detractors.[8] Callimachus himself praised Theocritus' Idyll XI in no uncertain terms[9] and we can also gather that the Syracusan poet was involved in the literary disputes of his day from the evidence furnished by the end of the *Heracliscus* (Idyll XXIV), where in the last two lines he asks the god to ensure that the poet, like himself, will prove victorious over his adversaries. Moreover, as we saw, it appears probable that Idyll XIII (the *Hylas*) and part of Idyll XXII (*Polydeuces and Amycus*) were recast by Apollonius in his own traditional style and included in the *Argonautica*, though clearly with no improvement on the originals.

Theocritus' claim to fame rests primarily upon his bucolic poetry, in which most of his outstanding dramatic, descriptive and lyric qualities are displayed. The question arises of whether he was truly the first bucolic poet in Greek literature, for early traces of the idyllic spirit can be found as far back as the *Odyssey* and the choral odes of Stesichorus.[10] An unknown ancient scholiast, with whom the scholia of Theocritus begin, assigns the origins of bucolic poetry not to poets earlier than Theocritus but to cult, to the festivals of Artemis and, more particularly, to the festival of Artemis in Syracuse, in which countrymen competed in song.[11] This does not appear probable, but even if the birth of bucolic poetry did not depend on cult, folk songs sung at festivals and upon many other occasions may well have been its origin. In fact, to this day singing matches at country gatherings continue to exist in Sicily and in Greece.

However that may be, we know of no pre-Theocritean bucolic poetry worthy of the name, although certain poets like Anyte, Lycophronides (early third century) or Leonidas of Tarentum made use of rustic themes. For the essence of bucolic poetry is the portrayal of musical and poetic rustics, the subject-matter of whose songs is love, and the description of the idyllic landscape, which is a suitable 'poetic' setting for the love motif. It is proper, therefore, to assume that it was Theocritus who, under the influence of the mimes of Sophron, drew his inspiration from the ordinary practice of Sicilian and other herdsmen and elevated traditional bucolic poetry to a highly skilled art-form. And the response this poetry provoked was indeed understandable in the Hellenistic world, where big-city life had developed together with all the yearning for the tranquillity and the peace of the countryside it usually brings with it.

It should, however, be borne in mind that in spite of the influence of Sophron, Theocritus' *merae rusticae* are far more idealized than his highly realistic urban mimes. Though the Theocritean rustic mimes—Idylls I, III, IV, V, VI, VII, X and XI[12]—differ from one another, they all portray musical and poetic rustics in the same spirit. Thus in Idyll I (*Thyrsis*) a goatherd asks Thyrsis to sing the song of the strange love and death of the mythical Sicilian herdsman Daphnis, the archetype of all bucolic poetry. Among the presents which are promised in order to persuade Thyrsis to sing is a splendid rustic bowl belonging to the goatherd; the long description of the bowl, in which the carved figures are filled with life and movement (a typical Alexandrian ecphrasis) serves as counterpart to the song of Thyrsis, who in the end receives the gift as a reward for his song.

Idyll III (the *Comos*), is a dramatized monologue in which an unnamed goatherd, after entrusing his goats to Tityrus, serenades Amaryllis, with whom he is in love. The tone is one of patronizing humour, as features of the urban *comos* and the *paraclausitheron* are transferred to a rustic setting.

Idyll IV, which is wholly dramatic, depicts in realistic terms—so different from Virgil's idealized shepherds—a gossipy conversation between Corydon, a cowherd, and Battos, a goatherd. The offensive-defensive opening leads to a friendly close; the tone is crude, earthy and, finally, characterized by much harsh teasing and proverbial utterances.

In Idyll V we have once again the description of the meeting of two herdsmen, Comatas and Lacon. But this is not a friendly meeting. Mutual antipathy gradually intensifies as they accuse, revile and ridicule one another before they agree to compete in a singing match in which Comatas is triumphant. The theme of Idyll VI like that of XI, is the love of Polyphemus for Galatea.

Idyll VII occupies a very special position among the rural mimes of Theocritus and is one of the undisputed masterpieces of Greek poetry. It is a narrative in the first person which describes a walk of the poet—who appears under the pseudonymn of Simichidas—with two friends to a farm in Cos, where they attend a harvest festival of Demeter. On their way in the midday heat (κατὰ μεσημβρίαν), with all its 'supernatural' connotations, they meet the goatherd Lycidas—obviously the nickname of a fellow poet we cannot identify[13]—and, after exchanging views on poetry, Simichidas and he each sing a song in appreciation of the other (Simichidas' song could, in fact, have formed the plot of a non-bucolic mime), after which the two poets part company and the three friends arrive at the farm. The poem ends with a magnificent description of the lush and peaceful setting of Demeter's festival. No other Greek poet has described so ex-

quisitely a hot day in high summer, except perhaps for Angelos Sike-
lianos, some 1600 years later, in his poem *Thalero*.

Idyll VII gave rise to the theory of the *masquerade bucolique*, according to
which Theocritus and his fellow-poets formed a religious or literary
society in Cos whose members assumed the nicknames of shepherds. This
is highly improbable, for by contrast with the idealized shepherds of
Virgil, most of the herdsmen and farmers of Theocritus are far too
realistically portrayed to be 'masks' for Alexandrian poets.[14]

Idyll X (the *Reapers*) deals not with herdsmen but with the reapers
Milon and Boukaios; the latter is in love with a dark, slender girl named
Bombyka. As a relief from his suffering he sings about her—parts of his
naive song of praise are meant to amuse the refined reader—and Milon,
after complimenting him, sings a reapers' working song, which is raised to
the level of sophisticated poetry.

Finally Idyll XI (the *Cyclops*), which, as we can see from Callimachus'
Epigram 64, was admired even by that most austere of critics, is addressed
to Theocritus' doctor friend, Nicias. It presents in a narrative frame the
uncouth and physically repulsive Polyphemus alleviating with song his
hopeless love for the nereid Galatea. The stupidity of that semi-bestial
figure lends scope to the poet's humour, which, however, is delightfully
good-natured. Philoxenus' famous dithyramb *Cyclops*, in which Polyphe-
mus was presented singing to the lyre, was one of Theocritus' sources.

Idylls VIII and IX, which are bucolic singing contests between Daph-
nis and Menalcas, are clearly spurious. In the former, elegiac couplets
(33–60) have been inserted between the hexameters, and in the latter,
which is exceedingly short (only thirty-six lines long), the adjudicator
himself, a figure familiar from Virgil's *Eclogues*, sings a song of his own.

Idylls IV and V are the least artificial of Theocritus' bucolic idylls; as
the scene is laid in Magna Graecia, it is perhaps reasonable to assume that
they represent early examples of his art, even if written after his departure
for the east. Idyll X is next to these in realism, for the rest of the *merae
rusticae* are much more artificial. Thus in Idyll I the treatment of bucolic
life is sublimated and generalized, and in Idyll VII the pastoral element
serves merely as a framework for the poem of Thyrsis. In a sense, this
holds good for Idyll XI too, which is a parody of, and a satire on, conceits
and motifs of contemporary love elegies, as well as of certain fashions and
practices of contemporary life. But Theocritus' satire is always friendly
and good-natured, originating in a keen sense of humour and not in the
indignation that springs from moral earnestness.

In the ideal bucolic world Theocritus presents, which accentuates the
timelessness of the poems, the idyllic landscape occupies a very special
place. It is, in fact, one of his most important contributions to literature.
This is a modest landscape with no vast vistas and with nothing strange or
surprising about it. Amiable, graceful, and deliberately vague it nearly

always displays the same features—a fountain, a murmuring stream, a rocky cave, a meadow where flocks wander, trees whose branches murmur in the breeze and whose foliage lends protection against the sun, a rustic altar, some rude images of pastoral divinities, the shrill song of the cicada, at a distance the sweep of a bay or a chain of mountains. And this is in keeping with the poet's vagueness in his delineation of character; it lends a certain lyricism to his verse which counterbalances, in a sense, its artificiality and its conventional qualities.

Moreover, it should be pointed out that the idyllic setting is seldom described all at once, in narrative form. It is introduced gradually, partly in the introduction and partly in the dialogue, so that by the time we reach the real core of the poems, the singing match, it stands alive before our eyes, with its peaceful pastoral atmosphere 'which induces meditation to sink into somnolence'. Reference should also be made to Theocritus' free use of the pathetic fallacy, for inanimate nature is repeatedly invited to take part in the suffering and the feelings of his heroes.

The Alexandrians, who had experienced the fatigue and the complications of big-city life, with all the yearning for the simplicity and the peace of the countryside it engenders, readily responded to Theocritus' poetry —indeed, were probably to a great extent responsible for its creation. There is little reason to think that any of Theocritus' bucolic poems (not even Idylls IV, V, VI, and XI, which have an ostensibly southern Italian setting) were written before the poet left for the East. In fact, most of them contain details, often botanical, that connect them with Cos and the eastern Mediterranean world, and they all indicate a longing for the tranquillity of country life. But alongside this idealized atmosphere and the sophistication of the *merae rusticae*, we find in them many elements of crude realism and even of impropriety and obscenity.[15] And it is this fusion of the two that the Alexandrians admired and honoured.

The non-pastoral mimes share many of the features of the bucolic, though on the whole they are more realistic. The three surviving town mimes (Idylls II, XIV and XV) have long been recognized as masterpieces of inspired realism, and in its own way their poetry is as great as, if not greater than, that of the country mimes.

Idyll II (the *Sorceresses*) is probably set in Cos and uses the New Comedy motif of the young girl who is abandoned by her lover. The whole poem is a dramatic monologue of the heroine, Simaetha, who practises at night the magic love charms current among the uneducated people of those days in the hope of bringing back her lover, the handsome and unscrupulous athlete Delphis, who conquered her and then disappeared. The psychology of love is admirably portrayed, with all its alternating outbursts of desire, tenderness and hatred. Simaetha is one of the most real and most moving love-sick heroines that poetry has created. At the same time the poem avoids all display of erudition and, though a town mime, shows a wonderful feeling for nature—as one would have expected from Theocritus—at the end of the poem, when Simaetha is left alone and pours out her heart to the moon.

Idyll XV (the *Women Participating in the Adonis Festival*) has Alexandria as its setting. It presents two Syracusan women who are on their way to see the festival of Adonis, which is held in the garden of the Palace of the Ptolemies, and to hear an Argive woman who sings a song in his honour. After a magnificently realistic opening scene in Praxinoa's home, the women reach and enter the palace garden with difficulty because of the crowds and the soldiers in the streets. The poem consists of three independent scenes—not a word is said about the poet himself—and everything comes to life in the uninterrupted and lively chatter of the women. The character drawing is brilliant, and the touches of humour and of subtle realism are superb. Idyll XV is a masterpiece, one of the brightest gems in the history of Greek poetry.

The third town mime, Idyll XIV (*Aeschinas and Thyonichos*), is also related to Alexandria and once more shows a close affinity with New Comedy because it deals with the maltreatment of a sweetheart and disappointed love. It is certainly less alive and cruder than Theocritus' other two town mimes and contains much flattery of Ptolemy II, who is described as very generous towards his free mercenaries; he is 'well-disposed, a lover of art, of an amorous disposition, most sweet in manner, aware of those who are his friends, and even more of those who are his enemies, generous to many, not refusing to give when asked for help, as is proper for a king' (ll. 59ff.).

The other poems of Theocritus have little in common with his country and town mimes. Of these we have already come across Idyll XVI (the *Charites*), addressed to Hiero, and Idyll XVII, the panegyric to Ptolemy, 'two masterpieces in the art of begging and flattery', as they have been called; they are laureate verse encomia rather than hymns to a deified ruler. In Idyll XVII reference is also made to the recent establishment of the cult of Ptolemy Soter and Berenice, but there is no suggestion that the ruling royal pair, Ptolemy Philadelphus and Arsinoë, are deified. They are, of course, effusively praised, as is the *pax Ptolemaea*, and of especial interest is the poet's desire to justify the incestuous marriage of the king and his sister by comparison with the union of Zeus and Hera. On the other hand, in Idyll XVI, in which Hiero, the tyrant of Syracuse, is praised, the appeal for patronage is even more obvious; side by side with this, however, we find much lively verse and a beautiful eulogy to peace. In both of these poems Theocritus transposes the manner and matter of choral lyric into hexameters in true Alexandrian manner.

Idyll XII (the *Aites*, the *Favourite*), is a short homosexual love poem composed in Ionic dialect and in hexameters, and four other pieces—Idylls XIII, XXII, XXIV and XXVI—are hymns or short epics, for the distinction is not always easy to draw.[16] The first, Idyll XIII, which is more of an epic idyll than an idyllic *epyllion*, tells in exquisitely lyrical terms how the water-nymphs kidnapped Hylas when the Argonauts had beached their ship in Cius, thus giving the reason why Heracles did not follow them to Colchis. The second, Idyll XXII (the longest of Theocritus' poems), is a hymn to the Dioscuri Castor and Polydeuces. It falls into two parts, the first dealing with the boxing victory of Polydeuces over Amycus,[17] the barbaric king of the Berbycians, and the second with Castor's battle with Lynceus when carrying off the Leucippides. The third, Idyll XXIV, is the *Heracliscus*, which we now know is a hymn, and not an *epyllion*, as was hitherto thought.[18] This is the most charming poem of this group, notable for its elegance and its vigour. It falls into two distinct parts. The first describes, with reference to Pindar's first Nemean Ode and Paean XX,[19] how the infant Heracles kills the two snakes that visit his cradle, while in the second, in which the erudite element prevails, Tiresias foretells the whole career of the hero until his admission to the circle of the gods. The last two lines contain an invocation to Heracles and an appeal to the god, as we have seen, to ensure that the poet, Theocritus himself, will prove victorious over his adversaries. The un-heroic treatment of a heroic subject, the studied naivety and the good-natured humour of the *Heracliscus* make it a perfect example of Alexandrian poetry at its best. The fourth, Idyll XXVI, describes the fate of Pentheus at the hands of his mother Agaue and her sisters Ino and Autonoa at the Bacchanals. It is a very short piece, which has been interpreted in several ways—as a hymn to Dionysus, as a poem composed for the initiation of a boy at the Mysteries of Dionysus, as an exercise devoid of any serious intention and even as an emotional outburst following a performance of Euripides' *Bacchae*.[20]

In his constant experimentation and search for innovation Theocritus also tackled in Idyll XVIII, which is addressed to Helen, the old traditional form of the epithalamium. The Sapphic epithalamia were apparently in the poet's mind when composing this idyll, but from his metre, technique, erudite allusions and humour a completely new creation emerged which has a distinct flavour and peculiar charm of its own.

Finally, in Idylls XXVIII, XXIX, XXX and XXXI Theocritus imitated the Lesbian poets of the early sixth century B.C., Sappho and Alcaeus, in both dialect and metre. Idylls XXIX, XXX and XXXI are παιδικά, dealing with homosexual love (the last, recently retrieved in a papyrus from Arsinoë, is very mutilated), but XXVIII (the *Distaff*), which was written to accompany the gift of a distaff to the wife of the poet's friend Nicias, is a short masterpiece cast in asclepiadeans *a majore*, whose lyricism and elegance are superb.

About the epigrams of Theocritus, twenty-two of which have survived, we shall speak in Chapter 12.[21]

In true Alexandrian fashion, love plays a central role in the poetry of Theocritus, for most of the agents of his mimes and his hymns are in love, be they great heroes of the past like Heracles or an uncultured shepherd, to say nothing of his *paidika* poems and Idyll XII. The variety of lovers we meet in his writings is indeed extensive. Some justify their weakness by referring to divine precedents; some are frank and crude to the point of grossness; others, like Daphnis in Idyll I, are idealistic beyond comprehension; and we are even presented with the clownish love of the Cyclops for Galatea in Idyll XI, *à la fois risible et émouvant*, as Legrand puts it.[22] But it is only on the unhappy moments of love that Theocritus concentrates, and there is hardly any psychological analysis of the lover's feelings in his country mimes. On the other hand, in one of his town mimes, Idyll II, Theocritus proves himself a master in the analysis of the psychology of love when dealing with Simaetha, the young girl whom the handsome, heartless athlete Delphis has dazzled, conquered and abandoned.

In the portrayal of love, perhaps more than in any other aspect of his poetry, Theocritus displays his astonishing versatility and his capacity for seeing both sides of the picture, the serious and the amusing, the lyrical and the prosaic, the humble and the heroic; for he can both identify himself with the suffering lover and at the same time appear to be an *irrisor amoris*.

True to his age, Theocritus was constantly striving after innovation. Thus he elevated the folk song into highbrow poetry; he transferred town scenes to the countryside (Idyll III); he introduced the techniques of drama into epic (Idyll XXII) and of New Comedy into the mime (Idylls II and XIV); he transposed the manner and matter of choral lyric into hexameters (Idylls XVI, XVII and XVIII); he varied the heroic beat of the hexameter to suit his bucolic idylls; he recast Ionic lyric love songs into hexameters (Idyll XII); he used lyrical metres, *kata stichon*, as narrative verse (Idyll XXVIII);[23] he presented works with deliberately loosely connected scenes (Idylls XV and XXIV); he humanized the great traditional figures of mythology (Idylls XIII and XXIV) and so forth.

In spite of the contrived and, in many ways artificial elements that abound in his poetry, Theocritus never over-emphasizes his learning. His lyricism is delightfully fresh and his humour alive, ranging from good-natured fun to subtle irony and the crudest belly-laugh. Moreover, he is a master of description, avoiding all long and tedious details and concentrating on a few deft strokes to characterize his subjects. His minute observations have been seen as in keeping with the spirit of science that was coming into its own in those days.

But Theocritus is also a flatterer. The deeds of Hiero are compared with those of Achilles and Ajax. Ptolemy Philadelphus is said to be braver than Achilles and Diomedes, and, as we have seen in the encomium to Ptolemy (Idyll XVII), his praises are sung quite unrestrainedly: nor does

Theocritus forget to compliment Queen Arsinoë in Idyll XV. This is understandable in an age when all art was at the service of the king and especially at the service of the Ptolemies. Occasionally, the poet borders on sentimentality, especially when speaking about friendship and love. There is no political passion in his works and no patriotism in the conventional sense, but local pride is evident, as well as a peaceful affection for the idyllic beauty of his native land (Idyll XVI, ll. 82f.).

Theocritus uses the dactylic hexameter for all his poems with the exception of Idylls XXVIII, XXIX, XXX and XXXI, which are in Aeolic metres. In the bucolic mimes various devices modify the heroic character of his verse.[24] In his hexameter works, with the sole exception of Idyll XII, which is written in Ionic, the dialect used is a literary Doric mixed with elements of the epic diction, which may reflect the Syracusan origin of the poet. This was well suited to bucolic and was adopted by his successors in that genre.

Theocritus is by far the greatest of the three major Alexandrian poets and unquestionably a key figure in the history of Greek—indeed, of Western—poetry. Callimachus may be technically superior and may have the honour of being the major innovator of poetry in the Alexandrian age, but, with the exception of his epigrams, his immaculate verse is too heavily burdened by erudition and his frigidity often off-putting. Apollonius Rhodius, on the other hand, in spite of his brilliant treatment of Medea's love in Book III of his *Argonautica* and of some extremely attractive genre scenes, is on the whole too stodgy, and there are long passages of intolerable boredom.

By contrast with these, the warmth of Theocritus' personality, his capacity to enjoy the beauty of life and nature, his exquisite mixture of romance and realism and his delightful humour, touched with tenderness, are captivating to a degree and explain the influence he exercised upon posterity and the large number of the poems spuriously attributed to him. (Nor should his influence upon certain aspects in the development of the Greek epigram be forgotten.) For not only were his Greek successors in bucolic poetry, Moschus and Bion, influenced by his verse, and Virgil, his great admirer and imitator, but the whole of Western pastoral poetry rightly considers him its father.

HERODAS

Herodas (or Herondas, for the exact form of his name is still a matter of dispute) is a poet whose work is closely related to that of Theocritus. His date is also uncertain; one reference to Ptolemy III Euergetes[25] (247–221 B.C.) appears to be relatively clear; this would place him one generation after Theocritus. Nor is the city of his birth known, even though his poems point to the eastern Mediterranean and partly to Cos.

He wrote *mimiambi*, literary mimes in iambic scazons and in the Ionic dialect, eight of which and the beginning of a ninth have been retrieved in an Egyptian papyrus.[26] These are short, subtle, realistic pieces with a particular emphasis on the seamy side of life. But the faithful representation of daily life which he is after and in which he excels[27] is cast in a form that is anything but realistic. Like Theocritus, he wrote only for the select few with a literary background, for Herodas' mimes were meant to be read or perhaps acted in solo performances, but not to be produced on the stage.

The subjects are typical mime themes. Thus the first, the *Bawd*, deals with the procuress Gyllis, who visits Meretrice, a married woman whose husband (or perhaps lover) has gone to Egypt, and tries to persuade her to become the mistress of a young athlete. Meretrice declines politely but firmly and dismisses the procuress with a cup of wine. The second, the *Pimp*, an entertaining parody of a trial speech in the grand style, most probably borrowed its motif from New Comedy. The speech is delivered in court by Battarus against a trader who is accused of housebreaking and of attempting to abduct one of his house-girls. The portrait of the vulgar and mercenary pimp is perhaps the author's masterpiece.

Mimiambus III, the *Schoolmaster*, is by far the most harmless of Herodas' works. In it an angry mother, Metrotime, exasperated by the pranks of her incorrigible son, brings him to a dry schoolmaster, Lampriscus, to have him flogged, and flogged he is. Mimiambus IV, the *Women Worshippers*, is of much greater interest. In this poem two women and a maid-servant (who is mute) bring their simple offerings to the temple of Asclepius at Cos and are lost in admiration at the temple's magnificent statues and paintings.[28] Both these women, the short-tempered Cynno and her naive friend Coccale, as well as the oily sacristan, the *neocoros* of the temple, are admirably portrayed.

The fifth, the *Jealous Mistress*, depicts Bitinna ordering off her unfaithful slave–paramour to be flogged and then hastily fetching him back to be branded. He is granted a provisional pardon, however, through the flattering entreaties of her maid, Cydilla. Mimiambus VI, the *Private Conversation*, is a cynical conversation between two friends, Metro and Coritto, which takes place when the first calls on the second to ask for some information. The seventh, the *Shoemaker*, portrays Cerdon, a fashionable shoemaker, selling his wares to exacting and excitable lady customers. The portrait of Cerdon, who is alternately unctuous and defiant, is masterly. Mimiambus VIII, the *Dream*, tells of a farmer — perhaps Herodas himself — who recounts a dream in which his goat was torn to pieces by worshippers of Dionysus and how he won the prize in the contest that followed. Herodas may be referring here to his literary battles, to his harsh critics (the Callimacheans?) and to his hopes of ultimate recognition as the successor of Hipponax. Unfortunately, the reconstruction of several important passsages of this mime is problematic.

Of the ninth and last surviving *mimiambus*, *Women Breaking the Fast*, only a fragmentary introduction exists, which brings to mind the beginning of Theocritus' Idyll XV.

There is keen observation in the sketches of Herodas, and many of the scenes are amusing, but they do not compare with the poetic excellence of Theocritus; neither in lyricism, nor in lightness of touch, nor in human sympathy, nor in subtle humour do they approach the Syracusan master. Herodas never seems to become involved in his sketches. Aloof and impersonal, he directs no anger, disgust or pleasure at his characters. If there is any subjective note in his pieces, it is one of detached and ironic depreciation. What should also be pointed out, to his honour, is that by contrast with Theocritus and Callimachus, in the writings of Herodas there is hardly any flattery.

Herodas must have been only one among many authors of such poetic mimes, now lost.

The popular spoken mime

Unfortunately, in this field there is a lamentable lack of material, and such as we have belongs to a considerably later period. However, evidence exists of the popularity the spoken mime enjoyed throughout the Hellenistic age.

The one spoken popular mime which has survived comes from an Oxyrhynchus papyrus of the second century a.d., but the compositions it contains, a mime and a farce, are assigned to late Ptolemaic or early Imperial times. The theme of the mime is the same as that of the fifth *mimiambus* of Herodas, a slave who refuses to yield to the demands of a jealous mistress. The details of the action remain obscure, and it has even been suggested that the papyrus contains merely the outline of a play, the basis on which the company could improvise as they pleased. The coincidence with Herodas has been interpreted by some scholars as indicating a popular adaptation and expansion of the earlier *mimiambus*, and by others (and this appears more probable) as merely the independent treatment by both mimes of a traditional subject.

What we can gather from the little available evidence is that side by side with isolated scenes from actual life, known as *paegnia*, there existed other, longer spoken mimes with plots, known as *hypotheseis*,[29] which are also thought to have served as models for the Romans Laberius and Publilius in Sulla's day. That such *hypotheseis* existed much earlier than the late Ptolemaic times can be also seen from a third-century terracotta lamp, found in Athens,[30] on which three actors are represented and the following inscription appears: Μιμολόγοι. Ὑπόθεσις Ἑκυρά (Actors of spoken mimes. The plot: The Mother-in-Law).[31]

The sung mime

About the sung mime we are somewhat better informed, for new discoveries (though few, fragmentary and mostly late) give us some idea of the popular verse, devoid of any moral purpose, which went under the name of mimody.

According to the philosopher and musical theorist Aristoxenus of Tarentum (c. 375–360 B.C.), mimody was divided into two types, hilarody and magody.[32] The first was a tragic burlesque, the second a comic burlesque. Performers of hilarody took part in the *agones thymelikoi* of those days, and they appeared dressed in white, wearing golden crowns and accompanied by a flute player. Theirs was a sober performance. On the other hand, magody was accompanied by a tambourine and cymbals and indulged in lascivious dancing rhythms.[33] There is no evidence that hilarody was influenced by the southern Italian *phlyakes*, but there can be little doubt about their similarity.

Mimody, as a short literary form, reflects the same Hellenistic aversion to the long poem that turned the epic into the *epyllion*. By shortening tragedy into hilarody and comedy into magody—and, of course, by changing their character to suit a wider and mixed Hellenistic audience —mimody catered for the impatience and fatigue of big-city life.

No examples of hilarody have survived from the early Alexandrian age, but an important fragment of what appears to be magody has been retrieved in an Egyptian papyrus of the second century B.C., as well as another minor fragment which was found inscribed on the door of a temple in Marissa, between Gaza and Jerusalem.

The former is known as the Alexandrian Erotic Fragment or *Fragmentum Grenfellianum*. This is probably not a fragment at all[34] but a complete composition, which gives the emotional appeal, largely in excited dochmiacs, of a deserted *hetaera* who pleads outside her lover's house to be taken back again into his affections. Its free metrical construction reminds one of the chanted arias of the later Euripidean plays; but with this rather pretentious metrical structure is combined the simple spoken *koine* of the second century B.C. The subject, also taken from daily life—one more abandoned girl, like Simaetha of Theocritus' Idyll II or the deserted girls we meet in New Comedy—is treated seriously and presented in the setting of a strange *paraclausitheron* in which the girl, and not the man, pleads outside the closed door of her lover. But as the door remains closed, threats follow the entreaties; these are followed in turn by further attempts at reconciliation, but all in vain. The absence of rhetoric and erudition makes it an attractive piece, which explains why mimody was so successful with its audiences. The Alexandrian Erotic Fragment also suggests that lyric poetry, and not only tragedy and comedy, should be considered one of the ancestors of mimody.

The short fragment from the temple door at Marissa is dated about 150 B.C. and shows a *hetaera* conversing with a lover who has been locked out. It is thought that the piece was sung as a solo. It confirms the statement of Athenaeus[35] that all Phoenicia was full of the so-called 'Locrian songs' which had adultery for their theme.

OBSCENE, SATIRICAL AND HUMOROUS VERSE

Cynaedoi

Magody, comic burlesque accompanied by Oriental instruments and obscene dancing, leads us to the wider sphere of 'shameless' poetry, known as cynaedology. The distinction between the two is not always clear, and in a certain sense they overlap, but whereas magody always had a plot, an *hypotheseis*, no matter how elementary, the *cynaedoi* were *paegnia* and did not need to have one.

Cynaedoi, the 'shameless' poems, were always composed in Ionic metres —hence their performers were called either *cynaedologoi* or *Ionicologoi*[36]— and were originally accompanied by music and sung by mimic dancers. Their subjects were indecent and their verses full of improper ambiguities, parodies and obscenities, whose purpose (not unlike that of some music-hall or cabaret songs of our own day) was to amuse a wide and unrefined public.

Originally, this poetic genre was beyond the pale of literature, and its origins can be traced at least as far back as Theodore of Syracuse, who lived before Aristotle,[37] but it came into its own in the early Hellenistic age. The names of two famous exponents of musical *cynaedoi* should be mentioned: Simos of Magnesia (c. 320 B.C.) and Lysis, also probably from Magnesia (c. 300 B.C.). Such was their popularity that the two kinds of mimody came to be distinguished by their names, *simodia* (Σιμῳδία) meaning hilarody and *lysodia* (Λυσῳδία) magody; but nothing of their work survives.[38]

This vigorous, amusing and obscene poetry was introduced into the realm of literature by two distinguished Alexandrian poets, Sotades of Maroneia and Alexander the Aetolian, at whose hands it shed its musical accompaniment and began to be composed *kata stichon*.[39] We know of the names of others who followed their example, but again no examples of their work have survived.

The man who was universally considered the master in that field was Sotades of Maroneia in Crete, who lived in the time of Ptolemy Philadelphus (beginning of third century B.C.). According to Athenaeus,[40] when in Alexandria Sotades ridiculed Lysimachus to amuse Ptolemy II, and when in Antioch he attacked Ptolemy II to amuse Lysimachus. But he enraged Ptolemy II Philadelphus when he wrote disparagingly about his marriage to his sister Arisinoë II—in the Macedonian tradition marriage between brother and sister was acceptable, but it shocked the other Greeks—and as a result he was drowned in the sea at the king's command.

Sotades invented the *versus sotadeus*, a minor Ionic metre which allowed great variations[41] and became the standard verse for *cynaedoi*. Some of the titles of his works—*Descent to Hades, Priapus, On Belestiche* (a mistress of Ptolemy II), *Amazon, Adonis* and *Ilias* (a transcription of the *Iliad* into sotadeans)—have survived, as well as a few fragments from them.[42] In these we find biting humour and a succinct casting of maxims into verse. The sotadeans preserved by Stobaeus are commonly thought to be unauthentic. Although Quintilian did not consider the works of Sotades suitable to be taught at school, they were widely read till the end of antiquity.

Among the imitators of Sotades one who deserves mention is Cleomenes, the boxer from Magnesia, after whom the *metrum cleomacheum*, an Ionic dimeter, was named.[43]

Silloi and the *spoudogeloion*

Of a much more serious nature were the *silloi*, the lampoons in hexameters, whose origins can be traced back to Xenophanes of Colophon (sixth century B.C.)[44] and whose development was influenced by the *spoudogeloion* (σπουδογέλοιον) of the Cynics, which attacked dogmatic philosophers and parodied Homer and other poets. From the few surviving fragments and from such information as we can gather from other sources, the basic characteristics of sillography were the use of the hexameter, the attacks on significant men (mainly philosophers), the use of alliterative puns and of words with ambiguous meaning and the constant parody of Homeric verses.

The greatest representative of sillography was Timon of Phlius (c. 320 –230 B.C.) the one-eyed Sceptical philosopher—he never tired of referring to himself as Cyclops—who had spent a part of his youth in poverty, earning his living as a dancer; he then studied in Megara with Stilpon and later with Pyrrhon of Elis, the founder of Greek Scepticism, for whom he always expressed admiration and affection.

Most famous of his many writings were his *Silloi* in three books, which were lampoons against the dogmatic philosophers, for Timon was quick to observe men's weaknesses (so say the records) and skilled at turning them into ridicule. The work was apparently cast in the form of a *Nekyia* or

'Descent to Hades', where violent arguments among the philosophers of the past were described, as well as a dialogue between the poet himself and Xenophanes. The *Silloi* was clearly no popular poem, for to appreciate its satire a fairly comprehensive knowledge of the history of philosophy was necessary, no matter how much Timon sneered at the learned academic society of the Alexandrian Museum. The few surviving fragments show Timon to have been an able parodist of Homer and a writer with a gift for creating new words. Even in the few lines of his we now have, sixty *hapax eiremena* occur, and a passion for monstrous compounds is evident which betrays the influence of comedy. Timon also composed *indalmoi* ('images'? 'fantasies'?) in elegiacs, *kynaedoi* and even tragedies and satyr plays now lost, to say nothing of his many philosophical prose writings.[45]

Silloi of the same nature as Timon's were also composed by two of his contemporaries, Crates of Thebes and Bion the Borysthenite. Crates of Thebes (c. 365–285 B.C.) was a Cynic who first attended in Athens the lectures of Bryson of the Megaric School but was soon converted to Cynicism by Diogenes of Sinope. He led a wandering life in the company of his wife, propagating voluntary poverty and independence and consoling people in distress.[46] He is said to have been the first to revise the verses of famous poets giving them a Cynical flavour. In these parodies he not only 'corrected' the mistaken (according to his principles) viewpoint of his originals but also supplied a moral if none existed. His most famous effort in this field was his parody of Homer, called *Pera* (the *Wallet*), in which this outward symbol of the Cynic credo gave its name to a sort of Utopia. He is also credited with composing tragedies of a very lofty character.[47]

Bion the Borysthenite (c. 325–255 B.C.) was the son of a freedman and of a *hetaera* of Borysthenes (Odessa). He was sold into slavery when he was young because of a fraud perpetrated by his father but, as the slave of the rhetorician Bion, he received a good education, was later set free and inherited the fortune of his master. He studied in Athens in both the Peripatos and the Academy but was more strongly influenced by Crates of Thebes and Theodoros the atheist and hedonist. He imitated the caustic humour, the criticism of convention and the shamelessness of the Cynics and wandered from town to town lecturing for money and preaching the Cyreniac doctrine that happiness is achieved by adapting oneself to circumstance. His writings, of which only a few shreds have survived, were composed in a highly eclectic style and later influenced Roman satire.[48]

There are no traces of true *silloi* after the days of Timon of Phlius, but the line of development clearly leads from sillography to the satires of Menippus of Gadara (first half of third century B.C.). He was a slave at Sinope who became a pupil of the Cynic Metrocles, bought his freedom and acquired the Theban franchise. The Menippean satires were characterized by a mixture of prose and verse, but it is uncertain whether the verse was original or comprised quotations from other poets.

Menippus was the originator of the σπουδογέλοιον, the serio-comic style, in which humorous expression was given to philosophical views. The aim of this mixture of the earnest and the droll was *ridentem dicere verum*. Marcus Aurelius calls Menippus 'a mocker of man's ephemeral existence'. His works are unfortunately lost, but he had Greek and Roman imitators, among them Varro, Seneca (in his skit on Claudius) and Lucian, and from their writings it is possible to gain some idea of the original which they followed. Of his works—which included the *Nekyia* (in which he imitated Crates), the *Diathekai*, the *Symposium*, the *Diogenous Prasis* and others—the *Nekyia* can be partly reconstructed; it appears that the poet described there how he visited the Underworld in order to find Tiresias and to ask him which life was best. In it he ridiculed rich and despotic rulers and parodied those serious works that told of a journey to Hades, like the descents of Orpheus, of Heracles and so on.

Menippus, who spared nobody, used various settings for his satires (banquet scenes, ascents to heaven, auctions) and seems to have had no compunction. With the Atticist renaissance his satires seem to have been forgotten until Lucian of Samosata (born c. A.D. 120) discovered this discarded compatriot of his. But he influenced Meleager of Gadara (c. 100 B.C.), and Varro's *Saturae Menippeae* are adapted from his. In Latin the Menippean satire, which is distinguished by Quintilian as a separate sort of satire (Inst. 10.1.95), is represented by Varro, Seneca and Petronius and descends to Martianus Capella (fifth century A.D.) and to the French *satire Ménippée*.[49]

Epic parodies

Finally, a word must be added here about the epic parody, a poetic genre which seems to have flourished in the Alexandrian world. Its origins are very old, probably going back to the *Margites* (eighty century B.C.?) and certainly to the *Batrachomyomachia* (probably end of sixth–beginning of fifth century B.C.). But the tradition of Homeric parody which runs through comedy from Cratinus (mid-fifth century B.C.) to Diphilus (born c. 360–350 B.C.), and which was later taken over by the sillographers and the gastronomists, was accorded the status of an independent genre, with a separate place of its own in competitions, by Hegemon of Thasos (mid-fifth century B.C.).[50] Among his works the *Gigantomachia* achieved fame.

In the Hellenistic Age, together with the good use of epic parody made by the sillographers and the satire of the Cynics, we also find the genre employed for trivial subjects like the *Deipna*, in which provocative verses described all kinds of spicy dishes and delicacies. In these the *Deipna* followed in the footsteps of comedy, which, since Epicharmus, had indulged in such gastronomic description.

The most distinguished of these gastronomic satirical poets was Archestratus of Gela (c. 350 B.C.), a contemporary of Aristotle, who was called 'the Hesiod or the Theognis of the gourmets'. But the *Deipnon Attikon* of Matron of Pitane (second half of the fourth century B.C.) was also well-known; the first line of this was a parody of the opening of the *Odyssey*:

Δεῖπνα μοι ἔννεπε Μοῦσα, πολύτροπα καὶ μάλα πολλά.

Some of these poems, like the *Deipnon* of Timarchidas of Lindos (c. 100 B.C.), were at least eleven rhapsodies long.

POPULAR MORALIZING VERSE

All that has come to light of the popular verse which eschewed any moral purpose and was intended to amuse a wide and less well-educated audience is, as we have seen, anonymous. But the period also had a popular moralizing verse, about which the papyri have enlightened us and whose significance we now understand. Among the moralists two deserve mention: Cercidas of Megalopolis and Phoenix of Colophon.

Cercidas of Megalopolis (c. 290–c. 220 B.C.) was a successful politician and lawgiver who played a leading role in the troubled political life of the Peloponnese during the third century. Outside politics he attained fame as a Cynic philosopher and poet. Only nine short fragments of Cercidas' verse have been preserved in literary sources, of which one is an extract from his *Iambi*. It shows that the work was composed in choliambic or *scazon* metre and that it attacked luxury. But substantial remains of his best-known work, the *Meliambi*,[51] poems lyrical in form with a satirical content, proved that Cercidas was an acute critic of his society and an original metrist. Though belonging to the wealthy governing class, he voiced the grievances of the poor and took his Cynic creed seriously, exhorting his fellow men to mend their ways while there was yet time. He also scolded the gods for the unjust distribution of earthly goods.

His style recalls that of the prose diatribe—supposed to be the invention of Bion the Borysthenite—which, however, he combines with other features deriving from the dithyramb, Old Comedy and the writings of Timon of Phlius. In his mixture of the serious and the light-hearted one can clearly see the influence of Crates of Thebes, whose example was also followed by Menippus of Gadara at roughly the same time. The language of the *Meliambi* is a literary Doric which avoids local peculiarities.

Cercidas has also been suggested as the author of an anthology of moralizing verse preserved in several papyri and possibly of some of the pieces written in scazons.[52] He is said to have had the first two books of the *Iliad* buried with him and to have framed a law that boys should learn the second book by heart.

Phoenix of Colophon (third century B.C.) was also the author of moralizing choliambics and of a poem, *Coronistae*, which was based on a Rhodian beggar's song, sung while travelling around with a crow. Of these Athenaeus has preserved five quotations, some coming from the *Ninos*, a poem about the mythical glutton. The new *iambus* fragment of twenty-two lines retrieved from a papyrus,[53] which attacks the perversity of the rich, has not prompted a reappraisal of Phoenix's poetic powers. It shows that his subject-matter was for the most part commonplace and that his enduring concern was to moralize about the failings of the rich and the sufferings of the poor. Phoenix is thought to have lived a little earlier than Callimachus; since there is some coincidence of themes between the two, the latter's *iambi* may owe something to those of Phoenix.

The other additions to the moralizing verse of the period are inconsiderable and disappointing. They include a few *gnomai* (prudential maxims) of a shadowy figure called Chares and fragments of some moral rules which, since the end of the fifth century B.C., have been spuriously attributed to Epicharmus.

CHAPTER 11

Lyric Poetry and Hymnography

It is true to say that from the third century onwards secular lyric poetry is mainly represented by the epigram. Few, short and totally unimportant are the surviving fragments of Hellenistic lyric poetry in the traditional sense of the term; they are nearly all anonymous and very poor indeed as poetry.[1] Secular lyrical poetry was no doubt dealt the death-blow by the independent and spectacular development of music in the Alexandrian age; it was no longer combined with words but was performed by individual virtuoso instrumentalists.

On the other hand, religious lyrical hymns continued to be composed, for though the Olympian and other deities had lost the importance they once had in the Classical world, festivals continued to be celebrated — often magnificently — and these provided suitable incentive for the composition of new religious hymns, which were sometimes chanted side by side with well-known older ones.[2] As far as we can gather, their literary value was on the whole very low. These new and numerous[3] Hellenistic religious hymns can be classified, according to the deities involved, into cult hymns to old Hellenic gods, hymns to deified members of ruling royal houses and hymns to Egyptian and other non-Greek deities.

The most important of the first group have been retrieved on inscriptions found in Epidaurus and Delphi. From Epidaurus six poems of an otherwise unknown modest poet, Isyllus (c. 320 B.C.), have come to light. Among them is a paean to Apollo and Asclepius in ionics and a hymn to Asclepius in hexameters, in which the poet thanks the god for defending Sparta against the attack of King Philip.[4]

From Delphi we have a paean by Philodamus of Scarphea (c. 324 B.C.), celebrating Dionysus with true Bacchic enthusiasm.[5] It is significant because of the evidence it provides of the interpretation of the worship of Apollo and Dionysus at Delphi. Next to this comes a paean to Apollo by Aristonous, a Corinthian cytharode (c. 222 B.C.),[6] for which he was granted certain privileges by the Delphians. A dactylo-epitrite hymn to Hestia by the same poet has also survived.

From Delphi we also have two further paeans to Apollo,[7] the first of which is composed by an unknown Athenian and the second by Limenius (c. 128/127 B.C.?). In the latter the paeonic rhythm predominates, and it ends with a wish for loyalty to Rome. Both these paeans have little to commend them as poetry, but they are unusually important texts because they are accompanied by musical notation.

To these should be added a dactylic paean to Asclepius from an inscription in Erythrea[8]—this is a few decades older than Isyllus—the paean of Macedonius to Apollo and Asclepius, found near the Asclepeium in Athens,[9] a hymn to Zeus of Dicte from Palaeokastro in Crete[10] and a hymn to the Dictaen Dactyls from Eretria.[11]

The adulation of the Hellenistic kings and conquerors goes back to the fourth century B.C., as can be seen from the paeans of Hermocles of Cyzicus[12] in honour of Antigonus and Demetrius Poliorketes and from the processional song of Duris, whose theme is the return of Demetrius from Corcyra. In it the 'god present' is honoured by the obliteration of all the other gods.[13] To these should be added a badly damaged papyrus from Chicago, which probably includes a hymn to Arsinoë II Aphrodite.[14] So much only has survived of the cult hymns to deified Hellenistic monarchs, but the output must have been considerable in view of the court flattery current in those days and the fact that the monarch was patron of all art. A clear distinction must be drawn, however, between cult hymns on the one hand and panegyrics or encomia on members of a ruling royal house on the other—poems like Theocritus' panegyric on Ptolemy II (Idyll XIX) or even Callimachus' *Ektheosis Arsinoes*—which cannot be classed among the former, even though they may speak of the deification of the monarch.[15]

Greek hymns were also composed to celebrate the 'new' Egyptian and other non-Egyptian deities. Thus we have an inscription from Delos containing sixty-five hexameters, composed by one Maeistas (end of third century B.C.),[16] which introduce the aretalogies (the poems in which the achievements ($\dot{\alpha}\varrho\varepsilon\tau\alpha\acute{\iota}$) of a god are described) of Serapis. Along with this appear the aretalogies in praise of the goddess Isis—they form a special branch of literature—of which the one in hexameters found in Andros, a most striking piece of mystic poetry of the days of Sulla,[17] and the one in trimeters from Cyrene should be singled out.[18]

Stobaeus, confusing the name of the city of Rome ($'P\grave{\omega}\mu\eta$) with the word for strength or courage ($\dot{\varrho}\acute{\omega}\mu\eta$) preserved in a section of his florilegium *On Courage* ($\Pi\varepsilon\varrho\grave{\iota}$ $\dot{\alpha}\nu\delta\varrho\varepsilon\acute{\iota}\alpha\varsigma$)[19] a hymn by Melinno on Rome. Its date is a matter of dispute, but it seems probable that it belongs to the first half of the second century, when the worship of the *Dea Roma* was fast gaining ground.[20] A paean on Titus Flaminius, part of which Plutarch has preserved, should also be mentioned here.[21]

Hymnography survived well into the Roman period, when colleges of *hymnodoi* were formed and the growth of superstition brought back the magic hymn. But hymnography was also invaded by prose as early as the fourth century B.C., though it is not until the second century A.D. that we find a good prose example, in the *Hieroi Logoi* of Aelius Aristeides.

Finally, two further religious hymns should be mentioned here, although they are literary and not cult hymns: the *Hymn to Zeus* by Cleanthes and the *Hymn to Eros* by Antagoras of Rhodes.[22] Cleanthes (331–232 B.C.), the distinguished philosopher, was the son of Phanias of Assos and a disciple of Zeno of Citium, whom he succeeded as head of the Stoic School from 263 to 232. His religious fervour pervaded the sober philosophy of Zeno, for he considered the universe to be a living thing, with God (Zeus) as its soul and the sun as its heart. In ethics he stressed disinterestedness and believed that evil thoughts were worse than evil deeds. Most famous of his works is his *Hymn to Zeus*, which is composed in hexameters and bears witness to true poetic inspiration and religious fervour. With this hymn begins the tradition of the philosophic–religious hymn, which was furthered by the Neo-Platonists and which we best know from the hymns of Proclus.

Antagoras of Rhodes (third century B.C.), who spent part of his life with Antigonus Gonatas in Macedonia, was not only a hymnographer but also an epic poet credited with a *Thebais*, and an epigrammatist.[23] Seven lines of his hymn to Eros have been preserved by Diogenes Laertius; it was a learned Alexandrian compilation of the myths associated with the birth of the god.[24]

Further names of poets of this period who wrote literary hymns are known, but nothing of their work survives.

CHAPTER 12

Alexandrian Epigrams, Technopaegnia and Priapea

THE ALEXANDRIAN EPIGRAM

All the major changes that lead from the Classical to the Hellenistic epigram took place in the course of the fourth and at the beginning of the third century B.C. For it was then that the impressive archaic and Classical restraint of feeling, so prominent in the epitaphs of the Persian Wars, gave way to a freer expression of emotion and that the size of the epigram, both sepulchral and dedicatory, was expanded. At the same time we also observe the appearance of the literary epigram, a short composition cast in the form of an epigram but not meant to be inscribed on a real monument.

These major changes in the scope and character of the Greek epigram were due partly to the influence of rhetoric and partly to that of tragedy, which infused personal emotions into its verses; even more were they the consequence of the intrusion of convivial poetry into the collections of genuine epigrams taken down from monuments in the late fifth and the fourth century.[1] Thus not only did purely fictitious epitaphs and votive inscriptions come to be composed—compositions known as epideictic ('for display'), like many of those we find in the *Peplus Aristotelicus* about mythical heroes and long-dead historical figures—but also epigrams on works of art and even epitaphs on dead animals began to appear.

Plato, as we have seen, made use of the epigram as a vehicle for erotic poetry, and he used it with supreme delicacy and power; from then onwards this brief literary form assumed a function which traditionally belonged to lyrical poetry. And in this guise, that of lyrical occasional poetry, it was further developed and expanded in the hands of the great Alexandrian epigrammatists of the third century B.C. until it became the most inclusive and the most popular kind of Hellenistic verse. Any moment, any phase of everyday life became the subject of this brief

and pointed literary form, which soon conquered the courts of the
Hellenistic monarchs, their great centres of learning like the Museum and
its libraries, all festivals and all private gatherings. Literary criticism, flattery
of kings and queens, admiration or censure of poets and artists, humorous
remarks or stinging satire were all expressed in epigrams, and Ptolemy II
even commissioned poets to celebrate in that literary form the discoveries
of his natural scientists. But whether refined, witty, obscene, insulting or
flattering, it rarely survived the occasion for which it was composed, for it
aimed at a sharp but fleeting impression. The Alexandrian epigram is
quite in keeping with the delight in delicacy and brevity which charac-
terizes the greater part of surviving highbrow Alexandrian poetry. It has
rightly been compared with the Hellenistic engraved gems that express
the same pleasure in the miniature and, at that time of increasing luxury,
had also become extremely fashionable.

In the third century B.C. two schools of epigrammatists appeared: the
Ionian School, centred on Samos and Alexandria, and the Doric School,
whose main representatives came from the Doric-speaking areas of the
Greek world—the Peloponnese, southern Italy and Thebes. The activi-
ties of both seem to have ceased rather early, at about 240 B.C. After that
date the epigram declined both in the east and in the west, and the minor
epigrammatists who continued writing fused in an eclectic manner ele-
ments from both those schools, which—and this should be stressed—no
matter how different, still had much in common. It was not until the end
of the second and the beginning of the first century B.C. that the Phoeni-
cian School of epigrammatists emerged, which, with poets like Antipater
of Sidon, Meleager of Gadara, Philoxenus and Archias of Antioch, gave
the epigram a new lease of life.

Numerous are the names of the Alexandrian epigrammatists we know
—approximately sixty were included in the *Garland* of Meleager[2]—but
the exact dates of many are uncertain, and several with the same name
(Dionysios, Theaetetus or Diotimus) cannot always be distinguished
from one another. Moreover, a relatively large number of anonymous
Alexandrian epigrams has survived—fifty-seven alone come from Melea-
ger's *Garland*[3]—which does not make matters easier, as their dates are
unknown and among them small masterpieces can be found[4] which have
been plausibly attributed to known poets.[5]

In view of all this intractable material, the best we can do is to concen-
trate on the major figures of the two schools, about whom we have a
reasonable amount of information and whose art left its imprint upon the
age. Poets not known primarily as epigrammatists (with the exception of
Theocritus and Callimachus, who are masters in that field) will not be
examined in this chapter.

The Ionian School of epigrammatists

The most brilliant epigrammatists of the Alexandrian age belong to the Ionian School, which was more social, more sophisticated and more versatile than the Doric, engaging in all the familiar categories of the epigram—the epitaph, the dedication, the erotic, the literary, the dramatic, the moralizing, the sympotic and the scoptic—even if love and wine seem to have been its main concern.[6]

Two of the forerunners of the Ionian School should be singled out, Plato and Theocritus of Chios. About Plato, who pointed the way to the Alexandrians by introducing the erotic element into the epigram, we have already spoken.[7] Theocritus of Chios (fourth century B.C.), on the other hand, the opponent of Theopompus, revived in his epigrams against Aristotle and Hermias the pugnacious attacks aimed at specific persons which had lain dormant since the days of Simonides.[8] In his footsteps followed many distinguished Alexandrian poets.

The leader of the Ionian School was Asclepiades of Samos (c. 320–280 B.C.), whom we have already met in Theocritus' Idyll VII, under the pseudonym of Sikelidas.[9] Though Samian in origin, he spent at least part of his life in Egypt, whose sophistication he seems to have enjoyed. He was not only an epigrammatist, for we hear of lyrical[10] and hexameter poems which he composed; these are now lost, however.

Of the approximately forty epigrams ascribed to Asclepiades in the *Anthology*, thirty-three are indisputably genuine; the attribution of the remainder is shared by other poets, most frequently Posidippus.[11] They reveal a witty, urbane personality interested in wine and love and well-acquainted with the Alexandrian *demi-monde*, the world of the *hetaerae*. His main subject is heterosexual love, which he treats with great delicacy but without the deep emotion that accompanies a single and exclusive affection. With striking simplicity of language and great metrical skill Asclepiades succeeds in fusing the quintessence of the love elegy with that of the drinking song in his epigrams, some of which read like miniature mimes. (One of his achievements was the introduction into love poetry of many of the erotic themes and symbols which have become part of world literature.) There are no real or imaginary epitaphs among the poems of Asclepiades, but he wrote on the works of earlier poets, a type of epigram which goes back to the fourth century.[12] There is an interesting epigram praising Antimachus' *Lyde*, which corroborates the information we have that Asclepiades was one of Callimachus' detractors and on the side of the long, 'turgid' poem.

All that is best in the Alexandrian epigram can be found in the works of Asclepiades, and this explains the influence he exercised over practically all contemporary and subsequent epigrammatists, most notably Posidippus and Callimachus.

Posidippus of Pella (c. 280 B.C.) was one of the two Macedonian poets of the period—Posidippus the New Comedy poet being the other—but, like so many distinguished writers of his day, he gravitated towards Alexandria. Thirty epigrams attributed to him have survived, dealing mostly with feasting and love; they reveal his indebtedness to Asclepiades,[13] and they treat sex with brisk, ironic realism. But we have also satirical or scoptic verses from his pen and three important formal dedicatory epigrams, two for the temple of Aphrodite Arsinoë on the promontory of Zephyrion, east of the city of Alexandria, and one for the Pharos.

It has been suggested that Posidippus studied in the Stoa, but though two of his epigrams show some philosophical colour, there are no grounds for that belief. He was publicly honoured by the Aetolians in 280[14] and probably by the Delphians,[15] the latter perhaps for celebrating in verse the defeat of the Gauls who had attacked Delphi in 279.

Posidippus did not compose epigrams exclusively. He also wrote an *Aethiopia*, an *Asopia* and elegies, of which only a badly mutilated fragment from one (*On Old Age*)[16] has survived on two writing tablets found in Egypt. Whether the so-called *Epithalamion on Arsinoë* found in papyrus is by Posidippus or not is a matter of dispute.[17]

Posidippus' main achievement is in the same field as Asclepiades—a number of his poems can be paired with those of Asclepiades, and six share an attribution—but he is poorer in inventiveness and less delicate in expression. Nonetheless, his vigour renders him attractive and far superior to his many imitators.

The third poet whom Meleager grouped with Asclepiades and Posidippus is Hedylus of Samos (c. 270 B.C.), a somewhat shadowy figure. He came from a literary family, for both his mother, Hedyle, and his grandmother, Moschine, were poetesses and probably of Athenian origin. Ten of his epigrams have survived, of which three are included in the *Anthology*. He shares with Asclepiades and Posidippus a liking for convivial epigrams, and with the latter a delight in scoptic verse on the gluttonous (this is why he is so frequently quoted by Athenaeus). He also wrote on an *automaton* dedicated at the temple of Aphrodite Arsinoë at Zephyrion, which is evidence that he too must have spent some time in Egypt.

Hedylus is capable of sentiment, as his epitaph on Theon reveals,[18] and he was also able vividly to present contemporary bohemian life;[19] but the field in which he excels is that of the scoptic, satirical epigram. Though vigorous, humorous and sensitive, the quality of his work is uneven and clearly inferior to that of the two great epigrammatists with whom he is closely associated. (However, wine seems to have been of considerably greater importance to him than to either of the others.)

Epigrams were not the only works of Hedylus. He also wrote elegies[20] and prose works now lost.

Next to Asclepiades, Callimachus[21] (c. 305–c. 240 B.C.) is by far the most important epigrammatist of the Alexandrian age. He may not be quite as simple and direct as the Samian poet, but he is equally vigorous and even more concise in his diction. Meleager, who included him in his *Garland* of epigrams, calls his work 'the sweet . . . myrtleberry of Callimachus, always full of sharp honey' (ἡδὺ . . . μύρτον Καλλιμάχου στυφελοῦ ἀεὶ μέλιτος), referring, it is thought, to his stringent economy of words. Two of the poet's epigrams — approximately sixty survive[22] — relate to the poet's family and to himself, the second being a fictitious epitaph on himself, in which, as we have seen, he describes how he wishes posterity to remember him; others reflect his connection with Egypt and the court of the Ptolemies and probably also his early days as a schoolmaster.

Callimachus' epigrams can be classed according to their subjects into erotic, sepulchral, dedicatory and epideictic.[23]

He is at his best in his erotic and his sepulchral epigrams. The former, some fifteen in number, differ from those of Asclepiades (although Callimachus borrows from them) because they are all homosexual and none is obscene.[24] They reveal great delicacy and depth of feeling when dealing with the tragic side of love — the one[25] that is related to Asclepiades' epigram on Nicagoras[26] is exquisite — and display a striking variety of form and tone. For Callimachus is capable of mixing the most heterogeneous elements in his erotic verse: anecdotes,[27] literary views,[28] even a funerary note, as in his tragic Cleonicus epigram.[29] But when speaking about his own love-life a self-conscious intellectualism bordering on frivolity seems to seize him.

Roughly eighteen Callimachean epitaphs have survived, of which only a few are fictitious, including the one for his own grave noted above. They transmit a deeply felt emotion and display simplicity and, often, an enviable brevity, the latter most notably in the almost eliptical statement lamenting the death of the twelve-year-old boy Nicoteles[30] — a magnificent achievement. Among Callimachus' epitaphs we also meet the use of dialogue (so that the epigrams assume the form of miniature dramas),[31] as well free compositions which contain thoughts suggested by the death of a friend or by the text of a funerary inscription. Most famous of this group is the one on his fellow poet Heracleitus of Halicarnassus,[32] but there is also a beautiful one on the tragic death of Melanippus and his sister Basilo.[33]

Short masterpieces are found not only among the poet's erotic and sepulchral verse; Callimachus is also a master of the dedicatory and the epideictic epigram — there is a beautiful one on a tragic mask of Dionysus hanging in a schoolroom[34] — and there are others with a literary or moralizing content[35] in which the same economy of language and the same firm metrical structure are displayed. The only form of epigram in which Callimachus did not engage was the sceptic.

The influence of Callimachus as an epigrammatist was very great indeed. It is probable that even in his lifetime there existed a recognized collection of his epigrams, which Pliny the Younger[36] and Martial[37] later knew; even later they seem also to have been read in schools.[38]

We may pass over a number of minor epigrammatists like Theaetetus the Cyrenean, who was praised by Callimachus,[39] or Diotimus, with whom Aratus commiserates for being reduced to teaching children,[40] and come to the last important representative of the Ionian School, Dioscorides (c. 240 B.C.), a younger contemporary of Callimachus about whose life we know nothing. Some forty of his epigrams have reached us, which fall essentially into four groups, erotic, literary and theatrical, funerary and epideictic.

The love poems of Dioscorides, which are fairly equally divided between homosexual and heterosexual love, are lively, ironical, realistic and much more obscene than those of Asclepiades. Of greater interest are his literary and theatrical pieces, seven of which are about famous ancient and contemporary poets—Sappho, Anacreon, Thespis, Aeschylus, Sophocles, Sositheus and Machon; individually and as a class they were much imitated.[41] Side by side with these we also find learned 'defences', and among them the defence of the daughters of Lycambes whom Archilochus had so violently attacked four centuries before.[42] Among his funerary epigrams, which form a series of lively and informative vignettes reflecting the Egyptian background, can be found three 'Spartan' poems —in fact, they are more narrative than funerary—in which Dioscorides celebrates in a romantic manner the ancient heroism of the Spartans. His small group of epideictic epigrams is of lesser significance. He has verses on 'inventors' like Hyagnes and Atys, paradoxical anecdotes and even one more ecphrastic epigram on the famous statue of a cow by Myron,[43] about which thirty such poems have survived. Among his writings he has also one hate poem.[44]

Though Dioscorides draws on the epigrams of his predecessors,[45] especially those of Asclepiades, Callimachus and Leonidas of Tarentum, his work has both novelty and variety—but regrettably little poetic inspiration. Dioscorides probably represents the end of an age of intense development of the Alexandrian epigram, for there are no significant local Egyptian exponents of that genre till the late Imperial period, and even then they are in no respect outstanding.

Of the anonymous epigrams retrieved in papyri which can be claimed by the Ionian School, the most noteworthy are the lament for the poet Philicus of Corcyra, whom we have already met,[46] and two pieces connected with the royal house of the Ptolemies, both of the late third century.[47] The first describes a *nymphaeum* (fountain-house) dedicated to Arsinoë III (?), and the second celebrates Ptolemy IV Philopator as a patron of letters and a warrior on the occasion of the dedication by him of the temple to Homer.

The Alexandrian epigrams on stone are few and mostly funerary. It is useless to speculate if any of these anonymous works are by known poets. One or two are remarkable, like the moving third-century sextain on Philoxenus[48] or the one treating the sad theme of the young woman dying in childbirth.[49]

To the reign of Ptolemy III Euergetes (246–221 B.C.) belong the funerary poems found in inscriptions from Apollonopolis Magna (Edfu), at the foot of each of which is the name of their poet, Herodes.[50] As a poet Herodes is otherwise unknown and is by no means impressive.

The lapidary inscriptions, which, as one would have expected, are mostly funerary, show the superiority of the third over the second century B.C. and do not compare as poetry with the works of the known Alexandrian epigrammatists.

The Doric School of epigrammatists

The poets of the Doric School of epigrammatists came, as we have seen, from the Doric areas of Greece proper, or from the west, and wrote chiefly in Doric. Their writings are straightforward and objective, eschewing on the whole the two most popular subjects of the Ionian School, love and wine.

Erinna of Telos (end of fourth century B.C.), the remarkable young talent who established the *epyllion*, as we have seen, can be seen as a precursor of this school. Although Pliny's statement which credits Erinna with an epigram on dead animals cannot be accepted,[51] her epigram on a picture of Agatharchis[52] indicates that she points the way to epideictic epigrams on works of art which the Alexandrian Doric epigrammatists practised.[53]

The Doric School is initiated by two extraordinary women, Anyte of Tegea and Nossis of Locri.[54] Anyte (c. 300 B.C.), who was a native of Tegea, seems never to have travelled beyond Naupactus. She shows herself to be an accomplished composer of quatrains, for which she has a marked preference, and is thought both to have introduced idyllic descriptions of landscape into the epigram[55] and to have invented the fictitious epitaph on animals. The latter became fashionable; such epigrams, or valedictory poems on animals in inscriptional form, were composed not only by many important Hellenistic poets like Leonidas, Simmias, Mnasalces and Meleager but also later by Byzantine poets.

Some twenty genuine epigrams by Anyte have survived, most of which appear to be pure literary exercises. Twelve are graceful mock-epitaphs on pet animals—the most dainty is on a cricket and a cicada;[56] there is a beautiful memorial to a charger killed in battle;[57] and a charming epigram on children playing with a bridled goat,[58] which Ovid imitated in his

Metamorphoses[59]—and most of the others are nature lyrics filled with quiet, pure emotions. Anyte shares many common themes with Mnasalces and Nicias, the friend of Theocritus.[60] She also composed hexameter poems and lyrics now lost, and was even called the 'female Homer' (Ὁ θῆλυς Ὅμηρος).[61]

Nossis (c. 290) was a native of Epizephyrian Locri and a near contemporary of Anyte. Of her epigrams twelve have come down to us, but only one[62] is amorous in tone, in spite of the fact that Meleager in his *Garland* classifies her as an erotic poetess; her admiration for Sappho, with whom she compares herself in her own fictitious epitaph,[63] also seems to imply this. Like Anyte, she is also called a *melopoios*, a lyrical poetess, so it appears probable that her other poetry was lyrical and that it had a pronounced erotic flavour. However, nothing is known about it, although some scholars have connected it with the 'Songs called Locrian' (τὰ Λοκρικὰ λεγόμενα ᾄσματα), which are said not to have differed from the songs of Sappho and Anacreon.[64]

Eight of Nossis' epigrams, which are all in quatrains, concern women; some are dedications, including a joint dedication of a robe woven by the poetess and her mother, Theuphilis, to Hera at Croton,[65] and others are on portraits. Among the latter we find one speaking of the impression a portrait makes upon the viewer, not only of what it looks like.[66] Nossis is also the poetess who introduced the *apophthegma*, the pithy saying, into the epigram.[67]

Closely connected with the poetry of Anyte is that of Mnasalces of Sicyon (c. 260 B.C.), but he hardly equals her in charm. Seventeen epigrams of his have been transmitted in the *Anthology*, mainly dedications and epitaphs, but there are also quatrains on animals among them and one on a temple of Aphrodite,[68] as well as a solitary love poem,[69] which appeals to a vine to wait to shed its leaves on Antileon when he goes to sleep under it. An eighteenth epigram of Mnasalces has been preserved in Athenaeus,[70] in which Arete is presented mourning at the side of Hedone. This is a variation, with minimal alterations, of a quatrain by Asclepiades on the monument of Ajax;[71] it shows the Sicyonian poet to be a man with Stoic leanings acquainted with the teachings of Cleanthes.[72] In the works of Mnasalces there are further contacts with Asclepiades as well as with Nicias and Callimachus.

A satirical attack by Theodoridas in the form of an epitaph[73]—perhaps composed while Mnasalces was still alive—refers to him as *elegeiopoios* (which probably means simply 'epigrammatist') and derides his bombast and his plagiarisms. The first of these charges may refer to lyric compositions now lost. It is true that most of Mnasalces' work has little originality and limited poetic value.

Theodoridas of Syracuse (second half of third century B.C.) attacked not only Mnasalces with a sepulchral epigram[74] but also Euphorion,[75] the latter probably after his death.[76] The majority of his eighteen epigrams that survive are simple and often beautiful dedications and epitaphs in the early Hellenistic manner, most of which read like true inscriptions. Some are located in Magna Graecia, others in northern Greece and possibly in Ephesus and Cyprus. Two of Theodoridas' poems seem to draw on Leonidas of Tarentum,[77] but, like so many other poets of his age, he also borrowed from Callimachus. Some of the metres employed are unusual, a practice favoured in the second half of the third century.

Theodoridas is also credited with a poem on Eros,[78] a dithyramb called the *Centaurs*,[79] iambic and hexameter poems[80] and possibly cynaedic songs.[81]

A representative of the Doric School who must be singled out is Perses of Thebes (c. 300 B.C.?), whose exact date is uncertain but whose style places him among the early Hellenistic epigrammatists.[82] Eight of his epigrams have survived, of which some are sepulchral and some dedicatory, all apparently written as real inscriptions. Two of these actually describe the reliefs under which they were carved.[83] Though more emotional than similar poems in the Classical era, they are restrained and dignified and have been called the counterparts in poetry of the reserved and impersonal sculptured Attic tombstones. A good example of these is an epigram on a representation of Mnasylla and her husband Aristoteles mourning over a portrait of their daughter Neotima, who died in childbirth.[84]

We must now turn to Theocritus (c. 300–c. 260 B.C.), who is one of the most distinguished representatives of the Doric School. His epigrams pose many problems, and it is interesting to note that they were not included in the *Garland* of Meleager.[85] Those which can be considered genuine with some degree of certainty—for even among the twenty-two transmitted in the bucolic manuscripts and also found in the *Anthology* some do not appear to be authentic—are of excellent quality, particularly, as one would have expected, those in which nature is described. The majority fall into groups of sepulchral and dedicatory inscriptions, a number of the latter being inscriptions for statues of poets.

Sixteen of Theocritus' epigrams are in elegiacs, of which six are on rustic themes, but there are also epigrams in other metres, often recognizable as a literary homage. The fictitious epitaph on Hipponax, for instance, is written in delightful choliambics. Epigram IV,[86] which is eighteen lines long, can hardly be called an epigram. It is more of a short elegy, describing a precinct of Priapus and including a petition to the god to cure a lover of Daphnis of his passion.

Theocritus is clearly one of the greatest epigrammatists of the Alexandrian era and one whose influence was felt for centuries.

From the pen of Nicias of Miletus (c. 280 B.C.), the medical friend of Theocritus, eight epigrams have survived. Theocritus addressed to him

Idylls XI and XIII and composed an epigram for a statue of Asclepius which Nicias dedicated;[87] he also sent his wife a gift of a distaff accompanied by Idyll XXVIII. In his turn, Nicias, a true 'scion of the Muses' (ἱερὸν ἔρνος Μουσῶν), as Theocritus calls him, responded, and the two first hexameters of the poem he sent in answer to Idyll XI have been preserved at the beginning of the Theocritean scholia to that idyll. In fact, they paraphrase a famous Euripidean fragment.[88]

Nicias is said to have been a schoolfellow of Erasistratos of Ceos, one of the greatest Hellenistic doctors. His friendship with Theocritus was struck at Cos, where Nicias was a student of medicine—probably at the then flourishing school of Praxagoras[89]—and Theocritus was spending some time with Philetas and his circle.

With the exception of two, all the surviving epigrams of Nicias are inscriptional. Of the two non-inscriptional epigrams, one is on an insect caught by a boy and the other is an exhortation to a bee to devote itself sedulously to making honey.[90] Nicias' epigrams are competent but of little distinction.

But the real master of the Doric School, and one of the greatest epigrammatists in the entire history of Greek poetry, is Leonidas of Tarentum (c. 275 B.C.). Cephalas included in his *Anthology* more epigrams by Leonidas than any other poet except Meleager, and this is probably also true of Meleager's *Garland*. Yet in spite of the substantial body of Leonidas' work which has survived—approximately a hundred epigrams[91]—we know very little about him. All we can gather is that he led the life of a poor wandering poet in the first half of the third century B.C.[92]—there is something of the Cynic in his insistence on his poverty—and that he probably never visited Egypt and the Ptolemies, for there is no mention of them in his verse.[93]

The majority of the epigrams of Leonidas are dedicatory and sepulchral, and they are mostly fictitious. The absence of wine and love from his poetry is striking, the one surviving *eroticon*[94] being purely rhetorical. His epigrams refer mostly to the world of humble workers and craftsmen —fishermen, sailors, builders, shepherds, weavers or flute players—who allegedly dedicate their tools and implements to the gods or find some strange death. The style of these epigrams is highly elaborate, full of grand and recondite compound words or technical terms and cast in mannered and rhetorical sentences. The metres used are preponderately elegiac, often burdened by a heavy spondaic element, but there are also some in iambics.

Leonidas has a tendency to choose deliberately strange subjects—such as the four sisters who all die in childbirth and whose father soon after dies of sorrow, or the sailor, half-eaten by a swordfish, and thus buried half in the earth and half in the water—and to idealize the underprivileged classes. Sympathetic indeed is his treatment of the humble workmen,

whose simple tools are elevated to a higher sphere through their qualifica-
tion by grand and pompous adjectives.

The influence of Anyte is evident in Leonidas' portrayal of nature,[95] and
his epigrams frequently resemble those of Nicias and others, though in
such instances it is hard to say who was the borrower and who the
originator. But themes and patterns, when adopted—if they were
adopted—were enlarged and enriched by the poet of Tarentum.

Though many of Leonidas' epigrams are heavy, baroque and romantic
(they have even earned him the unjust description of 'a competent ver-
sifier [but] hardly ever more than that'),[96] some real pearls can be found
among them, like the famous *lalageusa mea* which Cicero admired,[97] or the
splendid verses on the goat that ate the vine, whose root remained intact
to produce the wine for the libation to be poured at that goat's sacrifice.[98]

In certain fields Leonidas is clearly an innovator, for it was he who first
introduced the grandiloquence of the Asianic style to the epigram—a
literary form strikingly restrained and sparse until his day—and it was he
who first composed satirical epigrams in the form of dedications.[99]
Moreover, he initiated the *priapea*[100] and among them those that point to
the Latin *priapea*.[101] Following the lead of Erinna, he also composed
ecphrastic epigrams on works of art, like the one on Myron's cow and that
on Apelle's picture of Aphrodite; and following in the footsteps of Nossis,
he included *apophthegmata* in his verse.[102] He also included a fable in one of
his epigrams.[103]

Leonidas' influence on subsequent epigrammatists was greater than
that of any other—it can be traced to the sixth century A.D.—and his
influence was felt in Rome. Propertius and Ovid imitated him, and even
under wall paintings of Pompeii epigrams of his were found inscribed. It is
sad that his epitaph for his own tomb[104] foresees a bitter death away from
his homeland, a thing he deeply regrets.

As already mentioned, about 240 B.C. the great days of the Alexandrian
epigram were over. It has been suggested that when the Greeks' desire for
freedom was roused once more at the end of the third century B.C. and the
Aetolian League, with Sparta at its side, faced Macedon in the War of the
Allies (220–217), epigrams proclaimed once again Spartan ideals, Spar-
tan courage and heroic Spartan death. With that revival of the 'Doric
spirit' have been connected the epigrammatists Tymnes, Nicandros,
Damagetos, Hegesippos, Hegemon, Phaenos, Chaeremon and Alcaeus of
Messene, to say nothing of Dioscorides.[105] Unfortunately, we know too
little about most of these poets—we are in the dark about even the exact
dates of some of them—to be able to accept that suggestion without
reservation, and it is impossible to elaborate upon it here. However, one
point emerges clearly: the most striking and most original epigrammatist
of that group was Alcaeus of Messene, to whom, passing over the other
rather shadowy figures, we must now come.

Alcaeus of Messene (c. 200 B.C.) is the most important of the *epigonoi* of the great epigrammatists of the Ionian and the Doric Schools. He has been called the leader of that anti-Macedonian and pro-Spartan 'chorus of epigrammatists'[106] and is the only poet of the *Anthology* to have used the epigram as a political weapon, thus giving it a fresh mission. And that literary weapon was dreaded even by generals and kings.

About twenty of Alcaeus' epigrams have survived, including several biting lampoons on Philip V of Macedon (221–179 B.C.), whom, at an earlier stage of his life, the poet had admired. One of them, Plutarch tells us,[107] was sung throughout Greece. But the king's fierce retort, threatening Alcaeus with crucifixion, has also survived.[108] Alcaeus succeeded in angering not only King Philip but also Titus Flamininus with the epigram he wrote on the Thessalians who had fallen at the battle of Cynoscephalae (197 B.C.) — they are the speakers in that epigram[109] — because he gave the Romans and their general second place after the Aetolians in that victory. Later, when Flamininus solemnly proclaimed the freedom of the Greeks at the Isthmian Games of 196 B.C., Alcaeus made amends for that slight in a short but effective epigram[110] in which he purposely repeated, slightly altered, a line from the earlier poem.

Alcaeus' non-political epigrams are of the usual types — real and fictitious epitaphs, some on great poets (Homer, Hesiod, Hipponax), dedications and one on eunuch priests of Cybele,[111] who escaped from lions by beating their timbrels. The only love poems are three to young men,[112] the last to a young athlete whom Alcaeus fears Zeus may take as his cupbearer like Ganymedes.

Alcaeus' are the earliest invective epigrams we know of in the style which was later taken up by Catullus and cultivated by so many lampoonists after him. He is also said to have composed invective iambics, but they are now lost. He will be remembered, however, as the last epigrammatist of the Alexandrian age to have shown any true originality.

As we have seen, the Alexandrian epigram was essentially a phenomenon of the third century and the first half of the second century B.C., starting with Asclepiades of Samos and Anyte of Tegea and ending with Dioscorides and the most important *epigonos*, Alcaeus of Messene. In the latter half of this period Alexandria yielded place of honour as the centre of epigrammatic poetry to Syria, where Antipater of Sidon and later Meleager of Gadara perpetuated and renovated the epigrammatic tradition.

TECHNOPAEGNIA

Technopaegnia is a modern name for poems which are designed to display the author's skill especially by means of the shapes they make on the page, which portray the subjects of the poems. In such works poetry borrows from painting a visual element, a technique which has been possible only since poets first wrote verse to be read and not primarily to be heard.

Technopaegnia seem to have become popular at the beginning of the third century B.C. Five figurative poems have survived: three (in the shape of an axe, a pair of wings and an egg) have been attributed to Simmias of Rhodes; one (in the shape of a shepherd's pipe) has been spuriously attributed to Theocritus; and one (in the shape of an altar) is the work of Dosiadas of Crete. As would be expected, a variety of metres are used to achieve the desired shapes through the length of the lines on the page. Two of the surviving poems, the pseudo-Theocritean *Pipe* and Dosiadas' *Altar*, seem to delight in their obscure language, for they are rich in glosses, riddles and periphrasis. The *technopaegnia* were the culminating points of Alexandrian *katatechnon* (studied artificiality). It has been assumed that *technopaegnia* and other such literary games were played in the circle of Philetas in Cos,[113] but there is no proof whatsoever of this.

Simmias (or Simias) of Rhodes (c. 300 B.C.) has been credited with the invention of this art. He was a skilful poet and grammarian who wrote three books of *Glossae* and four books of poems of varying character. Fragments survive of a hexameter poem on Apollo[114] and of an epic called *Gorgo*, as well as of a hexameter poem called Μῆνες (*Months*), which is thought to have served perhaps as a model for Ovid's *Fasti*. Some lyrical fragments by Simmias have also survived and seven epigrams, of which four are of uncertain ascription. The three genuine ones are in the epideictic manner of the time and indicate some relationship with Anyte.[115] But Simmias is best-known today through his *technopaegnia*—his *Axe* (with which Epeios fashioned the Wooden Horse of Troy), his *Wings* (of Eros) and his *Egg* (of a swallow). Their language is a studied Doric dialect with a leaning towards rare and obscure words and dark expressions, most notably in the *Egg*.

About Dosiadas of Crete (beginning of second century B.C.) we know nothing.[116] The only work of his which survives is the *Altar*, a *paegnion* composed in a literary Doric dialect which purports to be a dedication by Jason. The *Altar* is full of riddles (γρῖφοι), for its language is obscure and allusive and its metres are mixed. It was later imitated by Basantios, who lived in the days of Hadrian.[117]

These Alexandrian *paegnia*, later imitated by the Romans,[118] are one more expression of the spirit of those early Hellenistic days which, in its desire to be playful, erudite and novel, indulged in the rare, the unusual and the obscure.

PRIAPEA

In the Alexandrian age we also meet, for the first time, the *priapea*, short poems honouring Priapus, the god of fertility, whose verses are full of coarse sensuality. (They are better known to us from their Latin counterparts.)[119] The spread of the cult of Priapus in the Hellenistic world is responsible for their appearance; the extent of its popularity can be seen from the inclusion of Priapus next to Dionysus in the great procession (the Πομπή) organized by Ptolemy II Philadelphus and described by Callixenus.[120]

It has been suggested that graffiti inspired by priapean religious practices gave rise to the poetic genre of the *priapea*.[121] As far as we can see, we first meet Priapus in poetry in an epigram of Hedylus,[122] where he is presented as the god to whom Niconoe, 'a scion of the Graces and the *Erotes*',[123] dedicates her faun skin and her golden pitcher. But it was Leonidas of Tarentum—inspired by Anyte's charming epigram[124] in which she presents the humble effigy of a god (Hermes) standing alone in the windy countryside and aiding wayfarers—who established the fashion of the *priapea*.[125]

Traditionally, Euphronius of Chersonesus (third century B.C.), the poet and teacher of Aristophanes of Byzantium, is considered to be the 'inventor' of the genre, but that is far from certain.[126] Euphronius is also occasionally included in the Pleiad of the dramatic poets.[127] Of his poems only a fragment of a *priapeum* has survived.[128] His commentaries on Attic comedy are often quoted in the Aristophanic scholia and by later lexicographers.

SECTION II

The Greco-Roman World:
The Transition to Classicism
(146 B.C.–A.D. 100)

Introduction

When Rome conquered and destroyed Carthage at the end of the Third Punic War (146 B.C.) she became more deeply involved in the rivalries of the Hellenistic kingdoms and finally subjugated them all. Thus the kingdom of the Seleucids, which had gradually been reduced to a small area by the attacks of Egypt, Rome and Parthia, was finally annexed to the Roman Empire by Pompey in 62 B.C.; the last of the Ptolemies, Caesarion, the son of Julius Caesar and Cleopatra, was executed at Octavian's command in 30 B.C., Egypt having already become a Roman dependency. Of the smaller Hellenistic kingdoms which had developed in the period between Alexander's death and the expansion of Rome to the east, some were suppressed by Rome, while others were reduced to the status of client kingdoms; Hiero II and Attalus I of Pergamum, who had joined the Roman cause, survived.

As part of the Roman state Greece entered upon a period of peace — the *pax Romana*—such as she had never known before in her history. After the collapse of the Achaean League in 146 B.C. the Roman Senate appointed a commission to reorganize Greece as a Roman dependency. Corinth, the centre of resistance, was destroyed, and the national and regional federations were abolished; some favoured cities like Athens and Sparta retained their rights as *civitates liberae*, but other Greeks were mostly subjected to tribute, although they enjoyed some form of self-government.

The period of Roman republican administration was not a happy one for the Greek world. Plundered by its rapacious administrators and tax collectors, the Greek cities turned to Mithridates in the hope of shaking off the Roman yoke. But the First Mithridatic War (88–84 B.C.) had disastrous effects upon them, for central Greece was left practically in ruins, to say nothing of the confiscations and exactions with which Sulla punished the disloyal cities. There was also the damage caused by pirates, who pestered the seas until they were finally suppressed by Pompey (67 B.C.). The poor resources of the Greek lands were further drained by the requisitions made by both Caesar and Pompey for their armies, whose struggle for world power was fought on Greek soil (48 B.C.); subsequently, so extensive were the requisitions and levies which Anthony imposed in 31 B.C. that Octavian had to take swift action to forestall general famine after the battle of Actium. However, although economic conditions did not greatly improve under the Empire, as commerce decreased and much of the land was abandoned to pasture, the Greek cities were fortunate in having a series of munificent philhellenic emperors on the throne for nearly a century after Domitian's death (96 A.D.).

Seeing no future before them during that long period of political stability, the Greeks became content to dwell in contemplation of the glories of the past. The spirit and the material for great new poetic works were absent, and it was left to the Roman poets to celebrate the grandeur of Rome. If we are to follow the course of Greek literature in those centuries, it should be borne in mind that after the conquest of the Romans in the east not only the political but also the cultural and literary centre of the Greco-Roman world removed to the west, to Athens and to Rome itself. Alexandria, Antioch and Pergamum, all the great eastern Hellenistic centres declined.[1] Thus from the middle of the second century B.C. we see Athens becoming once again the centre of Greek culture and learning; she retained her status until the city's destruction by Sulla, when, in spite of the tokens of friendship later offered by Augustus, she withdrew into the life of a quiet university city until the time of Justinian.[2]

It should also be noted that side by side with Athens, from about 100 B.C. Rhodes emerged as an important centre of Greek education. It was there, in that home of rhetoric, sculpture and painting, that Cicero and Caesar studied—to mention only two great names—and Dionysius Thrax and Posidonius taught.

But undoubtedly the most significant occurrence for the further development of Greek letters was that Rome herself was gradually drawn into the orbit of Greek culture and into the cult of Athens on which later Atticism relies. From the second century B.C. all Greek literary, philosophical and rhetorical movements found their representatives in Rome, and their battles were fought there, most significantly the bitter dispute about style in prose and even about Classical or Alexandrian poetry.[3]

One need not rehearse here the long line of distinguished Romans who were proud of their Greek education, nor labour the fact that from the second century B.C. to study in Athens was the pride of the Roman aristocracy, that Greek poetry and prose were recited in Roman theatres, that Roman libraries included Greek books and that many Romans composed works in Greek or gave Greek titles to their works. In fact, from 196 B.C. Roman cultural philhellenism became a real political power. It is also true that from Sulla's time the Romans looked down upon the *Graeculi* and the *assentatores* of those days, but in return they increasingly admired the 'ancient' Greeks for their intellectual achievements and their moral fibre. And this is the reason why Classicism, of which Atticism is such an important expression, was welcomed in Rome.

For the Romans saw in Classicism a superior moral ethos that celebrated especially 'courage' and 'truthfulness' and that they considered the exact opposite of Alexandrian servility and unreliability. In the use of Attic Greek they believed they could rediscover the ancient moral virtues; with Roman support the language was revived by Caecilius and Dionysius of Halicarnassus as the desirable form for literary prose, for many were the distinguished Romans who were enemies of the Asianic laxity and profuseness.

Needless to say, pure Atticism was never achieved, particularly not by the Atticists of the first generation;[4] we must wait until the second century A.D. for Attic purism to prevail, thus solving, in a sense, the problem of ἑλληνίζειν (the use of correct Greek) of the early Hellenistic scholars. The consequences of this victory for Atticism were far-reaching; unfortunately, they were not beneficial to the literature and the life of the Greeks. It proved a *damnosa hereditas* bequeathed to the Greek nation by its Roman conquerors, for the victory of Classicism on Greek soil marked the beginning of a new and lesser era in Greek letters.

At the same time, Roman literature, encouraged by the influence of the Greeks, reached in this period a splendour far superior to its Hellenic counterpart. Catullus, Propertius, Virgil, Horace and Ovid stand far above any of the Greek poets of their day. By fusing the Greek and the Roman, the Classical and the Alexandrian, into a living whole, they reached the last great peak that ancient poetry attained.

It is significant, however, and in a sense surprising, that the influence of Roman poetry upon the Greek poets was negligible. So great was the authority of the Hellenic poetic tradition that, no matter how exhausted, it pursued its own course, totally unaffected by the great Roman revival. Greek poetry, as far as we can judge from the scanty material at our disposal, follows on the whole in the footsteps of the highbrow, restrained Alexandrians, with two notable exceptions, the *Lament on Adonis*, spuriously attributed to Bion, and the *Lament on Bion*, wrongly assigned to Moschus, on which the influence of the Asianic style is evident. On the other hand, references in contemporary literature indicate that a reaction had already set in against the over-refined and fastidious Alexandrian style,[5] although this is not evident from the extant texts.

In the period of transition to Classicism the poet's education began to fall into line with that of the orator, and it is significant that poetry became established as one of the subjects to be studied not only in the schools of grammar but also in the schools of rhetoric, just as Theophrastus had earlier suggested.[6] We are therefore faced—and this, alas, holds good until the end of the Byzantine world—with the thankless task of distinguishing between poets who are creative, artistic personalities and those who are mere versifying schoolmasters or simply students writing exercises. Regrettably, the majority belong to the last two groups.

The transition from the Alexandrian to the Classicist age is, with the exception of the epigram, one of the poorest periods in the entire history of Greek poetry; nor did the Callimachean effort to renovate poetry through short, scholarly and highly finished works find many followers after the end of the third century B.C. In fact, as already mentioned, in the following two centuries a change in taste is evident, a swing to long, mythological and historical epics and encomia, probably a consequence of the shifting of the political and cultural centre of the Hellenistic world from Egypt to Asia, from the Ptolemies to the Seleucids and the Attalids.[7]

Many opportunities still existed for new poetry to be composed and publicly recited. The cities continued to organize festivals at which epic and lyric works were performed, and dramatic poetry, even if sung only in extracts, still formed part of the many theatrical competitions (ἀγῶνες θυμελικοί). At the same time, poetry was also read at private meetings, and this practice became increasingly fashionable, especially in Rome.

The Callimachean experiment had, of course, a striking revival in Rome in the first century B.C., when Parthenius brought the Gospel to the west and the *cantores Euphorionis*,[8] Catullus and half a dozen other poets and critics took up Callimachus and his teachings as the example of true art and established them in Rome. But that afterglow too did not last long, for in the days of Augustus Virgil and his new epic art, which drew once again on the anti-Callimacheans, won the day. Direct Callimachean influence disappeared for ever from creative poetry, even though the reputation of the Cyrenean poet lasted until the end of the age of Classicism.

CHAPTER 13

The Depletion of the Poetic Tradition

PASTORAL POETRY

Real bucolic poetry ends with Bion of Phlossa[1] (a settlement near Smyrna), who apparently lived at the end of the second century B.C. According to the anonymous lament on his death, he spent most of his life in Sicily and died of poisoning. The only complete work attributed to him (a number of fragments have also survived) is the *Lament on Adonis*, and even that attribution has been challenged by modern scholarship. Nevertheless, the *Lament on Adonis* is a remarkable romantic poem of the end of the second century, probably destined for recitation at one of the festivals of Adonis which were held yearly in various parts of the Greek world and, as we know from Theocritus,[2] with great splendour in Alexandria. It is the best surviving example of the Asianic style, full of pathos, to which poetry, and indeed all art, turned after the end of the third century B.C.

In the description of the love and loss of the goddess Venus the tone is one of studied sentimentality permeated by a stifling, half-irrational passion. Like Theocritus, Bion uses the refrain, but it is a long step from the vivid, realistic mimes of the Syracusan poet to this last sentimental outcry of bucolic poetry on the death of Adonis, in which not even the chronological order of the events described is observed. The dialect is Doric, and the hexameter is not carefully employed. However, in spite of its drawbacks, it is a striking poetic achievement.

Strongly influenced by Bion's *Lament on Adonis* is the *Lament on Bion*, a poem on the death of the poet composed by one of his pupils, a Greek from Italy who lived in the days of Sulla. It is another of the very rare examples of the Asianic style in Greek poetry; though laden with literary allusions —Milton's *Lycidas* imitates it—it displays real feeling and contains at least six of the most beautiful lines written in Greek (99–104), describing the transitory quality of human life.

To this period probably also belongs the *Boukoliskos*, a rustic mime spuriously attributed to Theocritus,[3] in which an unnamed oxherd complains that he has made advances to the town-dweller Eunica, who has rejected him with insolence,[4] and the *Megara*,[5] a duet in hexameters between Megara and Alcmene, the wife and the mother of Heracles, on the sorrows endured because of the hero's absence and a dream which seems to portend evil to him and his brother Iphicles. (Moschus has been wrongly credited with this poem.)

Of the works spuriously attributed to Theocritus, the most important is undoubtedly the *Fishermen* (Ἁλιεῖς), which must be assigned to this period, to judge by its subject-matter and its language, whose rhetorical, antithetical treatment reminds one of the Cynics and of the circle of Dion of Prusa. The poem deals with the humble life of two old fishermen and relates a dream of one of them in which he caught a golden fish. In his superstitious interpretation of the dream we can observe the Oriental influence which gradually permeated Hellenistic life. The response of the fisherman's friend to the dreamer's interpretation is an indication of the pessimism of the time and the poverty that the economic deadlock of the end of the first century had caused; but it also reflects realistic Greek reaction to Oriental superstition.[6] The poem conveys that incommunicable sense of nature which rounds and softens the toilsome days of the poor and the aged and combines many of the elements in which the Alexandrian bucolics and epigrams excel. It also illustrates how the poetry of Leonidas of Tarentum and the Alexandrian tendency to describe a studied simplicity of life influenced the longer works of this period.

Finally, mention should be made of the important fragment of a poem on Pan and Echo, found in a papyrus of the third century A.D.[7] It has been attributed to Euphorion, Bion, Nicander and even Nestor of Laranda, but neither its authorship nor its exact date can be fixed with any degree of certainty. It appears, however, that Virgil's Sixth Eclogue (13f.), if not based on this very poem, shares with it a common ancestor. In the poem Dionysus seems to have engaged Pan to play a contest, but the satyrs, led by Silenus, have stolen Pan's pipe. Pan makes a new one but has difficulty in producing from it any semblance of harmony. Doubtless Pan triumphed over the satyrs in the end.

EPIC POETRY

Legendary–historical and encomiastic epics

Legendary–historical and encomiastic epics continued to be composed in this period, but only the names of a few poets and some insignificant fragments have survived.

Of the poets the best-known (through Cicero's speech *pro Archia Poeta*) is Aulus Licinius Archias (c. 118–62 B.C.), who wrote on the Cimbrian and the Mithridatic Wars celebrating Marius and Lucullus and whom Cicero hoped to persuade to write about his Consulate. Born in Antioch, Archias came to Rome before 100 B.C., where Lucullus obtained for him the citizenship of Heraclea; later, under the *Lex Plautia Papiria*, Archias acquired Roman citizenship which, when contested, was successfully defended by Cicero. Archias also improvised in verse and wrote epigrams,[8] but identification of the forty-one epigrams in the Greek *Anthology* headed 'Archias' is not possible, as some or all may belong to the elder Archias.[9]

Other shadowy figures of this period are Thyillos, whom Cicero also hoped to persuade to write an epic about his Consulate;[10] Boethos of Tarsus, the author of an epic on the battle of Philippi who was charged by Strabo with being 'both a bad poet and a bad citizen';[11] Theodoros, who is reputed to have composed an epic on Cleopatra; Nicanor of Hierapolis, who lived in the days of Augustus and was much admired[12] (he was even called the 'new Homer'); Callistratus, whom Lucillius attacked;[13] and Heracleides Ponticus the Younger. From inscriptions of the first century B.C. we can glean merely the names of Agathocles, Apollonius, Protogenes and Chrysippus, all poets of encomiastic epics; and we even have fourteen lines of an anonymous epic on the battle of Actium in a papyrus in the British Museum.[14]

During the Hellenistic age, and in this period in particular, thousands of epic verses were composed, and a very large number must have been recited at public performances. That they all disappeared is a consequence partly of their inferior quality and partly of their connection with persons and events that, after the Roman conquest of the east, no longer interested the public or flattered influential men.

The didactic epic

Didactic verse also flourished, but it can hardly be called poetry. It still made use of the dactylic hexameter, as can be seen from the now lost astronomical works of Maximus (second century A.D.) and Dorotheus (first century A.D.) or the poem on wifely dutifulness by Naumachius (early second century A.D.), of which Stobaeus cites portions, but it also employed a variety of other metres. Thus the grammarian Heracleides Ponticus (c. A.D. 50), a pupil of Didymus Chalcenteros, examined in his *Leschai (Λέσχαι)* grammatical problems in Sapphic and Phalaecian hendecasyllables; Andronicus of Crete, Nero's favourite doctor, wrote his medical poem on antidotes against poisonous animals in elegiacs;[15] and Anubion his astrological work in comic iambic trimeters.

The fashion for using comic iambic trimeters for didactic poetry was apparently set by Apollodorus of Athens (born c. 180 B.C.), the son of Asclepiades, a scholar of great learning and varied interests. He was a pupil of Aristarchus but left Alexandria probably in 145/4 B.C., when Ptolemy VIII Physcon drove the scholars out of Egypt. After a stay at Pergamum, he came to Athens. The Χρονικά or Χρονικὴ σύνταξις, in which he employed the comic iambic trimeter, dealt in considerable detail with successive periods of history, important incidents, philosophical schools and the life and work of individuals from the fall of Troy (c. 1184 B.C.) to 144 B.C. This work, which was dedicated to Attalus II of Pergamum and which served as the main chronological handbook of the Imperial age[16]— it was based on the chronological researches of Eratosthenes—is now lost except for isolated citations. Apollodorus also wrote mythological, theological, geographical, critical, grammatical and exegetical works, but the Γῆς περίοδος or Περὶ γῆς, a geographical guidebook in comic trimeters which has been attributed to him (of which only fragments survive) is probably a later forgery.[17]

In this tradition follows the Περιήγησις (*Periegesis ad Nicomedem regem*) of Pseudo-Scymnus, the longest surviving didactic poem from the period, as well as the didactic iambic verses of Simylus, of which again only a few moralizing fragments survive.[18] Pseudo-Scymnus in his Περιήγησις, an unpoetic geographical summary which was written in about 90 B.C., gives in 747 iambic trimeters an account of a coasting voyage of Europe, which is followed by a similar account of the Pontus. They are both dedicated to Nicomedes II Epiphanes of Bithynia (147–95 B.C.). The author is unknown,[19] but as the Περιήγησις was once thought to be the work of Scymnus of Chios (c. 185 B.C.), he is now known as Pseudo-Scymnus.[20]

Other didactic works of the period dealt with philosophy, the wanderings of birds, fish and other such subjects.[21] Hardly any of these deserve the name of poetry, but they are interesting inasmuch as they are the link that joins Alexandrian didactic poetry with the abundant (and hopeless) didactic verse of the Byzantine world.

ELEGIAC POETRY

If the epic poetry of this period displays a distinct anti-Callimachean tendency, the Callimachean school of poetry had an important and influential representative in Parthenius of Nicaea (first century B.C.), the son of Heracleides and Eudora, who was greatly admired as an elegist and was ranked with Callimachus.[22]

Parthenius was taken prisoner by the Romans during the Third Mithridatic War and was sent to Italy (73 B.C.?), where he was freed. There, acting as 'the prophet of the Callimachean school', he influenced the *poetae novi* and, according to Macrobius,[23] was also Virgil's teacher in Naples. In his Callimachean views he was apparently an extremist, for he even dared to call the *Iliad* 'muck' and the *Odyssey* 'mud',[24] something Callimachus himself had the good sense never to do.

Of his various works only the names and a few fragments have survived. Among his elegies were two, the *Lament on Arete* and the *Encomium on Arete*, that were dedicated to the memory of his wife, a lament on the poetess Archelais and an elegy on Crinagoras, most probably the distinguished epigrammatist.[25] But he composed *epikedia* for others too. We also know of at least one poem in hexameters[26] and of various others about whose metre we are uncertain.[27] It is thought that his poem *Myttotos* (the name of a spicy dish of cheese, honey and garlic) served as model for the pseudo-Virgilian *Moretum* and that his treatment of the legendary Scylla of Megara in his *Metamorphoses* was used by the author of the *Cyris*.[28] From his few surviving fragments Parthenius emerges a soulless imitator of Callimachus and Euphorion, an impression that stands in direct opposition to his reputation in antiquity, when he was thought to be a master of the gentle and sad description of unrequited love.

We also possess extracts from a prose work by Parthenius, the *Sufferings of Love* (᾽Ερωτικὰ Παθήματα), a collection of love stories which he composed to furnish his patron, the poet and politician Cornelius Gallus, with themes for epics and elegies. The thirty-six love stories—for most of which our one manuscript appends a list of the names of the authors who have recorded them—are full of violence and treachery. Very much in the spirit of Euphorion's successors, they display all the characteristics of later Hellenistic love poetry, with its morbid tendency towards dramatic sentimentality.

As we have seen, Parthenius influenced greatly the Roman poets of his time, most prominently Catullus, Gallus and Virgil but also probably Calvus and Cinna. His reputation lasted for centuries; Hadrian had his tomb repaired and even Nonnus was acquainted with his writings.[29]

To the circle of Parthenius—for he had a great circle of friends, admirers and pupils—belong Simylus and the emancipated slave of Cato the Younger, Butes, of whose elegies we possess insignificant fragments. Among the elegiac poets of the period one should also record Marcus, who was attacked by Lucillius,[30] Boethos of Sidon,[31] who lived in the days of Augustus, and Gaius.[32] To us all that remains is their names.

THE EPIGRAM

The epigram, which was cultivated by Greeks and Romans alike,[33] surpasses all other poetry of this period. In subject-matter it differs little from that of the Alexandrian age, but in manner it is more conventional and artificial, a result of the increasing influence of rhetoric. It is worth remarking that after the end of the second century B.C. the amatory epigram, and in particular the pederastic, goes out of fashion, with the notable exception of the work of Philodemus and Argentarius, and that the favours of the Imperial household are now mainly sought through epigrams.

Variety characterizes the language and the metres of these epigrammatists, for they use both a literary Ionic and a literary Doric dialect, as well as a mixed diction, and their verse was cast in elegiacs, hendecasyllables, pentameters, iambic trimeters and scazons—the last two in their satirical epigrams; they even revived the epigram in hexameters after a long silence during the Alexandrian age.[34]

The period opens with three noteworthy Phoenician poets, Antipater of Sidon, Meleager of Gadara and Philodemus of Gadara, so that scholars often speak of a Phoenician School of epigrammatists which came to succeed that of Alexandria. But this is hardly correct, for their epigrams differ little from those of other contemporary poets who were not of Phoenician origin.

Antipater of Sidon (c. 130 B.C.) is not a poet of power or originality. Some eighty epigrams of his are included in the *Anthology* and one more has turned up in a papyrus,[35] but the majority are artificial epitaphs, copies of earlier pieces. However, some fine phrases can be found in them, and his two poems on the destruction of Corinth by the Romans[36] are full of feeling; we also learn from Cicero that he was a fluent improviser,[37] and he was later imitated by Meleager in his amusing address to his tombstone.[38] Antipater was also a poet of elegies.[39]

Far superior, a true master of the epigram, was Meleager of Gadara (c. 95 B.C). He was a poet and philosopher who lived in Tyre and retired to Cos, of which he was made a citizen, in his old age. His Menippean satires, Cynic discourses in prose mingled with verse, are lost, but the Greek *Anthology* contains about 130 epigrams attributed to him, nearly all erotic. They infuse amorous feeling into the traditional forms of epitaph and dedication, displaying liveliness, elegance and skill but little genuine emotion. Many are adaptations of the works of earlier epigrammatists, especially Asclepiades, Rhianus and Callimachus; it should be noted that the influence of Leonidas of Tarentum is almost completely absent. The language of Meleager is somewhat flamboyant, betraying the impact of

Asianic rhetoric, but his metres are fastidiously controlled. Perhaps the most beautiful of his extant poems is his long epigram—almost a short poem beyond the scope of an epigram—in twenty-three hexameters on spring.[40] He had many imitators up to the sixth century A.D.

Meleager is also the compiler of one of the oldest[41] and most influential anthologies of epigrams, the *Garland*, which was dedicated to one Diocles (probably Diocles of Magnesia, the author of a compendium of philosophers, on which Diogenes Laertius drew). It was called the *Garland* because he compared the forty-seven poets he included in his anthology with flowers, but the choice is made with little apparent appropriateness. (The view has been put forward that Meleager compiled the *Garland* in order to include his own epigrams in it.)[42] Its full scope and contents are not recoverable from the extant Palatine *Anthology*, the basis of which it formed.

Philodemus (c. 110–c. 40/35 B.C.) came from the same city as Meleager but probably died at Herculaneum. He came to Rome in about 75, where he enjoyed the favour and powerful friendship of the Pisones; in Naples and Herculaneum he had a circle of brilliant young students around him and devoted himself chiefly to popularizing Greek philosophy, viewing it from the Epicurean standpoint. His works covered a wide field—ethics, theology, psychology, logic, aesthetics and rhetoric. He influenced many learned and distinguished Romans of his day: Cicero had genuine respect for him, and Horace mentions him.[43] Some twenty-five of his epigrams survive, mostly love epigrams, often indecent (indeed, lewd) but in keeping with the fashion of his day. In them we can see that rhetoric, with its metaphors and sound effects, is gaining ground on the epigram. In fact, the subject-matter of both Meleager and Philodemus has much in common with the Latin love elegy, but the tone is more realistic and the subjectivity of the Latin love elegy is absent. No prose works of Philodemus were known until several rolls of papyri containing fragments of his writings were discovered among the ruins of L. Calpurnius Piso Caesoninus' villa at Herculaneum. It is also known that Piso had presented Philodemus with a magnificent villa at Herculaneum, where it is thought the poet died.

At the turn of the century Crinagoras of Mytilene infused new life into the epigram. This innovator was sent from his home town as an ambassador to Rome, first to Caesar in 45 B.C. and then to Augustus in 26/25 B.C. He was a client of Octavia, Augustus' sister, and introduced a new trend in the writing of epigrams by moving away from traditional rhetorical themes into a whole new range of topics associated with daily life. His epigrams also reflect affairs of state in the most prominent ranks of Roman society and contain personal reactions to realities which are not often found in the verse of that period. Yet on the whole he is more interesting for his connections with others than for his own sake. The language of

Crinagoras is vigorous, though often unpolished, and his metres usually rough.

To the Augustan period also belongs Marcus Argentarius, who has been characterized as the 'gayest of the Greek epigrammatists'.[44] He has been plausibly identified with the eccentric, Latin-speaking, Greek rhetorician Argentarius known to the elder Seneca;[45] the ironical spirit of the thirty-seven surviving epigrams which have been ascribed to the poet has much in common with what we know about the rhetorician—that he was a fluent, witty and often malicious speaker. Like his master Meleager, Argentarius is capable of expressing with equal facility a variety of moods in a variety of styles. He is elegant, picturesque and lucid and, with the exception of Crinagoras, stands far above the other epigrammatists of his day. As a humorist and punster he precedes Lucillius and Martial.

We must now turn to Philip of Thessalonica (c. A.D. 40), not because his surviving work is in the least distinguished but because he compiled a second *Garland*, a supplement to the *Garland* of Meleager, in which Greek epigrams were included basically in alphabetical sequences. Philip's anthology began where Meleager's ended, probably in the first decade of the first century B.C. and extended to the principate of Gaius (A.D. 37–41). Like Meleager's *Garland*, it was used by Constantine Cephalas in the tenth century A.D. in his compilation of the Greek *Anthology*.

Some eighty of Philip's own epigrams were included in his *Garland*, mostly dull adaptations of earlier Greek pieces. His style is generally Leonidean, distinguished only by a large number of new word formations. He has been rightly described as 'a second-rate dealer in second-hand materials'.[46] We know nothing about Philip's life except that he was one of the men who sought or enjoyed patronage at the Imperial court.

The epigrammatists included in the *Garland* of Philip (other than Philodemus, Crinagoras and Argentarius, none of whom is distinguished) fall into two main groups: first, those whose style is more or less straightforward and who choose conventional themes, such as Adaeus, Antiphanes, Antistius, Diodorus of Sardis and Erucius of Cyzicus—the latter noteworthy only for his bitter attack on Parthenius[47] and for a touching poem on a Greek woman captured by the Romans,[48] which may refer to his mother; and second, those who reflect the influence of Leonidas of Tarentum, like Maecius, Zonas, Antiphilus of Byzantium and Bianor. Their Leonidean style is characterized by the coining of words and extravagantly picturesque phrase-making applied to the description of commonplace objects and by the description of uncommon events. The most accomplished of the Leonideans are Maecius and Zonas, about whose life we know nothing; and it should be added that Antiphilus of Byzantium wrote at least one epigram of great charm,[49] which describes the memory of a happy sea journey or 'holiday' at sea.

A third and lesser group of competent but unimportant epigrammatists who are included in the *Garland* of Philip are men like Antipater of Thessalonica, Pompeius, Julius Polyaenus, Isidorus and Mundus, on whose work we need not elaborate here.

Finally, two epigrammatists of the days of Nero should be singled out, Leonidas of Alexandria and Lucillius. Leonidas was an astronomer who also composed ἰσόψηφα epigrams (epigrams whose lines produced equal numbers if the letters were assumed to be metrical symbols), a studied extravaganza of little poetic value. Of his three books of epigrams, some forty poems have survived.[50] Lucillius, on the other hand, who was patronized by Nero, is credited with over a hundred poems in the *Anthology* and seems to have specialized in mocking his contemporaries. Some of the poems are very funny — like the one about the two deaf men who choose a deaf man as the arbiter of their dispute,[51] or the thief who steals everything, including the detective[52] — while others are coarse, like the mimes of his day. Lucillius satirizes not only individuals but also types, and he is the first epigrammatist who specializes in bringing his poem to a sharp, humorous point in the last line, a punch line. As befits his satire, his language is colloquial, but at the same time cultivated. His work, reminiscent of Petronius and the *Apocolocynthosis*, strongly influenced Martial and other later epigrammatists.

Finally, it should be noted that some of the anonymous epigrams inscribed on stone that belong to this period are indeed impressive.[53]

DRAMATIC POETRY

In the period of transition to Classicism there was no noteworthy drama. This was due partly to the anti-theatrical attitude of Stoic, Platonic and Pythagorean philosophy and partly to the great success of the mime, which from Sulla's day conquered the theatre.[54] Moreover, the epideictic orations of the Sophists, which were held in the theatre and combined spectacle and literature (so theatrical was their delivery) to a certain extent took the place of real drama.

In compensation for this the reading of tragedies and comedies became more usual and, of course, much more frequent than their performance on the stage,[55] where only excerpts of plays were now mostly sung or acted. The earliest recorded instance of this new venture was at the Pythian contest at Delphi in 194 B.C., when Satyros of Samos offered Apollo 'Dionysus, a song with a chorus, and a lyre piece from Euripides' *Bacchae*' (ᾆσμα μετὰ χοροῦ Διόνυσον καὶ κιθάρισμα ἐκ Βακχῶν Εὐριπίδου)[56] instead of the traditional complete play.

However, in spite of these developments, inscriptions testify to the fact that productions of whole plays continued in various parts of the Greek world, and a long list of names of tragic and comic poets, as well as the titles of new works which were victorious at contests, have come down to us,[57] though we know nothing more about them. It is also interesting to note that not only Greeks but also Romans, such as Asinius Pollio (76 B.C.–A.D. 4) or Pliny the Younger (A.D. 61–112), tried their hand at composing Greek tragedies, and that on great occasions, like the Saecularia of 17 B.C., Greek tragedies were also acted in Rome.

The inscriptional evidence at our disposal shows that comedy was more popular than tragedy in those days. Of the various names of comic poets which have come down to us and about whose life and works we unfortunately have no further information, the Athenian Diomedes, son of Athenodorus, should be mentioned. He was honoured in Athens—a statue to him was set up in the theatre of Dionysus[58]—as well as in Epidaurus, and he was made an honorary citizen of Pergamum,[59] which indicates that his plays must have been widely appreciated. But in spite of his success among his contemporaries, his writings did not enter the realm of literature.

An unexpected development of this period is the revival of the satyr play and the popularity it seems to have enjoyed. We learn (once again from inscriptions) that tragedians in many parts of the Greek-speaking world composed satyr plays[60] and that these were occasionally performed before the tragedies,[61] but about their nature we are ignorant. This revival of the satyr play also explains why Cicero's brother, Quintus, tried to establish the genre in Rome[62] and why in Horace's *Ars Poetica* (220ff.) it is treated at such length.

Not only tragedians but Sophists and philosophers also engaged in writing tragedies, which were meant to be read and not acted, a practice which continued in the subsequent period of Classicism. Such were the tragedies of Nicolaus of Damascus, the Chancellor of Herod the Great of Judea (c. 75 B.C.),[63] or those of Scopelianus (c. A.D. 100), the distinguished orator of the days of Hadrian, who also wrote an epic Γιγαντία[64] (about which we know nothing),[65] or those of Isagoras and his teacher Chrestos, both Sophists of the Second Sophistic who prided themselves on improvising, even in verse. The rhetorical tragedies of Seneca or even Lucian's *Tragodopodagra* give us some notion of what those plays must have been like.

THE MIME AND THE PANTOMIME

In spite of all that we hear about tragedy, comedy and the satyr play during this period, all three were virtually dead, for as literary forms they belonged to the past. It was the mime and the pantomime that dominated the scene. In the latter a dancer represented traditional themes in dumb-show, supported by instrumental music and a chorus. It was a highly sophisticated type of entertainment, performed on the public stage or in private houses; though demoralizing, it was not coarse as the mime was. The mime, as we have seen, had already expanded from one simple scene (the Παίγνιον) to a skeleton play with a plot (the Ὑπόθεσις) in the Alexandrian era. This was further developed in the Imperial age and some distinguished representatives of the mimodrama are cited, the most important of whom was Philistion of Nicaea.

Philistion (c. A.D. 5), who is also sometimes described as a native of Sardis or Magnesia, is considered the most famous poet of mimes in late antiquity and often wrongly quoted as the inventor of the mimodrama. His *Ardalion*, an officious, meddlesome man overwhelmed with work who never succeeded in finishing anything, remained a standard comic type for centuries. The jokes and the humour of Philistion later formed the nucleus of a collection of jokes called *Philogelos*, and his dicta, together with the gnomes of Menander, were compiled under the title *Comparison of Menander and Philistion* (Σύγκρισις Μενάνδρου καὶ Φιλιστίωνος).

Papyrus finds have rendered a few minor fragments of such mimes.[66] In one, written in vaguely rhythmical prose with one short metrical interval, the subject is the rescue of a Greek woman named Charition from an Indian king who is about to sacrifice her to Selene. It is a farce with much low humour in it that makes fun of the *Iphigenia in Tauris* of Euripides[67] and serves as an example of the mime of the Imperial age, and more generally of the kind of literature which was then popular.

The pantomime also came into its own in that age, for the mime gradually declined into pantomime (παντόμιμος ὄρχησις), which, of course, required not poets but actors. Whereas the mimes drew much of their material from fantastic adventures and from everyday life, the panto-mime, which can be classified as tragic and comic, drew on mythology and, in particular, on the erotic motifs of tragedy. Later libretti were written for some of them.

The popularity of the pantomime was so great that neither the strictures of the Church Fathers nor the attacks of philosophers, nor even the strict orders of the emperors Trajan and Justinian succeeded in suppressing it. It survived until the very end of antiquity.

LYRIC POETRY AND HYMNODY

Lyric poetry continued to be composed, but practically none of it has survived.[68] The main reason for its disappearance is that collections of melic verse ceased to be made because it was difficult to copy the musical notation that accompanied the songs, and, if copied, it was not readily understood by the ordinary reader.

Thus we know of only a few obscure names of melic poets, some, like Amphicles of Rheneia (middle of second century B.C.) or Myrinos (second century B.C.), retrieved from inscriptions, and some, like Eutychides or Meliton, because they were attacked in epigrams;[69] but about their works we know nothing.

In compensation for this, a small number of mostly anonymous poems and fragments of poems have been gleaned from inscriptions and papyri, none of which is of significance,[70] with the possible exception of the impressive Isis hymn found at Andros (it belongs, as we saw, to the time of Sulla)[71] and a group of four further Isis hymns composed by one Isidorus in the first century B.C. for the temple of Isis Hermouthis at Medinet Madi in Fayyum. Two of these are in hexameters, while the others are in elegiacs—all are between thirty and forty lines long—recounting the praises of Isis and of the deified Amenemhet III. They are perhaps the last noteworthy items of late Ptolemaic verse composition; Isidorus is a hack craftsman who expressed himself in set formulae.[72]

HELLENISTIC JEWISH POETRY

A few words must be added here about the Hellenistic Jewish poetry in Greek which we meet in this period but whose origins are clearly earlier.

A Jewish literature in Greek appeared when, in the Alexandrian age, the Jews came under Greek influence, which was felt most forcefully by those of the Diaspora, especially those Jews established in Alexandria, who were linguistically Hellenized to the point of having their religious books translated into Greek. The purpose of these Jewish writings in Greek seems to have been twofold: first, to propagate the Hebrew faith and, second, to prove that the Hellenized Jews were not 'barbarians' but could participate in Greek philosophical thought and express themselves in Greek literary forms. Nonetheless, some of this Hellenized Hebrew poetry, such as the psalm or the prophetic speech, retained the traditional Jewish literary forms.

In the form of psalms we have the eighteen so-called *Psalms of Solomon*, which are not considered genuine works of Solomon but are so described to distinguish them from the Psalms of David. They were composed in the second half of the first century B.C., after the capture of Jerusalem and the death of Pompey (48 B.C.), to which they allude. It is a matter of dispute whether the *Psalms of Solomon* were originally composed in Greek or in

Hebrew—they have also been translated into Syriac and Coptic—but no matter which their original language, they are literary works with deep religious feeling, rich imagery and powerful similes.

Only scanty relics of the Hellenistic Jewish epic and dramatic poetry have survived, belonging to three writers—Philon the Elder (first century B.C.), Theodotus (end of second century B.C.) and Ezechiel (second century B.C.)—about whom we have already spoken.[73] Of the Hellenistic Jewish *pseudepigrapha*, the most important are the *Sibylline Oracles*, supposedly spoken by the Babylonian sibyl, a problematic corpus in which it is difficult to distinguish between the oracles of Jewish and those of Greek origin. That monstrous body of verse has a long history which starts with Heracleitus,[74] who tells of the sibyl whom the god compels to utter the truth, and ends with Jewish and Christian propaganda expressed in the form of prophecies. The collection consists of 4200 hexameters of various dates and is preceded by a prologue which points to the fifth century A.D. Nonetheless, a substantial core of the work consists of Jewish material belonging to the period about 170–145 B.C.[75] The disguise of the sibyl was adopted to demonstrate the priority of the religion of the Jews over the beliefs of the pagan world and to give authenticity to the prophecies about the fall of paganism.

Closely connected with the Jewish sibylline poetry is the *Orthodox Doctrine*, which consists of verses assigned to various Greek poets—Homer, Hesiod, Linus (or Callimachus), Aeschylus, Sophocles, Euripides, Philemon, Menander and Diphilus. Of special interest are the fictitious lines attributed to Orpheus that are presented as the bard's testament to his son Musaeus, in which he revokes his older belief in a pantheon and proclaims his faith in the one true God.

Of the collections of maxims in verse that have been preserved, *Menander's Maxims* (Γνῶμαι Μενάνδρου) are the most interesting; they include 150 general statements and practical advice about life, among which are many of purely Jewish origin, whereas the root of others can be traced back to Menander himself.

Finally, mention should also be made of the didactic poem of Pseudo-Phocylides, cast in 230 hexameters and called Γνῶμαι or Ποίησις ὠφέλιμος whose author seems to have known the Old Testament. It probably belongs to the first century A.D.—its date is a matter of dispute[76] —but includes much older Greek and Jewish gnomic material, though hardly any certain Christian teachings. Because of the moral and practical advice it offered (ὑποθῆκαι), it was much read, even in the Middle Ages.

The Greco-Roman World:
The Age of Classicism (A.D. 100–330)

Introduction

The age of Classicism (A.D. 100–330) is marked, as we have already seen, by the active interest taken by the Roman emperors in the Greek east, an interest which was first aroused in the days of Augustus but developed fully when the Empire felt secure in the west.

In the first century Vespasian (A.D. 69–79) had helped the Greek revival by crushing the Jews and establishing state-supported chairs of rhetoric, grammar, medicine and law, and not long after Stoic–Academic eclecticism was accepted by the Court. Hadrian (A.D. 117–38) and Antoninus Pius (A.D. 137–61) gave further support to philosophy, and Marcus Aurelius (A.D. 161–80) established in Athens four 'official' chairs of philosophy for the four recognized schools—the Academy, the Peripatos, the Stoa and the Garden of Epicurus—which was almost equivalent to founding a state university in that city.

In the second century the philhellenism of the Roman emperors turned more markedly from Asia Minor to Greece proper, and in particular to Athens, which Hadrian repeatedly visited and enriched with gifts and magnificent buildings.[1] At the same time nearly all the great cities and sanctuaries of Greece received impressive additions in the way of monuments and public buildings, the ruins of some of which are visible to this day.

Alexandria was, of course, still considered the second city of the Empire after Rome; but between the second and fourth centuries it was overshadowed by the cultural revival of Athens and the cities of Asia Minor, even though it was in Alexandria that the best pagan thought was appropriated by Clement, Origen and the Christian school and that the new religious mysticism emerged. The city remained, however, untouched by the Second Sophistic, the most important literary movement of those days.

The *pax Romana*, which had started with Augustus, was broken in A.D. 175 by the Costoboci, a northern tribe which raided central Greece but was forced by the local militia to retire beyond the Roman frontier. This first hint of northern interference was followed later by a more serious invasion, launched by the Goths in about 250. Though the walls of the city of Athens were rebuilt at Valerian's command and other fortifications were put up across the Isthmus, the Goths captured and pillaged the city of Athens in 267 and ravaged much of the land until they were ultimately repulsed beyond the Danube. Greece escaped another Gothic invasion for over a century.

When in 285 the Empire was divided by Diocletian into an eastern and a western half the Emperor took up his residence in the East at Nicomedia, from where closer contact with the critical frontiers of the Danube and the Tigris was possible and where the republican traditions of Rome were not so powerfully felt. Early in the next century Constantine, who reunited the two halves, fixed the capital of the Empire in the East and between 325 and 330 enlarged the old city of Byzantium to form his Christian New Rome, Constantinople.

With the transference of the capital of the Roman Empire from Rome to Constantinople and the Imperial favour shown to Christianity, a new era began in both the life and the literature of the Greeks.

If we now turn to the literature of the period, we shall observe that the Imperial age was primarily the age of prose and that the decline of poetry and philosophy made the Sophists and rhetoricians the educators of Greece and the carriers of its values. Yet in spite of the fact that the Sophists of the Second Sophistic looked down on contemporary verse — they were avid students of Classical poetry, above all that of Homer and tragedy[2] — poetry had a considerable place in the rhetorical schools. For the view was widely held that the composition of verse helped the orator[3] and that, except for the metre, there was no essential difference between prose and poetry.[4]

A result of this was that a rhetorical education now came to be considered indispensable to the poet, a development (whose origins lay, as we have seen, in the previous period) which in its turn brought about the blurring and almost complete dissolution of the traditional divisions of poetry — already shaken since the Alexandrian age — as well as of the traditional distinction between a poetic and a prose vocabulary.[5]

No manuals on the writing of poetry or on its topics have survived from late antiquity,[6] so we must turn to those on rhetoric, from which we can glean a good deal of information.[7] There we see that of the *progymnasmata* (instructions or exercises) suggested for oratory, three of those dealing with epideictic oratory are also related to poetry. These were basically three: the ecphrasis, excercises meant to teach the orator and the poet how to describe places, seasons, feasts, works of art and other such subjects; the *ethopoeia*, instructing him how to present the imaginary actions of persons[8] or of inanimate objects,[9] and the encomium, guiding the student how to proceed in the praise of living men,[10] of lands and of gods.[11] A fourth, the *synkrisis*, hardly concerns poetry. Of these four *progymnasmata*, though the *ethopoeia* was considered important, for it sought to develop a 'pathetic–ethical' style,[12] the encomium was the most significant. Quite apart from any literary considerations, the 'Encomium to the Emperor' (Βασιλικὸς λόγος) and the 'Salutary Address to an Official (or an Envoy)' (Προσφωνητικὸς λόγος) had great practical significance, as through them a city or an individual could secure money and protection; similar in a sense but less effective was the 'Farewell Address'. As all these encomia, when cast in verse, were composed for special occasions and usually by third-rate poets, it is not surprising that they are nearly all lost.[13] The best such surviving encomiastic poetry is in Latin and belongs to the next period.[14]

To the ecphrasis, the *ethopoeia*, the encomium and the *synkrisis* two further forms of 'rhetorical' poetry should be added, both of which, of course, already had a very long and noble history—the lament and the epithalamium, of which no noteworthy examples from this period have survived.[15]

As would be expected, the relation between poetry and rhetoric was that of reciprocal influence—as Fronto (c. 100–c. 160) put it: *Plerumque ad orationem faciendam versus, ad versificandum oratio magis adiuvat.*[16] For poetry, especially that of Homer, Euripides and Menander, provided oratory with material for festive orations and subjects for *progymnasmata*, as well as stylistic devices and vocabulary; and rhetoric in its turn restored to poetry all the artistic devices it had borrowed from verse in an earlier and greater age. For it was from poetry that the great Sophists of the fifth century B.C., in their endeavour to teach political virtue and to increase the powers of the mind, had taken over all their artistic devices and artifice— figures of speech, dramatic effects and so on—and used them in their artistic prose.

So it came about that the spirit of the prose of the late Hellenistic orators and romance writers invaded poetry with its unbridled exuberance, its taste for the baroque and its erotic sensuality; its influence encouraged a bombastic style with precious adornments and little originality. But poetry, though debased, was still alive. Poets still wandered from city to city, declaiming their verse at public assemblies and national games;[17] poetic competitions were still held, and, as inscriptions inform us, the *thymelikoi agones* can be attested till well into the third century A.D. It is of some interest to note that not only rhetoricians but also some philosophers of the third century engaged in composing verse. Such were the two peripatetic philosophers Ammonios and Ptolemaios, who were considered the most learned men of their day[18] but of whose verse nothing has survived. The poetry composed was mainly epics, mythological and didactic, epigrams, anacreontics, hymns, and a few erotic lyrics (in fact, the longest mythological epic ever written in Greek, the *Heroic Theogamies* of Peisander of Laranda, was composed then).

CHAPTER 14

The Decline of Lyric Poetry

DIDACTIC POETRY

In the second century A.D. didactic poetry seems to have flourished. For us it is represented by the works of Dionysius Periegetes, Oppian, Pseudo-Oppian and Babrius.

Dionysius Periegetes, 'the Guide', lived in Hadrian's time[1] and wrote the *Periegesis of the Inhabited World (Περιήγησις τῆς Οἰκουμένης)* in 1186 hexameters on the Callimachean pattern, describing in pseudo-epic style the known world, chiefly after Eratosthenes. One of the two acrostics traced in the poem (ll. 109–34) indicates that the author came from Alexandria.[2] The arrangement of the *Periegesis* is probably based on the pattern set in his geographical poem by Alexandros Lychnos of Ephesus, who was characterized by Cicero as *poeta ineptus* but *non inutilis;*[3] in style the influence of Callimachus and Apollonius Rhodius can be traced. In spite of its many omissions and errors, Dionysius' work was used for centuries as the main schoolbook for teaching geography. It was translated into Latin by Avienus and Priscianus, and commentaries were written on it.

To Dionysius have also been attributed the *Ὀρνιθιακά* (also ascribed to Dionysius of Philadelphia) and the *Vita Chisiana.*[4]

Oppian of Corycos in Cilicia (late second century A.D.) is the author of the *Halieutica*, a poem in five books on fishing. It is dedicated to an Emperor Antoninus, who is addressed together with his son and his co-regent, so it must have been composed under Marcus Aurelius Antoninus and Commodus between 177 and 180.[5] Its 3500 polished hexameters reflecting the Callimachean technique were greatly admired and it is said that the Emperor Caracalla presented the poet with a gold piece for each verse.

In its own way the *Halieutica* is a remarkable poem, for it is full of information on the habits of fish (Books I–II) and methods of fishing and even includes a vivid account of whale fishing (Books III–V).

The information is, of course, second-hand — there is little new scientific knowledge in it — but the poem is attractive, containing a number of mythological and other digressions, as well as striking similes and local allusions (such as a reference to a Cilician mountain climb).[6]

Among Oppian's sources we know only of Leonidas of Byzantium (mid-second century A.D.),[7] but his debt to Callimachus, Apollonius Rhodius and particularly Nicander is evident. In his turn Oppian exercised some influence on the *Cynegetica*, on Triphiodorus and on Nonnus.[8]

The *Cynegetica*, an inferior work on hunting, has also been attributed to Oppian of Cilicia, but it is the work of another author of the same name, Oppian of Apamea in Syria (second–third century A.D.), and differs from the *Halieutica* in language, metre and style. The *Cynegetica*, which is dedicated to Caracalla, (ll. I, iff.) deals with the 'inventors' of hunting, the huntsman's helpers, his hounds and horses, describes various wild animals from the lion to the hare and the methods used in their chase and names the four-legged animals that should not be hunted. Its source is probably some Hellenistic prose treatise on the subject, but there is much the author has borrowed from Nicander and Oppian's *Halieutica*. The style is harsh; there are a number of striking linguistic mistakes; and the construction of the hexameter is loose. It has been suggested that Oppian's use of alliteration may owe something to the influence of Syriac poetry.[9]

Collections of animal fables had existed since the days of Demetrius of Phalerum,[10] but the taste for these developed in late antiquity, when they formed part of the exercises of the schools of rhetoric.[11] There was a famous such collection of the second century A.D. compiled by Nicostratus, now lost; for us this literary genre is represented by Babrius.

Babrius (c. A.D. 100) was probably a Hellenized Roman who lived in the East and who composed, not later than the second century A.D.,[12] his version of Aesop's *Fables* in choliambic metre,[13] to which he added novelistic and paradoxographical material, as well as anecdotes.

Originally, the work probably consisted of ten books,[14] but in the preface of Avianus, the Roman fabulist (A.D. 400), and in the best of our manuscripts only two appear, of which the second is incomplete. The presentation of the fables is light and pleasing — perhaps the best of them is *The Sick Lion, the Fox and the Stag* — and the language, which is close to the *koine*, with an Ionic colour, and the metre, in which the stress accent begins to play a part, are well adapted to the subject-matter. The total number of the fables, which at some stage were arranged in alphabetical order according to the first letter of each fable, has been brought up to 137 from various sources.

This collection enjoyed great popularity; it was used in schools,[15] was translated into Latin and was paraphrased in prose and verse in the Middle Ages.

A number of other didactic poems (and some of great length) were composed in the age of Classicism on medical, astrological, grammatical, horticultural and metrical subjects. Some of these were well-known in late antiquity, but only a few minor fragments have survived.[16]

MYTHOLOGICAL AND HISTORICAL EPICS

If the second century had cultivated didactic poetry, the preference of the third was clearly for the vast mythological and historical epic; not infrequently the same poet tried his hand at both.

Nestor of Laranda in Lycia, who lived in the reign of Septimus Severus (A.D. 193–211) and was given Roman citizenship, was one such poet. He wrote an Ἰλιὰς λειπογράμματος, in each of the twenty-four books of which one letter of the alphabet did not appear, and a mythological epic in hexameters called *Metamorphoses*.[17] He also composed a historical epic, *Alexandrias*, on Alexander the Great, and two didactic medical works, the *Alexikepos* (Ἀλεξίκηπος) on healing plants, and the *Panakeia* (Πανάκεια), as well as a hymn on the Dioscuri. One of his sources was Nicander of Colophon.

Nestor was a smooth versifier, if we are to judge from the surviving fragments of the *Metamorphoses*,[18] in which the use of dactyls is profuse. His reputation must have been extremely good, for he was honoured in Rome, Ostia, Paphos, Ephesus and Cyzicus with busts or statues, and the orator Menander recommends his *Metamorphoses*.[19]

A figure of greater importance than Nestor was his son, Peisander of Laranda, who composed the *Heroic Theogamies* (Ἡρωϊκαὶ Θεογαμίαι), the longest epic ever written in Greek. It was a huge mythological encyclopaedia in sixty books, which spoke of the marriages of the gods and their love affairs with humans, starting with the marriage of Zeus with Hera. It was well-known for its flowing style. It appears that this new long epic dealt the final blow to the older cyclic epics, which for centuries had been known mainly from summaries.[20] It is interesting that Virgil was among the sources which Peisander used; the increasing interest of the Greek-speaking East in Virgil is also attested by the Virgil papyri of that period that have been retrieved[21] and by the translation of the *Georgics* into Greek by Arrianos.[22] The *Suda* also mentions prose works written by Peisander.

Dionysius (third–fourth century A.D.) is perhaps the last important poet of this group. He is the author of the *Bassarica*, at least fourteen books long, and of a *Gigantias*. The *Bassarica*, which dealt with the myth of Dionysus and his campaign in India, is the most important of a series of roughly contemporary epics dealing with Dionysus on which Nonnus later drew.[23] The *Gigantias* spoke of the battle of the Giants over Pallene and described the return of Heracles from Troy to Cos, as well as the stealing of the Cattle of the Sun by Alcyoneus. The influence of Nicander on Dionysius can also be traced.[24]

Other epic poets of the period are Soterichus of Oasis, Arrianos, Triphiodorus and Zoticos. Soterichus of Oasis in Egypt (c. A.D. 300) lived under Diocletian and composed *Patria, Bessarica*, an epic on Dionysus in four books, a second mythological epic, on Ariadne, *Calydoniaca* and a poem on the capture of Thebes by Alexander called *Python (Πύθων)* or *Alexandriakos*. He also composed in verse a life of Apollonius of Tyana, the Neo-Pythagorean sage, and he is credited by the *Suda* (probably wrongly) with an encomium on Diocletian.[25] No trace of his work has survived.[26]

The achievements of Alexander the Great, which had captured the imagination of the Hellenistic and Greco-Roman world, were also cast in verse by Arrianos (whose date is uncertain and who should be distinguished from the historian Flavius Arrianus of Nicomedia) in his *Alexandreia*, an epic in twenty-four books. He is also credited with an epic on Attalus of Pergamum, but no trace of either work has survived. Arrianos, as already mentioned, translated into Greek Virgil's *Georgics* and may well be the author of an epigram written on the nail of the Sphinx.[27]

We now know from a papyrus of the third century A.D.[28] that Triphiodorus — the traditional transcription Tryphiodorus is incorrect, as the name derives from the Egyptian goddess Triphis[29] — belongs to the third and not to the fourth or fifth century, as was previously thought. He was a grammarian and epic poet born in Panopolis in Egypt, where the goddess Triphis was worshipped, and, in his handling of the hexameter, was a precursor of Nonnus, whom he also seems to have influenced. His only surviving work, *The Capture of Troy*, in 961 hexameters, draws on the second book of Virgil's *Aeneid*,[30] to say nothing of the Homeric epics and the prose mythological handbooks and summaries then current. (It appears now probable that Quintus of Smyrna drew on Triphiodorus and not the reverse, as had been previously thought.) The poem opens with the construction of the Wooden Horse, into whose belly the Greeks climb, and then proceeds to relate Simon's stratagem and the arrival of the Horse in Troy. This is followed by a long prophecy by Cassandra warning the Trojans, after which the Greek fleet returns and, at a signal given by both Simon and Helen, the warriors descend from the Horse. Scenes of massacre fill the rest of the poem.

The poetry of Triphiodorus is neither original nor inspired, and it lacks all homogeneity. It is therefore not surprising that it exercised no noteworthy influence.

To Triphiodorus are also attributed a number of works now lost, among them the *Marathoniaca*, the *Story of Hippodamea* and an Ὀδύσσεια λειπογράμματος, in each of the twenty-four books of which one letter of the alphabet did not appear; the poet in this is no doubt imitating the Ἰλιὰς λειπογράμματος of Nestor of Laranda.

Finally, we know that Zoticos (c. A.D. 270) wrote the Platonic myth of the Atlantis in verse.

Papyrus finds have made it abundantly clear that a number of other such epic works existed, some inspired by the Trojan Cycle.[31] Among them are a fragment in hexameters attributed to Pancrates, describing a lion hunt in which Hadrian and Antinous took part;[32] an anonymous life of Apollonius of Tyana; a poem on Bokchoris, the Egyptian king of the Twenty-Fourth Dynasty (720–715 B.C.), whom the Greeks considered one of the six great Egyptian lawgivers; a poem on the Persian War of Diocletian (A.D. 284–316) and Galerius;[33] and so forth. Such was the vogue for hexameter poems that on the right leg of the so-called Memnon in Upper Egypt an otherwise unknown poet, Areios, Ὁμηρικὸς ποιητὴς ἐκ Μουσείου, immortalized his name by inscribing his hexameters.[34]

Of all these perhaps the most interesting is a fragment of an epic, *On the Creation*, which has been retrieved in a papyrus,[35] a poem grand in conception and forceful in execution. It is also an interesting item of hermetic theology, whose ultimate purpose was probably the narration of the historical founding of a particular city.[36]

Quite apart from the literary value of all these epics, what becomes clear is that the long epic against which Callimachus had fought so fiercely finally won the day in the Greek-speaking East, even if now and again a 'follower of Callimachus' is mentioned. The victory was complete, for perhaps in no other period of the history of Greek poetry did so many long mythological and historical epics appear, pointing the way to the voluminous works of Quintus Smyrnaeus and Nonnus which followed.

DRAMA AND THE MIME

Although drama fell short of the popularity that hymns and epigrams enjoyed in this period, there is evidence of a dramatic revival in the days of Hadrian and the Antonines,[37] of new tragic and comic poets and of famous actors—even actors of Old Comedy are cited![38]—although nothing of their works has survived. To the few names of those obscure playwrights that have been collected from various sources (names like M. Pomponius, M. P. Bassulus, *T. Aἴλ. Αὐρηλ. Ἀπολλώνιος Ταρσεὺς καὶ Ἀθηναῖος κωμῳδός*, or Oinomaos) we must add those of Apuleius[39] and the Sophists of the Second Sophistic who engaged in writing plays—Scopelianus, Niketes of Smyrna and his pupil Isagoras, whom we have already met,[40] and

Philostratus the Elder, the last credited by the *Suda* with no less than forty-three tragedies and fourteen comedies, as well as a work in three books on tragedy.[41] It is of interest that in the so-called Hadrianic Renaissance even the guilds of the actors were reorganized.

As in the previous period, most of the plays composed in the age of Classicism were written to be read and not acted,[42] an approach to drama which, in fact, can be traced as far back as Aristotle's *Poetics*.[43] Public performances were, on the whole, limited to excerpts of older plays, which were recited or, more usually, sung after they had been set to new music because the original musical accompaniment of their melic parts had perished,[44] as Dio of Prusa informs us.[45] (His evidence is confirmed by an interesting inscription of the first half of the second century A.D. found recently in Isthmia.[46] In it one Themiston from Miletus is honoured for being 'the first and the only one'—a claim which is patently untrue[47]—to use the dramas of Euripides and Sophocles and the poems of Timotheus in his musical compositions.) Such concert performances, we know, were also given by *tragodoi* in the Odeion of Herodes Atticus in Athens, the Athenian festival of Dionysus having degenerated by the first century A.D. into 'a form of dancing unworthy of its classical glory'.[48] By the second century the production of new tragedies and comedies ceased, as we can see from Pseudo-Lucian, who tells us: 'New poetry in honour of Dionysus, comedies and tragedies, has ceased to be composed; so they serve contemporary man by producing those of the past.'[49]

Naturally, solo scenes from drama—for such were the 'revivals' of many older plays—could not command wide audiences, so it is not surprising that the mime and the pantomime increasingly gained ground until they held full sway on the stage. Their popularity was such in the age of Classicism that they were even included in the celebrations organized in honour of Hadrian when he assumed power. A prologue of one of these mimes has survived,[50] but, as with other surviving fragments of Imperial mimes,[51] it has no literary value.

LYRIC POETRY

Few examples of the lyrical poetry of this period have come down to us. They are on the whole poor and unimportant pieces, mainly hymns, many of which are cast in hexameters.

Of these the most noteworthy are by Mesomedes of Crete (first half of second century A.D.), a freedman of Hadrian, who composed a *prooemium* to the Muse Calliope and short hymns on Helios, Nemesis, Nature and Isis, mainly in apapaestic metres and with no myths included. Of interest for the history of ancient music is the musical notation which accompanies the text of three of these.[52] Mesomedes also wrote a few other short lyrical poems, one addressing the Adriatic Sea, two on a sun clock, an ecphrasis of a sponge, one on a mosquito and one on a swan. To these should be added two short pieces found in the *Anthology*,[53] of which the first is a riddle. All the poetry of Mesomedes is cast in a literary Doric dialect.

Side by side with the works of Mesomedes we find a group of anonymous hymns on Zeus, Isis, Serapis, Apollo, Asclepius, Hecate, Fortuna and Dionysus, retrieved in papyri that belong to the second and third centuries A.D. and hardly worthy of the name of poetry.[54] Equally negligible are the fourth-century hymns on Pan, the Sun, Typhon, Hermes, the Moon, Diana-Luna, Hecate and Aphrodite,[55] collected from magic papyri.

To the age of Classicism also belongs the last of the surviving Isis aretalogies found on Ios (second or third century)[56] and the hymns composed by the Sophists of the Second Sophistic, Pausanias, Philostratus and Aelius Aristeides, of which only a few shreds have come down to us.[57] Aristeides, who also wrote prose hymns and epigrams,[58] informs us that he started writing poetry in Rome, 'inspired by Apollo',[59] but continued composing verse during his prolonged illness, often at night and even in his dreams. Of the Sophists Hippodromos (second–third century A.D.) is also credited with lyrical *nomes*[60] and Menander (third century A.D.) with undefined poetry, now lost.[61]

Apart from hymns, the lyric poets of the Imperial age seem to have been mainly concerned with love poetry,[62] but only the names of some such obscure writers have survived and no trace of their works.[63] The fragments of poems other than hymns which the papyri have rendered are few and unimportant; they include a strange, anonymous *Visit to the Underworld*, a poem of the end of the second century A.D., in which a man is described descending to the Underworld to converse with a woman who must formerly have been his wife or his mistress. The details of the journey, which are gruesome and horrible, diverge considerably from the traditional pattern of descents to the Underworld.[64]

The papyri have also saved from oblivion fragments of *Metamorphoses* by an unknown poet, remarkable for the long, compound adjectives found in them;[65] two anonymous sailors' songs of the second and third centuries A.D., the first being an invitation to ocean-going and Nile sailors to compete in songs comparing ocean and Nile[66] and the second a song of a Rhodian sailor upon his return to his native island;[67] two drinking songs (*scolia alphabetica*);[68] a *cantus lugubris*;[69] and a mimic monody in the style of the Alexandrian (Grenfell) Fragment,[70] which shows that in the first centuries A.D. this kind of poetry was not dead. It deals with the lament of a maiden who complains that her lover has abandoned her and has joined the gladiators.

As can be seen, lyric poetry, which for long years was in utter decline, was not revived in the Imperial age. To this age also belongs the beginnings of the new Christian religious poetry which will be dealt with in Chapter 16.

THE EPIGRAM

The age of Classicism marked the end of the ancient epigram. By the close of the third century A.D. it was practically dead, though it was revived in the fourth by Palladas. However, in spite of the fact that it had little of merit to boast of, it continued to be popular in the early part of the period, and even Roman emperors like Trajan (A.D. 98–117) or Hadrian (A.D. 76–138) wrote epigrams in Greek.[71]

The virtual disappearance of fictitious epitaphs and dedications was a characteristic of the age, while emphasis was given to the erotic epigram, which was cast in an unrestrained and vulgar manner. At one level this furthered the tradition of the so-called 'Phoenician School' of epigrammatists, but playful eroticism gave way to flagrant sensuality and pleasantry to crude vulgarity. This 'Oriental strain' which invaded the epigram is most evident in the writings of Straton of Sardis (c. A.D. 130) and of his near-contemporary, Rufinus of Samos (c. A.D. 150).[72]

Straton of Sardis made a collection of pederastic epigrams, the *Mousa Paidike*, which comprises the works of many authors, as well as roughly a hundred pieces of his own. It forms the backbone of Book XII of the Palatine *Anthology*. In these the sheer carnal sensuality is frequently offensive, for the verses are often coarse and mawkish; even when the epigrams display considerable dexterity of form, only very occasionally does a spark of true poetry emerge.[73] The epigrams of Rufinus of Samos combine an even cruder sensuality and a shameless realism with a much less well-developed sense of form.

Together with the carnal eroticism prevalent in the epigram of those days, we can also trace the continuation of a sceptic trend—it has also a didactic touch about it—which had started in Nero's time. This is represented by the writings of Philon of Byblos (c. A.D. 100?), Antiochus of Aigai (c. A.D. 100), Apollinarius (c. A.D. 100), Ammianus (c. A.D. 120) and Lucian (not Lucian of Samosata but an otherwise unknown writer of uncertain date).[74] At the same time, we also find the odd and usually dull epigram from the pen of men distinguished in other fields, such as Dionysius of Halicarnassus, the Sophist (c. A.D. 125), Heliodorus of Emessa (third century A.D.), Philostratus of Lemnos (A.D. 170–250), Nestor of Laranda (c. A.D. 210) and Diogenes Laertius (c. A.D. 225), to say nothing of various other obscure writers like Euodos (second–third century A.D.) or Eupithios (third century A.D.). Finally, mention should be made of Nicodemus of Heraclia (first or second century A.D.), who composed ἀνακυκλικὰ ἐπιγράμματα, epigrams which could also be read backwards.[75]

Judged as a whole, the epigram of this period allowed greater linguistic and metrical freedom. The hexameter, which had been revived in the previous period, continued to be employed, and prose words were now often introduced into the poetic diction, just as poetic words began to penetrate the prose writings of those days.[76]

Of the epigrams collected from inscriptions, an interesting group are those carved on the so-called statue of Memnon in Egypt, some of which have already been mentioned.[77] They are *proscynemata* of visitors who 'heard Memnon's voice' when dawn struck the huge seated stone form. Among them are the epigrams of two poetesses, Julia Balbilla,[78] who prided herself on royal descent, and Caecilia Treboulla,[79] and a beautiful epigram by one Asclepiodotus.[80]

In the age of Classicism we also meet with collections of epigrams, such as the one compiled by Diogenes Laertius called *Pammetros* (that is, epigrams composed in all kinds of metres), which included epigrams on famous men on which he drew for his own biographies of the philosophers, and the anthology of epigrams compiled by the grammarian Diogenianus in the days of Hadrian.[81] Nor should a number of epitaphs found on inscriptions of this period be overlooked,[82] some of which are truly beautiful verse.[83]

Related to the epigrams (and also transmitted in the same *Codex Palatinus*) are the so-called *anacreontea*, short poems in anacreontic metre dealing with wine and love in a light-hearted manner. The Hadrianic period also contributed to these trivia,[84] but as they really became fashionable from the fourth century onwards, they will be examined in Chapter 15, which covers the following period.

The Period of Transition from the Ancient World to the Middle Ages
(A.D. 330–641)

Introduction

The administrative reforms of Diocletian (284–305) and Constantine the Great (306–37) gave the Empire a new lease of life, but it was the transference of the capital from Rome to Constantinople and the Imperial favour increasingly shown to Christianity which set it on a new path.

Constantine's policy of religious tolerance and of a closer relation with Christianity clearly shows that a great turning-point had been reached in the history of the world and that the Greco-Roman civilization was becoming medieval, a change that signifies, among other things, the triumph of mysticism and the fall of rationalism, that mainstay of Classical culture. The preponderance of the Greek element in the new capital and in the Eastern provinces of the Empire, as well as the importance of the Greek language and Greek literature (which since the days of Hadrian had been recognized as the 'universal' language and literature) gradually led to the full Hellenization of the state, though in law, diplomacy and military matters the Roman tradition long held its own.

It is true that Alexandria remained an important centre for philosophy, scholarship, mathematics, astronomy and medicine until the sixth century and that the Alexandrian school played a most important part in the theological disputes of the first centuries; it is also true that Athens retained her significance as the centre of philosophy and rhetoric until Justinian closed her philosophical schools in 529.[1] But no matter how prominent those ancient seats of learning may have been, and although new substantial ones had sprung up—cities like Nicomedia, Tarsus, Berytus and Thessalonica—Constantinople was the glory of the Empire in the East. She was meant to combine Roman valour and Hellenic learning and was enriched from the start with all that art and letters could offer. Moreover, the splendid fortifications that Theodosius II (408–50) gave 'The City' enabled it to withstand all barbaric attacks for a thousand years.

The Council of Nicaea (325), representing the Roman world united under a single emperor, set the foundations of orthodoxy. But orthodox

Christianity was not yet entirely triumphant. It was still possible for the Emperor Julian (361–3) to revert to paganism—although the experiment showed that paganism was a dying force—and a number of heresies were yet to appear, all of which the Church managed to overcome successfully.

The fifth century saw the end of the Western Empire, battered by the barbarian onslaught. After the abdication of Romulus Augustus in 476 and the death of Julius Nepos in 480 no one in the West bore the title of emperor. The Empire in the East fared better. Visigoths, Huns and Ostrogoths each crossed the Danube, but in the end they sought their fortunes in the West. It was not until the Vandals established themselves in Africa (439) that Roman supremacy at sea was challenged.

Of the heresies, the most dangerous for the Empire was the Monophysite doctrine, introduced by an obscure archimandrite, Eutyches, which promulgated the single nature of Christ. The fourth Ecumenical Council at Chalcedon (451) crushed Eutyches, but its condemnation of Monophysitism had far-reaching political consequences. For from the bitterness then sown was reaped, nearly two centuries later, the easy Arab conquest of Syria and Egypt, economically, artistically and culturally the two most important provinces of the Empire in that period.

At the beginning of the sixth century Byzantium was again in great difficulties. The Persians renewed the war in the East, and Slavs and Bulgarians were penetrating south of the Danube; moreover, the capital was in the throes of the quarrels between the Circus factions, the Greens and the Blues. A strong administration was necessary to face the crisis, and this was supplied by the reign of Justinian, which owes much to the all-powerful influence of the Empress Theodora as well as to the able generals and capable ministers then in office.

The oustanding feature of the years between 518 and 610 is Justinian's attempt to reclaim for Rome many of the lands occupied by the barbarians in Africa, Italy and Spain. But this great undertaking in the West caused him to neglect the East, and the Empire was menaced by the Persians. At the same time, the frontier of the Danube gave way before the attacks of Huns, Slavs and Avars. Constantinople could not wage war on two fronts, and Asia, in which she had her heart, had to be saved. So the grand Western policy of Justinian, which had drained the Empire's resources, was abandoned.

The reign of Justinian is a decisive epoch in the history of civilization. Writers of talent—historians like Procopius, Agathias, John of Ephesus and Euagrius; poets like Paul the Silentiary and Agathias; theologians like Leontius of Byzantium—kept alive the tradition of Greek literature, and Christian poetry reached its peak in the person of Romanos the Melodist. Moreover, all kinds of constructions—bridges, castles, palaces, walls of cities, churches—were erected, many of them marvels of skill and magnificence; and jewels, fabrics, ivories and manuscripts of unique splendour were also produced.

But Justinian's two greatest creations were, beyond doubt, the codification of Roman law, known as the *Corpus Juris Civilis*, and the building of the cathedral of Santa Sophia, whose splendour outshone 'even the temple of Solomon'. They were both inspired by the principles of Imperial and Christian magnificence in which the emperor believed.

The Persian War, which was renewed under Chosroes II (590–628), brought the enemy to Chalcedon, opposite Constantinople. Again the whole Empire cried for a saviour. This time he came from Africa in the person of Heraclius, son of the exarch of Carthage, who overthrew the tyrant Phocas and founded a new dynasty. He felt his mission to be a religious undertaking, and throughout his reign (610–41) his religious concern was paramount.

Supported by the indomitable courage and energy of the Patriarch, Sergius, Heraclius faced the vigorous attacks of Persians and Avars, who almost captured Constantinople itself (626), and finally carried the war into the lands of the fire-worshippers. The kingdom of the Sassanids was crushed forever (629) and the Holy Cross was brought back from Ctesiphon to Jerusalem. The suzerainty of Byzantium was also established over the Slavs, who by then had filled the Balkan peninsula.

But the beginning of the seventh century was marked by a momentous and, for Byzantium, ominous event—the birth of Islam. For the tribesmen of Arabia were then for the first time united by a common faith, the Muslim, and it was during the reign of Heraclius that their armies attacked and wrested Palestine and Syria from the Empire; a few years later Egypt was lost. The over-taxed, persecuted Monophysite heretics made no attempt to preserve the Imperial dominion.

Thus by the death of Heraclius Church and State, the twin centres of Byzantine life, were indissolubly linked, and the enmity for Persia which Constantinople had inherited from Rome gave place to perennial hostility towards Islam.

If we now turn to the literary culture of the Eastern Empire, we shall observe that during this period great changes came about in the education of the young. Thus in the fourth century the *gymnasium* and the institution of the *ephebia*, which had been revived during the Hadrianic Renaissance, ceased to function, and with them interest in athletics and sports passed away.[2]

But although when Christianity triumphed[3] Christian virtues took the place of the teachings of ancient philosophy and the Christian sermon that of the Stoic–Cynic diatribe, boys at school were taught to venerate and to imitate the ancient authors. Naturally, to write correct ancient Greek became increasingly difficult as in its evolution the spoken language kept diverging from Classical usage; but precisely because of this the closer a contemporary author or poet approximated to the ancients, the more he was esteemed because the object was to reproduce the diction and style of the models. A result of this was that many 'educated' men were able to turn out some kind of verse for an epitaph, an epithalamium or even a panegyric, but this verse can hardly be called poetry.

It might appear strange in a Christian society that even the Fundamentalists should admit that boys should learn the pagan classics at school, and that when Julian debarred the teaching of pagan poets and philosophers to Christians the action aroused a storm of protest which resulted in the recasting of the Scriptures in Classical forms to replace the Classical authors in schools. Even the great Fathers of the Church in the fourth and fifth centuries admitted the significance of the classics and by so doing conferred on them ecclesiastical authority, such was the prestige of ancient Greek literature.

In poetry, as in all other aspects of life, the years between 300 and 641 were a period of transition from the ancient world to the Middle Ages. The traditional division of poetry into epic, lyric and dramatic, which had already become less rigid in the Hellenistic world, visibly decreased until it disappeared completely in the seventh century. At the same time it should be noted that the last florescence of the Second Sophistic in the fourth century was even less propitious for poetry than the First had been in the second century. It not only attacked poetry directly[4] but also promoted further fossilization by imposing on it the principles of rhetoric. As a result, a large number of utterly insignificant works were created.

Another damaging influence of those days was the new world of Oriental ideas which was developing side by side with the advance of Christianity and which soon permeated poetry. The formlessness and profuseness it encouraged can best be seen in the fifth-century Egyptian school of mythological epic and, most notably, in Nonnus. It is indeed interesting to observe that Upper Egypt and the Thebaid, which till the third century A.D. were a cultural backwater, became in the fifth one of the most productive sources of Greek poets in the whole Empire, men who cultivated verse which has been called 'the last flowering of ancient Greek poetry'.[5] One has only to remember Pamprepius, Cyrus, Nonnus and Triphiodorus, who came from Panopolis, or Christodorus, who came from Coptos, to mention only a few known names, to recognize the aptness of the description. There were also numerous other poet–grammarians from Byzantine Egypt, who spent their lives wandering from city to city writing panegyrics, invectives, epics (*patria*) or epithalamia in search of fame and fortune. But the appeal of their poetry must have been strictly limited, for it has all disappeared without trace.[6]

Yet the sudden revival of the grand mythological epic in this period is impressive and in a sense unexpected, be it the more restrained 'Ionian' epic of Asia Minor, as seen in the *Posthomerica* of Quintus Smyrnaeus, or the more profuse and buoyant epic from Africa, represented by the works of Nonnus and his school. Also noteworthy is the revival of the epic ecphrasis, which deals with the great Christian achievements like the construction of the church of Santa Sophia or grand pagan allegorical paintings like the Cosmos of the winter baths of Gaza. This period also produced a florescence of the epigram, both pagan and Christian,[7] that in the days of Justinian had a liveliness and variety that it had not attained since the days of Meleager, even though the influence of the rhetorical panegyric and the rhetorical ecphrasis was predominant.

The period is a remarkable one in the history of Greek metrics. For the most decisive event in the history of Greek metrics, the gradual disappearance of the distinction between long and short vowels, a process which had started in the later Hellenistic age, was completed by about A.D. 400, when the varying lengths of vowels were reduced to an absolute equality, and they were pronounced just as in modern Greek. As a result of this, quantitative metres (those in which rhythm depended on the difference between the long and short syllables) disintegrated, although learned poets continued to write verse in such metres up to the fifteenth century. As would be expected, the earliest false quantities in the verse of educated writers occur in the works of Christians like Methodius (c. 311), Arius (c. 250–c. 336) and Gregory of Nazianzus (329–89),[8] who addressed a public that did not have an ear for quantitative rhythms.

The placing of word accents at regular positions in the line also appeared at roughly the same time as quantitative distinctions began to decline.[9] The ancient musical character of the three Greek accents (acute, grave and circumflex) was gradually lost and was substituted by a fully dynamic quality—they developed into full stress accents—a phenomenon first apparent in the avoidance of an accentuated final syllable in the pentameters of Antipater of Sidon (c. 130 B.C.). Later the regulation of accents spread to almost all kinds of quantitative verse, until from about A.D. 500 the fixing of accents and the set number of syllables in a line determined the new Byzantine metrical system that we find in Christian religious and folk poetry, when the former abandoned the use of ancient metres. In this manner, and by grouping such 'regulated' lines into strophes, a great variety of rhythmical effects was achieved. But the early development of this new rhythmic system, which is a milestone in the history of Greek poetry, remains obscure. It was perfected by the days of Justinian. At that time it could not have been more than a century old.

After Justinian came a period of utter decline in Greek metrics. The only important event was the introduction of the fifteen-syllable line, the *politikos stichos*,[10] into literature, which, down to the present day, has been the principal metre of Greek poetry. The first traceable instance of the use of this metre in the period under consideration appears in an acclamation to the Emperor Maurice (582–602). Its origins, however, are a matter of dispute.[11]

With Synesius (c. 370–c. 414) polymetry came to an end. After his time we find in use only the three oldest and most common metres—the hexameter, the elegiac couplet and the iambic trimeter—and, rarely, the anacreontic, for verse of a lyrical character. It is of interest that the strictest of all forms of the hexameter was introduced in the fifth century by Nonnus, and that he was followed in this by his school up to the seventh century. But it should also be noted that the year 500 marked the end of the 'living' hexameter. This most ancient and noble Greek metrical form, which enjoyed a life of roughly two thousand years, ceased thereafter to be used in any living verse, though of course it continued to be employed as a 'museum piece' to the end of the Byzantine empire and even after.

From the seventh century on, the predominant 'ancient' metre was the paroxytone twelve-syllable line, which poets had developed out of the iambic trimeter by regulating the number of syllables and by placing the accents at set positions in the line. This made it possible for quantity to be disregarded without damage to the rhythm,[12] as we see it in the poetry of George the Pisidian (seventh century A.D.) and his followers.

But even earlier, from the fourth to the sixth century, iambic poetry was steadily gaining ground at the hexameter's expense. By the year 500 the iambic trimeter was used for most traditional epic subjects, a further indication that the feeling for the style and ethos of epic poetry was rapidly declining. Characteristic is the example of Marianus (c. A.D. 500), who recast in iambics a number of famous Alexandrian hexameter and elegiac poems, such as the *Idylls* of Theocritus; Callimachus' *Hecale, Aetia*, hymns and epigrams; Apollonius' *Argonautica*; Aratus' *Phaenomena*; and Nicander's *Theriaca*. The spread of iambic poetry can also be seen from the iambic prologues we meet in poems composed in other metres. By the end of the sixth century the iambic prologue had become almost obligatory.[13]

In religious poetry we see the last embers of ancient lyrical hymnody, inspired by Neo-Platonism and evident in the hymns of Proclus and Synesius (c. 370–c. 414)—the content of the latter is Christian—as well as the end of the hexameter hymn, as seen in a surviving collection of eighty-seven 'Orphic' hymns that indicates a revival of interest in Orphic mysticism in the fourth century.

But the centre of religious poetry was clearly Christian hymnography, composed according to the metrical rules of the new rhythmical system. Heretical at first and later orthodox, this genre was inspired by admiration for the martyrs of the Church and by deep devotion to its mysteries. As it treated of subjects which were popular and at the same time the province of the official state religion, it was the most lively and perhaps the most significant body of verse created in those days. The language of this Christian poetry blended traditional Attic Greek, as it was taught in the schools of rhetoric and grammar of the time, with many of the spoken forms, and fell into two main types. The first, which flourished in the fourth and fifth centuries, consisted of short, laudatory hymns of various metrical patterns, known as *troparia*;[14] the second, the *kontakion*, is an elaborate metrical sermon accompanied by music which developed in the sixth and seventh centuries.

In conclusion, attention should be drawn to the fact that it was in this period that all theatrical performances ceased. There is no inscriptional evidence to suggest that the *thymelikoi agones*, in which full plays — usually revivals of 'old' plays[15] — were acted, continued beyond the third century. Solos[16] and chorus songs from plays continued to be performed publicly, but, as in the Greco-Roman world, it was the mime and the pantomime, as well as performances at the circus and the hippodrome, that captivated the crowd. It is therefore not surprising that the attacks of the Fathers of the Church and the laws promulgated by Anastasius I (491–518) and Justinian I (527–65) were directed mainly against the mime and the pantomime. Information exists about theatrical performances which took place in the fourth and fifth centuries;[17] they also continued into the sixth century, as can be seen from the *Apologia Mimorum* of Choricius (probably written before 524), an epigram of Agathias on an actress and a notice in Menander Protector's autobiography (sixth century). But all free public performances of plays, be they ancient drama, mime or pantomime, seem to have ceased soon after Justinian's prohibitive law of 524.[18] So ended the long and noble tradition of ancient drama, which was not to be revived in the Greek world until the seventeenth century, in Venetian-occupied Crete.

A close examination of Byzantine literature shows that in Byzantium no prose or verse works were ever written with the intention of being acted on the stage. There were, of course, older dramatic dialogues, like that of the Patriarch Proclus (434–7) on the Virgin,[19] or those written by Methodius, bishop of Olympus (d. 311), in opposition to the Gnostics; we know that the *Thaleia* of Arius (c. 250–c. 336) — now almost completely lost — was a popularization of his heretical doctrines conceived to counterbalance the pagan stage, and that the *Antithaleia* was written to vitiate Arius' heretical success; and we even hear of a pantomime mystery play from the days of Maurice (591).[20] But all these works were meant to be read and not to be acted, as was the case with the *Tragodopodagra* or the *Okypous* of Lucian; the lost play *Susanna* with which St John of Damascus (c. 675–c. 749) is credited; or the *Christus Patiens*, that cento of the eleventh–twelfth centuries; or the later *dramatia*, short, allegorical dramatic pieces, of Michael Haploucheir (twelfth century), Theodoros Prodromos (twelfth century) and Manuel Philes (fourteenth century).

Nor can the *Nepter* (the *Washing of the Feet*) — which is performed to this day in church in Jerusalem and Patmos — in any sense be called a play, for the words spoken are those of the Scriptures. As has been aptly said, Byzantine poetry, just like Byzantine painting, lacks one dimension—the dramatic. In Byzantium it was the colourful liturgy of the Orthodox Church and the rich pageantry of the palace ceremonies that took the place of dramatic performances and satisfied the natural craving of the people for impressive spectacle. The Mystery Plays belong to the West.[21]

It has been said that in Byzantine literature a 'deep, dark chasm' of two centuries—from Heraclius to the Restoration of the Images (641–843) —separates the ancient world from the Middle Ages.[22] For poetry this is not quite true, for though the secular poetry of that period is indeed poor—the poorest in the history of medieval Greek poetry—Christian verse flourished. *Troparia* and canons, as we shall presently see, were produced in abundance, and some of them had great popular appeal, if not much poetic merit. So Christian religious poetry can be called the bridge that spans the 'chasm'.

Even from these brief observations it becomes clear that the period of transition from the ancient to the medieval Greek world, from Constantine to Heraclius, is one of the most important in the history of Greek poetry.

CHAPTER 15

Secular Poetry

THE EPIC

Mythological, didactic, historical and encomiastic epics continued to be composed in this period, as well as epic ecphrases. Most impressive is the sudden revival of the mythological epic, but the florescence of the epic ecphrasis is also noteworthy. Epic encomia, in which, as we have seen, the iambic trimeter had gained ground at the expense of the dactylic hexameter since the fifth century, were numerous. These cannot always be clearly distinguished from the historical epics, as historical events, battles, sieges and so on were often introduced and described in detail to celebrate the achievements of a living emperor or general.

The four types of epic poetry we meet in this period had best be treated separately.

The mythological epic

Two kinds of mythological epic flourished in those days, the first in Asia Minor and the second in Egypt. The epic of Asia Minor is represented by one large work, the *Posthomerica* of Quintus Smyrnaeus, which has been called 'the last glimmer of the Ionian Homeric tradition'. It uses old 'Ionian' mythological material; in style it is on the whole restrained, favouring straightforward descriptions and avoiding metrical artifice. On the other hand, the Egyptian school (for here we have a movement with several representatives) is the last ancient Greek school of epic poetry. It was founded by Nonnus and delights in bombastic description, unbridled sensuality and ingenious metrical devices. A powerful Oriental element is also evident.

THE EPIC OF ASIA MINOR

Quintus of Smyrna (third–fourth century) aspired to complete the story of the *Iliad* and to connect it with the *Odyssey* in a long epic now known as the *Posthomerica*, composed some thousand years after the Homeric epics were committed to writing. All the information we can gather about his life is that he lived in the vicinity of Smyrna and was a free man.[1] If a new fourth-century papyrus of a hexameter poem called Ὅρασις Δωροθέου (now in the Bibliotheca Bodmeriana of Geneva, papyrus Bodmer 29), which bears the name Quintus, is by Quintus Smyrnaeus, then we must assume that at some point of his life he became a Christian.[2] The date of Quintus is uncertain. Modern research believes that he probably belongs to the third century and certainly lived before Nonnus, by whose metrical and other innovations he is not affected.[3]

The *Posthomerica* are divided into fourteen books, called *logoi*, to which there is no *prooemium*. They deal with the death of Penthesilea, Memnon and Achilles (I–III); the funeral games held in honour of Achilles and the death of Ajax (IV–V); the exploits of Eurypylus and Neoptolemus (VI–VIII); the battle under the walls of Troy and the arrival of Philoctetes (IX); the death of Paris and the last attack of the Greeks, the construction of the Wooden Horse, Simon's ruse, the death of Laocoön, Cassandra's prophecies and the capture of the city (X–XIII). The epic ends with the departure of the Greeks, the storm they meet with on their way home, and the death of the Locrian Ajax (XIV).

The connection between the stories Quintus relates is loose. The true unit of composition is the book, the *logos*, which has its own dramatic interest. The only exceptions are the heroic achievements of Neoptolemus and Eurypylus, which break through the framework of the *logos*, but, though placed in the middle of the work, they do not form a structural centre.

Quintus drew on a large number of sources, the Homeric epics and their scholia, Sophocles, Euripides, Apollonius Rhodius and other Hellenistic poets now partly or fully lost, as well as on geographical, medical and mythological prose works. What is surprising is that he does not seem to know the cyclic epics, with the one possible exception of the *Aethiopis*.

It is a matter of dispute among scholars whether Quintus drew on Latin sources and, more specifically, on Virgil, Ovid or Seneca.[4] It should be borne in mind, however, that, as can be seen from the number of Latin papyri, the penetration of Latin poetry into the Greek-speaking East does not really begin until the fourth and fifth centuries.[5]

The language of the *Posthomerica* is basically Homeric but is blended with many elements from later poetic diction; the influence of Greek, as spoken in the poet's own day, has also been traced. The metre is basically the Homeric hexameter, unaffected by any of the Callimachean refinements or the devices of Nonnus. But the style of Quintus is flat and lifeless. He uses too many colourless adjectives, participles and similes; he repeats the same words too often, for his vocabulary is not rich, and, in spite of considerable restraint, indulges in rhetorical conceits. Thus the influence of rhetoric is evident in the set subjects introduced into the narrative—the battle, the embassy, the burial, the tempest—and in the manner in which they are treated; it is also evident in the speeches, which fall into common types of rhetorical exercises—the *agon*, the eulogy, the invective, the exhortation, the consolation—to say nothing of the many didactic and moralizing passages.

As a result of this moralizing tendency, everything in the narrative is presented as noble and irreproachable—full *semnotis* is observed. Paris is no playboy but a worthy successor of Hector; Achilles' passion for Penthesilea is disposed of in a few lines; the rape of Cassandra is treated with great discretion; the story of Oenone (one of the best episodes in the poem) is seen as a conjugal drama and not as a tragedy of love; and Helen is kept well in the background.

But in spite of this, Quintus does not succeed in infusing any true moral significance into his work, nor is he helped by his gods, who, in Homeric manner, indulge in their own passions. Moreover, in his confused theology, in which the supremacy of Fate is asserted (VII, 70–1), elements of stoicism and fatalism are blended with hints of Neo-Platonism and a preference for the salvation of those of noble birth. The much discussed passage which is thought to indicate Christian influence upon the poet (VII, 87–9) has assumed a new interest since the recent appearance of the Dorotheos papyrus.

Very different assessments have been made of the poetry of the *Posthomerica*, ranging from the remarkably high opinion of Sainte-Beuve to complete condemnation; what is beyond dispute is that the poet's slavish devotion to Homer deprives the verse of freshness and the narrative of vigour. The characters are like shadows, lacking depth or dramatic life. But there are redeeming features, such as the frequent references to nature in the similes or the presentation of the gentler side of the warrior after the battle is over (seen in the sudden love of Achilles for the dead Penthesilea), which give a warmth and directness that point to personal observation by the poet and not to the study of books. It has been remarked that a great defect of Quintus is that whereas Homer and Virgil present men fighting, working and struggling and leave the reader to feel with them, the poet of Smyrna explains their feelings—and does so in the most conventional manner. Real poetic excellence, such as in the Deidamia episode of Book VII, is rarely achieved. Furthermore, it is fair to add that Quintus, to his credit, avoids formless bombast and the unbridled sensuality which invaded poetry and prose in the following century.

The influence which the *Posthomerica* exercised upon subsequent Greek poetry is negligible, nor can Quintus be said to have created in any sense a school, as Nonnus did later on.

THE 'ORPHIC' *ARGONAUTICA*

Between Quintus Smyrnaeus and Nonnus should be placed the *Argonautica*, which are attributed to 'Orpheus'. This is probably a work of the fourth century—the date is a matter of debate—when the name of 'Orpheus' again came to the fore, for we find assigned to him not only mythological and didactic epics but also religious hymnic poetry,[6] all in hexameters. In all probability, this should be associated with the Platonic School's revival of interest in Orphic mysticism which we meet in the fourth century.

The *Argonautica*, whose author is unknown, deals with the journey of the Argonauts in 1400 hexameters. In many ways it echoes the *Argonautica* of Apollonius Rhodius but has none of the romantic or dramatic qualities of the Alexandrian epic, nor any of its poet's descriptive ability. The central figure is Orpheus, who, in spite of his prayers, sacrifices and long speeches, is not brought to life. The author's main interest seems to lie in geography. Perhaps it should be added that the best part of this insignificant poem is the taking of the Golden Fleece (ll. 890–1022).

A few fourth-century fragments of other mythological epics attributed to 'Orpheus' have also survived, but they are of little interest.[7]

NONNUS OF PANOPOLIS

Undoubtedly the most important and influential secular poet of the early Christian centuries was Nonnus. He was born in about A.D. 400 in Panopolis in Upper Egypt, the home of many poets of those days. He studied in Berytus and later lived in Alexandria, where he wrote his major work, the *Dionysiaca*.[8] If the *Metabole*, a paraphrase of St John's Gospel in hexameters, was truly composed by Nonnus, it must be assumed that later in life he became a Christian. However, he had not joined the Christian Church when he composed the *Dionysiaca*, as can be seen from the great store he sets by the practice of mystery cults.[9]

The *Metabole* belongs to a series of adaptations of the Bible into classical verse, similar to those composed by Apollinarius in the second half of the fourth century, when Julian forbade Christians to study classical authors at school. It must have been composed after A.D. 431, for the Virgin is frequently called *Theotokos*, the Mother of God, which presupposes the Ecumenical Council of Ephesus (431). It should be noted that the attribution of the *Metabole* to Nonnus is based mainly on the similarity of its language and metre to those of the *Dionysiaca*, because in the manuscript tradition that work is also ascribed to the philosopher Ammonius of Alexandria (third century A.D.).

Nonnus' *magnum opus*, the *Dionysiaca* (the *Adventures of Dionysus*), consists of forty-eight books; the author had aspired to compose a poem as long as the *Iliad* and the *Odyssey* put together. Its date has not been determined with certainty. The latest we can assign it to is A.D. 470,[10] for it was clearly composed before the *Encomium Heraclii ducis*,[11] which belongs to that year. It deals with the story of the god Dionysus from his birth to his apotheosis, with special reference to his Indian campaign. As we have seen, Dionysus and his achievements were a subject much treated by later epic poets (Dionysius, Soterichus, Scopelianus and others) but Nonnus surpassed them all in both fertility of description and absence of decorum.

The work falls into four parts. Books I–XII deal with the prehistory and youth of the god; Books XIII–XXIV with his campaign in India; Books XXV–XL with his battles with the Indians; and Books XLI–XLVIII—with Dionysus' triumphant return to the Greek world, his final arrival in Phrygia and his ascent to his throne in the heavens. This long narrative is expanded with numerous episodes, most of which treat of Dionysus' amorous exploits. Such are those describing his passion for Ampelos (Books X–XI), who is killed while hunting and in whose memory the vine is created; for the fair nymph Nicaea (Books XV–XVI); for Beroë (Books XLI–XLIII); for Ariadne (Book XLVII); and finally for Pallene and Aura (Book XLVIII). It might be worth mentioning here that Nonnus was the last ancient Greek poet who dealt with homosexual love. Not until the days of Cavafy (1868–1933) did it re-emerge in Greek verse, for the Christian sense of decorum was such that for a full fifteen centuries homosexuality was barred from all Greek poetry.

Nonnus was a well-read man and drew on many sources. Most evident among them are Homer, the Homeric Hymns, Pindar and the tragedians; and of the Alexandrians, Callimachus, Apollonius, Lycophron, the bucolic poets, Euphorion, Nicander and Parthenius. He also used the *Bassarica* of Dionysius, Quintus Smyrnaeus, Oppian, Pseudo-Oppian's *Cynegetica*, the 'Orphic' hymns, Herodotus and Plato, and even Latin sources like Ovid and Claudian.[12] Moreover, he was acquainted with law, medicine and the natural sciences—he was interested, for example, in the elephant (XXVI, 297) and in the origin of purple dye (XL, 306)—and was conversant with Neo-Platonism, Orphism, various eastern mystery cults and magic; it is even thought that in Book XLVIII (834) he may be referring to Christianity.

As would be expected, the tone throughout this gigantic poem is uneven, ranging from the idyllic, as we see it in the description of the rape of Europa, to the cosmic dementia of the Typhon's battle. Nor is it surprising that the *Dionysiaca* falls into many disconnected parts that obscure the central theme, which is how Dionysus wins the sky through his achievements. There are, in fact, many obvious additions,[13] and many of the battle scenes seem to have been put together out of independent individual bits, like mosaics. Intensity and not clarity is the poet's aim, for Nonnus was clearly a fast and superficial worker who probably never revised his work; this is apparent from the frequent contradictions and the many episodes which are out of place, to say nothing of the double versions which appear in the narrative.[14]

In the *Dionysiaca* the influence of epideictic oratory and of the late Hellenistic novel are all too evident.[15] Thus development and the realistic portrayal of character are lacking. As in any rhetorical encomium, Dionysus is intended to be a subject of praise, and no attempt is made to involve the reader in the trials of a hero who is in the process of working out his destiny. The poet simply narrates a series of deeds and accomplishments which the reader is asked to admire. Nonnus' Dionysus is perfection praised, by contrast with Homer's Achilles, whose human limitations are the focus of interest. Denying himself the field of character development, Nonnus resorts to *ethopoeia*, in which the speaker gives vent to various rhetorical sentiments that are generally appropriate for each occasion. The result is that the speeches of the *Dionysiaca* are set pieces, lacking dramatic and individual psychological insight.

The erotic element in the work has also been influenced by the encomium. It serves as a vehicle for the praise of the god; it is part of his 'Triumph' and it stands in marked contrast to Apollonius' treatment of love, which is made the very mainstay of the plot of the *Argonautica*. The encomiastic nature of the *Dionysiaca* also favours the use of certain rhetorical devices, like *deinotes*, achieved through the paradox, or the use of *synkrisis*, in which the realms of literature and mythology, and not that of nature, are the stuff of comparison.

It has rightly been said that the *Dionysiaca* represents a full adaptation of the old epic genre to the requirements of a new taste, which results in what might be called a grand epic encomium. For there can be little doubt that its main purpose is encomiastic, and that the author is conscious of his role as a major poet of the Second Sophistic who finally succeeds in effecting a reconciliation between two long warring elements, the poetic and the rhetorical. But the rhetorical is undoubtedly the dominant partner.

The style and language of Nonnus also reflect the tendencies of his day. He is careless both in his use of language and in his descriptions. Formlessness and lack of measure, probably due to Oriental influences, are his major faults, and he indulges in periphrasis, repetition, antithesis, anaphora, asyndeton, alliteration and assonance, as well as in plays on words, so that the general effect is very close to that of the Asianic rhetorical style. Moreover, his similes are limited (in their place he indulges in *synkrisis*), and he avoids rare words and the usual Homeric epithets.

The erotic element in which he delights is crude, unbridled and often morbid, for necrophilia,[16] sadism[17] and masochism[18] also appear, to say nothing of pederasty. In fact, Nonnus displays all the late Hellenistic lasciviousness as we know it from the love romances, the epigram and the Latin elegies of Maximianus of Eretria (sixth century A.D.). He is at his best in sentimental passages, such as those describing the story of Nicaea or the lament for Ariadne.

The greatest contribution of Nonnus to Greek poetry was certainly in the field of metrics, where he created a whole school. In the hexameter his influence was felt up to the seventh century A.D. and even later. Thus in his hexameters he avoids hiatus and never has two consecutive spondees; he frequently employs the trochaic caesura in the third foot and always accentuates one of the two ultimate syllables of the line, as well as one of the two ultimate syllables before a caesura. Thus in a sense Nonnus is a forerunner of the rhythmic versification based on the placing of accents which the Byzantine religious poets were to develop so fully. Most of these refinements are, of course, based on the Callimachaean rules of the hexameter; Nonnus' own rhythmic accentual additions were clearly inspired by the practice of Imperial artistic prose, which observed set accents at the end of its *clausulae*.[19] (At this point it should perhaps be added that the so-called 'Nonnian style' should not be seen as the creation of one man but as a long development influenced by the changes in pronunciation of Greek which came about during the *koine* period and by the fact that certain features of this style already appear in the Oppians and even in Quintus Smyrnaeus.)

To Nonnus a *Gigantomachia*, now lost, should also be probably ascribed.[20]

The influence of Nonnus on the modern world is negligible. The only poets worth mentioning who underwent his influence are Giambattista Marino, the friend of the Cretan Vitsentzos Kornaros, and his pupil Antonio Bruno, both great masters of the baroque.[21]

THE 'SCHOOL' OF NONNUS

When dealing with the poetry of this period it is usual to speak of the 'epic school' of Nonnus. In actual fact, the poets who are grouped under that heading depend on Nonnus chiefly in the matter of metrics; in subject-matter they draw on a variety of sources—including much Ionian–Homeric material—and they differ widely in style. Of these, two must be considered here: Musaeus and Colluthus.

Musaeus, a grammarian and probably a Christian,[22] wrote the highly romantic *epyllion, Hero and Leander*,[23] which has been called the 'last rose of the Greek garden'.[24] The story—that of the great love affair between Leander and Hero and of how the former was drowned while swimming the Hellespont to reach her—was not created by Musaeus. It probably derives from some Hellenistic source[25] (on which Ovid also drew in

Heroides 17 and 18). The influence of Achilles Tatius and of Nonnus is also evident, the latter especially in the hexameter, in which, however, Musaeus is less strict. The poem is competent and has romantic grace, and it influenced a number of much later poets, among them Marlowe, Byron, Schiller and Grillparzer. It is the best creation of the 'school of Nonnus'. Musaeus has also been credited with the *Love of Alphaeus and Arethusa*,[26] but its authenticity is not certain.

Musaeus is followed by Colluthus (fifth century A.D.), whose only surviving work, the *Rape of Helen*, tells in 394 hexameters the story of the judgement of Paris and of the Trojan prince's meeting with Helen, who follows him chiefly out of a desire to see a new country! The poem ends with young Hermione's lamentation when she finds that her mother has left. This is a poor and derivative work which draws on Homer, the Alexandrians—for example, Echo and the idyllic landscape (ll. 116f.) or the bucolic description of Paris (ll. 107f.)—and Nonnus. Similarity with Catullus[27] has also been traced, which may well be due to a common source.

Colluthus is credited with the composition of other, longer epics, the *Persica* and the *Calydoniaca* in six books, as well as with epic encomia.

As would be expected, a number of other mythological epics were composed in this period, of which only small fragments have survived.[28] We also know the names of various unimportant poets whose works have perished and who need not be mentioned here.

The didactic epic

Few and unimportant are the didactic epics of this period that have survived; some are composed in hexameters and others in iambic tri-meters. The combination of grammarian and poet that favoured didactic poetry became common in those days, as is evident from the names of Christodorus Illustrius from Coptos, Antiochus (against whom Libanius wrote an oration),[29] Seleucos of Emesa, Eudaimon, Dioscoros of Myra and others.[30] However, none of their poetic works has passed the test of time, which indicates that their quality must have been low.

Among the few extant didactic poems of those days the *Lithica*, whose theme is precious stones, should be singled out. It is an anonymous work, probably of the late fourth century, that, like the *Argonautica*, goes under the name of 'Orpheus', though it has hardly anything to do with Orphism. In 800 hexameter lines it presents the mythical Orpheus explaining to Theodamas, the son of Priam, the mystical value of jewels and their use in magic. The poem is based on a prose work on precious stones attributed, among others, to the 'magician' Damigeron (second century A.D.), which was also translated into Latin in the twelfth century. The *Lithica* has the distinction—its only distinction—of being the last Greek didactic poem to be composed in dactylic hexameters.

Two further didactic poems of those days should perhaps be mentioned here. The first is the *Chrestomathia*[31] of Helladios of Antinoöpolis (fourth century A.D.), which deals with Attic linguistic usages and Attic antiquities (Photius has preserved a long section from it) and the *Apotelesmatica (Astrological Influences)* by Manethon, the astrologist (fourth century A.D.), which in six books examines the stars and their influence upon men. Of these, three (Books II, III, and VI) seem to belong to the early third century and the rest, to the fourth or even later.

Related to didactic poetry are the Chaldean Oracles, which were highly esteemed among Neo-Platonists. It is thought that their author was the theurgist Julianus, who lived in the days of Marcus Aurelius (A.D. 161–80), but their hexameter remnants include later material which combines Pythagorean, Platonist and Stoic elements with Oriental views.

Finally, mention should be made once again of the Sibylline Oracles,[32] which, as we have seen, belonged to Jewish–Hellenistic culture, even if certain elements can be traced as far back as Heracleitus. We must return to them again here because that monstrous corpus took its final shape in the fifth century, when blatant forgeries and Christian influences were added. This, combined with the prophecy of the Cumaean Sibyl in Virgil's fourth eclogue, conferred on all the 'sibyls' a position in Christian literature and art similar to that of the Old Testament prophets.

Historical epics and epic encomia

Eulogistic poetry had, of course, a very old and noble history going back to Simonides and Pindar; and in the Alexandrian era it had enjoyed a renewed florescence in the hands of Theocritus and Callimachus. In the Imperial age it was the Second Sophistic that gave it a new lease of life, when it handed over to verse all the set rules which the rhetorical prose encomia employed in celebrating the 'achievements' or the persons of emperors, generals and other important government officials. This gradually became a more common practice, so that even men of minor status were often thus praised.

Most of these verse encomia are now lost, but from such examples as have survived the loss does not seem to be grave. They rarely rise above the rhetorical commonplaces of the day. However, the boundary between the rhetorical epic encomia and the historical epics of the time are not clear,[33] for both describe in some detail the military and other achievements of living men whom they set out to eulogize.

In those days the writers of such encomiastic or historical epic poetry were numerous, ranging from emperors and empresses like Julian or Eudocia to the most undistinguished schoolmasters. This versifying occasionally proved a most lucrative occupation, as was the case with John the Lydian (sixth century A.D.), who was paid out of public funds at the rate of a *solidus* for each line and was given a rich wife as a reward for the encomium he composed to celebrate the praetorian prefect Zoticus![34]

There can be no question of citing here the names of the authors of so many undistinguished lost works. As examples of the surviving Greek encomiastic poetry of this period the fragments may serve of an *epikeidion* (a funeral oration in verse) delivered on the death of a professor of the university of Berytus (fourth century),[35] or of an encomium on Heraclius, the general of Emperor Zeno (fifth century),[36] or of the so-called *Encomium Ducis Romanis* (fifth century),[37] which is a combination of a panegyric and a petition. In the *epikeidion* we see the use of the iambic prologue which was usual in those days, and in the mutilated hexameters of all the fragments many empty words of praise, profuse sentimentality, commonplace expressions and poor metrical technique.

If we are to see the epic encomium and the historical epic of this period at their best, we must turn to Latin poetry, to Claudius Claudianus (c. A.D. 365–404), one of the most important literary figures of waning antiquity (he also wrote Greek verse),[38] and Flavius Cresconius Corippus (sixth century A.D.), who, to quote Wilamowitz, 'was Roman only in language'.[39]

The celebration in verse of the military achievements of the early Byzantine emperors was not unusual. It followed in the footsteps of similar court epics in honour of the Hellenistic kings.[40] Closely connected with these are the *patria*, the histories of different cities in epic form, of which, again, painfully little has come down to us. Thus we hear that the Emperor Julian (A.D. 361–3) wrote a panegyric in honour of Emperor Constantius[41] and that Callistion celebrated Julian's Persian War in which he had taken part as *Protector domesticus*. We also know of the *Isaurica* by Christodorus of Coptos, which were composed to celebrate the submission of the Isaurians by Anastasius I (A.D. 491–518) in 497. But of all these next to nothing survives.

Christodorus of Coptos (fifth–sixth century A.D.) was a prolific epic poet. Besides the *Isaurica* he has been credited with a number of *patria*, mythological–historical epics on the foundation of Constantinople, Thessalonica, Miletus, Nacle, Tralles and Aphrodisias, as well as with the *Lydica*, in which the mythological history of Lydia was treated. Moreover, he composed the *Ixeutica*, a poem on how to trap birds, and three books of epigrams. He is also thought to have composed a verse account of the miracles performed by St Cosmas and St Damian, but the attribution is uncertain. Of all these works only one long, colourless ecphrasis in 416 hexameters has survived[42] and two sepulchral epigrams.

A near-contemporary of Christodorus was Pamprepius of Panopolis (A.D. 440–84), an ugly, dark-skinned grammarian who became involved in the intrigues of Illus against the Emperor Zeno (474–91) and was finally executed in an Isaurian castle where he had taken refuge when luck turned against him. Like Christodorus, he wrote panegyrics and encomia in hexameters and iambic trimeters in praise of the 'virtues' of high officials of the Empire, as well as other occasional poetry, now all lost. The *Suda* also credits him with *Isaurica Katalogaden*, which, however, may not have been in verse.

The fragments of two poems retrieved on a sixth-century papyrus have also been attributed to Pamprepius, but their authorship remains uncertain.[43] The first, in honour of one Patricius Theagenes, is insignificant; but the second, describing an autumnal day, though incomplete, is one of the most impressive poems of late antiquity. Although the influence of rhetoric upon it is evident—its structure follows a recognized literary type, the *ecphrasis synezeugmene*, 'that which combines things and seasons'[44]—there is tenderness and grandeur as the poet 'sings of the hours and tells their actions', that is, describes the activities of country life appropriate to the successive stages of a single day. The portrayal of the shepherd driving his herds to shelter against the background of a storm in the early morning, though admittedly laborious, is nonetheless majestic.

The Empress Eudocia, the beautiful and highly educated wife of Theodosius II (408–50), was also among those who composed epic encomia. Well-known is the one on her husband's victory over the Persians in 429, part of which has survived. She knew by heart and recited long stretches of Homer and also composed *Homerokentronas* (patchworks of Homeric tags).[45] After she had fallen out of favour, and during her exile in Jerusalem, where she also died, she cast in verse certain books of the Old Testament.

One of the protégés and favourites of Empress Eudocia was Cyrus of Panopolis (fifth century A.D.), who, after a brilliant public career during which he occupied the highest court and state offices, was banished when the empress went into exile, and was later appointed bishop of Kotyaeon in Phrygia, where he spent the rest of his life. Of his works only a few epigrams have come down to us, but he was known chiefly as an epic poet.[46] Photius speaks of an epic encomium in iambic trimeters which he wrote in honour of the Dux Marcianus, later Emperor Marcian (450–7).

Many other poets of those days are also reputed to have composed epics in iambic trimeters, among them Hermeias of Hermoupolis and the grammarian Hermapollon, who compiled *patria* of Egyptian Hermoupolis and Alexandria. A sixth-century(?) iambic epic on Heracles' labours, of which 211 lines have come down to us,[47] may also be worth mentioning.

But perhaps no better example exists of the popularity of the iambic trimeter in the fifth and sixth centuries than the work of Marianus, the son of Marsyas, a Roman, who lived in Palestine in the reign of Anastasius I (491–518). Later he came to Constantinople, where, according to the *Suda*, he became consul, *praefectus* and *patricius*. Marianus engaged in the long and futile task of recasting in iambic trimeters many famous Alexandrian hexameter and elegiac poems, like the *Idylls* of Theocritus, Callimachus' *Hecale*, *Aetia* and epigrams, Apollonius' *Argonautica*, Aratus' *Phaenomena* and Nicander's *Theriaca*! The literary value of these adaptations must have been minimal, for not a word has survived. The only verses we have from Marianus' pen are six second-rate epigrams. One of these, however, celebrating a hot spring called the Bath of Love,[48] seems to have suggested the last two of Shakespeare's sonnets, probably through the medium of a French or Italian translation.[49]

The last and most significant representative of the early Byzantine epic encomium is George the Pisidian. He lived in the reign of Heraclius (610–41) and was deacon and keeper of the archives (*chartophylax*) of the church of Santa Sophia in Constantinople. His poetry falls into two groups, historical and religious. He wrote a salutation to Heraclius in eighty-nine trimeters when the latter ascended the throne, accompanied the emperor on his Persian campaigns and celebrated his victories in three poems, the *Persian Campaign of King Heraclius*, a work of 1093 iambic lines, the *Heraclias*, in 471 iambics, and the *Recovery of the Holy Cross*, a short work of 116 verses.

He also wrote a long epic encomium in 541 trimeters on the Patriarch Sergius, entitled *On the Attack of the Avars on Constantinople and the Miraculous Saving of the City by the Virgin*, and a panegyric on the Patrikios and Governor Bonos in 168 trimeters.

George the Pisidian did not confine himself to panegyrics but engaged in writing other kinds of poetry as well, mainly of a religious nature.[50] He also wrote a satirical poem on an ugly man called *Alypios* and epigrams on religious and secular subjects.[51]

As a poet George the Pisidian is a man of limited inspiration and hardly any originality, faithfully following, wherever possible, the set rhetorical prescriptions. In spite of the discrimination with which he uses his rich vocabulary, the gross and uncouth flattery of his encomiastic poetry and the sweeping epic descriptions forced into the narrow confines of the twelve-syllable iambic verse make for a strained style. Furthermore, his didactic and moralizing poetry contains too much monkish wailing over the inevitability of sin and the vanity of life. True humanity is missing. Yet he was much admired in his own day and compared to advantage with Homer and Euripides, which illustrates clearly the extent of the decline of poetic feeling in seventh-century Byzantium.[52]

In spite of the Pisidian's limited poetic genius, he was in a sense a

milestone in the history of Greek poetry because of his full adaptation of
the iambic trimeter to the new metrical rules which turned it into the
Byzantine twelve-syllable line. Thus while adhering closely to the rules of
ancient prosody, he accentuated the eleventh syllable of his iambic verse
and rigorously retained a caesura after the fifth or seventh syllable. He
also avoided both an accent on the seventh syllable if a caesura was to
follow it and *enjambement*. Nearly all subsequent poets up to the days of
Manuel Philes (fourteenth century)[53] who used the iambic trimeter fol-
lowed these rules and developed them further. In his hexameters Pisides
was influenced by Nonnus, of whose metrical followers he is often consi-
dered the last representative.

The epic ecphrasis

The encomiastic spirit we have met in the epic encomia on 'notable' men
seems to have pervaded the epic ecphrasis in its description of 'celebrated'
monuments.

The ecphrasis appears in this period in two forms: first, as a group or
'crown' of short epigrams treating individually various parts of the same
monument; second, as long independent poems on the whole monument.
To the first kind belong the epigrams of Cyzicus of Book III of the
Palatine *Anthology*[54] and the Statues of Athletes in the Hippodrome of
Constantinople,[55] while to the second belong the ecphrases of Christo-
dorus of Coptus, Paul the Silentiary and John of Gaza.

The ecphrasis of Christodorus of Coptus is on the eighty statues of gods,
heroes and famous men that decorated the sumptuous *gymnasium* of Zeux-
ippus in Constantinople which was destroyed by fire during the Nika
revolt in 532. The poem constitutes Book II of the Greek *Anthology* and has
been called 'an elegant piece of rhetoric'. In reality it is completely lifeless;
it does not convincingly depict the works of art it sets out to describe and
so is of no help even to the art historian. The diction of Christodorus is
'Homeric', but metrically he displays the influence of Nonnus. It is
interesting to note that he also alludes to Virgil's *Aeneid*.[56]

The greatest exponent of the epic ecphrasis in all Greek poetry is clearly
Paul the Silentiary (sixth century A.D.), one of the most distinguished
poets of the days of Justinian. Paul was a *silentiarius*, a gentleman-usher, at
the court of Justinian and a member of a most active literary circle. He
composed seventy-eight epigrams,[57] which Agathias included in his
anthology, but his best-known work is the *Description of the Church of the
Hagia Sophia* in 887 hexameters, to which the *Description of the Ambon*, the
pulpit, in 275 hexameters is an appendix; both are preceded by iambic
prooemia. The exact description of the architectural details, the successful
similes, the vivid imagery, the wealth of light and colour and the sensuous

quality of the verse have earned this ecphrasis the distinction of being called 'the last victory of poetry over rhetoric'.[58] In metre and style Paul depends on Nonnus—his periphrases, pathos and baroque structure of sentence reflect the work of the earlier poet—but points of contact also exist between his poetry and that of Callimachus, Triphiodorus, Colluthus and Musaeus.

The poetry of Paul the Silentiary was well-received in its day—the ecphrasis of Santa Sophia was officially recited on 6 January 563, upon the occasion of the second inauguration of the Great Church[59]—and was also much admired later. It follows the tradition of the panegyric inaugural speech which leads from Dion and Aristeidis to Photius. It should be seen as both a panegyric to the emperor and to the Patriarch Eutychios and a description of a great work of art.[60]

A pagan pendant to Paul's Christian ecphrasis is the description of an allegorical mural painting in the winter baths of Gaza by his contemporary John of Gaza. The baths were built in about 536, and the painting represents the *cosmos*, the universe. The poem consists of 703 hexameters in the Nonnian style, preceded by an iambic prelude, and treats, in a dull and uninspiring manner, of sixty figures, among them *Aion, Ouranos, Helios, Atlas, Arete, Sophia, Bythos* and the winds. The work of John of Gaza has its place in the history of Greek poetry because it is the first known ecphrasis to describe allegorical representations. Six insignificant anacreontic poems have also come down to us from John of Gaza's pen.

Epic *ethopoeia*

Rhetoric in those days was very much concerned with exercises in *ethopoeia*, the delineating of character in both prose and verse. The subjects chosen for such rhetorical exercises, when executed in verse, were chiefly mythological. Their main importance in the history of poetry is that they helped in the development of the ethical–pathetic style, which culminated in the 'school' of Nonnus.[61]

LYRIC POETRY

There is painfully little lyric poetry that has come down to us from this period of transition; the extant material is represented chiefly by the epigram, which in Byzantium became the main vehicle of secular lyricism. In religious lyric hymnography the preponderant metre was the hexameter, as can be seen from the hymns of Proclus and the collection of so-called 'Orphic' hymns. Some religious verse has also been found on magic papyri,[62] but neither that nor the few flat occasional poems (epithalamia, *epikeidia* and so on)[63] that have survived are worth lingering over. They only testify to the lamentable decline of lyricism in those days. Of not much greater value are the trifling anacreontics which became fashionable from the fourth century on.[64]

Religious–philosophical hymnic poetry

In the field of religious–philosophical poetry the most impressive achievement is that of Proclus (A.D. 410–85),[65] who was born in Xanthus in Lycia but later came to Athens, where he became head of the Athenian Neo-Platonic school. Proclus wrote several philosophical treatises, commentaries on works of older philosophers, scientific works and literary works, among which an important position is held by his seven religious hexameter hymns on divinities—on Helios, Aphrodite, the Muses, all the gods, Lycian Aphrodite, Hecate and Janus, and Athene. They are fervent prayers for enlightenment and for guidance in rising above the errors of life. In language and metre they are reminiscent of the school of Nonnus, but their mystic, dualistic spirit comes close to that of Christianity. The syncretic theosophy of the period is perhaps best expressed in the hymns of Proclus, with which the long and glorious tradition of pagan hymnography ends.

Close in spirit to the hymns of Proclus and probably close in date, though perhaps somewhat older, is the *Orphic Book of Hymns* (’Ορφέως ὕμνοι πρὸς Μουσαῖον). This includes eighty-seven hexameter hymns on gods—among them Attis and Adonis—and divine personifications like *Physis* (Nature), *Nomos* (Law) and so on, all of little poetic merit. Their origin has been connected with the fourth-century revival of interest in Orphic mysticism shown by the Platonic School and, more particularly, by the Pergamene centre of Neo-Platonic theurgy. But the influence of Stoic philosophy is also noticeable.

The lament *On Human Life* by George the Pisidian, about whom we have already spoken, closes the list of 'lyrical' works of this period. It is composed in ninety Nonnian hexameters and to a great extent depends on Gregory of Nazianzus; further, it demonstrates the total confusion then prevailing in the traditional distinctions of poetry and confirms that the ancient lyrical metres were dead.

The epigram

The period of transition is one in which the epigram, which had been practically extinct in the second and third centuries, came again to the fore. The revival becomes evident in the Christian epigrams of Gregory of Nazianzus (329–89), with whom we shall deal below,[66] as well as in the vigorous verses of Palladas.

The revived pagan epigram, which flourished chiefly in the days of Justinian I (527–65), followed closely in the footsteps of its Hellenistic predecessor and often chose the same subjects—love, wine, marriage, death, riddles, jokes and so forth. But with the close of the period these erotic and convivial subjects were suppressed, never to appear again in the course of Greek epigrammatic poetry.

Scholars have found it strange that in a Christian age so many epigrams pagan in spirit should have been written. Agathias, who himself indulged in both Christian and secular verse, gives the only valid answer in the preface to his *Cycle*: that the literary genre itself demands certain pagan subjects.

Palladas (c. A.D. 360–415) was an embittered and violent grammarian who for long lived in Alexandria and whose main complaints seem to have been poverty and his wife. Though a pagan and an admirer of the philosopher Hypatia, he attacked pagans and Christians alike.[67] His epigrams, roughly 160 in number, are mainly hortative and epideictic; in some a satirical streak is also evident. But there is a marked absence of the erotic element. In language Palladas abides by the epic diction, but his metres, besides hexameters and elegiacs, are also iambic trimeters.

Although, together with Gregory of Nazianzus, he is the leading figure in the revival of the epigram and for centuries was widely read, Palladas cannot be said to have founded a school or to have been an innovator of that literary genre. An interesting isolated phenomenon of this period is the epigrammatist Metrodorus, who lived in the days of Constantius (337–61) and cast thirty-one mathematical problems in the form of epigrams.[68] There could hardly be a greater misuse of that poetic genre.

A few words should be added here about the famous 'last oracle' supposed to have been given by the god of Delphi to the physician Oribasius, Julian's *quaestor*, in 363, which is often mentioned as marking the end of the pagan world:'Tell this to the King: the decorated court has fallen to the ground, Phoebus no longer has a cell nor laurel of prophecy nor babbling fountain; even the chattering water has dried up.' There can be little doubt that this is a forgery composed by a Christian between 397 and 426, based on Gregory of Nazianzus,[69] to demonstrate the futility of Julian's belief in the oracle of Delphi. It should not be seen as a melancholy lament for the irrevocable past.[70]

Mention has already been made of the epigrams of Claudius Claudianus, Cyrus of Panopolis, Proclus, Marianus and Christodorus of Coptos, none of which offers anything noteworthy or new, so we need not return to them here.

We must now come to the days of Justinian I (527–65), in which a remarkable new florescence of epigrammatic poetry becomes evident, which turned once again for its models and its imagery to the Hellenistic age. No matter how traditional or conventional they may have been, Agathias and his friends maintained that they were embarking on something new,[71] that they were changing the character of a poetry neglected since the days of Palladas by resurrecting in it the stylistic and metrical features that Nonnus had popularized. In fact, all they succeeded in doing was to add to the epigram an element of verbosity and elaboration, no doubt a product of the influence not only of the late epic but also of rhetoric and of erotic epistolography, to which they also turned for inspiration. Nor should it be forgotten that there existed in those days a living background of contemporary inscriptional epigrams,[72] mainly honorific, sub-literary verse, against which their work, which also includes genuine inscriptional poems, should be judged.[73]

The most important sixth-century epigrammatist is Paul the Silentiary, whom we have discussed above in connection with the ecphrasis. Eighty-two of his epigrams have survived, about half of which are erotic (including *Arcana Veneris*); the others being dedicatory, sepulchral, epideictic, hortatory and sympotic. It is surprising that Paul, the writer of the grand Christian ecphrasis on Santa Sophia, should compose the most sensual epigrams of all his time. His work follows the well-known motifs and patterns of the Hellenistic age, but contacts with the poetry of Horace, Propertius and Ovid have also been traced, although these may be attributable to common sources. There is nothing new in the style of Paul's epigrams, but there are elegance and wit, as well as erudition, which to a certain extent justify the title he has been given of 'the last representative of the great tradition of the Greek epigram'.

Of the epigrammatists of Justinian's days the second in distinction is Agathias (A.D. 530–82), the son of Memnonius, who was born in Myrina in Asia Minor, studied in Alexandria and practised as an advocate in Constantinople; he married the daughter of Paul the Silentiary and became a functionary of the Imperial court.

Agathias wrote a *History of the Reign of Justinian*, which remained unfinished, and was a member of a circle of poets close to Justinian's court, interested mainly in the occasional poem or epigram. He published a collection of these by his contemporaries under the title of *Cyclos* (*Cycle*), in which he included 100 of his own poems, arranging his compilation in seven books according to subject.[74] It was probably published not later than 567,[75] and from it the Greek *Anthology* took most of the epigrams written later than Philip's *Garland*.

Agathias too depends heavily on the Hellenistic epigrammatic tradition for his themes and diction, in which, however, he tends to be overelaborate. In spite of the fact that the subjective element is suppressed and a didactic, moralizing colour emerges, his love poems are his best (and shortest) works. Many of the rest—epitaphs, dedications and sceptic, convivial or descriptive poems—are long-winded, recalling brief elegies rather than epigrams. Agathias is a good versifier, but there is lack of wit and originality in his writing. Nevertheless, his love poem on Rhodanthe, the *Swallows*, must be admitted to be a short masterpiece.[76] The prologue to Agathias' collection, in 133 lines, throws an interesting light on the literary movement of the time.

Other epigrammatists of Agathias' circle were Julian the Egyptian, who composed epitaphs and descriptive poems—no less than six of these on the celebrated statue of a cow by Myron—and whose full dependence on the epigrammatic tradition can also be seen from poems in the *Anthologia Palatina*,[77] in all of which he deals with Lais as an old woman dedicating her mirror to Aphrodite; Macedonius the Consul, from whose work forty-nine epigrams have survived and whose dependence on Leonidas of Tarentum is obvious; and Leontius Scholasticus, a lawyer whose twenty-four surviving epigrams are trifling examples of occasional verse (he seems to have enjoyed writing verse about the paintings of dancers which apparently lined the streets like modern theatre posters).[78]

Besides these there are many lesser epigrammatists of those days, the listing of whose names, naturally, we must forgo.[79] The period closes with the epigrams of George the Pisidian, who has already appeared earlier in these pages. In his poems the erotic element is fully suppressed and Christian thought brought to the fore, for it is chiefly churches, religious vessels, icons, saints and holy relics that he chooses to write about; secular subjects are less numerous. In metre George's preference is for the iambic trimeter, which henceforward ousts from the epigram the traditional elegiac couplet and the less frequent hexameter. In the suppression of the erotic element and in his preference for the iambic trimeter (as transformed into the Byzantine twelve-syllable line) George the Pisidian points the way in which most subsequent Byzantine epigrammatists were to follow.

The *anacreontea*

The ancient anacreontic metre was also adapted to the 'new' medieval pronunciation of Greek by the regular accentuation of the fourth foot of anaclastic Ionic dimeters, though in this period ancient quantities were still observed as a kind of 'poetic orthography', which the eye, but not the ear, could follow.[80] The so-called *anacreontea* are a collection of fifty-nine short pieces of varying date and merit which have come down to us as a consequence of the care of Constantine Cephalas (early tenth century).[81] At least a third of these belong to the period under consideration and do not differ greatly in tone and spirit from their contemporary epigrams.

Similar are the trifling anacreontics we saw attributed to John of Gaza and those by Procopius and Julian the Egyptian. Nor is the quality of those composed by George the Grammarian (beginning of sixth century — his beloved subject was the different roles the rose played in ancient mythology — or the grammarian Akolouthos[82] any better.

An art like Anacreon's defies imitation. In all later experiments charm gives way to insipidity and love to a crude enjoyment of wine, women and song. Even the metres chosen — the catalectic iambic and the anaclastic Ionic dimeter — give a monotonous humdrum effect. These later anacreontics are also partly responsible for the false view, which was long current, that Anacreon was a debauched, bibulous old man. Strangely enough, they gave rise to whole literary movements in the modern world, like the German or the French 'Anacreontic Movements'.

CHAPTER 16

Christian Poetry

We must now turn to Christian poetry, whose origins can be traced as far back as the Apostolic age but whose first literary works belong to the period under consideration. For it was only after the Council of Nicaea (325) and the transference of the Roman Empire's capital to Constantinople (A.D. 330) that it developed into verse with artistic claims.

The deep piety and spiritual ethos of this early Christian poetry stands in direct contrast to the lascivious frivolity of much of contemporary pagan verse. These elevated qualities, together with the social significance of the new religious poetry, give it an important position in the history of Greek literature—indeed, in the history of the Greek people. For the Byzantine Church, which developed its whole literature in Greek,[1] and the Imperial palace, representing the state, were the two major poles around which medieval Greek life came to revolve.

Such was the authority of the ancient literary tradition that Christian men of letters studied the Classical authors without being offended by their heathen impiety. It is therefore not surprising that Christian poetry, following the Classical examples, was initially also composed in Classical metres—admittedly, with certain liberties—even though these were already obsolete as a result of the changes in pronunciation of Greek which came about during the *koine* period of the Greek language (300 B.C.–A.D. 300). This poetry was not meant to serve liturgical purposes, so it never reached a wider Christian audience. Its main object was to edify and entertain a limited number of highly educated men. For a poetry that would meet the needs of the Christian service, one which could be heard and felt as verse by a congregation of mainly uneducated people, the Christians turned to the new rhythmical metrical system that soon dominated the scene. It was according to the rules of this system that all Christian liturgical poetry was composed, the poetry that constitutes the greatest literary achievement of the Byzantine Greeks.

The religious verse composed in ancient metres and that cast in the new rhythmic metrical system are best treated separately.[2]

CHRISTIAN POETRY IN ANCIENT METRES

The oldest instance of a Christian poem composed in Classical metres which has reached us is probably a prayer by Clement of Alexandria (c. A.D. 150–c. 215), who after studying theology and philosophy in several places, became a pupil of Pantaenus, the head of the Catechetical School of Alexandria, whom he succeeded in 190. In 202 he fell victim to persecution and was forced to flee. Although regarding the ideas of Greek philosophy as a 'divine gift to mankind', he believed that the only true 'gnosis' (religious knowledge or illumination) was that which presupposed the faith of the Church. His *Prayer to Christ the Saviour* (Ὕμνος τοῦ Χριστοῦ Σωτῆρος) in anapaestic monometers and dimeters is found at the end of the *Paedagogus*, one of his chief books dealing with Christian life and manners. Poetically, the hymn is of little value, as its short lines stagger under the weight of numerous adjectives and attributes, and the metaphors and symbols employed are commonplace.

Fragments of two other minor early Christian poems in Classical metres have also been found on papyri.[3] The first, *On The Trinity*, belongs to the third century and is also composed in anapaestic monometers, while the second, *On Christ*, is a work of the fourth. The most interesting feature of the latter is its metre, partly anapaestic and partly accentual, for it points to that fusion of quantitative and accentual rhythms which later spread to the iambic and anapaestic metres, changing the entire character of Greek poetry.

Of greater significance than any of the aforementioned poems is the *Partheneion* (the *Maidens' Song*) by Methodius, bishop of Olympus, who met with a martyr's death in 311. It appears at the end of his prose work *Symposium* or *On Virginity*, where he celebrates virginity in opposition to Plato who had praised Eros in his *Symposium*. Methodius' *Partheneion* is a hymn to Christ the Bridegroom, in which the Mother of God, the Queen of Virgins, and the Church, promoter of virginity, are also glorified. It consists of twenty-four strophes of loose iambic lines, all joined by an alphabetic acrostic and ending in the same refrain. The *Partheneion* of Methodius, though neither great nor original poetry—it draws for its images and symbols on the Scriptures—displays considerable feeling. In the history of Greek poetry it is of some importance because it is the first Greek forerunner of the *kontakion*, the greatest achievement of Byzantine liturgical poetry, about which we shall presently speak.

The dominant figure in the whole field of Christian poetry in Classical metres is undoubtedly Gregory of Nazianzus (c. A.D. 329–c. 390), the only one of the great Cappadocian fathers who was also a poet. With his friend, Basil of Caesarea, he shared an Athenian education and, later in life, an enthusiasm for Origen and asceticism. During the Council of Constantinople (381) he became bishop of the capital, but his impractical politics raised a storm against him. Too sensitive for politics, he retired to his family estate in Cappadocia, where he spent much of his time writing poetry, 'to shackle thus my own want of moderation', as he himself tells us.[4]

As a writer Gregory's greatness lies in his rhetorical prose. His forty-four[5] orations and 244 letters are full of Classical allusions as they cast Christian content in Classical forms. His vast poetic output, consisting of 400 poems (almost 17,000 lines) also shows a full mastery of school models that any pagan contemporary would have envied. Part of this corpus is theological, dealing with dogmatic and moral problems, in which, as would be expected, a marked didactic tone prevails. Another and more interesting section of his verse consists of the so-called 'historical poems', the best of which are those about the author's own life. A third important section are his 254 epigrams, all of a personal nature.

All Gregory's poetry is in quantitative metres—hexameters, elegiacs, iambics and anacreontics (the latter was no longer sung as a 'lyrical' metre). Occasionally, he uses more than one metre in the same work, as in the much quoted *On the Genuine Books of Scripture* (περὶ τῶν γνησίων βιβλίων τῆς δεοπνεύστον Γραφῆς).[6]

Of his poetical works the longest and most significant is the one entitled *On His Own Life* (περὶ τὸν ἑαυτοῦ βίον).[7] It consists of 1949 iambic trimeters and is not only an important source for the author's biography but also a landmark in the history of poetic autobiography.[8] In it Gregory speaks of his own life, from his birth to his departure from Constantinople, and offers an apology for his conduct in that city. Rhetorical pathos fills those verses, but true feeling and an elegiac touch here and there break through the conventional crust.

Gregory's feelings appear even more clearly in two of his other biographical poems. The first, 600 hexameters long, goes under the title *On Things Concerning Himself* (περὶ τῶν καθ' ἑαυτόν)[9] and the second, called *Lament on the Sufferings of His Own Soul* (Θρῆνος περὶ τῶν τῆς ἑαυτοῦ ψυχῆς παθῶν) is cast in 175 elegiac couplets; both have been compared with St Augustine's *Confessions*. The second is also responsible for much of the monkish wailing on the inevitability of sin we meet in later laments or addresses 'to one's own soul', for it served as the example *par excellence* of that 'lyrical' genre of Byzantine poetry.

Gregory has been also held up as the originator of the paraenetic alphabet, because of a much admired and frequently copied 'alphabet'.[10] Much esteemed also were the gnomic quatrains spuriously attributed to him which consist of iambic lines expressing pithy sayings with a common Stoic and Christian moral content and have something in common with Menander's *Monosticha*.[11] It has now been proved that

Gregory is not the author of the alphabet[12] and that the Christian paraenetic alphabet can be traced back before his days, as the *de Moribus Christianorum* found on a third century papyrus indicates.[13] The literary genre probably derives from alphabetically ordered collections of gnomes (maxims) of great men.[14] Nevertheless, it was the authority of Gregory of Nazianzus that encouraged so many distinguished men—among them Neilos, Elias Synkellos, Ignatius, Leo the Wise, Constantine the Sicilian, Symeon Metaphrastes and Theodore Prodromos—to develop that literary genre in iambic trimeters, anacreontics and political verses.[15]

Gregory has also long been considered the initiator of the new rhythmic metrical system in Byzantine religious poetry. For the *Evensong*[16] and the *Exhortation to the Virgins*,[17] both early Christian poems composed in the new rhythmic metrical system, were thought to be by him and were also considered the oldest examples of poetry written in that style.[18] More recent research has shown that beyond doubt they should be regarded as spurious[19] and that older examples exist.

It is natural (and not unusual) that to great names of the past lesser works should be attributed; such is the case with the *Christus Patiens*, the drama on the Passion of Christ which was believed to be a work by Gregory but has been proved to be a second-rate Euripidean cento of the eleventh or twelfth century.[20]

Numerous and important are Gregory's 'Christian' epigrams—254 in number, all of a personal nature and some of real beauty (for example, those on his friend Basil, his mother Nonna, his brother Caesarion; epitaphs on the pagan Greek world he abandoned and so on)—which constitute the eighth book of the Greek *Anthology*. They revived that literary genre after two centuries of almost complete obscurity and also helped in establishing thereafter the iambic trimeter as its standard metre.

In spite of the important position Gregory of Nazianzus occupies in the history of Greek poetry, the quality of his verse is at its best second-rate. It is long-winded, and the flat and moralizing didactic tone that prevails tends to become tiresome. For this reason, and because of his learned language and metres, Gregory's poetry remained aloof from the people and was never put to ecclesiastical use. It is the great stature of that Cappadocian Father and the approachable, edifying content of much of his verse, rather than its novelty, arresting imagery or lyricism, that are responsible for the considerable influence it exercised upon subsequent Byzantine writers.

A contemporary of Gregory of Nazianzus was Apollinarios of Laodicea (c. A.D. 310–c. 390), who was condemned by the second Ecumenical Council of Constantinople (381) as heretical because of his Christological teachings. When Julian the Apostate (361–3) prohibited teaching of pagan authors' works to Christians as a punishment, Apollinarios transcribed the

150 Psalms of the Old Testament into dactylic hexameters, so that they could be used in schools as a substitute—a strange and hopeless undertaking (stylistically, nothing short of a disaster) which, however, indicates how powerful the Classical tradition still was in those days. (An even less successful experiment was that of Ammianos (fourth-century A.D.), who, following in the footsteps of Apollinarios, also paraphrased the Psalms in hexameters.)[21]

After Gregory of Nazianzus the Christian poet second in importance who used Classical metres was Synesius of Cyrene (c. A.D. 370–c. 414). He came from a distinguished Cyrenean family and was educated in Alexandria under the philosopher Hypatia, so was well-versed in Neo-Platonic philosophy. He became a Christian and later bishop of his home town, Cyrene—the latter against his will—but never abandoned his Neo-Platonic beliefs or his wife.[22]

He is at his best in his nine hymns (a tenth attributed to him is spurious), which were never meant to be chanted in church. Also important are his 165 letters and his rhetorical discourses *On Kingship* and *Dion*, the latter being a powerful attack on the contemporary decline of human culture. Synesius' hymns are written in a literary Doric dialect and in ancient lyric metres—anapaestic monometers and Ionic dimeters and trimeters—and express a mixture of Christian and Neo-Platonic views. In spiritual and moral qualities they compare well with the hymns of Proclus, their pagan counterpart. They are inspired poems, composed to be accompanied by music.[23] It is in the hymns of Proclus and Synesius that we meet the end of the ancient tradition of hymnography.

To the latter part of this period belongs Sophronius (c. A.D. 560–638), Patriarch of Jerusalem, one of the protagonists in the Monothelite controversy. His literary activities embrace homilectics, hagiography and poetry, which he cast in anacreontics. Unfortunately, his anacreontic poetry is as dry and as empty of feeling as his dogmatic sermons; it also betrays the influence of the *kontakion*, the metrical sermon, which, as we shall see, had reached full maturity in his days.

Sophronius has also been said to be the inventor of the *triodion*—several poets claim that distinction—the shorter form of canon which has only three odes, and he has even been credited with having composed some poetry according to the new rhythmical metrical system, mainly short *troparia*, but this is equally uncertain.[24]

Three further insignificant anacreontic poems[25] should be mentioned because traditionally they have been attributed to Maximus Confessor (A.D. 580–662), the distinguished theologian who has been called 'the last independent thinker of the Eastern Church'. According to S. G. Mercati, however, they are in reality works of the Cretan Maximus Margunios (1549–1602).[26]

We have said that George the Pisidian[27] did not confine himself to panegyrics but also engaged in poetry of a religious nature. His best work of this kind is the one entitled *On the Vanity of Life*, which is produced after the manner of Ecclesiastes and cast in 262 hexameters. The longest is the *Hexameron*, in 1894 twelve-syllable iambic lines, a theological composition on the Creation.[28] He also wrote a polemical poem in iambics against the heretic Severus of Antioch and a hymn on the Resurrection of Christ.

Finally, attention should be drawn to two early Christian poems, the paraenetic alphabet *de Moribus Christianorum*[29] mentioned above and the fourth-century alphabet *On Christ*,[30] because of the metrical peculiarity they display in combining ancient quantitative with rhythmical accentual metres. This strange fusion indicates that we are moving from the one metrical system to the other; in a sense, these poems are the bridge joining the two.

CHRISTIAN POETRY IN THE NEW RHYTHMIC METRES

Although for many centuries Christian religious verse continued to be composed sporadically in Classical metres, all important poetry written for liturgical purposes was cast in the new rhythmic metrical system. These hymns and prayers had a wide appeal, and many of them were also chanted privately in Christian homes.

The variety of rhythms developed by the new metrical system from the second to the fourth century is astonishing. Though relying on different linguistic principles which sprang from the new pronunciation of Greek, they compare favourably with the great wealth of rhythms developed between the eighth and the fourth centuries B.C., when quantity was their base.[31]

Unfortunately, the details of the development of Byzantine religious poetry in the new rhythmic system escape us, for only a small part of what was then composed has reached us, and that consists mostly of anonymous hymns.[32] We can speak only in very general terms of three major stages in this evolution: the first, extending from the fourth to the sixth century, was a period of preparation, in which short hymns and prayers (the so-called *troparia*) abounded; the second, from the sixth to the eighth century, was the peak of Byzantine hymnography and is the one in which the *kontakion* (the metrical sermon), the greatest achievement of Byzantine poetry, reaches maturity; and the third, from the eighth to the thirteenth century, was undoubtedly a period of decline, even though the last and most popular form of liturgical poetry, the canon, a long-winded cycle of eight odes, established itself then and dominated the scene.

If we are to approach Byzantine religious poetry in the right spirit, we should bear in mind that the inspiration of its writers was confined strictly within the limits prescribed by dogma and that the theological ideas expressed derive more from Neo-Platonism[33] than from the teachings of Christ and the Apostles. Every work of art, accordingly, was considered as emanating from the Super-Essential (the *Hyperousios*) and as rendered apprehensible through the inspiration of the artist. The hymns sung in the liturgy were therefore seen by Orthodox Christians as mere reflections of the songs of praise sung by the angels to God, faint copies of the originals. The orthodox view of the worshippers of icons of Christ, the Virgin and the Saints was similar; the icons were thought to be rough images of their divine originals in heaven.

One more important fact should be pointed out: we cannot, unfortunately, hope to establish today the exact texts of many early liturgical poems, to reach the *ipsissima verba* of those poets; for over the centuries a great number of variants—often variants of equal quality—have been introduced into our texts by spirited psalmodists chanting the hymns in church or by 'inspired' (or careless) later scribes.

The period of preparation

The Byzantine rhythmic hymns developed from the hymns of the synagogue.[34] The singing of hymns, like the chanting of psalms, was a practice of the temple and the synagogues and therefore familiar to the early generations of Christians. It is, however, of interest to note that the singing of hymns at certain hours of the day was also a custom of the pagan Greeks, as inscriptions from Epidaurus show.[35]

At first, only psalms and short doxologies (phrases in which the whole congregation joined—'hallelujah', 'amen', 'hosanna', 'Kyrie eleison' and other similar ones) were chanted. Later the nine Odes from Scripture were introduced into the service, and finally a place was given to new laudatory hymns.[36] These, known as *troparia*,[37] were first admitted in large cities and in the face of fierce opposition on the part of the monks and the more austere religious circles, who condemned any music added to the Lord's prayers.

We possess few early Christian hymns. Among them are the famous *Christ is Risen from the Dead* (Χριστὸς ἀνέστη ἐκ νεκρῶν),[38] *O Joyful Light* (Φῶς ἱλαρόν),[39] traditionally attributed to the martyr Athenagoras (second century A.D.) and the *Glory to God in the Highest Heaven* (Δόξα ἐν ὑψίστοις Θεῷ),[40] all of which give the impression that they were composed in rhythmical prose rather than rhythmic verse, an impression also given by all the hymns found in the New Testament.[41] In these very short compositions the boundaries between the two are not always clear.

However, there are other hymns which were doubtless composed in verse, like the hymn on the Holy Trinity, retrieved on a third-century papyrus,[42] which is also the oldest datable fragment of Christian rhythmic verse, or the three anonymous Epiphany *troparia*[43] found on a fourth-century papyrus. Such are also the two famous hymns included in the liturgy of St John Chrysostom, the *Hymn of the Cherubims* (Οἱ τὰ Χερουβὶμ μυστικῶς εἰκονίζοντες) and the *Partaking of thy Mystic Supper* (Τοῦ δείπνου σου τοῦ μυστικοῦ);[44] and no doubt the *Evensong*[45] wrongly attributed to Gregory of Nazianzus, about which we have already spoken, is very old. A great number of early *troparia* must have been destroyed by the 'purists' and the monks, for only a very few have come down to us.[46]

The development of Orthodox hymnography was promoted by the success that Gnostic and heretical hymns enjoyed, which attracted many Christians to the services in which they were chanted. Such were the hymns of second-century Gnostics like Basilides and Valentinus, or Bardesanes (154–222) and his son Harmonius, or of heretics like Nepos[47] or Arius (fourth century), whose Syriac-speaking followers were also the first to establish antiphonal choirs. We have already mentioned the fame of the latter's liturgical drama *Thaleia*, which was composed to compete with the pagan theatre[48] and was refuted by the *Antithaleia*.

Of all this early unorthodox output only two inferior poetic works in Greek have survived, the fragment of a Gnostic hymn by Valentinus in dactylic metres[49] and the so-called 'Psalm of the Naassenes',[50] a Gnostic sect, the Hebrew equivalent of the Greek Ophites.

The Orthodox hymns, many of which must originally have been mere ecstatic improvisations,[51] multiplied and by the fourth century seem to have become so numerous and so heterodox that the Council of Laodicea prohibited 'all private songs' from being chanted in church (ἰδιωτικοὺς ψαλμοὺς λέγεσθαι ἐν ταῖς ἐκκλησίαις);[52] it allowed only appointed chorists to sing such hymns as were found in the books of the church (ἀπὸ διφθέρας).[53] Thus hymns not based on passages from the Scriptures were excluded from the services, a prohibition which must have restricted the scope of early hymnodists to reiterate or elaborate on passages from the canticles and the Psalms. However, the flow of inspiration does not seem to have dried up.

An important group of short anonymous hymns in lines of equal length (κατὰ στίχον) and a few in short strophes have come down to us[54] that in all probability belong to the end of the fifth century; they represent the fully developed *troparion*. One of these, the *Incorporeal Nature*, has also been found on a sixth-century papyrus (giving a *terminus post quem*)[55] and is chanted to this day in the Greek Orthodox Church. But as another of them, consisting of a strophe composed in lines of unequal length, has been found inscribed in a catacomb in Kertch[56] and is dated A.D. 491, we cannot tell which kind of *troparion*, the isostichic or the strophic, is the

older. For many years both types of hymn continued to be composed side
by side.

In this group of *troparia* we find phrases borrowed from the *Prayer for the
Dead* (Εὐχὴ τοῦ τρισαγίου)[57] and invocations to the Virgin, the prophets,
the patriarchs, the Apostles and the martyrs, as well as references to the
Day of Judgement. Simplicity and directness characterize their style, but
no flights of imagination are evident. The majority of them belong to the
ἀπόδειπνον of Lent, and the view has been put forward that the *kata
stichon* hymns (consisting usually of eleven-syllable lines)[58] were first writ-
ten in monasteries of Syria and Palestine to be recited by the monks
without musical accompaniment during their long hours of prayer.

As the attribution of the *Joyful Light* to the martyr Athenagoras has been
rightly challenged,[59] the oldest surviving *troparia* that can be assigned to an
author are those by Auxentius (fifth century). They are very short indeed
and have been transmitted via his *Vita*. (Cardinal Pitra grouped them
together to make one continuous hymn of seven stanzas,[60] a very doubtful
compilation.) Auxentius draws heavily on the Psalms and, to a lesser
degree, on the rest of the Scriptures.

To the fifth century also belong Anthimos and Timocles, both writers of
troparia,[61] of whose work nothing has survived. The first is said to have
been Orthodox, whereas the second was a Monophysite, but both had a
big following in Constantinople. Furthermore, Symeon the Stylite, the
Thamastoreites (521–96?), is credited with three short hymns inspired by
the violent earthquake of 577,[62] and to Emperor Justinian I (527–65) is
attributed the celebrated *troparion* The Only-Born (Ὁ μονογενής),[63] which
paraphrases in verse the Constantinopolitan Symbol of the Creed,[64] with
the addition of doxological formulae and a prayer for salvation. It was
composed in 536.

The names of three more early melodists or poets, Marcianus, Jo-
hannes Monachos and Seta, have survived, but nothing of their work, and
that of a poetess, Martha (sixth century), the mother of Symeon the
Stylite, the Thamastoreites, who also wrote her son's biography.

Troparia continued to be composed and to evolve for many centuries
side by side with the other and grander forms of religious poetry that
gradually developed.

The golden age of Byzantine hymnography (sixth to eighth centuries)

The sixth century not only gives us more, and more evolved, *troparia*, but
also the fully developed *kontakion*, the metrical sermon accompanied by
music which is the greatest achievement of Byzantine literature.[65] Its
origins, however, clearly go back to the fifth century.

A *kontakion* generally consists of between eighteen and twenty-four metrically identical stanzas (called *oikoi*), which are preceded by a short prelude (called a *koukoulion*) in a different metre.[66] The first letters of the stanzas form an acrostic, which frequently includes the name of the poet. The last line of the prelude introduces a refrain, with which all the following stanzas end. The length of the stanzas can be anything from four to eighteen lines long. We do not know how the *kontakion* was delivered, but from the surviving texts we gather that the main body of the metrical sermon was chanted from the pulpit by the preacher after the reading of the lesson, while a choir or perhaps even the whole congregation joined in the refrain. The length of many *kontakia*—some extend to thirty-two and even forty stanzas—and the 'epic' character of some point to a kind of recitative. The music which accompanied the early *kontakia* is now lost, but it was clearly closely integrated with the metres, the same tune being repeated with every stanza.[67]

The oldest datable *kontakia* are attributed to Romanos the Melodist and belong to the years 537–55, which represent the peak of this literary genre. But a number of more 'primitive' examples have survived which may well be considered older and to which we shall presently return.

It has been suggested with much cogency that the stimulus for this new Byzantine literary genre, like the stimulus for the new rhythmical metrical system, was provided by foreign literature, in all probability Syriac. For the basic elements that characterize the *kontakion* can be traced in three important types of Syriac poetry of the early Christian centuries, the *memrā*, the *madrāsā* and the *sugītā*.[68] There is nothing similar to these Syriac forms in Greek literature of the same period. In fact, the only surviving Greek writings which can be considered 'forerunners' of the *kontakion* are either translations from the Syriac, like the Greek metrical translations of Ephraem,[69] or works directly influenced by Syriac literature, like the *Partheneion* of Methodius[70] and the *Dialogue between Mary, Gabriel and Joseph*[71] attributed to the Patriarch Proclus (434–46). We may assume that it was the Syriac poets of the fourth century, Ephraem, Narsai, Cyrillona and Jacob of Serug, who, unhampered by the weight of Classical Greek tradition, gave a new impulse to Byzantine religious poetry, since Gregory of Nazianzus, Synesius and their contemporaries had failed in the endeavour to unite Classical forms with the Christian spirit in their verse.

The Syriac poets thus provided the model into which the Greeks of the fifth and sixth centuries infused new life. By combining the metrically primitive lines of the *memrā* and the endless *strophomythia* of the *sugītā* with the variety and the refrain[72] of the *madrāsā*, the Byzantine poets fashioned the long and disciplined strophes of their *kontakia*, in which argument and form are clearly and closely integrated in a manner which is essentially

Greek. Moreover, they added the prelude, the *koukoulion*, which appears to be a purely Greek creation.

Undoubtedly, the most impressive achievement of the Greek writers is the metrical perfection and variety they introduced. The metres, as with the *troparia*, are governed by the stress accent and the number of syllables in each line; but the great variety of 'pattern strophes' they thus composed —thirty-nine are attributed to Romanos alone—reveal a wealth of rhythmic effects which is indeed impressive. The true precursors of these rhythms were, of course, the isocolons in which the rhetoric of late antiquity delighted and the rhythmic period endings found in the fourth-century Greek prose.[73] But there is nothing comparable there with the regulated accents within a *colon* which we meet in the fully developed *kontakia*.

That literary genre reached its peak in the sixth century in the hands of Romanos the Melodist, but a number of less well-developed and anonymous *kontakia* have survived, so it is reasonable to assume (though it cannot be proved) that they represent the early stages in its development, because their metres are primitive and irregular in regard to outer and inner correspondence, their structure faulty, their diction crude and their dialogue extremely undeveloped; in fact, some are so elementary that they can hardly be called 'metrical sermons' at all. Perhaps the earliest of these is *The Lawless Pursued Me* (*Εθήρευσάν με ἄνομοι*),[74] which has been attributed to the fifth century.[75] It is a crude work, in which Christ speaks about his persecutors; it is cast in rough strophes that do not correspond properly and contains linguistic errors and an unorthodox use of the alphabetic acrostic.

Further steps in the development of the *kontakion* can be seen in the *New Song* (*Ἆσμα καινόν*),[76] a *canticum* composed for Palm Sunday which draws heavily on the Scriptures; the *Rulers of the Jews* (*Ἄρχοντες Ἑβραίων*),[77] composed for Good Friday; and the short *kontakion The First Man* (beginning *Ταῖς χερσί*).[78] All these are works of the fifth century.

It is only when we reach the end of the fifth century and the beautiful *canticum On Adam* (*Εἰς τὸν πρωτόπλαστον*)[79] that the literary genre reaches full maturity. For there we find all the elements of the fully developed metrical sermon, the *koukoulion*, full external and internal metrical correspondence, acrostic, refrain, dramatic presentation of the subject and a didactic tone. It is a truly successful poem, with lively imagery and deep religious feeling.

We must now examine a group of fully developed *kontakia*, *On the Departed*, whose subject and treatment suggest a relatively early age, certainly one earlier than Romanos. Two of these are anonymous,[80] but the third, if we can trust the acrostic, is by a poet named Anastasios, who has not yet been convincingly identified.[81] Directness and sincerity characterize all three of the *cantica*; the one by Anastasios became very popular and probably served as a model for the famous *kontakion* of Romanos *On Life in the Monastery*.[82]

To the same period we should also assign a short *kontakion* entitled *On the Virgin Mary*,[83] composed for the 'Beifest' of the Virgin Mary of 26 December and therefore written before 530–50, when the great triple Christological festival of 24–6 December was divided into three separate feasts, the Annunciation, Christmas and Epiphany. It has a fourfold alphabetic acrostic in the Syrian tradition[84] and was probably one of the sources of the celebrated *Akathistos Hymn*. Equally old is a mutilated *kontakion, On the Prophet Ilias*,[85] the only extant *canticum* in Greek in which a full Syrian *strophomythia* (a dialogue in which each speaker declaims for a whole strophe) is found. None of these works can claim to be impressive poetry, but they are all important steps in the evolution of the metrical sermon, leading to the *Akathistos Hymn* and the great *cantica* of Romanos.

The most famous of all surviving *kontakia* is the anonymous *Akathistos Hymn*,[86] the only one chanted complete in the Greek Orthodox Church to this day. It celebrates the Annunciation of the Virgin and the birth of Christ and consists of two *koukoulia* and twenty-four strophes bound by an alphabetic acrostic. Metrically it is unique, as the main body of the poem is formed from alternating strophes of two different lengths, the longer one celebrating the Annunciation of the Virgin and the shorter one the birth of Christ. The longer strophes also include the so-called 'Salutations of the Virgin' (Χαιρετισμοὶ τῆς Θεοτόκου), which consist of repeated addresses to Mary each beginning with 'Hail' (Χαῖρε). In all probability, this is a Syriac device[87] which was taken over by the Greeks. Syriac influence is also evident in the deliberate use of rhyme found in the pairs of lines of equal length of the 'Salutations'. This and the *canticum On Judas*, attributed to Romanos, are the only examples in the whole of Greek poetry of the use of rhyme before the conquest of Greek lands by the Franks of the Fourth Crusade (1204).[88]

The *Akathistos Hymn* (so called because it is chanted before a standing congregation)[89] has been attributed by modern scholars to authors separated by as many as five centuries: Apollonios of Laodicea (fourth century), Romanos the Melodist (sixth century), the Patriarch Sergius (seventh century), George the Pisidian (seventh century), Georgios Sikeliotis (seventh–eighth century), the Patriarch Germanos I (eighth century), the Patriarch Photius (ninth century) and others. Although most of these attributions are little more than arbitrary guesses, the field can be narrowed down by acknowledging that any attribution before the Third Ecumenical Council of Ephesus (431), when Mary was recognized as the Mother of God (*Theotokos* as opposed to a *Christotokos*), can be precluded; any date after the middle of the seventh century is equally impossible because the Persian Fire, and not Islam, is the 'enemy of Christianity' in the poem and because the influence of the *Akathistos* upon Byzantine literature begins to be evident then. Moreover, as the hymn is a celebration both of the story of the Nativity and of that of the Annunciation, it most probably belongs to the period before the common Festival of the Annunciation and the Nativity was divided into two separate feasts by Justinian I, the one to be celebrated on 25 March and the other on 25 December.

But even if we narrow the possible dates of composition, the author remains uncertain. The traditional attribution to the Patriarch Sergius is not substantiated—perhaps only the second *prooemium* (the celebrated *Τῇ ὑπερμάχῳ Στρατηγῷ*) comes from his pen[90]—nor is the attribution to Romanos convincing.[91] However that may be, the *Akathistos*, with the exception of the second *prooemium*, should most probably be ascribed to the days of Justinian I; so fully finished a *kontakion* could hardly belong to an earlier age. Furthermore, the Christological issues concerning the Incarnation of the Word that we find in it[92] also point to the sixth century, for theological issues do not appear in Byzantine religious poetry before the days of Justinian I.[93]

Like most Byzantine *kontakia*, the *Akathistos* also draws on the Scriptures and on a number of famous prose sermons, but it retains a striking individuality. With bold similes the poet succeeds in blending the overwhelming mystery of the Incarnation of the Word with the softer note of the cult of the Virgin; and the varied and intricate rhythms employed are enhanced by the music of the words. It should also be added that in the *Akathistos* the literary genre of the 'Salutations of the Virgin' reaches its peak,[94] even if the profuse and rhetorical praises of Mary attain a pitch of rather studied exuberance.

As we learn from the *synaxarion*[95] of the Festival of the *Akathistos* (the Saturday of the fifth week in Lent), this hymn was chosen by the Patriarch Sergius as the thanksgiving hymn to the Mother of God for the salvation of the city of Constantinople from the Avars in 626; and it was then that the second celebrated *prooemium* was added. This turned the whole poem into a thanksgiving hymn for victory and salvation, and it has been repeatedly used as such to this day. The literary qualities of the poem and the wide popularity of the cult of the Virgin in the East explain the far-reaching influence the *canticum* had upon subsequent Greek literature. It was quoted to satiety, copied and recast in iambic trimeters and political fifteen-syllable lines; modern Greek paraphrases of it exist; and it even influenced Byzantine and post-Byzantine art, especially between the fourteenth and sixteenth centuries, as is evident from the paintings of Mistras and Mount Athos and even from frescoes as far north as Romania.

To the days of Justinian belongs the greatest of all Byzantine poets, Romanos the Melodist. Little is known about his life; even the century in which he lived has long been hotly disputed.[96] It is likely that he was born in Syria, in the city of Emesa, and that he was of Jewish origin. As a young man he served as deacon at the Church of the Resurrection in Berytus, before coming to Constantinople during the reign of Anastasius I (491–518), where he was attached to the Church of the Virgin in the Kyrou quarter of the city.

According to the legend preserved in the *Life of St Romanos*,[97] he was miraculously endowed with the gift of writing *kontakia*. He is said to have composed about a thousand *cantica* for various festivals of the Christian calendar—naturally, a number not to be taken literally. After his death he was canonized as a saint of the Orthodox Church, but we do not know when. His fame as a musician and poet must have been established in his lifetime, for in a hymn later composed to celebrate his festival we are told that he was known to the emperor and to the palace circle. There is no indication, however, that he ever occupied an official position at court.

We do not know when Romanos died, but his *kontakion On the Ten Virgins II* (No. 48)[98] refers to the violent earthquakes of 9 July 552 and 15 August 555, so he must have survived beyond the middle of the sixth century. The beautiful *prooemium* to his *canticum On the Crucifixion* (No. 21), in which he speaks of approaching death (Ψυχή μου, ψυχή μου τί καθεύδεις/ τό τέλος ἐγγίζει), probably indicates that the poet lived to an advanced age, but in all probability he died before 24 December 562, for the *kontakion* that was composed for the second inauguration of Santa Sophia is not by him, as one would have expected had he been alive.[99]

Eighty-two *cantica* attributed to Romanos have survived, besides a few insignificant fragments and one short κατὰ στίχον prayer. Thirty-four of these are on the person of Christ, the rest dealing with other figures of the New and Old Testaments, martyrs and saints of the Christian Church and other religious subjects. A great number of the *kontakia* ascribed to Romanos appear to be spurious (probably all those on martyrs and saints),[100] for it has been proved that the acrostics were frequently falsified so as to include the name of the poet. The Christological *kontakia* are undoubtedly his most important compositions, though striking examples of his art can also be found among the *cantica* on other figures of the New and Old Testaments. Opinions would no doubt differ as to which are the best, but *On the Nativity* (No. 1), *On the Presentation in the Temple* (No. 4), *On Mary at the Cross* (No. 19) and *On the Resurrection VI* (No. 29) would be a reasonable selection.

The poet often composed more than one *kontakion* for the same festival; on the Resurrection of Christ, for example, we have six which are ascribed to him. Among the extant genuine *cantica*, however, we find no rehandling or recasting of the same material in another metrical form (*Umarbeitung*) executed by the poet himself.

The language of Romanos is the Atticizing 'literary *koine*' or Hellenistic Greek, which does not escape the influence of the simple spoken language nor that of the Scriptures, with their many Jewish-Greek elements. His style is marked by simplicity, dignity and emotional directness, the sentences moving in short and uninvolved phrases well-adapted to the intricate metres of which he is a master. As already mentioned, in one *kontakion* only, *On Judas* (No. 17), does he make use of rhyme, following the example of the *Akathistos*.

Romanos is a true poet, the one great poetic figure in Byzantine literature. In his grand Christological *kontakia* there is a sense of supreme exaltation and seriousness. His mind is steeped in arresting biblical images (he often uses biblical passages as illustrations); his metaphors are sharp, his similes striking, his comparisons bold, and he coins frequent successful maxims. Moreover, in the treatment of his subjects there is vivid dramatization; monologues are introduced to reveal the inner mind of his agents and dialogues to explain the motives of their actions. But perhaps the greatest quality of his major *kontakia* is the felicity of their structure. Many of them are conceived on two or even three levels of action — the heavens, the world of the living and the world of the dead — where the whole pageantry of Christ, the Apostles, the Virgin, the patriarchs of the Old Testament and martyrs and saints of the Church are presented alive before our eyes in a fervour of religious awe and Christian hope.

It is proper, however, to add that not all his *kontakia* are successful. The poet occasionally erupts into passion, piling contempt and abuse on the betrayers of the Lord.[101] Moreover, some, especially those with an epic rather than a dramatic impulse, tend to be excessively long and tedious, as, for example, *On the Three Children* (No. 46). And now and then dogmatic or exegetical digressions occur, always tiring but even more so when introduced by a man like Romanos, who had no real philosophical or theological training.

The most important sources of Romanos are the Old and New Testaments, the Apocrypha and certain *martyria* and *vitae* of martyrs and saints. Second to these, and of special interest for the moralizing and dogmatic passages, are the writings of famous Fathers of the Church such as Basil, Gregory of Nysa, Basil of Seleucia, Chrysostom and others. Whether or how far Romanos depended on the Greek translations of Ephraem remains an open question.[102]

The poetry of Romanos has been greatly admired since Cardinal Pitra first published a number of his works. Certain critics have considered some of his writings masterpieces of world literature.[103] There is no doubt that their merits are many and that in his hands the *kontakion* reached its peak. In religious poetry he represents the spirit of expansion and innovation which characterizes the era of Justinian in so many other fields. The ancient world, with all it had thought and felt, was passing away. But in the solemn surroundings of the Byzantine churches, with their brilliant mosaics and flickering candles, it was Romanos who gave new life to the long and glorious tradition of Greek poetry; it was he who revived the dramatic element and handed it down to the medieval Greeks in the strophes of his great *kontakia*, for which he has been fittingly called Θεορρήτωρ, the 'Orator of the Lord'.

In all probability, to the sixth century also belongs the *kontakion On Lazarus* by an otherwise unknown melodist, Kyriakos,[104] which is close in spirit and technique to the works of Romanos. Of historical interest (for poetically the quality is low) is also the anonymous *kontakion* composed to celebrate the second inauguration of the church of Santa Sophia and later chanted at the inauguration of other churches, including that of the Holy Sepulchre when restored by Heraclius.[105]

Important *kontakia* continued to be composed well into the seventh century and even later. Of the two celebrating the *Assumption of the Virgin Mary*, one is by an anonymous author[106] and the other by the melodist Cosmas,[107] from whose pen no other work has survived. They both presuppose an official festival of the Assumption of the Virgin, which was first established in the reign of the Emperor Maurice (582–602). Furthermore, the important anonymous *cantica On the Transfiguration*,[108] *On the Raising of the Holy Cross*[109] (which refers to the capture of the Holy Cross by Chosroes II in 614) and *On the Holy Fathers*[110] belong to the days of Heraclius (610–41).

This last work is of extraordinary significance, not only because of its quality but also because it is the only example of 'heretical' hymnography that has survived. It draws, often verbatim, on the famous *Ekthesis* of the Emperor Heraclius, which was issued as a 'Symbol of Faith' in 638 and celebrates the Holy Fathers of the Ecumenical Councils that defined the true dogma until 640. It is known that the *Ekthesis* was repudiated by Heraclius himself shortly before his death, when he became convinced that his Monothelite religious policy had failed (so this *kontakion* must be dated between 639 and 640), and that later the Patriarch Sergius and all his Monothelite followers were condemned as heretical. However that may be, the literary qualities of this *canticum* corroborate the view that the suppression of heretical literature has probably deprived us of many inspired and beautiful writings.[111] That to this day the *kontakion On the Holy Fathers* is chanted in church—if only in part—in honour of the Fathers of the Council of Nicaea (who no doubt would have disapproved wholly of the theological views of its author) is one more example of the irony of fate.

The new metres—and therefore melodies—employed by the post-Justinian poets of *kontakia* are relatively few. But usually, even when using well-known older metres and melodies, they added an *ideomelon koukoulion* (a prelude in a new metre and melody). There is much that is lively and arresting in their poetry, even though, as with the melodists of the days of Justinian, they relied heavily on the Scriptures and on the writings of the early Fathers of the Church.

Finally, to the religious poetry of roughly this period belongs a chronological–eschatological work by the monk Theophanios, called Χρονικὸν σύνταγμα περὶ συντελείας αἰῶνος ἤτοι κόσμου. It is a work of about A.D. 700 and speaks about the end of the world and the seven ages of man.[112]

As we shall see, practically all the hagiographical *kontakia*, most of them anonymous and of no literary value, with which the literary genre of the *kontakion* comes to an end belong to the days after the death of Heraclius and therefore to the subsequent period, when the great days of religious poetry were over.

Part Three

THE BYZANTINE WORLD

SECTION I

From Heraclius to the Restoration of the Images (641–843)

Introduction

The features which were to characterize the course of Byzantine history were assumed by the Eastern Roman Empire at about the middle of the seventh century. For it was then that the Slavs overran the Danube provinces and penetrated into Greece, that the greater part of Italy was lost to the Lombards and that the Pope became free to step into the shoes of the absent emperor. At the same time in the East the ancient hostility towards Persia gave way to enmity towards Islam, which lasted until the twentieth century. The heart of the empire was now in the Greek-speaking lands of Asia.

The house of Heraclius succeeded in holding back the initial attacks of the Arabs south of the Taurus, and though northern Africa fell to the Mohammedans in 697 and a Bulgarian kingdom was founded between the Danube and the Balkans, Constantinople stood firm as the protectress of Christianity and the Greek cultural tradition. During the reign of Leo III (A.D. 717–41) the Arabs, who had taken to the sea, were forced to abandon their supreme attack against the capital of the empire, but the Church historians never forgave that emperor for being the first to suppress the images. However, many of the iconoclast successors of Leo III won the respect of large numbers of their subjects.

The deadly icon controversy continued for over a century until the Empress Theodora, as regent for Michael III, secured in 843 the final victory of the image worshippers. Notwithstanding the unbridled fury of the monks and their many supporters, it can justly be said that the iconoclasts, though causing considerable damage to art and learning by their attacks on monasticism, gave the Empire a new and improved civil and military organization; their reforms of Imperial finance and their endeavour to make justice accessible to all should be particularly stressed.

The icon controversy, which shook the Empire to its foundations, falls into two distinct parts. During the first the issue was mainly theological, for the reverence paid to the holy images seemed to the iconoclasts to be

idolatrous and bigoted, while the icon worshippers believed that to forgo
the help of corporeal things was presumptuous, since even the Son of God
himself had taken a body and was the living image of the invisible God;
moreover, it was maintained that, as St Basil had stressed, 'honouring the
image led to the prototype'. The second part of the controversy assumed a
more pronounced political character. For the monks, who were the main
supporters of the icons, tried to break down the traditional Caesaro-
papism of Eastern Rome, whereas the emperor wished to crush their
ambitions and to be the master in the empire. In the end all that the icon
worshippers achieved was an assurance that the emperors would no
longer try to alter the Christian Church by Imperial decree. Nor was that
any longer important, since all theological development of the Church
ceased when she emerged from the icon controversy, having become, in a
full sense, the Orthodox Church.

The poetry of this period from Heraclius to the triumph of Orthodoxy
was on the whole poor. In the context of religious verse these years saw the
end of the great days of the *kontakion*, which were followed by a marked
decline of that literary genre until its end in the eleventh century. The
death-blow of the *kontakion* was probably dealt by the canon, the third
important kind of Christian poetry, which emerged in the second half of
the seventh century and whose origins can be traced as far back as the
sixth. In the canon music was more important than words, and this had
the effect of diminishing its poetic vigour. Moreover, the great length of
the canon brought about an agonizing search for variety, an expansion of
traditional religious motifs and a marked weakening of expression, and
often a display of erudition is evident which makes its style artificial and
stilted. Nevertheless, the canon soon became extremely popular and was
given a prominent place in the enlarged and embellished post-iconoclast
liturgy. It is proper to stress that in spite of all its shortcomings, the
emergence of this literary genre constitutes a landmark in the history of
Greek poetry because it gave the Greeks not only the main body of their
religious verse but also some of their most revered and beloved ecclesias-
tical hymns.

In this period, side by side with the leading representatives of the
canon—men like Andrew of Crete, St John Damascene or Cosmas of
Maiouma—we also meet Cassia, the most distinguished poetess of the
Byzantine world. Her religious verse is greatly superior to her secular
poetry, and in it we find one real short masterpiece, her hymn to Mary
Magdalene.

The period is also rich in *troparia*, short, independent laudatory hymns,
which differ widely in poetic merit; and it is also the one in which a new
minor form of liturgical poetry, the *syntomon* (short hymn) appeared. This
consists of several strophes (usually between four and nine) that were
inserted between the lines of psalms and of other religious poems; for that

reason it was also called the *sticheron*. Kyprianos is thought to have first composed such *stichera* in the eighth century.

We need not linger over the very inferior religious poetry in anacreontics that we come across once again. Perhaps only Arsenios' poem *On Easter Sunday* is worthy of mention as the first in which the anacreontic rhythm relies solely on the placing of accents within the line, ancient prosody being wholly disregarded. (This initiates what are known as the 'Byzantine anacreontics'.) It should also be noted that much Byzantine religious poetry of this period was translated into Syriac and other foreign languages.[1]

In secular poetry the leading figure of those days was clearly Theodore the Studite, that passionate champion of the icons and reformer of Greek monastic life. He also composed a great deal of liturgical poetry—short *kontakia*, canons, *triodia*, *troparia* and so on—which, however, is of little poetic value. His major contribution to verse is in the field of the epigram, to which he brought a fresh spirit. For in his epigrams Theodore presents, in a straightforward, simple manner, various moods and aspects of monastic life, genuine first-hand 'medieval' impressions and emotions not contingent on any weary literary tradition. Thus he brought new life to Byzantine secular poetry, which had lain dormant since the days of George the Pisidian, and he is the link between the seventh century and the new florescence of Greek lay poetry that we meet in the tenth.[2]

Just as in every other period of Byzantine history, along with Theodore the Studite we find a number of minor epigrammatists, emperors, churchmen and simple laymen, who treat of a variety of religious and other subjects but regrettably achieve little distinction.

Finally, a word should be added here about the short dramatic work of Ignatius the Deacon, *Adam, Eve and the Serpent*, not because of its poetic merits but because of the form of a dialogue in which it is cast, a form unusual in Byzantine poetry. It was no doubt meant to be read and not to be acted.

CHAPTER 17

The Supremacy of Religious Poetry

RELIGIOUS POETRY

Verse composed in ancient metres

During this period Christian poetry continued to be composed in ancient metres, mainly anacreontics and iambics. The tendency to superimpose on each line a system of regulated accents, which George the Pisidian introduced into his iambics, also persisted. Unfortunately, the surviving anacreontic religious verse is scanty and of limited value, as can be seen from the works of its three main representatives, Elias Synkellos, Michael Synkellos and Bishop Arsenios.

Of Elias Synkellos (eighth century?), who was secretary to the Patriarch of Jerusalem, two minor derivative poems have survived, an *Anacreontic of Contrition* (Ἀνακρεόντειον Κατανυκτικόν) and a *Lament on Himself* (Θρηνητικὸν εἰς ἑαυτόν).[1] Of Michael Synkellos (c. 761–846), a monk of the famous Palestinian monastery of St Sabbas and later a *synkellos*[2] to the Patriarchs of Jerusalem and Constantinople, we have only one poor work, an alphabetic acrostic, *On the Restoration of the Venerable and Holy Icons* (Εἰς τὴν ἀναστήλωσιν τῶν σεπτῶν καὶ ἁλίων εἰκόνων). Finally, from the pen of Arsenios, bishop of Corfu (ninth century), comes a much better poem, *On Easter Sunday*.[3] This consists of fourteen strophes of irregular length and displays considerable freshness in its description of spring, in which the influence of Theocritus, Bion and Leonidas of Tarentum can be traced. Moreover, as already mentioned, it has the distinction of being the first poem in which anacreontic rhythms rely solely on the placing of the accents within the line, initiating the so-called 'Byzantine anacreontics' or eight-syllable line.

To the religious poetry of this period we should also add an iambic poem by Andrew of Crete (c. 660–740), in which he speaks about his retraction from Monothelitism, into which he had lapsed in A.D. 712.

It is a work of little merit 128 lines long and dedicated to the deacon Agathon.

Undoubtedly, the most important religious poetry composed in ancient metres in those days are the three iambic canons attributed to St John Damascene, about which we shall speak below, in the section dealing with the canon.[4]

Verse composed according to the rhythmic metrical system

With the exception of the three aforementioned iambic canons attributed to St John Damascene, all other significant religious poetry of this period was composed in the Byzantine rhythmical system. Unfortunately, great confusion and uncertainty exists in this field: first, because most of the surviving works are anonymous and therefore cannot be dated with any accuracy; second, because several contemporary poets of the same name existed, about whom we know nothing more than their names, so it is impossible to ascribe surviving works to them with any degree of accuracy; and third, because the majority of the canons and a great number of *kontakia* and *troparia* have not yet been critically edited, to say nothing about a considerable number that have not yet been published at all. Consequently, the treatment of this most important period in the history of Greek poetry will have to be summary and incomplete. We shall limit ourselves to the most important representatives of each genre of the religious poetry of those days, about whom certain information can be gathered, and to a few significant anonymous works.

THE *TROPARION*

The *troparion*, the independent short hymn, continued to flourish during the seventh, eighth and ninth centuries. In fact, a considerable increase in such short hymns of praise becomes evident, enhanced by the introduction of new feasts of saints into the Christian calendar and by the lengthening of the service. In the seventh and eighth centuries, which were days in which religious music proliferated, a large number of new melodies were composed to accompany *troparia* that became known as *idiomela* or *automela* (hymns with their own melody); at the same time *troparia* called *prosomoia* (hymns to be accompanied by the same melody as others) were written to be chanted to old, popular tunes. *Troparia* were usually chanted at the beginning and end of a *kontakion* or a canon and often between the odes of the latter. Their length varied, for some were monostrophic compositions of only a few lines, whereas others consisted of several longer strophes. They all have a pronounced laudatory and lyrical character. Many *troparia* have a fixed place in the service and a special function, as can be seen from the liturgical books in which they were included. This gave them a number of more specific names by which they were known, but neither their place nor their function in the liturgy changed their character or created different kinds of poetry we need distinguish. They are all *troparia*, short hymns of praise of roughly the same nature accompanied by music.

Such are the *apolytikon*, the principal *troparion* of the day celebrating the feast or saint commemorated in the calendar, which is sung at the end of Vespers and *Orthros* (hence the name *apolytikon*, 'dismissal hymn'); the *hypakoe*, chanted in the morning office after Psalm CXVIII and also, later, after the third ode of a canon;[5] the *mesodion*, chanted between the biblical odes; the *theotokion* in honour of the Virgin; the *stavrotheotokion* celebrating Mary at the Cross; the *martyrikon* in honour of the martyrs; the *necrosemon*, a hymn on the departed; the *megalynarion*, a song of praise beginning with the word *megalynon* ('magnify'); the *eulogitarion*, beginning with the phrase εὐλογητὸς εἶ Κύριε ('praised be the Lord'); the φωταγωγικόν, starting with the word φῶς Κύριε ('Lord, light'); the *makarismos*, starting with the word Μακάριοι ('blessed'); the *katebasia*, sung after the monks have stepped down from their pews; the *kathisma*, a *troparion* chanted before a seated congregation; and so forth.

It would be idle to list here the names of all the poets of *troparia* belonging to this period which we find in the liturgical books of the Orthodox Church and in various medieval manuscripts, for we know nothing more about most of them, and several bore the same name.[6] What appears certain, however, is that all the major religious poets of those days (known mainly from their canons)—men like Andrew of Crete, St John Damascene, Kosmas of Maiouma, Theophanes Graptos, Theodore the Studite or Joseph of Thessalonica, and Cassia, the one distinguished poetess of Byzantium—also composed *idiomela troparia*; but, with few exceptions, there is no agreement among scholars over which of those attributed to them in the liturgical books are genuine[7] and which are the works of less distinguished poets of the same name. It is clear from the study of this large corpus of short, laudatory hymns that not one of the poets developed a truly personal voice that could lend individuality to his verse. Their poetry, labouring under a heavy dependence on passages of Scripture and seldom rising above the common rhetorical laudations of the Byzantine sermons, lacks all originality. Their impact must have been more musical than poetic.

In closing this brief account of the *troparion* of this period we must single out the beautiful short hymn, *On Mary Magdelene*, composed by Cassia (850), which to this day is sung in the Orthodox Church on Easter Tuesday. It is rightly classed among the masterpieces of Christian Greek poetry.[8] Noteworthy also is her *troparion* which compares the rule of Augustus with that of Christ,[9] and her Lauds (αἶνοι) for the morning office of 31 December, an *idiomelon* in which rhyme and *parechesis* are dexterously combined.

In spite of their many shortcomings, a large number of the *troparia* we find in the liturgical books were translated into foreign languages and many still continue to be chanted in various Orthodox churches.

THE DECLINE AND END OF THE *KONTAKION*

After the death of Heraclius (641) the literary genre of the *kontakion* began to decline rapidly, and this process continued until the eleventh century, when *kontakia* ceased to be composed.

In their great days (the sixth and the first half of the seventh century) *kontakia* were elevated metrical sermons of considerable length, in which dialogue and references to the Scriptures added dignity and drama. In the period under consideration they degenerated either into short, encomiastic hymns about saints and martyrs or into long, rambling, hagiographical biographies. They ceased to be homilies in verse. In the short encomiastic hymn (usually between ten and twelve strophes long) the saint is frequently addressed directly by the poet and exuberantly praised. The style is pompous and the diction purist, delighting in the coining of encomiastic epithets and indulging in platitudes. The influence of the late Hellenistic and early Byzantine prose encomium is evident, though all the traditional *topoi* are rarely observed. On the other hand, the long, rambling biographies — they extend on occasion to thirty-two long strophes! — are full of fantastic miracles worked by saints, described in a dry, flat style reminiscent of the miracle narratives which invaded hagiography after the sixth century. Both types often draw on the Apocryphal New Testament and on the *Lives* of saints, and their aim is not only to praise the martyrs but also to edify the faithful.

Moreover, new melodies, and therefore new metrical patterns, were on the whole no longer composed for *kontakia*, so the words of these later creations were usually cast to fit famous older melodies and metres like the *Tranoson* (*Τράνωσον*), the *Hoi en pasei te Ge* (*Οἱ ἐν πάσῃ τῇ γῇ*) or the *Ten Edem Bethleem* (*Τὴν Ἐδὲμ Βηθλεέμ*). In fact, such was the popularity of certain older melodies in those days that we also meet the strange practice of recasting the words of genuine lesser *kontakia* by Romanos into metrical patterns that made it possible for them to be chanted to the accompaniment of one of his celebrated melodies which had become popular.

The reasons for the decline of the *kontakion* in this period are not clear,[10] but the view that this was at least partly due to the decision of the Council of Troullos (692) that made preaching in prose obligatory on all Sundays and festivals appears plausible.[11] The development and increasing popularity of the canon and the shifting of taste to more 'erudite' texts[12] most probably also contributed to that decline.

To this period, and indeed to the two inferior types of hagiographical *kontakia* we have distinguished, must be assigned nearly all the *cantica* on saints spuriously attributed to Romanos, as well as the numerous and mainly anonymous *kontakia* on saints and martyrs which we find in the extant *kontakaria*, the medieval collections of *kontakia* which continued to be compiled in Greek monasteries until the fourteenth century.[13]

As is the case with the poets of the *troparia*, the poets of later *kontakia*, whose names are found in the acrostics, are hard to identify and difficult to date with any accuracy. Such are, for instance, Gabriel, Georgios, Ioannikios, Theodoros, Abbas, Arsenios, Joseph, Leon, Stephanos, Symeon, Paulos, Elias or Ioannes,[14] who remain for us, as Krumbacher puts it, 'nothing more than empty names'.[15] It is equally hard to assign to a known poet any of the many anonymous *kontakia* that have come down to us because their uniformity of style precludes any reasonably certain attribution. In this vast corpus of dull religious poetry a spark of true poetry appears in only a few exceptions, the most notable being the *kontakion* by Domitios (an otherwise unknown poet), *On the Birth of St John the Baptist*. It probably belongs to the seventh century and, as one of the manuscripts indicates, its acrostic was at some stage changed so that the name Romanos was substituted for Domitios, that of the true author.

In those days *kontakia*, like *troparia* and canons, were composed both in the East and in the West, and, naturally enough, at the three great centres of medieval religious poetry, the monasteries of St Sabbas in Palestine, St John Studios in Constantinople and St Basil in Grotta Ferrata, near Rome. Of the three the monastery of St John Studios can claim the greatest number of melodists, and modern scholarship has even spoken of a Studite school of poetry, which it has undeservedly called 'the last "original" school of composers of *kontakia*'.[16] Among the melodists of that 'school' the place of honour is held by Theodore the Studite, the great champion of the icons; after him his brother Joseph of Thessalonica and the famous branded monks, Theodoros and Theophanes the Graptoi, should be mentioned, all of whom distinguished themselves chiefly as poets of canons.[17]

Though the *kontakion* in this second and lesser stage of its life can make no claim to literary excellence, it is certainly worthy of study from a linguistic, historical and hagiographical point of view. In the post-iconoclast enlarged and embellished liturgy only small sections of famous older *kontakia* were included—usually the *prooemium* and the first strophe—which were inserted among the odes of canons. It is most probable that the florid music of the canons was to a great degree responsible for the final suppression of the *kontakion*, whose tunes were simple and repetitive and therefore less impressive.

THE CANON

It can hardly be questioned that the most important event in the history of Greek literature of those days was the emergence of the canon, the third major form of Christian religious poetry in Greek. In its fully developed form this was a hymn cycle of nine odes, of which the second was later suppressed except in Lent. Each ode usually consisted of between three and four stanzas,[18] and each was composed in a different metre and accompanied by a different melody. Though the name 'canon' (whose etymology is a matter of dispute)[19] prevailed, in the acrostics we also find the terms *poiema, hymnos, threnos, melos* and *melisma*.

The canon appears fully-fledged in the eighth century. Andrew of Crete (died 740) is traditionally considered its inventor, but its origins can be traced as far back as the sixth century.[20] Its development is closely connected with the chanting of the biblical odes in the *Orthros*, the morning office, which corresponds to Matins and Lauds in the West. The number of the biblical canticles was originally fourteen, as can be seen from the *Codex Alexandrinus*, the early fifth-century manuscript of the Greek Bible, but during the sixth century the Church of Jerusalem reduced them to nine, a lead which Constantinople followed shortly after. At the same time in Palestinian monasteries the practice was established of chanting short stanzas (*troparia*) between the verses of the biblical canticles, and by the end of the sixth century the Church of Jerusalem introduced the singing of nine odes in three groups, as well as the chanting of independent hymns after each group. It is probable that in one papyrus that can be dated to the second half of the seventh century[21] we have traces of an early stage in the development of the canon, for it contains hymns to the eighth and ninth biblical odes.[22] In the course of the eighth century the number of *troparia* composed to accompany each biblical canticle increased, and the name 'ode' was probably transferred from the biblical ode to these. Finally the biblical odes disappeared,[23] and their place was taken by this new hymn cycle, the canon. This development is corroborated by the famous *Megas Canon* composed by Andrew of Crete, whose 250 stanzas correspond to the lines of all nine biblical odes. Soon, however, the second ode of this ninefold hymn cycle was omitted because of its mournful character.[24] Thus the usual type of canon consisting of eight odes came into existence.

As time advanced, the connection of a canon with the biblical odes became increasingly loose and even completely disappeared, as can be seen from certain canons of Johannes Mauropous. Moreover, the original penitential quality of the canon, as expressed in the *Megas Canon*, was also abandoned, and a new laudatory type developed, which was composed to celebrate the great festivals of the Christian calendar as well as those of the lesser martyrs and saints. It was not long before shorter canons (known as *diodia*, *triodia* and *tetraodia*) were composed, which consisted, as their name indicates, of two, three or four odes. The restriction of the cantillation of the biblical odes at Lent, which was a time of penance, was responsible for this development. The number of the odes was then reduced to three from Monday to Friday and to four on Saturday.[25]

With the introduction of the canon, music began to play an increasingly important part in the service, and this led to a decline in poetry. For not only did each ode of a canon have its own tune,[26] but various *troparia* (*theotokia*, *stavrotheotokia* and so on), each with its own melody, as well as *stichera*[27] also accompanied by their own music, were inserted between the lines of the canons. For in the eighth and ninth centuries we have a further revival of Christian religious music, which may be associated with the florescence of Arabic music, centred in those days on Damascus, the home of all three major representatives of the canon — Andrew of Crete, St John Damascene and Cosmas of Maiouma. It is of interest to note, for example, that the composition of no less than 690 new melodies is attributed to Andrew of Crete and 531 to St John Damascene alone.[28]

The canons developed and reached maturity in the climate of the violent theological and political battles which characterized the icon controversy; it is therefore not surprising that they turned dogma into prayer and concentrated on presenting the orthodox religious views in a spirit of jubilation. However, as already noted, the poetry of the canons is greatly impaired by their length and by the frequent inclusion of elements relating to the biblical canticles whose place they came to take. This is also partly the reason for the frequent lack of unity and the absence of any true sequence of thought in those long hymn cycles. Many of the canons have acrostics — some of these are even in iambics or elegiacs — and some of the odes have refrains. The language of the canons is on the whole of a stricter Atticizing kind than that of the *kontakia*, and this tends to make their style stilted and artificial, especially where the iambic metre is used in the text instead of the flowing Byzantine rhythmical verse. This turn to more 'Classical' elements is clearly connected with the revival of interest in Classical studies that emerged in the days of Photius.

Canons, like *kontakia* and *troparia*, were naturally composed at the three major centres of Byzantine religious poetry already mentioned — the monasteries of St Sabbas, St John Studios and St Basil. Whether they originated in the monastery of St Sabbas, as has been suggested, or elsewhere, we cannot know. What is certain is that the *Typikon*[29] of St Sabbas is the one that brought about the renewal of the liturgical books, and in this the canon played a prominent part. Unfortunately, as already stated, the whole field of the canon has not yet been satisfactorily examined, so a full account of the history of this important literary genre cannot at present be given.[30] We shall therefore limit ourselves to the few major figures about whose poetry we can gain a reasonably accurate picture and who, as far as we can see, were imitated by numerous other minor writers.

The oldest important representative of the canon is St Andrew of Crete (c. 660–740), who is also traditionally (though wrongly) considered to be the inventor of that form. A native of Damascus, he became archbishop of Gortyna in Crete in about 692. During the icon controversy he was on the side of the icon worshippers, but in 712 he lapsed into Monothelitism, though he retracted his allegiance to it the following year. About this 'mistake' and his return to orthodoxy he speaks in the iambic poem dedicated, as we saw, to the deacon Agathon.[31] It is also thought that he composed his most famous poem, the *Megas Canon*, in penitence for that error. Andrew distinguished himself as both poet and orator, and a considerable number of his homilies have survived; but it is for his *Megas Canon* that he is chiefly remembered. This vast, rambling hymn cycle consists of nine odes in which he fuses praise of the Divinity with passages of confession and contrition. Though true feeling not infrequently breaks through the constant dependence on the Scriptures, the many repetitions and references to older religious verse dampen the poetry.

Together with the *Megas Canon* we find in the liturgical books a number of other lesser canons attributed to him — *On St Anne, On the Birth of the Virgin, On Lazarus,* several entitled *On the Mother of God*[32] — as well as short *idiomela*. He always included penitential odes in his canons, which are all characterized by their length. He must also have been extremely productive as a composer of music, for, as we have seen, in the books of the Church no less than 690 melodies are ascribed to him.[33]

St John of Damascus (c. 675–c. 749) is considered the most celebrated representative of the canon. Little is known of his life, and such sources as exist conflict considerably. Born into a rich Christian family of Damascus, he succeeded his father as the chief representative (*Logothetes*) of the Christians to the Caliph. He was later compelled to abandon this office because of his faith and withdrew in about 716 to the monastery of St Sabbas, near Jerusalem, where he became a priest. During the iconoclast controversy he was a strong defender of the images, which enhanced his authority in the orthodox world; he also wrote three discourses on the subject.

St John was a prolific writer in both verse and prose. His great dogmatic treatise, the *Fount of Wisdom* (Πηγὴ γνώσεως), which he supplemented with other dogmatic writings, had an immense influence on the Christian Church. He also composed a number of polemical, moral and ascetic treatises, homilies, lives of saints and biblical commentaries. All through the Middle Ages his works were used by the Greeks and the Slavs, though they were never commented on, nor did they lead to the formation of a school. In modern times too they have retained their influence over the thought of Eastern theologians. Much of St John's reputation rests on his erudition, for his command of earlier Christian literature and the Aristotelian tradition, as filtered through the Neo-Platonists and the Christian commentators, makes him greatly superior to any of his contemporaries.

To St John Damascene is also attributed the addition to the liturgical books of the *Octoechos*[34] (the *Book of Eight Modes*),[35] a collection of hymns devoted to the Common of the Season, arranged for eight consecutive days. This attribution, however, does not appear to be accurate; St John was probably the reviser and not the author of that famous book.[36]

St John was a prolific hymnographer. He composed canons in both quantitative and rhythmic metres, and he can claim to have revived ancient metres for works designed for the liturgy. Among the most famous hymns that go under his name are three iambic canons on the Nativity, the Epiphany and Pentecost, in which we find a system of superimposed set accents in the line. The authenticity of the last has been rightly challenged from the Middle Ages on, one Johannes of Arclas (otherwise unknown) claiming to be its author.[37] But the most celebrated of all his poetry is his *Easter Canon*, which is composed in the Byzantine rhythmic metrical system and which has been called the 'Golden Canon', or the 'Queen of Canons'. The liturgical books contain twelve more canons assigned to him, among them *On the Sunday of Antipascha, On the Assumption, On the Dormition of the Theotokos*, as well as a number of *troparia*.[38]

The poetry of St John involves many problems of authenticity. Certain scholars have assigned to him a large number of canons and *idiomela* (no less than ninety) which have come down to us under the name of Ioannes Monachos,[39] and there are hymns published under his name that others believe to be the writings of Johannes Mauropous (eleventh century).[40]

The poetry of St John Damascene is influenced by the verse of Gregory of Nazianzus, whom he greatly admired and on whose works he wrote extensive commentaries. Its fame is clearly due to the author's reputation as a theologian of the Eastern Church and as a musician. For his famous iambic canons, the pride of his poetic output on which extensive commentaries were written, if genuine, are composed in a stilted pedantic style whose artificial Atticizing diction is obscure, even preposterous.[41] Moreover, the dependence on older religious poetry and the constant references to passages of Scripture—too frequently the same ones— tend to be tiresome. More natural and flowing is the language and style of his great *Easter Canon*, in which true poetry shines here and there and the deep religious feeling that permeates it is not buried under a heavy crust of erudition. However, a common defect of the hymns of St John Damascene is that they constantly strive after decorative effect and frequently indulge in exposition of the main Christian doctrines of the Trinity and the Incarnation; nor is Mariology absent.

St John Damascene is also credited, by no less an authority than Eustathius, Archbishop of Thessalonica (twelfth century), with the composition of a full 'Euripidean' drama called *Susanna*, no trace of which has survived.[42]

After St John Damascene, Cosmas of Maiouma, also known as Cosmas Melodos or Cosmas of Jerusalem (born c. 700), is considered the most significant author of canons. As a young, orphaned boy he was adopted by the father of St John Damascene and brought up with him. The two were educated by a gifted Sicilian monk called Cosmas, who was also a poet and musician (whence springs a certain confusion regarding the authenticity of some of the poetry of the younger author).[43] Like his foster-brother, Cosmas entered the monastery of St Sabbas, near Jerusalem, and in 743 became the bishop of Maiouma in Phoenicia.

Cosmas composed canons — full canons as well as *triodia* and *diodia* — and *idiomela*, shorter hymns for various Christian festivals. The most famous of his works are his canons in honour of great Christian festivals such as Easter, the Nativity and the Exaltation of the Cross, of which fourteen were incorporated in the liturgical books of the Eastern Church. Most striking of these is his famous *Canon on Easter Sunday*.

Cosmas was also a great admirer of the poetry of Gregory of Nazianzus, on which he wrote commentaries, and his verse, like that of St John Damascene,[44] is burdened with erudition, references to Scripture and to the doctrine of the Church. Though on the whole more spontaneous, dogmatic views often freeze the poetic impulse and the artificial structure of the verse not infrequently disfigures the clarity of the thought. However, the hymns of Cosmas of Maiouma were much admired and greatly imitated in the medieval Greek world.

Next to these three leading figures mention should be made of Germanos I (c. 634–733), who is considered one of the chief promoters of the literary genre of the canon.[45] Descended from a noble Byzantine family, he joined the clergy of Santa Sophia, played a leading role in the Quinisext Council (692) and was appointed to the metropolitan see of Cyzicus. It seems that, ceding to the threats of the Emperor Philippicus, he signed the declaration against the Sixth Ecumenical Council; but he soon withdrew from Monothelitism and in 715 was elected Patriarch of Constantinople. His vigorous opposition to the iconoclasts resulted in his deposition in 725, when he retired to Platonium, where he died at a very advanced age.

Germanos was prolific both as a prose writer and as a poet. Of his prose works some historical writings, homilies and dogmatic letters have come down to us; the majority seem to have perished at the hands of the iconoclasts. On the other hand, much of his poetry has survived, but the problems of authenticity are once again grave. Thus we find in the Church's liturgical books about two dozen canons and more than a hundred *stichera* that go under the name of Germanos, but there is no unanimity among scholars as to which of these should be attributed to the

Patriarch Germanos I.[46] However that may be, none of the poetry which has come down under that name is of real distinction or displays any originality. If the Patriarch Germanos I was truly instrumental in establishing the canon in Byzantine religious poetry, it must have been due to his authority as Ecumenical Patriarch and gifted musician.

We must now turn to the famous monastery of Studios[47] in Constantinople, which, after being reorganized by the great monastic reformer Theodore the Studite, in the ninth century became the real centre of liturgical poetry and music of the Empire.

Of the Studite melodists the most famous composer of canons was Theophanes Graptos (c. 775–845), so called, so the story goes, because at the command of the Emperor Theophilos he and his brother Theodoros were branded on the forehead with iambic trimeters as a punishment for their resistance against the breakers of the images.[48] Before coming to the monastery of Studios, Theophanes spent twenty-two years of his life as a monk at that most important Eastern centre for religious music, the Laura of St Sabbas in Palestine; he had also visited Rome as a member of an embassy to the Pope. After the end of the icon controversy he was appointed metropolitan of Nicaea.

Theophanes Graptos was an astonishingly productive poet. The liturgical books of the Eastern Church attribute to him no fewer than 162 canons and nineteen *idiomela*. Although the authenticity of many of these has been challenged, there still remains a large body of poetry that must have come from his pen. But quantity does not usually favour quality. The verse of Theophanes is long-winded, bombastic and dry. Moreover, it is derivative and burdened with doubtful erudition. Here too music must have been more effective than words in establishing his fame as a melodist of the Eastern Church.[49]

Another distinguished member of the Studite circle of melodists and poets was Theodore the Studite (759–826) himself, that uncompromising theologian and gifted organizer of monastic life. The son of pious parents, he soon embraced religious life; he was ordained priest and later made abbot of Saccudium in north-western Asia Minor. In 799 Theodore and his monks moved to the deserted monastery of Studios in Constantinople, which they turned into a great centre of monastic reform. Theodore became the leader of the Zealot party in the Orthodox Church, which refused to make any concessions to temporal power, and as a result he was twice banished and imprisoned. His subsequent vigorous opposition to the iconoclasts caused him to be banished for a third time. He died in the Prince's Islands and is recognized as a saint by the Eastern and Western Churches.

Theodore's works include a large collection of important letters, many of them 'open letters', a 'Short' and a 'Long Catechesis', an 'Exposition of the Liturgy of the Presanctified', spiritual orations, a list of canonical penances, several polemical works against the iconoclasts and, as already noted, verse cast in 'erudite' and rhythmical metres.

About his *troparia* and *kontakia* we have already spoken, and his epigrams will be dealt with later.[50] Here we must examine his canons. Theodore and his brother, Joseph of Thessalonica, took a leading part in the revision of the *Triodion* and the extension of the *Parakletike*. In the former several canons have been transmitted under his name, and others are assigned to him of which a number have not yet been published, as, for example, the canons *On the Mother of God, On Christ, On St Theodore Stratelates*. Naturally enough, the authenticity of several has been challenged, among them that of the famous canon *On the Restoration of the Images*, a violent attack on the image breakers which has been ascribed to Theodore the Younger (mid-ninth century), later an abbot of the monastery of Studios.[51]

The liturgical poetry of Theodore the Studite is greatly inferior to his epigrams. His canons and *triodia*, like his *kontakia*, are bombastic and dry, delighting in a lame erudition and indulging in the formation of compound adjectives. But it is only fair to stress that beneath the crusted surface of the verse one feels true devotion burning. There is a marked difference between the pseudo-Atticizing style of his *triodia* and canons and the clear, workmanlike Greek of his epigrams.[52]

Of the Studite composers of canons third in importance is Joseph of Thessalonica (762–832), the brother of Theodore. Following the family tradition, he also became a monk at an early age and was persecuted and banished with his brother. In 807 he was appointed Metropolitan of Thessalonica but was once more exiled and suffered a martyr's death at the hands of the iconoclasts in 832. He was canonized by the Eastern Orthodox Church.

Joseph was highly regarded as an orator and a poet. Several of his homilies and panegyrics have survived, and he collaborated with his brother Theodore in the revision of the *Triodion* and the extension of the *Parakletike*. In the liturgical books of the Church a large number of poems are attributed to Joseph—canons, *triodia*, *troparia*—but the problems of authenticity are once again grave, as confusion between his writings and those of the synonymous Joseph the Hymnographer (816–86) is inevitable and constant. Many of his *triodia* in the *Triodion* are genuine, as are those poems that have come down under his name in the *Pentekostarion* and the *Parakletike*. Judged by these, the poetry of Joseph of Thessalonica does not seem to differ much from that of his brother, either in kind or in quality. Its fame clearly depended on the reputation of the author as a champion of orthodoxy and as a musician.

Side by side with these well-known names of hymnographers belonging to the period under examination we find in the liturgical books, as well as in medieval manuscripts, the names of several composers of canons whose dates are not certain and whose works are of little distinction, although in the tradition of the Church some are held to be poets of merit. Such on the whole secondary and often shadowy figures are Anatolios, Arsenios, Theodoros Graptos, Elias II, Patriarch of Constantinople, Johannes Palaiolauriotes, Endokimos, Klemes, Theodoros of Smyrna, Georgios of Nicomedia, Georgios of Amastris, Andrew the Blind and others, on whom we need not elaborate.[53]

A few words should be added here about Georgios the Hymnographer (eighth–ninth century?), for in the liturgical books we find twelve canons and one *idiomelon* that go under his name. A number of these hymns were composed in honour of the Virgin Mary, and there are others that have not been published. It is, however, a matter of dispute whether or not all the works bearing his name are by the same Georgios. Though he seems to have enjoyed considerable fame as a melodist of the Church, his verse is of little literary merit.

In this period of poetic decline it is some consolation to turn to the poetry of Cassia (also known as Cassiane or Eikasia) (c. 810–65), about whose *troparia* and Lauds we have already spoken.[54] Cassia, who is undoubtedly the most distinguished poetess of the Greek Middle Ages, was the offspring of a noble family—her father was a *Candidatos* at the imperial court—who, after the end of the icon controversy, became a nun.[55] Later, in about 843, she founded a convent, where she spent the rest of her life composing religious music and poetry.

The problems concerning the authenticity of her works are highly involved, but what appears to be unquestionably genuine is her canon *On the Departed*, as well as the *tetraodion* for Easter Sunday, perhaps her best surviving longer work. The poetry of Cassia is much more impressive than that of her contemporary ecclesiastical poets. In it we meet both depth of feeling and vividness of imagery and, not infrequently, adroitly employed rhetorical embellishments. About her secular poetry, her gnomes, we shall speak in the following chapter.

It may be worth adding that to the ninth century belong two other poetesses who also engaged in writing religious verse—Thecla[56] and Theodosia.[57] However, their achievements were greatly inferior to those of Cassia.

The poetry of the canons of the days between Heraclius and the Restoration of the Images is on the whole disappointing. The lack of originality, the slavish dependence on the Scriptures, the length and the linguistic erudition with which it is burdened dampen the deep religious feeling that permeates it, nor do the rhythmical metres in which most of it is cast help the clarity of expression. One cannot help but feel that it was the respect the leading melodists of those days commanded as champions of Orthodoxy and supporters of the icons that earned them their reputation as great poets during the Middle Ages. To this hypothesis must also be added their undeniable skill as melodists at a time when, as we have seen, music assumed a leading role in the enlarged post-iconoclast liturgy.

THE *SYNTOMON*

The *syntomon*, another new form of liturgical poetry, also emerged in this period. It was a prayer roughly fifty lines long, which fell into strophes (usually not less than four and not more than nine). These were initially inserted between the lines of the psalms and later between the lines of other, longer liturgical poems, a practice that also gave the *syntomon* the name of *sticheron*.[58] As with the *troparion*, if the melody that accompanied the *syntomon* was new, it was also called an *idiomelon*. The strophes of the *sticheron* were sometimes joined by an acrostic, which was occasionally falsified to accommodate the insertion of the name of a well-known religious poet. (Thus *stichera* have been attributed even to Romanos, who lived before the *syntomon* was invented!) Unfortunately, the poetic achievement of this literary genre is disappointing, as there is hardly any originality in its verse.

Kyprianos (first half of eighth century), a contemporary of St John Damascene who probably also came from Palestine (or Syria), is considered to have been the inventor of the *syntomon*.[59] He must have been a prolific writer, for the *Menaea* include a number of his *idiomela*, and twenty-three unpublished canons have been found which go under his name.[60] A large number of *stichera* are included in the liturgical books of the Orthodox Church, many of which are ascribed to leading poets of the Church like Theodore the Studite, Joseph of Thessalonica or Cassia.

SECULAR POETRY: A PERIOD OF OBSCURITY

The period from Heraclius to the Restoration of the Images marks the time of the poorest secular poetry in the entire history of Byzantine literature. Literary historians speak of a 'void' that followed George the Pisidian and persisted until the ninth century, when we come across the beginnings of a revival, of which the central figure was Theodore the Studite, in his role as an epigrammatist.

Theodosius the Grammarian (mid-eighth century), who is probably to be identified with the scholiast of religious poetry of the same name, may be considered a forerunner of this revival. He was the author of a poem on a siege of Constantinople by the Arabs in which (erroneously) the name of Heraclius appears. In all probability it deals with the siege of 717, during the reign of Leo III (the Isaurian). This is also supported by the fully regulated accents we find in the eighty iambic trimeters of the poem.

About the life and the liturgical verse of Theodore the Studite we have already spoken.[61] His true poetic achievement, however, lies with his epigrams, which are usually addressed to his fellow monks and are free of all rhetorical adornment and the customary literary conventions.[62] In a spirit of true devotion and humility he admonishes those who have chosen the monastic life; he strives to protect them from various temptations and sins and to help them in a practical manner. But, side by side with epigrams dealing with monastic life, he also wrote others on saints, icons, holy relics and churches, as well as a number of epitaphs. The language of Theodore's epigrams is workmanlike and simple; clichés are avoided, as well as *enjambement*; nor do we find allusions to antiquity or mythology. Their metre is always the twelve-syllable Byzantine iambic line. In the poetic wilderness of those days they claim a place of honour, but that does not mean that they are of significance in world literature, nor did they exercise any noticeable influence on the further development of the Greek epigram.

We know of four more epigrammatists of this period who should be noted: Cassia, the Emperor Theophilus and two Patriarchs of Constantinople, St Methodius and St Ignatius.

Cassia we have already met as a composer of religious verse, but she was also a gifted epigrammatist and writer of gnomic verse. In her gnomic sentences, which are perhaps modelled on the pseudo-Menandrean *Monosticha*, she speaks about friendship; these are followed by a poem of twenty-seven trimeters, all of which begin with the word μισῶ ('I hate'), in which social customs and human habits are examined and judged in a very sound manner. Her epigrams touch on a variety of subjects: woman, luck, beauty, wealth, stupidity, the unreliability of the Armenians and so on. She also wrote a series of verses on the nobility of monastic life. In her secular poetry Cassia shows dexterity and sensitivity, but she also follows the beaten track in making use of traditional motifs. However, no matter what her shortcomings may be—scholars have seen in her writing a touch of feminine *médisance*—we must wait many centuries before we again come across any noteworthy Greek poetry from a woman's pen.

Strangely enough, Theophilus (829–42), who was given a good liberal education and showed real interest in art and letters, is known as an epigrammatist only from the twelve trimeters he is said to have composed to be branded on the foreheads of the learned monks, the brothers Theodore and Theophanes, who were vigorous icon worshippers and were thereafter known as Graptoi ('inscribed upon').[63] The story runs that the command was accompanied by the words: 'And if the verses are bad, do not bother'! We hear of no other works by Theophilus.

We need not linger over the insignificant epigrams of the long-suffering

Patriarchs of Constantinople, Methodius (843–47) and Ignatius (847–58),[64] who also wrote second-rate liturgical verse. We must close this chapter with Ignatius the Deacon, who lived in the first half of the ninth century and who, after serving as deacon and *skeuophylax* (storekeeper) of Santa Sophia in Constantinople, was appointed Metropolitan of Nicaea. His prose works—patriarchal biographies, sermons and letters—do not concern us here. Such of his secular poetry as survives includes a verse paraphrase in tetrameters of Aesop's *Fables*, based on Babrius;[65] a gnomic *alphabetos*, consisting of twenty-four iambic trimeters,[66] in which the vanity of life, and the terror of the Last Judgement are treated; and a short dramatic dialogue, *Adam, Eve and the Serpent*, intended for reading and not for acting in church and hence treated as a 'secular' work.

To Ignatius the Deacon we must also ascribe the poor lament in Byzantine anacreontics *On the Death of Paulus his pupil*, as well as the epigrams in the Palatine *Anthology*,[67] of which the first three are sepulchral and the last an introduction to the edition of his works. Hitherto they were attributed to Ignatius μαγίστωρ τῶν γραμμάτων (second half of ninth century),[68] to whom only one epigram in the Palatine *Anthology* should be assigned.[69] Ignatius also compiled a collection of twenty-four moral and religious maxims, which he cast in iambics and arranged in alphabetical order.[70]

Of all the extant works of Ignatius the Deacon, his unassuming dramatic dialogue, *Adam, Eve and the Serpent*, is the most interesting because it constitutes a revival of the literary form of the dialogue in the ninth century, which should be considered in conjunction with the revival of interest in Classical drama.[71] Though his verse is on the whole poor, here and there a spark of true feeling emerges, as well as some pleasing learning.

SECTION II

From the Restoration of the Images to the Fourth Crusade (843–1204)

Introduction

The Amorian dynasty (820–67) was marked by the defeat of the Byzantines in the West—Sicily fell to the Arabs, and Venice pursued her independence—but it was also marked by success in the East, where the Arabs were pushed to a frontier line that reached from Armenia to northern Syria. Irregular raids were frequently made along that new frontier, but mutual understanding and respect were achieved, the conditions roughly reflected in the epic cycle of Digenis Akritas.

In art and learning the Amorian period displays a definite revival, and the renewed missionary activities of the Orthodox Church, represented by Cyril and Methodius, the Apostles of the Slavs, carried their civilizing effects to the Slavs of Moravia. Finally, the conversion of Bulgaria (864) brought Byzantine influence to bear on that most immediate enemy of the Empire. In this period there were several Slav risings, and Symeon the Great (893–927) extended the frontiers of the Bulgarian state southward into Greece, the Bulgarian raids reaching to the Isthmus. When the Second Bulgarian Empire (1186–1258) was ultimately subdued it was succeeded by Serb domination in the Balkan peninsula.

In the middle of the ninth century the momentous break with Rome took place, caused by the clashing ambitions of Pope Nicholas the Great and the spirited Patriarch Photius. This fatal dispute was to have great and far-reaching effects, especially after the Patriarch Michael Cerularius manipulated the final schism and established the full separation of the Eastern and the Western Christian Churches (1054).

The Macedonian dynasty (867–1057) marks the apogee of Byzantine glory. It abandoned the innovations of the iconoclasts and returned to the ancient heritage of Rome. The law of Justinian was restored, and with the rule of a series of great soldier-emperors—Nicephoros Phocas, John Tzimisces and Basil II, the Bulgar-Slayer—Crete, Syria and Mesopotamia were won back from the Mohammedans, and the Bulgars were finally crushed. The Byzantine Empire reached its furthest limits. At the same time Vladimir, Prince of Kiev (972–1015), was baptized, and the conversion

of Russia to Christianity began. But with the death of Basil II the great-
ness of Byzantium began to wane, as the struggle between the capital
and the provincial magnates increased, lessening the power of the army; a
losing battle was also waged against the Church, which was absorbing
more and more land for its tax-immune monasteries.

The time of the Macedonian dynasty was also an important period in
the development of education, learning, literature and art. The High
School of Constantinople became once again the centre of the Empire's
intellectual activities and a 'universal' encyclopaedic knowledge was
encouraged. One has only to remember men like Photius (ninth century),
Leo VI (the Wise), his son Constantine Porphyrogenitus (tenth century)
and Michael Psellus (ninth century)—to say nothing of their cultural
environment—to realize how extraordinarily elevated the intellectual
level of the Macedonian renaissance was. It should also be credited
with creating the conditions that were to favour the later revival of art and
letters in the days of the Comnenes and the Angeli. Nor should the
churches and palaces built during the Macedonian dynasty, notable for
their splendid proportions and balanced schemes of decoration, go un-
mentioned.

A few years after the end of the Macedonian dynasty the Seljuk Turks
triumphantly entered the military and political scene. At Manzikert
Byzantium suffered a blow at their hands (1071) from which it never fully
recovered. But in spite of this, the Eastern Empire enjoyed under the
Comnenian dynasty the last brilliant period of its history. The Seljuks and
the Petzenegs were repulsed, the Normans were defeated and the Crusad-
ers of the First Crusade (1095–9) were successfully dealt with. But the
price paid to Venice for her help, free trade throughout the Empire, was
disastrous, and the complete change in Byzantine policy which marked
the reign of Manuel I (1143–80) ended by making enemies of all the
Empire's allies. At the same time, the defeat of Myriokephalon in Phrygia
(1176) destroyed all hopes of reconquering Asia Minor from the Seljuk
Turks.

The Comnenian House was replaced by the incapable Angeli, and the
Western Powers, attracted by the splendour of the Byzantine emperors
and enraged by their diplomacy, now waited for an opportunity to humili-
ate them and to pillage Constantinople. This was provided by the Fourth
Crusade (1204) and by internal Byzantine disputes. The Crusaders' fleet,
guided by the greed of Venice, turned from its original purpose and sailed
to restore the fallen ruler Isaak II Angelos. A popular anti-Latin rising
followed; Isaak II and his son met their death; and the Crusaders
assaulted Constantinople, which they captured on 13 April 1204. A
disastrous sacking of the city followed.

A sunset glow pervaded the court of the later Comnenes. Art and letters
flourished; up to the last minute poets, historians and philosophers of

ancient Greece were studied and inspired the writers and artists of those days. Most evident was the imitation of the ancient language, which, in its endeavour to achieve Attic 'purity', became artificial, grandiloquent and entirely removed from the spoken, living tongue. But side by side with this there appeared a new literature in the spoken idiom, a literature no longer anonymous (as were the Digenis epic cycle or the folk songs) but partly autobiographical and partly critical of the times and their society—the typical product of a large-city community that begins to express itself articulately.

The Byzantine renaissance of the twelfth century—encyclopaedic knowledge was the order of the day; specialization had not yet set in— should also be seen as part of the general Western renaissance of the twelfth century, when the Latin classics were revived, as well as jurisprudence and philosophy, and the earliest of the universities appeared.[1]

In the history of Greek literature the period from the Restoration of the Images to the Fourth Crusade is one of paramount importance because it is marked by a general revival of poetry and because, from the tenth century onwards, the beginnings of modern Greek poetry can be traced both in diction and in metre.

At first, during the Macedonian period, there was once again considerable activity in the field of hymnography. The dominant figure was Joseph the Hymnographer (c. 816–86) who, coming from Syracuse, initiated the school of southern Italian and Sicilian poets; somewhat later emerged Symeon the Mystic (c. 949–1022), a man of striking originality, second in inspiration only to Romanos the Melodist. He was also the first to employ the fifteen-syllable line in long, purely religious hymns. The field can also boast of a remarkable representative of religious poetry in ancient metres in Johannes Geometres Kyriotes (c. 970). But later, in the days of the Comnenes and the Angeli, religious poetry declined so markedly that it has been called 'the poorest period in liturgical verse in the whole history of Byzantium'. This is due to the fact that by the eleventh century religious feeling had waned, and the attention of the Church, court and society had turned to the dogmatic quarrels between the Roman Catholic and Greek Orthodox Churches. But there was an even greater obstacle to its further development: the Greek Church liturgies had been completed; all the feast days had acquired their hymns, and there was no room left for more, so the ecclesiastical authorities decreed that no new additions should be allowed. The parodies of religious verse which begin to appear in the eleventh century testify to this decline.[2] In the West, however, Greek hymnography continued until the twelfth century; its centre was the Orthodox monastery of Grotta Ferrata near Rome.[3]

In this period there was a striking revival of the taste for the epigram, which reached maturity in the tenth century with the writings of Johannes

Kyriotes and its peak in the eleventh century with those of Christophoros of Mytilene and Johannes Mauropous. The interest in that literary genre can also be seen from the *Anthologia Palatina*, that large collection of pagan and Christian epigrams which is based on the compilation made by Constantine Cephalas in the early tenth century. It stands out as an example of the fine literary taste of the tenth century and of its love for compilations.

Side by side with the epigram a new lease on life was also given to the ecphrasis, the epic encomium, the 'elegy' of complaint (of course, no longer composed in elegiacs), the verse chronicle (now cast in fifteen-syllable political verse), as well as to various kinds of occasional poetry (including riddles), in which the crude, ironical side of the Byzantine mind also becomes evident.

But not all the 'erudite' poetic output of those days is praiseworthy, for we come across much soulless, moralizing and didactic verse that is hardly worthy of the name of poetry and the lamentable endeavour to revive in verse the tradition of the late Hellenistic prose romances of Achilles Tatius and Heliodorus. The 'erudite' Byzantine verse romances composed then are rightly considered the nadir of medieval Greek literature. However that may be, all this poetic activity demonstrates the revival of interest in metrical compositions.

Without doubt, the two milestones in the history of Greek poetry that mark this period are, first, the appearance in personal poetry of the fifteen-syllable political verse which was to become the most popular metre in the modern Greek world, and, second, the emergence of verse composed in the vernacular, which is rightly considered the beginning of 'modern Greek' poetry.

It has been argued that the oldest datable surviving examples of the use of political verse[4] in personal poetry are six short laments of the tenth century. The earliest three commemorate the death of Leo VI (912),[5] and they are followed by two epitaphs on Christopher (died 959), the eldest son of Romanos Lecapenos,[6] and a poem on the death of Constantine VII Porphyrogenitus (959), which has been attributed to Symeon Metaphrastes.[7] It should, however, be borne in mind that the dating of each of these poems is based on the assumption that it was written at a time close to the death it laments and that at least one of the poems for Leo VI was intended to be sung, for it has a model signature and the name of the melody (the *heirmos*, Ἄρχων τοῦ κόσμου), according to which it should be chanted. Moreover, only the two epitaphs on Christopher are written wholly in narrative political verse, as the others have refrains of seven or eight syllables at intervals, which means that they were conceived as strophic compositions and were probably also accompanied by music.

It has also been pointed out that probably earlier in date than those six

Imperial laments — though this cannot be proved — is the 'Calendar on Spring' found in the *Book of Ceremonies* by Constantine Porphyrogenitus.[8] It is also composed in political verses, and as it is part of a traditional ceremony, it would be fair to assume that it was written before 959, the year Constantine Porphyrogenitus died, though how long before we cannot tell.

If the fifteen-syllable line was used for epitaphs on Leo VI the Wise (886–912), the penitential alphabet attributed to Leo[9] and composed in the same metre[10] may well be genuine; this would make it the first personal poem in political lines we have and one with no connection with a musical accompaniment. And not much later than this must be placed the penitential alphabets in political verses attributed to Symeon Metaphrastes (tenth century)[11] and to his contemporary Nicephoros Ouranos, who was Magister in Antioch.[12] All these poems would be earlier than Symeon the Mystic (c. 949–1022), who is traditionally considered the first to have used the fifteen-syllable line in long, purely religious hymns.

The origin of the fifteen-syllable line, the political verse, is a matter of dispute. Many distinguished scholars argue that it had a popular origin, whereas others maintain that it had a learned one and was due to a creator who combined existing rhythms or to an adapter who revived in rhythmical terms a quantitative metre which had died long before. No convincing solution has as yet been given.[13] But no matter what the origin of that most important metre, it was used in the period under consideration for religious, didactic and court poetry because it was a medium which gave the impression of sincerity, and was considered an effective way to stimulate memory. It must be admitted that the use of the fifteen-syllable line for court poetry seems rather strange in view of the fact that it became an important means of expression for illiterate and half-literate members of society. Highly educated men like Psellus, Eustathius or Tzetzes looked down upon it, though they chose to employ it for didactic purposes. It may well be that the use of the political verse in ceremonial poetry sung by the Demes in the Hippodrome made its connection with the royal family possible.[14]

Shortly after the appearance of the political verse in purist personal poetry we also find it being used in personal poetry composed in the vernacular. And this, of course, is different from acclamations and folk songs in a 'spoken idiom' which have been traced, as we saw, as far back as the days of Justinian (527–65) and Maurice (582–602). Such are the four Ptochoprodromic poems, with their vigorous, coarse humour; the *Spaneas*, by an anonymous author, which consists of advice given by a courtier to a young prince; and the *On His Imprisonment* of Michael Glykas, begging the emperor to release him from an unjust punishment. They are all cast in fifteen-syllable verses and fall within the orbit of the court.[15]

Earlier than these, in the ninth century, we find the beginnings of the great epic Akritic Cycle, which apparently originated in Commagene or Euphratasia but then spread from the deserts of Syria to the Russian steppes, and from Asia Minor and the islands of Cyprus and Crete to the remote western Greek colonies of southern Italy. Of this cycle today we possess only a small number of isolated folk songs, no longer in their original linguistic form, and half a dozen versions of two verse romances which have been joined together and are known as the *Epic of Digenis Akritas*; they range from the fourteenth to the seventeenth century.

The linguistic material we can lay our hands on in this epic cycle is, of course, very important. In one version of the epic—the Escorial—and in the so-called *Ballad of Armouris* the language is close enough to the spoken idiom of its day; but it cannot be considered as genuine as the vernacular of the Ptochoprodromic and other demotic personal poems of the Comnenian age, which may be taken as the first reasonably true linguistic 'demotic' documents we have, even though there too the influence of purist diction can be traced. This is due to the fact that all extant poems of the Akritic Cycle (the ballads and the *Epic of Digenis*) have gone through a long period of oral transmission which has changed their original linguistic form. However, in spite of this, most historians of modern Greek literature regard the Akritic Cycle as the 'beginnings' of modern Greek demotic literature.[16]

Judged as a whole, the significance of this body of poetry in the vernacular is twofold: first, in it we find at last the first serious reaction against the ancient and all-powerful tradition of Atticism, whose effects upon the development of Greek poetry were disastrous; second, it demonstrates clearly the existence of a widespread oral poetry in the mid-Byzantine era through which so many extant Byzantine poetical works in the vernacular seem to have passed, even if some may have originated as written texts, the creations of pen-poets. For it has been proved that much oral poetry originates in written texts, which, once taken over by oral singers, are adapted to the circumstances of their recitation and thus often greatly changed.[17] Moreover, the existence of this widespread oral poetry in the Greek world had in its turn a considerable effect upon the style of later pen-poets, even upon very great ones like Vitsentzos Kornaros or Solomos.

In conclusion, it should be added that in the metrics of this period we also find the anacreontic line used no longer as part of a strophic system but instead as a simple narrative *kata stichon* verse, with regulated accents on the fourth and seventh syllables (one of the forms of the so-called Byzantine eight-syllable line).

CHAPTER 18

Religious Poetry

VERSE COMPOSED IN ANCIENT METRES

A few minor poems in ancient metres, mainly epigrams on religious subjects, have survived from the writings of the Patriarch Methodius of Syracuse (843–7) and the Patriarch Ignatius (died 878), who also wrote hymns in rhythmic metres.[1] Photius himself (c. 820–c. 893), that central figure of the Byzantine renaissance of learning, whose stormy patriarchate marked the beginning of the schism between the Eastern and Western Churches, also found the time to compose three anacreontic alphabets in praise of the Emperor Basil I (867–86)[2] and a *Prayer to Christ and the Virgin* in iambics.[3] They are insignificant as poetry, as are his works in rhythmical metres;[4] this is not surprising, for apparently verse meant little to that great man of letters, if we are to judge by the almost complete absence of poetical texts from his *Bibliotheca* or *Myriobiblion*. Some epigrams have also been attributed to him, but their authenticity is doubtful.

From the poetry of the patriarchs we may now turn to a royal poet, Leo the Wise (886–912). He was a pupil of Photius and a man of scholarly tastes, but he was as weak and colourless in his poetry as he was in his royal career. Among his varied verse compositions (for he wrote hymns in rhythmic metres, occasional poems and epigrams)[5] we find in anacreontics an *Ode of Contrition* with an alphabetic acrostic[6] and, in iambics, an equally uninspired *Encomium on Clement of Ancyra*.[7]

A contemporary of Leo the Wise was Metrophanes, metropolitan of Smyrna (c. 855), who was twice exiled and anathematized by the Pope for opposing the Union of the churches. Only one anaemic anacreontic poem of his, *On the Trinity*, has survived.[8]

Putting all this second-rate verse aside, we can now come to a leading figure of Byzantine literature, Johannes Geometres Kyriotes (born c. 920).[9] In the religious poetry of this period he ranks second to Joseph the Hymnographer, who never composed verse in ancient metres. Johannes

Geometres started his career as a *protospatharios*, a court official, and was subsequently made Metropolitan of Melitene; probably late in life he became a monk at the monastery of Kyrou in Constantinople, from where he acquired the name Kyriotes.[10] He was a man of wide education and culture who unstintingly praised ancient Greek literature and philosophy, but his outlook was distinctly Christian, religious and patriotic feelings being the most prominent features of his works. In the modern literary world Johannes Geometres' reputation rests on the large group of epigrams and other occasional poems he composed,[11] but in Byzantium he was known largely for his hymns to the Mother of God, which were considered masterpieces.

Five of these have survived. Four are in elegiacs, and in an appendix to these, written in iambics, the poet tells us that he chose that metre because the nobler hexameter expressed the 'divine', whereas the humbler pentameter expressed the 'human' nature of the Virgin. The fifth hymn is an *alphabetos* in hexameters, in which all the words of each line begin with the letter of the acrostic, a bone-dry *tour de force*. There is no doubt that the four hymns in elegiacs are permeated by a deep religious feeling and that the warm personality and wide culture of this author counterbalances to a great extent their classicizing diction and conventional metrical form. But the profuse use of rhetorical embellishments make his style studied and often frigid, and this is not helped by the juxtaposition of unconnected epithets; moreover, the author delights in the play of words.

Besides his hymns to the Mother of God, Johannes Geometres composed a *Prayer* (Εὐχή) and a *Confessional Poem* (᾿Εξομολόγησις), as well as an *Encomium on St Panteleëmon* in 1042 iambic trimeters, all much inferior to his secular poetry. He also paraphrased in iambics the nine odes of the Old Testament and tried his hand at didactic verse, writing an etymological lexicon in twelve-syllable iambic lines.[12] Needless to say, a lexicon in verse may be a remarkable feat but it is not poetry. A collection of ninety-nine epigrams celebrating ascetic life, called *Paradeisos*, has also been attributed to him, but their authenticity has rightly been challenged.[13]

We are now certain—for many years his date was a matter of dispute —that Symeon Metaphrastes belongs to the tenth century and that he was *Logothetes* in the reign of the Emperors Nicephoros Phocas (963–9), John Tzimisces (969–76) and Basil II (963–1025). He probably ended his life as a monk and was later canonized as a saint of the Church.[14]

Famous as a hagiographer and well-known for his work on the *Menaea*, his orations, his anthologies from the writings of great Fathers of the Church and his letters, we also find him composing religous verse, some of which he cast in Byzantine twelve-syllable iambics. Such is a prayer to be said before taking Holy Communion and a *synaxarion* on the Crucifixion.[15] We also know of iambic poems that he composed on the Incarnation and the Apostles in the form of questions and answers, but these have not yet been published.[16] His other religious poetry consists of canons, *stichera* and *troparia* in rhythmic metres, as well as three moralizing alphabets in fifteen-syllable lines, which, if genuine, should be among the oldest examples of religious–moral poetry cast in that metre.[17]

Among the hymns of Symeon the Mystic (c. 949–1022), the distinguished Byzantine theologian and mystic who was the first to use the fifteen-syllable line in religious hymnic poetry, eight are cast in anacreontics and fifteen in iambic trimeters.[18] They differ little in style, theological views or mystical experiences from his other poetry in political verse, which constitutes roughly half of his writings; we shall discuss Symeon the Mystic as a poet when dealing with them.[19] However, one point should be made here, that the hymn *On the Death of a Fellow Monk*[20]—probably on the death of Symeon's spiritual father, Eulabes—is a short masterpiece in iambics, one of the few poems Byzantine literature can boast about.

Another successful epigrammatist who also composed religious verse in ancient metres was Christophoros of Mytilene (c. 1000–50). About his life we know nothing more than that he was a proconsul and a *patrikios* and that he served as a judge ($K\varrho\iota\tau\dot{\eta}\varsigma$) in Paphlagonia. Although his epigrams and other short poems are among the best in Byzantine literature, his religious poetry in ancient metres is excessively dry. He is considered the inventor of the new literary genre of the verse calendar.[21] He composed such calendars both in ancient metres (iambics and hexameters) and as Church poetry in the form of *stichera* and canons.[22] His verse calendar in iambic couplets commemorates day by day the various saints of the Church. It is a monstrously dry catalogue of names, yet, strangely enough, parts of it were included in the *Menaea* of the Church. Christophoros is credited with the composition of a second verse calendar, this time in hexameters, which assigns one line to every day of the year, celebrating the various saints. Sections of this dreary digest have also found their way into the *Menaea*. Christophoros is also the author of the *synaxarion*[23] in iambic couplets included in the *Menaeon* of 18 December, the Feast of the Holy Fathers, a further example of a long, dry list of names (those of the offspring of Adam), bereft of all feeling.

St Neilos (c. 1004), the founder of the monastery of Grotta Ferrata near Rome which was to become the centre of religious poetry in the West, also wrote religious poetry which has not yet all been published. In iambics he composed, as far as we know, one poem on St Paul.[24]

From the pen of another distinguished epigrammatist, poet and scholar, Johannes Mauropous (eleventh century), we also have one canon in iambics, *On the Virgin Mary*.[25] It is a minor work, greatly inferior to his many rhythmical canons (which will be examined below)[26] and to his many remarkable epigrams and occasional poems,[27] a number of which are on religious subjects—the birth of Christ, Lazarus, the Dormition, St

John Chrysostom, St Nicholas and so on.[28] The one on an icon of the Weeping Madonna should be singled out for its beauty.[29]

Among Mauropous' epigrams we also find a series describing portable icons with inscriptions explaining the subjects represented.[30] (We have similar though less successful series of the same kind by Christophoros of Mytilene, Theodoros Prodromos, Manuel Philes and others.)

To Emperor Alexius I (1081–1118) is attributed[31] an iambic prayer 100 lines long, grouped according to its content into quatrains. On metrical and other grounds this inferior poem has been condemned as spurious.[32] It is probably the work of some priest of the court who composed it for the emperor to include in his prayers, hence it came to be called a 'prayer of the Emperor Alexius I'.[33] No trace of inspiration can be found in it.[34]

Finally, to the period of the Comnenes belongs the *Protokouropalates* (Head of the Palace Guard), Georgios Skylitzes (twelfth century), who wrote a long introductory poem in iambics[35] to the *Holy Armoury* (Ἱερὰ Ὁπλοθήκη), a prose work by Andronicos Kamateros.[36] It deals with true dogma and attacks, among others, the Roman Catholics, praising at the same time the work of Kamateros. Skylitzes also wrote religious poetry in rhythmical metres.[37]

In closing it should be noted that parodies of religious verse, which started in the eleventh century and which demonstrate its decline, were also composed in ancient metres, as is evident from the poem by Michael Psellus (1018–97) attacking a fellow monk in 297 iambics.[38] It is similar in spirit to that author's coarse attack on another fellow monk, Jacob, which he cast in the form of rhythmical religious poetry.[39]

VERSE IN RHYTHMIC METRES: RELIGIOUS POETRY IN DECLINE

We shall not re-examine in further detail those undistinguished Studite melodists and poets 'of uncertain date'—Theodoros of Smyrna, Theodore the Younger, Arsenios, Georgios of Nicomedea, Antonios, Basileios and others—who mark the decline and end of the *kontakion* in the East, some of whom most probably belong to this period. It suffices to repeat what one author has justly said about their work, and then dismiss them:

> A common quality of all those poets is bombastic diffuseness, many newly coined adjectives and many empty words. . . . In one hymn, for example, attributed to Theodore the Studite (obviously the Younger), we find 104 epithets compounded with φῶς, φάος and similar words.[40]

The *kontakaria* (medieval collections of *kontakia*) of Patmos, Sinai and

Mount Athos are full of such inferior *kontakia* (many of which are anonymous), no doubt influenced by the Studite School;[41] and many are the inferior similar canons found in medieval manuscripts and in the books of the Church.

For us the period opens with Joseph the Hymnographer (c. 816–86), the most prominent and prolific figure in the hymnography of the middle Byzantine years. He was born in Syracuse, but his family, fleeing from the Saracens, came to the Peloponnese and later moved to Salonica. There, at a very early age, Joseph joined the monastery of Latomos as a monk but later left to come to Constantinople, where he was ordained priest. In 841 he was sent to Rome to report on the icon controversy but on his way fell into the hands of pirates and was taken to Crete. When freed, he returned to Constantinople, only to be banished to the Crimea when the Patriarch Ignatius lost his throne (858). However, he returned once again to the capital, and we know that he was appointed *skeuophylax* of Santa Sophia. After his death he was canonized as a saint of the Orthodox Church.

Joseph wrote numerous canons, *triodia*, *kontakia*, *stichera* and other *troparia*, some accompanied by music he himself composed and others set to older melodies. His productivity is astonishing if one thinks of his adventurous life, for he composed over 200 canons on saints—from the most prominent to the most obscure—and on various Christian festivals, to say nothing of his other religious verse that floods the books of the Church.

Although he often used acrostics including his name, the authenticity of many works attributed to him has been contested. It is thought, probably rightly, that a number of these belong to Joseph of Thessalonica, the brother of Theodore the Studite, especially those hymns found in the *Triodion*, the *Pentekostarion* and the *Parakletike*.[42]

Joseph was greatly admired by his contemporaries and by the later Byzantine and post-Byzantine Orthodox world. He was considered the hymnographer *par excellence*—later religious poets wrote hymns in his honour—and to this day in certain Church circles some of his canons, like the one on the festival of the *Akáthistos*, that on earthquakes and that on the Assumption, are considered masterpieces.[43] Nevertheless, in spite of the clarity of his style and the impressive variety of his rhythms, Joseph's hymns are unquestionably long-winded, repetitive and derivative. On the whole, the modern reader does not readily respond to them.

The Patriarch Photius (c. 820–93) also composed religious poetry in rhythmical metres, but it is flat and conventional and in no way superior to his verse in ancient metres.[44] Not all of it has survived,[45] and the authenticity of some of the canons that go under his name has been challenged. He is credited with four canons on the Virgin,[46] two on the Virgin and the Trinity,[47] one on the Transfiguration[48] and one on St Irene.[49] He also wrote a didactic canon on the ages of man and *stichera* on Methodius.[50]

A remarkable figure, contemporary with Photius, is Leon Choerosphactes (c. 824–c. 920), also known as Leon Magistros. A highly educated man, versed in philosophy, astronomy and medicine, an *anthypatos* and *patrikios*, he served as the Emperor's special envoy, but was later accused of high treason and banished. Leon Choerosphactes engaged in theological writings—mainly exegetical compilations—and poetry. He composed a *Summary of Theology* (Χιλιόστιχος Θεολογία) in 1000 verses (a work now lost),[51] hymns in rhythmical metres, which include at least one *kontakion*,[52] ecphrases, epigrams and other occasional verse.[53] We know that Arethas of Caesarea (c. 850–c. 944?), that worldly prelate, theologian, scholar and bibliophile, attacked Leon's *Summary of Theology*, calling it the work of a 'Hellene', a pagan. However, a number of his *idiomela* and one *doxasticon* found their way into the *Menaea*.[54] It is still a matter of dispute which of the hymns in the books of the Church that go under the simple name Leon should be attributed to him and which, if any, to Leo the Wise.

We have already noted the scanty and unimportant verse composed by the Patriarch Ignatius in ancient metres.[55] He was much more productive in rhythmical verse, and no fewer than seventeen canons of his have survived, all included in the liturgical books of the Church.[56] Unfortunately, lacking all originality, they are not much superior to his erudite verse.

Marcus of Hydrous (c. 890), who enjoyed a high reputation as a melodist in his day, belongs to the second half of the ninth and the beginning of the tenth century. He is also included in the list of famous melodists compiled by Kallistos Xanthopoulos in the fourteenth century.[57] Of his writings only five odes of one canon have so far been published;[58] composed at the command of Leo the Wise, they were to be added to the celebrated *tetraodion* by Cosmas Maioumas, chanted on Good Friday, to form a full canon with nine odes. They display fine poetic feeling.

A contemporary of Marcus of Hydrous was Anastasios Quaestor (τραυλός: the 'Stammerer') (c. 900), who also wrote some secular poetry but was best-known for his liturgical verse. He composed a canon on repentance and others on various festivals of the Church—the Annunciation, the Presentation at the Temple, Palm Sunday and so on. Some of these are lost, and others, in which he apparently mixed iambics with rhythmical metres, have not been published.[59] Nikodemos Hagiorites includes in his Θεοτοκάριον (collection of hymns to the Virgin) two canons by him.[60] A number of hymns under the name of Anastasios are found in the liturgical books, but they cannot be attributed to the Stammering Quaestor with any certainty.[61] The famous *kontakion On the Departed*, which has the name Anastasios in its acrostic, is in all probability not one of his works.[62]

Two royal poets follow, Leo VI (the Wise) and his son, Constantine Porphyrogenitus. Leo VI, about whose poetry in ancient metres we have already spoken,[63] also wrote a number of *idiomela* and eleven morning prayers (ἑωθινὰ ἀναστάσιμα).[64] It has been argued that all hymns found in the Church books under the title Λέοντος τοῦ δεσπότου should be attributed to him, but this has not been universally accepted. We also know of a canon and other poems by Leo VI which have not been published.[65]

Leo VI typifies the renewed scholarly interests and encyclopaedic spirit of those days; they nonetheless, found their best expression in his son, Constantine Porphyrogenitus (912–59). Constantine spent most of the years of his Imperial impotence, when Romanos Lecapenus had seized power, in scholarly research, writing and organizing the compilation of a series of important encyclopaedic works. His own prose works are of great significance but, unfortunately, not his poetry. Of this only eleven *exaposteilaria* have survived[66] and one *troparion*,[67] all of very little interest.

Symeon Metaphrastes (tenth century) also engaged in poetry in rhythmical metres, which is no less conventional than his verse in classical rhythms.[68] It consists of several canons and *stichera*, most of which can be found in the books of the Church;[69] but the problems of their authenticity have not yet been solved.[70]

One *idiomelon*, five canons and eight *kontakia*[71] have been attributed to the hymnographer Gabriel (tenth century?), but it is by no means certain if they all belong to Gabriel of the Euergetidos Monastery[72] or if some should be assigned to the earlier Studite Gabriel. Most of these remain unpublished.

To the tenth century also probably belong a number of shadowy figures like Basileios Pegoriotes, Basileios Kyrios and Monachos and Theodoros Diakonos, on whom we need not dwell.[73]

Christophoros of Mytilene (eleventh century), the distinguished epigrammatist,[74] also tried his hand at religious rhythmical verse. Thus, side by side with his dry verse calendars in iambics and hexameters,[75] he also embarked on the composition of a long calendar in rhythmical metres, consisting of three *stichera* and one canon for each month of the year. In the *stichera* he commemorated the saints of the month day by day; in the canon which followed he repeated, in a more compact manner, the list of the saints already enumerated.[76] The poetic standard of this complex work is unfortunately very low indeed, though superior to that of his verse calendars in classical metres.

It is rather strange that whereas parts of his dismal verse calendars in iambics and hexameters found their way into the *Menaea*, not a line of his rhythmical calendar is to be found there. Nonetheless, it is clear that it made its mark, for it served as a pattern for subsequent imitators of equally flat verse calendars, like those by the monks Sergios, Gregorios, Michael and Arsenios (whose dates are unknown).[77] Even Theodoros Prodromos (died c. 1166) followed in the footsteps of Christophoros of Mytilene and composed the one Byzantine verse calendar of some artistic merit.[78]

Johannes Mauropous (eleventh century), whose canon in iambics has already been discussed,[79] is one of the most important poets of this period and one of the most attractive personalities in Byzantine literature, for he combined simple piety with a wide, humane culture. Born in Paphlagonia in about 1000, he was appointed to the Chair of Rhetoric in the refounded University of Constantinople in 1045 but a few years later became a monk at the Petra monastery and then Metropolitan of Euchaita in Pontus. He returned to the capital and to a monastic life in his old age.

Of the writings attributed to him, which comprise a collection of epigrams upon various subjects,[80] religious poetry in rhythmical and ancient metres, thirteen homilies, a lexicon in verse,[81] the life of a saint and letters, the most impressive are the 150 liturgical hymns in accentual rhythms. The most important of these fall into two groups, one consisting of twenty-eight canons on Christ and the other of sixty-seven on the Virgin. Side by side with these we find twelve canons on St John the Baptist and forty-four others on various saints of the Church. It is of interest that among the saints celebrated are two famous hymnodists, St John Damascene and Joseph the Hymnographer, on the latter of whom he composed no less than eight canons. Not all of the hymns attributed to Johannes Mauropous are genuine,[82] and unfortunately only a small part of them has been published. Much further research on the canons of this important author is necessary to provide us with a fuller picture of his poetry.

The accentual hymns of Johannes Mauropous are among the most successful of that genre. Though, like most canons, they are protracted, derivative and full of quotations from the Scriptures, we often find in them touches of true lyricism, fresh, arresting imagery and striking comparisons — for example, the Virgin 'clad in her virtue' is compared with a Byzantine empress dressed in her ceremonial gown,[83] and Peter is compared with the moon 'that reflects the light of the sun'. But on the whole his style is laboured, with too many figures of speech and metaphors, the former sometimes reaching the point of tongue-twisters through the use of alliteration.[84] Nevertheless, the canons of Johannes Mauropous were admired by his contemporaries, and although the liturgical books of the Church had already assumed their final form before the eleventh century, room was found in them for some of them. We find two on St Theodore Triron in the *Triodion*, one on the Virgin and one on the Angel Protector in the *Horologion* and a further canon on the Virgin in the *Euchologion*. Most of his hymns are simple prayers, παρακλητικοὶ ὕμνοι, asking for the help of

God or a saint in a case of sickness or some other need; they were not composed with the aim of finding a place in the liturgy.

Totally unimportant, as far as we can see, is the religious poetry of Michael Psellus (1018–97), the famous philosopher, historian, monk and man of letters who played a leading role in the political history of the Empire in the eleventh century and in his old age returned, more from necessity than choice, to monastic life. Psellus proved to be a pliant, time-serving courtier, whose immense literary output touched on most branches of knowledge, from grammar to medicine. Of his religious poetry in rhythmical metres, only an office in honour of Symeon Metaphrastes has been published;[85] some other liturgical verse of his has been traced, but still lies buried in manuscripts.[86] He was also, as we have seen, the inventor of the parody of religious verse both in ancient and rhythmical metres.[87]

Whereas by the eleventh century productivity in the field of religious poetry had dwindled in the East, in the West the Orthodox monastery of Grotta Ferrata developed, from the tenth century onwards, into a true centre for fresh religious verse. It should, however, be noted that the hymns produced there had no influence whatsoever upon the Orthodox liturgy. Strictly speaking, the list of Italo-Byzantine poets starts earlier than the tenth century with Joseph the Hymnographer, a native of Syracuse, and with Marcus of Hydrous.[88] But it came into its own with St Neilos (died 1000), the founder of the monastery of Grotta Ferrata, who brought to the fore the religious poetry of the West. He was born at Rosano, became a monk at an early age and joined the Roman Catholic Church. He composed his poetry in Greek; from his pen we have an office (ἀκολουθία) in honour of St Benedict, some *kontakia* and the poem on St Paul in iambic verses already mentioned.[89] Much of his work remains unpublished.

St Neilos was followed by Paul of Grotta Ferrata (eleventh century), who wrote *kontakia* (and probably also canons), and by Bartholomaeus (died 1050), an abbot of Grotta Ferrata, clearly the most prolific and perhaps the most significant of that group of religious poets. We have thirty canons and seventeen *kontakia* from his pen, as well as *stichera* and *idiomela* for Christ, the Virgin and various saints of the Eastern and Western Churches. He also composed an office in honour of St Neilos, the founder of the monastery.

Other less important eleventh-century poets from Grotta Ferrata were Leontios, who succeeded St Bartholomaeus as abbot of that monastery, Lucas, Arsenios and probably one Stephanos. They all wrote canons in honour of various saints of the Church.[90] The activities of the Grotta Ferrata poets can be followed until well into the twelfth century, when Johannes of Rosano (died 1181) composed his canon in honour of Bartholomaeus.

The quality of this Italo-Byzantine poetry is on the whole unimpressive, suffering from the faults that we find in nearly all later Byzantine religious verse; it is long-winded, lacks originality and is repetitive. Perhaps the greatest contribution the Grotta Ferrata poets made was to give the *kontakion*, which was practically dead in the East by the end of the tenth century, a new lease on life for roughly another two centuries in the West.

The century of the Comnenes is poor indeed in religious verse; in fact, no Byzantine period has less liturgical verse to show.[91] Only a few names need be mentioned here. First, Johannes Zonaras (twelfth century), the historian, lexicographer and expert in canon law, who became a monk after serving as a high court official in the reign of Alexius I (1081–1118). Among his writings, which include lives of the saints and commentaries on liturgical poems, one canon only has been found, *On the Mother of God*;[92] we also know of a hymn on the Holy Ghost which is now lost.

Zonaras is followed by the *Protokouropalates* Georgios Skylitzes, who lived in the reign of Manuel I (1143–80) and whose iambic poem on the *Holy Armoury* of Andronikos Kamateros we have already noted.[93] In rhythmical verse he composed an office on the stone, on which Christ is said to have been anointed by Joseph of Arimathea after he was brought down from the Cross, and which was taken to Constantinople in 1169. He also wrote two canons, one on St George and one on St Demetrius. The former was included in the *Menaea* but was later exchanged for one on the same saint by the hymnographer David (fourteenth century).

To the twelfth century belongs the hagiographer Nicolaos Kataskepanos—named after the monastery of Kataskepe, where he was a monk—under whose name go a number of canons on the *Theotokos* and a giant canon on repentance, 1000 strophes long, as well as forty *kathismata*. Unfortunately, the quality of his verse does not match its impressive quantity.

We come finally to Eustathius, Archbishop of Thessalonica (1125–c. 1195), that most noble product of the twelfth century, who tried his hand at religious verse. Among the many and varied works—grammatical, literary, theological, pastoral, historical and occasional—that great pastor and teacher wrote we find a lengthy prose commentary on St John Damascene's canon on Pentecost,[94] which indicates his interest in religious verse, and a canon on St Demetrius.[95] He also recast an existing office on St Alpheius and his brother.[96] However, like so many great scholars, Eustathius is not in any real sense a poet.

There is, of course, still a considerable body of religious poetry of this period, mostly anonymous, which has not yet been published. To judge from such samples as one has seen in manuscripts, the quality is on the whole low.

PARODIES OF RELIGIOUS VERSE

As already mentioned, by the eleventh century hymnography had lost its significance in the East. Religious feeling had declined and Church, court and society were absorbed by the dogmatic quarrels between the Greek Orthodox and Roman Catholic Churches. The parodies of religious poetry which began to appear are clear proof of this decline. The man who initiated this crude, indecent kind of humorous verse was no less a figure than Michael Psellus, referred to above,[97] who gave the form of a long canon, complete with acrostic and musical accompaniment, to a coarse attack on a fellow monk named Jacob, whom he accused of drunkenness.[98] This canon was an answer to a short iambic epigram Jacob had written in which Psellus was charged with having left the monastery of the Bithynian Olympus to which he had retired because he did not find 'his goddesses' there (according to the myth, Zeus left Olympus for the same reason). This kind of crude parody of religious verse continued for many years in Byzantium; we even have such a poem on urine (said to be an *aide memoire* written for the benefit of medical students) whose authorship is claimed by many writers—Blastares, Planudes, Maximus Blemmydes, even Photius! This trend culminated in the fourteenth-century *Mass of the Beardless Man* ('Η ἀκολουθία τοῦ Σπανοῦ), in which the whole liturgy is parodied in a most indecent and vulgar manner.[99]

Side by side with scurrilous parody we also find parody of religious verse whose purpose was truly to aid memory. Such is the work of Niketas of Serrae (c. 1100) on the titles of the pagan gods and of others on other subjects.[100]

RELIGIOUS POETRY IN POLITICAL FIFTEEN-SYLLABLE VERSE

Until recently Symeon the Mystic (c. 949–1022) was considered the first writer to use political verse in personal poetry. We have seen that that is not true.[101] Nevertheless, it remains certain that Symeon (also known as Symeon the Younger or the New Theologian) was the first poet to make extensive use of the political verse in genuine religious poetry, for the penitential alphabets we have seen are moralizing verse rather than true religious poetry.

A native of Paphlagonia, Symeon came to Constantinople, where his uncle was a palace official; after his uncle's death he tried to enter the

Studios monastery as a novice but was rejected on the grounds of his youth. At the age of twenty-one he experienced an overwhelming mystic vision, which influenced the rest of his life. Later, in 977, he finally succeeded in joining the Studios monastery as a monk but was soon expelled because of his strange views and mystical experiences and his extreme devotion for his spiritual father Eulabes and the novice Niketas Stethatos. He subsequently entered the neighbouring monastery of St Mamas, where he was ordained priest and then made abbot, but he was ousted from that monastery too because of his mystical teachings and the cult of his spiritual father Eulabes which he endeavoured to introduce after that monk's death. This led to Symeon's banishment from the capital. He died in exile, although permission had been granted for him to return to Constantinople.

Drawing on the traditions of the earlier Church, particularly on Pseudo-Dionysius and Maximus Confessor, Symeon built up a systematic theory and practice of mysticism, culminating in direct perception of the Divine Light. This mystical union with God, which was both spiritual and carnal, led — so he believed — to a complete rebirth of man, which left no trace of sin within him. In his hymns Symeon constantly exhorted his fellow monks to be pure so that they may experience this rebirth and then act as mediators between man and his Creator. All later Byzantine mysticism is built on the groundwork he laid down.

Symeon was a prolific writer whose views are expressed in a body of thirty-four catechisms, numerous theological and other works and fifty-eight hymns describing ecstatic experiences. Of these, thirty-five are in political fifteen-syllable verse;[102] the rest are written, as we saw, in Byzantine anacreontics and twelve-syllable iambics. Occasionally, he mixes his metres in the same piece, and some of his poems are cast in dialogue form. One is in the form of an alphabet.[103] There can be little doubt that Symeon is very loose in his use of all three metres,[104] but the relative proficiency with which he employs the fifteen-syllable line suggests an earlier body of poetry in that metre.

Symeon's verse — amounting to 10,700 lines — was collected and published after his death by his devoted pupil Niketas Stethatos and goes under the title *Loves of Divine Hymns* ("Ἔρωτες τῶν θείων ὕμνων), a title which betrays the influence of Pseudo-Dionysius Areopagetes. None of Symeon's hymns was composed for liturgical purposes; nor do the hymns constitute an organized system of mystical theology. They are spontaneous expressions of the author's strange visions, which seem to concentrate on a storm of inner light 'that broke in the mind, bringing about a union with God'.[105]

It is not surprising that the many wanton passages in which Symeon speaks of his love and his desire for fusion not only with the spirit but also with the body of Christ provoked a violent reaction and the wrath of the more conservative circles of the Church. Hymn 15 in particular has been considered blasphemous and excessively offensive, for there, among other things, the poet says: 'The hand of Christ, the foot of Christ become my hand and my foot. . . . It is truly a marriage that takes place, an unspeakable divine marriage . . . again I repeat, in carnal delight each one joins with the Lord.'

Nor were the passages in which Symeon accuses himself of the gravest crimes and the most shameful behaviour—adultery, sodomy, prostitution, perjury, theft, envy, hatred of his brothers, avarice, recklessness, the corruption of children[106]—seen by his contemporaries in the right light, although they were written in a spirit of self-abasement and contrition, true to the long and honoured tradition of Byzantine penitential poetry. They were taken at face value and therefore regarded as incriminating and shockingly offensive. In vain did his friend and pupil Niketas Stethatos try to explain their real meaning in the commentaries he later wrote. Symeon was condemned in the eyes of the Church—and condemned for ever.

The language of Symeon's hymns is on the whole simple—clearly not the spoken idiom of their day—with a sprinkling of rare and obsolete words and a few new ones formed by analogy. The poet makes abundant use of figures of speech (rhetorical questions, anadiplosis, correspondence and so on) and also employs *enjambement*, which is rare in Byzantine fifteen-syllable lines. His imagery is generally conventional, but now and again something fresh and arresting emerges, like the bishop who is presented as 'the official copy (seal) of God' ($\dot{\varepsilon}\varkappa\sigma\varphi\varrho\acute{\alpha}\gamma\iota\sigma\mu\alpha\ \Theta\varepsilon o\tilde{v}$),[107] the image of man 'imprisoned in the chains of his carnal passions'[108] or God entering Symeon's cell 'like a star rising in the night'.[109] Nevertheless, he is also long-winded and repetitive, and although absolute sincerity shines through his verses, their loose syntax and unpolished rhythms prevent them from rising to the realm of great poetry. However, Symeon's unusual personality marks him out as one of the few Byzantine religious poets who is original, and is rightly considered the most arresting figure in Byzantine religious poetry after Romanos. In the fossilized monotony of his contemporary verse he chose the living fifteen-syllable line as a suitable vehicle for expressing his tortured heart and established it in the field of personal poetry, turning it into a narrative rhythm capable of expressing deep and moving mystic experiences. In the poetic dearth of the mid-Byzantine period he truly shines forth 'like a star rising in the night'.

To the religious poetry in political verse of this period two works by Michael Psellus and one by the Patriarch Nicolaos III Grammatikos (1084–1111) must be added. In one of his two works Psellus addresses the Emperor Michael VII Doucas (1071–8) and deals in 300 lines with the rubrics of the psalms ($E\dot{\iota}\varsigma\ \tau\grave{\alpha}\varsigma\ \dot{\varepsilon}\pi\iota\gamma\varrho\alpha\varphi\grave{\alpha}\varsigma\ \tau\tilde{\omega}\nu\ \psi\alpha\lambda\mu\tilde{\omega}\nu$);[110] in the second, in 243 lines, he treats of the *Hexaemeron*, the birth of Adam, his exile and the Antichrist (Περὶ ἑξαημέρου καί εἰς τὴν γέννησιν τοῦ Ἀδὰμ καὶ εἰς τὴν ἐξορίαν αὐτοῦ καὶ περὶ Ἀντιχρίστου).[111] Both poems are of a didactic, religious nature and poetically unimportant. As didactic and equally unimportant as poetry is the poem by the Patriarch Nicolaos III Grammatikos, whose subject is fasting.[112]

CHAPTER 19

Secular Poetry

VERSE IN THE PURIST IDIOM

Epigrams, riddles, oracles and other occasional poetry

The epigrams of this period represent some of the best Byzantine 'lyrical' poetry. To a great extent they consist of versified, short, rhetorical panegyrics or ecphrases. Side by side with these we also find playful thoughts antithetically expressed and verse riddles. The somewhat longer occasional poems are in many respects similar to the epigrams.

As already noted, the growing interest in the epigram can be seen in the work of Constantine Cephalas (early tenth century), the palace official who compiled that important anthology of Greek epigrams covering the whole history of the literary genre up to his day on which the Greek *Anthology* was later based. Cephalas is not the first Byzantine Greek after Agathias (sixth century)[1] to have compiled an anthology of epigrams. We know of two more collections, a short one by a Thessalian who was in the service of Leo the Wise (886–912), known as the *Sylloge Euphemiana*, and an even shorter anonymous collection[2] which includes the epigrams of Johannes Geometres (tenth century). Cephalas drew on the older collections of Meleager, Philip, Straton, Diogenianus and Agathias and on copies from monuments of epigrams made by Magistros Georgios. He also included epigrams of his contemporaries, such as Ignatius, Kometas, and Constantine the Rhodian. This great collection, with its invaluable material, which was not completed by its author—who either died or abandoned the task[3]—no doubt gave an impetus to the composition of further epigrammatic poetry. The anthology of Cephalas, like all the important older ones that precede it, has been lost as a whole, but many hundreds of the poems these anthologies contained have survived in two extant compilations, the *Anthologia Palatina*[4] and the *Anthologia Planudea*. The latter is the work of the monk Maximus Planudes, who produced his own anthology before 1301, neatly arranged into seven books with complex subdivisions and based on the anthology of Cephalas, as well as on other sources.[5] He omitted all the epigrams he considered risky, as would be expected from a monk.[6]

Naturally, we must limit ourselves to the most important epigrammatists of the period.

First comes a truly distinguished man, Leon (ninth century), known as the Philosopher (ὁ φιλόσοφος) or the Mathematician (ὁ μαθηματικός), who in the reign of Theophilus (829–42) gave public lectures in the Church of the Forty Martyrs in Constantinople and was later enthroned as Metropolitan of Thessalonica. When, in the reign of Michael III (842–67), Caesar Bardas organized the University of Constantinople Leon was appointed head and taught philosophy there. (Among his pupils was Arethas, the learned archbishop of Caesarea.)

Leon's mathematical activities, which do not seem to have been free of astrological and magical fantasies, do not concern us here.[7] What interests us is a number of epigrams he composed,[8] mainly on the mathematical, astronomical and philosophical books he had acquired; among them there is also one strange and apparently improper epigram addressed to his mother.[9]

Leon Choerosphactes (c. 824–c. 920) follows, whose religious verse we have already seen.[10] He has been credited with twenty-eight epigrams dealing with a variety of subjects—Lucian, the *Batrachomyomachia*, philosophers like Plato, Aristotle or Porphyrius, St Basil, the Archangel Michael and others—in one of which Leon thanks his teacher Photius for giving him 'the milk of divine knowledge'.[11] They are followed by a long poem in which he defends himself against the accusation of not being a true Christian and a short iambic piece in which he complains that education, honour and the fear of God have disappeared from the world.[12]

Five lyrical poems by Choerosphactes have also survived. The first, which is mutilated, is on his daughter, Theoctiste, and is in iambics, arranged in two-line strophes; the rest are anacreontic alphabetical odes, two on the marriage of the Emperor Leo the Wise, one on a bath built in the emperor's 'courtyard' and one on Augusta Helen, the wife of 'young Constantine' (Constantine VII Porphyrogenitus).[13]

A contemporary of Leon Choerosphactes, Ignatius (*Μαγίστωρ τῶν γραμμάτων*) (c. 875), also wrote a few epigrams, in one of which he tells us that he 'brought to light the art of grammar, which had sunk in the sea of oblivion', and an anacreontic poem on his pupil, Paulus.[14] They are all second-rate verse.

Ignatius is followed by Kometas (ninth century), an ugly hunch-back grammarian who is the author of several lesser epigrams and short occasional poems. The longest of these, in fifty-seven hexameters, is on the

Raising of Lazarus;[15] more interesting are three others that complain how difficult it was in those days to find a text of Homer.[16]

The Patriarch Photius (c. 820–c. 893) is credited with a few epigrams (whose authenticity has been challenged)[17] and with three dry anacreontic odes with an alphabetic acrostic in honour of the Emperor Basil I.[18]

Leo the Wise (886–912), that diligent pupil of Photius,[19] was also the author of a few epigrams—on the Roman months, on certain books, on animal fights in the Circus and so on[20]—and of a few insignificant *karkinoi* (verses that can be read either from left to right or from right to left), not all of which are genuine.[21] He also wrote a poem in 231 iambic lines on his father, Basil I, whose authenticity has been challenged.[22]

In the Palatine *Anthology* we also find one epigram[23] by Anastasios Quaestor, whose religious poetry we have noted.[24] It consists of fourteen hexameters and speaks about Christ on the Cross and the meaning of the Crucifixion, whether in the thought of man or portrayed in a picture. It is a strained but sincere short poem.[25]

To the turn of the ninth century belongs an anonymous collection of twenty-nine epigrams and other short occasional poems.[26] They appear to be the work of a single man and are all of a religious nature, the great majority dealing with icons, a genre, as we have seen, continuously cultivated since the fourth century and well represented in the first book of the Greek *Anthology*. Strictly speaking, these poems are not ecphrases but encomia and prayers, and two of them [27] are long, dogmatic expositions of roughly fifty lines. They are all composed in iambics and in a literary idiom which, for metrical convenience, also employs vernacular words and forms, a practice we meet in Byzantine religious poetry as far back as the days of Romanos. From a poetic point of view they have little to recommend them.

We must now turn to the three leading epigrammatists of the middle Byzantine period.

First of these is Johannes Geometres Kyriotes (tenth century), about whose life and religious poetry we have already spoken.[28] Of his many epigrams and other occasional poems the most interesting are those dealing with contemporary historical events and the experiences of his own life. Such are the sepulchral epigrams on the Emperors Nicephoros Phocas and John Tzimisces, the epitaph on the Patriarch Polyeuchtos, those on the Bulgarian war and the revolt of Bardas Skleros and the one on the great comet that appeared in 975. Particularly interesting is the poem in which he describes his journey from Constantinople to Selymbria, passing through lands ravaged by war, and the picture he gives of the suffering peasants.[29] Less attractive are his epigrams on celebrated literary, historical or religious figures of the past—ancient poets, orators, philosophers and historians, Fathers of the Church and saints. As well as these we also find others on artistic, geographical or mythological subjects—the Muses, Mount Olympus, the river Meander, Athens, Constantinople, certain churches and so forth—as well as on subjects common in rhetorical exercises, like spring, summer, the noble horse. He also composed *ethopoeia* and riddles. The least original of his epigrams are those on common Christian subjects (the Nativity, the Baptism of Christ, the Holy Cross, the Apostles) and those on objects of cult, icons and so on.

In his epigrams and other occasional poems, whose length varies from one line to a hundred, Johannes Geometres uses hexameters, elegiacs and iambic trimeters. They are far above the usual run of Byzantine poetry, frequently vigorous and often original—a striking example is the comparison of the hand of the Emperor Nicephoros Phocas with the river Pactolus, known to have carried gold in its stream—but they are not free of rhetorical embellishments, which add a cold, conventional touch. Johannes Geometres also tried his hand at didactic verse, composing an etymological lexicon in iambics.[30]

The second major epigrammatist of this period is Christophoros of Mytilene (c. 1000–50), whom we have also met as a religious poet.[31] One hundred and forty-five epigrams and other short occasional poems of his have survived, composed mainly in iambic trimeters and occasionally in hexameters. Their subjects vary. We find addresses to emperors, like Romanos III, Michael IV the Paphlagonian, Michael V Kalaphates and Constantine IX Monomachos; congratulatory verses to Patriarchs; poems of sympathy, such as those to the Emperor Michael upon losing his throne or to the Metropolitan Demetrius of Cyzicus on his gout. Next to these we find poems of advice—for example, the one to the orator Menas, who had taken to drink—sepulchral epigrams, and the inevitable rhetorical exercises, such as those on the four seasons, the sparrow, the virtues of the ant, as well as riddles. Finally, we also come across a series of epigrams and short occasional poems on religious subjects (the Baptism of Christ, various saints) and works of art (a bronze horse in the Hippodrome, a picture of the Forty Martyrs).

The secular verse of Christophoros of Mytilene is indeed impressive. It is a relief to come upon it after the mass of soulless verse that burdens Byzantine literature. He can often hold his own even by comparison with the best epigrammatists of antiquity, as, for example, his delightful epigram-riddle on the snow shows;[32] his poem on the Baptism of Christ is praiseworthy[33] and that on the death of his sister Anastasia[34] truly moving. The epigrams of Christophoros, with their wit, elegance and delicacy of feeling, have been much admired and seem to have influenced subsequent Byzantine epigrammatists, like Johannes Mauropous, Theodoros Prodromos and Manuel Philes.[35]

The third distinguished epigrammatist of the middle Byzantine years is Johannes Mauropous (c. 1050), who was also, as we have seen, a significant and prolific religious poet.[36] We have from his pen a number of epigrams and occasional poems, often similar to those of Christophoros of Mytilene, who in several instances appears to have served as his model. Thus we have the inevitable epigrams on religious subjects and works of art (on an illuminated *Evangelium*, on holy icons, on a portrait of the emperor at Euchaita), verses satirizing bad poets, sepulchral epigrams (among which there is one for his own tomb) and attractive poems about personal experiences. Such are the poems he wrote when he sold his house upon leaving Constantinople and the one on the new house he bought when returning to the capital, or the poetic epistle he composed on his first acquaintance with the Imperial family.

The secular poetry of Johannes Mauropous has delicacy of feeling and charm, and his simple piety and wide, humane culture shine through the verses. Perhaps in none other of his works do these qualities emerge in a more captivating manner than in the beautiful prayer to Christ to save Plato and Plutarch from damnation, 'for both clung close to your laws in word and deed'.[37] Mauropous also tried his hand at didactic verse.[38]

Michael Psellus (1018–97), that strange, many-sided man,[39] also engaged in composing epigrams, riddles and occasional poems, some of them meant to be funny. As the problems of authenticity associated with his work are far from solved,[40] we shall only mention here those that can be attributed to him with some degree of certainty. Not all have been published.

Thus we have a long poem in 446 iambics on the death of Skleraina,[41] the mistress of the Emperor Constantine IX Monomachos (1042–54), one in 108 iambics addressed to the Emperor Isaac I Comnenus (1057–9),[42] a short one to the king,[43] one on the Twelve Apostles,[44] an epigram on the banner of the Emperor Constantine IX Monomachos and one on a *protosyncellos* (originally a bishop's 'cell-mate', later merely a court title), whose name is not given. These are followed by a long poem on epilepsy and a professedly playful poem on scabies, from which the poet suffered, which is unique in the literature of the world. At its best all this is third-rate poetry. On the other hand, Michael Psellus is considered to be one of the best authors of verse riddles. Eighteen go under his name, and they are followed by a group of five others with the common title *Aulikalamos*.[45] (The solution to these five riddles is given in an iambic poem by Nicephoros Prosuchos (twelfth century), a minor poet who became *Praetor* of Greece and the Peloponnese in 1182. A few more iambic occasional poems have survived from the pen of Nicephoros Prosuchos, a hymn on Mary the Egyptian and some epigrams.[46] The fashion for composing riddles was also taken up by Eustathios Macrembolites (second half of twelfth century), best-known as the author of a wretched prose romance called *Hysmene and Hysmenias*, excerpts from which have survived. Eustathios' eleven riddles[47] can claim neither charm nor wit.

Finally, thirty iambic couplets on virtues and vices, arts and sciences have also been wrongly ascribed to Psellus, which probably belong to an otherwise unknown poet called Paniotes.[48]

A greatly superior poet was Constantine the Sicilian (first half of tenth century), a scholar belonging to the circle of Leo the Wise. Like his royal patron, he composed occasional poetry in which the pessimistic side of Byzantine life emerges, so forcefully expressed in the alphabets of contrition. Such is his lament in anacreontics on the death of his parents and brothers, who were drowned during a storm at sea. The poem has a moving simplicity, free from all Byzantine bombast. Not without charm too is a short anacreontic love poem ('Ὠδάριον ἐρωτικόν), which was probably set to music. But a third anacreontic composition attributed to him, about a young man who is in love with a girl who either is, or intends to become, a nun, is indeed dull. (Its authenticity has been challenged.)[49] Constantine the Sicilian also composed three strange polemical poems against his teacher, Leon the Philosopher.[50]

A contemporary of Constantine the Sicilian was Constantine the Rhodian (first half of tenth century), best-known for his ecphrasis on the Church of the Holy Apostles in Constantinople,[51] which he wrote at the command of Constantine VII Porphyrogenitus. He also composed minor epigrams, three of which have been included in the Greek Anthology.[52]

The period of the Comnenes opens with The Muses, a poem composed by no less a man than the Emperor Alexius I Comnenus (1081–1118), the inaugurator of that important period of restoration and reform in the history of Byzantium. It consists of 448 iambic lines, full of colourless moral and religious advice, much of which goes back to Isocrates. But it also includes interesting personal observations and warnings against the lawyers, orators and civil servants of those days, as well as views on the Crusaders of the First Crusade. The poem, which is introduced by fifty-three iambic verses by another hand, displays considerable metrical accuracy, which corroborates the view that 'educated men from the tenth century onwards were taught to write "proper" iambic verses'.[53] It was probably written shortly before the emperor's death.

A talented epigrammatist of the Comnenian period, and one who, in a sense, is a link between Johannes Mauropous and Theodoros Prodromos, is Nicolaos Kallikles (turn of eleventh–twelfth centuries). He was a leading physician of his day, a professor of medicine in Constantinople— he even attended the Emperor Alexius I—a good epigrammatist and a composer of occasional poems. He wrote a number of epitaphs, among which is one for the common tomb of Sebastos Georgios Palaeologus, his wife and son, cast in the form of a dialogue between the tomb and a passer-by,[54] epigrams on living men and others on religious works of art, like the cross of Anna Porphyrogenita, daughter of the Emperor Alexius

I, a fragment of the Holy Cross belonging to the Empress Irene or a picture of the Second Coming in the palace. He is also credited with longer occasional poems, including one on the months of the year, giving six lines to each month; a poem on the Emperor John II Comnenus (1118–43); one on the Empress Irene (died 1126), who abandoned the throne to enter a nunnery, called *To the Roses*; and a long sepuchral poem on Doceana, who was related to Isaac Comnenus (1057–9).[55] The authenticity of some of these is doubtful.[56]

Many were the epigrammatists of this period, mostly occasional, insignificant writers. Two, however, should be singled out: Theophylactos of Ochrid (eleventh–twelfth century) and the famous jurist Theodoros Balsamon (fourteenth–fifteenth century), forty-five of whose epigrams have been published.[57]

A lively complaint against society and the Church of Cyprus has come down to us, written by Nicolaos Mouzalon (c. 1110), Archbishop of Cyprus and later Patriarch of Constantinople, on his resignation from the see of Cyprus. His accusations have considerable force, and he does not indulge in self-pity.[58] Greatly inferior is a similar poem, written by Nicetas, Bishop of Corcyra, a near-contemporary of Mouzalon, in which he complains about his resignation from the see of Corcyra. It consists of 310 iambic lines and is cast in the conventional tone of a lament.[59] He also composed an introduction in forty-three political verses to his commentary on the ascetic chapters of the ascetic–mystical work of Maximus Homologites (580–662).

The most prominent literary figure of the Comnenian age and the best epigrammatist was undoubtedly Theodoros Prodromos (died c. 1166), a man whose output is astonishingly varied. Little is known about his life. He was probably a teacher in the Patriarchal School of Constantinople and apparently very poor, if we are to judge from the many requests for patronage found in his verse and from a special category of poems in vernacular Greek attributed to him as Ptochoprodromos ('poor Prodromos'). If these poems really are from his pen, we can see how hard his life as a poor intellectual must have been ('Cursed be learning, my Christ, and cursed those who wish to be educated,' he exclaims); and it seems he had a nagging and unpleasant wife.[60] It is thought that he probably ended his life as a monk, having assumed the name of Hilarion.

Theodoros Prodromos was clearly a man of wide culture, who moved at ease in the Classical tradition and whose rationalist standpoint was unaffected by theological preconceptions. His poems include a large number of epigrams (he was, in fact, the most fertile epigrammatist and composer of short occasional poems of the eleventh and twelfth centuries). Most of them are on religious subjects—on various saints and Fathers of the Church, on books of the Old Testament, on the four Gospels, the Nativity and so on. Relatively few—and these are the best—are on secular subjects: a pair of lovers carved on a gem, an armless man who is cast into the sea. Among them can be found epitaphs in the traditional form of a dialogue between a tomb and a passer-by. In some of his epigrams Theodoros is mordant, indecent and vulgar; among them are the sixteen he wrote on an old man called Machaon who married a much younger wife.[61] Influenced by the fashion of his day, he also composed riddles.

His occasional poetry is frequently typical 'begging poetry' addressed to kings, queens and princes of the royal house and to influential dignitaries of state and Church whose help he hoped to enlist. Side by side with these we meet encomiastic poems, whose aim, once again, was to get something in return, and sepulchral verses on royalty (on John II Comnenus (1118–43) and his wife Irene, on their son, Sebastocrator Andronicos), as well as polemical verse like that attacking one Bardas. Many of his works—and, indeed, some of the works of his contemporary Johannes Tzetzes or by Manuel Philes, who lived later—indicate the patronage of letters which we meet in Byzantium and is also known from other sources. Of Prodromos' many occasional poems two should be singled out, one on his departure for Trebizond because of its content and the other on Nabbatos because of the strange form of an echo poem in which it is cast.[62]

Prodromos, following in the footsteps of Christophoros of Mytilene,[63] also composed two verse calendars. The first is in iambic trimeters and has one line for each day of the year commemorating the saint of the day; the second is in iambic quatrains and has, as we have noted, the distinction of being the only Byzantine verse calendar that can boast of some grace and feeling.[64]

This strange and versatile author also tried his hand at a lament in hexameters, called *Verses of Indignant Complaint at the Lack of Honour Shown to Reason.* In it he vents his rage at the scanty appreciation which his learning receives and, in conclusion, jokingly takes leave of all books and scholarship:

> ἔρρετ᾽ ἐμοῦ βιότοιο ἀπόπροθεν, ἔρρετε βίβλοι.
> Get out of my life, away, to Hell all books.[65]

But though epigrams and shorter occasional poems form an important part of Theodoros Prodromos's poetic output, he did not limit himself to these. He composed a verse romance, *Rhodanthe and Dosicles*[66] (a very inferior work); the *War of the Cat and Mice,*[67] a dramatic parody in twelve-syllable lines; an astrological poem in 593 fifteen-syllable lines,[68] addressed to the daughter-in-law of John II Comnenus; and probably a set of 'begging poems' in the vernacular known as Ptochoprodromic poems, of which we shall speak later.[69] Prodromos also wrote a large number of prose works, which include dialogues after the manner of Lucian on philosophical and literary subjects, grammatical works, commentaries on the hymns of St John Damascene and Cosmas of Maiouma, letters and speeches, not all of which have been published.

It should, however, be borne in mind that this remarkable man, who was probably one of the first to break through the stifling Classical literary tradition which went back for roughly two thousand years and to write on everyday life in the language of the people, addressed himself, as did all writers of the twelfth-century renaissance, to a coterie; hence some of his works are hard to understand.

An important contemporary of Theodoros Prodromos was Johannes Tzetzes (c. 1110–80), who will be dealt with in the section on didactic poetry,[70] as he is the author of the largest body of didactic verse in Byzantine literature; even some of his occasional poems, like the *Carmina Iliaca* (also known as *Antehomerica, Homerica Posthomerica*), are more didactic than straightforward verse. Johannes Tzetzes wrote a number of occasional poems about the personalities and events of his times, some of them attacking his enemies. Not all of them have been published, and some have been lost. Among them one deserves special mention because of its form. It is a ladder poem on the death of Manuel Comnenus (1143–80), consisting of ninety-one iambic lines, in which the last word of every verse is found at the beginning of the following line, thus forming the rungs of the climbing ladder.[71] Ladder poems have a long history going back to the verse letter of Polybius to Demetrius of Syria.[72] In the case of Tzetzes the form is supposed to lift the tragic pathos ninety steps high!

In the East the occasional poetry of this period closes with two laments. The first is by the Archbishop of Bulgaria, Hephaestos (end of twelfth century), and is a minor anacreontic poem on the death of his brother, Demetrius;[73] the second is the celebrated *Lament on the Decline of the City of Athens* written by Michael Choniates, also known as Michael Akominatos (c. 1150–1213), the last Orthodox bishop of Athens before the city was conquered by the Franks of the Fourth Crusade in 1205. Michael, who was the elder brother of the historian Niketas Choniates, bewails the complete absence in contemporary Athens of any of her traditional artistic or intellectual life and, in thirty flat but moving iambic lines, sings of her plight.[74] Michael Choniates also wrote some other verse, including an epic in 457 hexameters called *Theano*, some short poems of religious content and one riddle, a σχέδος[75]—all totally insignificant.

If we now turn to the West, we find that the southern Italian and Sicilian poets form an interesting group in the middle of the Byzantine period.[76] They all belong to the twelfth and thirteenth centuries and are a further proof of the prosperity of the Greek colonies of Magna Graecia until well into the Middle Ages. Moreover, they show that in the days of the Comnenes there was a revival of the Greek element there under the rule of the last Norman kings and their successor, Frederick II of Hohenstaufen.

We have already examined briefly the role of the Greco-Italian poets in the field of religious poetry.[77] Their activities in secular verse are no less interesting. Their most important representative was Eugenios of Palermo (c. 1130–1203), a Sicilian Greek statesman, mathematician and poet. He held various high offices under the Norman kings of Sicily, was imprisoned in Germany by Henry VI and finally returned to southern Italy as an official of the Holy See. He is the author of a poem written from prison, in which he laments his fate—a Western counterpart to the poems of Glykas and to those of Sachlikis, to which we shall turn later[78]—and of twenty-four other occasional pieces, many of which are epigrams and among which a panegyric on King William I (died 1166) or II (died 1189) can be found.[79] As his prose works show, Eugenios is an interesting representative of the trilingual culture (Greek, Latin and Arabic) of Norman Italy.

Next to Eugenios comes Georgios of Callipolis (twelfth century), keeper of the archives of the city of Callipolis in Calabria. His occasional poetry includes an interesting dialogue between the Emperor Frederic II and the city of Rome, a poem on the Emperor John III Vatatzes, various epigrams on religious and other subjects, as well as verses on the early death of a son of the *Domesticus* of Callipolis.[80]

Other members of this group of Greco-Italian poets are Roger of Otranto, Johannes of Otranto, Theodore of Callipolis, Eugenios the Philosopher and Johannes Grassos, all writers of epigrams on various religious and secular subjects and occasional poems of minor significance. The verse of these Greco-Italian poets, which is all cast in iambics, is no outstanding literary achievement, but it is of interest in the history of Greek literature because it shows the total dependence of the West on the Byzantine poetry of the East and throws considerable light on the historical conditions of the southern Italian and Sicilian world of the twelfth and thirteenth centuries.

Satirical and humorous verse

Byzantine humorous and satirical verse is characterized by a biting sarcasm directed against people and things wholeheartedly disliked. There is little good-natured fun or playful humour, such as is found in the ancient world and reappears later in modern Greek poetry. Thus in the epigrams of Constantine the Rhodian[81] (first half of tenth century) we find vulgar and crude attacks on Leon Choerosphactes, one of which even consists of complete lines formed from one gigantic compound word. Examples are:

$$Ἀλλαντοχορδοκοιλεντεροπλύτα$$
$$ὀρνιθοχηνονηττοπερδικοπράτα.$$

Another strikes at Theodore the Paphlagonian, drawing its similes from the life of the pigs and once again using long, vulgar compound words which the author considers witty. Of similar vulgarity and brutality are the answers which Theodore the Paphlagonian gave in verse to Constantine's attacks.[82]

The satirical poetry of Michael Psellus is also bitter and abusive when, as we have seen, he attacks a fellow monk in a poem cast in the form of liturgical poetry;[83] even worse is the one in which he strikes at a Jew whom he hates (κατὰ τοῦ Σαββαΐτα). Here the author outdoes himself, filling more than 300 iambic lines with abuse, 'a veritable dictionary of swear-words', as the poem has been called.[84] Nor does Psellus' poem on scabies, already mentioned,[85] display greater wit or refinement.

Besides his many other literary activities, Theodoros Prodromos (died c. 1166) also found time to write satirical and humorous verse. Among his epigrams and occasional poems are one on a lusty old woman[86] and one on a long-bearded old man (which almost succeeds in being witty).[87] To these should be added the sixteen abusive and obscene poems on Machaon, the aged man who married a young wife.[88] Of the satirical poetry in the vernacular attributed to Prodromos and of his 'amusing' pseudo-dramatic parody, the *War of the Cat and the Mice*, we shall speak later.[89] What can be said at this point, however, is that, when playful, Prodromos' humorous and satirical verse in the erudite language is derivative and when ironical, vulgar.

There are a number of anonymous satirical or humorous epigrams or short poems, some of which probably belong to this period, whose quality is poor indeed; we need not linger over them.[90] In general, this crude outpouring of abuse and bitter irony has little in it that is really amusing or witty and only proves how misunderstood were the character and mission of humorous verse in those days.

The ecphrasis

The full-scale poetic ecphrasis (as opposed to the short epigram), which had reached its peak in the sixth century in the hands of Paul the Silentiary, was revived in the ninth by Leon Choerosphactes.[91] To him should be attributed the ecphrasis on the hot springs at Pythia in Bithynia (Εἰς τὰ ἐν Πυθίοις θερμά), which was long thought to be the work of Paul the Silentiary.[92] The poem consists of 190 seven-syllable lines (hemi-iambics) and is more a paradoxical didactic work than a pure ecphrasis; its purpose seems to be to point out the strange and wonderful qualities of the springs.[93] In every respect it is a minor work.[94]

Far more important is the ecphrasis of the Church of the Holy Apostles by Constantine the Rhodian (first half of tenth century), which was composed at the command of the Emperor Constantine VII Porphyre-genitus between the years 931 and 944. (Constantine was a native of Lindos on Rhodes, and all we know about his life is that he became a notary and chaplain to the Imperial court.) Before proceeding to the actual description of the monument, the poet speaks about the 'seven wonders of Constantinople', his own poetic ability (for he had an inflated idea of himself), the emperor's virtues and the beauty of the capital city. When finally he comes to the church itself, his descriptions are neither clear nor precise, perhaps because of the inexactitude of the older sources he used;[95] however, such information as we can gather about the structure and decoration of that famous and totally destroyed building is welcome. It seems that an ecphrasis of Santa Sophia followed, which has been lost.[96] The best part of the poem is the description of Constantinople (ll. 321ff.), where a number of successful similes and some original ideas appear. What is striking is the poet's extreme hostility towards the pagan past. All ancient works of art are deprecated; Homer is called 'impudent' (θρασύς) and Orpheus is accused of having sung 'of the evil breed of daemons', whereas the author's own poetry, we are told, sounds like 'the clear song of the nightingale'. Needless to say, Paul the Silentiary's ecphrasis stands head and shoulders above Constantine the Rhodian's feeble endeavour.[97]

Side by side with these full-scale ecphrases a very large number of ecphrastic epigrams have survived, as we have seen,[98] for nearly all the epigrammatists of this period indulged in that literary genre when dealing with icons and other religious subjects. Some of them are of considerable length.

The epic encomium

The panegyric epic encomium, which had lain dormant since the days of George the Pisidian (seventh century), was also revived in this period.

Unknown is the author of a feeble epic encomium on Basil I (867–86), cast in 321 twelve-syllable lines, of which the first sixty are lost.[99] Much more important is the work of a Constantinopolitan deacon, Theodosius Diaconos (mid-tenth century), *The Capture of Crete* (Ἅλωσις Κρήτης), composed in 1039 iambic trimeters.[100] It deals, in five 'hearings' (ἀκούσματα), with the capture of Crete by Nicephoros Phocas in 961 — the island had fallen into the hands of the Arabs and pirates — and the further victories of Byzantine arms in Syria, culminating in the conquest of Aleppo. The tone is that of a panegyric, an encomium on the military achievements of the emperor to whom the poem was dedicated in about 963, after he had ascended the throne. The poet compares Nicephoros with the great men of antiquity and accuses Homer of dealing with minor events which he presents as of great importance. The army of the Greeks that conquered Troy, Theodosius says, was unimportant and its leaders, men like Achilles and Ajax, weak. If Homer wished to speak of truly great events, he should have sung of the streams of blood that flowed in Crete. It must be confessed that in spite of much hopeless bombast and chronicle-like narration, there are passages of true poetry in this work; nevertheless, on the whole, it is inferior to the panegyrics of George the Pisidian.

The anonymous cento of Homeric tags on the famous Byzantine general Georgios Maniakis need not detain us long. That brave warrior, after fighting the Arabs in Syria and in Sicily (to this day in Syracuse the 'Castel Maniaki' retains his name) and later the Arabs and Normans in southern Italy, was drawn to rebel against the Emperor Constantine IX Monomachos (1042–54) and led an army against the capital. He was killed in the decisive battle of 1043, which this poet describes in a cento of 'Homeric' hexameters.[101]

Finally, we must turn once again to the versatile Theodoros Prodromos (died c. 1166), who engaged in composing panegyric verse on emperors, princes and other powerful men of Church and state, always in the hope of getting something in return. The group of these works opens with poems celebrating the victories of the Emperor John II Comnenus (1118–43), the capture of Castamon and so on. These are followed by poems celebrating the marriage of that emperor to Irene, the marriage of John, son of the Sebastocrator Andronicos Comnenus, and the marriage of Prince Alexis, and there are others on the Empress Irene Doukena and others. Of special interest is the panegyric on the marriage of the Emperor Manuel Comnenus (1143–80) to Bertha von Sulzbach (1146) and on the engagement of a niece of Manuel Comnenus to the half-brother of the German king Conrad III.[102] Unfortunately, this output of panegyric court poetry is very inferior as literature because flattery, and not poetic composition, is its purpose.

The verse chronicle

The casting of history in verse is, as we have seen, a very old Greek practice. One has only to remember the *Persica* of Choerilos of Samos, the numerous *patria* of the ancient cities or the 'historic' encomia on Hellenistic monarchs and early Byzantine emperors to realize how far back the tradition goes and how consistent it was. But this period has something new to offer—a world chronicle in verse, starting from the Creation and reaching up to the days of its author, much on the pattern of the Byzantine prose world chronicles, which started with John Malalas (c. 491–c. 578).

Such is the *Historical Synopsis* of Constantine Manasses (second half of twelfth century), the poet and orator who served as a government official and later entered the Church and became Metropolitan of Naupactus.

His *Synopsis* is composed of 6733 fifteen-syllable verses and deals with the history of the world from the Creation to the death of Nicephoros Botaniatis in 1081. It is dedicated to Princess Irene, sister-in-law of the Emperor Manuel I Comnenus (1143–80) and marks a new attempt to dress universal history in an attractive garb. In content it is entirely derivative, drawing on Dionysius of Halicarnassus, Johannes Lydos, Johannes of Antioch, Pseudo-Symeon and others and, very occasionally, on sources not accessible to us. Moreover, the historical approach is superficial; it moves on the same popular level as the work of Georgios Monachos and Glykas. The narrative is adorned with set speeches, images, literary allusions, mythological references, similes and descriptive passages, handled with verve and considerable taste (hence its popularity, which is attested by the large number of manuscripts we have of that work, as well as by the existence of a prose paraphrase in vernacular Greek and an old Slavonic translation in Bulgarian of 1350). Manasses ends his work with a gross compliment to the Comnenes; he claims that he has not extended his poem to include their reign because their achievements are an ocean of great deeds across which not even Heracles could have sailed.

Manasses also wrote a Ὁδοιπορικόν, a traveller's diary, in some 800 twelve-syllable lines, describing his adventures on a diplomatic mission to Antioch, Jerusalem and Tripolis, which he visited in about 1161, having been sent by Manuel I Comnenus. It is an interesting work in a passable 'epic' style, with many lively descriptions. He also wrote didactic astrological works,[103] ecphrases and other poetry, some of it not yet published. About his verse romance, *Aristandros and Callithea*, we shall speak later,[104] and there is no reason to linger over his short poem in fifty-two political lines on the life of Oppian the Cilician.[105] A moralizing didactic poem of 916 political lines has also been attributed to him, but it probably belongs to one of his imitators.[106]

Among the historical poems of the period may be counted the long, unpublished poem in iambic trimeters composed by Constantine Stilbes (end of twelfth century) on the great fire of Constantinople, which ravaged the city in 1198.[107] Hardly anything is known about the life of its author, who apparently served as a teacher in the Orphanage of the Holy Apostles which Alexius I Comnenus[108] (1081–1118) had founded in the capital. Some insignificant prose works by the same author have also survived, as well as an unimportant poem in fifty-five trimeters on the death of one of his pupils.

Didactic verse

It is not very surprising that in this period, characterized by the revival of learning, a large number of didactic poems should have appeared. Their subjects are heterogeneous and often unsuitable for verse, and the metres employed vary; they include the iambic twelve-syllable line, the fifteen-syllable political line and rhythmical accentual verse.

The list of didactic poets starts with no less a man than the Patriarch Photius (c. 820–c. 893), who composed a canon in rhythmical verse the first ode of which deals with the ages of man.[109] Photius had many followers who wrote didactic poems in the form of Church hymns, of which Niketas, Bishop of Serrae and later Metropolitan of Heraclea (c. 1100), was the most prolific. His verse treated of grammatical, lexicographical and geographical subjects and was composed for the benefit of schoolchildren.[110] But other well-known writers, like Theodoros Prodromos[111] and the historian Johannes Zonaras[112] (first half of twelfth century), followed in his footsteps. Of scurrilous and didactic parodies of religious poetry we have already spoken.[113]

Johannes Mauropous (eleventh century), whose other poetic activities we have examined,[114] chose to write an etymological lexicon in 476 iambic lines, treating of 325 items grouped under four headings (sky and air, man, animals and plants), whose etymology he gives.[115] He composed this, as he himself tells us, 'to find relief from other bitter labours'. On the whole, the work is permeated by a Christian outlook, but traces of older discussions between Stoics and Alexandrians on the nature of language—on whether it developed φύσει or θέσει—can be detected. The influence of the Alexandrian grammarian Philoxenus (first century B.C.) is also apparent, with whose explanations Mauropous often agrees.

A near contemporary of Mauropous was Constantine Manasses (eleventh century), whose other verse we have discussed[116] and who composed a moralizing didactic poem of little merit in 916 fifteen-syllable political lines.[117]

Michael Psellus (1018–97) also contributed long works to the field of didactic verse, if only as *parerga*. The most important of these is his *Compendium on Law*, in iambic and political verses, which he composed for the benefit of his royal pupil, Michael Doucas (Σύνοψις τῶν νόμων διὰ στίχων ἰάμβων καὶ πολιτικῶν πρὸς τὸν Βασιλέα Μιχαὴλ τὸν Δούκαν) and in which he explains a large number of Latin and other legal terms.[118] This is followed by another didactic poem on the Psalms, and a third on rhetoric, in 483 fifteen-syllable lines, addressed to Constantine IX Monomachos,[119] in which dialectal and rare words are treated. He also wrote on medicine, grammar, geometry and other subjects.[120]

Constantine Manasses (second half of twelfth century), whom we have met as the author of a verse chronicle dedicated to Princess Irene, also wrote for the benefit of that *Sebastokratorissa* an astronomical poem of 593 fifteen-syllable lines. It deals with the influence of the planets on the earth and on the lives of men.[121] To Manasses has also been attributed (wrongly) another anonymous didactic, moralizing work, 916 political lines long.[122]

But the most prolific didactic poet of the Byzantine world was undoubtedly Johannes Tzetzes (c. 1110–80).[123] Strictly speaking, his vast didactic output has no place in a history of Greek poetry because the use of verse was for him a mnemonic device and not the outcome of any poetic inspiration. Nevertheless, Tzetzes' works are of interest for his many citations of lost commentaries, handbooks and, occasionally, works of ancient literature (as, for example, the poems of Hipponax which he embedded in his writings).

Johannes Tzetzes was born in Constantinople of a family that had seen better days. He received a good education and was appointed secretary to a provincial governor but was dismissed because of a scandal involving the governor's wife. After working for a time as a secretary, he gained a poor livelihood for the rest of his life by writing and teaching, although he enjoyed for a while the patronage of a lady of the Imperial house and had the sons of distinguished men as his pupils. Late in life he was attached to a monastery but not as a monk. Tzetzes, whose erudition was certainly impressive, was a vain and touchy man. When reduced by poverty to selling his library he claimed that he could rely on his memory, which, unfortunately, frequently let him down.

The best-known and longest of his didactic works is the *Histories* or *Chiliades*—the author himself called it *Βίβλος ἱστοριῶν*[124]—which is a versified commentary on his letters in 12,674 fifteen-syllable lines. In this he elucidates 660 points of mythology, history, literary history and geography alluded to in his 107 letters (some of which are mere rhetorical models and not missives). The *Chiliades* contain much information not available elsewhere, but Tzetzes' careless and hasty way of working causes him to make some unbelievable mistakes. He confuses the Nile and the Euphrates, for instance, and his reliance on his memory, of which he was so proud, makes much of it suspect. In fact, Tztezes' mania for commentaries was such that he provided his own *Chiliades* with marginal scholia, which are partly in verse, political and iambic. As an appendix to the *Chiliades* he also composed three short poems that constitute a bitter attack on the Eparch Kamateros.[125]

The bulk of his other didactic verse consists of commentaries on various ancient Greek poets from Homer to Oppian,[126] but we also find a paraphrase of the entire rhetorical corpus of Hermogenes[127] (its original title was probably *Λογισμοί*); a commentary on Porphyrius' introduction to Aristotle's categories; a poem on allegory called *Χρονικὴ Βίβλος*, not the whole of which has survived;[128] one on tragic poetry; two on metres; one on the differences found in poets[129] (*Περὶ διαφορᾶς Ποιητῶν*); and a theogony which refers to Homer and Hesiod.[130] Some of them are composed in iambic trimeters, others in fifteen-syllable lines. Undoubtedly, the most striking is his long allegorical commentary on the *Iliad* and the *Odyssey*, dedicated to the Empress Irene and consisting of roughly 10,000 political verses.[131] To these should be added his instructions in verse about dramatic and bucolic poetry, which preserve some of the literary theory of antiquity.

Most of these writings are by-products of Tzetzes' activities as a teacher and were either used as textbooks by himself or written on the order of distinguished patrons. They give us a picture of what a scholar—or, rather, book-worm—of twelfth-century Byzantium found of interest. Not all of his works have been published.[132]

A much less well-known figure than Johannes Tzetzes is his older brother, Isaak (born c. 1108), who shared Johannes' interest in Classical studies but apparently had a penchant for metrics. From his pen we have only a didactic poem on the Pindaric metres,[133] preceded by an iambic *prooemium*. The authenticity of two other works that have been attributed to him, verse scholia to Lycophron's *Alexandra*[134] and a didactic astronomical poem,[135] has been challenged.

Theodoros Prodromos (died c. 1166) also engaged in didactic poetry. He composed in the form of a canon a poem on *Equivalents* (Περὶ Ἀντιστοίχων),[136] an astronomical poem in 593 fifteen-syllable lines, in which he speaks about the planets,[137] as well as an allegorical poem on the twelve months of the year, with various dietetic suggestions.[138]

A contemporary of Theodoros Prodromos, Johannes Zonaras, whom we have already met,[139] wrote also in the form of a canon a poem describing various heresies, including those of the Bogomils and of the 'Latins',[140] and Lucas Chrysovergis, Patriarch of Constantinople (1156–69) composed a poem in political verses on fasting (Περὶ Διαίτης).[141]

Finally, a younger contemporary of Theodoros Prodromos, Johannes Kamateros (twelfth century), Archbishop of Bulgaria, wrote an astronomical poem in 1351 iambic lines which he dedicated to the Emperor Manuel Comnenus (1143–80), who was greatly interested in astronomy. The author names as his sources the Babylonian astronomers Selech and Meslas—he knew their works at second-hand—and deals with the planets, the zodiac, the qualities of the stars and their influence on men's lives.[142] (There are other Byzantine astronomical poems which have not yet been published.)

The verse romance

The romantic novels of the late Hellenistic world, in particular those of Achilles Tatius (second century) and Heliodorus (third century?), were, it appears, read and enjoyed by Byzantine scholars; for centuries, however, no new ones were written, as they hardly fitted into a Christian frame of reference. But in the mid and late twelfth century, when Classical models were again more freely copied and pagan thought was more readily accepted, new romantic novels were written which relied slavishly on their Hellenistic predecessors. Their themes were always the adventures of a pair of lovers, separated and united again after a series of terrifying episodes; their setting was invariably the ancient, pre-Christian world; and they always contained descriptive set pieces, like letters, trial scenes, speeches or capture by pirates.

We have three such poor, derivative works in verse, from the last of which only excerpts have survived. Two of them are in iambic trimeters, the third in fifteen-syllable lines, for the feeling for the appropriateness of form to content had long been lost. (In fact, the surviving medieval verse romances in purist Greek are rightly considered the nadir of Byzantine poetry.)[143] The author of the first of these is Theodoros Prodromos, that indefatigable writer whom we have met so often before. It is called *Rhodanthe and Dosicles*, after the names of its heroes, and consists of 4614 iambic trimeters. It is divided into nine books and is the longest of Prodromos' works. The plot is involved: Dosicles, who is in love with Rhodanthe, elopes with her from the city of Abydos, but the couple is captured by pirates on Rhodes. The lovers are parted; Rhodanthe is sold as a slave in Cyprus, while Dosicles is condemned to be sacrificed to the gods. He is luckily freed, however, and reaches Cyprus, where he is reunited with Rhodanthe and where, advised by the Delphic oracle, the two fathers of the lovers arrive. They find their children and all return together to Abydos, where the young couple are married.

The narrative is long, unwieldy, pretentious and barbaric,[144] and the involved and implausible development of the plot demonstrates Prodromos' complete inability to compose a verse romance. In spite of this, the novel was admired, read and copied by Prodromos' pupil, Nicetas Eugenianos (second half of twelfth century).

About Nicetas Eugenianos we know practically nothing. Following the outline of Prodromos' plot, he wrote the novel *Drosilla and Charicles*, a work of 3641 trimeters, which he also divided into nine books. But in a number of details he followed other, older writers, for he draws liberally on the bucolic poets, Musaeus, various epigrammatists of the Greek *Anthology*, the anacreontics, Heliodorus, Achilles Tatius and Longus. The result of this is that Eugenianos' work has many weak, romantic passages and many descriptions in the style of the Second Sophistic. His humour, moreover, wherever it appears, is certainly not civil. Judged as a whole, this novel has nothing original or attractive about it.[145]

We come last to the novel of Constantine Manasses (died c. 1187), *Aristandros and Callithea*, which was composed in fifteen-syllable lines and divided, once again, into nine books. Only excerpts from it survive,[146] in which we find moralizing passages and maxims, and from this we can surmise that the same motifs were used that are found in the older verse romances. In this work, as in his verse chronicle, the *Historical Synopsis*, Manasses employs many images and adopts the same moralizing attitude towards treachery, envy and slander.[147]

Verse dialogues and drama

At the end of the eleventh century the monk Philippos Monotropos (Solitarius) (c. 1095) cast in the form of a dialogue his moralizing work *Dioptra* (*The Mirror of Virtue*).[148] It consisted of four books, each roughly 1700 fifteen-syllable lines long, in which Body and Soul argue in a series of questions and answers. This work, which became very popular (it has even been translated into modern Greek) was preceded by an introduction in iambics and was enlarged by the addition of a fifth book called Κλαυθμοί, (*Lamentations*), which also circulated independently.

All other dialogues of this time, minor works with externally dramatic form, were also intended to be read and not to be performed on the stage.

An example of the Byzantine short, dramatic verse dialogue we have already met in the ninth century in the dialogue on the Fall (Στίχοι εἰς Ἀδάμ) written by Ignatius the Deacon.[149] The genre was revived in the twelfth century by Theodoros Prodromos who composed two such sketches. The first is the *War of the Cat and the Mice* (Κατομυομαχία), a dramatic parody inspired by the pseudo-Homeric *Batrachomyomachia*.[150] In structure, however, it is a miniature drama in five acts with a chorus, a messenger and a *deus ex machina* in the form of a beam that falls from the roof, kills the cat and saves the mice. The work, composed in iambic trimeters, is a parody not only of the dignity (σεμνότης) of ancient tragedy but apparently also of contemporary events and political figures that cannot be identified.[151] It has little to recommend it.[152]

The second is the moralizing dialogue *Friendship in Exile* (Ἀπόδημος φιλία), in which a debate is held between Friendship (Φιλία) and a guest (Ξένος). It is also composed in iambic trimeters. The argument runs that Friendship has been driven out of life and, on the advice of her servant Stupidity, has joined up with the courtesan Enmity. The usefulness of Friendship and the disadvantages of Enmity are then demonstrated with mythological examples. This boring trifle has been rightly called a 'thoroughly schoolmasterish exercise'.[153]

A contemporary of Theodoros Prodromos was Michael Haploucheir (twelfth century), about whom nothing is known. We have from his pen a short sketch (a δραμάτιον, as it is called) 122 trimeters long, in which a farmer (Ἀγροῖκος), a sage, Fortune (Τύχη), the Muses and a chorus take part. Fortune is praised by the farmer, but she is condemned, along with the Muses, by the sage, who complains about his poverty. The Muses finally promise him wealth, but he doubts that the promise will be kept.[154] In this dialogue a crude kind of humour appears, not dissimilar to that which we find in the demotic poems attributed to Theodoros Prodromos.

At this point we must briefly examine the play *Christus Patiens* (Χριστὸς Πάσχων), the only full-length Byzantine dramatic work that has survived, which has been traditionally but wrongly attributed to Gregory of Nazianzus.[155] In actual fact, it is an uninspiring cento of the eleventh or twelfth century by an unknown author, consisting of 2640 verses (all iambic trimeters except for the anapaests of lines 1461 ff.), clearly meant to be read and not to be acted.[156] The play begins with Christ's ascent to Golgotha and ends with the Resurrection and the Lord's appearance at the house of Mark's mother. The chorus, consisting of women of Galilee, does not sing but speaks in iambic trimeters. The central figure of the piece is Mary, not Christ, who is kept in the background and about whom we only hear from others. There is hardly any plot and no dramatic tension, the largest part of the play consisting of messengers' speeches and lamentations.

Its author draws on Scripture and the Apocryphal Gospels for both his subject and his diction; occasionally he also draws on well-known early Byzantine religious poetry. He also uses numerous lines, half-lines and formulae from Classical and Hellenistic plays. Most of this material is Euripidean, taken and adapted from the *Hecuba, Medea, Orestes, Hippolytus, Troades, Bacchae* and *Rhoesus*, but lines can be traced which are Aeschylean —from the *Agamemnon* and the *Prometheus*—and some from Lycophron's *Alexandra*; there must be others deriving from plays now lost. All this should not be judged in the light of a modern view of plagiarism. It is typical, 'praiseworthy' Byzantine imitation of the classics, which dominates much highbrow Byzantine writing;[157] and the play must have been widely read if we are to judge by the vast number of manuscripts in which it is transmitted.

In conclusion, perhaps a few words should be added here about the *Scenario from Cyprus* which has been lately discovered and which was thought to support the existence of Byzantine passion plays.[158] This has nothing to do with Byzantine drama and is one more illustration of the fact that the Lusignans, who ruled the island from 1192 to 1489, wished to impose on their Greek subjects in Cyprus the dramatization of Holy Week which was traditional at home.[159]

POETRY COMPOSED IN THE VERNACULAR

We must now turn to poetry composed in the vernacular, which makes its appearance in this period. The earliest examples are connected with the

Akritic Epic Cycle, to which, according to most scholars, the origins of modern Greek poetry can be traced.[160]

The Epic Cycle of Digenis Akritas

Of all the frontiers of the Byzantine Empire the most unsafe and the most frequently assaulted was the eastern. There the Persians, who were defeated by Heraclius, were succeeded by the Arabs, their conquerors. The struggle of Byzantium with the Arab world lasted from the seventh to the eleventh centuries, and the turning-point came in the middle of the ninth, when Byzantium, from a position of defence, took the offensive. By the tenth century the Byzantine armies had penetrated deep into Syria, and shortly afterwards the eastern front reached stalemate. A kind of friendly coexistence came about between Arab and Greek and lasted until the onslaught of the Seljuk Turks, which completely changed the picture in the Middle East.

In order to conduct this perennial war with the Arabs, the Byzantine Empire had organized its provinces into military governments called *themata*, each with a general (*strategos*) at its head. Facing the Byzantine military provinces of Cappadocia and Mesopotamia, the Muslim world had its own organization. The emirs of Erzurum and Melitene or of Mosul kept a large number of soldiers under their standards to protect the frontiers of the caliphate. Thus from the Black Sea to the deserts of Syria stretched a double line of enemy posts with armed men under the command of *strategoi* or emirs.

The Byzantine military leaders of those days did not boast of blind submission to their sovereigns in Constantinople, and the emirs too, taking advantage of the decline of the caliphate, led the life of independent princes, contracting alliances as they pleased; subordinates on both sides imitated their chiefs. In this state of universal disorder Christian and Muslim adventurers found a way of creating small, virtually independent principalities between the two powers, and bands of irregular and marauding forces — the *apelatai* of the Akritic Cycle — were also formed. The Middle East resounded with stories of their feats of arms and with the fame and glory of this or that individual.

So away from Constantinople, with her highly polished court, her formal bureaucracy, her endless theological disputes and her scholarly tastes, in the turbulent provinces of the East environment and conditions were conducive to the birth of an epic cycle, and it was there, between the ninth and the eleventh centuries, that the Akritic Cycle came into being. The central figure in this cycle is Basil Digenis Akritas, whose very name indicates the strange, mixed life of those Byzantine provinces. For 'Akritas' signifies a man protecting the limits (the *akra*) of the Empire, and

'Digenis' means the offspring of two races. Basil Digenis Akritas is said to have been the son of a Saracen father and a Greek mother who belonged to the noble Doucas family. This heroic figure is naturally represented in idealized terms, huge in stature, unsurpassed in the skills of wrestling and hunting, a man of keen intelligence and unique valour, who even challenges *Charos* (Death) to wrestle with him 'on the marble threshing-floor'. In fact, Digenis, as presented in the Akritic Cycle, is the personification of Greek heroic manhood, and in his physical and psychological make-up one discerns the qualities traditionally attributed to Alexander the Great and the mythological Heracles. It is not improbable that a real historical person looms behind the figure of Digenis Akritas, but none of the identifications made so far is convincing.[161]

Although it probably originated in Commagene or Euphratesia, this epic cycle captured the imagination of the people and spread from the burning deserts of Syria to the frozen Russian steppes and even reached the remote Greek colonies of Magna Graecia. From the vigorous Akritic Cycle of the mid-Byzantine period we possess today only a relatively small number of ballads and half a dozen versions dating from the fourteenth to the seventeenth centuries of a long poem known as the *Epic of Digenis Akritas*, as well as four Russian versions, none of which goes further back than the fourteenth century.

We will first examine the Akritic ballads and then proceed to the *Epic* itself.

THE AKRITIC BALLADS

As early as the ninth century we hear from Arethas of Caesarea of singers of heroic ballads, whom he calls 'wandering beggars, like cursed Paphlagonians, who now make up songs about the adventures of famous men and sing them for pennies from door to door';[162] the existence of such singers is confirmed by Theophanes Continuatus.[163] However, with the sole exception of the *Song of Armouris*, no Akritic ballads were committed to writing before the nineteenth century. This means that for many years these songs survived as oral poetry, handed down from generation to generation and transmitted from place to place. In the course of this process, as would be expected, they have been considerably transformed both in content and in linguistic form; nevertheless, they can easily be identified by their subjects and by the names of persons known in Byzantine history. The majority of these ballads come from Asia Minor (especially the Pontus) and the islands of Cyprus, the Dodecanese and Crete. The most important are the following.

First, the *Song of Armouris*. This consists of 201 fifteen-syllable lines (in the Leningrad version) and deals tersely with the epic motif of the son who frees his father from captivity. It is a masterpiece of its kind and, having been committed to writing in the fifteenth century, has suffered few changes in its original form. This makes it the oldest poem we have in the vernacular, a genuine example of a mid-Byzantine heroic ballad. H. Grégoire has connected this song with the victories of Michael III (842–67) of the Amorian dynasty, who avenged the defeat of his father Theophilus and the fall of Amorion in Phrygia (838).[164] A version of it is still sung in Cyprus.

Second, the ballads of Andronikos and Constantine. The origins of this group of ballads seem to go back to the eleventh century and to be rooted in true historical events. According to Grégoire, they are directly connected with the Doucas family, and in particular with Andronikos and Constantine Doucas, who were much honoured by the army and loved by their followers in Constantinople.[165] Of this group three should be singled out. The *Song of Andronikos*, which varies in length between fifty and sixty fifteen-syllable lines according to different versions, tells the tale of a brave young man who breaks free from captivity and sets out to find his father. This he achieves, but the two nearly engage in a fight before recognizing one another. The *Song of the Prisoner* treats of the same subject as the *Song of Andronikos* and is considered by some scholars to be the oldest of the group. The *Song of Porphyris* survives in more than thirty versions, varying in length between forty and fifty political lines. It deals with Porphyris (probably short for Porphyrogenitus), a young Cappadocian who boasts that he is greater than the emperor. Captured at the emperor's command, he is forced to march in fetters before the castle, in which the maiden whom he loves is living. At her instigation, he breaks his shackles, kills a large number of his pursuers and frees himself.

Third, the ballads on the death of Digenis. More than 1100 ballads on this subject are known, and some are of extreme beauty,[166] true hymns of manly courage and dignity. They have been called 'the epitaph of the heroes of all ages'.[167]

Finally, the well-known modern Greek folk song, *The Castle of the Beautiful Maiden* (*Τὸ Κάστρο τῆς Ὡριᾶς*), of which 140 versions exist, has also been connected with the fall of Amorion in 838 and therefore considered to be among the important surviving Akritic songs.[168]

Side by side with these oustanding ballads a vast number of lesser ones have come down to us whose origins are thought to go back to the ninth, tenth and eleventh centuries. They give a vivid picture of the spirit prevailing on the eastern borders of the Byzantine Empire in those days and of the ceaseless fighting between Arab and Greek. Of these lesser songs special mention should perhaps be made of the *Song of Theophylactos*, whose hero is thought to be the father of the Emperor Romanos Lecapenus (919–44). We shall deal later with the ballads that derive from the text of the *Epic of Digenis Akritas*.[169]

Before leaving the Akritic ballads, their impressive simplicity and vigour should be stressed; they stand in direct contrast to the anaemic so-called 'epic', whose literary qualities are minimal.

THE *EPIC OF DIGENIS AKRITAS*

The term 'epic' has rarely been more misapplied than in the case of the so-called *Epic of Digenis Akritas*, which is clearly in no sense an epic and is not even a single unit. It consists of two separate verse romances (probably originally the work of two different poets mechanically joined together), whose mid-Byzantine archetypes are now lost. All we have today are five later Greek versions in verse and one in prose, which range from the fourteenth[170] to the seventeenth centuries, and three prose Slavonic versions, as well as the fragment of a fourth; none of these is older than the fourteenth century.

The Greek versions are the following. First, that of Grotta Ferrata of the late thirteenth or early fourteenth century, which consists of 3749 non-rhyming fifteen-syllable lines and is divided into eight books. Second, that of Trebizond of the sixteenth century, 3180 political lines long and divided into ten books. The beginning is missing and it has several gaps.[171] Third, the Andros verse version (also known as the Athens version because the manuscript was brought to the National Library in Athens) of the sixteenth century, 4778 political lines long. It is also divided into ten books and in every respect is very close to that of Trebizond. Fourth, the Escorial version of the sixteenth century, which has only 1867 political lines and whose language is 'vernacular', in many respects close to that of the ballads; its fifteen-syllable lines are often broken into half-lines, the so-called *tsakismata*, or overflow of the metre. Fifth, the Oxford rhyming version of the seventeenth century, in 3095 rhyming fifteen-syllable lines —the only one which makes use of rhyme—which is signed by Ignatios Petrides, a Chiot monk, and dated 25 November 1670. Sixth, the Andros prose version, which is little more than a rendering into prose of the one of Andros in verse. It was composed by the Chiot Meletios Vlastos in 1632 and is now in the library of the University of Thessalonica. We also know that Caesarios Dapontes[172] (1711–84) saw on Mount Athos two more copies of the *Epic of Digenis Akritas*—one of them with miniatures—which are now lost,[173] and no doubt other written variants that have not survived must have circulated in the Greek world.

Of the four Russian versions (one consists only of titles of chapters and a few extracts from a burnt sixteenth-century manuscript once in the Mušin-Puškin Collection) none goes further back than the fourteenth or fifteenth century;[174] and it should be noted that there are differences between them and their Greek counterparts.[175]

Although the several Greek versions of the Digenis epic differ in language and in the number and sequence of the episodes included, as well as in many details, they all have virtually the same plot. This falls into two parts, corresponding to what can be called the 'Song of the Emir' and the 'Romance of Digenis Akritas'.[176] In outline it runs as follows.

In the first part, the 'Song of the Emir', a raiding Arab emir of Greek origin—he was captured by the Arabs as a child and brought up in the Mohammedan faith—kidnaps from her Cappadocian home the daughter of a Byzantine prince of the Doukas family. The young girl's brothers pursue the emir, defeat him in battle and force him to return to Byzantine territory. There he is converted to Christianity and marries the girl he kidnapped. A son is born of this union, whom they name Basil Digenis Akritas. Later, after many adventures, the emir returns to Arab lands and brings back with him his mother and the rest of his family, as well as many Arab followers who all become Christians and establish themselves permanently within the boundaries of the Byzantine Empire.

The second part, the 'Romance of Digenis', starts with descriptions of Digenis' childhood, education and training in the use of arms. Such is the young boy's ability and courage that on his very first hunt he kills a lion and two bears. The story of the manhood of Digenis is then recounted—his various adventures with bands of marauding outlaws (the *apelatai*) and his courtship of Eudocia, the daughter of a Byzantine border baron. He wins her love, and she runs away from her home to live with him in the wild border lands. There Akritas engages in killing bandits and in imposing law and order. The fame of his exploits spreads and even reaches the emperor, who visits him and admires a display of his prowess.

A long section follows in which Basil narrates a number of his adventures—the narrative moves from the third to the first person—including an affair he had with the daughter of an Emir, how he rescued Eudocia from the attack of a dragon and his single-handed combat with the formidable Amazon, Maximo, who tried in vain to seduce him after her defeat.

Digenis then proceeds to build a great castle with a splendid garden near the river Euphrates—the narrative returns to the third person—and descriptions of his life there follow, which include many strange details. Finally, at the age of thirty-three (the age at which Alexander the Great died) he falls seriously ill and, in a speech to Eudocia, recalls the happy life they have spent together. As she prays for his recovery, he expires, and she drops dead beside him. His funeral and tomb are also described—the latter recalling the famous tomb of Cyrus the Great at Pasargadae,[177] and the poem ends with a moralizing passage on the vanity of life and worldly glory.

The link between the two parts of the poem, the 'Song of the Emir' and the 'Romance of Digenis', is tenuous and external. They seem to have been joined together because the first deals with the father of Digenis and mentions the birth of Basil. Beyond this there is little the two have in common. The differences, in fact, are marked, for whereas in the 'Song of the Emir' the narrative flows smoothly and uninterruptedly, and true historical events can be traced in it,[178] in the 'Romance of Digenis' plot and background are purely fictitious, moulded on the pattern of the late Hellenistic romances, and the narrative is highly episodic, shifting from the third to the first person and back again to the third. Moreover, Akritas' lineage on his mother's side is given differently in the two sections. It appears probable, therefore, that the two parts of the epic were not the work of the same man and perhaps were not even fully contemporary. Nor do we know when the two were joined. This probably took place at the stage of the poem's history when, as it appears, it went through a period of oral transmission, about which we shall speak presently.

If we now turn to the sources of the *Epic of Digenis Akritas*—and for this purpose let us examine it as a whole—we shall see that no single existing Akritic ballad can have served as a source. The central figure, Digenis Akritas, is, of course, the hero of many, and two groups of such songs—those dealing with the snatching of the bride and those describing his death—cover ground common to parts of the epic; but direct dependence on the ballads cannot be shown.[179] On the other hand, there is a group of ballads that no doubt derives fully or partly from the text of the epic and supports the view that it must also have gone through a period of oral transmission. Most noteworthy of them are *The Palace of Digenis* (᾿Ακρίτας κάστρον ἔκτιζε),[180] *The Daughter of the Brave King* (῾Η κόρη τοῦ Λεβέντη Βασιλιᾶ),[181] and *The Snatching of the General's Daughter* (Τρεῖς ἄρχοντες ἐκάτσασιν νὰ φᾶσιν καὶ νὰ πιοῦσιν),[182] which derive from the descriptions of the palace and garden of Digenis in the epic,[183] descriptions that depend in their turn on Achilles Tatius.[184]

The dependence of the epic on passages of Achilles Tatius is only one of the many references to Classical, Hellenistic and Byzantine literature that have been traced in the texts and which prove that the original poets of the 'Song of the Emir' and the 'Romance of Digenis Akritas' were learned men and not illiterate, wandering singers. How else can one explain the quotations from Homer, the Homeric Hymns, Pindar, Arrian, Pseudo-Callisthenes' *Life of Alexander*, *Genesis*, the *Life of Barlaam and Ioasaph*, as well as the Herculean myths, to mention only a few striking examples?[185]

At the same time, important points of contact have been detected between the erudite romances of Eustathios Macrembolites and Theodoros Prodromos (both of the twelfth century),[186] as well as passages common to late Byzantine verse romances, like *Callimachus and Chrysorrhoe*, *Lybistros and Rhodamne*, the *Achilleis*, and even *Imberios and Margarona*, to say nothing of moralizing allegorical poems like Meliteniotes' *On Wisdom* (fourteen century). Naturally, none of these could have served as a source of the original works from which all the extant versions of the epic derive. The only plausible explanation is that during a period when the epic went through a stage of oral transmission some of these passages were grafted on to it by oral singers, whose repertoire included those 'later' poems. For the tendency of oral poets to mix materials at their disposal for the sake of variety or in order to avoid a pause in their recitation is well-known;[187] it is equally probable that points of contact with texts such as the romances of Eustathios Macrembolites and Theodoros Prodromos are due to later pen-poets, who elaborated upon the oral texts after they were committed to writing.

It has also been observed that many episodes we meet in the Akritic Cycle have their counterparts in Oriental narratives. For the Arabs also had their national epic, which celebrated the feats of their emirs and other heroes; so it is not surprising that many of their deeds, so similar to those of the Akritic warriors, found their way into narratives like the romances of Sayyid Battal and Köroglou, the Arabic prose novel of Dhât al Himma, the romance of Antar, the *Arabian Nights* and even Firdūsī's *Book of the Kings*.[188]

It is also worth mentioning that the adventures and deeds of the Greeks and Arabs of Euphratesia reached the West through the Crusaders and can be traced in the Latin verses on the First Crusade, the *Niebelungenlied*, the *Cid* and the achievements of Roland and William Tell.[189]

As already noted, such historical data as can be detected in the epic belong to the first part, the 'Song of the Emir'. Apart from the general background and the historical truth of a reconciliation of sorts between Arabs and Greeks that we find in it, we come across the hanging stone in the mosque of Palermo,[190] and the names Ambron for the emir's grandfather, Chrysoberges or Chrysocherpes for his father and Karoes for one of his uncles. All three, though somewhat transformed, are names of men connected with the Paulician movement.[191] The Paulicians, members of a sect of the Byzantine Empire, had operated under the emirs of Melitene, the greatest of whom was Omar-ibn-al-Aqta, known in the Byzantine world as Amer or Ambros. His nephew, who was also an emir of Melitene, came over to the Byzantine side and fought against the Mohammedans. According to Arab sources, shortly after about 935–40 a whole tribe, the Banu Habib, crossed the borders, established themselves in Byzantine territory and took part in the war against the Muslims.

Equally interesting is the mention of Neman's Sacred Kerchief,[192] which in about 944 was given by the people of Edessa to the Byzantine Greeks, who brought it to Constantinople. It is said that it had been received by King Abgar of Edessa from Christ's own hands and that traces of the Lord's features could be discerned on it.[193]

These figures and events of the ninth and tenth centuries, though transformed, have crept into the 'Song of the Emir', so it would be reasonable to assume that the song itself in its original form was not composed much later. In fact, one could readily agree with those scholars who see it as a product of the mixed Byzantine–Arab culture of the eastern provinces of which Melitene was the capital.

On the other hand, in the 'Romance of Digenis' no historical events can be detected; background and setting are totally fictitious. Nevertheless, a number of names have crept in that, though in most cases greatly altered, seem to be those of real historical figures, some of whom may hark back to a very distant past. Such are the Emperors Basil[194] and Romanos,[195] Joannakes, Philopappous, Kinnamos, the Amazon Maximo and Melimitzes. The Basil mentioned is probably Basil I (867–86), the Romanos probably Romanos I Lecapenus (919–44)[196] and the Joannakes probably Armenian Jiachnoukas, who was powerful in Mesopotamia in about 900.[197]

Much more surprising and less probable is the identification of Philopappous, whom we meet in the Akritic ballads, with the last king of Commagene, Antiochus Philopappus, who died in exile in Athens. The ruins of the monument he set up there between A.D. 114 and 116 still crown the Hill of Philopappus, south-west of the Acropolis of Athens. It is known that the family of Antiochus Philopappus lost its kingdom to the Romans in A.D. 72, during the Parthian Wars, and that the country did not readily submit to its conquerors. It has therefore been suggested that the last king of Commagene (or another king of the same name) became a symbol of liberty and of the local dynasty of rulers, and that in the course of the first century A.D. an epic was woven around his name which was handed down from generation to generation until the ninth century, when parts of it were incorporated into the *Epic of Digenis Akritas*. But though debased in the new epic cycle in which he was portrayed—Philopappous appears in the Akritic ballads in humble roles, those of a servant or a proxy—he still retains something of his former stature, for he knows a magic secret and teaches Digenis how to construct his musical instrument, the magic *thambouras*.[198]

Kinnamos has been identified with the Parthian leader, Cinnamus, who was crowned king of Persia in A.D. 40 but later abdicated. He is said to have been popular in Mesopotamia, and Josephus mentions him with praise,[199] so it is thought that his exploits may have been sung by both Persians and Greeks and were later drawn into the epic.

The battle with an Amazon in the 'Romance of Digenis' clearly derives from the adventures constructed around the life of Alexander the Great,[200] but the name Maximo is peculiar, being a diminutive for Maximilla, a Roman name rare in the Greek world. Strangely enough, in Sebastoupolis –Heracleopolis of the Pontus an inscription has been found in honour of a priestess Maxima, also called Amazonis (Μάξιμα ἡ καὶ ᾽Αμαζονὶς . . . ματρῶνα στολάτα).[201] This inscription was carved at the command of her husband Julios Potitos, a state official, in about A.D. 199. H. Grégoire has suggested that the name of that inscription 'from the land of the Amazons' caught the imagination of the people and passed into local folk songs and folk tales, where it became fused with the Amazons of the Alexander romance. It is an ingenious but improbable theory.

Last, Melimitzes, the leader of Maximo's band of *apelatai*, has been identified by Grégoire and Adontz[202] as the famous Byzantine–Armenian Melias, who lived in the reign of Leo VI (886–912) and was a friend of the Doucas family; he was the founder and first *strategos* of the theme of Lykandus.

Thus the epic cycle of Digenis Akritas may perhaps help us to trace relics, no matter how transformed, of Hellenistic and early Byzantine epics and folk songs, which were probably lost and forgotten when the achievements of later Christian and Muslim warriors overshadowed the deeds of their heroes. The older heroes, it is suggested, were then deflated and ridiculed, just as Charlemagne was ridiculed in the late *chansons de geste* and the chivalrous romances.

What emerges from this study of the strange, confused and confusing *Epic of Digenis Akritas* is that in order to solve its problems we must assume three important stages in its history.

The first is that of the original texts, of the 'Song of the Emir' and the 'Romance of Digenis', which were apparently not composed by the same man and were clearly the works of educated, 'erudite' pen-poets, who were familiar with the classics. Moreover, the knowledge these poets show of the geography and life of the eastern borders of the Empire suggests that even if Constantinopolitan by birth, they must have lived at least part of their lives in the East.

The second stage which must be assumed is that during which the erudite written texts passed into the world of oral poetry, for unmistakable characteristics of oral composition can be detected in the surviving versions. These are the suppression of the names of the original poets; the entirely episodic structure of a simple story, with the inevitable transposition of episodes and lines in the different versions; the variety in the sizes of those versions; narrative inconsistencies; lack of *enjambement*; conventional descriptions of battles, castles and adventures of love; the detailed presentation of garments, armour, horses' harnesses and so on; the shifting of the narrative from the third to the first person; contamination from other poems that were part of the oral poet's repertoire; and the independent creation of short folk songs from detached parts of the longer oral versions.

But perhaps the clearest proof that the *Epic of Digenis Akritas* passed through a period of oral transmission is the Escorial version itself, which can be nothing other than the product of direct dictation by a wandering Cretan ballad singer, who was trying to recite from memory in the musical recitative that still survives in Crete. Its disorder, the innumerable omissions, additions of irrelevant tags from ballads, the repetitions of the same lines, phonetic confusions, the use of formulae,[203] the way the words overflow the metre and the manner in which the metre breaks off into half-lines — the τσαχίσματα of the modern Greek folk songs — fully substantiate this view. Note also the beginning of the Andros versions: 'My dearest and beloved child, you have demanded many times that I should make known *in writing* all the exploits of Digenis Akritas, and I have obeyed your words . . .', from which it is clear that Eustathius,[204] its composer, and Manuel, for whom the text was written, had heard oral versions of the Digenis epics, some of which may well have been prose folk tales similar in genre to the extant Russian prose version.

We do not know when this transition from written texts to the world of oral poetry took place, but it must have been during this period of the epic's history that it was split into various versions, which gradually became contaminated with other oral material. It is possible that the Paulician elements found in our texts may be due to such contamination, and the same may be true of elements that are also found in the texts of the Arab epic or even of items like the Kerchief of Edessa. But what should be borne in mind is that some of these contaminations may derive from oral poems older in origin than the Digenis epic, and therefore they cannot be used as *termini* for dating the archetype, although many scholars have attempted to do this. Moreover, it was probably at this stage of the poem's history that the 'Song of the Emir' was joined to the 'Romance of Digenis' by oral singers to whose repertoire both belonged, just as at this stage the epic must have given birth to a number of 'younger' Akritic ballads, as well as to folk tales about Digenis based upon it.

The existence of a widespread oral poetic tradition — for how else could the Akritic ballads and the epic have wandered from Commagene to Magna Graecia? — is of great importance to the history of later Greek poetry; this is the earliest instance of it that we can attest with some certainty.

The third and last presumed stage in the history of the *Epic of Digenis Akritas* is the one in which some of the oral versions circulating in the Greek world were committed to writing and then elaborated upon by pen-poets (the latter not being the case with the Escorial version). It is these pen-poets who subdued certain characteristic elements of oral poetry, like the frequent use of formulae,[205] and introduced many new ones from other poems they knew; among them were probably elements from the erudite twelfth-century Byzantine verse romances and Meliteniotes' Εἰς τὴν Σωφροσύνην (*On Wisdom*). How complete the transformation of a poem can be in the hands of a pen-poet is well illustrated in the Oxford rhyming version of the Digenis epic, which in form has little in common with the original source. It is at this final stage of the poem's history that the pen-poets also divided their texts into eight or ten books and added the introductory verses.

What must be stressed once again is that we can now be certain that poems orally transmitted often originate in written texts,[206] and that each recitation of an orally transmitted poem should be considered an independent composition. For oral poets deliberately change or add lines and episodes in every recitation of the same poem, not because their memories are unreliable but because they consider that this modification is creative and because it flatters their pride as 'poets'.[207]

In view of this practice, which must be seen as an important feature in the transmission of the texts, we cannot tell what was the exact linguistic form of the original 'Song of the Emir' and 'Romance of Digenis'. Of the extant versions, the most conservative linguistically is the Trebizond, from which the Andros version differs little. Most demotic in diction and closest to the language of the ballads is the Escorial version. The Oxford rhyming version and the prose version of Andros, belonging to the seventeenth century, are of less linguistic interest.

Judged as poetry, both parts of the *Epic of Digenis Akritas* are disappointingly poor. Scholars of medieval and modern Greek, who have been fascinated by this strange and unusual composition, have greatly overrated its poetic qualities and have unjustifiably dubbed it 'the epic of medieval and modern Greece'. Except for the choice of great warriors as its central heroes and its reflection of the belligerent atmosphere of the eastern Byzantine provinces in the ninth and tenth centuries, there is nothing that is 'epic' about it; nor should we lose sight of the fact that the central motif of the work is 'erotic'. It is for their own personal glory and not *ad majorem gloriam* of Hellenism or Orthodox Christianity that the emir and Digenis battle. In no way can it be said to depict the battle of Christianity against Islam. Furthermore, there is little that can be called dramatic in the plot (or plots), and there is no subtlety in the character drawing (as is the case with most works dealing with figures that become 'typical' in a literary tradition). Finally, no doubt because of the period of oral transmission through which the epic passed, all the extant versions lack unity of structure, and details give rise to long digressions not unlike those found in Byzantine chroniclers and hagiographers. The simplicity and austerity of the folk songs is missing.

It would be unfair, however, not to admit the existence of some felicitous imagery and the liveliness of some of the dialogue, even if it is too often inclined to be sententious. There is also a clear appreciation of cultural values and religious tolerance.

In conclusion, it should be noted that though the *Epic of Digenis Akritas* can be seen as the forerunner of the erudite verse romances that appeared in the days of the Comnenes, it had hardly any influence on subsequent medieval and modern Greek literature. Such influence as it exercised is detectable in the heroes of late Byzantine verse romances in the vernacular[208] and very slightly in Kostis Palamas and some of his successors.[209]

The Ptochoprodromic poems and other verse in the vernacular

We must now examine the other works written in the vernacular that appeared in this period. Though second-rate as poetry, they are of capital significance in the history of Greek literature. Together with the Akritic poems, they are the oldest documents we possess written in a language closely approximating to the spoken idiom of those days; from them stems the tradition leading to the great Cretan poetic renaissance and through that to modern Greek poetry. It should be noted, however, that the idiom used in these works is not a pure form of the Greek spoken in the days of the Comnenes. It was influenced to some extent by the pseudo-Atticism of learned Byzantine writers, who were always keen to display their erudition by using the words, grammar and syntax of former and greater periods of Greek literature, from Homer to the early Fathers of the Church.

The earliest examples of personal verse in a spoken idiom are four vivid, satirical poems known as Ptochoprodromic poems; for all the poetry composed in the vernacular we have seen so far is that of 'impersonal' folk songs and one anonymous version — the Escorial — of the *Epic of Digenis Akritas.*

The first of these Ptochoprodromic poems has come down to us in one manuscript only[210] and consists of 274 non-rhyming fifteen-syllable lines. It begins by thanking the Emperor John II (1118–43) for his generosity (in appreciation of which the poet wrote this poem). The author then proceeds to describe the misery which his ill-tempered and querulous wife inflicts upon him and the hunger he suffers as a result of poverty and her heartless behaviour. He concludes by stressing that if the emperor does not come to his aid, he will soon die of hunger. The poet's intention is to amuse his patron and, by raillery and banter, to elicit financial support. The well-known trick of assuming a confidential tone is also used. The humour is often coarse and in bad taste, but the family scenes described are lively and even truly comic.

The second poem, consisting of 117 non-rhyming fifteen-syllable lines, is addressed to the *Sebastocrator* (probably a son of the Emperor John II) and describes the poverty and misery of the poet's home. It is intended to amuse the prince and at the same time to elicit his pity. But the tone is forced — there is nothing in it of the biting satire and buffoonery of the first Ptochoprodromic poem — and the list of household needs is pedantic and boring. This poem has come down to us in two manuscripts,[211] which display considerable differences in the sequence and fullness of the narrative, a fact that probably points to a period of oral transmission through which the poem may have passed.

The third poem, which is in 447 non-rhyming fifteen-syllable lines, attacks Byzantine monastic life. It is addressed to the Emperor Manuel Comnenus (1143–80) and describes the greed of the abbots and the suffering of timid monks and novices at their hands. As satire, this is clearly the best of the four Ptochoprodromic poems and is in keeping with much Byzantine derision of monastic life and with the Comnenes' views on monasteries, on which they tried to impose order, though with little success. It has come down in no less than seven manuscripts,[212] and the variants and changes we meet in them once again support the view that at some stage it too was probably transmitted orally.[213]

The fourth and last Ptochoprodromic poem is also addressed to 'The Emperor'—we do not know which emperor—and consists of 292 non-rhyming fifteen-syllable lines in one version and 167 in another. It is a virulent attack on learning and teaching by a hungry scholar who, disgusted with a scholar's life, sings the praises of other professions and of the happy life of merchants and artisans. The line

ἀνάθεμα τὰ γράμματα, Χριστέ, καὶ ποὺ τὰ θέλει
Cursed be learning, my Christ, and cursed those who wish to be educated

has become proverbial. Once again, the financial help of the Emperor is solicited. The fact that this poem has survived in five manuscripts,[214] with variations similar to those of the second and third Ptochoprodromic poems, suggests an oral phase in its transmission.

These four humorous works[215] are social documents of great importance that throw light on the life of lower bourgeois society in the twelfth century. Particularly attractive are the realistic touches through which we get a glimpse of the life and bustle of the capital city, including the cries of the street vendors, and the impression the poems give of the freedom of thought that prevailed in those times, the spirit of the renaissance of the Comnenes which was cut short by the Fourth Crusade in 1204. These poems contain elements similar to those we meet at that time in the West, when city life was developing, universities were being founded and an intellectual proletariat appeared for the first time. From a literary point of view, however, they are certainly not in the least remarkable, for they are undisciplined, long-winded and full of trivialities and obscure passages.[216]

The problem of their authorship also remains unsolved. The first editors, A. Koraes, E. Miller and E. Legrand, attributed them to Theodoros Prodromos, the well-known man of letters of the twelfth century of whom we have already repeatedly spoken,[217] but neither the language nor the circumstances of Prodromos' life justify this ascription. Later it was suggested by S. Papademetriou and G. Hatzidakis that there were two or even three authors with the name Prodromos, among them a monk named Hilarion, and that at least two were responsible for the Ptochoprodromic poems in the vernacular.[218] The theory has also been put forward that later in life Theodoros Prodromos became a monk. None of these views is tenable, nor are the linguistic differences found in the four poems such as to substantiate the hypothesis of multiple authorship.[219]

The most plausible view is that the Ptochoprodromic poems were originally written texts addressed to important patrons, emperors and *sebastocratores* and that they were drawn into the orbit of oral poetry because their subjects—the evil wife, the poverty-stricken father, the greedy abbot, the hungry scholar—were suitable for popular humorous recitations. In the course of their oral career their lively humour and coarseness may even have been heightened and thus a whole genre of low 'beggar poetry' came into being in which others followed and among them men of distinction such as Manuel Philes.[220] Whether some or all of the original written texts addressing the emperors and the *Sebastocrator* were the works of one man named Prodromos or of more than one we cannot know with any certainty; nor can we ascertain the exact form of the Greek in which they were originally written. As Theodoros Prodromos was known for petitionary poems of a similar sort, some unknown writers' works could easily have been attributed to him; they may even have placed their words in his mouth. It is of interest to observe, however, that the beginnings of the poems, the dedications to the patrons and many of the endings point to a much more educated form of Greek than that in which the main 'humorous' narratives are composed.[221] To Theodoros Prodromos have also been wrongly ascribed seven short love poems composed in the vernacular and cast in political verses. They are transmitted in a manuscript of the fifteenth century and display a kind of simple charm not unlike that of the folk songs.[222]

The two other poems that are connected directly with the Comnene court, the *Spaneas* and Michael Glykas' *On His Imprisonment*, are of less importance than the Ptochoprodromic poems.

The *Spaneas* is difficult to date with precision. Its true title is Διδασκαλία Παραινετική (*Didactic Exhortation*), and it consists of advice given by an elderly courtier, possibly a member of the Imperial house, to a young prince. It is an outline of court morals and etiquette which draws heavily on all the commonplace advice of the Pseudo-Isocratean *Ad Demonicum*, a work much read by the Byzantine Greeks. The author also draws heavily on the Scriptures, hence the poem presents a fusion of Christian and pagan views on virtue.

The title *Spaneas* (*The Beardless Man*) has given rise to much controversy; it has been thought to refer either to the author of the poem or to the person to whom it is addressed. Alexius Comnenus, the eldest son of the Emperor John II (1118–43), has been suggested as the author, but this and other suggestions[223] are unfounded. Nor is it probable that the young prince to whom it is addressed is a son of the sister of Emperor John II and the Sicilian 'Caesar', John Roger.[224]

The *Spaneas* is known from roughly twenty manuscripts and in many versions, varying from 200 to 670 fifteen-syllable lines. One[225] is in a relatively purist form of Greek, and there are also two Russian versions. The number and kind of the variants point once again to a period of oral transmission.

Michael Glykas (c. 1160), a native of Corfu, is a well-known man of letters who wrote a world chronicle, theological works and letters, all in the purist idiom. As a young man he was cast into prison on a charge unknown to us and wrote a poem in the vernacular (which, however, is mixed with erudite elements), *On His Imprisonment*, in which he described the hardships he was suffering. Through it he tried to elicit clemency from the Emperor Manuel I (1143–80), explaining that his predicament was due entirely to a neighbour's slander. The poem was written in 1158–9[226] and, according to a note in the manuscript, Glykas was condemned to be blinded. The penalty could not have been carried out because we find him later free and continuing his career as an author.

Glykas draws on the Scriptures, and the poem contains reflections on the changes of life, as well as some humorous passages (for example, ll. 270ff.). The didactic element, which often comes to the fore, is enhanced by the many proverbs quoted in the demotic.

Glykas seems to have had a predilection for short, pithy sayings, for he also put together a separate collection of proverbs, together with their theological interpretations.

Satires against abbots and monks were popular in the Middle Ages. We find one in the poem *The Philosophy of the Drinking Monk*, which consists of 118 non-rhyming political lines and is probably contemporary with the Ptochoprodromic poems. It is a piece of gross irony that parodies the liturgy and quotes the Scriptures in singing the praises of drink. There is much that is shocking and deplorable about it.[227]

SECTION III

From the Conquest of Constantinople
by the Franks to the Fall of the City
to the Turks (1204–1453)

Introduction

There can be little doubt that by 1204 the Greeks and the Latins hated each other heartily and considered one another heretics and political opponents. This violent antipathy flared up to an unprecedented degree when the Fourth Crusade captured and sacked Constantinople and established on the ruins of the Byzantine Empire several Latin states, the empire of Constantinople, the kingdom of Thessalonica, various baronies in central Greece and the principality of the Morea in the Peloponnese. But it was Venice that took the lion's share and, by establishing her rule over the most important islands and naval bases, became the commercial mistress of the eastern Mediterranean.

However, the great mass of the people and the clergy remained faithful to Orthodoxy, and the resistance of the Byzantines against the Franks created three new Greek states — the empire of Nicaea under the Lascarids, the empire of Trebizond under the great Comnenes and the despotat of Epirus under the Comnenoi–Angeloi — whose main objects were to drive the Latins away and to reunite the empire. It was then that the modern national concept of Hellenism developed.

It was the empire of Nicaea that took the lead under Theodore Lascaris (1204–22) and especially under the able rule of John Vatatzes (1222–54), and so the Greek states eventually overthrew the fragile edifice of the Crusades and liberated most of the Byzantine populations from the Western yoke. Thus in 1222 the Franks lost the kingdom of Thessalonica, and in 1261 the armies of Michael VIII Palaeologus, who had usurped the throne of Nicaea, recaptured Constantinople. The Franks stayed longer in central Greece and the Peloponnese, until finally the principality of the Morea became the despotat of the Morea, fief of the younger sons of the dynasty of the Palaeologues. But Venice kept Crete till 1669 and a hold on the Ionian Islands until much later.

The Byzantine state, as restored in 1261, was but a pitiful remnant of an empire. The new dynasty of the Palaeologues was faced with huge difficulties: a double battle in the West and in the East, the ascending power of feudal aristocracy and the development of Western cities as centres of a trading bourgeoisie. Moreover, the period of expansion of the medieval economy had ended, and population growth was declining. From 1301, when the Turks won their first victory over the Byzantine armies at Baphaeum, Asia Minor was practically abandoned to its fate, and, in spite of the efforts of several great sovereigns, Byzantium sank slowly to its ruin. Hemmed in by the Turks on the east and the Serbian kingdom on the west, the Empire was gradually reduced to the capital and the surrounding countryside, until at last, after a valiant resistance, Constantinople itself fell to the Ottoman Turks in 1453, and the Roman Empire of the East was no more. The last tragic emperor, Constantine XI (1448–53) died a heroic death in defence of the city and so became a symbol of Hellenism and Orthodoxy throughout the long centuries of Turkish domination that followed.

Thus ended the Byzantine Empire, and there can be no question that it was the Fourth Crusade, with its 'act of international brigandry' (as the capture of Constantinople in 1204 has been called) and the despotism, vandalism and barbaric rapacity of its leaders, that brought about the Empire's downfall. During the thousand years and more of its glorious existence, during which it combined and evolved the Classical Greek, Roman and Christian traditions, it had kept the Muslim world at bay until Western civilization had developed and it spread the seeds of culture to the Slav world and to the peoples of the Middle East. In its death agony Byzantium sent out to the West forerunners of the great Western European Renaissance, thus fulfilling its literary and intellectual mission.

The despotat of the Morea and the empire of Trebizond survived the Fall of Constantinople by only a few years. When Trebizond succumbed to the Turks in 1461 the last memory of Byzantine greatness disappeared.

The empire of Nicaea became briefly a centre of letters and learning, for its emperors called to their court Greek scholars from many parts of Greece, encyclopaedists, historians and learned churchmen. The court of Nicaea has rightly been seen as the bridge that joins the renaissance of the Comnenes with that of the Palaeologues, but in the field of poetry nothing of significance was produced; nor can the empire of Trebizond or the despotat of Epirus boast of any noteworthy poetry.[1] The scanty and feeble poetry that developed in those three free Greek states never established a character of its own and can in no way be distinguished from the mainstream of development of Byzantine literature.

Strangely enough, in Constantinople after 1261, in spite of political, economic and military crises, literary and spiritual life flourished to a surprising degree. This florescence constitutes the so-called renaissance of the Palaeologues, when the classics were once again diligently studied and the high schools were reorganized. Several members of the Imperial family have left literary works of their own, among them Manuel II Palaeologus (1391–1425) and John VI Cantacuzenus (1341–55); distinguished historians appeared; philosophers, humanists, scholars, jurists, *savants* and even poets of some merit, like Manuel Holobolos and Manuel Philes, were active, to say nothing of the Church and the whole Hesychast movement. It is true that little agreement existed between the distinguished members of the renaissance of the Palaeologues, for Unitarian fought against Anti-Unitarian, and Platonist against Aristotelian. And it should not be forgotten that all those learned men were under the yoke of the classics, which in a sense stifled originality.

By contrast with this highbrow Constantinopolitan conservatism— which, incidentally, is evident even in the despotat of Mystras where, because of its isolation, some new ideas did develop—a new movement was initiated by simple people who were not cramped by the heavy hand of tradition. Thus the living language appeared in a number of interesting works, especially in the lands where the Frankish occupation had broken down the Byzantine system of education and Frankish models were at hand. Such are the verse romances in the vernacular, verse chronicles, like the *Chronicle of the Morea*, sonnets and short lyrics, all composed in a diction close to that spoken in the area of their origin. But we shall speak about these in detail later.[2]

Most of the poems composed in the demotic of this period are anonymous and appear in several versions, evidence of the wide diffusion of oral poetry, which is anonymous and delights in reshaping the works it transmits.[3] As was the case with the *Epic of Digenis Akritas*, many of the versions of such orally transmitted works were later committed to writing and then elaborated upon by pen-poets, who produced their own more sophisticated versions, some of which also made use of rhyme.

The existence of a widespread oral poetry in the Greek-speaking world of the late Byzantine period is of great significance in the history of Greek poetry, even if some of the works thus transmitted originated in written texts. For in many respects it determined the style of this new poetry in the vernacular—a poetry meant to be heard and not read—which, as already noted, in its turn had a direct influence upon the style of subsequent pen-poets when they composed their own original works in writing.

CHAPTER 20

Religious Poetry

In this chapter we shall not retain the distinction between religious poetry composed in ancient metres, rhythmic verse and political lines that has been observed up to this point, for there is very little indeed composed in ancient rhythms and fifteen-syllable lines, and such of it that exists is the work of poets who wrote mainly in rhythmical metres.

With the eleventh century, as we have seen, the freshness and vigour of Byzantine religious verse comes to an end. Nonetheless, a number of poets continued to be active in the East, composing *troparia*, *stichera* and canons, until the fall of Constantinople to the Turks.

The decline of religious poetry was accompanied in the thirteenth and fourteenth centuries by the development and expansion of the music chanted in church. It was then that the melodies of a simple, more or less syllabic type gave way completely to melismatic melodies, the simple recitative delivery to a kind of coloratura chanting.[1] The names of a series of distinguished church musicians belonging to the last centuries of the Byzantine world are known, among them John Glykas, Manuel Chrysaphes and Johannes Koukouzelis,[2] but only a few melodies of those then composed found their way into the liturgical books of the Church, which had by then become fully stereotyped.

The period opens with the Patriarch Germanos II (1222–40), one of the most vigorous opponents of the Union of the Churches. He ascended the patriarchal throne in Nicaea at the invitation of the Emperor John III Vatatzes (1222–54) and died in 1240. From his pen we have one canon in rhythmical verse on the seven Ecumenical Councils—in the *Menaea* of 11 October—and, in political verse, a poem on repentance.[3] *Pentekostaria*[4] are also attributed to him.[5] It is possible that some of the poems in the liturgical books going under the simple name Germanos may be by him.

Nicephorus Blemmydes (c. 1197–c. 1272) follows, one of the few noteworthy religious poets of the period. This remarkable scholar and man of letters left Constantinople after the Latin conquest of 1204 and joined the Church in Nicaea, where he also became tutor to Theodore II

Doucas Lascaris (1254–8) and the teacher of the historian Georgios Acropolites. He later became abbot of a monastery near Ephesus and was offered, but refused, the Ecumenical throne.

Blemmydes was a central figure in the intellectual life of the empire of Nicaea and wrote many works on philosophy, theology, geography, medicine, rhetoric, education and other subjects. But he also engaged in religious poetry, composing canons in iambics (the most important of these is on Gregorios Thaumatourgos), *stichera*,[6] verses on the Psalms and other occasional poems on religious subjects, which have not yet been published.

The Emperor Theodore II Doucas Lascaris was one of the most interesting men of his time. Among his many activities as statesman and writer—for he wrote dogmatic and pastoral theological works, orations and letters—he also found time to compose religious poetry. Of this the best are his canons on the Virgin, although they lack originality.[7]

Another patriarch of the empire of Nicaea, Arsenios Autoreianos (1255–60 and 1261–7), later Ecumenical Patriarch, also tried his hand at religious poetry. A Constantinopolitan by birth, he was sent to Rome to negotiate the Union of the Churches and later, as Patriarch, twice crowned emperor the usurper Michael VIII Palaeologus (1259–61 and 1261–82). After an eventful life he died in exile in 1273. Arsenios is the author of an anacreontic poem on Easter and the canon for the Ψυχοσάββατον (All Souls' Day), which is chanted in the Orthodox Church on the Saturday of the week before Pentecost.[8] Both are conventional and derivative works. To Arsenios is also ascribed the office of the Εὐχέλαιον (the Unction), but this attribution has rightly been challenged.[9]

Manuel Holobolos (c. 1240), the well-known orator and philosopher, also experimented in the field of religious poetry. He was in the service of Michael VIII Palaeologus, but his sympathy for John Lascaris resulted in his mutilation and retirement to a monastery. However, in 1267 he was offered the rectorship of the patriarchal high school in Constantinople but was later punished again for opposing the emperor's policy on the Union of the Churches. It is not known when he died.

The main body of his verse consists of twenty hymns in fifteen-syllable lines addressed to the Emperor Michael VIII—they are panegyric poems of the ceremony of the *Prokypsis*—in which various Christian festivals are explained. Their composition was part of Holobos's official duties when, as Church Orator, he had to receive the emperor, and they are full of servile court flattery.[10] More attractive are his shorter poems in iambics, a hymn on an image of St Mary the Egyptian, *monosticha* on the Passion of the Lord and on a holy relic of St John Chrysostom, two sepulchral epigrams and some other unimportant light verse.[11] Manuel Holobolos' interest in poetry can also be seen in his prose works, which include commentaries on the Alexandrian *technopaegnia* and other poems. Mention should also be made of Mattheos Blastaris (c. 1335), the well-known author on canonical law and various controversial dogmatic problems of his day, who composed no less than six hundred and fifth-three *troparia* and *stichera*, not one of which is an *idiomelon*.

The most important figure in the religious poetry of this period is undoubtedly Nicephoros Kallistos Xanthopoulos (died c. 1335). All we can gather about his life is that he served as a priest in the Church of Santa Sophia in Constantinople, whose great library he used assiduously, and that he died as a monk, having assumed the monastic name of Neilos.

His major work is an ecclesiastical history, but he also tried his hand at hagiography, exegetical and grammatical works, homilies and poetry. Xanthopoulos' liturgical poetry, with the exception of one prayer composed in eight-syllable lines,[12] is all cast in rhythmical verse and consists of a canon on the Ζωοδόχος Πηγή (the Virgin as Fountain of Life) included in the *Pentekostarion*,[13] several prayers to the Mother of God, all of which have alphabet acrostics, and some *megalinaria* on the Virgin and on saints. One of the prayers to the Virgin is cast in the form of 'Salutations to the Virgin' (χαιρετισμοί)[14] and has all the words of each of its twenty-four long stanzas starting with the same letter of the alphabet, a veritable *tour de force*.

More voluminous is his non-liturgical religious verse and his secular poetry, composed mainly in iambics. It comprises didactic poems in the form of catalogues of emperors, patriarchs, dignitaries of the Church and state, the Apostles, the saints of the calendar year and the hymnographers,[15] There is also a summary of the historical sections of the Old Testament (Σύνοψις τῆς θείας Γραφῆς),[16] a supplement to this in the form of a synopsis of Jewish history according to the Maccabees and Flavius Josephus (Συνοπτικὴ πρὸς θείαν Γραφήν)[17] and a description of the Fall of Jerusalem (Ἅλωσις Ἱερουσαλήμ)[18] as well as a long work in 2700 iambic lines on the life and miracles of St Nicholas of Myra, not yet published. Xanthopoulos, following the tradition of Theodore the Studite and the distinguished epigrammatists of the middle Byzantine years, also composed epigrams and short occasional poems on religious subjects, such as the *Akathistos Hymn*, or gems with representations from the Scriptures, amulets, icons of saints and so on.[19] He also wrote commentaries on the *Octoechos* and on various aspects of religious poetry.

The poetry of Nicephoros Kallistos Xanthopoulos, even though of significance in the literature of the declining Empire, has little to excite the modern reader; it lacks originality and, in spite of its sincerity, has nothing arresting about it.

The list of religious poets of the Byzantine Empire closes with the royal poet Manuel II Palaeologus (1391–1425). This widely cultured man, who fought persistently to save the threatened Empire from the Turks, left a number of speeches, theological works, treatises on the duties of a king, letters and some poetry, not all of which have been published. Of his verse, the canon entreating the Mother of God (κανὼν παρακλητικός) should be singled out for its sincerity and feeling.[20] He also composed a thanksgiving poem on the occasion of Bajazet's defeat,[21] as well as *megalinaria* for the Saturday of Holy Week and a *Lament of the Virgin*.[22]

It would be unfair to close this account of Byzantine religious poetry without adding a few words about the moving lyrical *Lament of the Virgin*, the *Epitaphios Threnos*, which is chanted to this day in church on the evening of Good Friday. Little is known about its date and authorship, but it probably existed in some form as early as the ninth century, although it was not incorporated into the actual service until the thirteenth or fourteenth century, and some parts of it may well be even more recent.[23] Its distinctive character lies in the lyrical rather than narrative treatment of the material, enhanced by the music that accompanies it. Precedents for the *Epitaphios Threnos* can be found in earlier homilies as well as in the *Christus Patiens* and the *Acta Pilati*.[24]

Side by side with the *Epitaphios Threnos*[25] a number of beautiful such lamentations of the Virgin exist in the vernacular and some in an erudite form of Greek,[26] the earliest of which probably belong to the fourteenth century.[27]

Even after the Fall of Constantinople religious poetry continued to be composed, as can be seen from the works of Mattheus Camariotes[28] (died 1490), Nicolaos Malaxos[29] (fifteenth century) and Johannes Plousiadenos,[30] also known as Joseph of Methone (2nd half of fifteenth century), but it is inferior poetry, the last dying gasp of a long and noble tradition.

Looking back on the whole course of Byzantine religious poetry, which we must now leave, it is proper to stress that Byzantine hymnography not only constituted the greatest literary achievement of the Greek Middle Ages but also accomplished an important historical mission. In the Greek world it kept Christian feeling and national consciousness alive in the face of the numerous barbarian invasions that ravaged the Empire and during the long years of servitude under the Turks that followed. Moreover, it sustained and consoled the Greeks and inspired them to regain their religious and national independence. To the east, to the west and to the north it scattered the seeds that grew into the literature and culture of other peoples—the Russians, the southern Slavs, the Romanians, the Syrians, the Copts and the Armenians—and it exercised paramount influence over Christian art and a noticeable influence over the development of later Greek poetry.

CHAPTER 21

Secular Poetry

POETRY IN THE PURIST IDIOM

Epigrams, didactic verse and other occasional poems

With the possible exception of Manuel Philes, Byzantine 'lyrical' poetry has little to be proud of in this period, which opens with two Cypriot poets who are among the very few Byzantine 'provincial' poets we know by name.

The first is Constantine Anagnostes (thirteenth century), one of the earliest writers to use both the purist and the spoken idiom in his verse,[1] to whom are attributed some epigrams[2] and two short poems. One expresses in the purist idiom the author's gratitude to an otherwise unknown secretary, Constantine, while the other addresses in the demotic a son or pupil of his named Paul.

The second Cypriot poet is Georgios Lapithis (thirteenth century), who enjoyed the patronage of the Lusignans. He wrote a long, didactic, moralizing work in 1491 political verses, which is metrically faulty and includes many boring trivialities. as he hands out advice to the state, society and the family of his day. He draws on Isocrates and the Scriptures and only occasionally expresses some views of his own.[3]

Poets and scholars of this period were still interested in the epigram, despite its obvious decline, and among them Maximus Planudes (c. 1255–c. 1305) occupies a prominent position. That distinguished scholar, who was equally at home in literature, mathematics and theology, was also one of the few Byzantine men of letters to have had a thorough acquaintance with Latin and to have translated Latin authors into Greek. Educated in Constantinople, Planudes became successively an Imperial secretary, a monk in Constantinople and titular abbot of a monastery near Scutari. Sent on a diplomatic mission to Venice, he was arrested for a time by the Venetians and on his return journey was even captured by pirates. He taught many of the fourteenth-century Byzantine humanists and was a pioneer in bridging the intellectual gap between East and West.

Planudes was not a poet himself,[4] but he has a place in the history of Greek poetry because of the celebrated anthology he compiled. This, as we have seen, is based on the *Anthology* of Constantine Cephalas (tenth century)[5] but includes supplementary material; it is divided into seven books, with complex subdivisions. His choice of poems was determined by moral criteria and the taste of his time rather than by true poetic excellence, all erotic epigrams being excluded and others considered obscene expurgated. The poems not in the Palatine *Anthology* that are included in the Planudean are some 400 in number.[6]

The *Anthology* of Planudes[7] had a considerable influence on the later Byzantine epigram, as can be seen from the work of Manuel Philes. Thereafter its influence can be followed in Italy and the West, where it was much read, edited and annotated from the beginning of the fifteenth century.[8]

Manuel Philes (c. 1275–c. 1345), a central figure in the poetry of this period and its most distinguished epigrammatist, was to the Palaeologues what Theodoros Prodromos was to the Comnenes—the typical Byzantine court poet. He was a native of Ephesus who held a court appointment in Constantinople and took part in diplomatic missions to Persia, Russia, the Arab world and possibly even India. Later he fell from grace and was imprisoned. It is clear that he was in touch with many important men of his day, but his constant soliciting and flattery of those in power indicate a man of lower social status.

Philes is one of the most productive Byzantine authors and one of the rare medieval Greek writers who wrote poetry almost exclusively. His surviving verse amounts to some 25,000 lines! His favourite metre is the twelve-syllable iambic line, which he employs with strict new metrical rules.[9] He also wrote hexameters and fifteen-syllable political verse. Eschewing the vernacular, he composed exclusively in erudite literary Greek.

The bulk of Philes' work consists of short occasional poems, epigrams on stock religous themes like icons, votive offerings, liturgical books, ecclesiastical vessels and so on, or on stock rhetorical subjects like the rose, the sun, the moon, the sea. Side by side with these we find poems on works of art (pieces of sculpture, gems, seals); requests to all and sundry (emperors, patriarchs, princes) for furs, wine, fodder for his horse, game; encomia on benefactors, full of revolting flattery; complaints about his poverty; epitaphs; and descriptive pieces. Most of these poems are on actual objects and for actual occasions, but he also composed some purely fictitious pieces, like the one on an allegorical representation of the twelve months of the year or the poem describing the wedding of Alexander, which is nothing more than a paraphrase of Lucian's *Herodotus s. Aetion*.

Most of Philes' occasional poems are relatively short, but there are also two groups of longer works, the first consisting of 'didactic' poems and the second of dramatic dialogues.

Of the first the most important is the one entitled *On the Qualities of Animals* (Περὶ ζῴων ἰδιοτήτων), which draws on Aelian and is dedicated to the Emperor Michael IX Palaeologus (1295–1320). It consists of 2015 iambic trimeters and deals with a series of important birds, quadrupeds and fish, as well as some fabulous animals like the onocentuaros or the unicorn. This is followed by a much shorter piece describing the elephant (Σύντομος ἐλέφαντος ἔκφρασις) and a work entitled *On Plants*, which is composed of brief, independent poems on corn, the grape, the rose and the pomegranate.

There are three dramatic dialogues. Though called *dramatia*, they have nothing to do with drama. The first is a dialogue between a living man and the soul of a dead man; at the end the dead man's wife also joins in. Its 240 fifteen-syllable lines form twenty-four strophes, linked by an alphabetic acrostic, and are supposed to serve as a consolation for death. The second, in 602 iambic trimeters, is a pseudo-dramatic dialogue between the parents, widow, brother and servant of an unidentified dead man. It has been suggested that the dead man is Andronicus Palaeologus (1282–1328) and that the meeting-place is his grave. They all speak once only, expressing their love, sorrow and admiration for the deceased, and the poem concludes with the father reciting, at the end of his speech, the epigram carved on the tomb. The work is bereft of all action and life.[10] The third is a dramatic *ethopoeia* in 966 iambic trimeters and is a panegyric in dialogue form on the great *domesticus* Johannes Kantakouzenos. The participants in this piece are the poet himself, *Nous* (the spirit), Johannes Kantakouzenos and a chorus of virtues that acclaims the celebrated man. The poem falls into 138 flat strophes. Philes also transcribed the *Akathistos Hymn* into fifteen-syllable lines, a vain and useless undertaking.

Manuel Philes is at his best in his shorter works. His longer poems are protracted and boring. For in spite of his unquestioned technical skill as a versifier, he has no true poetic vein. His work is pedestrian, and he repeats motifs (even entire passages) in poem after poem. It is thought that he probably had a stock of honorific addresses ready, to which he added a line or two specifying name and occasion. His poetry is of interest for the incidental information it contains on prosopography, art history and several other subjects. There is little doubt that the *Anthology* of Maximus Planudes exercised a great influence over Philes' work,[11] and he can safely claim the title of being the last noteworthy Byzantine epigrammatist.[12]

The return to Classicism in the days of the Palaeologues is also evident in the use of the hexameter in the poetry of Theodoros Metochites (died 1332). Metochites was the chief minister and friend of the Emperor Andronicus II (1282–1328), on whose fall he retired to the monastery of

Chora (now the Kariye Cami), which he had earlier had restored and decorated with the finest examples of late Byzantine fresco painting. Theodoros Metochites was a renowned polymath and champion of Church Union. His works, many still unpublished, include paraphrastic commentaries on Aristotle, speeches, rhetorical exercises, panegyrics, a handbook of astronomy, miscellaneous philosophical, historical and literary essays, letters and poems.

In verse we have twenty long hexameter poems—consisting in all of no fewer than 9188 lines —on events and personalities contemporary with the author. From them we learn about Theodoros' monastic life, his library, his sincere interest in culture, his own personal difficulties and his fervent desire that his literary output should not be lost at his death; among them we also find epitaphs on Irene and Michael, the wife and son of Andronicus II (1282–1328), encomiastic poems on Fathers of the Church, as well as a strange didactic poem on 'The Mathematical, and especially the Harmonic form of Philosophy' (Περί τοῦ μαθηματικοῦ εἴδους τῆς φιλοσοφίας καὶ μάλιστα περὶ τοῦ ἁρμονικοῦ). The main interest of Metochites' verse lies in the information it gives, and not in its poetic quality, which is poor.[13]

Verses have also survived from the pen of Nicolaos Kabasilas[14] (mid-fourteenth century), the last great mystic of Byzantium, and from that of Nicephoros Gregoras, (born 1295),[15] the great late Byzantine polyhistor.

In the year 1392 a poem was composed in 759 political lines and in a fairly erudite diction on the fall of Constantinople to the Franks and the recapture of the city by the Greeks. The author, who is unknown, draws on the historians Niketas Choniates and Georgios Akropolites and, after dealing with the recapture of the city by the Greeks, proceeds to give an account of ecclesiastical affairs from the reign of Michael VIII Palaeologus (1261–82) to that of Andronicus II (1282). Though of little artistic or historical value, it is noteworthy for expressing the spirit of the times.[16]

To the fourteenth century also belongs the verse chronicle of Ephraem (c. 1313),[17] which in 9588 twelve-syllable lines deals with Roman and Byzantine history from the early Empire to 1261 but covers in detail only the Comnenes, the Angeli and the empire of Nicaea. As all the sources of this chronicle can be traced, it holds little interest for the historian[18] and none for the lover of poetry.

Mention must also be made of four minor fourteenth-century poets, all of whom composed accentual anacreontics in which quantity is entirely disregarded. These are Johannes Katrares, author of a vivid attack on the orator Neophytus;[19] Marcus Angelos, who wrote on Eros and even saw the magnetic needle as pointing to the north because of the love of the magnet for the axis of the world;[20] Johannes Comnenos of Sozopolis, who composed a reasonable poem on confessing his own sins;[21] and Stephanos Sgouropoulos, a *protonotarios* in Trebizond, whose major work, 300 eight-syllable lines long, is in honour of the Emperor Alexius III of Trebizond (1350–90). He also composed some other minor occasional poems.[22]

Of much greater significance is the monstrous allegorical poem of 3060 fifteen-syllable lines on temperance (*Εἰς τὴν Σωφροσύνην*) by Theodoros Meliteniotes (died c. 1395), the astronomer, theologian and poet who held a succession of high offices among the patriarchal staff at Constantinople. It describes in romantic–allegorical terms an imaginary journey to the realm of Temperance (*Σωφροσύνη*), guided by Temperance herself, who is presented as a beautiful virgin. She leads him first to her magnificent garden, which has seven obstacles (*φρούρια*) protecting its entrance that offer the poet the opportunity to display his vast knowledge of mythology and natural science. Eventually he reaches the castle of Sophrosyne and, after a detailed description of it, comes to the culminating point of the poem, the bed of Temperance, which is made of gold, silver and precious stones. Here Meliteniotes excels himself, giving a veritable dictionary of mineralogy in verse and an alphabetical catalogue of stones in the manner of Pliny. We are then led back to the garden, whose beauty is described in detail, decorated as it is with statues of great men of the pagan and Christian past and all the pagan gods, which once again incite the writer to display his erudition. Finally, the beauty of the mistress of the castle, Sophrosyne herself, is described, and it is explained that the garden is Paradise and the obstacles at the entrance the difficulties man finds in trying to practise temperance.

This monstrosity in verse may have a place in the history of Western allegorical–moralizing poetry, but to the modern reader it gives neither aesthetic satisfaction nor useful knowledge. The descriptions of the palace and garden bring to mind the similar, though less elaborate, descriptions of the Byzantine demotic verse romances and of the *Epic of Digenis Akritas*. It is possible that parts of Meliteniotes' vast poem may have passed into Byzantine oral poetry and there contaminated versions of the verse romances *Callimachus and Chrysorrhoe, Libystros and Rhodamne, Belthandros and Chrysantza*[23] and even the epic of Digenis.[24]

As is the case with Byzantine religious poetry, the list of writers of epigrams and short occasional poems closes with the royal author Emperor Manuel II Palaeologus (1391–1425).[25] Among his secular verse, which is slight, a lively attack in anacreontics on a garrulous, uneducated man, which illustrates the poet's lighter side, deserves mention.

Finally, in closing this group, a word should be added about an anonymous idyll of the first half of the fifteenth century consisting of sixty-three hexameters[26]—like the idyll composed by Maximus Planudes,[27] it draws on Theocritus and Virgil—and about the verse riddles which seem to have been popular up to the end of the Empire. The tradition of verse riddles is old, of course, as can be seen from the fourteenth book of the Greek *Anthology*, but it is of interest that a collection of twenty-five iambic verse riddles has survived from this final period of Byzantine literature.[28] Their authorship is unknown and their literary quality, unfortunately, poor.[29]

POETRY IN THE VERNACULAR

Historical and descriptive poems

Three historical and one short descriptive poem were also composed during this period in free Byzantine lands.[30] The first is the *Lament on Tamerlane*, an anonymous work in ninety-six fifteen-syllable lines which relates how Sultan Bajazet was forced to raise the siege of Constantinople in 1402, when the Mongols invaded Asia Minor, and how he was defeated by them at the battle of Ancora (1403), after which they indulged in savage massacres and pillaging. The author appears to have been an eye-witness at the battle of Ancora, hence his lively descriptions. He was also a man of some education, for he gives an 'erudite' linguistic touch to his narrative.[31] (An echo of the same events can also be found in modern Greek folk songs.)[32]

The last attempt of the West to come to the rescue of the Greeks when they were hard-pressed by the Turks ended with the defeat at Varna in 1444, and this is the subject of the second historical poem, the *Battle of Varna*. It was at this conflict that the young king of Poland, Vladislav, was killed; the Hungarian hero, John Hunyadi, was forced to retreat with the Western Crusaders, and all hope of help from the West was lost. The poem describes the battle in 465 political lines, and the author states that, hidden in a forest, he followed it, overcome by terror. However, the description seems more like a rhetorical exercise than a true report, and it appears to have been written long after the battle.[33] Two similar versions of this poem have survived. The first (probably the original) goes under the name of Zotikos Paraspondylos and the second under that of Georgios Argyropoulos. It is, of course, possible that both drew on a lost original. Paraspondylos, who was a high official of the Empire but no man of letters, states that all he wishes to do is to describe accurately the tragedy he witnessed.[34]

The third of the historical poems is short and totally unimportant, telling in very simple language of the love life of the Empress Theodora, wife of Justinian I (527–65). It has come down to us via a thirteenth-century manuscript[35] but must derive from an older work.[36]

The descriptive poem is called *A Narrative on Famous Venice* (Διήγησις τῆς φουμιστῆς Βενετίας) and is homage paid by an anonymous poet to the Mistress of the Adriatic in eighty-four fifteen-syllable lines. The majestic monuments of the city—the Church of St Mark, the Palace of the Doges and so on—are lavishly praised by the simple versifier, who also reveals a certain hankering after the wealth and power of the West. An interesting feature of this fifteenth-century work, which was clearly composed before the Fall of Constantinople and in lands that were not under Frankish rule,[37] is that it makes partial use of rhyme.[38]

Allegories and popular moralizing verse

Allegorical and moralizing verse was, as we have seen, composed throughout the Greek Middle Ages. One has only to remember the importance attached to the moralizing works of Gregory of Nazianzus, and the various 'laments' addressed by poets to their own souls, not to mention the edifying aspect of Church hymns and of Byzantine didactic verse, to realize how popular it was.

But the purist language of much of this poetry prevented it from reaching the populace, so a series of works in the vernacular emerged that catered for the uneducated. A number of these took the form of alphabets, such as the fourteenth-century *Penitential and Edifying Alphabet on this Vain World*, the first *contemptus mundi* in vernacular Greek,[39] while others were cast in different poetic forms.[40] Their literary value is limited, so we need not linger over them, with one possible exception—*The Sinner's Prayer*[41] which, though only sixteen lines long, is a direct and moving piece.

More ambitious are two other relatively short anonymous poems, *The Tale of Consolation about Good and Bad Fortune* (thirteenth century) and *The Story of Ptocholeon* (fourteenth century?), on both of which Frankish influence can be traced.

The first relates, in 756 political lines, how an unhappy young man sets out to reach the Castle of Ill Fortune in the hope of finding out why she is so harsh with him. On his way he meets a handsome young man, Time, who gives him an introduction to her. From Ill Fortune's residence he is led to the home of Good Fortune, where he is finally released from his troubles. In this tale, which seems to depend on the verse romance of *Libystros and Rhodamne*[42] the personifications are highly artificial and the moral drawn at the end (do not be fatalistic; man is master of his fate) commonplace. Nevertheless, the narrative—all in the first person—is not without some interest.[43]

The Story of Ptocholeon, of which we have five versions of varying length, the longest consisting of 853 trochaic eight-syllable lines, derives from an Oriental (perhaps Indian) story. It runs thus: a rich and wise old man loses all his property in a raid by corsairs and, at his own request, is sold by his children into slavery. At the palace where he comes to serve he displays his wisdom and his knowledge of precious stones and of human and animal nature and even reveals that the king, his master, is not legitimate. He is then sent back to his own country, covered with riches and glory, the moral being that honesty wins the day. The story, which has a mixture of Oriental and Western elements, can be traced in the *Eracle* of Gautier d'Arras (thirteenth century), in the Russian song of Ivan and in a Turkish legend. The language of *The Story of Ptocholeon* and the use of a less common metre, trochaic octasyllables, point to a relatively early date; the several surviving versions indicate that it was popular[44] and probably passed through a period of oral transmission.

Although, strictly speaking, they are not moralizing poetry, a few words should be added here about the so-called *Oracles of Leo the Wise*.[45] Many pagan ideas and practices had, as we know, survived throughout the Middle Ages and, among them, a belief in the influence of the stars on human destiny and of omens drawn from various natural phenomena. Even emperors had astronomers in their entourages, whose advice they sought, and serious Byzantine historians make mention of dreams, visions and prophecies, so it is not surprising that such things played an even greater role in the life of simple people. Most of these prophecies that exercised so great an influence on popular thought and imagination were, naturally, *vaticinia post eventum*. A surviving collection of such oracles in popular form, probably belonging to the late fourteenth or the fifteenth century, is ascribed (wrongly, as we have seen) to Leo the Wise (886–911). It consists of 461 octasyllable trochaic lines that fall into five sections and bewail the vices and misfortunes of the Empire, foretelling its doom; at the end the arrival of Antichrist is announced, during whose reign all miseries shall prevail. As much of their content derives from the rehandling and misunderstanding of older material now lost, much of it is incomprehensible today.[46]

Animal stories

In late Byzantine popular literature we find a series of works on animals and plants that differ from the famous older *Physiologos*,[47] the medieval manual of natural science and source of so many marvellous stories. Whereas in the older *Physiologos* the treatment was mystic–allegorical, in the popular animal stories the approach is light-hearted and satirical, concentrating on the strange or amusing qualities and habits of various beasts. It suffices to remember the myths of Aesop to realize how old and how widely enjoyed this literary genre has been among the Greeks.

The popular late Byzantine *Physiologos* probably belongs to the early fifteenth century and consists of 1131 political lines whose metre is lame — at two points the metre breaks off and sections in prose are inserted—

and whose language is dry and dead. Divided into forty-nine sections, it deals first with the animals of the earth (the elephant, the snake, the stag and so on), then with two creatures of a 'double nature' (the centaur and the satyr) and finally with the animals of the air (for example, the dove, the pelican, the phoenix). The *Physiologos* professes to retain a 'popular scientific character', but a number of strange stories distorted by popular imagination and the most fantastic etymologies of the names of animals are included; certain allegorical and satirical elements deriving from the old 'erudite' *Physiologos* can also be traced in it. Two manuscripts of this strange work exist, both belonging to the sixteenth century, in which traits of many redactors can be found; they point to a period of oral transmission for this poem too.[48]

The Playful Tale about Quadrupeds,[49] which can be dated with certainty to 1364 (ll. 11ff.) also draws on the *Physiologos*. In 1082 political lines and a mixed erudite and popular diction it describes a meeting of all the animals at the invitation of the lion, their king. After swearing friendship with one another, each of them speaks, presenting his own merits and the defects of one of the others. At the end the lion announces that the truce is over and that they can continue with their old hostilities; a bloody battle ensues until night brings an end to the slaughter. The didactic element is obvious, but it is mixed with burlesque, humorous and obscene passages, and there are political, religious and social allusions, such as the attacks on the Jews and the Roman Catholics (ll. 385f.).[50]

The anonymous *Poulologos*,[51] a poem about birds, corresponds to the *Playful Tale about Quadrupeds* and may well have drawn on it. Several versions of it exist, the longest of which, in 670 political lines, is composed in a vigorous, flowing, vernacular diction. The anonymity of the poem and the several surviving versions point to a period of oral transmission.

In the *Poulologos*[52] the king of the birds, the eagle, invites his plumed fellows to the marriage of his son. The guests, who appear in pairs, once again sing their own praises and disparage the others. Finally, the eagle intervenes and threatens that if they continue fighting, he will send the hawk and the falcon to attack them. At this the birds cease quarrelling and turn to eating and drinking, so that both marriage and poem have a happy ending. The *Poulologos* is, in a sense, an *ornithologicum compendium* which includes humorous and obscene passages as well as allusions to the Church and the political and social circumstances of the later Empire.[53] It is difficult to date the poem with any precision; it may well be the oldest of the surviving late Byzantine animal stories.[54]

Finally, among the animal stories we find the *Synaxarion of the Estimable Donkey* (Συναξάριον τοῦ τιμημένου Γαϊδάρου), whose title is meant to be comic, as a *synaxarion* is the life of a saint. It deals with three of the favourites in animal stories—the wolf, the fox and the donkey. The two former are friends and gossips who try to deceive, kill and devour the donkey. However, during a rough sea journey the donkey succeeds in tricking and drowning both of them. This poem, whose theme may be very old, has come down to us in two versions, one of the fifteenth and a longer one, of Cretan origin, of the sixteenth century.[55]

The romances of love and chivalry that belong to this period will be treated in Chapter 22, which deals with Greek poetry under the Franks, for though we know nothing about their authors or their provenance, Western medieval chivalry has had such a marked influence upon them that clearly they must be examined there. The pure Byzantine literary tradition ends in 1204 in the lands occupied by the Franks, just as it ends in 1453 in those conquered by the Turks. But its aftermath is, of course, clearly felt and constitutes the thread that runs through all later Greek poetry until the liberation of Greece in the nineteenth century.

Part Four

THE GREEKS UNDER
THE FRANKS
AND THE TURKS

The Greeks under the Franks
(1204–1797)

Introduction

After the conquest of Constantinople by the Franks in 1204 the Crusaders became involved in disputes about the Imperial throne and finally decided to divide the Empire among themselves. A new Latin emperor was to be elected with control over a quarter of the Empire, and the remainder was to be divided so that one half went to the Venetians, who got the lion's share, and one half to the Crusaders.

The Latin empire of Constantinople lasted only fifty-seven years, but some of the Venetian and the Frankish states that arose as a consequence of the Fourth Crusade continued to exist for two or three hundred years, so that in a sense the history of the Greek lands lost its unity and became the story not of one but of many separate states.

Of the units that thus arose three mainly concern us here, the Morea, Crete and Rhodes, to which a fourth must be added, Cyprus, which had earlier fallen into Frankish hands(1191); for it is in these four Frankish-occupied areas that Greek poetry flourished, and it is there—particularly on Crete—that the development of the history of Greek poetry must be traced. The others, the kingdom of Thessalonica (1204–23), the duchy of Athens (1205–1460), the duchy of the Archipelago (1207–1566), the County Palatine of Cephalonia (1194–1483) and other minor Latin states have little to show in this respect.

The principality of Achaia (1205–1432) in the Morea had a long and involved history lasting more than two centuries, into which we naturally cannot go. It must suffice to say that Geoffrey de Villehardouin, with only a few hundred soldiers, won the whole of the Peloponnese in a single battle and that he acknowledged the king of Thessalonica as overlord. The ruins of the baronial castles in the lands which he had won and which he had partitioned among his followers can still be seen. Venice kept the ports of Modon and Croton and the Byzantine Greeks retained Monemvasia. This was soon lost to the Franks, only to be regained together with Mistra and Old Maina (1262), acquisitions that paved the way for the restoration of Byzantine rule in the Peloponnese. For by 1432, apart from a few points held by Venice, the whole of the peninsula was reconquered by the Byzantine emperor, though this reconquest did not last long, the despotat of the Morea falling to the advancing Turks in 1461.

The Western French culture which the Franks introduced to the Peloponnese had its effect upon Greek poetry, as we shall see. For although the exact local origin of the late Byzantine verse romances is unknown, there can be little doubt that oral Provençal poetry, which was most probably introduced into Greek lands, had a significant effect upon them (some are pure adaptations into Greek of Provençal originals); and it was a poet of mixed Frankish and Greek origin (a *gasmoulos*) who probably composed the Greek version of the *Chronicle of the Morea* for the benefit of Greek-speaking Frankish aristocrats and of those Greeks who collaborated with them. This new poetic upsurge in the spoken idiom was no doubt also helped by the fact that in the Frankish-occupied Greek lands Byzantine Church-sponsored, 'erudite' Greek education had broken down, and the spoken idiom, which had already started to emerge from obscurity in the Comnenian period, came into its own.

If we now turn to Venice, of all her possessions (1204–1797)—and it should be remembered that Venetian sovereignty was not always clearly defined, for she acquired influence and control in the absence of formal administration—Crete was the most important. This she purchased in 1204 and held, despite many insurrections, until 1669, when the island was seized by the Turks. Venice sent colonists to Crete, which was divided into feudal fiefs, and the Orthodox Church was occupied by the Latin clergy. As a result of the harsh policy of the Mistress of the Adriatic, not only the natives but also the colonists were alienated, so that revolt followed revolt throughout the thirteenth and fourteenth centuries until privileges similar to those that the Venetian aristocracy enjoyed were ceded to the Cretan aristocracy. This brought a measure of order to the island. Gradually, as the old feudal system declined, Venice softened her rule, especially after the loss of Cyprus and in the face of the approaching Turkish danger.

An almost homogeneous Cretan society, at least in the cities, was thus formed by the last quarter of the sixteenth century, for many of the Venetian colonists had adopted Greek dress and speech, and there were many conversions to the Orthodox faith.[1] This new mixed society, in which the Greek element became increasingly prominent, gradually acquired considerable wealth; as usual, culture followed in the footsteps of economic expansion. Thus it came about that at the turn of the sixteenth century in the towns, and most prominently in the capital, Candia, civilized life developed that was similar to that of many advanced Italian cities. Academies of writers and artists were established (notably the Academia dei Stravaganti); theatrical performances were given; tournaments were held; and poetry, scholarship, iconography and architecture flourished.[2] Of special significance for the history of Greek poetry is the first appearance of the use of rhyme in Crete, in the work of Stephanos Sachlikis (died c. 1403), which is attributable, no doubt, to the influence of Italian poetry.

Indicative of this new spirit of expansion was the flourishing Greek Cretan colony in Venice, which at that time was about 6000 strong and had its own Orthodox church of St George. At the same time special endowments were set up by wealthy Greeks to facilitate the education of their countrymen, the most famous being the Collegio Flanginis, the *Flanginianòn Hellenomuseion*, in Venice, established in 1664; and the practical usefulness of a Paduan medical degree should not be underrated (Padua was for long under Venetian control), as the medical school sustained a flow of students from the East.[3]

Unfortunately, all the cultural activities of Crete, some of which persisted even during the long siege of Candia (1648–69), came to an end when the island fell to the Turks in 1669 and those men of art and letters who survived came as refugees to the Ionian Islands or the West.

But Crete was not the only significant Venetian possession in the Greek world. Modon and Croton—'the right eye of the Republic'—the Euboea, a number of Aegean islands, Maina, Nauplia, important points on the western coast of Greece, and the Ionian Islands were for long years under her rule. In fact, the defence of the Christian Aegean had fallen to Venice, which, as a result, had to engage in several wars against the Ottoman Empire, in the course of which the entire Peloponnese was conquered in 1685–7 and the Parthenon was bombarded and destroyed during a siege of Athens (1687). Tenos, the last island that Venice held in the Aegean, was lost to the Turks in 1715, but she kept the Ionian Islands until 1797, when they were captured by the French of Napoleon.

Not only the Venetians but also the Genoese became masters of islands in the Aegean Sea—Chios through the Genoese chartered company of the Giustiniani (1304–1566), the rich island of Lesbos through the Gattilusio family and lesser islands which they held for years. And the Knights of St John, who had lived in Cyprus since the fall of the Holy Land to the Muslims (1291), in 1309 occupied the island of Rhodes and the neighbouring islands, which they governed until 1522, when the Turks captured Rhodes and they were forced to withdraw to Malta.

Moreover, the great eastern island of Cyprus, which was captured by Richard Lionheart in 1191 on his way to join the Third Crusade, was finally ceded to Guy de Lusignan, the last king of Jerusalem, who installed on the island a number of Franks. The kingdom of Cyprus was ruled by the Lusignans until 1473, when it passed into the hands of the Venetians. It remained in their possession (with a brief interval of Genoese occupation) until 1571, when it fell to the Turks. But though Cyprus was dominated by the Franks for centuries, the feeling of the people remained

Greek, as the many risings against their conquerors show. As in the Morea, in Cyprus there were few French barons, and many seem to have become bilingual, adopting the Greek language and Greek customs.

The Frankish occupation, which left many traces upon the countryside in the form of great castles and isolated towers, made little mark upon the Greek people and their institutions. The attempts to reunite the Churches of Rome and Constantinople were fruitless. Conquerors and conquered never really amalgamated; the newcomers—Italians, Frenchmen, Catalans, Navarrese, Germans and Flemings—did not come in sufficient numbers to obtain a firm grip on the country. Their strongholds remained a series of garrisons in foreign lands. However, the social life of that feudal society, with its brilliant courts and gay tournaments, was a bright one, and the Greeks, except for those on the islands of Crete and Cyprus, seem to have accepted the Frankish occupation with docility.

Although the Franks made no great impact on the language and the social life of the Greeks, their influence upon Greek poetry was significant, for they left their mark on the late Byzantine verse romances, on lyrical poetry, on the verse chronicles and, most prominently, on the great period of Cretan poetry (the sixteenth and seventeenth centuries), as well as on that of the Ionian Islands. (As already mentioned, the use of rhyme should be regarded as one of the important contributions of the Franks to Greek verse.) Through these channels they influenced significantly the course of Greek poetry.

CHAPTER 22

Verse Romances and Historical Poems

ROMANCES OF LOVE AND CHIVALRY

We have already seen the influence and, in a sense, the first 'revival' of the late Hellenistic romances in the *Epic of Digenis Akritas* and, of course, more fully in the insipid, erudite twelfth-century romances of Theodoros Prodromos, Nicetas Eugenianos, Constantine Manasses and Eustathios Macrembolites. We must now examine a further interesting development of this literary genre in a group of romances of love and chivalry that were composed between the mid-thirteenth and the mid-fifteenth centuries. They are all anonymous and are cast in the vernacular and in political verses; we have no evidence to indicate where they were written.

What characterizes this group of verse romances is that Western medieval chivalry has had a marked influence upon them, although they draw on the Byzantine literary tradition[1] and Oriental elements are not absent.[2] Behind their heroes, who are vassals of Love and some of whom have foreign names, stands the ideal type of the French cavalier created by Chrétien de Troyes and his successors, which, taken over by the so-called 'second chivalry' and the medieval French romance, was transplanted to Greek soil when the conquests of the Fourth Crusade had created a favourable climate for its expansion. Their tournaments, their adventures in distant lands, their heroes bring us close to the world of the *roman courtois* and the ballads of the Arthurian Cycle.

But although Frankish is the dominant influence that helped to shape these Byzantine medieval romances,[3] a strong Oriental influence is evident in the fairy-tale motifs used (most notably those of the *Thousand and One Nights*); nor should that of modern Greek fairy-tales and folk songs — most prominently that of the *Katalogia* (*καταλόγια*), the love songs — be underrated or the part played by the erudite Byzantine literary tradition. For the authors of these romances knew those of the Second Sophistic and their Byzantine erudite counterparts, and their works have many elements in common with them—as, for example, the ecphrasis, the detailed description of castles, gardens and works of art. As we shall see, there are many clear signs—the anonymity of the works, their poetic technique, the several versions in which some appear and the contamination with other works or with one another—that suggest that this whole group of poems probably went through a period of oral transmission, even if some or all of them originated in written texts.

The surviving late Byzantine verse romances can be conveniently grouped under the following three headings: original verse romances; Greek translations of Western romances; and pseudo-historical romances with something of a 'nationalist' colouring.

Original verse romances

This group consists of six pieces, in five of which increasing Frankish influence can be traced, starting with *Callimachus and Chrysorrhoe* and culminating in *Phlorios and Pliatzaphlora*.

The sixth of this group, the *Achilleis*, whose debt to Frankish models is also indisputable, at the same time owes something to the *Epic of Digenis Akritas* and the Alexander romance, and this leads us to a somewhat purer 'Greek' atmosphere; but, as has often been said, there is nothing of a Greek 'nationalist' spirit in it.

Callimachus and Chrysorrhoe is probably the oldest of the surviving verse romances in the demotic. It consists of 2605 political lines and has come down to us in only one manuscript. An outline of the story runs as follows. The young prince Callimachus frees the beautiful princess Chrysorrhoe from the Castle of the Ogre, where she has been kept a prisoner, and kills the fierce ogre who is guarding her. The two fall in love, but they are soon parted when an evil witch leads a king (his name is not given) to that enchanted palace; he carries Chrysorrhoe away after causing Callimachus to fall into a deadly torpor as a result of eating a magic apple he is offered. Callimachus is eventually restored to life by his two brothers and sets out in search of Chrysorrhoe, whom he finds in the palace of the king who has siezed her and who has also fallen deeply in love with her. To be close to Chrysorrhoe, Callimachus agrees to be employed as the king's gardener, which enables the two lovers to meet at night, but they are soon found out. Finally, when the identity of Callimachus as a prince is discovered, the king has compassion upon him, sets the two lovers free and arranges for them to get married.

It is clear that the atmosphere of this romance, whose poetic merits are few, is that of a fairy-tale, but it is doubtful if the poem was widely known. The author himself is unknown, though indirect evidence, deriving from a poem of Manuel Philes, suggests that it may be the work of Andronicos

Palaeologos, a cousin of the Emperor Andronicos II (1282–1328), and that it was composed between 1310 and 1340.[4] The knowledge of Byzantine court etiquette and the somewhat conservative form of Greek employed, as well as the lack of any pronounced Western influence may well support this view.

Belthandros and Chrysantza, the second of these verse romances, is very different in character and style. It is a shorter work, consisting of only 1348 political lines, and describes how Belthandros, unable to endure his father's harsh rule, leaves his country and comes to Tarsus. Close to that city he finds the *Erotokastron*, the Castle of Love, where he is informed that he will fall in love with the princess Chrysantza. At a beauty contest held there he chooses a beautiful young girl; no sooner has he made his choice, however, than everything disappears from his sight, as in a dream. He then continues his journey and eventually reaches Antioch, where he enters the service of its king, only to find that the king's daughter is Chrysantza, the very girl he chose at the beauty contest of the *Erotokastron*. As foretold, the two fall in love and meet secretly, to the king's great displeasure. However, the fury of the king is appeased when he is made to believe that Belthandros is in love not with his daughter but with her maidservant, whom he is obliged to marry; but the marriage is not consummated. In the end Belthandros escapes from Antioch and, taking Chrysantza with him, reaches his homeland, where they are both joyfully received.

The poem is full of Western elements, as is evident from the names Belthandros, Rhodophilos and Philarmos (which seem to derive from Bertrand, Rodolphe and Willerm), the reference to hawking, the Castle of Love, the king of Antioch and so on; for this reason a model from Provence has been suggested on which the romance's unknown Greek author may have drawn. But we cannot overlook the fact that many Greek elements — and important ones—are also there, such as the appearance of the late Hellenistic figures of *Tyche* (*Fortuna*) and Eros, the beauty contest (a purely Byzantine practice),[5] the 'Byzantine' luxury of the *Erotokastron*, the fact that Chrysantza is called a *Porphyrogenitus* and others. And there are certain passages in the poem that are reminiscent of modern Greek folk songs.

It is difficult to assign a date to this well-constructed, if not poetically arresting, work. It is noteworthy that in it Antioch, which fell to the Mohammedans in 1269, is still in Christian hands. This probably means that an earlier version of the same story went back to the thirteenth century.[6] The anonymity of the poem, the simplicity of its diction—it is composed in a simpler form of Greek than the *Callimachus and Chrysorrhoe* —the points of contact with the *Libystros and Rhodamne* and with modern Greek folk songs, indicate that this work too has probably been through a period of oral transmission.

Libystros and Rhodamne is the most important and the longest of these romances of chivalry.[7] The narrative, which is in the first person, is rather involved and is related by young Klitovos to Queen Myrtane, his first love.

On a long journey Klitovos meets Libystros, a Latin prince of the land of Libandros, who, after dreaming an allegorical dream, leaves his country and comes to the *Argyrokastron*, the Silver Castle, where he falls in love with Rhodamne, the daughter of its king and master. Libystros attaches his messages of love to arrows, which he shoots on to the castle terrace— much of the poem is taken up by these love letters—and so finally wins the princess over, and the two get married. But shortly after Berderichos, king of Egypt, seizes Rhodamne and carries her away with the help of a witch, and Libystros sets out across the world to find her. During these peregrinations he meets Klitovos, and the two continue the search together until they come across the witch who helped the king of Egypt to kidnap Rhodamne. She gives them magic horses to cross the sea, and they finally find the princess, whom they bring safely back to the Silver Castle. After the reunion of Libystros with Rhodamne, Klitovos marries her sister Melanthia, who dies two years later. He then returns to his homeland and to Queen Myrtane, to whom he relates the story.

In this romance the atmosphere is totally different from that of the Hellenistic and the Byzantine novels. Klitovos and Libystros are not shadowy, pseudo-ancient heroes, 'descendants of the young men who frequented the Hellenistic *gymnasia*', but warriors (καβαλλάριοι)[8] like the Western knights. As has been noted, if they were transferred to Provence, they would be at home with the heroes of troubadour fiction. Thus, Libystros wears no beard; his hair is cut in Frankish fashion; he carries a falcon. In both dress and independence of character Rhodamne is a Frankish and not a Byzantine princess. But these details and much else that is Frankish are fused in this poem with clear Byzantine elements, such as the allegorical figures of the months and the virtues (included in imitation of Eustathios Macrembolites), the Court ceremonial and certain descriptions of nature—which, incidentally, are not unlike those found in modern Greek folk songs.[9]

The narrative flows easily in spite of the complicated structure—we have two pairs of lovers and two narrators, Klitovos and Libystros—and has a clear lyrical bent; in metre and language it is close to modern Greek. We know nothing about its author, who must have come from some area (like Cyprus or Crete) where there was a strong Frankish influence; but there are no clear dialectal elements in the badly transmitted text that could help us in locating it. It probably belongs to the end of the four-teenth or the beginning of the fifteenth century.[10]

The *Libystros and Rhodamne* also appears to have gone through a period of oral transmission, as the anonymity of the poem, the two differing ver-sions of the story we have, the badly transmitted text and the contaminations with other verse romances (like the *Belthandros and Chrysantza*) and with modern Greek folk songs suggest.

In *Imberios and Margarona*, the fourth of these tales of chivalry, Western influence is evident indeed. It has rightly been called a Greek version of the twelfth-century French story *Pierre de Provence et la Belle Maguelonne*, attributed to Bernard de Tréviers, which enjoyed great popularity and of which many Western variations exist. It may well have been known in Frankish-occupied Morea in the thirteenth century where it was perhaps recast in Greek. The view has also been put forward that it was brought to Greek lands by the Cistercian monks, who since 1211 had occupied the monastry of Daphni, near Athens, a monastery which, according to one tradition, was 'founded' by Imberios and Margarona. But this is much less probable. However that may be, in the Greek version many purely Greek elements can also be found, and even the hero himself is an Orthodox Greek trained in the classics.

The story is the following. Imberios, the son of a king of Provence and a brave and well-educated cavalier, after defeating a foreign knight in a tournament, leaves Provence in pursuit of further glory. At Anapli (Nauplia) he wins and marries the Princess Margarona as the result of a victory at a tournament and then escapes with her to return to Provence. On their way Imberios is captured by pirates when trying to retrieve a precious talisman an eagle has snatched away from him, and he is sold to the king of Egypt as a slave. Margarona continues her journey alone and reaches Provence, where, in despair at the loss of her husband, she builds a nunnery by the sea. In due course the eagle brings the snatched talisman to Provence; at the sight of it Margarona believes her husband to be dead. But Imberios manages to escape from Egypt and, after further adventures, reaches France, where he is given shelter in the very nunnery that Margarona has founded. There husband and wife recognize one another, and the joyful news reaches the palace. For long years thereafter they reign happily over their people in Provence.

We have two Greek versions of *Imberios and Margarona*, one in 862 political lines, probably the work of a Cretan poet of the late fifteenth century, and a later one in 1046 rhyming fifteen-syllable couplets. Though poetically unimportant, this verse romance was much loved and was published several times from the sixteenth century onwards. Once again, the anonymity of the poem, the multiple versions, the identical scenes, words and phrases which are found in other of our verse romances (notably *Phlorios and Pliatzaphlora*)[11] point to a period of oral transmission. Naturally, after it was finally committed to writing once again pen-poets elaborated on it, as the rhyming version clearly shows.

But perhaps Western influence is most clearly evident in the fifth tale, that of *Phlorios and Pliatzaphlora*. It is a Greek rendering of a story found in many European literatures, all the versions of which go back to the twelfth-century French original, *Floire et Blanchefleur* (on which Boccaccio's *Filocolo* is also based). The Greek romance is a rehandling and enlargement of the Tuscan *Il cantare di Fiorio e Biancifiore*.

The romance tells the tale of a childless cavalier and his wife who visit the Sepulchre of St James in Spain to pray for a child. In answer to their prayers, the cavalier's wife becomes pregnant, but on their way home they are attacked by the Saracen king, Philip; the cavalier is killed and his spouse taken prisoner and forced into the service of the Saracen queen. In due course she becomes the queen's friend, but when she gives birth to her child, a boy they name Phlorios, she dies. Meanwhile the Queen herself has borne a daughter named Pliatzaphlora; when the two children become adults they fell in love with one another, but the king is opposed to their marriage, so Phlorios is sent away to another king's court. At Phlorios' departure Pliatzaphlora gives him a magic ring that will lose its brightness whenever she is in danger. When the king fraudulently succeeds in condemning Pliatzaphlora to death by burning, Phlorios becomes aware of the danger through the magic ring and comes swiftly to her rescue. The King then sells Pliatzaphlora into slavery, and once again Phlorios is made aware of the danger and hurries to help her. This time he is too late, however; she has been carried away. So Phlorios sets out in search of her and reaches first Alexandria and then Babylon, where Pliatzaphlora is the slave of an emir. The two young lovers are united once again and meet secretly, but they are betrayed by a magic fountain whose water flows through the tower which is Pliatzaphlora's prison. Upon learning this, the angry emir decides to burn them both alive, but the fire will not burn. At last the emir is informed of the noble birth of Phlorios and, as it emerges that they are related, liberates both the lovers, agrees to their marriage and sends them back to Spain. There a second marriage ceremony takes place, and all the people of that kingdom are converted to Christianity. Phlorios ends by becoming king in Rome.

We have two versions of the story in Greek, one in 1796 and one in 1874 political lines, both probably belonging to the end of the fourteenth or the beginning of the fifteenth century. Their style is verbose, and the language is mixed with erudite and demotic elements, indiscriminately used. There is much dialogue in the narrative and a great number of figures of speech. As poetry it is an inferior work, perhaps the worst of all the surviving verse romances. The contaminations with *Spaneas*,[12] *Imberios and Margarona* and certain folk songs, the anonymity of the poet, the two different versions, the loose narrative and the repetitions all point, once again, to a period of oral transmission.

The *Achilleis*, the last of this group, has come down to us in three versions, the longest of which consists of 1820 political lines. According to this romance, a king of the Myrmidons has a son called Achilles, a great warrior who is also well versed in Greek literature. He wishes to distinguish himself in battle and this he does, pursuing the fleeing enemies of his father to the walls of a distant castle. There he sees the daughter of the enemy king—her name is not given—with whom he immediately falls in love. He makes peace with her father and, promising to become the slave of the God of Love, whom he has previously spurned, sends a love letter to the young princess. Meanwhile, Love, appearing in the form of a bird, wounds the princess with his arrow, and the two young lovers secretly escape. Her infuriated brothers pursue them, but they are defeated in battle by Achilles. However, a reconciliation comes about, and the young couple celebrate their marriage, after which Achilles' father holds a tournament, in the course of which Achilles defeats a Frankish cavalier. Thereafter that 'admirable young man, the glory of the Greeks', lives happily, hunting lions and other wild beasts, until his wife falls ill and dies. Soon after, he dies of grief.

The longest of the three versions[13] has a 'later' addition[14] in which the Trojan War is described. In this Achilles takes part; in order to bring an end to the fighting, it is arranged that he shall marry the sister of Paris. During the marriage ceremony, which takes place in the cathedral of Troy, Achilles is assassinated; the Greeks once again attack and sack the city of Troy in order to avenge the death of their hero.

It is amusing to see that at the end of this version (ll. 1798ff.) the poet says that he is acquainted with the writings of Homer, Aristotle, Plato and Palamedes.[15] He knew nothing of Greek poetry or mythology, of course. Achilles is presented as a handsome Western knight wandering 'in foreign lands' in search of adventure, and the whole spirit of the poem is that of chivalry. What adds something of a 'Greek' colour to this romance is the influence which the *Epic of Digenis Akritas* and, to a much lesser degree, the Alexander romance have had upon it. Like Digenis, Achilles is a marvellously precocious child and a man of gigantic powers who defeats all his opponents, slays lions and other wild beasts and dies almost simultaneously with his beloved wife. It is true that all these motifs are also found here and there in various other epic and romantic narratives, but the appearance of so much that is common to the Digenis epic and the *Achilleis* is striking.

There are also other Greek elements in the *Achilleis*, such as the ecphrasis (the description of the garden and the fountain), the *pittakia*, the love letters, the invocation to Eros and the subordinate position of woman (which, of course, has little to do with the *amour courtois* of French poetry). But what is certain is that there is nothing that indicates a 'national' Greek spirit in the poem. The three versions we possess clearly go back to one original, probably of the fourteenth or early fifteenth century. These variants, the anonymity of the poem, the points of contact with other demotic songs and verse romances again suggest a period of oral transmission.

Before leaving this body of Frankish-influenced romances of the fourteenth and fifteenth centuries, what should be stressed is the important position which they occupy in the course of Greek poetry, although they are inferior works from a literary point of view. For it was this Western-influenced verse that brought new life to the waning Byzantine poetic tradition which, with very few and unimportant exceptions, had clung for centuries, in sterile imitation, to over-used Classical and Hellenistic patterns and to a stilted pseudo-Atticist diction of various shades. The new poetic forces which were released seem to have sprung, on the one hand, from the disintegration of the fossilized Byzantine educational system in the Frankish-occupied lands and, on the other, from the appearance in the new Frankish courts established on Greek soil of Western troubadours with their inspiring poetry, which was taken over by Greek singers. For the Latinized Greek aristocracy that then emerged and collaborated closely with the Frankish conquerors and the *gasmouli* (the offspring of mixed marriages) must have been thirsting for such entertainment in the Greek language.

As we have seen, perhaps with the sole exception of *Callimachus and Chrysorrhoe*, it is impossible to determine the exact provenance of the Frankish-influenced Greek romances—the Morea, the Aegean islands, Rhodes, Cyprus, Crete?—but what is certain and should be stressed is that this poetry, in spite of all the Western elements it contained, did not break away completely from its Byzantine roots, nor from the Oriental features which the Byzantine tradition had absorbed.[16] It simply furthered the Greek poetic tradition by imbibing the new spirit of the *romans courtois*, with their knights errant, their adventures in foreign lands, their tournaments, their idealized notion of love, their beautiful princesses so free in spirit, their feudal allegiances and their romantic feeling for nature, in which the pathetic fallacy plays no small part. Another important point is that this new poetry developed and amplified the Greek oral poetic tradition that had flourished in Byzantium since the days of the Akritic Cycle[17] and had made use of the spoken idiom—by no means the least of the services it rendered. For if Greek poetry survived and was handed down to Crete and to the singers of the bleak years of Turkish domination, its resilience was due in no small measure to the oral singers of the late Byzantine centuries who, mostly uneducated men themselves, addressed uneducated, largely illiterate audiences and so had to use a living demotic tongue to be understood; for in oral poetry no audience accepts a language it cannot follow.[18] Thus the old erudite diction was gradually ousted from most Greek verse.

The new impetus that was given to Greek poetry in the demotic and reached its apex in seventeenth-century Crete (when it was cruelly interrupted by the conquest of the island by the Turks in 1669) passed on, as we shall see, to the Ionian Islands, and from there to Greece proper after her liberation. So it is fair to say that modern Greek poetry owes a great debt to the injection of life that it received from the West, the first important examples of which are the late Byzantine verse romances we have just examined. They represent one of the channels through which Greek poetry flowed on its way from the Middle Ages to the modern world.

Greek translations of Western romances

Brief mention should also be made of three late Byzantine verse translations of Western works. It is doubtful if they deserve a place in the history of Greek poetry, for, unlike the previous group of verse romances, they are not adaptations of Western works in which a fusion of Frankish and Greek elements is achieved but straightforward translations that have had no influence whatsoever upon the development of Greek poetry.

First, there is the Greek translation, in 853 political lines, of the romance *Apollonius of Tyre*—probably a work of the late fourteenth century. This well-known story spread widely in the West when translated from the original Latin version into most major European languages and influenced, among others, Chaucer and Shakespeare. It is probably of Hellenistic Greek origin,[19] but the medieval Greek poem under discussion here has no direct dependence on it. It is, as the title clearly says, μεταγλώττισμα ἀπὸ λατινικὸν εἰς τὸ ῥωμαϊκόν, a translation from Latin into Greek ('Latin' here meaning 'Western'). In all probability, it is a translation of a Tuscan version of the story.[20]

In the Greek poem Apollonius, his wife and his daughter are involved in many adventures. They are parted, believe each other dead and, at the end, are happily reunited. The action takes place in the Greek East, in Antioch, Cyrenaica, Ephesus, Tarsus and Mytilene. The only liberty the Greek translator takes is to elaborate on certain religious and moralizing passages of the poem, which he presents in the light of Orthodox Byzantine piety.

A second Greek version of the same story, in 1894 rhyming political lines, has survived, which was first printed in Venice in 1534 and reprinted several times. Some of these editions bear the words Ποίημα ἀπὸ χειρὸς Κωνσταντίνου Τεμένεω ('A poem written by Constantine Temenes'), and others mention one Gabriel Akontianos as author. The part played by these men in the rhyming version of *Apollonius of Tyre* has not been clarified. The version itself depends on the rehandling of the original story by the Florentine Antonio Pucci (1309–88), which had enjoyed considerable popularity and on which even modern Greek folk tales have been shown to be based.

The romance of *Apollonius of Tyre* has little in common with the tales of love and chivalry which we have examined; it is more reminiscent of the romances of Xenophon of Ephesus and Achilles Tatius.[21]

Second, we have the *Trojan War*, a translation of a large part of the *Roman de Troie* of Benoît de Sainte-Maure (twelfth century), a poem of 30,000 lines. It is long work, clumsy in expression, which, however, survives in many manuscripts, a fact that indicates a wide circulation.[22]

Third is *The Old Knight*, a short, dry version in literary Greek of the French romance *Guiron le Courtois*, whose real name was *Palamède*. It is cast in 306 political lines and gives only snatches of the story that belongs to the circle of King Arthur and the Knights of the Round Table; the Greek translator took his story from an Italian version by Rusticano di Pisa (c. 1272–98).

In those days not only were translations limited to Western works but Greek works were transposed into a simpler form of Greek, as can be seen from the hopeless *Translation of the Iliad*—this is not a translation of the Homeric text but one of Johannes Tzetzes 'Allegories of the Iliad'—composed by Constantine Hermoniacos in eight-syllable lines at the command of John II, Despot of the Epirus (died 1335).

Pseudo-historical romances

Finally, we come to the *Life of Alexander* and *The Tale of Belisarius*, two pseudo-historical romances with a 'national Greek' character which, as they belong to this same circle of verse romances, must be dealt with here.

The *Life of Alexander* (dated 1388) is an anonymous metrical version, in an erudite form of Greek, of the Hellenistic romance of Pseudo-Callisthenes. It derives directly from the ancient text[23] and speaks about the birth of Alexander, his education under Aristotle, the taming of Bucephalus, his wars against the 'Romans' and the Persians, various heroic achievements of the Macedonian king, numerous adventures in legendary lands, the wonders he came across in India and, finally, his death at the hands of two traitors who poisoned him.

We also have a later rhyming version of the *Life of Alexander* in the demotic, which was often reprinted from 1529 onwards in Venice, as well as a prose version in many redactions from the same or a slightly earlier period (about 1500). To these should be added the late seventeenth-century demotic prose version known as the *Chap-Book* (Φυλλάδα) *of Alexander the Great*, which enjoyed great popularity. As would be expected, a number of strange and marvellous stories became associated with the personality of the Macedonian king. It is through these Byzantine versions of Alexander's life that his achievements spread to the Balkans and to the peoples of the Middle East.

The Tale of Belisarius, again an anonymous work, is a pathetic narrative in demotic Greek dealing with the life and the sad end of Belisarius, the great general of Justinian I (527–65). Around that important historical figure legends and fantastic stories are woven, among them the tale that Belisarius also led his army against Britain and returned to Constantinople in triumph, bringing back as a prisoner the king of England! The poem makes Belisarius the subject of the courtiers' envy, so that in the end, in spite of his great military successes, they persuade the emperor to imprison and to blind him.

The Tale of Belisarius has survived in three versions.[24] The oldest, probably dating from the fifteenth century, consists of 556 fifteen-syllable lines, whereas the second, in 997 rhyming political verses, was printed in Venice in 1525. The third, in 840 political lines, is attributed to Emmanuel Georgillas (c. 1500), the Rhodian poet.[25]

Both these poems, with their pseudo-historical and 'national' character and their fantastic and popular content, are interesting examples of the kind of poetry that was enjoyed in the late Middle Ages in the East. No doubt other similar ones, now lost, must have existed. Their object was to excite the curiosity of their audiences and to stir in their hearts the 'heroic' spirit and a sense of wonder.

HISTORICAL POEMS

Of the three noteworthy historical poems of this period, *The Chronicle of the Morea*, an anonymous work of more than 9000 political lines dealing with the establishment and the development of Frankish rule in Greece is by far the most important. It starts with the year 1095 (the year of the First Crusade) then, skipping the Second and the Third Crusades, covers in detail the Fourth Crusade and what ensued in the Peloponnese until 1292, when the text breaks off.

We have versions of the *Chronicle of the Morea* in four different languages —Greek, French, Italian and Aragonese. Except for the Aragonese, which we know was commissioned by Juan Fernandez de Heredia, Grand Master of the Knights Hospitallers in the last decade of the fourteenth century, and which draws on both the French and the Greek versions, it is a matter of dispute which of the others is the original or from what original, now lost, they all derive.[26] The most promising view appears to be that they all go back to a French narrative which was probably longer than the surviving French account, the *Livre de la Conqueste de la Princée de l'Amorée*.[27]

Of the four multilingual narratives of the *Chronicle*, only the one in Greek concerns us here. The five manuscripts that transmit it fall into two families, representing two distinct versions which have been published separately.[28] It is of interest that the slightly later and shorter of the two suppresses many anti-Greek elements of the earlier and longer one and gives, as we shall see, clear indications that it has gone through a period of oral transmission.

The *Chronicle of the Morea* reflects the cultural and political life of the Frankish-occupied Peloponnese and, at the linguistic level, a very special mixed diction in which spoken Greek is fused with erudite Greek elements and Frankish words and terms. What must be concluded is that the Greek of the *Chronicle* was not spoken but is 'translation Greek'.[29] It is clear that the original Greek redactor must have belonged to the milieu of the fourteenth-century Frankish masters of the Morea, and must have composed his work for the benefit both of Hellenized members of the French aristocracy and of Greek nobles who, politically and culturally, had gone over to the side of the Franks. The suggestion has been made that he may have been a *gasmoulos*, the offspring of a mixed marriage between a Frank and a Greek, whose religion was Roman Catholic.

The *Chronicle* is, in a sense, of a 'popular' nature, designed to appeal and to excite to acts of prowess, just as were the Provençal *chansons de geste*, the *Chanson d'Antioch* or the *Chanson de Jerusalem*, which were composed at the beginning of the twelfth century and are concerned with the Crusades. In the first part the poem deals at considerable length with the Fourth Crusade and the fall of Constantinople to the Franks in 1204. But the greatest and most important part of the poem is dedicated to the princes of the Morea, whose reign is presented in a somewhat legendary manner and with many errors and confusions. The favourite here is Guillaume de Villehardouin (1245–78), who was defeated at the battle of Pelagonia (1259), was taken prisoner and finally became a vassal of the Emperor Michael VIII Palaeologus (1261–82). It was the battle of Pelagonia that put an end to French ambition in the Morea.

Though poetically a dry text—and the Greek version is even drier than the French—one can see how the feudal organization of the Morea and its court, the achievements of brave knights, the battles, the towns as commercial centres and the position of the Church as described in the *Chronicle* could exercise a fascination on the men of the fourteenth and fifteenth centuries. However, for us today its significance lies not in its poetic charm but in the historical and linguistic information it provides.

As with the verse romances, the shorter of the two Greek versions,[30] even if not an oral composition, has clearly gone through a period of oral transmission,[31] and this explains why the anti-Greek elements found in the longer pen-version are here suppressed. The wider and purely Greek audience to which it was addressed would not readily accept them. The Western oral tradition of poetry, which was introduced to the courts of the Greek lands under Frankish occupation, enhanced and furthered the

Byzantine oral tradition that flourished in the days of the *Epic of Digenis Akritas*.

The second historical poem from the Frankish occupation of Greek lands is the *Chronicle of Tocco*. The beginning is missing, but the body of the poem is long enough (3923 fifteen-syllable lines) and is written in an unassuming vernacular. It is a kind of family epic of the Frankish ruling house in the Epirus by an unknown author, which starts at the death of Leonardo I Tocco (1375–7) and continues until the beginning of the war over Glarentza (1426–7) that Carlo I Tocco waged with the Palaeologues. The earliest of the two manuscripts in which it is transmitted belongs to the early fifteenth century.[32] As poetry it is negligible.

The third is a brief work called *The Song of Henry of Flanders*, consisting of between forty and sixty rhyming political lines (for several versions of it have survived) of Cretan or Corfiot origin. It deals with the Emperor Henry of Flanders (1206–16), who succeeded his brother Baldwin I of Flanders, the first Latin emperor of Constantinople, when the latter was taken prisoner by the Bulgars. The poem, as we have it today, is a fifteenth-century work, but it clearly derives from a much older song in honour of Henry of Flanders, who was celebrated by Franks and Byzantine Greeks alike.[33]

About the *Ballad of Arodaphnusa* we shall speak in our discussion of Cypriot poetry under the Franks.[34]

CHAPTER 23

Poetry from the Aegean Islands, Rhodes, Cyprus, Crete and the Ionian Islands

We must now abandon the division of poetry according to poetic genres—verse romances, historical poems and so on—and examine the entire poetic output of certain Greek areas under Frankish rule so as not to lose sight of its special 'local' character, which, of course, is most notable in Crete and the Ionian Islands but can also be traced in certain Aegean islands, on Rhodes and in Cyprus.

THE AEGEAN ISLANDS

It is in the fifteenth and sixteenth centuries that love poems with a distinct personal note appear in Greek. They retain, of course, much of the colour of the folk song, but love is their theme, and in character they have much of the subjective personal quality found in the chivalrous verse of France and Italy, an element totally absent from the pure Byzantine tradition. It has therefore been rightly postulated that these songs are the outcome of Western influence upon Greek poets.

Rhodes has been suggested as the place of origin of some of these[1]—in one of them Rhodes is mentioned by name—but other Aegean islands that were long under Frankish rule could lay an equal claim to the title, as they were also lands in which a fusion of Byzantine with Western cultural elements took place; for side by side with a Western approach to love, allusions to Byzantium are found in these songs (references to the emperor and the mercenaries of the Byzantine Empire and so forth).

Two important collections of such love poems have survived, to which a third, shorter one of less significance should be added. The first is known by the name *Erotopaegnia* (*Love Games*) and has been transmitted in a fifteenth-century manuscript now in the British Museum.[2] It contains 112 short poems — 714 unrhyming political lines in all — some of which have been arranged into four incomplete alphabets, obviously the work of some 'later' redactor. The most complete of these alphabets is responsible for the title *The Alphabet of Love* by which the whole collection is sometimes known.

Lines 140–330 of the *Erotopaegnia*, known as 'The Song of the Hundred Words', form a short narrative in which a young girl poses a hundred questions to the young man who courts her and promises that if he answers them, she will embrace him. After the first ten answers, which are all love songs, she embraces him, and after nine more she succumbs and becomes his mistress, only to be cruelly abused and mocked for her weakness. The rest of this collection of love poems is hard to arrange in groups and they contain mostly complaints about the suffering which love causes. In style and verse they have much in common with the folk songs, but they are more outspoken and much more passionate, combining Western sentimentality with Eastern sensuality.

The second collection of such love songs comes from a late fifteenth- or early sixteenth-century Vienna manuscript[3] and is known as *Popular Songs*. It consists of 153 short pieces (154 if we are to include *The Seduction of the Young Girl*) 853 political lines long in all, of which some are rhyming couplets. These show that rhyme, which first appears in modern Greek poetry in the writings of the Cretan Stephanos Sachlikis (1332–c. 1403), soon spread to the rest of the Frankish-occupied Greek world.[4]

The *Popular Songs*, none of which can be older than the fifteenth century, are similar to the *Erotopaegnia* in sentiment and composition. Some retain the freshness of the folk song, while others are more sophisticated and less arresting.

The last collection of love poems which has survived comes from a Neapolitan manuscript[5] and is, on the whole, similar in character and quality to the two previous ones. It consists of six anonymous pieces, ranging from six to ninety-eight verses in length, of which four are cast in eight-syllable lines, while the other two are in the usual political verse. They seem to come from the same milieu as the *Erotopaegnia* and the *Popular Songs* and are probably of the same date.

Though considered by some scholars to be part of the *Popular Songs*,[6] *The Seduction of the Young Girl* (also known as *The Ballad of the Young Girl and the Young Man: Ῥιμάδα κόρης καὶ νιοῦ*) should be treated separately, for it is a remarkable, independent poem of which we have two versions, the longer in 191 political lines. In a lively and captivating manner it describes the love affair of a frivolous young man and a pure young girl, who eventually gives in and allows him to enter her bedroom. After conquering her, the young man abandons her and the poem closes with the girl's despair and the curses she hurls at his head. In diction *The Seduction of the Young Girl* is close to the folk songs but has a deeper, realistic sensuality; it clearly comes from a more sophisticated milieu than that of the folk songs and one in which morals were slacker. It has been suggested that its origin may be Cretan. Of interest are the 'reversals of nature' we find in it, which are reminiscent of Alexandrian poetry,[7] as well as the curses of the young girl, similar to those in the folk song *The Curse of the Deserted Maiden*.[8] The poem, probably the work of a fifteenth-century pen-poet, passed into oral poetry and was widely sung in many versions in the Dodecanese, the Cyclades and Corfu. Certain passages betray contaminations with the famous Cretan pastoral *The Shepherdess*.[9]

RHODES

If doubts have been rightly expressed about the Rhodian origin of the *Erotopaegnia*, there can be no doubts about the poetry of Emmanuel Georgillas (also known as Λιμενίτης), who lived and wrote in Rhodes at the end of the fifteenth century, when the island was ruled by the Knights of St John (1308–1522). Though Western culture was clearly prevalent among the Knights themselves, the population of the island continued to be Greek-speaking, so it is not surprising to find there a Greek poet of some ability. Unfortunately, we know nothing more about Emmanuel Georgillas except that he was a Roman Catholic and that he lost many members of his family during the terrible plague that ravaged Rhodes in 1498–9, a calamity which he describes in his poem *The Plague of Rhodes* (Θανατικὸν τῆς ῾Ρόδου). This consists of 644 rhyming political verses and is a simple narrative of faulty structure, for the poet jumps from one topic to another in a monotonous diction burdened by too many compound words. Its limited literary qualities are further vitiated by the moralizing tone the author assumes; for he considers the visitation of the plague a punishment for the sins of the people of Rhodes and mixes lamentation with tiresome exhortation to return to a purer life. Yet in spite of all this, he is a poet with a distinct personal voice, a rare quality in those days, and we find in his work interesting information about the society and the mores of fifteenth-century Rhodes. He blossoms particularly when he gives a detailed description of the great Rhodian ladies and of their dress.

To Emmanuel Georgillas has also been attributed, as we have seen, the rhyming version of *The Tale of Belisarius*[10] and (probably wrongly) a poem called *The Capture of Constantinople*,[11] which laments the fall of the city to the Turks and appeals to the powerful rulers of the West for help.

CYPRUS

From the days of the Lusignans in Cyprus (1192–1473) we have two interesting folk songs, both of which have survived in more than one version, *The Ballad of Arodaphnusa* and *Chatzinis and Arete*. The first deals with the 'murder' of Arodaphnusa (whose real name was Giovanna Dalema), a mistress of King Peter I (1359–69), by Queen Eleanora, his wife. As we know from the *Chronicle of Machaeras*,[12] Arodaphnusa was not murdered but cruelly tortured by the queen, an event which took place in 1369; so the folk song cannot have originated much later.

Chatzinis and Arete speaks of a young girl who is seduced by an Egyptian called Chatzinis; after complaining to 'the king' about it the two are happily married (in some versions Arete marries the king). The Cypriot version, published by Émile Legrand, has definite poetic merits. The editor dates the original of the poem to about 1460, connecting it with the Egyptian soldiers who were sent by the Sultan of Egypt to Cyprus to help Jacques de Lusignan to regain his throne.

From the first half of the fourteenth century we also have a long poem by Georgios Lapithis known as *The Duties of the Citizen*, which, in 1490 political lines, gives moral and practical advice; it is a work of no literary value.

Greatly superior to this in every respect is the anonymous *Lament on the Fall of Constantinople* (second half of the fifteenth century), which must have been composed shortly after the city fell to the Turks in 1453. In 118 political lines it describes in a naive but moving manner how the sad news reached Greece and Crete, how the great city was ruined and sacked, how noble men and women, monks and nuns, were enslaved and how churches were profaned; the heroism of the last Emperor is stressed and the poem culminates in the tragic lines: 'The angels and the saints no longer protect us!' The language used is a common demotic and the tone very close to that of the folk songs. Because of its allusions to Crete, it was earlier thought to be a Cretan work, but it has recently been shown to be Cypriot. Its literary value is unquestionable.

Just before the fall of Cyprus to the Turks in 1571 a series of beautiful love poems was composed which contains lyrics that are clearly among the most attractive of early modern Greek literature. The poems are composed in Italian hendecasyllables in the local idiom of the island and employ a variety of Renaissance forms—those of the sonnet, the octave, the *terzina*, the *canzone*, the *sestina*, the ballade, the *barzeletta* and so on. Italian influence is preponderant; some of these poems are direct imitations of Petrarch or of his followers—such as J. Sannazzaro (1456–1530) and P. Bembo (1470–1547)—while others, which are not quite imitations, are in the spirit of Petrarchism. The poet of these extraordinary works, who raised the local dialect to a true literary level, is the first to express in modern Greek many of the finer shades of the amorous feeling known from the Renaissance of the fifteenth century. The prevailing atmosphere in these poems is one of extreme sophistication and presupposes a highly refined and educated society, a milieu totally different from that of the folk songs. Unfortunately, the love poems of Cyprus, which represent one of the highest points of Renaissance literature in the Greek world, had no sequel after the Turks conquered the island.

Shortly before Cyprus fell to the Turks Malta was besieged by an Ottoman expeditionary force (1571). On that memorable siege and the resistance of the Knights of St John we have a short Cypriot poem of seventy-two rhyming political lines attributed to Solomon Rhodinos, who was both a poet and a painter. This unimportant work must have passed on to the world of oral poetry, for several versions of it exist, coming from various parts of Greece. (On the same siege, as we shall see, a long poem was also written by the Cretan poet Antonios Achelis, which is an adaptation from the Italian.)[13]

Solomon Rhodinos also composed a *Lament on Cyprus*, which, in 906 rhyming political lines, vividly describes the massacres and the pillaging that followed the conquest of the island by the Turks and laments the great calamity. It considers that the sins of the people of Cyprus are responsible for their sufferings and has much in common with the folk songs and the laments on the Fall of Constantinople. From this poem derives another short ballad, *The Capture of Cyprus by the Turks*.

In the field of religious poetry Frankish-occupied Cyprus has a few interesting items to show, of which the poems *On Good Friday* and *On the Resurrection* are the most noteworthy. On the other hand, the so-called *Cyprus Scenario* does not indicate the existence of Byzantine Passion Plays.[14]

The conquest of Cyprus by the Ottoman Empire in 1571 brought to an end all literary activity on the island except for the folk songs. The one notable exception is a poem by the Cypriot archimandrite Joachim Kantzellieris[15] (mid-seventeenth century) on the Turkish–Venetian War of 1645–69, an event about which the Cretan poets Anthimos Diakrousis Tzanes Bounialis and Athanasios Skleros also wrote.[16]

CRETE

We must now turn to Cretan poetry, the greatest literary achievement of the Greeks under the Franks. This can be divided into three periods: the first, extending from the conquest of the island by the Venetians to the fall of Constantinople to the Turks (1204–1453), is still predominantly Byzantine in character, but Western influence begins to be felt; the second, covering the years 1453 to 1590, is marked by the rapid development of a distinct Western Cretan flavour; and the third, running from 1590 to the fall of the island to the Turks in 1669, known as the golden age, is the one that finally gave birth to a 'Renaissance poetry' of a high standard.

The beginnings of Cretan poetry (1204–1453)

The oldest traceable examples of modern Greek verse on Crete are folk songs belonging to the epic cycle of Digenis Akritas; they were probably brought to the island by veterans of the Byzantine armies and by other Greeks who were established there after Crete was reclaimed from the Arabs by Nicephoros Phocas in 961. Some are still to be heard among the *Rizitika Tragoudia*, so called because they are sung in the foothills (the 'roots') of the White Mountains.[17] Another group of old Cretan folk songs—some of which are older than the fall of Constantinople to the Turks—belongs to the days of the Venetian occupation of the island.[18] They can be distinguished from those composed under Turkish domination because they are shorter and more restrained, because they make no use of rhyme and because no words of Turkish origin can be found in them.

In the early days of Venetian domination some of the Byzantine verse romances in the vernacular were also sung on Crete. It has even been argued, as we have seen, that at least one of these, the *Belthandros and Chrysantza*, may have been composed on the island; later adaptations of others, such as the *Imberios and Margarona*, into rhyming couplets were certainly made there.

We know little about the beginnings of personal poetry in Venetian-occupied Crete. For us it appears fully-fledged in the works of three remarkable poets, Stephanos Sachlikis, Leonardos Dellaportas and Marinos Falieros.

Stephanos Sachlikis (born before 1332; died c. 1403), we now know, can be safely considered the first representative of Cretan poetry.[19] This strange man, who 'preached morality through the self-indulgent descriptions of his own immorality', was born in Candia in the first half of the fourteenth century, neglected his studies and squandered his fortune (he came from a well-to-do family) and his youth in pursuing the pleasures of the flesh. This eventually landed him in jail, where he wrote some of the most virulent attacks on the prostitutes of Candia, most of whom he knew personally, as well as vivid descriptions of life in prison and the vile habits of his gaolers. Later, after he was released from prison, he wrote his autobiography, Ἀφήγησις Παράξενος (*A Strange Narrative*), in 908 political verses, in which he informs us that having left prison and being unable to live in the country with boorish peasants, he returned to Candia, where he worked as a lawyer, complying with the corrupt habits of his colleagues. It was then that he also wrote a poem of advice (Ἑρμηνεῖαι) addressed to young Phrantzeskis, the son of one of his friends, in which he warns him to avoid prostitutes, playing at dice and wandering in the streets at night.

Sachlikis was a man of great intelligence and no morals. He depicts with verve the colourful habits of Cretan society, his realism touching on cynicism when he speaks about the underworld of Candia. The influence of the Byzantine poetic tradition is evident in the use of the fifteen-syllable line and in the impact of Byzantine satirical precedents like Ptochoprodromos, Glykas and the *Spaneas*; but much more decisive was the influence upon him of Italian fourteenth-century poetry and, in particular, of the personal autobiographical and moralizing verse then fashionable, such as that of Antonio de' Beccari da Ferrara (1315–c. 1370) or Francesco di Vannozzo of Padua (c. 1335–90). But no matter how many or how varied the influences that shaped his poetry, Sachlikis retained a striking personal quality in his work; to this fact, doubtless, is due the influence he exercised in turn upon other satirical writers. This can be traced, for example, in one of the two anonymous Cretan poems entitled *Praise of Women* and *Life of Noble Women and most Honourable Ladies*, both works probably of the sixteenth century.[20]

Sachlikis' work is a landmark in the history of Greek poetry, for in his writings we find the first use of rhyme in modern Greek. Rhyme, as we have seen, originated in Syriac poetry,[21] was taken over by the Christian Latin poets of North Africa, from where it wandered to Spain, Provence and Italy, and was finally brought by the Crusaders to the Greek world.[22] Sachlikis experiments with rhyme in the poem on his imprisonment, using it sporadically in two, three, four and occasionally five consecutive lines, just as it was employed in the *frottola*, a kind of popular Italian song of the period. In others of his works he makes use of the rhyming couplet in an admirably finished form, which indicates that he cannot have been the first to try out rhyme in Greek. Older, less polished experiments must have existed which are now lost.[23] However, we cannot go far wrong if we assume that the use of rhyme was introduced into Greek poetry in the course of the fourteenth century and, more precisely, in the second half.

This sudden florescence of rhyme, most notably of the rhyming couplet, at the turn of the fourteenth century is indeed remarkable and clearly due to Italian influence; just as striking is the speed and completeness with which it replaced the older, non-rhyming political verse. In fact, the rhyming fifteen-syllable couplet—the *distichon*—soon came to be regarded as a separate unit of thought as well as of metre, and many such beautiful, independent couplets were fashioned, some of which are proverbial to this day.

A further important consequence of the new dates that have been calculated for Sachlikis is that we must now accept the existence of a well-developed Cretan poetic diction as early as the fourteenth century, a diction whose basis is the common Greek vernacular of the period, mixed with erudite and Cretan dialectal elements.

A near-contemporary of Sachlikis was Leonardos Dellaportas (c. 1350–c. 1420). He was born in Candia and, though Greek Orthodox in religion, devoted his life to the service of the Venetian republic as soldier, lawyer and ambassador. At an advanced age, on account of a natural child he had acquired, he was cast into jail, and it was there that he wrote most of the 4000 verses of his poetry.

Of his four extant poems—all poor as poetry—the most important is a dialogue with Truth (personified as a beautiful young woman) in 3166 political lines, in which the poet defends himself against the accusations of his enemies. To console and sustain the wronged poet, Truth relates edifying stories from the Scriptures and from Classical antiquity.

The other three of Dellaportas' works are of a religious or moralizing nature. The first, 800 lines long, is on the Passion; the second is a poem of contrition (Περὶ ἀνταποδόσεως) in 150 lines; and the last is a shorter prayer on Christ and the Virgin (Λόγοι παρακλητικοί).

Dellaportas' works (which were only discovered recently),[24] written so soon after the verse of Sachlikis, show how swiftly and how fully the new Cretan poetry began to flourish in the second half of the fourteenth and the beginning of the fifteenth century; moreover, they demonstrate clearly how traditional Byzantine features—the moral, religious and didactic tone,[25] the fifteen-syllable non-rhyming line[26] and the common spoken diction enriched by erudite and dialectal elements—were fertilized by the contact with the West.

Recent research[27] has also shown that a third significant poet, Marinos Falieros (c. 1395–c. 1474), whose date was long a matter of dispute, belongs to the end of the first period of Cretan poetry. Much concerning this writer is still obscure, and we have as yet no satisfactory edition of his works. However, we know that he was the son of a noble family with feudal holdings and that he married Fiorenza Zeno, the only daughter of the Lord of Andros, by whom he had several children. He also served as *supracomitus*, fitted out a galley for the defence of Crete and was a member of committees instituted to fix the taxation levied on the Jews and the extraordinary taxation to be levied for the fortification of Crete after the fall of Negroponte (1470).

Five poems have come down to us under his name, of which two are erotic dream poems closely akin to each other, two are didactic (admonitory or consolatory verse) and one is a short lament for the Virgin in dramatic form.

The two erotic poems, in which the poet transposes personal experiences into the world of dreams, are by far the most attractive, especially the first, the *Dream of Love* ('Ἐρωτικὸν Ἐνύπνιον),[28] among whose 130 rhyming fifteen-syllable lines amusing and humorous touches can be found. The second, called *History and The Dream* ('Ἱστορία καὶ Ὄνειρον), is much longer (748 political rhyming lines) but less rewarding. Both betray the influence of Italian erotic poetry, most notably that of Leonardo Giustiniani (c. 1410), whose *canzonette* had circulated widely in Italy during the fifteenth century. On the other hand, in Falieros' didactic poetry the influence of Byzantine didactic verse is evident, most prominently that of the *Spaneas*, with its commonplace 'wisdom'.

The *Lament on the Passion and the Crucifixion* (Θρῆνος εἰς τὰ πάθη καὶ τὴν Σταύρωσιν) is a dialogue in 404 rhyming political lines, written with true feeling. It is the first 'dramatic' account of the Passion in modern Greek, but, like all other surviving laments on the Virgin,[29] was not meant to be acted. The 'scenic' instructions found in the manuscript are given simply to help the reader.

The poetry of Marinos Falieros, most of which appears to have been composed between the years 1420 and 1430, has a pleasing spontaneity and a lively diction and makes good use of rhyme.

To the early 15th century also belongs an anonymous[30] poem, *On Expatriation* (Περὶ Ξενιτείας), which has survived in two versions, the longest in 548 political lines. It has much in common with the folk songs on the same subject, the hardships and the sorrows of life away from home. The poem, consisting of several short, independent parts, is not unlike the late Byzantine *Alphabet on Expatriation*.[31] Roughly contemporary with the poem *On Expatriation* is the religious verse of Johannes Plousiadenos (1429–c. 1500), about which we have already spoken.[32]

Strange indeed is the absence of any stage of experimentation in this early awakening of Cretan personal poetry, which emerged fully-fledged and immediately became established. The new diction—a mixture of spoken, erudite and Cretan dialectal elements—imposed itself fully, and the use of rhyme ousted all unrhyming verse from the literary scene suddenly and completely. It is characteristic that the word *rhimadoros* ('rhyme maker') came to mean 'poet' and *rhimada* ('rhyming') to mean 'poetry'.[33]

As we now know that the sudden florescence of Cretan poetry, whose able representatives were Sachlikis, Dellaportas and Falieros, emerged before the fall of Constantinople to the Turks (1453), the older view that 'educated' refugees from Byzantium after the Fall were responsible for the awakening of Cretan literature is no longer tenable. Recent research in the Cretan archives now in Venice has shown beyond doubt that this was a local, spontaneous florescence, a product of the fertilizing contact of the Cretan writers with the West, which infused new life into the waning Byzantine poetic tradition. Thus revived and transmuted, it continued its course.

The development and expansion of Cretan poetry (1453–1590)

In this period the language, metre and rhyme of Cretan poetry was further developed by fresh contacts with the West. In content it is predominantly didactic (in a broad sense) and satirical.

Of the didactic poets, the most important is Bergadis (c. 1500)—the name is a Greek form of the Venetian Bragadin—about whose life we know nothing. In his poem *Apokopos* —so called after the first line: *Μιὰν ἀπὸ κόπου νύσταξα* . . . ('Once, because I was tired, I felt inclined to sleep')—he describes a dream in which he descends to Hades, is asked if the living remember the dead and, in a satirical vein, answers that they are soon forgotten. The departed then express their desire to return to the world of the living and give him various messages for those they love— which, however, the frightened poet never delivers when he returns to the light.

Many folklore elements are mixed with Eastern allegories in this pessimistic poem, and, of course, Italian influence is evident.[34] Some striking descriptions of the beauty of the world of the living and of a shipwreck probably depend on an as yet unidentified Western source. The purpose of the poem is neither strictly didactic nor religious. It simply sets out to express the sad reality that life is transitory and that for the dead there is room neither in the world nor in the memory of the living. The language, once again, is a close-knit mixture of spoken, erudite and Cretan dialectal elements and the versification almost faultless. The *Apokopos* has the distinction of being the first book in spoken Greek to be published in Venice (1519). It ran to several editions.

A contemporary of Bergadis was Georgios Houmnos (end of fifteenth century), probably a notary of Chandax. Shortly before 1493 he cast in unpolished rhyming political verses a Byzantine prose collection of apocryphal biblical stories which he called *Κοσμογέννησις* (the *Creation*). In spite of their deep religious feeling, they have little literary value but are interesting as an example of the close link between the developing Cretan poetry and the dying Byzantine literary tradition.

To the end of the fifteenth century also belongs Andreas Sklentzas, scion of a well-known family of Cretan men of letters who became a

Roman Catholic monk and wrote religious verse. His most important poem is on Mary Magdalene, but his hymns and prayers to Christ, the Holy Ghost, the Mother of God, and St Francis are also noteworthy, as well as a poem on death. He also translated into Greek the Latin Prayer to the Holy Communion by St Thomas Aquinus.

A minor didactic poem of those days, known as *The Speech of the Dead King*, has also survived; in it the anonymous poet describes how once, because of the rain, he took refuge in a ruined chapel where the skeleton of a dead king appeared to him and told him how glorious he had been in life but that everything was lost at his death, and how this turned the poet's thoughts to repentance and to the Day of Judgement.[35]

The rhyming version of the romance *Apollonius of Tyre*, which is attributed to the Cretan poet Gabriel Akontianos (end of fifteenth century), and about which we have already spoken (p. 543), also belongs here. It is of special interest because of the influence it had on Vitsentzos Kornaros.

On the devastating earthquake that caused havoc in Crete in 1508 — also described by the Duke of Crete, Ieronymus Donatus, and by others — we have a poem by Manolis Sklavos called *The Disaster of Crete* ('Η Συμφορὰ τῆς Κρήτης). We know nothing about the poet, who relates in an animated manner the panic of the inhabitants, the litanies held by the clergy, the gathering outside the city of all who escaped alive in Candia and the terrible storm that followed the earthquake. He then sings the praises of the former beauty of the island and attributes the calamity to the sins of the Cretans, who, he warns, should they not repent, will fall under the sword of the Turk. We also have two short poems, *Complaints*, about the same earthquake, the longest in fifty rhyming political lines, describing what followed the catastrophe in Sitia.

At the end of the Middle Ages and particularly during the sixteenth century a series of works was written on *Charos* (Death) and on life after death in both East and West. In the Greek East the dominant feature of these poems seems to be a vigorous reaction against the lax morals that contact with the West was introducing to the lands under Frankish occupation. Such is, in a sense, the poem of Johannes Pikatoros (beginning of sixteenth century), a native of Rethymnon, called *Lament on Bitter and Insatiate Hades* ('Ρίμα θρηνητικὴ εἰς τὸν πικρὸν καὶ ἀκόρεστον Ἅδην), on which the influence of Bergadis' *Apokopos* can also be traced. Pikatoros describes, in 563 rhyming political verses, how in a dream he reached Hades, where dead kings, noblemen, young men, girls and children lay weeping and speechless, their joints full of worms. Full of indignation at the sight, he discussed death and original sin with Charos, his guide. Various interpretations of life after death are given, in which views from antiquity, the Scriptures, Greek folk songs and Western writings are fused. The poet is imaginative and displays considerable power in his descriptions.

To the beginning of the sixteenth century, as we have already mentioned, also belong two fairly short, anonymous, anti-feminist satirical works, the *Praise of Women* (Ἔπαινος γυναικῶν) and the *Life of Noble Women and Most Honourable Ladies* (Συναξάριον τῶν εὐγενικῶν γυναικῶν καὶ τιμιωτάτων ἀρχοντισσῶν). The first makes fun of the faults of young, unmarried girls, of married women and of widows, while the second tries to prove how evil women are and how inferior to men. Both draw on Italian poetry, and neither has any literary value.

The satirical and didactic spirit of the times also found expression in animal fables, that popular Byzantine literary genre. Thus the Byzantine *Synaxarion of the Estimable Donkey* was recast in rhyming couplets by an unknown Cretan poet and printed in Venice in 1539 as *The Delightful Tale of the Donkey, the Wolf and the Fox*. The dialect is pure Cretan and there is some fine humour in it as the donkey outwits the fox and the wolf and throws them into the sea. Less successful is the anonymous fable *The Cat and the Mice*, in which a cat pretends he is dying in order to trap some simple-minded mice.

Just as the *Lament on the Passion and the Crucifixion* by Marinos Falieros[36] was meant to be read and not to be acted, so too was the anonymous sixteenth-century *Prayer to the Passion of Christ* (Λόγοι παρακλητικοὶ εἰς τὰ πάθη τοῦ χριστοῦ), which casts in dialogue the Betrayal of Judas, the last Supper and the Judgement of Christ. On the whole the poet followed Matthew and, less closely, St John and the Apocrypha; the poem ended with the Crucifixion and a lament for the Virgin, now lost. It has little literary but some linguistic interest.

The period closes with two historical poems, one on the siege of Malta (1565) and one on the capture of Cyprus by the Turks (1571).

The *Siege of Malta* is an unpolished but interesting work by an otherwise unknown poet from Rethymnon, Antonios Achelis (second half of sixteenth century), describing the siege of the island by the Turks in 1565, which the Knights of St John successfully resisted. By and large, this is a poetic version, in Cretan vernacular, of Marino Fracasso's Italian prose description of that event; occasionally, however, Achelis abandons his source and adds episodes otherwise unknown and similes drawn from Latin and Italian poetry. A definite 'patriotic', anti-Muslim spirit prevails.

The second, the *Lament on the Fall of Cyprus to the Turks*, as yet unpublished, has much interesting information to offer on the conquest of the island by the Turks and on the Battle of Lepanto which followed (1571).[37] Certain linguistic elements in this anonymous poem seem to point to a Cretan author.

Judged as a whole, the poetic output of this second period of Cretan poetry is by no means outstanding. Though colourful and brave in its experimentation, it has many linguistic and metrical infelicities and too great a dependence on earlier Byzantine or contemporary Italian models. This is, of course, understandable (indeed, inescapable), faced as it was with the end of the Byzantine Empire, increasing contact with the West, the spread of the use of rhyme and, not least, the beginning of printing, which was to give Greek poetry a totally new complexion. However, its faults notwithstanding, the verse of this period made considerable strides and opened the way to the golden age of Cretan poetry that followed.

The golden age of Cretan poetry (1590–1669)

The new age which began at the end of the sixteenth century and continued until the fall of the island to the Turks was inaugurated by a pastoral poem, *The Shepherdess*, then moved on to the greatest achievement of Cretan literature, the drama, and concluded with the long and impressive verse romance, the *Erotokritos*, whose influence upon the further development of modern Greek poetry can hardly be overrated.

PASTORAL POETRY

As a precursor to Cretan pastoral poetry one should consider *The True Shepherd* ('Ο πιστικὸς Βοσκός), a free rendering into the Cretan idiom, by an unknown poet, of the famous Italian pastoral tragi-comedy *Pastor Fido* by G. B. Guarini (1538–1612). This noteworthy free translation, cast in 'Italian' eleven- and seven-syllable verses, retains something of the characteristic Western lyricism of the original.[38]

True Cretan pastoral poetry finds its first and, as far as we know, its only expression in *The Shepherdess*, the work of an unknown poet. When first published in 1627, it appeared under the name of one Nicolaos Drymetinos, who does not seem to be the real author.

The story is naive and simple: a young shepherd falls deeply in love with a beautiful shepherdess, whom he accompanies to the cave where she lives with her father. There, her father being absent, the young lovers spend some happy days together, and then the shepherd leaves, promising to return within a month. However, falling ill, he is obliged to break his promise, and when he returns three months later he is informed that the shepherdess has died of grief. Unable to find consolation, the young man wanders across the hills lamenting his misfortune.

This tale is clearly based on an Italian model—Cretan mores did not tolerate lovers living in open sin—which has not yet been identified. The Greek version, which runs to 476 eleven-syllable rhyming lines (some of them rather clumsy), is in a simple Cretan dialect and has a certain graceful naivety that counterbalances the sloppy sentimentality of the story. It was much admired by Greeks and foreigners alike and was even translated into Latin in the seventeenth century. Extracts from the poem —even the complete poem and a version of it partly recast into fifteen-syllable lines—were chanted in the Aegean islands and in other parts of Greece.

THE CRETAN THEATRE

The majority of the works of the Cretan golden age are dramatic: they are considered the apex of 'Greek renaissance' literature.

The existence of plays composed and acted in Crete presupposes a suitable social milieu for such artistic activities, and this was basically the bourgeois class, whose economic development in the sixteenth and seventeenth centuries enabled it to share with the nobility the patronage of the arts, much on the pattern of Venice and other Italian cities. In Italy this patronage was practised to a great extent through the establishment of academies, which were societies of educated men with scholarly and artistic pursuits.[39] During the sixteenth and seventeenth centuries one of the important purposes of these Italian academies was the support and promotion of drama, which they achieved by encouraging their members to write plays and by arranging for them to be publicly read or performed. Such performances were given at first in the palaces of the nobility or in improvised theatres and later in wooden theatres specially constructed for that purpose. The only criterion for joining these academies was a desire for education. There was no barrier to men who did not belong to the nobility or who were not Italian by birth or Roman Catholic by faith.

Recent research has shown that in Crete in the second half of the sixteenth and in the second quarter of the seventeenth century three such academies were founded on the Italian pattern: the Accademia de Vivi in Rethymnon, founded in about 1555, the Accademia dei Stravaganti in Candia, most probably founded in about 1590, and the Accademia dei Sterili in Chania, established in about 1632. Most important of these was the Accademia dei Stravaganti,[40] for the Vivi had apparently a very short and undistinguished life[41] and the Sterili perished soon after it was founded, when the Turks captured the city in 1645.[42] It can hardly be doubted that it was the Accademia dei Stravaganti that provided the stimulus and a suitable milieu for the development of the Cretan theatre —as, indeed, for the development of the entire Cretan literature of the golden age.

We know, for example, that John Mourmouris, to whom Georgios Chortatsis dedicated his *Erophile*, was a member of the Accademia dei Stravaganti, and we hear of meetings held in the home of the nobleman Matteo Zeno, at which Italian and Greek poems were probably also recited. Such meetings were no doubt frequented by the intelligentsia of Candia, which could boast of a remarkable number of scholars, lawyers, doctors and churchmen, many of whom were educated in Italian universities (most notably that of Padua) from the middle of the sixteenth century onwards.[43] It is these men who, having become acquainted with Italian literature and, in particular, with Italian drama, aspired to transplant it to Crete and, like their Italian models, to use the spoken idiom as their literary language. It should be remembered that by the sixteenth century the Cretan vernacular had become the mother tongue of the majority of Venetian settlers in Crete, a great number of whom had also joined the Orthodox Church.

It has been argued that Cretan drama, which emerges with such fully developed works as those of Chortatsis, must have gone through an earlier stage of development, now lost. It is not impossible that Cretan 'Mystery Plays' may have been acted,[44] and one should assume that travelling companies of the Commedia dell'Arte visited Candia from Venice. But the roots of the Cretan theatre do not lie with such 'popular' performances. They must be sought in Renaissance Italian tragedy, with its long monologues, pompous dialogue and gruesome scenes of horror, and in the Commedia Erudita as fertilized by comic scenes taken over from the Commedia dell'Arte. The Cretan theatre started with translations and adaptations of those fully developed Italian tragic and comic plays, and that is the reason why from the very beginning it was a fully fledged, mature theatre. That is also why all the kinds of plays performed in Italy in those days—tragedy, comedy, pastoral and religious plays—appeared simultaneously on the Cretan stage.

The remarkable man who introduced the theatre to Crete and elevated the local idiom into a suitable literary language for drama was Georgios Chortatsis (c. 1595), a contemporary of Shakespeare. He came from a noble family of Rethymnon, studied in Italy and was well versed in Classical (particularly Latin) and Italian literature. He was a gifted, versatile man who, drawing on Italian models, composed at least three plays: the *Erophile*, a sanguinary tragedy; the *Katzourbos*, written in the style of the sixteenth-century Italian Commedia Erudita; and the *Gyparis* (or *Panoria*), a pastoral play. All were types of drama fashionable in Italy in those days, and all three plays were apparently written between the years 1590 and 1600.[45]

His most ambitious work is the tragedy *Erophile*. It treats of the love of Erophile, daughter of King Philogonus of Egypt, for Panaretos, a prince of the court, whom she secretly marries. Her father, upon discovering this, kills the young man and offers Erophile his head and his hands. In despair the heroine kills herself; the king is slain by her attendants. The immediate prototype of this gruesome drama is the Italian tragedy *Orbecche* by G. B. Giraldi (1504–1573), which was published in 1547; but Chortatsis also drew on Tasso's tragedy *Il Re Torrismondo* (1587)[46] and reduced the number of scenes of horror. However, the play remains horrific enough, for the *Erophile*, following closely the notions of sixteenth-century Italian tragedy, suffers from its weaknesses: the scenes of horror presented on the stage, the endless rhetorical monologues and dialogues, the excessive length (five long scenes) and the profusion of gnomic elements. On the other hand, it should be noted that the versification—basically the rhyming fifteen-syllable line—is faultless, that there is considerable nobility of feeling and that, in spite of the cold and restrained language, touches of true lyricism break through. These are to be found mainly in the scenes of passionate grief, into which elements from traditional Cretan laments have been introduced.

The *Erophile*, true to pattern, also contains chorus songs. In that of the first act the power of Eros is fêted in rhyming eleven-syllable lines in what appears to be a paraphrase of the celebrated Sophoclean chorus in the *Antigone* (ll. 781ff.); this probably derives from some Italian translation or paraphrase of the Greek. Here, for the first time, we see clearly the original Classical Greek influence returning to Greek poetry through a Western model. Love takes his place, with Pride, Wealth, the Sun and Death, in the set pieces given to the chorus; these figures and the lesser ones of Virtue, Daring and Hope are in keeping with the convention of the sixteenth century emblematists who influenced Western poetry.

Though the modern viewer of the play finds it unendurably long—it has been acted repeatedly in modern Greece—and though neither the delineation of character nor the dramatic tension (which reaches its peak in the fourth act, when father and daughter face one another) is impressive, the Cretans, for whom it was written, must have enjoyed it; for it was often performed in Candia, and it ran into several editions when printed. Moreover, popular adaptations of it were made to be acted in other parts of Greece, and it even became part of the Carnival festivities in many Greek islands.

The *Katzourbos* (or perhaps *Katzarapos*) is the poet's most mature work and certainly the best of the three Cretan comedies that have survived. Its plot is simple: young Nicholas is in love with Cassandra, whom her foster-mother wants to marry off to an old man called Armenis, from whom she hopes to get money. In the end it emerges that Armenis is the father of Cassandra, and so the two young lovers get married without further opposition. The story is thin, but the stage is filled with a series of comic types—the *miles gloriosus*, the courtesan, the pedantic schoolmaster, the gluttonous slave, thieves and clowns—all drawn from the sixteenth-century Italian Commedia Erudita.[47] At the same time the swift action, the lively language and metre and, not least, the humour make the *Katzourbos* a remarkable comedy of its kind.

The versatility of Chortatsis as a dramatic poet can be seen from the *Gyparis* (or *Panoria*), a pastoral play at which he also tried his hand. The plot is similar to those of numerous Italian *tragicommedie pastorali*, with the peculiarity that we have two pairs of lovers: Gyparis loves Panoria, and his friend Alexis loves Athousa. The two shepherdesses, true to the goddess Artemis, refuse the love of the shepherds and will not be persuaded to marry them by either the old woman, Phrosyne, or Panoria's father, Giannoulis. Finally, the shepherds pray to the goddess Aphrodite; her son, Eros, shoots the two young shepherdesses with his arrows and thus brings about a favourable solution.

The whole subject is taken originally from ancient mythology (from the *Metamorphoses* of Ovid), but Chortatsis' immediate source is Luigi Groto's *La Calisto*, published in Venice in 1583.[48] The conventional pastoral setting of the Italian play is completely changed in the Cretan adaptation, in which there are no metamorphosed gods, no nymphs and no Arcadia. Here we have Cretan shepherdesses and Cretan names, and the action takes place in Crete. For, as has been pointed out, unlike their courtly Italian counterparts, the realistic Cretan spectators did not wish to escape into an Arcadian dream world. Their own shepherds were too close at hand for that to be at all possible. However, Chortatsis' descriptions of country life are fresh, and there is a pleasing simplicity about this play. That pastoral plays and poems were enjoyed in Crete can also be seen from the Cretan translation of G. B. Guarini's *Pastor Fido* and from *The Shepherdess*, about which we have spoken.[49]

For all three of his dramatic works Chortatsis composed *intermedia*. For those of the *Erophile* he drew mainly on Tasso's *Gerusalèmme Liberta*, for those of his comedies, on Ovid and ancient mythology. These elaborate *intermedia* indicate that the Cretan audiences, like their Italian counterparts, were bored by the long conventional plays and found relief in the spectacle, the dance and the music of the *intermedia*.[50]

Chortatsis is undoubtedly the greatest Greek dramatist of the sixteenth century; with the possible exception of the author of *The Sacrifice of Abraham*, he towers head and shoulders above all the others. Versatile, capable of composing tragic, comic and pastoral tragi-comic plays alike, he lifted the Cretan spoken idiom into the realm of literature and was a true master of versification. His language, it is true, is more precise and more vivid in his lighter plays than in the *Erophile*, which has, one always feels, a frigid, artificial element about it. In the use of the fifteen-syllable line, in which he mainly composed his plays, he is superbly adept, employing a variety of rhythms different from those of folk songs, as well as *enjambement*, which adds fluidity to his rhythms. Chortatsis, the poet who revived drama in Greek after the silence of so many centuries, can be fairly called a landmark in the history of Greek poetry.

The only other Cretan dramatist whose name we know is Joannes Andreas Troilos (c. 1640), who, like Chortatsis, also came from Rethymnon. No further details about his life are known, and only one play of his has survived, *King Rhodolinos*, which was printed in Venice in 1647.[51] The play deals with Rhodolinos, king of Memphis, who is tortured by the conflicting claims of love and friendship, and ends with the deaths of Aretousa, the princess he loves, Rhodolinos himself, his sister Rhododaphne and his friend, Trosilos, king of Persia. The tragedy is an adaptation of Tasso's late tragedy *Il Re Torrismondo* (1587). Troilos simplified the action, exchanged ten scenes of the original for eleven of his own, replaced the chorus songs with new ones, three of which are in the form of sonnets —among the best early modern Greek sonnets we have—and idealized the plot of the original. *King Rhodolinos* has few of the virtues of the *Erophile*, by which it was influenced in the handling of the language and the verse, and most of its faults.

The third and last tragedy, which has traditionally been considered Cretan,[52] is the *Zenon*, about whose author we are in the dark. It follows, in a servile manner, the *Zeno* of the British Jesuit Joseph Simon, which was written in Latin and published in 1648. The Greek *Zenon* must have been composed shortly after. Recent research has shown persuasively that this tragedy of blood and thunder, which follows the rules prescribed for the dramatic works of the Jesuits, was written and performed in Zakynthos in 1682–3.[53] It deals with the intrigues of Zeno, the Byzantine emperor (474–91), and his cousin Longinus to secure the throne and with their final punishment—Longinus is killed and Zeno buried alive—and has no merits except for smooth versification and a few passable lyrical passages. It is the only surviving Greek tragedy of that period with a historical plot.

Besides the *Katzourbos* of Chortatsis, two more Cretan comedies have survived, one by the poet Marcos Antonios Foscolos and the other, called *Stathis*, by an unknown comedian. *Stathis* was written before 1648, the year in which the siege of Candia (Mega Kastro) by the Turks began.[54] The plot more or less follows the lines of *Katzourbos*, except that here we have two pairs of lovers instead of one—Chrysippos and Lamprousa on the one hand and Pamphilos and Phaedra on the other. The old lover (in this case the Dottore, a rich lawyer), the obstacle in the lovers' path, makes an appearance in this play too, as does the recognition of the lost child (Chrysippos, who is a child of Stathis, Phaedra's father) that brings about the happy ending and the marriage of both pairs of lovers.

Much of the development is difficult to follow, for it appears that we do not have the original but a later abridgement in three acts of what must have been a five-act comedy. However, in spite of its shortcomings, we find a number of beautiful verses in *Stathis*. The two *intermedia* of this play have also survived, one including a combat between Christian knights and Turks and the other an episode of the Trojan War.

The last of the Cretan plays is the *Fortunatos*, which has come down to us in an autograph manuscript of its author, Marcos Antonios Foscolos (died 1662),[55] and was composed and acted shortly before May 1663,[56] during the great siege of Candia by the Turks (1648–69). The author apparently held an important position in the Cretan community of his day. The influence of *Katzourbos* is evident once again, both in the general structure of the play and in individual scenes and characters. In the *Fortunatos* the rival of the young lover, Fortunatos, is an old doctor, Louras, with whom Melia, a miserly woman, wants to marry her daughter Petronela. In the end it emerges that Fortunatos is the lost son of old Louras, who, delighted at finding him, consents to his marriage with his beloved Petronela. Once again we meet in this play the *miles gloriosus*, the pedantic schoolmaster, the gluttonous servant, the busybody and so on. The four *intermedia* of the *Fortunatos* have also survived, whose subject is the judgement of Paris. If not in poetic merit, at least in structure and theatrical economy *Fortunatos* is superior to *Katzourbos*.

Apart from the three complete Cretan comedies we have examined, others were written in those days on Crete which are now lost or from which only fragments have come down to us. Undoubtedly, they were all modelled on Italian plays. Thus we have the prologue of an unknown comedy which consists of a speech by Aphrodite[57] and a strange survival of a dialogue at the end of the fairy-tale *The Forgotten Betrothed*.[58] This seems to derive from a comic dialogue in verse between Fiorentinos and Dolceta, apparently part of a Cretan play that in its turn depended on Francesco Cieco's *Mambriano* (published in 1509).[59]

Needless to say, the ultimate source of all these Cretan comedies is New Comedy, and in particular Menander, whose influence returned to Crete through Plautus, Terence and the Italian Commedia Erudita. It is moving indeed to observe Greek influence re-introduced to Greece through the West in this devious manner. The second type of Italian comedy, the Commedia dell'Arte, which had such wide circulation and such success in Italy in the seventeenth century, seems to have been unknown in Crete except, of course, for such of its elements as it had handed over to the Commedia Erudita.

To complete the picture of the Cretan theatre, we must now turn to the anonymous religious play *The Sacrifice of Abraham*, which is the pearl of the dramatic literature of that period. It is a dramatization of the Old Testament episode recounted in *Genesis* 22, which it follows closely.

An Angel visits Abraham in his dream and brings him God's command to sacrifice his only child Isaac in order to demonstrate his faith. Abraham, though deeply distressed, is prepared to obey in silence, but Sarah bursts out in unrestrained lamentation when she hears about it. However, a vague hope, which is specified towards the end of the play, helps her to bear the weight of her grief. Isaac is then led to the summit of the mountain where the sacrifice is to take place—the journey lasts three whole days—and Abraham is able to induce him to accept the role of victim without a murmur. At the critical moment the Angel appears once again and orders Abraham to replace his knife in its sheath. They then return exultant to their home, where they are received by a deeply moved Sarah, and they thank God for His mercy.

The immediate prototype of this Cretan play is *Lo Isach* of Luigi Groto (1586). But the Greek version is in every respect superior to the insignificant Italian original, as indeed to the French and Italian plays on the same subject by Théodore de Bèze and Feo Belcari. The Cretan writer has omitted the chorus songs and the prologue of the original and has even abandoned the traditional division into acts; the action is determined by his analysis of the characters, which is profound and perceptive. They move us by their entirely human qualities.

Moreover, there are passages (such as Sarah's laments or Isaac's waking) that are infused with a tender lyricism; nor is Isaac's candour, filial love and attachment to his mother 'lyrically' less moving. The whole episode is so artfully presented that when Abraham has replaced his knife in its sheath the relief we experience is transformed into a feeling of grateful joy. This is no primitive work, nor has it about it anything of the traditional, static representation of episodes from Holy Writ. There is warmth not only in the characters of the play but also in its language and its rhythms. It contains none of the cold, 'aristocratic' and learned elements of the *Erophile*'s diction, and it is much closer to true folk verse — metrical *enjambement* is greatly restricted — in its admirable 1144 fifteen-syllable lines. The main defect of *The Sacrifice of Abraham* is its prolixity, so frequent in Cretan plays; the same ideas sometimes find expression in two and even three similar ways. Nonetheless, it is one of the most powerful plays written in modern Greek.

The author of *The Sacrifice of Abraham* is unknown, but a number of scholars are inclined to attribute the play to Vitsentzos Kornaros,[60] the poet of the *Erotokritos*, an attribution by no means certain. This religious drama soon became popular, as can be seen from the many editions to which it ran after its first publication in 1696; it was not only widely read but also acted at popular festivals, and there are those in Crete who still know it all by heart. It was also translated into Serbian and, surprisingly enough, into Turkish!

THE 'HEROIC' VERSE ROMANCE

If Georgios Chortatsis is the most important Cretan dramatist, Vitsentzos Kornaros (1553–1617) is the greatest of all the Cretan poets and one of the most significant and influential figures in the entire course of Greek poetry.

Recent research has shown that Vitsentzos was most probably the son of Jacob Kornaros, a Venetian–Cretan aristocrat, and that he was born near Sitia. Later, when he married Marietta Zeno, he came to live in

Candia, where he joined the Accademia dei Stravaganti. When the great plague broke out in Crete in 1591—it lasted until 1593—he was one of the few members of the nobility who did not leave the city but stayed on there and served as *Provveditóre all Sanita* (an office responsible for health and welfare) during that crisis. Among the Cretan archives now in Venice documents have been found written in Vitsentzos' own hand. They are in Greek but transcribed in the Latin alphabet, so we must assume that the poet did not attend a Greek school and that his formal education was Italian, as would be expected of a Roman Catholic Venetian nobleman, even if linguistically Hellenized. Kornaros probably died in 1617 and was survived by two daughters.[61]

The only Greek work we can attribute with certainty to Vitsentzos Kornaros is the *Erotokritos*, which is rightly considered the masterpiece of Cretan poetry and a milestone in the history of Greek literature. It is a 'heroic' verse romance—it has sometimes been wrongly called an epic— of more than 10,000 rhyming fifteen-syllable lines and is divided into five parts, a division probably due to the influence of Renaissance drama, for the poem has a distinct dramatic character and delights in dialogue. The story, which, as the poet tells us in his introduction, deals with 'the power of love' and 'the trials of arms' runs as follows.

Erotokritos, the son of Pezostratos, a councillor of King Heracles of Athens, falls in love with the king's daughter Aretousa, whom he serenades night after night. Aretousa, intrigued and enchanted by the beautiful songs, falls in love with her unknown admirer. After a fight with the king's men, Erotokritos decides to travel abroad in the hope of forgetting Aretousa; but this he finds impossible, and, upon returning to Athens to see his father who has fallen ill, discovers that she is also in love with him. Subsequently, at a tournament which King Heracles proclaims to cheer up his downcast daughter and in which lords and princes from various lands take part, Erotokritos is the victor and receives the crown of victory from Aretousa's hands. After various secret meetings between the two young lovers, Erotokritos asks the king, through his father, for the hand of Aretousa in marriage. The king, infuriated at this request, which he considers an affront, exiles the young lover and decides to give his daughter in marriage to the prince of Byzantium. At Aretousa's stubborn refusal, he casts her into a dark dungeon, together with her faithful nurse Phrosyne. There she stays, unyielding, for three whole years, until the king of Wallachia, Vladistratos, attacks King Heracles and Athens. The city is about to fall to the Wallachians when Erotokritos, transformed by a magic philtre into a dark-skinned knight, arrives in time to challenge and kill the Wallachian king in single combat. In reward, he asks for the hand of Aretousa, which is gratefully granted, and, after testing her fidelity, Erotokritos takes a further magic potion and regains his normal appearance. A moving scene of reunion ensues, and the two lovers are married with the king's blessing, to reign happily ever after over the kingdom of Athens.

The story is not original. Kornaros took it from the French prose romance of Pierre de la Cypède, *Paris et Vienne*, which had been published in 1478 and had enjoyed great popularity.[62] The Cretan poet probably used an Italian translation, which he adapted to suit the taste of the Cretan world of the sixteenth and early seventeenth centuries. This is evident both in the character of his heroine Aretousa, who, unlike her French prototype, never escapes to live openly in sin with her lover, and in the outcome of the story, which in the Cretan version is a consequence of the courage of the hero and not of his cunning, as in the French. Moreover, in the French original there are five tournaments, whereas in the Greek there is only one, and that is not an accurate description, for it is a mixture of the joust, in which the participants were not meant to hurt one another but simply to strike at their opponents' helmets, and the combat on foot, in which lances and shields were used (when on horseback the combatants held no shields). It should further be remarked that the battle between Athens and the Wallachians is an addition of the Cretan poet.

Paris et Vienne may have given the story to Kornaros, but it was not his only source. There is ample evidence of the influence of Italian Renaissance poetry and, in particular, Ariosto's *Orlando Furioso* and the emblem literature of the West; for it was in the sixteenth and seventeenth centuries that the emblem writers rejuvenated the older conceits of poetry, especially in their treatment of love.[63] And side by side with his Western sources, the influence of Chortatsis, of the Cretan folk songs and even of certain Byzantine verse romances has been traced.

The setting of the *Erotokritos* is that of the Latins in the Levant but transposed to an 'ideal' antiquity, in which the sun, the moon and the stars are worshipped and Greek names take the place of Frankish, Turkish, Slavonic and Wallachian ones, all of which betray the influence of the Renaissance. For there can be little doubt that the princes who appear in the poem are modelled on the Frankish dukes and marquises of medieval and post-medieval Greece and that Athens is the Athens of the *Sire d'Athènes* and has nothing to do with Classical Athens; Byzantium, the Slavs, the Turks, the Wallachians are as the Venetians, and not the Greeks, had seen them.

Special significance is conferred by the poet on the clearly symbolic combat of Book II between the Caramanite Spidoliondas and the Cretan Charedemos. This reflects the struggle between Venetian Crete and Turkey and not the 'perennial struggle between Greeks and Turks', as many Greek scholars maintain. It is important to distinguish between what the Greeks later read into the lines of *Erotokritos*, when it became for them a 'national' poem, and what Kornaros' intention was. Though at many points the *Erotokritos* reflects the Cretan civilization and life of its day—its serenades, its amorous escapades, its admiration for courage, the significance of virginal purity in woman—and this was to a very large extent Greek, the allegiance of the poet was clearly Venetian. Nor should it be forgotten that the grand tournament of Book II was set for 25 April, the national Venetian festival, and that there is no attack against a Frank in the whole of the poem like those we find, for example, in the writings of Marinos Tzanes Bounialis.

The *Erotokritos* must be dated, on the poet's own testimony, before 1587, when he came to live in Candia. Later, of course, Kornaros may have revised the poem; to such a revision, it has been argued, belongs the combat in Book II between the Cretan and the Caramanite.[64] The excellent finish of the verse and the mastery of its diction, as well as the mature approach to life apparent in the poem, indicate that the author was not a youth experimenting with poetry. However, if *Erotokritos* was concluded as early as 1587, it is indeed surprising that it was published in Venice in 1713, so long after the poet's death, when many other inferior Cretan works had gone into print much earlier.

The *Erotokritos* sets great store by true love, friendship, courage and patriotism, and this is the reason for its later popularity among the Greeks. Of these, true love is at the centre of the poem—which is what one would have expected of a love romance—but it is a love less subtle than the chivalrous love of the Middle Ages. No room is left for doubt, jealousy or self-pity; not even death can come between the lovers, for then 'What the bodies have not accomplished, the souls will accomplish in Hades.' The poet feels a special warmth towards Aretousa, his heroine, who is thirteen or fourteen years old and whom he presents as blossoming from an innocent child into a woman obsessed by passion—a full-blooded passion that has nothing sick, mystical or metaphysical about it.

Much of Kornaros' love imagery depends on the *emblemata amatoria* which were then circulating in the West and which had promoted an emblematic way of thinking among poets. Thus in *Erotokritos* Love is presented not only in the old, traditional manner as the boy archer or the blindfolded and wanton boy, but also as Love the Cook, Love the Schoolmaster, Love the Soldier, Love the Spider, Love the King and Love at the Cart's Tail, to mention only a few of the love images we find in the poem. At the same time, the lover's heart—here the influence of the *emblemata sacra* is evident—is represented not only as transfixed by arrows but also as having a deep-rooted tree in it, as thrust into the furnace of love, as equipped with many eyes keeping vigil and so on. This clearly shows that Kornaros was both thinking emblematically and writing for a Western-educated, if Greek-speaking, audience that could appreciate his emblematic imagery.

Side by side with the erotic, we also find in *Erotokritos* a distinct didactic element. The aphorisms and the proverbs found in its verses are abundant, and the author takes great pains to stress the suffering and danger involved in the amorous passion, as well as the inevitable clash between love and wisdom, passion and common sense. In fact, both King Heracles and the nurse, Phrosyne, represent wisdom, the first in a harsh, the other in a compassionate manner, and Erotokritos' friend Polydoros signifies restraint and practicality. At the end of the poem love and wisdom are reconciled, of course, but only after much suffering and the passage of time.

Character drawing in *Erotokritos* is simple and, to a certain extent, 'typical'—Erotokritos is *the* Brave, True Lover, Aretousa *the* Pure, Devoted Maiden—but it is not naive, and it is well served by the poet's use of dialogue, from which rhetoric and bombast are mercifully absent.

But the true virtues of *Erotokritos* are its diction and its versification. In both these fields Kornaros is a master. The language he uses is, naturally, rooted in the spoken Cretan idiom of his day but enriched by a number of fully absorbed erudite elements that have shed all trace of pedantry. It is without doubt the most fluent and the most lyrical Greek poetic diction since the end of the ancient world. At the same time, the skill and variety achieved in the use of the fifteen-syllable line is astonishing. It flows freely, with a melodious quality often reminiscent of Solomos and Seferis, the greatest masters of that verse. Moreover, the use of rhyme is remarkable for its novelty, its freshness and its accuracy.

There is a plastic and yet subtle quality in the style of Kornaros, enlivened by the constant use of dialogue, and the tone of the narrative is restful, for it is pitched neither too high nor too low. From time to time it is adorned with passages of calm, deep lyricism reminiscent of the best folk songs. The similes are also striking, though it must be admitted that not many are original. Classical Greek, Latin and Renaissance poetry have all contributed to that noble stock. It is indeed interesting to note that one of these, comparing a falling warrior with a flower cut down by the plough in the field (Book IV, ll. 1889ff.) comes from Homer (VIII, 306–8) via Stesichorus via Virgil and Ariosto![65] There is also a moderate use of allegory in the *Erotokritos*.

Kornaros is a good story-teller, for his descriptions are accurate—they always insist on the concrete—his lyricism is burdened by no sloppy sentimentality and his repetitions (admittedly numerous) are always introduced with attractive variations. In fact, there is an ease, a nobility and a human dignity about the *Erotokritos* which is reminiscent of the atmosphere of the Renaissance and of Ariosto. There are also, of course, a number of shortcomings, the most prominent of which is prolixity: the dialogues and lamentations are too long; there are too many battle scenes; and there are sections, like the tournament of Book II, that fail to hold the reader.

The *Erotokritos* has been assessed by Greek and foreign scholars and critics in the most diverse terms possible, ranging from the complete condemnation of Adamantios Koraes[66] to the outspoken praise and admiration of Georgos Seferis in his remarkable essay, *Erotokritos*.[67] It certainly exercised a special fascination upon the Greeks, who learned of it from the refugees who came to the Peloponnese and the Ionian Islands after the fall of Candia in 1669. That Western knightly romance became a 'national' poem and its hero a symbol of suffering Hellenism; surprisingly enough, he was exalted side by side with the traditional 'national heroes', Digenis Akritas and Alexander the Great, the great symbols of Hellenic heroism. Innumerable cheap editions of *Erotokritos* appeared, and the poem was widely recited and acted during the carnivals held in villages and towns throughout Greece. It was also translated into Romanian and Turkish and even recast into 'erudite' Greek by Dionysios Photeinos (1818) for the benefit of the Phanariots. Naturally, the poem had its widest circulation in Crete, where people knew large sections (and even its entire 10,000 lines) by heart; many were the lines that became proverbial or household words.[68]

But, above all, it was a great source of inspiration for Solomos, who picked up from it the thread of a living Greek poetry and handed it over to the Greeks after the liberation of Greece from the Turks. How extensive the influence of Kornaros has been on subsequent modern Greek poetry can be seen from the works of poets as diverse as Palamas, Krystallis and Seferis, who are all indebted to him. Thus it is true to say that Vitzentzos Kornaros is a major landmark in the history of Greek poetry and the culminating point of the Byzantine trend that started with the epic cycle of Digenis Akritas. After him a hundred years of full poetic decline followed.

HISTORICAL POEMS

The golden age of Cretan poetry closes with the poem of Athanasios Skleros (died 1664), the *War of Crete* (also known as *Lament of Crete*), which deals with the great war of 1645–69 between Venetians and Turks until the author's death in 1664.[69] The *War of Crete* is composed in fifteen-syllable lines and in an erudite diction—which is not surprising in a man as learned as Athanasios Skleros, who had studied in Venice and Padua and was awarded a doctorate in philosophy and medicine. As the author was an eye-witness to many of the events he describes, his poem is an interesting historical source, even if devoid of true poetic merit.[70]

The capture of Crete by the Turks and the ravaging of the island that followed is also deplored by Gerasimos Palladas (died 1717) in his *Lament of Crete*, composed in popular fifteen-syllable lines. Palladas was a highly educated priest who left the island after the Turks seized Candia in 1669. He later became Metropolitan of Adrianople and Patriarch of Alexandria. He wrote various philosophical and theological works, most of which have not been published, as well as minor religious and patriotic poems, of which the *Lament of Crete* is the best. Most moving are the passages which depict the despair of the Cretans at seeing their churches turned into mosques and stables and the sufferings and shipwrecks of the escaping refugees.[71]

The fall of Crete to the Turks was also described in a long metrical chronicle by one of the most important Cretan exiles who took refuge in the Ionian Islands, Marinos Tzanes Bounialis. He came from Rethymnon and lived in Crete till the capitulation of Candia (1669), when he escaped to Corfu and composed his chronicle. It consists of 12,000 rhyming political verses full of much interesting and horrifying information, the most striking of which is his eye-witness account of the capture of Rethymnon. Marinos Tzanes Bounialis is acquainted with the work of Anthimos Diakrousis,[72] on which he draws, and probably also with *La Guerra di Candia* of Andrea Valiero. By contrast with Valiero, his point of view is Greek, for he equates the Turks with the Franks and underlines the important part played by the Greeks during that war.

The literary claims of Bounialis are admittedly few, for he is a clumsy verse writer and a monotonous narrator, much in the Byzantine style; one would think that he remained untouched by the spirit of the Renaissance which excited so many of his compatriots. However, there are numerous moving lines in his narrative, most notably those describing the sorrows of a Cretan in exile. Bounialis also published in Venice (1684) a pamphlet of inferior religious verse.

A few words should be added here about some minor quasi-historical Cretan poems, some of which passed into the oral tradition and became popular folk songs. Such are *The Sultan's Wife* (also known as *The Daughter of the Pope*), which enjoyed great popularity in the islands, for some twenty versions of it have been traced. It deals with a Cretan girl, Eugenia Vergitzi, who was enslaved at the age of three, when Rethymnon fell to the Turks, and who later became a favourite wife of the Sultan Mohamet IV (1648–87).[73] Another is the so-called *Sack of Parikia*, the capital of the island of Paros, which in 673 rhyming eleven-syllable lines (the end is missing) describes how the Turkish fleet ravaged the Cyclades in 1668 and destroyed Parikia. Its poetic value is limited, but it should not be underrated as a historical source.[74] Finally, we have *The Song of Sousa*, a short seventeenth-century poem about a young Cretan girl who falls in love with a Turk and whom her brother kills to defend the honour of his family. This song was sung on many Greek islands.[75]

The fall of Candia to the Turks in 1669 put an abrupt end to all cultural life on Crete. Waves of refugees to the Morea and the Ionian Islands took the Cretan poems (and thus the seed of the further development of Greek poetry) to Zante, Cephalonia and Corfu. A dark cloud of suffering fell on the island which was to continue for centuries, inspiring a new series of revolts against its new and harsher masters, the Turks.

Cretan poetry—mainly that of the oral tradition—did not die, however. It continued to flourish underground and only occasionally emerged in the open, as with the *Song of Daskalogiannis* by Pantzelios, which deals in 1034 rhymed political lines with the disastrous revolt of the Sphakiots in 1770, and the shorter anonymous *Tower of Alidakis*, which belongs to the same period. The hopes and sufferings of the Cretans found expression in many anonymous folk songs and couplets down to the twentieth century.[76]

Scholars have maintained that with the *Song of Daskalogiannis* a new tradition started,[77] one which later embraced the historical songs of the Greek War of Independence (1821–8) and all others recounting, in a stark vivid narrative, the local and national history of the Greeks. These, they believe, were songs with a modern sense of history that developed side by side with the 'hauntingly elegiac and deeply moving oral tradition of lyrico-balladic klephtic panegyrics and laments drawn from the lives of the *armatoloi* and the Klephts and the brave bands of palikars' that fought against the Turks in the Peloponnese and mainland Greece.[78]

The significance of the Cretan revival in poetry is remarkable indeed and constitutes a landmark in the history of Greek literature. For through their contact with the West the Cretan poets fertilized the waning Byzantine poetic tradition, introduced the use of rhyme, revived drama in Greek after many centuries of silence and developed a rich and supple poetic diction which, had not the island fallen to the Turks, would have probably become the common modern Greek literary language. But that disaster condemned it to remain the gifted vehicle of expression of a provincial literature, and the main stream of Greek writing was obliged to struggle on for centuries in an effort to shape a Pan-Hellenic literary diction.

But it should also be admitted that on the whole Cretan literature is a literature born of the translation and adaptation of Italian models, though these were rarely followed in a servile or mechanical spirit.[79] Nor should it be forgotten that the Cretan poetic achievement has been grossly overrated by many modern Greek critics, who ignore the fact that, with few exceptions, the modern reader is bound to find the Cretan works long-winded and, if he is not truly interested in the history of Greek poetry, tedious. If we compare them with the great contemporary literature of the West, we are bound to acknowledge that they are inferior and provincial.

THE IONIAN ISLANDS

After the fall of Cyprus and Crete Venetian territory was limited to the Ionian Islands, apart from a brief period of Venetian rule in the Peloponnese from 1684 to 1714. As a result of this, much closer contact was established between Venice, the centre of Greeks of the Diaspora, and the Ionian Islands, so that Greek poetry composed in both has much in common.

As would be expected, the Greeks who had fought in Crete on the Venetian side fled with them to Venice or took refuge in the Heptanese when the island was conquered by the Turks, bringing with them their songs and many manuscripts of Cretan literary works.[80] Thus the Cretan poetic tradition was transplanted to the Ionian Islands, at first in the hands of the Cretan refugees but soon afterwards in those of the Heptanesians.

It is true, of course, that even before the arrival of the Cretan refugees the Ionian Islands had literary works of their own and that Cretan influence was felt before 1669, but the value of these works is restricted. Thus, apart from the writings of the Corfiot Iakovos Trivolis (sixteenth century), who lived in Venice and about whom we shall speak below,[81] we have the awkward theatrical work of the Zakynthian Theodoros Montseleze, *Eugena*, published in 1646, and the translation by Michael Soumakis of G. B. Guarini's *Pastor Fido* (1568) in fifteen-syllable lines reminiscent of Cretan poetry;[82] and it is even probable that the anonymous 'Cretan' drama *Zeno*, which was performed in Zakynthos in 1682–3, is not Cretan but the work of a Zakynthian poet.[83]

A Cephallonian by birth, the poet Anthimos Diakrousis (seventeenth century)—he later retired as a monk, assuming the name of Akakios— wrote *The Account in Verse of the Terrible War of Crete*. Diakrousis probably lived part of his life in Crete, for he wrote in a Cretan dialect mixed with Cephallonian idiomatic usages. His verse chronicle, 1400 rhyming political lines long, relates the preparations of the Turks for their attack on Crete, the capture of Chania, Rethymnon and Candia, as well as the terrible sufferings of the Cretans at the hands of their Muslim conquerors. He concludes with a lamentation 'on miserable Crete'. There is little inspiration and no originality in Diakrousis' work, which is reminiscent of a Byzantine chronicle, although here and there it takes on the colour of a folk song.

Another Cephallonian poet who deserves mention is Petros Katsaitis (seventeenth–eighteenth century), who lived in the Morea and, when taken prisoner by the Turks, was sent to Crete. He later returned to Cephallonia, where he composed all three of his surviving works. The first, the *Lament on the Peloponnese*, is a metrical chronicle in rhymed hendecasyllables dealing with the fall of the Peloponnese to the Turks in 1715; the other two, the *Iphigenia* and the *Thyestes*, are tragedies written in 1720. Both these plays are cast in fifteen-syllable lines and treat, in five acts, of the well-known ancient myths. There is little action in them, little lyricism and no clash of characters; nor are they original, for they are based on the Italian tragedies on the same subjects and bearing the same titles by L. Dolce (1508–68). They must be seen as a feeble continuation in the Ionian Islands of the Cretan dramatic tradition. Other such works were probably written there in the course of the seventeenth century which are now lost.

Rimades (minor popular poems) were, of course, composed until much later in the Heptanese. Examples are *The Child Crucified by the Jews*, which was inspired by an event that took place in Zante in 1712 and captured the popular imagination, or the *Song of Captain Manettas*. From Zante also probably comes the humorous poem *An Old Man should not Marry a Young Girl*.

Poetry composed in ancient Greek also made an appearance in the Ionian Islands, as is evident from an anthology entitled *Fresh Flowers Just Culled from the Prairie of the College of Corfu*, published in Venice in 1766. They are feeble patriotic and religious verses in the Byzantine tradition collected by Jeremias Kavvadias, a professor in the College of Corfu. Their main interest lies in the fact that they demonstrate that the Greeks of the Heptanese struggled to protect and foster their Greek heritage in spite of the Venetian occupation of their islands.

CHAPTER 24

The Greeks of the Diaspora

The Greeks who came to live in Italy after the fall of Constantinople to the Turks (1453) were on the whole bilingual, and those who received a formal Italian education mastered Latin. Those who were, or wished to be, professional scholars also studied ancient Greek, for this was, of course, in keeping with the spirit of the Renaissance as well as with their national pride as descendants of the ancient Greeks.

A number of such scholars composed poetry in ancient Greek. The most popular poetic form they employed was the elegiac epigram, as inherited from Byzantium but also as influenced by Renaissance and post-Renaissance Western poetry. As a result, many of these short poems were strange and affected, full of allegorical figures and obscure mythological allusions. On the whole, they are found scattered and isolated in the larger works those scholars composed,[1] but occasionally small collections were published, like the one called *Epigrams* by Janus Lascaris (1445–1535), which appeared in Paris in 1527. Their poetic value is minimal.

But the Greek scholars of the Diaspora did not engage only in the composition of epigrammatic poetry. They also wrote hymns, odes, dedications and other occasional verse in ancient metres and in Classical Greek, in which the fusion of Byzantine and Western humanism can be traced. On the whole, this poetry is artificial and stilted, but occasionally an inspired piece appears, like the famous *Hymn to Plato* by Marcus Moussouros (1470–1517), which he prefixed to his Aldine *editio princeps* of the complete works of Plato, dedicated to Pope Leo X. This has been undeservedly dubbed by some scholars 'the finest piece of poetry written in the Greek language since antiquity'.[2]

Of the lesser scholar-poets, mention should be made of Demetrios Moschos (c. 1470), who wrote in hexameters a poem called *The Carrying Off of Helen*, which he dedicated to Louis XII of France; Antonios Eparchos (1492–1571), who, in his *Lament on the Catastrophe of Greece*, appeals to Francis I of France and Charles V of Spain to help the Greeks; and Leonardos Philaras (died 1673), known in his day as the 'Christian

Pindar', the most famous of whose works was an *Ode in Honour of the Immaculate Conception of the Mother of God*.[3] To these should be added the stilted scholarly poems of the great Chiot Roman Catholic humanist and scholar Leon Allatios (1588–1669). The most important is *Hellas* in 754 iambic trimeters.

The Greeks of the Diaspora also composed verse in the vernacular,[4] and several minor works of a patriotic nature have survived, like the *Conquest of Constantinople*, wrongly attributed to Emmanuel Georgillas, or an anonymous poem in 1410 rhyming lines addressed to Charles V of Spain, soliciting his help against the Turks. Side by side with these we find other poems fully in the Byzantine tradition, like the moralizing works of Gioustos Glykos (c. 1520), the verses of Tzanes Ventramos (c. 1540), two anonymous dialogues between Man and Death published in Venice in 1586,[5] the verses of Nicolaos Sophianos (c. 1540), the distinguished scholar, grammarian and educationalist, and above all the poetry of Markos Dephanaras (c. 1540).

Marcos Dephanaras wrote *The Story of Suzanna*[6] in 376 rhyming political lines, and a long didactic work in 788 rhyming political lines entitled *Didactic Words of a Father to his Son*, which draws on Marinos Falieros.[7] To Depahanaras has also been attributed, though wrongly, the poem *Birth, Exploits and Death of Alexander the Macedonian*, an otherwise unknown version of the *Romance of Alexander*.

A noteworthy figure among the poets of the Diaspora is Iakovos Trivolis (died 1547–8), the son of a noble Corfiot family who lived part of his life in Venice. From his pen we have two poems, *The Story of Tagiapetra* and *The History of the King of Scotland and the Queen of England*. The first deals, in rhymed octasyllabic lines, with the exploits of John Anthony Tagiapetra, a Venetian captain who fought against the Muslim pirates in the Adriatic and was killed in 1553. The work is full of the rhetorical devices and mannerisms of contemporary Italian poetry and also makes use of many Italian words. The second, cast in rhyming political verses, is based on Boccaccio's *Decameróne*, though it does not follow its model blindly and also draws on one of Boccaccio's anonymous imitators. Unfortunately, there is nothing in Trivolis even remotely reminiscent of Boccaccio's fine style and wit; it is surprising that his inferior poetry became popular among the Greeks and ran into several editions.[8]

Venetian victories over the Turks inspired another Greek poet, Tzanes Koronaios (c. 1520), to write, in roughly 4500 rhyming political lines, *The Exploits of Mercurius Bouas* (Bouas was a Greco-Albanian captain who had served in the Venetian forces during the Italian wars of 1495–1517). It is more of a panegyric than a historical narrative and has no poetic merit.

The life of the *stratioti*, the *Greci erranti*, who were employed as mercenaries by the powerful kings of the West, also captured the imagination of the poets of those days. Thus Leonardos Phortios (early sixteenth century) wrote a poem *On Military Art* in 912 octasyllable rhyming lines, and Manolis Blessis (c. 1564) published in Venice in 1564 *The Poems of Manoli Blessi*, in both of which much information about the adventurous life of those mercenaries is given. Manolis Blessis, who was a *stratioti* himself, also wrote a long poem called *The Conquest of Nicosia*, in which he mourns the fall of that 'second Venice' to the Turks and the fate of the *stratioti* who must now seek other patrons.[9]

A few collections of minor poems by different authors should also be mentioned, such as the *Collection of Poems in Greek, Latin and Italian in Honour of Our Lady the Protectress (de la Guarde)*, published in Bologna in 1601, the *Flowers of Helicon Culled on the Occasion of the Doctorate of Apostolos Raspis*, published in Venice in 1680, or the *Flowers of Piety on the Assumption of the Virgin*, published in Venice in 1708. Of the three, the last is by far the most interesting. It includes prose and poetry ·in Classical Greek, Latin and modern Greek of twelve students of the 'Greek College of Venice', founded in 1662 by Thomas Flanginis for young Greeks who wished to receive a Western education. There is a noteworthy spirit of patriotism in those writings, among which is a sonnet that foresees the Greek War of Independence. It is one of the oldest modern Greek sonnets and is considered the first 'patriotic' modern Greek poem, a link between the laments on the Fall of Constantinople, and the *Thourios* of Rhegas Pheraios. Another interesting sonnet in this collection is a satire on the genre of poems *invita Minerva*, which is a precursor of the satirical poems we shall later find in the Ionian Islands. As has so aptly been said, in the *Flowers of Piety* we can see 'modern Greek poetry trying out its wings'.[10]

Closer to the popular feeling were certain works on historical events of the seventeenth and eighteenth centuries, like the *Lamentation and Complaint of the City of Athens on the Death of her Noble Citizen Michael Limbonas*, composed by the Cretan priest Antonios Bouboulis (seventeenth century), or the *Calamity and Servitude of the Morea*, by the Epirot Manthos Ioannou (c. 1718), describing the conquest of the Morea by the Turks in 1718.

Finally, fleeting mention should be made of modern Greek verse translations of ancient and Renaissance works by Greeks of the Diaspora, most noteworthy of which are the paraphrase of the *Iliad* by Nicolaos Loukanis (seventeenth century) and the anonymous translation into political lines of Boccaccio's *Theseid* (early sixteenth century). On the whole, these verse translations have little literary value except perhaps for the *Theseid*, which has some successful passages, in spite of its clumsy versification.

In view of the great difficulties and the poverty which the Greeks of the sixteenth and seventeenth centuries faced, it is much to their credit that they succeeded in saving so much of their Byzantine and ancient heritage. They worked unsparingly for the renaissance of Greece, and it is largely they who sowed the seeds of the later movement for Greece's liberation.

SECTION II

The Greeks under the Turks
(1453–1829)

Introduction

With the fall of Constantinople to the Turks in 1453 the Greek nation found itself faced with the greatest difficulties, as all Greek lands were under barbarous Turkish or self-seeking Frankish domination. Yet the Greeks, though defeated, were not a subjugated people, for they clung to the faith and the traditions of their ancestors.

The most fertile parts of the conquered lands were distributed as fiefs to Turkish pashas, beys and agas, who formed from them a feudal military organization; but as the Turks were unable to manage peoples whose language they did not understand and whose religion was different from their own, local Christian authorities were established and gradually special privileges were even granted to certain areas which enabled the Byzantine heritage to survive.

The Turks did not attempt any wholesale conversion of the Greeks to Islam. As an insurance against a Catholic Western Crusade to deliver the eastern lands immediately after the fall of Constantinople, the Patriarch was re-enthroned and the freedom of Orthodox Christian worship 'guaranteed'. But in actual fact the Patriarchate came more and more under the control of the Turkish authorities, and most churches, including the great cathedral of Santa Sophia, were converted into mosques.

The major distinction made between Muslims and Christians was the payment of the *haratch*, or capitation tax, by every male unbeliever over ten years of age; and Christians had to pay twice the duty paid by a Muslim on imports and exports. But the real hardship arose as a consequence of the various exactions of the provincial governors, so that many Christians escaped either to Venetian territory or overseas. Thus by about 1700 the population of the mainland was reduced to roughly 1,500,000 souls.

The organization of the janissaries, the *corps d'élite* of the Turkish army which was recruited entirely from Christian children, was a source of appalling distress. One boy out of every five, or one from every Christian family, was taken by the officers of the sultan, a terrible tribute which lasted until 1676. Nor was the plight of Christian women, cast forcibly into the harems of the Turks, less barbarous.

Yet, in spite of all these cruel circumstances, the number of Greek renegades was limited, no doubt largely as a result of the influence of the Church. For in those bleak days the Church came to play a leading political role; it became the champion of not only Orthodoxy but also of Greek nationalism, its clergy, a clergy militant, always taking the lead in the many risings against the Turks.

The sixteenth and seventeenth centuries were perhaps the most critical for the Greeks. For in the eighteenth century the steady decline of Turkish administration, which had begun in the seventeenth century, made it possible for them greatly to improve their general conditions. Taking advantage of the inefficiency and the corruption that were encountered everywhere in the Ottoman Empire, their resourcefulness and ingenuity succeeded in capturing all the commerce and the maritime trade of the eastern Mediterranean, which resulted in the re-emergence of many flourishing Greek communities. Thus it became possible for education to be organized and subsidized once more and for Greeks who had studied in the West to return to their own country and to help it on the road towards a new life.

For with the Fall of Constantinople the light of learning that had shone in so many centres of the empire—Constantinople, Mystras, Trebizond —had been extinguished. Most of the scholars had already left for the West, carrying with them the seeds of the Renaissance; the class of educated and cultured men had virtually disappeared from Greece; schools were closed down, and for centuries it was left to the poorly educated Orthodox clergy to keep the embers of learning alive and to sustain the hope of a national resurrection. Thus out of the ruins of that broken world a number of centres of learning and schools were gradually established, most important of all the Patriarchal School in Constantinople—later known as 'The Grand School of the Nation'—and, under its aegis, those of Joannina, Chios, Athens, Moschopolis, Thessalonica, Zagora, Arta, Patmos, Siatista, Ambelakia, Adrianople, Dimitsana, Smyrna, and Kydoniae. To these the Greek scholars returning from the West, known as the 'Teachers of the Nation', brought the ideas of the Enlightenment and of the French Revolution which prepared the Greeks for their War of Independence.

Of special import for the development of Hellenism were the Danubian principalities, as Wallachia and Moldavia were not conquered by the Turks but were tributary states protected by the Porte, whose princes were crowned by the Patriarch of Constantinople. Large groups of their inhabitants spoke the Greek language, and schools and colleges were organized on the Byzantine pattern of education. The true significance of these was that in them Western ideas and methods of teaching were freely introduced; this fusion of Western with traditional Byzantine elements was a real blessing for the Greeks, who, it should be remembered, were also faced with the prohibition on printing Greek books in the Ottoman Empire.[1]

But no matter how important peripheral centres like the Danubian principalities may have been, the true centre of Hellenism throughout the period of Turkish domination was the Ecumenical Patriarchate of Constantinople. About it, in the quarter of the city called Phanar, a Greek aristocracy gathered—partly descended from the old Byzantine nobility and partly consisting of successful merchant princes—which clung to the old traditions. These men, known as the Phanariots, were seen by all as the leaders of the Greeks. They formed a separate society, isolated from the Turks, and the Patriarchate itself gradually fell under their influence. Many of them collaborated with the sultan and, because of their education (a number had studied in the universities of the West and especially at that of Padua), exercised considerable power within the Ottoman Empire. Fiscal agents of the sultan, administrators of the public treasure, ambassadors to foreign courts, Dragomans of the Porte and of the Fleet and last but not least princes (Hospadars, Voivoids, beys) of the Danubian principalities were often members of those distinguished Phanariot families.

A considerable number of Phanariots played an important role in the intellectual and literary life of the Greeks from the seventeenth to the first quarter of the nineteenth centuries, encouraging education, founding libraries, publishing books abroad and, because of their knowledge of French, bringing the Greek world into closer contact with French literature and thought. Although their linguistic and literary views were on the whole narrow-minded and conservative and their faults numerous and often grave, what cannot be denied is the important part they played in laying the foundations of the spiritual and intellectual renaissance of the modern Greeks. Unfortunately, in creative literature and especially in poetry they have little to show, nor were they ever able to grasp the beauty and the vigour of the folk songs of their day, which expressed the feelings of the people in their own spoken idiom and which were undoubtedly the only really important poetry created during that period in Greek lands occupied by the Turks.

With the outbreak of the Greek War of Independence in 1821 the social, political and literary activities of the Phanariots come to an end. The great majority of these were obliged to leave Constantinople; some came to Greece and took part in the War of Independence, while others became established in the West.

Among the rising enemies of Turkey, Russia was to exercise the most decisive influence upon Greek affairs, for Russian agents appeared in various parts of European Turkey to prepare their fellow Orthodox

Christians for the day of their liberation. In 1770 the brothers Orlow, with a small Russian force, landed in the Peloponnese, but such Greco-Russian forces as were mustered were defeated by the Turks at Tripolitza. By the Treaty of Kiutschuk Kainardji (1774) the Russians obtained international sanction for the rights of the Orthodox Christians of the Ottoman empire, and in 1783 a commercial treaty concluded between Russia and Turkey gave the Greeks the right to trade under the Russian flag. The struggle for Greek independence was not the outcome of Russian policy, however, but the result of the rapidly rising national self-consciousness among the Greeks themselves.

The French Revolution of 1789 was a powerful stimulus to the Greeks in their striving for liberty. Everywhere there were signs of Greek nationalism, which cannot be dissociated from the merging of the literary and Classical revival of the eighteenth century with the ideas produced by the Enlightenment and with those of the French Revolution.

It is true that at the Congress of Vienna (1814–15) the statesmen of Europe had agreed on a conservative system in Europe and could not afford an upheaval in the Balkans. But the Quadruple Alliance did not include any guarantee of the Ottoman Empire, while the Holy Alliance implicitly excluded any such idea. However, in spite of appearances, the Levant was in no state of tranquillity. Serbia had been in revolt since 1804 and local officials of the Ottoman Empire, like Mehmet Ali in Egypt and Ali Pasha in Joannina, were striving after independence; in 1814 the *Philike Hetairia*, a society for promoting Greek patriotic sentiment and providing the Greeks with arms, was founded. The activities of the Klephts, the freedom-loving Christians who had taken to the mountains and preyed upon the Turks, and the *armatoloi*, the Christian *gendarmerie* that joined them, also contributed to the Greek struggle for independence.

The signal for the Greek revolt was given in March 1821, and in April a spontaneous rising in the Peloponnese, led by the clergy, the primates (land-owners and magistrates) and chieftains, began. Thus started the War of Independence of the Greeks, which, after four centuries of barbarous Eastern domination, was to liberate a small part of the Greek lands and to give birth to the new Greek state.

CHAPTER 25

The Survival of the Byzantine Heritage

LAMENTS ON THE FALL OF CONSTANTINOPLE AND ATHENS

The period opens with laments upon the Fall of Constantinople (1453). And this is not surprising, for in the history of the world few events had such a momentous effect upon a people as the Fall of Constantinople had upon the Greeks, the city they saw as the last bulwark of freedom and Orthodox Christianity.

Many such laments have survived,[1] some of which we have already seen, such as the Cypriot *Anaklema* (*Lament*)[2] or *The Capture of Constantinople*, wrongly attributed to the Rhodian poet Emmanuel Georgillas.[3] Most moving of all, of course, is the famous folk song on the last mass in Santa Sophia, about which we shall speak later.[4] Mention should also be made here of the anonymous *Lament of the Four Patriarchates*, in which the patriarchates of Constantinople, Alexandria, Antioch and Jerusalem mourn the fall of Byzantium in a repetitive composition of little originality dated about 1500.

The fall of Athens to the Turks in 1456 was mourned in the anonymous *Lament on the Fall of Athens*, a short poem of sixty-eight political lines which refers to the old glory of Athens and describes the massacres and the devastation which followed the capture of the city.[5] Laments of minor literary significance were also composed on the fall of other Greek cities to the Turks.

MODERN GREEK FOLK SONGS

The folk songs have a place of their own in modern Greek literature, because of their great poetic merits and the influence they exercised upon the course of modern Greek poetry.

Folk songs usually represent an early stage in the development of a people's literature,[6] and they are, on the whole, anonymous. Moreover, they are modified and adapted as they travel from the area in which they originate to others that adopt them and as they are handed down orally from generation to generation. A result of this is the emergence of many versions of the same folk song, some of which often have a different dialectal tinge. As frequently observed, although folk songs may express more clearly and more directly the character of a people than most personal poetry, they rarely have the power to educate or elevate a nation, for they are not addressed to the elite, to the intellectual leaders of a society, nor do they offer new or unusual interpretations of life which could open new horizons to their audience. In the Greek world, because of its historical and geographical circumstances, we meet with the strange and unusual coexistence of developed personal poetry and unsophisticated folk songs, a parallel life which can be traced from the Middle Ages to the middle of the nineteenth century.

As with all bodies of anonymous verse—another such example is early Byzantine religious poetry—it is impossible to date modern Greek folk songs with any accuracy or to follow their development even in outline. The only exceptions are the historical folk songs, which we must assume were composed shortly after the events they refer to. Furthermore, the use of rhyme (which, as we have seen, was introduced to Greek poetry in the fourteenth century) may be considered a *terminus post quem* for the rhyming folk songs.[7]

Two further points should also be noted: first, women played an important part in the composition of modern Greek folk songs, most notably the lullabies and dirges, for Greek men do not lull their children to sleep, nor do they chant laments at funerals; second, as already mentioned,[8] a number of folk songs originated in written texts which at some stage passed into the world of oral poetry and were then chanted by professional singers (in Cyprus known as ποιητάρηδες, 'poets'). Many such professional singers, often blind, existed in eighteenth-century Greece.[9]

The Greek folk songs, whose heyday was the eighteenth century, can be conveniently divided into the following groups: historical folk songs; folk songs proper ('those which accompany all expressions of people living a natural or civilized life'), such as carols, lullabies, working songs, wedding songs, love songs, dirges; narrative folk songs, known in Greek as *paraloges* from the medieval Greek word παρακαταλογή ('melodramatic delivery');[10] and the Klephtic ballads.

Historical folk songs

The historical folk songs which have survived are relatively few and, unfortunately, cannot serve as reliable historical sources, for popular imagination distorts historical events, and the original songs have often been greatly changed in the course of their oral transmission.

A few of the surviving historical folk songs go back to the Middle Ages, like the satirical song on the Emperor Maurice (582–602),[11] the song attacking Phocas the Tyrant (602)[12] or the one on the escape of Alexius Comnenus in 1081.[13] Side by side with these, a number of the Akritic ballads we have already examined[14] could also be considered historical songs in a broader sense. On the other hand, it is a matter of dispute whether the verses on the fall of Adrianople[15] constitute a genuine folk song referring to the capture of the city by the Turks in 1361.

Of all the surviving historical folk songs undoubtedly the most moving are those lamenting the fall of Constantinople in 1453;[16] among them the one on the last mass in Santa Sophia[17] should be singled out, of which several versions exist, ranging from eleven to eighteen political lines. Its tragic lyricism is deeply moving, and particularly noteworthy are the last two lines addressed to the Virgin, in which a note of optimism about the future of the Greek and Orthodox Christianity emerges at that dark historical moment, a ray of hope so different from the pessimistic *Oracles of Leo the Sage* that were circulating shortly before the fall of the city.[18] As has been aptly remarked, 'It is the song of a defeated, but not of a subjugated people.'[19]

Among the later notable historical folk songs are those that tell of the slaves carried away by the fierce pirates Horuk and Hairedin Barbarossa (sixteenth century),[20] of the trials of the Peloponnesians at the hands of the Albanians after the rising of 1769,[21] of the battle of the Souliots against Ali Pasha in 1792[22] and of the drowning of the beautiful Kera Phrosyne and seventeen other women in the lake of Joaninna[23] at the command of that cruel tyrant. A number of the Klephtic ballads are also, strictly speaking, historical songs, but their epico-lyric, panegyric character, which is so different from the flat, factual, narrative tone of the other historical folk songs, has influenced literary historians to group them separately.[24]

Historical folk songs with a 'new historical sense'[25] continued to be composed until the end of the Greek War of Independence (1821–9), but in them the cult of personal heroism which we know from the Klephtic ballads has disappeared, and in its place we find patriotism and religion celebrated in an abstract and impersonal manner.[26] Nonetheless, some of these are moving; one example is *The Condemned Cretan*,[27] composed in 1830, when, at the end of the War of Independence, Crete was excluded from the Greek lands to be liberated from the Turks.

Folk songs proper

Many are the occasions which gave rise to Greek folk songs proper—
certain days of the year, marriages, village festivals, departures, family
life, work and death. Thus carols were composed for 1 January and
1 March (a practice which went back to antiquity);[28] working songs were
produced by millers,[29] sailors and shepherds; marriage songs and dancing
songs were composed for all parts of wedding festivities; love songs,
lullabies, dirges and songs of departure (*τῆς ξενητεᾶς*), full of the bitter-
ness of life in foreign lands, were created. In fact, there are songs for
practically every public and private occasion, all characterized by a depth
of feeling, a natural grace and a freedom of imagination that are indeed
impressive.

Out of all this remarkable output it is worth lingering for a little over
three groups, the lullabies, the love songs and the dirges, which provide an
admirable insight into Greek character. In the lullabies one can see the
depth and delicacy of feeling of the Greek mother and the firm belief of the
Greeks in family life. In the love songs the power of their passion and the
shades of feeling expressed are deeply moving, as they sing of the first
experience of love, of the long delays between the meetings of lovers, of the
envy caused by rivals and of death caused by a broken heart; of a son's
confession to his mother that he is in love with a girl whom he is too shy to
approach, of a mother's intervention to persuade a young girl to marry her
son, of marriage brokers and helping friends; of love charms, of young
girls led astray, of secret meetings at the village spring, of serenades and
swift exchanges in the street, of the placing of bets and so forth. These love
songs are fresh and simple, full of lively images and plain symbols. They
often have a playful charm and invariably strike a tone which has been
described as 'pure and modest, without being prudish'. At the same time
it should be pointed out that in these songs woman is not idealized as she is
in the West but is seen on the whole as an instrument of delight or
destruction. Some of the love songs are very short, between four and seven
lines, and some (the *lianotragouda*) are only couplets, among which the
Cretan *mantinades* have a special place.

Finally, we come to the dirges (*μοιρολόγια*), which, as we have seen,
are the work of women, often of famous professional mourners
(*μοιρολογίστρες*). New ones are no longer composed, but old and famous
dirges are still chanted at village funerals to this day. Among them the
laments of the Maina should be singled out. They are usually composed in
eight-syllable lines and are characterized by a pronounced realism. Per-
haps the most moving and most lyrical of these are the dirges on children
that occasionally take the form of a dialogue between the mourner and the
dead child.

In these laments Hades, the Underworld, is presented as a dark, mouldy place in which the shades of the dead wander about, longing for the light of day and seeking to steal from Death the key of the Underworld's gate in order to escape and return to the warmth of the sun. *Charos*, Death himself, is often represented as an old man, lean and severe, who will, however, deign to play quoits or to take a meal with the young man he is about to carry away. More often he is represented as a proud horseman astride a black horse, carrying on the back of his saddle the souls of the dead as he leads them to the Spring of Forgetfulness, the equivalent of the ancient river of Lethe. Popular imagination has also represented him dining with his wife, the *Charondissa*, or even as having a mother who is sorry for the dead he is carrying away.

We must now come to the couplet, the δίστιχο or λιανοτράγουδο, as it is called in modern Greek, which is the only form of folk poetry that is still alive in Greece. Its origins lie not in antiquity[30] but in the Middle Ages, when from the tenth and particularly from the thirteenth century onwards the couplet became a popular, short, independent strophe, and series of them were strung together to form alphabets or other, longer poems. Many such couplets were and still are improvised at festivals, weddings and other social gatherings for the entertainment of the guests; others are snippets of longer poems — often the beginnings of poems — that have become detached because of their succinct expression of a thought. They embrace many sides of life, usually pronouncing views on love and friendship, family life and politics. The gnomic and apophthegmatic nature of many must be stressed; in them the wisdom of ages seems to be concentrated. But satirical and even purely nonsensical couplets exist.[31] Of great beauty and variety are the Cretan rhyming love couplets, the so-called μαντινάδες. The great majority of the couplets are cast in the fifteen-syllable line[32] and are accompanied by music. A number of these originally did not rhyme, but they have been altered so as to fit into a rhyming scheme.

The *paraloges*

From a literary point of view, the *paraloges*, long, narrative folk songs, are superior to the folk songs proper and represent a more mature stage in the development of folk poetry.[33] In a way, they are similar to the ballads of northern and western Europe, though they are not composed in stanzas and do not always employ rhyme. In them epic is fused with lyrical elements, and the use of dialogue is usual; many have a tragic ending. In their verses we meet great warriors, kings and princes, young lovers, the dangerous water-nymphs (νεράϊδες), the Fates (Μοῖρες), ghostly and daemonic figures, the fierce Little Folk (καλλικάντζαροι) and other creations of popular imagination.

A special and particularly lively group of these are connected with the Akritic Cycle, about which we have spoken;[34] in them an epic, heroic spirit is evident, and love plays no part. Most beautiful and most widespread among them are *The Dead Brother*[35] and *The Bridge of Arta*,[36] in which the tragic element predominates. The most authentic version of the latter goes under the title *Hair's Bridge* and comes from Asia Minor. In both the deep family feelings of the Greeks are clearly evident.

From Asia Minor we must come to the islands if we are to find the well-known erotic *paraloges*. One that exists in many versions and must have been very popular is *Chartzianis*, otherwise known as *The Sun-Born Maiden*,[37] in which the hero, dressed as a woman, is admitted to the room of his beloved. The other well-known erotic *paraloges* are *The Abandoned Girl*[38] and *The Maid of Honour* (κουμπάρα) *who becomes a Bride*. There are, of course, several others with a young girl as their central figure, all probably originating in the islands and belonging to the thirteenth, fourteenth and fifteenth centuries. In these the influence of the Franks is often discernible.

Among the erotic *paraloges* there are those that have as their heroine an unfaithful wife or a mistress and not a virgin. These have been attributed to Crete, because of the relaxation of morals on that island after the arrival of the Franks; their environment is reminiscent of that of the poetry of Sachlikis. From the islands also comes a group of lovely folk songs connected with the sea, like the *Master North Wind* (Κὺρ Βοργιᾶς)[39] and *The Travelling Girl*.[40]

If we turn from the islands to consider Greece proper, we shall find another set of *paraloges* and ballads, among them the so-called 'tragic group', of which *The Murderous Mother*,[41] which dates back to before the sixteenth century, is the most famous. Many of the Greek *paraloges* spread beyond Greece to the lands of the Serbs, the Bulgars, the Romanians and right to northern Europe.[42]

The Klephtic ballads

As has already been mentioned, the Klephts were the freedom-loving Christians who, unable to endure Turkish oppression, took to the mountainous regions north of the Isthmus, where they led a semi-independent existence. They preyed upon the Turks and even, when driven to extreme necessity, upon the more peaceful populations of the plains, a practice that earned them the title of the Klephts ('Bandits').

In the second half of the sixteenth century, in order to combat these mavericks, the Ottoman Empire organized a Christian *gendarmerie* known as *armatoloi* ('bearers of arms').[43] Many of these, upon falling into disfavour with their masters, took refuge in the mountains and joined the bands of Klephts. Thus from the second half of the seventeenth century — but particularly in the course of the eighteenth and the first half of the nineteenth century — the Klephts became the forerunners in the struggle for Greek independence.[44] Their fight against the Turks was uneven and the circumstances in which they lived extremely harsh, so that a true heroic spirit developed among them and a fine contempt for death — both admirably reflected in their poetry.

The Klephtic ballads developed in mainland Greece, and in the eighteenth century they represented the final and supreme stage in the evolution of modern Greek folk poetry. They can be separated into two groups, one dealing with the achievements or the death of an individual Klepht and the second with the life of the Klephts in general.[45] Of the two, the first is poetically greatly superior and probably the older.[46]

The true spirit of Klephtic poetry is more evident in the ballads that deal with the achievements or the death of an individual Klepht. Such are the songs about the heroes Boukouvalas, Stathas, Melionis, Kitsos, Zidros, Stournaris, Gyftakis or the heroine Despo.[47] In these the spirit of freedom is celebrated, above all the inspiring self-respect and dignity of the man who is prepared to sacrifice everything in the name of freedom and who, when gravely wounded, asks his comrades to kill him so that he may not fall into the hands of his enemies. There is a striking absence of all conventional patriotism in these poems and of any reference to religion, and their lyricism is very sparse. Moreover, they are free from all exaggeration — a virtue we did not meet in the Akritic ballads — and from all horrifying descriptions of wounds or death.

The language and technique of these ballads is in keeping with the pragmatic simplicity of their content. They are short (usually roughly ten to twenty lines long) and apospasmatic, and they always include snippets of dialogue. Their simple, forceful language relies mainly on verbs and concrete nouns; the decorative adjective is avoided. A characteristic feature is their pronounced epico-lyric panegyric character. Some of these songs were composed by poets who followed the Klephts to the mountains, while others were composed by Klephts themselves.[48]

On the other hand, the songs of the second group, those that deal with the life of the Klephts in general, though richer in lyrical elements (the pathetic fallacy is ubiquitous) are compositions 'in cold blood' and are full of abstractions. Their subjects are on the whole conventional — the death of the chief Klepht, the Klephts' weapons, the Klephts' fatigue, the Klephts' hopes — and though their technique is considerably more developed, they are not as interesting as the songs of the first group. Among them is a notable series of songs that deal with battles between mountains, a motif that goes back to antiquity, as we know from a fragment of Corinna found on a second-century papyrus in which Mount Helicon and

Mount Cithaeron are fighting.[49] Such battles of mountains in Greek folk songs have survived in Crete and in Carpathos,[50] but the most famous of all is the Pan-Hellenic ballad of *The Battle between Mount Olympus and Mount Kisavos*.[51]

Klephtic poetry flourished until the days of the Greek War of Independence (1821–9). When the whole Greek nation rose to shake off the Turkish yoke, the Klephtic bands merged with the other warriors, and this brought about the end of Klephtic life and Klephtic balladry. After the liberation of Greece, when the areas in which the Klephts mainly operated were incorporated in the new Greek kingdom, such poetry continued to be composed for a few decades in Macedonia and the Epirus, but it soon died out there too. In liberated Greece a few poems inspired by the Klephtic tradition were composed in the nineteenth century, dealing with the adventures of well-known brigands like Davelis, Doulas or Constantellos, but they are of no literary value.

The main characteristic of all Greek folk songs is their simplicity in expressing emotions and in describing material things; by contrast with the Akritic songs, exaggerations are avoided. The diction is also in keeping with this simplicity, for it has short periods and no inversions and avoids rare words. The snippets of dialogue, which are an integral part of the style of Greek demotic songs, are also clear and to the point. A frequent element in their technique which must be noted is the repetition of the same word or of synonymous words in the two halves of the fifteen-syllable line,[52] the line they most frequently use. *Enjambement* is rare, as is the use of rhyme except in the couplets, the *lianotragouda*. It should also be mentioned that there are many recurring formulae and set descriptions.

The sadness of the tone of many modern Greek folk songs is striking, and this is enhanced by the plaintive airs to which many of them are sung. For it must be remembered that the demotic songs were always accompanied by music and often by dance.[53] The Klephtic ballads in particular are sung according to a peculiar strophic system which embraces a line and a half as a unit. In other songs the singer often breaks the line by inserting small, independent units called *gyrismata* or *tsakismata*, which give variety to the song.

Greek folk songs have been the object of much admiration since C. Ch. Fauriel first collected and published a number of them in the nineteenth century. One has only to remember the unqualified praise of a man like Goethe. But perhaps their greatest claim to glory is that they served as the main source of inspiration and guidance for the revival of modern Greek poetry since the liberation of Greece. The emergence of Solomos and the Ionian School of poetry—most notably Valaoritis—is inconceivable without them, and so is that of the New School of Athens and Palamas; and from there the line leads directly to Sikelianos, Kazantzakis and Seferis.

PERSONAL POETRY UNDER THE TURKS

The first and darkest period (1453–1600)

The social and political circumstances of the Greeks during the first century and a half after the Fall of Constantinople and the lack of contact with the West caused complete literary stagnation among all those living under Ottoman domination. In that period of transition—in which, as has been aptly said, 'an old world was dying and a new one was being born, and both death and birth take place in suffering'[54]—it was the Orthodox Church that kept guard over the ruins of Byzantine culture: hence the prevalence of the erudite linguistic tradition in all writings, except for the scanty poetic output, which was all cast in a mixed linguistic idiom and in political verse.

We have already spoken about the anonymous laments on the Fall of Byzantium. We must now turn to such personal poetry as appeared on that impoverished literary scene, which was dominated by theology. It is on the whole didactic and historical verse, whose poverty of imagination is striking and whose main interest is linguistic; circumstances did not favour lyrical inspiration, nor was there a true Byzantine lyrical tradition for those writers to develop further.

The best-known poet of this period is Georgios Aetolos (c. 1525–80), who was born in Corinth and lived much of his life in Constantinople, where it is thought (but this is not certain) that he directed the Patriarchal School. His most interesting work in verse is his *Collection of Aesopian Myths*, which consists of short, independent poems cast in rhyming fifteen-syllable lines. Its literary value is minimal. Of even less significance are his other three known poems, two eulogies on Michael Kantakouzenos, a rich Greek who collaborated with the Turks and was known as the 'Son of Satan',[55] and *The History of Peter the Lame*.

Of greater interest is the long poem, *The Establishment of the Patriarchate in Moscow*, composed in 1620 political lines by Arsenios, bishop of Elasson (c. 1548–1625). It is an almost epic description of the adventures encountered by the Ecumenical Patriarch, Jeremias, and the author when they visited Russia in 1588 in order to establish in Moscow the Russian Patriarchate. Unfortunately, its poetic merits are very limited.

Three poems about the life and deeds of the Wallachian national hero, Michael the Brave (1558–1601), have also survived. The first is by the Epirot Stavrinos Vestiares (died c. 1613) and is called *The Exploits of Michael the Brave*. It is interesting to note the influence of the folk songs and of the Akritic cycle upon it. The second is by Georgios Palamides (c. 1607) and bears the title *History of Michael the Brave*. It is in 1378 rhyming political lines and betrays the influence of Tasso's *Gerusalèmme Liberata*. Michael is presented there not as a Greek but as a great Christian Crusader. The third, a much longer poem (2860 rhyming political lines) called *The History of Wallachia*, is by Mattheos, Metropolitan of Myra (died 1624). It is a continuation of the work of Georgios Palamides and deals with Wallachian history from 1601 to 1617, presented with much moralizing and didacticism. Though it has no literary value, it is of some interest because it includes a lament on the Fall of Byzantium in which, for the first time, we meet the view directly expressed that, if the Greeks are to regain their liberty, they should rely not on foreign aid but on their own resources, which must be reorganized.

That this approach found a response among the poet's contemporaries can be seen from the *Lament* attributed to Synadinos (born 1600), a priest from Serrae, which in 160 rhyming political lines and in a biblical style, grieves over the misfortunes of the Greeks. The poem incorporates part of Mattheos' lament, echoes of which can also be found in other poems.[56]

The period of religious humanism (1600–69)

The period 1600 to 1669 was characterized by the vigorous reaction of the Orthodox Church against Roman Catholic propaganda—especially that of the Jesuits—and Turkish oppression. It was in these years that the Greek clergy came to realize that the education of the Greeks was the best means of achieving its religious and patriotic ends. A number of great Ecumenical Patriarchs took the lead in this movement, and friendly relations were established with the Protestant countries. But, in spite of this anti-Catholic attitude, many of the Greeks pursued their studies in Italian universities and, returning to their homes, aspired to introduce the 'new' Western ideas to the Greek world, which in many respects were opposed to the old, traditional, 'Byzantine' views. Nonetheless, a literature based on Western Classicism was not to see the light in Turkish-occupied Greek lands before the eighteenth century.

This period of religious humanism is marked by the complete absence of any noteworthy poetry —indeed, of any *belles-lettres* in the Turkish-occupied Greek world. Only a few men of the Church continued to compose insignificant hymns and the odd unimportant poem—the works of savants but not of poets—such as the epigrams and the iambic verses *On the Monastery of Kiev, its Holy Relics and Vessels* by Meletios Syrigos (1590–1664), the verses of Nectarios, Patriarch of Jerusalem (1607–76) or those of Paisios Agiapostolitis, Metropolitan of Rhodes (died 1601). In this poetic desert mention should perhaps also be made of Mattheos Kolitzis (c. 1610), who wrote a curious short poem called *The Life of False Demetrius*, dealing, in faulty but lively verses, with the battles between

Muscovites and Poles in the years 1605–6. and some totally unimportant romances in verse. The most popular of these was *The Story of the Jewess Markada*, published in Venice in 1668 (it ran into many editions), which recalls in parts certain folk songs and the Cretan pastoral *The Shepherdess*.[57]

Harbingers of the Greek revival (1669–1750)

In character and quality no great change is noticeable in the Greek poetry of these years in the lands under Turkish occupation. We need not linger over totally insignificant odes and hymns on the Classical pattern, like those by Antonios Koraes, the grandfather of Adamantios Koraes, or occasional poems like that by an otherwise unknown priest, Paul, on the *Restorations of the Church of St Menas* in Crete or certain unimportant laments. Nor do the satirical dialogue *The Stable* by Neophytos, abbot of the monastery of St Sabbas in Bucharest, or the short anonymous poem *The Husband's Vengeance*, treating of a story similar to that which inspired both Byron and Victor Hugo in their poems entitled *Mazeppa*, show any greater literary merit.[58]

To get some notion of the poetry of this period we must turn to two longer poems of the middle of the eighteenth century, *The Battle of the Elements* by J. Rizos Manes (born 1716), a Constantinopolitan doctor, and the *Bosporomachia* by Momars (c. 1752), an Austrian Embassy interpreter in Constantinople, which were much admired and read in those days. The latter was even revised, so it is said, by the Patriarch Kallinikos.

The Battle of the Elements is an allegorical poem which, in 200 seven-syllable lines, describes how Earth, who gazes vainly at her reflection in the water, is brought back to her senses by the flood; the *Bosporomachia* deals with a dispute between the two banks of the Bosporus over the question of which is the more beautiful. Its roughly 4000 rhyming political lines are a materpiece of prolixity and tedium. Both these works were influenced by contemporary French poetry and in their turn exercised a considerable influence upon the Phanariots.

Far more important than Rizos Manes or Momars was Caesarios Dapontes (1711–84), who was considered the leading literary figure of the eighteenth century. He was born on the island of Skopelos and was educated in Constantinople, Bucharest and Jassy; later he became secretary to two princes of Moldavia, Constantine and John Mavrogordato. He was later cast into jail by the Turks; when released, and after an unhappy marriage, he became a monk on Mount Athos. He subsequently left the Holy Mountain for eight years, allegedly to raise funds for his monastery, but finally returned there and devoted himself to writing until his death. He himself tells us: 'In my adventurous life I have seen both Heaven and Hell.'

Dapontes is the most prolific and best-known poet of the eighteenth century. His works, not all of which are published, embrace religious, historical, geographical and didactic writings, as well as myths, hymns and other occasional poetry. Most of these are cast in flowing fifteen-syllable lines but not all should be considered poetry—he himself would have agreed with this—as, for instance, the long work of 30,000 lines on Byzantine history or his commentaries on the liturgies.

Of his poems, the best are *The Mirror of Women* and *The Garden of Graces*. The first, consisting of many thousands of lines (it fills 900 printed pages) he wrote when in prison; it deals with the evil doings and other activities of biblical and historical women. But there are also digressions speaking of his own adventures and of events of his day. The verses are on the whole poor and the rhymes faulty, but there is in them much interesting material for the linguist, the folklorist and the historian. *The Garden of Graces* is also a long poem—it runs to 6000 fifteen-syllable lines—and is a veritable hotch-potch of unconnected elements from the poet's life, myths, miracles, hymns and extracts from other authors, including Classical authors like Herodotus, Plutarch and Athenaeaus. Occasionally, a faint spark of poetry appears in these lines, as, for example, in the passages describing the beauty of solitude and of monastic life.

The language of Dapontes is mixed, ranging from that of erudite liturgical poetry to that of everyday speech. In spite of his limited education, he believed and proclaimed that the Greeks could regain their liberty only through learning. He thus leads us to the next period, that of the Greek revival.

The Phanariots (1750–1821)

In the second half of the eighteenth century and up to the outbreak of the War of Independence the general Greek reading public continued to enjoy the products of Cretan literature, such as the *Erotokritos*, *The Sacrifice of Abraham*, *The Shepherdess*, as can be seen from the several editions to which those works ran. On the other hand, the Phanariot elite was drawn to the fashionable literature of the West, mainly French but also Italian, German and English.[59] The influence of the Phanariots was such that the production and circulation of translations of Western works far exceeded those of original Greek works–the second half of the eighteenth century is called the 'Age of Translations'—which came to be looked down upon as unworthy and below the desirable literary standards.

There can be little doubt that these translations broadened the Greek literary horizon, for the Phanariot poets were on the whole poor amateur versifiers, most of whom have been forgotten, as they rarely published their works. By and large their verses were included in private collections and anthologies, in which poems, folk songs, letters and translations rubbed shoulders, or circulated in manuscript copies. Though all these versifiers were not, strictly speaking, Phanariots by birth, they were all Phanariots in spirit and used the language of the Constantinopolitan writers, which on the whole had a marked purist tendency and in metre occasionally broke away from the traditional fifteen-syllable line.

Among the Phanariot poets whose names we know, two are worthy of note: Alexandros Kalphoglou (1725–95), whose erotic poetry was much admired in its day; and Alexandros Mavrogordato (1754–1819), a Grand Dragoman of the Porte and later Prince of Moldavia, who took refuge in Russia when the Russo-Turkish War of 1785 broke out (he is perhaps the best representative of that group). He published a well-known anthology called *The Bosphorus in Borysthenes* (Dnieper), which includes, among other frigid and elaborate works, a poem praising the spoken idiom, something very rare among the distinguished Phanariots.

To these two poets can be added Constantine Manos (born 1777), writer of a pastoral idyll, *Cleanthes and Aurocome*; Michael Perdikaris (1766–1828), a writer of verse satires in which the influence of Lucian is evident; and Georgios Sakellarios (1767–1838), a doctor from Kozane who composed didactic, patriotic and lyrical verse and is the first Phanariot poet in whose work the influence of English poetry (*The Nights* by Young) can be traced.[60] There are also the odes written upon the birth of the *Aiglon*, the son of Napoleon I, odes with a pronounced patriotic content, the best-known author of which was Apostolis Arsakis (1792–1874).[61]

The forerunners of modern Greek poetry

Three poets of note belong to the eve of the Greek War of Independence, all of them influenced by the Phanariot tradition: Rhegas Pheraios (or Velestinlis), Athanasios Christopoulos and Joannes Velaras.

Rhegas Pheraios (1757–98) was born at Valestino (the ancient Pherae) and was the son of a wealthy family. In his stormy life he served as a schoolmaster at Kissos on Mount Pelion, took refuge from the Turks at the monastery of Vatopedi on Mount Athos, mastered French and German in Constantinople, Jassy and Bucharest, served at the courts of the Danubian princes, founded a society to promote Greek patriotic sentiment and to provide the Greeks with arms, and, believing that the French Revolution would shortly lead to action in the Balkans, went to Vienna to organize the movement among exiled Greeks and their sympathizers. From there he published Greek translations of foreign works in the common tongue and formed a collection of national songs which, though not published until after his death, was passed from hand to hand in manuscript, arousing patriotic enthusiasm everywhere in Greece. His work was cut short, for he was handed over to the Turks by the Austrian government and was executed in 1798.

He is remembered for his *Thourios* (*War Song*), the Greek version of the *Marseillaise*, paraphrased by Byron as 'Sons of the Greeks arise!'. This poem, which is not remarkable poetry, displays such fervent patriotism and is so genuine and direct that it can still move the modern Greek reader. It was sung with almost equal passion by Greek, Romanian, Albanian and Slav—the freedom and the union of all the Balkans was Rhegas' dream—and many a hero and martyr died with it on his lips.[62]

Joannes Velaras (1771–1823), son of an Epirot merchant, was born in Cerigo and educated in Janinna and then in Padua and Bologna, where he studied medicine. Though drawn to the liberal ideas of the French Revolution and the early Napoleonic Wars, when he returned to Epirus he joined the entourage of Veli, the son of Ali Pasha, as his private doctor.

Velaras was not only a doctor, but also a man well versed in the classics—he translated parts of Thucydides (Book II), Plato's *Crito* and the *Batrachomyomachia* into demotic Epirot Greek—an amateur botanist and, above all, a poet who wrote lyrical and satirical verse, fables and 'characters' (the 'Liar', the 'Glutton', the 'Envious Man' and so on), the latter in the style of La Bruyère. His lyrics are short, fresh and straightforward but frequently derivative[63]—there is clear evidence of the influence of the eighteenth-century drawing-room bucolics—and in diction and metre often faulty. However, they brought a new breath of life to Greek personal poetry and a lyricism inspired by nature (most notable is his song *The Spring*) that had been missing from Greek verse since the days of Cretan poetry; in fact, some of his longer rhyming erotic poems are very reminiscent of Cretan *mantinades*. The freshness of Velaras' poetry is attributable chiefly to his language, which is an uncompromising Epirot dialect, often recalling the liveliness and spontaneity of the folk songs. For he applied in his poetry the extreme demotic linguistic views he had expressed in his small book *Romeike Glossa* and to comply with them even trimmed down words and phrases of the purist tradition.

In his vivid satirical works he attacks the social evils of his time with a view to both entertaining and improving his fellow man. The absence of malice in them is refreshing. Velaras, above all other Phanariot poets, points to the modern Greek revival, as the poets of the Ionian School later expressed it.[64]

Athanasios Christopoulos (1772–1847), the son of a priest, was born in the Macedonian town of Kastoria. He was educated first in Bucharest and then in Budapest and Padua, where he studied law and medicine. Later he returned to Constantinople and the Danubian principalities, where he served at the courts of Prince Alexander Mourouzis and Prince John Karatzas as a tutor and legal adviser. Finally, he was appointed Grand Logothete and judge at the courts of Bucharest and Jassy.

Christopoulos was a prolific writer of legal, religious, philosophical, medical and political works, but he is remembered chiefly as a poet.[65] His first literary work was a poor patriotic play called *Achilles*, which has the distinction of being the first non-Cretan modern Greek play to be printed.[66] Greatly superior and far more popular were his lyrical poems, erotic and convivial in character, which earned him, undeservedly, the title of the 'New Anacreon'. The influence of French and Italian poetry and of the Anacreontics upon these facile and monotonous poems is more than evident; his is a verse in which skin-deep flirtation instead of true erotic passion and a conventional 'Bacchic' approach to the virtues of wine prevail. (It is indeed difficult to understand why the poetry of Christopoulos was so widely admired beyond the small Phanariot courts, with their atmosphere of *politesse* and ceremony, and was even translated into French and German. A collection of his lyrics was the first book of verse to be printed in Athens.)[67]

The language of Christopoulos is simple and fluent and close to the spoken idiom, and this no doubt accounts for a great part of his popularity and for the influence he exercised upon later Greek poetry. One further point should perhaps be added: no patriotism is evident in his verse—a rare phenomenon in the poetry of those days.

All these three precursors of modern Greek poetry had the common virtue of employing the spoken idiom in various degrees of purity in their works and thus at last breaking free from the oppressively erudite Phanariot linguistic tradition. In this Velaras was the most successful, and that is the reason why his influence upon subsequent Greek poetry superseded that of all other Greek writers outside Crete.

Rhimades

In the eighteenth and early nineteenth century unpretentious 'historical' poems of a patriotic nature circulated in the Greek world. They nearly all dealt with the resistance of the Greeks against the Turks, but they must be distinguished from the Klephtic ballads, as they were not true folk songs but inferior 'personal' poetry that occasionally passed for brief spells into the realm of oral poetry. This can be seen from the use of rhyme in some of them, which gave them the name *rhimades* ('rhyming poems').

Such are the 'historical' poems about Lambros Katsonis (1752–1804), the celebrated Greek corsair who fought against the Turks,[68] or the two Epirot poems on Ali Pasha called *The Genealogy of Ali Pasha* and *The Lament on Ali Pasha*. It should be noted that the Byzantine genre of the lament continued to be cultivated, as is evident from the *Lament of Roumeli* and the *Rising of the People of Smyrna against the Notables* (an event which had taken place in 1788), both of which are insignificant as poetry. Another poem which enjoyed some popularity in those days because of its 'patriotic' content was *The Story of the Lord and Spatharios Staurakis*, which deals with an agent of the Danubian princes who was put to death by the Turks. Finally, to complete the picture, *The History of Maina, its Habits, Villages and Products*, attributed to Nikitas Siphakos, and two equally inferior poems dealing with the disputes of the Demogerontes (town councillors) of Smyrna should also perhaps be mentioned. In the light of such a dearth of poetic creativity, it is perhaps not surprising that the works of Athanasios Christopolous and Joannes Velaras should have been considered masterpieces by their contemporaries.

Part Five

MODERN GREECE
(1829–1940)

Introduction

The Greek literary revival of the eighteenth century, which was connected largely with ideas produced by the Enlightenment and the French Revolution, soon led the Greek people and their clergy to revive their old dream of freedom. The Greeks, because of the Klephts and the *armatoloi*, had never, in fact, been fully disarmed, and by the end of the eighteenth century these bands had become more daring than ever; nor did the Greek and Albanian sailors, particularly those of the islands of Hydra and Spetsai, feel any fear of the Turkish navy. Moreover, as we have seen, in 1814 the secret society *Philike Hetairia*, whose object was revolutionary, was founded in Odessa, and by 1819–20 its activities had become united with the general movement for liberation.

The signal for the revolution of the Greeks against the Turks was given in March 1821 by a raid upon Jassy and Bucharest from Russian territory; after a long and bitter struggle the liberation of a small part of the Greek world was achieved in 1829. We need not describe the many acts of heroism and self-sacrifice which marked those years, nor the cruelty of the Turks and the wholesale destruction and massacres perpetrated by them.

After the assassination of President Kapodistrias in 1831 and after many painful negotiations, the throne of Greece was finally given to the seventeen-year-old Otto, son of the philhellene King Ludwig I of Bavaria, in 1832. It was agreed that the northern frontier of the new kingdom should run from the Gulf of Volos in the east to the Gulf of Arta in the West; of the islands, only Euboea and the Cyclades were ceded to Greece, whose capital was transferred from Nauplia to Athens in 1834.

Much was achieved in the first ten years of 'Bavarian' rule, but the leaders and veterans of the Revolution were not satisfied. Even after the king, having come of age, began to preside over his Cabinet, police supervision, burdensome taxation and officious administration persisted; this led to the bloodless coup of 1843, which forced the monarch to grant a constitution in 1844. At the same time a new generation of politicians emerged, nurtured at the University of Athens under the principles of the

French Revolution, and in October 1862 risings in Acarnania, followed by insurrections in Nauplia and elsewhere, forced the royal court into exile at Bambers, where the king died four years later. He was succeeded by George I, a young Danish prince, in 1864, when with England's consent the union of the Ionian Islands with Greece also took place.

Otto and his queen, Amalia, took over a small country with a ruined economy and an illiterate people which for centuries had been living under Oriental rule and together tried to lay the foundations of a state based on Western principles. Within thirty years the population and naval traffic had doubled, and foreign trade had more than quadrupled. Moreover, Athens, once a backward Turkish village, had grown into a small city and the Piraeus had been transformed from a fishing village into a busy port.

The revival of the Byzantine Empire, known as the 'Great Idea' which would liberate and embrace all Greeks still under the Turkish yoke, was uppermost in the hearts of the Greek nation during Otto's reign; it dominated all political and literary life. Around the court in Athens now clustered many lively Greek elements, drawn to that new centre of Hellenism from Constantinople, the Danubian principalities, Trieste, London and the Heptanese. A fresh intellectual life was thus born in Greece, which expressed itself in poetry in the so-called Old School of Athens, or 'School of the Greek Romantics', that developed side by side with the more Western and sophisticated School of the Ionian Islands.

The reign of George I (1864–1913) marked a great step forward in the political and social development of Greece, which was achieved in the face of a series of severe international and national crises. Such were the Cretan revolutions of 1866 and 1870 against the Turks; the creation of a Greater Bulgaria by the Treaty of San Stephano in 1878 (fatal for the fulfilment of the Greek national aspirations in European Turkey); the capture of eastern Roumelia by Bulgaria in 1885, where a population of about 250,000 Greeks were living; and the new insurrection by the Cretans in 1896 that brought about the intervention of Greece and her severe defeat by the Turks in 1897. Since the liberation of the country Greek national pride had never been more deeply wounded than in 1897, and a dark cloud of guilt and shame hung over the Greeks until the victorious Balkan Wars of 1912–13.[1]

The upsurge of Greek national pride that followed the victories of the Balkan Wars—in which Turkey and Bulgaria, the traditional enemies of Hellenism, were defeated—can hardly be overrated. Consequently, there followed once again the revival of the 'Great Idea', whose realization now appeared almost feasible.

The reign of George I, during which the Ionian Islands, Thessaly, southern Epirus and finally Crete had been incorporated into Greece (the population of the country had been trebled, its density doubled and communications had been developed)[2] was also the one in which city life gradually emerged in Greece; for the reign of King Otto had known only village communities, even if some bore the names of cities glorious in antiquity, like Athens, Sparta or Thebes. As was to be expected, this new urban spirit was manifest in the works of the younger writers. In poetry it clearly emerged in the verse of the poets of the 1880s and was prevalent in that of their successors.

The Demotic Movement which developed in the late 1880s and which sought to return the Greek language, Greek intellectual life and Greek education to its contemporary roots, was undoubtedly the most significant cultural event of the reign of George I. The ground for this was prepared by the pioneer work of a group of enlightened men, among whom three should be noted; the historian Constantine Paparrigopoulos, the folklorist Nicholas Politis and the Neo-Hellenist at the École des Langues Orientales of Paris, Émil Legrand.

The result of the pioneer work of these men was to turn the tide of interest towards contemporary Greek life and the language spoken by the people. But it was not until John Psycharis (1854–1929) assumed the leadership of the Demotic Movement that it acquired Pan-Hellenic significance and broadened out to embrace most aspects of Greek intellectual and artistic life. For from its original concern with language it came to examine and encourage all forms of popular art—music, architecture, painting and dancing—as well as literature and education in the real sense of the word.

The roots of the modern Greek language question go as far back as the first century B.C., when Atticism turned the tide against the developing form of Hellenistic *koine* Greek and established the view that 'correct' Greek—not only from a grammatical, but also from a 'moral' point of view—was that used by the Attic authors of the fifth and the fourth century B.C. This 'correct' Greek was gradually introduced into all Hellenistic schools of rhetoric and grammar; later, supported by the Church and the State, it was adopted by the schools of the Byzantine Empire and survived, *mutatis mutandis* (for a mixture of the Atticizing written language with the developing spoken modern Greek idiom was inevitable), as the Greek taught at school until the liberation of Greece in the nineteenth century.

There were, of course, several attempts made by enlightened men to strike a compromise between the written, 'static' Atticizing idiom and the 'evolving' spoken Greek, but none was universally accepted until Adamantios Koraes (1748–1833), the distinguished classical scholar, put forward his own, which became the basis of the official Greek language, the *katherevousa*, which modern Greece adopted when the new Greek kingdom was established. During the nineteenth century Koraes' *katherevousa*, which was much closer to Attic than to spoken Greek, prevailed and was 'improved' and further 'purified' by a large number of Greek authors and men of letters. The *katherevousa* became virtually a different language from that of everyday speech; many purists were writing in what was, in effect, 'bad' ancient Greek, a practice which was considered patriotic and demonstrated, in their view, the continuity of the Greek tradition and of the Greek nation. Against the dead weight of this and other such stilted educational views, the Demotic Movement of the eighties reacted; needless to say, at the linguistic level, which remained the basis of the whole controversy, the struggle was not easy. To fight that long, uninterrupted and glorious tradition which embraced the Greek classics, the Gospels and the writings of the Fathers of the Church, demanded both courage and a powerful scholarly armoury. In neither of these was Psycharis found wanting.

The effect of the Demotic Movement upon the intellectual life of the Greeks, as indeed upon their educational system, can hardly be exaggerated. On poetry, which is our main concern here, it exercised an unparalleled liberating and rejuvenating influence, for it inspired a group of younger poets to cut loose from the Romantic past and to found the New School of Athens, which brought life back to waning Greek poetry.

King George I, who for fifty years had handled his excitable Mediterranean subjects with remarkable northern calm, was murdered in Salonica in 1913 and was succeeded by his son Constantine I. The reign of Constantine I (1913–22) was eventful and, on the whole, unhappy both for the sovereign and for the Greek nation. Constantine ascended the throne at the peak of his glory, when he was leading the Greek armies, whose commander he was, from triumph to triumph during the Balkan Wars. But universal adoration soon turned into mistrust and then into a violent hatred on the part of at least half the nation when, during the First World War, he endeavoured to keep Greece neutral against the advice of his Prime Minister, Elephtherios Venizelos. A series of political crises led to a full-scale revolution by Venizelos and to the exile of the king in 1917. He was succeeded by his second son, Alexander, when Greece joined the Entente and fought on her side against the Central Powers and her old traditional enemies, Turkey and Bulgaria.

The end of the First World War nearly saw the realization of the Greek dream, the 'Great Idea'. Greek armies, standing on soil which they controlled, were literally outside the walls of Constantinople, and practically the whole of Hellenism was embraced within the boundaries of a free Greek State.[3] It was a far cry from the shameful defeat of 1897, and the elation felt by the whole Greek nation was immense.

But fatigue had also set in. The country was exhausted by war and by prolonged mobilization, and the accidental death of King Alexander on 25 October 1920 fatally revived the issue of his successor. It was then that Venizelos's opponents combined to defeat him at the elections of Novem-

ber 1920—a turning-point in modern Greek history—and, after a plebi-
scite which was held immediately and from which the Venizelists ab-
stained, King Constantine was restored to his throne.

The revival of Turkish power under Kemal Pasha and the enmity of
France and Italy would probably have deprived even a Venizelist Gov-
ernment of the full harvest of the Treaty of Sèvres. But now, under her new
leadership, Greece was clearly heading for disaster. And this finally came
in 1922, when the exhausted Greek armies, within 100 kilometres of
Ankara, were driven out of Asia Minor by Kemal Pasha and his soldiers.
Smyrna was burnt down by the infuriated Turks, and a wave of roughly a
million Greeks, destitute and demoralized, sailed across the Aegean from
their homes in Asia Minor to find refuge in a shattered Greece.

The consequence of this disaster haunted Greek politics for fifteen years
or more. We need not go into those tragic events which forced King
Constantine to abdicate in 1922 and which resulted in the execution of six
of his Ministers; nor need we elaborate on the political disputes between
republicans and royalists and the lamentable interventions of the army
that took place before the final proclamation of Greece as a Republic on
24 March 1924.

What is important for the understanding of the further development of
Greek poetry is the complete collapse of all the old, traditional values
which followed the defeat of 1922, those very values which had inspired
and sustained Greeks since their great War of Independence (1821–9).
For the Asia Minor disaster of 1922 was a major turning-point in Greek
history, which was naturally reflected in Greek letters, for it consti-
tutes the end of the 'Great Idea' and all that it stood for in modern Greek
history and life.

The general sense of futility and lack of orientation, enhanced by
further internal political troubles, continued until 1928, when Venizelos
resumed the leadership of his old party and, on 3 July, took office again,
forming a Government. Once more, his record during four and a half
years of power (1928–32) was one of striking success in foreign policy
but growing difficulties at home. Nevertheless, it was thanks to this
enlightened and courageous statesman, the man who had almost brought
the 'Great Idea' to its fulfilment, that new and more realistic national
ideals were established. These can be summarized as hard work to deve-
lop all that was good within the boundaries of post-war Greece, and the
decision to abandon the ancient dream of expansion and of Greek power
in the eastern Mediterranean.

These realistic and balanced goals restored emotional stability to the
country, and much of the despair and the sense of futility aroused by the
Asia Minor disaster dissipated. Moreover, the influx of the refugees, in
spite of the great social, political and financial problems it had created,
had also introduced a considerable increase in manpower and a new

creative impulse into Greece. The sad past was swiftly sinking into obscurity. It is not surprising, therefore, that in those years a new group of writers emerged — poets, prose writers and critics — who in the course of the 1930s brought about a full revival of modern Greek letters and, in particular, modern Greek poetry.

But the currency crisis of 1931 finally caused the downfall of Venizelos. The end of his administration was followed by much political instability and by fresh (and unfortunate) interventions of the army until 1935, when George II, the eldest son of King Constantine, was returned to the throne after a plebiscite in which 97 per cent of the votes were said to have been cast in favour of the restoration of the monarchy. But in August 1936 General J. Metaxas, taking advantage of an accidental appearance of strength among the Communists, dissolved the Chamber and declared martial law. The dictatorship thus inaugurated remained unshaken until Metaxas died in January 1941, after successfully defending Greece against the Italian attack and before the onrush of the German invaders.

However, in spite of the Metaxas dictatorship and the dark clouds of war which were massing, the late 1930s can be seen as a period of national revival of both the economic and the intellectual life of the country. The self-confidence and pride which were then regained led to the successful resistance against the Italian attack of 1941 and to the proud opposition against the Axis occupation of Greece during the bleak years of 1942–4.

CHAPTER 26

The Old School of Athens: The Greek Romantics

It was in the capital of the new Greek state—first Nauplia and then Athens—that a turbulent mixture of dialects and traditions rubbed shoulders, that the first poetic school of liberated Greece, known as the Old School of Athens, or the 'Greek Romantics',[1] emerged. The most important educated class of Greeks that clustered around the Athenian-Bavarian court were the Phanariots, and to them fell the task of helping the new state to develop socially and intellectually. The debt of the Old School of Athens to that group of learned men cannot be over-rated.

The poets who flourished in Athens between 1830 and 1880 are read very rarely today, and modern Greek criticism on the whole considers them a closed chapter in the history of Greek literature. Nevertheless, they constitute an important aspect of the cultural life of the first fifty years of the free Greek state and have therefore a claim to be remembered and studied.

The Old School of Athens falls into three distinct periods: the first covers the years 1830 to 1850; the second extends from 1850 to 1870; and the final, the period of decline, spans another ten years. In fact, Kostis Palamas, the distinguished poet and critic, has called Achilles Paraschos's poem on Lord Byron, which he recited at Missolonghi in 1880, 'the swan song of the Greek Romantics'.

In the decade 1820–30, which roughly coincides with the Greek War of Independence, we find a few precursors of the Old School of Athens, the most noteworthy of whom are Jakovos Rizos Neroulos (1778–1850) and Jakovos Rizos Rangavis (1779–1855). Neroulos was a Phanariot, born in Constantinople, who came to Athens and served as minister of Education in the Greek Government, and as Greek Ambassador to the Porte. He is the author of the well-known prose comedy, *Korakistika*,[2] which attacked the linguistic view of Koraes; two dead, Classicizing tragedies, *Aspasia* and *Polyxene*; a mock-heroic poem, *The Stolen Turkey* (in which he imitates

Boileau's *Lutrin*); some soulless lyrics; and two flat comedies, *The Questionable Family* and *The Fear of the Newspapers*.

Jakovos Rizos Rangavis was less ambitious than his cousin, Neroulos. He wrote third-rate lyrics on love, solitude and social injustice, as well as some hopeless Classicizing tragedies. He also translated into modern Greek works of Alfieri, Corneille, Racine and Voltaire.

Along with these two writers, we find during the Greek War of Independence a number of versifiers (they can hardly be called poets) who wrote verse to inspire or to celebrate the warriors fighting for the freedom of the Greeks. In these writings—some are in the style of traditional folk songs, whereas others are in a more ambitious 'purist' style—many references are made to ancient glorious achievements, such as Marathon or Thermopylae, or to great men of antiquity, such as Themistocles and Pelopidas. The best-known of these versifiers are K. Kokkinakis, P. Kallas (also known as Tsopanakos) and S. Bougioukles.

A similarly uncouth mixture of patriotism and Romanticism prevails in the much more sophisticated, though scant, poetry composed by Spyridon Trikoupis (1788–1873), the distinguished statesman and historian of the Greek War of Independence.

THE INITIAL STAGE OF THE OLD SCHOOL OF ATHENS (1830–50)

The initial stage of the Old School of Athens was characterized by the effort to reconcile the simple 'tender melancholy' and the 'spoken idiom' of the Phanariot poetic tradition with the growing claims of the Classical Greek past and the erudite linguistic elements that were gaining ground among the educated classes in liberated Greece. At the same time, rhetorical grandiloquence, political issues and ponderous subjects became more and more fashionable. Politics began to permeate poetry (many of the better-known poets were also leading journalists and political pamphleteers); patriotism became rampant; and the influence of French literature mounted, especially that of Béranger, Lamartine and Victor Hugo.

Panagiotis and Alexandros Soutsos

The poet who introduced Romanticism to the modern Greek world was Panagiotis Soutsos (1806–68), son of a noble Phanariot family, who was born in Constantinople and educated first at the Chios High School and later in Paris, Padua and Venice. His long lyric–dramatic work, *The Traveller*, published in 1831 in Nauplia, was inspired, as he himself tells us, 'by the cloudy horizons of northern Europe'. It describes how the traveller and the maiden, Ralou, part, fail at first to recognize each other upon meeting once more, lose their senses and finally commit suicide, exchanging heart-rending words of love as they die. It is indeed surprising that this sloppy, highly Romantic work met with such immediate success that it ran into seventeen editions, each containing increasingly 'purified' diction to comply with the Classicizing demands of the age. In fact, as we can see from his pamphlet, *New School of the Written Word*, the poet himself came to believe that modern Greek poetry should aim at returning to pure Attic Greek if it were to be worthy of the Classical tradition.

Panagiotis Soutsos also wrote lyrical poems, which he published in 1835 in a book called *Guitar*, as well as plays and novels. His lyrical poems consist of love and drinking songs and of some patriotic and satirical verse. Written under the influence of the French Romantics and of Athanasios Christopoulos, they are not without merit; but his four plays, *Messias*, *Euthymios Vlachavas*, *The Unknown* and *Karaiskakis* (the last is perhaps the best of the four), are negligible. He also cast some of Aesop's fables into verse. It is quite evident that as the poet grew older and made increasing use of a more pronounced 'purist' diction, the quality of his poetry declined.[3]

Panagiotis Soutsos may have introduced Romanticism to the Athenian scene, but it was his older brother, Alexandros Soutsos (1803–63), who came to be considered the leading figure during the early stages of the Old School of Athens. Like Panagiotis, Alexandros was born in Constantinople and was educated at the Chios High School and later in Paris. He took part in the Greek War of Independence and participated vigorously in the politics of liberated Greece, as a result of which he was stoned, imprisoned and repeatedly exiled. He died penniless in a hospital in Smyrna. When exiled from Greece he travelled widely and even visited the American continent.

Alexandros Soutsos introduced another significant aspect of Romanticism to the Athenian literary scene—the passion for political freedom and social justice. His most interesting poems are his *Satires*, in which he fiercely attacked everything he considered despotic and illiberal, from Capodistria—he even called his murderers 'tyrannicides'—to King Otto and Queen Amalia, the Bavarian advisers of the king, the Greek politicians, who, he believed, 'were at the service of foreign powers', the flattering courtiers, corrupt European diplomats and the 'privileged few' who oppressed the 'deserving many'. Of his satires, which circulated widely, the best are *The First Satires*, published in 1827; *The Panorama of Greece*, published in 1828; and *The Mirror of Greece*, which appeared in print in 1845. All reflect the influence of Béranger.

As a lyrical poet, Alexandros Soutsos was less successful. His two most ambitious works in this field are *The Wanderer*, a pale imitation of Byron's *Childe Harold*, containing much autobiographical material and many political assaults, and the epico-lyrical *Greece Fighting the Turks*, an unsatisfactory poem dealing with the War of Independence, which was nevertheless much admired in its day. His verse plays, *The Profligate*, *The Prime Minister* and *The Untameable Poet*, as well as his minor verse are very inferior works indeed; nor does *The Exile*, written in bombastic prose, reach a high standard.

The language of Alexandros Soutsos is a mixture of spoken and 'purist' elements. It is often flabby, tending increasingly towards 'purism' with the passing of the years. His trochaic verses he groups into stanzas and varies by introducing shorter lines. Because he treated with passion of patriotic and political subjects that fired the imagination of his contemporaries, he was highly esteemed in his day, both as a satirist and as a lyrical poet. For the Greek of today, his lyrical verse seems lifeless, but his satires still retain much of their verve and provide an admirably sharp and often witty picture of Greek society during the reign of King Otto.[4]

Alexandros Rizos Rangavis

Another leading figure of the initial stage of the Old School of Athens was Alexandros Rizos Rangavis (1809–92), the son of Jakovos Rizos Rangavis. Born in Constantinople, he accompanied his father to the Danubian principalities, Odessa and Munich, where he studied at the Bavarian Military Academy. After having served as an officer in the Bavarian artillery, he came to Greece, where he was successively appointed Foreign Secretary, Professor of Archaeology at the University of Athens and Ambassador to Paris, Washington and Berlin.

Alexandros Rangavis was not only a remarkable man of action, but also an indefatigable man of letters. His complete works (which include writings on grammar, metrics, archaeology, history, mathematics, military matters, lexicography, plays, lyrical verse, translations of ancient Greek, German, French and Italian poetry, novels and short stories) amount to nineteen volumes, all published in his lifetime. But poetry was the passion of his life, and it was as a poet that he wished to be remembered.

Rangavis embarked on his literary career as a Romantic writer. As might be expected, he was profoundly influenced by French and German Romantic writers, though this influence was partly concealed under a 'popular' Greek veil of 'demotic' diction and heroic names for his protagonists. His later works are marred by the frigid, erudite linguistic elements which penetrated his writing, with an increasingly stultifying effect.

In 1831 Rangavis published a highly Romantic poem called *Demos and Helen*, in which Demos, a young Klepht, rescues a Greek girl, Helen, from the Turks, falls in love with her and decides to marry her. But an old hermit, whom they ask to perform the marriage ceremony, refuses to officiate, and the infuriated Demos kills him. It eventually emerges that Demos is the hermit's son and Helen Demos' sister; hence the old man's refusal. In spite of many faults, this exuberant work stands head and shoulders above anything written until then by a Greek Romantic poet.

In 1837 Rangavis published his first collection of verse, under the title *Various Poems*, which was soon followed by a second volume with the same name. They include lyrical, epic, dramatic and satirical works, as well as translations from French and German. The influence of the German Romantics is evident, most notably in the *Woman Traveller*; nor is the Byronic spirit absent, as can be seen from the play *Phrosyne* and from the longer metrical narrative *Laoplanos* (*The Man who Leads Men Astray*). These collections reflect much of the enthusiasm, the immaturity and the confusion of contemporary Athenian society.

It is generally agreed that Rangavis's best poem is *The Voyage of Dionysus*, a lyrical narrative published in 1864. Cast in elegant five-line stanzas and in an incisive, though frigid, 'purist' language, it deals with the mythical encounter of the god Dionysus with the Tyrrhenian pirates. *The Swift Hawk*, published in 1871, is seen as his second best poem, while of his numerous tedious plays *The Thirty* is considered the most successful. Other works of Rangavis that can be singled out are the poem *She* (᾽Εκείνη); the comic verse play *The Bald Man's Wedding*, which is not free from political undertones; and the short lyric *The Klepht*, which, set to music, is sung by the Greek army on parade even today.

His critics have called Alexandros Rangavis 'a Phanariot with a coating of German philosophy', ' frigid neo-Classicist' and 'an author delighting in rhetoric', and there is an element of truth in all these accusations. But at the same time considerable inspiration, an attractive variety of form and rhythm and a certain restrained grace cannot be denied in the best of his works, to say nothing of his burning patriotism.

This distinguished representative of the Greek Romantics lived to see the entire course followed by the Old School of Athens to its decline; and he was enlightened enough to realize when its days were over and to welcome the emerging New School of Athens, especially the poetry of Georgios Drosinis. His own verse, with its pretentious images, its trenchant archaic language, its patriotic fervour and its numerous Classical references, though a noteworthy phenomenon in the history of modern Greek literature, exercised no influence whatsover upon the subsequent generations of Greek poets.[5]

The linguistic problem that troubled Alexandros Rangavis—the increasing significance attached by Athenian society to the 'purist' forms of

Greek—also harassed two other noteworthy romantic poets, Zalocostas and Orphanidis.

Georgios Zalocostas

Georgios Zalocostas (1805–58) was born in Syrrakion in the Epirus and educated in Livorno. Returning to Greece, he took part in the Greek War of Independence and in the famous sally of Missolonghi of 1824. From his early youth he had been passionately fond of painting and poetry, and it was with the latter that he made his name.

The lengthy epico-lyrical works of Zalocostas deal with historical events connected mainly with the War of Independence. They are, as would be expected, highly patriotic, but also full of rhetoric and bombast. Of these the best are *The Khan of Gravia* and *Missolonghi* (the former is greatly superior to the latter); but mention should also be made of *The Sword and the Crown, Photos and Phrosso, The Last Night*, and *The Mouth of Preveza*.

Far more moving are his shorter lyrics, some of which are among the best Greek poems composed in the first half of the nineteenth century. Love, nature and the sorrow of death are the main sources of Zalocostas's inspiration, the last particularly familiar to a man who lost both his parents on the same day and witnessed the death of a beloved older brother and seven of his own children. His contemporaries greatly admired his poems *The Moon, The Partridge* and *The Poet*, as well as two translations he had made from the Italian called *Her Departure* and *The Kiss*. For the modern reader there can be little doubt that *The North Wind that Freezes the Little Lambs* is his most moving lyric. It was composed on the death of his fourth son.

Zalocostas wrote in both the demotic and the *katharevousa*—his most successful works are composed in the former—and employed other metres besides the traditional fifteen-syllable line. The influence of contemporary Italian poetry upon his work is clear, and it is this acquaintance with Italian literature that enabled him to appreciate the poetry of Solomos and to serve as one of the tenuous early links between the Old Athenian School and the School of the Ionian Islands. Though there is little depth of thought or perfection of form in the often naive verse of Zalocostas, its directness and its lyrical sincerity are appreciated even today.

Theodoros Orphanidis

A much lesser talent than Georgios Zalocostas, Theodoros Orphanidis (1817–85), was born in Smyrna, studied botany in Paris and later became a distinguished professor of botany at the University of Athens. He appeared on the literary scene in 1836 with a collection of politico-satirical poems called *Menippos*, in which the influence of Alexandros Soutsos, whom Orphanidis greatly admired, is paramount. However, his facile and faulty verses and his often vulgar personal attacks do not compare with the satires of Soutsos. The same disappointing qualities also appear in the poetry he published in 1840 in the short-lived satirical periodical *The Archer* (Ὁ Τοξότης), of which he was the editor.

Orphanidis also produced longer, more ambitious epico-lyrical compositions, the best-known of which are *The Man Without a Fatherland, Chios Enslaved* (dealing with an uprising of the Chiots against the Genoese in the fourteenth century) and *Saint Menas* (describing the Turkish massacre of the Chiots in 1822). He also published a mock-heroic poem called *Tiri-Liri* ('senseless babble') or *The Shooting Season on the Island of Syros* in 3000 fifteen-syllable lines. In spite of its flabby versification, it is his most interesting work because of its comic scenes and its gibes at well-known men and ideas of those days.

In view of the poor quality of Orphanidis's verse, it is surprising that he was awarded several prizes at the Athenian poetry competitions,[6] and that he was also invited to serve as one of their adjudicators.

Joannes Karasoutsas

Joannes Karasoutsas (1824–73) was also born in Smyrna a few years after Orphanidis but spent most of his life in Athens, desperately struggling to make a living as a teacher of French. At the age of fifty, unable to go on, he committed suicide, a fact hardly noticed by the Athenian literati. As a young man, Karasoutsas published two volumes of verse, *The Lyre* and *The Suckling Muse*, the second of which he dedicated to Alexandros Rangavis, whom he greatly admired. He continued writing and developing his art in the 1840s and 1850s; his best poetry can be found in the slender volumes *Melodies of Dawn* and *Barbitos*, which he published in 1846 and 1860 respectively.

Karasoutsas, who has a clear sense of rhythm and form, used an austere 'purist' diction—he composed only one poem in the spoken idiom, and that at the age of eighteen—in which a marked elegance, real feeling and warmth glow beneath the glacial surface. His subjects—love, freedom, nature, the Christian faith, his Ionian homeland—are all treated with passion, but never in an exaggerated manner. He shows great sensitivity to colours, perfumes and the shifting qualities of light. His human, gentle, personal voice is a welcome change from the harsh, declamatory outcry of so many of his fellow poets.

Demosthenes Balabanis

Perhaps the best Greek Romantic poet of the early Old School of Athens was Demosthenes Balabanis (1824–54), who was born in Karytaina in the Peloponnese and studied medicine in Athens. Throughout his short life he was deeply interested in literature and published verse in various periodicals and anthologies, though never a complete volume of poetry; he also wrote some prose.

The purist form of Greek, which he used in most of his works, is handled with striking elegance, and his imagery is precise and clear; even when a streak of rhetoric appears, it is never excessive or bombastic. In his few poems in the demotic he draws frequently on folk songs, which lends them vigour and life. *The Klepht's Grave* is considered his best poem.

Elias Tantalidis

Elias Tantalidis (1818–76) was born in Constantinople, where he lived and worked as a teacher at the theological seminary in Chalke. Though he lost his eyesight at an early age, he never lost his gaiety and love of life, composing playful as well as erotic and other Romantic verse. He is considered the last of the 'Phanariot poets', and a member, in a broad sense, of the school of the Athenian Romantics. We have three collections of his verse, the *Playful or Various Poems*, the *Private Verses* and the *Songs*, of which the first, published in 1839, is the best.

Stephanos Koumanoudis

Stephanos Koumanoudis (1818–99) was born in Adrianople, studied classics in Germany and France and, on arriving in Greece, was appointed Professor of Latin at the University of Athens. His contribution to modern Greek literature was in the field of literary criticism rather than in original writings, but as a young man he used to compose poetry, an activity he occasionally indulged in even later in life. In 1851 he published his best-known work, a comic 'epic' poem called *Stratis Kalopicheiros*, which to the modern reader appears long and tedious. His finest work is a series of sonnets, *On Venice*, which, though full of Romantic nostalgia, are noteworthy for their linguistic restraint and their clear imagery.

THE MIDDLE YEARS OF THE OLD SCHOOL (1850–70)

The third quarter of the nineteenth century saw the peak of the Old School of Athens. Its initial year, 1850, was a landmark in the history of modern Greek poetry, for the influential poetry competitions were then established in Athens. The first and most important of these was the Rallis Competition, which was held under the aegis of the University of Athens and continued till 1861. Soon after that the Voutsinas Competition was instituted, a more enlightened but less prominent literary event, which persisted until 1877. Others of lesser significance followed later.[7]

To ensure their success, generous benefactors contributed substantial sums of money for prizes, and leading men of letters were appointed to serve as judges. Before long, all the established poets and most of those emerging submitted their works for consideration in the hope of being awarded a Rallis or a Voutsinas prize.

Originally, no poetry was accepted in these competitions unless written in the 'purist' language. But this restriction was lifted in 1862,[8] and three years later Achilles Paraschos ventured to submit poems composed in the demotic. However, it was not until 1873 that the first prize was awarded to a collection containing poems in the spoken idiom, *The Voice of My Heart* by D. G. Kambouroglou, about which we shall speak when dealing with the precursors of the New School of Athens.[9]

As the 'purist' diction became increasingly fashionable in the Athenian educated circles of the forties, fifties, sixties and seventies of the nineteenth century, and as it was a prerequisite for any entries to the poetry competitions until 1862, it naturally permeated the writings of the Romantic poets of the day. And this diction affected not only those who emerged in the fifties and sixties but also established poets like Panagiotis and Alexandros Soutsos, Alexandros Rangavis, Zalocostas and Orphanidis. The result was deplorable, for what finally evolved was an artificial mixture of spoken and obsolete, academic words and usages and a stilted, frozen, pseudo-archaic style that in due course (and not unexpectedly) provoked a violent reaction.

During this period the influence of Western European Romantic poetry, which had been felt since the early days of the School, was greatly enhanced, particularly that of Victor Hugo, Lamartine, Alfred de Musset, Young (whose *Nights* were translated into modern Greek several times) and Byron. At the same time many lesser Romantics began to make an impression, especially those who delighted in evoking the horrors of the deathbed and the tombstone—and in unbridled rhetoric. This trend, coupled with the uncontrollable patriotism of those days, lowered the standard and dampened the originality of much Greek poetry. It eventually led to the decline and end of the Old School of Athens, whose tenets in its heyday had spread beyond the capital to Syros, Patras and Nauplia, even as far as Constantinople and Smyrna. In fact, the literature of Athens redounded throughout the world of Hellenism, and even the Ionian Islands and their much more evolved and sophisticated School did not escape its impact.

Two new major figures appeared on the literary scene during the second period in the life of the Old School of Athens: Demetrios Paparrigopoulos and Spyridon Vasiliadis.

Demetrios Paparrigopoulos

Demetrios Paparrigopoulos (1843–73), the son of the distinguished historian Constantine Paparrigopoulos, was born in Athens and studied law, but from an early age he was deeply interested in philosophy, publishing philosophical essays which revealed his restless and pessimistic spirit. He also composed much epico-lyrical poetry, and his first collection of verse, called *Sighs* (*Στόνοι*), won the first prize at the Voutsinas Competition of 1866; his second collection, *The Swallows*, was also awarded a prize. Paparrigopoulos composed poetry until his early death; he also wrote prose plays, which make poor reading.

With the exception of a few patriotic poems, such as *Arkadi* and *The Greek Flag*, inspired by the uprising of the Cretans against the Turks in 1866, and a poem attacking Napoleon III for opposing the liberation of Crete, all his other verse bewails the sorrow and futility of life. Paparrigopoulos often chose his subjects from antiquity—as, for example, his *Orpheus* or *Pygmalion*. In his despair, which amounts to a death wish, he is not unlike Leopardi;[10] during his lifetime and long after his death his pessimistic but poignant poem, *The Lamp of the Cemetery of Athens*, was widely acclaimed and committed to memory by a number of educated Greeks.

The language of Paparrigopoulos is academic, pretentious and highly rhetorical, and his versification is often faulty. Nevertheless, his despair and his conviction that life is nothing more than a vale of tears, because genuine, are despondently moving.

Spyridon Vasiliadis

Spyridon Vasiliadis (1844–73), a contemporary and friend of Paparrigopoulos, was born in Patras, studied law in Athens and died in Paris. In contrast to his gloomy friend, he had a gay and optimistic disposition, being, as his contemporaries said, 'more of an artist and less of a thinker'.

His poetic career was very brief, for he published his first book of verse, *Images and Waves*, which was awarded a prize at the Voutsinas Competition in 1866, only seven years before his death. In 1873 he brought out a second book of poems, *Winged Words*, in which, abandoning his earlier Romantic themes of death, tombs and tears, he turned to the ancient world for inspiration.

Vasiliadis felt a deep contempt for Byzantium, which he considered 'rotten and degenerate', but he greatly admired ancient Greek literature and the modern Greek folk songs and even sought to combine elements of both in his verse. But in this he was not successful; his modern detractors claim, with some justification, that he had 'all the faults of the Greek Romantics and few of their virtues'; that he is superficial, rhetorical, repetitious and exuberant; that his diction is lax and his metres faulty. Nevertheless, he enjoyed considerable popularity in his day and was admired for the patriotic fervour of his verse and its attacks on social injustice.

Vasiliadis also wrote tragedies and other plays in prose, as well as literary criticism. Of his plays, the most successful was *Galatea*, which was translated into French (Sarah Bernhardt even contemplated acting in it).

Demetrios Bernardakis

The one poet of the Old School of Athens who distinguished himself as a dramatist was Demetrios Bernardakis (1834–1907). Verse plays had often been composed, as we have seen, by Phanariot poets such as Athanasios Christopoulos, Rizos Neroulos and Jakovos Rizos Rangavis, by most of the more eminent Athenian Romantic poets and by some of the precursors of the Ionian School.[11] Some of these had been performed in such far-flung places as Bucharest, Jassy, Odessa, Zante and Athens. But after the Cretan theatre came to an end in 1669, we must turn to Demetrios Bernardakis if we are to find modern Greek poetic drama of any merit.

Though of Cretan origin, Bernardakis was born in Mytilene. He studied in Germany and was later appointed Professor of History at the University of Athens, where he eventually came into conflict with his colleagues and retired to Lesbos, where he died. It should be noted that he played a leading part in the language dispute which had flared up in the 1880s; he wholeheartedly supported the demotic.

Early in life he began composing poetry and even as a student submitted works to the poetry competitions,[12] though with no success. In 1856, however, he was awarded a prize for his epico-lyrical piece, *Eikasia* (a bad poem inspired by Byzantine history), which followed the composition of an equally unappealing epico-lyrical comic *epyllion*, the *Graomyomachia* (Γραομνιομαχία).

Bernardakis then turned to drama, in which he was much more successful. His first important work in this field was *Maria Doxapatri*, based on a story from the Frankish rule of the Morea. It was submitted to the Rallis Competition in 1857 but failed to receive a prize. The play bears witness to a strong Shakespearean influence, though its plot is purely Romantic and its language cold and formal.

When Bernardakis returned from Germany to Greece he 'recovered from the mist of Romanticism'—these are his words—and looked to ancient Greece and Byzantium for inspiration. The product of this new turn was a large body of plays: *Cypselidae* (in which a chorus also appears), *Merope, Euphrosyne, Fausta, Antiope* (as yet unpublished) and *Nicephoros Phocas*. Of these, *Merope* and *Fausta*, which was a great success on the Athenian stage, stand head and shoulders above the others, though they too belong to a theatre which, on the whole, is poor in character drawing and decidedly untheatrical in terms of language and speech patterns. Though he represents a definite advance in modern Greek poetic drama and his success encouraged others to follow his lead,[13] Bernardakis marks the tail-end of an age that was swiftly vanishing, and his plays were soon forgotten when the New School of Athens came into its own.

Before leaving the second stage in the life of the Old School of Athens it should be noted that most of the poets who had won fame before the 1850s continued to write and publish poetry well into the 1860s. At the same time numerous lesser figures emerged, whose works are as voluminous as they are unimportant. Because they exerted no influence on the course of Greek poetry, we shall limit ourselves to a fleeting mention of the most important names: Timoleon Ambelas (1850–1926); Antonios Antoniadis (1836–1912); Alexandros Byzantios (1841–98); Kleon Rangavis (1842–1917), who was a son of Alexandros Rangavis; and Angelos Vlachos (1838–1920).[14]

THE END OF THE OLD SCHOOL (1870–80)

The 1870s marked the decline and end of the Old School of Athens, in spite of the beneficial influence the Ionian School of poetry had begun to exercise upon it through the writings of Laskaratos and Valaoritis. For the funereal gloom of the lesser side of the Romantic Movement,[15] the stultifying archaic diction and the rhetorical exuberance that increasingly prevailed—to say nothing of blatant linguistic errors—brought about a violent reaction which is also evident in the attacks levelled by the judges of the poetry competitions against the works submitted for judgement and the parodies of Romantic poetry that started to appear.[16]

There were two further reasons for the decline of the School: first, the development of journalism in Greece as an independent profession no longer connected with literature caused the demise of the old political-literary ideal as conceived by Béranger, Lamartine, Hugo and Byron and espoused by the older Greek Romantics; second, a large, new, educated class of women emerged which no longer responded readily to the crude patriotic spirit or the politically oriented satire of the older Greek Romantics but hankered after a more gentle Romanticism, such as they found in the translations of Lamartine or Heine.

But what shook the Old School of Athens to its very roots and greatly contributed to its downfall was the violent attack launched on it by Emmanuel Roidis, the brilliant critic and author of the satirical novel *Pope Joan*. Influenced by the views of Hippolyte Adolphe Taine,[17] he put forward the view that the contemporary Greek environment and the 'historical moment' were not conducive to the creation of true poetry. In this he was challenged by Angelos Vlachos, but he quickly retaliated with a lively essay, *On Modern Greek Poetry*,[18] in which he convincingly condemned all Greek Romantic poets except Achilles Paraschos and Aristotelis Valaoritis as derivative, inconsequential and without merit. Roidis had studied philosophy and aesthetics in Germany. His well-founded, trenchant arguments provoked many men of letters to join in the discussion, which eventually led to the downfall of the School.

By 1870 nearly all the older well-known Romantic poets of the Athenian School had passed away. The dominant figures of the seventies were two brothers, Achilles and Georgios Paraschos (the former one of the major Greek Romantic poets), and they are the only poets worth mentioning, for their several minor contemporary poetasters offered nothing of any value to Greek poetry.

Achilles and Georgios Paraschos

Achilles Paraschos (1838–95), the leading figure during the last days of the Old School of Athens, was born in Nauplia, the son of Chiots whose true name was Nasakis. He was brought up in Athens, where he received a very limited education, but his striking personal appearance—he was called the ideal image of a poet—and his facile sentimental verses soon made him the *enfant gâté* of Athenian society. He was greatly and universally admired. Halls, corridors and even adjoining streets were packed whenever he gave a public recitation. He was also one of the few poets who made money out of the sale of his books of verse. His funeral was attended by 'the whole of the city of Athens'.

Like most Greek Romantics, Achilles Paraschos found in love, the fatherland and death his main sources of inspiration. Byron, Lamartine and Ossian were the foreign poets who influenced him most, though he knew their works only in translation.

In 1881 Paraschos published three volumes of his *Complete Works*, and two more came out in 1904, after his death. They include epic and epico-lyrical poems, such as *Alphredos*, *The Unknown*, or *Satan and Christina*; purely lyrical works, which he divided into patriotic, erotic, elegiac and pedagogical themes, naming them *Laurels*, *Myrtles*, *Willows* and *Grass*; as well as a mixed group, which he called *Leaves*. Their emotional exuberance is extreme, often bordering on the ridiculous, and an unbridled grandiloquence characterizes his rather superficial verse. Of his erotic poems, *Reminiscences* and *The Relics of Love* were famous in his lifetime. Judged by modern standards, perhaps his most effective poems are *Two Services*, the *Elegy on Canaris*, *On Princess Alexandra*, *In the Days of King Otto*, *On the Death of a Maiden* and *The Old Leader*. Paraschos also wrote a moving poem about the death of King Otto, although he had fought against the king in the revolution of 1863 which deposed him.

In spite of all his shortcomings, his lack of education, his faulty diction —he wrote an 'impure purist Greek and an impure demotic Greek'—and his often limping metres (he composed some of the worst fifteen-syllable lines ever written), Paraschos's poetry has a natural flow and feeling, and his verses express the mood of the time. In fact, so personal is his voice that although his poetry can be ridiculed, it could never be imitated. In short, Achilles Paraschos was the culmination of all that the Old School of Athens typified.

The last Athenian Romantic poet worthy of mention is Georgios Paraschos (1832–86), the older brother of Achilles. He never published a collection of poems in his lifetime, but two of his lyrics, the *Eothinon* (*The Song of Dawn*) and *The Guard* were awarded prizes by the Ministry of Defence for the best patriotic poetry. Other poems, such as *Arkadi*, on the heroic resistance of the Cretans against the Turks in the monastery of Arkadi in 1866, and the *Hymn to George I*, were universally acclaimed. He also translated the *Iliad* into 'purist' modern Greek.

Georgios Paraschos's poetry was mainly patriotic and erotic, reflecting the influence of Byron and Lamartine. Its feeling is warm, its imagery vivid and its diction mixed; but it is in good taste. The modern reader responds to his verse more readily than to that of his younger brother.

With Georgios and Achilles Paraschos, the real life of the Old School of Athens came to an end. This school of poetry, with its often intolerably stilted *katherevousa*, its pseudo-Byronic airs, its long-winded rhetoric, its hackneyed patriotism and its funereal Romanticism, in which spurned heroes, disillusioned lovers, the deathbed and the grave appeared far too frequently, passed completely away in the 1880s, when a fresh assessment of national values and the great linguistic and cultural movement known as the Demotic Movement started to gather momentum. This trend directed the attention of the Greek nation to the School of the Ionian Islands, where the spoken idiom was being used successfully (it would also foster the emergence of the New School of Athens). Until that time, with the notable exception of Solomos and Valaoritis, the Ionian poets had not received the Pan-Hellenic recognition enjoyed by their Athenian counterparts.

CHAPTER 27

The School of the Ionian Islands

Since the fifteenth century the Ionian Islands had been under the direct control of Venice, and in a way each island tried to be a microcosm of her mistress. The nobility owned all the land, controlled the monopolies and spoke Italian among themselves; such Greek as they knew was colloquial and ungrammatical. Their culture was Italian, and their sons were almost all educated at Italian universities, where not a few won distinction.

The position of the nobles remained economically, if not politically, unaltered down to the 1860s, except for an interlude in 1797 when the Revolutionary Army of France took temporary possession of the Heptanese. The *libri d'oro*, in which the nobility were inscribed, were then burned, but the islands were speedily occupied by the Russians, who restored their privileges to the nobles. This policy was retained by the English during the period of British 'protection' (1815–64).

Though Italian linguistically and culturally, the Ionian aristocracy was almost all of the Orthodox faith; as religion was a strong feature in the determination of national sentiment, this counted for much. In the Greek War of Independence the majority declared themselves solidly for Greece and bitterly resented the non-intervention policy of the English Government. Most of the islands' inhabitants, who worked the estates of the Ionian aristocrats, were of Greek stock, and their numbers were supplemented during the eighteenth and nineteenth centuries by settlers from the mainland seeking refuge from the Turks. Nor should the older settlers, who had arrived after the fall of Crete in 1669, be forgotten.

The small, independent state of the Ionian Islands continued to exist until 1863 when, with the accession of the new dynasty to the Greek throne, Great Britain consented to the union of the islands with Greece. It is evident that historical conditions favoured the independent development of the Ionian School of poetry, which flourished alongside the Old School of Athens.

THE FORERUNNERS OF THE IONIAN SCHOOL

The precursors of Solomos, who point the way to the diction and metres of the Ionian School, were mostly centred on Zante. Their emergence is due mainly to the Cretan literary tradition imported by the Cretan refugees; also to the Venetian editions of Cretan works which were readily available in Zante and Corfu; and, to a certain extent, to the influence of the poetry of Athanasios Christopoulos and Joannes Velaras, which had become popular all over the Greek-speaking world.

These very minor poets fall into three groups. The first consists of authors of light-hearted erotic and anacreontic lyrics such as were written then in the West, the best of whom were Stephanos Xanthopoulos (c. 1670), Andreas Sigouros (1722–75) and Thomas Danelakis (c. 1790); the second group, whose most prominent representatives were Nicolaos Koutouzis (1746–1813) and Antonios Martelaos (1754–1819), engaged in political satire inspired by the ideas of the French Revolution and attacked both the local aristocracy and the foreign masters of the Heptanese; and the third, by far the most interesting group, was made up of satirical playwrights, whose object was to establish a theatre in Zante.[1] They started with adaptations of Cretan plays like the *Erophile* or the *Sacrifice of Abraham*, but soon proceeded to compose short, 'original' pieces about 200 lines long, based on Cretan works like the *Erotokritos* or the *Gyparis*. Side by side with these new one-act plays, others were performed, dealing with comic scenes from everyday life—the law courts, weddings and so on that enlivened Zante's gay carnival. These were, *mutatis mutandis*, not unlike the ancient mimes (though, clearly, no connection between the two exists).

Towards the end of the eighteenth century more ambitous plays began to be composed. They were inspired by Italian models, vigorous social satires, usually ridiculing local or visiting eccentrics. The most successful authors of these were Savogias Sourmelis (c. 1770), whose comedies, *The Charlatans* and the *Men of Morea*, were greatly appreciated, and Demetrios Gouzelis (1773–1842), a more versatile dramatist, who also wrote plays on ancient subjects, such as *Phidias and Damon* or *Dionysius the Tyrant*. Nonetheless, his mordant contemporary comedy, *Chasis*, written in a vivid Zantiot dialect, is by far his best work.[2]

The contribution of these poets to the School of the Ionian Islands lies mainly in their lively diction and their varied 'Italian' metres, which they also blended with Greek folk-song rhythms, eschewing the monotony of the dominating fifteen-syllable line.

The revival of verse drama in the Heptanese runs parallel to the similar efforts of the Phanariots in the Danubian principalities and in Odessa.

Though less ambitious, it is certainly more alive and more entertaining. It was in the wake of such literary activities that the Ionian School emerged, which infused new life into Greek poetry.

THE MAJOR POETS OF THE IONIAN SCHOOL

The Ionian School may be conveniently divided into two periods. The first covers the years 1821–88, from the outbreak of the Greek War of Independence to the appearance of the Demotic Movement; the second, the years 1888–1912, when Lorentzos Mavilis, the last distinguished Ionian poet, fell fighting the Turks in Epirus.

The founder and greatest representative of this school is Dionysios Solomos, whose views and personality dominated all the poets of the Heptanese, with the notable exception of Andreas Kalvos. The circumstances of Kalvos's life and his aloof and difficult character led him to follow a different path. All that can be said about the Ionian School as a whole, therefore, has very little relevance to his work.

Solomos and his successors were true products of the nineteenth century and did not escape the impact of the political and literary currents then sweeping the West. Thus patriotism became one of the major characteristics of the whole School, lying at the root of much of its poetry. And as Greek nationalism was closely connected—indeed, fused—with the Orthodox faith, a religious element runs through the literature of the School and, in certain instances, takes a deeper mystic turn.

Nor could the Ionian poets escape the concern with love, death and the beauty of nature which the Romantic Movement was spreading across Europe. But the Ionians exercised remarkable restraint and refinement in handling these subjects, with the prominent exception of Valaoritis, who had also turned to Epirot folk songs for inspiration.

As would be expected, the influence of Italian poetry on their writings was profound. Nevertheless, there can be little doubt that the dominant trait of the poets of the Heptanese, and the greatest service they rendered to Greek poetry, was their choice of the vernacular as the language of their verse. They developed it with unerring sensitivity to sound, rhythm and association of words, so that when the New School of Athens finally emerged in the 1880s as the champion of the demotic it had to turn to them for guidance and support. Cretan literature, some folk songs and the simple poetry of Christopoulos and Velaras were all Solomos had to look to when he embarked on his great venture of writing national poetry in the spoken idiom. And this he managed to do in the face of the erudite Phanariot tradition and the enormous prestige of Koraes and his 'halfway house' to ancient Greek.

In 1842 C. Ch. Fauriel published his *Chansons grecques populaires*, whose effect upon the School was paramount. Not only did the book provide the Ionian poets with a mine of linguistic and other material, but its admirable introduction also encouraged them in their mission by making it clear that Greek poetry should be composed in the spoken language if it were to command the admiration of the West. Thus inadvertently Fauriel became one of the 'fathers' of the Ionian School—and, indeed, of all modern Greek poetry worthy of the name.

Nor should the interest which the Ionian poets took in literary criticism be overlooked. For they became deeply involved in both Italian and German aesthetic philosophy, which affected their own work considerably. No comparable intellectual drive existed among their contemporaries of the Old School of Athens, for all their Western contacts and models.

In spite of the fundamental differences between the two schools and the unquestionable superiority of the Ionians, it would be unfair to say that the literature of the Greek capital left no imprint upon them. 'Purist', Romantic Athens radiated a Pan-Hellenic fervour, which the Ionian Islands did not escape, and its effects were felt increasingly by their lesser poets as the years went by.

In retaliation, the Ionian poets began to exert a much deeper and more creative influence upon the poetry of Athens in the 1870s, when the writings of Valaoritis and, to a lesser degree, of Laskaratos imposed themselves on the Greek nation. Ironically, it was Valaoritis, with his exuberant and Romantic verse, who dealt the Athenian Romantics a severe blow when he convinced the young Palamas that the demotic should be the language of verse. In Palamas's footsteps, as we shall see, the whole of the New School of Athens followed.

However, the direct legacy of Solomos was soon to peter out. After his immediate successors (of whom Julios Typaldos is the most significant) little new blood sustained its impact. One last creative outburst came at the end of the first period of the School with the profuse and baroque poetry of Valaoritis, who introduced new vigour by drawing on the folk songs of Epirus.

At the end of the nineteenth century a spark of true poetry from the Heptanese flared again in the works of Markoras and Lorentzos Mavilis. Though an old man by then, Markoras finally became a universally accepted literary figure, and Mavilis's polished verse was read and enjoyed by the whole of educated Greece. There were also, of course, a number of lesser figures, who wrote in the twilight of the School.

The heroic death of Mavilis in 1912 marked the end of the School of the Ionian Islands, to which Greece owes an inestimable debt. Without the genius of Solomos and the enthusiasm of his followers, the cold, dead weight of 'purist' diction would have stifled Greek poetry, and Palamas and the New School of Athens might never have emerged.

Andreas Kalvos

It is convenient to begin this study of the major Ionian poets with Andreas Kalvos (1792–1869), for, as we saw, he stands apart from the rest of the school. He was born in Zante, the son of Joannes Kalvos, a strange and restless character who had tried his hand as a soldier, a sailor and a merchant. His mother, Adriane Roukani, came from a noble Zantiot family. She was soon abandoned by her husband, who left the island and established himself with his two sons in Livorno, when the poet was only ten. There Andreas went to school but, owing to his father's poverty, was unable to pursue university studies. The broad education he managed to acquire was due entirely to his own initiative and hard work.

At the age of twenty Kalvos went to Florence, where he met Hugo Foscolo (who was also a Zantiot and son of a Greek mother) and, through him, a number of the leading Italian men of letters. With Foscolo he visited Switzerland and later England, but the two men parted on unfriendly terms, as both were highly strung and quarrelsome. After the break with Foscolo, Kalvos remained in England, tutoring and translating in order to make a living. He led a tempestuous life and eventually married an English girl whose name is not known. She gave him a daughter, but both mother and daughter died, and Kalvos left England.

In 1821 we find him in Switzerland, where, excited and inspired by the outbreak of the Greek War of Independence, he composed and published in 1824 his first book of Greek poems, *The Lyre*—ten patriotic odes. He published another ten odes two years later in Paris, and this is all the poetry he ever wrote in Greek. In 1826 he decided to return to Greece but soon left the mainland for Corfu, where he stayed for twenty-five years, working as a teacher, translator and correspondent. (For a while he even occupied the chair of philosophy at the Ionian Academy.) But Kalvos's aloof and quarrelsome nature and the fits of melancholy to which he was prone did not make him popular in Corfu. It is remarkable that although he and Solomos lived in the same small town for twenty-three years, no contact between the two poets has ever been reported.

In 1852 Kalvos returned to England, where he married again. His second wife, Charlotte Augusta Wadams, was a teacher who directed her own boarding school for girls in Louth, in Lincolnshire. Kalvos taught mathematics and modern languages to his wife's boarders; he pursued his own studies and continued with his translations[3] until his death in 1869, always a difficult, unhappy and unlucky man.

Andreas Kalvos was a polygraph. He wrote tragedies, odes, articles and lectures; he translated theological and scientific works and compiled dictionaries.[4] None of these is in Greek, except for the twenty odes published in Lausanne and Paris in 1824 and 1826 respectively, which alone concern us here.[5]

Nearly all Kalvos's poems were inspired by events connected with the Greek War of Independence, so it is not unfair to say that it was the Greek Revolution that turned him into a major Greek poet. When he set out to write Greek verse he was faced with the same problems as Solomos but approached them in a less creative manner. In diction, no doubt influenced by Foscolo, he chose the spoken idiom as his basis and tried to enrich it with 'very ancient words and linguistic usages'. The result is a mechanical juxtaposition of incompatible elements (no real fusion is achieved), which often startles but never delights. Such vigour as his language retains is due to the demotic vocabulary, for he had the sense not to cut himself off completely from the living roots of Greek. In metre he created a new kind of strophe, consisting of four lines of seven syllables and one of five, inspired by Italian models and by what he must have thought were Classical metrics. He never made use of rhyme.[6]

The structure of Kalvos's odes is simple and carefully planned, varying in length from ten to thirty-nine stanzas. The general ideas which he wishes to express are illustrated with a flow of images. Some of them have great power and originality, as, for example, 'the hours falling like drops of fire from the sun into the sea of eternity', or 'the circling sun ceaselessly enfolding like a spider with its light and with death'. The poet is most concerned with the moral world of man, with justice, courage, freedom, virtue and self-sacrifice, all of which are inspired and illustrated by incidents of the Greek War of Independence. It is the tragic side of moral excellence that interests him most, and in his *Ode to Death* he achieves a true tragic vision. Though the heroism and sufferings of the Greeks—all contemporary events—are his main sources of inspiration, there is one noteworthy exception, his ode to his native island, Zante. This is perhaps the most moving of his poems, as it is the work of an exile looking back on the life and beauty of his homeland.

A true child of his time, Kalvos uses the classic conventions of mythology, obscure archaic names for modern places and so on, as well as various Romantic motifs recalling Ossian and Young. The conflict between the austere classicist structure and tone of his odes with the softer, Romantic outbursts are no small part of the attraction of his poetry. But the odes of Kalvos have other, more substantial virtues: considerable grace, tenderness and power unmarred by undue repetition or rhetorical verbosity. They also include many epigrammatic lines.

Kalvos may not have achieved the fusion of the living and the traditional attained by Solomos, but he is greatly superior to any other poet of his generation.[7] Yet his work failed to impress his contemporaries and exercised no influence upon the further development of Greek poetry. It was quickly forgotten and remained so until Palamas revived his memory in a notable lecture in 1889. Today he is the only 'purist' poet—if 'purist' he can be called—who is read and admired by the younger generations of Greeks.

Dionysios Solomos

Dionysios Solomos (1798–1857), the founder of the School of the Ionian Islands, was born in Zante in 1798. He was the son of Count Nicholas Solomos and a young servant girl, Angelici Nikli, such liaisons being frequent and readily tolerated in the Heptanese in those days. As a young man Count Nicholas had married Marnetta Kákni, a lady of good family, and had had by her a son, Robert, and a daughter, Helen. But after his wife's death and when practically on his own deathbed he married Angelici, an act which led to the legitimization of Dionysios and his younger brother, Demetrios. Immediately after the count's death Angelici remarried, giving the poet a second half-brother, Joannes Leontarakis. Such was the involved and unhappy family background of Dionysios Solomos.

Dionysios lived with his mother in Zante until the age of ten, when he was sent to Italy to be educated, first in Venice and Cremona and then at the University of Padua, where he graduated in law. More important than his legal studies were Solomos's private literary pursuits in Italy and his contact in Milan with many distinguished literary figures, such as Monti, Manzoni and Foscolo.

In those days, Solomos took a passionate interest both in the battle between Neo-Classicists and Romantics which was invading Italy and in the problems of language which were so closely connected with the Italian literary disputes. On this subject the ideas of the French Enlightenment seem greatly to have impressed him, especially the views that education should be based on the national tongue and that primitive 'popular' creations, such as folk songs, were of capital significance.

When in Italy he also started composing poetry in Italian. These poems, of which *La distruzione di Gerusalèmme* is the most ambitious, were on religious themes and betray the influence of Manzoni's *Inni sacri*. They also show how early religious sentiment came to the fore in Solomos's life. It was to deepen with the years, fusing with his fervent patriotism to become one of the main traits of his personality and of his work.

At the age of twenty he returned to the Heptanese after a ten-year absence. The period of creativity that followed can be divided into two distinct parts. The first covers the years he spent in Zante, during which time he developed his art and began mastering Greek as a literary medium for his poetry. The second embraces the years he spent in Corfu, where his Greek poetry attained full maturity.

THE ZANTE PERIOD (1818–28)

During his first years after his return to Zante, Solomos started to experiment with Greek verse. A number of his short early lyrics have survived. They are composed either in short Italian lyrical stanzas or in the rhyming Greek political fifteen-syllable line, which betrays the influence of Cretan poetry. For it was to Cretan poetry that Solomos had to turn for guidance when writing in Greek—and, more specifically, to the *Erotokritos* and *The Shepherdess*, both of which were popular in Zante. Apart from a few folk songs, this was the only Greek poetry in the spoken idiom that he could lay his hands on. Many of these slender lyrics, most famous of which is *The Little Fair-Haired Girl*, circulating in manuscript copies, became widely admired on the island, and some were also set to music.

Among his very first experiments in Greek were a few brief translations from Italian poetry; they are of little merit. Much more important for his career were the Italian poems he continued to compose on a variety of subjects—odes on Aphrodite, Satan or St Dionysios. Some of them were published in 1822 in Corfu by the poet's friend, Strandi, in a book entitled *Rime improvvisate*. This book was well enough received in the Heptanese, but its chief importance lies in the fact that the reputation it earned for its author induced Spyridon Tricoupis to visit Solomos that year and to urge him to undertake the grand project of his life, that of becoming the 'Dante of Greece'. For Tricoupis, the distinguished diplomat, orator and historian of the Greek War of Independence, had deeply felt the need for a national poet who would sing the exploits of the revolution and help to unify the Greeks.[8]

The enthusiasm which had seized all classes in Zante in the early years of the war infected Solomos too.[9] But a spark was needed to kindle the flame, and this was supplied by Tricoupis's visit. Thus 1822 marks the first significant turning-point in the life of the poet—indeed, the first significant landmark in the development of Greek poetry since the fall of Crete in 1669.

The result of Tricoupis's contact with Solomos was truly amazing, for a few weeks after their meeting the poet composed his celebrated *Hymn to Liberty*, which established his reputation both in Greece and in the West. The poem was first published in Missolonghi in 1824 and was immediately translated into Italian and French. It consists of 158 four-line stanzas of alternately rhyming trochaic verses which celebrate the power and beauty of liberty. But it is clearly the work of a young man experimenting. Too often rhetoric dulls the lyrical outbursts, and the structure of the poem is faulty. Moreover, flagrant borrowings from Dante, Ariosto, Monti, Manzoni, Parini, Foscolo and Byron have been pointed out by modern critics and cast a shadow on the originality of parts of the work. Nevertheless, Solomos's fame spread rapidly all over Europe. Hugo, Lamartine, Chateaubriand and Manzoni applauded his poetry, and even Goethe is said to have called him the 'Byron of the East'.

The fact that Solomos, like Byron, 'woke up and found himself famous' did not help his early poetry. This can be seen from his ode *On the Death of Lord Byron*, which was composed in 1824, shortly after the *Hymn to Liberty*, and is rightly considered the worst of all his works. There are a few brilliant passages in this long, rambling poem, but on the whole it contains more rhetoric than poetry and little cohesion.

When the first volume of Fauriel's *Chansons grecques populaires* appeared in 1824, its learned introduction, as we have seen, came to provide Solomos with constant inspiration in the hard task he had undertaken. The young poet continually referred to it and thus the influence of Fauriel upon Solomos and through him upon the course of Greek poetry can hardly be overrated.[10]

In the following year (1825) Solomos wrote his famous epigram on Psara. Nothing could be in greater contrast to the long-winded ode *On the Death of Lord Byron* than these four succinct, powerful lines which portray the tragedy and the glory of the island. Not since the days of Simonides had such great patriotic epigrammatic poetry been written in Greek.

In 1826, Solomos wrote a fine lyric, *The Poisoned Girl*, a dignified and sincere defence of his friend, Maria Paraskevopoulos, who had committed suicide because of her desperate love for her Italian music teacher. It indicates a great advance in the narrative lyrical art of the poet and marks the final stage of his development, approaching the threshold of great poetry.

To the poet's Zantiot period also belong the beginnings of two major works which were never concluded, *Lambros* and *The Free Beseiged*. Between 1823 and 1825 Solomos put together *The Dialogue*, his only extant completed prose work, which expresses his linguistic credo. As might be expected, he passionately defends the spoken idioms against the pedantic purists and those, like Koraes, who wished to sail a middle course.

Another example of Solomos's demotic prose has survived in the *Woman of Zante*, a strange sketch for a long satirical poem which was never completed. In this work we can see the ardour and venom which appear in Solomos's satires, for he wrote satires (or their outlines) throughout his life.[11] His early playful satires on a doctor, Roides, composed in 1824 give way to the much sharper *Dream*, written in 1826 at the death of the usurer John (and not, as hitherto thought, Anthony) Martinengo. Then comes the real malice of the *Woman of Zante*, which is followed by another violent satire connected with the sad family lawsuit which was to cloud the poet's life. Examination of Solomos's papers has revealed plans for a number of other satires which were never finished.

After ten years in Zante, Solomos was beginning to feel the need for a change. So at the close of 1828 he left for Corfu, the capital of the Heptanese and the seat of the Lord High Commissioner's Government.

THE CORFU PERIOD (1828–57)

When Solomos reached Corfu the English and the Ionian nobility were on the best of terms. The gay Anglo-Ionian circle led by the Adamses received him in their midst, praised his poetry and showered compliments upon him. The next five years on the island were probably the happiest of the poet's life.

His first poem that we know from this period is *The Nun*, composed when Anna Maria Georgomila took the veil in 1829. It is perhaps his deepest religious poem and also the first in which the influence of German poetry is apparent.

At the same time Solomos began once again to work at intervals on his *Lambros*, the full-length Byronic poem he had started in Zante. This was to take the form of a long, dramatic epic in the Italian *ottava rima* of Ariosto,[12] except for some inserted lyrical songs. Based on an actual event, the plot is highly melodramatic, punctuated with incest, insanity, graveyards and ghosts in the worst Romantic manner. Though the prose summary of *Lambros* is rife with these gothic elements, the fragments of the poem which have survived are impressive, especially *Easter Eve*, *The Prayer of Maria* and *The Revelation to Lambros* in the deserted church. These fragments indicate a great advance both in language and in content, for though patriotism is not absent, the poet's main concern is the inner riches and horrors of the spirit and the harmony of nature. In this they point to the great compositions which were to follow, *The Cretan*, *The Free Besieged* and *The Shark*. It should be noted that the two lyrical songs which were to be included in *Lambros*—*The Mad Mother* and *The Brother and Sister*—belong to the pre-Tricoupis period; their rhythm and musicality are astonishing, considering their date of composition.

In Corfu Solomos turned once again to the study of Cretan poetry and, in particular, the *Erotokritos*. In 1833, under the influence of its form, he began work on *The Cretan*, the first of the longer compositions which mark the highest level of his art, in which every line is tooled to perfection. Thus 1833 is another milestone in the development of his craft and of modern Greek poetry in general.

The poem tells the story of a Cretan youth who escapes with his fiancée in a small boat after his family has been slaughtered on the island by the Turks. The raging storm suddenly ceases, and the sea 'takes all the stars unto her breast'. From the moon's floating reflection a 'Lady of the Moon' rises before the young man's eyes. The astonished Cretan tells the lady of his misery, and her soft eyes fill with tears. One teardrop falls on the youth's hand, which he has raised in reverence. From that moment his hand can no longer kill; it is to be the hand of a beggar whom no passer-by can refuse. The Lady of the Moon vanishes as suddenly as she appeared, accompanied by a sound whose sweetness defies description. But when at length the boat reaches the shore the Cretan finds that his fiancée is dead.

Though Solomos abandoned *The Cretan* in 1834, the considerable fragments we have betray the enormous pains the poet took over every word. The use of the political fifteen-syllable line in that poem is exquisite, hardly surpassed to this day.

During this time Solomos became embroiled in a dispute with his half-brothers over his father's will. An ugly lawsuit ensued in which the poet was compelled to brand his mother as a liar and a harlot in order to save his fortune. This act nearly drove him insane, for as a child he had been devoted to her. Finally, the long and painful affair ended in 1838, in favour of Dionysios and his brother Demetrios, but at a terrible cost, for the poet never recovered fully from the ordeal.

In spite of all his troubles, Solomos did not cease work on his poetry, especially on the most ambitious of all his undertakings, the one he considered his life's work, *The Free Besieged*. This poem occupied him from his early years in Zante until about 1849. It underwent three radical revisions, involving changes of metre and arrangement, but was never completed. The kernel of the poem, the heroic defence and ultimate fall of Missolonghi in 1826, remains the same throughout, but in each revision it is treated from a different angle, corresponding to the changing views and maturing personality of the poet.

The first draft was for a lyrical poem entitled *The Debt* or *The Brothers by Adoption*. It was probably to be a straightforward glorification of the heroes, with little symbolism or esoteric meaning attached to it. We know that Solomos conceived the idea when he was living at the Villa Strani, outside the town of Zante, and had looked northward to Missolonghi during the long and agonizing siege and had listened to the ceaseless cannonade—an experience he never forgot.[13]

This first draft was put aside when the poet went to Corfu and conceived a grander, deeper spiritual treatment of the same theme. In metre too the change was significant; he abandoned short, lyrical stanzas, which were unsuitable for the epic quality of the subject, and employed the same rhyming political verse he had used in *The Cretan*. Thus in the second draft Solomos moved away from mere historical or narrative poetry and raised his sights to embrace the sphere of tragic drama in the Schillerian sense: the conflict of the rational soul with the mindless forces of matter. The temptation of the senses and the intimidation of the spirit became his central themes. Turk and Arab, symbolizing brute force, strive to demoralize the besieged Greeks and to lure them to surrender with the promise to spare them if they renounce Christianity. Their hopes of relief dashed, their spirits flag, and nature, clothed in all the loveliness of spring, joins in to weaken their resolution. But reason is victorious, and the stubborn endurance of the besieged frees them absolutely. When the great moment of the sortie arrives they go forth to their triumph and their death.

A considerable portion of the second sketch has survived, though mostly in isolated couplets or single lines of powerful originality and beauty. It is by far the most important of the three drafts.

In 1844, Solomos embarked on a new venture in his struggle to master his poetic medium. He abandoned the rhyming couplet, replacing the more conventional jingle of rhyme with richer and more musical diction. He first employed this new style in the third sketch of *The Free Besieged*. Only fifteen short fragments have survived, together with an appendix containing almost double that number of variants and alternative versions.

Much of the third draft is taken from the second, but the execution of the recast passages is most impressive. Not since the days of Callimachus had such technical perfection in Greek verse been achieved, and without the cold detachment that so often mars Callimachean poetry.

The poetic ideas which govern the second and third sketches of *The Free Besieged* and of the later *Shark* sprang to a large extent from Solomos's study of German aesthetic criticism and philosophy, which he read in Italian translation.[14] Most of all he admired Schiller; in his works he saw—as is evident from his *Thoughts* (Στοχασμοί) on *The Free Besieged*— the ultimate expression of all that his life stood for. A fatal quest for the perfect synthesis of content and form haunted him as he grew older; it goes far to explain the limited amount of verse he wrote or allowed to survive, as do the numerous erasures, alterations and marginal notes found in his manuscripts after his death.

Though Solomos never ceased to write poetry in Italian, a new flowering of his Italian poetry occurred between the years 1847 and 1851. This is not surprising, since Solomos found such difficulty in shaping spoken Greek into a medium fit for the expression of the highest ideals. Of the Italian poems he composed at this time, the sonnet *On Orpheus* and the poem *Sappho* are of great interest, as is the prose sketch, *L'Usignolo e lo Sparviere*. Several such prose sketches have survived, which are further attempts to find suitable forms in which to convey the Schillerian motif of the victory of the spirit over matter and brute force.

By 1849 Solomos seems to have given up working seriously on *The Free Besieged*, but the search for the ideal harmony between form and substance always obsessed him. The inspiration to try this once more in Greek was provided by a tragic accident which happened in Corfu two years earlier. A young English soldier had gone for a swim at dusk and had been attacked and killed by a shark. Prompted by this incident, Solomos began composing his *Porphyras (The Shark)* in 1847, along lines similar to those of all his Schillerian poetry.

He presents the young soldier alone in the utter peace of a calm sea. Just when the experience of a mystic union of peace and beauty releases a fountain of joy in the young man's heart, when the individual and nature are in complete accord, the 'tiger of the sea' attacks him, and a terrible battle ensues. Thus, as is typical of Solomos, happiness and knowledge are achieved only when death is at hand. The shark, like the Turk or the hawk, symbolizes the unthinking savagery without which the soul cannot rise to perfection.

A few short, magnificent fragments of the poem are all that have survived, but it is said that those who heard Solomos reciting a whole version of it were deeply impressed.

Solomos did not, however, confine his experimentation to the *Porphyras*. He was also engaged in other major compositions, such as the *Carmen seculare*, in which he was to depict the contemporary condition of the Greek nation and to visualize its future, and *The Eastern War*, inspired by the hope which the Greeks had experienced when the Crimean War broke out and Hadjipetros rose in Epirus against the Turks.[15] Of the former, a few excellent fragments exist, which show unusual technical perfection with end-stopped political lines. Of the latter, we have only a few verses composed in 1854. They are probably the last we have from the poet's hand. It is perhaps fitting that his final Greek poem, like the *Hymn to Liberty* with which he first achieved fame, should be of a patriotic nature.[16]

Among his last Greek poems the *Epigram on Frances Frazer*, the beautiful young daughter of Sir John Frazer, the Permanent Secretary to the High Commissioner, should be singled out. It was composed in 1849 and published by the poet himself on single sheets, only one of which has survived. It is a small masterpiece, illustrating the deep agony Solomos experienced in his later years in trying to communicate with the divine and to find an answer to the great metaphysical problems that obsessed him. In the virginal chastity of Frances Frazer he saw an element of the divine and felt that he had at last come into contact with at least one expression of it in the purity of the girl's soul, 'shaped by the Angels'.

Solomos's last public triumph was not in Greek but in Italian, the *Navicella Greca*. This poem describes a gallant confrontation between a small Greek ship and the flagship of the British fleet, which was blockading the Piraeus in 1849, during the so-called Don Pacifico affair. It was recited by the poet himself in the Great Hall of the Ionian Academy and was greeted with prolonged applause. A few days later he sustained a cerebral stroke, and later in the year yet another, which confined him to his bed. He died in February 1857 and was given a magnificent funeral.

After his death the *Found Remains* (as they were tactfully called) of Solomos's poetry were published by J. Polylas. Throughout Greece there was great disappointment at the small amount of poetry found among his papers. Rumours circulated that Solomos's envious elder brother, Robert, had destroyed much of his work, but they were clearly unfounded, as can be seen from the manuscripts which have survived. From these we can ascertain beyond doubt that Solomos's struggle to create out of a crude spoken idiom a suitable poetic diction for his highly sophisticated ideal was the real reason why he never concluded any of his major works. He worked every line to exhaustion in order to convey the subtle shades of his lyricism. His very high standards never allowed him to get far beyond small pieces, often complete in themselves but always fitting into the prose sketches of longer, unfinished works. It is even possible that he destroyed some of his work himself when it did not meet with his approval.[17]

Certain aspects of Solomos's poetry deserve to be underscored, for they constitute his legacy to later Ionian poets and, to a certain extent, to modern Greek poetry in general. The first of these is his overwhelming patriotism, which runs right through his poetry to the concluding lines of *The Eastern War*.[18] This is not only conceived in conventional, Romantic, nineteenth-century, nationalistic terms; it also emerges as a deep and enlightened love for anything truly Greek—customs, festivals, the spoken language, the sense of honour and pride, perhaps most of all the Orthodox Church.

This brings us to the deep religious feeling characteristic of so many of Solomos's poems. The profound mysticism evident in his first Italian religious poems deepens into a great liberating force in *The Free Besieged* and then shifts to an agonizing preoccupation with the mystery of life and the inability to find a key to it, as expressed in the beautiful *Epigram on Frances Frazer*.

With the possible exception of *The Woman with the Shawl* in one of his Italian sketches, from which we may even infer carnal desire, all of Solomos's portraits of women are highly idealized. Of the three types of women which appear in his poetry—the mother, the lover and the chaste virgin, all noble and refined figures—it is to the last that Solomos feels most attracted. All the poet's ethereal feminine characters are clad in a symbolic, Romantic garment; they are but symbols (in the Schillerian sense) through which to reach ideal beauty, both moral and aesthetic, and ultimately the truth. A cruder, physical attraction to the opposite sex never emerges in the poetry of Solomos; it should be remembered that he never married.[19]

Another important aspect of the poet's work is his treatment of nature. Once again, we find a symbolic, spiritual approach which deepens with the years. In the serenity and beauty of nature—Solomos always stressed that he preferred the calm to the stormy sea—he came to see the splendour and harmony of the universe, and in the 'fountain of joy' which the peace of nature releases in man, the beginning of the true spiritual awakening of the individual. The purely idyllic touch of his earlier poetry and the more superficial approach to the external wonders of nature were soon abandoned, to be replaced by an interpretation of the deeper spiritual message behind its lovely façade, as expressed in *The Free Besieged* and *Porphyras*.

But undoubtedly his most important characteristic, and the greatest service he rendered to Greek poetry, was his choice of the demotic as the language of his verse. Through his patient labour over the years, his musical ear, his exceptional flair for the selection and collation of words, he gave dignity and a new meaning to the spoken idiom. His impact on the language of poetry, first among the Ionian poets and then, after the Demotic Movement of the 1880s, on all subsequent Greek poets, was enormous. As has so often been said, 'no one has a better right to be styled the 'Dante of the Modern Greek Parnassus'.

Nor should Solomos's contribution to the field of metrics be under-rated. By successfully introducing a number of Italian metres into Greek, he helped, more than any other poet, to break down the monotony of the traditional popular Greek metres. His dependence on Italian poetry was not, of course, limited to metrics alone. Its influence, especially on his early work, was immense, while that of Dante and Petrarch (to mention only the two Italian literary giants he most admired) has been traced throughout his writings.

Finally, a word should be added about his deep interest in aesthetic literary criticism, which is a further legacy he bequeathed to his Ionian successors.[20]

Solomos has rightly been seen by all students of Greek poetry as one of the great milestones in its course from Homer to the present day. For it was Solomos and Solomos alone who restored Greek verse to the realm of great art and saved it from degenerating into mere rhetorical verbiage. Few men can claim to have affected so profoundly the entire development of a national literature with such a small corpus of fully finished verse. Indeed, prophetic were the words of Gerasimos Markoras, who said, shortly after the poet's death. 'The coming generations will get to know and honour Solomos more, because our glorious poet did not sink into the darkness of the past, but stood at the doorway of the future.'[21]

Julios Typaldos and lesser successors of Solomos

The Ionian poet who followed most closely in Solomos's footsteps was Julios Typaldos (1814–83). He was born in Cephalonia of a Greek father, whose family was originally of Italian stock, and an Italian mother, a Veronese countess, Terèsa Ringetti. He was educated in Verona and Corfu and at the universities of Padua, Florence and Pisa, where he studied law. He later served in the Ionian law courts as a judge, and he died in Corfu, having spent fourteen years in retirement in Florence when the Ionian Islands were annexed to Greece.[22]

Typaldos was a friend and great admirer of Solomos, to whom he dedicated his *Poems*, the one slender book of verse he published in his lifetime. In his lyricism we find something of the refinement and idealizing tendency of the older poet, but nothing even remotely approaching the depth or the technical perfection of Solomos's mature work. Typaldos's small output—a few of his poems are still unpublished—is notable for its patriotic feeling and restful simplicity. No symbolism burdens the verse, and no boisterous rhetoric cheapens it. The successful use of synizesis, the relative absence of harsh consonants and the lavish use of rhyme makes his lines extremely musical, but his colourless diction and his facile rhymes add a softness bordering on insipid sweetness.

His most highly praised lyric is *The Creation of the Imagination*, a poem on the ideal woman with whom he was perpetually in love but never met. Some of his less ambitious verse is more successful, such as *The Escape*[23] or *The Two Flowers*, which were set to music and became very popular in their day.

Of his patriotic poems, *Rhegas* is the most interesting, presenting Rhegas Velestinlis as an idealized bard who, with his songs, incites the Greeks to fight for their independence. In this work, as in many of his other patriotic poems (most prominently in *The Condemnation of the Klepht*), his debt to folk song is evident.

Most moving is the poet's serene approach to death, as portrayed in *The Two Flowers* or *The Little Child and Charos*, for which Goethe's *Erlkönig* served as a model. Any intimation of horror is avoided, and only the sad beauty of death's eternal peace is suggested. But Typaldos was equally aware of nature's indifference to the suffering of man, and this he expressed forcibly in *The Mad Girl*, in which echoes of Leopardi can be traced. In only one poem, *The Death of Hamko*, did Typaldos abandon his usual serenity to describe in wild, realistic terms the death of Ali Pasha's fierce mother in the torment of her final criminal moments.

In his maturer years Typaldos did not escape the influence of the Athenian Romantics, as witnessed by his later patriotic poems, such as the *Ode on the Union of the New Greek Provinces with Greece in 1881* or the *Ode on the Death of the Philhellene Lenormant*. However, in his verse erudite and blatant patriotic elements were transmuted and absorbed, and thus rendered less offensive.

Finally, it should be mentioned that Typaldos also translated a large part of Tasso's *Gerusalèmme liberata* into modern Greek.

With the exception of Typaldos, Solomos's immediate successors were all lesser poets and need not detain us for long. Among them one might single out the Zantiot, Antonios Matesis (1794–1875), a friend and admirer of Solomos, who also began his literary career by writing verse in Italian. His Greek poetry is, on the whole, light-hearted—it comprises satires, anacreontics and idylls—striking an occasional serious note when the subject is the death of a warrior or a friend. His poor vocabulary and faulty rhymes finally succumbed to the influence of the Athenian 'purists', which clearly did not improve his poetry.[24]

Passing mention should also be made of Antonios Manousis (1828–1903), who appeared on the literary scene with a long poem called *The Blind Girl*, which was followed by two collections of verse, *Sighs* and *Lyrical Poems*. They are full of platitudes and also betray the deadening influence of the Athenian Romantics. The same burden weighs on the work of the Corfiot, G. K. Romas (1796–1867), whose first collection of poems, *The Flowers*, earned him the title of the 'Young of the Heptanese'.

A more forceful personality was that of the Cephalonian P. Panas (1832–96), who translated Ossian into unrhymed political lines. In his *Works of Idleness*, his only book of original poems, some literary satires are worthy of comment, but he too bears witness to the impact of the Athenians.

Finally, a few words should be added here about Georgios Tertsetis (1800–74), the Zantiot scholar and friend of Solomos, whose mediocre poetry attracted attention in the nineteenth century. (Solomos had also taken an interest in his early work, as can be seen from their correspondence.) His language is a reasonable example of the spoken idiom; but his works, whether inspired by Greek antiquity (*Corinna and Pindar, The Wedding of Alexander the Great and of the Macedonian Generals at Sousa in Persia*) or by contemporary history (*The 25th of January, 1833* or *The Dream of the King*) are flat and verbose and are hardly ever read today. As a man of character and as the person who induced Theodore Kolokotronis to write his memoirs, he has an important place in the literary life of nineteenth-century Greece, but not as a poet.

One of the important legacies Solomos bequeathed to the Ionian writers was his interest in aesthetics and literary criticism. Jaovos Polylas (1825–96) took up the torch in this field and, until the days of Kostis Palamas, was undoubtedly the most important modern Greek critic.

Polylas was born in Corfu and was one of the few distinguished Ionian men of letters who did not receive his education abroad. However, after his marriage he spent two years in Naples, where, accompanied by his ailing wife, he studied literature at the university. His interest in literature and philosophy was profound, and it was mainly through his translations into Italian of major German aesthetic writers that Solomos was introduced to their views. But Polylas was not only a scholar; he was also a man of action. After the union of the Heptanese with Greece, he repeatedly represented Corfu in the Greek Parliament, and he was active as a journalist until the end of his life.

Polylas's most important critical work is his edition of Solomos's poems and his admirable introduction to them. His critical writings influenced a number of Greek poets, both in the Ionian Islands and in Athens, and these justify his place in an account of the history of Greek poetry, though his own original verse is meagre and unimportant. He made his mark, however, by translating such classics as the *Iliad*, the *Odyssey* and *Hamlet* into modern Greek.[25]

Aristotelis Valaoritis

We must now turn to Aristotelis Valaoritis (1824–79), who, after Solomos, is without doubt the most impressive poet of the Ionian School. He was born in Leucas, into a family which came from Epirus and had fought for generations against Turkish oppression. He was educated first in Leucas and Corfu and then in Geneva, Paris and Pisa, where he graduated from the university in law. Handsome, rich, with a romantic, liberal nature, he became passionately involved in the Italian and Hungarian struggles against Austria, as well as in many colourful amorous escapades. He settled down in 1852, when he married Eloisia Typaldos, and returned to live on Leucas. He represented his native island first in the Ionian Parliament and then, after the union with Greece, in the Greek Parliament, where he repeatedly won wide acclaim.

Valaoritis's early poems were written in *katherevousa* and remain unpublished to this day. Soon, however, he followed the example of Solomos and turned to the spoken idiom. The first fruit of this change appeared in 1847, in a collection called *Works in Verse* (Στιχουργήματα), but he later disowned these adolescent poems and never published them again. His mature poetry dates from the *Commemorations* (Μνημόσυνα), published in Corfu in 1857 and enlarged in a second edition to include a number of new important poems. They consist of patriotic and personal verse, many of which are on the deaths of friends and relatives of the poet. Of the patriotic poems, *Thanasis Bagias, Samuel, The Escape, The Rock and the Wave* and the celebrated *Ode On Patriarch Gregory V*[26] deserve special mention; of the pure lyrics, those that stand out are *The First of March, Kalogiannos, The Uprooted Tree, The Wild Vine* and the moving elegy *On the Death of my Daughter, Nathalie.*

But without doubt the most important poem included in the second edition of *Commemorations* is *Astrapogiannos*, a long epico-lyrical work about a young Klepht, Lambetis, who kills his wounded leader, Astrapogiannos, at the latter's command and carries his head away to prevent its falling into the hands of the Turks. Later Lambetis himself is wounded and dies on the spot where he buried his leader's head. In this highly romantic adaptation of the Klephtic ballads, the forceful imagery and arresting rhythms are memorable.

Valaoritis's first major work, *Kyra Phrosyne*, appeared in 1859. It is a lyrico-dramatic poem in four cantos, whose subject is the love affair of

Mouchtar, son of the notorious Ali Pasha of Jannina, and the beautiful
Christian woman, Phrosyne. Ali fell in love with Phrosyne, and when she
did not respond to that old man's advances he had her drowned in the lake
of Jannina. This is the least successful of Valaoritis's longer poems. Ali
Pasha is presented as a satanic Byronic hero; the melodramatic outbursts
are intolerable; and there is little distinction made between the charac-
ters. However, two lyrics included in that work became famous in their
day—*Like a Yellow Dried Leaf* and *What a Kiss that Was*—and are still
pleasing, in spite of their romantic exaggeration.

Kyra Phrosyne was the work of a young man who had not yet mastered his
medium and was still under the spell of Byron and Victor Hugo. Ten
years later Valaoritis published his *Athanasios Diakos*, which many critics
consider his masterpiece. It was conceived as an epic and deals with the
death of Athanasios Diakos, a man of prodigious courage who was finally
captured and roasted on a spit by the Turks during the Greek War of
Independence. The poem consists of six cantos, in which platitudes and
conventional ringing rhetoric abound. The hero is a highly idealized
symbol of Greek heroism, and even the structure of the poem is faulty, the
first five cantos being devoted entirely to the battle of Alamana which
preceded Diakos's death. Yet in a strange way something of the heroic
breath of true Klephtic poetry pervades the verse, and the dramatic
element is not unsuccessfully developed. Nor should certain sensitive
descriptions of nature be overlooked, as well as some passages in which
horror is masterfully evoked.

Valaoritis also left a long, unfinished work called *Photeinos*. This is
clearly the best and most balanced of his poems, although judgement of
unfinished works is always dangerous and unfair. Its subject is taken from
the early Frankish occupation of the Heptanese and a rising of the Greek
inhabitants of Leucas against their conquerors. Photeinos, the hero, retires
to the mountains with his daughter and plans the revolution. An aged
champion of freedom, he is presented as gentle, humane and determined.
The whole poem, whose verse is terse, lively and free of bombast and
mock-heroic rhetoric, centres on this warm, proud character. Valaoritis is
also reputed to have composed another long poem, *The Blind Chormobitis*,
which was lost during one of his journeys from Athens to Leucas. Only a
small fragment of it survives.

Valaoritis set out to uphold the tradition of the Klephtic folk songs of
Epirus in personal, 'sophisticated' poetry, and it is true that he succeeded
in bringing into modern Greek poetry something of the simplicity and
vigour of these songs. But being a romantic by nature, and living in a
period of Greek history when unbridled patriotism was the norm, he fell
prey to mock-heroic rhetoric and the Romantic penchant for deathbeds
and tombstones, both alien to Klephtic folk songs, though very much part
of the Athenian School, whose influence Valaoritis did not avoid. The real

weakness of his poetry is that it matured very little and very slowly over the years. One can hardly believe that twenty-two years separate the composition of the *Commemorations* and the *Photeinos*.

Nevertheless, although Valaoritis did not escape the sick sentimentality of his period, his work has two important virtues: its language and its metres. He expressed himself in simple, straightforward, demotic diction, which was free of extreme dialectical elements, even if it is not exciting on the whole; and he took considerable care over his metres. He developed the political line and explored many of its possibilities and variations. He experimented most successfully with the popular eleven-syllable line with a caesura after the sixth and an accent after the fourth syllable. In his lyrics he also used shorter Italian metres.

As already mentioned, Valaoritis was one of the links that connected the School of the Ionian Poets with that of the Athenian Romantics. Though he took much from the latter, in turn he also gave much back. In fact, he beat the Athenians at their own game, for his romantic excesses caused a violent reaction even in the capital. His poetry was parodied and attacked by the leading critics of the day (with the notable exception of Roidis). In finding fault with Valaoritis, the Old School poets found themselves under fire for their use of the same mannerisms and devices; the death-blow had been dealt.

Aside from his contribution to the collapse of the Athenian Romantics, perhaps Valaoritis's greatest direct gift to modern Greek poetry was his decision to write in the demotic. For we know that it was the demotic poetry of Valaoritis that stimulated Palamas to use the spoken idiom for his own verse, and the other founders of the New School of Athens soon followed his example.

Andreas Laskaratos

Another important link between the Ionian Islands and Athens is Andreas Laskaratos (1811–1901), the Cephalonian satirist. He was born in the town of Lixouri and was educated in Cephalonia, Corfu, Zante, Paris and Pisa, where he graduated in law. One of his teachers in Corfu was the poet Andreas Kalvos, who took an interest in the young man's poetry. In Zante Laskaratos met Solomos, whom he greatly admired and whose influence is evident in his early lyrics.

After finishing his studies Laskaratos returned to Cephalonia, where he practised law, but he soon withdrew to his small country estate, where he spent his time farming, writing and reading. In 1846 he married Penelope Korgialeniou and shortly afterwards was forced, for financial reasons, to move his family to Argostoli, the island's capital. In 1856 Laskaratos published the prose work *The Mysteries of Cephalonia*, which provoked a storm that clouded the rest of his life, for in it he attacked the duplicity and corruption of Cephalonian society and of the clergy. As a result, he was accused of heresy and was excommunicated by the Church. Consequently, he left for Zante and then for England, where he spent three years in exile.[27] After his return to the Heptanese he embarked on the edition of a satirical journal, *The Lamp* ('Ο Λύχνος), which again caused a sensation and landed him in jail for a few months. In the troubled years which followed his return from England Laskaratos visited Athens repeatedly and became acquainted with the leading Greek men of letters, who gradually came to know and respect him, as did all his earlier detractors on the islands. Thus at the end of his life even the Church withdrew its anathema; honoured by all, Laskaratos died in 1901 at the age of ninety.

Laskaratos was a man of great integrity. He is remembered mainly for his satirical works, both in prose and in verse; his lyrical poetry is scanty and weak. As a satirist, he first emerged with some daring, youthful verse called *The Indecent Poems* (Άσεμνα), which circulated in manuscript among his friends but were never published.[28] The first verse satire he published was *Lixouri*, in which he makes fun of the inhabitants of that town, who quarrelled violently over a pier that was to be built in the harbour. As his model, he used Tassoni's *La séchia rapita* (a work of the seventeenth century), which he adapted to local circumstances. There is a good sense of fun in it, and the language is racy and demotic.

Contemporary with *Lixouri* is another, more biting political satire, *The Gun Boat* (Βάρκα Κανονιέρα), in which Laskaratos compares liberty with a woman of loose morals familiar to everyone in Cephalonia under the nickname 'the Gun Boat'. Laskaratos's political views were conservative; he was opposed to the liberals who advocated the union of the Ionian Islands with Greece, whom he succeeded in outraging, just as he had outraged the conservatives and the Church with his *Mysteries of Cephalonia*. *The Gun Boat*, as well as the majority of the short satirical and lyrical poems of that period, were published later (in 1872) in a book entitled *Verses* (Στιχουργήματα), which does not spare the rich, the poor or the Church. Among them a few purely playful poems can be found, such as his well-known sonnet *On Love*, and one tender and beautiful sonnet on the portrait of his wife, which he wrote during his exile in London, when she and their children had remained behind in Cephalonia. Very much in the tradition of the Italian satirists Berni, Manro or Caporali, Laskaratos is more playful than vicious. The humourist in him is more evident than the social reformer, though he thought of himself as a critic of society. (In his footsteps followed other Cephalonian satirists, such as Georgios Molfetas (1871–1916), who for twenty-four years published the satirical journal *Zizanio*.)

Laskaratos wrote in a highly personal literary diction, in which erudite elements are fused with the local vernacular; it was clearly to this and not to his ability as a versifier that Palamas and his contemporaries referred when they called him the 'harbinger' (*προάγγελος*) of the new Greek poetic development and considered him one of the heirs of Solomos, for his metres are often faulty.

Laskaratos also wrote essays, polemical articles and short stories, which were collected after his death and published under the title *Habits and Ideas of Cephalonia* (*Ἤθη, ἔθιμα καὶ δοξασίες τῆς Κεφαλλονιᾶς*); a series of character sketches in the manner of Theophrastus, published under the title *Ecce Homo*; translations into Greek of foreign works; and a long autobiography in Italian.

Gerasimos Markoras

After Julios Typaldos the most distinguished successor of Solomos was Gerasimos Markoras (1826–1911). Born in Cephalonia, he was educated in Corfu at the Ionian Academy (Andreas Kalvos was one of his teachers) and later in Italy, where he read law. However, true to the Heptanesian aristocratic tradition, he devoted his three years in Italy to literary rather than to legal studies. Upon returning to the Ionian Islands, he married and settled down in Corfu as a gentleman farmer. But his wife soon died, and he lived from then on with his sister, about whom he wrote the moving sonnet called *Two*. Though he was a fervent supporter of the union of the Ionian Islands with Greece, he played no part in the local political disputes. Instead he devoted his whole life to poetry and took a lively interest in the literary, musical and theatrical life of Corfu.

It was his friendship with Solomos that helped Markoras to develop his own art; and he also emulated the older poet's desperate pursuit of perfection in form, as is evident from the variety of metres he used. His shy and unassuming nature prevented him from publishing anything until the death of Solomos—he never even read his verse to his master—when he emerged with *The First Saturday of the Souls* (*Τὸ Πρωτοσάββατο*), commemorating the great poet's death. Later he contributed poems to the local papers until 1890, when his first collection of verse, *Poetic Works*, was printed. This was followed eight years later by a second book entitled *Short Journeys*. As soon as his *Poetic Works* appeared, Markoras was acclaimed as a major poet by the supporters of the New School of Athens. For by 1890 the Demotic Movement had gathered momentum, and Markoras's diction excited and delighted the leading Athenian poets and critics.

Markoras' longest work, *The Vow*, composed in 1875, is considered his best and most important poem. It is cast in rhyming political lines and treats of the tragic love of a young Cretan girl, whose betrothed is killed during the Cretan uprising of 1866. Although conceived in exuberant

Romantic and patriotic terms, it is a moving piece of poetry, with some fine imagery and a good command of the spoken language.

Markoras composed no narrative poetry after *The Vow* but dedicated himself to lyrical and satirical verse and to translations from Classical Greek, German and Italian poets. He is at his best in his short lyrics. Like most representatives of the Ionian School, he chose as his favourite themes patriotism, love and death. His sympathy for the simple people of the countryside is endearing, and the gentle melancholy which pervades his poems is never oppressive. Today the Greek reader responds less readily to his patriotic verse, such as the famous *Our Castles*, written when the fortifications of Corfu were demolished prior to the union with Greece, or *The Arrival of George I*, which celebrated the King's arrival in Greece in 1864. His lyrics, especially *Julietta Gartzoni* and *The Complaint of the Dead Girl*, are far more appealing.[29]

Lorentzos Mavilis

The last flash of true lyricisim from the Ionian Islands is to be found in the poetry of Lorentzos Mavilis (1860–1912). He was born in Ithaca, of a Spanish father and a Corfiot mother, and was educated in Corfu and Germany, where his philosophical studies enhanced his natural idealism. He was a good linguist and has left a number of translations, some even from Sanskrit.

Mavilis was also a great patriot, who fought in Crete in 1896, in Epirus in 1897 and was killed as a volunteer in Jannina during the First Balkan War in 1912. As a member of the House of Representatives in 1909, he supported the use of the demotic as the official language.

He wrote little original poetry, but his exquisite sonnets, of which *Lethe* and *The Olive Tree* are his masterpieces, secure him a special place in the modern Greek pantheon. He worked hard on his verse, transforming into true poetry much of his practical wisdom and philosophical thought. His fully finished lines have nothing laboured about them, his inspiration always depending on his own experience. He is the greatest sonnet writer in modern Greek poetry, and though there is something 'Parnassian' about the form of his sonnets, their human tone and personal involvement temper that impression. They were published in Alexandria in 1915, after his death.[30]

Finally, it should be added that there were several minor Heptanesian poets who, after writing some rather conventional verse in their youth, abandoned literature for other pursuits. Of these, Gerasimos Mavrogiannis (1823–1906), Elizabethios Martinengos (1832–85) and Georgios Martinellis (1836–96) are the most noteworthy.

CHAPTER 28

The New School of Athens

THE FORERUNNERS OF THE NEW SCHOOL

The final death-blow to the Old School of Athens was dealt, as we have seen, by the Demotic Movement which flared up in Greece in the 1880s. This is not the place to elaborate on the nature or the significance of this movement or on the momentous effects it had upon Greek life. It must suffice to repeat that it started in support of the spoken idiom as opposed to the stilted archaic forms of the written 'official' language; but it soon broadened out from a purely linguistic battle into a reaction against the weight of the whole archaic tradition, preaching a return of literature, art, politics and social life to their modern Greek roots. The movement became more active and more effective when Giannis Psycharis (1854–1929), the distinguished linguist and Professor of Modern Greek at the École des Langues Orientales in Paris, became its leader.[1] Its influence upon the Athenian literary scene cannot be overrated; and in it lie the true roots of the New School of Athens.

But before proceeding to the major representatives of the New School we must examine four of its important precursors, Georgios Bizyenos, Aristomenis Provelengios, D. G. Kambouroglou and Johannes Papadia-mantopoulos. They foreshadow the new poetry that was to flourish in the eighties but were never free of the shadow of the past, even after the New School became established and was influencing their own work.

Georgios Bizyenos (1849–96) was born in a small village of Thrace called Biza and was educated in Constantinople—he was a pupil of the poet Elias Tantalidis—and later in Germany, where he studied philosophy. In 1873, still very young, he published his first collection of poems, called *Poetic First Fruits*, in which a remarkable command of the spoken idiom is evident; and in the next year he published a totally insignificant play called *Codrus*, dealing with the mythical king of Athens of that name. Ten years later, in London, he published *Attic Breezes*, in which he collected his early as well as his later poetic output, consisting of epico-lyrical, erotic and satirical works, in the first of which the patriotic element is stressed. In 1892 he had a serious nervous breakdown and spent the last four years of his life in a lunatic asylum.

The poetry of Bizyenos is superior to that of any of his contemporary Athenian Romantics. His demotic diction (when he chooses to employ it) is racy, though often prosy, and his use of rhetoric sparse; and his allegories and personifications are readily graspable; but his lyricism is on the whole dull. Bizyenos also wrote philosophical essays and short stories, some of which are superior to his verse.

Aristomenis Provelengios (1850–1936) was a poet of less power and much less originality than Bizyenos. He was born on the island of Siphnos and was educated in Germany, where he studied philosophy. He too appeared on the literary scene very young, with a poor, archaizing play called *Theseus*, in which the influence of Alexandros Rangavis, whom Provelengios greatly admired, is evident. His poetry consists of lyrical and epico-lyrical works, as well as a number of lifeless verse plays. To the end of his life he wavered between the 'purist' and the spoken diction, and even when using the latter, the influence of the former is evident. Delicacy and a colourless nobility characterize his poetry, which is well in keeping with the nostalgia for the past and for the beautiful things out of reach which he so often wrote about. The best of his collections of verse is *Autumnal Harmonies*, which includes poems of love, nature and science.[2]

D. K. Kambouroglou (1852–1942) is better-known as a historian, a folklorist and an essayist than as a poet. Yet his book of inferior verse, *The Voice of my Heart*, was awarded a prize at the University Poetry Competition of 1873 and is a landmark in the history of modern Greek poetry, both because it was the first collection that included poems in the demotic to receive a prize and because of its light-hearted and amusing tone, so different from the conventional, funereal floods of tears and rhetorical pomposity of the Greek Romantics. That book of unimportant verse and the satirical poem which Kambouroglou wrote in 1874, parodying the Athenian Romantics—it was favourably mentioned at the Athenian poetry competion of that year—indicate that the Old School of Athens was coming to an end.

Johannes Papadiamantopoulos (1856–1910), better known under his French pen-name of Jean Moréas, was born in Athens, studied in Germany, Italy and France and died in Paris. His best poetry was, of course, written in French; about this we shall not speak, as it belongs to the history of French literature. But he started his remarkable literary career as a Greek poet by publishing a few short poems in Athenian literary periodicals and calendars of the time and then, in 1878, issued one collection in Greek, under the title *Vipers and Turtledoves*. In this book poems in an inflated Romantic and 'purist' style rub shoulders with more direct and restrained verse in the spoken idiom which, though second-rate, foreshadows the poetry of the eighties. After *Vipers and Turtledoves* Papadiamantopoulos gave nothing more to Greek literature.

THE 'GENERATION OF THE EIGHTIES'

It was in the 1870s, roughly ten years before Giannis Psycharis appeared on the literary scene and the Demotic Movement had come into its own, that a group of spirited young writers, reacting against the sickly sentimentality, the mock-heroic patriotism and the stilted diction of most of the Greek Romantics, decided to embark on a new kind of poetry. They were greatly encouraged, as we have seen, by the enlightened criticism of Emmanuel Roidis and the guidance given to them by Nicolaos Politis, as well as by the appearance, between 1876 and 1880, of three new, forward-looking literary periodicals in which they could publish their works — *Hestia, Rabagas* and *Don't Lose Yourself (Μὴ χάνεσαι)*.[3] As the last two were satirical publications, they provided an excellent incentive for those young writers to compose light-hearted verse and so move away from the ponderous, pretentious poetry of those days.

The leading figures of this group, known to Greek literary criticism as the 'Generation of the Eighties', are Nikos Kambas, Georgios Drosinis, Kostis Palamas, Johannes Polemis and Georgios Strategis. Around them clustered a number of other young poets, among whom Georgios Souris and Demetrios Kokkos should be singled out, who soon followed a different course.

As some of these poets spoke French and were interested in the literary life of France, their attention was drawn to the Parnassians, whom they came to admire as anti-Romantic writers. The Parnassian spirit, which countered Romantic exuberance and offered something balanced and new, they soon aspired to transfer to the Greek literary scene, and for this purpose they chose François Coppée, Sully Prudhomme,[4] and T. Banville as their models; Leconte de Lisle and Théophile Gautier, the true fathers of the Parnassian Movement, they discovered much later.

Thus, following the French lead (even if in France the Parnassian Movement was already at an end), the Greek Parnassians eschewed rhetoric and grandiloquence and turned to more homely subjects, to the joys and sorrows of everyday life; they also began to employ more varied and agile rhythms than those of the Greek Romantics, who had used to satiety the traditional fifteen-syllable and eight-syllable lines.

In the course of time the early light-hearted and often naive verse of these poets gave way to more serious and ambitious creations, which were published in *Hestia* and also collected in small, independent books. This group of young writers—the 'Generation of the Eighties'—constitutes a turning-point in the history of Greek poetry, for it is they who infused new life into the moribund Greek verse and in due course wrote some of the masterpieces of modern Greek literature.

The influence of the Parnassians, once introduced to the Athenian scene, did not limit itself to the younger poets. Old and established writers like Bizyenos and Provelengios also began to feel its impact, and it persisted in Greece until the end of the nineteenth century. It would also be true to say that some of the most distinguished poets of the 'Generation of the Eighties', such as Drosinis and Polemis, never succeeded in freeing themselves from it. However, to the credit of the Greek Parnassians it should be noted that in spite of their French models, they retained in their verse a truly Greek flavour and developed a note of optimism which is absent, on the whole, from their French counterparts.

The young poets of the 1880s met at first with a violent and bitter attack on the part of the old order. For a long time they were mocked—Achilles Paraschos dubbed them *Paidarellia*, ('Silly Youngsters')—and serious literary criticism either took little notice of them or roundly condemned them. Undaunted, they continued their work, however, and when Psycharis became the acknowledged leader of the Demotic Movement and the maturer works of Drosinis and Palamas appeared, they began to be taken seriously and finally won the day, saving Greek poetry from what appeared to be certain death.

Nicolaos Kambas

The first of the 'Generation of the Eighties to publish a volume of verse was Nicolaos Kambas (1857–1932), in 1880. He was born on the island of Lesbos and studied law at the University of Athens. During his studies he became passionately interested in literature and was the main agent in introducing the whole group to the French Parnassians. His early light-hearted verse he published in the satirical periodicals *Don't Lose Yourself* and *Rabagas*, his later poems in his one and only book, *Verses*. His poetry is clearly second-rate, some of it in the demotic and some in the *katherevousa*, and his literary activities were limited to the years 1877–83, for he soon abandoned literature to devote himself to a legal career in Alexandria. He is accorded a place in this history of Greek poetry in recognition of the fact that it was mainly through him that young Palamas and Drosinis were initially informed about the literary life of France.

Georgios Drosinis

Georgios Drosinis (1859–1951) was born in Athens (his family came from Missolonghi) and was educated in Athens and Leipzig, where he studied law and literature. After returning to Greece he became editor of the literary journal *Hestia* (1888–94), from which position he was able to help the younger Greek Parnassians, and later Director of Education at the Ministry for Education and a member of the Academy of Athens.

Drosinis started publishing verse in the satirical journal *Rabagas* and later, in 1880, brought out his first book of poems, *The Spider's Web*, which is a landmark in the history of the New School of Athens. For in it the beneficial influence of the French Parnassians[5] can clearly be seen in the appealing restraint of tone, the simplicity of language and the choice of subjects from everyday life; lamentations and mock-heroic patriotism are eschewed.

The Spider's Web was followed in 1881 by a second collection of verse called *Stalactites*, and a few years later by a third, *Idylls*, in which the author's admiration for folk songs becomes evident. Interest in modern Greek folk songs and modern Greek folklore was to become one of the salient features of the early period of the New School of Athens, and it was Drosinis who first successfully demonstrated this.[6] The *Idylls* also have the distinction of being the first of Drosinis's books that did not include a single poem in the 'purist' diction.

During the course of his long life Drosinis published thirteen collections of poems.[7] His main sources of inspiration were love and country life, with all the colourful aspects of Greek village life. His muse is serene and controlled and never indulges in stormy emotions, nor is there any real development in his art over the years. Moreover, whenever he touches on philosophical topics—and this is rare—the freshness of his verse seems to suffer. However, much to his credit (and in spite of the traceable impact of the Parnassians, Goethe, Heine and later German lyrical poetry, as well as of Theocritus and the Anacreontics, to mention only the more obvious influences he underwent), his poetry retains a pronounced modern Greek character.

Of the thirteen collections Drosinis published, three deserve special mention: *Darkness Full of Light* (Φωτερὰ Σκοτάδια), *Closed Eyelids*, and *Night will be Falling*, in which the poet can be seen at his best. The last, as opposed to the other two, consists not of independent works, but of a sequence of eighty short poems describing, in idealized terms, life in a Greek village in the company of a beloved woman. Here Drosinis's gentle lyricism reaches its peak, for everything—churches, fountains, fruit-laden trees, autumn rain, cloudy March nights, the harvest, the vintage and so on—achieves an idyllic serenity and a concrete beauty of its own, as though lit by the love of the woman who accompanies the poet.

Although the best poetry of Drosinis can be found in the three collections singled out above, there are a number of beautiful or famous individual poems in some of his other books, such as *Evensong* in *Calm* (*Γαλήνη*), or *The Greek Earth* in *The Amaranths* (*Ἀμάραντα*). Patriotism, which inspired *The Greek Earth*—a poem every Greek schoolboy knows by heart—is also responsible for inspiring some of Drosinis's best poetry, most notably the poem *How Many Generations have Passed Away*, which in a restrained and moving manner describes the spirit of the Greeks during the Balkan Wars of 1912–13.[8]

The accusation levelled by many modern Greek critics at Drosinis that 'his poetry is only fit for schoolchildren' is totally undeserved. He is not only noteworthy for having introduced the Parnassian spirit into Greek poetry and for having been the leader of the anti-Romantic group until Palamas took over; he is also a writer of quality who can delight the unbigoted poetry lover with much of his frugal and well-turned verse.

Drosinis's literary activities did not limit themselves to original poetry. They embraced prose—he wrote short stories and one novel—translations of Classical Greek and Western works, as well as a large number of critical and other articles in newspapers and journals.[9]

Kostis Palamas

The major figure of the 'Generation of the Eighties' is undoubtedly Kostis Palamas (1859–1943). A son of Judge Michael Palamas, he was born in Patras. When he was barely seven he lost both his parents and was placed in the keeping of his father's elder brother, Demetrios, a schoolteacher in Missolonghi, the home town of the Palamas family.

His uncle's home, in which the poet lived until he was seventeen, was strange and gloomy; from the very beginning Kostis felt isolated there and 'wrapped up inside himself'.[10] When he finished school in Missolonghi, which he considered a nightmare, he was sent to Athens to study law at the University, but his real interest was literature, and this, as well as growing financial difficulties, lured him away from his legal studies so that he never acquired a law degree. In order to secure a living, Palamas embarked on a journalistic career, which was responsible for much of his early literary criticism and was his only source of income until 1897, when he was appointed Secretary to the University of Athens, a post he held for thirty years. In 1887 he married Maria Valvi, with whom he had been in love for many years, and of that marriage three children were born. When he died in 1943, during the German and Italian occupation of Athens, his majestic funeral, attended by thousands of admirers, was a national event.

When Palamas arrived in Athens he soon became the centre of a circle of young writers who were experimenting, as we have seen, in the field of poetic diction[11] in reaction to the Greek Romantics. Under the influence of the French Parnassians and of modern Greek folklore studies, he proceeded to publish his early verse in the avant-garde periodicals *Don't Lose Yourself* and *Rabagas*, poems in which patriotism played an important part. These he later included in his first book of verse, *The Songs of my Homeland*, which appeared in 1886.[12] Although they were works of little merit, the young Palamas received many encouraging letters from distinguished scholars and writers, and further appreciation poured in when his *Hymn of Athene* was awarded the prize at the Philadelpheios poetry competition of 1889.[13] The lavish praise heaped on this poem of little originality, uncouth diction and no metrical subtlety clearly shows the impoverished state of poetry in Greece at the time. Nor was Palamas's next collection of poems, *The Eyes of my Soul*, published in 1892, a great advance on the first. In it the poet struggled to infuse new life into the ancient world by blending Classical themes with Christian and modern Greek imagery.

It was not until 1897, when Palamas circulated his *Iambs and Anapaests*, that he came into his own and all the potential and the vigour of his poetry became evident. For poetic symbols now took the place of long, rambling descriptions, and important subjects appeared on which he was later to elaborate, such as the fusion of Pagan and Christian elements in modern Greek life or the significance and the beauty of the demotic language, which were treated in a straightforward and restrained manner.

The years 1897 to 1915 were the great creative years of Palamas, for it was then that he published his three major works — *Life Immovable* (1904), *The Dodecalogue of the Gypsy* (1907) and *The King's Flute* (1910) — as well as three further important collections of poems, *The Sorrows of the Lagoon* (1912), *City and Solitude* (1912) and *Altars* (1915). It should be remembered that at that time the struggle for the establishment of the Demotic Movement was at its peak, and whereas Psycharis, Eftaliotis and Pallis supported it wholeheartedly from abroad, it was Palamas who fought the real battle in Athens, always running the risk of losing his post as Secretary to the University of Athens (such was the bigoted fury of the 'purists' against him) which was his only source of income.[14]

In 1898 the poet's youngest child, Alkis, died at the age of five. This tragedy inspired the composition of *The Grave*, a cross between an elegy and a lament, notable for its exquisite lyricism and musicality and for its successful fusion of elements from the popular laments with sophisticated personal verse.

In 1903 Palamas also tried his hand as a dramatist by writing *The Trisevgeni* (*The Most Noble*), a prose play beyond the scope of this book. It should be noted, however, that its pronounced poetic diction competes with the vigour and beauty of Palamas's verse. In the same year he composed the *Hymn of Greeting to the Tragic Muse*, which was recited at the Royal Theatre as an introduction to a festive production of Aeschylus' *Oresteia* in a demotic translation that provoked violent demonstrations among the students, during which two people were killed. Such were the passions the Demotic Movement had stirred.

Life Immovable is considered by many critics to be the most significant collection of poems to appear in Athens since the liberation of the country from the Turks. It includes two of the most ambitious longer works of Palamas, *The Palm Tree* and *The Ascraean*, and a number of excellent shorter lyrics, among which the sequence of sonnets called *Fatherlands* and the epigrammatic *Hundred Voices* stand out. In it we also find a part of the *Greetings of the Sun-Born*, the first truly Symbolist poem composed in modern Greek.[15]

The Palm Tree, cast in thirteen-syllable *ottava rima*, is also a Symbolist poem, which gives expression to a series of reflections on the place of man (indeed, the place of every living thing) in the universe. The central image, from which the poem derives its name, is a tall palm tree that gives life and death to the small blue flowers that grow in its shade. The imagery is rich, drawn mainly from nature, but the symbolism, though pretty clear, was vigorously attacked for its obscurity when the poem appeared.

The Ascraean, originally conceived as part of a longer work, *The Great Visions*, which was never completed, sets out to explore the relationship of man with Mother Earth, and for that reason the poem is named after Hesiod, the native of Ascra and author of the *Works and Days* whose 'continuator' Palamas purports to be. To establish this, the motif of death and rebirth, one of the favourite motifs of Palamas's poetry is introduced, and the handing over of Hesiod's lyre to Palamas is meant to symbolize the rebirth of ancient Greek poetry in the works of the modern demoticist poets. The ending of the *Ascraean* (a work of 666 fifteen-syllable lines) includes some of the most beautiful verses Palamas ever wrote.

Life Immovable established the poet's reputation, not only in the Greek world of letters,[16] but also beyond the confines of Greece. But it was only in 1907, when he published *The Dodecalogue of the Gypsy*, undoubtedly his greatest and most influential work, that he was universally acclaimed as a great poet.[17] The poem consists of twelve cantos, cast in a mixture of free verse and regular metres, whose structure is loosely knit; through them a number of metaphysical and social problems — ideas of cosmogony, of the relation of man and nature, of death and rebirth — are interwoven. The unity of the poem lies in its central figure, the gypsy, a symbol whose Protean character seems to embody 'the poet's thousand loves'. This gypsy hero is primarily a symbol of freedom and art, for in the Greek world gypsies are considered wanderers, citizens of no country, adherents of no religion, free spirits with a strong musical bent. He is capable of comradeship but unable to fit in with his fellow men. He tries his hand at various jobs and arts but finds them all constricting, just as he finds love constricting and deceptive when he experiences it with a young gypsy woman.[18] Thus disillusioned, he moves away from all conventional forms of happiness until he finds a mysterious violin, which once belonged to an old hermit, and plays on it. The music he makes rejuvenates the gypsy himself and also enchants the children who cluster around him, whereas the older men rage at it. Thus the gypsy—here Palamas himself—is a real *vates*, a prophet-poet addressing the future, such as the Greek world had not known since antiquity.

But even this relatively clear outline of the gypsy's part in the *Dodecalogue* is by no means easy to follow. For the gypsy symbolizes not only freedom, art and Palamas himself; like most of the poet's shifting symbols, he also symbolizes several further notions—Greek, Western man and free man in general. This complex gypsy cannot compromise—the influence of Nietzsche is evident here—and finds his freedom incompatible with the social environment in which he lives. So he voluntarily destroys all the values he has tried to serve—fatherland, religion and love—and sinks to 'the lowest steps of the ladder of evil'. There he finally finds his wings, 'his former great wings' and, with the help of the old hermit's violin, raises all the values he has condemned to their proper elevated status again, to a superior 'intellectual' world. The new generation, the offspring of 'fearless man' (the man of iron will-power) and of the 'never-smiling girl' (who symbolizes science) are those who will build the new world, the New Olympus. Thus the *Dodecalogue of the Gypsy*, finishing on an optimistic note in keeping with the belief of the nineteenth century in science, presents Palamas, the prophet-poet, foretelling a bright future for the Greeks and for mankind in general.

In the *Dodecalogue of the Gypsy* all the virtues and all the shortcomings of Palamas's poetry are evident. There is a splendid wealth of imagery and a great mastery of rhythm and sound; and the dedication of the poet to his mission as a Greek cannot fail to impress. But it is true to say that there is also much that is formless and vague, an inability to create sharply defined characters and to construct successfully dramatic scenes; nor are the arguments introduced ever followed to their logical conclusion. The grafting of image upon image, which no doubt owes much to the technique of the French Symbolists, is indeed impressive, but the fluidity of Palamas's shifting symbols is baffling and damages the artistic illusion. Moreover, there are few novel philosophical ideas in the poem. However, this remarkable work is a landmark not only in the writing of Palamas, but also in the history of modern Greek literature, for with it we see modern Greek poetry moving away at last from a narrowly national sphere into the wider world of international thought and aspiration.

Palamas's second major work, *The King's Flute*, appeared in print complete in 1910. The years 1904–8, when the body of the poem was composed and partly published, were the most dramatic period in the struggle between Bulgars and Greeks in Turkish-occupied Macedonia, when an irregular warfare was raging under the eyes of the crumbling Ottoman Empire. This struggle inspired Palamas to write his twentieth-century epic, for which he chose as hero the Byzantine emperor Basil II, the 'Bulgar-Slayer' (Βουλγαροκτόνος), who in the tenth century had destroyed the Bulgarian empire that had threatened Byzantium.

In this epic Basil II is once again a shifting symbol, representing the historical figure of the emperor, Greek heroism in general—the continuity of the Greek heroic spirit having been inspired no doubt by Constantine Paparrigopoulos' *History of the Greek Nation*—and the poet himself. It is interesting that Palamas chose Athens and the Parthenon, not Constantinople and Santa Sophia, as symbols of the continuity of Greek history; and this he was able to do because in 1018 Basil II came to the Parthenon, which had been converted long before into the majestic Church of Our Lady, to offer thanksgiving to God for his victory over the Bulgars.

The King's Flute owes its name and its beginning to a strange incident related in the medieval chronicle of Pachymeres[19] which had excited the imagination of the poet. There we are told that Michael Palaeologus, prior to the recapture of Constantinople from the Franks in 1259, found in the ruined church of St John the Evangelist, near the walls of the city, the relics of a man's body with a shepherd's pipe in his mouth. A lettered stone close by indicated that the coffin of the corpse, now resting against a wall, was that of Basil II, the 'Bulgar-Slayer'. Palamas worked out this story to serve his own ends. He conceived the king's flute as another form of epic muse, whose song could span the ages and through the story of the past give its prophetic message for the future of the Greeks.

The poem consists of twelve cantos and two prologues and is composed in non-rhyming fifteen-syllable lines, the traditional heroic metre of the 'epic' of Digenis Akritas and of the Klephtic folk songs.[20] Cantos 3, 4, 5 and 6, which form the core of the epic story, are given over to descriptions of Basil's achievements and to his long, triumphant march through Greece at the head of his armies in order to reach Athens and the Parthenon. One cannot fail to admire the quantity and variety of historical, mythological, folkloric and geographical material of which the poet has made use, or indeed his linguistic skill and originality in linking modern Greece with her historical past at every step of this long journey.

Between Canto 9, when Basil confesses his sins to the Mother of God, and the end of Canto 11, there are long and incoherent sections of Byzantine history, descriptions of Constantinople and details about the life of the emperor. At the same time a number of short, independent prayers, reminiscent of Byzantine *theotokia*,[21] sustain the undertone of the devotional atmosphere.

As these confessions proceed, the historical figure of Basil II, the ruthless warrior who reflects many of the characteristics of Nietzsche's Superman, gradually recedes and merges with the person of the poet, so that in Canto 11 the emperor's prayers become Palamas's vision of the future. The theme of decline and revival emerges once again, and we are told that new worlds—Europe, America and the East—will succeed Byzantium and that new creeds—capitalism and socialism—will take the place of the old religions. Finally, a new, 'ideal' world will arise, where only 'true values' will reign supreme. For the present, however, the poet stresses, the heroic example of Basil II remains valid, for men always seek a leader, and war and force are the powers which destroy or sustain a state. The poem thus ends on an epic note, for it is the heroic spirit that Palamas hopes to kindle in the Greeks. Canto 12 is but a short epilogue of fifty lines which brings us back to the initial scene of the ruined chapel of St John the Evangelist, where the corpse crumbles to the ground and the flute lies silent, 'a reed to be thrown away'.

As with most of Palamas's longer compositions, the structure of *The King's Flute* is apospasmatic, episodic in the derogatory sense. Here too, as in the *Dodecalogue*, the poet is incapable of creating a concrete, tangible central figure, for, as we have seen, the symbol of Basil II shifts from the historical person to the abstract notion of heroism and finally to the person of the poet. Moreover, there is no novel or coherent approach to the major problems of war and peace, of nationalism and humanity as a whole, of life and death; and the style is much too profuse, burdened by too many adjectives and too much metaphor.

It is only fair to stress, however, that there are a number of excellent poetic passages in this work, such as the First Prologue and the descriptions of the Prince's Islands and of the Empress Theodora, of Athens and the Parthenon, of the quality of the Attic light. Nor should the linguistic and the metrical achievement of Palamas go unmentioned, for he transposed into personal poetry a large number of obscure demotic words, created many new, compound ones and explored with admirable dexterity all the possible variations in the use of the fifteen-syllable line. That metrical achievement alone would ensure a prominent place for *The King's Flute* in modern Greek poetry, to say nothing of the poem's rich imagery and wealth of historical, mythological, geographical and folkloric information that has been transmuted into real poetry. Finally, it should be noted that this is the only twentieth-century European epic to have been composed so far.

The great creative period of Palamas continued until roughly 1915, when he published *Altars*, in many of the poems of which we find reflected the spirit prevailing in Greece during the First World War; they are notable for the depth of their humane feelings.[22] To this period also belong the collections *Harsh and Timid Verses*, *Pentasyllables*, *Sentimental Whisperings*,

The City and Loneliness, *The Sorrows of the Lagoon* and *Satirical Exercises*; with the exception of the last, which consists of criticism of the political and social life of Greece, all share a certain sadness and a tendency to look back on youth with nostalgia.

In many of these volumes poems of extraordinary power and beauty are included, such as *The Satyr and the Naked Song* in *The City and Loneliness* and the introductory poem to *Pentasyllables*, though *The Sorrows of the Lagoon* is the most effective as a complete collection. In it the poet returns to the scenery of his childhood, the sad, flat lagoon that stretches before Missolonghi, and the majority of the poems are personal recollections or incidents from the poet's own town.[23]

Between the years 1915 and 1917 a second series of *Pentasyllables* was composed, and these were followed by a collection of 102 sonnets, the *Dekatetrasticha*, *The Evening Fires* and *Poems of a Single Form* and by a second series of *Sentimental Whisperings*, in which, once again, a preoccupation with the past is evident and a sad note is struck on the whole.

Palamas was elected a founder member of the Academy of Athens and was honoured as a Chevalier de l'Ordre de la Légion d'Honneur by the French Government. When he retired from his post as Secretary to the University of Athens in 1928 he devoted himself to the preparation of his unpublished or uncollected poems. A result of this was the appearance in 1930 of the remarkable collections *Timid and Harsh Verses*, *Prose Paths*, *The Cycle of Tetrastichs* and *Music to a New Accent*, followed in 1931 by *Passages and Greetings* and, in 1935, in spite of the stroke he suffered in 1933, by *The Nights of Phemios*. In these collections, and especially in *Timid and Harsh Verses*, real masterpieces can be found, such as the poems *The Madman's Song*, *The Swan and Leda*, *Vanna* or *Thomas*. (But side by side with these outstanding works there is a considerable amount of 'old man's' poetry.) Finally, in 1935, Palamas surprised his admirers by publishing in the journal *Nea Grammata*[24] his *Homeric Hymn* cast in a modern version of the heroic hexameter and conceived against the background of the Homeric *Hymn to Demeter*. After the poet's death a further collection of poems, *The Evening Fires*, was published, which included *The Great Garden*, a beautiful, sad poem which suggests that at the end of his life—the exact date of the poem's composition is unknown—Palamas was disillusioned and had seen all the dreams for which he had worked remain unfulfilled.

It is hard to overrate the significance of Palamas in the revival of modern Greek poetry. By rejecting the Romantics and the 'purist' form of Greek, he infused new life into Greek poetry; he led a group of his contemporaries and all the younger poets who followed him into a fresh world of literature in which all the possibilities of the modern Greek language and its rhythms were explored. Together with these, he scrutinized and put at the service of modern Greek verse not only ancient and medieval Greek poetry, history, mythology and folklore and the Greek landscape, but much of the great literature and philosophy of the West as well. Nor should his brilliant literary criticism or his prose writings, among which his short stories occupy a place of honour, be overlooked.[25]

Palamas is primarily a lyrical poet. The dramatic and the epic element, though naturally not absent from his major works, are hardly as developed in him. The wealth, sharpness and originality of his imagery, his unerring feeling for sound and rhythm, his deep sincerity and his ability to fuse the great past with the present of Greece secure for him an outstanding position in nineteenth- and twentieth-century Western poetry. It is true to say, however, that like most authors who have written a great deal—his output was gigantic—he tends to be repetitive, and like most Greeks of his generation he did not always eschew rhetorical exuberance and a tendency to abstraction.

Johannes Polemis

Johannes Polemis (1862–1924), the third important member of the 'Generation of the Eighties', was a poet of much less power and scope than either Palamas or Drosinis. His family came from the island of Andros, but he was born in Athens, where he also studied law; later he read philosophy in Paris. After his return to Greece he served in the Ministry of Education, became Secretary of the School of Fine Arts and founded the Society of Greek Playwrights.

Polemis started composing poetry at the age of thirteen and, like most members of his generation, later came under the influence of the French Parnassians, from which he never escaped. But side by side with this, older Romantic trends, though admittedly muted, are evident in his works. Polemis's first poems appeared in *Rabagas* and *Hestia*, but from 1883 he proceeded to publish nine collections of his own[26] and an anthology of poetry for children called *The Child's Muse* (1914). His lyrical verse enjoyed great popularity in his lifetime and was awarded the first prize at the Philadelpheios Competition of 1888 and the National Prize for Letters ('Ἀριστεῖον Γραμμάτων) in 1918.

Polemis's poetry is mainly lyrical. He also wrote some weak verse plays (one-act plays, on the whole) and translated into modern Greek a few *Idylls* of Theocritus, Euripides' *Electra* and Victor Hugo's *Hernani*. His verse is facile and shallow. There are no thrilling flights of imagination and no true psychological insight to liven up his writings, whose diction and rhythms, though pleasing enough, are never exciting. The best of Polemis's poems can be found in his collections *The Old Violin*, whose title poem is deeply moving, and *The Broken Marbles*.[27]

Georgios Strategis

The last and least influential of the leading figures of the 'Generation of the Eighties' was Georgios Strategis (1860–1938), who was born on the island of Spetsae and studied law in Athens, Paris and Berlin. After a brief sojourn in Alexandria he came to live and to work as a lawyer and notary in the Piraeus.

Like all the other young poets of the 1880s, he published his first works in the periodical *Don't Lose Yourself* and then proceeded to the edition of his first collection of poems, called *Rhododendrons*, in 1880. Eleven years later he achieved a Pan-Hellenic reputation with his poem *Eros and Psyche*, which was composed in the 'purist' idiom and was awarded the prize of the Philadelpheios Poetry Competition.

However, the Demotic Movement and the example of Palamas and Drosinis induced him to compose 'modern' poetry in the demotic, though he never succeeded in freeing himself completely from the influence of Achilles Paraschos. Patriotic enthusiasm characterizes the verse of Strategis, much of which sings of an idealized Greece and great Greek achievements, but the inspiration is on the whole weak, the tone pale and the form never fully worked out. Of the seven collections he published[28] (for he also wrote short plays of no literary value and a short story in the Tsakonian dialect, and he translated plays from French and German), the best are *Home Songs* (*Τραγούδια τοῦ Σπιτιοῦ*, 1889) and *What the Waves Say* (1919).[29]

The lesser poets

Of the lesser poets of the 1880s, Georgios Souris and Demetrios Kokkos are the most noteworthy, both of whom distinguished themselves in the composition of light-hearted, humorous verse. Modern Greek poetry, which is so rich in lyrical verse, has little satirical or humorous verse to boast of. Of the products of the Old School of Athens, only the *Satires* of Alexandros Soutsos are worthy of mention, and those of the School of the Ionian Islands, only the humorous poems of Andreas Laskaratos. The New School of Athens is a little richer in this respect, for besides the *Satirical Exercises* and the *Dekatetrasticha* of Palamas, it can also claim the writings of Souris and Kokkos, the best of which are by no means negligible. On the other hand, the satirical verse on Greek political life of Sophocles Karydis (died 1893) and of Kleanthes Triantaphyllos (died 1889) is hardly worthy of mention.[30]

Georgios Souris (1852–1919) was born in Syros, where he attended the local high school and, after a short stay in Russia, studied classics at the

University of Athens but failed to get a degree. By 1873 he had begun to publish humorous poems and soon joined the company of Kambas, Drosinis, Palamas and Polemis. In 1883 he embarked on publishing his own weekly satirical verse journal, *Romios*, which he continued to edit single-handedly until 1918.[31] Side by side with the vast humorous panorama of Greek political, social and artistic life on which he focuses in *Romios*, Souris also wrote much other light-hearted verse, as well as short verse comedies.[32] No other writer succeeded in grasping more accurately or more vividly the idiosyncracy of the modern Greek character than Souris. His diction is mixed—demotic and erudite elements happily rub shoulders—his versification and rhymes excellent and his mixture of sparkling wit and biting social criticism arresting. His patriotism, his lyrical gift and his good-natured sense of fun made him very popular during his lifetime, and he was greatly honoured by the state at his death. Especially moving are the issues of *Romios* which appeared during the Balkan Wars of 1912–13. It is true to say that much of his humour is dated, however.

Passionate and monolithic natures like that of Psycharis condemned Souris for 'not hating and not loving anything too much'. Palamas called him 'wingless' and even K. Demaras in his *History of Modern Greek Literature* accuses him of a lack of 'social responsibility' and of a 'deeper sense of duty'. Not a word of this holds good; there can be little doubt that Greece would have been a much happier place if she had had civilized writers, less passionately involved and more good-natured, who could laugh at things and at themselves, as Souris did.

Demetrios Kokkos (1856–91), whose family came from Naxos, was born in Andritsaina in the Peloponnese, studied law in Athens and served at the Greek consulate in Trieste. He died young; he was killed by a lunatic who thought that Kokkos had ridiculed his father in one of his musical plays.

Kokkos emerged as a poet with verse published in *Rabagas, Don't Lose Yourself* and the newspapers *Asty* and *Acropolis*. Later he brought out four collections,[33] in which his penchant for humorous poetry is given rein, as well as his ambivalence towards the 'purist' and the demotic dictions. However, as a humorous and lyrical writer and as a social and political critic, he stands far below Souris. He enjoyed greater success as a writer of musical comedies of manners (Κωμειδύλλια), the music for which he also composed.[34] The most notable was *The Luck of Maroula*, which he wrote in collaboration with Demetrios Koromelas (1850–98), a prolific theatrical writer.

It would be misleading to imply that all Greek poets of the last decades of the nineteenth century belonged to the same group or that they were all under the influence of the French Parnassians. Two striking examples of complete independence are Alexandros Pallis and Argyris Eftaliotis, who were both intimately connected with the early stages of the Demotic Movement, though they spent most of their lives away from Greece.

Alexandros Pallis (1851–1935), whose family came from Epirus, was born in the Piraeus. At an early stage he interrupted his classical studies at the University of Athens and turned to commerce, spending most of his life in India and England. However, he never ceased to be deeply interested in contemporary Greek literary developments and, becoming a friend of both Psycharis and Palamas, was one of the leading champions of the demotic cause.

He engaged in the editing and translation of Classical Greek and Western European works,[35] as well as of the New Testament, the last giving rise to a violent reaction on the part of most conservative Greeks. Of his translations, the most famous is that of the *Iliad* into fifteen-syllable lines reminiscent of the demotic folk songs. It was awarded the prize of the French Society for the Promotion of Hellenic Studies and constitutes a milestone in the early development of the Demotic Movement. (It has only recently been superseded by a translation by Nikos Kazantzakis and Johannes Kakridis.) But Pallis was not only an editor and a distinguished translator of texts; he was also a poet in his own right. He composed poetry for children, published in 1889 in a collection called *Little Songs for Children*, which is included, together with his other occasional poetry, in a book entitled *Empty Walnuts*, published in 1915. The diction of Pallis's poetry is a robust demotic, influenced by folk songs, and his lyricism is fresh and lively, in spite of a didactic streak that runs through his writings.[36]

Kleanthes Michaelidis (1849–1923), who adopted the pen-name of Argyris Eftaliotis, was born in Mytilene and, like Alexandros Pallis, engaged early in life in commerce and spent most of his days in India and England. When initiated by Pallis into the Demotic Movement, he abandoned his early 'purist' linguistic views and became one of the most passionate demoticists and followers of Giannis Psycharis. He also became involved in translations and produced a full translation of the Homeric *Odyssey* into modern Greek—but he did not limit himself to that. He wrote original poetry of his own, distinguishing himself as a sonnet writer,[37] as well as a history of modern Greece, a play and, above all, noteworthy short stories.

Eftaliotis's language is a powerful, fully fledged demotic, and his verse is well-turned, but in the course of time his inspiration seems to have waned, giving way to an anti-lyrical realism.

Both Eftaliotis and Pallis, who were such influential figures in the early stages of the Demotic Movement, retained their intransigent linguistic views to the end, as only men living abroad and away from the realities of Greek life could afford to do. It was this distance from the Athenian literary scene that enabled them to follow in their poetry a course so different from the one that was being shaped in those days in Greece under the leadership of Palamas and Drosinis.

THE POETS OF THE TURN OF THE CENTURY

The *Noumas* Group

At the turn of the century a second group of young poets emerged who were all followers and admirers of Palamas. The new avant-garde journal of those days was *Noumas* (1903–24), and as most of these poets published their work in it, they are also known as the *Noumas* Group of poets.

The leading figures of this group were J. Zervos (1874–1944); K. Karthaios, the pen-name of K. Lakon (1878–1955); R. Golfis, the pen-name of D. Demetriades (1886–1957); N. Petmezas, who also wrote under the pen-name Lavras (1873–1952); and Markos Tsirimokos (1872–1939). All are minor poets,[38] who need detain us only for a moment. The service they rendered modern Greek poetry was that they explored the linguistic and rhythmical possibilities of demotic diction in personal, lyrical verse. They also translated a number of Classical Greek and Western masterpieces into a racy, popular language, which, however, seldom rose above the ideals of the first 'heroic' decade of the Demotic Movement and its blind emulation of folk songs. It should be added that Markos Tsirimokos introduced into modern Greek poetry certain traditional French forms, such as the *triolet*, the *villanelle* and the *dizain*.[39]

The influence of Symbolism

Much more important than the *Noumas* Group was a second set of poets, who also appeared on the literary scene at the turn of the century and nearly all of whom were influenced by the French Symbolists. Like the Parnassian Movement, Symbolism arrived in Greece when it was practically dead in France; it came in four successive waves, covering the years 1892–1905, 1905–15, 1915–25 and 1931–40.

Symbolism was brought to Athens in 1892 by Stephanos Stephanou (1868–1944), a minor poet and dramatist and, for a while, Director of the Royal Theatre, who published a slender book of Symbolist verse called *The Rose's Dream*. This caused a considerable stir in the Athenian world of letters, and a long and heated discussion followed among the literati, with the result that no less a man than Kostis Palamas[40] was eventually won over to Symbolism and, with him, a group of gifted young poets such as

Constantine Hadjopoulos, Johannes Gryparis and Johannes Kambysis. Miltiades Malakasis and Lambros Porphyras were also drawn to Symbolism, but to a lesser degree, whereas Kostas Krystallis, who belonged to the same group, remained totally unaffected by it. So great was the impression made by this new poetic creed that it was espoused even by Greeks living abroad, such as Apostolos Melachrinos in Constantinople.

It was not only to Baudelaire, Mallarmé and Verlaine that Greek poets and poetry lovers turned for guidance; they were also attracted by the decadents of Symbolism, men like Jules Laforgue (1860–87) and the Belgian Maurice Maeterlinck (1862–1949). The notions of a *poésie pure* and of *ars gratia artis* met with a warm enough reception for two progressive literary magazines to be founded, *Techne* (1898–9) and *Dionysos* (1901 –2), which championed these views. However, in spite of this enthusiasm among the young, the Greek poets of the turn of the century never became Symbolists in the true sense of the word, for they adopted mainly the stylistic technique of their French and German models rather than the music of their words or their abstract thoughts. We must come to the next generation of Greek poets, the so-called 'Generation of 1905' and, to a greater degree, that of the 1920s, to trace a deeper and more creative influence of Symbolism.

Judged as a whole, the impact of Symbolism upon modern Greek poetry was clearly beneficial, for, without losing its Hellenic character, it was enriched by the use of free verse and became more musical and more subtle. Before long the ridicule and hostility with which the old guard had greeted the Symbolists gave way to silent acceptance and then to admiration.

We must now briefly examine the major representatives of this new group of poets.

The senior member, Constantine Hadjopoulos (1868–1920), was born in Agrinion and, as a boy, was adopted by S. Staikos, whose fortune he later inherited. He studied law at the University of Athens, practised as a lawyer for some years in Agrinion and then devoted himself exclusively to literature. During one of his visits to Germany he met the Finnish writer Sanny Hägmann, whom he eventually married. It was in Germany that he became acquainted with the German Symbolists who so profoundly affected his writing.

Hadjopoulos was active as a poet and as a writer of prose, as well as a translator of several German, Russian and Scandinavian authors. For a time he also edited the periodicals *Techne* and *Dionysos*. At first he contributed poems to various journals under the pen-name Petros Vasilikos, but later he published four collections of poems under his own name. Of these, *Simple Ways* ('Απλοῖ τρόποι) (1920) and *Night Legends* (Βραδυνοὶ θρύλοι) (1920) are the best.[41]

Hadjopoulos is a melancholy, elegiac poet with a soft and melodious voice, whose imagery is not truly Greek but misty and northern European.[42] And yet his 'northern' Symbolism, in which the dream prevails over the allegory, had a considerable effect upon contemporary Greek poetry. Moreover, his literary criticism, his short stories and his Symbolist novel, *Autumn*, secure for him an important place in modern Greek letters.

Kostas Krystallis (1868–94), one of the few distinguished poets of that generation who remained totally unaffected by Symbolism, was born in the village of Syrrakion in Epirus, the birthplace of the poet Georgios Zalocostas.[43] As a schoolboy in Jannina he published his first poem, *The Shades of Hades*, a long, uncouth, Romantic work, which was so full of hatred for the Turks that he was obliged to flee for his life from Turkey (Jannina was then still part of the Ottoman Empire) and take refuge in Greece. In 1889, a poor persecuted shepherd boy, he reached Athens and began work as a typesetter. He was later employed by the Peloponnesus Railway Company at a meagre wage, but his poor health soon gave way, and he died of consumption at the age of twenty-six. Literature was Krystallis's passion, and in his short life he managed to produce five books of poems.[44] After his death a sixth was issued, in which various individually published works were collected. He also wrote a number of short stories.

Krystallis is one of the most genuinely 'Greek' figures of modern Greek poetry. He is the bucolic poet who sings of the countryside in 'idealized-realistic' terms. He extols the seasons, the times of day, the purity and freedom of life in the hills, with a shepherd's disdain for the flat, hot plains. His language is a robust and unadulterated demotic, punctuated by a number of dialectal expressions and full of the rhythms and the spirit of Epirot folk songs. It is clear that this pictorial poet—he was certainly not a 'thinker'—was much impressed in the early stages of his career by Valaoritis and later by Theocritus, as he came to see him.

What made his poems so attractive and so popular at the turn of the century were their moving expression of the deep nostalgia of the expatriot and their escapist rejection of harsh urban reality. Krystallis is rightly seen as one of the poets who helped most in establishing the use of the demotic in modern Greek literature and as one of the few modern Greek writers who was untouched by any foreign influence.

Mention should also be made of Constantine Manos (1869–1913), the distinguished politician and author, who was born in Athens and studied law in Leipzig and Heidelberg and, later, literature at Oxford. He was also teacher of Greek and reader to the Empress Elisabeth of Austria; he took part in the uprisings in Crete against the Turks and in the 'Macedonian Struggle' against the Bulgarians; he became a member of the Greek Parliament; and he was finally killed in the Balkan Wars.

As a student Manos published his only book of verse, a collection of playful love lyrics called *Words of the Heart,* which was awarded first prize in the Philadelpheios Competition; but he continued to compose and publish verse in various literary journals until the end of his life, and there is much that remains unpublished. Manos is by no means an outstanding poet, but he holds his own among his contemporaries.

On the other hand, Miltiadis Malakasis (1869–1943) is one of the most impressive lyrical poets of this group, ranking second only to Gryparis. He was born in Missolonghi, studied law at the University of Athens, spent much of his life in France, travelled widely in the West and was awarded the National Prize for Arts and Letters.

His poetry, which is scattered throughout various journals and collected in several volumes which he himself published, falls into two distinct periods. In the first, which covers the years 1898–1910, the influence of Jean Moréas is paramount; he was a poet whom Malakasis greatly admired and whose *Stances* he translated into modern Greek. He owed to Moréas the brevity and harmony of much of his own verse, the suggestive lyrical outbursts as well as the occasional lighter touches that lend elegance and refinement to his writing. It was during this first period that Malakasis also wrote a weak one-act play called *The Mistress of the Tower* (1904). In the second period, extending from 1910 until his death, Malakasis lived and worked under the shadow of Palamas, whose book *The Sorrows of the Lagoon* seems to have brought the widely travelled and Westernized poet back to his Greek roots, to Missolonghi and the robust Rumeliot life. This he described in his two best books of verse, *The Asphodels* (1918) and the *Songs of Missolonghi* (1920), which contain his masterpieces, *Batarias, Takis Ploumas* and *The Little Nightingales Say So.*

The poetry of Malakasis is remarkable for its lightness of touch, the dancing quality of its rhythms and the musicality of its language. But it is also unquestionably superficial, with little passion and no interest in the serious concerns of life, except for love. Even there, the tragic side of Eros is never broached; for all that love be unrequited, it is presented as a soft, gentle emotion. It is true that the passage of time, so often referred to, sheds a graceful melancholy upon much of Malakasis's verse, but one cannot help feeling that in this too there is something artificial and conventional. Only in his Missolonghi poems, and especially those dealing with the violinist Batarias, does a manly, Rumeliot vigour permeate his verse, giving it an almost epic ring, which one feels is both original and sincere.

There can be little doubt that the most gifted and the most significant poet of the first post-Palamas generation was Johannes Gryparis (1872–1942). He was born on the island of Siphnos and was educated first in Constantinople and later at the University of Athens, where he read classics. His classical and other literary and philosophic studies he subsequently furthered in Italy, France and Germany.

He started his career as a schoolmaster in Constantinople, where he also became the co-editor of the literary journal *Philological Echo*. When he settled in Greece permanently he continued to teach, though for a while he joined the Greek civil service and also served as Director of the National Theatre. Like Malakasis, he was awarded the National Prize for Arts and Letters.

Gryparis, who was also a gifted painter, was not a prolific writer. He ceased to publish original verse early in life, preferring to translate Classical Greek and other European masterpieces. His translation of the complete works of Aeschylus into modern Greek is famous, to say nothing of his renderings of parts of Sophocles, Homer, Catullus and Goethe.

Though his earlier poems show a debt to the Parnassians, especially Heredia and Théophile Gautier, Gryparis later borrowed the techniques of the Symbolists. To the first period belong his faultless sonnets, known as *Scarabs*, and his eleven-syllable poems called *Terracottae*. To the second belong the *Intermedia* (1899–1901), in which his verse becomes freer and more musical and his images more strikingly suggestive. Gryparis also made use of legends drawn from popular tradition and medieval writings, as can be seen from his *Tryphon and Chrysophrydi* and his well-known poem *The Pedlar* (ʽΟ Πραματευτής). In 1919 Gryparis collected and published all his earlier poetry in the only book he issued in his lifetime, *Scarabs and Terracottae*; but more poems, some of them oustanding, were found among his papers after his death and are now included in his *Collected Works*.

Gryparis played an important role in the development of modern Greek poetry. It is he who fostered the tradition inaugurated by Palamas and the Demotic Movement through his extensive knowledge of ancient Greek literature, folk songs and peasant folklore. The general impression we gain from his poetry is that of a terse style uncluttered by adjectives or unusual words but vibrant with striking images, metaphors and similes and perfectly finished. An admirer and follower of Psycharis, he managed to shape a frugal and restrained diction—a rare accomplishment in those days—in spite of his coining of many compound words. His effect upon subsequent poets, especially Angelos Sikelianos,[45] was remarkable.

Spelios Pasagiannes (1874–1910), another interesting poet of this group, was born in the village of Castania, near Sparta. Although he initially intended to study medicine in Athens, he soon interrupted his studies to devote himself to literature. He also travelled to broaden his education but fell ill and, like Krystallis, died young.

Pasagiannes began his literary career by contributing verse and short stories to various journals, including *Techne*, and quickly succumbed to the Symbolist devices and techniques which its editors, Hadjopoulos and Gryparis, were then propagating. During his short life Pasagiannes did not publish a book of his own verse, but after his death his brother,

Kostas, brought out a volume of his collected poetry called *Echoes* (1920).[46] This includes the series by the same name, which is, in fact, a single work, as well as two further groups of poems, *The Cowherd* and *The Tearful Girl* (Ἡ Δάϰρυνη).

The main interest of Pasagiannes's verse is linguistic, for he wrote a robust, pronounced demotic, full of idiomatic usages and rare words.[47] However, in spite of his vivid imagination and his sure grasp of the picturesque, he never goes beyond simple lyrical descriptions, which are occasionally unpleasantly flabby, and his metres are often faulty. No deep thoughts can be found in his verse, which gives the impression that it stopped short at the point of experimentation. Nevertheless, his language did have some impact on later poets and can even be traced in the poetry of Sikelianos and Melachrinos.[48]

Johannes Kambysis (1872–1901), another poet of this group who died young, was born in Korone in the Peloponnese, studied law in Athens and then travelled to Germany to further his education. In his short life he produced prose plays, short stories, dramatic and lyrical poems and translations; and, in collaboration with Constantine Hadjopoulos and others, he founded the periodical *Dionysos*. He is better-known as a play-wright—his best play, *The Mother's Ring*, was repeatedly and successfully produced in Athens—and as a short-story writer than as a lyrical poet. His poetry, consisting of three dramatic poems (*In the Clouds*, *The East* and *Aregiannos*) and two collections of lyrics (*The Shadow of Wisdom* and *The Book of Fragments*), is dominated by a Romantic symbolism and betrays a true poetic talent, though it never reached maturity.[49]

Zacharias Papantoniou (1877–1940), who was born in Karpenissi and who abandoned his medical studies to dedicate himself to art and letters, stands, in a sense, apart from the poets of this group; he was less of a Symbolist and more of an eclectic than any of the others. After taking up journalism and serving as a *nomarch* (Prefect of Department), he became Director of the National Picture Gallery and was later awarded the National Prize for Arts and Letters for his distinguished art criticism and his other writings.

Papantoniou left four books of poetry: a weak verse play called *The Dead Man's Oath* (1929); *The Swallows* (1920), a book of poems for children; and two collections of lyrics, *War Songs* (1897) and *Divine Gifts* (1928). In 1923 he published *Prose Rhythms*, a book of poems in prose, a hybrid literary genre of which he is the most important Greek representative. *War Songs* is a young man's work, patriotic and sensitive but totally immature. On the other hand, in *Divine Gifts* he appears as a mature and calm observer of nature and of human life, deeply pessimistic but without a trace of bitterness or despair.[50]

Last but not least of this group is Lambros Porphyras (1878–1932), the pen-name of Demetrios Sypsomos, whose family came from the island of

Chios. He finished his secondary education in the Piraeus, where he lived most of his life as a recluse, associating only with a few men of letters and with humble fishermen and workmen, in whose company he enjoyed drinking. It was his poor health and shy nature that led him to withdraw from society and to refrain from furthering his studies.

Even as a schoolboy Porphyras composed verse. His first poem appeared in 1894 in an obscure and short-lived magazine called *Stadium* (1894–5); but his truly creative years were the first decade of the twentieth century, and he included most of the poems of those days in his collection *Shadows* (1920). More of his work was published after his death, in a volume called *Musical Voices*.[51] The poetry of Porphyras is refined and musical, pervaded by a sincere sadness. It is not surprising that, as a great admirer of Verlaine and Moréas, he was also attracted to Symbolism. Porphyras's world is a gentle world of landscapes and seascapes, in which trees and waves, wind and rain and simple folk are depicted with a restrained lyrical nobility. He wrote a few autobiographical poems, such as the well-known *The Journey*, in which Annoula, a girl with whom the poet was in love, appears, or *Lacrimae rerum*, written about his sister, or *Now and Never*. However, it is true to say that this soft, lyrical world of Porphyras has little depth and often verges on sentimentality. There is no linguistic or metrical originality in his work—his language and rhymes are conventional—nor can any development be traced in it.

THE DEMOTIC MOVEMENT AND GREEK POETRY COMPOSED OUTSIDE GREECE

The beneficial influence of the Demotic Movement upon modern Greek poetry spread beyond the boundaries of the country and was felt by Greek writers living in Constantinople, Smyrna and elsewhere in the Ottoman Empire. The channel through which the new linguistic and literary views that had conquered Athens were disseminated to the Greeks in Turkey were the various Athenian journals and the literary periodicals of Constantinople, most prominently *Philological Echo* and *Zoe* (1902–9, 1919–22), whose editor was Apostolos Melachrinos. Gradually, it came about that many of the older Romantic poets abandoned their original 'purist' diction, adopted the demotic and turned to the tenets of Symbolism, while new poets emerged, keen to follow modern trends. With the end of the First World War and the defeat of Greece at the hands of the Turks in 1922, all these writers were obliged to leave their homes and came to live in Greece, where they continued their literary activities. The most noteworthy of these were Apostolos Melachrinos (1883–1952) and Homeros

Bekes (1886–1972) from Constantinople; Michael Argyropoulos (1862–1949), Angelos Semeriotis (1870–1944), Alexandros Photiadis (1870–1943) and Stelios Seferiadis (1873–1951) from Smyrna; and Apostolos Mammelis (1876–1935), also from Asia Minor. The Demotic Movement also affected much of the poetry being written in Cyprus.[52]

Of this group, Apostolos Melachrinos[53] should be singled out, for he developed into one of the most important Greek Symbolists. Born in Brăila in Romania, he was educated in Constantinople and lived most of his life there. He published two collections of poems, *The Way Leads* (1904) and *Variations* (1909), and translated plays of Euripides and Aristophanes into modern Greek. He was a great admirer of Mallarmé and of Gryparis. The musicality of his verse is its finest quality; he aspired to become the Greek Mallarmé but did not have the capacity to distinguish between the serious and the trivial aspects of language. However, he can claim to have written one of the best poems in modern Greek, *It is Raining*. He was never able to repeat the achievement.

THE SECOND POST-PALAMAS GENERATION
('THE GENERATION OF 1905')

The year 1905 can be considered an important landmark in the history of modern Greek poetry, for it was roughly then that a new group of gifted poets appeared on the literary scene. The three most distinguished were Angelos Sikelianos, Nikos Kazantzakis and Kostas Varnalis; but others should be mentioned, such as Soteris Skipis, Markos Avgeris, Romos Philyras and Napoleon Lapathiotis, as well as two noteworthy poetesses, Myrtiotissa and Emily Stephanou Daphne. Initially, the impact of Symbolism was felt by all these poets to a greater or lesser degree, but the major figures were quick to break free and soon found their individual voices.

Angelos Sikelianos

The central figure of the second post-Palamas generation is undoubtedly Angelos Sikelianos (1884–1951). Born on the island of Leucas and later sent to Athens to study law, he never completed his studies. In 1906 he married the American Eva Palmer, who put her wealth at his disposal, so that Sikelianos could travel widely and develop his natural gifts.

Sikelianos was an avid, though undisciplined, reader; what resulted from his studies was the fusion of traditional Greek and advanced Western cultural elements which can be traced in his poetry. He also developed a strange personal, mystical philosophy, which permeated his longer writings and took concrete shape in the movement known as the 'Delphic Idea'. This movement owed its name to the fact that Sikelianos came to regard Delphi as one of the great sources of wisdom and of inspiration derived from the 'Orphic tradition', as he conceived and interpreted it. He strove to give the movement's esoteric teachings expression in the form of lectures, poems and essays; but the most significant of these attempts was a plan to found a university at Delphi which would serve as an international centre of spiritual and communal learning. The immediate consequences of the 'Delphic Idea' were two festivals held at Delphi in 1927 and 1930, which brought in their wake not only the financial ruin of the Sikelianos couple, but also the collapse of their marriage. They divorced shortly after, and the poet was condemned to poverty and to a city life in Athens, where he never felt at ease.

Sikelianos later married again, and his second wife, Anna, gave him sustained moral support and comfort during the last years of his life. But the privations and horrors of the war had undermined his health; he died in 1951, after a prolonged illness, broken in body, though not in spirit.

Sikelianos wrote both lyrical and dramatic poetry, which should be examined separately.

THE LYRICAL POETRY

After publishing some early lyrics in the avant-garde periodicals of those days, *Dionysos*, *Noumas*, *Zoe* and *Akritas*, Sikelianos composed his first important work, *The Visionary*, in 1907.[54] It is an autobiographical poem, written in free verse, and describes in ecstatic terms the poet's first contact with nature during adolescence and early manhood. It is a true hymn to the Greek countryside and country life, which is transformed at the end from a paean to physical vigour and beauty, as the poet feels the urge to be lifted 'among the stars'.

In order to find the 'true source of life . . . his original self', Sikelianos tried to identify more and more with the Greek tradition, as he understood it. This is the subject of his second long, lyrical poem, *The Prologue of Life*, written some ten years after *The Visionary*. It consists of five parts (five 'Consciousnesses', as he called them), each made up of rhapsodic hymns.[55] There Dionysus is seen as the essential principle of everything — rock, flower, animal and human being — and the poet, having realized the 'meaning' of the 'Biological God' he has met,[56] proceeds to tackle the four major problems in life, those of 'my earth', 'my race', 'woman' and 'faith'. He illuminates them as an 'initiated person' and forces them to comply with his central demand, that of personal creativeness. *The Prologue of Life* includes many felicitous descriptions, though they are often encumbered by symbols drawn from the Orphic and Pythagorean traditions;[57] but, by contrast with *The Visionary*, Sikelianos here makes poor use of free verse and resorts too frequently to similes.

Though one may have certain qualms about *The Prologue of Life*, no reservations are possible with respect to the admirable series of lyrics which Sikelianos published in 1915 in his book *Verses*. They display a perfect mastery of form, a virile, harmonious language—profuse but not rhetorical—a rare depth of feeling and brilliant, novel imagery. They are perhaps the best poems Sikelianos ever wrote, and among them are some masterpieces, such as *The First Rain, Pan, Pantarkes, Thalero, John Keats* and *Dante's Mother*, poems that would do honour to any literature.

After 1919 Sikelianos embraced a completely 'visionary mode' of creation.[58] The first major work in which this is evident is *The Mother of God*, a poem which he never concluded; it is a mystical hymn to Mother Nature, seen as *natura naturans perpetuam divinitatem*.[59] The completed part consists of 275 rhyming fifteen-syllable couplets, which fall into five sections. It begins by describing the pain which death evokes and proceeds to celebrate love and nature's capacity for rebirth; finally, it acclaims 'cosmic knowledge' and the supreme joy that it can give. The 'Mother of God' is none other than the 'great primeval image of Mother Nature', but with the shifting quality of Sikelianos's symbols it gradually comes to be identified with the Mother of God and the creative capacity of Eternal Earth, as well as the figure of Eternal Woman.

However confused (and, at the same time, over-simplified) this pattern of thought may be, reflecting the poet's struggle to reduce the many-faceted reality of life to a few basic, original 'units', it is sustained by musical, forceful diction and by excellent imagery. The poem was inspired by the death of Sikelianos's sister, to whom he was devoted.

His next major work was *The Easter of the Greeks*, which was also never finished; only eleven long sections of it were published, all cast in rhyming four-line stanzas. The poet himself tells us that he wished to express his direct spiritual contact with the great 'subconscious religious world', which can be found 'in the depths of any time',[60] and for that purpose he chose the Christian 'myth'. Typically, however, he did not limit himself to this but fused with it Greek mythological elements, like the *Hymn to Helen* or the *Song of the Argonauts*, hoping that by a synthesis of pagan and Christian components he could achieve a unified, metaphysical approach to the mystery of the cosmos through a universal and eternal myth.[61]

Needless to say, Sikelianos did not achieve what he set out to do, and the pagan and Christian elements are not always happily blended; for example, the Annunciation of the Virgin by a fully armed Eros and the comparison of Mary with Semele are not in the best of taste. But, as in most of Sikelianos's poetry, the diction is vivid and virile, the imagery evocative and many of the daring similes arresting, even though the tone is far from being uniform.

A third major lyrical work of Sikelianos, the *Delphic Word*, consisting of four independent songs, was written to propagate the 'Delphic Idea'. The poetry in this piece is incidental and fragmentary and does not compare with the successful parts of *The Mother of God* or of *The Easter of the Greeks*.

Of much greater significance—indeed, of the greatest significance in the history of modern Greek poetry—are some of the shorter lyrics which Sikelianos composed in the 1930s, of which *The Sacred Road*, *Lilith*, *The Study of Death*, *The Greatest Lesson* and *The Attic Song* should be singled out. These poems differ greatly in content, form and tone but all show Sikelianos at the peak of his 'second springtime'. *The Sacred Road* is clearly the best poem of all. It is the only work in which Sikelianos succeeded in putting his mystical philosophy across in a simple, moving manner. And this he achieved by starting from a concrete, personal experience (a meeting with a gypsy and two bears on the way to Eleusis), which he used as a springboard from which to rise to his general abstractions about the universe.

A few words must be added about Sikelianos's erotic poetry, in the course of the composition of which, he tells us,[62] he moved from 'fragmentation' (that is, a departure from the original divine unity whose very kernel was *sexus*) to a full union with the 'flame of love', the 'God'. The whole process starts with *The Hymn of the Great Return* and culminates in *The Study of Death*; but an important landmark in this erotic journey is the poem *Lilith*, in which the form of the woman whom Sikelianos loved reawakened in him the 'mystic primeval picture of the Feminine'.

The poems that Sikelianos grouped under the title *Epinicean Odes II* were all written after the Italian attack on Greece in 1940. Of these, *Kleisoura*, *The Stygean Oath*, *The Unwritten Poem* and *The Story of Solon* are outstanding. In some, the patriotic element, in others the political-social element prevails. Perhaps the most moving poem which Sikelianos wrote during the Second World War was the one on the death of Kostis Palamas, which he recited at the poet's funeral in 1943.

THE DRAMATIC WORKS

The dramatic works of Sikelianos are greatly inferior to his lyrical poetry. Drama is clearly not his medium, for the most attractive side of his tragedies is their lyricism; in structure, dramatic conflict and characterization they are faulty. Moreover, they are not appropriate vehicles for his strange, mystical philosophy, which only burdens and confuses them.

In 1932, as an introduction to his tragedies, Sikelianos wrote *The Dithyramb of the Rose*, an allegorical work in dialogue form containing the same message to mankind that we find in his major lyrical works: a call for purification and for a direct, esoteric, mystical union with the 'God', attained after an arduous 'climb'. The tragedies which followed—*The*

Sibyl (1940), *Daedalus in Crete* (1943), *Christ in Rome* (1946), *The Death of Diogenes* (1947) and the unfinished *Asclepios*—reflect both in their structure and in their use of a chorus, the pattern of Classical Greek tragedy. For Sikelianos aimed at heroic grandeur, which he tried to create by making a heroic decision the core of all his plays. They are concerned with the basic problems of freedom versus tyranny (seen, from another angle, as the individual against the state) and man's fall from unity. These, he believed, were both contemporary and eternal issues.

In his plays Sikelianos made no concession to the modern theatre, nor did he wish to speak as a twentieth-century man. His was the voice of eternity addressing 'sick' and 'enslaved' humanity and showing it the way to salvation. His message was optimistic: mankind could, if properly guided, regain an 'undivided life' and thus be 'free' and 'healthy' again.

There can be little doubt that Sikelianos's writings contain no organized philosophical thought and that their major virtue is their exquisite lyricism. Yet in all fairness it should be admitted that his vague, impracticable visions, which became entangled with the world of the subconscious and many elements of established religions, add a further dimension to his poetry, something of the metaphysical and heroic, a sometimes titanic grandeur. After Palamas, he is perhaps the greatest poet of modern Greece. It is a pity that the rhetorical quality of much of his poetry does not lend itself to translation. That is the main reason why he is so much less well-known in the West than Cavafy, Seferis and Elytis.

If the early roots of his poetry can be traced to Whitman, Nietzsche, Palamas, D'Annunzio and Claudel, to say nothing of Pasagiannis, he certainly soon outgrew them and established his own distinct voice and style. Among his many admirers and followers were Kazantzakis, Varnalis, Avgeris, Kambanis, Douras, Karzis and Takis Varlas. In some of them the poetic flame did not burn long, and in others it turned to prose; his most faithful disciple was perhaps Takis Varlas.

Nikos Kazantzakis

Nikos Kazantzakis (1883–1957) was born in Heracleion, in Crete, where he also received his elementary education. Later he studied at the Franciscan High School in Naxos and then law at the universities of Athens and Paris.

During his life he travelled widely and lived for some time in Vienna and Berlin, where he became acquainted with the misery and social unrest of post-war Germany. His travels included journeys to the Soviet Union, Japan, China and Spain, where he was a press correspondent during the Civil War in 1936. England he visited as a guest of the British Council during the first months of the Second World War. The rest of the war he spent in Greece and, when the country was liberated from the Axis powers, he became involved in politics, establishing a socialist group and serving for a short time as Minister without Portfolio in the Greek Government. In June 1945 he left Greece and settled permanently in Antibes, in the south of France, where he continued writing and supervising the editions and the translations of his works. Taken ill on his way to visit China in 1957, he died in Freiburg and was buried at his birthplace, Heracleion.

Kazantzakis was a many-faceted and restless man. At first he believed in an aristocratic nationalism, as professed by Ion Dragoumis, but during his stay in Berlin he turned to the revolutionary Communist ideas in vogue after the end of the First World War. It was then that he wrote the *Asketike* (his *Ascetic Exercises*, later published under the title *Salvatores Dei*), which he considered the 'seed' from which all his later work 'grew'.[63] Subsequently, after his three visits to the Soviet Union (1925–9), he denied his former social and political views and turned to nihilism. Repudiating the 'prophets' who had possessed his mind—Nietzsche, Buddha and Marx—Kazantzakis adopted Odysseus as his prototype and hero.

Kazantzakis distinguished himself and won an international reputation as a prose writer and a poet; but his many remarkable works in prose—novels, philosophical treatises, plays, critical essays and travel books—are beyond the scope of this book.[64]

This writer made his appearance on the Greek literary scene in 1908 with a prose play called *The Master-Builder*,[65] in which the influence of Nietzsche is evident, enhanced by a deep sensuality; for the notion of the Superman haunted him from early youth until the end of his life. Kazantzakis, whose emotional and religious worlds were the constant prey of doubt, was also haunted by the figure of Christ; after a visit to Mount Athos he wrote a verse play called *Christ* in 1915. This was followed in 1922 by two further tragedies, *Buddha* and *Odysseus* (the former in prose and the latter in verse), which illustrate a new spiritual orientation wrought largely by his experiences in post-war Germany, his acquaintance with Oswald Spengler's views on the end of the civilizations and the effect which the Asia Minor disaster of 1922 had upon him.

Before the Second World War Kazantzakis composed three new tragedies, *Nicephoros Phocas* (1928) in verse, *Melissa* (1937) in prose and *Julian the Apostate* (1939) once again in verse; in the post-war years (1944–9), when engaged in writing his novels, he also composed a number of plays on ancient and modern, mythological, biblical and historical figures, as can be seen from their titles: *Prometheus the Fire-Bearer*, *Prometheus Bound* and *Prometheus Released* (these form a trilogy), *Kapodistrias*, *Kouros* (or *Theseus*), *Constantine Palaeologus*, *Sodom and Gomorrah* and *Christopher Columbus*. Of these *Sodom and Gomorrah*, *Kouros* and *Christopher Columbus* are in prose.[66] In all his verse plays he favours the ten- and the twelve-syllable iambic line, and he has a lively, racy diction, but they are wanting in lyricism.

Throughout Kazantzakis's dramatic output one can easily trace the various writers and philosophers who impressed him in the course of his life, most prominently Nietzsche with his Superman and Bergson with his *élan vital*. But despite this, and although he poured much of his anguish into his tragedies as he grew older—even more than into his novels—one cannot help feeling that somehow there is little real difference between them. He seems always to take up the same tragic theme, which he develops with certain variations: the solitary hero who confronts the many; the man who knows the 'great secret' (as the poet calls it) 'that the struggle is in vain' but who is also convinced that he must battle on to the end. It matters little if this man is called Julian, Constantine Palaeologus, Kapodistrias or Christopher Columbus.

But if we are to judge Kazantzakis as a poet, we must turn to his great 'philosophical' epic, the *Odyssey*, which he considered his most important work and which established his international reputation as an author. He worked on it for years; in its finished form this astonishing poem consists of 33,333—the number was symbolic for Kazantzakis—seventeen-syllable iambic verses, divided into twenty-four rhapsodies. It embodies his whole approach to life. Kazantzakis's *Odyssey* continues the story of Odysseus from the point where Homer's *Odyssey* (or perhaps one should say, Tennyson's *Ulysses*) left off. For the hero Odysseus, discontented with daily life in Ithaca, leaves the island on his last journey, accompanied this time by a small number of comrades, all social outcasts. After various adventures in Sparta, from where he abducts Helen, in Crete, where a conspiracy dethrones King Idomeneus, in Egypt, where, as in Crete, a working-class revolution breaks out, he reaches the sources of the Nile, and there, after long and solitary contemplation, he builds his own ideal city. But on the very day of its official inauguration the city is destroyed by a volcano. A second period of contemplation follows, during which Odysseus becomes convinced that there is no god, there is neither virtue nor justice in life, a conviction that for him is equivalent to complete freedom.

Thus unfettered by any religious, moral or social bonds, he sets out for his long and final journey to the South Pole, in the course of which he meets the 'great leaders of the Souls', Buddha, Christ, Lenin and others, all presented in thin disguise. He compares his nihilistic liberty with their teachings and, finding his own views superior, sails on 'to the waters of No Hope with Death at the tiller'. And indeed at the South Pole he is shipwrecked on a large iceberg, where, surrounded by all his friends (who somehow turn up), 'his great mind . . . fluttered with empty wings . . . upright through the air . . . and freed itself from its last cage, its freedom'.

The Odyssey clearly represents Kazantzakis's own journey through the world of thought; Odysseus is none other than the poet himself in epic masquerade. Once again, we find the ideas expressed in *Asketike*: solitary contemplation is the only means of achieving philosophical freedom after all ethical and social conventions have been overthrown. In a world where no god, no virtue and no justice exist—a completely nihilistic world—one should follow one's own vision, for that constitutes the only true freedom.

The poet mocks all human accomplishment and denies man any hope. What should be noted, however, is that Kazantzakis's nihilism does not curb his insatiable desire for action, nor his admiration for the human mind. These passions are the only divinities which he acknowledges. 'I do not love man. I love only the flame that devours him,' he proclaims with inhuman callousness. The only positive value that the poet seems to accept is art (the 'song') because it expresses the personal vision, the individual dream.[67] It goes without saying that the poet's views are advanced with considerable poetic licence and a number of contradictions. Moreover, Kazantzakis shows himself to be as dogmatic as any of the religions or theories he wishes to overthrow. The contradictions are a consequence partly of the disparate quality of the works he admired but not all of which he fully digested; for snatches of Plato, Sir Thomas More, Nietzsche, Marx, Freud, Spengler and Bergson, to mention only a few of the more obvious names, appear and reappear in the lines of this long epic.

It has been argued that the literary achievement of Kazantzakis's *Odyssey* lies mainly in its rich and sonorous language. This is overwhelming, certainly; it contains words that are rare, unknown and idiomatic, as well as a number that have sprung from the poet's own fertile imagination. The outcome is a diction which aims at a monumental effect but has no homogeneity and frequently degenerates into a pseudo-heroic, taunting virility—what Kostis Palamas called 'empty provocation' (ἄδειο νταϊλίκι). Moreover, the deliberately primitive atmosphere which the poet tries to create stands in direct contrast to the sophisticated philosophical thoughts and arguments which he puts forward and the abundant allegories which he uses. The style too, with its wealth of pictorial detail and protracted scenes, frequently gives the impression that Kazantzakis is simply padding out his lines—as does the metre chosen, the seventeen-syllable line, which too often sounds like an ordinary fifteen-syllable line with two more syllables limply tacked on.

However, in all fairness it must be said that there are episodes whose poetic effect is undeniable; that there is much novel and powerful imagery and several moments of lyrical, 'apocalyptic' beauty. Modern Greek poetry has unquestionably been much enriched by this formidable epic.

While he was working on the *Odyssey* (that is, from about 1933 to 1939), Kazantzakis also wrote a series of cantos, poems in *terza rima*, which are his only lyrical works (if lyrical they may be called). They are dedicated to people who played an important part in the formation of his personality, ranging from Dante and El Greco to his parents and close friends. He set out to compose twenty-four, as there were twenty-four rhapsodies in his *Odyssey*, and called them playfully 'the twenty-four bodyguards of the *Odyssey*'. They were printed after his death under the title *Tertsines*.

A discussion of Kazantzakis as a poet would not be complete without mention of his important translations into modern Greek, the most significant of which are the *Iliad* and the *Odyssey*, prepared in collaboration with Johannes Kakrides. His versions of Dante's *Divine Comedy* and the first part of Goethe's *Faust* are equally noteworthy. It is beyond the scope of this book to deal with Kazantzakis's turn to the novel in the last ten years of his life, which established his fame and proved him to be a great and a versatile writer.

Kostas Varnalis

The third leading figure of the second post-Palamas generation is Kostas Varnalis (1884–1974), who was born in Pyrgos in Bulgaria. He was educated in Philippopolis and at the universities of Athens and Paris, where he studied classics, philosophy and sociology. He then worked as a schoolmaster, first in the Greek schools of Bulgaria and later in Greece, and also engaged in journalism. In 1959 he was awarded the Lenin Prize for Peace.

The early poetry of Varnalis, which has a pronounced sentimental flavour, was influenced by the Parnassians, by the Symbolists and, most strikingly, by Palamas. But the poet soon abandoned these models, turned to Greek antiquity for inspiration and developed a sensuous, Dionysiac quality and a deep musicality in his verse, as well as a sharp, satirical tone expressed in playful, agile rhythms.

His first collection of poems, *The Honeycombs* (1905), is immature, for Varnalis did not find his own voice until he went to Paris to further his studies in 1919 and was won over by dialectical materialism and Marxism. This is clearly evident in the two collections he subsequently published, *The Light that Burns* (1922), a work in dramatic form cast in both prose and verse,[68] and *The Enslaved Besieged* (1927), whose title was chosen in deliberate contrast to Solomos's *Free Besieged*. The poetry of both these books is clearly politically engaged; nonetheless, its lyrical intensity and excellent workmanship secure for Varnalis an important place in modern Greek poetry. Poems like *The Mother of Christ*, *Magdalen*, *The Sorrows of the Virgin* and *Dialogue Between Man and Woman* are no mean achievements and show the author at his best. In *The Enslaved Besieged* Varnalis forcefully puts across his anti-war and anti-idealistic views, and his satire and scorn reach their peak. Another memorable poem is his well-known *Those in the Hands of Fate* (Οἱ Μοιραῖοι), which was published in 1921 in the magazine *Neolaia* (*Youth*). After 1931 he issued only one more book, *Poems*, which has rightly been characterized as 'social art'; for it includes poems attacking the bourgeoisie, satirizing war, singing the praises of peace and, in *The Leader*, calling for a social revolution. He also put all his caustic wit at the service of politics, as evidenced by the poems *The Ballad of Kyr Mentios* or *The Good Citizen*.

The language of Varnalis is robust and vivid, his lyricism virile and his versification excellent. There can be little doubt that his feelings for the underprivileged are sincere. Although politically committed, his poems are neither conventional nor in any way crude propaganda, and this is indeed a rare achievement.[69] He also wrote some good literary criticism, short stories and memoirs.

The lesser poets

The remaining poets of this group require only brief mention. Soteris Skipis (1881–1951) was a prolific poet (he published seventeen collections of verse!) but facile and careless. Initially, he fell under the sway of the Symbolists. Napoleon Lapathiotis (1893–1944), whose life ended in suicide, was a low-key poet, full of nostalgia and despair, and a great admirer of Walter Pater and Oscar Wilde. Markos Avgeris (1884–1973), whose real name was George Paraskevopoulos, was more of a critic than a lyrical poet, but his collection *The Songs of the Table* scored a success. And finally, Romos Philyras (1889–1942), the pen-name of J. Economopoulos, who spent the last two years of his life in a lunatic asylum, poured out his disillusionment with life and his anti-heroic attitude to the point of indulging in self-mockery.

Much more important are the two poetesses, Myrtiotissa and Emily Stephanou Daphne, who appeared on the Greek literary scene with true claims to art. For although poetry had been composed by a number of educated women, both in the Phanariot circle and in the Ionian Islands, as well as in Athens after the liberation of Greece,[70] they have all justly been consigned to oblivion. We must go back as far as Cassia[71] in the ninth century before we find a Greek poetess worthy of the name.

Myrtiotissa (1883–1968), the pen-name of Theone Dracopoulos, the daughter of a Greek diplomat, was born in Constantinople and educated in Athens. As she had an unruly and emotionally charged nature, she hated school and fervently desired to become an actress; her family being opposed to this, she turned instead to writing confessional, passionate and erotic poetry. She entered into many intense amorous relationships, two of which were with leading poets, Kostis Palamas and Lorentzos Mavilis.

It was for the latter that she wrote her best love lyric, called *I Love You*, a modern Greek classic.

Myrtiotissa's diction is simple and musical; her metres are lively; and she succeeds in turning commonplace confessions into convincing and moving poems, for they stem from deeply felt personal experience. Literary critics have called her poetry a 'brave cry of sensuality'. Occasionally, however, there are touches of bitter sarcasm in her verse, reminiscent of Karyotakis, as there are in her sequence *Comico-Tragic Continuity*. Myrtiotissa published six volumes of verse[72] and translated Euripides' *Medea* into modern Greek.

By contrast, Emily Daphne (1887–1941) led a quiet, conventional life. She was born in Marseille and educated in Athens, and she taught at the Arsakeion High School for Girls. She was the wife of a minor poet, Stephanos Daphnes, whose real name was Thrasyboulos Zoiopoulos. Emily Daphne wrote one-act plays (her *Gloria Victis* was awarded a prize), short stories and a novel, but she is remembered most for her lyrical verse. The delicacy of her feeling, the pleasing variety of her rhythms and the noble simplicity of her diction reserve for her a firm place among the writers of her generation.[73]

In closing this brief survey of the 1905 group of poets it should be noted that it was through their support that *Hegeso* (1907–8), the first (if short-lived) Greek magazine dedicated exclusively to poetry, appeared on the scene. Moreover, it was also largely because of the interest in literature provoked by these poets that the Phexi Library (1914–17), directed by John Zervos, was established, in which the modern Greek classics were published, as well as a number of translations of great European writers.

THE 'COSMOPOLITAN POETS' (1915–25)

The next group of poets to emerge can be called the 'cosmopolitan poets'. By 1915 the second wave of Symbolism had ceased to be a beneficial influence upon Greek poetry, and the initial impact of the Demotic Movement had spent itself. Young writers were restless and were feverishly looking for something new. Once again, they turned to the West for guidance, and it was the 'cosmopolitan spirit', expressed in France as a yearning for travel and escape, that captured their fancy. Thus pure, lyrical Symbolism, so vital in the first fifteen years of the twentieth century, gave way to a descriptive, *fantaisiste* literature between 1915 and 1925.

On the whole, those years can be seen as a period of decline in modern Greek poetry, no doubt largely because of the bitter political struggles

which tore Greek society apart during and after the First World War and
the great national disaster of 1922, with the social and cultural upheaval it
brought in its wake. Nor is the pessimistic and anti-heroic spirit which
spread all over Europe after the end of the First World War less respon-
sible for the escapist tone which permeated Greek writing in the 1920s. It
is also worth bearing in mind that Athens itself was rapidly growing into a
worldly metropolis, so that big-city life became a reality and soon came to
be seen as another means of escape from an everyday, humdrum, 'provin-
cial' existence.

The search for the exotic and for escape was also blended with crude
eroticism and sloppy neo-Romanticism, the roots of which can be traced
to the French *poètes maudits* and the lesser Belgian Symbolists. This second
wave of Symbolism, which arrived in Greece during the course of the First
World War, expressed itself in a lesser escapist poetry. It found its prime
advocate in Constantine Karyotakis and remained fashionable until his
death in 1928.

Strictly speaking, the Greek 'cosmopolitan poets' fall into two groups:
first, those who had actually experienced sophisticated cosmopolitan life,
such as K. Ouranis, A. Doxas or N. Kavvadias; and second, those known
as the 'coffee-house cosmopolitans',[74] poets who spent long hours in
Athenian cafés dreaming of extended trips abroad, travels to Vladivostok
or to remote African sites, but who had never actually stepped out of
Greece. Such were Orestis Laskos, Alexandros Baras and Caesar Emma-
nuel, who has also been called the poet of 'Athenian night-life between the
wars'.[75] The impact of Constantine Cavafy upon these poets must be
mentioned, for the verse of that strange, isolated man was beginning to be
known in Athens in the 1920s and to affect the poetry of the young. His
Ithaca became their symbol, for in it the journey and not the port of arrival
was the significant thing.

The writer who inaugurated Greek 'cosmopolitan' poetry was Kostas
Ouranis (1890–1953). He was born in the small town of Leonidion in the
Peloponnese, studied in Nauplia, Constantinople, Geneva and Paris, and
spent much of his time travelling abroad. For a period of his life he also
served in the Greek consular service and as press attaché at various Greek
embassies.

Ouranis, who was touched by the second wave of Symbolism to reach
Greece, had a true lyrical gift centred on real or imaginary impressions of
his travels, but his technique is poor. His best poems are to be found in his
collections *Spleen* (1911) and *Those Who Feel Nostalgia* (Νοσταλγοί) (1920).
In the first there are still traces of a considerable re-working of Baude-
laire's morbidity, whereas in the second can be found scenes from the
poet's visits to France, England, Spain, Holland and Belgium, viewed
through a veil of nostalgia and melancholy. Ouranis also recorded his
delight in travel in charming books on his experiences abroad.

The Romantic, 'cosmopolitan' spirit of Ouranis opened the way to several other poets. The next step was taken by Angelos Doxas (1900–) the pen-name of Nicolaos Dracoulides, a psychoanalyst who also found time to write several collections of poems, novels, essays and literary criticism. In one collection, *Libation to the Wind* (1927), to which Palamas wrote an introduction, he gives vignettes of Parisian life between the wars that alternate between confession and crude display. Some of these verses are graceful, but others are pure journalistic gossip, recounting tales of the Métro or the bistro and of transitory erotic escapades, while parading 'fashionable' (often vulgar) women's names like Toto, Zozo, Ninette, Lucy and so forth.

'Cosmopolitan' poetry came truly into its own with Nikos Kavvadias (1910–75), who was born in Harbin, Manchuria, took to the sea at an early age and travelled widely as an officer in the Greek merchant navy. At the age of twenty-four he published his first book of poems, *Marabou* (1934), which took the Greek literary scene by storm. His debt to Ouranis is obvious; his verse has technical faults and lacks metrical variety; but he opened a new and wider world to modern Greek poetry, the underworld of the great international harbours and the dirty tramp steamers that plough the seas with their mysterious cargo of crude, brutal and exotic experiences. Every aspect of this complex cosmos is presented with true humanity and understanding, even the attraction of evil and immoral pleasures.

The only other collection of poems which Kavvadias published, *Mist*, appeared in 1947.[76] In spite of their greater maturity and a clear improvement in their poetic technique, these poems are much less fresh than their predecessors, for they are no longer coloured by the dreams of youth. Kavvadias brought to fulfilment what Ouranis had started in 1915; he is rightly considered the best exponent of Greek 'cosmopolitan' poetry.

The lesser side of 'cosmopolitan' poetry, the 'armchair school of escapism', is represented by Laskos, Baras and Emmanuel.[77] Orestis Laskos (1908–), born in Eleusis, was a true bohemian, wavering between the cinema, the stage and poetry; A. Baras (1906–), a native of Constantinople who was educated in Athens, was sensitive, ironical and a follower of Cavafy; and Caesar Emmanuel (1902–70), an Athenian-born classical scholar and schoolmaster, delighted in the nightlife of Athens. All three, rather than travelling abroad, indulged in long and exciting imaginary journeys, and 'instead of extolling the bucolic countryside, wrote of night clubs, music halls and bars, substituting the "romantic" sounds of the violin for the jazz band and Venus for Josephine Baker'.[78] Their descriptions are characterized by unexciting metres and flat language reminiscent of the theatrical reviews and the sloppy, sentimental magazines popular in those days.[79]

Alexandros Baras, the most skilful and most humorous of the three, in his amusing poem *Cleopatra, Semiramis and Theodora* even introduced a ship's captain who committed suicide by jumping from the bridge into the sea in full uniform, thus achieving a double 'escape' through travel and through death.

OTHER POETS OF THE 1920s

Telos Agras

Telos Agras (1899–1944), the pen-name of Evangelos Ioannou, is the link between the early 'cosmopolitan' poets and Constantine Karyotakis, the most important poet of the 1920s. He was born in Thessaly, studied law at the University of Athens and served at the Ministries of Tourism and Agriculture, as well as in the National Library. He was killed by a stray bullet in the streets of Athens at the end of the war. In 1940 he was awarded the National Prize for Poetry.

Telos Agras was both a poet and a literary critic. In his lifetime he published only two books of verse, *The Bucolics and the Encomia* (1939) and *Weekdays* (1940). His later poems, which had appeared in various magazines, were collected posthumously in a volume entitled *The Roses of the Day*, published in 1965.

Agras's early poems reflect the influence of Jean Moréas and of Jules Laforgue, but he soon found his own voice, that of a musical, melancholy dreamer who moved in an unreal world and on whom the monotony of life weighed heavily. Perhaps his best lyrics are those that portray, in a less gloomy mood, the picturesque side of some Athenian neighbourhoods. Though his language is neither original nor rich, his sense of form and rhythm are well-developed, especially in the posthumously published works.[80]

Constantine Karyotakis

Constantine Karyotakis (1896–1928), the most significant and influential poet of the 1920s, whose verse is haunted by a death wish expressed more clearly than any other writer the oppressed and agonized spirit of those days, as it struggled for escape from the strain of everyday reality through travel and even through death.

He was born in Tripolis, in the Peloponnese, and studied law at the University of Athens. He later joined the Greek civil service and made several trips abroad, in the course of which he visited Paris and Berlin. But he ended up by committing suicide in the small provincial town of Preveza, where he found life intolerable.

Karyotakis's first collection, *The Suffering of Man and Things*, appeared in 1918 and was followed in 1919 by a second volume called *Banishing Pain* (Νηπενθῆ). Both books were awarded prizes at the Philadelpheios Competition (which, incidentally, was by then regarded as old-fashioned by the younger writers). In 1927 he issued his third and last collection, *Elegies and Satires*, which established his reputation. He also translated French and German poetry into modern Greek. Karyotakis's sources can be traced to the French Renaissance poets, from François Villon to Mathurin Régnier, as well as to the late Symbolists, from Jules Laforgue to Laurent Tailhade, whose clever, satirical poetry until then was unknown in Greece.[81] Of the Greek poets, Cavafy, Varnalis and especially Malakasis impressed him.

It has been pointed out that the pessimistic poetry of D. Paparrigopoulos[82] and Karyotakis had much in common; although that may be true, the former is bombastic and philosophically inclined, whereas Karyotakis is restrained, prosy, caustic and lonely. When Karyotakis's pessimism sank to embittered depths, he turned to satire as an outlet, attacking certain writers as well as the whole tradition of modern Greek letters. He was also a strident anti-feminist, his hatred provoked by the deceitful character he ascribed to the women he had loved. (In this connection it should perhaps be added that he is said to have suffered from a distressing venereal disease.)

Pastoral scenes were never attractive to Karyotakis, the city dweller. At most he was drawn to the trees in city streets, the grass growing between stones in a courtyard, potted plants and autumn leaves rustling on the pavements. City realism entered Greek poetry with Cavafy; this Karyotakis took over from him and turned into a new kind of bourgeois realism, depicted in terms of the civil service, the office and red tape. Karyotakis's verse is largely confessional in tone, and though his visual imagery is weak, blurry and abstract, his lines are rich with acoustic images. His diction is a strange mixture of elements taken from both demotic and *katherevousa* but blended with considerable charm. His versification is conventional, as is his use of rhyme, yet there is originality and fluidity in his rhythms.

Karyotakis's nightmare verse was not innovative enough to rejuvenate Greek poetry; with it ended the tradition that started in 1915 with the escapist, 'cosmopolitan' poetry of Ouranis. What seems to have excited his contemporaries most was the note of familiarity it struck. Karyotakis's suicide at the age of thirty-two created a sensation, and a whole army of lesser poets emerged who tried to imitate his pessimistic verse. Of these dubious heirs, with their unbalanced language, their denial of moral values and their conviction that misery and disillusion were a kind of divine gift, only one name need be mentioned—that of M. Zotos (1905–32).[83] This unfortunate trend in Greek literature continued till the mid-1930s, even after Seferis[84] had initiated, with his poem *The Turning-Point*, the new poetry which was to flourish in that decade.

After Myrtiotissa and Emily Daphne, it is not until the 1920s that we find poetry worthy of the name composed by women. Among them two stand out: Maria Polydouri and Lili Iakovidou.[85]

Maria Polydouri

Maria Polydouri (1902–29) was born and grew up in Kalamata. Soon after completing her secondary education, driven by her tempestuous and revolutionary nature, she escaped secretly from her home and ran away to Athens. She started reading law and working as a civil servant but never completed her legal studies, for after her father's death she went to Paris, where her frail health gave way under the stress of the undisciplined and exuberant life she led. She returned to Greece and died of consumption in utter poverty at the state hospital, Soteria.

A major event in Polydouri's life was her passionate and tragic love affair with the poet Constantine Karyotakis, which inspired her most beautiful love lyrics, *Your Hands*, *The Return* and, above all, *Only Because You Loved Me*. After Karyotakis deserted her, and especially after his death, he became for her the symbol of passionate love which transcended the real man of flesh and blood.

But Polydouri did not write love lyrics on Karyotakis alone; she also addressed some to one Georgiou, who was her fiancé for a short time, and there is even one, called *Come My Sweet Boy*, on the poet Giannis Ritsos, who was then very young.

Polydouri's poetry is exclusively erotic. Her world is devoted solely to amorous passion, which is often seen sinking into the lengthening shadow of death. Nothing else seems to have touched her, not even the gigantic national disaster of 1922, nor the changing ideals of her own generation. But the tragic intensity of her poems, her courage, intellectual honesty and musical sense of rhythm, make the best of her verse remarkable and counterbalance its extemporaneous quality, the lack of variety in her subject-matter and her rather flat and unexciting diction. She is perhaps the finest of contemporary Greek poetesses.[86]

Lili Iakovidou-Patrikiou

Lili Iakovidou-Patrikiou (1899–   ) was born and educated in Athens, where she studied law and started publishing poems in *Noumas* in 1922. Her lyricism is centred on her quasi-religious devotion to Kostis Palamas, whose art dominates her own verse. Her greatest gift was that through her warm and sensitive approach she was able to express purely cerebral concepts as emotional experience. She idealized love, and her gratitude flowed out to the things that moved her in life. As she matured, she brought her diction and technique more up to date, but she was never able to free herself from the shadow of Palamas, so evident in her book *Earth Without Water* (1969), a protracted elegy on the death of her daughter, modelled on Palamas's *Grave*. Lili Iakovidou-Patrikiou has also published critical essays on various Greek writers, several plays, received the National Prize for Poetry and two prizes from the Academy of Athens.[87]

Religious trends in the poetry of the 1920s

Alongside the pessimistic, escapist, 'cosmopolitan' verse of the 1920s, we also find poetry of a religious vein. This is not, as one might have expected, the outcome of despair; it stemmed from a positive religious impulse, accompanied by a certain amount of philosophical speculation. In it we meet a belief in man and in traditional moral values which stands in direct contrast to the decadent, hopeless attitude of Karyotakis and his followers, though it must be admitted that as literature it is clearly inferior. The most important representatives of this trend are Takis Papatzonis and Georgios Douras.

Takis Papatzonis (1895–1976) was born in Athens, studied law and French literature and was employed by the Ministry of Finance as an economist. He joined the Roman Catholic Church in 1916 and was later elected to the Academy of Athens. The poems he had published in various literary magazines he collected in three books, *Selections I* (1934), *Ursa Minor* (1944) and *Selections II* (1962),[88] to which he added some new ones. He also translated into modern Greek a number of works of eminent foreign writers, including some by Edgar Allan Poe, and wrote a few short stories.

Papatzonis's religious poetry has a mystic elation fused with a wordly awareness, from which even irony is not absent. But it is firmly rooted in the dogma of the Catholic Church, even when Papatzonis abandons conventional, straightforward exposition and moves into an almost pantheistic world, described in apocalyptic terms. In his diction the spoken idiom blends with religious terms, and his versification is extraordinarily free.

The poetry of Georgios Douras (1895–1965) is far less impressive than that of Papatzonis. Born in Alexandria and educated in Volos and

Athens, where he read law, Douras soon came under the sway of Angelos Sikelianos. More conservative in versification and diction than his mentor, he engaged in a neo-Christian poetry that proclaims his faith with fervour. In the course of time—for between 1918 and 1962 he published twelve collections of poems—the tone of his poetry became more gentle.[89]

Finally, we should not leave the twenties without noting that *Nea Hestia* (1928–   ), the literary periodical, was founded in 1928 by the distinguished novelist and playwright, G. Xenopoulos, and is continued by Petros Haris of the Academy of Athens. It developed into the longest-lived and perhaps the most influential literary journal of modern Greece.

CONSTANTINE CAVAFY

Before proceeding to the writers of the 1930s and the new vitality which they infused into contemporary Greek verse, we must turn to Constantine Cavafy (1868–1933), the Alexandrian poet who created an independent poetic province of his own.

The son of a successful merchant, he was born in Alexandria, educated in England and then returned to live in the city of his birth, where he worked for long years as a clerk in the Irrigation Service. Living outside Greece, he remained quite unaffected by the developments that were taking place in Athens. The Demotic Movement and all that the New School of Athens was achieving did not touch him; he was even rather cynical about the ascendancy of Palamas. What did influence him, however, was the aestheticism and the Romantic exoticism and decadence fashionable in the late nineteenth-century literature of the West. In an unadorned, personal style, he composed his own hedonistic, disillusioned, wordly-wise, often ironical but always deeply humane poetry. He is the most original of all the modern Greek poets.

Cavafy, who divided his own poetry into three categories—philosophical,[90] hedonistic and historical—developed his art by proceeding from subjective to increasingly objective representation. By 1893, as his poem *Candles* shows, he had abandoned the Romantic nature imagery and the imitative themes of his early verse and had moved into a more subtle, more alive, metaphorical landscape. By the following year he had also perfected the three modes that were to dominate his work throughout his maturity: narrations, which recorded an episode or outlined a character; dramatic monologues, which made use of historical figures (usually minor, peripheral ones), who served as metaphors for perennial attitudes; and first-person didactic monologues.

Cavafy, who spent most of his life away from Europe, had no secure sense of an established background, so he turned to a half-lost and broken past, which he brought to life by the force of his genius. This was his 'mythical' Alexandria, which he created during the years 1911–21 and which gave him the symbols and myths he needed; for the tavern life of contemporary Alexandria and the special interest it held for him did not call on all his gifts.[91] Through his 'mythical city', which he conceived as pleasure-loving, witty, tolerant, lazy, artistic and refined, he could step outside the narrow world of Romantic decadence and become universal.

This poetic evocation of Alexandria, in both its contemporary and its ancient manifestations, started with the famous poem *The God Abandons Anthony*. The process followed Cavafy's earlier preoccupation with cities as personal and communal metaphors and later broadened to embrace other 'mythical' cities of the Hellenistic world[92]—Antioch, Seleucia, Sidon, Beirut and so on and, in his later years, Sparta and Byzantium. Thus the poet projected a view of Greek history across eighteen centuries (he had always been deeply interested in history and in his youth had wished to become an historian). But it should be noted that neither the great age of Hellas, nor the Greek War of Independence, nor subsequent modern Greek history ever became subjects for his subtle poetry.

The poems dealing with Cavafy's 'mythical' Alexandria describe specific moments in its history from which lessons of universal validity were drawn; for he saw in many famous episodes examples of recurring human problems, and he had the ability to extract something of ecumenical interest from historical records. Moreover, he attributed a particular way of life to imaginary characters, clothed in the trappings of history, which furthered his design to dramatize his myth. Whenever he returned to the Alexandria of his own times—and this he did increasingly towards the end of his life, when he decided to expose his 'real' self—he restricted himself largely to a particular erotic world at a prescribed moment in the recent past; he described meetings in the dark entrances of taverns, in shops that sell perfumes and ties, in ordinary bedrooms or in cafés where old men drag out their boredom and young men arrange assignations for the gratification of their unnatural desires.

Cavafy saw Hellenism as the only measure of civilization among barbarians aspiring to rise above their station in history. In his view, progress for barbarians meant to be Hellenized (even if in his poem *Returning from Greece* he does not seem to disdain mixing with the barbarians). Although he may have accepted, and may even have been attracted by, the mixture of Greek and Oriental elements, it was the pure Greek civilization he respected. And he felt an especially passionate devotion to the Greek language as a symbol of the highest culture. To be Greek and to speak Greek was for him, as we can see in his *Poseidonians*, the greatest of blessings. As he expanded his picture of Hellenism to include the Sparta of about 222 B.C. and Byzantium from 1078 to 1453, we see him also focusing on the state as it disintegrates, still serving as an example of enduring Hellenic attitudes, in particular of pride in self and nation. In this broader picture Cavafy presented the Greek experience in a more complex and comprehensive manner than that afforded by his Alexandrian image, though the Alexandrian way of life remained for him the touchstone for judging the quality of experience of all other historical periods.

From the world of Hellenism Cavafy reached out in his last years to a more universal image of the human predicament, one that expressed his tragic view of life in both ideological and historical terms. Few poets have conveyed more clearly and more subtly the tragic isolation of modern man or the deadening effects of boredom; and he looks upon the human condition with a detached irony, accompanied by a deep sympathy and understanding for the victims of that blind power called Life or Fate, and especially for those who have the courage to see themselves and their hopeless circumstances for what they are. It is important to realize that the poems which Cavafy wrote after 1910 build on each other, supplement and complete one another, so as to create a more or less general metaphor, and they do so in a way that permits the expression of the poet's final, detached illumination.

Perhaps the most important sources of Cavafy's inspiration were erotic passion and, closely connected with it, distress at the passage of time. His love, tyrannical and often painful, was for young men: for Cavafy was a homosexual, and his attraction to homosexuality was enhanced by the knowledge that it was forbidden. The handsome young men whom he idealized and often placed in historical settings in his poems were for him the 'heroes of pleasure' (οἱ γενναῖοι τῆς ἡδονῆς), the physical perfection and sensual possibilities of the male body being what he most cherished. On the other hand, the passage of time, which brings an early end to youth, the symbol of love and beauty, was a source of deep despair for the poet, who could not bear old age, as we can see from his poem *The Souls of Old Men*. In fact, his perfect *ephebes* had to die young—it was an aesthetic demand—and this explains the number of elegant sepulchral poems he wrote immortalizing their beauty. For he believed that the handsome young dead, like exquisite erotic experiences, can live on in aesthetic images and that their memory is the greatest hymn to youth, beauty and love. To achieve this was, for Cavafy, the true mission of poetry, an understandable attitude for an aesthete who was tortured by time and death, as they swept all he valued into oblivion.

One theme which seems to have weighed upon Cavafy is the isolation which he believed all men feel, which in its turn induces a sense of incarceration. He maintained that this condition of feeling trapped and imprisoned is unavoidable, that it comes about imperceptibly and that it is all the more tragic because men, to the end, refuse to give up hope. His poems *The Walls, The Windows, Trojans, The City* and even *Waiting for the Barbarians* deal with this subject. But Cavafy could laugh at the human predicament, as he did in his poems *Envoy from Alexandria* and *In a Township of Asia Minor*, even if his laughter was bitter.

Cavafy was clearly a fatalist and a pessimist who saw a vacuum behind all appearances; this explains why he never stood in awe or admiration before the great men of his own day or of the past. What he did make abundantly clear through his poems was that the qualities he truly admired and honoured were courage, human dignity and self-respect. And his notions of these qualities, which demand endurance and the absence of the slightest trace of self-pity, are all the more noteworthy because they are founded on no religious belief, nor do they expect any success or reward. It is basically a brave decision that sustains them, as we can see in his remarkable poems *Thermopylae, Those who Fought for the Achaean League, The God Abandons Anthony, Come O King of the Lacedaemonians,* and *Che fece . . . il gran refuto.* In the last the poet stresses the significance of making one's own decisions independently of what is considered right or wrong, and in *The God Abandons Anthony* and *Come O King of the Lacedaemonians* that pity and self-pity are the greatest enemies of dignity. The other side of the picture—the tragic and comic aberration—appears in his poems *Satrapy* and *From the School of the Renowned Philosopher.*

Not only does Cavafy point out the futility of all worldly greatness (in *King Demetrius* and *Manuel Comnenos,* for example), but he also notes how hubristic self-reliance can be, such as that of Caesar in *The Ides of March* or of Mithradates in *On the March to Sinope.* For Cavafy the moral balance is weighted on the side of those who face their destiny with courage and wisdom rather than with arrogance or with an excess of cynicism; he knows that Caesar, Mithradates, Artemidorus or Theodotus are all protagonists of the human drama played throughout history.

As might be expected, Cavafy was opposed to any state-sponsored religion; this is the reason why Julian the Apostate is made the butt of scorn and mockery for both heathen and Christian. At the same time, the power of religion *vis-à-vis* aestheticism is admirably expressed in one of his finest poems, *Myris, Alexandria 340 A.D.,* as well as in his *Theatre of Sidon,* for a dogmatic, militant and moralizing Church is bound to challenge the delicate balance of the aesthetic life.

Cavafy is also a great master in the use of irony. Many of his poems illustrate the vanity of the purely human state and its defencelessness before fate and death. His irony is such that he sometimes reverses the situation and shows that the deluded opinions of man may add glory and glamour to an occasion. Moreover, his ironical survey of human actions shows real compassion and sympathetic understanding, as is evident in his beautiful *Alexandrian Kings.* Much of his dramatic irony—*King Claudius* is a good example of this—is based on the assumption that the reader knows the historical facts and can appreciate another side of the historical moment, as in *When the Watchman saw the Light*.

Though Cavafy treated a wide range of subjects, he particularly liked those in which there was an element of paradox or contradiction, or those which illustrated a discord in men themselves or between their hopes and their actual circumstances. It was less the ironies of life than its enigmas that engaged him. He would probe a subject until he found in it some insoluble conflict, and then he would present the conflict as an individual, dramatic crisis. He rarely told a story. His concern was with the core of a situation, with the human factors that worked within it and with the riddles that it raised.

Cavafy's re-creation of the past gives us his own special vision. The dignity of history enabled him to exercise his full talents and to move away from his poems of modern life, with their insistence on the vagaries of the sexual appetite and their morbid and defeated moods. His concern with the past was not an escape from life, but a more complete interest in it, a means of seeing perennial issues in their true perspective. He soon came to see that past and present have the same abiding qualities and that human nature presents the same problems and paradoxes in all periods. Through his dramatic handling of this material he was able to enter many strange corners of the human soul; so firm was his grasp of the essentials of reality that he seems always to have dealt with issues of fundamental importance.

Cavafy's straightforward style, divested of all adornment, his diction, a strange, personal mixture of 'refined' spoken elements and 'purist' words and usages, his conversational rhythms, with their sparing use of rhyme (he hated anything that brought poetry close to music), lent his writings simultaneously the grace of verse and the freedom of prose. This and an epigrammatic, gnomic element which he cultivated are well-suited to the didactic thread that runs right through his poetry. For beyond the form in which the poems are cast one can discern a forceful didacticism in them all, no matter how indirectly it may be hinted at. In his own way Cavafy renovated and furthered the noble tradition of didactic verse that begins with no less a figure than Hesiod. His poetry, which is dominated by a note of refined melancholy, proceeds to tell us all that we are supposed to know, leaving little room for the active participation of the reader's imagination in the artistic experience. There is little suggestion of, and no room for, the dream.

Cavafy never offered a volume of his work for sale during his lifetime. He published only in broadsheets or in pamphlets printed exclusively for distribution among his friends and relatives. He also published poetry in two Alexandrian literary magazines of the day, *Nea Zoe* and *Grammata*. After his death his archives revealed much unpublished work—sixty-eight complete poems, all dating from before 1928. They have all been published since.[93]

In 1926 the Greek dictator Pangalos awarded Cavafy the Order of the Phoenix, but full recognition came slowly and only after the poet's death. Cavafy is now universally and rightly acclaimed as a major twentieth-century poet, and his influence upon contemporary Greek verse continues to be paramount.

THE POETS OF THE 1930s[94]

The influence of Constantine Karyotakis continued to be felt well into the 1930s, but the poetry of his sterile imitators could lead nowhere. The change in the literary climate came about only after Georgos Seferis published his first collection of poems, *The Turning-Point* (Στροφή) in 1931. The poetic revival which established itself with Seferis had been foreshadowed a few years earlier in the work of two minor poets, Theodoros Dorros and Niketas Rantos (the pen-name of N. Kalamaras). It was they who, in defiance of any traditional form, gave free rein in their verse to 'subconscious elements that are not checked by reason'. But their insignificant writings were soon forgotten.

The true protagonists in the further development of modern Greek poetry in the 1930s were Georgos Seferis and Odysseus Elytis, both Nobel Prize winners, whose influence became widely felt. They were followed by P. Prevelakis, G. Sarantaris, A. Drivas, D. Antoniou, A. Matsas, A. Embirikos, N. Engonopoulos and N. Gatsos. The last three, together with Elytis, introduced Surrealism to Greek poetry. Together with these poets, who were obviously not all of equal merit, the thirties also produced two distinguished, politically committed poets belonging to the Left, Giannis Ritsos and Nicephoros Vrettakos. At the same time the literary magazine, *Nea Grammata* (1935–40), edited by G. Katsibalis, made its appearance, greatly encouraging the new poets to publish their verse and thus acquire self-confidence.

Georgos Seferis and the influence of T. S. Eliot

Georgios Seferiadis (1900–71) the son of Stylianos Seferiadis (a noted barrister, Professor of International Law at the University of Athens and himself a poet),[95] was born in Smyrna. When war broke out in 1914, the family moved to Athens and from there Seferiadis was sent to Paris to study law. He then joined the Greek diplomatic service and was appointed attaché to the Greek Foreign Ministry in 1926.

His first book of poems, *The Turning-Point*, published in 1931 under his pen-name, Seferis, is a landmark in the course of modern Greek poetry. The affinity of this work with that of the French Symbolists, especially Mallarmé and Valéry, is very evident; they had captured the imagination of the young man and had become the models on which he had first aspired to fashion his own writing. This volume marks the beginning of the fourth and most beneficial wave of Symbolist poetry to affect Greek verse.

In several of Seferis's poems of this period the motif of transitory and frustrated love recurs, and the poignancy of many of them is accentuated by the use of metaphors which are essentially conceits, not unlike the kind of imagery that appealed to the Metaphysical poets: 'the fruitless voice withered', 'the magnet of your hair', 'the blade of your silence'. Moreover, the frequent use of *technical* as opposed to *natural* imagery characterized his early poetry, as well as a deep interest in musical effects through rhyme and metre quite in keeping with the principles of French Symbolism. The poet's experimentation with musical effects reached its highest point in *The Discourse of Love*. It is concerned with the feelings and thoughts which follow the separation of lovers and is the most important poem of *The Turning-Point*—and, indeed, of his whole early period. It is also interesting because it reveals that even before Seferis came into contact with modern English poetry he was already making use of a technique fundamental to the poetry of T. S. Eliot and Ezra Pound; the conscious adaptation of motifs from an established literary work, together with verbatim quotations whose purpose was to enlarge the poet's own vision. For *The Discourse of Love* cannot be fully understood unless it is seen against the background of the famous Cretan verse romance *Erotokritos*,[96] whose love scenes emphasize, supplement or, by contrast, lend tragic depth to the five movements of Seferis's poem. *The Discourse of Love* represents the highest point of lyricism which Seferis ever reached.

With *The Cistern*, a long, pessimistic, philosophical poem written in 1932, the years of experimentation come to an end. We now pass to a work, *Mythical Story* (Μυθιστόρημα), which is at the core of Seferis's poetry, not only in terms of chronology but also in terms of theme and form. It is the culmination of trends in thought and expression developed throughout the early period, and his subsequent poetry derives rather than deviates from this centre. It is also the most important work in terms of Seferis's relationship with modern English poetry because it was written during the period when he was absorbed in the writings of T. S. Eliot. Seferis increasingly felt that metrical lyricism, rhythmical speech and embellished verse no longer sufficed, no longer served a purpose. Valéry had taught him precision, the need to express things in almost mathematical terms, yet Valéry remained to the end enchantingly and musically lyrical. Seferis moved away from this model to follow the lead of Eliot and Pound, who demonstrated that it was possible to compose free verse in a descriptive, quasi-prosaic language informed by supra-historical sense of time and space, creating thus a new kind of poetry, more direct and more convincing than traditional poetry, with its ornamented grandiloquence. Nothing like this had happened in Greek poetry before.

Mythical Story is one long poem divided into twenty-four sections. It is a moving deeply pessimistic sequence of images and thoughts that illustrates, comments upon, the Greek scene as it emerged after the end of the catastrophic war against Turkey in 1922 and the expulsion of the Greek population from Asia Minor. Like all great poetry, it can be enjoyed at many levels, the personal, the national, the human. For the young Seferis the loss and destruction of Smyrna, his home town, was a wound that was never to heal. From that day he lost faith in all great achievements; he saw life as a crumbling edifice, a condemned structure destined to fall into ruins, a pitiful memorial to a beautiful, mythical past. And he was not alone in this. His whole generation was profoundly disillusioned when it saw the dreams and labours of four centuries come true with the signing of Treaty of Sèvres in 1920—the Treaty placed both sides of the Aegean in Greek hands—and then suddenly, in less than two years, shatter and perish in the flames of the Asia Minor disaster. In this national calamity Seferis perceived the intervention of fate, an ancient curse at work, the one that destroys all human dreams.

The persona that speaks in *Mythical Story* is a modern Ulysses, set apart from his weaker companions, the modern Argonauts, by his sensitivity to his condition. (The mixture of the ancient myths should not trouble us; it is deliberate.) The poem demonstrates Seferis's sympathy with the new, so-called 'mythical' school in England.[97] But though Seferis is in full sympathy with it, certain differences are also apparent. In Joyce, for example, the disparity between the contemporary and the ancient is largely presented through an exaggerated contrast between various episodes from the *Odyssey* and their modern counterparts. In this respect, Joyce's modern *Odyssey* is a parody of its model; often a humorous and antithetical contrast is achieved by means of irony. Seferis's *Odyssey*, on the other hand, is rather a reworking of relevant aspects of the classic in a contemporary context, and there is little, if any, irony in his version. His method is selection and re-statement rather than 'transformation', as it is with Joyce. Seferis's protagonist is not a duplicate of Odysseus; he is characterized in terms of similarity rather than ironic contrast. The distinction between antiquity and contemporary Greece is reflected in the fact that the modern hero is not heroic, as his predecessor was, and that he does not reach his Ithaca.

The general landscape of *Mythical Story* is that of a Greek *Waste Land*: dry rocks, naked islands, old, disused harbours, broken oars, battered wrecks washed ashore, a few scattered pine trees, deserted shores, low-backed mountains, a scarcity of water, a longing for coolness, dried-up wells, mutilated statues, solitary hovels under a sun that empties the eye sockets and strips the face down to the bone. This side of Greece appears for the first time in Greek poetry in the verse of Seferis, transposed in a dream that assumes the fascination of a nightmare. *Mythical Story*, the Greek *Waste Land*, may have originated in the flames of Smyrna and the Asia Minor campaign, but it developed into one of the great European poems, capturing and splendidly expressing the general mood of frustration and fatigue that followed the end of the First World War.

All Seferis's later works, *Log Book I* (1940), *Exercise Book* (1928–37), *Log Book II* (1944), *The Thrush* (1947) and *Log Book III* (1955), rise from the same central point of anguish, though each is a new poetical event, a new version of the 'rhapsody of bitterness', as Greek critics have called his poetry.

In *Log Book I* we also find *The King of Asine*, Seferis's masterpiece. In it he uses the golden burial mask of the king of Asine as a symbol of the void, of the weight of the vacuum left by those we love, who pass so strangely through and out of our lives, a motif which haunted him from his early youth. Over the void we lovingly set a golden burial mask and carry it with us to our grave. Here again, in a true Symbolist manner, the contraries are fused; life and death are joined, for death is carried by us during our lifetime, and our love gives life to the dead.

The Second World War drew Seferis away from Greece. After the Germans occupied Athens he followed the Greek Government into exile and became a 'refugee' in a series of countries: Egypt, South Africa, Syria. New lands unfolded before his eyes, a vast panorama of dark, soft, cruel self-seeking men—or so he saw them. At a time as garishly dynamic, as criminally 'heroic' as that of the Second World War, the poet's quiet humanity remained intact. He continued to be an enemy of the sweeping gesture, the thundering slogan embraced by so many others, but his disillusionment with life seems to have deepened. Perhaps this is nowhere more clearly expressed than in his poem *Last Stop*, which he wrote in an Italian harbour after he had boarded the ship that was to bring him back to Greece at the end of the war in 1944.

His first post-war poem is *The Thrush* (*Κίχλη*) and longing for happiness permeates this highly pessimistic work, which was written on the island of Poros in 1946. Just off the shore of that island a small ship called the *Thrush* had been sunk by the Germans in 1941. The shattered relic of its hull could be seen through the water, and the funnel still protruded out of the sea. Life and death, light and darkness were again united in this symbol, the seed from which stem all the other images and ideas (personal, historical and mythological) in the poem. *The Thrush*, somewhat like a musical composition, falls into three parts, each of which develops the central motif expressed in the Silenus–Midas epigram: 'It is better not to know and not to feel.' Thus the memories of home and of childhood give way to those of youth and erotic delight and they, in their turn, to those of the coarsening of body and soul. These then lead into the last part of the poem, which is a discourse on life and death in which both are united once more.

In the late 1940s Seferis left Greece again, this time for the East. Having been promoted to the rank of Ambassador, he headed the Greek Embassies to Lebanon, Syria and Iraq from 1953 to 1956. During this period he also visited Cyprus twice. These trips to Cyprus made a deep impression on the poet. In a sense, they renewed his emotional relationship with Greece because they coincided with the outbreak of the Cypriot struggle for independence. As Seferis himself wrote, he found that in Cyprus 'the miracle still works.' The experience proved to be a lyrical and spiritual rebirth for the poet. This is evident in the last volume of poems, *Log Book III*, which includes some of his most powerful and original work, such as *Helen, Engomi* and *On the Outskirts of Kyrenia*. Finally, mention should be made of his *Three Secret Poems*, published in 1966, perhaps the most esoteric of all his works.

The many virtues of Seferis's poetry secured for him the Palamas Prize of the Academy of Athens in 1956 and the Nobel Prize for Literature in 1963. And these virtues are indeed impressive: purity of diction, directness of description, brilliant and original imagery, variety and subtlety in the use of rhythm, all of which he developed and helped his contemporaries to further. The battle against the dead weight of the Classical past and the bombastic rhetoric of the early Greek Romantics was really won only in the 1930s, through the achievement and the leadership of Seferis. He responded admirably to the challenge posed by the long and glorious tradition of Greek poetry. He was not crushed by it, nor drawn to a sterile imitation; instead he conveyed, in novel and arresting terms, his personal world and much of the spirit of his age. Yet the world of Seferis is on the whole a world of despair, and this is the basic weakness in his poetry. There is no Ithaca for Seferis's Odysseus to reach or even to long for. Moreover, there is hardly any irony or wit, not a flicker of humour, to relieve the grand tragic picture. In dead earnest the poet moves from one bleak landscape to another, from one cry of despair to the next, grasping fully and brilliantly expressing the aesthetic quality of life but always groping in vain for an acceptable moral order, something that might give 'meaning' and 'significance' to existence.

The post-Seferis generation

As this book does not deal with any living poets, because they are too close to be assessed properly, the discussion of the post-Seferis generation will be limited to Georgios Sarantaris and Anastasios Drivas, who both died young, victims of the Second World War, and Alexandros Matsas.

Georgios Sarantaris (1908–41) was brought up and educated in Italy; at an early age he was greatly influenced by Ungaretti. When he came to live in Greece in 1932 he spoke little Greek, but he soon became passionately involved in Greek literary life. His philosophical bent for morals and metaphysics found expression in his poetry, whose lyricism is arresting. Its gentle sadness has been compared with the 'melancholy of a beautiful day'.[98] Perhaps his best poem is *The March* (*'Εμβατήριον*), a highly lyrical and humane piece recalling the early poets of the Ionian Islands. Even in his erotic poetry the feeling is more spiritual than sensual.

Anastasios Drivas (1899–1942), on the other hand, was deeply affected by the work of Sarantaris, but he lacked his idealism and spirituality, being mostly concerned with nature and landscape and very little with man. His later work owes much to Odysseus Elytis and even more to the poetry of Éluard and Jouve, which Elytis had translated into modern Greek. He was a poet of modest inspiration but had the rare virtue of not being confessional.

Alexandros Matsas (1911–69) stood apart from any poetic trend or group of his contemporary poets. Gentle, aristocratic (he served in the Foreign Office and his last post was that of Ambassador to Washington) and with affinities with Cavafy, he wrote about Greek nature and Greek history in his own unconventional manner. He also posed many dark, human problems in his verse, to which he gave no answer. Matsas left three tragedies on classical subjects, of which *Clytemnestra* and *Jocasta* (particularly the chorus songs) represent a noble effort to revitalize ancient forms and myths by invoking a modern lyrical sensitivity.

The Surrealists

In 1935, the year in which Seferis published his *Mythical Story*, Andreas Embirikos published the *Hypsikaminos* (*The Kill of High Heat*), which introduced Surrealism to the Greek literary world. As with the Parnassian Movement and Symbolism, Surrealism came belatedly to Greece, for ten years had already passed since André Breton, the founder of the movement, had published his celebrated *First Manifesto*.[99]

Of the leading Surrealists, Embirikos, Elytis, Engonopoulos and Gatsos, we shall speak only about the first, as the others are still living. There is no doubt that Odysseus Elytis, who has just been awarded the Nobel Prize for Literature, is the most eminent of the group—indeed, he is one of the leading contemporary poets and has an important place in the poetic pantheon of Greece; nonetheless, it was Andreas Embirikos (1902–76) who brought 'orthodox' surrealism to the Greeks. *The Kill of High Heat* is cast not in verse but in prose and consists of a series of phrases without any rational or emotional connection, composed according to the principles of automatic writing. Like so many products of this method, it has no literary value, except for some random lines which foreshadow the poet as he appears in the *Hinterland* ('Ενδοχώρα), published two years later in 1937. This includes poems composed between 1934–7, whose strange, exotic, erudite language can be considered a real contribution to modern poetic diction.

Embirikos is the first 'Dionysiac' poet after Sikelianos. His erotic passion as expressed in verse is both 'primitive' and modern, but Surrealistic strangeness destroys much of the aesthetic effect. To its credit, Embirikos's poetry is purged of low hedonism or sick sensuality. One of his best poems is called *Strophes Strophalon* (*The Turning of the Propellers*), a lyrical hymn to an ocean liner (indeed, to Greek seamanship) fitting for a poet who belonged to one of the leading Greek shipping families.

CONCLUSION

Such is, in outline, the development of modern Greek poetry between the 1880s, when Palamas and his contemporaries injected new life into Greek verse, and 1940. Needless to say, most of the leading writers of the 1930s continued to produce poetry during and after the Second World War; some are still publishing fine verse to this day.

Nearly three millennia separate Homer and Seferis; the Greek nation has experienced many dramatic turns of fortune during those years. Yet throughout the centuries every generation of Greeks has expressed its joys and its sorrows in verse—frequently in verse of outstanding originality and beauty. Poetry written in Greek not only constitutes the longest uninterrupted literary tradition of the Western world, but it has also provided the various forms in which Western man has voiced his emotions and many of his finest thoughts. In several of these genres—the epic, the lyric, the dramatic—the achievements of the Greeks have yet to be surpassed. It is a happy augury that better poetry has been written in Greek in the last century than in the fourteen centuries that preceded it; moreover, as the Nobel Prizes for Literature awarded to two Greek poets within the last few years acknowledge, by surrendering its political and purely national aspirations, Greek poetry has again attained universal validity and significance.

NOTES

LIST OF ABBREVIATIONS

AP	*Anthologia Palatina*
APl	*Anthologia Planudea*
Beck, *GBV*	H. G. Beck, *Geschichte der byzantinischen Volksliteratur*, Munich, 1971
Beck, *KTLBR*	H. G. Beck, *Kirche und theologische Literatur im byzantinischen Reich*, Munich, 1959
Bergk, *PLG*	T. Bergk, *Poetae Lyrici Graeci*, 4th edn., Leipzig, 1882
Burs. *Jahresb.*	*Bursians Jahresbericht (Jahresbericht über die Fortschritte der klassischen Altertumswissenschaft*, Berlin–Leipzig et alibi, 1875–
BZ	*Byzantinische Zeitschrift*
Christ–Paranikas, *AGCC*	W. Christ and M. Paranikas, *Anthologia Graeca Carminum Christianorum*, Leipzig, 1871
CIG	*Corpus Inscriptionum Graecarum*
Diehl, *ALG* (*ALG²*, *ALG³*)	E. Diehl, *Anthologia Lyrica Graeca*, 2nd edn., Leipzig, 1936; 3rd edn. (vol. 1, sections 1–3), rev. R. Beutler, Leipzig, 1949–52
Dölger, *BDIR*	F. Dölger, *Byzantinische Dichtung in der Reinsprache*, 2nd edn., Salonica, 1961
Edmonds, *FAC*	J. M. Edmonds (ed.), *Fragments of Attic Comedy*, vols. 1–3, Leyden, 1957–61
Gow–Page, *HE*	A. S. F. Gow and D. L. Page (eds.), *The Greek Anthology: Hellenistic Epigrams*, vols. 1–2, Cambridge, 1965
Gow–Page, *GPh*	A. S. F. Gow and D. L. Page (eds.), *The Greek Anthology: The Garland of Philip and Some Contemporary Epigrams*, vols. 1–2, Cambridge, 1968
Heitsch, *GDRK*	E. Heitsch (ed.), *Die griechischen Dichterfragmente der römischen Kaiserzeit*, vols. 1, 2nd edn., and 2, Göttingen, 1963–4
Hunger, *HPLB*	H. Hunger, *Die hochsprachliche profane Literatur der Byzantiner*, vol. 2, Munich, 1978
IG	*Inscriptiones Graecae*
Jacoby, *FGH*	F. Jacoby (ed.), *Fragmente der griechischen Historiker*, Berlin, 1923
Kaibel, *CGF*	G. Kaibel (ed.), *Comicorum Graecorum Fragmenta*, vol. I, i, Berlin, 1889

Kaibel, *EG*	G. Kaibel (ed.), *Epigrammata Graeca ex Lapidibus*, Berlin, 1878
Kleine Pauly	K. Ziegler, W. Sontheimer (eds.), *Der Kleine Pauly, Lexicon der Antike*, vols. 1–5, Stuttgart–Munich, 1964–75
Kock, *CAF*	T. Kock (ed.), *Comicorum Atticorum Fragmenta*, vols. 1–3, Leipzig, 1880–8
Krumbacher, *GBL*	K. Krumbacher, *Geschichte der byzantinischen Literatur*, 2nd edn., Munich, 1897
Legrand, *Collection de monuments*	E. Legrand, *Collection de monuments pour servir a l'étude de la langue néo-hellénique*, vols. 1–19, Paris, 1869–72 (n. s. = série 1–7, Paris, 1874–5)
Lobel–Page, *PLF*	E. Lobel and D. L. Page, *Poetarum Lesbiorum Fragmenta*, Oxford, 1955
Maas, *FBKP*	P. Maas, *Frühbyzantinische Kirchenpoesie* (*Kleine Texte*, 52–3), Berlin, 1931
Maas–Trypanis, *SRMCG*	P. Maas and C. A. Trypanis, *Sancti Romani Melodi Cantica Genuina*, vol. 1, Oxford, 1963
Maas–Trypanis, *SRMCD*	P. Maas and C. A. Trypanis, *Sancti Romani Melodi Cantica Dubia*, vol. 2, Berlin, 1961
Meineke, *FCG*	A. Meineke (ed.), *Fragmenta Comicorum Graecorum.*, vols. 1–5, Berlin, 1839–57
Migne, *PG*	J. P. Migne, *Patrologiae Cursus Completus*, Series Graeca, Paris, 1857–
Mus. Helvet.	*Museum Helveticum*
Nauck, *TGF*	A. Nauck (ed.), *Tragicorum Graecorum Fragmenta*, 2nd edn., Leipzig, 1889
Notices et extraits de la Bibliothèque Nationale	*Notices et extraits des manuscrits de la Bibliothèque Nationale (Royale) et d'autres bibliothèques*, Paris, 1787–
Olivieri, *FCGM*	A. Olivieri (ed.), *Frammenti della commedia graeca e del mino nella Magna Graecia*, vol. 1, 2nd edn., Naples, 1946; vols. 2–3, 2nd edn., Naples, 1947
Pack, *GLLT*	R. A. Pack, *The Greek and Latin Literary Texts from Greco-Roman Egypt*, Ann Arbor, 1952 (2nd edn. 1965); Berlin, 1970
Page, *GLP*	D. L. Page, *Greek Literary Papyri*, London, 1942 (Loeb)
Page, *LGS*	D. L. Page, *Lyrica Graeca Selecta*, Oxford, 1968
Page, *PMG*	D. L. Page (ed.), *Poetae Melici Graeci*, Oxford, 1962
Palamas	Κωστῆ Παλαμᾶ, Ἅπαντα, vols. 1–16, Athens, n.d.
Pap. Oxy.	Oxyrhynchus Papyri, eds. B. P. Grenfell and A. S. Hunt, 1898
Pauly–Wissowa, *REkA*	A. Pauly, G. Wissowa and W. Kroll, *Real-Encyclopädie der klassischen Altertumswissenschaft*, vols. 1–, Stuttgart, 1893–
Pitra, *AS*	J. B. Pitra, *Analecta Sacra Spicilegio Solesmensi Parata*, vols. 1–8 (vol. 6 is missing), Paris, 1876–88
Powell, *CA*	I. V. Powell (ed.), *Collectanea Alexandrina*, Oxford, 1925
Rhein. Mus.	*Rheinisches Museum*
Röm. Mitt.	*Römische Mitteilungen*
Schmid–Stählin, *GL* (*GL*, 2⁶, 1; *GL*, 2⁶, 2)	W. Christ, W. Schmid and O. Stählin, *Geschichte der griechischen Literatur bis auf die Zeit Justinians*, Part 1, vols.

1–5, 5th edn., Munich, 1929–48; Part 2, first half, 6th edn., Munich, 1920; Part 2, second half, 6th edn., Munich, 1924

SIG   W. Dittenberger, *Sylloge Inscriptionum Graecarum*, 3rd edn., Leipzig, 1915–24

Snell, *TGF*   B. Snell (ed.), *Tragicorum Graecorum Fragmenta*, vol. 1, Göttingen, 1971

Suda   A. Adler (ed.), *Suidae Lexicon*, vols. 1–5, Leipzig, 1933–8

West, *IEG*   M. L. West, *Iambi et Elegi Graeci*, vols. 1–2, Oxford, 1971–2

Wien. Stud.   *Wiener Studien*

PART ONE: ANCIENT GREECE

Section I: From the Mycenaean World to the Persian Wars (c. 2000–490 B.C.)

Introduction

1 No precise date can be given for the arrival of the first Greeks, but by the beginning of the second millennium B.C. they had undoubtedly reached the southern Balkan peninsula.
2 These three and a half centuries, known as the Dark Age of Greece, are usually divided thus: Sub-Mycenaean, c. 1120–1025 B.C.; Protogeometric and Geometric, c. 1025–700 B.C.

Chapter 1: Epic Poetry

1 Following universal practice, the book numbers of the *Iliad* are given in Roman numerals in this study and those of the *Odyssey* in Arabic numerals.
2 G. S. Kirk, *The Language and Background of Homer*, 2nd edn., Cambridge, 1967, p. 186.
3 From Minoan Crete we now know of several representations of lyre players using the seven-stringed lyre; there also exists a small figure of a lyrist dated c. 2500 B.C. and originating from the Cyclades. From a later date is the picture of a seated lyrist playing a five-stringed lyre on the wall of the *megaron* of Nestor's palace at Pylos (see M. L. Lang, *The Palace of Pylos in Western Messenia*, Princeton, 1969, vol. 1, pl. 126).
4 *Oime* is the oldest Greek name for a song or poem that we know.
5 The commonest version of Homer's life is to be found in the *Lives of Homer* (T. W. Allen, *Homeri Opera*, 2nd edn., Oxford, 1946, vol. 5, pp. 184f.), which were compiled from Hellenistic times onwards but which contain elements from the Classical period. Also well-known is the line about the seven cities that claimed to be Homer's birthplace: Smyrna, Chios, Colophon, Ithaca, Pylos, Argos and Athens (*AP*, bk. 16, no. 297). Different versions of this line exist; see Schmid–Stählin, *GL*, vol. 1, pp. 88, 89n. 2.
6 Bergk, *PLG*, fr.6 = Paus., 9.9.5. Callinus refers to Homer as the author of the *Thebaid*.
7 A. Parry, *The Making of Homeric Verse*, Oxford, 1971.
8 See P. Mazon (in collaboration with P. Chartraine and P. Collart), *Introduction à l'Iliade*, Paris, 1942, p. 236.
9 This probably originated in the vengeance motif for a relative or member of the household; see C. A. Trypanis, *Rhein. Mus.*, vol. 106, 1963, p. 289. On all these, see more details in C. A. Trypanis, *The Homeric Epics*, Warminster, Wilts, 1977, pp. 12f.
10 See p. 72.
11 *de Sub.*, 9.13.

12 Enough linguistic and other evidence exists to prove that both the Homeric epics in their final form are Ionian creations, which accords with the other information that we have about the Ionian origin of Homer.

13 See G. S. Kirk, *The Songs of Homer*, Cambridge, 1962, pp. 316f.

14 See Parry, *The Making of Homeric Verse*, pp. 118f.

15 This list, which is extensive when complete, shows that a large part of the epics must have been composed after 700 B.C.

16 Other such excellent 'descriptive' similes are to be found at XXII, 21f., where Achilles is compared with the Dog Star; XXII, 93f., where Hector is compared with an angry snake; VI, 503f., where Paris is compared with a stallion.

17 Roughly speaking, each of the first two kinds occupies one-fifth of the poems, whereas the last occupies three-fifths of the entire two epics.

18 D. B. Monro, *Homer: Iliad*, 4th edn., Oxford, 1903, vol. 2, pp. 307f.

19 Examples are IX, 556f., and XVII, 605f. This interweaving of themes and clauses is a result of the paratactic nature of Homeric poetry, which tends to state logically subordinate ideas as separate, grammatically co-ordinated propositions.

20 On the Homeric styles, see Kirk, *The Songs of Homer*, pp. 159f.

21 See G. P. Shipp, *Studies in the Language of Homer*, Cambridge, 1953, pp. 18f.

22 The phenomenon known as the 'double simile' probably arose after the epics had been committed to writing, when parallel, independent similes, put side by side for alternative use in recitation, were joined together.

23 Even the epithets by which he is described are non-anthropomorphic: ἀστεροπητής 'god of lightning'; νεφεληγερέτα 'cloud-gatherer'; πατὴρ ἀνδρῶν τε θεῶν τε 'father of men and gods'.

24 *Rep.*, 606e.

25 *Op.*, 630.

26 Lines 23–35.

27 There is too much in Hesiod's poetry that is personal to the poet for us to accept the idea that his poems were ever in the repertoire of rhapsodes. Moreover, the laboured quality of much of the composition has rightly been said to suggest the painful task of writing rather than the unfettered ease of oral creation. Alphabetic writing was, of course, known in Hesiod's day. See L. H. Jeffery, *The Local Scripts of Archaic Greece*, Oxford, 1961, p. 68.

28 *Sphragis* is the inclusion of the poet's name in his own work.

29 The authenticity of the *Theogony* has been repeatedly but wrongly challenged ever since Pausanius (9.314).

30 Recent research into certain parts of the poem, such as the *Titanomachia*, has revealed a marked difference between Homeric and Hesiodic hexameter poetry. In the latter a number of recurring patterns in words and themes has been observed. But the poem as a whole cannot be forced into a scheme of ten-verse units, as has been attempted by, for example, H. Schwabel, *Serta Philologica Aenipontana*, Innsbruck, 1961, p. 69.

31 *Theog.*, 120f.

32 The term *Ehoiai* derives from the formula ἢ οἵη (or the like) that introduced the names of mortal women who were loved by gods.

33 Cf. lines 11–24 and *Theog.*, 225.

34 See Schmid–Stählin, *GL*, vol. 1, p. 533.

35 *Op.*, 504–35.

36 *Theog.*, 686–712.

37 For this reason Hesiod has rightly been considered an excellent source of information about archaic Greece.

38 According to them, even certain passages in Homer that contained catalogues of names — like the Catalogue of the Nereids in *Iliad*, XVIII — could for that reason be taken as spurious.

39 The story of Hesiod's meeting and contest with Homer was probably an invention of Alcidamas, the fourth-century rhetorician and Sophist, inspired by *Op.*, 650–60; see M. L. West, in *Classical Quarterly*, vol. 17, 1967, pp. 433f.

40 The Μεγάλαι Ἠοῖαι (*Great Ehoiai*), which were genealogical; the Μελαμπόδια

(*Melampodia*), probably an account of famous seers; the Κήυχος Γάμος (*Marriage of Keyx*), which told of a prince of Trachis who entertained Heracles; the Αἰγίμιος (*Aegimius*), which appears to have narrated, in two books, the battle between Aegimius, the ancestor of the Dorians, and the Lapithae (it is also attributed to Cecrops of Miletus); the Χείρωνος Ὑποθῆκαι, which concerned the advice of Chiron to Achilles; the Ἀστρονομία (*Astronomy*), which told of the rising and setting of the principal stars; and the Ὀρνιθομαντεῖαι (*Augury by Birds*), the Μεγάλα Ἔργα (*Great Works*) and the Κάμινος or Κεραμεῖς (cf. *Pollux*, 10.85) are also attested. Of all these poems, only a few fragments have come down to us.

41 The word *hymnos* is of uncertain origin (see E. B. Boisacq, *Dictionnaire étymologique de la langue grecque*, 3rd edn., Heidelberg, 1938) and in the widest sense comprises all kinds of religious poems: paeans, dithyrambs, *prosodia*, *parthenia* and *hyporchemata*. The earliest composers of hymns of whom we hear are Olen, Pamphos, Orpheus and Musaeus (cf. Paus., 9.27.2; 1.22.7; 5.7.8), all of them shadowy figures of uncertain date.

42 It tells us that Apollo was born several days after his twin sister Artemis, and it attributes Leto's difficulties in finding a place for her confinement to the terror felt by the world of not Hera's vengeful anger but the new god's appalling power.

43 Cf. Thuc., 3.104; Aristoph., *Birds*, 575. It is attributed by Didymus the Grammarian to the rhapsode Cynaethus of Chios (schol. to Pindar, *Nem.*, 2.1), who is said to have been the first to recite Homer in Syracuse in the Sixty-Ninth Olympiad (504–501 B.C.).

44 It has the appearance of Attic work of the fifth or fourth centuries B.C.

45 It is probably Alexandrian.

46 On Homeric Hymns, see G. S. Kirk, in *Yale Classical Studies*, vol. 20, 1967, p. 167.

47 See G. L. Huxley, *Greek Epic Poetry from Eumelos to Panyassis*, Cambridge, Mass., 1969.

48 See *Oxford Book of Greek Verse*, no. 94.

49 277d; cf. 22c.

50 Proclus, probably the Neo-Platonist philosopher who died in A.D. 485, wrote a *Chrestomathia*, or handbook of literature, including an account of the Cycle, with summaries of its constituent poems. His work, which is probably a résumé of yet another, older epitome of the poems, is lost; but we have fairly full extracts from it in the *Bibliotheca* of Photius (Patriarch of Constantinople, A.D. 858–67 and 878–86) and other Byzantine works.

51 Aristotle was the first to limit the works of Homer to the *Iliad* and the *Odyssey*, though even he admitted also the spurious mock-epic *Margites*, a view that later gained general acceptance. The real implication in calling these poems 'Homeric' is that they date from a time when it was not thought worthwhile to record the author's name.

52 2.117.

53 4.32; see p. 73.

54 The title of the poem is unexplained. It is thought to suggest either that it was composed in Cyprus or that Aphrodite, the Cypriot goddess, played a large part in it.

55 Of the various other early epics known to us, some may well have been included in the Cycle. Their remains are collected in the old and inadequate edition of G. Kinkel, *Epicorum Graecorum Fragmenta*, Leipzig, 1877, which is supplemented by Allen, *Homeri Opera*, vol. 5.

56 See A. Severyns, *Le cycle épique dans l'école d'Aristarche*, Paris–Liege, 1928.

57 See pp. 367 and 371.

58 It is noteworthy that not a single papyrus fragment has been identified.

59 Cf. Hes., *Scutum*, 27–56.

60 *Olymp.*, 4.2.

61 4.32.

62 Jacoby, *FGH*, vol. 2: fr. T.5. The *Tabula Borgiana*, a Greek inscription of the Roman period, names in a list of epics a *Danaides*, allegedly of 6500 verses (Kinkel, *Epicorum Graecorum Fragmenta*, vol. 1, p. 4).

63 The story of the Argonauts was also treated in the so-called Naupactian epic (*Naupactiaca*), which was not a poem about Naupactus but one recited at a festival there. The

Naupactiaca, about which we know very little, has been attributed to Carcinus of Naupactus (seventh to sixth century B.C.) but, more frequently, to a nameless Milesian poet.

64 See Huxley, *Greek Epic Poetry*, pp. 83f.

65 See W. G. Forrest, in *Bulletin de correspondance hellénique*, vol. 80, 1956, p. 43, n. 3.

66 With the problematical exception, be it said, of the lost Musaean and Onomacritean hymns. A large body of hymnic, purificatory, oracular and theogonical poetry passed under the name of Musaeus, which became attached to many epic hexameters, mostly anonymous; see H. Diels, *Die Fragmente der Vorsokratiker*, 6th edn., ed. W. Kranz, Berlin, 1951, no. 2. But Musaean poetry does not bear the marks of high antiquity; cf. Huxley, *Greek Epic Poetry*, p. 114.

67 *Thes.*, 28.

68 Paus., 10.28.2; an otherwise unknown poem called *Atthis*, attributed to one Hegesinous, is also quoted by Pausanius.

69 For the view that twelve does not become the canonical number of Heracles' labours much before the Hellenistic period, see F. Brommer, *Herakles*, Münster, 1953.

70 Cf. Callim., *Ep.*, 6.

71 Gilbert Murray, *Ancient Greek Literature*, 4th edn., London, 1907, p. 70. The following are earlier: the *Foundation of Colophon* and the *Colonization of Elea*, composed by Xenophanes of Colophon (c. 510 B.C.), and perhaps the *Smyrneis* of Mimnermus (c. 630 B.C.). West, *IEG*, vol. 2, pp. 163f.; Jacoby, *FGH*, vol. 3: fr. C, 545–7; Schmid–Stählin, *GL*, vol. 1, pp. 543f.

72 Allen, *Homeri Opera*, fr. 3.

73 See Jeffery, *The Local Scripts of Ancient Greece*, pp. 235–6.

74 There were, we know, other comic battle pieces, such as the *Spider Fight* and the *Crane Fight*.

75 See Schmid–Stählin, *GL*, vol. 1, pp. 228f.

76 Under the same name are also preserved some much later poems, such as the *Argonautica*, the *Lithica* and a number of hymns to various gods, about which we shall speak later.

77 See pp. 321f.

78 See p. 361.

Chapter 2: Lyric Poetry

1 This process has been observed in the ballad poetry of the English and the Scots, among others, and in modern Greek folk poetry. Its relevance to the case of Homer has been discussed in Chapter 1.

2 See A. R. Burn, *The Lyric Age of Greece*, London, 1960, pp. 26of.

3 See p. 61.

4 Aristot., *Poet.*, 1448.b.32. Indications of the part played by such invective in the cult of Demeter are seen in the Homeric *Hymn to Demeter*, when the jokes of the girl Iambe amuse the mourning goddess, and in the *gephyrismoi* of the procession to Eleusis.

5 His whole life probably falls within the first two-thirds of the seventh century B.C. See F. Jacoby, in *Classical Quarterly*, vol. 35, 1941, pp. 97f., in answer to A. A. Blakeway, *Greek Poetry and Life*, Oxford, 1936, pp. 534f., and Pauly–Wissowa, *REkA*, suppl. 11, pp. 136f.

6 Diehl, *ALG*³, no. 6 (6).

7 Diehl, *ALG*³, no. 64 (63).

8 This legend probably arose from a misunderstanding of the word *kypsantes* ('hanging their heads'), which Archilochus used to describe the family's humiliation.

9 R. Merkelbach and M. L. West, in *Zeitschrift für Papyrologie und Epigraphik*, vol. 14, 1974, pp. 97f.; the authenticity of this fragment has been challenged—see T. Gelzer, in *Mus. Helvet.*, vol. 32, 1975, pp. 12f.; R. B. Kamerbeek, in *Mnemosyne*, vol. 29, 1976, pp. 113f.; J. Ebert and W. Luppe, in *Zeitschrift für Papyrologie und Epigraphik*, vol. 16, 1975, pp. 223f.

10 *AP*, vol. 7, no. 351 (= Gow–Page, *HE*, pp. 1561–2).

11 3 *Pyth.*, 2.99.

12 Diehl, *ALG³*, no. 112 (103).

13 Diehl, *ALG³*, no. 104 (84).

14 Diehl, *ALG³*, no. 118 (85).

15 *Theog.*, 121.

16 Diehl, *ALG³*, no. 77 (77).

17 See F. Lasserre and A. Bonnard, *Archiloque*, Paris, 1958, Testimonia 7.

18 Pindar, *Olymp.*, 9.1.

19 See A. Hauvette, *Archiloque, sa vie et ses oeuvres*, Paris, 1905, pp. 266f.

20 Diehl, *ALG³*, no. 29 (20).

21 Diehl, *ALG³*, no. 24a (16.18.17).

22 Diehl, *ALG³*, no. 45 (49).

23 Diehl, *ALG³*, nos. 77 (85.87)–78 (86).

24 *Suda*, s.v.

25 He proclaimed that man should die at sixty (Diehl, *ALG³*, no. 6 (6)), to which Solon answered, 'Not at sixty, but at eighty' (Diehl, *ALG³*, no. 22 (20.21.18)).

26 Diehl, *ALG³*, nos. 12a–13 (14).

27 Tithonus (Diehl, *ALG³*, no. 4 (4)); the sun's magic bowl (Diehl, *ALG³*, no. 10 (12)).

28 *Foundation of Colophon* (Diehl, *ALG³*, no. 12 (9)); Strabo, 633.

29 Diehl, *ALG³*, no. 1 (13).

30 Diehl, *ALG³*, no. 3 (4).

31 Lobel–Page, *PLF*, fr. 55.

32 The poet himself uses the word 'seal' (σφϱηγίς), but its significance here is doubtful.

33 On Greek homosexuality, see K. J. Dover, *Greek Homosexuality*, London, 1978.

34 See lines 1365f.; U. Köhler, in *Athenische Mitteilungen*, vol. 9, 1881, pp. 1f.; cf. E. Harrison, *Studies in Theognis*, Cambridge, 1902, p. 261.

35 See C. F. Russo, *Rendiconti della reale accademia dei Lincei*, 7th series, 1955.

36 P. Friedländer and H. H. Hoffleit, *Epigrammata: Greek Inscriptions in Verse from the Beginnings to the Persian Wars*, Berkeley, 1948, p. 53.

37 For sepulchral epigrams (of the seventh century), see, for example, Friedländer and Hoffleit, *Epigrammata*, p. 1; for dedicatory epigrams (c. 750–650 B.C.), *ibid.*, p. 10; for epigrams on road signs, *ibid.*, p. 149.

38 15.694c.

39 Page, *PMG*, no. 909.

40 We know from excavations on Crete and Pylos that this instrument was in use from the late Minoan age onwards, although the Greeks attributed its invention to Terpander.

41 Alcaeus was not the only member of his family who went into exile. His brother Antimenidas seems to have suffered the same fate and to have entered service as a mercenary under Nebuchadrezzar, king of Babylon. Upon his return 'from the ends of the earth', Alcaeus wrote a poem about him, celebrating his victory over a foe of gigantic stature.

42 This image of the ship of state has a long and varied history embracing, *inter alia*, Greek tragedy, the *Theognidea*, the speeches of Pericles (as reported by Thucydides), Plato's *Republic* and Horace, *Odes*, 1.14. The image has also been revived in modern times. But Alcaeus is here probably not speaking of the state in the sense of the later *politeia* but of his own political group, caught in the storm of a struggle for power.

43 I should like to take the opportunity here to publish an emendation to Lobel–Page, *PLF*, fr. 130 (G2)27, which Paul Maas made but, as far as I know, has never been published. ἄμεινον is emended to ἄϱμενον (cf. Hes., *Op.*, 786).

44 Such are the lines celebrating the death of the tyrant Myrsilus (fr. 39 (29)), which served Horace as a model for his ode *Nunc est bibendum*, on the death of Cleopatra.

45 Diehl, *ALG²*, no. 86 (20).

46 *Odes*, 1.10.

47 Lobel–Page, *PLF*, fr. 347 (Z23); Diehl, *ALG²*, no. 94 (39).

48 *Op.*, 582f.

49 3.12.

50 ⌣ — ⌣ — ⌣ | — ⌣ ⌣ — | ⌣ —
    ⌣ — ⌣ — ⌣ | — ⌣ ⌣ — | ⌣ —
    ⌣ — ⌣ — — ⌣ ⌣
    — ⌣ ⌣ — ⌣ ⌣ — | ⌣ — —

For example, Diehl, *ALG²*, no. 120 (Lobel–Page, *PLF*, fr. 6 (A6), 9f.):
καὶ μή τιν'ὄκνος μόοκος ἀμμέων
λάχη·πρόδηλον γὰρ μέγ'ἀέθλιον·
μνάσθητε τὼ πάροιθα μόχθῳ·
νῦν τις ἄνηρ δόκιμος γενέσθω.
Cf. D. S. Raven, *Greek Metre*, London, 1962, §138.

51 Lobel–Page, *PLF*, frs. 119 (F5), 326 (Z2).
52 *de Imit.*, 2.2.8.
53 Lobel–Page, *PLF*, frs. 102, 137.
54 Thus, for example, she mocks Andromeda for being captivated by a rustic lass who 'did not know how to draw her rags about her ankles' (Lobel–Page, *PLF*, fr. 57.3).
55 Lobel–Page, *PLF*, fr. 96.
56 Lobel–Page, *PLF*, fr. 1.
57 Lobel–Page, *PLF*, fr. 31.
58 *de Sub.*, 10.
59 Cf. Diehl, *ALG²*, no. 63 (55): 'Pure Sappho of the dark tresses and the honey-sweet smile'.
60 24.8.
61 Catullus' imitation, Lobel–Page, *PLF*, fr. 105c, is also in terms that suggest that the context of the Greek poem was erotic:
idem cum tenui carptus defloruit ungui /nulli illum pueri, nullae optavere puellae (LXII, 43–4).
62 Diehl, *ALG²*, no. 94 (52).
63 Lobel–Page, *PLF*, fr. 44.

64 — ⌣ — ⌣ | — ⌣ ⌣ — | ⌣ — —
    — ⌣ — ⌣ | — ⌣ ⌣ — | ⌣ — —
    — ⌣ — ⌣ | — ⌣ ⌣ — | ⌣ — —
    — ⌣ ⌣ — —

For example, Sappho, Diehl, *ALG²*, no. 4 (3) (Lobel–Page, *PLF*, fr. 34):
ἄστερες μὲν ἀμφὶ κάλαν σελάναν
ἂψ ἀποκρύπτοισι φάεννον εἶδος,
ὄπποτα πλήθοισα μάλιστα λάμπη
γᾶν ἐπὶ παῖσαν
Cf. Raven, *Greek Metre*, §136.

65 Lobel–Page, *PLF*, fr. 55.
66 *de Sub.*, 10.
67 The tradition lasted until the days and the person of Horace.
68 Critias, Diehl, *ALG³*, no. 8 (1); H. Diels, *Die Fragmente der Vorsokratiker*, 6th edn., ed. W. Kranz, Berlin, 1951, no. 88.B4.
69 Diehl, *ALG²*, no. 37 (54).
70 See p. 570.
71 ⌣ ⌣ — ⌣ — ⌣ — — (Anac., Diehl, *ALG²*, no. 43 (63), 7: ἄγε δηΰτε μηκέτ'οὕτω). This is used as 'stichic' length, with the alternative form ⌣ ⌣ — — ⌣ ⌣ — —. For the glyconics (— ⌣ | — ⌣ ⌣ — | — —) and the pherecrateans (— ⌣ | ⌣ — ⌣ ⌣ — | —), see Raven, *Greek Metre*, pp. 88, 90.
72 Page, *PMG*, no. 43; Athen., 12.5.33f.
73 See pp. 406f.
74 Both, Page, *GLP*, no. 1.
75 Pap. Oxy. 2370.
76 See H. Färber, *Die Lyrik in der Kunsttheorie der Antike*, Munich, 1936, pp. 7f.
77 Paus., 9.22.3.
78 Herod., 6.76f.; Polyaen., 8.33.

79 $\breve{\underset{\smile\smile}{}}|—\smile\smile—|\overset{\smile}{—}—$; cf. Raven, *Greek Metre*, p. 92.

80 Paus., 2.20.8.

81 Page, *PMG*, no. 1.

82 Paus., 4.4.1.

83 The paean seems originally to have been a hymn addressed to Apollo, but it was used at an early stage for other purposes on military, sympotic or other public occasions. In the Hellenistic age paeans were addressed to successful individuals and gods other than Apollo.

84 Page, *PMG*, no. 16.

85 Page, *PMG*, no. 1.

86 Page, *PMG*, no. 5.

87 Page, *PMG*, no. 56.

88 Page, *PMG*, no. 39.

89 Page, *PMG*, no. 89.

90 Diehl, *ALG²*, no. 98 (25); Page, *LGS*, no. 218.

91 2.38.

92 3.744.

93 *Aen.*, 4.522.

94 10.1.62.

95 Pap. Oxy. 2617; D. L. Page, *Supplementum Lyricis Graecis*, Oxford, 1974, pp. 5f.

96 C. M. Bowra, *Greek Lyric Poetry*, 2nd edn., Oxford, 1961, pp. 121f.

97 Page, *LGS*, addenda, p. 268; Page, *Supplementum Lyricis Graecis*, pp. 5f.

98 Cic., *Tusc. Disp.*, 4.33.71.

99 Although a couplet honouring Harmodius and Aristogiton, the tyrannicides, is attributed to him, it is not necessarily genuine; while his (genuine) epitaph on Hippias' daughter shows his affection for the house of Pisistratus.

100 Page, *PMG*, no. 4.

101 Page, *PMG*, no. 17.

102 Page, *PMG*, no. 89.

103 Those most likely to be genuine are Diehl, *ALG²*, nos. 79, 83, 85, 91. The attribution to Simonides of two inscriptions found in the Athenian *agora* (Diehl, *ALG²*, nos. 88 (90)a, 88b) is very questionable.

104 Page, *PMG*, no. 38.

105 Plut., *de Glor. Ath.*, 3.

106 *de Imit.*, 2.2.6.

107 Page, *PMG*, no. 542.

108 Pap. Oxy. 2432; Page, *PMG*, no. 36.

109 Diehl, *ALG²*, no. 79.

110 *Pyth.*, 7; unless Timodamus of Acharnae (*Nem.*, 2) was an Athenian.

111 See, for example, *Isthm.*, 1.3.4; cf. Polyb., 4.31.

112 Fr. 106 (Bowra).

113 *Pyth.*, 4.

114 Three surviving fragments (Snell, *TGF*, frs. 76, 77, 78) probably come from this dithyramb.

115 *Pyth.*, 8.

116 Snell, *TGF*, fr. 70; Snell, *TGF*, fr. 81 probably also belongs to the same poem.

117 *Pyth.*, 10.

118 For example, *Ol.*, 4, 8, 10.

119 *Ol.*, 1.

120 For example, *Pyth.*, 6, or *Nem.*, 8.

121 Strophe and antistrophe are metrically identical but not so the epode. All strophes and antistrophes within a poem, as well as all epodes, follow the same metrical pattern.

122 Rhythmically, the Pindaric epinician odes can be divided into two classes, which may be called Dorian and Aeolian, but each single poem has its own metrical individuality.

123 As in *Ol.*, 2.

124 On the rhythms, see P. Maas, *Greek Metre*, trs. H. Lloyd-Jones, Oxford, 1962, §§53–5.
125 See H. Fränkel, *Wege und Formen frühgriechische Denkens*, 2nd edn., Munich, 1962, p. 366.
126 Cf. *Ol.*, 13.13.
127 Cf. *Ol.*, 10.20.
128 *Nem.*, 3.41.
129 Fr. 21 (Bowra).
130 *Pyth.*, 1.41.
131 *Ol.*, 1.
132 Hor., *Carm.*, 4.2.
133 *Ol.*, 2.56–8; *Pyth.*, 2.72–3; *Nem.*, 3.80–2.
134 Snell, *TGF*, fr. 3, 23f.
135 Odes 18 and 19.
136 18.
137 See pp. 121f.
138 See pp. 233f.

Section II: From the Persian Wars to the Death of Alexander (490–323 B.C.)

Chapter 3: Tragedy

1 West, *IEG*, no. 120; Diehl, *ALG*³, no. 77.
2 Cf. Herod., 1.23. The paeans of Xenocritus of Locri Epizephyrii, a poet older than Stesichorus, which dealt with heroic themes (Pseudo-Plut., *de Mus.*, 10.1134e) do not seem to have been real dithyrambs; nor does any ancient writer ascribe dithyrambs to Stesichorus.
3 *Suda*, s.v. Λάσος.
4 As well as dithyrambs, of which he was a pioneer, he composed hymns (see text, Page, *PMG*, nos. 364f.).
5 See E. B. Buschor, *Satyrtänze und frühes Drama*, Munich, 1943–5.
6 The contest between the dithyrambic choruses at various other Athenian festivals — like the Thargelia or the Panathenaea — was always a tribal one.
7 Marm., *Par.*, 46.
8 Diehl, *ALG*², no. 79.
9 Pindar, frs. 60–77 (Bowra).
10 *Odes*, 15–21.
11 Other names associated with the earlier school of dithyrambic poets were Kekeides, Pontacles and Nicostratos.
12 See pp. 233f.
13 For a full presentation of the main theories about this vexed problem, see A. W. Pickard-Cambridge, *Dithyramb, Tragedy and Comedy*, 2nd edn., rev. T. B. L. Webster, Oxford, 1962; M. Pohlenz, *Die griechische Tragödie*, vols. 1, 2, 2nd edn., Göttingen, 1954; A. Lesky, *Die griechische Tragödie*, 4th edn., Stuttgart, 1968 (trs. H. A. Frankfort, London, 1965).
14 *Poet.*, 4.1449a.9f.
15 *Poet.*, 4.1449a.21f.
16 *Poet.*, 4.1448b.24f.
17 6.67.
18 S.v. Arion.
19 Published by H. Rabe, in *Rhein. Mus.*, vol. 63, 1908, p. 150.
20 S.v. οὐδὲν πρὸς τὸν Διόνυσον; s.v. also Arion.
21 Cf. Aristot., *Poet.*, 3.1488a.29f. The conflicting claims of Dorians and Athenians to have founded tragedy can be traced back as far as Charon of Lampsacus (sixth–fifth century B.C.).

22 Buschor, in his *Satyrtänze und frühes Drama,* put forward the theory that the dancing daemons with fat bellies and buttocks depicted in many archaic vase paintings are the true satyrs. But they are nowhere directly so called, so his theory, which involves complicated inferences and is otherwise unsupported, cannot be accepted with any certainty.

23 Line 220.

24 On the existence of a non-choral mummery in honour of the Attic Dionysus of Eleutherae, and for a full discussion of its combination with 'tragic' choruses, see Pickard-Cambridge, *Dithyramb, Tragedy and Comedy,* pp. 120f.

25 *Poet.,* 4.1449a.9.

26 *Orat.,* 26.316d.

27 In the *Poetics* too (4.1449a.9f.) Aristotle maintains that the starting-point of dialogue lay in the opposition of the leader, the *exarchon,* and the chorus.

28 On the interpretation of *hypocrites,* the term by which the actor was known in later times, have been based various theories about the origin of tragic dialogue. But all are very doubtful. The meaning 'answerer', which has been read into the word, is by no means certain and cannot be reconciled with passages such as Pindar, fr. 140b (Snell). Similarly, passages such as Plato, *Tim.,*·72b, seem to demand a translation such as 'interpreter' or 'explainer'. On this question, see A. Lesky, *Studi in onore di U. E. Paoli,* Florence, 1955, p. 469; M. Pohlenz, in *Hermes,* vol. 84, 1956, p. 69; and G. F. Else, in *Wien. Stud.,* vol. 72, 1959, p. 75.

29 See p. 123.

30 See B. Snell, *Die Entdeckung des Geistes,* 3rd edn., Hamburg, 1955 (trs. T. C. Rosenmayer, New York, n.d., pp. 90f.).

31 No early northern Peloponnesian choral experiment seems to have achieved a form that we would recognize as drama. See W. Kranz, *Geschichte der griechischen Literatur,* 4th edn., Bremen, n.d., p. 135, n. 1.

32 Aristot., *ap. Them.,* 26.316d.

33 Hor., *Ars Poet.,* 275f.

34 Snell, *TGF,* vol. 1, p. 63.

35 Kranz, *Geschichte der griechischen Literatur,* p. 135, n. 1.

36 The first unambiguous appearance of 'satyrs' is in the satyr plays such as Euripides' *Cyclops* and Sophocles' *Ichneutae* and in representations in art of scenes from satyr plays (cf. F. Brommer, *Satyrspiele,* 2nd edn., Berlin, 1959). Like the *sileni,* they are spirits of wild life in woods and hills; see H. J. Rose, *Handbook of Greek Mythology,* 2nd edn., New York, 1953, p. 156. They are bestial in their desires and behaviour and bear physical signs of their animal nature.

37 Paus., 2.13.5.

38 Diosc., in *AP,* bk. 7, no. 37.

39 Diog. Laert., 2.133.

40 *Corpus Inscriptionum Atticarum,* vol. 2, p. 973.

41 See A. W. Pickard-Cambridge, *The Dramatic Festivals of Athens,* 2nd edn., rev. J. Gould and D. M. Lewis, Oxford, 1973, pp. 233–4. E. G. Turner published in *Mus. Helvet.,* vol. 33, 1976, pp. 1f. (dedicated to Bruno Snell on his eightieth birthday, June 1976), Papyrus Bodmer XXVII, which includes a fragment of a satyr play on the confrontation of Heracles and Atlas. It is a λειπογράμματον text, without a sigma, which points to a later date. It may, however, be the later recasting of an earlier piece.

42 Cf. W. Aly, 'Satyrspiel', in Pauly–Wissowa, *REkA,* vol. 2A, pp. 235f.

43 When they appeared as hunters, reapers, shepherds or other rustic characters, as was frequently the case, they doubtless wore appropriate items of clothing in addition to the purely satyric dress.

44 The satyric dance was called σίκιννις, but the derivation of the word and the form of the dance are unknown to us.

45 The comparison which was drawn in antiquity between this figure and Socrates was based not only on their common ugliness but also on a shared irony and wisdom.

46 Cf. Vitruv., 5.6.9; Diosc., in *AP,* bk, 7, no. 412.

47 On the Athenian dramatic performances, see Pickard-Cambridge, *The Dramatic Festivals of Athens*, pp. 57f.

48 On all such festivals, as well as those of Collytus, Eleusis and Icaria, see Pickard-Cambridge, *The Dramatic Festivals of Athens*, pp. 57f., 177f.

49 See W. Kranz, *Stasimon*, Berlin, 1933, esp. chs. 1, 4.

50 Cf. Pap. Oxy. 2256, 3.

51 See Pickard-Cambridge, *The Dramatic Festivals of Athens*, pp. 177f.

52 For information about the architecture of the ancient theatre, see Pickard-Cambridge, *The Dramatic Festivals of Athens*.

53 Aristot., *Eth. Nic.*, 3.1; Clement., *Alex. Strom.*, 2.461.

54 Marm., *Par.*

55 But see H. Lloyd-Jones, in *Journal of Hellenic Studies*, vol. 76, 1956, p. 55; and D. Page, in J. D. Denniston and D. Page, *Agamemnon*, Oxford, 1957, p. xv.

56 Plut., *Quaest. Conv.*, 715e; Aristot., *Ran.*, 1021.

57 Those who consider that the words of the chorus (ll. 686f.) are irrelevant because it must be ignorant of Eteocles' motives (cf. Kurt von Fritz, *Antike und moderne Tragödie*, Berlin, 1962, p. 214) disregard the fact that the author's only real allegiance is to the audience, not to the agents of his play, and look for a total logic and a verisimilitude foreign not only to Aeschylus but also to Homer.

58 Pap. Oxy. 2256, fr. 3.

59 See A. Lesky, *A History of Greek Literature from Homer to the Age of Lucian*, trs. J. Willis and C. de Heer, London, 1966, p. 252.

60 W. Schmid, for example, in his great *Literaturgeschichte* considers it an anonymous work written under the influence of the Sophistic movement; Schmid–Stählin, *GL*, vol. 3, pp. 281f.

61 See Lesky, *A History of Greek Literature*, p. 255.

62 In the eleventh Pythian ode of Pindar, however, Clytaemnestra also kills Agamemnon with her own hand, and in the story as reported in the *Odyssey* she probably did the same. On Aeschylus' sources, see E. Mazon, *Eschyle*, 6th edn., Paris, 1953 (Budé series), introduction.

63 See W. Headlam, in *Journal of Hellenic Studies*, vol. 26, 1906, pp. 268f.

64 Diog. Laert., 2.133.

65 Aristot., *Poet.*, 1449a.16.

66 See P. Wiesmann, *Das Problem der tragischen Tetralogie*, Zurich, 1929.

67 Accounts in later sources of Aeschylus' contributions in this field are highly suspect. Cf. Pickard-Cambridge, *The Dramatic Festivals of Athens*, pp. 180f.

68 *Inst. Or.*, 10.1.66.

69 *Frogs*, 82.

70 *de Prof. Virt.*, 7.

71 The Telephus trilogy (?) (see *Suda* and *IG*, vol. 2², insc. 3091) seems to contradict the view that he never composed a connected trilogy.

72 Donat., on *Ter. Andr.*, 297.

73 *Rhein. Mus.*, vol. 3, 1829, p. 68.

74 Herod., 9.71.

75 *Philosophie der Religion*, vol. 16, 1, p. 133; *Aesthetik*, vol. 2, 2, p. 1.

76 For example, *Eumenides*, 585f.

77 Line 27.

78 See A. Wasserstein, in *Gnomon*, vol. 32, 1960, p. 178.

79 Aristoph., *Frogs*, 82.

80 Lesky, *History of Greek Literature*, p. 296.

81 *Poet*, 4.

82 Even the titles of the Sophoclean plays (not, of course, invented by the poet himself) suggest that this peculiarity of his drama was recognized in the ancient world. Of the seven surviving plays, six are named after the central figure. On the other hand, epigraphical evidence shows that on at least one occasion Sophocles wrote a connected trilogy, the *Telepheia*, parts of one play from which, the *Assembly of Achaeans*, have been identified from papyri; see Page, *GLP*, nos. 3, 21, with bibliography, and

D. Page, in M. Platnauer (ed.), *Fifty Years (and Twelve) of Classical Scholarship*, Oxford, 1968, p. 90.

83 See B. M. W. Knox, *The Heroic Temper*, London, 1964, pp. 3f.

84 The influence of the Sophists on Sophocles has generally been overrated. Though undoubtedly a traditionalist and closer in spirit to Aeschylus than to Euripides, Sophocles did not, and could not, escape the influence of the Sophists' far-ranging scepticism.

85 The concept to which Sophocles gives the word *Dike* has no single-word equivalent in English. It means neither 'justice' nor 'retribution' in any modern sense, but rather a principle of order and regularity; see H. D. F. Kitto, *Sophocles, Dramatist and Philosopher*, London, 1958, pp. 50f.

86 At the same time the poet shows that it is sheer folly to neglect those of the divine laws which we do not know simply in order to follow *ad hoc* man-made laws, as, for example, Creon attempts to do in the *Antigone*.

87 Examples are the Ismene scene in the *Antigone* and the Creon scene in *King Oedipus*.

88 Highly educated *hetaerae* such as Aspasia were neither Athenian nor well-respected.

89 Tycho von Wilamowitz-Moellendorff, in his book *Die dramatische Technik des Sophokles*, Berlin, 1917, stressed the dramatic significance of the single scene, which he regarded as more important than the unity and coherence of the play as a whole. Thus he argues the subordination to the effect of the single scene of not merely plot but character drawing as well.

90 The compression of events off the stage during a choral ode is, however, rarely such as to provoke a sense of improbability.

91 His masterpiece of this genre is the duet sung by Oedipus and the chorus in the *King Oedipus*, as the hero emerges, blinded, from the palace.

92 Certain scholars believe that Sophocles was the first to introduce the messenger speech to the Attic theatre. In Aeschylus there is only one real example of the form, the description of the Persian defeat at Salamis in the *Persians*. The end of Oedipus' sons, as related in the *Seven Against Thebes*, hardly amounts to a messenger speech.

93 It is difficult for us to comprehend the ancient sensitivity that distinguished between the actual perpetration of a violent act, which was not to be presented on stage, and its results, often mangled bodies, which were shown to the audience. A special machine, indeed, the ἐκκύκλημα, was devised to bring the corpses on stage.

94 The author remembers Jean-Louis Barrault stressing, in a lecture entitled 'On the Theatre', just this point about the importance of spectacle in drama: 'What we carry away from the theatre when we leave a great production is the spectacle, not the words.'

95 Philochorus, fr. 21.

96 The point of the joke is lost for us.

97 Some scholars believe that this Euripides, who produced the plays after the poet's death, was not the son but the nephew of the poet.

98 Aristot., *Rhet.*, 2.6, and schol.

99 Plutarch, *Nic.*, 17.

100 For example, *Hecuba*, 1187, and Nauck, *TGF*, fr. 439.

101 See Schmid–Stählin, *GL*, vol. 3, pp. 759f.

102 Thuc., 2.35f.

103 See B. Snell, in *Philologus*, vol. 97, 1948, pp. 125f.

104 See pp. 178f.

105 A. Nauck, *Euripidis Perditarum Tragoediarum Fragmenta*, Leipzig, 1902, fr. 288.

106 G. Zuntz, *The Political Plays of Euripides*, Manchester, 1955, p. 31.

107 *ibid.*, pp. 6f.

108 Nauck, *TGF*, fr. 286.

109 See J. Diggle, *Euripides: Phaethon*, Cambridge, 1970, pp. 47f.

110 *de Hist. Conscr.*, 1.

111 See B. Knox, *Euripidean Comedy: The Rearer Action, Essays in Honour of Francis Ferguson*, New Brunswick, 1970; and A. Burnett, *Catastrophe Survived*, Oxford, 1971.

112 In the *Iphigeneia in Tauris* the action takes place in the far-off land of the Taurians; in

the *Helen*, among the Egyptians; and so on. This feature brings this group of plays very close to the tradition of fairy-tale plays discussed above.

113 See Burnett, *Catastrophe Survived, passim.*

114 2.112–20.

115 *Thesmoph.*, 850.

116 Aristot., *Pr.*, 19.15.

117 See Pherecrates, Kock, *CAF*, fr. 145; Pickard-Cambridge, *Dithyramb, Tragedy and Comedy*, pp. 38f.

118 *Thesmoph.*, 100; *Frogs*, 1301f.

119 K. Wessely, *Mitteilungen aus der Sammlung der Papyrus Erzherzog Reiner*, vol. 5, 1892, pp. 65f., with photographs; and D. D. Flaver, in *American Journal of Philology*, vol. 81, 1960, pp. 1f.

120 For example, *Ion*, 82–183.

121 For example, *Ion*, 859–922.

122 *Orest.*, 1369–502.

123 See Kranz, *Geschichte der griechischen Literatur*, p. 207.

124 And in modern times too Gilbert Murray has written: 'For sheer beauty of writing, for a kind of gorgeous dignity, that at times reminds one of Aeschylus, and yet is compatible with the subtlest clashes of mood and character, the *Trojan Women* stands, perhaps, first among all the works of Euripides.' *Euripides and his Age*, London, 1965 (rpt. of 2nd edn., 1947), p. 67.

125 See Murray, *Euripides and his Age*, pp. 76f.

126 Plutarch tell us (*Crassus*, 32) that after Crassus was killed by the Parthians his head was carried on stage during a performance of the *Bacchae* in Armenia.

127 E. R. Dodds, *The Greeks and the Irrational*, Berkeley–Los Angeles, 1968, p. 273.

128 Cf. *Orest.*, 917–22, and the peasant husband of Electra in the play of that name.

129 The traditional claim that he died as a result of an attack by wild dogs is, as has already been mentioned, not to be trusted.

130 The striking composition of the opening passage of the play may be due to the confusion of two of the poet's drafts; see Lesky, *A History of Greek Literature*, p. 396.

131 *Poet.*, 14.1454a.

132 See W. Ritchie, *The Authenticity of the Rhesus of Euripides*, Cambridge, 1964.

133 See p. 199.

134 Cf., for example, *Hippolytus*, 120; *Andromache*, 439, 1164f.; *Phoenician Women*, 86f.; *Children of Heracles*, 347, 735, 1341f.; *Iphigeneia in Aulis*, 394.

135 Nauck, *TGF*, fr. 311. Doubts about divine justice are, in fact, directly expressed in several places – for example, *Hippolytus*, 1102; *Medea*, 1112f.; *Heracles*, 342f.; *Ion*, 252f.; *Trojan Women*, 469; *Hecuba*, 408 – and when the powers of destiny are not personified, they work with no regard to *Aidos* or to Justice (cf. *Alcestis*, 983f.; *Helen*, 1212; *Iphigeneia in Aulis*, 1405; fr. 684, 1048). Euripides' anti-religious attitude is also evident in his attacks on priests, seers and oracles.

136 See Schmid–Stählin, *GL*, vol. 3, p. 702.

137 'Ἀνάγκη is sometimes presented as a goddess proper (*Hecuba*, 491f.), and the figure of *Tyche* is sometimes seen as equal to the gods (*Electra*, 890) and even above them (*Heracles*, 1314f.). In the *Iphigeneia in Tauris* the abstraction Χρεών ('what must be') is said to rule over both men and gods!

138 Fr. 480.

139 Also called the 'live-wire' notion of guilt; see Kitto, *Sophocles, Dramatist and Philosopher*, pp. 42f.

140 See W. Jaeger, *Paideia*, trs. G. Highet, Oxford, 1954, vol. 1, p. 4f.

141 See Pickard-Cambridge, *Dithyramb, Tragedy and Comedy*, pp. 38f.

142 Cf. K. J. Beloch, *Griechische Geschichte*, Berlin–Leipzig, 1925, vol. 4, pp. 493f.

143 *Poet.*, 13; 1452a.29.

144 *Gespräche mit Eckermann*, 28.3.1827, ed. E. Beutler, Zurich, 1948, p. 611.

145 *IG*, 2², inscs. 2318, 2319–23, 2325.

146 Diog. Laert., 3.6.

147 Athen., 14.617b.

148 Paus., 2.13.5.
149 *IG*, vol. 2², insc. 2325.
150 Snell, *TGF*, vol. 1, frs. 2,3.
151 *Suda*, s.v. Phrynichus.
152 Herod., 6.21.
153 Snell, *TGF*, vol. 1, fr. 1.
154 *Suda*, s.v.
155 Snell, *TGF*, vol. 1, fr. 1a.
156 *Suda*, s.v.
157 Athen., 1.3f.
158 *Suda*, s.v.
159 Line 33.
160 Diog. Laert., 2.133.
161 10.451c.
162 *Poet.*, 24; 1459b.30.
163 See C. Corbato, in *Dionyso*, vol. 11, 1948, p. 163.
164 *Amat. Narr.*, 14.
165 The transformation was probably no more than the refashioning of the old tragedy into a kind of fairy-tale.
166 See Lesky, *A History of Greek Literature*, pp. 411f.
167 Περὶ τραγῳδίας, 5 (probably by Michael Psellus), edited by R. Browning, Γέρας: *Studies presented to George Thomson*, Acta Universitalis Carolinae, 1963, pp. 67f.
168 Snell, *TGF*, vol. 1, pp. 155f.
169 See pp. 236f.
170 *Vita* of Euripides.
171 Cf. A. Croiset and M. Croiset, *Histoire de la littérature grecque*, 4th edn., Paris, 1928, vol. 3, pp. 394f.
172 On Carcinus, see T. B. L. Webster, *Fourth-Century Tragedy and the Poetics*, Wiesbaden, 1954, pp. 1f., 82, 300f; Diehl, in Pauly–Wissowa, *REkA*, vol. 20.
173 *IG*, vol. 2², insc. 2325, according to a probable restoration.
174 *Clouds*, 1264–5; *Thesmoph.*, 169; *Frogs*, 86.
175 Nauck, *TGF*, p. 770.
176 Aristot., *Poet.*, 6; 1450a.25.
177 *ibid.*, 6; 1450b.5.
178 *IG*, vol. 2², insc. 2320.
179 Cf. Aristot., *Poet.*, 14; 1453b.30; see also Plut., *de Glor. Ath.*, 7.
180 Snell, *TGF*, 1, pp. 227f.
181 *Rhet.*, 3.12; 1413b.12f.
182 See E. Vogt, in *Ant. Abendl.*, vol. 13, 1967, pp. 82f.
183 13.608d.
184 Snell, *TGF*, 1, pp. 215f.
185 According to Aristotle, Euripides did write a play of the same name.
186 Cf. A. Lesky, in *Gnomon*, vol. 23, 1951, pp. 141f.; G. Björck, in *Arktos*, n.s., vol. 1, 1954, p. 16.
187 See Lesky, *A History of Greek Literature*, p. 631 and n. 2.
188 See Ritchie, *The Authenticity of the* Rhesus *of Euripides*.
189 Cf. T. B. L. Webster, *Art and Literature in Fourth-Century Athens*, London, 1956, p. 32.
190 *ibid.*, p. 30.

Chapter 4: Comedy

1 What we see in Shakespeare, the phenomenon of a great poet composing both tragedies and comedies, was discussed in the ancient world (cf. Plato, *Symp.*, p. 223; *Philebus*, p. 50; *Laws*, p. 816) but was never practised.
2 The word τρυγῳδία, which we meet as a synonym of τραγῳδία in Aristophanes and Eupolis, is formed playfully after κωμῳδία, τρύξ, meaning 'dregs' or 'lees' of wine. Only later was it taken seriously.

3 On these, see A. W. Pickard-Cambridge, *Dithyramb, Tragedy and Comedy*, 2nd edn., rev. T. B. L. Webster, Oxford, 1962, pp. 132f. The humorous adoption of aliases on public occasions is a feature of many pre-literate societies.

4 Athen., 622.d. Their speech appears in iambics.

5 Athen., 8.384.

6 *IG*, vol. 2², insc. 2318.

7 It is hardly necessary to repeat here that Aristotle's linguistic argument connecting κωμῳδία with κώμη is implausible. Nor should his connection between comedy and the lighter poems of the epic age, such as the *Margites*, be taken seriously.

8 On these, see Pickard-Cambridge, *Dithyramb, Tragedy and Comedy*, pp. 305f.

9 *Poet.*, 3; 1448a.34.

10 Sosibius (c. 300 B.C.) was also enlisted (Athen., 621d,e; Jacoby, *FGH*, fr. 595.F.7), who speaks about the *deikelistai*, Spartan mummers who acted short farces dealing with everyday life, as well as the *phlyakes* of Tarentum and the *ethelontai* of Thebes. The Laconian dance *kordax* (*Pollux*, 4.104–5), Sicilian singing competitions (schol. Theocr., p. 2 (Wendel)) and the grotesque masks found at the sanctuary of Artemis Orthia, near Sparta, were also adduced to support the Doric ancestry of Attic comedy. But all the Doric pre-dramatic choruses of fat men, ugly women and so on, as archaeology has shown, have also an Attic ancestry; see *Kleine Pauly*, vol. 3, p. 283. Other theories about the origins of Attic comedy, such as those put forward by Varro (Kaibel, *CGF*, frs. 57f.) or Aristophanes (Kock, *CAF*, fr. 253), need not be discussed here.

11 Ecphantides, Kock, *CAF*, fr. 2, and schol. to Aristoph., *Wasps*, 54; also Aristot., *Eth. Nic.*, 4.6.1123a.20, with schol.

12 At the festival of the Lenaea, so intimately connected with comedy, we also hear of a procession of wagons from which the riders jeered at the bystanders. The scholiast of Aristophanes, *Knights*, 546, seems to include among these σκώμματα, songs of a ludicrous kind composed by poets.

13 *Poet.*, 5; 1449b.4.

14 Pickard-Cambridge, *Dithyramb, Tragedy and Comedy*, p. 173.

15 *ibid.*, pp. 183f.

16 *Suda*, s.v. Chionides; cf. *IG*, vol. 2², insc. 2325.

17 *Poet.*, 1449b.2.

18 Aeschin., 1.157.

19 These generalizations are based mainly on Aristophanes, so the structural features given may not be of great antiquity. For the names and details of the various parts of Old Comedy, see *Kleine Pauly*, vol. 3, pp. 281f., s.v. 'Komödie'.

20 Towards the end of the third century performances were given at Delphi by seven *choreutai* and later by even fewer; see A. W. Pickard-Cambridge, *The Dramatic Festivals of Athens*, rev. J. Gould and D. M. Lewis, 2nd edn., Oxford, 1973, p. 236.

21 Ἐπίρρημα in Old Comedy was a speech, commonly of trochaic tetrameters, spoken by the *coryphaeus* after the *parabasis*.

22 Characteristic is the passage in the *Knights* (230f.), in which Aristophanes says that none of the mask makers dared to produce a portrait of Cleon.

23 Attempts to restrict by legislation the vilification of living men seem to have been made; cf. schol. Aristoph., *Birds*, 1297, and schol. Aristoph. *Ach.*, 67.

24 In *Aristophanes*, Oxford, 1933, p. 6, Gilbert Murray put forward the view, based on Cornford's theory (F. M. Cornford, *The Origins of Attic Comedy*, London, 1914; rev. T. H. Gaster, Gloucester, Mass., 1968), that the *gamos* at the end of Old Comedy was the survivor of a ritual element in the Dionysiac *comos*.

25 On all these metres, see D. S. Raven, *Greek Metre*, London, 1962. On the comic iambic trimeter, in which more licence is allowed than in tragedy, see §29; on the trochaic tetrameter *catalectic*, used particularly as the metre of the chorus ἐπίρρημα, following the *parabasis*, §35; on the anapaestic tetrameter *catalectic*, commonly used in comic dialogue, §83; on the iambic tetrameters, §33 and §32; and on anapaestic dimeters, §85 and §79. It is, of course, impossible in a book of this nature to give a detailed analysis of all these metres.

26 Aristotle ascribes to Epicharmus and Phorius in Sicily and to Crates in Athens the first composition of plots (*Poet.*, 5).

27 Or, according to Aelian (*Nat. Hist.*, 6.51), the rival.

28 The term *mimos*, in its inclusive sense, embraces singers, dancers, jugglers, mimes, conjurors – all performers similar to those whom we see today in variety theatres and circuses.

29 Douris of Samos: Jacoby, *FGH*, fr. 76, F.72.

30 The *Suda* (s.v. Chionides) says that his work was performed eight years before the Persian Wars, which are assumed to have taken place in 480/79 B.C.

31 It is doubtful if the texts of Chionides' plays were preserved in Aristotle's day, for he says very little indeed about the first recorded comic poets in the *Poetics*.

32 Kock, *CAF*, fr. 2.

33 Hesichius, s.v. ἐϰϰεχοιϱιλωμένη.

34 *Serm.*, 1.4.1.

35 Pack, *GLLT*, no. 163.

36 Kock, *CAF*, fr. 71 of the *Thracian Women* suggests that Pericles had just escaped the danger of ostracism in 444/3 B.C.

37 Page, *GLP*, no. 196.

38 *Diff. Com.*, 7, 12.

39 Kock, *CAF*, fr. 199.

40 *Diff. Com.*, 14.

41 See Kaibel, *CGF*, p. 18.

42 Aristot., *Poet.*, 5; 1449b.5 and 9.1451b.8f.

43 Kock, *CAF*, fr. 157.

44 Kock, *CAF*, fr. 108.

45 Kock, *CAF*, frs. 42, 44.

46 Plut., *Pericles*, 32.

47 Diehl, *ALG*³, no. 3 (4.5).

48 Kock, *CAF*, fr. 82. The play is unnamed.

49 Kock, *CAF*, fr. 63, from the play *Phormophoroi*.

50 Kock, *CAF*, fr. 46, from an unnamed play.

51 Schol. Plat., *Apol.*, 19c.

52 Thuc., 2.27.

53 The name of the last son is uncertain.

54 *IG*, vols. 2², 3², no. 1740. In Athens after 508/7 the *Boule* (Council) consisted each year of fifty men chosen by lot from each of the ten *phylae* (tribes). Each group of fifty served as *prytaneis* for one-tenth of the year.

55 Much bibliographical information in R. Cantarella, *Aristophane*, Milan, 1949, vol. 1, pp. 135f.

56 See Kock, *CAF*, frs. 198, 222, and *Clouds*, 529, with schol.

57 Thus it was Philonides who trained the chorus for the *Wasps*, the *Frogs* and the now lost *Proagon* and *Amphiaraos*; his son produced the *Aeolosycon* and the *Cocalus* in 388.

58 A list of his plays is transmitted with his *Vita* in two manuscripts.

59 In the course of time this core of comedy degenerated and individual sections were left out.

60 The anapaests were often felt to be the most important part of the *parabasis* and are sometimes called the *parabasis* by themselves.

61 The *pnigos* was also called the *makron*.

62 In reality this 'oracle' is a maxim of political wisdom: an unscrupulous demagogue can be overthrown only by a more unscrupulous one.

63 This is an old myth motif, well-known from the story of Pelias and its dramatization by Euripides.

64 See M. Bieber, *History of the Greek and Roman Theatre*, Princeton, 1939, fig. 79.

65 Schol. *Clouds*, 522.

66 Kierkegaard, in the seventh thesis of his doctoral dissertation.

67 19c.

68 But it is also Plato who, seven years after the performance of the *Clouds*, presents

Aristophanes in the *Symposium* supplementing the arguments and the wisdom of Socrates.

69 At the same Lenaea Aristophanes had presented the *Proagon*, a play now lost, which dealt with the performance of actors before the tragic contest of the Dionysia.

70 In Athens citizens were given a small fee to act as jurymen. In this capacity they also fulfilled most of the functions of our judges. As all trials in which the state or its 'allies' were concerned were held before such courts, their political importance was considerable. The fee was raised by Cleon from two to three *obols*, which won all these small men to his side, and that is the reason why Aristophanes attacks them.

71 Concluded after the death of Cleon and of his great Spartan opponent Brasidas.

72 The subject of peace and war was also treated by the poet in two other lost plays, Γεωργοί and Ὁλκάδες.

73 See p. 174.

74 The design of the stage on which this play was acted is indeed problematic.

75 It has been argued that at that time 'the life of the peasant was not so far removed from that of the town dweller that it called for or underwent poetic transfiguration'; therefore all notion of the 'idyllic' or the 'pastoral' in the *parabasis* should be dismissed (A. Lesky, *A History of Greek Literature from Homer to the Age of Lucian*, trs. J. Willis and C. de Heer, London, 1966, p. 437). But this is certainly wrong, for the Athenians, cooped up for years in their city during the Peloponnesian War, most certainly longed for and idealized country life.

76 Kock, *CAF*, frs. 294–7.

77 The Thesmophoria was a women's festival in honour of Demeter common to all Greeks and regularly celebrated in autumn.

78 Telephus, dressed as a beggar, had snatched Orestes in order to secure a hearing from the Greeks.

79 There are two opening choruses in the play, but it is not clear whether these were intended to be separate or parts of the same one.

80 In *A History of Greek Literature*, p. 441.

81 See M. P. Nilsson, *Geschichte griechischer Religion*, 2nd edn., Munich, 1955–61, vol. 1, p. 799.

82 See A. Meder, *Der ath. Demos zur Zeit des peloponn. Krieges* (Diss.), Munich, 1938, p. 73, for a bibliography on the subject.

83 The same note is also occasionally found in the *Ecclesiazusae*, once in the *Clouds* and later in the plays of Menander.

84 While praising the healing god, Aristophanes does not miss the opportunity to challenge the honesty of the priests.

85 Though these themes were clearly borrowed by Menander from Euripides.

86 It might be interesting to note that the instruments that accompanied Aristophanes' plays were mainly the *aulos* and only occasionally the lyre (especially in the passages in which tragedy was parodied).

87 Hor., *Sat.*, 1.4.1; Quint., 10.1.65.

88 The *Suda* claims that he was only seventeen when he presented his first play, but this is scarcely credible.

89 *Suda*, s.v. Eupolis. The name Eupolis appears on a monument commemorating Athenians who fell at the Hellespont in a naval battle against the Lacedaemonians (*IG*, vol. 1², insc. 950, 52); we do not know if this is the name of our poet. About a privilege exempting poets from military service we otherwise know nothing; cf. Schmid–Stählin, *GL*, vol. 3, p. 113, n. 6.

90 The name is that of an Attic deme.

91 And if Pap. Soc. It. 1213 belongs to the Προσπάλτιοι, we probably have a further indication of the poet's concern with Pericles and his warlike measures.

92 See *Clouds*, 553.

93 Kock, *CAF*, fr. 54.

94 Kock, *CAF*, frs. 352, 361.

95 See schol. Juv., 2.91.

96 The story had already been refuted in antiquity by Eratosthenes; cf. Cic., *ad Att.*, 6.1.

97 See A. Körte, in *Hermes*, vol. 47, 1912, pp. 276f.
98 He is mentioned by Aristophanes in *Lysis.*, 801, together with Phormis, as an example of a brave soldier. He was also the victor of Oenophyta (457 B.C.). It has also been argued that this may be the Myrionides of whom we hear at the time of the Persian Wars. It is hard to decide, but the first proposition appears more probable.
99 Kock, *CAF*, fr. 94.
100 *Vit. Aristoph.*, 11; cf. Anon., *de Com.*, 10.
101 Platon., *Diff. Com.*, 15.
102 Anón., *de Com.*, 10.
103 Kock, *CAF*, fr. 58.
104 *IG*, vol. 2², insc. 2325, 63.
105 A play of that name has also been attributed to Aristophanes.
106 *IG*, vol. 2², insc. 2325, 64 *Φιλ* [ ].
107 *Poet.*, 2; 1448a.12.
108 15.699a.
109 15.698f.
110 See Athen., 15.698f.
111 See U. von Wilamowitz-Moellendorff, in *Kleine Schriften*, vol. 4, Berlin, 1971, p. 219.
112 Names of other poets of Old Comedy—not all of equal merit—are the following: Alcaeus, Apollophanes, Archippus, Aristonymos, Autocrates, Callias, Cantharus, Cephisodorus, Demetrius, Diocles, Leucon, Lysippus, Metagenes, Nicochares, Nicophrom, Philyllius, Polyzelus, Sannyrion, Strattis, Theopompus. According to the *Suda*, Autocrates also wrote tragedies, an exceptional case if the information is correct, for poets never composed both tragedies and comedies in antiquity.
113 The division of ancient Greek comedy into Old, Middle and New was challenged by W. Fielitz, *de Comm. Att. Bipartita*, Bonn, 1866, who was followed by Kock in the introduction to *CAF*, vol. 2, p. 12. But see O. Crusius, in *Philologus*, vol. 46, 1888, p. 606; G. Kaibel, in *Hermes*, vol. 24, 1889, pp. 57f.; and Ph.-E. Legrand, *Daos*, Lyons, 1910, pp. 4f.
114 They can be found in A. Körte, in Pauly–Wissowa, *REkA*, vol. 21, p. 1226.
115 8.336d.
116 See T. B. L. Webster, *Studies in Later Greek Comedy*, Manchester, 1953, pp. 98f., 139f., 174f., 208f., 217f. and *passim*.
117 On the other hand, according to the evidence of pottery, indecent jesting with old myths seems to have continued in the *phlyax* farce of the Greek west.
118 Alexis, in Kock, *CAF*, fr. 135.
119 See Aristot., *Poet.*, 1450a.25; 1451b.7.
120 Ἰατρός, Κηπουρός, Κιθαριστής, Κναφεύς, etc.
121 Ἀδελφοί, Δίδυμοι, Πρόγονοι, Ὁμοπάτριοι, etc.
122 Ἄσωτοι, Δυσέρωτες, Μοιχοί, Παιδεραστής, Παράσιτος, etc.
123 Βοιωτός, Βυζάντιος, Ζακύνθιος, Ποντικός, Κᾶρες, etc.
124 Γάμος, Εὔπλοια, Ὑδρία, etc.
125 See Satyr., *Vit. Eur.*
126 See Webster, *Studies in Later Greek Comedy*, p. 8.
127 Cf. Aesch., 1.157.
128 Eubulus, in Kock, *CAF*, frs. 104, 105; cf. Alexis, in Kock, *CAF*, fr. 237; and Heniochus, fr. 5.
129 Longer anapaestic systems are not rare; see Körte, in Pauly–Wissowa, *REkA*, vol. 21, p. 1265.
130 *Eth. Nic.*, 4.1128a.20.
131 Platon., 11.
132 Webster, *Studies in Later Greek Comedy*, pp. 37–49.
133 See K. J. Dover, in M. Platnauer (ed.), *Fifty Years (and Twelve) of Classical Scholarship*, Oxford, 1954, p. 146.
134 See Körte, *loc. cit.*
135 Kock, *CAF*, fr. 18.
136 Kock, *CAF*, fr. 122.

137 *Suda*, s.v. Of these, three at least at the Lenaea (*IG*, vol. 2², insc. 2325, 142).
138 Cf. Hor., *Serm.*, 1.2.101f., with Kock, *CAF*, fr. 67, and *Prop.*, 2.12, with Kock, *CAF*, fr. 41.
139 Anon., *de Com.*, 17; Kaibel, *CGF*, p. 9.
140 *Mor.*, 4.20.
141 Thus, for example, carnal love is seen as a crime against real love (Kock, *CAF*, fr. 70); life is said to be a kind of carnival (Πανήγυρις) (Kock, *CAF*, fr. 219); and old age is regarded as life's evening (Kock, *CAF*, fr. 228).
142 Gellius, *Noct. Att.*, 2.23.1.
143 Cf. G. Arnott, *Rhein, Mus.*, vol. 102, 1959, pp. 252f.
144 Kock, *CAF*, fr. 237, 206(?).
145 Kock, *CAF*, fr. 107.
146 Athen., 235e.

Chapter 5: Later Lyric, Elegiac and Epic Poetry

1 See pp. 121f.
2 The music that accompanied it was of the Phrygian type, and the normal accompanying instrument was the flute; both were considered 'orgiastic' and passionate.
3 See U. von Wilamowitz-Moellendorff, *Textgeschichte der griechischen Lyriker*, Berlin, 1900, pp. 11f.; H. Schönewolf, *Die jungattische Dithyrambos* (Diss.), Giessen, 1958.
4 See Athen., 8.364a; cf. Meineke, *FCG*, vol. 1, p. 76. The ascription of this fragment to Pherecrates has been challenged; see A. W. Pickard-Cambridge, *Dithyramb, Tragedy and Comedy*, 2nd edn., rev. T. B. L. Webster, Oxford, 1962, p. 39 and n. 1.
5 See Xen., *Mem.*, 1.4.3, and Pherecrates, fr. 145.
6 *AP*, bk. 4, nos. 1, 7.
7 Plato, *Laws*, 3, 700d.
8 See C. del Grande, *Ditirambografi*, Naples, 1946, pp. 59f.; P. Maas, in Pauly–Wissowa, *REkA*, vol. 11, pp. 479f.
9 See del Grande, *Ditirambografi*, pp. 64f.; W. Riemschneider, in Pauly–Wissowa, *REkA*, vol. 20, pp. 925f.
10 *Birds*, 1373–404.
11 *Gorg.*, 501e.
12 290f.; cf. schol.
13 Kock, *CAF*, fr. 209.
14 *Suda*.
15 Diehl, *ALG*, no. 7 (21).
16 Satyr., *Vit. Eur.*, fr. 39, col. 22.
17 Pseudo-Plut., *de Mus.*, 4.1132e.
18 *Rhet.*, 3.1413b.12.
19 Athen., 13.603d.
20 Athen., 13.602c.
21 See p. 197.
22 Diehl, *ALG*³, no. 2 (4).
23 Diehl, *ALG*³, no. 8 (1). It must have been composed shortly after Damaste's *On Poets and Sophists* and Alcidamas' *Mouseion*.
24 These are Πολιτεῖαι (probably a prose version of the Ἔμμετροι Πολιτεῖαι); Ἀφορισμοί (could be part of the Πολιτεῖαι); Περὶ φύσεως, ἔρωτος ἢ ἀρετῶν(?) and the Δημηγορικὰ Προοίμια
25 See pp. 91f.
26 See W. Peek, *Griechische Vers-Inschriften*, vol. 1, Berlin, 1955.
27 At the city's request, Euripides wrote a fine epigram on the Athenians lost in Sicily (Plut., *Nic.*, 17).
28 Diehl, *ALG*³, nos. 1 (1)–17 (6); U. von Wilamowitz-Moellendorff, *Hellenistische Dichtung in der Zeit des Kallimachos*, Berlin, 1924, vol. 1, p. 131; C. M. Bowra, *Problems of Greek Poetry*, Oxford, 1953. But see also W. Ludwig, *in Greek, Roman and Byzantine Studies*, vol. 4, 1963, pp. 59f.

29 Diehl, *ALG*¹, vol. 2, pp. 171f.; fr. 637 (Ross).

30 Diehl, *ALG*³, p. 64, 1–2.

31 See p. 76. Probably a new fragment by Choerilus of Samos is found in Pap. Oxy. 2814.

32 Hermesianax, fr. 7, 41–6; (Plut.) *Cons. ad Apoll.*, 9.106b.

33 Her. Pont., fr. 91 (Voss).

34 See K. J. Beloch, *Griechische Geschichte*, Berlin–Leipzig, 1925, vol. 4, p. 222. A papyrus from Hermoupolis, containing fragments of a commentary on the *Artemis* and the *Thebais* with seventeen lines from the text, confirms the view based on earlier fragments that several characteristics of academic Hellenistic poetry—for example, the interpretation of Homer, the contamination of myths and the obscure vocabulary— are already to be found in Antimachus, despite Callimachus' disparagement of his verse. See E. Barber, in M. Platnauer (ed.), *Fifty Years (and Twelve) of Classical Scholarship*, Oxford, 1954, p. 272.

35 If Pap. Milan. 17 contains excerpts of the *Artemis*, the poem was written in hexameters, and its recording of the cults and titles of the goddess recalls the *Hymn to Artemis* of Callimachus.

36 See M. Puelma, in *Philologus*, vol. 101, 1957, pp. 90f.

37 *AP*, bk. 9, no. 63, and bk 12, no. 168.

38 See P. Brandt (ed.), *Corpusculum Poesis Epicae Graecae Ludibundae*, Leipzig, 1888, vol. 1, p. 114.

39 The word *epyllion* (ἐπύλλιον), meaning 'short poem', is found only once in an ancient author (Athen., 2.65a); cf. J. Heumann, *de Epyllio Alexandrino* (Diss.), Leipzig, 1904, p. 7. Its employment to signify a short poem written in hexameter verse is wholly modern and has been generally adopted for convenience.

40 *AP*, bk. 7, no. 712. The view expressed by M. L. West, in *Zeitschrift für Papyrologie und Epigraphik*, vol. 25, 1977, pp. 95f., that no poetess of that name existed is totally unconvincing. See also S. P. Pomeroy, *Zeitschrift für Papyrologie und Epigraphik*, vol. 32, 1978, pp. 17f.

41 Diehl, *ALG*², nos. 1a, 13.

42 This, if we are to judge from later surviving examples, was usually a narrative poem of between roughly 100 and 600 hexameters, whose subject was generally an episode taken from the life of a mythical hero or heroine, the love motif being particularly prominent in the later instances; see M. M. Crump. *The Epyllion from Theocritus to Ovid*, Oxford, 1931.

43 *AP*, bk. 7, no. 190; Plin., *Nat.*, 34.57.

44 Diehl, *ALG*², nos. 11, 142 (130).

45 *AP*, bk. 6, no. 352; J. Geffcken, in *Neue Jahrb. für das klass. Altertum*, vols. 39–40, 1917, p. 104.

46 *AP*, bk. 7, no. 11.

47 See Beloch, *Griechische Geschichte*, vol. 6, p. 494.

PART TWO: THE HELLENISTIC AGE

Section I: The Alexandrian Age (323–146 B.C.)

Introduction

1 The term *Hellenismus* was coined by J. C. Droysen to denote the period extending from Alexander the Great down to Augustus. Other scholars have used the term to indicate periods of different lengths. In this book the Hellenistic age will be considered as covering the years 323 B.C. to A.D. 330.

2 At the same time the Hellenistic rulers showed an enlightened indulgence of and support for foreign local religions, in particular the Ptolemies and the Attalids.

3 See C. H. Roberts, in *Mus. Helvet.*, vol. 10, 1953, pp. 264f.

4 R. Pfeiffer, *History of Classical Scholarship*, Oxford, 1968, vol. 1, p. 96.

5 See P. M. Frazer, *Ptolemaic Alexandria*, Oxford, 1972, vol. 1, pp. 316f.

6 We now know from Pap. Oxy. 1241 that the first great librarians were Zenodotus, Apollonius Rhodius, Eratosthenes, Aristophanes of Byzantium, Apollonius the Eidographos and Aristarchus.

7 See H. Diels, *Poetarum Philosophorum Fragmenta*, Berlin, 1901, pp. 173f. A zoo was set up then, for the first time, in the gardens of the palace of the Ptolemies, in which rare and colourful animals of the East were exhibited.

8 According to Menecles of Barca, Alexandria became the teacher of Greece in the arts and sciences through the refugees who fled then from the Museum (Jacoby, *FGH*, fr. 270.F.9); see Frazer, *Ptolemaic Alexandria*, vol. 1, p. 86.

9 According to a doubtful tradition, Mark Antony gave the Pergamene library, which is said to have contained 200,000 books, to the Alexandrian Museum to make up for losses caused by fire during Caesar's siege in 47 B.C. (Plut., *Ant.*, 58).

10 On the Museum, see Müller-Graupe, in Pauly–Wissowa, *REkA*, s.v. 'Museum'; U. von Wilamowitz-Moellendorff, *Hellenistiche Dichtung in der Zeit des Kallimachos*, Berlin, 1924, vol. 1, pp. 16of.; G. Faider-Feytmans, *Hommages à Joseph Bidez et à Franz Cumont*, Brussels, 1949, pp. 97f.; Frazer, *Ptolemaic Alexandria*, vol. 1, pp. 312f.

11 An interesting story is told by Galen (17.A.607, Kühn). Ptolemy III borrowed from Athens the state manuscript of the tragedians, on the pretext that he wished to copy it, but never gave it back. He returned instead a careful copy of it, together with a cargo of wheat, and forfeited the security of fifteen talents that he had given.

12 The productions of the pinacographical type are an outcome of this cataloguing and listing undertaken in the Alexandrian Library. The lists of approved writers of the past prepared by Aristophanes of Byzantium and by Aristarchus (see Quint., 1.4.3) are the ancestors of the later 'canons' of authors, although these cannot be traced to a specifically Alexandrian origin; see Pfeiffer, *History of Classical Scholarship*, vol. 1, pp. 203f.

13 The origins of philological science go back to the Peripatetic School. Aristotle was the pioneer as far as Greek erudition is concerned. See J. B. Bury, in *The Hellenistic Age*, Cambridge, 1925 (New York, 1968), p. 23.

14 The Alexandrians by no means succeeded in amassing in their libraries all the writings of the great Classical authors. They did not even have all the plays of Euripides, the most popular of the 'old' dramatists in those days, and many of the plays of Old Comedy were missing, to mention only two striking examples. See also Frazer, *Ptolemaic Alexandria*, vol. 1, p. 323.

15 A notable exception was, of course, Ion of Chios.

16 The same applies to the poets of the golden age of Alexandrian poetry. Aratus believed that he was well-versed in astronomy; Eratosthenes was a mathematician; Nicias, the doctor friend of Theocritus, and Nicander were knowledgeable about medicine; Callimachus, Lycophron, Alexander the Aetolian, Apollonius Rhodius and Rhianus were grammarians, lexicographers, literary critics and literary historians—to mention only some of the leading poets of those days.

17 Such are the Asclepiadean, Sotadean, Archebulean and Phalaecean metres, among others. These were units of Classical lyrical strophes detached from their contexts and used as narrative verses (*kata stichon*).

18 Lines 341–4 of Menander's *Dyskolos* make one wonder how large a role love really played in the lives of the poor.

19 As we have seen, the idyllic spirit (but in a different sense) first emerged in the Homeric epics—in the description of Calypso's cave (5, 63–74), the garden of Alcinous (7, 112–32) and the harbour of Phorcys (13, 96–112).

20 How far the glorification of the slave had been taken in Hellenistic tragedy can be seen from the fact that the Athenian actor Alexander (first century B.C.), son of Cyrus, had a slave's mask on his tombstone. It was along those lines that the ebullient Plautine slave developed.

21 See also W. Ellinger, *Die Darstellung der Lanschaft in der griechischen Dichtung*, Berlin, 1975.

22 See K. Ziegler, *Das hellenistische Epos*, 2nd edn., Leipzig–Berlin, 1966, pp. 44f.
23 See A. P. Smotrytsch, in *Miscellanea di studi Alessandrini in memoria di A. Rostagni*, Turin, 1963, pp. 248f.
24 *Idylls*, 7.45f.
25 *AP*, bk. 12, no. 168.
26 Fr. 1 (Pfeiffer).
27 *AP*, bk. 7, no. 2.
28 Seé E. A. Barber, in *The Hellenistic Age*, New York, 1970, p. 36.
29 See E. V. Hansen, *The Attalids of Pergamon*, Ithaca, N.Y., 1947, pp. 243f. Pergamene scholarship came into its own in the second century B.C.
30 Of the great Alexandrians, perhaps only Aratus, Rhinton, Euphorion and probably Leonidas of Tarentum never visited Alexandria.
31 Festivals such as the Alexandria, the Ptolemaia, the Seleucia, the Demetria, the Eumenia and so on.
32 See G. M. Sifakis, *Studies in the History of Hellenistic Drama*, University of London Classical Studies, no. 4, London, 1968, pp. 99f.

Chapter 6: New Comedy

1 See T. B. L. Webster, *Greek Theatre Productions*, London, 1956, pp. 74f.
2 The influence of Euripides upon Middle Comedy was also very extensive, of course, as we have seen. The profound admiration of the New Comedy poets for Euripides can also be seen from what they themselves say about him. Cf. Philemon (Kock, *CAF*, fr. 130): 'If really, as some say, the dead can still feel, I would hang myself to see Euripides'; Diphilus (Kock, *CAF*, fr. 60): 'the golden Euripides'; and so on.
3 See B. Knox, *Euripidean Comedy: The Rearer Action, Essays in Honour of Francis Ferguson*, New Brunswick, 1970, pp. 68f.
4 A. Körte, *Hellenistic Poetry*, trs. J. Hammer and M. Hadas, New York, 1929, p. 22.
5 The travesty of the myths that we find in New Comedy is one of the compensations that Middle Comedy offered for the suppression of political satire.
6 Cf. Menander, *Epitrepontes*, 543f. (Körte).
7 Terence, in his prologue to the *Andria*, characteristically states that Menander composed the *Maiden of Andros* and the *Maiden of Perinthos*, but that he who knows the one also knows the other, as they are so similar in content.
8 This is also reflected in the titles of the plays. The Flute Player, the Painter, the Soldier, the Arcadian, the Boeotian Women and others also came to acquire definite associations.
9 Cf. Menander, 714 (Körte).
10 Philemon (Kock, *CAF*, fr. 89) tells us that if we brought 30,000 foxes together, they would all be the same, whereas in a similar number of men we would find as many individual personalities.
11 This can be seen from famous lines such as Philemon's (Kock, *CAF*, fr. 135): 'I am a man and nothing human is alien to me' (ἄνθρωπος εἰμὶ καὶ οὐδὲν ἀνθρώπινον ξένον μοι ἔστιν).
12 Theophrastus defined comedy as 'a change in private affairs involving no disaster' (Kaibel, *CGF*, fr. 57).
13 See E. Fraenkel, *Plautinisches im Plautus, Philologische Untersuchungen*, vol. 28, 1922.
14 The image of life as a play was used by New Comedy and the Stoics, who held that to each man Fate assigns a role, which he must fulfil as well as possible.
15 *IG*, vol. 14, insc. 1184.
16 Some of these may be alternatives, for when a play was revived, as frequently happened with Menander's plays after his death, it was occasionally renamed.
17 Cf. T. B. L. Webster, *Studies in Menander*, 2nd edn., Manchester, 1960, pp. 24f.
18 *IG*, vol. 14, insc. 1183 (Test. 61c, Körte). Aristophanes' admiration is also evident in his saying: ὦ Μένανδρε καὶ βίε, πότερος ἄρ' ὑμῶν πότερον ἀπεμιμήσατο (Syrianus on Hermogenes, 2.25, Rabe = Test. 32, Körte). However, the endless chaos, political and social, of his times is not portrayed in Menander's plays.

19 See J. M. Jacques, *Ménandre*, vol. 1, *La Samienne*, Paris, 1971 (Budé).

20 A new papyrus find has given us a new scene from the *Misoumenos*; see E. G. Turner, in *Bulletin of the Institute of Classical Studies*, University of London, Supplement 17, 1965.

21 Pack, *GLLT*, pp. 75f.

22 On this, see T. B. L. Webster, *Studies in Later Greek Comedy*, 2nd edn., Manchester, 1970, pp. 208f.

23 Plautus used the *Dis Exapaton* for his *Bacchides*, the *Synaristosai* for his *Cistellaria*, the first *Adelphi* for his *Stichus* and an unidentifiable play for his *Aulularia*.

24 *Andr.*, 18. Terence used the *Andria* and the *Perinthia* for his own *Andria*; the *Eunuchus* and the *Kolax* for his *Eunuchus*; the second *Adelphi* and the Menander original of the same name for his *Heauton Timoroumenos*.

25 Only 140 lines are missing; see Jacques, *Ménandre*, vol. 1.

26 For the dating of Menander's plays, see Webster, *Studies in Menander*, pp. 103f.

27 Plut., *Mor.*, p. 853 (2) (A. Körte, *Menander, Reliquiae*, Leipzig, 1959, vol. 2, p. 8, Test. 41).

28 The division of Menander's plays into plays of reconciliation and those of social criticism, and the further classification into intrigue plays and single-character plays (cf. Webster, *Studies in Menander*, p. 109), is not convincing, for these qualities often overlap.

29 *Epitr.*, 33; *Per.*, 71; *Dysk.*, 230.

30 Each name acquires a distinct association: young men are called Moschion, Gorgias, Chaereas; older men, Lades, Demeas, Smicrines; Pamphile, Plangon and Glycera designate young girls or women; and so on. Certain plays of Menander have three or four names in common, but similarity of name does not necessarily imply a similarity of character.

31 Fr. 749 (Körte).

32 Fr. 486 (Körte).

33 Fr. 430 (Körte).

34 Fr. 613 (Körte).

35 Ter., *Heaut.*, 77. On this, see M. Pohlenz, in *Hermes*, vol. 78, 1943, p. 270.

36 Fr. 484 (Körte).

37 Cf. Quint., 10.1.69; 71.

38 On these, see *Menandri Sententiae*, ed. S. Jaekel, Leipzig, 1964, and W. Görler, Μενάνδρου Γνῶμαι, Berlin, 1963.

39 *Flor.*, 16; cf. Quint., 40.1.72.

40 *Suda*, Anon.; Kaibel, *CGF*, p. 9.

41 Strabo, 14.671.

42 *IG*, vol. 2², insc. 3073.

43 Page, *GLP*, nos. 61, 64, 69; see also the *ostraca* in J. G. Milne, in *Journal of Hellenic Studies*, vol. 43, 1923, pp. 40f.

44 See Webster, *Studies in Later Greek Comedy*, p. 133.

45 See G. Jackmann, *Problemata* 3, Berlin, 1931, p. 229. The one value Philemon seems to honour is friendship; otherwise his moralizing does not go beyond the polite commonplaces of the Athenian society of his day.

46 Cf. H. Dohm, *Mageiros*, Munich, 1964, pp. 122f.; for example, Kock, *CAF*, fr. 79, fashioned on Euripides' *Medea*.

47 For example, Callimedon the Crab (Kock, *CAF*, fr. 42); Seleucus' tiger (Kock, *CAF*, fr. 47); and so on.

48 Apul., *Flor.*, 16.

49 Quint., *Inst.*, 10.1.72; Apul., *Flor.*, 16; Aul. Gell., *Att. Noct.*, 4.17.1.

50 *IG*, vols. 2², 3², insc. 10321.

51 See Webster, *Studies in Later Greek Comedy*, p. 173.

52 See G. Kaibel, in Pauly–Wissowa, *REkA*, vol. 2, p. 2852; Apollod. (57); and Webster, *Studies in Later Greek Comedy*, pp. 225f.

53 *Suda*.

54 The original of Plautus' *Epidicus* has also been ascribed to Apollodorus, but without certainty. See Webster, *Studies in Later Greek Comedy*, p. 242.

55 See Webster, *Studies in Later Greek Comedy*, pp. 236f.
56 Aul. Gell., *Att. Noct.*, 2.23.1.
57 See H. von Heintze, in *Röm. Mitt.*, vol. 68, 1961, pp. 8of.
58 *IG*, vol. 2², insc. 1320.
59 Athen., 14.658f.

Chapter 7: Alexandrian Elegy

1 Ph.-E. Legrand, *La poésie alexandrine*, Paris, 1924, p. 143.
2 The fullest and most sensible discussion of the matter can be found in A. A. Day, *The Origins of Latin Love Elegy*, Oxford, 1938. On the 'novelistic' element in Alexandrian elegy, see C. del Grande, in *Miscellanea di studi Alessandrini in memoria di A. Rostagni*, Turin, 1963, pp. 225f.
3 See Schmid–Stählin, *GL*, vol. 2, p. 118.
4 The view that this group was organized into a fictitious bucolic society is untenable; cf. A. Gercke, in *Rhein. Mus.*, vol. 48, 1887, pp. 602f.
5 The information in Athenaeus (13.5526; cf. Aelian, *Var. Hist.*, 9.14) that Philetas was excessively thin is clearly a misunderstanding based on what his detractors said about his 'slender' and 'short' poetry.
6 *AP*, bk. 6, no. 210 is by the homonymous Philetas of Samos.
7 Cf. Schol. Flor. Callim., fr. 1, 12–15 (Pfeiffer).
8 See G. Scheibner (in F. Zucker's *Menander's Dyskolos*), D. Akademie d. Wissenschaften zu Berlin, *Schriften der Sektion für Altertumswissenschaft*, 1965, pp. 103f.; G. Scheibner, in *Philologus*, vol. 111, 1967, pp. 129f.; Hollis, *Classical Quarterly*, vol. 26, 1976, pp. 147f. But R. J. Carden, *Bulletin of the Institute of Classical Studies*, University of London, 16, 1969, pp. 29f., argues much more convincingly for Euphorion as the author.
9 The *Miscellaneous Glosses*, or *Miscellanea* (Ἄτακτοι Γλῶσσαι, Ἄτακτα), was the most famous of Philetas' prose works. It was a lexical compilation explaining rare words and technical terms. Thirty fragments survive. Extracts from the work were also used as a school text, and Aristarchus is said to have attacked it. Strabo (3.168) also assigns to Philetas a work with the title Ἑρμηνεῖαι (*Interpretations*), which was in all probability a prose work.
10 It is thought that Book I told of the loves of shepherds, Book II of the loves of heroes and historical figures and Book III of those of poets and philosophers; see C. del Grande, in *Miscellanea di studi Alessandrini*, p. 227.
11 The name ending in '–ion' suggests a courtesan.
12 Powell, *CA*, frs. 2, 3.
13 For the opposite view, see R. Heinze, in Berichte der Sächs Akademie, vol. 81, 1919, 1, p. 127. It is worth noting that three times in the fragment the poet addresses Leontion herself. It is unlikely, however, that he used this device throughout the poem.
14 See O. Crusius, in Pauly–Wissowa, *REkA*, vol. 5, p. 2281.
15 Powell, *CA*, fr. 4.
16 Hence called 'the Aetolian', to distinguish him from Alexander the Ephesian.
17 See p. 300.
18 These are composed in the *versus sotadeus*, a minor Ionic metre that allowed great variation.
19 Powell, *CA*, fr. 7.
20 On this literary form, which was popular in the Alexandrian age, see Crusius, in Pauly–Wissowa, *REkA*, vol. 5, p. 2282. Its origins go back to Aeschylus; see Schmid–Stählin, *GL*, vol. 1, 2, pp. 189f.
21 It has been suggested that these are related to Agathon's *Antheus*, which it reflects; see C. Corbato, in *Dioniso*, vol. 11, 1948, p. 163.
22 See Schmid–Stählin, *GL*, vol. 1, 2, pp. 189f.
23 See Crusius, *loc. cit.*
24 The *Diegeseis* (*Expositions*), a late prose work which gave the arguments of the poems of Callimachus, contains much valuable information about the *Aetia*. Thus it gives the subjects of the last few *aetia* of Book III and possibly of all Book IV. Fragments of

three separate *Diegeseis* have been found in papyri, all presumably going back to a common source (cf. R. Pfeiffer, *Callimachus*, Oxford, 1949, 1953, vol. 2, p. xxviii and n. 1).
25 *AP*, bk. 7, no. 42.
26 Cf. also Cic., *Somn. Scip.*
27 Fr. 75 (Pfeiffer).
28 Fr. 178 (Pfeiffer).
29 Fr. 43 (Pfeiffer).
30 Moreover, the end of Book III, which closed with the cult of Euthycles, the Olympic victor from Epizephyrii Locri, shows that Callimachus did not exclude the historical period from the *Aetia*.
31 This is very much in keeping with the prose writings of Callimachus, which extended to the semi-scientific field of paradoxography and included a number of lists of 'marvels' or 'curiosities'–natural objects, historical and mythological events and so on. The *Aetia* are therefore very important to our understanding of the intellectual interests of third-century Alexandria, among other things.
32 Catull., 66.
33 See Pfeiffer, *Callimachus*, vol. 1, *passim*; vol. 2, p. xli.
34 It has also been suggested that political differences may have exacerbated the dispute; see A. P. Smotrytsch, in *Miscellanea di studi Alessandrini*, pp. 255f.
35 See K. Ziegler, *Das hellenistische Epos*, 2nd edn., Leipzig–Berlin, 1966, pp. 1f.
36 Unfortunately, given the evidence we have, it is impossible to reconstruct this famous quarrel between Callimachus and Apollonius.
37 If, as is probably, the *Chiliades* and the *Cup Thief* of Euphorion were influenced by Callimachus' *Ibis*, a series of prophecies or mythical punishments may have been included in it.
38 On the *epyllion*, p. 240 and pp. 278f.
39 Cf. Ovid, *Met.*, 8.620f.; Pseudo-Virgil, *Moretum*, and so on.
40 Unfortunately, that is all that can be said with certainty about that famous poem. Many are therefore the questions which remain unanswered. Did Theseus describe to Hecale any of his previous labours in the course of their conversation? What space was accorded to the actual fight with the bull? What were the circumstances of Hecale's death? How was that strange night scene, in which birds are the speakers and an old crow narrates ancient Athenian stories, connected with the rest of the poem? All this and much more has, for the time being, to remain problematic.
41 On the new fragments from this and other Callimachean poems, see 'New Fragments of Callimachus: A Bibliographical Note', added to C. A. Trypanis, *Callimachi Fragmenta*, London, 1958 (Loeb), when the book was last reprinted (1979).
42 It is only fair to stress that even in the Homeric Hymns the religious element had already given way to 'a short story in verse'.
43 We shall examine them again in Chapter 12, pp. 329f.
44 Besides the *Pinakes*, Callimachus wrote many other works in prose; for example, a *Chronological Register of the Athenian Dramatic Poets*, a study of Democritus' writings and language, numerous encyclopaedias (about nymphs, birds, games, winds, rivers and so on), collections of *paradoxa* and glosses.
45 Diehl, *ALG*, 2² 6, pp. 82f.
46 *ibid.*; see K. Ziegler, in Pauly–Wissowa, *REkA*, vol. 18B, p. 1141 (no. 3); F. Susemihl, *Geschichte der griechischen Literatur in der Alexandrinerzeit*, Leipzig, 1891–2, vol. 1, pp. 465f.
47 See P. M. Frazer, *Ptolemaic Alexandria*, Oxford, 1972, vol. 2, p. 1090, n. 459.
48 Pseudo-Long., *de Sub.*, 33.5.
49 See R. Merkelbach, in *Miscellanea di studi Alessandrini*, pp. 469f.
50 *ibid.*
51 See pp. 294f.
52 *AP*, bk. 11, no. 130.

Chapter 8: The Alexandrian Epic

1 These, as we have seen, were considered genuine works of Hesiod by the Alexandrians, and that is why a considerable number of fragments from the works of these Hesiodic *epigonoi* have been retrieved in papyri, by contrast with the *Cycle*, from which not a scrap has turned up in Egypt. The sharp distinction drawn by the Alexandrians between Homer and the epic *Cycle* is clearly responsible for this.

2 See K. Ziegler, *Das hellenistische Epos*, 2nd edn., Leipzig–Berlin, 1966.

3 Ziegler's attempts to reconstruct their content and style by comparison with the *Annales* of Ennius, the Pergamene sculptures, Hellenistic historiography and the poetry of Nonnus and his 'school' has been challenged. See E. Barber, in M. Platnauer (ed.), *Fifty Years (and Twelve) of Classical Scholarship*, Oxford, 1968, p. 281.

4 The later Alexandrians and the Romans had a preference for love stories.

5 See p. 272.

6 *AP*, bk. 9, no. 545.

7 See Ziegler, *Das hellenistische Epos*, pp. 1f.

8 Powell, *CA*, pp. 72f.; W. Schubart and U. von Wilamowitz-Moellendorff, in *Berliner Klassikertexte*, vol. 5, 1, Berlin, 1907, pp. 68f.

9 Powell, *CA*, pp. 71f.

10 See A. Körte, *Hellenistic Poetry*, trs. J. Hammer and M. Hardas, New York, 1929, p. 164.

11 The following prose works of Euphorion are cited: *About the Isthmian Games*, *About the Aleuadae*, *About the Makers of Songs* and a lexicon to Hippocrates.

12 *AP*, bk. 6, no. 679; bk. 7, no. 651.

13 Powell, *CA*, frs. 8, 9 probably come from the *Curse* or the *Cup Thief*.

14 Powell, *CA*, frs. 44, 51; cf. Lucian, *Hist. Conscr.*, 57.

15 Powell, *CA*, fr. 92.

16 Of the three new fragments (Page, *GLP*, fr. 121) of Euphorion, one describes Heracles bringing Cerberus from Hades; the second probably comes from the *Curse* or the *Cup Thief*; and the third, from a different source (see A. Barigazzi, in *Aegyptus*, vol. 27, 1947, pp. 1–2, 53f., and in *Athenaeum*, vol. 26, 1946, pp. 1–2, 34f.) is longer but hardly more attractive. The roll to which the third fragment belongs had poems of Euphorion arranged alphabetically; the end of the *Thrax* and the beginning of the *Hippomedon Maior* remain. The former dealt with two unhappy love stories, summarized by Parthenius (13 and 26). For the latest fragments of Euphorion, see Pap. Oxy. 2219 and 2220; B. A. van Groningen, *Euphorion*, Amsterdam, 1977; and R. J. Carden in *Bulletin of the Institute of Classical Studies*, University of London, 16, 1969, pp. 29f., who discusses the fragment of the *epyllion* wrongly attributed by G. Scheibner to Philetas. See also p. 727, n.8.

17 Tusc., 3.45. The most interesting and important of the extant Latin *epyllia* is the Pseudo-Virgilian *Ciris*. It probably belongs to the school of Cornelius Gallus; see M. M. Crump, *The Epyllion from Theocritus to Ovid*, Oxford, 1931, pp. 154f.

18 Moschus is treated here to provide a fuller picture of the Alexandrian *epyllion*.

19 He is called a grammarian by the *Suda*, but no traces of evidence to support this description survive. The identification with the Moschus mentioned by Athenaeus (11.485e) as author of a work on Rhodian words is very improbable.

20 The authenticity of the *Europa* has sometimes been challenged on metrical grounds because, by contrast with the *Runaway Love* and Moschus' bucolic fragments, it does not conform to Callimachean metrical rules.

21 Similar to the *Runaway Love* in character is another short, elegant poem called *Love the Honeycomb Stealer*, wrongly attributed to Theocritus (19).

22 *AP*, bk. 4, no. 200.

23 On these, see pp. 349f.

24 These were the summaries of thirty-six stories in prose dedicated to Cornelius Gallus, for him to use in his poetry.

25 The history of the Latin *epyllion*, which was so profoundly influenced by the Alexandrian and post-Alexandrian *epyllion*, falls into three periods, from each of which a few striking examples survive. The first period is that of Catullus and his school, of which

Catullus, 64, *Peleus and Thetis*, is a brilliant example; the second is that of the early years of Virgil and of Cornelius Gallus, of which *Eclogue VI* and the pseudo-Virgilian *Ciris* (a work of the school of Gallus, if not by Gallus himself) are representative *epyllia*; and the third is the period of the great Augustans, from which we have Virgil's beautiful *Aristaeus*, with which Book IV of the *Georgics* ends, and the *Metamorphoses* of Ovid. The latter, consisting of a long series of *epyllia* worked into a single large volume, gives us some idea of the content of many lost Alexandrian and Roman *epyllia*. See Crump, *The Epyllion from Theocritus to Ovid*, p. 135. On the view that *Eclogue VI* is an *epyllion*, see Crump, *loc. cit.*, p. 174. See also W. Wimmel, *Kallimachos in Rom, Hermes Einzelschriften*, no. 16, Wiesbaden, 1960.

26 Apollonius Rhodius probably left the headship of the Library and Alexandria for Rhodes in about 246/5 and never returned; see P. M. Frazer, *Ptolemaic Alexandria*, Oxford, 1972, vol. 1, pp. 332f.

27 A *Vita* reports that Apollonius later returned to Alexandria, won great success with his complete epic—for the first version apparently consisted only of the first two books—became head of the Library and was buried beside Callimachus. This misinformation is probably the result of a confusion with the younger Apollonius (the Eidograph), who was Eratosthenes' second successor in the administration of the Library (cf. Pap. Oxy. 1241).

28 We know of prose works by Apollonius on Hesiod, Archilochus and Antimachus, as well as a tract, *Against Zenodotus*.

29 The Alexandrian interest in *aetia* (causes) is thought to have been the stimulus for the composition of so many *ktiseis* poems in the Hellenistic world. It has been argued that these *ktiseis* poems of Apollonius were *epyllia* and full-blown epics, and that Theocritus, Callimachus and Apollonius were the inventors of the Alexandrian *epyllion* (Crump, *The Epyllion from Theocritus to Ovid*, p. 19). But this view is untenable if we remember the *epyllia* of Erinna and Philetas.

30 *AP*, bk. 11, no. 275.

31 From the brilliant Homeric similes down to the solemn choruses of tragedy descriptions of nature are introduced primarily to illustrate a human condition and not for their own sake—with the possible exception of the celebrated Colonus chorus in Sophocles' *Oedipus at Colonus*, pp. 668f.

32 Theocritus, 13.

33 Idyll 22.

34 Short Alexandrian epics, *epyllia* of an erotic character, had no doubt pre-existed Apollonius' *Argonautica*.

35 On the gods in Apollonius and their retention of their divine qualities in spite of everything, see P. Händel, in *Miscellanea di studi Alessandrini in memoria di A. Rostagni*, Turin, 1963, pp. 363f.; and, of course, H. Herter, in *Jahresbericht über die Fortschnitte der klass. Altertumswissenschaft*, vol. 284, 1944–5, pp. 278f., and L. Klein, in *Philologus*, vol. 86, 1931, pp. 18f.

36 It has been pointed out that the *Argo* undertook a return journey as well as an outward one, which burdened the poet. Odysseus and Aeneas have an enormous advantage over Jason.

37 His interest in the geography of the west, for which he drew on the historian Timaeus and a geographer, Timagetus, is striking.

38 Virgil said, of course, that it was easier to steal his club from Hercules than a single line from Homer.

39 See R. Heinze, *Virgils epische Technik*, 4th edn., Stuttgart, 1957.

40 See Schmid–Stählin, *GL*, 2⁶, 1, p. 140.

41 The number of important Callimachean followers we know of is very limited: Philetas, Theocritus, Callimachus himself and Euphorion in the third century; Moschus and Bion in the second; and Parthenius in the first.

42 Plut., *Lys.*, 18.8.

43 Pap. Oxy. 2520.

44 On the very poor quality of Choerilus' poetry, see Hor., *Epist.*, 2.1.233, and Porphyrio, the scholiast of Horace's *Ars Poetica*, *Ars. Poet.*, 357.

45 See Diehl, *ALG²*, 6, p. 104; Athen., 6.253d.
46 He also composed a *Perseid*.
47 See Ziegler, *Das hellenistische Epos*, p. 23f.
48 See E. A. Barber, in *The Hellenistic Age*, Cambridge, 1925, p. 49.
49 Thus Philon the Elder (c. 200 B.C.) composed an epic *On Jerusalem Περὶ τὰ Ἰεροσόλυμα*, of which twenty-four lines have survived, and Theodotus (date unknown) was the author of the epic *On the Jews* (*Περὶ Ἰουδαίων*), whose exact content is a matter of dispute. The fragment of forty-seven hexameter lines which has survived refers to events in *Genesis*, 33.34, in a simple epic style.
50 Book 4, especially 6.1.
51 He produced an edition of the *Iliad* and the *Odyssey* that was considered more conservative than that of Zenodotus.
52 Powell, *CA*, frs. 66–76.
53 3.1f.
54 If, as suggested, he is not the poet who wrote an epic on Cleopatra, his date is unknown. See E. Diehl, in Pauly–Wissowa, *REkA*, vol. 5A, p. 1809.
55 See C. O. Brink, *Horace on Poetry*, Cambridge, 1963.
56 He also composed epigrams and a hymn on Eros. See Powell, *CA*, fr. 120; and K. J. Beloch, *Griechische Geschichte*, Berlin–Leipzig, 1925, vol. 4, p. 508.
57 Ziegler, *Das hellenistische Epos*, pp. 53f.
58 See Powell, 'Epica Adespota', in *CA*, and the new papyri fragments.
59 Plat., *Phaedr.*, 267a.
60 See H. Diels, *Poetarum Philosophorum Fragmenta*, Berlin, 1901, p. 171.
61 *AP*, bk. 9, no. 507.
62 In spite of a separate title (*Προγνώσεις διὰ σημείων*: Forecasts by Weather Signs), it is an integral part of the poem.
63 Varro of Atax, Cicero, Germanicus and Avienius all translated the *Phaenomena* into Latin.
64 A pupil of Callimachus, who wrote geographical works full of marvels and fables.
65 Four lines of this have survived, in which he praises Aratus; see *Vit. Arat.*, 1, p. 55 (West), p. 79 (Maas). Cf. Frazer, *Ptolemaic Alexandria*, vol. 2, p. 4090, n. 459.
66 See also Page, *GLP*, no. 124; Heitsch, *GDRK*, vol. 2, pp. 23f., no. 64; Pack, *GLLT*, no. 1873, on a second-century A.D. papyrus describing features of the flora of Egypt in connection with the rise of the Nile.

Chapter 9: Alexandrian Drama

1 In the great dramatic competitions of the Hellenistic cities a place was usually accorded to the revival of 'old' plays (*παλαιαί*). In the case of tragedy these were most frequently revivals of Euripidean plays; in that of comedy, the plays of Menander. Side by side with these competitions, dithyrambs of Timotheus and Philoxenus were also performed, and parts of old epics were recited. The winners of the competitions competed among themselves for the title of victor victorum. Apart from these grand theatrical competitions, numerous smaller shows (*ἐπιδείξεις*) took place, in which poets, orators and musicians performed.
2 See T. B. L. Webster, in *Miscellanea di studi Alessandrini in memoria di A. Rostagni*, Turin, 1963, p. 540.
3 See G. M. Sifakis, *Studies in the History of Hellenistic Drama*, University of London Classical Studies, no. 4, London, 1968. pp. 1f.
4 Athen., 5.203e.
5 The most important of the many theatrical guilds (*σύνοδοι*) that were active in those days were the Guild of Athens, on the pattern of which all the others were fashioned, the Guild of the Isthmus and the Ionian Guild. They had sections residing permanently in various Hellenistic cities; and privileges such as the *ἀσυλία* (inviolability) or the *ἀσφάλεια* (a guarantee of personal safety) were granted to their members by certain Hellenistic rulers who were keen to ensure that their festivals were magnificently celebrated. The members of these guilds, the *technitai*, as they were

called, claimed to be servants of Dionysus; although they were often men of low moral reputation, they were not only well-paid but were also often honoured by decrees and statues, as inscriptions from Delphi and Delos indicate. See Sifakis, *Studies in the History of Hellenistic Drama*, pp. 99f.

6 Thus, for example, Lycophron has been credited with sixty-four tragedies, Homeros of Byzantium with forty-five, Sosiphanes with seventy-three, Philicus with forty-two and Timon of Phlius with sixty tragedies and thirty satirical plays.

7 The names of these are in K. Ziegler, in Pauly–Wissowa, *REkA*, vol. 6A, p. 1970. See also F. Schramm, *Tragicorum graecorum hellenisticae quae dicitur aetatis fragmenta* (Diss.), Münster, 1929.

8 See A. W. Pickard-Cambridge, *The Dramatic Festivals of Athens*, 2nd edn., rev. J. Gould and D. M. Lewis, Oxford, 1968, pp. 101f., in particular pp. 124f.

9 On the Pleiad, see F. Stoessl, in Pauly–Wissowa, *REkA*, vol. 21, pp. 191f.

10 His views on poetry—known to us through the summary of Philodemus—are said by Porphyrion to have been adopted in essentials by Horace in his *Ars Poetica*; see C. O. Brink, *Horace and Poetry*, Cambridge, 1963.

11 This, about one-third of the play, is found in Book 9 of Eusebius' *Preparatio Evangelica*, which draws on Alexander Polyhistor's (105 B.C.) book on the Jews. It should be remembered, however, that the *Exagoge* was not written by a Greek and may therefore not be a sound basis on which to draw firm conclusions about Greek tragedy contemporary with it. See Ziegler, in Pauly–Wissowa, *REkA*, vol. 6A, p. 1979; B. Snell, *Szenen aus griechischen Dramen*, Berlin, 1971, pp. 170f; and A. Kappelmacher, in *Wien. Stud.*, vol. 44, 1924–5, p. 69.

12 See p. 301.

13 This was replaced in Roman times by the *pulpitum*. We meet the *proskenion* in Delos in 282 B.C.; cf. *IG*, vol. 11, insc. 158, A, 67–9.

14 Cf. Vitruv., 5.7.2; Pollux, 4.123. Thus we read in *Problem. Aristot.*, 19.48: 'Under the influence of the hypo-Dorian and the hypo-Phrygian modes we are inclined to action, which is not appropriate to the chorus. For the chorus is an inactive observer of events; for its only function is to display a friendly attitude to those who are on the stage at the same time.'

15 On the introduction of the *onkos* masks, see T. B. L. Webster, in *Hesperia*, vol. 29, 1960, p. 258.

16 Aristot., *Poet.*, 1456a.26.

17 Crass., 33.3.

18 See Sifakis, *Studies in the History of Hellenistic Drama*, p. 122.

19 See W. Beare, *The Roman Stage*, 2nd edn., London, 1955, pp. 19, 199f. In Menander's *Dyskolos* we can see the last stage in the development of the Greek comic chorus, which became a *comos*, a band of revellers, who entered between acts and appeared again at the end of the play, and who had nothing to do with the plot.

20 See R. Browning, in Γέρας, *Studies Presented to G. Thomson*, Prague, 1973, pp. 67f., §5.39: Πρῶτος δὲ Ἀγάθων τὸν ὑποδώριον τόνον εἰς τραγῳδίαν εἰσήνεγκεν καὶ τὸν ὑποφρύγιον. The author is probably Michael Psellus.

21 For the actors the musical modes used were the hypo-Dorian and the hypo-Phrygian, which urged men to action; that used for the chorus was mainly the mixo-Lydian, a quiet, mournful kind of music suitable for passive chorus songs.

22 See S. Eitrem, L. Amunsden and R. P. Winnington-Ingram, in *Symbolae Osloenses*, vol. 31, 1955, pp. 1f.

23 Pap. Oxy. 2439.

24 See Webster, in *Miscellanea di studi Alessandrini*, p. 540.

25 A Delphic inscription (*SIG*, no. 648) has been cited in support of this; it speaks of a κιθάρισμα ἐκ Βακχῶν Εὐριπίδου.

26 *AP*, bk. 5, no. 137.

27 See Webster, in *Miscellanea di studi Alessandrini*, p. 39. Cleopatra, whom we have seen listed with comic and tragic actors in Delos in 268 B.C., was a trick dancer.

28 Nero (Suet., *Ner.*, 21) 'sang' tragedies—which obviously means parts of tragedies. See K. Latte, in *Eranos*, vol. 52, 1954, pp. 125f. An inscription of the second century

A.D. from Isthmia (published by O. Bronner, in *Hesperia*, vol. 22, 1953, p. 192) speaks of Themison as 'the first and only one to use dramas of Euripides and Sophocles and the poetry of Timotheus in the production of musical and lyrical compositions'. Themison, if the reading is correct, won ninety-four victories. He was obviously not the only man to make use of such material.

29 See Sifakis, *Studies in the History of Hellenistic Drama*, p. 79.
30 This is, of course, a Classical practice going back to Phrynichus' *Melitou Halosis* and Aeschylus' *Persians*.
31 Moschion also wrote a *Telephus*. His style, though uneven, shows considerable boldness. See Nauck, *TGF*, frs. 812–16; Schramm, *Tragicorum graecorum hellenisticae quae dicitur aetatis fragmenta*, p. 63. A fragment from an unknown tragedy on the origins of civilization (thirty-three lines long) has survived. It recalls in some points Aeschylus' *Prometheus Vinctus*, 436f.
32 This has been supported by Ziegler in his article 'Tragödie', in Pauly–Wissowa, *REkA*, vol. 6A, p. 1976.
33 See D. L. Page, *Actor's Interpolations in Greek Tragedy*, Oxford, 1935.
34 Cf. Homer, *Iliad*, XVIII, 87.
35 Nauck, *TGF*, fr. 818.
36 On this, see St Josifovic, in Pauly–Wissowa, *REkA*, suppl. 11, pp. 888–930.
37 The *Orphanos* may have been a play with entirely fictitious characters.
38 According to W. Schubart, who draws this conclusion from Hibeh Papyri no. 30, 23 (vol. 1, London, 1906).
39 Hephest., Ench., p. 30.21 (Diehl, *ALG*, 2², 6, pp. 158f.).
40 See Page, *GLP*, no. 90; K. Latte, in *Mus. Helvet.*, vol. 11, 1954, pp. 1f. The metre had been used before by Simias, but as far as we know no other poem was ever composed solely in lines of this metre.
41 Page, *GLP*, no. 90.
42 One short but striking fragment of these has survived that speaks of the transitory quality of human happiness (Nauck, *TGF*, frs. 819–20).
43 Schol. Aristoph., *Thesmoph.*, 1059.
44 Page, *GLP*, no. 105(b).
45 *Proceedings of the British Academy*, vol. 35, 1950, p. 1.
46 See K. Latte, in *Eranos*, vol. 48, 1950, p. 136, who proves beyond doubt that diction and metre are Hellenistic. On the discussion about the date and the structure of the play, see A. Lesky, *Das hellenistische Gyges-Drama: gesammelte Schriften*, Berne–Munich, 1966, pp. 204f.
47 1.8–12.
48 See p. 303.
49 R. A. Coles, in *Bulletin of the Institute of Classical Studies*, University of London, no. 15, 1968, pp. 100f.
50 It is true that the fourth century cannot be precluded.
51 Twenty lines of this play have survived (Nauck, *TGF*, frs. 821–4). The conquest of a cruel barbarian at the hands of a Greek hero was a favourite subject of the old satyr play.
52 7.173.
53 *AP*, bk. 7, no. 707.
54 On satyr masks, see T. B. L. Webster, in *Bulletin of the Institute of Classical Studies*, University of London, suppl. no. 14, 1962, pp. 143f.
55 There can be no doubt that the *Menedemus* was a satyr play, for Silenus appears addressing his children in the extant fragments (Nauck, *TGF*, frs. 817–18).
56 See Nauck, *TGF*, frs. 810–11; see also B. Snell, *Scenes from Greek Drama*, Berkeley, 1964, chs. 5, 6. The *Agen* has also (but certainly wrongly) been attributed to Alexander the Great.
57 See Sifakis, *Studies in the History of Hellenistic Drama*, pp. 124f.
58 Cf., for example, Athen., 14.664a. His claim that he was acquainted with more than eight hundred plays of Middle Comedy (Athen., 8.336d) indicates that a very large number of comedies had found their way into the Alexandrian Library.

59 See T. B. L. Webster, in *Classical Quarterly*, n.s. 2, vol. 46, 1952, pp. 13ff.

60 *AP*, bk. 7, no. 708.

61 See A. S. F. Gow, in *Miscellanea di studi Alessandrini*, p. 528. There can be no doubt that Gow's emendation of κηφῆνα to κύφωνα in line 3 is correct.

62 Such collections appear in the fourth century B.C.—for example, those of Theocritus of Chios and Demetrius of Phalerum. The ancestry of the genre may be seen in some parts of Xenophon's *Memorabilia*; Olivieri, *FCGM*, vol. 2.

63 *AP*, bk. 7, no. 414.

64 Kaibel, *CGF*, frs. 183f.; Olivieri, *FCGM*, vol. 2, pp. 7f.

65 Kaibel, *CGF*, fr. 190.

66 Kaibel, *CGF*, fr. 192; cf. T. B. L. Webster, *Hellenistic Poetry and Art*, New York, 1964, pp. 126f.

Chapter 10: The Literature of Popular Entertainment

1 In a wider sense the Greeks regarded as mimes all kinds of entertainers—singers, dancers, jugglers, conjurers and so forth—who performed at banquets or in the market-place. In the Alexandrian age they were classed according to their skills.

2 See E. A. Barber, in *The Hellenistic Age*, Cambridge, 1925, p. 59.

3 Athenaeus, for example, speaks of a dramatic entertainment in Sparta called *deikelon*, in which the actor represented various characters, such as a fruit thief or a foreign doctor.

4 A. Körte, *Hellenistic Poetry*, trs. J. Hammer and M. Hadas, New York, 1929, p. 279.

5 It is impossible to reconstruct any one of the mimes of Sophron from the fragments that survive. Their titles (the *Tunny Fisher*, the *Messenger*, the *Sempstresses, Women Spectators at the Isthmian Games* and so on) show that Sophron set out to depict scenes from everyday life.

6 See W. C. Headlam and A. D. Knox, *Herodes*, Cambridge, 1922, p. xxv.

7 *Id.*, VII.45f. Of Theocritus' poems not one exceeds 300 lines; only two are longer than 200 lines and twenty are under 100 lines long.

8 Schol. Flor., 5.5: R. Pfeiffer, *Callimachus*, 2 vols., Oxford, 1949, vol. 1, p. 3.

9 *Epigr.*, 64.

10 See p. 105. In prose this can be traced back to Xenophon, when he compares the diligent with the idle man, and, of course, to the splendid beginning of Plato's *Phaedrus*.

11 On ancient traditions assigning the origins of bucolic poetry to cult, see H. Beckby, *Die griechische Bukoliker*, Meisenheim/Glan, 1975, pp. 347f.

12 Idylls VIII and IX are probably spurious; they indicate how soon Theocritus was imitated.

13 On suggestions for poets who may be hiding under the 'mask' of Lycidas, see J. H. Kühn, in *Hermes*, vol. 86, 1958, p. 66; see also A. Cameron, in *Miscellanea di studi Alessandrini in memoria di A. Rostagni*, Turin, 1963, pp. 291f.

14 See M. Puelma, in *Mus. Helvet.*, vol. 17, 1960, p. 144.

15 These appear much more forcefully to the modern reader, whose notion of the 'idyllic', the 'bucolic' and the eclogue is tainted by the pastorals of the Renaissance and the shepherds and shepherdesses of the eighteenth century.

16 Theocritus, Callimachus and Apollonius could be considered jointly responsible for the development, if not for the birth, of the Alexandrian *epyllion*.

17 In this part Theocritus had Homeric Hymn 33 in mind.

18 This is evident from the mutilated last lines and a marginal note retrieved in a sixth-century papyrus from Antinoe; see A. S. Hunt and I. Johnson, *Two Theocritus Papyri*, Oxford, 1930.

19 Paean XX (Snell).

20 See B. A. van Groningen, in *Miscellanea di studi Alessandrini*, pp. 338f.

21 As with most great poets, a number of spurious works have been attributed to Theocritus with which we need not concern ourselves here. These are: the *technopaegnion Syrinx*, Idylls VIII and IX (about which we have spoken), Idyll XIX (the

Kyriokleptes), Idyll XX (the *Boukoliskos*), Idyll XXI (the *Fishermen*), Idyll XXIII (the *Lover*), Idyll XXV (*Heracles the Lion Killer*) and Idyll XXVII (the *Oaristys*).

22 In *La poésie alexandrine*, Paris, 1924, p. 83.

23 His epigrams also display a variety of metres.

24 Most important of these is the use of the bucolic diaeresis, the word ending that precedes the fifth metre of a hexameter line. The fourth metre must be a dactyl, and the caesura preceding a diaeresis is usually the *kata triton trochaeon* or the *penthemimeral*.

25 In *Mimiambus* 1.30.

26 First published by F. G. Kenyon in 1891.

27 It has been suggested that Herodas was influenced by Apelles' book on art, which claimed that art should strive after an 'absolute illusion of reality' and that 'the common man was the best judge of art' (*vulgum diligentiorem iudicem quam me praefero*, Plin., *Nat. Hist.*, 25.84). See Salona Luria, in *Miscellanea di studi Alessandrini*, pp. 394f.

28 In this *mimiambus* forty-one out of the ninety-five verses (19–38, 56–78) are dedicated to 'art criticism', in which the 'absolute illusion of reality', in the terms of Apelles' book on art, is stressed and praised.

29 The distinction between παίγνια and ὑποθέσεις is drawn by Plutarch in *Symp. Quaest.*, 7.4.712e; see also O. Crusius, *Herondas*, ed. min., 5th edn., 1914, pp. 146f.

30 See Schmid–Stählin, *GL*, 2⁶, p. 201.

31 There is also a dialogue with a drunkard (Powell, *CA*, p. 181; Page, *GLP*, no. 74) on an *ostracon* of the second or the first century B.C. — if the dating is correct — that should also be examined in this connection.

32 On the alternative names *simodia* and *lysodia*, see p. 320.

33 See Schmid–Stählin, *GL*, 2⁶, p. 202.

34 See Barber, in *The Hellenistic Age*, p. 62.

35 15.679b.

36 See C. Wachsmuth (ed.), *Corpusculum Poesis Epicae Graecae Ludibundae*, Leipzig, 1885, vol. 2, p. 27. According to Schmid–Stählin, *GL*, vol. 2⁶, 1, p. 202, the name derives from the Ionian origin of this genre.

37 See Aristot., fr. 515 (Rose); *Suda*, s.v. Sotades.

38 It is thought that they were also set to music composed by others.

39 Cf. Strabo, p. 648.

40 16.620f.

41 This was later used by the Romans for didactic poetry.

42 See Diehl, *ALG*, vol. 2², 4, pp. 186f., nos. 1–18; Powell, *CA*, pp. 238–45.

43 See Crusius, *Herondas*, p. 130.

44 Four books of *silloi* have been attributed to Xenophanes, but the exact meaning of the term *silloi* in connection with him is a matter of dispute. See Wachsmuth, *Corpusculum Poesis Epicae Graecae Ludibundae*, vol. 2, p. 62.

45 Fragments in H. Diels, *Poetarum Philosophorum Fragmenta*, Berlin, 1901, pp. 173f.; V. Brochard, *Les Scéptiques grecs*, 2nd edn., Paris, 1923.

46 He became so universally loved that people wrote on their doors 'Welcome to Crates, the good spirit' (Julian, *Or.*, 6.201b).

47 Fragments in Diels, *Poetarum Philosophorum Fragmenta*, pp. 216f.; Nauck, *TGF*, frs. 809–10.

48 C. Wachsmuth, *Sillographi Graeci*, Leipzig, 1885, pp. 73–7.

49 Wachsmuth, *Corpusculum Poesis Epicae Graecae Ludibundae*, vol. 2, pp. 78–85; see R. Helm, *Lucian und Menippus*, Berlin, 1906; J. Wight Duff, *Roman Satire*, Berkeley, 1936, ch. 5.

50 By some he is described as a poet of Old Comedy (cf. Aristot., *Poet.*, 2.14448a.12). The competition was part of the *Thymelikoi Agones*.

51 Pap. Oxy. 1082.

52 See A. D. Knox, *The First Greek Anthologist*, Cambridge, 1923.

53 A Heidelberg papyrus, inv. 310 (Pack, *GLLT*, no. 1605).

Chapter 11: Lyric Poetry and Hymnography

1 Such are, for example, a short, elegaic fragment on the Golden Age (Pack, *GLLT*, no. 1388; Powell, *CA*, p. 131; Diehl, *ALG*, vol. 2², 6, p. 88, no. 1; Page, *GLP*, p. 462); an angry speech of a Hellenistic king (Pack, *GLLT*, no. 1389; Powell, *CA*, p. 131; Diehl, *ALG*, vol. 2², 6, p. 89, no. 2(1); Page, *GLP*, p. 462); and so on. Other miserable surviving fragments appear to be exercises: for example, Pack, *GLLT*, no. 1266; Powell, *CA*, p. 185; Pack, *GLLT*, no. 1516; Powell, *CA*, p. 187; Diehl, *ALG*, vol. 2², 6, p. 204; Page, *GLP*, p. 412.

2 We know, for example, that the *Paean to Asclepius* by Sophocles was chanted down to the Imperial age; see P. Maas, *Epidaurische Hymnen*, Schriften der Konigsberger Gesellschaft der Wissenschaften, 9.5, 1933, p. 155.

3 Several inscriptions from various cult centres record the names of hymnic poets and the honours paid to them for their compositions, and Ptolemaic and Roman papyri from Egypt attest to the same practice.

4 Powell, *CA*, pp. 132–6; Diehl, *ALG²*, vol. 2, 6, pp. 113–18; Maas, *loc. cit.*; and U. von Wilamowitz-Moellendorff, in *Philologische Untersuchungen*, vol. 9, 1886, p. 1f.

5 Powell, *CA*, pp. 165; Diehl, *ALG*, vol. 2², 6, pp. 119f. The metre displays the predominance of choriambic trimeters and glyconics.

6 Powell, *CA*, pp. 162f; Diehl, *ALG*, vol. 2², 6, pp. 134f. It is in regular stanzas of glyconics and pherecrateans.

7 Powell, *CA*, pp. 141f; Diehl, *ALG*, vol. 2², 6, pp. 172f. On their date, see also G. M. Sifakis, *Studies in Hellenistic Drama*, University of London Classical Studies, no. 4, London, 1968, pp. 89, 92.

8 F. Sokolowski, *Lois sacrées de l'Asie Mineure*, Paris, 1955, p. 24b.

9 Powell, *CA*, pp. 138f.; Diehl, *ALG*, vol. 2², 6, pp. 127f.

10 Powell, *CA*, pp. 160f.; Diehl, *ALG*, vol. 2², 6, pp. 131f.

11 Powell, *CA*, pp. 171f.

12 Athen., 15.697a.

13 Athen., 6.253d; Powell, *CA*, pp. 173; Diehl, *ALG*, vol. 2², 6, pp. 104f.

14 Powell, *CA*, fr. 82; Pack, *GLLT*, no. 1279.

15 The ancient theorists—Theon., *Progymn.*, 8 (Waltz); Menander, Περὶ ἐπιδεικτικῶν, 2 (9.129) (Waltz)—consider the hymn to be a special form of the encomium, and they draw distinctions between various kinds.

16 Powell, *CA*, p. 68; *IG*, vol. 15/4, insc. 1299.

17 See W. Peek, *Der Isis-hymnos von Andros und verwandte Texte*, Berlin, 1930.

18 See D. Müller, *Aegypten in die griechischen Isis Aretalogien*, Berlin, 1961.

19 Stob., *Ecl.*, 3.7.12.

20 See C. M. Bowra, in *Journal of Roman Studies*, vol. 47, 1957, p. 21.

21 Powell, *CA*, p. 173; Diehl, *ALG*, vol. 2², 6, p. 107.

22 These should be distinguished from the literary hymns of a Theocritus or a Callimachus, who used the form of the hymn as an excuse for writing occasional poetry.

23 See P. von der Mühl, in *Mus. Helvet.*, vol. 19, 1962, pp. 2f.

24 Powell, *CA*, p. 120; see Fr. Lasserre, *La figure d'Eros dans la poésie grecque*, Lausanne, 1946, pp. 133f.; von der Mühl, *loc. cit.*, pp. 28f.

Chapter 12: Alexandrian Epigrams, Technopaegnia and Priapea

1 See R. Reitzenstein, *Epigramm und Skolion*, Giessen, 1893. Plato is the first author who can be proved to have used such a collection; see A. Körte, *Hellenistic Poetry*, trs. J. Hammer and M. Hadas, New York, 1929, p. 355.

2 See Gow–Page, *HE*, vol. 2, pp. 718f.

3 See Gow–Page, *HE*, vol. 1, 1, pp. 199f.

4 For example, *AP*, bk. 5, no. 135.

5 See, for example, R. Reitzenstein, in Pauly–Wissowa, *REkA*, vol. 6, p. 89, who attributes *AP*, bk. 5, no. 135 to Posidippus.

6 It has been said that the Ionian School was close to the thought of Epicurus and

Aristippus, whereas the Doric was closer to the Stoics, with their pantheism (H. Beckby, *Anthologia Graeca*, Munich, 1957–8, vol. 1, pp. 24f.), but the distinction is hardly so sharp.

7 See p. 237.

8 Diehl, *ALG²*, no. 99 (169), the famous sepulchral scoptic epigram on Timocreon the Rhodian.

9 The name Sikelidas remains unexplained. Some scholars believe that it is a patronymic, his father being named Sikelos or Sikelidas. On the possibility of his being a *Proxenos* of the Delphians in 276, see C. A. Trypanis, in *Classical Review*, vol. 2, 1952, pp. 67f.

10 Two lyrical metres, the greater and the lesser asclepiad, bear his name.

11 Asclepiades and Posidippus wrote many epigrams on the same subjects, and it has been suggested that together with Hedylus they published their epigrams in a book called *Soros* (see R. Reitzenstein, *Epigramm und Skolion*). The suggestion is not convincing; such literary collaboration is otherwise unknown in antiquity.

12 See M. Gabathuler, *Hellenistische Epigramme auf Dichter* (Diss., Basle), Leipzig, 1937.

13 Posidippus borrows actual lines and parts of lines from Asclepiades and Callimachus.

14 *IG*, vol. 9, insc. 1; see O. Weinreich, in *Hermes*, vol. 53, 1918, pp. 434f.

15 See Trypanis, *loc. cit.*, pp. 75f.

16 See H. Lloyd-Jones, in *Journal of Hellenic Studies*, vol. 83, 1963, pp. 77f.

17 See Fr. Lasserre, in *Rhein. Mus.*, vol. 102, 1959, pp. 222f.; R. Keydell, in *Kleine Pauly*, vol. 4, pp. 1075f.

18 Athen., 4.176c; Gow–Page, *HE*, vol. 1, no. 10.

19 Athen., 11.473a; Gow–Page, *HE*, vol. 1, no. 6.

20 Strabo, 14.683, criticizes for its geography an elegy of Hedylus dealing with a flight of deer from Cilicia to Cyprus.

21 See also pp. 273f.

22 Some with alternative ascriptions do not seem likely to be genuine.

23 Fictitious sepulchral and dedicatory epigrams are often classed among the epideictic.

24 Only one epigram attributed to Callimachus is connected with a woman, Conopion (*AP*, bk. 5, no. 23), and that is probably spurious.

25 *AP*, bk. 12, no. 134.

26 *AP*, bk. 12, no. 135.

27 *AP*, bk. 6, no. 336.

28 *AP*, bk. 13, no. 43.

29 *AP*, bk. 12, no. 71.

30 *AP*, bk. 7, no. 453.

31 *AP*, bk. 7, no. 522.

32 *AP*, bk. 7, no. 80. One epigram only of Heracleitus the Halicarnassian survives (*AP*, bk. 7, no. 465). It is about a young woman who died in childbirth, together with one of her twin children. It reveals deep emotion, which makes us regret the loss of that poet's other 'nightingales', as Callimachus calls his poems.

33 *AP*, bk. 7, no. 517.

34 *AP*, bk. 6, no. 310.

35 *AP*, bk. 7, no. 89, for example, is a short story with a moral told in eight elegiac couplets.

36 *Epist.*, 4.3.4.

37 4.23.

38 Athen., 16.699c.

39 *AP*, bk. 9, no. 565.

40 *AP*, bk. 11, no. 436.

41 See P. M. Frazer, *Ptolemaic Alexandria*, Oxford, 1972, vol. 1, p. 599.

42 See p. 84.

43 *AP*, bk. 9, no. 734.

44 *AP*, bk. 11, no. 363.

45 See Gow–Page, *HE*, vol. 1, Dioscorides, III, IV and *passim*.

46 Page, *GLP*, no. 106.
47 Page, *GLP*, nos. 105a, 105b.
48 W. Peek, *Griechische Grabgedichte*, Berlin, 1960, no. 192.
49 *ibid.*, no. 180.
50 *ibid.*, nos. 164, 165.
51 *Nat. Hist.*, 34.57; see Gow–Page, *HE*, vol. 2, p. 101; see also p. 240.
52 *AP*, bk. 6, no. 352.
53 See p. 336.
54 The period is rich in poetesses. We have already met Hedyle, the mother of the epigrammatist Hedylos, and Moiro of Byzantium, mother of the Alexandrian tragic poet Homeros. Two epigrams by the latter survive (Gow–Page, *HE*, vol. 1, p. 145), both of an idyllic nature.
55 *AP*, bk. 9, nos. 313f.
56 *AP*, bk. 7, no. 190.
57 *AP*, bk. 7, no. 208.
58 *AP*, bk. 6, no. 313.
59 10.121f. See C. A. Trypanis, in *Classical Philology*, vol. 65, 1970, p. 52.
60 This persuaded Reitzenstein (*Epigramm und Skolion*, p. 123; Pauly–Wissowa, *REkA*, vol. 6, pp. 84f.) that the three could be considered the true 'leaders' of the Doric School of epigrammatists.
61 *AP*, bk. 9, no. 26.
62 *AP*, bk. 5, no. 170.
63 *AP*, bk. 7, no. 718.
64 Clearchus, in Athen., 14.639a. See also U. von Wilamowitz-Moellendorff, *Hellenistische Dichtung in der Zeit des Kallimachos*, Berlin, 1924, vol. 1, p. 135.
65 *AP*, bk. 6, no. 265.
66 *AP*, bk. 6, no. 353.
67 *AP*, bk. 5, no. 170.
68 *AP*, bk. 9, no. 933.
69 *AP*, bk. 12, no. 138.
70 4.163.
71 *AP*, bk. 7, no. 145.
72 Some modern scholars have considered it a parody; cf. J. Geffcken, *Griechische Epigramme*, Heidelberg, 1916, p. 125, but see also T. B. L. Webster, *Hellenistic Poetry and Art*, New York, 1964, p. 229.
73 *AP*, bk. 13, no. 21.
74 *ibid.*
75 *AP*, bk. 7, no. 406.
76 In this strange epigram Euphorion is said to have been buried by the walls of the Piraeus (Πειραϊκοῖς . . . παρὰ σκέλεσιν), whereas we know that he died and was buried in the east, in Antioch or Apamea (*Suda*).
77 *AP*, bk. 7, nos. 479, 732.
78 Athen., 11.175f.
79 Athen., 15.699e.
80 Athen., 6.229b; 7.302c.
81 *Suda*, s.v. Sotades.
82 See the long discussion—though it leads to no definite conclusion—in Gow–Page, *HE*, vol. 2, pp. 446f.
83 *AP*, bk. 7, nos. 445, 730.
84 *AP*, bk. 7, no. 730.
85 See R. J. Smutny, *The Text History of the Epigrams of Theocritus*, Berkeley, 1955.
86 *AP*, bk. 9, no. 437.
87 *AP*, bk. 6, no. 337.
88 Nauck, *TGF*, fr. 663.
89 See M. Wellmann, in Pauly–Wissowa, *REkA*, vol. 11, p. 334, s.v. Erasistratos.
90 This epigram may also have served as an inscription for an ornamental relief or a picture.

91 Besides the epigrams in the *Anthology*, one more is to be found in Stobaeus and another in a papyrus (Page, *GLP*, no. 107 (3)).

92 The date of Leonidas is indicated by *AP*, bk. 6, nos. 129, 131, which are dedications of loot from battles against the Lucans in 281 B.C., *AP*, bk. 6, no. 130 probably referring to the victory of Pyrrhus over Antigonos Gonatas in 273 B.C.; *AP*, bk. 9, no. 25, which refers to Aratus' *Phaenomena*, should be after 273.

93 From his epigrams we can gather that he probably visited Epirus, Athens, Cos and Asia Minor; see R. Keydell, in *Kleine Pauly*, vol. 3, pp. 568f.

94 *AP*, bk. 9, no. 563.

95 *AP*, bk. 9, no. 326; *APl*, no. 230.

96 See Gow–Page, *HE*, vol. 2, p. 307.

97 *AP*, bk. 10, no. 1; Gow–Page, *HE*, vol. 1, no. 85.

98 *AP*, bk. 9, no. 99.

99 *AP*, bk. 6, nos. 293, 298, 305.

100 *APl* (B), no. 261; Gow–Page, *HE*, vol. 1, no. 84; cf. also *APl* (A), no. 236; Gow–Page, *HE*, vol. 1, no. 83.

101 See n.100.

102 *AP*, bk. 7, nos. 472, 736; Stob., *Flor.*, 120.9.

103 9.99.

104 *AP*, bk. 7, no. 715.

105 See Beckby, *Anthologia Graeca*, vol. 1, pp. 33f.

106 On the complicated relationship of Alcaeus with the Macedonians and his enmity towards Sparta, see F. W. Walbank, in *Classical Quarterly*, vol. 37, 1943, pp. 1f.

107 *Flam.*, 9.

108 *APl*, no. 266.

109 *AP*, bk. 7, no. 247.

110 *APl*, no. 5.

111 *AP*, bk. 6, no. 218.

112 *AP*, bk. 12, nos. 29, 30, 64.

113 Schmid–Stählin, *GL*, 2^6, 1, p. 125.

114 To this poem belong the verses in Pap. Michigan 3.139 = Pack, *GLLT*, no. 1458.

115 Gow–Page, *HE*, vol. 1, nos. 1–3. *AP*, bk. 7, no. 202.

116 He was thought to be a contemporary of Theocritus and has even been identified with the historian of the same name who wrote *Cretika*. But his date is later; see *Kleine Pauly*, s.v. Dosiadas.

117 A. S. F. Gow, *Bucolici Graeci*, Oxford, 1962, p. 184.

118 See P. Maas, in Pauly–Wissowa, *REkA*, vol. A9, pp. 103f.

119 We have in Latin a collection of eighty anonymous *priapea* (F. Buecheler and W. Heraeus, *Petronii Saturae et Liber Priapeorum*, Berlin, 1922, pp. 149–72), as well as some more that are attributed to Tibullus and Virgil.

120 Athen., 5.203e; see also Frazer, *Ptolemaic Alexandria*, vol. 1, p. 207.

121 See H. Herter, in *Kleine Pauly*, vol. 4, p. 1131.

122 *AP*, bk. 6, no. 292.

123 In Alexandrian poetry the one god Eros degenerates into many young *erotes*, who are the forefathers of the Pompeian cupids and of the *putti* we find decorating so many nineteenth- and twentieth-century theatres.

124 *AP*, bk. 9, no. 314.

125 See p. 339.

126 See Herter, *loc. cit.*

127 Choirob. on Heph., p. 236.

128 Powell, *CA*, frs. 176f.

Section II: The Greco-Roman World: The Transition to Classicism (146 B.C.–A.D. 100)

Introduction

1 It should be remembered that it was in these eastern centres, and most prominently in Antioch and Pergamum, that the Asianic style had come into its own, not only in rhetoric, but also in poetry, sculpture and architecture. Its greatest surviving achievement is the Pergamum Altar.

2 The gifts and favours then bestowed upon the city of Athens by lesser eastern rulers should also be noted. Such were the services rendered by monarchs like the Attalids, Nicomedes, king of Bithynia, Ariarathes V and Ariobarzanes II of Cappadocia, and Herodes of Judea.

3 Rome had its followers of the Asianic style (Hortensius, the younger Cicero and the orators of the early Imperial centuries); its Atticists (Brutus, Calvus, Calidius); and a middle party (Cicero in his maturer years), which fused elements of both the Asianic and the Atticist styles and which finally won the day. And in Sulla's time, as already mentioned, Alexandrian poetry was brought to Rome by Valerius Cato and Parthenius, influencing Catullus and the Roman elegists and retaining its vigour — as can be seen from Virgil, Horace himself and Ovid — even after Horace and Augustus had taken the side of Classicism.

4 The first representative of Atticism in the Greek world was Dion of Prusa (born c. A.D. 40), a friend of the Romans. Vespasian (A.D. 69–79) appointed professors of Greek and Roman rhetoric (Suet., *Vesp.*, 18), Quintilian being the first Imperial professor. This support of higher education was limited to Rome, but it inclined the state-directed education towards a taste for Classicism, as in the private schools of rhetoric and grammar in the days of Augustus and Tiberius the Asianic tendency was still prevalent; see Schmid–Stählin, *GL*, 2⁶, 1, p. 317.

5 See, for example, Pseudo-Longinus, *de Sub.*, 33.4; Luc., *de Hist. Consc.*, 57; Antipatros of Thessalonica, *AP*, bk. 11, no. 20; *AP*, bk. 11, nos. 321, 322; and Schmid–Stählin, *GL*, 2⁶, 2, p. 230, n. 9.

6 In the Introduction to Section III (*The Age of Classicism*) we shall elaborate on this; see pp. 365f.

7 It has been argued that this was responsible for the emergence in all spheres of the Asianic style, which strove after grand works full of shapeless pathos, by contrast with the Alexandrian, which was refined and decorative, promoting discipline and strict form. We cannot be certain that the birth of this style, which was disliked by so many influential Romans, was the consequence of Oriental influence; see K. Ziegler, *Das hellenistische Epos*, 2nd edn., Leipzig–Berlin, 1966, pp. 12f.

8 Euphorion was considered one of the great 'Callimacheans'.

Chapter 13: The Depletion of the Poetic Tradition

1 The most important bucolic poet of this period is Moschus, about whom we have already spoken (see pp. 282f.)

2 15.

3 20.

4 See A. S. F. Gow, *Theocritus*, Cambridge, 1950, vol. 2, pp. 364f.

5 A. S. F. Gow, *Bucolici Graeci*, Oxford, 1952, pp. 146f.

6 'Dreams are but lies'; 'Seek the flesh of fish, lest you die of famine with all your dreams of gold.'

7 Heitsch, *GDRK*, vol. 1, pp. 17f.; Gow, *Bucolici Graeci*, pp. 168–70.

8 Cic., *Div.*, 1.79.

9 Cf. *AP*, bk. 9, no. 91. See F. Susemihl, *Geschichte der griechischen Literatur in der*

Alexandrinerzeit, Leipzig, 1891–2, vol. 1, p. 900; T. Reinach, *de Archia Poeta* (Diss.), Paris, 1890.

10 See A. Hillscher, *Jahrbücher für klass. Philologie*, suppl. 18, 1891, p. 403.

11 Page 674.

12 See E. Rohde, in *Kleine Schriften*, Tübingen, 1901, vol. 1, p. 336.2; A. Raubitschek, in *Hesperia*, vol. 23, 1954, pp. 317f.; L. Robert, in *Revue des études grecques*, vol. 68, 1955, p. 210.

13 *AP*, bk. 11, no. 136.

14 See F. G. Kenyon, in *Revue de philologie*, vol. 19, 1895, pp. 77f.

15 See Heitsch, *GDRK*, vol. 2, pp. 7f.

16 P. M. Frazer, *Ptolemaic Alexandria*, Oxford, 1972, vol. 1, p. 457.

17 Text in C. Müller, *Fragmenta Historicorum Graecorum*, Paris, 1848–70, vol. 1, pp. 449f. See Schwarz, in Pauly–Wissowa, *REkA*, vol. 1, pp. 2855f.; and F. Atenstädt, in *Rhein. Mus.*, vol. 82, 1933, pp. 115f. On the other hand, B. Niese, in *Hermes*, vol. 44, 1909, pp. 161f., and L. Pareti, in *Atti della Regia Accademia delle Scienze di Torino*, vol. 45, 1909–10, pp. 229f., believe the Γῆς περίοδος to be a genuine work by Apollodorus.

18 A. Meineke, in *Historia Critica Comicorum Graecorum*, Berlin, 1839, pp. xiiif., distinguishes this didactic poet Simylus from the comic poet of the same name (Meineke, *FCG*, vol. 2, fr. 444). Whether the author of the elegy on Tarpeia (Diehl, *ALG*, vol. 2², 6, p. 102f.)—which should perhaps be dated earlier than the Augustan age—is the same or not is a matter of dispute; see K. Müller, in *Mus. Helvet.*, vol. 20, 1963, pp. 114f.

19 It has been attributed by A. Diller (see *Transactions of the American Philological Association*, vol. 86, 1955, pp. 276f.) to one Pausanius of Damascus (cf. Const. Porph., *Them.*, 1.2).

20 Text in K. Müller, *Geographi Graeci Minores*, Paris, 1885–61, vol. 1, pp. 196f.

21 Thus Demetrius of Troizen wrote on philosophy; Pancrates of Arcadia, Caicalus of Argos and Poseidonius of Corinth on fish; and Pseudo-Boio on the wanderings of birds; see Schmid–Stählin, *GL*, vol. 2⁶, 1, pp. 330f.

22 Pollianus, *AP*, bk. 11, no. 130.

23 *Sat.*, 5.57.

24 Erycius, *AP*, bk. 7, no. 377.

25 Other titles of his elegies were: *Aphrodite*, *Bias* (a friend of the poet, on whom he composed a lament), *Delos* and *Leucadiai*. Fragments have also survived of a *Lament on Timandros*.

26 *Erot.*, 11.4.

27 The titles of these are: *Anthippe*, *Lament on Auxithemis*, *Eidolophanes* (Εἰδωλοφανής), *Heracles*, *Iphiclus*, *Metamorphoses*, *Propempticon* and *Myttotos*.

28 This has been vigorously contested by A. Ehlers, in *Mus. Helvet.*, vol. 11, 1954, pp. 65f.

29 Dion., 26.357.

30 *AP*, bk. 11, no. 135.

31 See *AP*, bk. 9, no. 248.

32 See Lucian, as. 55.

33 The Hellenistic fashion for epigrams was taken over by the Romans, and it developed until we hear of epigrams by almost everyone who pretended to culture—Cicero, Caesar, Augustus, Maecenas, Tiberius, Seneca, Petronius and so on—as well as anonymous collections and attacks against unpopular emperors.

34 See A. Wifstrand, *Von Kallimachos zu Nonnos*, Lund, 1933, pp. 155f.

35 Page, *GLP*, pp. 454f.

36 *AP*, bk. 7, no. 493; bk. 9, no. 151.

37 *de Or.*, 3.194.

38 *AP*, bk. 7, no. 428; cf. bk. 7, no. 427.

39 As can be seen from *AP*, bk. 7, no. 428.16—and *AP*, bk. 6, no. 219 seems to confirm this—for it is a short elegy rather than an epigram.

40 *AP*, bk. 9, no. 363.

41 It was not the oldest such anthology; see Gow–Page, *HE*, vol. 1, p. xvi.

42 For the date of the *Garland* it is significant that Meleager's compatriot Philodemus is missing; see Gow–Page, *HE*, vol. 1, pp. xvf.

43 *Serm.*, 1.2.120.
44 By G. Highet, in the *Oxford Classical Dictionary*, Oxford, 1970, s.v. Argentarius.
45 *Controv.*, 9.3(26),12–13.
46 Gow–Page, *GPh*, vol. 2, p. 329.
47 *AP*, bk. 7, no. 377.
48 *AP*, bk. 7, no. 368.
49 *AP*, bk. 9, no. 546. On Antiphilus, see K. Müller, *Die Epigramme des Antiphilos von Byzanz*, Berlin, 1935.
50 He has also been identified with a grammarian of Tiberius' reign; see H. Usener, *Kleine Schriften*, vol. 2, Leipzig, 1913, and A. Linnenkugel, *de Lucillo Trahaeo*, Paderborn, 1928.
51 *AP*, bk. 9, no. 251.
52 *AP*, bk. 11, no. 177.
53 Such are, for example, *IG*, vol. 12, insc. 5.739 of the first century B.C. (see U. von Wilamowitz-Moellendorff, *Hellenistische Dichtung in der Zeit des Kallimachos*, Berlin, 1924, vol. 2, p. 300.3) or the epitaph from Gaul, in *Inscriptiones Graecae Sicilae et Italiae*, no. 2508 (ed. Kaibel).
54 In those days the general Greek public took increasing pleasure in purely musical performances, and many theatres were used more frequently as gathering places for the public (they were occasionally even called *ecclesiasteria*) or for performances of mimes, pantomimes and pseudo-naval battles than as suitable settings for the presentation of new dramatic works.
55 See E. Rohde, *Der griechische Roman*, 3rd edn., Leipzig, 1914, p. 371, n.1.
56 *SIG*, no. 648B 3; see G. M. Sifakis, *Studies in the History of Hellenistic Drama*, University of London Classical Studies, no. 4, London, 1968, p. 96. The solo singer was called τραγῳδός which explains the modern Greek word for song, τραγούδι. See S. Menardos, Ἀφιέρωμα εἰς Γ. Χατζηδάκιν, Athens, 1921, pp. 15f., and S. Kyriakides, Αἱ ἱστορικαὶ ἀρχαὶ τῆς δημώδους Νεοελληνικῆς Ποιήσεως, Salonica, 1954.
57 On these, see Schmid–Stählin, *GL*, 2⁶, 1, pp. 333f.
58 *IG*, vol. 2², insc. 4257.
59 *IG*, vol. 4, insc. 1146, and *SIG*, no. 728K 34.
60 Such were Theodotus, Polemon, Sophocles, Aristomenes, Ariston, Diogenes, Dionysius and others, all otherwise unknown.
61 See J. Frei, *de Certam. Thymelicis*, Basle, 1900, p. 21.
62 See O. Kern, in *Athenische Mitteilungen*, vol. 19, 1894, pp. 100f.
63 Only one gloss and one fragment (Stob., *Ecl.*, 3.14.7) of his have survived. See A. Körte, in Pauly–Wissowa, *REkA*, vol. 17, p. 362, and Jacoby, *FGH*, frs. 90f, 132.
64 It probably disappeared because of its inferior quality.
65 On Scopelianus, see Dornseiff, in Pauly–Wissowa, *REkA*, vol. 3A, pp. 580f. On the poetry of the Sophists of the Second Sophistic, see F. G. Welcker, *Die griechische Tragödien*, Bonn, 1841, vol. 3, pp. 1322f.; Rohde, *Der griechische Roman*, pp. 332f.; E. Norden, *Die antike Kunstprosa*, Leipzig–Berlin, 1915–18, p. 886; and W. Schmid, *Der Atticismus*, Stuttgart, 1887–97, vol. 1, p. 214.
66 See Page, *GLP*, pp. 332f.
67 Page, *GLP*, pp. 336f.
68 It should be noted that from the first century B.C. the *aulodia*, the song accompanied by the *aulos*, disappears from the thymelic competitions (ἀγῶνες θυμελικοί); see Frei, *de Certam. Thymelicis*, p. 28.
69 Lucillius, *AP*, bk. 11, no. 133; bk. 9, no. 143.3; bk. 11, no. 246, where Meliton is also accused of having written a 'rotten' drama called *Niobe*.
70 See Diehl, *ALG*, vol. 2², 6, pp. 202f.; Page, *GLP*, nos. 92, 93; Heitsch, *GDRK*, vol. 1, pp. 34f.
71 See W. Peek, *Der Isis-hymnos von Andros und verwandte Texte*, Berlin, 1930.
72 See Frazer, *Ptolemaic Alexandria*, vol. 1, p. 671. On the aretalogies, the poems that describe the achievements of the god (which the god himself often relates), see

D. Müller, *Ägyptien und die griechische Isis-aretalogien*, Berlin, 1961, and E. Norden, *Agnostos Theos*, Leipzig, 1923, pp. 183f.

73 The text of the Philon fragment in A. Ludwich, *de Philonis Carmine Greco-Iudaico, Königsberg Univ. Programm*, 1900. The text of the Theodotus fragment in A. Ludwich, *de Theodoti Carmine Graeco-Iudaico*, Regimontii, 1899.

74 H. Diels, *Die Fragmente der Vorsokratiker*, 6th end., ed. W. Kranz, Berlin, 1951, no. 22B.92.

75 See Frazer, *Ptolemaic Alexandria*, vol. 2, pp. 708f.; Editions: A. Rzach, *Oracula Sibyllina*, Vienna, 1891; A. Kurfess, *Sibyllinische Weissagungen*, Munich, 1951 (a selection).

76 On this, see Schmid–Stählin, *GL*, vol. 1, 1.299f.

Section III: The Greco-Roman World: The Age of Classicism (A.D. 100–330)

Introduction

1 In Rome too Hadrian founded the *Athenaeum*, on the pattern of the Alexandrian Museum, as a centre of Hellenic learning.

2 See E. Rohde, *Der griechische Roman*, 3rd edn., Leipzig, 1914, p. 357.

3 Nicagoras called poetry 'the Mother of the Sophists' (Philostr., *Vit. Soph.*, 620), and Polemon considered poetry more important than prose (Philostr., *Vit. Soph.*, 539).

4 See Menander, 3.341 (Spengel). Aelius Aristeides tells us that orators can replace poets (*Address to the Gods*, frs. 37–46) (Keil).

5 See W. Schmid, *Der Atticismus*, Stuttgart, 1887–97, esp. vol. 4, pp. 66of. This was also partly helped by the tradition of the Menippean satires, in which both prose and verse were used.

6 See Toivo Viljamaa, in *Commentationes Humanarum Litterarum Societatis Scientiarum Fennica*, vol. 42.4, 1968, p. 17.

7 The earliest is by Theon (first century A.D.), which is incomplete and represents the final form of the *progymnasmata*, the instructions on rhetorical exercises. We glean a considerable amount of information from Hermogenes of Tarsus (c. A.D. 160–225), whose textbooks were widely used and expanded in Byzantine times. See H. Gärtner, in *Kleine Pauly*, vol. 2, p. 1082.

8 If dealing with the actions of a dead person, it was called *eidolopoeia*.

9 This was called *prosopopoeia*.

10 The encomium, praise of living men, has, as we have seen, a long history going back to Pindar and Simonides. But its precise and final rules seem to date from the second and third centuries A.D.; see Kroll, in Pauly–Wissowa, *REkA*, suppl. 7, pp. 1131.

11 The encomium or hymn to a god has, of course, its own age-old tradition, based on religious and philosophical views, to which the poetry of the Imperial age did not do justice. Examples in Heitsch, *GDRK*, vol. 1, pp. 165f. (nos. 47–50). The most important surviving example belongs to the fourth century A.D. Heitsch, *GDRK*, vol. 1, pp. 82f. (no. 24). On this see J. Bidez, *Revue de philologie*, n.s. vol. 27, 1903, p. 81.

12 Such examples are *AP*, bk. 9, nos. 451–80, and Heitsch, *GDRK*, vol. 1, nos. 21, 26, 37, 42.

13 Examples in Heitsch, *GDRK*, vol. 1², nos. 16, 27, 31.

14 This consists of the encomia composed by Claudian (c. A.D. 395), Sidonius Apollinaris (born c. A.D. 430), Corippius (sixth century A.D.) and Priscianus (sixth century A.D.).

15 Unfortunately, the encomia (or ἔπαινοι), ethopoeiae and so on that have survived in papyri from this period are fragmentary on the whole and negligible as poetry. The reader may find them conveniently collected in Page, *GLP*, and Heitsch, *GDRK*.

16 *Ep.*, 3.16.

17 Rohde, *Der griechische Roman*, pp. 371f.; A. Boulanger, *Aelius Aristide*, Paris, 1923, pp. 42f.
18 Longinus, in Porph., *Vit. Plot.*, 20; Philostr., *Vit. Soph.*, 2.27.4, p. 118.1 (Kayser).

Chapter 14: The Decline of Lyrical Poetry

1 This is stated in the acrostic of lines 513–32. See U. Bernays, *Studien zu Dionysius Periegetes*, Heidelberg, 1905, pp. 12f.; and U. von Wilamowitz-Moellendorff, *Kleine Schriften*, vol. 2, p. 219.
2 Acrostics have been traced as far back as the third century B.C.; see Schmid–Stählin, *GL*, 2⁶, p. 677, no. 4.
3 *ad Att.*, 1.20; 6.22.7.
4 The *Vita Chisiana* is edited by A. Colonna, in *Bolletino dei Comitato per la Preparazione dell' Edizione Nazionale dei classici Greci a Latini*, n.s. vol. 5, 1957, pp. 9f.
5 The *Halieutica* was also known to Athenaeus (1.13b).
6 IV, 65f.
7 See R. Keydell, in *Hermes*, vol. 72, 1937, pp. 430f.
8 See R. Keydell, in Pauly–Wissowa, *REkA*, vol. 15, pp. 695f.
9 See E. Norden, *Die antike Kunstprosa*, Leipzig–Berlin, 1915–18, pp. 834f.
10 Schmid–Stählin, *GL*, vol. 2⁶, 1, p. 677.
11 See A. Hausrath, in Pauly–Wissowa, *REkA*, vol. 6, pp. 170f.
12 Cf. Pap. Oxy. 1249, and the *epimythium* of fable 43.
13 In this he followed the lead of Callimachus, but his choliambics betray the Imperial age, when the last syllable was generally long and the penultimate accented.
14 So the *Suda* informs us.
15 See L. Radermacher, in *Rhein. Mus.*, vol. 57, 1902, pp. 142f.
16 For example, we know of the Ἰατρικά in forty books by Marcellus Sidus, who lived in the days of Hadrian (Heitsch, *GDRK*, vol. 2, p. 16), of the astrological work in seven books by Antiochus of Athens (c. A.D. 300), which later became famous among the Arabs, and so on. On a didactic poem on plants of the second century A.D. and one on metres of the third century A.D., see Heitsch, *GDRK*, vol. 1, pp. 203f. On the pseudo-Pythagorean *Carmen Aureum*, probably of the second century A.D., see P. van der Horst, *Les vers d'or pythagoriciens* (Diss.), Leyden, 1932.
17 Fragments of which are to be found in *AP*, bk. 9, nos. 128(?), 129, 364, 536, 537.
18 Nestor's surviving fragments in H. Düntzer, *Die Fragmente der epischen Poesie der Griechen*, Cologne, 1840–2, vol. 2, p. 105; see Keydell, in Pauly–Wissowa, *REkA*, vol. 17, p. 125.
19 Spengel, *Rhet.*, 3.393.
20 See A. Severyns, *Le cycle épique dans l'école d'Aristarque*, Paris, 1928, pp. 75f.
21 See Pack, *GLLT*, nos. 2300–12.
22 Peisander's few surviving fragments in Heitsch, *GDRK*, vol. 2, pp. 44f. On Peisander, see Keydell, in Pauly–Wissowa, *REkA*, vol. 36, p. 145.
23 For fragments of such epics on Dionysus retrieved from papyri, see H. Cronert, in *Archiv für Papyrusforschung*, vol. 2, 1902–3, p. 351.
24 Text of considerable surviving fragments in Heitsch, *GDRK*, vol. 1, pp. 60f (no. 19). On Dionysius, see O. Crusius, in Pauly–Wissowa, *REkA*, vol. 5, p. 294.
25 See Weinberger, in Pauly–Wissowa, *REkA*, vol. 5, second series, pp. 1231f.
26 There is no support for the attribution of Page, *GLP*, no. 542 (Heitsch, *GDRK*, p. 79) to Soterichus.
27 *CIG*, vol. 4, no. 700 (Kaibel, *EG*, no. 1015).
28 Pap. Oxy. 2946.
29 See Keydell, in Pauly–Wissowa, *REkA*, vol. A7, p. 178.
30 See Keydell, in Pauly–Wissowa, *REkA*, vol. 13, second series, p. 179.
31 See Pack, *GLLT*, nos. 1417 (Page, *GLP*, no. 133), 1418 (Page, *GLP*, no. 137), 1461.
32 Heitsch, *GDRK*, vol. 1, pp. 51f. Pancrates of Alexandria had suggested to Hadrian that a kind of lotus should be named after his favourite Antinous, implying that it had grown from the blood of a lion that the emperor had killed near Alexandria.

33 Page, *GLP*, pp. 542f.; Heitsch, *GDRK*, vol. 1, pp. 79f.
34 Kaibel, *EG*, no. 1009.
35 Page, *GLP*, pp. 544f.
36 See also B. Wyss, in *Mus. Helvet.*, vol. 6, 1949–50, p. 194.45.
37 See K. Münscher, in *Philologus*, suppl. 10, 1907, pp. 539f.; Schmid–Stählin, *GL*, 2⁶, 2, p. 685.
38 Athen., 3.82.115b.
39 *Flor.*, 9.37.
40 See p. 358.
41 The Sophists of the Second Sophistic honoured tragedy, which they considered helpful to their art. Nicagoras called tragedy 'the mother of Sophists', and even Hadrian himself is quoted as an example of a poet who failed to attain the grand style because of his excessive use of tragedy in his *Metamorphoses*. On tragedies composed by the Sophists, see F. G. Welcker, *Die griechische Tragödien*, Bonn, 1841, vol. 3, pp. 1322f.; E. Rohde, *Der griechische Roman*, 3rd edn., Leipzig, 1914, pp. 37f.; W. Schmid, *Der Atticismus*, Stuttgart, 1887–97, vol. 1, p. 40.
42 See p. 357. Such was the practice with the plays of Nicolaus of Damascus (c. 65 B.C.) who is credited with both tragedies and comedies.
43 26.146a.12. See also F. Mehmel, *Vergil und Apollonius Rhodius*, Hamburg, 1940, p. 20.23.
44 This, as we have seen, had already begun in the second century B.C. (see p. 357 and *SIG*, no. 36488).
45 19.5: ἰαμβεῖα, τούτων μέρη διεξίασιν ἐν τοῖς Θεάτροις, τὰ δὲ μαλακώτερα ἐξερρύηκε, τὰ περὶ τὰ μέλη.
46 See O. Bruneer, in *Hesperia*, vol. 22, 1953, p. 192; and K. Latte, in *Eranos*, vol. 52, 1954, pp. 125f.
47 See p. 299.
48 See Philostr., *Vit. Apol.*, 4.21.; Dio, *Chrysostom*, 11.9; Schmid, *Der Atticismus*, vol. I, p. 40.14. The actors who performed such excerpts from tragedies were clad in full dramatic costume.
49 Demosth., enc. 27.
50 Heitsch, *GDRK*, vol. 1, p. 12, no. 12.
51 For example, Page, *GLP*, nos. 77–9.
52 See K. von Jan, *Musici Scriptores Graeci*, Leipzig, 1895, pp. 454f., and suppl. 1899, pp. 40f. (2nd edn. of both 1962).
53 *AP*, bk. 14, no. 63; *APL*, no. 323.
54 Texts in Heitsch, *GDRK*, vol. 1², pp. 165f.
55 Texts in Heitsch, *GDRK*, vol. 1², pp. 180f.
56 See P. M. Frazer, *Ptolemaic Alexandria*, Oxford, 1972, vol. 1, p. 804.
57 Of the hymns of Pausanius (see Menander, *Rhet. Gr.*, 3.341, Spengel) nothing survives; of those by Philostratus Flavus only two short anapaestic compositions, one on Thetis and a song of Achilles to Echo, have come down to us (Philostr., *Heroicus*, 2.208, and 213, Kayser); and of Aristeides' hymns to Asclepius, Athene, Pan, Hecate, Achelous, Hermes, Dionysus, Heracles and Asclepius, Aisepus, the nymphs and Artemis Thermaia, only a few tiny scraps have escaped destruction (Aristeid., 50.4; 50.31; 50.38–40; 50.45, Keil). On the 'poetry in prose' of Aristeides, see A. Boulanger, *Aelius Aristide*, Paris, 1923, pp. 300f.; W. F. Lenz, in *Rivista di cultura classica e mediovale*, vol. 3, 1961, pp. 156f.; and A. Hölfer, *Der Sarapishymnus des Aelius Aristeidis*, Stuttgart–Berlin, 1935 (= *Tübinger Beiträge zur Altertumswissenschaft*, vol. 27, 1935).
58 50.46 (Keil).
59 50.31 (Keil). He wrote a paean of two strophes and an epode.
60 Philostr., *Vit. Soph.*, p. 620.
61 Menander, 3.341. The 'poet and Sophist' Falernus (second–third century A.D.) had an epigram of his own inscribed on the right leg of the Memnon in Egypt (Kaibel, *EG*, no. 994).
62 Maximus Tyrius, *Diss.*, 29, p. 388.11 (Holbein). See also Philostr., *Epist. Erot.*, 68.

63 See Schmid–Stählin, *GL*, 2⁶, 1, p. 201.
64 See Page, *GLP*, no. 94.
65 Page, *GLP*, no. 95.
66 Page, *GLP*, no. 97.
67 Page, *GLP*, no. 98.
68 Heitsch, *GDRK*, vol. 1², pp. 38f.
69 Heitsch, *GDRK*, vol. 1², pp. 42f.
70 Heitsch, *GDRK*, vol. 1², pp. 44f.
71 Epigrams by Trajan, *AP*, bk. 9, no. 338, bk. 11, no. 418; epigrams by Hadrian, *AP*, bk. 6, no. 332; bk. 7, no. 674; bk. 9, nos. 137, 387, 402.
72 R. Keydell, in *Hermes*, vol. 80, 1952, pp. 498f., places Rufinus after Straton and before Ausonius; see also M. Boas, in *Phililogus*, vol. 73, 1914–16, pp. 1f.
73 For example, *AP*, bk. 12, no. 18: ψυχῆς ἔστιν ἔρως ἀκόνη; *AP*, bk. 12, no. 31: καιρὸς ἔρωτι φίλος; and so on.
74 See Helm, in Pauly–Wissowa, *REkA*, vol. 26, pp. 1739f., and G. Setli, *Gli epigrammi di Luciani*, Turin, 1892.
75 *AP*, bk. 6, nos. 314–20; bk. 9, no. 53.
76 See Schmid, *Der Atticismus*, esp. vol. 4, pp. 660f. The origins of this should probably be traced back to the Menippean satires (third century B.C.), in which both prose and verse were used in the same works.
77 Kaibel, *EG*, nos. 988–1014.
78 Kaibel, *EG*, nos. 988–90, 991(?), 992(?).
79 Kaibel, *EG*, nos. 1001–3. On the poetesses of the Imperial period, see M. L. West, *Die griechische Dichterrinnen der Kaiserzeit: Kyklos*; R. Keydell, *Zum neunzigsten Geburtstag*, Berlin–New York, 1978, pp. 101f.
80 Kaibel, *EG*, no. 993.
81 *Suda*, s.v. Diogenianus.
82 Collected by Kaibel in *EG*, and by W. Peek in *Griechische Vers-Inschriften, Grab-Epigramme*, Berlin, 1955, vol. 1.
83 Such are, for example, Peek, *loc. cit.*, no. 1897 (no. 450 in W. Peek, *Griechische Grabgedichte*, Berlin, 1960), a beautiful epitaph of the second century from Hermopolis Magna; or Peek, *Griechische Vers-Inschriften*, nos. 447, 459.
84 See O. Crusius, in Pauly–Wissowa, *REkA*, vol. 1, 2, pp. 2045f. The best edition is that of C. Preisedanz, *Carmina Anacreontea*, Leipzig, 1912.

Section IV: The Period of Transition from the Ancient World to the Middle Ages (A.D. 330–641)

Introduction

1 The Parthenon was turned into a Christian church between 426 and 485. (Alison Frantz, in *Dumbarton Oaks Papers*, vol. 19, 1965, pp. 185f., argues for a later date.)
2 Christianity, like the medical profession of those days, opposed all physical culture. It should be remembered that Theodosius I abolished the Olympic Games in 394. See J. Geffcken, *Der Ausgang der griechisch-römischen Heidentums*, 2nd edn., Heidelberg, 1929.
3 By 400 the battle was won. By the seventh century no pagans were living in Constantinople. According to R. Keydell, in Pauly–Wissowa, *REkA*, vol. 18, 3, p. 414, the last pagan poet of whom we know was born in 448.
4 See Julian, *Misop.*, pp. 433, 13f. (Hertlein); Eunap., *Vit. Soph.*, p. 92 (Boissonade).
5 By A. Cameron, in *Historia*, vol. 14, 1965, pp. 470f.
6 See Cameron, *loc. cit.*
7 On the Christian epigrams, see A. D. Komines, in *Revue des études sud-est européenes*, vol. 7, 1969, p. 577.

8 See P. Maas, *Greek Metre*, trs. H. Lloyd-Jones, Oxford, 1962, p. 14.

9 On the Byzantine metres, consult Dölger, *BDIR*, pp. 51f.

10 It consists of fifteen syllables, with a caesura after the eighth syllable. Its basic form is: x× x× x× x×//x× x× x× x. There is no difference between long and short syllables, and the accents are dynamic (*καὶ πῶς θρασὺς ὁ τὴν αἰδῶ προβεβλημένηνἔχων*). At the beginning of the two half-lines we may have x× instead of x×. Occasionally, such freedom is allowed that only in the ending of the line is the exact placing of the accent observed. See T. Stavrou, *Νεοελληνικὴ Μετρική*, Athens, 1930, pp. 63f.

11 See Krumbacher, *GBL*, pp. 792, 650; P. Maas, *BZ*, vol. 21, 1912, p. 29. According to D. S. Robertson, in *Classical Review*, vol. 57, 1943, pp. 8–9, the first political verse is found in Procopius, *Hist. Arc.*, 15.25–7, but this does not appear probable. The origins of the fifteen-syllable verse are discussed in a later chapter; see pp. 454f.

12 See P. Maas, in *BZ*, vol. 12, 1903, p. 268; W. Cronert, in *Philologus*, vol. 84, 1929, p. 157.

13 See A. D. Cameron, in *Classical Quarterly*, n.s. vol. 200, 1970, pp. 119f.; R. Browning, in *BZ*, vol. 63, 1970, p. 368.

14 On the various meanings of the word *troparion*, see Sophocles' *Greek Lexicon of the Roman and Byzantine Periods* s.v. *troparion*. As we shall see, the isostichic hymns are of great importance among them.

15 Cf. Pseudo-Lucian, *Demosth.*, enc. 27.

16 See Schmid–Stählin, *GL*, vol. 2⁶, p. 333. The modern Greek word *τραγούδι* ('song') owes its origin to such solos from tragedy that were sung independently, as has already been mentioned.

17 See G. I. Theocharides, *Beitrage zur Geschichte des byzantinischen Profantheater im 4 und 5 Jahrhundert* (Diss., Munich), Salonica, 1940.

18 It is true that attacks on the mime and pantomime continued, and the ruling of the Second in Trullo Council (692) was probably directed against them.

19 Migne, *PG*, vol. 65, pp. 736f.

20 Theoph. Simokates, p. 187.29 (C. de Boor). We are also told that the iconoclast emperors 'favoured' the theatre, whatever that may mean.

21 It has repeatedly been advanced that the Western religious plays (the Mystery Plays, the Passion Plays and the Miracles) had their origins in Byzantium. This is not true. They originated, it appears, in Rome (see M. S. de Vito, *L'origine del dràmma liturgico*, Rome, 1938). Nor is the recently discovered *Cypriot Scenario* anything more than a revival by the Lusignans in Cyprus of the French dramatization of Holy Week. In the Byzantine Church, in spite of what Liutprand says ('Santa Sophia was turned into a theatre'; Liutprand, *Relatio de Legatione Constantinopolitana*, 9 (p. 149, Dümmler), such performances never went beyond the division of parts in certain hymns and sermons. See G. La Paina, in *Speculum*, vol. 11, 1936, pp. 171f., and Dölger, *BDIR*, p. 16.

22 Krumbacher, *GBL*, p. 12.

Chapter 15: Secular Poetry

1 See Quint. Smyrn., *Posthomerica*, 12.308f., and Tzetzes, schol., in *Posthomerica*, 282.

2 This is a strange narrative in which the pagan *Δωρόθεος* becomes a Christian and assumes the name *'Ανδρέας*. At the end we find: *Τέλος 'Οράσεως Δωροθέου Κοίντου τοῦ ποιητοῦ* (The information was given to me by Professor Olivier Reverdin of Geneva.)

3 As a fairly certain *terminus post quem*, Oppian's *Halieutica* can be given—a work, as we have indicated, dedicated to Caracalla—on which the *Posthomerica* draws; and as a probable *terminus ante quem*, there is Calchas' prophecy (13.334–41), in which Rome and not Constantinople is said to be the capital of the world and which is therefore to be dated before A.D. 330. See F. Vian, *Quintus de Smyrne*, Paris, 1963–9, vol. 1, p. xxi (Budé); also in *Revue de philologie*, vol. 28, 1959, pp. 50f., and *Recherches sur les Posthomerica de Quintus de Smyrne*, Paris, 1959, pp. 28f.

4 See R. Keydell, in *Gnomon*, vol. 33, 1961, p. 278.

5 See Pack, *GLLT*, nos. 2300–12.

6 See p. 396.
7 See Schmid–Stählin, *GL*, 2⁶, 2, p. 984.
8 Cf. Nonnus, *Dionys.*, 1.13, and *AP*, bk. 9, no. 198.
9 For example, IV.31; XII.142, 171; XLVI.363.
10 See R. Keydell, in Pauly–Wissowa, *REkA*, vol. 17, p. 904; I have not seen the work of R. Dostalova-Jenistova, in *Listy Filologické* (1956), which dates the *Dionysiaca*.
11 Heitsch, *GDRK*, vol. 1², p. xxiv.
12 See R. Keydell, in *Burs. Jahresb.*, vol. 272, 1941, p. 39; and G. D. Ippolito, in *Rivista di filologia*, vol. 90, 1962, p. 300.
13 For example, XVIII.174b–196a; XX.256–60; XLIV.35–122; XLVIII.258–301.
14 For example, XXII.187–217, 320–53. The best-finished parts of his work are Books I–X; the least polished are the battle scenes of Books XXII, XXIII, XXVII, XXVIII, XXIX, XXX, XLIII.
15 See E. D. Lasky, in *Hermes*, vol. 106, 1978, pp. 357f.
16 XXXV.27.
17 XXXIV.266f.
18 XVI.38.
19 See P. Maas, *Greek Metre*, trs. H. Lloyd-Jones, Oxford, 1962, §§ 89–100.
20 *AP*, bk. 9, no. 198.
21 See Keydell, in Pauly–Wissowa, *REkA*, vol. 17, p. 918.
22 On the date of Musaeus, for long a matter of dispute, see Keydell, in Pauly–Wissowa, *REkA*, vol. 16, p. 768.
23 See T. Gelzer and C. Whitman, *Musaeus, Hero and Leander*, London, 1975 (Loeb), p. 299.
24 H. Keochly, *de Musaei Grammatici Codice Palatino (Festgabe Philologenversammlung Heidelberg, 1865 = Opuscula Philologica*, vol. 1, Leipzig, 1881, pp. 447–68), p. vii.
25 See Page, *GLP*, pp. 512f.
26 *AP*, bk. 9, no. 362.
27 64.31f.
28 For example, Page, *GLP*, pp. 544f. and Heitsch, *GDRK*, vol. 1, p. xli.
29 *Or.*, 39 (Foerster).
30 See Schmid–Stählin, *GL*, 2⁶, 2, p. 1077, n. 3; R. Reitzenstein, *Geschichte der griechischen Etymologika*, Leipzig, 1897, p. 313.
31 A *chrestomathia* is a book containing a summary of useful knowledge.
32 See p. 361.
33 See T. Nissen, in *Hermes*, vol. 75, 1940, pp. 298f.
34 *de Magg*, 3.27.
35 Heitsch, *GDRK*, vol. 1², no. 30; Page, *GLP*, no. 138.
36 Heitsch, *GDRK*, vol. 1², no. 34; Page, *GLP*, no. 144.
37 Heitsch, *GDRK*, vol. 1², no. 36; Page, *GLP*, no. 143.
38 Claudian's Greek poems are all lost except for two fragments of a *Gigantomachia* that have been ascribed to him (ed. J. Koch, Leipzig, 1893) and some epigrams under his name in the *Palatine Anthology*.
39 *Die Kultur der Gegenwart*, Leipzig, 1912, p. 278.
40 See K. Ziegler, *Das hellenistische Epos*, pp. 14f.
41 Julian, *Or.*, 1 (p. 25, Hertlein).
42 *AP*, bk. 2, 1–416.
43 Heitsch, *GDRK*, vol. 1², pp. 111f., no. 3.
44 Apthonius, 37.17.
45 See A. Ludwich, *Eudociae Augustae Procli, Lycii, Claudiani Reliquiae*, Leipzig, 1897, and in *Rhein. Mus.*, vol. 37, 1882, pp. 206f; G. Sattler, *de Eudociae Homerocentonibus*, Programm, K. B. humanistischen Gymnasiums in Bayreuth, Bayreuth, 1804. The oldest cento in Greek poetry belongs to the second century A.D. (see Hunger, *HPLB*, p. 98), but centos, echo poems, ladder poems and poems with strange phrases like acrostics running through them, of which Byzantine literature contains certain examples, are παίγνια rather than poetry; see Hunger, *HPLB*, pp. 98f.
46 See Schmid–Stählin, *GL*, 2⁶, 2, pp. 960f.

47 See B. Knös, in *BZ*, vol. 17, 1908, pp. 397f.

48 *AP*, bk. 9, no. 627.

49 See F. A Wright, *A History of Later Greek History*, 2nd edn., London, 1951, p. 397.

50 See pp. 412f.

51 See Hunger, *HPLB*, vol. 2, p. 159; Krumbacher, *GBL*, p. 711.

52 Cf. A. Baumgartner, *Geschichte der Weltliteratur*, Freiburg, 1905, vol. 4, pp. 538f.

53 See P. Maas, in *BZ*, vol. 12, 1903, pp. 287f.

54 See H. Meyer, *de Anthologiae Palatinae Epigrammatis Cyzicensis* (Diss.), Königsberg, 1911, who dates the epigrams of Cyzicus to this period.

55 *AP*, bk. 16, nos. 335–87. See A. Cameron, *Porphyrius the Charioteer*, Oxford, 1973, pp. 96f.

56 See R. G. Austin, *Aeneidos*, 2, Oxford, 1964, vol. 2, p. 289.

57 See p. 405.

58 W. Peek, in Pauly–Wissowa, *REkA*, vol. 18, pp. 2366f.

59 See P. Friedländer, *Johannes von Gaza und Paulus Silentarius*, Leipzig–Berlin, 1912, p. 110.

60 On the ecphrasis on the hot springs in Pythia, wrongly attributed to Paul the Silentiary, see p. 481.

61 Examples of such uninspired epic *ethopoeia* from this period can be found in *AP*, bk. 9, nos. 451–580 (*Τίνας ἀν εἴποι λόγους* — 'what would so-and-so have said in certain circumstances?'); in Heitsch, *GDRK*, nos. 21, 26, 37, 38; or in the *rhesis* of Achilles' shade found on a diptych in Cairo. See O. Crusius, in *Philologus*, vol. 64, 1905, pp. 144f.

62 See Heitsch, *GDRK*, vol. 1², pp. 179–97. Such are, for example, the hymns on Pan, the Sun, Typhon, the Moon, Hecate, Aphrodite and so on.

63 See Heitsch, *GDRK*, vol. 1², pp. 85, 146f.

64 See pp. 406f.

65 The hymns of Synesius, in many ways equally impressive, will be treated in Chapter 16.

66 See pp. 409f.

67 See *AP*, bk. 9, nos. 773, 180–3; *AP*, bk. 11, no. 384.

68 *AP*, bk. 14, nos. 116–46. See P. Tannery, *Revue des études grecques*, vol. 6, 1893, pp. 59f.; Schmid–Stählin, *GL*, 2⁶, 1, p. 159, n. 1.

69 *Orat.*, 5.52 (Migne, *PG*, vol. 35, p. 704).

70 See G. Wolff, *de Novissimum Oraculum Aetate*, Berlin, 1854, p. 44, C. M. Bowra, *On Greek Margins*, Oxford, 1970, pp. 233f. Text in Georgius Cedrinus, 1, p. 304a (p. 532, Bonn).

71 See *AP*, bk. 4, nos. 3, 114.

72 See, for example, *AP*, bk. 7, nos. 551, 560, 561, 568, 597 and so on.

73 See L. Robert, in *Hellenica*, vol. 4, 1948, pp. 34f.; Cameron, *Porphyrius the Charioteer*, pp. 65f.

74 The earlier collections by Meleager and Philip were compiled not according to subject but according to the names of the poets represented.

75 See A. Cameron, *Agathias*, Oxford, 1970, pp. 13f.

76 *AP*, bk. 5, no. 237.

77 *AP*, bk. 6, nos. 18–20.

78 Cf. Agathias, *AP*, bk. 5, no. 297.5–6; D. Wienreich, in *Sitzungsberichte der Heidelberger Akademie der Wissenschaften*, vol. 1, 1944–8, pp. 8of., 104f.

79 Even an epigram of Damascius has survived (*AP*, bk. 7, no. 553); he was one of the seven Neo-Platonist philosophers who took refuge at the Persian court when Justinian I closed the philosophical schools of Athens in 529.

80 As we shall see, in the ninth century anacreontics ceased to observe quantity completely. Then not only the penultimate syllable but also the fourth foot was regularly accented. In the fourteenth century more regular accents were introduced into the line; see Dölger, *BDIR*, p. 56.

81 *AP*, Parisin. Gr., suppl. no. 384; see p. 471.

82 Bergh, *PLG*, vol. 3, no. 1097. The name has been emended by H. Weil to Colluthos.

Chapter 16: Christian Poetry

1 The Byzantine Church, although it developed its literature in Greek, never hindered the evolution of new Christian literatures in other tongues such as Aramaic, Armenian or Coptic.

2 Krumbacher (in *GBL*) draws a distinction between liturgical poetry to be chanted in church and religious poetry in general. But the distinction is not always clear.

3 Texts in Heitsch, *GDRK*, vol. 1, pp. 157f.

4 2.1.39, v. 34f. All the poetry of Gregory of Nazianzus is in Migne, *PG*, vol. 37, pp. 397f. and vol. 38, pp. 10f.

5 One is considered spurious.

6 1.1.12.

7 2.1.11. New edition of the *De Vita sua* by Chr. Jungck, Heidelberg, 1974.

8 See G. Misch, *Geschichte der Autobiographie*, Berne, 1949, vols. 1–2, pp. 612f. and L. Niedermeier, *Unterschwungen über die antike poetische Autobiographie* (Diss.), Munich, 1919, pp. 32f.

9 2.1.1.

10 Migne, *PG*, vol. 37, pp. 908f.

11 Migne, *PG*, vol. 37, pp. 928f.

12 It was H. L. Davids (*De Gnomologiën van Sint Gregorios van Nazianze* (Diss.), Nijmegen–Utrecht, 1940) who first pointed this out. See also R. Keydell, in *Atti VIII Congresso Internazionale di Studi Bizantini*, 1951, vol. 1, pp. 134f.

13 Heitsch, *GDRK*, vol. 1², p. 161. A. Harnack, in *Sitzungsberichte der Königlich Preussischen Akademie der Wissenschaften zu Berlin*, vols., 33–4, Berlin, 1900, pp. 986f.; Harnack dates the *de Moribus Christianorum* to between 250 and 330. See also on the paraenetic alphabets the views of A. N. Anastasievic, *Die parainetische Alphabete in der griechischen Literatur*, Munich, 1905.

14 See L. Sternbach, in *Wien. Stud.*, vol. 13, 1891, pp. 57f. On the Christian Homeric cento of Bishop Patrikios, see Hunger, *HPLB*, p. 100, and *AP*, bk. 1, no. 119.

15 See Krumbacher, *GBL*, p. 718.

16 1.1.32.

17 1.2.3.

18 See Krumbacher, *GBL*, p. 661.

19 See R. Keydell, in *BZ*, vol. 43, 1950, pp. 334f.

20 See Schmid–Stählin, *GL*, 2⁶, 2, p. 1420; see also p. 490.

21 Krumbacher, *GLB*, p. 654.

22 To this day married clergymen are not appointed bishops by the Orthodox Church.

23 See J. Kroll, in *Die Antike*, vol. 2, 1926, p. 279.

24 See M. Paranikas, in *Sitzungsberichte der Bayerischen Akademie der Wissenschaften*, Munich, 1870, 2, pp. 53f.; A. Baumstark, in *Oriens Christianus*, n.s. vol. 5, 1915, pp. 201f.

25 Migne, *PG*, vol. 91, pp. 1417f.

26 S. G. Mercati, *Annales de l'Institut de Philologie et d'Histoire Orientales et Slaves* (Brussels), vol. 2, 1934, pp. 619f. (*Mélanges Bidez*).

27 See p. 400.

28 About the *Hexameron* E. Bouvy, a sensitive critic, wrote that it is 'une oeuvre littéraire de mérite. Il y a de la verve et des élans lyriques; les pensées sont élevées' (*Poètes et mélodes*, Nîmes, 1886, p. 167). It has also been translated into Armenian and Slavonic.

29 Heitsch, *GDRK*, vol. 1², pp. 161f.

30 Heitsch, *GDRK*, vol. 1², pp. 160f.

31 See P. Maas, *Greek Metre*, trs. H. Lloyd-Jones, Oxford, 1962, pp. 1, 13f.

32 For a list of the names of Byzantine religious poets, see E. Follieri, *Initia Hymnorum Ecclesiae Graecae*, vol. 5,1b, Vatican, 1966, pp. 251f.

33 More specifically, from Plotinus and Proclus, as brought into conformity with Christian dogma by Dionysius the Areopagite.

34 See M. Simonetti, *Memorie dell'Accademia dei Lincei, Classe di Scienze Morale*, vol. 8, 4, fasc. 6, 1953; Dölger, *BDIR*, p. 42 and n. 16.

35 *IG*, vol. 4, insc. 2.

36 See E. Pandelakis, in Θεολογία, vol. 16, 1938, pp. 5f.
37 The name *troparion* comes from *tropos*, meaning musical mode or style, and in this context signifies a short hymn in a certain musical mode. For the various meanings of the word *troparion*, see Sophocles, *Greek Lexicon of the Roman and Byzantine Periods*, s.v. *troparion*.
38 Christ–Paranikas, *AGCC*, p. 90.
39 Christ–Paranikas, *AGCC*, p. 40.
40 Christ–Paranikas, *AGCC*, p. 38.
41 See J. Schattemann, *Studien zum neutestamentlichen Prosahymnus*, Munich, 1965.
42 Heitsch, *GDRK*, vol. 1², pp. 159f. The musical notation that accompanies this text is also the oldest Christian music that we possess; see E. Wellesz, *A History of Byzantine Music and Hymnography*, Oxford, 1949, p. 129.
43 G. Bickell, *Mitteilungen aus der Sammlung der Papyrius Erzherzog Reiner*, Vienna, 1887, vol. 2, p. 83. On the view that these are verse and not rhythmic prose, see J. Kunz, in *BZ*, vol. 41, 1941, pp. 40f. The papyrus is well-fingered, which indicates that the texts were often used in church services.
44 Maas, *FBKP*, p. 11. About both of these Kedrenus (1.684) says, 'It was ordained that they should be chanted' in the reign of Justinus II (565–78), which means that they must be much older.
45 Christ–Paranikas, *AGCC*, p. 29.
46 Part of one has even been found on a fragment of Egyptian pottery, see S. Petrides, in *Écho d'Orient*, vol. 3, 1899–1900, pp. 361f.
47 Euseb., *Hist. Eccl.*, 7.24.4.
48 See Athanasius, Migne, *PG*, vol. 26, pp. 16f.; P. Maas, in *BZ*, vol. 18, 1909, pp. 511f.
49 See U. von Wilamowitz-Moellendorff, in *Hermes*, vol. 34, 1899, pp. 218f.
50 Christ–Paranikas, *AGCC*, p. 32.
51 See J. Kroll, in *Die Antike*, vol. 2, 1926, pp. 259, 264; also *Acts of the Apostles*, 4.24.
52 Canons 15, 59.
53 The order was renewed by the Council of Braga in 553.
54 See Maas, *FBKP*, pp. 2f.; C. A. Trypanis, in *BZ*, vol. 65, 1972, pp. 334f.
55 Maas, *FBKP*, p. 4.
56 Maas, *FBKP*, p. 10.
57 A. Baumstark, *Liturgie comparée*, 3rd edn., rev. B. Botte, Chenetogne, 1953, ch. 4.
58 The eleven-syllable line with the stress on the antepenultimate foot is an old metre, probably originating in the fifth century; see Maas, in *BZ*, vol. 18, 1909, p. 320.
59 See F. Dölger, in *Die Antike und Christentum*, vol. 5, 1936, p. 17.
60 Pitra, *AS*, vol. 1, no. 23, and Migne, *PG*, vol. 114, pp. 1416.
61 Cedrinus, p. 349C (Bonn).
62 The text of one in Christ–Paranikas, *AGCC*, p. xxxiii.
63 The text in D. Plazidus de Meester, *Die Göttliche Liturgie unseres hl. Vaters Johannes Chrysostomus*, Munich, 1938, p. 34.
64 Cod. Just. 1.1.7.
65 The word *kontakion* first appears in the ninth century and derives from the *kontos*, the *rotulus* on which the manuscript of the poem was rolled. The Byzantine poets of the sixth century called their metrical sermon by a number of other terms, such as *hymnos*, *epos*, *ode*, *psalmos* and *deesis*. On the *kontakion*, see P. Maas, in *BZ*, vol. 19, 1910, pp. 285f.; J. Grosdidier de Matons, *Romanos le Mélode*, Paris, 1977, pp. 3f.
66 This seems to follow the example of the prologue in comic iambics, which was 'obligatory' in the sixth century for poems in other metres; see R. Browning, in *BZ*, vol. 63, 1970, p. 368.
67 Such musical notation as we have goes back only as far as the thirteenth century.
68 On these, see A. Baumstark, *Geschichte der syrischen Literatur*, Bonn, 1922, pp. 39f.; R. Duval, *La littérature syriaque*, Paris, 1904; Fr. Feldman, *Syrische Wechsellieder von Narses*, Leipzig, 1896, p. 4.
69 On these, see J. Assemani, *Ephraem Syri Opera*, vols. 1–4, Rome, 1732–46; S. I. Mercati, *Ephraem Syri Opera*, vol. 1, Rome, 1915.
70 See p. 409.

71 See Migne, *PG*, vol. 65, pp. 721–58; see also A. Kirpitschnikow, in *BZ*, vol. 1, 1892, pp. 527f., and R. Fletcher, in *BZ*, vol. 51, 1958, pp. 55f.

72 It should be noted, however, that acrostics can be traced back to Greek literature of the third century B.C. and the Psalms; see E. Vogt, in *Antike und Abendland*, vol. 13, series 1, 1967, p. 80.

73 See E. Norden, *Die antike Kunstprosa*, Leipzig–Berlin, 1915–18, pp. 843, 861f.

74 Pitra, *AS*, vol. 1, pp. 484f.

75 P. Maas, *Kleine Schriften*, Munich, 1973, pp. 363f.

76 Pitra, *AS*, vol. 1, pp. 476f.

77 Pitra, *AS*, vol. 1, p. 482; Maas, *Kleine Schriften*, pp. 361f.

78 Maas, *FBKP*, p. 13.

79 Maas, *FBKP*, pp. 16f. Obviously, the fragment from a *kontakion* entitled *On Daniel* (Pitra, in *AS*, vol. 1, pp. 291f.) is also very old.

80 See C. A. Trypanis, in *Wiener byzantinische Studien*, vol. 5, 1968, pp. 65f., 73f.

81 Trypanis, *loc. cit.*, pp. 51f.

82 Maas–Trypanis, *SRMCG*, no. 55. All numbering of the cantica of Romanos that follow is that of the Maas–Trypanis edition.

83 Trypanis, in *Wiener byzantinische Studien*, vol. 5, 1968, pp. 161f.

84 See E. Bouvy, *Poètes et Mélodes*, Nîmes, 1886, p. 332; cf. also *Psalms*, CXIX, IX, X, XV, XXXIV and so on.

85 Maas, *FBKP*, pp. 21f.

86 Text and bibliography, Trypanis, in *Wiener byzantinische Studien*, vol. 5, 1968, pp. 17f.

87 Cf. H. Chase, *Texts and Studies*, vols. 1–3, Cambridge, 1891, pp. 168f.

88 See p. 554.

89 As distinct from the *kathismata*, which are hymns inserted between the odes of a canon and are sung before a seated congregation.

90 We know of no other poetical work that has been attributed to Sergius.

91 See Trypanis, in *Wiener byzantinische Studien*, vol. 5, 1968, pp. 17f.

92 *Prooemium* 1.3–7; Strophe O.1–6.

93 P. Maas, in *BZ*, vol. 15, 1906, p. 24.

94 The hymn to the Virgin by Johannes Geometres Kyriotes, with its effusive salutations, is clearly greatly inferior (Migne, *PG*, vol. 106, pp. 855).

95 A *synaxarion* is a short account of a saint or feast.

96 See Maas–Trypanis, *SRMCG*, p. xv, n. 5.

97 H. Delehay, *Propylaeum ad Acta Sanctorum*, Brussels, 1902, pp. 95f.

98 All numbers are those of the Maas–Trypanis edition.

99 See Trypanis, in *Wiener byzantinische Studien*, vol. 5, 1968, pp. 139f.

100 On these, see Maas–Trypanis, *SRMCD*, nos. 186f.

101 The most striking example of this is Maas–Trypanis, *SRMCG*, no. 17, *On Judas*.

102 See P. Maas, in *BZ*, vol. 23, 1923, pp. 451f.; K. Krumbacher, *Miscellen zu Romanos, Abhandlungen der philos.-philol. und der histor. Klasse der K. Bayer. Akademie der Wissenschaften*, Munich, 1907, vol. 25, 3, pp. 78f.; Grosdidier de Matons, *Romanos le Mélode*, pp. 254f.

103 See Beck, *KTLBR*, p. 426: 'einige seiner Lieder sind Meisterwerke der Weltliteratur.'

104 Trypanis, in *Wiener byzantinische Studien*, vol. 5, 1968, pp. 79f.

105 *ibid.*, pp. 141f.

106 *ibid.*, pp. 127f.

107 *ibid.*, pp. 117f.

108 *ibid.*, pp. 105f.

109 *ibid.*, pp. 149f.

110 *ibid.*, pp. 87f.

111 This particular canticum clearly survived because the views that it expressed on the Trinity and the Incarnation were in accordance with those of the Council of Chalcedon and because, obeying the orders of the Council of 638, it made no mention of one or two 'energies' in the person of Christ.

112 Text and commentary by E. von Dobschutz, in *BZ*, vol. 12, 1903, pp. 534f.; see also Beck, *KTLBR*, p. 473.

PART THREE: THE BYZANTINE WORLD

Section I: From Heraclius to the Restoration of the Images (641–843)

Introduction

1 See J. Molitor, in *Oriens Christianus*, vol. III, 3, 4, 5, 6, 8, 1930–3, in six sequences.
2 See R. Browning, in *Revue des études grecques*, vol. 81, 1968, pp. 408, 409 n. 1. This should not be dissociated from the regeneration of interest in ancient Greek poetry that began in the first half of the ninth century in Byzantium.

Chapter 17: The Supremacy of Religious Poetry

1 They were composed for liturgical use and followed in the footsteps of Sophronius of Jerusalem (Beck, *KTLBR*, p. 604).
2 A *synkellos* is the 'provider and adviser' of a bishop.
3 The attribution of this poem to Michael Synkellos has been challenged. See Beck, *KTLBR*, pp. 503f.
4 See p. 440.
5 The stanzas of the odes of a canon were also called *troparia*.
6 Such are shadowy figures like Anatolios—to whom 100 religious poems are ascribed! —Byzantios, Georgios of Syracuse, Georgios Sikeliotis, Theodosius of Syracuse, Georgios of Amastris, Sergios the Hymnographer, Georgios the Hymnographer, Ephraem of Caria, Andreas Pyrros (the Blind) or Sykeotes, many of whose dates and literary output continue to be matters of dispute. And the problem becomes insuperable when we turn to the numerous anonymous *troparia* that constitute the majority of those that have survived and whose style has a baffling uniformity. See Beck, *KTLBR*, pp. 474f., 515f.
7 It is also thought that the *Anabathmoi* (antiphonal *troparia*) of the *Octoechos* may be a work of Theodore the Studite, but this is by no means certain. On the *Anabathmoi*, see L. Petit, *Dictionnaire d'archéologie chrétienne et de liturgie*, Paris, 1907f., s.v. *Anabathmoi*.
8 Christ–Paranikas, *AGCC*, p. 103.
9 Christ–Paranikas, *AGCC*, p. 104.
10 See the discussion on this in K. Mitsakis, *Βυζαντινὴ Ὑμνογραφία*, Salonica, 1971, vol. 1, pp. 546f.
11 See E. Wellesz, *A History of Byzantine Music and Hymnography*, 2nd edn., Oxford, 1971, pp. 204, 366.
12 This led to the revival of classical studies in Byzantium in the ninth century.
13 Their exact purpose remains unknown.
14 See K. Krumbacher, *Die Akrostichis in der griechischen Kirchenpoesie, Sitzungsberichte der philos.-philol. und der histor. Klasse der K. Bayer. Akademie der Wissenschaften*, Munich, 1903, pp. 631f.
15 K. Krumbacher, *Miscellen zu Romanos, Abhandlungen der philos-philol. und der histor. Klasse der K. Bayer. Akademie der Wissenschaften*, Munich, 1907, vol. 24, 3, p. 92. This vexed question cannot be fully discussed in a book of this nature. See, for certain views, Mitsakis, *Βυζ. Ὑμνογραφία*, pp. 510f., and Beck, *KTLBR, passim*. On the *kontakia* of Gregorios of Syracuse, see E. Mioni, in *Bolletino della Badia Greca di Grotta Ferrata*, vol. 1, 1947, pp. 202f.
16 See S. Mercati, *Encyclopedia Italiana*, 33 vols., Milan–Rome, 1929– , s.v. *contacio*. See also V. Lowe, 'A Group of Hagiographical Studite *Kontakia*' (unpublished thesis, University of Oxford), 1976.

17 Among the minor Studite 'melodists' of those days were Arsenios, Stephanos, Procipios, Isidoros, Antonios, Basileios, Gabriel, Nikolaos and others, who composed various kinds of poetry.

18 The stanzas of the odes of a canon were, as we have seen, also (wrongly) called troparia.

19 See A. J. Phytrakis, Ἡ Ἐκκλησιαστικὴ ἡμῶν Ποίησις, Athens, 1957, p. 46 n. 1, and Christ–Paranikas, *AGCC*, pp. 58f.

20 See H. Schneider, in *Biblica*, vol. 30, 1949, p. 260.

21 Rylands Papyrus 466. C. H. Roberts, *Catalogue of the Greek and Latin Papyri in the John Rylands Library, Manchester*, vol. 3, Manchester, 1938, pp. 28f.

22 These are two groups of hymns; the first consists of doxologies sung at Matins after the eighth canticle, and the second, the *Megalynaria* (the Magnificat *troparia*) is attached to the ninth.

23 The reading of the biblical odes continues to this day in certain monasteries, especially on Mount Athos.

24 This was due to the fact that the second ode of the canons was based on the canticle 'Give ear, O ye Heavens' (*Deuteronomy*, 32).

25 See H. Schneider, in *Biblica*, vol. 30, 1949, p. 267.

26 Therefore, naturally, also its own metrical pattern. These were based on the first strophe of each ode, which is known as the *heirmos* or *katabasia*.

27 On these, see p. 446.

28 See Phytrakis, Ἡ Ἐκκλησιαστικὴ ἡμῶν Ποίησις, p. 54.

29 The *Typikon* is the liturgical manual that indicates how the services should be recited during the ecclesiastical year.

30 Thus G. Schiro and A. Gonzanto point out that 355 canons, among which are included works of the greatest representatives of this literary genre, have not yet been critically edited; many are not published at all: see *Akten des XI internationalen byzantinistenkongresses* (Munich, 1958), Munich, 1960, pp. 539f.

31 See pp. 433f.

32 The canon on St Peter is not considered genuine; see Beck, *KTLBR*, p. 501.

33 Andrew of Crete is also considered by some to have introduced—by others, simply to have made use of—the third 'mode' in Byzantine music (ἦχος γ΄ and ἦχος πλάγιος γ΄). See G. Schiro, in Κρητικὰ Χρονικά, vol. 19, 1961, pp. 113f.

34 Also known as the *Parakletike*.

35 That St John was a productive composer of music can also be seen from the 531 melodies attributed to him; cf. S. Eustratiadis, Εἱρμολόγιον, Chennevieres-sur-Marne, 1932, p. ά.

36 See E. Werner, in *Hebrew Union College Annual*, vol. 21, 1948, pp. 211f., and the hymns of the *Octoechos* transcribed by H. J. W. Tillyard, in *Monumenta Musicae Byzantinae* III, V, Copenhagen, 1940–9.

37 Eustathios of Thessalonica expresses doubts about the authenticity of all three iambic canons. In the third, *On Pentecost*, preposterous words like Ἀκτιστοσυμπλαστουργοσύνθρονος are found, which cannot have come from the pen of St John Damascene. See also St Winkly, *The Canons of St John Damascene to the Theotokos* (unpublished thesis, University of Oxford), 1973.

38 These are *necrosema*.

39 See Beck, *KTLBR*, p. 485.

40 See W. Weyh, in *BZ*, vol. 17, 1908, p. 49; J. Hussey, in *Journal of Theological Studies*, vol. 47, 1946, pp. 200f.

41 See n. 37.

42 See K. N. Sathas, Ἱστορ. δοκίμιον περὶ τοῦ θεάτρου καί τῆς μουσικῆς τῶν Βυζαντινῶν, p. τοθ΄; Krumbacher, *GBL*, pp. 645, 675. P. Maas believes that a fragment has survived: ὁ ἀρχέκακος δράκων, πάλιν πλανᾶν ἔσπευδε τὴν Εὔαν ἐμέ. See Migne, *PG* 94, introduction to John Damascene's works; Eustath. in Dionys. Perieg., 976, and in the commentary on St John Damascene's canon on the Pentecost, *Spicilegium Romanum*, vol. 5, 2, 1842, p. 165.

43 Thus, for example, out of twenty-four works published under the name of Cosmas of

Maiouma in Migne, *PG*, vol. 98, pp. 456f., the authenticity of only fourteen has not been disputed; see Beck, *KTLBR*, p. 515.

44 See *Suda*, s.v. Ἰωάννης Δαμασκηνός.

45 G. Schiro, in Κρητικὰ Χρονικά, vol. 19, 1961, pp. 113f.

46 In certain manuscripts the *euchae* of the Great Hours and the Office of the Gonyclisia, as well as a variety of *troparia*, are ascribed to him, but their authenticity has also been challenged; see Beck, *KTLBR*, p. 475.

47 It was founded in 463 by a former Roman consul, Studios, and dedicated to St John the Baptist. Its monks became zealous upholders of Orthodoxy against the monophysites and iconoclasts. It became especially famous as a model of Eastern monasticism and for its school of copyists and artists.

48 The story is probably untrue, but an interesting detail given is that in order for the punishment to be the more severe the iambic trimeters were deliberately branded incorrectly!

49 One of the canons of Theophanes Graptos is in honour of St Romanos the Melodist; see S. Petrides, in *BZ*, vol. 11, 1902, pp. 363f.

50 See p. 447.

51 See Beck, *KTLBR*, pp. 495, 603.

52 One of the great desiderata for Byzantine studies is a full critical edition of the prose and verse works of Theodore the Studite. See Lowe, 'A Group of Hagiographical Studite *Kontakia*' (unpublished thesis, University of Oxford, 1976).

53 The classification of the great melodists varied according to the scholar and the date at which such work was undertaken. Thus, for example, the Venetian edition of the *Typikon* says (p. 15): 'First comes Cosmas of Maiouma, second St John Damascene, third Theophanes Graptos, fourth Joseph the Hymnographer.' Andrew of Crete and the Patriarch Germanos are not even mentioned. Nicephoros Callistos Xanthopoulos (fourteenth century), in his iambic poem on the greatest melodists, writes:
Οἱ τὰ μέλη πλέξαντες ὕμνων ἐνθέων ‖ ἡ λύρα τοῦ πνεύματος Κοσμᾶς ὁ ξένος, ‖ Ὀρφεὺς νεαρὸς ἡ Δαμασκόθεν χάρις ‖ καὶ Θεόδωρος, Ἰωσῆφ οἱ Στουδῖται ‖ ὄργανα τὰ κράτιστα τῆς μουσουργίας, ‖ ξένη τε σειρὴν Ἰωσῆφ ὑμνογράφος ‖ μέλος παναρμόνιον Ἀνδρέας Κρήτης ‖ καὶ Θεοφάνης ἡ μελιχρὰ κινύρα, ‖ Γεώργιος, Λέων τε Μᾶρκος, Κασία.
See Phytrakis, Ἡ ἐκκλησιαστικὴ ἡμῶν πρίησις, p. 62, n. 6.

54 See p. 54.

55 The story that she had taken part in a beauty contest from which the Emperor Theophilus was to choose a wife, and that her quick-witted answer to one of his remarks deprived her of the throne, does not appear to be true. See I. Rochow, *Studien zu den Werken und dem Nachleben der Dichterin Kassia*, Berlin, 1967 (*Berliner Byzantinistische Arbeiten*, 38) pp. 5f. Equally untrue is the story that some of the lines of her *troparion* on Mary Magdalene were written by the Emperor Theophilus, who visited her as she was composing it; see E. G. Pantelakis, Ἀφιέρωμα εἰς Γ. Χατζηδάκιν, Athens, 1921, pp. 150f. It is also untrue that she died on the island of Cassos, where her alleged grave was shown to visitors.

56 Thecla composed a canon on the Virgin, published in Nicodemos Hagioreites' Θεοτοκάριον, Venice, 1798, pp. 22f.

57 See J. B. Pitra, *Hymnographie de l'église grecque*, Paris, 1867; E. Emereau, in *Echo d'Orient*, vol. 25, 1926, pp. 179f.

58 The *stichera* correspond to the antiphons of the Western Church.

59 See G. Schiro, in *Bollettino della Badia greca di Grotta Ferratta*, vol. 3, 1949, pp. 132f., 195f.

60 See E. Eustratiades, in Νέα Σιών, vol. 30, 1935, pp. 689f., and vol. 31, 1936, pp. 5f.

61 See pp. 443f.

62 They can hardly be called 'religious' poetry, and for that reason they are treated in the section 'Secular Poetry'.

63 See Georgius Cedrenus, p. 521 (Bonn, pp. 115f.) and Krumbacher, *GBL*, p. 707, n. 1.

64 Texts in L. Sternbach, *Eos*, vol. 4, 1898, pp. 150f.; S. G. Mercati, in *Bessarione*, vol. 24, 1920, pp. 198f.

65 Published in an appendix to O. Crusius, *Fabulae Aesopeae*, Leipzig, 1897.

66 Its authenticity has been challenged; see C. F. Müller, in *BZ*, vol. 1, 1892, pp. 521f.

67 Bk. 15, nos. 29–31, 39.

68 See Krumbacher, *GBL*, p. 720.

69 Bk. 1, no. 109. See R. Browning, in *Revue des études grecques*, vol. 81, 1968, pp. 408, 410n.

70 Published by C. F. Müller, in *Rhein. Mus.*, vol. 46, 1891, pp. 320f.

71 See Browning, *loc. cit.*, pp. 401f.

Section II: From the Restoration of the Images to the Fourth Crusade (843–1204)

Introduction

1 Direct contact between Italy and Byzantium in the twelfth century seems to have been much more extensive than might have been expected.

2 Nicephorus Blemmydes (1197–c. 1272) even composed a poem on how to diagnose diseases by the colour of urine, which he set to the melody of a well-known religious hymn!

3 This period too is beset by the same problem as the previous one with regard to the identity of religious poets with the same name and of the works attributed to them. Moreover, a large number of important texts have not yet been published, and there are few critical editions. The wealth of material can be seen at a glance in E. Follieri, *Initia Hymnorum Ecclesiae Graecae*, vols. 1–4, Vatican, 1960–6 (*Studi e Testi*, 215). We shall of necessity limit ourselves to the major figures, about whom we have certain information.

4 In Byzantine Greek the word πολιτικός meant 'common', 'that which is in everyday use'. Eustathius (eleventh century) says that it came to be used in that sense shortly before his time. Later πολιτικὸς στίχος, political verse, had the same meaning as πεζὸς λόγος, prose (as opposed to poetry) in classical metres. See F. Dölger, in *BZ*, vol. 55, 1962, p. 360, and A. Heisenberg, *Dialekte und Umgangsprache im Neugriechisch*, Munich, 1918.

5 Published by I. Sevčenko, in *Dumbarton Oaks Papers*, vols. 23, 24, 1969, pp. 189f.

6 Published by L. Sternbach, in *Eos*, vol. 5, 1898–9, pp. 7f.

7 Sevčenko, *loc. cit.*

8 Bonn edition (1829), p. 366, nos. 9–11; p. 367, nos. 19–21. This song belongs to the type known as *chelidonisma*, although no swallow appears in it. On the type, see N. G. Politis, in Λαογραφία, vol. 3, 1912, pp. 649f., and S. Baud-Bovy, in Βυζαντινὰ καὶ Μεταβυζαντινά, vol. 1, 1978, pp. 23f.

9 In Cod. Vindob, theol. gr. 244 (Nessel), 2. It is as yet unpublished, as far as I know.

10 Its first line is: Ἀδὰμ τὸν πρῶτον ἄνθρωπον ἢ Εὔα τὸν ἐποῖχε, see Krumbacher, *GBL*, p. 720, who considers it spurious. See also M. J. Jeffreys, in *Dumbarton Oaks Papers*, vol. 28, 1974, p. 175.

11 Published in Migne, *PG*, vol. 114, pp. 131f. Its first line is: Ἀπὸ βλεφάρων δάκρυα ἀπὸ καρδίας πόνους. For other unpublished alphabets attributed to Symeon Metaphrastes, see Krumbacher, *GBL*, pp. 718f.

12 Published by A. Papadopoulos-Kerameus, in *BZ*, vol. 8, 1899, pp. 66f. Little is known about the life of Nicephoros Ouranos. See A. Ehrhard, in Krumbacher, *GBL*, p. 145; Papadopoulos-Kerameus, *loc. cit.*; and H. Delehaye, *Les saints stylites*, Brussels, 1923, p. 60. Also S. G. Mercati, in *Analecta Bollandiana*, vol. 68, 1950, pp. 121f. (= *Collectanea*, vol. 1, pp. 565f.). The literary genre of the penitential alphabet is, as we have seen, very old, going back to Gregory of Nazianzus, but not until this period were such alphabets cast in political verse.

13 A detailed discussion about the origin and nature of the fifteen-syllable political line can be found in Jeffreys, *Dumbarton Oaks Papers*, vol. 28, 1974, pp. 143f., in which all

the older views of S. Kyriakides, S. Baud-Bovy, J. Koder, L. Politis and K. Krumbacher, as well as all the evidence, are given. A brief, up-to-date bibliographical account of this appears in A. Kambylis, *Symeon Neos Theologos, Hymnen*, Berlin–New York, 1976, p. 345, n. 35. See also H. G. Beck, *Geschichte der byzantinischen Volksliteratur*, Munich, 1971, pp. 15f., and bibliography on p. xxi; and M. Alexiou and D. Holton, in *Mandatophoros*, vol. 9, 1976, pp. 22–4.

14 Jeffreys, *loc. cit.*, pp. 179f. On the acclamations, see E. H. Kantorowicz, *Laudes Regiae*, Berkeley–Los Angeles, 1958.

15 It should perhaps be added here that one Constantine Anagnostes, a Cypriot who lived before the thirteenth century, is the first known author to write verse both in the vernacular and in purist Byzantine Greek; see Krumbacher, *GBL*, p. 773.

16 See, for example, K. Demaras, A. Mirambel, B. Lavignani, B. Knös and L. Politis, in their histories of modern Greek literature. S. Baud-Bovy, in Ἑλληνικά, vol. 26, 1973, p. 13, postulates that the origins of the fifteen-syllable line may be sought in the Akritic Epic Cycle.

17 See B. Lord, *The Singer of Tales*, Cambridge, Mass., 1960, pp. 124f.; A. Parry, *The Making of Homeric Verse*, Oxford, 1971, *passim*.

Chapter 18: Religious Poetry

1 Published by L. Sternbach, in *Eos*, vol. 4, 1897, pp. 150f. For the hymns of Ignatius in rhythmic metres, see p. 462.

2 Migne, *PG*, vol. 102, pp. 573f.; Christ–Paranikas, *AGCC*, pp. 50f.

3 A. Lauriotes, in Ἐκκλησιαστικὴ Ἀλήθεια, vol. 28, 1895, pp. 220f.

4 See p. 461.

5 See p. 463.

6 Published by P. Matranga, in *Anecdota Graeca*, Rome, 1850, vol. 2, pp. 683f.; Migne, *PG*, vol. 107, pp. 309f.; Christ–Paranikas, *AGCC*, p. 48 (in the latter incomplete).

7 A few fragments of this in Migne, *PG*, vol. 107, pp. 665f.; also in Ἀλκαίου Ἱερομονάχου, Λέοντος Σοφοῦ Πανηγυρικοὶ Λόγοι, Athens, 1886, pp. 191f. On other poems by Leo VI, which are now lost, see P. Maas, in *BZ*, vol. 21, 1912, pp. 436f., and T. Nissen, *Die Anakreonteen*, Munich, 1940, pp. 56f.

8 See S. G. Mercati, in *BZ*, vol. 30, 1929, pp. 56f.

9 On his rhetorical and exegetical works, which do not concern us here, see Krumbacher, *GBL*, p. 735; Beck, *KTLBR*, pp. 553f.

10 On the name Geometres, see F. Dölger, in *BZ*, 1931, p. 410.

11 See pp. 473f.

12 See p. 485.

13 See A. Erhard, *Überlieferung und Bestand der hagiographischen und homiletischen Literatur der griechischen Kirche*, Leipzig, 1937f., vol. 1, pp. 155, 217, 340, who attributes them, probably correctly, to Neilus.

14 See Beck, *KTLBR*, p. 571.

15 Migne, *PG*, vol. 114, pp. 209–92.

16 Beck, *KTLBR*, p. 571.

17 See pp. 467f.

18 In some of his iambic hymns Symeon also introduces fifteen-syllable lines. On Symeon's metres, see A. Kambylis, *Symeon Neos Theologos, Hymnen*, Berlin–New York, 1976, pp. 333ff.

19 See pp. 468f.

20 Hymn No. 10 (Kambylis).

21 See P. J. Darrouzés, in *Revue des études byzantines*, vol. 16, 1958, pp. 59f.; H. Follieri, in *Analecta Bollandia*, vol. 77, 1959, pp. 254ff.

22 See p. 463.

23 A *synaxarion* is also the life of a saint or part of a *Menaeon*, the Book of the Church that gives, for each month, the office commemorating the saints.

24 See S. Gassisi, in *Oriens Christianus*, vol. 5, 1905, pp. 26f.

25 In the *theotokarion* (collection of poems in honour of the Mother of God) of St Nicodemus of Mount Athos (ed. S. Schoinas, Volos, 1974), pp. 196f.

26 See pp. 464f.

27 See pp. 474f.

28 Migne, *PG*, vol. 120, pp. 1119f.; P. de Lagarde and J. Bolligs, *Ioannis Euchaitorum Metropolitae quae in Codice Vaticano Graeco 676 supersunt, Abhandlungen der histor.-phil. Klasse der K. Gesellschaft zu Göttingen*, 28, 1881, Berlin, 1882.

29 No. 20 in Lagarde, *loc. cit.*

30 This is not a simple set of epigrams on saints, as suggested by Krumbacher, *GBL*, p. 738.

31 On his poem the *Muses*, see p. 476.

32 See Maas, in *BZ*, vol. 22, 1913–14, p. 369.

33 *Ibid.*

34 Maas, *loc. cit.*, writes that he published only a few strophes so that no one would ask for more!

35 Published by A. Demetrakopoulos, in Ὀρθόδοξος Ἑλλάς, Leipzig, 1972, pp. 26f.

36 On this, see Krumbacher, *GBL*, pp. 90f.

37 See Beck, *KTLBR*, p. 662.

38 Known as *In Monachum Sabbaitam*, published by E. Kurtz and F. Drexl, *Michaelis Pselli Scripta Minora*, vol. 1, Milan, 1936, pp. 220f.

39 See p. 467.

40 Krumbacher, *GBL*, p. 677 and n. 4. According to Krumbacher, the lowest level is reached in an anonymous hymn on St Eustathius (Cod. Patm. 212f., 161f.).

41 Lists of these in E. Mioni, *I kontakaria del Monte Athos*, Venice, 1936, and N. B. Tomadakis, Ῥωμανοῦ τοῦ Μελῳδοῦ Ὑμνοι, vols. 2, 3, Athens, 1954, 1957.

42 See Beck, *KTLBR*, p. 601.

43 Migne, *PG*, vol. 105, pp. 1020f., 1416f.

44 See p. 457.

45 See Pitra, *AS*, vol. 1, p. 438.

46 Published in Nicodemos Hagiorites, Θεοτοκάριον, Venice, 1898, pp. 9, 20, 33, 111.

47 Published by A. Papadopoulos-Kerameus, in *Pravoslavnyj Palestinskij Sbornik*, vol. 2, 1892, pp. 9f.

48 Published by A. Papadopoulos-Kerameus, Εἷς ὕμνος τοῦ πατριάρχου Φωτίου, Odessa, 1900.

49 Partly published by Pitra, *AS*, vol. 1, pp. 438f.

50 Christ–Paranikas, *AGCC*, pp. 90f. For further details, see E. Follieri, *Initia Hymnorum Ecclesiae Graecae*, Vatican, 1960–6, vol. 5,2, p. 305.

51 On his lost poetry, see T. Nissen, *Die Anakreonteen*, p. 55.

52 See E. Mioni, in *Byzantion*, vol. 19, 1949, pp. 127f.

53 See Beck, *KTLBR*, p. 595.

54 See Follieri, *Initia Hymnorum Ecclesiae Graecae*, vol. 5,2, p. 291; they go under the name of Leon Magistros.

55 See p. 457.

56 See Follieri, *Initia Hymnorum Ecclesiae Graecae*, vol. 5,2, p. 272.

57 A. J. Phytrakes, Ἡ ἐκκλησιαστικὴ ἡμῶν ποίησις Athens, 1957, p. 62, n. 6; see also p. 755, n. 54.

58 Τριῷδιον (edition of Ἀποστολικὴ Διακονία τῆς Ἐκκλησίας τῆς Ἑλλάσος), Athens, 1960, pp. 425f.; Christ–Paranikas, *AGCC*, pp. 196f.

59 See Beck, *KTLBR*, p. 605.

60 Venice, 1898; pp. 81 and 109.

61 Follieri, *Initia Hymnorum Ecclesiae Graecae*, vol. 5,2, p. 252. The Slavonic *Octoechos* includes *stichera* by Anastios Quaestor.

62 See C. A. Trypanis, in *Wiener byzantinische Studien*, vol. 5, 1968, pp. 51f.

63 See p. 457.

64 Migne, *PG*, vol. 107, pp. 300f.; H. F. Tillyard, in *Annual of the British School at Athens*, vol. 30, 1932, pp. 86f., and vol. 31, 1933, pp. 115f. On the *idiomela*, see Follieri, *Initia Hymnorum Ecclesiae Graecae*, vol. 5,2, p. 290.

65 See Beck, *KTLBR*, p. 547.
66 Christ–Paranikas, *AGCC*, pp. 110f.; Migne, *PG*, vol. 107, pp. 300f. We are told that there are eleven because after the Resurrection Christ appeared to eleven disciples.
67 Πεντηκοστάριον χαρμόσυνον, Rome, 1883, p. 469.
68 See pp. 458f.
69 See Follieri, *Initia Hymnorum Ecclesiae Graecae*, vol. 5,2, p. 304; also Pitra, *AS*, vol. 1, pp. 433f.; Migne, *PG*, vol. 114, pp. 219f.; C. Litzica, *Poesia Religiosa Bizantina*, Bucharest, 1889, pp. 51f.; A. Papadopoulos-Kerameus, in *BZ*, vol. 8, 1899, pp. 66f.
70 See Beck, *KTLBR*, p. 571. He also composed three moralizing alphabets in fifteen-syllable lines, on which see Migne, *PG*, vol. 114, pp. 131f., and Krumbacher, *GBL*, pp. 718–19.
71 Beck, *KTLBR*, p. 606f.; Follieri, *Initia Hymnorum Ecclesiae Graecae*, vol. 5, 2, pp. 258f.
72 C. Emereau, in *Écho d'Orient*, vol. 22, 1923, pp. 422f.; S. Petrides, in *Écho d'Orient*, vol. 8, 1905, pp. 298f.; A. Papadopoulos-Kerameus, in *BZ*, vol. 12, 1903, pp. 171f.
73 See Beck, *KTLBR*, p. 606. Nor should we linger over names like those of Theophanes Sikeliotes, Theosteriktos, Andreas Perros, Paulos of Amorion, Paulos of Xeropotamou, Georgios Hagiopolites, Euthymios Styriotes, Alexios of Nicea, all minor poets of those years whose religious poetry, even when identified, has nothing to recommend it.
74 See p. 474.
75 See p. 459.
76 Published in the Ὡρολόγιον of Venice in 1563 and the Ἐκκλησιαστικὸν Ἡμερολόγιον, Constantinople, 1887.
77 See Darrouzés, in *Revue des études byzantines*, vol. 16, 1958, pp. 73f.
78 Darrouzés, *loc. cit.*
79 See p. 459.
80 See p. 459.
81 See p. 485.
82 See J. Hussey, in *BZ*, vol. 44, 1951, pp. 278f.
83 Canon 6.121–5 (Follieri).
84 For example, on Peter II, Ode VI, strophe 5:
   Ὡς ἁγίων ἁγία, πανάμωμε,
   ἅγιον ἁγίων ἁγίως ἐγέννησας,
   ὃς ἐν ἁγίῳ Πνεύματι
   ἁγιάζει τοὺς σὲ ἁγιάζοντας.
85 By Kurtz and Drexl, *Michaelis Pselli Scripta Minora*, vol. 1, pp. 108f.; Migne, *PG*, vol. 114, pp. 199f.
86 See Beck, *KTLBR*, p. 541.
87 See p. 467.
88 See p. 462.
89 See p. 459.
90 On this group of Grotta Ferrata poets, see J. Schiro, *Innographi Italo-Greci*, vol. 1, 2, Grotta Ferrata, 1947.
91 Beck, *KTLBR*, pp. 662f.
92 Migne, *PG*, vol. 135, pp. 413f.
93 See p. 460.
94 Migne, *PG*, vol. 135, pp. 503f.
95 L. Fr. Tafel, *Eustathii Metropolitae Thessalonicensis Opuscula*, Frankfurt, 1832, pp. 166f.; Migne, *PG*, vol. 135, pp. 161f. Krumbacher, *GBL*, p. 540, locates a second canon by Eustathius, which Tafel, *loc. cit.*, published as prose.
96 Tafel, *loc. cit.*, pp. 136f.; Migne, *PG*, vol. 135, pp. 283f.
97 See p. 465.
98 Published by K. N. Sathas, in Μεσαιωνικὴ Βιβλιοθήκη, vol. 5, 1876, pp. 177f.
99 See Krumbacher, *GBL*, pp. 682, 809f.
100 See p. 485.
101 See pp. 454f.
102 Four further iambic hymns have beginnings or endings in political verse. Half of

Symeon's book of hymns (5352 lines) is in fifteen-syllable lines. On his use of that metre, see Kambylis, *Symeon Neos Theologos, Hymnen*, pp. 345f.

103 5 (Kambylis).

104 See J. Koder, *Syméon le Nouveau Théologien, Hymnes*, Paris, 1969, vol. 1, pp. 82f.; Kambylis, *Symeon Neos Theologos, Hymnen*, pp. 239f.

105 See K. Holl, *Enthusiasmus und Bussgewalt beim griechischen Mönchtum*, Leipzig, 1898, pp. 26f.

106 20.70f. (Koder).

107 58.65 (Koder).

108 27.96 (Koder).

109 22.5.155 (Koder).

110 Kurtz and Drexl, *Michaelis Pselli Scripta Minora*, vol. 1, pp. 389f.

111 *ibid.*, pp. 401f.

112 Published by J. Koder, in *Jahrbuch der Österreichischen Byzantinistik*, vol. 19, 1970, pp. 203f.

Chapter 19: Secular Poetry

1 See pp. 405f.

2 In Cod. Paris. Suppl. Gr., 352.

3 See R. Auberton, in *Revue des études anciennes*, vol. 70, 1968, pp. 56f.

4 Auberton points out (*loc. cit.*) that even the books of the *Palatine Anthology* that are considered to be derived from Cephalas' anthology (5, 6, 7, 9, 10, 11) may be later accretions around a Cephalas nucleus.

5 See C. Wendel, Pauly–Wissowa, *REkA*, vol. 20, pp. 2202f.

6 The best edition of the *Greek Anthology*, with copious indexes, a bibliography, introductions, translations and notes, is in four volumes, edited by H. Beckby, 2nd edn., Munich, 1967. For a good concise bibliography, see K. Preisdanz, in *Kleine Pauly*, vol. 1, p. 377.

7 See K. Vogel, in *Akten des XI internationalen byzantinisches Kongresses* (Munich, 1958), Munich, 1960, pp. 66of.; E. E. Lipšic, *Vizantijskij Vremennik*, vol. 2, 27, 1949, pp. 106f.; and J. L. Heiberg, in *Bibliotheca Mathematica*, n.s. 1, 1887, pp. 33f.; Krumbacher, *GBL*, pp. 621f.; J. Mau, in *Kleine Pauly*, vol. 3, p. 566 (Leon, 9).

8 *AP*, bk. 9, nos. 200–3, 214, 361, 578f.; bk. 15, no. 12; and possibly bk. 16, no. 387c.

9 *AP*, bk. 9, no. 361.

10 See p. 462.

11 In J. F. Boissonade, *Anecdota Graeca*, Paris, 1829–33, vol. 2, 1830, pp. 469f.: Migne, *PG*, vol. 107, pp. 663f.; see also L. Sternback, *Anthologia Planudea, Appendix Barberino-Vaticana*, Leipzig, 1890, pp. 84f. and E. Mioni, *Miscellanea*, vol. 1, Padua, 1978, pp. 69f. Four further epigrams may be found in G. Kolias, *Léon Cheorosphactés, magistre, proconsul et patrice*, Athens, 1939, appendix.

12 Matranga, in *Anecdota Graeca*, vol. 2, pp. 557f.

13 Matranga, *loc. cit.*, pp. 561f.; also in Bergh, *PLG*, vol. 3, pp. 355f. See also T. Nissen, *Die Anakreonteen*, Munich, 1940, pp. 59f.

14 The epigrams in *AP*, bk. 1, no. 109; bk. 15, nos. 29–31. The poem on Paulos in S. G. Mercati, in *BZ*, vol. 17, 1908, pp. 392f., and Matranga, in *Anecdota Graeca*, vol. 2, pp. 664f.; see also Nissen, *Die Anakreonteen*, p. 53.

15 *AP*, bk. 15, no. 40.

16 *AP*, bk. 15, nos. 36–8. Cf. *AP*, bk. 5, no. 265; bk. 9, nos. 586, 597; bk. 15, no. 40.

17 Krumbacher, *GBL*, p. 522.

18 Migne, *PG*, vol. 102, pp. 577f.

19 For his religious poetry, see p. 457.

20 Migne, *PG*, vol. 107, pp. 659f.

21 Migne, *PG*, vol. 107, pp. 665f.; cf. Krumbacher, *GBL*, p. 721.

22 Migne, *PG*, vol. 107, pp. 1130f. See A. Brinkmann, A. Lycopol, *Alexandri Lycopolitani contra Manichaei opiniones disputatio*. Leipzig, 1895, preface, p. xvi and p. 199 (the first sixty lines are missing), and Hunger, *HPLB*, vol. 2, p. 113. On other iambic poems

of Leo the Wise, now lost, see Nissen, *Die Anakreonteen*, pp. 59f. In the fourteenth and fifteenth centuries a collection of oracles circulated spuriously under Leo's name.

23 Bk. 15, no. 28.
24 See p. 462.
25 On other lay poetry by Anastasios Quaestor, see Beck, *KTLBR*, p. 605, as well as A. Papadopoulos-Kerameus, in Νέα Ἡμέρα, 2 (15), 9 (20), nos. 1422–3, March 1902.
26 Included in Cod. Ox. Barocci, 50f. 381–6, and published in R. Browning, in *Byzantion*, vol. 33, 1963, pp. 316f.
27 Nos. 14 and 16.
28 See pp. 475f.
29 Migne. *PG*, vol. 106, pp. 956f.
30 See p. 485.
31 See p. 463.
32 4.7 (Kurtz).
33 3 (Kurtz).
34 75 (Kurtz).
35 As Krumbacher has pointed out (*BLG*, p. 738), it is ironical that the mice which the poet abuses for infesting his house got their own back by badly damaging the only Grotta Ferrata manuscript in which his poems are transmitted.
36 See pp. 464f.
37 43 (de Lagarde).
38 See p. 485.
39 See p. 465.
40 See Krumbacher, *GBL*, pp. 439f.
41 Published by E. Kurtz and F. Drexl, *Michaelis Pselli Scripta Minora*, vol. 1, Milan, 1936, pp. 190f.
42 Published by Kurtz and Drexl, *loc. cit.*, pp. 45f.
43 Published by Kurtz and Drexl, *loc. cit.*, p. 49.
44 Published by Pitra, in *AS*, vol. 4, p. 496.
45 The riddles in Boissonade, in *Anecdota Graeca* vol. 3, 1831, pp. 429f. The *Aulikalamos* is also in Boissonade, *loc. cit.*, p. 453.
46 Published by M. Treu, *Eustathii Macrembolitae quae feruntur Aenigmata, Gymnasial-programm*, Breslau, 1893, pp. 10f., 33f.
47 Published by Treu, *loc. cit.* A study of the Byzantine riddles has been made by S. Lampros, in Δελτίον Ἱστορικῆς καὶ Ἐθνολογικῆς Ἑταιρείας, vol. 2, 1885–9, pp. 152f.
48 See Krumbacher, *GBL*, p. 441.
49 See Nissen, *Die Anakreonteen*, p. 70.
50 In Migne, *PG*, vol. 107, LXIf.
51 See pp. 481f.
52 *AP*, bk. 15, nos. 15, 16, 17.
53 See P. Maas, in *BZ*, vol. 22, 1913, p. 366.
54 No. 6 (Sternbach).
55 Published in L. Sternbach, *Nicolai Callicles Carmina*, Crakow, 1903.
56 See Krumbacher, *GBL*, pp. 744f.
57 See S. G. Mercati, in *Studi Bizantini*, vol. 1, 1925, pp. 175f.; K. Horna, in *Wien. Stud.*, vol. 25, 1903, pp. 165f.
58 Published by S. Doanidou, in Ἑλληνικά, vol. 7, 1934, pp. 110f.; cf. P. Maas and F. Dölger, in *BZ*, vol. 38, 1938, pp. 2f.
59 Published by S. Lampros, Κερκυραϊκὰ ἀνέκδοτα, Athens, 1882, pp. 23f.
60 It should be borne in mind that reliable inferences about the life of Theodoros Prodromos can hardly be made from the so-called Ptochoprodromic poems because the poetic persona may well vary from poem to poem.
61 Prodromos, in his use of the hexameter, has an otherwise unknown central caesura; see C. Gianelli, *Studi in onore di L. Castiglioni*, Florence, 1960–1, pp. 331f.

62 See Krumbacher, *GBL*, p. 756:
Στοᾶς ὁρῶ τὸ μῆκος ὡς μέγα μέγα,
ψυχρὸν ὕδωρ ἥδιστον ἐμφέρει φέρει,
καὶ γὰρ τὸ ῥεῖθρον ἄφωνον ῥέει ῥέει, etc.
Alexius II also composed at the age of thirteen an echo song on the death of his father Manuel Comnenus (died 1180), which shows how little the ethos of the various poetic forms was acknowledged in those days. See Krumbacher, *GBL*, p. 762, n.1.

63 See P. Darrouzés, in *Revue des études byzantines*, vol. 16, 1958, pp. 79f.

64 Migne, *PG*, vol. 133, pp. 1419.

65 *ibid.*

66 See p. 488.

67 See p. 481.

68 See p. 487.

69 See pp. 502f.

70 See pp. 486f.

71 Ἄναξ βασιλεῦ, σοῦ πεσόντος οὐ φέρω
καὶ μὴ φέρων τὸ πάθος αὐτὸς δακρύω,
καὶ δακρύων τὸ φίλτρον εἰς σὲ δεικνύω, etc.
Published by M. Magri, in *Bolletino del Comitato per la Preparazione di Edizioni Nazionali di Classici Greci e Latini*, vol. 9, 1961, pp. 73f.; and Matranga, in *Anecdota Graeca*, vol. 2, pp. 619f.

72 See C. Wunderer, in *Philologus*, vol. 54, 1895, pp. 430f.

73 Edited by Fr. Hanssen, in *Phililogus*, suppl. 5, 1889, pp. 221f.; see also Krumbacher, *GBL*, p. 762, n. 1.

74 Published by S. G. Mercati, *Εἰς μνήμην Σπ. Λάμπρου*, Athens, 1935, pp. 435f.

75 All published in S. Lampros, *Μιχαὴλ Ἀκομινάτου Χωνιάτου τὰ σωζόμενα*, vols, 1, 2, Athens, 1879–80. On Michael Akominatos, see G. Stadtmüller, *Michael Choniates, Metropolit von Athen*, Vatican, 1934.

76 On this group of poets, see S. Borsari and M. Gigante, *La parola del Passato*, fasc. 14–20, 1951; M. Gigante, *Poeti Italo-Byzantini del secolo XIII*, 1953 (texts); S. G. Mercati, in *BZ*, vol. 47, 1954, pp. 41f.; M. Gigante, in *Ἑλληνικά*, vol. 13, 1954, pp. 111f.

77 See p. 465.

78 See pp. 505 and 553f.

79 Published by M. Gigante, *Eugenii Panormitani Versus Iambici*, Palermo, 1964; see also S. Speck, in *BZ*, vol. 58, 1965, p. 82, and L. Sternbach, in *BZ*, vol. 11, 1902, pp. 406f.

80 See A. M. Bandini, *Manuscripts of the Laurentian Library (Catalogus Cod. Man. Bibl. Mediceae)*, Leipzig, 1961, his description of Cod. V.10.

81 See p. 476. On his ecphrasis, for which he is best-known, see pp. 481f.

82 Both Constantine the Rhodian's attacks and Theodore the Paphlagonian's answers are published in Matranga, *Anecdota Graeca*, vol. 2, pp. 624f.; see also P. Walters, in *Rhein. Mus.*, vol. 38, 1883, pp. 117f.

83 See p. 467.

84 Published by Kurtz and Drexl, *Michaelis Pselli Scripta Minora*, pp. 220f. Two poems, one of them in fifteen-syllable lines, attacking an unknown monk for his conceit, are not by Psellus, as has been suggested; see Krumbacher, *GBL*, p. 440.

85 See Krumbacher, *GBL*, p. 439.

86 *Κατά φιλοπόρνου γραός*. This has been incorrectly published by E. Miller under the name of Manuel Philes, in *Manuelis Philae Carmina*, Paris, 1857, vol. 2, pp. 306f.

87 Published by J. F. Boissonade, in *Anecdota Graeca*, vol. 4, pp. 430f.

88 See p. 478.

89 See p. 489.

90 On Byzantine humour, see also G. Soyter, *Griechische Humor von Homers Zeiten bis Heute*, 2nd edn., Berlin, 1961, pp. 92f., and M. J. Kyriakis, in *Βυζαντινά*, vol. 5, 1973, pp. 289f.

91 See pp. 462 and 472.

92 See S. G. Mercati, in *Rivista degli studi orientali*, vol. 10, 1924, pp. 212f.; P. Maas, in *BZ*, vol. 25, 1925, pp. 358f. The attribution to Leon Choerosphactes has been challenged by R. Anasti, in *Siculorum Gymnasium*, n.s. vol. 17, 1964, pp. 1f., who sees in lines 167–70 a reference to the icon controversy and considers the work a product of the days of Constantine V Copronymous (741–75).

93 See K. Prächter, in *BZ*, vol. 13, 1904, pp. 1f.

94 See Nissen *Die Anakreonteen*, pp. 62f.

95 Probably the ones that Cedrinus used (Bonn, vol. 1, pp. 563f.).

96 The information is gathered from lines 268f. and 282.

97 On Constantine Rhodius' epigrams and lyrical poetry, see p. 476.

98 See pp. 472f.

99 Edited by A. Brinkmann, in *Alexandri Lycopolitani contra Manichaei Opiniones Disputatio*, Leipzig, 1895, pp. xvif. See also G. Moravcsik, Εἰς μνήμην Κ. Ἀμάντου, Athens, 1960, pp. 1f.

100 Edited by Fr. Jacobs (Bonn, 1828) and M. M. Panayotakis, Θεόδωρος ὁ διάκονος καὶ τὸ ποίημα αὐτοῦ Ἅλωσις τῆς Κρήτης, Heracleion, 1960.

101 S. Lampros, Ἱστορικὰ Μελετήματα, Athens, 1884, pp. 152f.

102 Edited by E. Kurtz, in *BZ*, vol. 16, 1907, pp. 69f.; C. Welz, *Analecta Byzantina*, Leipzig, 1910; W. Hörandner, *Theodoros Prodromos, Gedichte*, Vienna, 1974 (*Wiener byzantinistische Studien* 11), nos. 3–6, 8.II, 15–19.

103 See pp. 485f.

104 See pp. 488f.

105 See A. Westermann, Βιογράφοι, Braunschweig, 1857, p. 67.

106 See Krumbacher, *GBL*, pp. 378f.

107 See J. Diethart, 'Der Rhetor und Didaskalos Konstantinos Stilbes' (unpublished Diss.), Vienna, 1971.

108 See Krumbacher, *GBL*, p. 762.

109 See Pitra, *AS*, vol. 1, pp. 441f.

110 Editions: W. Studemund, in *Anecdota Varia Graeca*, vol. 1, 1886, pp. 270f.; A. Westermann, Μυθογράφοι, Braunschweig, 1843, pp. 355f.; see also Krumbacher, *GBL*, pp. 587f.

111 See E. Miller, in *Annuaire de l'Association pour l'Encouragement des Études Grecques en France*, vol. 10, 1876, pp. 131f.

112 Zonaras wrote a poem on Mary in which the various heresies were described.

113 See p. 467.

114 See pp. 459, 464f., 474f.

115 R. Reitzenstein, *Geschichte der griechischen Etymologika*, Leipzig, 1897, pp. 173f.

116 See p. 483.

117 Published by E. Miller, in *Annuaire de l'Association pour l'Encouragement des Études Grecques en France*, vol. 9, 1875, pp. 23f.

118 Published by P. Zeppos, *Jus-Graecoromanum*, Athens, 1931, vol. 7, pp. 379f.; Migne, *PG*, vol. 122, pp. 925; Migne, *PG*, vol. 122, pp. 920f.

119 Published by Boissonade, in *Anecdota Graeca*, vol. 3, pp. 200f.

120 See Boissonade, *loc. cit.*, and in *Anecdota Graeca*, vol. 1, pp. 175f.; also Migne, *PG*, vol. 122, pp. 1075.

121 E. Miller, in *Notices et extraits de la Bibliothèque Nationale*, vol. 23, 1872, pp. 8f.

122 See O. Marzal, in *BZ*, vol. 60, 1967, pp. 249f.

123 For his occasional poems, see p. 479.

124 The title *Chiliades* is a legacy of the first editor, Gerbel (c. 1546).

125 The most recent edition of the *Chiliades* is that of P. A. M. Leone, *Ioannis Tzetzae Historiae*, Naples, 1968; see also W. Hörandner, in *Byzantion*, vol. 39, 1969, pp. 108f. To the same group of didactic poems as the *Chiliades* belongs a late anonymous poem in 211 twelve-syllable lines on the labours of Heracles; see B. Knös, in *BZ*, vol. 17, 1908, pp. 397f.

126 Not all Tzetzes' commentaries on ancient poetry are in verse. He also wrote scholia on Homer, Aristophanes, Lycophron and others in prose. The verse commentaries were for amateurs, whereas the prose ones were for scholars.

127 Excerpts in C. Waltz, *Rhetores Graeci*, Stuttgart–Tübingen, 1832–6, vol. 3, pp. 670f.; J. A. Cramer, *Anecdota Graeca e Codd. Manuscriptis bibliothecarum Oxoniensium*, Oxford, 1835–7, vol. 4, pp. 1f. See C. Wendel, in Pauly–Wissowa, *REkA*, vol. 8A, p. 1990.

128 See H. Hunger, in *Jahrbuch der Oesterreichischen byzantinischen Gesellschaft*, vol. 4, 1955, pp. 13f.

129 See Kaibel, *CGF*, vol. 1, pp. 34–49.

130 Edited by I. Bekker, *Abhandlungen der K. Alkademie der Wissenschaften*, Berlin, 1840, and Matranga, in *Anecdota Graeca*, vol. 2, pp. 577f. See also H. Hunger, in *BZ*, vol. 46, 1953, p. 302.

131 The *Iliad* (6632 lines long), edited by J. F. Boissonade, Paris, 1851. The *Odyssey* (3109 lines long), edited by H. Hunger, in *BZ*, vol. 48, 1955, pp. 4–48; vol. 49, 1956, pp. 249f.

132 There is no full edition of Tzetzes. Recent editions exist of a few of his works, however. General information on these can be found in W. Hörandner, in *Byzantion*, vol. 39, 1969, pp. 108f., and Hunger, *HPLB*, pp. 117f. For older bibliographies, see Krumbacher, *GBL*, pp. 526f.; C. Wendel, in Pauly–Wissowa, *REkA*, vol. 7A, pp. 1959f.; Dölger, *BDIR*, pp. 23f.; W. O. Schmitt, in *Kleine Pauly*, vol. 5, pp. 1031f.; R. Browning, in *Past and Present*, vol. 28, 1964, pp. 14f.; F. Dölger, *Geschichte der Textüberlieferung der antiken und mittelalterlichen Literatur*, Zurich, 1961, vol. 1, pp. 25f.

133 Published by J. A. Cramer, *Anecdota Graeca e Codd. Manuscriptis Bibliothecae Regiae Parisiensis*, Oxford, 1839–41, vol. 1, pp. 59f.

134 This has also been attributed to Johannes Tzetzes or has been considered the common work of both brothers.

135 See Krumbacher, *GBL*, p. 761.

136 Published by Miller, in *Annuaire de l'Association pour l'Encouragement des Études Grecques en France*, vol. 10, 1876, pp. 131f.

137 Published by Miller, in *Notices et extraits de la Bibliothèque Nationale*, vol. 23, 1872, pp. 1f.

138 Published by B. Keil, in *Wien. Stud.*, vol. 11, 1889, pp. 94f.

139 See p. 466.

140 See Krumbacher, *GBL*, p. 682.

141 Published by S. Lampros, in *Νέος Ἑλληνομνήμων*, vol. 16, 1915, pp. 200f.

142 Published by L. Weigl, in *Programm Progymnasium Frankenthal*, 1908.

143 See E. Rohde, *Der griechische Roman*, 3rd edn., Leipzig, 1914, pp. 554f. See also Hunger, *HPLB*, vol. 2, pp. 119f.

144 Published by R. Herscher, *Scriptores Erotici Graeci*, Leipzig, 1859, vol. 2, pp. 289f.

145 Published by Herscher, *loc. cit.*, pp. 437f.; see S. Delegeorgis, in *Neo-Hellenika*, vol. 2, 1975, pp. 21f. Nicetas Eugenianos also wrote a monody on Theodoros Prodromos; see S. G. Mercati, in *Studi bizantini e neoelleniki*, vol. 4, 1935, pp. 222f.

146 Published by Herscher, *loc. cit.*, pp. 555f.; O. Mazal, in *Wiener byzantinistische Studien*, vol. 4, 1967; E. T. Tsolakis, *Συμβολὴ στὴ μελέτη τοῦ ποιητικοῦ ἔργου τοῦ Κωνσταντίνου Μανασσῆ καὶ κριτικὴ ἔκδοση τοῦ μυδιστορήματος και Ἡρίστανδρον καὶ Καλλιστιν*, Salonica, 1967. Our knowledge of this romance has recently been extended by another 765 verses in a Viennese and a Munich manuscript, in which the erotic element is stressed. See Hunger, *HPLB*, vol. 2, p. 126 and nn. 91, 92. On the moralizing, didactic poem that copies Manasses (Cod. Paris, Gr. 2750), see O. Mazal, in *BZ*, vol. 60, 1967, pp. 249f.

147 One more Byzantine romance has survived from this period. It is the prose work of Eustathios Macrembolites (second half of the twelfth century) entitled *Hysmine and Hysminias*, a crude imitation of Achilles Tatius.

148 Published by E. Auvray, *Bibliothèque de l'École des Hautes Études*, fasc. 22, Paris, 1875; S. Lauriotis, in *Ὁ Ἄθως*, vol. 1 (1919), Athens, 1920; and E. S. Shuckburg, in *Emmanuel College Magazine*, nos. 2–3, 1894. Latin translation in Migne, *PG*, vol. 127, pp. 701. See also W. Hörandner, *Ἀκροθίνια*, Vienna, 1964, pp. 23f.

149 See p. 448.

150 Only one manuscript (Marcianus gr. 524) attributes the *Catomyomachia* to Theodoros Prodromos. This work has been correctly compared with the *Σχέδη μνός*, another humorous work by Prodromos, in prose, about a battle between a cat and a mouse.

151 See H. Hunger, in *Byzantina Vindobonensia*, vol. 3, 1968, pp. 55f.
152 Published by H. Hunger, *Der byzantinische Katz-Mäuse-Krieg. Theodoros Prodromos, Katomyomachia*, Vienna, 1968.
153 Published by Fr. Dübner, in G. Wagner (ed.), *Euripides Fragmenta*, Paris, 1846, pp. 83f.; it is republished in Migne, *PG*, vol. 133, pp. 1321f.
154 Published by M. Treu, in *Gymnasial-Programm*, Waldenburg (Schles.), 1874; Matranga, in *Anecdota Graeca*, vol. 2, pp. 622f.; P. Leone, in *Byzantion*, vol. 39, 1968, pp. 251f.; see also S. G. Mercati, in *Byzantion*, vol. 18, 1948–9, pp. 197f. This same *dramation* of Haploucheir has been incorrectly attributed to Johannes Tzetzes by Krumbacher, *GBL*, p. 534.
155 See p. 411.
156 Published by J. E. Brambs, Leipzig, 1885; also in Migne, *PG*, vol. 38, pp. 731f., and A. Tuilier, *La passion du Christ, Tragédie*, Paris, 1969, who wrongly attributes it to Gregory of Nazianzus (see H. Hunger, in *Gnomon*, vol. 43, 1971, pp. 127f.), an attribution that has recently been supported by other scholars; see J. Grosdidier de Matons, in *Travaux et mémoires*, vol. 5, 1973, pp. 363f., and Q. Cantarella, in *Atti del III Congr. Intern. Studi sul drama antico* (1969), Rome–Syracuse, 1970, pp. 405f. Hunger, *HPLB*, vol. 2, pp. 102f., does not exclude the possibility that it is a work of Prodromos.
157 See H. Hunger, in *Dumbarton Oaks Papers*, vols. 23–4, 1969–70, pp. 15f.
158 See S. Baud-Bovy, in *Byzantion*, vol. 13, 1938, pp. 321f., and A. Vogt, in *Byzantion*, vol. 6, 1931, pp. 37f.
159 See Dölger, *BDIR*, p. 16.
160 See B. Knös, *Histoire de la littérature grecque*, Stockholm–Göterborg–Uppsala, 1962, p. 49; L. Politis, *A History of Modern Greek Literature*, Oxford, 1973, p. 22; K. T. Demaras, Ἱστορία τῆς Νεοελληνικῆς Λογοτεχνίας, 6th edn., Athens, 1975, pp. 19f.
161 H. Grégoire, for instance, suggested that Digenis Akritas was none other than the Tourmarches Diogenis who, according to the chronographer Theophanes (463, de Boor), was killed in 788 fighting the Arabs. On this and other suggestions, see Grégoire, Διγενὴς Ἀκρίτας, New York, 1942, p. 36; A. J. Syrkin, *Poema o Digenise*, Moscow, 1964, pp. 81f.; also in *Vizantijskij Vremennik*, vol. 18, 1961, pp. 124f.; K. Sathas and É. Legrand, *Les exploits de Digénis Acrites*, Paris, 1875, pp. 101f. The only mention of Akritas in Byzantine literature is a passing reference in the Ptochoprodromic poems; see D. C. Hesseling and H. Pernot, *Poèmes Prodromiques en grec vulgaire*, Amsterdam, 1910, vol. 3, p. 164.
162 In a scholion on a passage of Philostratus' *Life of Apollonius*. See S. Kougeas, in Λαογραφία, vol. 4, 1913, pp. 236f.; cf. also *Vita Stephani Jun.*, Migne, *PG*, vol. 100, pp. 1169f.
163 72 (Bonn). On such singers of ballads, see also G. K. Spyridakis, in Ἀρχεῖον Πόντου, vol. 16, pp. 263f., and in Ἑλληνικά, vol. 11, 1957, pp. 275f.
164 Originally, Grégoire believed that the son of Armouris was the son of one of the generals taken prisoner at the fall of Amorion (see Grégoire, in *Byzantion*, vol. 7, 1932, pp. 291f.); later he changed his mind and postulated that the son of Armouris was Michael III himself (see Grégoire, in *Revue des études grecques*, vol. 46, 1933, pp. 29f.). For other identifications, see Beck, *GBV*, pp. 54f.
165 On this and other views, see Beck, *GBV*, pp. 57f.
166 Such, for example, is no. 78 in N. Polites, Ἐκλογαὶ ἀπὸ τὰ τραγούδια τοῦ Ἑλληνικοῦ Λαοῦ, 3rd edn., Athens, 1932.
167 The original of one of these is thought to belong to the seventh century (636), consequently to a time before the Akritic Cycle came into being. See S. Impellizzeri, in *Atti del Museo Pitré*, vol. 1, 1950, pp. 5f., especially pp. 24f.; Beck, *GBV*, p. 50.
168 It is also known as Τὸ κάστρο τῆς Μαροῦς (*The Castle of Marou*). See G. K. Spyridakis, in *Akten des XI internationalen Byzantinistenkongresses* (Munich, 1958), Munich, 1959, pp. 581f. The text in S. Baud-Bovy, *La chanson populaire grecque du Dodécanèse*, vol. 1, *Les textes*, Paris, 1936, p. 276.
169 See p. 496.
170 Father Petta, librarian of Grotta Ferrata, now dates the Grotta Ferrata text to the second half of the thirteenth or the beginning of the fourteenth century; see L. Politis,

in *Atti del Convegno Internationale sur Tema: La poesia epica e la sua formazione*, Rome, 1970 (Accademia Nazionale dei Lincei, anno 367, 1970, quaderno 139), p. 554.

171 This was the first manuscript of the *Epic of Digenis* that was discovered; it was found in Trebizond in 1858 and is now lost.

172 See p. 598.

173 See S. Lampros, *Collection de romans grecs*, Paris, 1880, p. 99, and H. Grégoire, *Διγενὴς Ἀκρίτας*, New York, 1940, p. 40.

174 On these see Beck, *GBV*, pp. 67f.

175 Translations of the Russian texts in P. Pascal, *Byzantion*, vol. 10, 1935, pp. 301f. (French); H. F. Graham, in *Byzantinoslavica*, vol. 29, 1968, pp. 51f. (English); and P. Kalonaros, *Βασίλειος Διγενὴς Ἀκρίτας*, Athens, 1970, vol. 2, pp. 257f. (modern Greek, based on P. Pascal's translations).

176 See Beck, *GBV*, pp. 72f.

177 Escorial version, lines 1667f.

178 Such, for example, is the spirit of reconciliation between Arabs and Greeks that we find at the end of the 'Song of the Emir', which corresponds to historical actuality and can also be traced in certain Akritic ballads, like the *Song of Armouris*.

179 Of those dealing with the bride-snatching, one group presents Digenis snatching away his own bride at the moment when she is about to be married to another man; a second group presents other warriors trying to snatch away the bride of Digenis. In some of these we come across certain strange details, like the versions that present Digenis' mother as a nun or a Jewess. See Beck, *GBV*, p. 89.

180 P. Kalonaros, *Βασίλειος Διγενὴς Ἀκρίτας*, Athens, 1970, vol. 2, p. 248, no. κδ΄.

181 *ibid.*, p. 231, no. ιβ΄.

182 *ibid.*, p. 229, no. ια΄.

183 *ibid.*, pp. λγ΄–λδ΄, with footnotes.

184 A15.1–8.

185 On the literary sources of the epic, see H. Grégoire, in *Byzantion*, vol. 6, 1931, pp. 490f., *Compte rendu du IIIe Congrès International des Études Byzantines*, Athens, 1932, pp. 281f., *Διγενὴς Ἀκρίτας*, New York, 1940, pp. 142f.; see also O. Schissel, in *Neophilologus*, vol. 27, 1942, pp. 143f.; Kalonaros, in *Βασίλειος Διγενὴς Ἀκρίτας*, vol. 2, pp. ε΄f., also see *Πρακτικὰ Ἀκαδημίας Ἀθηνῶν*, vol. 18, 1943, pp. 33f., and in *Γράμματα*, vol. 3, 1943, pp. 236f.; S. Impellizzeri, in *Atti del Museo Pitré*, vol. 1, 1950, pp. 82f.; Syrkin, *Poema o Digenise*, pp. 67f.

186 See pp. 487f.

187 See A. B. Lord, *The Singer of Tales*, Cambridge, Mass., 1960, p. 120.

188 On these, see H. Grégoire, in *Byzantion*, vol. 7, 1932, pp. 371f., in *Byzantion*, vol. 11, 1936, pp. 571f., *Διγενὴς Ἀκρίτας*, pp. 142f., in *Byzantion*, vol. 16, 1944, pp. 527f., in *Bulletin de la Classe des Lettres de l'Académie Royale de Belgique*, vol. 5, 17, 1934, pp. 463f.; H. Grégoire and R. Goosens, in *Zeitschrift der Deutschen Morgenl. Gesellschaft*, vol. 13, 1934, pp. 213f.; R. Goosens, in *Byzantion*, vol. 9, 1934, pp. 303f.; S. Kryiakides, in *Byzantion*, vol. 11, 1936, pp. 563f.; V. Christides, in *Byzantion*, vol. 32, 1962, pp. 549f.; M. Canard, in *Byzantion*, vol. 10, 1935, pp. 283f., and *Byzantion*, vol. 12, 1937, pp. 183f.; S. Impellizzeri, in *Annali della Scuola Normale Superiore di Pisa*, vol. 2, 11, 1942, pp. 221f.

189 See Sathas and Legrand, *Les exploits de Digenis Acrites*, p. 129; A. Hatem, *Les poèmes des Croisades*, Paris, 1932; H. Grégoire, *Διγενὴς Ἀκρίτας*, pp. 156f.

190 Grotta Ferrata I, 101. See Beck, *GBV*, pp. 72, 78. This is thought to refer to the hanging coffin of Aristotle, on which Hankal reports; see W. Hasluck, *Christianity and Islam*, Oxford, 1929, p. 17. Palermo fell to the Arabs in 831 and was conquered by the Normans in 1071.

191 Chrysocherpes is thought to refer to Chrysocheir and Karoes to Karbeas, both names of important Paulician warriors.

192 Grotta Ferrata, III, 150.

193 On the historical background of the 'Song of the Emir', see H. Grégoire, in *Byzantion*, vol. 5, 1930, pp. 327f., and in *Byzantion*, vol. 8, 1933, pp. 534f.; see also N. Adnotz, in *BZ*, vol. 29, 1929–30, pp. 198f.

194 Grotta Ferrata, IV, 973.
195 *Andros and Trebizond*, 1368, 1663.
196 H. Grégoire, in *Byzantion*, vol. 6, 1931, p. 495; R. Goosens, in *Byzantion*, vol. 7, 1932, p. 311.
197 H. Grégoire, *Mélanges N. Jorga*, Paris, 1933, pp. 382f., believes that the reference is to Johannes the Cappadocian, the powerful minister of Justinian I, who was much loved in the land of his birth.
198 An Athenian folk song and a local tradition bear witness to a single-handed combat between Philopappous and Digenis on the very hill of Philopappus. See G. Kambouroglou, Ἱστορία τῶν Ἀθηνῶν, Athens, 19, vol. 1, p. 393.
199 *Ant. Jud*, 20.63f.
200 See A. Pallis, Ἡ Φυλλάδα τοῦ Μεγαλέξαντρου, Athens, 1935, p. 139; Strabo, IA, p. 503f. (Meineke); Procopius, 4.4 (Bonn).
201 See G. Manganaro, in *Akten des XI Internationalen Byzantinistenkongresses* (Munich, 1959), Munich, 1960, pp. 325f. The inscription is now lost.
202 Adnotz, in *BZ*, vol. 29, 1929, p. 86; H. Grégoire, in *Revue des études grecques*, vol. 46, 1933, pp. 29f., and in *Byzantion*, vol. 8, 1933, pp. 79f.
203 On these in the Digenis epic, see Lord, *The Singer of Tales*, pp. 207f. It is important to remember that the formulaic structure that we know from Homeric poetry and much other oral verse is not indispensable and is, in fact, not used at all in many orally transmitted poems. See W. Eberhard, in *Folklore Studies*, vol. 5, 1955, pp. 57f.
204 Not Eustathios Macrembolites, as A. Chatzes maintained in Ὁμηρικαὶ Ἔρευναι, vol. 1, Athens, 1930. See H. Grégoire, in *Byzantion*, vol. 6, 1931, p. 483, and S. Kyriakidis, in Λαογραφία, vol. 10, 1929, pp. 624f.
205 On the scarcity of formulae, see M. Jeffreys, *Digenis Akritas Manuscript Z*, Δωδώνη, Ἐπετερὶς Φιλοσ. Σχολῆς Πανεπιστημίου Ἰωαννίνων, Joannina, 1967.
206 See Lord, *The Singer of Tales*.
207 See C. A. Trypanis, in *BZ*, vol. 56, 1963, pp. 1f.
208 See J. B. Bury, *Romances of Chivalry on Greek Soil*, Oxford, 1911, pp. 20f.
209 See Beck, *GBV*, pp. 384f. Some 'archaeological memories' of Digenis have been traced in ceramics from the excavations of the Agora of Athens and perhaps in a representation on a relief from Salonica. See S. Pelekanides, Μελέτες Παλαιοχριστιανικῆς καὶ Βυζαντινῆς Ἀρχαιολογίας, Salonica, 1977, pp. 145f., and A. Frantz, in *Hesperia*, vol. 11, 1941, pp. 9f.
210 The Parisinus 396 of the thirteenth or early fourteenth century.
211 The Parisinus 396 and the Hierosol. Sabait. 415.
212 On these, see Beck, *GBV*, p. 102.
213 This does not mean, of course, that it was originally an oral composition.
214 See Beck, *GBV*, p. 103.
215 On Byzantine humour in general, see G. Soyter, *Humor von Homers Zeit bis Heute*, and in *BZ*, vol. 52, 1959, pp. 357f.; see also M. J. Kyriakis, 'Satire and slap-stick in seventh and twelfth century Byzantium', Βυζαντινά, vol. 5, 1973, pp. 289f.
216 It is now certain that they are less significant for our knowledge of the spoken idiom of the twelfth century than was earlier thought to be the case.
217 See pp. 447f.
218 The manuscripts attribute poems I and II to Θεόδωρος Πρόδρομος. Poems III and IV are attributed by some manuscripts to the same poet and by others to Ἱλαρίων Πρόδρομος or to Πτωχοπρόδρομος. In 1.70 his wife calls him Πτωχοπρόδρομε, and in II,101 the poet speaks about a Πτωχοπροδρομᾶτον.
219 See E. Kurtz, in *BZ*, vol. 10, 1901, pp. 244f.; Hesseling and Pernot, *Poèmes Prodromiques en grec vulgaire*, pp. 8f.; and Dölger, *BDIR*, p. 15, n. 6.
220 Other such poems have been published by A. Maiuri, in *BZ*, vol. 23, 1914–19, pp. 397f. The five published by S. Papademetriou, in *Létopis, Istoriko-filologičeskago obščestva pri novorossijskom Universitetě*, viz. Otd. Odessa, vol. 8, Byzantine Section, no. 4, 1899, pp. 1f., are not by Theodoros Prodromos.
221 See Beck, *GBV*, p. 104.
222 Published by É. Legrand, in *Revue des études grecques*, vol. 4, 1891, pp. 70f.

223 See J. Kallitsunakes, in Πρακτικὰ 'Ακαδημίας 'Αθηνῶν, vol. 40, 1965, pp. 56of.
224 See Politis, *A History of Modern Greek Literature*, p. 27.
225 Cod. Maroc. VII, 51.
226 Krumbacher, *GBL*, p. 807.
227 Published by E. Legrand, in *Receuil de chansons populaires grecques*, Athens–Paris, 1874, vol. 1, pp. 2f., and S. Lampros, in Νέος 'Ελληνομνήμων, vol. 1, 1904, p. 433.

Section III: From the Conquest of Constantinople by the Franks to the Fall of the City to the Turks (1204–1453)

Introduction

1 The poets Constantine Loukites and John Lazarpoulos of Trebizond, as well as Johannes Apokaukos, Metropolitan of Naupactus (died 1230), in the despotat of Epirus, are totally insignificant versifiers.
2 See pp. 535f.
3 See Lord, *The Singer of Tales*, pp. 68f.

Chapter 20: Religious Poetry

1 See E. Wellesz, *A History of Byzantine Music and Hymnography*, 2nd edn., Oxford, 1971, pp. 325f.
2 See Krumbacher, *GBL*, pp. 676f.
3 Published by K. Horna, in *Programm des Sophien-Gymnasiums in Wien*, 1901–2, pp. 13f.
4 A *Pentekostarion* is a *troparion* to be chanted during the fifty Paschal days.
5 Published by A. Papadopoulos-Kerameus, in *Vizantijskij Vremennik*, vol. 13, 1906, pp. 488f. See also E. Follieri, *Initia Hymnorum Ecclesiae Graecae*, vols. 1–4, Vatican 1960–6, vol. 5, 2, p. 260.
6 His *stichera* and the iambic canon on Gregorios Thaumatourgos have been published by A. Heisenberg, *Nicephori Blemmydae Curriculum Vitae*, Leipzig, 1892, pp. 122f., and J. B. Bury, in *BZ*, vol. 6, 1897, pp. 526f.
7 Published in Migne, *PG*, vol. 144, pp. 777f.; Nicodemus Hagioreites, Θεοτοκάριον (Volos, 1974), pp. 98f. (this is based entirely on the Salutations to the Virgin of the *Akathistos* hymn), and C. Leggeris and K. Paraskeuopoulos, 'Ωρολόγιον τὸ Μέγα, Athens, 1898, pp. 536f. On Theodore Lascaris, see J. B. Papadopoulos, *Théodore II Lascaris, empéreur de Nicée*, Paris, 1908.
8 The anacreontic poem on Easter in Migne, *PG*, vol. 140, pp. 937f., the Canon for All Soul's Day, in B. Koutloumousianos, Πεντηκοστάριον Χαρμόσυνον, Athens, 1959 (edition of the 'Αποστολικὴ Διακονία).
9 The office of the Εὐχέλαιον is included in the *Euchologion*. On it, see Beck, *KTLBR*, p. 703. In the Θεοτοκάριον of Nicodemus Hagioreites (Volos, 1974), pp. 70f., there is a canon on the Virgin by one 'Αρσένιος μοναχός, which might well be the work of Arsenios Autoreianos, who spent part of his life as a monk. On other works attributed simply to Arsenios, see Follieri, *Initia Hymnorum Ecclesiae Graecae*, vol. 2, p. 255; we cannot know if some of these should be ascribed to him or to 'Αρσένιος Κερκύρας, 'Αρσένιος Κρυπτοφέρρης or, 'Αρσένιος Περγάμου.
10 Nineteen of these are published by J. F. Boissonade, in *Anecdota Graeca*, Paris, 1829–33, vol. 5, pp. 159f.; the twentieth is published by M. Treu, in *BZ*, vol. 5, 1896, pp. 546f.
11 The poem on the image of St Mary the Egyptian in E. Miller, *Manuelis Philae Carmina*, Paris, 1857, vol. 2, pp. 373f. On Holobolos, see Krumbacher, *GBL*, p. 770f., and Beck, *KTLBR*, p. 704.
12 M. Jugie, in *Byzantion*, vol. 5, 1929–30, pp. 376f.
13 B. Koutloumousianos, Πεντηκοστάριον Χαρμόσυνον, pp. 17f.
14 Published by Jugie, *loc. cit.*, pp. 357f.

15 The catalogues of the emperors and patriarchs published in Labbaeus, *Protrept. Hist. Byz.* (a precursor of the Paris Corpus).
16 Migne, *PG*, vol. 147, pp. 605f.
17 Migne, *PG*, vol. 147, pp. 623f.
18 Migne, *PG*, vol. 147, pp. 601f.
19 Some of these can be found in the small volume *Cyri Theodori Prodromi Epigrammata . . .*, Basiliae apud Ioannem Bebelium, 1536.
20 Only in Latin translation, in Migne, *PG*, vol. 156, pp. 107f. In Greek, the text in É. Legrand, *Lettres de l'empéreur Manuel Paleologue publiées d'après trois manuscrits*, Premier Fasc., Paris. 1893.
21 Published in Legrand, *loc. cit.*
22 See C. Emereau, in *Écho d'Orient*, vol. 23, 1924, pp. 408f.; V. Grumel, in *Écho d'Orient*, vol. 26, 1927, p. 343; Beck, *KTLBR*, p. 748. He also wrote a short, lively anacreontic poem satirizing a garrulous, uneducated man, published by P. Matranga, in *Anecdota Graeca*, Rome, 1950, vol. 2, 1850, p. 682.
23 See D. Pallas, in *Miscellanea Byzantina Monacensia*, vol. 2, Munich, 1965, pp. 55f., and M. Alexiou, in *Byzantine and Modern Greek Studies*, vol. 1, 1975, p. 119.
24 Alexiou, *loc. cit.*, pp. 121f.
25 J. Nikolaidis, Ἱερὰ Σύνοψις, Athens, n.d., pp. 506f.
26 On these, see B. Bouvier, *Le Mirologue de la Vierge*, Rome, 1976 (Bibliotheca Helvetica Romana, XVI).
27 See M. Manousakas, in *Mélanges Merlier*, vol. 2, 1956, pp. 49f.
28 See A. Bidel, in *BZ*, vol. 35, 1935, pp. 337f.
29 See Emereau, in *Écho d'Orient*, vol. 23, 1924, p. 414. For his poems that are included in the liturgical books, see Follieri, *Initia Hymnorum Ecclesiae Graecae*, vol. 2, p. 296.
30 See Beck, *KTLBR*, pp. 771f.; and M. Manousakas, in Ἀθηνᾶ, vol. 68, 1965, pp. 49f., and in *Revue des études byzantines*, vol. 17, 1959, pp. 28f.; as well as Follieri, *Initia Hymnorum Ecclesiae Graecae*, p. 278.

Chapter 21: Secular Poetry

1 See Krumbacher, *GBL*, p. 774.
2 On Anagnostes, see N. Bănescu, *Deux poètes byzantins du XIIIe siècle*, Bucharest, 1913.
3 Published by J. F. Boissonade, in *Notices et extraits de la Bibliothèque Nationale*, vol. 12, 2, 1831, pp. 1–74, and reprinted in Migne, *PG*, vol. 149, pp. 1002f.
4 On the single bucolic idyll that Planudes composed in 270 hexameters, drawing on Theocritus and Virgil, see M. Pontani, *Maximi Planudis Idyllium*, Padua, 1973. On a second such anonymous late Byzantine idyll, see J. Sturm, in *BZ*, vol. 10, 1901, pp. 433f.
5 See p. 471.
6 In modern editions they are printed in Book 16 of the *Greek Anthology*.
7 A few words should be added here on the recent research on the *Greek Anthology*. It now appears that we have two important apographs of the *Planudean Anthology* (British Museum Additional, 16409 and the incomplete Parisinus graecus, 2744), which help to illustrate a hitherto unsuspected stage in its composition. Moreover, we have a much smaller anthology of epigrams in Laurentianus XXXII.16 (at ff. 383r–384r), written in Planudes' own hand. This gives evidence of a project he was to handle on a much larger scale twenty years later. On *AP*, bk. 15, nos. 41–50, which come from a later twelfth- or thirteenth-century collection, consult R. Auberton, in *Revue des études anciennes*, vol. 70, 1968, pp. 69–70. The best and most modern complete edition of the *Greek Anthology* (which naturally includes Book 16 with the Planudes additions), is by H. Beckby, *Anthologia Graeca*, 2nd edn., Munich, 1965– (first edition, 4 vols. 1957–8).
8 On Maximus Planudes, see C. Wendel, in Pauly–Wissowa, *REkA*, vol. 20, pp. 2202f.; C. Wendel, in *Geschichte der Textüberlieferung der antiken und mittelalterlichen Literatur*, vol. 1, Zurich, 1961; W. O. Schmitt, in *Kleine Pauly*, vol. 4, pp. 890f.
9 See P. Maas, in *BZ*, vol. 12, 1903, pp. 295f. In Philes' hands the rules by which certain

syllables should be accented were extended, giving the verse a perfect schematic rhythm and balance. Thus, when the verse has a five-syllable caesura, the seventh and eighth syllables are not accented. But not even Philes dared disregard the now dead ancient quantities in his iambics, with the exception of the vowels α, ι, υ, which most Byzantine poets after Georgios Pisedes used indiscriminately as short or long.

10 On some other insignificant poems in dialogue form, see Hunger, *HPLB*, pp. 147f.

11 See Krumbacher, *GBL*, p. 728.

12 Manuel Philes' works are published by E. Miller, *Manuelis Philae Carmina*, vols. 1,2, Paris, 1855–7; E. Martini, *Carmina Inedita*, Naples, 1900; F. Dübner and F. S. Lehrs, *Poetae Didactici et Bucolici*, Paris, 1962; C. von Holzinger, in *BZ*, vol. 20, 1911, pp. 734f.

13 Two of the poems are edited by M. Treu, *Dichtungen des Grosslogotheten Theodoros Metochites*, Gymnasial-progr., Potsdam, 1895. On the other eighteen unpublished poems, see R. Guilland, in *Revue des études grecques*, vol. 35, 1922, pp. 82f., and *Études byzantines*, Paris, 1959, pp. 177f. On Theodoros Metochites, see Krumbacher, *GBL*, pp. 550f.; H. Hunger, in *BZ*, vol. 55, 1952, pp. 4f.; and H. G. Beck, *Theodoros Metochites: die Krise des byzantinischen Weltbildes im 14 Jahrhundert*, Munich, 1952.

14 A. Garzya, in *Bolletino Grotta Ferrata*, vol. 10, 1956, pp. 51f.

15 S. G. Mercati, in *Bessarione*, vol. 22, 1918, pp. 90f.

16 T. Gasparrini Leporace and E. Mioni, *Cento Codici Bessarionei*, Venice, 1968, no. 51. There is another short anonymous poem on the recapture of Constantinople by the Greeks in 1261; see S. G. Mercati, in *BZ*, vol. 36, 1936, pp. 289f.

17 Edited by A. Mai, Bonn, 1840; reprinted in Migne, *PG*, vol. 143, pp. 12f.

18 See O. Lampsidis, *Beiträge zum byzantinischen Chronisten Ephraem und seiner Chronik*, Athens, 1972.

19 Matranga, in *Anecdota Graeca*, vol. 2, 1850, p. 657; T. Nissen, *Die Anakreonteen*, Munich, 1940, p. 74. The poem has a curious 'ethnographic' quality, for Neophytus is accused of being of Wallachian descent, Albanian in appearance and Bulgar-Albano-Wallachian in his bearing! On Katrares' *Dialogue on Astrology*, see F. Jürss, in *BZ*, vol. 59, 1966, pp. 275f.; on his dramatic endeavours, see G. de Andrés, J. Irigoin and W. Hörandner, in *Jahrbuch der Österreichischen Byzantinistischen Gesellschaft*, vol. 23, 1974, pp. 201f.

20 Published by Nissen, *Die Anakreonteen*, pp. 76f.

21 Published by Boissonade, in *Anecdota Graeca*, vol. 3, 1831, pp. 456f.; see Nissen, *Die Anakreonteen*, p. 75.

22 Published by A. Papadopoulos-Kerameus, in Ἀνάλεκτα Ἱεροσολυμιτικῆς Σταχυολογίας, vol. 1, 1891, pp. 431f.; and T. Papatheodorides, in Ἀρχεῖον Πόντου vol. 19, 1954, pp. 262f.; see Nissen, *Die Anakreonteen*, p. 75.

23 See also Beck, *GBV*, p. 125.

24 The poem of Meliteniotes is published by M. E. Miller, in *Notices et extraits de la Bibliothèque Nationale*, vol. 19, 2, 1857, pp. 1f. On the poem, see F. Dölger, *Quellen und Vorbilder zu dem Gedicht des Meliteniotes Εἰς τὴν Σωφροσύνην* (unpublished Diss.), Munich, 1919; F. Dölger, *Miscellanea Giovanni Mercati*, vol. 3, Vatican, 1946, pp. 238f.; F. Dölger, in *Annuaire de l'Institut de Philologie et d'Histoire Orientales de l'Université Libre de Bruxelles*, vol. 2, 1934, pp. 515f.

25 See p. 515.

26 Published by J. Sturm, in *BZ*, vol. 10, 1901, pp. 433f.

27 See p. 518.

28 Published by Matranga, in *Anecdota Graeca*, vol. 2, 1850, p. 682.

29 Published by S. Lampros, in Δελτίον τῆς Ἱστορικῆς καὶ Ἐθνολογικῆς Ἑταιρείας τῆς Ἑλλάδος, vol. 2, 1885–9, pp. 152f.; see also Krumbacher, *GBL*, p. 766.

30 We shall deal with the *Chronicle of the Morea*, the *Chronicle of Tocco*, the *Song of Henry of Flanders* and the *Ballad of Arodafnusa* in Part Four, as they are the works of men living in lands under Frankish occupation.

31 Published by W. Wagner, *Medieval Greek Texts*, London, 1870, and *Carmina Graeca Medii Aevii*, Leipzig, 1874.

32 See Beck, *GBV*, p. 161.

33 See J. Moravcsik, *Görög kölemény a Várnai*, Budapest, 1935, pp. 579f.

34 Published by Moravcsik, *loc. cit.*; see also N. G. Svoronos, in Ἀθηνᾶ, vol. 48, 1938, pp. 163f. and Beck, *GBV*, p. 162.
35 Bodleianus Barocc., 18.
36 Edited by O. Lampsides, in Νέον Ἀθήναιον, vol. 3, 1961, pp. 17f.
37 See. B. Knös, *Histoire de la littérature néo-grecque*, Stockholm–Göterborg–Uppsala, 1962, p. 103.
38 The *Narrative on Famous Venice* is published by Wagner, *Carmina Graeca Medii Aevi*, pp. 221f.; P. K. Bouboulides, in Ἀθηνᾶ, vol. 69, 1967, pp. 181f.
39 It consists of 120 political lines that form twenty-four strophes joined by an alphabetic acrostic. Published by Wagner, *loc. cit.*; on this, see also G. T. Zoras, Νέα Ἑστία, vol. 55, 1955, pp. 1199f.; and Beck, *GBV*, p. 192.
40 See Knös, *Histoire de la littérature néo-grecque*, pp. 84f.
41 Published by É. Legrand, *Bibliographie grecque vulgaire*, Paris, 1880.
42 See pp. 538f.
43 Published by S. Lampros, *Collection de romans grecs*, Paris, 1880; see also G. A. Megas, in Λαογραφία, vol. 15, 1953, pp. 3f.
44 The various versions can be found in É. Legrand, in *Annuaire de l'Association pour l'Encouragement des Études Grecques en France*, vol. 6, 1872, pp. 53f.; Wagner, *Carmina Graeca Medii Aevi*, pp. 277f.; F. Dölger, in J. Schick (ed.), *Corpus Hamleticum*, I.5, and *Die Scharfsinnsproblem*, Leipzig, 1938, vol. 2, pp. 243f.; G. Zoras, Σπουδαστήριον Βυζαντινῆς καὶ Νεοελληνικῆς Φιλολογίας Πανεπιστκμίου, Athens, 1959.
45 See p. 463.
46 Published by É. Legrand, *Collection de monuments*, n.s. 5, Paris, 1875.
47 See Knös, *Histoire de la littérature néo-grecque*, pp. 150f.
48 Published by Legrand, in *Collection de monuments*, vol. 16, 1875; see also F. Sbordone, *Physiologus*, Milan, 1936, pp. 303f.; M. Goldstaub, in *Philologus*, suppl. 8, Leipzig, 1899–1901, pp. 339f.; C. Gidel, *Nouvelles études de la littérature grecque moderne*, Paris, 1878, pp. 401f.; and D. Kaimakis, *Der Physiologus nach der ersten Redaktion*, Hain, 1974.
49 In some manuscripts the title of the work is not παιδιόφραστος which means 'playful', but πεζόφραστος, 'written in popular speech'.
50 Edition in Wagner, *Carmina Graeca Medii Aevi*, pp. 141f.; see also Gidel, *Études sur la littérature grecque moderne*, Paris, 1866, pp. 303f.; S. Xanthoudides, *Byantinische-neugriechische Jahrbücher*, vol. 5, 1926–7, pp. 348f.; V. Šandrovskaja, in *Vizantijskij Vremennik*, vol. 9, 1956, pp. 211f., and *Vizantijskij Vremennik*, vol. 10, 1957, pp. 181f.; and V. Tsiouni, Παιδιόφραστος διήγησις τῶν τετραπόδων, Munich, 1974.
51 The attribution of the *Poulologos* to Prodromos by the Cod. Constant. Sereil, 35, of the year 1461 is not to be trusted.
52 Editions in Wagner, *Carmina Graeca Medii Aevi*, pp. 179f.; Zoras, Σπουδαστήριον Βυζ καὶ Νεοελληνικῆς Φιλολογίας τοῦ Πανεπιστημίου Ἀδηνων, 1956, and in Ἐπετηρὶς Ἑτ. Βυς. Σπουδῶν, vol. 30, 1960–1, pp. 150f. A full edition of the versions in S. Krawczynski, Ὁ Πουλολόγος, Berlin, 1960; see also P. Bouboulides, in Ἀθηνᾶ, vol. 67, 1964, pp. 133f.
53 See Beck, *GBV*, p. 174. The word *poulologos* means 'ornithologist'.
54 The reference to the compass (see Knös, *Histoire de la littérature néo-grecque*, p. 154) gives the early fourteenth century as a *terminus post quem*.
55 Edition in Wagner, *Carmina Graeca Medii Aevi*; also L. Alexiou, in Κρητικὰ Χρονικά, vol. 9, 1955, pp. 81f.

PART FOUR: THE GREEKS UNDER THE FRANKS AND THE TURKS

Section I: The Greeks under the Franks (1204–1797)

Introduction

1 See W. Miller, *Essays on the Latin Orient*, Cambridge, 1921, pp. 189f.
2 On the Cretan academies, theatrical performances, tournaments and so on, see N. M. Panayotakis, in *Θησαυρίσματα*, vol. 5, 1968, pp. 45f. and 73f.
3 See W. H. McNeill, *Venice, the Hinge of Europe, 1081–1797*, Chicago, 1974, pp. 228f.

Chapter 22: Verse Romances and Historical Poems

1 See J. B. Bury, *Romances of Chivalry on Greek Soil*, Oxford, 1911, p. 23.
2 Because of the Frankish influence, these romances are examined in this chapter, although some of them — perhaps all of them — may not have originated in lands that were conquered by the Crusaders.
3 We know, for example, that Boniface, king of Salonica, was accompanied by Rambaud de Vaqueiras, a troubador from Provence, who afterwards boasted in one of his letters in verse that he addressed to his patron that he had 'helped him to conquer the Empire of the East and the kingdom of Salonica, the island of Pelops and the duchy of Athens'. See W. Miller, *Essays on the Latin Orient*, Cambridge, 1921, p. 59.
4 See B. Knös, in *Ἑλληνικά*, vol. 17, 1962, pp. 274f.
5 See Krumbacher, *GBL*, p. 715.
6 The contact with Meliteniotes' *Εἰς τὴν Σωφροσύνην* is no *terminus ante quem*, for, as with the *Epic of Digenis Akritas*, the contamination probably took place during the period of oral transmission of the romance after 1397.
7 It is transmitted in five manuscripts, which shows that it was a fairly popular story.
8 *Kaballarioi* means 'horsemen'. The Greeks had no word for 'knight-errant', but they coined a verb that expressed a similar notion, *kosmoanagyreuein*, meaning to roam the world on a quest.
9 See K. T. Demaras, *Ἱστορία Νεοελληνικῆς Λογοτεχνίας*, 6th edn., Athens, 1975, p. 28.
10 Henri Grégoire thought that the names Berderichos and Libystros referred to the Emperor Frederick II (1194–1250) and to Louis IX (1215–70) and was therefore inclined to attribute the poem to the thirteenth century. But this does not appear probable. See B. Knös, *Histoire de la littérature néo-grecque*, Stockholm–Göterborg–Uppsala, 1962, p. 120. Nor does the contamination of parts of this romance by Meliteniotes' *Εἰς τὴν Σωφροσύνην* help us in dating the poem because it may be due to a period of later oral transmission. See Beck, *GBV*, p. 125.
11 See E. Kriaras, in *Akten XI Internationalen Byzantinistenkongresses* (Munich, 1958), Munich, 1960, pp. 269f. There he suggests that *Imberios and Margarona* is a later work than *Phlorios and Pliatzaphlora*. But thanks to contaminations introduced by successive singers, it is impossible to draw conclusions about the dates of such works.
12 See p. 504.
13 In Cod. Neapol. III, B.27 (251), dated 5 May 1520.
14 See Beck, *GBV*, p. 130.
15 See K. Mitsakis, in *BZ*, vol. 59, 1966, pp. 5f.; P. Speck, in *Jahrbücher Österreichische byzantinische Gesellschaft*, vol. 18, 1969, pp. 89f.
16 It is well in this respect to remember the wise words of Charles Diehl: 'Aux barons

français, venus conquérants, la civilisation grecque semble avoir donné plus qu'elle n'a reçu d'eux.'

17 In Greece, of course, though it cannot be followed uninterruptedly, it goes back to the Homeric epics and to Hesiod.

18 Hence in the language of these verse romances (even in the later forms that they took when committed to writing and elaborated upon by pen-poets) we find many pronounced demotic linguistic elements, as, for example, the abundant use of the diminutive, long compound words, the mixture of a synthetic with an analytic syntax and so on.

19 See E. Rohde, *Der griechische Roman*, 3rd edn., Leipzig, 1914, pp. 435f.

20 See Beck, *GBV*, pp. 136f. We know that Antonio Pucci (died 1383) wrote a long version of this story, *I storia d'Apollonio*, which enjoyed widespread popularity.

21 See E. Klebs, *Die Erzählung von Apollonius aus Tyre*, Berlin, 1899; E. Perry, *The Ancient Romances*, Berkeley–Los Angeles, 1967, p. 294.

22 An edition of this work has been prepared by Mrs E. M. Jeffreys and Professor M. Papathomopoulos of Jannina.

23 For certain other sources, see R. Merkelbach, *Die Quellen des griechischen Alexanderromans*, Munich, 1954.

24 The Western versions of the *Tale of Belisarius* by Rotrou (1609–50) and Marmontel (1723–99) are independent of these Byzantine poems. (I have not seen A. F. van Gemert, in *Folia Neohellenica*, vol. 1, 1975, pp. 45–72.)

25 See p. 550.

26 The best account is that of G. A. Spadaro, in *Siculorum Gymnasium*, vol. 12, 1959, pp. 125f.; see also M. J. Jeffreys, in *BZ*, vol. 68, 1975, pp. 304f., who believes that the original was Greek.

27 See especially D. Jacoby, in *Journal des Savants*, 1968, pp. 133f.

28 J. Schmitt, *The Chronicle of the Morea*, London, 1904.

29 On the Greek of the *Chronicle of the Morea*, see M. J. Jeffreys, in *BZ*, vol. 68, 1975, pp. 304f., and in *Dumbarton Oaks Papers*, vol. 27, 1973, pp. 165f., where the 'formulae' that appear in the text are discussed; G. N. Hatzidakis, Μεσαιωνικὰ καὶ Νέα Ἑλληνικά, Athens, 1905, vol. 1, pp. 515f.

30 Paris. Gr. 2898.

31 As lines 1340–3, 1349–56 and 2898 (Schmitt) show; see C. A. Trypanis, in *BZ*, vol. 56, 1963, pp. 1f.

32 Edited by G. Schirò, Τὸ χρονικὸν τῶν Τόκκων, τὰ Ἰωάννινα κατὰ τὰς ἀρχὰς τοῦ ιε΄ αἰῶνος, Jannina, 1965. See also G. Schirò, in *Rivista di studi bizantini*, vols. 2–3, 1965–6, pp. 119f.

33 Published by M. J. Manousakas, in Λαογραωία, vol. 14, 1952, pp. 3f.; see also M. J. Manousakas, in Λαογραφία, vol. 15, 1954, pp. 336f.

34 See p. 551.

Chapter 23: Poetry from the Aegean Islands, Rhodes, Cyprus, Crete and the Ionian Islands

1 Rhodes has been suggested because it was the island on which Western and Byzantine culture often fused. This is, of course, even more true of Crete, but the absence of any Cretan dialectal elements from these poems precludes a Cretan origin.

2 Brit. Mus. add. 8241.

3 Vind. Th. Gr. 244.

4 See pp. 553f. According to G. Morgan (in Κρητικὰ Χρονικά, vol. 14, 1960, p. 35), rhymed political lines in original folk songs do not appear until the beginning of the eighteenth century.

5 Cod. Neapol. III, B.27.

6 The reason for this is that it is transmitted in the same Viennese manuscript (Vind. Th. Gr. 244) of the late fifteenth or early sixteenth century. However, it is also transmitted independently in Ambrosianus Y, 89 supp.

7 Theocrit., 1, 132f.

8 No. 128a (Polites).

9 Editions: É. Legrand, *Bibliothèque grecque vulgaire*, vol. 2, Paris, 1881; H. Pernot, *Chansons populaires grecques de XVe et XVIe siècle*, Paris, 1931, pp. 72f. See also S. Baud-Bovy, *Le chanson populaire grecque du Dodécanèse*, Geneva, 1961, pp. 201f.

10 See pp. 544f.

11 See p. 587.

12 §§ 234f. (Dawkins).

13 See p. 559.

14 See Dölger, *BDIR*, p. 16.

15 See E. Kriaras, in *Κρητικὰ Χρονικά*, vols. 15–16, 1963, pp. 399f.

16 See pp. 572f.

17 These are either feast songs (*Τραγούδια τῆς τάβλας*) or journey songs (*Τραγούδια τῆς στράτας*), and they differ from the rest of Cretan folk poetry in that they are sung only by choruses of men—never by a soloist or by women—and without musical accompaniment.

18 See S. Alexiou, *Κρητικὴ Ἀνθολογία*, Herakleion, 1969, pp. 237f.

19 Hitherto he was placed in the fifteenth century, but recent research in the Cretan archives, now in Venice, by M. J. Manousakas and A. F. van Gemert has shown beyond doubt that he was born before 1332. This, and the important consequences drawn from this discovery, were part of a paper given by those two scholars at the Fourth International Conference of Cretan Studies held in Herakleion in August 1976, which is still unpublished. I wish to thank Professor M. J. Manousakas for allowing me to refer to the results of their important research in this book.

20 See p. 559.

21 See W. Meyer, in *Abhandlungen d. philos.-philol. Klasse der Bayerischen Akademie der Wissenschaften*, vol. 17, 2, 1885, pp. 370f.

22 The only two early examples of the use of rhyme in Greek are the *Akathistos* hymn and Romanos' *kontakion* on Judas.

23 An example in which the poet experiments with the use of rhyme—employing the same rhyme in two or three consecutive lines and, occasionally, rhyming couplets—is the poem *On Expatriation* (*Περὶ τῆς Ξενιτείας*). See W. Wagner, *Carmina Graeca Medii Aevi*, Leipzig, 1874, pp. 203f.

24 It was discovered by M. J. Manousakas, who is also preparing an edition of Dellaportas' work.

25 It appears that Dellaportas' *Dialogue*, in which he denies his guilt, is an answer very much in the moralizing Byzantine style to the work of Sachlikis who, also writing in prison, admits his own guilt with self-satisfaction.

26 Rhyme appears in Dellaportas' work only three times—in two three-line units and in one four-line unit that use the same endings.

27 See A. F. van Gemert, in *Θησαυρίσματα*, vol. 14, 1977, pp. 7f.

28 The title is that given to the work by the modern editor.

29 See M. J. Manousakas, *Mélanges Octave et Melpo Merlier*, Athens, 1952, vol. 2, pp. 3f. Another anonymous work of the sixteenth century in 112 rhyming political lines, called *Prayer to the Passion of Christ* and cast in dramatic form, is also meant to be read and not acted; see Manousakas, *loc. cit.*

30 According to J. Kallitsounakis, *Πρακτικὰ Ἀκαδημίας Ἀθηνῶν*, vol. 1, Athens, 1933, the author of this poem is probably a monk named Alexios.

31 See G. Zoras, *Σπουδαστήριον Βυζ. καὶ Νεοελλ. Φιλολογίας Πανεπιστημίου Ἀθηνῶν*, Athens, 1955.

32 See p. 516.

33 But it was not until the eighteenth century that rhyme reached the Cretan folk songs (see n. 4), so old and so powerful was the island's non-rhyming tradition.

34 Even Dante has been quoted as one of *Apokopos'* sources.

35 Edition: M. J. Manousakas, in *Ἐπετηρὶς Φιλοσοφικῆς Σχολῆς Πανεπιστ. Θεσσαλονίκης*, vol. 8, 1963, pp. 295f.

36 See p. 556 and n. 29.

37 On this, see T. Tzedakis, in *Κρητικὰ Χρονικά*, vols. 15–16, 1961–2, pp. 156f. A full

edition of this interesting work is being prepared by M. J. Manousakas and C. A. Trypanis.

38 Another translation of the *Pastor Fido* was prepared by Soumakis (1658), from the Ionian Islands; but it is greatly inferior to the anonymous Cretan translation.

39 On these, see G. Gabrieli, in *L'Accademia in Italia, Accademie e Biblioteche d'Italia*, vol. 1, 1927–8, pp. 6f; W. Cochrane, *Tradition and Enlightenment in the Tuscan Academies, 1690–1800*, Rome, 1961.

40 See N. M. Panagiotakis, in Θησαυρίσματα, vol. 5, 1968, pp. 83f.

41 See N. M. Panagiotakis, Πεπραγμένα Γ΄ διεθνοῦς Κρητικοῦ Συνεδρίου, Athens, 1947, vol. 2, pp. 232f.

42 We also know of the Assicurati, a similar academy later established on Corfu.

43 It is interesting to see the description of this society in Foscoles' *Fortunatos* (ll.91–3): 'honoured, glorious and famous in the world/for its courage in battle, for its erudition/ and for everything else'.

44 No such Cretan 'Mystery Play' to be acted has survived.

45 See M. J. Manousakas, in Κρητικὰ Χρονικά, vol. 17, 1964, pp. 271f.

46 See M. J. Manousakas, in Κρητικὰ Χρονικά, vol. 13, 1959, pp. 73f. As we shall see, *Il Re Torrismondo* also served as a model for Andreas Troilos' *King Rodolinos*.

47 When Chortatsis was young, Ruzzante, Calmo and Giancarli, three talented poets and actors, were renewing in Venice the conventional Commèdia Erudita. Many of the new elements they introduced were taken over by Chortatsis.

48 The view that Luigi Groto's *Calisto* was the source of the *Gyparis* has been challenged by A. Sachinis in ᾿Αθηνᾶ, vols. 73–4, 1974, pp. 24f.

49 See pp. 560f.

50 M. J. Manousakas, Κρητικὰ Χρονικά, vol. I, 1947, pp. 525f.

51 Only one copy of this edition is known to have survived, which is now in the Gennadios Library in Athens (printed works MGL 72, B).

52 We cannot be certain that its author was Cretan.

53 A. Evangelatos, in Θησαυρίσματα, vol. 5, 1968, pp. 177f.

54 M. J. Manousakas, in Κρητικὰ Χρονικά, vol. 1, 1947, pp. 55f.

55 See A. L. Vincent, in Θησαυρίσματα, vol. 4, 1967, pp. 53f., and in Θησαυρίσματα, vol. 5, 1968, pp. 119f.

56 See G. Morgan, in Κρητικὰ Χρονικά, vol. 8, 1954, pp. 61f.

57 See G. Morgan, in Κρητικὰ Χρονικά, vol. 9, 1954, pp. 69f.

58 Of this many versions have survived, see M. J. Manousakas, ῾Η Κρητικὴ Λογοτεχνία κατὰ τὴν ἐποχὴν τῆς Βενετοκρατίας, Salonica, 1965, pp. 39f.

59 *ibid.*, p. 40, n. 2.

60 The first to attribute *The Sacrifice of Abraham* to Kornaros was St Xanthoudides, in the introduction to his monumental edition of the *Erotokritos*; see also L. Politis, ᾿Αφιέρωμα στὴ μνήμη τοῦ μανόλη Τριανταφυλλίδη, Athens, 1960, pp. 357f. If, however, the work was written, and not simply copied, in 1635, it cannot be by Kornaros, who was dead by then.

61 A sonnet by Andrea Kornaros on the death of his brother Vitsentzos is included in MS N. A. 436, f. 43n, of the Central National Library of Florence.

62 This was first pointed out not by N. Cartojan, *Accademia Romanâ. Memoriile sectiunii literare*, series 3, vol. 7, 1934–6, mem. 4, Bucharest, 1935, pp. 83f. (see also *Revue de littérature comparée*, vol. 16, 1936, pp. 265f.), but by Christophoros Philetas in the nineteenth century; see A. Angeloglou, in *Anglo-Greek Review*, vol. 6, 1953, pp. 145f.

63 It is also interesting to note the appearance in the *Erotokritos* of the Italian literary device of 'love at a distance', as when Aretousa falls in love simply through hearing the song of Erotokritos, or at the end, when he asks for her hand in marriage. Compare for example, Dante, *Purg*; 22.17; Petrarch, *Rime*, 52.103.

64 Other scholars date the composition of *Erotokritos* between 1640 and 1660; see L. Politis, *A History of Modern Greek Literature*, Oxford, 1973, p. 66, and the 'Introduction to L. Politis' 3rd edition of the *Erotokritos*, pp. 12f. (Athens, 1976), where the date of the poem is discussed.

65 See p. 105.

66 Άτακτα, Paris, 1828, vol. 1, p. 180. He considers it inferior even to the poetry of Ptochoprodromos.

67 Ὁ Ἐρωτόκριτος, Athens, 1946 (now in Δοκιμές, 2nd edn., Athens, 1962, pp. 207f.)

68 'It was the most popular reading of the Levant from the sixteenth to the nineteenth century.' W. Miller, *Essays on the Latin Orient*, Cambridge, 1921, p. 198.

69 Three other poems on the same subject exist, composed by Anthimos Diakrouses, a Cephalonian; Tzanes Bounialis, a Cretan in exile, and the Cypriot Joachim Kantzerllieris.

70 Edition: K. Sathas, Ἑλληνικὰ Ἀνέκδοτα, vol. 2, Athens, 1867.

71 Edition: M. Petrou-Messogitis, in Ἐπετηρὶς Ἑταιρείας Κρητικῶν Σπουδῶν, vol. 2, 1939.

72 See p. 575.

73 M. J. Manousakas, in Κρητικὰ Χρονικά, vol. 5, 1951, pp. 349f.

74 Edition: E. Kriaras, in Ἀθηνᾶ, 48, 1938, pp. 53f.

75 M. I. Douglerakis, in Κρητικὰ Χρονικά, vol. 9, 1955, pp. 334f. The so-called *Song of Kapetan Manettas*, a long poem of the seventeenth century about Captain Manettas and his adventures and family troubles, is most probably not by a Cretan, but by a poet from the Ionian Islands. See A. Katsuros, in Λαογραφία, vol. 18, 1959, pp. 432f.

76 On the poems of Michalis Vlachos (1705), Karamousas, Yannaronikolas and Moros, see G. Morgan, in Κρητικὰ Χρονικά, vol. 14, 1960, pp. 35f.

77 A. B. Lord, *The Heroic Tradition of Greek Epic and Ballad: Hellenism and the First Greek War of Liberation*, Salonica, 1976, p. 91.

78 See also G. Morgan, in Κρητικὰ Χρονικά, vol. 14, 1960, pp. 35f., on the non-rhyming political lines of Michalis Vlachos, which are older than the *Song of Daskalogiannis*.

79 The Cretan poets often used more than one Italian model for their works, introduced various local Cretan elements into them and never transferred from the West anything that would shock Cretan sensitivity.

80 Thus is came about that the *Erotokritos* was published in Venice in 1713, and that in 1725 Edward Harley, second Earl of Oxford, bought on Corfu a manuscript of the *Erophile* (British Museum, MS Harleian. 5644), the only known copy until very recently.

81 See p. 578.

82 See P.-P. Ioannou, *Probleme der neugriechischen Literatur*, vol. 3, Berlin, 1960, pp. 141f.

83 See p. 565. On the recently found and as yet unpublished poem on the capture of Cyprus by the Turks, which might be either Cretan or Corfiot in origin, see p. 559.

Chapter 24: The Greeks of the Diaspora

1 Scholars who indulged in this kind of epigrammatic poetry are Michael Apostolis (c. 1422–80), Johannes Argyropoulos (1434–86), Marcus Moussouros (1470–1517), Demetrius Moschus (c. 1470), Matthaios Debaris (1505–81), Michael Sophianos (died 1565) and Phrangiskos Portos (1510–81). A small selection is in L. Politis, Ποιητικὴ Ἀνθολογία, vol. B. Athens, 1965, pp. 140f. On these authors see Knös, *Histoire de la litterature néo-grecque*, pp. 295f.

2 See D. J. Geanakopolos, *Byzantium and the Renaissance: Greek Scholars in Venice*, Cambridge, Mass., 1962.

3 There is also the amusing case of the Chiot Georgios Koressios, Professor of Greek at Pisa, who wrote a poem in 432 ancient Greek elegiacs on the Florentine ball game called *calcio*, published in Venice in 1611. Greek scholars also wrote and published poems in Latin, some of whom, like Michael Marullus Tarchaniotes (died 1500) acquired great fame. Even Ronsard wrote a poem on his death entitled *Epitaph de Marulle*.

4 A religious play called *David* in the Chiot spoken idiom, the work of an unknown Chiot Jesuit living in Rome, has been published by Th. Papadopoulos, Athens, 1979, as the present book went to the printer. Its literary value is minimal.

5 See P. K. Bouboulidis, in Ἐπετηρὶς Ἑταιρείας Βυζαντινῶν Σπουδῶν, vol. 25, 1955, pp. 284f.
6 Probably an amplified version of the short Byzantine poem with the same title.
7 See pp. 555f.
8 See E. Kriaras, *Probleme der Neugriechischen Literatur*, vol. 3, Berlin, 1960, pp. 62f.
9 To Manolis Blessis, that soldier-poet, a number of other lesser poems have been wrongly attributed; see B. Knös, *Histoire de la littérature néo-grecque*, Stockholm–Göteborg–Uppsala, 1962, p. 315.
10 New edition of the *Flowers of Piety* by J. Vlachogiannis, Athens, 1950. Other collections of poems by various authors followed on the *Flowers of Piety*, of which only the *Anthology in Honour of Georgios Ipomenas*—all poems are in ancient Greek—need be mentioned. Edition in Πανδώρα, December 1868.

Section II: The Greeks under the Turks (1453–1829)

Introduction

1 All Greek ecclesiastical and other books were printed in the West, in Venice, Frankfurt, Cologne, Paris, Rome and Oxford. In 1634 some totally unimportant printing appeared secretly in a few monasteries of the Balkans. In 1682 a printing house was set up in Jassy.

Chapter 25: The Survival of the Byzantine Heritage

1 See K. Demaras, Ἱστορία τῆς Νεοελληνικῆς Λογοτεχνίας, 2nd edn., Athens, 1955, pp. 53f.
2 See p. 551.
3 See p. 550.
4 See p. 589.
5 Edition: E. Destounis, St Petersburg, 1881; also in G. A. Babaretos (ed.), Βασικὴ Βιβλιοθήκη, vol. 1, Athens, 1955.
6 See N. G. Politis, Γνωστοὶ ποιηταὶ δημοτικῶν ἀσμάτων (Διαλέξεις Φιλολογικοῦ Συλλόγου Παρνασσοῦ 1), Athens, 1916, p. 45. Second edn., Athens, 1925.
7 The dating and provenance of the various famous modern Greek folk songs is a matter of dispute. Thus, according to S.P. Kyriakides, (Αἱ ἱστορικαὶ ἀρχαὶ τῆς νεοελληνικῆς δημοτικῆς ποιήσεως, 2nd edn., Salonica, 1954) the *Paraloges*, the narrative folk songs, appeared at the end of the ancient world, and their origin can be traced in the isolated sung parts of ancient Greek tragedy, which had then become very popular (see Libanius, *Or.*, lxiv, *pro saltatoribus*, vol. 4, p. 493 (Foerster)) and from which the modern Greek word τραγούδι, song, originates.
At the same time S. Baud-Bovy (in *La chanson populaire grecque du Dodécanèse*, Geneva, 1936) maintains that the first appearance of the erotic element in Greek folk songs should be assigned to the twelfth century and the Dodecanese. The songs, whose heroines are unfaithful wives or mistresses, he assigns to thirteenth- or fourteenth-century Crete, and to the sixteenth century and mainland Greece the songs of the so-called 'tragic group', like the well-known *Murderous Mother* (no. 41, Politis). Unfortunately, these speculations cannot be confirmed.
8 See p. 575.
9 C. Fauriel mentions one Gavoiannes from Thessaly, who wandered from village to town singing popular folk songs 'like a modern Homeric bard'. *Chansons populaires de la Grèce moderne*, Paris, 1924, vol. 1, p. xc.
10 See S. Kyriakides, in Λαογραφία, vol. 12, 1948, p. 473, and Αἱ ἱστορικαὶ ἀρχαὶ τῆς δημώδους Ἑλληνικῆς Ποιήσεως, Salonica, 1934, pp. 7f.
11 See Krumbacher, *GBL*, p. 792.
12 Krumbacher, *GBL*, p. 793.
13 Page 251 (Politis).

14 See pp. 492f.

15 No. 1 (Politis).

16 See K. Demaras, Ἱστορία τῆς Νεοελληνικῆς Λογοτεχνίας, 6th edn., Athens, 1975, pp. 50f.

17 No. 2 (Politis).

18 See p. 524.

19 Cf. N. G. Politis, Ἐκλογαὶ ἀπὸ τὰ τραγούδια τοῦ Ἑλληνικοῦ λαοῦ, 7th edn., Athens, 1978, p. 12.

20 No. 3 (Politis).

21 No. 4 (Politis).

22 No. 5 (Politis).

23 No. 6 (Politis).

24 See pp. 592f.

25 Which, according to A. B. Lord, begins with narratives like the *Song of Daskalogiannis* by Pantzelios; see p. 574.

26 See Politis, Γνωστοὶ ποιηταὶ δημοτικῶν ἀσμάτων, pp. 19f., 34f.

27 No. 18 (Politis).

28 Athen., 8.295–360, speaks about the ancient *coronisma* and *chelidonisma*, the latter sung to celebrate the return of the swallows. It is interesting that the modern Greek *chelidonisma*, sung on 1 March, should start with exactly the same words as the ancient Greek one: Ἦλθεν ἦλθεν χελιδόνα. See Fauriel, *Chansons populaires de la Grèce moderne*, vol. 1, pp. xxviii, cix.

29 The modern Greek millers' song also starts with exactly the same words as the ancient Greek song.

30 The similarity of modern Greek 'contests', where people compete with improvised couplets, with the exchanges between Comatas and Lacon in Theocritus V should not mislead us, nor the occasional identity of the contents of such couplets with ancient Greek poetry; for example, A. Passow, *Popularia Carmina Graeciae Recentioris*, Leipzig, 1860, p. 407, no. DXXVIII, and Musaeus, *Hero and Leander*, 94–5 (Ludwich). See S.P. Kyriakides, Ἡ γένεσις τοῦ διστίχου καὶ ἡ ἀρχὴ τῆς ἰσομετρίας, Salonica, 1947, and G. Soyter, in Λαογραφία, vol. 8, 1921–5, pp. 386f.

31 For example, Soyter, *loc. cit.*, p. 426.

32 But we also have couplets in other metres, like the iambic or trochaic seven- and eight-syllable line, or the iambic thirteen-syllable line.

33 See S. Kyriakides, Λαογραφία, Athens, 1965, vol. 1, pp. 48f.

34 These are the *Armouris*, the *Son of Andronikos*, *Porphyris*, *Beauty's Castle*, the *Dead Brother*, the *Bridge of Arta* and the songs on the *Death of Digenis*.

35 No. 92. (Politis). This swift and vigorous narrative—a masterpiece of its kind—speaks of a mother who lies sick in bed; her nine sons have died, and her one daughter is married and living in Babylon. The last of her sons, the dead brother, rises from his grave and brings his sister back to their mother on horseback.

36 No. 89 (Politis). It treats of the primitive idea that in order to make a building strong, an animal or a man should be sacrificed, so that the 'soul', with its superhuman powers, may protect it. Many bridges and aqueducts are associated with a similar myth: for example, the bridge of Spercheios, the bridge of the Saros in Cilicia, the Maiden's Bridge in Chios and so on. See J. C. Lawson, *Modern Greek Folklore and Ancient Religion*, Cambridge, 1910, pp. 262f.

37 No. 74 (Politis).

38 No. 82 (Politis).

39 No. 88 (Politis).

40 No. 476 (Passow).

41 No. 41 (Politis).

42 See W. J. Entwistle, *European Balladry*, Oxford, 1939, pp. 309f., 316f.

43 Christians were forbidden to carry weapons in the Ottoman Empire.

44 On the Klephts and the *armatoloi*, see K. Paparrhegopoulos, Ἱστορία τοῦ Ἑλληνικοῦ Ἔθνους, 6th edn., Athens, 1932, vol. 5.2, pp. 134f., 140f.

45 A good selection of both these groups can be found in the publication by the Academy

of Athens, Ἑλληνικὰ Δημοτικὰ Τραγούδια (Δημοσιεύματα τοῦ Λαογραφικοῦ Ἀρχείου 7), Athens, 1962, vol. 1, pp. 183f., 271f.

46 See J. M. Apostolakis, Τὸ κλέφτικο τραγούδι, Athens, 1950, p. 88; M. Vitti, *Canti del ribelli Greci*, Florence, 1956, p. 30.

47 Both N. Politis and the selection of the Academy of Athens have classed the *Song of Despo* among the historical folk songs, as it refers to a known event which took place on 23 December 1803.

48 See Fauriel, *Chansons populaires de la Grèce moderne*, vol. 1, pp. xcf., and N. G. Politis, Λαογραφικὰ Σύμμεικτα, Athens, 1920, vol. 1, pp. 225f.

49 See p. 101.

50 See Ἀκαδημία Ἀθηνῶν, Ἑλλην. Δημοτικὰ Τραγούδια, vol. 1, pp. 286f.

51 No. 23 (Politis).

52 The correspondence of content and form has been stressed by S. Kyriakidis in Ἡ γένεσις τοῦ διστίχου καὶ ἡ ἀρχὴ τῆς ἰσομετρίας, Salonica, 1947.

53 Of these folk dances, the *syrtos* can be traced back to the first century A.D. cf. *IG*, vol. 7, insc. 2712, lines 66f.

54 B. Knös, *Histoire de la littérature néo-grecque*, Stockholm–Göteborg–Uppsala, 1962, p. 394.

55 Michael Kantakouzenos, who was also a patron of the arts, was finally executed by the Turks. A minor poem on his death is published by É. Legrand, *Recueil de poèmes historiques. . . .* , Paris, 1877.

56 See G. Zoras in Ἐπιθεώρησις Ἑλληνο-Ἰταλικῆς πνευματικῆς κοινωνίας, vol. 2, 1939, pp. 150f.

57 See p. 560. To this period also belongs the rhyming Oxford version of the *Epic of Digenis Akritas*, composed by the Chiot monk Ignatios, about which we have spoken. See p. 494.

58 On these, see T. Veneris, Χριστιανικὴ Κρήτη, Athens, 1912, pp. 379f.; É. Legrand, *Collection de monuments*, vol. 7, Paris, 1869, and vol. 12, Paris, 1904; É. Legrand, *Bibliothèque grecque vulgaire*, vol. 2, Paris, 1881.

59 The first translation of a Shakespearean play appeared in 1789; it was *Romeo and Juliet*. Towards the end of the period under consideration of the British poets it was Young, 'Ossian' and Byron who were the most popular. On these see Knös, *Histoire de la littérature néo-grecque*, pp. 607f.

60 Two more poets should perhaps be mentioned, both mainly known for their bad translations: Georgios Roussiadis (1783–1854), who translated the *Iliad* into modern Greek, and Dionysios Photcinos, who made an even worse translation of the *Erotokritos* into a purist form of Greek.

61 On the Phanariot poets, see L. I. Vranouzis (ed.), Βασικὴ Βιβλιοθήκη, Athens, 1956, and Knös, *Histoire de la littérature néo-grecque*, pp. 607f.

62 The best edition is by Fauriel, in his *Chansons populaires de la Grèce moderne*.

63 His famous lyric *The Little Bird*, for example, is an imitation of a poem by Danelakis, and his *Enchanted Tree* derives from Boccaccio; see Knös, *Histoire de la littérature néo-grecque*, p. 639.

64 See K. Palamas, Τὰ πρῶτα Κριτικά, Athens, 1913, p. 69 (Ἅπαντα, vol. 2).

65 See L. Politis, *A History of Modern Greek Literature*, pp. 107f.

66 In Vienna, in 1805.

67 In 1825. His poems Βάκχος τρυγητής and Φίλε Στέφανε, νὰ ζήσῃς were widely admired.

68 Several versions of this exist, the longest of which is in 125 rhyming twelve-syllable lines.

PART FIVE: MODERN GREECE (1829–1940)

Introduction

1 These followed the so-called 'Macedonian Struggle', when Greece was trying to protect those of her people who were living in Macedonia from organized Bulgarian raids.
2 The Corinth Canal was opened in 1893, and nearly 4000 kilometres of road and over 1000 kilometres of railway were constructed.
3 The population of Venizelist Greece had swollen from under 3,000,000 to 6,500,000.

Chapter 26: The Old School of Athens: The Greek Romantics

1 Not all the Greek Romantic poets belong to the Old School of Athens, for some of the best-known representatives of the School of the Ionian Islands were also distinguished 'Romantic' poets.
2 *Korakistika* is a children's game, in which the syllable–*ko* is added after each syllable of a word: for example, *λέκο-γωκο* and so on.
3 *Π. Σούτσου, Ποιήματα*, Athens 1915 (*Βιβλιοθήκη Φέξη*).
4 *'Α. Σούτσου, "Απαντα*, Athens, 1963 (*ἐπιμέλεια Ν. Κοντομιχάλη*); *'Α. Σούτσου, "Απαντα*, Athens, 1916 (*Βιβλιοθήκη Φέξη*).
5 See Palamas, *"Απαντα*, vol. 2, pp. 404f.
6 See p. 619.
7 Such were the Philadelpheis, the Lassanaios and the Pantelideios competitions. On all these, see G. Valetas, in *Νέα Ἑστία*, vol. 263, 1937, pp. 1819f.; P. Markakis, *Μελέτες*, Athens, 1947; K. Demaras, in introduction to *Οἱ ποιηταὶ τοῦ ιθ´ αἰῶνος* (*Βασικὴ Βιβλιοθήκη*, vol. 12), pp. *κα´* f.; K. Papapanos, *Οἱ ποιητικοὶ διαγωνισμοὶ καὶ ἡ δημοτική μας γλῶσσα*, Athens, 1973.
8 See K. Demaras, *Ἱστορία τῆς Νεοελληνικῆς Λογοτεχνίας*, 4th edn., Athens, 1968, p. 340.
9 See p. 649.
10 See Palamas, *"Απαντα*, vol. 10, pp. 267f.
11 See pp. 627f.
12 See pp. 627f.
13 Such were A. Antoniadis (1836–1912), K. Berses (1845–81), P. D. Zanos (1848–1908) and A. Phatseas (1821–72), all of them inferior playwrights.
14 Angelos Vlachos, an Athenian by birth, was a man of great culture and intelligence who served as Minister of Foreign Affairs and as Greek Ambassador in several European countries. Though a minor poet, he played a major role in the intellectual life of his country as a critic and as a journalist at the turn of the century. His own books of poetry, *Dawn*, *Hours* and *Lyrical Poems*, were no important contribution to Greek literature, but his modern Greek translations of Lamartine, Heine, Sophocles, Shakespeare, Goethe and others were widely read and enabled many Greeks to become acquainted with the writings of those major poets. He was also enlightened enough to see the weaknesses of the Old School of Athens and to recognize the suitability of the spoken idiom for poetry.
15 It should not go unobserved perhaps that in the last years of the Old School of Athens we also meet with a wave of suicides by insignificant Romantic poets like John Raptarchis (1838–71) or Andreas Rhegopoulos (1821–89).
16 Those by Panayotis Panas and Gregorios Kambouroglou should be noted particularly.
17 Hippolyte Adolphe Taine (1828–93), the French historian of literature, had advanced the deterministic theory that heredity, environment and the historical moment were responsible for the character of a writer and his work.

18 See E. Rhoidis, *Περὶ συγχρόνου 'Ελλ. Ποιήσεως* in *῞Απαντα 'Εμμ. 'Ροΐδη* (ed. E. P. Photiadis), Athens, 1960, vol. 2, pp. 368f.

Chapter 27: The School of the Ionian Islands

1 The first theatre was built in Zante in 1750.

2 On other, less significant precursors of the Ionian School, see B. Knös, *Histoire de la littérature néo-grecque*, Stockholm–Göteborg–Uppsala, 1962, pp. 635f.

3 He even had a hand in the translation into Greek of the Anglican Prayer Book.

4 On these, see G. Zoras, *Andrea Calbo, Opere Italiane*, Rome, 1938.

5 In 1830 a poem circulated in Corfu under the title *Hymn to the Olive*, in the same unusual metre as the other odes by Kalvos. It may well be by the poet of *The Lyre*, though there is no proof of this.

6 There are, of course, considerable variations of this basic metric pattern in his strophes. Modern Greek critics have seen in Kalvos's stanza a further elaboration of the two half-lines which go to make the political fifteen-syllable line.

7 Modern Greek critics have often called the odes of Kalvos 'Pindaric'. Needless to say, there is absolutely no justification for this adjective. The idea that great events should be rendered immortal by great poetry and the concern with morality—both characteristic of Kalvos—are common to much Classical poetry and are not exclusively Pindaric.

8 Letter by Tricoupis, dated 6 June 1859, published in Zante in 1903.

9 Solomos has often been attacked for not actively participating in the Greek Revolution. It appears that physical (as opposed to moral) courage was not one of his qualities. He did not respond to repeated invitations to visit Greece both during and after the Revolution; nor was he ever initiated in the Zante branch of the 'Friendly Association' (the secret society for promoting the liberation of Greece), despite a widespread belief to the contrary.

10 In the second volume of Fauriel's monumental work, Solomos's *Hymn to Liberty* and other examples of modern Greek poetry in the demotic were included.

11 See L. Politis, *῾Η γυναῖκα τῆς Ζάκυνθος*, Athens, 1944, pp. 13f.

12 The same metre had already been used in Greek in thirteenth- and fourteenth-century Cypriot love poems, based on Frankish models introduced to the island by the Venetians. See T. Siapkara Pitsillides, *῾Ο Πετραρχισμὸς στὴν Κύπρο*, 2nd edn., Athens, 1976, p. 56.

13 He was deeply moved by the sight of some women from Missolonghi who had taken refuge in Zante and went around the city after dark begging for food and bandages for the wounded, for they were ashamed to be seen in the daylight.

14 Solomos knew Italian, French and English but did not read German fluently. We know now, from his own papers, of the vast number of German philosophical and literary works that he studied in translation, which embraced much of classical and Romantic German poetry and the philosophical and aesthetic works of Fichte, Schelling, Hegel and Schiller. See Politis, *῾Η γυναῖκα τῆς Ζάκυνθος*, p. 227.

15 There is also a sketch for a long poem on the Byzantine general Nicephoros Bryennios.

16 Solomos's patriotism during his last years was just as fervent as in his youth, as can also be seen from the epigram he wrote on King Otto sailing past Corfu in 1850.

17 See R. Levesque, *Solomos*, Athens, n.d., pp. 28f.

18 Strangely enough, this was accompanied by a gradual swerve in his political views from ardent liberalism to full conservatism. The author of the *Hymn to Liberty* even reached the point of suggesting that the time was not ripe for the Heptanese to be united with Greece!

19 He has been accused of homosexual tendencies, but this claim has never been substantiated.

20 The evidence of L. Politis (*Γύρω στὸ Σολωμό*, Athens, 1958, *passim*) to defend Solomos's fragmentary compositions in the light of modern 'disjointed' lyricism is unconvincing. Although many of his extant fragments form a complete lyrical entity,

they were not conceived as independent units, but as parts of a wider, *continuous* framework never completed. Solomos was not trying to introduce a new kind of 'shattered', eliptical expression; he aimed at whole works, which he was unfortunately unable to conclude because of the very high standards he set himself and because of the inadequacies inherent in the spoken language of his day as a vehicle for poetry.

21 See Politis *Γύρω στὸ Σολωμό*, vol. 2, p. 157f., (edition *Στοχαστῆ*).

22 It is very strange that in spite of his unquestionable patriotism, Typaldos, like Solomos and Laskaratos, maintained that the union of the Heptanese with Greece in 1864 was premature.

23 This poem is said to have been composed for his wife, Leonora, who left her first husband to marry him.

24 Matesis's one noteworthy work is his prose play, *The Basil* (*Ὁ Βασιλικός*), on a local Zantiot theme.

25 Another noteworthy Ionian critic and translator of ancient and foreign works into modern Greek was Georgios Kalosgouros (1849–1902). He was also responsible for the development of the thirteen-syllable line in Greek. See Palamas, *Ἅπαντα*, vol. 2, p. 58.

26 The poet was given a real ovation when he recited his ode on the Patriarch Gregory V at the unveiling of the statue of that martyred prelate. This was also the first occasion on which poetry in the demotic was heard at an official ceremony within the precinct of the University of Athens and, as such, constitutes a landmark in the history of Greek literature.

27 It is reported that upon an earlier visit to England in 1854 he taught Greek and Italian at Cambridge. I could not ascertain whether this was Classical or modern Greek.

28 Later in life he tried to collect the copies and to destroy them.

29 On Markoras, see K. Palamas, *Τὰ Πρῶτα Κριτικά*, Athens, 1913, pp. 48f.

30 Under the title *Λορέντζος Μαβίλης, Τὰ Ἔργα*. A second edition was published in 1923. On Mavilis, see C. Paraschos, *Μορφὲς καὶ Ἰδέες*, Athens, 1938, pp. 211f., and in *Ἰόνιος Ἀνθολογία*, vol. 12, March 1938.

Chapter 28: The New School of Athens

1 In 1888 Giannis Psycharis published *My Journey*, ostensibly a series of travelling impressions, but really intended to awaken the dormant linguistic consciousness of the Greek nation. It was then that the real battle flared up.

2 Three more of his books of lyrical verse should be mentioned, entitled *Poems* (1896), *Poems* (1916) and *Facing the Infinite* (1926).

3 The last two were satirical periodicals, *Rabagas* edited by Kleanthis Triantaphyllos and Blasis Gabrielides, two distinguished Constantinopolitan journalists, and *Don't Lose Yourself* by Blasis Gabrielidis alone.

4 In fact, Prudhomme's *Reliquaire* and Coppée's *Stances et poèmes* became their Gospels.

5 It is indicative of the Parnassian influence that in *The Spider's Web*, instead of an introduction Drosinis published a few lines of François Coppée.

6 Drosinis never ceased to be interested in folk songs. In his very last collection, *Embers in the Ashes*, he tried to introduce into personal poetry the 'quatrains' of demotic verse.

7 These are: *The Spider's Web* (1880); *Stalactites* (1881); *Idylls* (1885); *The Amaranths* (1890); *Calm* (1915); *Closed Eyelids* (1918); *Sword of Fire* (1912–21); *Halcyon Days* (1912–21); *Night will be Falling* (1915–22); *She Said* (1912–32); *The Departed Swallows* (1911–35); *Beauty's Lament* (1927); *Spark in the Ashes* (1940).

8 It is in the collection *Darkness Full of Light*. Some of his early and rather trivial songs, like 'The Almond Tree in Blossom', set to music, enjoyed Pan-Hellenic popularity.

9 His prose works, *Amaryllis*, *Erse* and *Country Letters*, are considered by some critics to be superior to his poetry.

10 See *Ἅπαντα*, vol. 4, p. 311.

11 The first poem of any merit Palamas published in the demotic was *The Violet*, inspired by Julia Despotopoulos, a friend of the poet in Missolonghi. It appeared in the *Attic Journal* of 1876.

12 Palamas' last poem in the purist idiom was published in 1885 and is named *Sleep*. See *Ἅπαντα*, vol. 9, pp. 13f.

13 Eight years later, in 1896, Palamas was invited to write the *Olympic Hymn* upon the revival of the Olympic Games as an international event. This, translated into Japanese, was also recited at the Olympic Games held at Tokio in 1964.

14 On those important battles see Palamas, *Ἅπαντα*, vol. 2, pp. 233f., and vol. 6, pp. 542f., 571f.

15 This poem, parts of which were published in 1901, was published complete in *Altars* in 1915.

16 To get an idea of the state of poetry in Greece at the beginning of the twentieth century, it suffices to say that of the 600 copies printed in the first edition of *Life Immovable*, less than thirty were sold during the first month of its publication.

17 The poem was published *in toto* in 1907, but Cantos 2, 3 and 4 had already been published in 1905, in the periodical *Noumas*, and other parts even earlier. The bulk of the work was composed between 1899 and 1903.

18 This probably has its roots in the poet's first experience of carnal love with a gypsy woman. See the poem *The Gypsy Woman* in the *Sorrows of the Lagoon*, and Palamas, *Ἅπαντα*, vol. 5, p. 182.

19 See Palamas, *Ἅπαντα*, vol. 5, p. 32.

20 There is one short passage in free verse and a few others in which slight variations of the fifteen-syllable line are evident.

21 See p. 435.

22 Poems from *Altars* that should be singled out are *The Land that does not Die, Autumn, Full Loneliness, Behind the Bars* and *Cassiane*.

23 The most famous of the poems included is *The East*, one of the greatest musical achievements in modern Greek poetry.

24 *Νέα Γράμματα*, 1935, pp. 121f.

25 See A. Sahinis, *Ἡ πεζογραφία τοῦ Παλαμᾶ*, Salonica, 1972.

26 These are *Poems* (1883); *Winter Flowers* (*Χειμώνανθοι*) (1888); *Alabasters* (1900); *The Old Violin* (1909); *Broken Marbles* (1918); *Poems of Peace* (*Εἰρηνικά*) (1919); *Heirlooms* (*Κειμήλια*) (1920); *Exotic Poems* (1921); *Evensong* (1922).

27 It might be worth while repeating here Palamas's characterization of Polemis's poetry: 'A shady, flowering garden in which the cricket sings, the owl laments, the daisies, the roses and the acacias are fragrant. There, under the April stars, shy maidens promise eternal love to those they love.' See also G. Katsimbalis, in *Νέα Ἑστία*, 15 April 1962; G. Themelis (ed.), *Βασική Βιβλιοθήκη*, vol. 24, Athens, 1957.

28 These are: *Rhododendrons* (1880), *Two Anniversaries* (1889), *New Poems* (1892), *Home Songs* (*Τραγούδια τοῦ Σπιτιοῦ*) (1889), *War Memorials and Commemorations* (1902), *Trophies* (1914), *What the Waves Say* (1918).

29 K. Palamas, *Γ Στρατήγη, Πενῆντα Χρόνια* Athens, 1927. G. Themelis, *Προβελέγγιος, Δροσίνης, Πολέμης, Στρατήγης, Καμπᾶς* (*Βασική Βιβλιοθήκη*, vol. 24), Athens, 1957.

30 On other negligible humorous poets who followed in the footsteps of Souris, see K. Demaras, *Ἱστορία Νέας Ἑλλ. Λογοτεχνίας*, 4th edn., Athens, pp. 409f.

31 At the very beginning he was helped by other poets like D. Kokkos and J. Polemis.

32 Such works are his *Eastern Question, The Blue Book, The Epidemic, Don Juan, The Penniless, The Periphery* and *He Does Not Qualify*. He also has many shorter, humorous works on social, political and artistic life, as well as a few lyrical and elegiac poems.

33 These are: *Laughs* (1880); *Memories and Hopes* (1886); *Poems* (1889); and *Daisies* (1891) (*Μαργαρῖται*).

34 These were: *Old Nicholas' Lyre, Captain Jacob* and *Uncle Linardos*. A fourth such play, *The Village Bride*, he left half-finished at his death.

35 He edited Sophocles' *Antigone* and Book XVIII of the *Iliad*, and he translated Euripides' *Cyclops* and Book I of Thucydides, as well as Shakespeare's *Merchant of Venice* and parts of Kant's philosophical writings. He also wrote an interesting travel book called *Brousos* and a number of critical articles.

36 On Pallis, see K. Palamas, *Ἅπαντα*, vol. 2, pp. 119f.

37 His sonnets, under the title of *Old Tunes*, were published in 1909. His other poem under the title *The Song of Life* also met with success.

38 Occasionally, they turned out a very good poem, as, for example, *The Pelegrinos or The Song of the Evening*, *The Cicada* or *The Greek Summer* by J. Zervos, or *The Songs of April* by R. Golfis.

39 See E. P. Voutierides, Ἱστορία τῆς Νεοελληνικῆς Λογοτεχνίας, 2nd edn., Athens, 1965, p. 292.

40 The first significant Symbolist poem written in Greece was Palamas' *The Greetings of the Sun Born* (see p. 656). It was followed by Gryparis' *Intermedia*.

41 The other two are *The Songs of Loneliness* (1898) and *Elegies and Idylls* (1898).

42 Prevalent are the curling mist, the hazy moonlight, the wind carrying dry leaves, birds that do not sing, rain, footprints in the forest, etc.

43 See p. 616.

44 These are *The Shades of Hades* (1886); *The Monk of the Missolonghi Pass* (1889); *Swallows* (1890); *Poems of the Countryside* (1891); *The Singer of the Village and the Fold* (1893); *Other Poems* (1896) was issued after the poet's death. Most of his poetry is in fifteen-syllable lines; only occasionally did he use the iambic thirteen-syllable line, the eleven-syllable line and the trochaic sixteen-syllable verse.

45 See pp. 672f.

46 In 1927 a second edition of *Echoes* appeared, containing several poems not included in the first.

47 It is of interest that the widely used term *malliaros* (hairy), meaning the user of a very pronounced demotic, was first coined by the writer J. Kondylakis, jokingly referring to Spelios Pasagiannes and his brother, Kostas, who both had long hair.

48 See pp. 672f.

49 See Petros Vasilikos (C. Hadjopoulos), Διόνυσος, 1902. On his prose plays, see D. Gounelas, Νέα Ἑστία, vol. 51, 1977, pp. 167f.

50 D. Goulas, Δυὸ μορφὲς τῆς Ῥούμελης, Athens, 1961; Νεοελληνικὰ Γράμματα, 167 (102.1940) is dedicated to him.

51 P. Haris, Ὅταν ἡ ζωὴ γίνεται ὄνειρο, 2nd edn., Athens, 1957. His collected poems are now published by G. Valetas, Athens (n.d.).

52 On modern poetry composed in Cyprus, see N. Kranidiotis, Ἡ Κυπριακὴ Ποίηση Athens, (n.d.), and Ὁ ἐθνικὸς χαρακτὴρ τῆς Κυπριακῆς Λογοτεχνίας Athens (n.d.).

53 On Melachrinos, see K. Ouranis, Δικοί μας καὶ ξένοι vol. 2, Athens, 1955; I. M. Panagiotopoulos, Τὰ πρόσωπα καὶ τὰ κείμενα, vol. 1, Athens, 1943; A. Karantonis, Εἰσαγωγὴ στὴ νεώτερη ποίηση, Athens, 1958, pp. 132f.

54 It was published in 1909.

55 The last of these, *The Consciousness of Personal Creativeness*, was added to the first four much later, in 1947.

56 See introduction to Λυρικὸς Βίος, ed. G. Savvides, vol. I, Athens, 1959, p. 30.

57 See Philip Sherrard, *The Marble Threshing Floor*, London, 1956, p. 135.

58 I am using the term in the Jungian sense, according to which the 'visionary mode' deals with experiences which do not belong to the realm of understanding, such as those found in the second part of Goethe's *Faust*. See C. G. Jung, 'Psychology and Literature', in M. Schrer, J. Miles and G. McKenzie, *Criticism*, 2nd edn., New York–Chicago–Atlanta, 1958, pp. 117f.

59 See introduction to Λυρικὸς Βίος, ed. G. Savvides, vol. I, p. 34.

60 See introduction to Λυρικὸς Βίος, ed. G. Savvides, vol. I, p. 35.

61 See E. P. Papanoutsos, Παλαμᾶς, Καβάφης, Σικελιανός, Athens (n.d.), p. 216, n. 64.

62 See introduction to Λυρικὸς Βίος, ed. G. Savvides, vol. I, pp. 44f.

63 He describes it as 'the method by which the soul rises from circle to circle until it attains the highest contact. The circles are five: Ego, Humanity, Earth, Universe, God. The last part of the theory is 'Action', and the last step up to redemption is 'Silence'. See P. Prevelakis, Ὁ ποιητὴς καὶ τὸ ποίημα τῆς Ὀδύσσειας, Athens, 1958, p. 79.

64 On these see P. Prevelakis, *loc. cit.*, and L. Politis, *A History of Modern Greek Literature*, pp. 220f.; P. Prevelakis, Ὁ Καζαντζάκης, Βίος καὶ Ἔργα, Athens, 1977.

65 It was published in 1910. His earlier plays, *The Day is Breaking* (which he submitted to a dramatic competition in Athens), *Until When* and *Phasma*, passed unnoticed. See D. Gounelas, Νέα Ἑστία, vol. 51, 1977, Christmas issue, pp. 166f.

66 His plays, except for his three early ones, are included in Ν. Καζαντζάκη, Θέατρο vols. 1–3, ed. Helen Kazantzakis, Athens, 1964–71. The early plays in Νέα Ἑστία 51, 1977, Christmas issue, pp. 166f.

67 The introduction, synopsis and notes to Kazantzakis' *Odyssey* in Kimon Friar's English translation can be of considerable help to the English-speaking reader of this formidable work.

68 He published this under the pen-name of Demos Tanalias.

69 Several of his poems are collected in Ποιήματα, Athens, 1964. See T. Malanos, Δειγματολόγιο, Athens, 1962.

70 On these, see A. Tarsoule, Ἑλληνίδες Ποιήτριες, 1857–1940, Athens, 1951; and Knös, *L'histoire de la littérature néo-grecque, passim.*

71 See p. 435.

72 These are *Songs* (1919), *Yellow Flames* (1925), *The Gifts of Love* (1932), *Cries* (1939) and two volumes of her *Anthology for Children* (1930), all in her collected works, Ἅπαντα, Athens, 1962.

73 The collections of verse she published are *Chrysanthemums* (1903), *The Golden Cups* (1923), *Argo* (1927).

74 See A. Karantonis, Προβολές, Α', Athens, 1965, pp. 20f.

75 *ibid.*, p. 35.

76 Both collections are now published together in the Galaxias series, Athens, 1961.

77 Though this book does not deal with living poets, these three must be included for the 'armchair school of escapism' to be represented.

78 Karantonis, Προβολὲς, Α', p. 34.

79 See Karantonis, Προβολές, Α', p. 36.

80 See A. Karantonis, Φυσιογνωμίες, Athens, 1960, vol. 2, p. 196.

81 This is the culmination of the second wave of Symbolism that influenced modern Greek poetry, which had started in 1915.

82 See p. 620.

83 See A. Karantonis, Νέα Γράμματα, Athens, 1935, vol. I, pp. 478f.; Telos Agras, P. Haris and C. Paraschos, in Νέα Ἑστία fasc. 16, 17, 18, 1928.

84 See pp. 694f.

85 Other poetesses who were to be active until much later but who started composing poetry in the twenties are Zoe Karelle, the pen-name of Chrysoula Argyriade (1901–   ); Rita Boume-Papa (1906–   ); Dialechte Zeugole (1907–   ); and Melissanthe, the pen-name of Hebe Skandalake (1910–   ).

86 Her most representative collection of verse is *The Trills That Fade* (1928).

87 The collections of Lili Iakovidou's poems are: *Hours Full of Light* (1932), *Forty Songs* (1936), *Skylarks* (1940), *Reference* (1957), *Earth Without Water* (1969), *Idols of the World* (1973). See also A. Karantonis, in Νέα Γράμματα, vol. I, 1935, pp. 241f.

88 In 1962 he collected all his poems in two volumes of the same title, *Selections I* and *II*.

89 All his poems written between 1921 and 1962 are published in *Poems 1921–1962*, Athens, 1968.

90 He does not belong, of course, to any of the known philosophical schools. See E. M. Papanoutsos, Παλαμᾶς, Καβάφης, Σικελιανός, Athens, n.d., pp. 97f.

91 See E. M. Keeley, *Cavafy's Alexandria*, Cambridge, Mass., 1976.

92 The process starts in 1912 with his poem *Philhellene*, but developed from 1917 onward and lasted till he died.

93 Ἀνέκδοτα Ποιήματα, 1882–1923, ed. G. Savvides, Athens, 1968.

94 This book ends with the beginning of the Second World War and does not deal with any of the living poets; the picture of the poets of the 1930s is therefore bound to be incomplete, as many of them are still alive and active.

95 See p. 672.

96 See p. 568.

97 'We keep the symbols and the names that the myth has brought down to us,' Seferis
writes, 'Suffice it we know that the typical characters have been changed in accor-
dance with the passage of time and the different conditions of our world. "This", as
Eliot has said speaking about Joyce, "is simply a way of controlling, of ordering, of
giving shape and a significance to the immense panorama of futility and anarchy
which is contemporary history." Instead of the narrative method, we now use the
mythical method.' See Anglo-Hellenic Review, Athens, June 1947, p. 501.

98 On Sarantaris, see A. Karantonis, *Φυσιογνωμίες, Δεύτερη Σειρά*, Athens, 1960,
pp. 197f.

99 In it André Breton defined Surrealism as 'a form of psychic automation, whereby
human expression is liberated from the confines of reason and established morals, as
well as a movement which in its metaphysical connotation bases its belief in the
superior reality of the dream and of those verbal and pictorial associations created by
the mind when it is allowed unbridled activity'.

BIBLIOGRAPHY

GENERAL BIBLIOGRAPHY

The following list makes no claim whatever to completeness.

For full bibliographical details for works cited in abbreviated form, see the List of Abbreviations, pp. 703–5.

HISTORY OF ANCIENT GREEK POETRY

Bowra, C. M., *Landmarks in Greek Literature*, London, 1966
Bowra, C. M., *Ancient Greek Literature*, London, 1966
Christ, W., Schmid, W., and Stählin, O., *Geschichte der griechischen Literatur bis auf die Ziet Justinians*, Pt. 1, 5th edn., Munich, 1929–48, Pt. 2, 6th edn., Munich, 1920, 1924
Croiset, A., Croiset, M., *Histoire de la littérature grecque*, 5 vols., 4th edn., Paris, 1928
Körte, A., *Die hellenistische Dichtung*, Leipzig, 1925; 2nd rev. edn., ed. P. Händel, Stuttgart, 1960
Kranz, W., *Geschichte der griechischen Literatur*, 4th edn., Bremen, n.d.
Legrand, É., *La poésie alexandrine*, Paris, 1924
Lesky, A., *A History of Greek Literature from Homer to the Age of Lucian*, trs. J. Willis and C. de Heer, London, 1966
Lesky, A., *Geschichte der griechischen Literatur*, 3rd edn., Berne, 1971
Mackail, J. W., *Lectures on Greek Poetry*, London–New York, 1926
Murray, G., *A History of Ancient Greek Literature*, 4th edn., London, 1907
Pauly, A., Wissowa, G., Kroll, W., *Real-Encyclopädie der klassischen Altertumswissenschaft*, Stuttgart, 1893–
Rose, H. J., *A Handbook of Greek Literature*, 4th edn., London, 1961
Susemihl, F., *Geschichte der griechischen Literatur in der Alexandrinerzeit*, 2 vols., Leipzig, 1891–2
Wilamowitz-Moellendorff, U. von, *Hellenistische Dichtung in der Zeit des Kallimachos*, 2 vols., Berlin, 1924; rpt. 1962
Wright, F. A., *A History of Later Greek Literature from the Death of Alexander in 323 B.C. to the Death of Justinian in A.D. 565*, London, 1932
Ziegler, K., and Sontheimer, W. (eds.), *Der Kleine Pauly, Lexikon der Antike*, 5 vols., Stuttgart–Munich, 1964–75

Bursians Jahresbericht (*Jahresbericht über die Fortschritte der klassischen Altertumswissenschaft*), Berlin–Leipzig et alibi, 1873– . The best bibliographical summary of Classical literature.

Editions of Classical Greek texts

The most consistently good are those published in the Teubner series (Leipzig) and the Oxford Classical Texts (OCT). Texts with parallel translations can be found in the Loeb Classical Library, London–Cambridge, Mass., 1912 (English); Collection des Universités de France (Budé series), Paris, 1920– (French).

Anthologies of Classical Greek poetry

Murray, G., Bailey, C., Barber, E. A., Higham, T. F., and Bowra, C. M. (eds.), *The Oxford Book of Greek Verse*, Oxford, 1962

Trypanis, C. A., *The Penguin Book of Greek Verse*, Harmondsworth, 1971

HISTORY OF BYZANTINE POETRY

Bardenhewer, O., *Geschichte der altkirchlichen Literatur*, 5 vols., Freiburg, 1913–32

Baynes, N. H., Moss, H. St L. B., *Byzantium*, 2nd edn., Oxford, 1949 (The chapters on Byzantine literature by F. H. Marshall and J. Mavrogordato)

Beck, H. G., *Kirche und theologische Literatur im byzantinischen Reich*, Munich, 1959 (*Handbuch der Altertumswissenschaft*, vol. 12, 2.1)

Beck, H. G., *Geschichte der byzantinischen Volksliteratur*, Munich, 1971 (*Handbuch der Altertumswissenchaft*, vol. 12, 2.3)

Dieterich, K., *Geschichte der byzantinischen und neugriechischen Literatur*, Leipzig, 1902

Dölger, F., in *Franz Dölger: zum 70. Geburstage*, 2nd edn., Salonica, 1961

Hunger, H., *Byzantinische Geisteswelt von Konstantin dem Grossen bis zum Fall Konstantinopels*, Amsterdam, 1967

Hunger, H., *Die hochsprachliche profane Literatur der Byzantiner*, 2nd vol. (*Handbuch der Altertumswissenschaft*, vol. 12, 5.2), Munich, 1978

Hussey, J. M., *Church and Learning in the Byzantine Empire*, Oxford, 1937

Impellizzeri, S., *La letteratúra bizantina da Constantino agli iconoclasti*, Bari, 1965

Krumbacher, K., *Geschichte der byzantinischen Literatur*, 2nd edn., Munich, 1897 (*Handbuch der Altertumswissenschaft*, vol. 9, 1); Greek translation by G. Soteriades, 3 vols., Athens, 1897–1900; rpt. 6 vols., Athens, 1964–5

Krumbacher, K., 'Greek Literature: Byzantine', in *Encyclopaedia Britannica*, 14th edn. (1911)

Montelatici, G., *Storia della letteratúra bizantina*, Milan, 1916

Pernot, H., *Études de littérature grecque moderne*, Paris, 1916

Runciman, S., *Byzantine Civilisation*, 3rd edn., London, 1948

Editions of Byzantine Greek texts

The most complete series of texts remains *Patrologia Graeca*, ed. J. P. Migne, 162 vols., Paris, 1857–66. The historical texts can be found in *Corpus Scriptorum Historiae Byzantinae*, ed., B. G. Neibuhr, 50 vols., Bonn, 1828–97. Some of the religious texts have been brought up to date in the series *Sources Chrétiennes*, Paris, 1956. See also Teubner and Budé series.

Anthologies of medieval Greek poetry

Βασική Βιβλιοθήκη, 48 vols., Athens, 1952–8; a broad anthology of verse and prose works, each volume with a separate title, introduction and bibliography.

Cantarella, R., *Poeti bizantini*, 2 vols., Milan, 1948
Trypanis, C. A., *Medieval and Modern Greek Poetry*, Oxford, 1951
Trypanis, C. A., *The Penguin Book of Greek Verse*, Harmondsworth, 1971

HISTORY OF MODERN GREEK POETRY

Augeris, M., Εἰσαγωγὴ στὴν ἑλληνικὴ ποίηση, 3rd edn., Athens, 1971
Baud-Bovy, S., *Poésie de la Grèce moderne*, Lausanne, 1946
Demaras, K. Th., Ἱστορία τῆς νεοελληνικῆς λογοτεχνίας (ἀπό τὶς πρῶτες ῥίζες ὡς τὴν ἐποχή μας), 6th edn., Athens, 1975 (translated into French and English)
Διαλέξεις Φιλολογικοῦ Συλλόγου Παρνασσοῦ περὶ Ἑλλήνων Ποιητῶν τοῦ ΙΘ´ αἰῶνος, 2 vols., 2nd edn., Athens, 1925
Hesseling, D. C., *Histoire de la littérature grecque moderne*, trs. from the Dutch by N. Pernot, Paris, 1924
Kampanes, A., Ἱστορία τῆς Νέας Ἑλληνικῆς Λογοτεχνίας, Athens, 1925; 5th edn. (1948), rpt. 1971
Karandonis, A., Εἰσαγωγὴ στὴ Νεώτερη Ποίηση, Athens, 1958
Karandonis, A., Γύρω ἀπό τή σύγχρονη ἑλληνική Ποίηση, Athens, 1961; both this and the above title in one volume, 5th edn., Athens, 1978
Keeley, E., Bien, P., *Modern Greek Writers*, Princeton, 1972
Knös, B., *L'histoire de la littérature néo-grecque: la période jusqu'en 1821*, Stockholm–Göteborg–Uppsala, 1962
Lavagnini, B., *La letteratúra neoellenica*, 3rd rev. edn., Florence–Milan, 1969
Manousakas, M. J., Ἡ Κρητικὴ Λογοτεχνία κατὰ τὴν ἐποχὴ τῆς Βενετοκρατίας Salonica, 1965; the same study in French in *L'Hellénisme contemporain*, vol. IX, 1955, pp. 95f.
Mastrodemetres, P. D., Εἰσαγωγὴ στὴ νεοελληνικὴ φιλολογία, 2nd edn., Athens, 1976
Mirambel, A., *La littérature grecque moderne*, Paris, 1953
Panagiotopoulos, J., Τὰ Πρόσωπα καὶ τὰ Κείμενα, 6 vols., Athens, 1943–55
Paraschos, K., Δέκα Ἕλληνες Λυρικοί, Athens, 1937
Pernot, H., *Études de littérature grecque moderne*, Deuxième Série, Paris, 1918
Politis, L., *A History of Modern Greek Literature*, Oxford, 1973
Politis, L., Θέματα τῆς Λογοτεχνίας μας, 2 vols., Salonica, 1976
Politis, L., Ἱστορία τῆς Νεοελληνικῆς Λογοτεχνίας, Athens, 1978
Sathas, K. N., Νεοελληνικὴ Φιλολογία. Βιογραφία τῶν ἐν τοῖς γράμμασι διαλαμψάντων Ἑλλήνων (1453-1821), Athens, 1868
Spyridakis, G., *La Grèce et la poésie moderne*, Paris, 1954
Thrylos, A., Κριτικὲς Μελέτες, 3 vols., Athens, 1924–5
Valetas, G., Ἐπίτομη Ἱστορία τῆς Νεοελληνικῆς Λογοτεχνίας, Athens, 1966
Vitti, M., *Storia della letteratúra neogreca*, Turin, 1971; Greek translation, Athens, 1978; German translation, Munich, 1972
Voutierides, E. P., Ἱστορία τῆς Νεοελληνικῆς Λογοτεχνίας, 2 vols., Athens 1924–7; 2nd edn., 1965
Voutierides, E. P., Σύντομη ἱστορία τῆς Νεοελληνικῆς λογοτεχνίας (1000-1930) Athens, 1933; 3rd edn., supplemented (1931-76) by D. Giakos, Athens, 1976

Anthologies of Modern Greek poetry

Apostolides, H. N., *Ἀνθολογία*, 2 vols., 2nd edn., Athens, 1967

Βασικὴ Βιβλιοθήκη, 48 vols., Athens, 1952–8; a broad anthology of works, in verse and prose.

Politis, L., *Ποιητικὴ Ἀνθολογία*, 7 vols., Athens, 1964–7

Trypanis, C. A., *Medieval and Modern Greek Poetry*, Oxford, 1951

Trypanis, C. A., *The Penguin Book of Greek Verse*, Harmondsworth, 1971

PART ONE: ANCIENT GREECE

Section I: From the Mycenaean World to the Persian Wars (c. 2000–490 B.C.)

CHAPTER 1: EPIC POETRY

THE HOMERIC EPICS*

Allen, T. W., *Homeri Opera*, 5 vols., Oxford, 1912–46

Ameis, K. F., Hentze, C., Cauer, P., *Homerus: Odyssee*, Amsterdam, 1964; *Ilias*, Amsterdam, 1965

Bethe, E., *Homer: Dichtung und Sage*, 3 vols., Leipzig–Berlin, 1914–27

Bowra, C. M., *Tradition and Design in the Iliad*, Oxford, 1930

Cauer, P., *Grundfragen der Homerkritik*, 2 vols., Leipzig, 1921–3

Chantraine, P., *Grammaire homérique*, 2 vols., I³, Paris, 1958 II, 1953

Focke, F., *Die Odyssee*, Stuttgart, 1943

Heubeck, A., *Der Odyssee-Dichter und die Ilias*, Erlangen, 1954

Kakrides, J. Th., *Homeric Researches*, Lund, 1949 (trs. of the original, J. Th. Kakrides, *Ὁμηρικὲς Ἔρευνες*, Athens, 1949)

Kakrides, J. Th., *Ὁμηρικὰ Θέματα*, Salonica, 1954

Kakrides, J. Th., *Ξαναγυρίζοντας στὸν Ὅμηρο*, Salonica, 1971 (*Ἡ Βιβλιοθήκη τοῦ Φιλολόγου*, ἀρ. 11)

Kirk, G. S., *The Songs of Homer*, Cambridge, 1962

Komnenou-Kakride, O., *Σχέδιο καὶ Τεχνικὴ τῆς Ἰλιάδας*, Athens, 1947

Komnenou-Kakride, O., *Σχέδιο καὶ Τεχνικὴ τῆς Ὀδύσσειας*, Salonica, 1969

Leaf, W., *Iliad*, London, 1960

Lesky, A., in Pauly–Wissowa, *REkA*, suppl. 11, pp. 687f. (Pub. separately 1967)

Lorimer, L. H., *Homer and the Monuments*, London, 1950

Mazon, P., *Introduction à l'Iliade*, Paris, 1942

Meister, K., *Die homerische Kunstsprache*, Leipzig, 1921

Merkelbach, R., *Untersuchungen zur Odyssee*, Munich, 1969 (2nd edn.)

Muehll, P. von der, *Kritisches Hypomnema zur Ilias*, Basle, 1952

*Out of the huge Homeric bibliography only a very few select titles can be mentioned here. For further titles, see A. Lesky, *Die Homerforschung in der Gegenwart*, Vienna, 1952; Pauly–Wissowa, *REkA*, suppl. 11; E. R. Dodds, in M. Platnauer (ed.), *Fifty Years (and Twelve) of Classical Scholarship*, Oxford, 1968, pp. 1f.

Nilsson, M. P., *Homer and Mycenae*, London, 1933
Page, D. L., *The Homeric Odyssey*, Oxford, 1955
Page, D. L., *History and the Homeric Iliad*, Berkeley, 1959
Parry, A., *The Making of Homeric Verse*, Oxford, 1971
Sanford, W. B., *Odyssey*, Oxford, 1958
Schadewaldt, W., *Iliasstudien*, Leipzig, 1938
Schadewaldt, W., *Von Homers Welt und Werk*, Stuttgart, 1959
Schwartz, E., *Die Odyssee*, Munich, 1924
Snodgrass, A. M., in *Journal of Hellenic Studies*, vol., 94, 1974, pp. 114f.
Trypanis, C. A., *The Homeric Epics*, London, 1976
Wace, A. J. B., Stubbings, F. H., *A Companion to Homer*, London, 1962
Webster, T. B., *From Mycenae to Homer*, London, 1958
Wilamowitz-Moellendorff, U. von, *Die Ilias und Homer*, Berlin, 1920
Wilamowitz-Moellendorff, U. von, *Die Heimkehr des Odysseus*, Berlin, 1927

HESIOD

Colonna, A., *Hesiodi Opera et Dies*, Milan, 1959
Colonna, A., *Le opere e i giorni*, Milan, 1968
Dornseiff, F., *Antike und alter Orient*, 2nd edn., Leipzig, 1959
Evelyn-White, H. G., *Hesiod, Homeric Hymns and Homerica* (Loeb), London, 1914; rev. edns., 1920, 1936
Fondation Hardt, *Hésiode et son influence: Entretiens sur l'antiquité classique VII*, Geneva, 1962; contains K. V. Fritz, *Hesiodisches im Hesiod*, G. S. Kirk, *Hesiod, the Theogony*, and other writings.
Fränkel, H., *Dichtung und Philosophie des frühen Griechentums*, 2nd edn., Munich, 1963, ch. 3
Groningen, B. A. van, *La composition littéraire archaïque grecque*, Amsterdam, 1958
Jacoby, F., *Hesiodi Theogonia*, Berlin, 1930
Krafft, F., *Vergleichende Untersuchungen zu Homer und Hesiod*, Göttingen, 1963
Mazon, P., *Hésiode* (Budé), Paris, 1928; last reprint 1951
Merkelbach, R., *Die Hesiod-Fragmente auf Papyrus*, Leipzig, 1957
Paulson, J., *Index Hesiodeus*, Lund, 1890
Pap. Oxy., vol. 28
Russo, C. F., *Hesiodi Scutum* (with commentary), Florence, 1950; 2nd edn., 1965
Rzach, A., 'Der Dialekt des Hesiodos', *Jahrbuch für klassische Philologie*, Suppl. 8, Leipzig, 1876
Rzach, A., *Hesiodi Carmina*, ed. maior with full *testimonia*, Leipzig, 1902; *ed. minor*, 3rd edn. (Teubner), Leipzig, 1913
Rzach, A., in Pauly–Wissowa, *REkA*, vol. 8, pp. 1167f.
Schwarz, J., *Pseudo-Hesiodea*, Leyden, 1960
Schwenn, F., *Die Theogonie des Hesiodos*, Heidelberg, 1934
Sellschopp, I., *Stilistische Untersuchungen zu Hesiod*, Hamburg, 1934
Solmsen, F., *Hesiod and Aeschylus*, Cornell Studies no. 30, Ithaca, NY, 1949
Solmsen, F., *Hesiodi Theogonia, Opera et Dies, Scutum* (OCT), Oxford, 1970
Troxler, H., *Sprache und Wortschatz Hesiods* (Diss.), Zurich, 1964
Walcot, P., *Hesiod and the Near East*, Cardiff, 1966
Waltz, P., *Hésiode, les travaux et les jours*, Brussels, 1909

West, M. L., *Hesiod: Theogony*, Oxford, 1966
West, M. L., *Hesiod: Works and Days*, Oxford, 1978
Wilamowitz-Moellendorff, U. von, *Hesiodos Erga*, Berlin, 1928, (omits *Days*)

THE HOMERIC HYMNS

Allen, T. W., Sikes, E. E., Halliday, W. R., *The Homeric Hymns*, 2nd edn., Oxford, 1936
Allen, T. W., *Homeri Opera*, 2nd edn., Oxford, 1946, vol. 5
Evelyn-White, H. G., *Hesiod, the Homeric Hymns and Homerica* (Loeb), London, 1936
Humbert, J., *Homère: hymnes* (Budé), 4th edn., Paris, 1959
Richardson, N., *Homeric Hymn on Demeter*, Oxford, 1974
Wünsch, R., in Pauly–Wissowa, *REkA*, vol. 9, pp. 140f.
Zumbach, O., *Neuerungen in der Sprache der homerischen Hymnen*, Winterthur, 1955

EPIC POETRY OTHER THAN THE HOMERIC AND THE HESIODIC

Abel. A., *Orphica*, Leipzig–Prague, 1885
Allen, T. W., *Homeri Opera*, vol. 5, Oxford, 1946
Bethe E., *Homer: Dichtung und Sage*, 2nd edn., Leipzig–Berlin, 1929, vol. 2, pp. 149f.
Brandt, P. (ed.), *Corpusculum poesis epicae Graecae ludibundae*, vol. 1, Leipzig, 1888
Forderer, M., *Zum homerischen Margites*, Amsterdam, 1960
Guthrie, W. K., *Orpheus and Greek Religion*, 2nd edn., London, 1953
Huxley, G. L., *Greek Epic Poetry from Eumelos to Panyassis*, Cambridge, Mass., 1969
Kern, O., *Fragmenta Orphicorum*, 2nd edn., Berlin, 1961
Kinkel, G., *Epicorum Graecorum fragmenta*, Leipzig, 1877, vol. 1
Kirk, G. S., *The Language and Background of Homer*, Cambridge, 1964
Marckscheffel, J. G. G., *Hesiodi, Eumeli, Cinaethonis, Asii et Carminis Naupactii Fragmenta*, Leipzig, 1840
Radermacher, L., in Pauly–Wissowa, *REkA*, vol. 13, p. 1705
Rzach, A., in Pauly–Wissowa, *REkA*, vol. 11, pp. 2347f.
Schwarz, J., *Pseudo-Hesiodea*, Leyden, 1960
Sévéryns, A., *Le cycle épique dans l'école d'Aristarque*, Paris–Liège, 1928
Welcker, F. G., *Der epische Cyclus*, 2 vols., Bonn, 1835–49 (2nd edn., 1865–82)
Wilamowitz-Moellendorff, U. von, *Homerische Untersuchungen*, Berlin, 1884

PHILOSOPHICAL EPICS AND PROVERBIAL POETRY

Bowra, C. M., *Early Greek Elegists*, Cambridge, Mass., 1938
Cornford, F. M., *Greek Religious Thought from Homer to the Age of Alexander*, 2nd edn., London, 1950, pp. 69f.
Diehl, *ALG³*, vol. 1, 1, pp. 63–74 (Xenophanes)
Diehl, *ALG³*, vol. 1, 1, pp. 57–60 (Phocylides)
Diehl, *ALG³*, vol. 1, 2, pp. 91–108 (Pseudo-Phocylides)
Diels, H., *Parmenides Lehrgedicht*, 2nd edn., in *Atene e Roma*, vol. 2, 1899, pp. 1f.

Diels, H., *Fragmente der Vorsokratiker*, 4 vols., 6th edn., ed. W. Kranz, Berlin, 1951, vol. 1, pp. 217–67f.

Fränkel, H., *Wege und Formen frühgriechischen Denkens*, 2nd edn., Munich, 1960, pp. 335f.

Fränkel, H., *Dichtung und Philosophie des frühen Griechentums*, 2nd edn., Munich, 1962

Gomperz, T., *Griechische Denker*, 4th edn., Berlin–Leipzig, 1922, vol. 1, pp. 187f.

Guthrie, W. K., *Orpheus and Greek Religion*, 2nd edn., London, 1953

Jaeger, W., *Die Theologie der frühen griechischen Denker*, 2nd edn., Darmstadt, 1964

Kranz, W., in *Sitzungsberichte der Deutschen Akademie der Wissenschaften zu Berlin*, Berlin, 1916

Untersteiner, M., *Senofane*, Florence, 1956

CHAPTER 2: LYRIC POETRY

IAMBIC POETRY

Diehl, *ALG*

West, *IEG*, vol. 1

ARCHILOCHUS

Crusius, O., in Pauly–Wissowa, *REkA*, vol. 1, pp. 487–507

Diehl, *ALG³*, vol. 1, 3, pp. 2–48

Hauvette, A., *Archiloque, sa vie et ses oeuvres*, Paris, 1905

Jacoby, F., in *Classical Quarterly*, vol. 35, 1941, pp. 97f.

Lasserre, F., Bonnard, A., *Archiloque: fragments*, Paris, 1958

Merkelbach, R., West, M. L., in *Zeitschrift für Papyrologie und Epigraphik*, vol. 14, 1974, pp. 98f.

Treu, M., in Pauly–Wissowa, *REkA*, suppl. 11, pp. 136f.

Treu, M., *Archilochos*, Munich, 1959

West, *IEG*, vol. 1, pp. 1f.

SEMONIDES OF AMORGOS

Diehl, *ALG³*, vol. 1, 3, pp. 49f.

West, *IEG*, vol. 2, pp. 96f.

HIPPONAX

Diehl *ALG³*, vol. 1, 3, pp. 80f.

Knox, A. D., *The Greek Choliambic Poets*, London, 1929

Masson, O., *Les fragments du poète Hipponax*, Paris, 1962

West, *IEG*, vol. 1, pp. 109f.

ELEGIAC POETRY

Bowra, C. M., *Early Greek Elegists*, Cambridge, Mass., 1938

Burn, A. R., *The Lyric Age of Greece*, London, 1960

Campbell, D. A., *Greek Lyric Poetry*, London, 1967

Diehl, *ALG³*, vol. 1, 1; vol. 1, 2; *ALG²*, vol. 2, 5, pp. 84–118
Hudson-Williams, T., *Early Greek Elegy*, Cardiff, 1926
West, *IEG*, vol. 2
Wilamowitz-Moellendorff, U. von, *Sappho und Simonides*, Berlin, 1913

CALLINUS

Diehl, *ALG³*, vol. 1.1, pp. 1–3
West, *IEG*, vol. 2, pp. 47f.

TYRTAEUS

Bowra, C. M., *Early Greek Elegists*, Cambridge, Mass., 1938
Diehl, *ALG³*, vol. 1, 1, pp. 4f.
Snell, B., *Tyrtaios und die Sprache des Epos, (Hypomnemata 22)*, Göttingen, 1969
West, *IEG*, vol. 2, pp. 149f.

MIMNERMUS

Diehl, *ALG³*, vol. 1, 1, pp. 48f.
Szádeczky-Kardoss, S., in Pauly–Wissowa, *REkA*, suppl. 11 (s.v. Mimnermos)
Szádeczky-Kardoss, S., *Testimonia de Mimnermibus, vita et carminin*, Szeged, 1959
Treu, M., *Von Homer zur Lyrik*, 2nd edn., Munich, 1968, pp. 279f.
West, *IEG*, vol. 2, pp. 81f.

SOLON

Diehl, *ALG³*, vol. 1, 1, pp. 20–47
Gundert, H., *Archilochos und Solon, Das neue Bild der Antike*, Leipzig, 1942, vol. 1, pp. 130f.
Jaeger, W., *Solons Eunomie, Sitzungsberichte der Deutschen Akademie der Wissenschaften zu Berlin*, Berlin, 1926, pp. 69f.
West, *IEG*, vol. 2, pp. 119f.
Woodhouse, W. J., *Solon the Liberator*, Oxford, 1938

THEOGNIS

Bowra, C. M., *Early Greek Elegists*, Cambridge, Mass., 1938, ch. 5
Burn, A. R., *The Lyric Age of Greece*, London, 1960, pp. 247f.
Carrière, J., *Theognis de Mégare*, Paris, 1948
Diehl, *ALG³*, vol. 1, 2, pp. 1–81
Hudson-Williams, T., *The Elegies of Theognis*, London, 1910
Kroll, J., 'Theognis Interpretationen', *Philologus*, suppl. 19/1, 1936
Raubitschek, A. E., in *Classical Philology*, vol. 58, 1963, pp. 136f.
Volkmann, H., in *Kleine Pauly*, vol. 5, pp. 262f.
West, *IEG*, vol. 1, pp. 172–242
Young, D., *Theognis* (Teubner), Leipzig, 1961, 2nd edn., 1971

EPIGRAM AND *SCOLION*

Beckby, H., *Anthologia Graeca*, 2nd edn., Munich, 1957–8
Bowra, C. M., *Greek Lyric Poetry*, 2nd edn., Oxford, 1961, pp. 373f.
Diehl *ALG*, *passim*

Friedländer, P., and Hoffleit, H. H., *Epigrammata: Greek Inscriptions in Verse from the Beginnings to the Persian Wars*, Berkeley, 1948
Lattimore, R., *Themes in Greek and Latin Epitaphs*, Urbana, 1962
Page, *PMG*, pp. 472–8.
Page, D. L., Epigrammata Graeca, Oxford, 1975
Peek, W., *Griechische Vers Inschriften*, vol. 1, Berlin, 1955
Peek, .W., *Griechische Grabgedichte*, Berlin, 1960
Reitzenstein, R., *Epigramm und Skolion*, Giessen, 1893
Reitzenstein, R., in Pauly–Wissowa, *REkA*, vol. 6, pp. 71f. (s.v. Epigramm)

MONODY (*CITHAROEDIA*)

Bowra, C. M., *Greek Lyric Poetry*, 2nd edn., Oxford, 1961
Page, *LGS*
Page, *PMG*
Page, D. L., *Supplementum Lyricis Graecis*, Oxford, 1974

TERPANDER

Page, *PMG*, pp. 362–3; cf. fr. 941
Wilamowitz-Moellendorff, U. von, *Timotheos Die Perser*, Berlin, 1903, pp. 92 f.; rpt. Hildesheim, 1970

ALCAEUS

Bowra, C. M., *Greek Lyric Poetry*, 2nd edn., Oxford, 1961, pp. 130f.
Crusius, O., in Pauly–Wissowa, *REkA*, vol. 1, pp. 1498f.
Diehl, *ALG²*, vol. 1, 4, pp. 86–159
Lobel–Page, *PLF*, pp. 112–29
Pack, *GLLT*, pp 10f.
Page, D. L., *Sappho and Alcaeus*, Oxford, 1955, pp. 147f.
Page, D. L., *Supplementum Lyricis Graecis*, Oxford, 1974, pp. 77f.
Pap. Oxy., nos. 2288–308
Treu, M., in Pauly–Wissowa, *REkA*, suppl. 11, pp. 8f.
Treu, M., *Alkaios*, Munich, 1952
Voight, E. M. *Sappho et Alcaeus*, Amsterdam, 1971

SAPPHO

Bowra, C. M., *Greek Lyric Poetry*, 2nd edn., Oxford, 1961, pp. 176f.
Diehl, *ALG²*, vol. 1, 4, pp. 3–85
Gallavotti, C., *Saffo e Alceo*, 2 vols., Naples, 1956–7; vol. 1, 3rd edn., 1962
Lobel, E., Σαπφοῦς Μέλη, Oxford, 1925
Lobel–Page, *PLF*, pp. 1f.
Page, D. L., *Sappho and Alcaeus*, Oxford, 1955, pp. 1f.
Page, D. L., *Supplementum Lyricis Graecis*, Oxford, 1974, pp. 74f.
Perrota, G., *Saffo e Pindaro*, Florence, 1936, pp. 3f.
Schadewaldt, W., *Sappho*, Berlin, 1950
Treu, M., in Pauly–Wissowa, *REkA*, suppl. 11, pp. 1222f.
Wilamowitz-Moellendorf, U. von, *Sappho und Simonides*, Berlin, 1913, pp. 17f.

ANACREON OF TEOS

Bowra, C. M., *Greek Lyric Poetry*, 2nd edn., Oxford, 1961, pp. 268f.
Crusius, O., in Pauly–Wissowa, *REkA*, vol. 1, pp. 2035–43
Diehl, *ALG²*, vol. 1, 4, pp. 161–92
Gentili, B., *Anacreonte*, Rome, 1958
Latte, K., in *Gnomon*, vol. 27, 1955, pp. 495f.
Michelangeli, A., *Anacreonte e la sua fortuna nei secoli*, Bologna, 1922
Page, *PMG*, pp. 171–235
Page, D. L., *Supplementum Lyricis Graecis*, Oxford, 1974, pp. 103f.
Wilamowitz-Moellendorff, U. von, *Sappho und Simonides*, Berlin, 1913, pp. 102–21

CHORAL LYRIC POETRY

ALCMAN

Bowra, C. M., *Greek Lyric Poetry*, 2nd edn., Oxford, 1961, pp. 16f.
Burn, A. R., *The Lyric Age of Greece*, London, 1960, pp. 180f.
Diehl, *ALG²*, vol. 2, 5, pp. 7–38
Garzya, A., *Alcmane, i frammenti*, Naples, 1954
Pack, *GLLT*, vol. 2, p. 42
Page, *PMG*, pp. 2–91
Page, D. L., *Alcman: The Partheneion*, Oxford, 1951
Page, D. L., *Supplementum Lyricis Graecis*, Oxford, 1974, pp. 1f.
Treu, M., in Pauly–Wissowa, *REkA*, suppl. 11, pp. 19f.

STESICHORUS OF HIMERA

Bowra, C. M., *Greek Lyric Poetry*, 2nd edn., Oxford, 1961, pp. 74f.
Diehl, *ALG²*, vol. 2, 5, pp. 48f.
Maas, P., in Pauly–Wissowa, *REkA*, vol. 3, A, p. 2458 (s.v. Stesichorus)
Meillier, C., in *Revue des études grecques*, vol. 91, 1978, pp. 12f.
Page, *PMG*, pp. 97–141
Page, D. L., *Supplementum Lyricis Graecis*, Oxford, 1974, pp. 5f.
Pap. Oxy., 2506, 2617–19.
Parsons, P. J., in *Zeitschrift für Papyrologie und Epigraphik*, vol. 26, 1977, pp. 7f.
Treu, M., in Pauly–Wissowa, *REkA*, suppl. 11, p. 1253
Vürtheim, J., *Stesichoros Fragmente und Biographie*, Leyden, 1919

IBYCUS OF RHEGIUM

Bowra, C. M., *Greek Lyric Poetry*, 2nd edn., Oxford, 1961, pp. 241f.
Diehl, *ALG²*, vol. 2, 5, pp. 48f.
Page, *PMG*, pp. 94–141
Page, D. L., *Supplementum Lyricis Graecis*, Oxford, 1974, pp. 44f.
Wilamowitz-Moellendorf, U. von, *Sappho und Simonides*, Berlin, 1913, p. 121

SIMONIDES OF CEOS

Boas. M., *De Epigrammatis Simonideis*, Amsterdam, 1905
Bowra, C. M., *Greek Lyric Poetry*, 2nd edn., Oxford, 1961, pp. 308f.
Diehl, *ALG²*, vol. 2, 5, pp. 61f.

Fränkel, H., *Dichtung und Philosophie des frühen Griechentums*, 2nd edn., Munich, 1962
Hauvette, A., *De l'authenticité des épigrammes de Simonide*, Paris, 1896
Kegel, W. J. H. F., *Simonides*, Gröningen, 1962
Page, *PMG*, pp. 238–323
Wilamowitz-Moellendorf, U. von, *Sappho und Simonides*, Berlin, 1913

PINDAR

Bowra, C. M., *Pindari Carmina* (OCT), 2nd edn., Oxford, 1947
Bundy, E. L., *Studia Pindarica*, 2 vols., Berkeley, 1962
Burton, R. W. B., *Pindar's Pythian Odes*, Oxford, 1962
Bury, J. B., *The Nemean Odes, The Isthmian Odes*, London, 1890–2
Dornseiff, F., *Pindars Stil*, Berlin, 1921
Farnell, L. R., *The Works of Pindar*, 3 vols., London, 1930–2; rpt., 1961
Finley, J. H., *Pindar and Aeschylus*, Cambridge, Mass., 1955
Fränkel, H., *Dichtung und Philosophie des frühen Griechentums*, 2nd edn., Munich, 1962, pp. 577f.
Gaspar, C., *Essais de chronologie pindarique*, Brussels, 1900
Gerber, D. E., *A Bibliography of Pindar, 1513 to 1966*, Princeton, 1969
Gildersleeve, B. L., *The Olympian and Pythian Odes*, 2nd edn., New York, 1890
Gundert, H., *Pindar und sein Dichterberuf*, Frankfurt a. Main, 1935
Kirkwood, G. M., in *Gnomon*, vol. 35, 1963, pp.130f.
Norwood, G., *Pindar*, Berkeley, 1945; rpt., 1956
Puech, M., *Pindare* (Budé), 4 vols., Paris, 1949–58
Schadewaldt, W., *Der Aufbau des Pindarischen Epinikion*, Halle, 1928; rpt. 1966
Schroeder, O., *Pindari Carmina* (*ed. major*), 3rd edn., Leipzig, 1930
Schwenn, F., in Pauly–Wissowa, *REkA*, vol. 20, pp. 1006f.
Snell, B., *Pindarus*, vol. 1, 4th edn., vol. 2, 3rd edn., Leipzig, 1964 (Teubner)
Turyn, A., *Pindari Carmina*, Oxford, 1952
Wilamowitz-Moellendorf, U. von, *Pindaros*, Berlin, 1922

BACCHYLIDES

Crusius, O., in Pauly–Wissowa, *REkA*, vol. 2, pp. 2793–801, supplemented by A. Körte, *REkA*, suppl. 4, pp. 58–67
Kenyon, F. G., *The Poems of Bacchilides*, London, 1897
Séveryns, A., *Bacchylide*, Paris, 1933
Snell, B., *Bacchylidis, Carmina cum Fragmentis*, 8th edn., Leipzig, 1961

Section II: From the Persian Wars to the Death of Alexander: (490–323 B.C.)

CHAPTER 3: TRAGEDY

DITHYRAMB AND TRAGEDY

Anderson, M. J. (ed.), *Classical Drama and its Influence: Essays Presented to H. D. F. Kitto*, London, 1965

Baldry, H. C., *The Greek Tragic Theatre*, London, 1971

Buschor, E., 'Satyrtänze und frühes Drama', *Sitzungsberichte der Bayerischen Akademie der Wissenschaften, philos.–hist. Klasse*, Munich, 1943, Heft 5

Else, G. F., *The Origins and Early Form of Greek Tragedy*, Harvard, 1965

Grande, C. del, Τραγῳδία, 2nd edn., Naples, 1962

Jens, W. (ed.), 'Die Bauformen der griechischen Tragödie', *Poetica*, Beiheft 7, Munich, 1971

Jones, J., *On Aristotle and Greek Tragedy*, London, 1962

Kitto, H. D. F., *Form and Meaning in Drama*, 2nd edn., London, 1960

Kitto, H. D. F., *Greek Tragedy*, 3rd edn., London, 1961

Kranz, W., *Stasimon*, Berlin, 1933

Lattimore, R., *The Poetry of Greek Tragedy*, Baltimore–London, 1958

Lesky, A., *Die griechische Tragödie*, 4th edn., Stuttgart, 1968; trs. H. A. Frankfort, London, 1965

Lesky, A., *Die tragische Dichtung der Hellenen*, 3rd edn., Göttingen, 1972

Lloyd-Jones, H., in *Cuadernos de la Fundactión Pastor*, vol. 13, Madrid, 1966, pp. 11–33

Lucas, D. W., *The Greek Tragic Poets*, 2nd edn., London, 1959

Norwood, G., *Greek Tragedy*, 4th edn., London, 1948

Patzer, H., *Die Anfänge der griechischen Tragödie*, Wiesbaden, 1962

Petersen, E., *Die attische Tragödie als Bild und Bühnenkunst*, Bonn, 1915

Pickard-Cambridge, A. W., *The Theatre of Dionysos*, Oxford, 1953

Pickard-Cambridge, A. W., *Dithyramb, Tragedy and Comedy*, rev. T. B. L. Webster, 2nd edn., Oxford, 1962

Pickard-Cambridge, A. W., *The Dramatic Festivals of Athens*, rev. J. Gould and D. M. Lewis, 2nd edn., Oxford, 1973

Pohlenz, M., *Die griechische Tragödie*, 2 vols., 2nd edn., Göttingen, 1954

Romilly, J. de, *La tragédie grecque*, Paris, 1970

Schadewaldt, W., *Monolog und Selbstgespräch, neue philologische Untersuchungen*, no. 2, Berlin, 1926

Schönewolf, H., *Der jungattische Dithyrambos* (Diss.), Giessen, 1938

Seeck, G. A., *Das griechische Drama (Grundriss der Literaturgeschichten nach Gattungen)*, Darmstadt, 1979

Trendall, A. D. and Webster, T. B. L., *Illustrations of Greek Drama*, London, 1971

Vernant, J.-P. and Vidal-Naquet, P., *Mythe et tragédie en Grèce ancienne*, Paris, 1977

Webster, T. B. L., *Greek Theatre Production*, London, 1956

Webster, T. B. L., 'Greek Tragedy', in M. Platnauer (ed.), *Fifty Years (and Twelve) of Classical Scholarship*, 2nd edn., Oxford, 1968

Wilamowitz-Moellendorff, U. von., *Einleitung in die griechische Tragödie*, Berlin, 1907; rpt. 1959

THE SATYR PLAY AND THE ORIGINS OF TRAGEDY

Aly, W., in Pauly–Wissowa, *REkA*, vol. 2A, pp. 235f. (s.v. Satyrspiel)

Brommer, F., *Satyrspiele: Bilder griechischer Vasen*, Berlin, 1944, 2nd edn., 1959

Buschor, E., 'Satyrtänze und frühes Drama', *Sitzungsberichte der Bayerischen Akademie der Wissenschaften, philos.–hist. Klasse*, Munich, 1943, Heft 5

Guggisberg, P., *Das Satyrspiel* (Diss.), Zurich, 1947

Lesky, A., *Die griechische Tragödie*, 4th edn., Stuttgart, 1968; trs. H. A. Frankfort, London, 1965

Pohlenz, M., *Das Satyrspiel und Pratinas von Phleius*, Göttingen, 1927

Steffen, V., *Satyrographorum Graecorum Reliquiae*, 2nd edn., Poznań, 1956

Webster, T. B. L., 'Monuments Illustrating Tragedy and Satyr Play', *Bulletin of the Institute of Classical Studies*, University of London, suppl. no. 20, 2nd edn., 1967

Ziegler, K., in Pauly–Wissowa, *REkA*, vol. 6A, pp. 1899f.

THESPIS

Else, G. F., *The Origins and Early Form of Greek Tragedy*, Cambridge, Mass., 1965, pp. 51f.

Lesky, A., *Die tragische Dichtung der Hellenen*, 2nd edn., Göttingen, 1972

Patzer, H., *Die Anfänge der griechischen Tragödie*, Wiesbaden, 1962, pp. 21f.

Pickard-Cambridge, A. W., *Dithyramb, Tragedy and Comedy*, rev. T. B. L. Webster, 2nd edn., Oxford, 1962, pp. 6of., 69f.

Pickard-Cambridge, A. W., *The Dramatic Festivals of Athens*, rev. J. Gould and D. M. Lewis, 2nd edn., Oxford, 1973

Snell, *TGF*, vol. 1, pp. 1–2

Stoessl, F., in *Gratzer Beiträge*, vol. 2, 1974, pp. 53f.

THE GREAT TRAGEDIANS

AESCHYLUS

Broadhead, H. D., *The Persians*, Cambridge, 1960

Denniston, J. D., Page, D. L., *Aeschylus: Agamemnon*, Oxford, 1957

Earp, F. R., *The Style of Aeschylus*, Cambridge, 1948

Fraenkel, E., *Aeschylus: Agamemnon*, 3 vols., Oxford, 1950

Griffith, M., *The Authenticity of Prometheus Bound*, Cambridge, 1977

Groeneboom, P., *Aeschylos: Perser*, 2nd edn., Göttingen, 1960

Hermann, G., *Aeschyli Tragödie*, 2 vols., Leipzig, 1852; 2nd edn., 1859

Hommel, H., *Wege zu Aischylos*, Darmstadt, 1974

Kitto, H. D. F., *Form and Meaning in Drama*, 2nd edn., London, 1960

Kraus, W., in Pauly–Wissowa, *REkA*, vol. 23, pp. 666f.

Kraus, W., *Strophengestaltung in der griechischen Tragödie*, vol. 1, *Aischylos und Sophokles*, Vienna, 1957

Mazon, E., *Eschyle* (Budé), 6th edn., Paris, 1953

Méautis, G., *Eschyle et la trilogie*, Paris, 1936

Mette, H. J., *Die Fragmente der Tragödien des Aischylos*, Berlin, 1959

Murray, G., *Aeschylus, The Creator of Tragedy*, Oxford, 1940

Murray, G., *Aeschyli Tragodiae* (OCT), 2nd edn., Oxford, 1955

Nauck, *TGF*

Nestle, W., *Die Struktur des Eingangs in der attischen Tragödie*, Stuttgart, 1930

Nestle, W., *Menschliche Existenz und politische Erziehung in der Tragödie des Aischylos*, Stuttgart, 1934

Owen, E. T., *The Harmony of Aeschylus*, Toronto, 1952

Page, *GLP*, pp. 2–11

Page, D. L., *Aeschyli septem quae supersunt tragodiae* (OCT), Oxford, 1972

Reinhardt, K., *Aischylos als Regisseur und Theologe*, Berne, 1949

Romilly, J. de, *La crainte et l'angoisse dans le théâtre d'Eschyle*, Paris, 1958

Romilly, J. de, *L'évolution du pathétique d'Eschyle à Euripide*, Paris, 1961

Rose, H. J., *A Commentary to the Surviving Plays of Aeschylus*, 2 vols., Amsterdam, 1957–8

Schroeder, O., *Aeschyli Cantica*, Leipzig, 1907

Smyth, H. W., *Aeschylean Tragedy* (Sather Lectures), Berkeley, 1924

Smyth, H. W., *Aeschylus*, London–Cambridge, Mass., 1926; vol. 2, rpt. 1957, with appendix by H. Lloyd-Jones containing the principal papyrus fragments (Loeb)

Snell, B., *Aischylos und das Handeln im Drama*, Leipzig, 1928

Solmsen, F., *Hesiod and Aeschylus*, New York, 1949

Stanford, W. B., *Aeschylus and his Style*, Dublin, 1942

Taplin, O., *The Stagecraft of Aeschylus*, Oxford, 1977

Thomson, G., *Prometheus*, Cambridge, 1932

Thomson, G., *Oresteia*, 2 vols., Cambridge, 1938 (incorporating the work of W. Headlam)

Thomson, G., *Aeschylus and Athens*, 2nd edn., London, 1946

Tucker, T. G., *Supplices*, London, 1889

Untersteiner, M., *Eschilo*, Milan, 1946–7

Verrall, A. W., *Eumenides*, London, 1908

Vürtheim, J., *Supplices*, Amsterdam, 1928

West, M. L., in *Journal of Hellenic Studies*, vol. 99, 1979, pp. 130f.

Wilamowitz-Moellendorff, U. von, *Aischylos: Oresteia*, 2 vols., Berlin, 1896

Wilamowitz-Moellendorff, U. von, *Aischylos – Interpretationen*, Berlin, 1914

Wilamowitz-Moellendorff, U. von, *Aischylos*, Berlin, 1914 (*ed. minor*, 1915, rpt., 1958)

SOPHOCLES

Blumenthal, A. von, 'Sophocles: Literature for 1936–1938', in *Burs. Jahresb.*, vol. 277, 1942

Blumenthal, A. von, in Pauly–Wissowa, *REkA*, vol. 3, A, 1927, pp. 1040f.

Bowra, C. M., *Sophoclean Tragedy*, Oxford, 1944

Carden, R. (contrib. W. S. Barrett), *Sophocles: The Papyrus Fragments*, Berlin–New York, 1974

Dain, A., Mazon, P., *Sophocle* (Budé), 3 vols., 2nd edn., Paris, 1955–60

Dawe, R. D., *Sophoclis Tragoediae* (Teubner), 2 vols., Leipzig, 1979

Diehl, E., *Supplementum Sophocleum*, Bonn, 1913

Ellendt, F., *Lexicon Sophocleum*, rev. H. Genthe, 2nd edn., Leipzig–Berlin, 1872; rpt. 1958

Jebb, R. C., *Sophocles*, Cambridge, 1883–96; rpt., text only, 1897; rpt. unaltered, 1902–8, 1962; each play separately, with translation, 1883 onwards; three further volumes, edited by A. C. Pearson, containing the fragments, Cambridge, 1917

Kamerbeek, J. C., *Ajax, Trachiniae*, Leyden, 1953

Kapsomenos, S. G., *Sophocles' Trachinierinnen und ihr Vorbild*, Athens, 1963

Kirkwood, G. M., *A Study of Sophoclean Drama*, Cornell Studies in Classical Philology no. 31, Ithaca, N.Y., 1958

Kitto, H. D. F., *Sophocles, Dramatist and Philosopher*, London, 1958

Kitto, H. D. F., *Greek Tragedy*, 3rd edn., London, 1961

Knox, B. M. W., *The Heroic Temper: Studies in Sophoclean Tragedy*, Sather Lectures, no. 35, Berkeley, 1964

Lesky, A., in *Anzeiger für die Altertumswissenschaft*, Innsbruck, 1949–61, vols. 12–14 (for bibliography)

Lesky, A., *Die tragische Dichtung der Hellenen*, 3rd edn., Munich, 1972

Lukas, D. W., *Greek Tragic Poets*, 2nd edn., London, 1959

Masqueray, P., *Sophocle*, 2nd edn., Paris, 1929

Nauck, *TGF*, pp. 131f.

Page, *GLP*, pp. 12–53

Pearson, A. C., *Sophocles* (OCT), Oxford, 1924

Radt, S., *Tragicorum Graecorum Fragmenta*, 4th vol., Göttingen, 1977

Reindhardt, K., *Sophocles*, 3rd edn., Frankfurt/Main, 1947

Romilly, J. de, *L'évolution du pathétique d' Eschyle à Euripide*, Paris, 1961

Schadewaldt, W., *Sophokles und das Leid*, 4th edn., Potsdam, 1948

Schneidewin, F. W., Nauck, A., *Sophocles*, 3 vols., rev. E. Bruhn and L. Radermacher, 10th edn., Berlin, 1909–14

Waldock, A. J. A., *Sophocles the Dramatist*, Cambridge, 1951, rpt., 1966

Webster, T. B. L., *Introduction to Sophocles*, Oxford, 1936

Weinstock, H., *Sophokles*, 3rd edn., Wuppertal, 1948

Wilamowitz-Moellendorff, T. von, *Die dramatische Technik des Sophokles*, Berlin, 1917

EURIPIDES

Arnim, H. von, *Supplementum Euripideum* (including Satyrus' *Vita*), Bonn, 1913

Austin, C., *Nova Fragmenta Euripidea in Papyris Reperta*, Berlin, 1968

Barrett, W. S., *Euripides: Hippolytos*, Oxford, 1964

Bond, G. W., *Hypsipyle*, Oxford, 1963

Breitenbach, W., *Untersuchungen zur Sprache der euripideischen Lyrik*, Stuttgart, 1934

Burnett, A. P., *Catastrophe Survived*, Oxford, 1971

Campbell, A. Y., *Helen*, Liverpool, 1950

Cantarella, R., *I Cretesi*, Milan, 1964

Dale, A. M., *Euripides: Alcestis*, Oxford, 1954

Dale, A. M., *Euripides: Helen*, Oxford, 1967

Denniston, J. D., *Euripides: Electra*, Oxford, 1939

Diggle, J., *Euripides: Phaethon*, Cambridge, 1970

Dodds, E. R., *Euripides: Bacchae*, 2nd edn., Oxford, 1960

England, E. B., *Euripides: Iphigeneia in Aulis*, London, 1891

Grube, G. M. A., *The Drama of Euripides*, London, 1961

Handley, E. W., Rea, J., 'Euripides' Telephus', *Bulletin of the Institute of Classical Studies*, University of London, suppl. 5, London, 1957

Kitto, H. D. F., *Greek Tragedy*, 3rd edn., London, 1961

Lesky, A., *Anzeiger für die Altertumswissenschaft*, vol. 16, 1963, pp. 129f. (bibliography)

Lesky, A., *Die tragische Dichtung der Hellenen*, 3rd edn., Munich, 1972 (with bibliography of recent work)

Lucas, D. W., *The Greek Tragic Poets*, 2nd edn., London, 1959

Méridier, L., Grégoire, H., Parmentier, L., Chapouthier, F., Meunier, J., Goossens, R. and Jouan, F., *Euripide* (Budé), 7 vols., Paris, 1923

Murray, G., *Euripides: Fabulae* (OCT), 2nd edn., Oxford, 1910

Murray, G., *Euripides and his Age*, 2nd edn., Oxford, 1946

Nauck, A., *Euripides*, 3rd edn., Leipzig, 1913–21

Nauck, *TGF*, supplemented by B. Snell, 2nd edn. Holdesheim, 1964

Nestle, W., *Euripides, der Dichter der griechischen Aufklärung*, Stuttgart, 1901

Norwood, G., *Essays on Euripidean Drama*, London, 1954

Owen, A. S., *Euripides: Ion*, Oxford, 1939

Page, *GLP*, pp. 54f.

Page, D. L., *Actors' Interpolations in Greek Tragedy*, Oxford, 1934

Page, D. L., *Euripides: Medea*, Oxford, 1938

Paley, F. A., *Euripides*, 3 vols., 2nd edn., London, 1872–80

Pap. Oxy., vol. 27

Pearson, A. C., *Euripides: Helen*, Cambridge, 1903

Pearson, A. C., *Euripides: Phoenician Women*, Cambridge, 1909

Platnauer, M., *Euripides: Iphigeneia in Tauris*, Oxford, 1938

Pohlenz, M., *Die griechische Tragödie*, 2nd edn., Göttingen, 1954

Rivier, A., *Essai sur le tragique d'Euripide*, Lausanne, 1944

Romilly, J. de, *L'évolution du pathétique d'Eschyle à Euripide*, Paris, 1961

Schwartz, E., *Scholia in Euripidem*, 2 vols., Berlin, 1887–91

Séchan, E., *Études sur la tragédie grecque dans ses rapports avec la céramique*, Paris, 1926, rpt. 1967

Strohm, H., *Iphigeneia in Tauris*, Munich, 1949

Way, A. S., *Euripides* (Loeb), 4 vols., London, 1912; rpt. 1959

Weber, L., *Euripides: Alkestis*, Leipzig, 1930

Webster, T. B. L., *The Tragedies of Euripides*, London, 1968

Wilamowitz-Moeliendorff, U. von, *Heracles*, 2 vols., 2nd edn., Berlin, 1895

Wilamowitz-Moellendorff, U. von, *Euripides: Ion*, Berlin, 1926

Winnington-Ingram, R. P., *Euripides and Dionysus*, Cambridge, 1948

Zuntz, G., *The Political Plays of Euripides*, Manchester, 1955

Zürcher, W., *Die Darstellung des Menschen im Drama des Euripides*, Basle, 1947

THE LESSER TRAGEDIANS

Page, *GLP*, pp. 136f.

Webster, T. B. L., *Fourth Century Tragedy and the Poetics*, Wiesbaden, 1954

Webster, T. B. L., *Art and Literature in Fourth Century Athens*, London, 1956, rpt., 1969

PRATINAS

Brommer, F., *Satyrspiele*, 2nd edn., Berlin, 1959

Dale, A. M., in *Eranos*, vol. 48, 1950, pp. 14f.

Nauck, *TGF*, pp. 726–8

Pickard-Cambridge, A. W., *Dithyramb, Tragedy and Comedy*, rev. T. B. L. Webster, 2nd edn., Oxford, 1962, pp. 17f., 65f.
Pohlenz, M., *Das Satyrspiel und Pratinas von Phleius*, Göttingen, 1927, pp. 298–321

CHOERILUS

Nauck, *TGF*, pp. 719–20

PHRYNICHUS

Blumenthal, A. von, in Pauly–Wissowa, *REkA*, vol. 20, pp. 911f.
Freymuth, G., in *Philologus*, vol. 99, 1955, pp. 51f.
Léoni, A., 'Quelques aspects de la vie de Phrynichos d'après les autres anciens', *Annales de la Faculté des lettres et Sciences Humaines d'Aix*, Série classique, vol. 47, 1967
Lloyd-Jones, H., in *Cuadernos de la Fundactión Pastor*, vol. 13, Madrid, 1966, pp. 11–33.
Nauck, *TGF.*, pp. 720f.
Stoessl, F., in *Mus. Helvet.*, vol. 2, 1945, pp. 148f.

ION OF CHIOS

Blumenthal, A. von, *Ion von Chios*, Stuttgart–Berlin, 1939
Diehl, E., in Pauly–Wissowa, *REkA*, vol. 9, pp. 1861f.
Jacoby, F., in *Classical Quarterly*, vol. 41, 1947, pp. 1f.
Webster, T. B. L., in *Hermes*, vol. 71, 1936, pp. 263f.

CRITIAS

Nauck, *TGF*, pp. 770–5
Powell I. U., and Barber, E. A., in *New Chapters*, vol. 3, 1933, pp. 148f.
Wilamowitz-Moellendorff, U. von, *Analecta Euripidea*, Berlin, 1895, pp. 161f.

ASTYDAMAS

Nauck, *TGF*, pp. 777–80
Wilamowitz-Moellendorff, U. von, *Aischylos-Interpretationen*, Berlin, 1914, pp. 238f.

CHAEREMON

Nauck, *TGF*, pp. 781–92
Rhesus: in all treatments of Euripides
Ritchie, W., *The Authenticity of the Rhesus of Euripides*, Cambridge, 1964 (reviewed by E. Fraenkel in *Gnomon*, vol. 37, 1965, pp. 228–41)

CHAPTER 4: COMEDY

OLD COMEDY

Anagnostopoulos, G. P., Γλωσσικὰ ’Ανάλεκτα, ’Αθηνᾶ, 36, pp. 1f., 1924
Austin, C. (ed.), *Comici Graeci: Comicorum graecorum fragmenta in papyris reperta*, Berlin, 1973
Bieber, M., *History of the Greek and Roman Theatre*, Princeton, 1939, rpt., 1961

Breitholtz, L., *Die dorische Farce, im griechischen Mutterland vor dem 5 Jahrh.*, Stockholm, 1960

Buschor, E., 'Satyrtänze und frühes Drama', *Sitzungsberichte der Bayerischen Akademie der Wissenschaften, philos.–hist. Klasse*, Munich, 1943

Cornford, F. M., *The Origins of Attic Comedy*, London, 1914; 2nd edn., rev. T. H. Gaster, Gloucester, Mass., 1968

Croiset, M., *Aristophane et les parties à Athènes*, Paris, 1906; trs into English, J. Loeb, London, 1909

Demiańczuk, J., *Supplementum Comicum*, Cracow, 1912; rpt. Hildesheim, 1967

Dittmer, A., *The Fragments of Athenian Comic Didascaliae Found in Rome*, Leyden, 1923

Dover, K. J., in M. Platnauer (ed.), *Fifty Years (and Twelve) of Classical Scholarship*, Oxford, 1968, pp. 123f.

Edmonds, *FAC*

Geissler, P., *Die Chronologie der altattischen Komödie*, Berlin, 1925

Gelzer, T., *Der epirrhematische Agon bei Aristophanes*, Munich, 1960

Gomme, A. W., *Essays in Greek History and Literature*, Oxford, 1937, pp. 249–95

Herter, H., *Vom dionysischen Tanz zum komischen Spiel*, Iserlohn, 1949

Jachmann, G., *Plautinisches und attisches, Problemata 3*, Berlin, 1931, pp. 3f.

Kaibel, *CGF*, vol. 1

Keller, G., *Die Komödien des Aristophanes und die athenische Volksreligion seiner Zeit*, Tübingen, 1931

Kock, *CAF*

Kock, T., *De Personarum Comicorum Introductione*, Breslau, 1914

Körte, A., in Pauly–Wissowa, *REkA*, vol. 11, pp. 1207f.

Krause, F., *Quaestiones Aristophaneae Scaenicae*, Rostock, 1903

Kunst, K., *Studien zur griechisch–römischen Komödie*, Vienna–Leipzig, 1919

Legrand, É., *Daos*, Lyon–Paris, pp. 64–324

Lever, K., The Art of Greek Comedy, London, 1956

Meineke, *FCG*

Murray, G., *Aristophanes*, Oxford, 1933

Neil, R. A., *Knights*, Cambridge, 1909

Oellacher, H., in *Wien. Stud.*, vol. 38, 1916, pp. 81–157

Olivieri, *FCGM*, vol. 1

Page, *GLP*, pp. 194f.

Pickard-Cambridge, A. W., *The Theatre of Dionysus at Athens*, Oxford, 1953

Pickard-Cambridge, A. W., *Dithyramb, Tragedy and Comedy*, rev. T. B. L. Webster, 2nd ed., Oxford, 1962

Pickard-Cambridge, A. W., *The Dramatic Festivals of Athens*, rev. J. Gould and D. M. Lewis, 2nd edn., Oxford, 1973

Platnauer, M., 'Comedy', in *New Chapters in the History of Greek Literature*, 3rd series, Oxford, 1933

Platnauer, M., *Antistrophic Variations in Aristophanes*, in *Greek Poetry and Life*, Oxford, 1936, pp. 241f.

Radermacher, L., 'Zur Geschichte der griechischen Komödie', *Sitzungsberichte der Österreichischen Akademie der Wissenschaften in Wien, philos.–hist. Klasse*, vol. 102, no. 1, 1925

Roggwiller, A. E., *Dichter und Dichtung in der attischen Komödie*, Zurich, 1926

Suss, W., *De Personarum Antiquae Comodiae Atticae Usu atque Origine*, Bonn, 1905
Webster, T. B. L., in *Classical Quarterly*, vol. 42, 1948, pp. 15ff.
Webster, T. B. L., *The Masks of Greek Comedy*, London, 1949
Webster, T. B. L., 'Monuments Illustrating Old and Middle Comedy', *Bulletin of the Institute of Classical Studies*, University of London, suppl. 11, 1961
Wehrli, F., *Motivstudien zur griechischen Komödie*, Zurich–Leipzig, 1936
Weiher, A., *Philosophen und Philosophenspott in der attischen Komödie*, Munich, 1913
White, J. W., *The Verse of Greek Comedy*, London, 1912
Wilamowitz-Moellendorff, U. von, *Aristophanes: Lysistrata*, Berlin, 1922; rpt. 1958
Wilhelm, A., *Urkunden dramatischer Aufführungen in Athen*, Vienna, 1906
Wüst, E., in Pauly–Wissowa, *REkA*, vol. 20, pp. 292–306

The early comedians

EPICHARMUS

Berk, L., *Epicharmus*, Groningen, 1964
Kaibel, *CGF*, vol. 1, pp. 188f.
Olivieri, *FCGM*, vol. 1
Pickard-Cambridge, A. W., *Dithyramb, Tragedy and Comedy*, rev. T. B. L. Webster, 2nd edn., Oxford, 1962, pp. 230f.

SOPHRON

Breitholtz, L., *Die dorische Farce im griechischen Mutterland*, Stockholm, 1960
Kaibel, *CGF*, vol. 1, pp. 188f.
Körte, in Pauly–Wissowa, *REkA*, vol. 3, A, pp. 1100–3
Olivieri, *FCGM*, vol. 2, pp. 59–143
Page, *GLP*, p. 328
Papyri Greci e Latini, Publicazioni della Società Italiana per la ricerca dei papiri greci e latini in Egitto, vol. 11, 1935, no. 1214
Pickard Cambridge, A. W., *Dithyramb, Tragedy and Comedy*, rev. T. B. L. Webster, 2nd edn., Oxford, 1962

CRATINUS

Demiańczuk, J., *Supplementum Comicum*, Cracow, 1912, pp. 30f.
Edmonds, *FAC*, vol. 1, pp. 15f.
Kock, *CAF*, vol. 1, pp. 11f.
Körte, A., in Pauly–Wissowa, *REkA*, vol. 11, pp. 1647f.
Meineke, *FCG*, vol. 1, pp. 43f; vol. 2, pp. 15f.
Pieters, J. T., *Cratinus*, Leyden, 1946

CRATES

Demiańczuk, J., *Supplementum Comicum*, Cracow, 1912, p. 30
Edmonds, *FAC*, vol. 1, pp. 152f.
Kock, *CAF*, vol. 1, pp. 130f.
Meineke, *FCG*, vol. 1, pp. 233f.

PHERECRATES

Demiańczuk, J., *Supplementum Comicum*, Cracow, 1912, pp. 66f.

Edmonds, *FAC*, vol. 1, pp. 145f.
Kock, *CAF*, vol. 1, pp. 145f.
Meineke, *FCG*, vol. 2, pp. 252f.

TELECLIDES

Demiańczuk, J., *Supplementum Comicum*, Cracow, 1912, p. 86
Edmonds, *FAC*, vol. 1, pp. 180f.
Kock, *CAF*, vol. 1, pp. 209f.
Meineke, *FCG*, vol. 2, pp. 361f.

HERMIPPUS

Demiańczuk, J., *Supplementum Comicum*, Cracow, 1912, p. 53
Edmonds, *FAC*, vol. 1, pp. 284f.
Kock, *CAF*, vol. 1, pp. 224f.
Meineke, *FCG*, vol. 2, pp. 380f.

The golden age of Old Comedy

ARISTOPHANES

Boudreaux, P., *Le texte d'Aristophane et ses commentateurs*, Paris, 1919
Coulon, V., *Aristophane*, (Budé) 5 vols., Paris, 1923–30
Dover, K. J., in *Lustrum*, vol. 2, 1957, pp. 52f. (bibliography)
Dover, K. J., *Aristophanic Comedy*, London, 1972
Dübner, F., *Scholia*, Paris, 1877; rpt. Hildersheim, 1969
Dunbar, H., *A Complete Concordance to the Comedies and Fragments of Aristophanes*, Oxford, 1883
Ehrenberg, V., *The People of Aristophanes*, 2nd edn., Oxford, 1951
Gomme, A. W., in *Classical Review*, vol. 52, 1938 pp. 97f.
Holzinger, K. von, *Plutus*, Vienna, 1940
Koster, W. J. W., *Scholia in Aristophanem*, Gröningen, 1960
Leeuwen, J. van, *Aristophanes Nubes, Equites, Plutus, Thesmophoriazusae, Ecclesiazusae, Pax, Aves, Lysistrata*, Leyden, 1892–1906
Mazon, P., *Essai sur la composition des comédies d'Aristophane*, Paris, 1904
Murray, G. *Aristophanes*, Oxford, 1933
Newiger, H. J., 'Metapher und Allegorie: Studien zu Aristophanes', *Zetemata*, vol. 16, 1957
Platnauer, M., *Peace*, Oxford, 1964
Radermacher, L., *Die Frösche*, Vienna, 1921; rpt. 1954
Rogers, B. B., *The Peace of Aristophanes*, London, 1866; *Frogs*, London 1902; *Ecclesiazusae*, London, 1902; *Thesmophoriazusae*, London, 1904; *Plutus*, London, 1907; *Knights*, London, 1910; *Clouds*, London, 1910; *Wasps*, London, 1915; *Birds*, London, 1920
Russo, C. F., *Aristofane: autore di teatro*, Florence, 1962
Starkie, W. J. M., *Wasps*, London, 1897; *Acharnians*, London, 1909; *Clouds*, London, 1911
Süss, W., in *Rhen, Mus.*, vol. 97, 1954, pp. 115, 229, 289f.
Taillardat, J., *Les images d'Aristophane; études de langue et de style*, 2nd edn., Paris, 1965

Todd, O. J., *Index Aristophaneus*, Cambridge, Mass., 1932
Wilamowitz-Moellendorff, U. von, *Aristophanes: Lysistrate*, Berlin, 1927; rpt. 1958

EUPOLIS

Demiańczuk, J., *Supplementum Comicum*, Cracow, 1912, pp. 43, 117
Edmonds, *FAC*, vol. 1, pp. 310f. (unreliable in Δῆμοι)
Geissler, P., *Die Chronologie der altattischen Komödie*, Berlin, 1925
Kock, *CAF*, vol. 1, pp. 258f.
Meineke, *FCG*, vol. 1, pp. 104f.; vol. 2, pp. 426f.
Page, *GLP*, pp. 202f.
Pap. Oxy., 1240
Papyri Greci e Latini, Publicazioni della Società Italiana per la ricerca dei papiri greci e latini in Egitto, vol. 11, 1935, p. 111, no. 1213, (Προσπάλτιοι)
Wilamowitz-Moellendorff, U. von, *Aristophanes: Lysistrate*, Berlin, 1927, pp. 44–51

PHRYNICHUS

Anon., *de Com.*, 10
Demiańczuk, J., *Supplementum Comicum*, Cracow, 1912, pp. 74f.
Edmonds, *FAC*, vol. 1, pp. 450f.
Kock, *CAF*, vol. 1, pp. 369f.
Meineke, *FCG*, vol. 2, pp. 580f.

PLATO

Demiańczuk, J., *Supplementum Comicum*, Cracow, 1912, pp. 76f.
Edmonds, *FAC*, vol. 1, pp. 488f.
Geissler, P., *Die Chronologie der altattischen Komödie*, Berlin, 1925
Giannini, A., in *Dioniso*, vol. 19, 1956, pp. 232f; vol. 22, 1959, pp. 189f.
Kock, *CAF*, vol. 1, pp. 601f.
Korte, A., in Pauly–Wissowa, *RFkA*, vol. 20, pp. 2537f.
Meineke, *FCG*, vol. 2, pp. 615f.

PHILONIDES

Demiańczuk, J., *Supplementum Comicum*, Cracow, 1912, p. 73
Edmonds, *FAC*, vol. 1, pp. 564f.
Kock, *CAF*, vol. 1, pp. 254f.
Meineke, *FCG*, vol. 2, pp. 421f.

HEGEMON OF THASOS

Brandt, P. (ed), *Corpusculum poesis epicae Graecae ludibundae*, Leipzig, 1888, vol. I, pp. 37f.
Edmonds, *FAC*, vol. 1, pp. 810f.
Kock, *CAF*, vol. 1, p. 700
Meineke, *FCG*, vol. 1, pp. 214f.; vol. 2, p. 743
Schachermeyr, E., in *Sitzungsberichte der Österreichischen Akademie der Wissenschaften in Wien*, vol. 247, no. 5, p. 5.
Wilamowitz-Moellendorff, U. von, in *Kleine Schriften*, Berlin, 1971, vol. 4, p. 219

MIDDLE COMEDY

Austin, C. (ed.), *Comici Graeci: Comicorum Graecorum fragmenta in papyris reperta*, Berlin, 1973

Dover, K. J., in M. Platnauer (ed.), *Fifty Years (and Twelve) of Classical Scholarship*, Oxford, 1968, pp. 96f.

Fraenkel, E., *De Media et Nova Comoedia Quaestiones Selectae*, Göttingen, 1912

Kock, *CAF*, vol. 2

Lever, K., in *Classical Journal*, vol. 49, 1953–4, pp. 167f.

Maidment, K. J., in *Classical Quarterly*, vol. 29, 1935, pp. 1f.

Meineke, *FCG*, vol. 1

Olivieri, *FCGM*, vol. 2

Page, *GLP*, pp. 230f.

Webster, T. B. L., in *Classical Quarterly*, n. s., vol. 2, 1952, pp. 13f.

Webster, T. B. L., *Studies in Later Greek Comedy*, Manchester, 1953

Webster, T. B. L., 'Monuments Illustrating Old and Middle Comedy', *Bulletin of the Institute of Classical Studies*, University of London, suppl. 11, 1961

Wehrli, F., *Motivstudien zur griechischen Komödie*, Zurich–Leipzig, 1936

Wilhelm, A., *Urkunden dramatischer Aufführungen in Athen*, Vienna, 1906

Celebrated poets of Middle Comedy

ANTIPHANES

Demiańczuk, J., *Supplementum Comicum*, Cracow, 1912, p. 8
Edmonds, *FAC*, vol. 2, pp. 162f.
Kock, *CAF*, vol. 2, pp. 12f.
Meineke, *FCG*, vol. 3, pp. 3f.

ANAXANDRIDES

Demiańczuk, J., *Supplementum Comicum*, Cracow, 1912, p. 7
Edmonds, *FAC*, vol. 2, pp. 161f.
Kock, *CAF*, vol. 2, pp. 135f.
Meineke, *FCG*, vol. 3, pp. 161f.

EUBULUS

Demiańczuk, J., *Supplementum Comicum*, Cracow, 1912, pp. 40f.
Fedele, D., in *Dioniso*, n.s., vol. 10, 1947, pp. 137f.
Kock, *CAF*, vol. 2, pp. 164f.
Meineke, *FCG*, vol. 3, pp. 203f.

ALEXIS

Demiańczuk, J., *Supplementum Comicum*, Cracow, 1912, p.7
Kock, *CAF*, vol. 2, pp. 297f.; vol. 3, p. 744
Meineke, *FCG*, vol. 3, pp. 382f.
Page, *GLP*, pp. 232f.

TIMOCLES

Demiańczuk, J., *Supplementum Comicum*, Cracow, 1912, pp. 88f.

Edmonds, *FAC*, vol. 2, pp. 6oof.
Kock, *CAF*, vol. 2, pp. 451f.
Körte, A., in Pauly–Wissowa, *REkA*, vol. 4, A. pp. 126of.
Meineke, *FCG*, vol. 3, pp. 59of.

CHAPTER 5: LATER LYRIC, ELEGIAC AND EPIC POETRY

LYRIC POETRY

Pickard-Cambridge, A. W., *Dithyramb, Tragedy and Comedy*, rev. T. B. L. Webster, 2nd edn., Oxford, 1962
Schönewolf, H., *Der jungattische Dithyrambos* (Diss.), Giessen, 1938
Wilamowitz-Moellendorff, U. von, *Timotheos, Die Perser*, Leipzig, 1903

DIAGORAS OF MELOS

Diehl, *ALG*², vol. 2, 5, pp. 126f.

MELANIPPIDES OF MELOS

Diehl, *ALG*², vol. 2, 5, pp. 153f.
Grande, C. del, *Ditirambografi*, Naples, 1946, pp. 37f.
Maas, P., in Pauly–Wissowa, *REkA*, vol. 15, pp. 422f.
Page, *PMG*, pp. 390–402

PHILOXENUS OF CYTHERA

Grande, C. del, *Ditirambografi*, Naples, 1946, pp. 66f.
Page, *PMG*, pp. 423–32

TIMOTHEUS

Diehl, *ALG*², vol. 2, 5, pp. 134f.
Edmonds, J. M., *Lyra Graeca* (Loeb), 3rd edn., London, 1940, pp. 28of.
Grande, C. del, *Ditirambografi*, Naples, 1946, pp. 83f.
Oellacher, H., *Papyrus Erzherzog Reiner*, n.s., vol. 1, 1932, p. 136
Schönewolf, H., *Der jungattische Dithyrambos* (Diss.). Giessen, 1938
Page, *PMG*, pp. 399f.
Wilamowitz-Moellendorff, U. von, *Timotheos, Die Perser*, Leipzig, 1903

LICYMNIUS OF CHIOS

Diehl, *ALG*², vol. 2, 5, pp. 131f.
Page, *PMG*, pp. 396f.

ELEGIAC AND EPIC POETRY

DIONYSIUS CHALCUS

Diehl, *ALG*³, vol. 1, 1, pp. 88f.
Garzya, A., in *Rivista di filologia e di instruzione classica*, vol. 80, 1952, pp. 193f.

Reitzenstein, R., *Epigramm und Skolion*, Giessen, 1893
Wilamowitz-Moellendorff, U. von, *Hellenistische Dichtung*, Berlin, 1924, vol. 1, pp. 97f.

CRITIAS

Diehl, *ALG*³, vol. 1, 1, pp. 94f.
Diels, H., *Fragmente der Vorsokratiker*, ed. W. Kranz, 4 vols., 6th edn., Berlin, 1951, no. 88
Nauck, *TGF*, pp. 770–5
Pack, *GLLT* pp. 254, 428, 452–3, 1456
Powell, I. U., Barber, E. A., *New Chapters in the History of Greek Literature*, 3rd series, Oxford, 1933, vol. 3, p. 148f.
Treu, M., in Pauly–Wissowa, *REkA*, vol. 9, A, pp. 1944f.

ANTIMACHUS

Diehl, *ALG*³, vol. 1, 1, pp. 100f.
Hiersche, G. R., 'Wörter und Formen der Fragmente erhaltenen hellenistischen Epik' (Diss.), Jena, 1952 (typescript)
Pap. Oxy., vol. 30
Puelma, M., in *Philologus*, vol. 101, 1957, pp. 90f.
Trüb, J., *Kataloge in der griechischen Dichtung*, Oberwinterthur, 1952, pp. 74f.
Wyss, B., *Antimachi Colophonii Reliquiae*, Berlin, 1936

ARCHESTRATUS

Brandt, P. (ed.), *Corpusculum Poesis Epicae Graecae Ludibundae*, Leipzig, 1888, vol. 1, pp. 114f.

ERINNA

Bowra, C. M., *Problems in Greek Poetry*, Oxford, 1953, pp. 151f.
Crump, M. M., *The Epyllion from Theocritus to Ovid*, Oxford, 1931
Diehl, *ALG*², vol. 1, 4, pp. 207f.
Latte, K., in *Nachrichten der Akademie der Wissenschaften in Göttingen philol.–hist. Klasse*, Göttingen, 1953, pp. 79f.
Maas, P., in *Hermes*, vol. 69, 1934, pp. 206f.
Pomeroy, S. P., in *Zeitschrift für Papyrologie und Epigraphik*, vol. 32, 1978, pp. 17f.
West, M. L., in *Zeitschrift für Papyrologie und Epigraphik*, vol. 25, 1977, pp. 95f.

PART TWO: THE HELLENISTIC AGE

GENERAL BIBLIOGRAPHY

Barber, E. A., *Hellenistic Poetry in the Hellenistic Age*, Cambridge, 1923
Barber, E. A., *The Cambridge Ancient History*, vol. 7, Cambridge, 1928, ch. 8, pp. 249f.
Barber, E. A., 'Hellenistic Poetry', and appendix by G. Giangrande, in M. Platnauer (ed.), *Fifty Years (and Twelve) of Classical Scholarship*, Oxford, 1968

Biese, A., *Die Entwicklung des Naturgefühls bei den Griechen und Römern*, 2 vols., Kiel, 1882–4

Cessi, C., *La poesia ellenistica*, Bari, 1912

Couat, A., *La poésie alexandrine sous les trois premiers Ptolémées*, Paris, 1882; English translation by J. Loeb, London, 1931

Herter, H., 'Das Kind im Zeitalter des Hellenismus', *Bonner Jahrbücher*, vol. 132, 1927

Herter, H., in *Burs. Jahresb.*, vol. 255, 1937, pp. 65–217

Herter, H., in *Burs. Jahresb.*, vol. 285, 1944–5, pp. 213–410

Knaack, G., in Pauly–Wissowa, *REkA*, vol. 1, pp. 1399–1407

Körte, A., *Hellenistische Dichtung*, Leipzig, 1925; trs. J. Hammer and M. Hadas, New York, 1929 (with bibliography)

Körte, A., and Händel, P., *Die Hellenistische Dichtung*, Stuttgart, 1960

Legrand, É., *La poésie alexandrine*, Paris, 1924

Meineke, A., *Analecta Alexandrina sive Commentationes de Euphorione Chalcidensi, Rhiano Cretensi, Alexandro Aetolo, Parthenio Nicaeno*, Berlin, 1843

Pfeiffer, R., *Ausgewählte Schriften*, Munich, 1960, pp. 148f.

Powell, J. U., Barber, E. A. (eds.), *New Chapters in the History of Greek Literature*, vol. 1, Oxford, 1921; vol. 2, Oxford, 1929; vol. 3, Oxford, 1933

Reizenstein, R., *Epigramm und Skolion*, Giessen, 1893

Rohde, E., *Der griechische Roman*, 3rd edn., Leipzig, 1914

Rostagni, A., *Poeti alessandrini*, Turin, 1916

Susemihl, F., *Geschichte der griechischen Literatur in der Alexandrinerzeit*, 2 vols., Leipzig 1891–2

Tarn, W. W., *Hellenistic Civilisation*, 2nd edn., London, 1930

Webster, T. B. L., *Hellenistic Poetry and Art*, New York, 1964

Wendland, P., *Die hellenistisch–römische Kultur in ihren Beziehungen zum Judentum und Christentum*, 3rd edn., Tübingen, 1912

Wilamowitz-Moellendorff, U. von, *Hellenistische Dichtung in der Zeit des Kallimachos*, 2 vols., Berlin, 1924

Wright, F. A., *A History of Later Greek Literature*, London, 1932

Section I: The Alexandrian Age (323–146 B.C.)

CHAPTER 6: NEW COMEDY

THE STRUCTURE AND PREOCCUPATIONS OF NEW COMEDY

Demiańczuk, J., *Supplementum Comicum*, Cracow, 1912

Edmonds, *FAC*

Fraenkel, E., 'Plautinisches im Plautus', *Philologische Untersuchungen*, vol. 28, 1922; Italian translation with important appendices, 1960

Gomme, A. W., *Essays in Greek History and Literature*, Oxford, 1937

Kock, *CAF*

Krysiniel-Jósefowicz, B., *De Quibusdam Plauti Exemplaribus Graecis, Philemo-Plautus*, Torún, 1949

Legrand, É., *Daos*, Lyons–Paris, 1910

Meineke, *FCG*

Murray, G., *Aristophanes*, Oxford, 1933

Page, *GLP*

Schroeder, O., *Novae Comoediae Fragmenta in Papyris Reperta Exceptis Menandreis*, Bonn, 1915

Webster, T. B. L., *Greek Theatre Productions*, London, 1956

Webster, T. B. L., 'Monuments Illustrating New Comedy', *Bulletin of the Institute of Classical Studies*, University of London, suppl. 11, 1961

Webster, T. B. L., *Studies in Later Greek Comedy*, 2nd edn., Manchester, 1970

THE POETS OF NEW COMEDY

MENANDER

Allinson, F. G., *Menander* (Loeb), London, 1951

Arnott, W. G., *Menander* (Loeb), vol. 1, Cambridge, Mass.–London, 1979

Barns, J. W., 'Misogynes', in *The Antinoopolis Papyri*, Part 2, no. 5, London, 1960, pp. 8–29

Bruhn, C., *Über den Wortschatz des Menander* (Diss.) Kiel, 1910

Capps, E., *Four Plays of Menander*, Boston, 1910

Dedoussi, C., *Samia*, Athens, 1965

Demiańczuk, J., *Supplementum Comicum*, Cracow, 1912, pp. 54f.

Dittmar, W., *Sprachliche Untersuchungen zu Aristophanes und Menander*, Leipzig, 1933

Dohm, H., *Mageiros*, Munich, 1964

Durham, D. B., *The Vocabulary of Menander*, Princeton, 1913 (Diss.)

Edmonds, *FAC*

Fraenkel, E., 'Plautinisches im Plautus', *Philologische Untersuchungen*, vol. 28, 1922, p. 374

Gomme, A. W., and Sanbach, F. H., *Menander, a Commentary*, Oxford, 1973

Handley, E. W., *The Dyscolos of Menander*, London, 1965

Handley, E. W., 'Dis Exapaton', *Bulletin of the Institute of Classical Studies*, University of London, suppl. 15, 1968

Jacques, J. M., *Dyscolos* (Budé), Paris, 1963

Jaekel, S., *Menandri Sententiae*, Leipzig, 1964

Kassel, R., *Menander: Sicyonius*, Berlin, 1965

Körte, A., *Menander: Reliquiae*, vol. 1, Leipzig, 1938 (with supplement by A. Thierfelder, 1957); vol. 2, ed. A. Thierfelder, 1959

Körte, A., in Pauly–Wissowa, *REkA*, vol. 15, pp. 707f.

Kraus, W., 'Menanders Dyscolos', *Sitzungsberichte der Österreichischen Akademie der Wissenschaften in Wien*, vol. 234, 1960

Leeuven, J. van, *Menandri Fabularum Reliquiae*, Leyden, 1919

Lloyd-Jones, P. H., *Dyscolos*, Oxford, 1960

Sandbach, F. H., *Menander, Reliquiae Selectae*, Oxford, 1972

Sehrt, A., *De Menandro Euripidis Imitatore*, Giessen, 1912 (Diss.)

Turner, E. G., 'New Fragments of the Misumenos of Menander', *Bulletin of the Institute of Classical Studies*, University of London, suppl. 17, 1965

Turner, E. G., in *Proceedings of the British Academy*, vol. 63, 1977, pp. 314f.

Webster, T. B. L., *Studies in Menander*, 2nd edn., Manchester, 1960

Webster, T. B. L., *An Introduction to Menander*, London, 1974
Wilamowitz-Moellendorff, U. von, *Menander: das Schiedsgericht*, 2nd edn., Berlin, 1958
Zucker. F., *Der Hellenismus in der deutschen Forschung 1938–48*, Wiesbaden, 1956, vol. 1

PHILEMON

Demiańczuk, J., *Supplementum Comicum*, Cracow, 1912, p. 717
Dietze, C. A., *De Philemone Comico*, Göttingen, 1901
Edmonds, *FAC*, vol. 3, pp. 2f.
Kock, *CAF*, vol. 2, pp. 478f.; vol. 3, pp. 749f.
Krysiniel-Jósefowicz, B., *De Quibusdam Plauti Exemplaribus Graecis, Philemo–Plautus*, Torún, 1949
Meineke, *FCG*, vol. 4, pp. 3f.
Page, *GLP*, no. 50
Rapisarda, E., *Filemone Comico*, Milan, 1939
Webster, T. B. L., *Studies in Later Greek Comedy*, 2nd edn., Manchester 1970, pp. 125f.

DIPHILUS OF SINOPE

Coppola, G., in *Atene e Roma*, n. s., vol. 5, 1924, pp. 185f.
Demiańczuk, F., *Supplementum Comicum*, Cracow, 1912, p. 40
Edmonds, *FAC*, vol. 3A, pp. 96f.
Friedrich, W. H., in *Zetemata*, vol. 5, Munich, 1953
Kock, *CAF*, vol., 2, pp. 541f.
Marigo, A., in *Studi Italiani di Filologia Classica*, 1907, pp. 375f.
Meineke, *FCG*, vol. 4, pp. 375f.
Webster, T. B. L., *Studies in later Greek Comedy*, 2nd edn., Manchester, 1970, pp. 152–83

APOLLODORUS OF CARYSTUS

Demiańczuk, J., *Supplementum Comicum*, Cracow, 1912, pp. 8f.
Edmonds, *FAC*, vol. 3A, pp. 184f.
Kock, *CAF*, vol. 3, pp. 280f.
Krause, E. F., *De Apollodoris Comicis*, Berlin, 1903
Kuiper, W. E. J., 'Two Comedies of Apollodorus of Carystus', *Mnemosyne*, suppl. 1, 1938
Meineke, *FCG*, vol. 4, pp. 440f.
Mras, K., in *Anzeiger der Österreichischen Akademie der Wissenschaften in Wien, philos.–hist. Klasse*, 1948, pp. 184f.
Page, *GLP*, no. 58
Posani, M. R., in *Atene e Roma*, series 3, vol. 44, 1942, pp. 141f.
Schadewaldt, W., in *Hermes*, vol. 66, 1931, pp. 1f.
Schuster, M., *De Apollodoris Poetis Comicis*, Vienna–Neustadt, 1907
Webster, T. B. L., *Later Greek Comedy*, 2nd edn., Manchester, 1970, pp. 205f.

POSIDIPPUS

Edmonds, *FAC*, vol. 3A, pp. 228f.

Heintze, H. von, in *Röm. Mitteilungen*, vol. 68, 1961, pp. 8of.
Kock, *CAF*, vol. 3, pp. 335f.
Körte, A., in Pauly–Wissowa, *REkA*, vol. 22, p. 426
Meineke, *FCG*, vol. 1, pp. 482f.

CHAPTER 7: ALEXANDRIAN ELEGY

Alfonsi, L. in *Miscellanea di studi alessandrini in memoria di A. Rostagni*, Turin, 1963, pp. 454f.
Barigazzi, A., in *Maia*, vol. 3, 1950, pp. 16f.
Crusius, O., in Pauly–Wissowa, *REkA*, vol. 5, pp. 2260–307
Day, A. A., *The Origins of Latin Love-Elegy*, Oxford, 1938
Gigante, M., in *Rivista di filologia classica*, vol. 82, 1954, pp. 67f.
Grande, C. del, in *Miscellanea di studi alessandrini in memoria di A. Rostagni*, Turin, 1963, pp. 225f.
Groningen, B. A. Van, *Euphorion*, Amsterdam, 1947
Heinze, R., *Ovids elegische Erzählung*, Leipzig, 1919 (*Berichte der Sächsischen Gesellschaft der Wissenschaften*, vol. 71, 7, 1919)
Pack, *GLLT*
Powell, I. U., *Collectanea Alexandrina*, Oxford, 1925
Puelma, M., in *Mus. Helvet.*, vol. 11, 1954, pp. 101f.
Rohde, E., *Der griechische Roman*, 3rd edn., Leipzig, 1914
Rostagni, A., *Scritti Minori*, vol. 2, pt. 2 (*Romana*), Turin, 1956, pp. 23f.
Skutsch, F., in Pauly–Wissowa, *REkA*, vol. 6, p. 1177 (s.v. Euphorion)
Webster, T. B. L., *Hellenistic Poetry and Art*, New York, 1964
Zimmermann, F., in *Hermes*, vol. 69, 1934, pp. 179–89
Zucker, F., *Der Hellenismus in der deutschen Forschung, 1938–48* Wiesbaden, 1956, vol. 1

ALEXANDRIAN ELEGY BEFORE CALLIMACHUS

PHILETAS

Barigazzi, A., in *Hermes*, vol. 84, 1956, pp. 162f.
Diehl, *ALG²*, vol. 2, 6, pp. 49–55
Ellenberger, O., *Quaestiones Hermesianacteae* (Diss.), Giessen, 1907
Kuchenmüller, G., *Philitae Coi Fragmenta Poetica* (Diss.), Berlin, 1928
Nowacki, A., *Philitae Coi Fragmenta Poetica* (Diss.), Münster, 1927
Pap. Oxy., 2260 (L. Alfonsi, in *Aegyptus*, vol. 34, 1954, pp. 211f.)
Powell, *CA*, pp. 90–6
Puelma, M., in *Philologus*, vol. 101, 1951, pp. 90f.
Wimmel, W., in *Hermes*, vol. 86, 1958, pp. 346f.

HERMESIANAX OF COLOPHON

Crusius, O., in Pauly–Wissowa, *REkA*, vol. 5, p. 2281
Diehl, *ALG²*, vol. 2, 6, pp. 56–64
Heibges, St., in Pauly–Wissowa, *REkA*, vol. 8, pp. 823–8

Heinze, R., *Ovids elegische Erzählung*, Leipzig, 1919 (*Berichte der Sächsischen Gesellschaft der Wissenschaften*, vol. 71, 7, 1919)

PHANOCLES

Diehl, *ALG²*, vol. 2, 6, pp. 71–3
Powell, *CA*, pp. 106–9

ALEXANDER AETOLUS

Diehl, *ALG²*, vol. 2, 6, pp. 74f.
Powell, *CA*, pp. 121–30

CALLIMACHUS THE CYRENIAN

Barigazzi, A., in *Hermes*, vol. 86, 1958, pp. 453–77
Bartoletti, V., in *Miscellanea di studi alessandrini in memoria di A. Rostagni*, Turin, 1963, pp. 262f.
Brink, K. O., in *Classical Quarterly*, vol. 40, 1946, pp. 11f.
Cahen, É., *Callimaque et son oeuvre poétique*, Paris, 1929
Cahen, É., *Les hymnes de Callimaque*, Paris, 1930
Capovilla, G., *Callimaco*, Rome, 1967
Colonna, A., in *Athenaeum* (Pavia), n.s., vol. 30, 1952, pp. 191f.
Coppola, G., in *Rendiconti dell'Accademia delle Scienze dell'Istituto di Bologna, Classe di sc. mor.*, 3rd series, vol. 7, 1932–3, pp. 30f.
Coppola, G., *Cirene e il nuovo Callimaco*, Bologna, 1935
Corbato, C., *Note Callimachee*, Trieste, 1958
Dawson, C. M., in *Yale Classical Studies*, vol. 11, 1950, pp. 1f.
Desrousseux, A. M., in *Revue des études grecques*, vol. 53, 1940, pp. 145f.
Eichgrün, E., *Kallimachos und Apollonios Rhodios* (Diss.), Berlin, 1961
Erbse, H., in *Hermes*, vol. 83, 1955, pp. 411–28
Fränkel, H., *Der kallimacheische und der homerische Hexameter*, Göttingen, 1926
Gallavotti, C., in *Studi Italiani di filologia classica*, n.s., vol. 11, 1934, pp. 81–96
Gallavotti, C., *Callimacho, il libro dei Giambi*, Naples, 1946
Gallavotti, C., in *Gnomon*, vol. 29, 1957, pp. 423f. (review of Pap. Oxy., vol. 23, 1956)
Gow–Page, *HE*, vol. 1, pp. 57f.; vol. 2, pp. 151f.
Herter, H., in Pauly–Wissowa, *REkA*, suppl. 5, pp. 184f.
Herter, H., *Kallimachos und Homer*, Bonn, 1929
Herter, H., in *Burs. Jahresb.*, vol. 255, 1937, I pp. 65f.
Herter, H., in *Burs. Jahresb.*, vol. 285, 1944–5, pp. 224f.
Heumann, J., *De Epyllio Alexandrino* (Diss.), Leipzig, 1904
Howald, E., *Der Dichter Kallimachos von Kyrene*, Erlenbach–Zurich, 1943
Howald, E., Staiger, E., *Kallimachos, Dichtungen*, Zurich, 1955
Kapp, I., *Callimachi Hecalae fragmenta* (Diss.), Berlin, 1915
Knox, A. D., in *Philologus*, vol. 81, 1926, pp. 241f.; cf. *Classical Review*, vol. 39, 1925, pp. 13f.
Krafft, F., in *Hermes*, vol. 86, 1958, pp. 471–80
Lapp, F., *De Callimachi Cyrenaei Tropis et Figuris* (Diss.), Bonn, 1965
Lavagnini, B., *Da Mimnermo a Callimaco*, Turin, 1950

Lobel, E., Pap. Oxy., vol. 23, 1956, pp. 89–96

Mair, A. W., *Callimachus* (Loeb), London, 1921

McKay, K. J., *Erysichthon, a Callimachean Comedy* (Diss.), Utrecht (Leyden), 1962

McKay, K. J., in *Mnemosyne*, vol. 16, 1963, pp. 243f.

Mühll, P. von der, 'Die Zeit des Apollonhymnos des Kallimachos', *Mus. Helvet.*, vol. 15, 1958

Pack, *GLLT*, pp. 28f.

Pfeiffer, R., *Kallimachos Studien*, Munich, 1922

Pfeiffer, R., *Die neuen Diegeseis zu Kallimachosgedichten*, Munich, 1934

Pfeiffer, R., *Callimachus*, 2 vols., Oxford, 1949, 1953

Puelma, M., *Lucilius und Kallimachos*, Frankfurt/Main, 1949

Puelma, M., in *Philologus*, vol. 101, 1957, p. 95

Rostagni, A., in *Rivista di filologia classica*, vol. 61, 1933, pp. 189f.

Schlatter, G., *Theokrit und Kallimachos* (Diss.), Zurich, 1941

Smotrytsch, A. P., in *Helicon*, vol. 1, 1961, pp. 661f.

Smotrytsch, A. P., in *Miscellanea di studi alessandrini in memoria di A. Rostagni*, Turin, 1963, pp. 249f.

Treu, M., in *Miscellanea di studi alessandrini in memoria di A. Rostagni*, Turin, 1963, pp. 273f.

Trypanis, C. A., *Callimachi Fragmenta* (Loeb), London, 1958, rpt., Cambridge, Mass.-London, 1975

Vico, G. de, *Giornale italiano di filologia*, vol. 6, 1953, pp. 252f.

Wilamowitz-Moellendorff, U. von, *Hellenistische Dichtung in der Zeit des Kallimachos*, Berlin, 1924

Wimmel, W., in *Hermes*, vol. 86, 1958, p. 349

Wimmel, W., 'Kallimachos in Rom', *Hermes Einzelschriften*, 16, 1960

ALEXANDRIAN ELEGY AFTER CALLIMACHUS

ERATOSTHENES OF CYRENE

Hiller, E., *Eratosthenis Carminum Reliquae*, Leipzig, 1872

Keller, G. A., *Eratosthenes und die alexandrinische Sterndichtung* (Diss.), Zurich, 1946

Maass, E., *Analecta Eratosthenica*, Berlin, 1883

Merkelbach, R., in *Miscellanea di studi alessandrini in memoria di A. Rostagni*, Turin, 1963, pp. 469f.

Olivieri, A., *Mythographi Graeci*, Leipzig, 1897, vol. 3, pt. 1

Powell, *CA*, pp. 58f.

Solmsen, F., in *Transactions of the American Philological Association*, vol. 78, 1947, pp. 252f.

Thalamas, A., *La géographie d'Ératosthène* (Diss.), Paris, 1921

CHAPTER 8: THE ALEXANDRIAN EPIC

Bühler, W., 'Die Europa des Moschos. Text, Übersetzung und Kommentar', *Hermes*, Einzelschriften, Heft 13, 1960

Carspecken, J. F., in *Yale Classical Studies*, vol. 13, 1952, pp. 33f.

Crump, M. M., *The Epyllion from Theocritus to Ovid*, Oxford, 1931

Drögemüller, H.-P., *Die Gleichnisse im hellenistischen Epos* (Diss.), Hamburg, 1956

Heinze, R., *Virgils epische Technik*, 4th edn., Stuttgart, 1957

Heumann, J., *De Epyllio Alexandrino* (Diss.), Leipzig, 1904

Huber, G., *Lebensschilderung und Kleinmalerei im hellenistischen Epos* (Diss.), Basle, 1926

Legrand, É., *La poésie alexandrine*, Paris, 1924

Lesky, A., in *Wien. Stud.*, vol. 63, 1948, pp. 22–68

Mayhoff, C., *Di Rhiani Cretensis Studiis Homericis*, Leipzig, 1870

Meineke, A., *Analecta Alexandrina*, Berlin, 1843

Powell, J. U., 'Epica Adespota', in *CA*, pp. 71f.

Radermacher, L., *Mythos und Sage bei den Griechen*, 2nd edn., Brünn–Munich–Vienna, 1938

Westerink, L. G., in *Mnemosyne*, vol. 13, 1960, pp. 329f.

Wilamowitz-Moellendorff, U. von, *Hellenistische Dichtung in der Zeit des Kallimachos*, Berlin, 1924

Ziegler, K., *Das hellenistische Epos*, 2nd edn., Leipzig, 1966

THE *EPYLLION*

EUPHORION

Alfonsi, L., in *Miscellanea di studi alessandrini in memoria di A. Rostagni*, Turin, 1963, pp. 454f.

Barigazzi, A., in *Athenaeum*, vol. 16, 1948, pp. 34f.

Barigazzi, A., in *Maia*, vol. 3, 1950, pp. 16f.

Barigazzi, A., in *Rivista di filologia e di istruzióne classica*, vol. 92, 1964, pp. 288f.

Bartoletti, V., *Papyri Greci e Latini*, vol. 14, Florence, 1957, no. 1390

Carden, R. J. D., in *Bulletin of the Institute of Classical Studies*, University of London, vol. 16, 1969, pp. 29f.

Crump, M. M., *The Epyllion from Theocritus to Ovid*, Oxford, 1931

Groningen, A. van, *Euphorion*, Amsterdam, 1977

Latte, K., in *Philologus*, vol. 90, 1935, pp. 129f.

Meineke, A., *Analecta Alexandrina*, Berlin, 1843, pp. 3f.

Page, *GLP*, pp. 486f.

Pap. Oxy., 2526

Powell, *CA*, pp. 28f.

Scheidweiler, E., *Euphorionis Fragmenta* (Diss.), Bonn, 1908

Skutsch, F., in Pauly–Wissowa, *REkA*, vol. 6, pp. 1174f.

Treves, P., *Euforione e la storia ellenistica*, Milan, 1955

Westerink, L. G., in *Mnemosyne*, vol. 13, 1960, pp. 329f.

THE LONG ALEXANDRIAN EPIC

APOLLONIUS RHODIUS

Ardizzoni, A., *Apollonio Rodio, Le Argonautiche, Libro III*, Rome, 1958; *Libro I*, Rome, 1967

Delage, E., *La géographie dans Les Argonautiques d'Apollonius de Rhodes*, Bordeaux–Paris, 1930

Eichgrün, E., *Kallimachos und Apollonios Rhodios* (Diss.), Berlin, 1961

Erbse, H., in *Hermes*, vol. 81, 1953, pp. 163–96

Faerber, H., *Zur dichterischen Kunst in Apollonios Rhodios Argonautica (Die Gleichnisse)* (Diss.), Berlin, 1932

Fränkel, H., *Die Handschriften der Argonautika des Apoll. Rhodios*, Göttingen, 1929

Fränkel, H., in *Mus. Helvet.*, vol. 14, 1957, pp. 1f.

Fränkel, H., in *Mus. Helvet.*, vol. 17, 1960, pp. 1–20

Fränkel, H., *Apollonius Rhodius* (OCT), Oxford, 1961

Fränkel, H., *Noten zu den Argonautika des Apollonios*, Munich, 1968

Gillies, M. M., *The Argonautica of Apollonios Rhodios, Book III*, Cambridge, 1928

Händel, P., 'Beobachtungen zur epischen Technik des Apollonios Rhodios', *Zetemata*, vol. 7, Munich, 1954

Herter, H., in *Rhein. Mus.*, vol. 91, 1942, pp. 310–26

Herter, H., in *Burs. Jahresb.*, 285, 1944–5, pp. 213–410

Hübscher, P. A., *Die Charakteristik der Personen in Apollonius Argonatika* (Diss.), Freiburg, 1936

Ibscher, R., *Gestalt der Szene und Form der Rede in den Argonautika des Apollonios Rhodios* (Diss.), Munich, 1939

Klein, L., in *Philologus*, vol. 86, 1931, pp. 18f.

Knaack, G., Pauly–Wissowa, *REkA*, vol. 2, pp. 126f.

Köhnken, A., *Apollonios Rhodios und Theokrit* (Diss.), Göttingen, 1965

Marxer, G., *Die Sprache des Apollonios Rhodios in ihrer Beziehung zu Homer* (Diss.), Zurich, 1935

Mehmel, F., 'Virgil und Apollonios Rhodios . . .', *Hamburger Arbeiten zur Altertumswissenschaft*, vol. 1, 1940

Merkel, R., *Apollonii Rhodii Argonautica* (Teubner), Leipzig, 1854

Mooney, G. W., *The Argonautica of Apollonios Rhodios*, London–Dublin, 1912

Mugler, K., in *Philologus*, vol. 96, 1944, pp. 1–17

Platt, A., in *Journal of Philology*, vol. 33, 1913, pp. 1f.; vol. 34, 1915, pp. 129f.; vol. 35, 1919, pp. 72f.

Powell, *CA*, pp. 4f. (fragments)

Seaton, R. C., *Apollonii Rhodii Argonautica*, Oxford, 1929

Vian, F., *Apollonios de Rhodes, Argonautiques, Chant III*, Paris, 1961

Wendel, C., *Scholia in Apollonium Rhodium Vetera*, Berlin, 1935

THE DIDACTIC EPIC

ARATUS

Erren, M., *Aratus, Die Phaenomena des Arates von Soloi*, Wiesbaden, 1967

Knaack, G., Pauly–Wissowa, *REkA*, vol. 2, pp. 126f.

Maass, E., *Arati Phaenomena*, Berlin, 1893

Maass, E., *Commentariorum in Aratum Reliquiae*, Berlin, 1898; rpt. 1954

Mair, G. R., *Callimachus, Lycophron, Aratus*, (Loeb), London, 1921

Martin, J., *Arati Phaenomena*, Florence, 1954

Martin, J., *Histoire du texte des Phénomènes d'Aratus*, Paris, 1956

Pfeiffer, E., *Studien zum antiken Sternglauben*, Leipzig–Berlin, 1916

NICANDER OF COLOPHON

Gow, A. S. F., and Scholfield, A. F., *Nicander*, Cambridge, 1953

Schneider, O., *Nicandrea*, Leipzig, 1856

CHAPTER 9: ALEXANDRIAN DRAMA

Beare, W., *The Roman Stage*, 2nd edn., London, 1977

Coles, R. A., 'A New Fragment of a Post-Classical Tragedy from Oxyrhynchus',
Bulletin of the Institute of Classical Studies, University of London, suppl. 15, 1968

Gabathuler, M., *Hellenistische Epigramme auf Dichter* (Diss., Basle), Leipzig, 1937

Holzinger, C. von., *Lykophrons Alexandra*, Leipzig, 1895

Latte, K., *Eranos 52*, 1954, pp. 125f.

Mair, A. W., *Callimachus, Lycophron, Aratus* (Loeb), London, 1921

Olivieri, *FCGM*, vol. 2

Page, D. L., *Actors' Interpolations in Greek Tragedy*, Oxford, 1935

Scheer, E., *Lykophronis Alexandra*, 2 vols., Berlin, 1881, 1908

Schramm, E., *Tragicorum Graecorum hellenisticae quae dicitur aetatis fragmenta . . .*
(Diss.), Münster, 1931

Sifakis, G. M., *Studies in the History of Hellenistic Drama*, London, 1968

Snell, B., *Scenes from Greek Drama*, Berkeley, 1964

Venini, P., in *Dioniso*, vol. 16, 1953, pp. 3f.

Völker, E. D., *Rhintonis Fragmenta*, Halis Saxonum, 1887

Webster, T. B. L., *Studies in Later Greek Comedy*, Manchester, 1953; 2nd edn., 1970

Webster, T. B. L., in *Hesperia*, vol. 29, 1960, p. 258 (introduction of *onkos* masks)

Webster, T. B. L., 'Monuments illustrating New Comedy,' *Bulletin of the Institute
of Classical Studies*, University of London, suppl. 11, 1961

Webster, T. B. L., *Hellenistic Poetry and Art*, New York, 1964

Wieneke, J., *Ezechielis Judei: Exagoge*, Munster, 1931

CHAPTER 10: THE LITERATURE OF POPULAR ENTERTAINMENT

THE MIME

THEOCRITUS

Beckby, H., *Die griechischen Bukoliker*, Meisenheim/Glan, 1975

Bignone, E., *Teocrito, studio critico*, Bari, 1934

Blumenthal, V., in Pauly–Wissowa, *REkA*, vol. 5A, p. 2001

Cataudella, Q., *Lycidas, Studi in onore di Ugo Enrico Paoli*, Florence, 1956

Cholmeley, R. J., *The Idylls of Theocritus*, 2nd edn., London, 1919

Dover, K. J., *Theocritus, Select Poems*, London, 1971

Erbse, H., in *Mus. Helvet*, vol. 29, 1965, pp. 232f.

Gallavotti, C., *Theocritus, quique feruntur Bucolici Graeci*, Rome, 1946

Gallavotti, C., *Lingua, tecnica e poesia negli idilli di Theocriti*, Rome, 1952

Giangrande, G., in *Archeologia classica*, vol. 37, 1968, pp. 491–533

Giangrande, G., in *Quaderni Urbinati di cultura classica* (Rome), vol. 12, 1971,
pp. 95–113f.

Gow, A. S. F., *Theocritus*, 2 vols., Cambridge, 1950

Gow, A. S. F., *Bucolici Graeci* (OCT), Oxford, 1952

Horstmann, A. E. A., *Ironie und Humor bei Theocrit* (Diss.), Meisenheim/Glan, 1976

Jachmann, G., in *Maia*, n.s., vol. 5, 1952, p. 161

Kühn, J. H., in *Hermes*, vol. 86, 1958, pp. 40–79

Latte, K., *Theocriti Carmina*, Iserlohn, 1948
Latte, K., *Zur Textkritik Theokrits*, Göttingen, 1949
Lawall, G., *Theocritus' Coan Pastorals*, Washington, D.C., 1967
Legrand, É., *Études sur Théocrite*, Paris, 1898; rpt. 1968
Legrand, É., in *Revue des études anciennes*, vol. 47, 1945, pp. 214f.
Legrand, É., *Bucoliques grecs*, vols. 1, 2 (Budé), Paris, 1946
Lembach, K., *Die Pflanzen bei Theokrit*, Heidelberg, 1970
Lindsell, A., in *Greece and Rome*, vol. 6, 1937, pp. 78–93
Meinke, W., *Untersuchungen zu den enkomiastischen Gedichten Theokrits*, (Diss.), Kiel, 1966
Monteil, P., *Theocritus, Idylles 2, 5, 7, 11, 15*, Paris, 1968
Ott, U., *Die Kunst des Gegensatzes in Theokrits Hirtengedichten*, New York, 1969
Petropoulos, D., in *Λαογραφία*, vol. 18, 1959, pp. 79–88
Puelma, M., in *Mus. Helvet.*, vol. 17, 1960, pp. 144–64
Rosenmeyer, T. G., *The Green Cabinet: Theocritus and the European Pastoral Lyric*, Berkeley–Los Angeles, 1969
Rossi, L. E., in *Giornale italiano di filologia*, n.s., vol. 2, 1971, pp. 13–24
Rossi, L. E., in *Studi italiani di filologia classica*, vol. 43, 1971, pp. 5–25
Rumpel, J., *Lexicon Theocriteum*, Leipzig, 1879
Sanchez-Wildberger, M., *Theokrit–Interpretationem* (Diss.), Zurich, 1955
Schlatter, G., *Theokrit und Kallimachos* (Diss.), Zurich, 1941
Wendel, C., *Scholia in Theocritum Vetera*, Leipzig, 1914
Wilamowitz-Moellendorff, U. von, *Die textgeschichte der griechischen Bukoliker*, Berlin, 1906
Wilamowitz-Moellendorff, U. von, *Bucolici Graeci* (OCT), 2nd edn., Oxford, 1914
Wilamowitz-Moellendorff, U. von, *Hellenistische Dichtung in der Zeit des Kallimachos*, Berlin, 1924, vol. 2, pp. 130f.
Williams, F., in *Classical Quarterly*, n.s., vol. 21, 1971, pp. 137–45

Herodas

Crusius, O., *Untersuchungen zu den Mimiamben des Herodas*, Leipzig, 1892
Crusius, O., *Die Mimiamben des Herodas*, Göttingen, 1893
Crusius, O., Herodas, 5th edn., 1914 (2nd edn. by R. Herzog, 1926)
Headlam, W. and Knox, A. D., *Herodas*, Cambridge, 1922
Knox, A. D., in *Philologus*, vol. 81, 1926, pp. 241f.
Knox, A. D., Herodas (Loeb), London, 1929
Kynaston, H., in *Classical Review*, vol. 6, 1892, pp. 85f.
Luria, S., in *Miscellanea di studi alessandrini in memoria di A. Rostagni*, Turin, 1963, pp. 394f.
Nairn, J. A., *The Mimes of Herondas*, Oxford, 1904
Nairn, J. A., Laloy, L., *Hérondas, Mimes*, Paris, 1928, rpt., 1960 (Budé)
Reich, H., *Der Mimos*, 2 vols., Berlin, 1903
Schmidt, V., *Sprachliche Untersuchungen zu Herodas*, Berlin, 1968

CHAPTER 11: LYRIC POETRY AND HYMNOGRAPHY

Bowra, C. M., in *Journal of Roman Studies*, vol. 47, 1957, p. 21
Diehl, E., *ALG²*, vol. 2, 6, *passim*

Maas, P., 'Epidaurische Hymnen', *Schriften der Königsberger Gesellschaft der Wissenschaften*, vol. 9, 5, 1933, p. 155
Mühll, P. von der, in *Mus. Helvet.*, vol. 19, 1962, pp. 2f.
Pack, *GLLT*, nos. 1266, 1388, 1389, 1516
Page, *GLP*, pp. 412, 462
Peek, W., *Der Isis-hymnos von Andros und verwandte Texte*, Berlin, 1930
Peek, W., *Griechische Versinschriften*, vol. 1, Berlin, 1955
Powell, *CA*, pp. 132f.

CHAPTER 12: ALEXANDRIAN EPIGRAMS, TECHNOPAEGNIA AND PRIAPEA

Basson, J., *De Cephala et Planude Syllogisque Minoribus*, Berlin, 1917
Beckby, H., *Anthologia Graeca*, 4 vols., Munich, 1957–8, 2nd edn., n.d.
Biese, A., *Die Entwicklung des Naturgefühls bei den Griechen und Römern*, Kiel, 1882–4
Brecht, F. J., in *Philologus*, suppl. 22, 1930
Dübner, F., Cougny, E., *Epigrammatum Anthologia Palatina*, 3 vols., Paris, 1864–90
Gabathuler, M., *Hellenistische Epigramme auf Dichter* (Diss., Basle), Leipzig, 1937
Geffcken, J., *Griechische Epigramme*, Heidelberg, 1916
Geffcken, J., in *Neue Jahrbücher für d. klass. Altertum*, vol. 39, 1917, pp. 88f.
Gow, A. S. F., *The Greek Anthology: Sources and Ascriptions*, Hellenic Society, suppl. paper no. 9, 1958
Gow–Page, *HE*
Harberton, V., *Meleager and the Other Poets of the Greek Anthology from Plato to Leonidas Alexandrinus*, London, 1895
Herrlinger, G., *Totenklage um Tiere in der antiken Dichtung (Tübinger Beiträge zur Altertumswissenschaft*, vol. 8), Stuttgart, 1930
Hezel, O., *Catullus und das griechische Epigramm* (Diss.), Tübingen, 1932
Kägi, P., *Nachwirkungen der älteren griechischen Elegie in den Epigrammen der Anthologie* (Diss.), Zurich, 1917
Keydell, R., (s.v. Epigramma) *Reallexikon für Antike und Christentum*, vol. 5, pp. 539f.
Kock, B., *De Epigrammatum Graecorum Dialectis* (Diss.), Göttingen, 1910
Lavagnini, B., *Lirici ellenistici: Asclepiade, Callimaco, Meleagro, Filodemo*, Turin, 1928
Luck, G., in *Mus. Helvet.*, vol. 11, 1954, pp. 170f.
Lumb, T. W., *Notes on the Greek Anthology*, London, 1920
Mackail, J. W., *Select Epigrams from the Greek Anthology*, New York–Bombay–Calcutta, 1906
Menk, A., *De Anthologiae Palatinae Epigrammatis Sepulcralibus* (Diss.), Marburg, 1884
Meyer, H., *De Anthologiae Palatinae Epigrammatis Cyzicenis* (Diss.), Königsberg, 1911
Paton, W. R., *The Greek Anthology* (Loeb), 5 vols., London, 1916–18
Peek, W., *Griechische Versinschriften*, vol. 1, Berlin, 1955
Peek, W., *Griechische Grabgedichte*, Berlin, 1960
Preisendanz, K., *Praefatio ad Anthologiam Palatinam*, Leyden, 1911
Preisendanz, K., in *Zentralblatt für Bibliothekswesen*, vol. 58, 1941, pp. 87f.

Prinz, K., *Martial und die griechische Epigrammatik*, Leipzig–Vienna, 1911

Prittwitz-Gaffron, E. von, *Das Sprichwort im griechischen Epigram* (Diss.), Giessen, 1911

Reitzenstein, R., *Epigramm und Skolion*, Giessen, 1893

Schmidt, L., and Reitzenstein, R., in Pauly–Wissowa, *REkA*, vol. 1, p. 2380 (s.v. Anthologie)

Schmidt, L., and Reitzenstein, R., in Pauly–Wissowa, *REkA*, vol. 6, pp. 71–111 (s.v. Epigramm)

Smutny, R. J., *The Text History of the Epigrams of Theocritus*, Berkeley, 1955

Stadtmüller, H. (ed.), *Anthologia Palatina* (Teubner), vol. 1 (I–VI), Leipzig, 1894; vol. 2, I (VII), Leipzig, 1899; vol. 3, I (IX, 1–563), Leipzig, 1906

Stella, L. A., *Cinque poeti dell'Antologia Palatina*, Bologna, 1949

Sternbach, L., *Meletemata Graeca*, Vienna, 1886

Waltz, P., *et al.*, *L'Anthologie grecque* (Budé), 13 vols., Paris, 1928

Weber, L., in *Hermes*, vol. 52, 1917, pp. 536f.

Webster, T. B. L., *Hellenistic Poetry and Art*, New York, 1964

Weinreich, O., 'Epigramm und Pantomimus', *Sitzungsberichte der Heidelberger Akademie der Wissenschaften*, Heidelberg, 1944–8, 1.

Weinreich, O., *Epigrammstudien*, Heidelberg, 1948

Weisshäupl, R., *Die Grabgedichte der griechischen Anthologie*, Vienna, 1889

Wendling, E., *De Peplo Aristotelico Quaestiones Selectae*, Strasbourg, 1891

Wifstrand, A., *Studien zur griechischen Anthologie*, Lund–Leipzig, 1926

Wilamowitz-Moellendorff, U. von, *Sappho und Simonides*, Berlin, 1913

Wilamowitz-Moellendorff, U. von, *Hellenistische Dichtung in der Zeit des Kallimachos*, Berlin, 1924, vol. 1, pp. 119f.

THE ALEXANDRIAN EPIGRAM

ASCLEPIADES

Gabathuler, M., *Hellenistische Epigramme auf Dichter* (Diss., Basle), Leipzig, 1937

Gow–Page, *HE*, vol. 1, pp. 44f.; vol. 2, pp. 114f.

Knauer, O., *Die Epigramme des Asklepiades von Samos* (Diss.), Tübingen, 1935

Ludwig, W., in *Mus. Helvet*, vol. 19, 1962, pp. 156f.

Ouvré, H., *Quae fuerint dicendi genus et ratio metrica apud Asclepiadem, Posidippum, Hedylum*, Paris, 1894

Peters, O. J., *Asklepiades von Samos* (Diss.), Leipzig, 1922

Puelma, M., in *Gnomon*, vol. 22, 1950, pp. 308f.

Reitzenstein, R., *Epigramm und Skolion*, Giessen, 1893

Reitzenstein, R., in Pauly–Wissowa, *REkA*, vol. 6, pp. 71f.

Stella, L. A., *Cinque poeti dell'Antologia Palatina*, Bologna, 1949

Tarán, S. L., *The Arts of Variation in the Hellenistic Epigram*, Leyden, 1979

Wallace, W. and M., *Asklepiades of Samos*, Oxford–London–New York, 1941

Wilamowitz-Moellendorff, U. von, *Hellenistische Dichtung in der Zeit des Kallimachos*, Berlin, 1924, vol. 1, pp. 146f.

POSIDIPPUS

Gow–Page, *HE*, vols. 1, 2

Lloyd-Jones, H., in *Journal of Hellenic Studies*, vol. 83, 1963, pp. 75f.

Ouvré, H., *Quae fuerint dicendi genus et ratio metrica apud Asclepiadem, Posidippum, Hedylum*, Paris, 1894
Page, *GLP*, pp. 444–9
Peek, W., in Pauly–Wissowa, *REkA*, vol. 18, pp. 438f.
Reitzenstein, R., *Epigramm und Skolion*, Giessen, 1893, pp. 96f., 163f.
Schott, P., *Posidippi Epigrammata Collecta et Illustrata* (Diss.), Berlin, 1905
Wallace, W. and M., in *Transactions of the American Philological Association*, vol. 70, 1939, pp. 191–202

HEDYLUS

Gow–Page, *HE*, vols. 1, 2
Ouvré, H., *Quae fuerint dicendi genus et ratio metrica apud Asclepiadem, Posidippum, Hedylum*, Paris, 1894
Wallace, W. and M., in *Transactions of the American Philological Association*, vol. 70, 1939, pp. 191–202
Webster, T. B. L., *Hellenistic Poetry and Art*, New York, 1964 ch. 2

ERINNA

Bowra, C. M., *Greek Poetry and Life: Essays Presented to Gilbert Murray*, Oxford, 1936, pp. 325f.
Gow–Page, *HE*, vols. 1, 2
Latte, K., *Nachrichten von der Akademie der Wissenschaften Göttingen, Phil.–hist. Kl.*, 1953, no. 3
Pomeroy, P., in *Zeitschrift für Papyrologie und Epigraphik*, vol. 32, 1978, pp. 17f.
West, M. L., in *Zeitschrift für Papyrologie und Epigraphik*, vol. 25, 1977, pp. 95f.

NOSSIS

Gow-Page, *HE*, vols. 1, 2
Luck, C., in *Mus. Helvet.*, vol. 11, 1954, pp. 182f.
Wilamowitz-Moellendorff, U. von, *Hellenistische Dichtung in der Zeit des Kallimachos*, Berlin, 1924 vol. 1, pp. 135f.

MNASALCES

Geffcken, J., in Pauly–Wissowa, *REkA*, vol. 15, pp. 2247f.
Gow–Page, *HE*, vols. 1, 2
Seelbach, W., 'Die Epigramme des Mnasalkes von Sikyon und des Theodoridas von Syrakus', *Klassische–Philologische Studien*, vol. 28, 1964
Webster, T. B. L., *Hellenistic Poetry and Art*, New York, 1964, pp. 229f.

THEODORIDAS

Gow–Page, *HE*, vols. 1, 2
Maas, P., in *Studi italiani di filologia classica*, n.s., vol. 15, 1938, p. 80
Peek, W., in *Philologus*, vol. 117, 1973, pp. 66f.
Seelbach, W., 'Die Epigramme des Mnasalkes von Sikyon und des Theodoridas von Syrakus', *Klassische–Philologische Studien*, vol. 28, 1964
Webster, T. B. L., *Hellenistic Poetry and Art*, New York, 1964, pp. 227f.

PERSES

Gow–Page, *HE*, vols. 1, 2

LEONIDAS OF TARENTUM

Bevan, E., *The Poems of Leonidas of Tarentum*, Oxford, 1931
Dawson, C. M., in *American Journal of Philology*, vol. 71, 1950, pp. 271f.
Geffcken, J., in *Jahrbücher für Philologie und Pädagogik*, suppl. 23, 1897, pp. 1f.
Gow–Page, *HE*, vols. 1, 2
Hansen, B., *De Leonida Tarentino*, Leipzig, 1914
Stella, L. A., *Cinque poeti dell'Antologia Palatina*, Bologna, 1949, pp. 77f.
Webster, T. B. L., *Hellenistic Poetry and Art*, New York, 1964, pp. 217f.
Wilamowitz-Moellendorff, U. von, *Hellenistische Dichtung in der Zeit des Kallimachos*, Berlin, 1924, vol. 1, pp. 193f.; vol. 2, pp. 103f.

ALCAEUS OF MESSENE

Edson, C., in *Classical Philology*, vol. 42, 1948, pp. 88–105
Reitzenstein, R., *Epigramm und Skolion*, Giessen, 1893, pp. 285f.
Wallbank, F. W., in *Classical Quarterly*, vol. 36, 1942, pp. 135f.; vol. 37 1943, pp. 1f.
Webster, T. B. L., *Hellenistic Poetry and Art*, New York, 1964, pp. 233f.

TECHNOPAEGNIA

Haeberlin, C., *Carmina Figurata Graeca*, Hanover, 1887
Maas, P., in Pauly–Wissowa, *REkA*, vol. 5A, pp. 103f.
Wilamowitz-Moellendorff, U. von, *Kleine Schriften*, Berlin, 1935– , vol. 5, 1, p. 502

SIMMIAS OF RHODES

Diehl, *ALG²*, vol. 2, 6, pp. 251f.
Fränkel, H., *De Simia Rhodio* (Diss.), Göttingen, 1915
Gow–Page, *HE*, vols. 1, 2
Maas, P., in Pauly–Wissowa, *REkA*, vol. 3A, pp. 159f.
Merkelbach, R., in *Aegyptus*, vol. 31, 1951, pp. 254f.
Merkelbach, R., in *Mus. Helvet.*, vol. 10, 1953, pp. 68f.
Notopoulos, J. A., in *American Journal of Philology*, vol. 62, 1942, pp. 281f.
Powell, *CA*, pp. 109f.

Section II: The Greco-Roman World: The Transition to Classicism (146 B.C.–A.D. 100)

CHAPTER 13: THE DEPLETION OF THE POETIC TRADITION

PASTORAL AND EPIC POETRY

Arland, W., *Nachtheokritische Bukolik* (Diss.), Leipzig, 1937
Atenstädt, F., in *Rhein. Mus.*, vol. 82, 1933, pp. 115f.
Cazzaniga, I., in *Studi classici e orientali*, vol. 10, 1961, pp. 44f.
Diehl, *ALG²*, vol. 2, 6, pp. 94f.
Diller, A., *The Tradition of the Minor Greek Geographers*, philological monographs published by the American Philological Association, no. 14, 1952

Diller, A., in *Transactions and Proceedings of the American Philological Association*, vol. 86, 1955, pp. 276f.

Ehlers, W., in *Mus. Helvet.*, vol. 11, 1954, pp. 65f.

Frazer, P. M., *Ptolemaic Alexandria*, 3 vols., Oxford, 1972, vol. 1, p. 457

Friedländer, P., *Das Problem des Klassischen und die Antike*, Leipzig, 1931, rpt., Stuttgart, 1933

Gow, A. S. F., *Bucolici Graeci* (OCT), Oxford, 1952

Heitsch, *GDRK*, 2nd edn., vol. 1, pp. 17f.

Hillscher, A., in *Jahrbücher für klassische Philologie*, suppl. 18, 1891, pp. 403f.

Kenyon, F. G., in *Revue de philologie, de littérature et d'histoire anciennes*, vol. 19, 1895, pp. 77f.

Legrand, É., *Bucoliques grecs* (Budé), vol. 2, Paris, 1946

Müller, K., *Geographici Graeci Minores*, 3 vols., Paris, 1855–61, vol. 2, pp. 102f.

Müller, K., in *Mus. Helvet.*, vol. 20, 1963, pp. 114f.

Niese, B., in *Hermes*, vol. 44, 1909, pp. 161f.

Pareti, L., in *Atti dell'Accademia delle Scienze di Torino, classe di scienze morali, storiche e filologiche*, vol. 45, 1909–10, pp. 229f.

Raubitschek, A., in *Hesperia*, vol. 23, 1954, pp. 317f.

Reinach, Th., *De Archia Poeta* (Diss.), Paris, 1890

Robert, L., in *Revue des études grecques*, vol. 68, 1955, pp. 210f.

Rohde, E., *Kleine Schriften*, 2 vols., Tübingen–Leipzig, 1901, vol. 1, p. 336, n.2.

Schrot, G., in *Kleine Pauly*, vol. 1, p. 905f.

Schwartz, in Pauly–Wissowa, *REkA*, vol. 1, pp. 2855f.

Susemihl, F., *Geschichte der griechischen Literatur in der Alexandrinerzeit*, Leipzig, 1891 2, vol. 1, p. 900

Wilamowitz-Moellendorff, U. von, *Reden und Vorträge*, 4th edn., Berlin, 1925, vol. 1, pp. 292f.

Ziegler, K., *Das hellenistische Epos*, Leipzig–Berlin, 1934; 2nd edn., 1966

ELEGIAC POETRY

PARTHENIUS

Cazzaniga, I., in *Studi classici e orientali*, vol. 10, 1961, pp. 44f.

Diehl, *ALG²*, vol. 2, 6, pp. 94f.

Gaselee, S., *The Love Romances of Parthenius and Other Fragments* (Loeb, with *Daphnis and Chloe*), London–New York, 1916 (several rpts)

Martini, E., *Mythographi Graeci*, Leipzig, 1902, vol. 2, sect. 1 (suppl)

Meineke, A., *Analecta Alexandrina*, Berlin, 1843 pp. 255f.

Pfeiffer, R., in *Classical Quarterly*, vol. 37, 1943, pp. 23f.

Rostagni, A., *Scritti Minori*, 2 vols., Turin, 1955–6, vol. 2, 2, pp. 49f.

SIMYLUS

Diehl, *ALG²*, vol. 2, 6, p. 102

BUTES

Diehl, *ALG²*, vol. 2, 6, p. 102

MARCUS

AP, bk. 11, no. 135

BOETHOS OF SIDON

AP, bk. 9, no. 248

THE EPIGRAM

Keydell, R., *Reallexikon für Antike und Christentum*, vol. 5, pp. 539f.

ANTIPATER OF SIDON

Gaertingen, H. von, Peek, W., *Hermes 76*, 1941, pp. 220f.
Gow–Page, *HE*, vol. 1, pp. 11–35; vol. 2
Setti, G., *Gli epigrammi degli Antipatri*, Turin, 1890
Waltz, P., *De Antipatro Sidonio* (Diss.), Bordeaux, 1906
Wifstrand, A., *Von Kallimachos zu Nonnos*, Lund, 1933, pp. 155f.

MELEAGER OF GADARA

Capra d'Angelo, P., *La poesia di Meleagro*, Cagliari, 1942
Garrison, D. H., in *Hermes Einzelschriften*, 41, 1978, pp. 71f.
Gow–Page, *HE*, vol. 1, pp. 214–53; vol. 2
Harberton, V., *Meleager and the Other Poets of the Anthology from Plato to Leonidas Alexandrinus*, London, 1895
Ouvré, H., *Méléagre de Gadara*, Paris, 1894
Radinger, K., *Meleagros von Gadara*, Innsbruck, 1895
Webster, T. B. L., *Hellenistic Poetry and Art*, New York, 1964, ch. 9

PHILODEMUS

Cichorius, C., *Römische Studien*, Leipzig, 1922, pp. 295f.
Dreyer, O., in *Kleine Pauly*, vol. 4, pp. 759f.
Gow–Page, *GPh*, vol. 1, pp. 350–69; vol. 2
Stella, L. A., *Cinque poeti dell'Antologia Palatina*, Bologna, 1949

CRINAGORAS OF MYTILENE

Cichorius, C., *Rom und Mytilene*, Leipzig, 1888
Gow–Page, *GPh*, vol. 1, pp. 198–231; vol. 2
Rubensohn, M., *Crinagorae Mytilenaei Epigrammata* (Diss.), Berlin, 1888
Weinreich, O., in *Wien. Stud.*, vol. 59, 1941, pp. 77f.
Weinreich, O., *Epigrammstudien*, Heidelberg, 1948

MARCUS ARGENTARIUS

Re, R. del, in *Maia*, vol. 7, 1955, pp. 184f.
Small, S. G. P., in *Yale Classical Studies*, vol. 12, 1951, pp. 65f.

PHILIP OF THESSALONICA

Cichorius, C., *Römische Studien*, Leipzig, 1922
Gow–Page, *GPh*, vol. 1, pp. 296–351; vol. 2
Hirsch, E., in *Wissenschaftliche Zeitschrift der Martin-Luther Universität*, Halle–Wittenberg, 1966, pp. 40f.
Peek, W., in Pauly–Wissowa, *REkA*, vol. 19, 2, pp. 2239f.

Other epigrammatists

Brecht, F. J., *Motiv-und Typengeschichte des griechischen Spottepigramms*, Leipzig, 1930

Cichorius, C., *Römische Studien*, Leipzig, 1922, pp. 325f. (Antipater of Thessalonica), and pp. 356f. (the youngest poets of the *Garland of Philip*)

Crupi, P., *L'epigramma greco di Lucillio*, Naples, 1964

Keydell, R., in *Philologus*, vol. 112, 1968, pp. 141f.

Linnenkugel, A., in *Rhetorische Studien* (Paderborn), vol. 13, 1926, pp. 52f.

Müller, K., *Die Epigramme des Antiphilos von Byzanz*, Berlin, 1935

Prinz, K., *Martial und das griechische Epigramm*, Leipzig–Vienna, 1914

Robert, R., *L'epigramme grecque* by A. E. Raubitschek, B. Gentili *et al.*, Geneva, 1968, pp. 181f.

Usener, H., *Kleine Schriften*

DRAMATIC POETRY

Frei, J., *De Certaminibus Thymelicis*, Basle, 1900

Kern, O., in *Athenische Mitteilungen*, vol. 19, 1894, pp. 100f.

Körte, A., in Pauly–Wissowa, *REkA*, vol. 17, pp. 362f. (s.v. Nikolaos)

Norden, E., *Die antike Kunstprosa*, Leipzig–Berlin, 1915–18, pp. 886f.

Rohde, E., *Der griechische Roman*, Leipzig, 1876, pp. 332f.

Schmid, W., *Der Atticismus*, 5 vols., Stuttgart, 1887–97, vol. 1, p. 214

Welcker, F. G., *Die griechischen Tragödien*, Bonn, 1841, vol. 2, pp. 1322f.

THE MIME AND THE PANTOMIME

Philistion

Eberhard, A. (ed.), *Philogelos: Hierocles et Philagrii Facetiae*, Berlin, 1869

Irmscher, J., *Philistion–Philemon: Festschrift Constantinescu-Iaşi*, Bucharest, 1965, pp. 19f.

Thierfeder, A., *Der Lachfreund von Hierokles und Philagrios*, Munich, 1968

Wüst, R., in Pauly–Wissowa, *REkA*, vol. 19, pp. 2402f.

LYRIC POETRY AND HYMNODY

Frazer, P. M., *Ptolemaic Alexandria*, Oxford, 1972, vol. 1, p. 671 (on the hymns of Isidorus)

Heitsch, *GDRK*, vol. 1², nos. 6, 8, 10

Müller, D., *Ägyptien und die griechische Isis–aretalogien*, Berlin, 1961

Norden, E., *Agnostos Theos*, Leipzig, 1923, pp. 183f.

Page, *GLP*, nos. 92, 93

Peek, W., *Der Isis-hymnos von Andros und verwandte Texte*, Berlin, 1930

Vanderlip, V. F., *The Four Greek Hymns of Isidorus and the Cult of Isis*, Toronto, 1972

HELLENISTIC JEWISH POETRY

Dodds, E. R., *Pagan and Christian in an Age of Anxiety*, Cambridge, 1965

Frazer, P. M., *Ptolemaic Alexandria*, Oxford, 1972, vol. 1, pp. 706f.

Kurfess, A., in *Zeitschrift für Neutestamentliche Wissenschaft*, vol. 38, 1939, pp. 171f.

Kurfess, A., *Sibyllinische Weissagungen*, Munich, 1951 (a selection)

Ludwich, A., *De Theodoti Carmine Graeco–Iudaico, Universitätsprogramm Königsberg*, 1899

Ludwich, A., *De Philonis Carmine Graeco–Iudaico Commentatio, Universitätsprogramm Königsberg*, 1900

Section III: The Greco-Roman World: The Age of Classicism (A.D. 100–330)

CHAPTER 14: THE DECLINE OF LYRIC POETRY

DIDACTIC POETRY

Dionysius Periegetes

Bernays, U., *Studien zu Dionysius Periegetes*, Heidelberg, 1905

Bernhardy, G., edition of Dionysius Periegetes with Eustathius' commentary, Leipzig, 1828

Knaack, in Pauly–Wissowa, *REkA*, vol. 5, pp. 915f.

Müller, K., *Geographici Graeci Minores*, 3 vols., Paris, 1855–61, vol. 2, pp. 103f.; fragments, p. xxvi.

Oppian of Corycos in Cilicia

Gow, A. S. F., in *Classical Quarterly*, vol. 18, 1968, pp. 6of. (on the *Halieutica*)

James, A. W., in *Hermes*, vol. 93, 1965, pp. 429f.

Keydell, R., in *Kleine Pauly*, vol. 4, pp. 315f.

Mair, A. W., *Opian, Colluthus and Tryphiodorus* (Loeb), London, 1928

Oppian of Apamea in Syria

Boudreaux, P., *Oppien d'Apamée, La Chasse* ('Οππιανοῦ Κυνηγετικά), Paris, 1908

Keydell, R., in *Kleine Pauly*, vol. 4, pp. 315f.

Mair, A. W., *Oppian of Apamea* (Loeb), London, 1928

West, M. L., in *Classical Quarterly*, vol. 13, 1963, pp. 57f.

Babrius

Crusius, O., in Pauly–Wissowa, *REkA*, vol. 2, pp. 2655f.

Crusius, O., *Babrii Fabulae Aesopeae* (Teubner), Leipzig, 1897

Dain, A., Πεπραγμένα τοῦ θ΄Διεθν. Βυζαντ. Συνεδρίου, vol. 3, 1958, pp. 101f.

Perry, B. E., *Babrius and Phaedrus* (Loeb), London, 1964

MYTHOLOGICAL AND HISTORICAL EPICS

Nestor of Laranda

AP, bk. 9, nos. 128 (?), 129, 364, 536, 537 (fragments of *Metamorphoses*)

Düntzer, H. (ed.), *Die Fragmente der epischen Poesie der Griechen*, Cologne, 1840–2, vol. 2, p. 105

Keydell, R., in Pauly–Wissowa, *REkA*, vol. 17, pp. 125f.

PEISANDER OF LARANDA

Heitsch, *GDRK*, vol. 2, pp. 44f.

Keydell, R., in Pauly–Wissowa, *REkA*, vol. 19, pp. 145f.

Sévéryns, A., *Le cycle épique dans l'école d'Aristarque*, Paris, 1928, pp. 75f.

DIONYSIUS

Crönert, W., in *Archiv für Papyrusforschung*, vol. 2, 1903, p. 351

Heitsch, *GDRK*, vol. 1², pp. 6of.

Keydell, R., in *Hermes*, no. 67, 1932, pp. 240f.

Knaack, in Pauly–Wissowa, *REkA*, vol. 5, pp. 924–5

Livrea, H., *Dionysii Bassaricon et Gigantidis Fragmenta*, Rome, 1973

Morel, W., in *Archiv für Papyrusforschung*, vol. 9, 1932, pp. 240f.

Wifstrand, A., in *Eranos*, vol. 28, 1930, pp. 102f.

Other epic poets

Cameron, A., *Claudian*, Oxford, 1970, pp. 478f.

Ferrari, L., *Sulla Presa di Ilio di Trifiodoro*, Palermo, 1962

Funaioli, G., in *Rhein. Mus.*, vol. 88, 1939, pp. 1f. (Triphiodorus)

Heitsch, *GDRK*, vol. 1², pp. 51f., 79

Kaibel, *EG*, p. 1009

Keydell, R., in Pauly–Wissowa, *REkA*, vol. 13², pp. 178f. (Triphiodorus)

Mair, A. W., *Oppian, Colluthus and Tryphiodorus* (Loeb), London, 1928

Orsini, P., in *Pallas*, vol. 21, 1974, pp. 3f.

Page, *GLP*, pp. 542, 544f.

Weinberger, G., *Tryphiodori et Colluthi Carmina* (Teubner), Leipzig, 1896

Wyss, B., in *Mus. Helvet.*, vol. 6, 1949, pp. 194f.

DRAMA AND THE MIME

Broneer, O., in *Hesperia*, vol. 22, 1953, p. 192

Heitsch, *GDRK*, vol. 1², p. 12, no. xii

Latte, K., in *Eranos*, vol. 52, 1954, pp. 125f.

Münscher, K., in *Philologus*, suppl. 10, 1907, pp. 539f.

Page, *GLP*, nos. 77–9

Rohde, E., *Der griechische Roman*, 3rd edn., Leipzig, 1914, pp. 37f.

Schmid, W., *Der Atticismus*, 5 vols., Stuttgart, 1887–9, vol. 1, p. 214

Welcker, F. G., *Die griechischen Tragödien*, Bonn, 1841, vol. 3, pp. 1322f.

LYRICAL POETRY

Baldini, G., in *Annuario del Liceo Gimnasio G. Carducci in Viareggio, 1929–32*, Pisa, 1932, p. 183

Boulanger, A., *Aelius Aristide*, Paris, 1923, pp. 300f.

Frazer, P. M., *Ptolemaic Alexandria*, Oxford, 1972, vol. 1, p. 804

Heitsch, *GDRK*, vol. 1², pp. 24, 38, 42, 44, 165, 180

Hölfer, A., *Der Sarapishymnus des Aelius Aristeidis*, Stuttgart–Berlin, 1935

Jan, C. von, *Musici Scriptores Graeci* (Teubner), Leipzig, 1895, pp. 454f.; supplement, 1899, pp. 40f.; 2nd edn. of both 1962

Kayser, K. L., *Philostratus, Heroicus*, Leipzig, 1870–1, vol. 2, pp. 208, 213

Lenz, W. F., in *Rivista di cultura classica e medioevale*, vol. 3, 1961, p. 156

Martelloti, G., *Mesomede*, Rome, 1929

Page, *GLP*, nos. 94, 97, 98

Pöhlmann, E., 'Griech. Musikfragmente', *Erlanger Beiträge*, vol. 8, 1960

THE EPIGRAM

Boas, M., in *Philologus*, vol. 73, 1914–16, pp. 1f.

Crusius, O., in Pauly–Wissowa, *REkA*, vol. 1, pp. 2045f.

Geffcken, J., in Pauly–Wissowa, *REkA*, vol. 4, 1 (2nd series), pp. 276f.

Helm, in Pauly–Wissowa, *REkA*, vol. 13, pp. 1739f.

Keydell, R., in *Hermes*, vol. 80, 1952, pp. 498f.

Keydell, R., in *Reallexikon für Antike und Christentum*, vol. 5, 1961, p. 539

Page, D., *The Epigrams of Rufinus*, Cambridge, 1978

Peek, W., *Griechische Vers-Inschriften, Grab-Epigramme*, Berlin, 1955, vol. 1

Peek, W., *Griechische Grabgedichte*, Berlin, 1960

Preisendanz, K., *Praefatio ad Anthologiam Palatinam*, Leyden, 1911

Preisendanz, K., in *Philologus*, vol. 75, 1919, pp. 476f.

Sandre, T., *Les épigrammes de Rufin*, Paris, 1922

Schmid, W., *Der Atticismus*, 5 vols., Stuttgart, 1887–9, vol. 4, pp. 660f.

Setti, G., in *Rivista di filologia classica*, vol. 20, 1892, p. 233

West, M. L., *Die griechische Dichterinnen der Kaiserzeit, Kyklos, R. Keydell, zum neunzigsten Geburtstag*, Berlin–New York, 1978, pp. 101f.

PALLADAS

Bowra, C. M., in *Classical Quarterly*, vol. 10, 1960, pp. 118f.

Cameron, A., in *Journal of Hellenic Studies*, vol. 84, 1964, pp. 54f.

Cameron, A., in *BZ*, vol. 57, 1964, pp. 279f.

Cameron, A., in *Classical Quarterly*, vol. 15, 1965, pp. 215f.

Cameron, A., in *Journal of Roman Studies*, vol. 55, 1965, pp. 17f.

Stella, L. A., *Cinque poeti dell'Antologia Palatina*, Bologna, 1949

Section IV: The Period of Transition from the Ancient World to the Middle Ages
(A.D. 330–641)
CHAPTER 15: SECULAR POETRY

THE EPIC

The mythological epic

QUINTUS SMYRNAEUS

Kakridis, P., *Κόϊντος Σμυρναῖος*, Athens, 1962
Kehmptzow, F., *De Quinti Smyrnaei fontibus ac mythopoeia*, Kiel, 1891
Keydell, R., in Pauly–Wissowa, *REkA*, vol. 24, pp. 1271f.
Paschal, G. W., *A Study of Quintus Smyrnaeus,* Chicago, 1904
Sainte-Beuve, C. A., *Études sur Virgile*, 4th edn., Paris, 1891
Vian, F., *Recherches sur les Posthomerica*, Paris, 1959
Vian, F., *Quintus de Smyrne, la suite d'Homère* (Budé), 3 vols., Paris, 1963–9
Way, A. S., *Quintus Smyrnaeus: The Fall of Troy* (Loeb), London, 1913
Zimmermann, A., *Quinti Smyrnaei Posthomericorum Libri XIV* (Teubner), Leipzig, 1891

THE 'ORPHIC' ARGONAUTICA

Abel, E., *Orphica et Procli Hymni*, Leipzig–Prague, 1885
Buse, H., *Quaestiones Hesiodeae et Orphicae*, (Diss.,) Halle, 1937
Dottin, G., *Les Argonautiques d'Orphée* (Budé), Paris, 1930
Hermann, G., *Orphica*, Leipzig, 1805
Kern, O., *Orphicorum Fragmenta*, Berlin, 1922
Keydell, R., in Pauly–Wissowa, *REkA*, vol. 18, pp. 1333f.
Ziegler, K., in Pauly–Wissowa, *REkA*, vol. 18, pp. 1254f. and 1321f.

NONNUS OF PANOPOLIS

Castiglioni, A., *Collectanea Graeca*, Pisa, 1911
Collart, P., in *Recherches d'archéologie, de philosophie et d'histoire* (Cairo), vol. 1, 1930, pp. 275f.
Golega, J. von, *Studien über die Evangelien Dichtung des Nonnos von Panopolis*, Breslau, 1930
Heidacher, H., *Quellen und Vorbilder der Dionysiaka des Nonnus* (Diss.), Graz, 1949
d'Ippolito, G., *Studi Nonniani*, Palermo, 1964
Keydell, R., in Pauly–Wissowa, *REkA*, vol. 17, pp. 904–20
Keydell, R., *Nonni Panopolitani Dionysiaca*, 2 vols. Berlin, 1959
Lasky, E. D., in *Hermes*, vol. 106, 1978, pp. 357f.
Ludwich, A., *Nonni Panopolitani Dionysiaka*, 2 vols., Leipzig, 1909–11
Peek, W., *Lexikon zu den Dionysiaka des Nonnos*, Hildesheim, 1974
Rouse, W. H. D., *Nonnus: Dionysiaca* (Loeb), 3 vols., London, 1940
Scheindler, A., *The Metabole*, Leipzig, 1881
String, M., *Untersuchungen zum Stil der Dionysiaka* (Diss.), Hamburg, 1966
Vian, F. and Chuvin, P., *Nonnos, Dionysiaca, Books 1–5*, Paris, 1976
Wifstrand, A., *Von Kallimachos zu Nonnos*, Lund, 1933, pp. 78f. (style of Nonnus)

THE 'SCHOOL' OF NONNUS

Bo, D., *Musaei Lexicon*, Hildesheim, 1966

Geltzer, T. and Whitman, C. H., *Musaeus* (Loeb), London, 1975

Keydell, R., in Pauly–Wissowa, *REkA*, vol. 16, pp. 767–9

Kost, K., *Musaios, Hero und Leander*, Bonn, 1971

Kost, K., *Krit. exeg. Kommentar zu Musaios und Ovid* (Diss.), Cologne, 1975

Livrea, E., *Colluto: Il Ratto di Elena*, Bologna, 1968

Ludwich, A., edition of Musaeus in H. Lietzmann (ed.), *Kleine Texte*, Bonn, 1912

Mair, A. W., *Oppian, Colluthus and Tryphiodorus* (Loeb), London, 1928

Malcovati, E. (ed.), *Museo*, Milan, 1947

Orsini, P., *Musée: Héro et Léandre* (Budé), Paris, 1968

Orsini, P., *Colluthus: L'enlèvement d'Hélène*, Paris, 1972

Schott, G., *Hero und Leander bei Musaios und Ovid* (Diss.), Cologne, 1957

Weinberger, W., *Tryphiodori et Colluthi Carmina* (Teubner), Leipzig, 1896

Weinberger, W. (with W. Kroll), in Pauly–Wissowa, *REkA*, vol. 2, 2, pp. 109f.

The didactic epic

Abel, E., *Orphica*, Leipzig–Prague, 1885

Heitsch, *GDRK*, vol. 1^2, pp. 203f. (on anonymous poets)

CHALDEAN ORACLES

Geffcken, J., *Das Ausgang des griechisch–römischen Heidentums*, 2nd edn., Heidelberg, 1929, pp. 84f.

Kroll, W., 'De Oraculis Chaldaicis', *Breslauer philologische Abhandlungen*, 7, 1894

SIBYLLINE ORACLES

Erbse, H., *Fragmente griech. Theosophie*, Hamburg, 1941

Keydell, R., in *Burs. Jahresb.*, vol. 272, 1941, pp. 22f.

Kurfess, A., *Sibyllinische Weissagungen*, Munich, 1951

Mras, K., in *Wien. Stud.*, vol. 28, 1906, pp. 43f.

Rzach, A., Χρησμοὶ Σιβυλλιακοί (*Oracula Sibyllina*), Prague–Vienna–Leipzig, 1891

Historical epics and epic encomia

AP, bk. 2, lines 1–416; bk. 7, nos. 697, 698 (Christodorus of Coptus)

AP, bk. 7, no. 557; bk. 9, nos. 136, 623, 808, 809; bk. 15, no. 9 (Cyrus of Panopolis)

AP, bk. 9, nos. 626, 627, 657, 668, 669; bk. 16, no. 201 (Marianus)

Baumgarten, F., in Pauly–Wissowa, *REkA*, vol. 3, 2, pp. 2450f. (Christodorus of Coptus)

Cameron, A., and Cameron, A., in *Journal of Hellenic Studies*, vol. 86, 1966, pp. 17, 21 (Marianus)

Frendo, J. D. C., in *Orpheus*, vol. 21, 1974, pp. 45f. (George the Pisidian)

Friedländer, P., *Johannes von Gaza und Paulus Silentarius*, Leipzig–Berlin, 1912, pp. 94f. (Christodorus of Coptus)

Heitsch, *GDRK*, vol. 1^2, pp. 111f. (Christodorus of Coptus)

Hercher, R., *Claudii Aeliani Varia Historia*, Leipzig, 1866, vol. 2 (George the Pisidian), pp. 601f.

Hunger, H., in *Dumbarton Oaks Papers*, vols. 23–4, 1969–70, pp. 23f. (George the Pisidian)

Kern, O., *Fragmenta Orphicorum*, Berlin, 1922

Keydell, R., in Pauly–Wissowa, *REkA*, vol. 18, pp. 1338f. ('Orphic' *Lithica*)

Keydell, R., in Pauly–Wissowa, *REkA*, vol. 18, pp. 409f. (Christodorus of Coptus)

Ludwich, A., *Eudociae Augustae Procli Lycii Claudiani Carmina Graecae rel.*, Leipzig, 1897 (Eudocia)

Nissen, T., in *Hermes*, vol. 75, 1940, pp. 298f. (George the Pisidian)

Page, *GLP*, no. 140

Pertusi, A., in *Aevum*, vol. 30, 1956, pp. 395f.

Pertusi, A. (ed. and trs.), *Giorgio di Pisidia: poemi*, vol. I, *Panegirici epici*, Ettal, 1959

Sternbach, L., in *Wien. Stud.* vol. 13, 1891, pp. 1f.; vol. 14, 1892, pp. 51f.

The epic ecphrasis

Bergk, *PLG*, vol. 3, 4 (the anacreontics)

Friedländer, P., *Johannes von Gaza und Paulus Silentarius*, Leipzig–Berlin, 1912

Keydell, R., in *Burs. Jahresb.*, vol. 230, 1931, pp. 134f.; vol. 272, 1941, pp. 47f.

Maas, P., in *BZ*, vol. 25, 1925, pp. 212f.

Mercati, S. G., *Rivista degli studi orientali*, vol. 10, 1923–5, pp. 212f.

Peek, W., in Pauly–Wissowa, *REkA*, vol. 18, pp. 2366f.

Thiele, in Pauly–Wissowa, *REkA*, vol. 9, 2, pp. 1747f.

Veh, O., *Prokop: Bauten*, Munich, 1977, pp. 306–80, 475–510

LYRIC POETRY

Religious–philosophical hymnic poetry

PROCLUS

Beutler, R., in Pauly–Wissowa, *REkA*, vol. 23, pp. 186f.

Voigt, E., *Procli Hymni*, Bonn, 1960

Wilamowitz-Moellendorff, U. von., 'Die Hymnen des Proklos und Synesios', *Sitzungsberichte der Preussischen Akademie der Wissenschaften zu Berlin*, Berlin, 1907, pp. 272f.

Zintzen, C., in *Rhein. Mus.*, vol. 108, 1965, pp. 71f.

ORPHIC HYMNS

Guthrie, W. K. C., *Orpheus and Greek Religion*, London, 1934, 2nd edn., 1952

Keydell, R., in Pauly–Wissowa, *REkA*, vol. 18, pp. 1321f.

Quandt, G., *Orphei Hymni*, Berlin, 1955, 2nd edn., Berlin, 1962

EPIGRAMS

Keydell, R., in *Reallexikon für Antike und Christentum*, vol. 5, 1961, pp. 536–77 (with bibliography)

Komines, A. D., *Τὸ βυζαντινὸν ἱερὸν ἐπίγραμμα καὶ οἱ ἐπιγραμματοποιοί*, Athens, 1966

PALLADAS

Bowra, C. M., *On Greek Margins*, Oxford, 1970, p. 264
Cameron, A., in *Journal of Hellenic Studies*, vol. 84, 1964, pp. 54f.
Cameron, A., in *BZ*, vol. 57, 1964, pp. 279f.
Cameron, A., in *Classical Quarterly*, vol. 15, 1965, pp. 215f.
Cameron, A., in *Journal of Roman Studies*, vol. 55, 1965, pp. 17f.
Franke, A., *De Pallada Epigrammatographo* (Diss.), Leipzig, 1899
Irmscher, J., *Realismus in der antiken Literatur: Palladas in Memoriam C. Daicoviciu*, Cluj, 1974, pp. 177f.
Peek, W., in Pauly–Wissowa, *REkA*, vol. 18, pp. 158f.
Stella, L. A., *Cinque poeti dell'Antologia Palatina*, Bologna, 1949
Zerwes, W., 'Palladas von Alexandrien' (unpublished Diss.), Tübingen, 1957

PAUL THE SILENTIARY

Corbato, C., *La poesia di Paolo Silenziario*, Trieste, 1951
Friedländer, P., *Johannes von Gaza und Paulus Silentiarius*, Leipzig–Berlin, 1912
Peek, W., in Pauly–Wissowa, *REkA*, vol. 18, pp. 2366f.
Veniero, A., *Paolo Silenziario*, Catania, 1916
Viansino, G., *Paolo Silenziario, epigrammi*, Turin, 1963

AGATHIAS

Cameron, A., in *BZ*, vol. 60, 1967, pp. 374f.
Cameron, A., *Agathias*, Oxford, 1970
Cameron, A. and Cameron, A., in *Journal of Hellenic Studies*, vol. 86, 1966, pp. 6f.; vol. 89, 1969, pp. 108f.
McCail, R. C., in *Mnemosyne*, vol. 4, series 21, 1968, pp. 76f.
McCail, R. C., in *Journal of Hellenic Studies*, vol. 89, 1969, pp. 87f.
McCail, R. C., in *Byzantion*, vol. 41, 1971, pp. 205f.
Tomadakis, N. B., *Φιλοσ. Σχολὴ Πανεπιστημίου 'Αθηνῶν, περ. Β΄*, vol. *Η΄*, 1957–8, pp. 157f. (on the epigrams on his mother)
Viansino, G., *Agatia Scolastico, epigrammi*, Milan, 1967

JULIAN

Hartigan, K. V., in *Eranos*, vol. 73, 1975, pp. 43f.
Thiele, G., in Pauly–Wissowa, *REkA*, vol. 10, pp. 12f.

MACEDONIUS

Cameron, A. and Cameron, A., in *Journal of Hellenic Studies*, vol. 86, 1966, p. 17

LEONTIUS

Cameron, A. and Cameron, A., in *Journal of Hellenic Studies*, vol. 86, 1966, pp. 14f.
Weinreich, O., in *Sitzungsberichte der Heidelberger Akademie der Wissenschaften*, vol. 1, 1944–8, Heidelberg, 1948, pp. 80f., 104f.

The *anacreontea*

Bergk, *PLG*, vol. 3, p. 1080 (John of Gaza); pp. 1098–108 (George the Grammarian); p. 1097 (Akolouthos)
Michelangeli, A., *Anacreonte e la sua fortuna nei secoli*, Bologna, 1922

Nissen, T., *Die byzantinischen Anakreonteen*, Munich, 1940
Preisendanz, C., *Carmina Anacreontea* (Teubner), Leipzig, 1912
Weber, L., *Anacreontea* (Diss.), Göttingen, 1895

CHAPTER 16: CHRISTIAN POETRY

CHRISTIAN POETRY IN ANCIENT METRES

CLEMENT OF ALEXANDRIA

Bardenhewer, O., *Geschichte der altkirchlichen Literatur*, 5 vols., Freiburg, 1913–32
Chadwick, H., *Early Christianity and the Classical Tradition*, Oxford, 1966
Heitsch, *GDRK*, vol. 1², p. 157

METHODIUS OF OLYMPUS

Bonwetsch, N., *Methodius*, Berlin, 1917, pp. 131f. (*Die griech. Christlichen Schrift-
steller der ersten drei Jahrhunderte*)
Christ–Paranikas, *AGCC*, p. 33
Pellegrino, M., *L'Inno del Simposio di S. Metòdio màrtire*, Turin, 1958

GREGORY OF NAZIANZUS

Ackermann, W., *Die didaktische Poesie des Gregorios von Nazianz*, Leipzig, 1903
Altaner, B., *Patrologie*, 5th edn., Freiburg, 1958 (with bibliography)
Bardenhewer, O., *Geschichte der altkirchlichen Literatur*, 5 vols., Freiburg, 1913–32,
vol. 3, pp. 216f.
Christ–Paranikas, *AGCC*, p. 23
Campenhausen, H. von, *Griech. Kirchenväter*, 2nd edn., Stuttgart, 1956, pp. 101f.
Jungck, C., *Gregor von Nazianz, de Vita Sua*, Heidelberg, 1974
Keydell, R., in *BZ*, vol. 43, 1950, p. 33
Lefherz, F., *Studien zu Gregor von Nazianz* (Diss.), Bonn, 1958
Migne, *PG*, vol. 37, pp. 397f.; vol. 38, pp. 11f.
Misch, G., *Geschichte der Autobiographie*, 3rd edn., Frankfurt/Main, 1950, vol. 1, 2,
pp. 383–402
Pellegrino, M., *La poesia di S. Gregorio Nazianzeno*, Milan, 1932
Phytrakis, A. J., *Tò Ποιητικὸν Ἔργον τοῦ Γρηγορίου τοῦ Ναζιανζηνοῦ*,
Athens, 1968
Puech, A., *Histoire de la littérature grecque chrétienne*, vol. 3, Paris, 1930, pp. 318f.
Tuilier, A., *Grégoire de Nazianze; la passion du Christ, Tragédie*, Paris, 1969
Wyss, B., in *Mus. Helvet.* vol. 6, 1949, p. 177

APOLLINARIOS OF LAODICEA

Altaner, B., *Patrologie*, 2nd edn., Freiburg, 1950, p. 271
Golega, J., *Der homerische Psalter*, Ettal, 1960
Lietzmann, H., *Apollinaris von Laodikea und seine Schule*, vol. 1, Tübingen, 1904
Ludwich, A., *Apollinarii Metaphrasis Psalmorum* (Teubner), Leipzig, 1912

SYNESIUS OF CYRENE

Keydell, R., in *Hermes*, vol. 84, 1956, p. 151

Lacombarde, Ch., *Synésios de Cyrène, Hymnes* (Budé), Paris, 1979, vol. 1
Terzaghi, N., *Synesii Cyrenensis Hymni et Opuscula*, 2 vols., Rome, 1939–44
Wilamowitz-Moellendorff, U. von, 'Die hymnen des Proklos und Synesios', *Sitzungsberichte der Preussischen Akademie der Wissenschaften zu Berlin*, Berlin, 1907, pp. 272f.

SOPHRONIUS

Christ–Paranikas, *AGCC*, pp. 43f.
Gigante, M., *Sophronii Anacreontica*, Rome, 1957
Migne, *PG*, vol. 87, 3, p. 3733
Nissen, T., *Die byzantinischen Anakreonteen*, Munich, 1940, pp. 27f.

MAXIMUS CONFESSOR (?)

Beck, *KTLBR*, pp. 436f.
Migne, *PG*, vol. 91, p. 1417

CHRISTIAN POETRY IN THE NEW RHYTHMIC METRES

ROMANOS AND THE *KONTAKION*

Bouvy, E., *Poètes et mélodes*, Nîmes, 1886
Cammelli, G., *Romano il Melode*, Florence, 1930
Grosdidier de Matons, J., *Romanos le Mélode et les origines de la poésie religieuse à Byzance*, Paris, 1977 (with good bibliography)
Grosdidier de Matons, J., *Romanos le Mélode*, Paris, 1977
Krumbacher, K., in *Sitzungsberichte der philos.–philol. und der histor. Klasse der K. Bayerischen Akademie der Wissenschaften*, Munich, 1898, vol. 2, pp. 69f.; 1899, vol. 2, pp. 3f.; 1901, pp. 693f.; 1903, pp. 551f.
Krumbacher, K., in *Abhandlungen der philos.–philol. und der histor. Klasse der K. Bayerischen Akademie der Wissenschaften*, Munich, 1907, vol. 24, 3, pp. 1f.; 1911, vol. 25, 3, pp. 252f.
Maas, P., in *BZ*, vol. 15, 1906, pp. 1f.; vol. 16, 1907, pp. 565f; vol. 19, 1910, pp. 285f.; vol. 24, 1923–4, pp. 1f.
Maas, P., *FBKP*
Maas, P., in *Byzantion*, vol. 14, 1939, pp. 381f.
Maas–Trypanis, *SRMCG*
Maas–Trypanis, *SRMCD*
Meyer, W., *Anfang und Ursprung der lateinischen und griechischen rhythmischen Dichtung: Gesammelte Abhandlungen zur mittellateinischen Rhythmik*, Berlin, 1905, vol. 2, pp. 1f.
Mioni, E., *Romano il Melode*, Padua, 1937
Mitsakis, K., *The Vocabulary of Romanos the Melodist* (Diss.), Oxford, 1964
Mitsakis, K., *Βυζαντινὴ Ὑμνογραφία*, Athens, 1971, vol. 1, pp. 357f. (with good bibliography)
Pitra, *AS*, vol. 1
Tomadakis, N. B., *Ῥωμανοῦ τοῦ Μελωδοῦ Ὕμνοι*, 6 vols., Athens, 1952–61
Trypanis, C. A., in *Byzantion*, vol. 36, 1966, pp. 560f.
Wellesz, E., *A History of Byzantine Music and Hymnography*, 2nd edn., Oxford, 1961, pp. 5f.

PART THREE: THE BYZANTINE WORLD

Section I: From Heraclius to the Restoration of the Images (641–843)

CHAPTER 17: THE SUPREMACY OF RELIGIOUS POETRY

RELIGIOUS POETRY

Verse composed in ancient metres

ELIAS SYNKELLOS

Christ–Paranikas, *AGCC*, pp. 47f.
Matranga, P., *Anecdota Graeca*, 2 vols., Rome, 1850, vol. 2, pp. 641f.
Nissen, T., *Die byzantinischen Anakreonteen*, Munich, 1940, pp. 46f.

MICHAEL SYNKELLOS

Nissen, T., *Die byzantinischen Anakreonteen*, Munich, 1940, pp. 48f.

ARSENIOS

Matranga, P., *Anecdota Graeca*, 2 vols., Rome, 1850, vol. 2, pp. 670f.

ANDREW OF CRETE

Beck, *KTLBR*, pp. 503f.
Dölger, *BDIR*, 39.56
Heisenberg, A., in *BZ*, vol. 10, 1901, pp. 505f.

Verse composed according to the rhythmic metrical system

THE *TROPARION*

Texts in *Horologion, Menaea, Parakletike, Pentekostarion, Theotokarion, Triodion*

Bardenhewer, O., *Geschichte der altkirchlichen Literatur*, 5 vols., Freiburg, 1913–32
Beck, *KTLBR*, pp. 262f.
Christ–Paranikas, *AGCC*, pp. 54f.
Maas, P., Mercati, S. G., and Gassisi, S., in *BZ*, vol. 18, 1909, pp. 309f.
Raes, A., in *Enciclopedia Cattòlica*, vol. 12, 1954, cols. 571f.
Wellesz, E., *A History of Byzantine Music and Hymnography*, 2nd edn., Oxford, 1971, pp. 146f.

THE DECLINE AND END OF THE *KONTAKION*

Bardenhewer, O., *Geschichte der altkirchlichen Literatur*, 5 vols., Freiburg, 1913–32, vol. 5
Beck, *TKLBR*, pp. 472f.
Bouvy, E., *Poètes et mélodes*, Nîmes, 1886
Gassisi, S., *Studi Liturgici III*, Grotta Ferrata, 1913
Grosdidier de Matons, J., *Romanos le Mélode*, Paris, 1977

Krumbacher, *GBL*, pp. 676f.

Krumbacher, K., 'Umarbeitungen bei Romanos', *Sitzungsberichte der philos.–philol. Klasse der K. Bayerischen Akademie der Wissenschaften*, Munich, 1899, 2, pp. 3f.

Krumbacher, K., 'Die Akrostichis in der griechischen Kirchenpoesie', *Sitzungsberichte der philos.–philol. und der histor. Klasse der K. Bayerischen Akademie der Wissenschaften*, Munich, 1903, pp. 55f.

Krumbacher, K., 'Miscellen zu Romanos', *Abhandlungen der philos.–philol. und der histor. Klasse der K. Bayerischen Akademie der Wissenschaften*, Munich, 1907, pp. 92f.

Lowe, V., 'A Group of Hagiographical Studite *Kontakia*' (unpublished Diss.), Oxford, 1976

Maas, P., in *BZ*, vol. 15, 1906, pp. 1f.

Maas–Trypanis, *SRMCD*

Mioni, E., *Romano il Melode*, Padua, 1937

Mioni, E., in *Bolletino della Badia Greca di Grotta Ferrata*, vol. 1, 1947, pp. 202f.

Mitsakis, K., *Βυζαντινὴ Ὑμνογραφία*, Athens, 1971

Tomadakis, N. B., *Ρωμανοῦ Μελωδοῦ Ὕμνοι*, Athens, 1952–61, vols. 1–4 and suppl. to vol. 4

Tomadakis, N. B., *Εἰσαγωγὴ εἰς τὴν Βυζ. φιλολογίαν*, vol. 2, *Ἡ Βυζαντινὴ Ὑμνογραφία καὶ Ποίησις*, Athens, 1965

THE CANON

Beck, *KTLBR*, pp. 262f.

Christ, W., in *Sitzungsberichte der philos–philol. und der histor. Klasse der K. Bayerischen Akademie der Wissenschaften*, Munich, 1870, pp. 75f.

Christ–Paranikas, *AGCC* (introduction)

Dölger, *BDIR*, pp. 28f.

Heiming, O., *Syrische Eniânê und griechische Kanones*, Munster, 1932

Krumbacher, *GBL*, pp. 673–9

Pantelakes, E. G., *Συμβολαὶ εἰς τὴν Ἑλλ. Χριστιανικὴν ποίησιν*, vol. 30, 1919, pp. 103–76

Papadopoulos, C. J., *Συμβολαὶ εἰς τὴν ἱστορίαν τῆς παρ᾽ ἡμῖν ἐκκλησιαστικῆς μουσικῆς, καὶ οἱ ἀπὸ τῶν ἀποστολικῶν χρόνων ἄχρι τῶν ἡμερῶν ἡμῶν ἀκμάσαντες ἐπιφανέστεροι μελῳδοί, ὑμνογράφοι, μουσικοὶ καὶ μουσικολόγοι*, Athens, 1890

Weyh, W., in *BZ*, vol. 17, 1908, p. 1f.

ANDREW OF CRETE

Altaner, B., and Stuiber, A., *Patrologie*, 7th edn., Freiburg, 1966, p. 534

Bardenhewer, O., *Geschichte der altkirchlichen Literatur*, 5 vols., Freiburg, 1913–32, vol. 5, pp. 152f.

Beck, *KTLBR*, pp. 500f.

Christ–Paranikas, *AGCC*, pp. 97f., 147f.

Heisenberg, A., in *BZ*, vol. 10, 1901, pp. 505f.

Kampanaos, S., *Νέα Φόρμιγξ*, vol. 2, 1922, pp. 3f, nos. 19–20

Mercenier, E., *A propos d'André de Crète, tome commémoratif du millénaire de la Bibliothèque Patriarchale d'Alexandrie*, Alexandria, 1953, pp. 170f.

Migne, *PG*, vol. 97, pp. 1306f., 1437f.

Nikodemos, Στέφανος τῆς ἀειπαρθένου, ἤτοι Θεοτοκάριον, ed. G. Musaios, Constantinople, 1894

Sanz, P., in *Jahrbuch der Österreichischen Byzantinischen Gesellschaft*, vol. 4, 1955, pp. 1f.

St John of Damascus

Texts in *Menaea, Parakletike, Pentekostarion*

Altaner, B. and Stuiber, A., *Patrologie*, 7th edn., Freiburg, 1966, pp. 526f.

Bardenhewer, O., *Geschichte der altkirchlichen Literatur*, 5 vols., Freiburg, 1913–32, vol. 5, pp. 51f.

Beck, *KTLBR*, pp. 476f.

Christ–Paranikas, *AGCC*, pp. 218f.

Emereau, C., in *Écho d'Orient*, vol. 22, 1923, pp. 434f; vol. 23, 1924, pp. 196f.

Hoeck, J. M., in *Orientalia Christiana Periodica*, vol. 17, 1951, pp. 5–60 (on the research on St John Damascene)

Hussey, J., in *Theological Studies*, vol. 47, 1946, pp. 200f.

Krumbacher, *GBL*, pp. 68f., 674f.

Lauriotes, S., *Ἀνέκδοτοι ἐκκλησιαστικοὶ ὕμνοι, Θεολογία*, vol. 9, 1931, pp. 340f.

Migne, *PG*, vol. 96, pp. 818–1408

Nauck, A., 'Canones Iambici cum Commentario et Indice Verborum', in *Bulletin de L'Académie Impériale des Sciences de St Petersbourg*, vol. 6, 1894, pp. 199f.

Tillyard, H. J. W., 'The Canon for Easter with Music from a Byzantine Hirmologus', *Laudate*, 1, 1923, pp. 61f.

Tillyard, H. J. W., *Monumenta Musicae Byzantinae*, Copenhagen, 1940–9, vol. 3, sect. 5 (transcription of the hymns of the *Octoechus*)

Winkley, S., 'The Canons of John of Damascus to the Theotokos' (unpublished Diss.), Oxford, 1973

Xydis, T., *Οἱ ἰαμβικοὶ κανόνες τοῦ Δαμασκηνοῦ*, Athens, 1948

Cosmas of Maiouma

Beck, *KTLBR*, pp. 515f.

Christ–Paranikas, *AGCC*, pp. 161f.

Lagarde, P. de, and Bolligs, J., *Iohannis Euchaitorum Metropolitae quae in Codice Vaticano Graeco 676 supersunt*, Berlin, 1882, p. 222

Lauriotis, S., in *Θεολογία*, vol. 9, 1931, pp. 340f.

Migne, *PG*, vol. 98, pp. 459f.; pp. 164f.

Papadopoulos-Kerameus, A., in *BZ*, vol. 14, 1905, pp. 519f.

Papadopoulos-Kerameus, A., *Ἀνάλεκτα Ἱεροσολ. Σταχυολογίας*, 5 vols., St Petersburg, 1891–8, vol. 2, pp. 164f.

Tillyard, H. J. W., in *BZ*, vol. 28, 1928, pp. 25f.

Germanos I

Altaner, B. and Stuiber, A., *Patrologie*, 7th edn., Freiburg, 1966, p. 535

Bardenhewer, O., *Geschichte der altkirchlichen Literatur*, 5 vols., Freiburg, 1913–32, vol. 5, pp. 48f.

Beck, *KTLBR*, pp. 473f.
Christ–Paranikas, *AGCC*, pp. 98f.
Dobschütz, E., *Christusbilder*, Leipzig, 1899, pp. 120f. (on the spurious canon on the Icon of Christ)
Krumbacher, *GBL*, pp. 66f.
Pitra, *AS*, vol. 1, p. xvi
Migne, *PG*, vol. 98, p. 453

THEOPHANES GRAPTOS

Texts in *Horologion, Menaea, Pentekostarion*

Christ–Paranikas, *AGCC*, pp. 236f.
Pitra, *AS*, vol. 1, pp. 408f.

THEODORE THE STUDITE

Beck, *KTLBR*, pp. 491f.
Christ–Paranikas, *AGCC*, pp. 83, 101f.
Gardner, A., *Theodore of Studium: His Life and Times*, London, 1905
Hausherr, I., *Saint Theodore Studite, l'homme et l'ascète*, Rome, 1926
Lowe, V., 'A Group of Hagiographical Studite *Kontakia*' (unpublished Diss.), Oxford, 1976
Migne, *PG*, vol. 99, pp. 1757f.
Pitra, *AS*, vol. 1, pp. 336f.

JOSEPH OF THESSALONICA

Texts in *Menaea, Parakletike, Pentekostarion*

Beck, *KTLBR*, pp. 505f.
Eustratiades, S., in *Μακεδονικά*, vol. 2, 1941–52, pp. 70f.
Johannou, P., in *Analecta Bollandiana*, vol. 65, 1947, pp. 134f.

GEORGIOS THE HYMNOGRAPHER

Beck, *KTLBR*, p. 519
Emereau, C., in *Écho d'Orient*, vol. 22, 1923, pp. 424f.
Pitra, *AS*, vol. 1, pp. 275f., 600
Toscani, T., and Cozza, I., *De Immaculata Deiparae Conceptione Hymnologia Graeca*, Rome, 1862
Vitali, F., *Anthologion*, Rome, 1783

CASSIA

Argyropolous, J., *Ἡ Κασσιανή, ὁ βίος καὶ τὸ ποιητικὸν ἔργον αὐτῆς*, Athens, 1924
Beck, *KTLBR*, p. 519
Christ–Paranikas, *AGCC*, pp. 103f.
Eustratiades, S., *Ἐκκλησιαστικὸς Φάρος*, vol. 31, 1932, pp. 92f.
Krumbacher, *GBL*, pp. 715f.
Krumbacher, K., in *Sitzungsberichte der philos.–philol. und der histor. Klasse der K. Bayerischen Akademie der Wissenschaften*, Munich, 1897, pp. 305f.

Maas, P., in *BZ*, vol. 10, 1901, pp. 54f.
Petridés, S., in *Oriens Christianus*, vol. 7, 1902, pp. 218f.
Psichari, J., *Quelques travaux de linguistique, de philologie et de la littérature hellénique*, Paris, 1930, vol. 1, pp. 951f.
Tillyard, H. J. W., in *BZ*, vol. 20, 1911, pp. 420f.

THE *SYNTOMON*

Texts in *Horologion, Menaea, Parakletike, Pentekostarion, Triodon*

Christ–Paranikas, *AGCC*, pp. lxxii, cxv

SECULAR POETRY: A PERIOD OF OBSCURITY

THEODOSIUS THE GRAMMARIAN

Hunger, *HPLB*, p. 113
Lampros, S. P., Ἱστορικὰ Μελετήματα, Athens, 1884, pp. 129f.

THEODORE THE STUDITE

Christ–Paranikas, *AGCC*, pp. 101f. (*stichera* and *idiomela*)
Garzya, A., in Ἐπετηρὶς Ἑταιρ. Βυζαντινῶν Σπουδῶν, vol. 28, 1958, pp. 11f.
Hunger, *HPLB*, p. 167
Migne, *PG*, vol. 99, pp. 1757f. (canons); pp. 1767 (the spurious canon on the Restoration of the Images)
Pitra, *AS*, vol. 1, pp. 336f.
Radošević, N. and Maksimović, L., in *Zbornik Radova Vizantološkog Instituta*, vols. 14–15, 1973, pp. 191f.
Speck, P., in *Helikon*, vol. 3, 1963, pp. 41f.
Speck, P., *Theodoros Studites Jamben auf verschiedene Gegenstände*, Berlin, 1968

THE EMPEROR THEOPHILUS

Bekker, I., *Theophanes Continuatus* (Bonn), pp. 104f.
Bekker, I., *Skylitzes–Kedrenos* (Bonn), vol. 2, pp. 114f.
Dindorf, L. (ed.), *Ioannis Zonarae Epitome Historiarum*, 6 vols., Leipzig, 1868–75, vol. 3, p. 409
Muralt, E., *Georgios Monachos*, St Petersburg, 1859, p. 714

ST METHODIUS AND ST IGNATIUS

Hunger, *HPLB*, pp. 143f.
Mercati, S., in *Bessarione*, vol. 24, 1920, pp. 198f.
Sternbach, L., in *Eos*, vol. 4, 1898, pp. 150f.

CASSIA

Beck, *KTLBR*, pp. 472, 519
Hunger, *HPLB*, p. 168
Krumbacher, K., 'Kasia', in *Sitzungsberichte der philos.–philol. und der histor. Klasse der K. Bayerischen Akademie der Wissenschaften*, Munich, 1897, 3, pp. 347–56
Psichari, J., *Quelques travaux de linguistique, de philologie et de la littérature hellénique*, Paris, 1930, vol. 1, pp. 951f.

Rochow, I., in *Helikon*, vol. 6, 1966, pp. 704f.

Rochow, I., *Studien zu der Person, den Werken und dem Nachleben der Dichterin Kassia*, Berlin, 1967

IGNATIUS THE DEACON

Boissonade, J. F., *Anecdota Graeca*, Paris, 1851, vol. 1, pp. 436f.

Browning, R., in *Revue des études grecques*, vol. 81, 1968, pp. 406f.

Dübner, Fr., in *Euripidis Fragmenta*, Paris, 1846, pp. 91f.

Gigante, M., in *Akten des XI. internationalen Byzantinisten Kongresses* (Munich, 1958), Munich, 1960, pp. 114f.

Hunger, *HPLB*, p. 143

Marenghi, G., in *Emerita*, vol. 25, 1957, pp. 457f.

Matranga, P., *Anecdota Graeca*, 2 vols, Rome, 1850, vol. 2, pp. 607f.

Migne, *PG*, vol. 117, pp. 1164f.

Müller, C. F., *Ignatii Diaconi Tetrasticha Iambica 53, versus in Adamum 143*, Kiel, 1886

Müller, C. F., in *Rhein. Mus.*, vol. 46, 1891, pp. 320f.

Section II: From the Restoration of the Images to the Fourth Crusade (843–1204)

CHAPTER 18: RELIGIOUS POETRY

VERSE COMPOSED IN ANCIENT METRES

JOHANNES GEOMETRES KYRIOTES

Migne, *PG*, vol. 106, pp. 855f. (hymns to the Mother of God); pp. 868f. (*Paradeisos*, paraphrase of the Cantica); pp. 889f. (encomium on St Panteleimon –incomplete)

Sajdak, J., *Joannis Kyriotis Geometrae Hymni in SS Deiparam*, Posen, 1931

Sternbach, L., in *Dissertationes classis philologicae Academiae Litt. Cracoviensis* (Cracow), 16, 1892, pp. 218f.

JOHANNES MAUROPOUS

For more bibliography, see p. 846

Schoinas, S., *Canon on the Virgin in Iambics: The Theotokarion of St Nicodemus of Mount Athos*, Volos, 1974, pp. 196f.

ST NEILOS

Beck, *KTLBR*, p. 607

Emereau, C., in *Écho d'Orient*, vol. 24, 1925, pp. 164f.

Gassisi, S., in *Oriens Christianus*, vol. 4, 1904, pp. 308f.; vol. 5, 1905, pp. 26f. (published separately, Rome, 1906)

Minasi, G., *San Nilo di Calabria*, Naples, 1892

MATTHEOS BLASTARIS

Paraschos, P. B., Ἅπαντα τὰ ὑμνογραφικὰ τοῦ Ματθαίου Βλαστάρη, Athens, 1980

VERSE IN RHYTHMIC METRES

JOSEPH THE HYMNOGRAPHER

Christ–Paranikas, *AGCC*, pp. 242–53

Cozza-Luzi, J., in *Bessarione*, vol. 5, 1889, pp. 429f. (on poems other than canons)

Eustratiades, S., in Ῥωμανὸς ὁ Μελῳδός, vol. 1, 1932–3, pp. 413f.

Eustratiades, S., in Θεολογία, vol. 13, 1935, pp. 172f.

Eustratiades, S., in Μακεδονικά, vol. 2, 1941–52, pp. 70f.

Follieri, E., *Initia Hymnorum Ecclesiae Graecae*, Rome, 1960–6, vol. 5, pt. 2, pp. 279f. (for poems found in liturgical books)

Kurtz, E., in *Zapiski of the Imperial Russian Academy of Sciences*, viii, vi, 1, St Petersburg, 1902, pp. 82f.

Migne, *PG*, vol. 105, pp. 925f. (canons)

Mioni, E., in *Bolletino della Badia Greca di Grotta Ferrata*, vol. 2, 1948, pp. 87–98, 177–92 (*kontakia*)

Oikonomides, N. A., in Ἀρχεῖον Πόντου, vol: 18, 1953, pp. 218f.

Papadopoulos–Kerameus, A., *Monumenta Graeca et Latina ad Historiam Photii Pertinentia*, St Petersburg, 1901, vol. 2, pp. 1f.

Pitra, *AS*, vol. 1, pp. 381f. (*kontakia*)

Tomadakis, E. I., Ἰωσὴφ ὁ Ὑμνογράφος, Βίος καὶ ἔργον, Athens, 1971

PHOTIUS

Beck, *KTLBR*, pp. 520f.

Christ–Paranikas, *AGCC*, pp. 50f.

Hergenröther, J., *Photius, Patriarch von Constantinopel, seine Leben, seine Schriften und das griechische Schisma*, 3 vols., Regensburg, 1867–9 (basic but old)

Krumbacher, *GBL*, pp. 73f.

Lauriotis, A., Ἐκκλησιαστικὴ Ἀλήθεια, 1895, no. 28, p. 220

Migne, *PG*, vol. 102, pp. 577f. (non-liturgical poems)

Nikodemos Hagiorites, Θεοτοκάριον, Venice, 1898, pp. 9f., 20f., 33f., 111f. (four canons)

Papadopoulos-Kerameus, A., in *Pravoslav. Palestinskij Sbornik*, vol. 11, 1892, pp. 9f. (the canons on the Trinity and on Mary, the Mother of God)

Papadopoulos-Kerameus, A., in *Lêtopis of the University of Odessa*, Byzantine Section, vol. 5, 1900, pp. 527f. (on the Transfiguration)

Pitra, *AS*, vol. 1, pp. 438f.

Ziegler, K., in *Kleine Pauly*, vol. 4, pp. 813f.

Ziegler, K., in Pauly–Wissowa, *REkA*, vol. 20, pp. 667f.

ANASTASIOS QUAESTOR

Beck, *KTLBR*, pp. 605

Bouvy, E., in *Écho d'Orient*, vol. 1, 1897–8, pp. 262f.

Ehrhard, A., *Überlieferung und Bestand der hagiographischen und homiletischen Literatur der griechischen Kirche*, Leipzig, 1937f., vol. 1, pt. 1, p. 436

LEO VI (THE WISE)

Idiomela in *Menaea, Pentekostarion, Triodion*

Beck, *KTLBR*, pp. 546f.

Christ–Paranikas, *AGCC*, pp. 105f. (the eleven morning hymns), p. 109 (one *idiomelon*)
Krumbacher, *GBL*, p. 721
Migne, *PG*, vol. 107, pp. 300f., 309f. (the anacreontic ode)
Moravcsik, G., *Byzantinoturcica*, 2nd edn., Berlin, 1958, vol. 1, pp. 400f. (general literature)
Nissen, T., *Die byzantinischen Anakreonteen*, Munich, 1940, pp. 65f. (the anacreontic ode)

CONSTANTINE PORPHYROGENITUS

Beck, *KTLBR*, p. 551
Christ–Paranikas, *AGCC*, pp. 110f.
Krumbacher, *GBL*, pp. 252f.
Lippold, A., in *Kleine Pauly*, vol. 1, pp. 1289f.
Moravcsik, G., and Jenkins, R., *de Administrando Imperio*, 2 vols., Budapest, 1949–62
Ostrogorsky, G., *Geschichte des byzantinischen Staates*, 2nd edn., Munich, 1952, pp. 224f.

LEON CHOEROSPHACTES, MAGISTER

Follieri, E., *Initia Hymnorum Ecclesiae Graecae*, Rome, 1960–6, vol. 5, pt. 2, p. 291
Mioni, E., in *Byzantion*, vol. 19, 1949, p. 127 (a *kontakion*)

CHRISTOPHOROS OF MYTILENE

Follieri, E., *I calendri in metro innografico di Christoforo Mitileneo*, 2 vols., Brussels, 1980

JOHANNES MAUROPOUS

Beck, *KTLBR*, pp. 555f.
Follieri, E., *Initia Hymnorum Ecclesiae Graecae*, Rome, 1960–6, vol. 5, pt. 2, pp. 274f. (the hymns found in the liturgical books and the *Theotokarion*)
Follieri, E., *Giovanni Mauropode metropolita di Eucaita, otto canoni paracletici a N. S. Gesú Cristo*, Rome, 1967
Gärtner, H., in *Kleine Pauly*, vol. 3, pp. 1096f.
Gudeman, in Pauly–Wissowa, *REkA*, vol. 9, 2, pp. 1750f.
Hussey, J., in *Journal of Roman Studies*, vol. 37, 1947, pp. 70f.
Hussey, J., in *BZ*, vol. 44, 1951, pp. 278f.
Krumbacher, *GBL*, pp. 171f., 740f.
Lagarde, P. de, and Bolligs, J., *Ioannis Euchaitarum Metropolitae quae in Codice Vaticano Graeco 676 supersunt*, Berlin, 1882
Lauriotes, S., Ἁγιορειτικὴ Βιβλιοθήκη, Volos, 1937 (twenty-one canons)
Migne, *PG*, vol. 120, pp. 119–1200
Moravcsik, G., *Byzantinoturcica*, 2nd edn., Berlin, 1958, vol. 1, pp. 334f.
Reitzenstein, R., *Geschichte der griechischen Etymologika*, Leipzig, 1897, pp. 173f.
Tomadakis, E. I., Ἰωσὴφ ὁ Ὑμνογράφος, Βίος καὶ ἔργον, Athens, 1971, pp. 234f.

THE ITALO-BYZANTINE POETS

St Neilos

Gassisi, S., in *Oriens Christianus*, vol. 5, 1905, pp. 26f.; published separately, Rome, 1906

Paul of Grotta Ferrata

Gassisi, S., in *Oriens Christianus*, vol. 5, 1905, pp. 74f.

Bartholomaeus

Giovanelli, G., *Gli inni sacri di S. Bartholomeo juniore*, Grotta Ferrata, 1955
Schiro, J., *Innografi Italo-Greci*, Grotta Ferrata, 1947 (critical work on all poets)

Johannes Zonaras

Migne, *PG*, vol. 135, pp. 413f.

Georgios Skylitzes

Petrides, S., in *Vizantijskij Vremennik*, vol. 10, 1903, pp. 46of.

Nicolaos Kataskepanos

Texts in Nikodemos Hagioreites, Θεοτοκάριον, Venice, 1898, pp. 76, 98

Beck, *KTLBR*, p. 639
Emereau, C., in *Écho d'Orient*, vol. 23, 1924, p. 414
Mercati, S. G., in *Studi bizantini*, vol. 3, 1931, pp. 299f.

Eustathius of Thessalonica

Beck, *KTLBR*, pp. 634f.
Gärtner, H., in *Kleine Pauly*, vol. 2, pp. 464f. (for further literature)
Krumbacher, *GBL*, pp. 536f.
Migne, *PG*, vol. 36, pp. 161f., 284f.
Tafel, L. F., *Eustathii Metropolitae Thessalonicensis Opuscula*, Frankfurt, 1832, pp. 136f., 167f; rpt. Amsterdam, 1964

PARODIES OF RELIGIOUS VERSE

Michael Psellus

Beck, *KTLBR*, p. 538
Gärtner, H., in *Kleine Pauly*, vol. 4, pp. 1210f.
Hunger, *HPLB*, p. 117
Kriaras, E., in Pauly–Wissowa, *REkA*, suppl. 11, pp. 1124f.
Krumbacher, *GBL*, pp. 433f.
Kurtz, E., and Drexl, F., *Michaelis Pselli Scripta Minora*, Milan, 1936, vol. 1, pp. 108f.
Migne, *PG*, vol. 14, pp. 199f.

RELIGIOUS POETRY IN POLITICAL VERSE

Symeon the Mystic

Beck, *KTLBR*, pp. 585f.
Beck, H.-G., in *BZ*, vol. 46, 1953, pp. 57f.
Hausherr, I., *Symeon le Nouveau Théologien*, Rome, 1928
Holl, K., *Enthusiasmus und Bussgewalt beim griechischen Mönchtum*, Leipzig, 1898
Kambylis, A., *Symeon Neos Theologos, Hymnen*, Berlin–New York, 1976 (includes a full bibliography)
Koder, J., in *Jahrbuch der Österreichischen Byzantinischen Gesellschaft*, vol. 15, 1966, pp. 153f.
Koder, J., *Syméon le Nouveau Théologien, hymnes*, 3 vols., Paris, 1969–73
Maas, P., *Aus der Poesie des Mystikers Symeon, Festgabe A. Ehrhard*, Bonn–Leipzig, 1922, pp. 328f.

Nicolaos iii Grammatikos

Koder, J., in *Jahrbuch der Österreichischen Byzantinischen Gesellschaft*, vol. 19, 1970, p. 203

CHAPTER 19: SECULAR POETRY

VERSE IN THE PURIST IDIOM

Epigrams, riddles, oracles and other occasional poetry

Johannes Geometres Kyriotes

Beck, *KTLBR*, pp. 553f.
Hörandner, W., in *Jahrbuch der Österreichischen Byzantinischen Gesellschaft*, vol. 19, 1970, pp. 109f.
Hunger, *HPLB*, p. 169
Migne, *PG*, vol. 106, pp. 901f. (epigrams)
Scheidweiler, F., in *BZ*, vol. 45, 1952, pp. 277f.

Christophoros of Mytilene

Hunger, *HPLB*, p. 171
Krumbacher, *GBL*, pp. 737f.
Kurtz, E., *Die Gedichte des Christophoros Mytilenaios*, Leipzig, 1903

Johannes Mauropous

Beck, *KTLBR*, pp. 555f.
Gudeman, in Pauly–Wissowa, *REkA*, vol. 9, pp. 1750f.
Hörandner, W., in *Jahrbuch der Österreichischen Byzantinischen Gesellschaft*, vol. 19, 1970, pp. 109f.
Hunger, *HPLB*, p. 169
Hussey, J. M., in *Journal of Roman Studies*, vol. 37, 1947, pp. 70f.
Hussey, J. M., in *BZ*, vol. 44, 1951, pp. 278f.
Krumbacher, *GBL*, pp. 171f.

Lagarde, P. de, and Bolligs, J., *Ioannis Euchaitorum Metropolitae quae in Codice Vaticano Graeco 676 supersunt*, Berlin, 1882; rpt. in Migne, *PG*, vol. 120, pp. 1039f.

Moravcsik, G., *Byzantinoturcica*, 2nd edn., Berlin, 1958, vol. 1, pp. 334f. (for further bibliography)

Reitzenstein, R., *Terentius Varro und Johannes Mauropous von Euchaita*, Leipzig, 1904

CONSTANTINE THE SICILIAN

Bergk, *PLG*, vol. 3, pp. 1084f.

Cramer, J. A., *Anecdota Graeca*, 4 vols., Oxford, 1839–41, vol. 4, p. 380 (the short romantic ode)

Krumbacher, *GBL*, p. 723

Matranga, P., *Anecdota Graeca*, 2 vols., Rome, 1850, vol. 1, pp. 555f.

Migne, *PG*, vol. 107, pp. lxif.

Monaco, G., in *Studi bizantini e neoellenici*, vol. 7, 1953, pp. 153f. (the lament on the death by drowning of his father and brothers)

Nissen, T., *Die byzantinischen Anakreonteen*, Munich, 1940, pp. 63f.

Reitzenstein, R., in Pauly–Wissowa, *REkA*, vol. 4, pp. 1033f.

NICOLAOS KALLIKLES

Hunger, *HPLB*, p. 171

Krumbacher, *GBL*, pp. 744f.

Sternbach, L. (ed.), *Nicolai Calliclis Carmina*, Cracow, 1903

THEODOROS PRODROMOS

Bernardinello, S., *Theodori Prodromi de Manganis*, Padua, 1972

Colonna, A., *Heliodori Aethiopica*, Rome, 1938, pp. 363f.

Diehl, C., *Figures byzantines*, 8th edn., Paris, 1927, vol. 2

Galavotti, C., in *Studi bizantini e neoellenici*, vol. 4, 1935, pp. 218f.

Galavotti, C., in *Atti dell'Accadèmia dei Lincei* III (*Rendiconti della classe di scienze morali, storiche e filologiche dell'Accadèmia dei Lincei*, vol. 4, 1949, pp. 357f.

Garzya, A., *Versi e un opusculo inediti di Michele Psello*, Naples, 1966

Gianelli, C., in *Analecta Bollandiana*, vol. 75, 1957, pp. 299f.

Gianelli, C., *Epigrammi di Teodoro Prodromo: Studi in onore di Luigi Castiglioni*, Florence, 1960, p. 333

Gulielmino, A. M., in *Siculorum Gymnasium*, n.s., vol. 27, 1974, pp. 121f.

Herscher, R., *Scriptores Erotici Graeci*, Leipzig, 1859, vol. 2, pp. 555f. (*Hysmine and Hysminias*)

Herscher, R., Κατομυομαχία, Leipzig, 1873

Hörandner, W., in *Byzantinische Forschugnen*, vol. 4, 1972, pp. 88f.

Hörandner, W., *Theodoros Prodromos, Historische Gedichte*, Vienna, 1974

Hunger, *HPLB*, vol. 2, pp. 128f., 144f.

Hunger, H., *Der byzantinische Katz–Mäuse–Krieg: Theodoros Prodromos, Katomyomachia*, Vienna, 1968

Krumbacher, *GBL*, pp. 751f.

Krumbacher, K., in *Jahrbuch der Österreichischen Byzantinischen Gesellschaft*, vol. 16, 1967, pp. 91f.

Markakes, P., Κατομυομαχία, Athens, 1955

Mathieu, M., in *Byzantion*, vol. 23, 1953–4, pp. 131f.

Mercati, S. G., in *Rendiconti dell'Accademia dei Lincei*, vol. 28, 1919, pp. 426f.

Migne, *PG*, vol. 122, p. 1075; vol. 133, p. 1419

Miller, E., in *Notices et extraits de la Bibliothèque Nationale*, vol. 23, 1872, pt. 2, pp. 1f.

Moravcsik, G., *Byzantinoturcica*, 2nd edn., Berlin, 1958, vol. 1, pp. 523f.

Sternbach, L., in *Wien. Stud.*, vol. 25, 1903, pp. 10f.

Sulogiannes, E., Στίχοι φερόμενοι ὡς πτωχοπροδρομικοὶ εἰς χειρόγραφον τοῦ ῾Αγ. ῎Ορους, Athens, 1968

Vilborg, E., *Achilleus Tatios*, Stockholm, 1955, p. xliv

JOHANNES TZETZES

Bekker, I., *Antehomerica, Homerica et Posthomerica*, Berlin, 1816, vol. 1

Bekker, I., in *Abhandlungen der Deutschen Akademie der Wissenschaften zu Berlin*, Berlin, 1840, pp. 147–69

Boissonade, J. F. (ed.), Paris, 1851 (*Iliad*, allegories)

Browning, R., in *Byzantion*, vol. 31, 1961, pp. 229f.

Browning, R., in *Past and Present*, vol. 28, 1964, pp. 14f.

Cramer, J. A., *Anecdota Graeca*, 4 vols., Oxford, 1835–7, vol. 3, pp. 302f.; vol. 4, pp. 1–148

Dölger, *BDIR*, pp. 23f.

Hörandner, W., in *Byzantion*, vol. 39, 1969, pp. 108f.

Hunger, *HPLB*, pp. 117f.

Hunger, H., in *Jahrbuch der Österreichischen Byzantinischen Gesellschaft*, vol. 4, 1955, pp. 13f.

Hunger, H., in *BZ*, vol. 48, 1955, pp. 4f.; vol. 49, 1956, pp. 249f.

Kaibel, *CGF*, pp. 34–49

Kiessling, M. T., *Historiarum Variarum Chiliades*, Leipzig, 1826; rpt. Hildesheim, 1963

Krumbacher, *GBL*, p. 526

Lehrs, F. S., *Hesiodi Carmina*, Paris, 1878

Leone, P. A. M., *Ioannis Tzetzae Historiae*, Naples, 1968

Magri, M. A., in *Bolletino del Comitàto per la Preparazione di Edizioni Nazionali di Classici Greci e Latini*, vol. 9, 1961, pp. 73f.

Matranga, P., *Anecdota Graeca*, Rome, 1850, vol. 1

Mercati, S., in *Byzantion*, vol. 18, 1946–8, pp. 197f.

Mercati, S., in *BZ*, vol. 44, 1951, pp. 416f.

Moravcsik, G., in *BZ*, vol. 49, 1956, pp. 33f.

Moravcsik, G., *Byzantinoturcica*, 2nd edn., Berlin, 1958, pp. 342f.

Petrides, S., in *BZ*, vol. 12, 1903, pp. 568f.

Positano Massa, L., *et al.*, *Commentarii in Aristophanem*, 3 vols., Groningen, 1960–2

Schmitt, W. D., in *Kleine Pauly*, vol. 5, 1031f.

Speck, P., in *Rhein. Mus.*, vol. 102, 1959, pp. 15f.

Walz, C., *Rhetores Graeci*, 9 vols., Stuttgart–Tübingen, 1832–6, vol. 3, pp. 670f.

Wendel, C., in *BZ*, vol. 40, 1940, pp. 23f.

Wendel, C., in Pauly–Wissowa, *REkA*, vol. 8A, pp. 1959f.

Satirical and humorous verse

Hunger, *HPLB*, pp. 149f.

Kyriakis, M. J., in Βυζαντινά, vol. 5, 1973, pp. 289f.

Soyter, G., *Griechischer Humor von Homers Zeiten bis Heute*, 2nd edn., Berlin, 1961, pp. 92f.

CONSTANTINE THE RHODIAN

Matranga, P., *Anecdota Graeca*, Rome, 1850, vol. 2, pp. 624f.
Wolters, P., in *Rhein. Mus.*, vol. 38, 1883, pp. 115f.

MICHAEL PSELLUS

Kurtz, E., and Drexl, F., *Michaelis Pselli Scripta Minora*, Milan, 1936, vol. 1, pp. 220f.
See also p. 847

THEODOROS PRODROMOS

Ahlborn, H., *Pseudo–Homer, der Froschmäusekrieg; Theodoros Prodromos, der Katz–Mäuse–Krieg*, 2nd edn., Berlin, 1968
Boissonade, J. F., *Anecdota Graeca*, 5 vols., Paris, 1829–33, vol. 4, pp. 430f.
Hunger, H., *Der byzantinische Katz–Mäuse–Krieg: Theodoros Prodromos, Katomyomachia*, Vienna, 1968
Miller, E., *Manuelis Philae Carmina*, Paris, 1857, vol. 2, pp. 306f.

The ecphrasis

LEON CHOEROSPHACTES

Anasti, E., in *Siculorum Gymnasium*, n. s., vol. 17, 1964, pp. 1f.
AP, bk. 4, no. 75
Kolias, G., *Leon Choerosphactes*, Athens, 1939
Maas, P., in *BZ*, vol. 25, 1925, pp. 358f.
Mercati, S. G., in *Rivista degli studi orientali*, vol. 10, 1924, pp. 212f.
Nissen, T., *Die Anakreonteen*, Munich, 1940, pp. 62f.

CONSTANTINE THE RHODIAN

Downey, G. M., *Constantine the Rhodian, his Life and Writings: Late Classical and Medieval Studies in Honour of A. M. Friend Jr*, Washington, D. C., 1955
Legrand, É., in *Revue des études grecques*, vol. 9, 1896, pp. 31f.

The verse chronicle

Bekker, I., edition of Constantine Manasses in the Bonn corpus, Bonn, 1837
Horna, K., in *BZ*, vol. 13, 1904, pp. 313f.
Miller, E., in *Notices et extraits de la Bibliothèque Nationale*, vol. 23, 1872, pt. 2, pp. 8f.
Tsolakis, E. T., *Συμβολὴ στὴ μελέτη τοῦ ποιητικοῦ ἔργου τοῦ Κωνσταντίνου Μανασσῆ καὶ κριτικὴ ἔκδοση τοῦ μυθιστορήματός του "Τά κατ' Ἀρίστανδρον καί Καλλιθέαν"*, Salonica, 1967

The verse romance

Boissonade, J. F., *Scriptores Erotici*, Paris, 1856
Cupane, C., *Atti dell'Accademia di Scienze, Lettere e Arti di Palermo*, series 4, vol. 33, 1973–4, pp. 243f.
Deligiorgis, S., in *Neo-Hellenika*, vol. 2, 1975, pp. 21f.

Gigante, M., in *Akten des XI. Internationalen Byzantinisten Kongresses* (Munich, 1958), Munich, 1960, pp. 168f.

Helfer, B., Niketas Eugenianos, ein Rhetor und Dichter der Komnenenzeit (unpublished Diss.), Vienna, 1972

Helm, R., *Der antike Roman*, Göttingen, 1956

Herscher, R., *Scriptores Erotici Graeci*, Leipzig, 1859, vol. 2

Hörandner, W., in *Byzantinische Forschungen*, vol. 4, 1972, pp. 55f.

Horna, K., in *BZ*, vol. 13, 1904, pp. 347f.

Hunger, *HPLB*, pp. 119f.

Mazal, O., in *Jahrbuch der Österreichischen Byzantinischen Gesellschaft*, vol. 15, 1966, pp. 231f.

Mazal, O., in *BZ*, vol. 60, 1967, pp. 249f.

Mazal, O., in *Wiener byzantinische Studien*, vol. 4, 1967 (edition Manasses)

Rohde, E., *Der griechische Roman*, 3rd edn., Leipzig, 1914

Schissel, O., *Der byzantinische Garten*, Vienna, 1942

Svoboda, K., in *Izvestija Bulg. Archaeol. Instituta*, vol. 9, 1935, pp. 191f. (on Nicetas Eugenianos in French)

Tsolakis, E. T., *Συμβολὴ στὴ μελέτη τοῦ ποιητικοῦ ἔργου τοῦ Κωνσταντίνου Μανασσῆ καὶ κριτικὴ ἔκδοση τοῦ μυθιστορήματός του "Τὰ κατ' Ἀρίστανδρον καί Καλλιθέαν"*, Salonica, 1967

POETRY COMPOSED IN THE VERNACULAR

The Epic Cycle of Digenis Akritas

Beck, *GBV*, pp. 60, 62

Dieterich, K., in *BZ*, vol. 13, 1904, pp. 53f.

Grégoire, H., *Διγενὴς Ἀκρίτας*, New York, 1942, pp. 219f.

Kalonaros, P. P., *Βασίλειος Διγενὴς Ἀκρίτας*, 2 vols., 2nd edn., Athens, 1970, vol. 2, pp. 207f.

Kyriakidis, S., *Ὁ Διγενὴς Ἀκρίτας*, Athens, 1926, pp. 35f.

Petropoulos, S., *Ἑλληνικὰ δημοτικὰ τραγούδια (Βασικὴ Βιβλιοθήκη*, 46.47), Athens 1958–9, vol. 1, pp. 1f.

Politis, N. G., *Ἐκλογαὶ ἀπὸ τὰ τραγούδια τοῦ Ἑλληνικοῦ λαοῦ*, 3rd edn., Athens, 1932, pp. 79–106

Rhomaios, K., in *Ἀρχεῖον Πόντου*, vol. 17, 1952, pp. 155–71: *Τὰ Ἀκριτικὰ τραγούδια τοῦ Πόντου*

Rhomaios, K., in *Κρητικα Χρονικά.*, vol. 7, 1953, pp. 394–408: *Ἡ Κρητικὴ παραλλαγὴ τοῦ Θανάτου τοῦ Διγενῆ*

Rhomaios, K., in, *Αρχεῖον Πόντου*, vol. 27, 1966, pp. 150–206

Trapp, E., *Studi classici in onore di Q. Cataudella*, Catania, 1972, vol. 2, pp. 637f.

The Epic of Digenis Akritas

Alexiou, S., *Ἀκριτικά*, Herakleion, 1979

Beck, *GBV*, pp. 48f.

Diehl, C., *Figures byzantines*, 8th edn., Paris, 1927, pp. 291f.

Grégoire, H., in *Byzantion*, vol. 5, 1929–30, pp. 327f.

Grégoire, H., in *Bulletin de la classe de lettres*, Académie Royale de Belgique, 1931, pp. 463f.

Grégoire, H., in *Byzantion*, vol. 6, 1931, pp. 481f.

Grégoire, H., in *Bulletin du IIIe Congrès International des Études Byzantines*, Athens, 1932, p. 281

Grégoire, H., in *Byzantion*, vol. 7, 1932, pp. 287f.

Grégoire, H., in *Byzantion*, vol. 8, 1933, pp. 572f.

Grégoire, H., *Mélanges N., Jorga*, Paris, 1933, pp. 383f.

Grégoire, H., in *Revue des études grecques*, vol. 46, 1933, pp. 29f.

Grégoire, H., *Mélanges Bidez*, Brussels, 1934, pp. 451f.

Grégoire, H., in *Bulletin de la classe des lettres*, Académie Royale de Belgique, 1936, pp. 224f.

Grégoire, H., in *Byzantion*, vol. 14, 1939, pp. 255f.

Grégoire, H., *Διγενὴς Ἀκρίτας*, New York, 1942

Grégoire, H. and Goossens, R., in *L'Antiquité Classique*, vol. 1, 1932, pp. 429f.; vol. 2, 1933, pp. 449f.

Hesseling, D. C., *Λαογραφία*, vol. 23, 1912, pp. 537f.

Impellizzeri, S., *Il Digenis Akritas, l'epopea di Bisanzio*, Florence, 1940

Kalonaros, P. P., *Βασίλειος Διγενὴς Ἀκρίτας*, 2 vols., 2nd edn., Athens, 1970

Knös, B., *Histoire de la littérature néo-grecque*, Stockholm–Göteborg–Uppsala, 1962

Kuz'mina, V. D., *Devgenievo Dejanie*, Moscow, 1962, pp. 3f.

Kyriakides, S., *Ο Διγενὴς Ἀκρίτας*, Athens, 1926

Kyriakides, S., *Ἀκριτικαὶ Μελέται, Miscellanea G. Mercati*, Vatican, 1946, vol. 3, pp. 1f.

Kyriakides, S., in *Akten des XI. Internationalen Byzantinisten Kongresses* (Munich, 1958), Munich, 1960, vol. 2, p. 1f.

Lampros, S., *Collection de romans grecs en langue vulgaire et en vers*, Paris, 1880, vol. 3

Legrand, É., *Les exploits de Basile Digénis Acritas, epopée byzantine publiée d'après le manuscrit de Grotta Ferrata*, 2nd edn., Paris, 1902

Mavrogordato, J., *Digenis Akrites*, Oxford, 1956

Meliarakis, A., *Βασίλειος Διγενὴς Ἀκρίτας*, Athens, 1881

Notopoulos, J. A., in *Λαογραφία*, vol. 17, 1958, pp. 451–3; vol. 18, 1959, pp. 423–31

Paschales, D., in *Λαογραφία*, vol. 9, 1926, pp. 305f.: *Οἱ Δέκα λόγοι τοῦ Διγ. Ἀκρίτα*

Politis, L., in *Atti del Convegno Internazionale sul Tema: La poesia epica e la sua formazione*, Rome, 1970 (Accademia Nazionale dei Lincei, anno 36? (1970), quaderno 139, pp. 551f.)

Rambaud, A., in *Revue des deux mondes*, vol. 4, 1875, pp. 922f.

Sathas, K., and Legrand, É., *Les exploits de Basile Digénis Acrites*, Paris, 1875

Syrkin, A. J., in *Vizantijskij Vremennik*, vol. 13, 1906, pp. 488f.

Syrkin, A. J., *Poema o Digenise Akrite*, Moscow, 1964

Trapp, E., *Digenis Akritas*, Vienna, 1971

Trypanis, C. A., in *Gnomon*, vol. 45, 1973, pp. 614f.

Zerlentes, B. G., *Εὐσταθίου πρός τινα Μανουὴλ προσφιλέστατον αὐτοῦ*, Athens, 1920

The Ptochoprodromic poems and other verse in the vernacular

The Ptochoprodromic poems

Beck, *GBV*, pp. 4f., 101f.
Hesseling, D. C., and Pernot, H., *Poèmes Prodromiques en grec vulgaire*, Amsterdam, 1910

The *Spaneas*

Beck, *GBV*, pp. 105f.
Papademetriou-Theodoride, N., in Ἑλληνικά, vol. 28, 1975, pp. 92f.
Wagner, W., *Carmina Graeca Medii Aevi*, Leipzig, 1874; rpt. in G. Zoras, Βυζαντινὴ Ποίησις, Βασικὴ Βιβλιοθήκη, Athens, 1956, vol. 1, p. 72
Zoras, G., in *Rivista di studi bizantini e neoellenici*, vol. 1, 1964, pp. 47f. (a new version from Epirus (Cod. Vat. Gr. 1831), which includes 229 previously unknown lines)

Michael Glykas

Legrand É., *Bibliothèque grecque vulgaire*, Paris, 1880–1913, vol. 1, pp. 18f.
Sathas, K., Μεσαιωνικὴ Βιβλιοθήκη, Venice, 1872–98, vol. 5, pp. 544f. (the collection of proverbs)
Tsolakis, E. T., Μιχαὴλ Γλυκᾶ στίχοι οὓς ἔγραψεν καθ᾿ ὃν κατεσχέθη καιρόν, Salonica, 1959
Wagner, W., *Carmina Graeca Medii Aevi*, Leipzig, 1874 (the proverbs)

Section III: From the Conquest of Constantinople by the Franks to the Fall of the City to the Turks (1204–1453)

CHAPTER 20: RELIGIOUS POETRY

Patriarch Germanos II

Follieri, E., *Initia Hymnorum Ecclesiae Graecae*, Rome, 1960–6, vol. 5, pt. 2, p. 260
Horna, K., in *Program des Sophien–Gymnasiums in Wien*, 1901–2, pp. 13f.
Papadopoulos-Kerameus, A., in *Vizantijskij Vremennik*, vol. 13, 1906, pp. 488f.

Nicephorus Blemmydes

Bury, J. B., in *BZ*, vol. 6, 1897, pp. 526f.
Heisenberg, A., *Nicephori Blemmydae Curriculum Vitae*, Leipzig, 1892, pp. 122f.
Hunger, *HPLB*, p. 162

The Emperor Theodore II Doucas Lascaris

Leggeris, C., and Paraskeuopoulos, K., Ὡρολόγιον τὸ Μέγα, Athens, 1898, pp. 536f.
Migne, *PG*, vol. 140, pp. 777f.
Nicodemus Hagioreites, Θεοτοκάριον, Volos, 1974, pp. 98f.
Papadopoulos, J. B., *Théodore II Laskaris, empéreur de Nicée*, Paris, 1908

Arsenios Autoreianos

Beck, *KTLBR*, p. 703
Follieri, E., *Initia Hymnorum Ecclesiae Graecae*, Rome, 1960–6, vol. 5, pt. 2, p. 255
Koutloumousianos, B., Πεντηκοστάριον Χαρμόσυνον, Athens, 1959 ('Αποστολικὴ Διακονία)

Manuel Holobolos

Beck, *KTLBR*, p. 704
Boissonade, J. F., *Anecdota Graeca*, 5 vols., Paris 1833, vol. 5, pp. 159f.
Krumbacher, *GBL*, pp. 770f.
Miller, E., *Manuelis Philae Carmina*, 2 vols., Paris 1855–7, vol. 2, pp. 373f.
Treu, M., in *BZ*, vol. 5, 1896, pp. 546f.

Nicephoros Kallistos Xanthopoulos

Cyri Theodori Prodromi Epigrammata . . ., Basiliae apud Ioannem Bebelium, 1536
Hunger, *HPLB*, pp. 172, 114
Jugie, M., in *Byzantion*, vol. 5, 1929–30, pp. 357f., 376f.
Migne, *PG*, vol. 147, pp. 65, 601–6, 623–32
Koutloumousianos, B., Πεντηκοστάριον Χαρμόσυνον, Athens, 1959, pp. 17f.
Papadopoulos-Kerameus, A., in *BZ*, vol. 11, 1902, pp. 43f.

Manuel II Palaeologus

Beck, *KTLBR*, p. 748
Emereau, C., in *Écho d'Orient*, vol. 23, 1924, pp. 408f.
Grumel, V., in *Écho d'Orient*, vol. 26, 1927, p. 343
Legrand, É., *Lettres de l'empéreur Manuel Paléologue publiées d'après trois manuscrits*, premier fasc., Paris, 1893
Matranga, P., *Anecdota Graeca*, Rome, 1850, vol. 2, p. 682

The *Lament of the Virgin*

Alexiou, M., in *Byzantine and Modern Greek Studies*, vol. 1, 1975, pp. 119, 121
Bouvier, B., *Le Mirologue de la Vierge*, Rome, 1976
Manousakas, M. J., *Mélanges Merlier*, Athens, 1956, vol. 2, pp. 49f.
Nikolaidis, J., Ἱερὰ Σύνοψις, Athens, n. d., pp. 506f.
Pallas, D., *Passion und Bestattung Christi, Miscellanea Byzantina Monacensia*, Munich, 1965, vol. 2, pp. 55f.

Mattheus Camariotes

Bidel, A., in *BZ*, vol. 35, 1935, pp. 337f.

Nicolaos Malaxos

Emereau, C., in *Écho d'Orient*, vol. 23, 1924, p. 414
Follieri, E., *Initia Hymnorum Ecclesiae Graecae*, Rome, 1960–6, vol. 5, pt. 2, p. 296
Hunger, *HPLB*, p. 211

Johannes Plousiadenos

Beck, *KTLBR*, pp. 771f.
Follieri, E., *Initia Hymnorum Ecclesiae Graecae*, Rome, 1960–6, vol. 5, pt. 2, p. 278

Hunger, *HPLB*, pp. 208f.

Manousakas, M. J., in *Revue des études byzantines*, vol. 17, 1959, pp. 28f.

Manousakas, M. J., in *'Aθηνᾶ*, vol. 68, 1965, pp. 49f.

CHAPTER 21: SECULAR POETRY

POETRY IN THE PURIST IDIOM

Constantine Anagnostes

Bǎnescu, N., *Deux poètes byzantins du XIIIe siècle*, Bucharest, 1913

Krumbacher, *GBL*, p. 774

Georgios Lapithis

Boissonade, J. F., in *Notices et extraits de la Bibliothèque Nationale*, vol. 12, 1831, 2, pp. 1–74

Migne, *PG*, vol. 149, pp. 1002f.

Maximus Planudes

Beckby, H., *Anthologia Graeca*, 2nd edn., Munich, 1965–

Hunger, *HPLB*, pp. 68f. (see also bibliography)

Migne, *PG*, vol. 20, pp. 2202f.

Schmitt, W. O., in *Kleine Pauly*, vol. 4, pp. 890f.

Wendel, C., *Geschichte der Textüberlieferung der antiken und mittelatlerlichen Literatur*, Zurich, 1961, vol. 1

Manuel Philes

Dübner, F. and Lehrs, F. S., *Poetae Didactici et Bucolici*, Paris, 1862

Holzinger, C. von, in *BZ*, vol. 20, 1911, pp. 734f.

Hunger, *HPLB*, pp. 114f.

Krumbacher, *GBL*, p. 728

Maas, P., in *BZ*, vol. 12, 1903, pp. 295f.

Martini, E., *Carmina Inedita*, Naples, 1900

Migne, *PG*, vol. 158, pp. 961f.

Miller, E., *Manuelis Philae Carmina*, 2 vols., Paris, 1855–7

Theodoros Metochites

Beck, H. G., *Theodoros Metochites: die Krise des byzantinischen Weltbildes in 14 Jahrhundert*, Munich, 1952

Guilland, R., in *Revue des études greques*, vol. 35, 1922, pp. 82f.

Guilland, R., *Études byzantines*, Paris, 1959, pp. 117f.

Hunger, *HPLB*, pp. 248f., 671f.

Hunger, H., in *BZ*, vol. 55, 1952, pp. 4f.

Krumbacher, *GBL*, pp. 550f.

Ševčenko, I., in P. A. Underwood (ed.), *The Kariye Djami*, Princeton, 1975, vol. 4, pp. 19f.

Treu, M., *Dichtungen des Grosslogotheten Theodoros Metochites*, Gymnasial–progr., Potsdam, 1895

ON THE FALL OF CONSTANTINOPLE AND THE RECAPTURE OF THE CITY

Müller, J., in *Sitzungsberichte der Österreichischen Akademie der Wissenschaften in Wien*, vol. 9, 1852, pp. 336f.

EPHRAEM

Lampsidis, O., *Beiträge zum byzantinischen Chronisten Ephraem und zu seiner Chronik*, Athens, 1971
Mai, A., *Ephraem*, Bonn, 1840; text rpt. in Migne, *PG*, vol. 143, pp. 12f.

JOHANNES KATRARES

Andrés, G. de, Irigoin, J., and Hörandner, W., in *Jahrbuch der Österreichischen Byzantinischen Gesellschaft*, vol. 23, 1974, pp. 201f.
Jürss, F., in *BZ*, vol. 59, 1966, pp. 275f.
Matranga, P., *Anecdota Graeca*, Rome, 1850, vol. 2, p. 657
Nissen, T., *Die byzantinischen Anakreonteen*, Munich, 1940, p. 74

MARCUS ANGELUS

Nissen, T., *Die byzantinischen Anakreonteen*, Munich, 1940, p. 76

STEPHANOS SGOUROPOULOS

Nissen, T., *Die byzantinischen Anakreonteen*, Munich, 1940, p. 75
Papadopoulos-Kerameus, A., Ἀνάλεκτα Ἱεροσολ. Σταχυολογίας, St Petersburg, 1891, vol. 1, pp. 431f.
Papatheodorides, T., in Ἀρχεῖον Πόντου, vol. 19, 1954, pp. 262f.

THEODOROS MELITENIOTES

Beck, *GBV*, p. 125
Cupane, C., in *Jahrbuch der Österreichischen Byzantinischen Gesellschaft*, vol. 27, 1978, pp. 1f.
Dölger, F., 'Quellen und Vorbilder zu dem Gedicht des Meliteniotes' (unpublished Diss.), Munich, 1919
Dölger, F., in *Annuaire de l'Institut de Philologie et d'Histoire Orientales de l'Université de Bruxelles*, vol. 2, 1934, pp. 515f.
Dölger, F., *Miscellanea Giovanni Mercati*, Vatican, 1946, vol. 3, pp. 238f.
Hunger, *HPLB*, pp. 119, 253f., 278
Miller, M. E., in *Notices et extraits de la Bibliothèque Nationale*, vol. 19, 2, 1857, pp. 1f.
Tiftixoglu, V., in *BZ*, vol. 67, 1974, pp. 1f.

VERSE RIDDLES

Krumbacher, *GBL*, p. 766
Lampros, S., Δελτίον τῆς Ἱστορικῆς καὶ Ἐθνολογικῆς Ἑταιρείας τῆς Ἑλλάδος, Athens, vol. 2, 1885–9, pp. 152f.
Matranga, P., *Anecdota Graeca*, Rome, 1850, vol. 2, p. 682

POETRY IN THE VERNACULAR

Historical and descriptive poems

LAMENT ON TAMERLANE

Beck, *GBV*, p. 161
Wagner, W., *Medieval Greek Texts*, London, 1870
Wagner, W., *Carmina Graeca Medii Aevi*, Leipzig, 1874

THE *BATTLE OF VARNA*

Beck, *GBV*, p. 162
Moravcsik, G., *Görög kölemény á Varnai csatárol*, Budapest, 1935
Svoronos, N. G., in *'Aθηνᾶ*, vol. 48, 1938, pp. 163f.

ON THE EMPRESS THEODORA

Lampsides, O., in *Néov 'Aθήναιον*, vol. 3, 1961, pp. 17f.

A *NARRATIVE ON FAMOUS VENICE*

Bouboulides, P. K., in *'Aθηνᾶ*, vol. 69, 1967, pp. 181f.
Knös, B., *Histoire de la littérature néo-grecque*, Stockholm–Göteborg–Uppsala, 1962, p. 103
Wagner, W., *Carmina Graeca Medii Aevi*, Leipzig, 1874, pp. 221f.

Allegories and popular moralizing verse

Dölger, F., in J. Schick (ed.), *Corpus Hamleticum*, vol. 1, part 5, *Die Scharfsinnsprobe*, sect. 2, Leipzig, 1938, pp. 234f.
Lampros, S., *Collection de romans grecs . . .*, Paris, 1880
Legrand, *Collection de monuments*, n.s., vol. 5
Legrand, É., in *Annuaire de l'Association pour l'Encouragement des Études Grecques en France*, vol. 6, 1872, pp. 53f.
Megas, G., in *Λαογραφία*, vol. 15, 1953, pp. 3f.
Wagner, W., *Carmina Graeca Medii Aevi*, Leipzig, 1874, pp. 277f.
Zoras, G., *Σπουδαστήριον Βυζαντινῆς καὶ Νεοελληνικῆς Φιλολογίας τοῦ Πανεπιστημίου 'Aθηνῶν*, Athens, 1956

Animal stories

PHYSIOLOGOS

Gidel, C., *Nouvelles études de la littérature grecque moderne*, Paris, 1878, pp. 401f.
Goldstaub, M., in *Philologus*, suppl. 8, 1899–1901, pp. 339f.
Kaimakis, D., *Der Physiologos nach der ersten Redaktion*, Hain, 1974
Knös, B., *Histoire de la littérature néo-grecque*, Stockholm–Göteborg–Uppsala, 1962, pp. 150f.
Legrand, *Collection de monuments*, vol. 16
Riedinger, R., in *BZ*, vol. 70, 1977, pp. 109f.
Sbordone, F., *Physiologus*, Milan, 1936

THE PLAYFUL TALE ABOUT QUADRUPEDS

Gidel, C., *Études sur la littérature grecque moderne*, Paris, 1866

Sandrovskaja, V. S., in *Vizantijskij Vremennik*, vol. 9, 1956, pp. 211f; vol. 10, 1957, pp. 18f.

Tsiouni, V., *Παιδιόφραστος διήγησις τῶν ζώων τῶν Τετραπόδων*, Munich, 1974

Wagner, W., *Carmina Graeca Medii Aevi*, Leipzig, 1874, pp. 141f.

Xanthoudides, St., in *Byzantinisch-neugriechischen Jahrbücher*, vol. 5, 1926–7, pp. 348f.

POULOLOGOS

Beck, *GBV*, pp. 173, 174

Bouboulides, P., in *Ἀθηνᾶ*, vol. 67, 1964, pp. 133f.

Krawczynski, S., *Ὁ Πουλολόγος*, Berlin, 1960

Wagner, W., *Carmina Graeca Medii Aevi*, Leipzig, 1874, pp. 179f.

Zoras, G., *Σπουδαστήριον Βυζ. καὶ Νεοελληνικῆς Φιλολογίας τοῦ Πανεπιστημίου*, Athens, 1956

Zoras, G., in *Ἐπετηρὶς Ἑταιρείας Βυζαντινῶν Σπουδῶν*, vol. 30, 1960–1, pp. 150f.

SYNAXARION OF THE ESTIMABLE DONKEY

Alexiou, L., in *Κρητικὰ Χρονικά*, vol. 9, 1955, pp. 81f.

Wagner, W., *Carmina Graeca Medii Aevi*, Leipzig, 1874

PART FOUR: THE GREEKS UNDER THE FRANKS AND THE TURKS

Section I: The Greeks under the Franks (1204–1797)

CHAPTER 22: VERSE ROMANCES AND HISTORICAL POEMS

ROMANCES OF LOVE AND CHIVALRY

Beck, *GBV*, pp. 117f.

Bury, J. B., *Romances of Chivalry on Greek Soil*, Oxford, 1911

Mazal, O. B., in *Jahrbuch der Österreichischen Byzantinischen Gesellschaft*, vols. 11–12, 1962–3, pp. 9f.

Mazal, O. B., in *BZ*, vol. 57, 1964, pp. 194f., 464f.

Mazal, O. B., in *Jahrbuch der Österreichischen Byzantinischen Gesellschaft*, vol. 14, 1965, pp. 83f.

Original verse romances

CALLIMACHUS AND CHRYSORRHOE

Beck, *GBV*, pp. 117f.

Hadjigiakoumis, M. K., *Τὰ μεσαιωνικὰ δημώδη κείμενα, συμβολὴ στὴν μελέτη καὶ τὴν ἔκδοσή τους*, Athens, 1977, vol. 1.

Knös, B., in *Ἑλληνικά*, vol. 17, 1962, pp. 274f.

Kriaras, E., *Βυζαντινὰ ἱπποτικὰ μυθιστορήματα*, Athens, 1955 (*Βασικὴ Βιβλιοθήκη*, 2) (*Καλλίμαχος, Βέλθανδρος, Ἰμπέριος, Φλόριος*)

Lampros, S., *Collection des romans grecs*..., Paris 1880, pp. 1f.

Megas, G. A., *Mélanges Merlier*, Athens, 1956, vol. 1, pp. 147f.

Pichard, M., *Le roman de Callimachos et Chrysorrhoé*, Paris 1956

BELTHANDROS AND CHRYSANTZA

Beck, *GBV*, pp. 120f.

Diehl, C., *Figures byzantines*, Paris 1918, vol. 2, pp. 320f.

Kriaras, E., *Silloge bizantina in onore di S. G. Mercati*, Rome, 1957, pp. 237f.

Legrand, É., *Bibliothèque grecque vulgaire*, vol. 1, Paris, 1880, pp. 125f.

Miliades, G., *Βέλθανδρος Χρυσάντζα*, Athens, 1925

LIBYSTROS AND RHODAMNE

Beck, *GBV*, pp. 121, 127f.

Diehl, C., *Figures byzantines*, Paris, 1918, vol. 2, pp. 337–53

Grégoire, H., in *Byzantion*, vol. 9, 1934, pp. 383–5

Lambert, J. A., *Le roman de Libistros et Rhodamné*, Amsterdam, 1935

Rotolo, V., *Libistro e Rodamne, romanzo cavalleresco bizantino*, Athens, 1965 (Italian translation and introduction)

Wagner, W., *Trois poèmes grecs du Moyen Age*, Berlin, 1881

IMBERIOS AND MARGARONA

Beck, *GBV*, pp. 143f.

Bees, N. A., 'Der französisch-mittelgriechische Ritterroman *Imberios und Margarona* und die Grundrung des *Daphni Klösters* bei Athen', *Texte und Forschunge zur byzantinisch–neugriechischen Philologie*, Berlin, 1924

Kriaras, E., in *Akten des XI. Internationalen Byzantinisten Kongresses* (Munich, 1958), Munich, 1960, pp. 269f.

Lampros, S., *Collection de romans grecs* ..., Paris, 1880, pp. 239f.

Legrand, É., *Bibliothèque grecque vulgaire*, vol. 1, Paris, 1881, pp. 283f.

Schreiner, M., in *Akten des XI. Internationalen Byzantinisten Kongresses* (Munich, 1958), Munich, 1960, pp. 556f.

Wagner, W., *Collection de monuments* ..., Paris, 1874, vol. 3

PHLORIOS AND PLIATZAPHLORA

Beck, *GBV*, pp. 140f.

Hesseling, D. C., *Le roman de Phlorios et Pliatza Phlora*, Amsterdam, 1919

Schmitt, J., in *BZ*, vol. 2, 1893, pp. 211f.

Wagner, W., *Medieval Greek Texts*, London, 1870, pp. 1f.

THE ACHILLEIS

Beck, *GBV*, p. 129
Hesseling, D. C., *L'Achilléide byzantine*, Amsterdam, 1919
Lampros, S., in *Νέος Ἑλληνομνήμων*, vol. 15, 1921, pp. 367f.
Mitsakis, K., in *BZ*, vol. 59, 1966, pp. 5f.
Schmitt, J., in *BZ*, vol. 2, 1893, pp. 212f.
Speck, P., in *Jahrbuch der Österreichischen Byzantinischen Gesellschaft*, vol. 18, 1969, pp. 89f.
Wagner, W., *Trois poèmes grecs du Moyen Âge*, Berlin, 1881, pp. 1f.

Greek translations of Western romances and other works

Beck, *GBV*, pp. 136f.
Breillat, P., in *Mélanges d'archéologie et d'histoire*, vol. 55, 1938, pp. 308f.
Ellissen, A., *Ὁ πρέσβυς ἱππότης, ein griechisches Gedicht aus dem Sagenkreis der Tafelrunde*, Leipzig, 1846
Iorga, N., in *Bulletin de la section historique de l'Academie Roumaine*, vol. 14, pp. 15f.
Janssen, A. A. P., *Narratio neograeca Apolonii Tyrii* (Diss.), Amsterdam, 1954
Jeffreys, E. D. and Jeffreys, M. J., in *Byzantine and Modern Greek Studies*, vol. 5, 1979, pp. 115f.
Klebs, E., *Die Erzählung von Apollonius aus Tyrus*, Berlin, 1899
Legrand, É., *Bibliothèque grecque vulgaire*, Paris, 1870, vol. 5
Maurophyrydis, D., *Ἐκλογὴ μνημείων τῆς νεωτέρας Ἑλληνικῆς γλώσσης*, Athens, 1866, pp. 257f.
Perry, E., *The Ancient Romances*, Berkeley–Los Angeles, 1967, pp. 294f.
Wagner, W., *Medieval Greek Texts*, London, 1870

Pseudo-historical romances

Cantarella, R., in *Studi bizantini e neoellenici*, vol. 4, 1935, pp. 153f.
Follieri, E., *Atti del Convegno Internazionale sul tema: La poesia epica e la sua formazione*, Accademia Nazionale dei Lincei, Rome, 1970, pp. 583f.
Holton, D., *Διήγησις τοῦ Ἀλεξάνδρου, The Tale of Alexander, the Rhymed Version*, Salonica, 1974 (*Βυζαντινὴ καὶ Νεοελλ. Βιβλιοθήκη* I.)
Knös, B., in *Eranos*, vol. 58, 1960, pp. 237f.
Merkelbach, R., *Die Quellen des griechischen Alexanderromans*, Munich, 1954
Reichmann, S., *Das byzantinische Alexandergedicht*, Meisenheim/Glan, 1963
Schreiner, H., in *BZ*, vol. 21, 1912, pp. 54f.
Veloudis, G., *Ἡ Φυλλάδα τοῦ Μεγαλέξανδρου*, Athens, 1977, (*Ἑρμῆς, Νέα Ἑλληνικὴ Βιβλιοθήκη*, 39)
Wagner, W., *Carmina Graeca Medii Aevi*, Leipzig, 1874
Wagner, W., *Trois poèmes grecs du Moyen Age*, Berlin, 1881

HISTORICAL POEMS

THE CHRONICLE OF THE MOREA

Adamantiou, A. I., *Τὰ Χρονικὰ τοῦ Μορέως, Δελτίον Ἱστορικῆς καί Ἐθνολογικῆς Ἑταιρ. τῆς Ἑλλάδος*, vol. 6, 1906, pp. 453f.

Beck, *GBV*, pp. 157f.

Buchon, J. A., *Chroniques étrangeres relatives aux expéditions françaises pendant le XIII siècle*, Paris, 1840

Buchon, J. A., *Recherches historiques sur la principauté française de Morée et ses hautes baronies*, vol. 2, Paris, 1845

Hatzidakis, G. N., Μεσαιωνικὰ καὶ Νέα Ἑλληνικά, Athens, 1905, vol. 1, pp. 515f.

Jacoby, D., in *Journal des Savants*, July–September 1968, pp. 133f.

Kalonaros, P., Τὸ Χρονικὸν τοῦ Μορέως, Athens, 1940

Knös, B., *Histoire de la littérature néo-grecque*, Stockholm–Göteborg–Uppsala, 1962, p. 97

Lurier, H. E., *Crusaders and Conquerors: The Chronicle of the Morea*, New York–London, 1964

Schmitt, J., *The Chronicle of the Morea*, London, 1904

Spadaro, G. A., 'Studi introduttivi alla Crònaca di Morea', I, *Siculorum Gymnasium*, vol. 12, 1959, pp. 125f.; II, *ibid.*, vol. 13, 1960, pp. 133f.; III, *ibid.*, vol. 14, 1961, pp. 1f.

THE CHRONICLE OF TOCCO

Manousakas, M. J., in Λαογραφία, vol. 14, 1952, pp. 3f.; vol. 15, 1954, pp. 336f.

Schirò, J., Τὸ χρονικὸν τῶν Τόκκων, τά Ἰωάννινα κατὰ τὰς ἀρχὰς τοῦ IB´ αἰῶνος, Jannina, 1965

Schirò, J., in *Rivista di studi bizantini*, vols. 2–3, 1965–6, pp. 119f.

Schirò, J., *Cronaca dei Tocco di Cefalonia*, Rome, 1975

CHAPTER 23: POETRY FROM THE AEGEAN ISLANDS, RHODES, CYPRUS, CRETE AND THE IONIAN ISLANDS

THE AEGEAN ISLANDS

Baud-Bovy, S., *La chanson populaire grecque du Dodécanèse*, Geneva, 1961, pp. 201f.

Pernot, H. and Hesseling, D., 'Ἐρωτοπαίγνια', *Chansons d'amour*, Paris–Athens, 1913

Pernot, H., *Chansons populaires grecques de XVe et XVIe siècles*, Paris, 1931

Wagner, W., Ἀλφάβητος τῆς ἀγάπης, *Das ABC der Liebe, Eine Sammlung rhodischer Liebeslieder*, Leipzig 1879

Zoras, G., Ἀνέκδοτα ποιήματα, Ἐπιθεώρησις (Rome), vol. 4, July 1940

Zoras, G., Ἀλφάβητος τῆς ξενιτείας, Σπουδ. Βυζ. καὶ Νεοελλ. Φιλολογίας Παν. Αθηνῶν, Athens, 1955

RHODES

Legrand, É., *Bibliothèque grecque vulgaire*, vol. 1, Paris, 1880, pp. 203f.

Michaelides, D. K., Δωδεκανησιακὸν Ἀρχεῖον, vol. 5, 1970, pp. 81f.

Papachristopoulos, C., Εἰς μνήμην Κ. Ἀμάντου, Athens, 1960, pp. 76f.

Wagner, W., *Carmina Graeca Medii Aevi*, Leipzig, 1874, pp. 32f.

CYPRUS

Baud-Bovy, S., in *Byzantion*, vol. 13, 1938, pp. 321f.

Boissonade, J. F., in *Notices et extraits de la Bibliothèque Nationale*, vol. 12, 2, 1831, pp. 1f.

Kriaras, E., *Τό ἀνάκλημα τῆς Κωνσταντινούπολης* (editions of the University of Salonica), Salonica, 1956

Kriaras, E., in *Κρητικὰ Χρονικά*, vols. 15–16, 1963, pp. 399f.

Legrand, É., *Bibliothèque grecque vulgaire*, Paris, 1890, vol. 2, pp. 58f.

Miller, E., and Sathas, K., in *Publications de l'École des Langues Orientales* (Paris), 2e série, vol. 3, 1882, pp. 1–2

Petropoulos, D., *Ἑλλ.Δημοτικὰ Τραγούδια*, Athens, 1958, pp. 98f.

Pharmakides, X., *Κύπρια Ἔπη*, Nicosia, 1926

Pitsillidès-Siapkaras, T., *Le Petrarchisme en Chypre, Poèmes d'amour en dialecte chypriote d'après un manuscrit du XVIe siècle*, 2nd edn., Paris, 1975 (Athens, 1976)

Prouses, K., in *Κυπριακὰ Γράμματα*, vol. 4, 1939, pp. 485f.

Sakellarios, A., *Κυπριακά*, Athens, 1891

Spyridakis, G. K. S., *Ἐπιστημονικὴ Ἐπετηρὶς Φιλοσ. Σχολῆς Πανεπ. Ἀθηνῶν*, Athens, 1955–6, pp. 423f.

Vito, M. S. de, *L'origine del drama liturgico*, Rome, 1938

Zoras, G., in *Νέα Ἑστία*, vol. 58, 1955, pp. 1073f.

Zoras, G., *Ἡ Κυπριακὴ φιλολογία κατὰ τὴν περίοδον τῆς Φραγκοκρατίας*, Athens, 1976., pp. 603f.

CRETE

Miller, W., *Essays on the Latin Orient*, Cambridge, 1921

The beginnings of Cretan poetry (1204–1453)

Alexiou, S., *Κρητικὴ Ἀνθολογία*, Herakleion, 1969

Bouboulidis, P., *Κρητικὴ Λογοτεχνία*, Athens, 1955 (*Βασικὴ Βιβλιοθήκη* I)

Embirikos, A., *La renaissance crétoise, XVIe et XVIIe siècles*, vol. 1, *La littérature*, Paris, 1960

Manousakas, M. J., *Ἡ Κρητικὴ Λογοτεχνία κατὰ τὴν ἐποχὴ τῆς Βενετοκρατίας*, Salonica, 1965

STEPHANOS SACHLIKIS

Cantarella, R., in *Μύσων*, vol. 7, 1938, pp. 74f.

Legrand, É., *Annuaire des études grecques*, vol. 5, 1871, pp. 201f.

Legrand, *Collection de monuments*, no. 15

Liubarskij, G. N., in *Κρητικὰ Χρονικά*, vol 14, 1960, pp. 308f.

Papademetriou, S. P., *Stephanos Sachlikis*, Odessa, 1896

Vitti, M., in *Κρητικὰ Χρονικά*, vol. 14, 1960, pp. 173f.

Wagner, W., *Carmina Graeca Medii Aevi*, Leipzig, 1874, pp. 62f.

LEONARDOS DELLAPORTAS

Manousakas, M. J., in *Πρακτικὰ Ἀκαδημίας Ἀθηνῶν*, vol. 29, 1954, pp. 32f.

Manousakas, M. J., in *Ἐπετηρὶς Ἑταιρείας Βυζαντινῶν Σπουδῶν.*, vol. 27, 1957, pp. 340f.

Manousakas, M. J., in *Κρητικὰ Χρονικά*, vol. 12, 1958, pp. 387f.

Manousakas, M. J., *Un poeta cretese ambasciatore di Venezia a Tunisi e presso i Turchi: Leonardo Dellaporta e i suoi componimenti poetici. Venezia e l'Oriente fra tardo Medio Evo e rinascimento*, Florence, 1966, pp. 283f.

MARINOS FALIEROS

Bakker, W. F. and Germert, A. F. van, *The ῾Ρίμα Παρηγορητική of Marinos Falieros, Studia Byzantina et Neohellenica*, Leyden, 1972, pp. 74f.

Gemert, A. F. van, *Marinos Falieros en tijn beide lief desdromen*, Amsterdam, 1973

Gemert, A. F. van, in *Θησαυρίσματα*, vol. 14, 1977, pp 7f.

Manousakas, M. J., *Mélanges Octave et Melpo Merlier*, Athens, 1956, vol. 2, pp. 51f.

Mystakides, B. A., in *Νέος Ποιμήν*, vol. 4, 1922, pp. 569f.

Schmitt, J., in *Δελτίον Ἱστορικῆς Ἐθνολογικῆς Ἑταιρείας*, vol. 4, 1892, pp. 291f.

Zoras, G., in *Ἐπιθεώρησις*, vol. 3, 1940, pp. 311f.

Zoras, G., in *Κρητικὰ Χρονικά*, vol. 2, 1948, pp. 39f., 213, 416f.

Zoras, G., in *Νέα ῾Εστία*, vol. 5, 1955, pp. 843f.

Zoras, G., in *Ἐπετηρὶς Ἑταιρείας Βυζαντινῶν Σπουδῶν*, vol. 26, 1956, pp. 41f.

Zoras, G., *Μαρίνου Φαλιέρου Ἱστορία καὶ ῎Ονειρον*, Athens, 1961

ON EXPATRIATION

Kallitzounakis, J., *Πραγματεῖαι τῆς ᾽Ακαδημίας ᾽Αθηνῶν*, vol. 1, Athens, 1935, pp. 1f.

Zoras, G., *Σπουδαστήριον Βυζ. καὶ Νεοελλ. Φιλ. Πανεπιστημίου ᾽Αθηνῶν*, 5th edn., Athens, 1953

Zoras, G., *῾Η ξενιτειὰ ἐν τῇ ῾Ελληνικῇ ποιήσει*, Athens, 1953

The development and expansion of Cretan poetry (1453–1590)

GEORGIOS HOUMNOS

Alexiou, S., in *Κρητικὰ Χρονικά*, vol. 17, 1964, pp. 183f.

Manousakas, M. J., in, *Ἐπετηρὶς Ἑταιρείας Βυζαντινῶν Σπουδῶν*, vol. 21, 1951, pp. 280f.

Marshall, E. H., *Old Testament Legends*, Cambridge, 1925

Megas, G. A., *Γεωργίου Χούμνου ἡ Κοσμογέννησις*, Athens, 1975

Pernot, H., *Études de littérature grecque moderne*, vol. 1, Paris, 1916, pp. 208f.

ANDREAS SKLENTZAS

Kakoulides, E., in *῾Ελληνικά*, vol. 20, 1967, pp. 117f.

Kavarnos, J. P., *Κρητικὰ Χρονικά*, vol. 4, 1950, pp. 7f.

GABRIEL AKONTIANOS

Helm, P., *Der antike Roman*, Göttingen, 1956

Klebs, E., *Die Erzählung von Apollonius aus Tyrus*, Berlin, 1899

Wagner, W., *Medieval Greek Texts*, London, 1870, pp. 57f.

MANOLIS SKLAVOS

Bouboulides, P., *῾Η Συμφορὰ τῆς Κρήτης τοῦ Μανόλη Σκλάβου*,

Σπουδαστήριον Βυζαντινῆς καὶ Νεοελληνικῆς Φιλολογίας Πανεπιστημ. Ἀθηνῶν, Athens, 1955
Wagner, W., *Carmina Graeca Medii Aevi*, Leipzig, 1874, pp. 53f.

JOHANNES PIKATOROS

Kriaras, E., Ἡ Ρίμα Θρηνητικὴ τοῦ Ἰωάννου Πικατόρου, Ἐπεητρὶς τοῦ Μεσαιωνικοῦ Ἀρχείου τῆς Ἀκαδημίας Ἀθηνῶν, vol. 2 1942, pp. 1f.
Pernot, H., *Études de littérature grecque moderne* Paris 1916, vol. 1, pp. 195f.
Wagner, W., *Carmina Graeca Medii Aevi*, Leipzig, 1874, pp. 224f.

THE PRAISE OF WOMEN AND THE LIFE OF NOBLE WOMEN AND MOST HONOURABLE LADIES

Koukoules, P., in Κρητικὰ Χρονικά, vol. 7, 1953, pp. 55f.
Krumbacher, K., in *Sitzungsberichte der philos.–histor. Klasse der königlichen Akademie der Wissenschaften*, Munich, 1905, 3, pp. 335f.

THE DELIGHTFUL TALE OF THE DONKEY, THE WOLF AND THE FOX

Alexiou, S., in Κρητικὰ Χρονικά, vol. 9, 1955, pp. 523f.
Gidel, A., *Études sur la littérature grecque moderne*, Paris, 1866, pp. 331f.
Wagner, W., *Carmina Graeca Medii Aevi*, Leipzig, 1874, pp. 124f.

THE CAT AND THE MICE

Bănescu, N., Εἰς μνήμην Σπυρίδωνος Λάμπρου, Athens, 1935, pp. 393f.

PRAYER TO THE PASSION OF CHRIST

Manousakas, M. J. and Parlangèli, O., in Κρητικὰ Χρονικά, vol. 8, 1954, pp. 109f.

ANTONIOS ACHELIS

Pernot, H., *Collection de monuments . . .*, 3e série, vol. 2, Paris, 1910
Pernot, H., *Gentil de Vendosme et Antoine Achelis, le siège de Malte*, Paris, 1910

LAMENT ON THE FALL OF CYPRUS TO THE TURKS

A full edition of this interesting work is being prepared by M. J. Manousakas and C. A. Trypanis.
Tzedakis, T., in Κρητικὰ Χρονικά, vols. 15–16, 1961–2, pp. 156f.

The golden age of Cretan poetry

PASTORAL POETRY

Alexiou, S., Ἡ Βοσκοπούλα, Herakleion, 1963
Alexiou, S., *Anonimo Cretense, La Voskopoula, a cura di S. Alexiou, A. Gentilini, M. Peri, F. M. Pontani*, Istituto di Studi bizantinie neogreci, University of Padua, Quaderni 9, 1975
Doulgerakis, E. I., in Κρητικὰ Χρονικά, vol. 10, 1956, pp. 253f.
Gabrieli, G., in *L'Accademia in Italia, Accademie e Bibliotheche d'Italia*, vol. 1, 1927–8, pp. 5f.
Joannou, P., Ὁ πιστικὸς βοσκός, *Der Treue Schäfer*, Berlin, 1962
Legrand, *Collection de monuments*, vol. 1, 3rd edn.

Pernot, H., *Études de la littérature grecque moderne*, Paris, 1916, vol. 1, pp. 271f.

Politis, L., *Θέματα τῆς λογοτεχνίας μας*, 2nd series, Salonica, 1976, pp. 53f.

THE CRETAN THEATRE

Manousakas, M. J., *Κριτικὴ βιβλιογραφία τοῦ Κρητικοῦ Θεάτρου*, 2nd edn., Athens, 1964

Manousakas, M. J., *Ἡ Κρητικὴ λογοτεχνία κατὰ τὴν ἐποχὴ τῆς Βενετοκρατίας*, Salonica, 1965, pp. 29f.

Mavrogordato, J., in *Journal of Hellenic Studies*, vol. 48, 1928, pp. 75f., 243 (postscript)

Politis, L., in L. Vassardaki, *The Modern Greek Theatre*, Athens, 1957

Politis, L., *Venezia e l'Oriente fra tardo Medioevo e Rinascimento*, Florence, 1966, pp. 225f.

Sathas, K. N., *Κρητικὸν Θέατρον*, Venice, 1879; 2nd edn. Athens, 1963

Solomos, A., *Τὸ Κρητικὸ Θέατρο, Ἀπὸ τὴ φιλολογία στὴ σκηνή*, Athens, 1973

Valsa, M, *Le Théâtre grec moderne de 1453 à 1900*, Berlin, 1960

GEORGIOS CHORTATSIS

Kriaras, E., *Γύπαρις, Κρητικὸν δράμα*, Athens, 1940

Kriaras, E., *Γ. Χορτάτση, Πανώρια*, Salonica, 1975 (*Βυζαντινὴ καὶ Νεοελληνικὴ Βιβλιοθήκη*, 2)

Marshall, F. H., *Three Cretan Plays: The Sacrifice of Abraham, Erophile and Gyparis*; also the Cretan pastoral poem, *The Fair Shepherdess*, with an introduction by John Mavrogordato, London, 1929

Politis, L., *Γ. Χορτάτση, Κατζοῦρμπος*, Herakleion, 1964

Sathas, K. N., *Κρητικὸν Θέατρον*, Venice, 1879

Xanthoudides, St., *Ἐρωφίλη, τραγωδία Γ. Χορτάτζη*, Athens, 1928

JOANNES ANDREAS TROILOS

Lowe, C. G., *Εἰς μνήμην Σπυρίδωνος Λάμπρου*, Athens, 1935, pp. 190f.

Manousakas, M. J., in *Ἑλληνικὴ Δημιουργία*, vol. 12, 1953, pp. 67f.

Manousakas, M. J., in *Ἀθηνᾶ*, vol. 59, 1955, pp. 343f.

Troilos, I. A., *Βασιλεὺς Ῥωδολῖνος, τραγωδία*, Venice, 1677. Photostatic reproduction with a Foreword by F. R. Walton and an Introduction by M. J. Manousakas

THE ZENON

Bouboulides, P., in *Κρητικὰ Χρονικά*, vol. 9, 1955, pp. 7f.; vol. 7, 1953, pp. 127f.

Evangelatos, A., in *Θησαυρίσματα*, vol. 5, 1968, pp. 177f.

Pouchner, W., in *Θησαυρίσματα*, vol. 17, 1980, pp. 206f.

Sathas, K. N., *Κρητικὸν Θέατρον*, Venice, 1879, pp. 1f.

Solomos, A., *Τὸ Κρητικὸ Θέατρο, Ἀπὸ τὴ φιλολογία στὴ σκηνή*, Athens, 1973

STATHIS

Alexiou, S., in *Κρητικὰ Χρονικά*, vol. 9, 1955, pp. 134f.

Anon., in *Θέατρο*, vol. 1, 1962, pp. 48f.

Manousakas, M. J., in *Κρητικὰ Χρονικά*, vol. 1, 1947, pp. 55f.; vol. 9, 1955, pp. 291f.

Martini, L., Στάθης, Κρητικὴ Κωμωδία, Salonica, 1976 (Βυζαντινὴ καὶ Νεοελληνικὴ Βιβλιοθήκη, 3)
Sathas, K. N., Κρητικὸν Θέατρον, Venice, 1879, pp. 103f.

MARCOS ANTONIOS FOSCOLOS

Jenkins, R. J. H., in *The Link*, vol. 1, 1938, pp. 29f.
Kriaras, E., Ἡμερολόγιον τῆς Μεγάλης Ἑλλάδος, Athens, 1935, pp. 131f.
Morgan, G., in Κρητικὰ Χρονικά, vol. 9, 1955, pp. 61f.
Spyridakis, G. K., in Ἑλληνικὴ Δημιουργία, vol. 12, 1958, pp. 91f.
Vincent, A. L., in Θησαυρίσματα, vol. 4, 1967, pp. 53f.; vol. 5, 1968, pp. 119f.
Xanthoudides, St., Μάρκου Ἀντωνίου Φωσκόλου Φορτουνᾶτος, Athens, 1922

FRAGMENTS

Manousakas, M. J., Ἡ Κρητικὴ λογοτεχνία κατὰ τὴν ἐποχὴ τῆς Βενετοκρατίας, Salonica, 1965, pp. 39f.
Morgan, G., in Κρητικὰ Χρονικά, vol. 9, 1955, pp. 69f.

THE SACRIFICE OF ABRAHAM

Antoniadis, S., Ἡ Θυσία τοῦ Ἀβραάμ, Κρητικὸν μυστήριον τοῦ 16ου αἰῶνος, Athens, 1922
Bakker, W. F., *The Sacrifice of Abraham*, Centre for Byzantine Studies, University of Birmingham, 1978
Kriaras, E., in Κρητικὰ Χρονικά vol. 1, 1947, pp. 227f.
Legrand, É., *Bibliothèque grecque vulgaire*, Paris, 1880, vol. 1, pp. 226f.
Manousakas, M. J., Ἡ Κρητικὴ Λογοτεχνία κατὰ τὴν ἐποχὴ τῆς Βενετοκρατίας, Salonica, 1965, pp. 43f.
Mavrogordato, J., in *Journal of Hellenic Studies*, vol. 48, 1928, pp. 75–96, 243 (postscript)
Megas, G., Ἡ Θυσία τοῦ Ἀβραάμ, κριτικὴ ἔκδοσις, rev. edn., Athens, 1954
Pernot, E., *Études de littérature grecque moderne*, Paris, 1916, pp. 231f.
Politis, L., Ἀφιέρωμα στὴ μνήμη τοῦ Μανόλη Τριανταφυλλίδη, Athens, 1960
Salaville, S., in Ἐπετηρὶς Ἑταιρ. Βυζαντινῶν Σπουδῶν, vol. 24, 1954, pp. 351f.
Tsantsanoglou, H., Βιτσέντζος Κορνάρος, Ἡ Θυσία τοῦ Ἀβραάμ (Εἰσαγωγὴ Ἄγγελου Τερζάκη), 2nd edn., Athens, 1974
Zoras, G., Περὶ τὰς πηγὰς τῆς Θυσίας τοῦ Ἀβραάμ, Athens, 1945

THE 'HEROIC' VERSE ROMANCE
VITSENTZOS KORNAROS

Alexiou, S., in Κρητικὰ Χρονικά, vol. 6, 1952, pp. 351f.
Alexiou, S., Ὁ Χαρακτὴρ τοῦ Ἐρωτοκρίτου, Herakleion, 1952
Alexiou, S., Βιτσέντσου Κορνάρου Ἐρωτόκριτος. Ἀνατύπωση ἀπὸ τὴν ἔκδοση Στ. Ξανθουδίδου, Εἰσαγωγὴ Λίνου Πολίτη, Athens, 1952; 2nd edn., 1968; 3rd edn., 1976
Alexiou, S., in Κρητικὰ Χρονικά, vol. 11, 1957, pp. 49f.
Alexiou, S., in Κρητικὰ Χρονικά, vol. 23, 1971, pp. 199f.
Alexiou, S., Βιτσέντσου Κορνάρου Ἐρωτόκριτος, Athens, 1980

Cartojan, N., *Poema cretană Erotocrit in literatura romanescă si izvorul ei necunoscut.* Academia Romanâ, Memoriile sectiunii literare, series 3, vol 7, 1935, pp. 83f.

Cartojan, N., in *Revue de littérature comparée,* vol. 16, 1936, pp. 265f.

Cartojan, N., in *Cultura neolatina,* vols. 4–5, 1944–5, pp. 122f.

Kriaras, M., Μελετήματα περὶ τὰς πηγὰς τοῦ Ἐρωτοκρίτου, Athens, 1938

Maspero, Fr., *Vincenzo Cornaro Erotokrito. Introduzione, traduzione e note (I Classici Bietti),* Milan, 1975

Mavrogordato, J., *The Erotokritos* (translation with an introduction by S. Gaselee), Oxford, 1929

Seferis, G., Ἐρωτόκριτος, Athens, 1946 (= Δοκιμές, 3rd edn., Athens, 1974, vol. 1, pp. 268f.)

Xanthoudides, St., Βιτσέντζου Κορνάρου, Ἐρωτόκριτος, Herakleion, 1915

HISTORICAL POEMS

ATHANASIOS SKLEROS

Petrou-Mesogitis, M., in Ἐπετηρὶς ἑταιρείας Κρ.Σπουδῶν, vol. 2, 1939, pp. 339f.

Sathas, K., Ἑλληνικὰ Ἀνέκδοτα, vol. 2, Athens, 1867

MARINOS TZANES BOUNIALIS

Xiroulakis, A., Ὁ Κρητικὸς Πόλεμος, Trieste, 1908

OTHERS

Doulgerakis, M. I., in Κρητικὰ Χρονικά, vol. 9, 1955, pp. 334f.

Katsuros, A., in Λαογραφία, vol. 18, 1959, pp. 432f.

Kriaras, E., in Ἀθηνᾶ, vol. 48, 1938, pp. 119f.

Manousakas, M. J., in Κρητικὰ Χρονικά, vol. 5, 1951, pp. 349f.

PANTZELIOS' SONG OF DASKALOGIANNIS

Laourdas, B., Τὸ τραγούδι τοῦ Δασκαλογιάννη, Herakleion, 1947

Legrand, É., *Recueil de poèmes historiques en grec vulgaire* . . ., Paris, 1877

Mango, C., in Κρητικὰ Χρονικά, vol. 8, 1954, pp. 44f.

Petropoulos, D., in Κρητικὰ Χρονικά, vol. 8, 1954, pp. 227f.

TOWER OF ALIDAKIS

Legrand, É., *Receuil de poèmes historiques en grec vulgaire* . . ., Paris, 1877

Tomadakis, N. B., Νεοελληνικά, δοκίμια καὶ μελέται, Athens, 1953, pp. 84f.

OTHER ANONYMOUS SONGS

Lord, A. B., *The Heroic Tradition of Greek Epic and Ballad. Hellenism and the First Greek War of Liberation,* Salonica, 1976, pp. 91f.

Morgan, G., in Κρητικὰ Χρονικά, vol. 14, 1960, pp. 35f.

THE IONIAN ISLANDS

THEODOROS MONTSELEZE

Vitti, M., *T. Montselese, Εὐγένα,* Naples, 1965

MICHAEL SOUMAKIS

Ioannou, P.-P., *Probleme der neugriechischen Literatur*, Berlin, 1960, vol. 3, pp. 141f.

ANTHIMOS DIAKROUSIS

Xiroulakis, A., *Ο Κρητικὸς Πόλεμος*, Trieste, 1908

PETROS KATSAITIS

Kriaras, E., *Κατσαΐτης, Ἰφιγένεια, Θυέστης, Κλαυθμὸς Πελοποννήσου, ἀνέκδοτα ἔργα*, Athens, 1950

RHIMADES

Katsuros, A., in *Λαογραφία*, vol. 18, 1959, pp. 432f.

Legrand, É., *Recueil de poèmes historiques en grec vulgaire . . .*, Paris, 1877

Wagner, W., *Carmina Graeca Medii Aevi*, Leipzig, 1874, pp. 348f.

CHAPTER 24: THE GREEKS OF THE DIASPORA

Bouboulidis, P. K., in *Ἐπετηρὶς Ἑταιρείας Βυζ. Σπουδῶν*, vol. 25, 1955, pp. 284f.

Follieri, E., *Il Teseida neogreco*, vol. 1, *Testi e studi byzantino-neohellenici*, Rome–Athens, 1959

Geanakoplos, D. J., *Greek Scholars in Venice*, Cambridge, Mass., 1962

Hesseling, C. D., *Charos, ein Beitrag zur Kenntnis des neugriechischen Volksglaubens*, Leipzig–Leyden, 1897

Irmscher, J., *J. Trivolis Ποιήματα*, Berlin, 1956 (*Berliner byzantinische Arbeiten*, vol. 1)

Karaiskakis, S., in *Λαογραφία*, vol. 11, 1934, pp. 1f. (Markos Dephanaras)

Knös, B., *Un ambassadeur de l'Hellénisme. J. Laskaris et la tradition greco-byzantine dans l'humanisme français*, Paris, 1945

Knös, B., *Histoire de la littérature néo-grecque*, Stockholm Göteborg–Uppsala, 1960, pp. 315f.

Kriaras, E., *Probleme der neugriechischen Literatur*, Berlin, 1960, vol. 3, pp. 62f.

Legrand, *Collection de monuments*, no. 13 (Trivolis); n. s. vols. 14, 17 (Leonardos Phortios)

Legrand, É., *Bibliothèque grecque vulgaire*, Paris 1881, vol. 2, pp. 123f. (Markos Dephanaras), pp. 144f. (Antonios Bouboulis); vol. 3, pp. 280f. (Manthos Ioannou)

Meschini, A., *Giano Laskaris, epigrammi greci*, Padua, 1976

Papadopoulos, T. I., *Ἀγνώστου Χίου ποιητῆ ΔΑΒΙΔ*, Athens, 1979

Politis, L., *Ποιητικὴ Ἀνθολογία Β'*, Athens, 1965, pp. 140f.

Rotolo, V., *Il carme 'Hellas' di Leone Allacci*, Palermo, 1966

Sathas, K., *Ἑλληνικὰ ἀνέκδοτα*, Athens, 1867, vol. 1 (Tzanes Koronaios)

Sathas, K., *Documents inédits relatifs a l'histoire de la Grèce au Moyen Age*, vol. 4, Paris, 1883, pp. LVIIf. (Manolis Blessis); vol. 9, Paris, 1890, pp. 262f. (Manolis Blessis)

Schmitt, J., in *Études de philologie néo-grecque*, Bibliothèque de l'École des Hautes Études, Paris, 1892, pp. 279f.

Tsourkas, A., *Gli scolari greci di Padova nel rinovamento culturale dell'Oriente Ortodosso*, Padua, 1958

Zoras, G., in Ἐπιθεώρηση (Rome), vol. 4, 1940 (Goustos Glykos)

Zoras, G., Ἐπιστημονικὴ Ἐπετηρὶς Φιλοσοφικῆς Σχολῆς Πανεπιστημίου Ἀθηνῶν, vol. 5, 1954–5, pp. 432f. (anonymous poem to Charles V of Spain)

Zoras, G., Σπουδαστήριον Βυζαντ.καὶ Νεοελλ. Φιλολογίας Πανεπιστημίου Ἀθηνῶν Athens, 1956

Section II: The Greeks under the Turks (1453–1829)

CHAPTER 25: THE SURVIVAL OF THE BYZANTINE HERITAGE

LAMENTS ON THE FALL OF CONSTANTINOPLE AND ATHENS

Apostolakis, G., Ἐπιστημονικὴ Ἐπετηρὶς Φιλοσοφ.Σχολῆς Πανεπιστημίου Θεσσαλονίκης, vol. 5, 1940, pp. 3f.

Demaras, K., Ἱστορία τῆς Νεοελληνικῆς Λογοτεχνίας, 2nd edn., Athens, 1955, pp. 53f.

Lampros, S., Μονῳδίαι καὶ θρῆνοι ἐπὶ τῇ ἁλώσει τῆς Κωνσταντινουπόλεως, Νέος Ἑλληνομνήμων, vol. 5, 1908, pp. 190–269, 341, 486, 491

Legrand, É., Bibliothèque grecque vulgaire, vol. 1, Paris, 1880 (E. Georgillas on the Fall of Constantinople)

Megas, G., in Λαογραφικὸν Ἀρχεῖον, vol. 8, 1956, pp. 3f.

Wagner, W., Medieval Greek Texts, London, 1870, pp. 141f.

Zoras, G., Βασικὴ Βιβλιοθήκη, vol. 1, Athens, 1955, pp. 53f. (Lament on the Fall of Athens)

Zoras, G., Περὶ τὴν ἅλωσιν τῆς Κωνσταντινουπόλεως, Athens, 1959

MODERN GREEK FOLK SONGS

Academy of Athens, Δημοτικὰ Τραγούδια, Athens, 1965, vol. 1

Apostolakis, J., Τὸ Δημοτικὸ Τραγούδι, Athens, 1929

Apostolakis, J., Τὸ κλέφτικο τραγούδι, Athens, 1950

Baud-Bovy, S., La chanson populaire grecque du Dodécanèse, Geneva, 1936

Baud-Bovy, S., Études sur la chanson cleftique, Athens, 1958

Beaton, R., Folk Poetry of Modern Greece, Cambridge, 1980

Demaras, K., Ἱστορία τῆς Νεοελληνικῆς Λογοτεχνίας, 4th edn., Athens, 1968, pp. 5f., 23f. and passim

Deter-Grohmann, I., Das neugriechische Volkslied, Munich, 1968, vol. 1

Entwistle, W. J., European Balladry, Oxford, 1939, pp. 309f., 316f.

Fauriel, C., Chansons populaires de la Grèce moderne, 2 vols., Paris, 1924–5

Georgiades, T., Der griechische Rhythmus: Musik, Reigen, Vers und Sprache, Hamburg, 1949

Ioannou, G., Τὰ δημοτικά μας τραγούδια, Athens, 1966

Ioannou, G., Παραλογές, Ἐπιμέλεια Γ. Ἰωάννου, Athens, 1970

Joannidu, M., Untersuchungen zur Form der neugriechischen Klagelieder (Diss.), Munich, 1938

Krumbacher, BLG, p. 792

Kyriakidis, S. P., in Λαογραφία, vol. 12, 1948, pp. 473f.

Kyriakidis, S. P., *Αἱ ἱστορικαὶ ἀρχαὶ τῆς δημώδους νεοελληνικῆς ποιήσεως*, 2nd edn., Salonica, 1947

Kyriakidis, S. P., *Ἡ γένεσις τοῦ διστίχου καὶ ἡ ἀρχὴ τῆς ἰσομετρίας*, Salonica, 1947

Lawson, J. C., *Modern Greek Folklore and Ancient Religion*, Cambridge, 1910, pp. 262f.

Lord, A. B., *Hellenism and the Greek War of Liberation*, Salonica, 1976, pp. 91f.

Lüdeke, H., *Neugriechische Volkslieder*, 2 vols., Athens 1947-64 (vol. 1 texts, vol. 2 translations)

Passow, A., *Popularia carmina Graeciae recentioris*, Leipzig, 1860

Petropoulos, D., *La comparaison dans la chanson populaire grecque*, Athens, 1954

Petropoulos, D., *Ἑλληνικὰ Δημοτικὰ Τραγούδια*, 2 vols., Athens, 1958

Politis, N. G., *Γνωστοὶ Ποιηταὶ δημοτικῶν ᾀσμάτων Διαλέξεις φιλολ. Συλλόγου Παρνασσός*, Athens, 1916, vol. 1, pp. 45f.

Politis, N. G., *Ἐκλογαὶ ἀπὸ τὰ τραγούδια τοῦ Ἑλληνικοῦ λαοῦ*, 6th edn., Athens, 1969

Soyter, G., in *Λαογραφία*, vol. 8, 1921-5, pp. 386f.

Vitti, H., *Canti del ribelli Greci*, Florence, 1956

Zambelios, S., *Ἄσματα δημοτικὰ τῆς Ἑλλάδος*, Corfu, 1852

PERSONAL POETRY UNDER THE TURKS

The first and darkest period (1453–1600)

GEORGIOS AETOLOS

Bănescu, N., *Un pòeme grec vulgaire relatif à Pierre le Boiteux de Valachie*, Bucharest, 1912

Legrand, É., *Bibliothèque grecque vulgaire*, Paris, 1896, vol. 8, pp. 1f. (text of Aesopic Fables)

Legrand, É., *Νέος Ἑλληνομνήμων*, vol. 9, 1912, pp. 252f.

Russo, D., *Studii istorice greco-române*, Bucharest, 1939, vol. 1, p. 37f.

ARSENIOS OF ELASSON

Kournoutos, G., in *Βασικὴ Βιβλιοθήκη*, vol. 44, Athens, 1953, pp. 73f.

Zambelios, S., *Καθίδρυσις Πατριαρχείου ἐν Ρωσσίᾳ*, Athens, 1859

Zambelios, S., in *Πανδώρα*, vol. 10, 1859–60, pp. 52f.

STAVRIANOS VESTIARES

Grecu, V., *Probleme der neugriechischen Literatur*, Berlin, 1960, vol. 3, pp. 180f.

Legrand, É., *Recueil des poèmes historiques . . .*, Paris, 1877

Russo, D., *Studii istorice greco-române*, Bucharest, 1939, vol. 1, pp. 114f.

GEORGIOS PALAMIDES

Legrand, É., *Bibliothèque grecque vulgaire*, Paris, 1881, vol. 2, pp. 183f. (history of Michael the Brave)

Russo, D., *Studii istorice greco-române*, Bucharest, 1939, vol. 1, pp. 145f.

Mattheos of Myra

Legrand, É., *Bibliothéque grecque vulgaire*, Paris, 1881, vol. 2, pp. 231f. (history of Wallachia)

Russo, D., *Studii istorice greco-române*, Bucharest, 1939, vol. 1, pp. 159f.

Synadinos of Serrae

Pennas, P., in *Σερραϊκὰ Χρονικά*, vol. 1, 1938, pp. 1f. (Lament), *Τὸ Χρονικὸν τοῦ Παπασυννοδινοῦ*.

The period of religious humanism (1600–69)

Meletios Syrigos

Kournoutos, G., in *Βασικὴ Βιβλιοθήκη*, vol. 44, Athens, 1953, pp. 91f.

Nectarios

Manousakas, M. J., in *Κρητικὰ Χρονικά*, vol. 1, 1947, pp. 291f.; vol. 7, 1953, pp. 163f.

The Story of the Jewess Mardada

Legrand, É., *Recueil de poèmes historiques* . . ., Paris, 1887

Harbingers of the Greek revival (1669–1750)

J. Rizos Manes

Legrand, *Collection de monuments*, vol. 7 (The Battle of the Elements)

Momars

Vranousis, L., *Οἱ Πρόδρομοι, Βασικὴ Βιβλιοθήκη*, vol. 11, Athens, 1956, pp. 31f. (*Bosporomachia*)

Caesarios Dapontes

Demaras, K., in *Βασικὴ Βιβλιοθήκη*, vol. 43, Athens, 1955, pp. 40f.

Legrand, É., *Bibliothèque grecque vulgaire*, vol. 3, Paris 1881 (edition of *The Garden of Graces* and sections of *The Mirror of Women*)

Vranousis, L. *Οἱ Πρόδρομοι, Βασικὴ Βιβλιοθήκη*, vol. 11, Athens, 1956, pp. 1f.

The Phanariots (1750–1821)

Knös, B., *Histoire de la littérature néo-grecque*, Stockholm–Göteborg–Uppsala, 1960, pp. 607f.

Vranousis, L., *Οἱ Πρόδρομοι, Βασικὴ Βιβλιοθήκη*, vol. 11, Athens, 1956, pp. 31f.

The forerunners of modern Greek poetry

Rhegas Pheraios

Daskalakis, A., *Rhigas Velestinlis*, Paris, 1937
Daskalakis, A., *Μελέται περὶ τοῦ Ρήγα Βελεστινλῆ*, Athens, 1964

Lampros, S., *Ρήγας, Βηλαρᾶς Χρηστόπουλος, Διαλέξεις περὶ Ἑλλ.ποιητῶν τοῦ ΙΘ´ αἰῶνος*, 2nd edn., Athens, 1925, vol. 1, pp. 53f.

Palamas, *Ἅπαντα*, vol. 2, pp. 17f.

Vranousis, L. (ed.), *Ρήγας Βελεστινλῆς Φεραῖος, Ἅπαντα*, 2 vols., Athens, 1963

JOANNES VELARAS

Babaretos, G. A. (ed.), *Ἅπαντα*, Athens, 1935

Lampros, S., *Ρήγας, Βηλαρᾶς Χρηστόπουλος, Διαλέξεις περὶ Ἑλλ.ποιητῶν τοῦ ΙΘ´ αἰῶνος*, 2nd edn., Athens, 1925, vol. 1, pp. 53f.

Palamas, K., *Τὰ πρῶτα κριτικά*, Athens, 1913, pp. 69f.

Tomadakis, N. B., *Ὁ Ἰωάννης Βιλλαρᾶς*, Athens, 1943

Vranousis, L., *Οἱ Πρόδρομοι, Βασικὴ Βιβλιοθήκη*, vol. 11, Athens, 1956, pp. 201f.

ATHANASIOS CHRISTOPOULOS

Christopoulos, A., *Λυρικά, Ἐρωτικά*, Paris, 1864

Lampros, S., *Ρήγας, Βηλαρᾶς Χριστόπουλος, Διαλέξεις περὶ Ἑλλ. ποιητῶν τοῦ ΙΘ´ αἰῶνος*, 2nd edn., Athens, vol. 1, pp. 53f.

Χρηστοπούλου, A., Ἅπαντα, Ἀναστύλωσε Γ. Βαλέτας, Athens, 1969

Χρηστοπούλου, A., Λυρικά, Ἐπιμέλεια Ἑ. Τσαντσάνογλου, Athens, 1970

Vranousis, L., *Οἱ Πρόδρομοι, Βασικὴ Βιβλιοθήκη*, vol. 11, Athens, 1956, pp. 79f.

Rhimades

Bouboulidis, P. K., in *Μικρασιατικὰ Χρονικά*, vol. 8, 1959, pp. 402f.

Henrichson, R. J. F., *Inbydelseskrift til den offentlige Examen i Odense Cathedralskole 1849*, Copenhagen, 1849

Karantzas, K., *Σμύρνης Τραγωδίες*, Athens, 1958

Kougeas, S., *Ἑλληνικά, Παράρτημα 4 (Προσφορὰ εἰς Στ.Κυριακίδην)*, Salonica 1953, pp. 364f.

Legrand, *Collection de monuments*, vol. 18

Legrand, É., *Recueil de poèmes historiques . . .*, Paris, 1877

Legrand, É., *Bibliothèque grecque vulgaire*, vol. 3, Paris, 1881, pp. 332f.

Magiakos, P. S., *Ὁ Λάμπρος Κατζώνης*, Athens, 1932

Maurer, G. L., *Das griechische Volk*, Heidelberg, 1835, vol. 3

Papacharalabos, G., in *Κυπριακαὶ Σπουδαί*, vol. 15, 1951, pp. 131f.

PART FIVE: MODERN GREECE (1829–1940)

CHAPTER 26: THE OLD SCHOOL OF ATHENS: THE GREEK ROMANTICS

THE INITIAL STAGE OF THE OLD SCHOOL OF ATHENS (1830–50)

Demaras, K. T., *Ποιηταὶ τοῦ ΙΘ´ αἰῶνος*, Athens, 1954, introduction (*Βασικὴ Βιβλιοθήκη*, vol. 12)

Politis, L., Ἑλληνικὸς ϱομαντισμός (1830–1880), Θέματα τῆς Λογοτεχνίας μας, 2nd series, Salonica, 1976, pp. 99f.

Rhoidis, E., Περὶ συγχρόνου Ἑλληνικῆς Ποιήσεως, Ἅπαντα, 5 vols., Athens, 1978, vol. 2, 286f.

Vlachos, A., Ἀνάλεκτα, 2 vols., Athens, 1901, vol. 2, pp. 5f.

PANAGIOTIS SOUTSOS

Demaras, K. T., Ποιηταὶ ΙΘ΄ αἰῶνος (Βασικὴ Βιβλιοθήκη, 12), Athens, 1954

Panagiotopoulos, I. M., Ὁ νεοελληνικὸς ϱομαντισμός, Τὰ πρόσωπα καὶ τὰ κείμενα, vol. 6, Athens, n.d., pp. 59f.

Tsokopoulos, G., Οἱ ἀδελφοὶ Σοῦτσοι, Διαλέξεις περὶ Ἑλλήνων Ποιητῶν τοῦ ΙΘ΄ αἰῶνος, 2nd edn., Athens, 1925, vol. 1, pp. 207f.

Vlachos, A., Ἀνάλεκτα, 2 vols., Athens, 1901, vol. 2, pp. 5f.

ALEXANDROS SOUTSOS

Α. Σούτσου, Ἅπαντα (ἐπιμ. Ν. Κοντομιχάλη), Athens, 1963

Α. Σούτσου, Ἅπαντα, Athens, 1916 (Βιβλιοθήκη Φέξη)

Tsokopoulos, G., Οἱ ἀδελφοὶ Σοῦτσοι, Διαλέξεις περὶ Ἑλλήνων Ποιητῶν τοῦ ΙΘ΄ αἰῶνος, 2nd edn., Athens, 1925, vol. 1, pp. 207f.

Vlachos, A., Ἀνάλεκτα, 2 vols., Athens, 1901, vol. 2, pp. 36f.

ALEXANDROS RIZOS RANGAVIS

Palamas, Ἅπαντα, vol. 2, pp. 404f.

Rangavis, A. Rizos, Ἅπαντα τὰ Φιλολογικά, τομ. Α΄, Λυρικὴ ποίησις, Athens, 1874

Zalokostas, E., Ἀλέξανδρος Ρίζος Ραγκαβῆς, Διαλέξεις περὶ Ἑλλήνων Ποιητῶν τοῦ ΙΘ΄αἰῶνος, 2nd edn., Athens, 1925, vol. 1, pp. 245f.

GEORGIOS ZALOCOSTAS

Demetrakopoulos, P., Γ. Χ. Ζαλοκώστας, Διαλέξεις περὶ Ἑλλήνων Ποιητῶν τῶν ΙΘ΄ αἰῶνος, 2nd edn., Athens, 1925, vol. 2, pp. 5f.

Lampros, S., Γεώργιος Ζαλοκώστας, Athens, 1868

Vlachos, A., Ἀνάλεκτα, 2 vols., Athens, 1901, vol. 2, pp. 110f.

Ζαλοκώστα, Γ. Χ., Τὰ Ἅπαντα, Athens, 1859

THEODOROS ORPHANIDIS

Ambelas, T., Θεόδωρος Ὀρφανίδης, Διαλέξεις περὶ Ἑλλ. Ποιητῶν τοῦ ΙΘ΄ αἰῶνος, 2nd edn., Athens, 1925, vol. 1, pp. 331f.

Ὀρφανίδου, Θεοδώρου, Τὰ Ἅπαντα, Athens, 1915 (Βιβλιοθήκη Φέξη)

JOANNES KARASOUTSAS

Demaras, K. T., Οἱ ποιηταὶ τοῦ ΙΘ΄ αἰῶνος, Athens, 1954 (Βασικὴ Βιβλιοθήκη, 12)

Paraschos, K., Δέκα Ἕλληνες Λυρικοί, 2nd edn., Athens, 1962, pp. 22f.

Vlachos, A., Ἀνάλεκτα, 2 vols., Athens, 1901, vol. 2, pp. 56f.

DEMOSTHENES BALABANIS

Demaras, K. T., Οἱ ποιηταὶ τοῦ ΙΘ΄ αἰῶνος, Athens, 1954 (Βασικὴ Βιβλιοδήκη, 12).

Elias Tantalidis

Tantalidis, E., *Παίγνια ἢ ποιήματα διάφορα ἐκδοθέντα ὑπὸ Ἰωσὴφ Μάγνητος ἐκ τῆς Ἐμπορικῆς Τυπογραφίας Ἡ Ἠώς*, Constantinople, 1839

Stephanos Koumanoudis

Bees, N., *Ἔμμετρα κείμενα Σ. Α. Κουμανούδη*, Athens, 1949
Βρεττοῦ, Ἡμερολόγιον, Athens, 1862

THE MIDDLE YEARS OF THE OLD SCHOOL (1850–70)

Demetrios Paparrigopoulos

Anninos, C., *Βασιλειάδης, Παπαρρηγόπουλος καὶ οἱ περὶ αὐτούς, Διαλέξεις περὶ Ἑλλ. Ποιητῶν τοῦ ΙΘ´ αἰῶνος*, 2nd edn., Athens, 1925, vol. 2, pp. 279f.
Palamas, *Ἅπαντα*, vol. 10, pp. 267f.
Παπαρρηγοπούλου, Δ., Ἅπαντα, 1867 (does not contain all his works)
Παπαρρηγοπούλου, Δ., Ἅπαντα, 1915 (*Βιβλιοθήκη Φέξη*)

Spyridon Vasiliadis

Palamas, *Ἅπαντα*, vol. 2, pp. 427f.
Vasiliades, S., *Παντοῖαι ποιήσεις, Ἀττικαὶ Νύκτες*, Athens, 1900, vol. 2

Demetrios Bernardakis

Michaelidis, M. I., *Βίος καὶ ἔργα Δημητρίου Ν. Βερναρδάκη*, Mytilene, 1909

Angelos Vlachos

Vlachos, A., *Ἠώς, συλλογὴ ποιήσεων πρωτοτύπων καὶ μεταπεφρασμένων*, Athens, 1857
Vlachos, A., *ῖ Ὧραι*, Athens, 1860
Vlachos, A., *Λυρικὰ ποιήματα*, Athens, 1875

THE END OF THE OLD SCHOOL (1870–80)

Rhoidis, E., *Περὶ συγχρόνου Ἑλληνικῆς ποιήσεως, Ἅπαντα*, 5 vols., Athens, 1978, vol. 2, pp. 286f.

Achilles Paraschos

Karandonis, A., *Ἀπὸ τὸν Σολωμὸ ὡς τὸν Μυριβήλη*, Athens, 1969
Palamas, *Ἅπαντα*, vol. 2, pp. 423f.
Xenopoulos, G., *Οἱ Παράσχοι, Διαλέξεις περὶ Ἑλλ. Ποιητῶν τοῦ ΙΘ´ αἰῶνος*, 2nd edn., Athens, 1925, vol. 2, pp. 167f.

Georgios Paraschos

Palamas, *Ἅπαντα*, vol. 2, pp. 411f.
Xenopoulos, G., *Οἱ Παράσχοι, Διαλέξεις περὶ Ἑλλ. Ποιητῶν τοῦ ΙΘ´ αἰῶνος*, 2nd edn., Athens, 1925, vol. 2, pp. 167f.

CHAPTER 27: THE SCHOOL OF THE IONIAN ISLANDS

THE FORERUNNERS OF THE IONIAN SCHOOL

Bouboulides, P. K., *Προσολωμικοί*, 3 vols., Athens, 1966–73
Laskaris, N. I., *Ἱστορία τοῦ Νεοελληνικοῦ Θεάτρου*, 2 vols., Athens, 1938–9
Protopappas-Bouboulides, G., *Τὸ Θέατρον ἐν Ζακύνθῳ ἀπὸ τοῦ ΙΖ´ μέχρι τοῦ ΙΘ´ αἰῶνος*, Athens, 1958
Sideris, G., *Ἱστορία τοῦ Νέου Ἑλληνικοῦ Θεάτρου*, Athens, n.d., vol. 1
Valsa, M., *Le théâtre grec moderne de 1453 à 1900*, Berlin, 1953

THE MAJOR POETS OF THE IONIAN SCHOOL

Zoras, G. T., *Ἑπτανησιακὰ Μελετήματα*, 4 vols., Athens, 1959–69

ANDREAS KALVOS

Bouvier, B., Calvos in *Modern Greek Writers*, eds. E. Keeley and P. Bien, Princeton, 1972, pp. 68f.
Demaras, K., *Οἱ πηγὲς τῆς ἔμπνευσης τοῦ Κάλβου* (*Ρομαντικὰ σημειώματα Γ´, ἀνάτυπο ἀπὸ τὴν Νέα Ἑστία*), Athens, 1946
Karandonis, A., *Ἀπὸ τὸν Σολωμὸ στὸν Μυριβήλη*, Athens, 1969
Νέα Ἑστία, Ἀφιέρωμα στὸν Κάλβο, vol. 40, 1946 (Christmas 1956)
Palamas, K., *Κάλβος ὁ Ζακύνθιος* (1888), *Ἅπαντα*, vol. 2, pp. 28f.
Paraschos, K., *Δέκα Ἕλληνες Λυρικοί*, 2nd edn., Athens, 1962, pp. 41f.
Pontani, F. M., *Ἀνδρέου Καλβου Ὠδαι*, Athens, 1970
Porphyres, K., *Ὁ Ἀνδρέας Κάλβος καρμπονάρος. Ἡ μυστικὴ δίκη τῶν καρμπονάρων τῆς Τοσκάνης*, Athens, 1975
Seferis, G., *Δοκιμές*, Cairo, 1944, vol. 1, 3rd edn., Athens, 1974
Sherrard, P., *The Wound of Greece*, London, 1978
Sofroniou, S. A., *Ἀνδρέας Κάλβος, Κριτικὴ μελέτη* preface by R. J. H. Jenkins, Athens, 1960
Vitti, M., *A. Kalvos e i suoi scritti in Italiano*, Naples, 1960
Vitti, M., *Πηγὲς γιὰ τὴ βιογραφία τοῦ Κάλβου* (*Ἐπιστολές* 1813–20), Salonica, 1963 (*Ἑλληνικά, Παράρτημα*, 15)
Zoras, G., *Κάλβου Ὠδαὶ μετὰ τῆς πρώτης γαλλικῆς μεταφράσεως ὑπὸ* St Julien *καὶ* Pauthier de Censay, Athens, 1962

DIONYSIOS SOLOMOS

Apostolakis, G. M., *Ἡ ποίηση στὴ ζωή μας*, 2nd edn., Athens, 1923
Beaton, R., in *Byzantine and Modern Greek Studies*, vol. 2, 1976, pp. 161f.
Brandenburg, J., *Solomos et l'Italie*, Rotterdam, n.d.
Coutelle, L., *Formation poètique de Solomos (1815–1833)*, Athens, 1977
Hadjigiakoumis, E., *Νεοελληνικαὶ Πηγαὶ τοῦ Σολωμοῦ* (Diss.), Athens, 1968
Jenkins, R., *Dionysius Solomos*, Cambridge, 1940
Konomos, Dinos, *Σολωμοῦ ἀνέκδοτα γράμματα στὸν Ἰωάννη Γαλβάνη*, Athens, 1950 (*Collection de l'Institut Français d'Athènes*, no. 72)
Kriaras, E., *Διονύσιος Σολωμός, Ὁ βίος, τὸ ἔργο*, Salonica, 1957; rpt. 1970
Lorentzatos, Z., *Γιὰ τὸ Σολωμό, τὴ λύρα τὴ δίκαιη*, Athens, 1974

Maronitis, D. N., *Δ. Σολωμός. Οἱ ἐποχὲς τοῦ Κρητικοῦ*, Athens, 1975

Νέα Ἑστία, vol. 104, 1978 (Christmas 1978, as well as Christmas 1943, dedicated to Solomos)

Νέα Γράμματα, vol. 2, 1936 (also dedicated to Palamas)

Palamas, *Ἅπαντα*, vol. 2, pp. 21f., 484f.

Palamas, Κ., *Διονύσιος Σολωμός. Ἐπιμέλεια Μ.Κ. Χατζηγιακουμῆ (Ἑρμῆς, Νέα Ἑλληνικὴ Βιβλιοθήκη, 9), Athens, 1970*

Politis, L., *Ὁ Σολωμὸς στὰ γράμματά του*, Athens, 1956

Politis, L., *Γύρω στὸ Σολωμό Μελέτες καὶ ἄρθρα (1938–1958)*, Athens, 1958

Politis, L., *Διονυσίου Σολωμοῦ Ἅπαντα*, 2 vols., Athens, 1948–60

Politis, L., *Αὐτόγραφα Ἔργα. Ἐπιμέλεια Λίνου Πολίτη*, 2 vols., Salonica, 1964 (*Ἀριστοτέλειον Πανεπιστήμιον Θεσσαλονίκης*)

Raizis-Byron, M., *Dionysios Solomos*, New York, 1972 (Twaynes's World Authors Series)

Stohastis, (ed.) *Γύρω στὸ Σολωμό*, 2 vols., Athens, 1925–7

Tsantsanoglou, H., *Μία λανθάνουσα ποιητικὴ σύνθεση τοῦ Διονυσίου Σολωμοῦ, Τὸ αὐτόγραφο τετράδιο Ζακύνθου ἀρ. II*, Salonica, 1978

Julios Typaldos

Konomos Dinos, *Ἅπαντα. Ἐπιμέλεια–εἰσαγωγὴ Ντίνος Κονόμος (Ἅπαντα Νεοελλήνων κλασσικῶν)*, Athens, 1970

Palamas, *Ἅπαντα*, vol. 8, pp. 285f.

Palamas, Κ., *Διαλέξεις περὶ Ἑλλήνων Ποιητῶν τοῦ ΙΘ´ αἰῶνος*, 2nd edn., Athens, 1925, vol. 2, pp. 127f. (*Ἅπαντα*, vol. 8, pp. 285f.)

Lesser successors of Solomos

Buchard, J., *Γεώργιος Τερτσέτης, Βιογραφικὴ καὶ φιλολογικὴ μελέτη (1800–1843)*, Athens, 1970

Palamas, Κ., *Γράμματα*, Athens, 1904, vol. 1, pp. 81f.

Stephanou, D., *Γ. Τερτσέτης, Διαλέξεις περὶ Ἑλλήνων ποιητῶν τοῦ ΙΘ´ αἰῶνος*, 2nd edn., Athens, 1925, vol. 2, pp. 35f.

Valetas, G., *Ἅπαντα Γ. Τερτσέτη, ἀναστύλωσε Γ. Βαλέτας*, Athens, 1966–7

Vellanitis, T., *Πολυλᾶς, Μαρκορᾶς καὶ ἡ Σχολὴ τῆς Κερκύρας, Διαλέξεις περὶ Ἑλλ. Ποιητῶν τοῦ ΙΘ´ αἰῶνος*, 2nd edn., Athens, 1925, vol. 2, pp. 35f.

Vlachos, A., *Ἀνάλεκτά*, 2 vols., Athens, 1901, vol. 2, pp. 83f.

Jakovos Polylas

Andreadis, A., *Ἰάκωβος Πολυλᾶς, Μαρκορᾶς καὶ ἡ σχολὴ τῆς Κερκύρας*, Athens, 1916

Palamas, *Ἅπαντα*, vol. 2, pp. 88f.

Valetas, G., *Ἰ. Πολυλᾶς Ἅπαντα τὰ λογοτεχνικὰ καὶ κριτικά, ἀναστύλωσε Γ. Βαλέτας*, 2nd edn., Athens, 1959

Aristotelis Valaoritis

Apostolakis, G. M., *Ἀριστοτέλης Βαλαωρίτης*, Athens, 1936

Nirvanas, P., *Α. Βαλαωρίτης, Διαλέξεις περὶ Ἑλλ. Ποιητῶν τοῦ ΙΘ´ αἰῶνος*, 2nd edn., Athens, 1925, vol. 2, pp. 91f.

Palamas, *Ἅπαντα*, vol. 8, pp. 161f.

Paraschos, C., *Μορφὲς καὶ ἰδέες*, Athens, 1938, pp. 99f.

Rhoidis, E., *Ἅπαντα*, 5 vols., Athens, 1978, vol. 2, pp. 407f.

Savvidis, G., *Φωτεινός*, Athens, 1970 (*Ἑρμῆς Νεα Ἑλλ. Βιβλιοθήκη*, 7)

Tarabout, Y., *La langue de Valaoritis*, Athens, 1970 (with good bibliography)

Valaoritis, A., *Βίος καὶ ἔργα*, 3 vols., Athens, 1907, (*Βιβλ. Μαρασλῆ*)

ANDREAS LASKARATOS

Karandonis, A., *Φυσιογνωμίες*, Athens, 1959, vol. 1, pp. 62f.

Laskaratos, A., *Ἅπαντα*, Athens, 1959

Laskaratos, A., *Βιογραφικά μου ἐνθυμήματα, Ἀνέκδοτη αὐτοβιογραφία, Εἰσαγωγή, κείμενο, πίνακες Ἀλ. Γ. Παπαγεωργίου*, Athens, 1966

Palamas, *Ἅπαντα*, vol. 2, pp. 81f.

Zervos, J., *Ἀνδρέας Λασκαράτος, Διαλέξεις περὶ Ἑλλήνων Ποιητῶν τοῦ ΙΘ´ αἰῶνος*, 2nd edn., Athens, 1925, vol. 1, pp. 279f.

GERASIMOS MARKORAS

Markoras, G., *Ἅπαντα, ἀναστύλωσε Γ. Βαλέτας*, Athens, 1950

Palamas, K., *Τὰ πρῶτα κριτικά*, Athens, 1913, pp. 48f.

Vellanitis, T., *Πολυλᾶς, Μαρκορᾶς καὶ ἡ Σχολὴ τῆς Κερκύρας, Διαλέξεις περὶ Ἑλλ. Ποιητῶν τοῦ ΙΘ´ αἰῶνος*, 2nd edn., Athens, 1925, vol. 2, p. 223

LORENTZOS MAVILIS

Ἅπαντα, Ἐπιμέλεια Μαρ. Μαντουβάλου, 2 vols., Athens, n.d.

Karandonis, A., *Τά ἔργα τοῦ Λορέντζου Μαβίλη*, Alexandria, 1915

Karandonis, A., *Φυσιογνωμίες*, Athens, 1959, vol. 1, pp. 72f.

Paraschos, C., *Μορφὲς καὶ ἰδέες*, Athens, 1938, pp. 211f.

Peranthis, M., *Δώδεκα Διαλέξεις*, Athens n.d., pp. 89f.

Peranthis, M., *Λ. Μαβίλης Ἅπαντα*, Athens, 1960 (*Ποίηση, μεταφράσεις, μελέτες*)

CHAPTER 28: THE NEW SCHOOL OF ATHENS

Νέα Ἑστία, Christmas, 1976, *Λογοτεχνία καὶ Δημοτικισμός*, pp. 1f.

Panagiotopoulos, I. M., *Ἡ σύγχρονη Ἑλληνικὴ Ποίηση, Τὰ πρόσωπα καὶ τὰ κείμενα*, vol. 1, Athens, 1943, pp. 7f.

THE FORERUNNERS OF THE NEW SCHOOL

ARISTOMENIS PROVELENGIOS

Palamas, *Ἅπαντα*, vol. 2, pp. 138f.

Karandonis, A., *Φυσιογνωμίες*, Athens, 1959, vol. 1, pp. 141f.

GEORGIOS BIZYENOS

Bizyenos, G., *Ἅπαντα, Ἐπιμέλεια Κ. Μαμώνη*, Athens, 1955

Palamas, K., *Βιζυηνὸς καὶ Κρυστάλλης, Διαλέξεις περὶ Ἑλλήνων Ποιητῶν τοῦ ΙΘ´ αἰῶνος*, 2nd edn., Athens, 1925, vol. 2, pp. 341f.

JOHANNES PAPADIAMANTOPOULOS (JEAN MORÉAS)

Gourmont, Jean de, *Jean Moréas*, Paris, 1905
Jouanny, R., *Jean Moréas, ecrivain grec. La jeunesse de Ioannis Papadiamantopoulos en Grèce (1856–1878)*, Paris, 1975 (*Bibliothèque des lettres modernes, 25*)

THE 'GENERATION OF THE EIGHTIES'

NICOLAOS KAMBAS

Βασικὴ Βιβλιοθήκη, vol. 24, ἐπιμέλεια Γ. Θέμελη, Athens, 1953
Valetas, G., Νίκος Καμπᾶς, Mytilene, 1936

GEORGIOS DROSINIS

Baud-Bovy, S., *Poésie de la Grèce moderne*, Lausanne, 1946
Karandonis, A., Φυσιογνωμίες, Athens, 1959, vol. 1, pp. 160f.
Levesque, R., *Domaine grec (1930–1946)*, Paris, 1947
Palamas, Ἅπαντα, vol. 2, pp. 130f.

KOSTIS PALAMAS

Demaras, K., Κωστῆς Παλαμᾶς, Ἡ πορεία του πρὸς τὴν τέχνη, Athens, 1947
Eklünd, B.-L., *The Ideal and the Real: A Study of the Ideas in Kostis Palamas' Δωδεκάλογος τοῦ Γύφτον*, Göteborg, 1972
Emrich, G., *Antike Metaphern und Vergleiche im lyrischen Werk des Kostis Palamas*, Amsterdam, 1974
Jenkins, R., *Palamas*, an Inaugural Lecture at King's College, London, 1971
Hourmouzios, A. Ὁ Παλαμᾶς καὶ ἡ ἐποχή του, 3 vols., Athens, 1943–60
Karandonis, A., Γύρω στὸν Παλαμᾶ, 2 vols., Athens, 1959–71
Karandonis, A., Κωστῆς Παλαμᾶς, Φυσιογνωμίες, Σειρὰ Δεύτερη, Athens, 1960, pp. 7f.
Karandonis, A., Κωστῆς Παλαμᾶς, Athens, 1980
Kasinis, K. G., Βιβλιογραφία Κωστῆ Παλαμᾶ (1911–1925), Athens, 1973
Katsimbalis, G. K., Βιβλιογραφία Κωστῆ Παλαμᾶ, Athens, 1943 (and suppl.)
Νέα Γράμματα, vol. 2, 1936 (also dedicated to Solomos)
Νέα Ἑστία, Κωστῆς Παλαμᾶς, vol. 34 (Christmas 1943)
Panagiotopoulos, I. M., Τὰ πρόσωπα καὶ τὰ κείμενα, Athens, 1944, vol. 3 (all dedicated to Palamas)
Papanoutsos, E. P., Παλαμᾶς, Καβάφης, Σικελιανός, Athens, 1949
Politou-Marmarinou, E. Ὁ Παλαμᾶς καὶ ὁ γαλλικὸς Παρνασσισμός (D.Phil.), Athens, 1976
Sykoutris, J., Ὁ Δωδεκάλογος τοῦ Γύφτου τοῦ Κ. Παλαμᾶ, Athens, 1976
Tsatsos, K., Κ. Παλαμᾶς, 3rd edn., Athens, 1966

For editions of Palamas works see:
Κωστῆ Παλαμᾶ, Ἅπαντα, 16 vols., Athens, 1962–9
Κωστῆ Παλαμᾶ, Ἀνθολογία, selection by G. K. Katsibalis and A. Karandonis, Athens, 1973
Κωστῆ Παλαμᾶ, Ἀλληλογραφία by K. G. Kasinis, vol. 1 (1875–1915), Athens, 1975; vol. 2 (1916–28), Athens, 1978

JOHANNES POLEMIS

Katsimbalis, G., *Νέα Ἑστία*, 15 April 1962
Palamas, *Ἅπαντα*, vol. 2, pp. 460f.

The lesser poets

GEORGIOS SOURIS

Karandonis, A., *Φυσιογνωμίες*, Athens, 1959, vol. 1, pp. 148f.
Karandonis, A., *Ἀπὸ τὸν Σολωμὸ ὡς τὸν Μυριβήλη*, Athens, 1969
Palamas, *Ἅπαντα*, vol. 2, pp. 446f.
Panagiotopoulos, I. M., *Τὰ πρόσωπα καὶ τὰ κείμενα*, Athens, n.d., vol. 6, pp. 158f.

ALEXANDROS PALLIS

Palamas, *Ἅπαντα*, vol. 2, pp. 119f.
Pallis A., *Λέκα Ἀρβανίτη, μαλλιαροῦ, Κούφια Καρύδια*, Liverpool, 1915
Triantaphyllides, M., *Μνημόσυνα. Ψυχάρης, Πάλλης, Ἐφταλιώτης*, Salonica, 1939–46
Triantaphyllides, M., *Ἅπαντα*, 5 vols, vol. 5, pp. 366f.

ARGYRIS EFTALIOTIS

Michaelides, K. M., *Ἀργύρης Ἐφταλιώτης*, Athens, 1930
Politis, L., *Ἀργύρης Ἐφταλιώτης, Θέματα τῆς λογοτεχνίας μας*, 2nd series, Salonica, 1976, pp. 132f.
Valetas, G., *Ἅπαντα Ἀ. Ἐφταλιώτη*, 3 vols., Athens, 1973

THE POETS OF THE TURN OF THE CENTURY

CONSTANTINE HADJOPOULOS

Hadjopoulos, C., *Ποιήματα*, Athens, 1956–7
Karandonis, A., *Φυσιογνωμίες*, Athens, 1959, vol. 1, pp. 227f.
Νέα Ἑστία, vol. 28, 25 October 1940
Νεοελληνικὰ Γράμματα, fasc. 193, 10 August 1940
Palamas, *Ἅπαντα*, vol. 2, pp. 221
Thrylos, A., *Κριτικὲς Μελέτες*, 3 vols., Athens, 1924–5, vol. 3, pp. 29f.

KOSTAS KRYSTALLIS

Ἅπαντα, Ἐπιμέλεια, εἰσαγωγὴ Μ. Περάνθη, 2 vols., Athens, 1959
Ἅπαντα, Πρόλογος-εἰσαγωγὴ, ἐπιμ. Γ. Βαλέτα, 2 vols., Athens, 1959
Karandonis, A., *Φυσιογνωμίες*, Athens, 1959, vol. 1, pp. 131f.
Palamas, K., *Ἅπαντα*, vol. 2, pp. 463f.
Palamas, K., *Βιζυηνὸς καὶ Κρυστάλλης, Διαλέξεις περὶ Ἑλλ. Ποιητῶν ΙΘ´ αἰῶνος*, 2nd edn., Athens, 1925, vol. 2, pp. 341f.

MILTIADIS MALAKASIS

Karandonis, A., *Φυσιογνωμίες*, Athens, 1959, vol. 1, pp. 131f.
Νέα Ἑστία, vol. 34, 1 January 1943
Palamas, K., in *Νέα Ἑστία*, vol. 44, 15 February 1953

Panagiotopoulos, I. M., *Τὰ πρόσωπα καὶ τὰ κείμενα*, Athens, 1949, vol. 5, pp. 13f.

Paraschos, K., *Δέκα "Ελληνες Λυρικοί*, 2nd edn., Athens, 1962, pp. 52f.

Thrylos, A., *Κριτικὲς Μελέτες*, 3 vols., Athens, 1924–5, vol. 3, pp. 45f.

Valetas, G., *"Απαντα, 'Αναστύλωσε καὶ ἔκρινε Γ. Βαλέτας*, 2 vols., Athens, 1964

JOHANNES GRYPARIS

"Απαντα τὰ πρωτότυπα μὲ τὰ μικρὰ μεταφράσματα. "Εκρινε Γ. Βαλέτας, Athens, 1952

Katsimbalis, G., *Βιβλιογραφία Ι. Ν. Γρυπάρη*, Athens, 1942 and 1944

Νέα 'Εστία, vol. 32, 1 July 1942

Panagiotopoulos, I. M., *Τά πρόσωπα καὶ τὰ κείμενα*, Athens, 1943, vol. 1, pp. 107f.

Panagiotopoulos, I. M., *'Ο ἄγνωστος Γρυπάρης*, Athens, 1954

Thrylos, A., *Κριτικὲς Μελέτες*, 3 vols., Athens, 1924–5, vol. 3, pp. 5f.

SPELIOS PASAGIANNIS

Karandonis, A., *Φυσιογνωμίες*, Athens, 1959, vol. 1, pp. 206f.

Pasagiannis, S., *"Απαντα, Ποιήματα, πεζογραφήματα, μεταφράσματα, γράμματα. 'Αναστύλωσε Γ. Βαλέτας*, Athens, 1965

ZACHARIAS PAPANTONIOU

Νεοελληνικὰ Γράμματα, fasc. 167, 1940 (dedicated to Z. Papantoniou)

Νέα 'Εστία, vol. 27, 1 April 1940

Panagiotopoulos, I. M., *Τὰ πρόσωπα καὶ τὰ κείμεναι*, Athens, 1943, pp. 121f.

Papantoniou, Z., *Τὰ Θεῖα δῶρα*, Athens, 1931

LAMBROS PORPHYRAS

"Απαντα, Λάμπρος Πορφύρας, ἔκρινε Γ. Βαλέτας, Athens, 1956

Haris, P., *"Οταν ἡ ζωὴ γίνεται ὄνειρο*, 2nd edn., Athens, 1957

Νέα 'Εστία, vol. 13, 1 January 1933

Panagiotopoulos, I. M., *Τὰ πρόσωπα καὶ τὰ κείμενα*, Athens, 1949, vol. 5, pp. 47f.

Paraschos, K., *Δέκα "Ελληνες Λυρικοί*, 2nd edn., Athens, 1962, pp. 66f.

Thrylos, A., *Κριτικὲς Μελέτες*, 3 vols., Athens, 1924–5, vol. 3, pp. 199f.

THE DEMOTIC MOVEMENT AND GREEK POETRY COMPOSED OUTSIDE GREECE

Karandonis, A., *Εἰσαγωγὴ στὴ Νεώτερη Ποίηση*, Athens, 1958

Karandonis, A., *"Αγγελος Σημηριώτης, Φυσιογνωμίες*, Athens, 1960, vol. 2, pp. 78f.

Ouranis, K., *Δικοί μας καὶ Ξένοι*, Athens, 1955, vol. 2 (on Melachrinos)

Panagiotopoulos, I. M., *'Απόστολος Μελαχρινός, Τὰ πρόσωπα καὶ τὰ κείμενα*, Athens, 1943, vol. 1, pp. 61f.

On modern poetry composed in Cyprus see:

Kranidiotis, N., Ἡ Κυπριακὴ Ποίηση, Athens, n.d.

Kranidiotis, N., Ὁ Ἐθνικὸς Χαρακτὴρ τῆς Κυπριακῆς Λογοτεχνίας, Athens, n.d.

THE SECOND POST-PALAMAS GENERATION (THE 'GENERATION OF 1905')

ANGELOS SIKELIANOS

Avgeris, M., Ἄγγελος Σικελιανός I, Ἡ ποίησή του. Τὸ Θέατρό του. Κριτικὸς ἀπόλογος, Athens, 1952

Demopoulos, T., Ὁ Διθύραμβος τοῦ Ρόδου, Athens, 1934

Karandonis, A., Παλαμᾶς, Καβάφης, Σικελιανός, (Βασικὴ Βιβλιοθήκη Ἀετοῦ), 1st series, Athens, 1955

Karandonis, A., Φυσιογνωμίες, Athens, 1960, vol. 2, pp. 108f.

Katsimbalis, G. K., Βιβλιογραφία Ἀ. Σικελιανοῦ, Athens, 1946; supplement, Athens, 1952

Νέα Ἑστία, Christmas, 1952, fasc. 611, pp. 1–24 (dedicated to A Sikelianos)

Papanoutsos, E. P., Παλαμᾶς, Καβάφης, Σικελιανός, 2nd edn., Athens, 1955

Paraschos, K., Δέκα Ἕλληνες Λυρικοί, 2nd edn., Athens, 1962, pp. 137f.

Sherrard, P., *The Marble Threshing Floor*, London, 1956

Sherrard, P., *The Wound of Greece*, London, 1978

Warner, R., and Frangopoulos, T. D. (trs.), *On the Greek Style: Select Essays in Poetry and Hellenism*, London, 1967

NIKOS KAZANTZAKIS

Izzet, A., *Nikos Kazantzaki, biographie avec un tableau chronologique établi par P. Prevelaki*, Paris, 1965

Janiaud-Lust, C., *N. Kazantzakis, sa vie, son oeuvre*, Paris, 1970

Karandonis, A., Φυσιογνωμίες, Athens, 1960, vol. 2, pp. 131f.

Panagiotopoulos, I. M., Τὰ πρόσωπα καὶ τὰ κείμεναι, Athens, 1943, pp. 38f.

Politis, L., *A History of Modern Greek Literature*, Oxford, 1973, pp. 220f.

Prevelakis, P., Ὁ ποιητὴς καὶ τὸ ποίημα τῆς Ὀδύσσειας, Athens, 1958; 2nd edn., 1977

Prevelakis, P., Τετρακόσια γράμματα τοῦ Καζαντζάκη στὸν Πρεβελάκη, Athens, 1965

Stanford, W. B., *The Ulysses Theme: A Study in the Adaptability of a Traditional Hero*, Oxford, 1954

Zographou, L., *N. Καζαντζάκης, ἕνας τραγικός*, Athens, 1960

KOSTAS VARNALIS

Malanos, T., Ὁ ποιητὴς Κώστας Βάρναλης, Alexandria, 1944

Varikas, V., Ὁ ποιητὴς Κώστας Βάρναλης, Athens, 1936

Varnalis, K., Ἅπαντα, 3 vols., Athens 1956–8

The lesser poets

SOTERIS SKIPIS

Karandonis, A., Φυσιογνωμίες, Athens, 1960, vol. 2, pp. 90f.

NAPOLEON LAPATHIOTIS

Diktaios, A., Ναπολέων. Λαπαθιώτης, Τὰ ποιήματα, Εἰσαγωγή, σχόλια, παρουσίαση, Athens, 1964

ROMOS PHILYRAS

Korphis, T., Ρῶμος Φιλύρας, Συμβολὴ στὴ ζωὴ καὶ τὸ ἔργο του, Athens, 1974

Paraschos, K., Δέκα Ἕλληνες Λυρικοί, 2nd edn., Athens, 1962, pp. 153f.

THE 'COSMOPOLITAN POETS' (1915–25)

KOSTAS OURANIS

Panagiotopoulos, I. M., Τὰ πρόσωπα καὶ τὰ κείμενα, Athens n.d., vol. 6, pp. 229f.

OTHER POETS OF THE 1920s

TELOS AGRAS

Karandonis, A., Φυσιογνωμίες, Athens, 1960, vol. 2, pp. 188f.
Νέα Ἑστία, vol. 8, 1928, fasc. 16
Stergiopoulos, K., Ὁ Τέλος Ἄγρας καὶ τὸ πνεῦμα τῆς παρακμῆς, Athens, 1962

CONSTANTINE KARYOTAKIS

Malanos, T., Ἕνας Ἡγησιακός. Συμβολὴ στὴ μελέτη τοῦ Καρυωτάκη, Alexandria, 1938
Panagiotopoulos, I. M., Τὰ πρόσωπα καὶ τὰ κείμενα, Athens, 1949, vol. 5, pp. 105f.
Paraschos, K., Δέκα Ἕλληνες Λυρικοί, 2nd edn., Athens, 1962, pp. 193f.
Peri, M., Sul linguaggio di Kariotakis, Padua, 1972
Savvidis, G. P., Ἅπαντα τά Εὑρισκόμενα, 2 vols., Athens, 1965–6
Savvidis, G. P., Κ. Γ. Καρυωτάκης. Ποιήματα καὶ Πεζά, Athens, 1972 (Ἑρμῆς, Νέα Ἑλλ. Βιβλιοθήκη, 21)

MARIA POLYDOURI

Μαρίας Πολυδούρη Ἅπαντα, ed. L. Zographou, Athens, n.d.

Religious trends in the poetry of the 1920s

TAKIS PAPATZONIS

Papatzonis, T., Ἐκλογή Α΄–Β΄, Athens, 1962

CONSTANTINE CAVAFY

Bowra, C. M., *The Creative Experiment*, London, 1949

Dallas, G., *Καβάφης καὶ ἱστορία. Αἰσθητικὲς λειτουργίες*, Athens, 1974

Dalver, R., *The Complete Poems of Cavafy*, New York–London, 1961

Delopoulos, G. K., *Καβάφη ἱστορικὰ καὶ ἄλλα πρόσωπα*, Athens, 1978

Forster, M., *Pharos and Pharillon*, London, 1926, pp. 91–7

Karandonis, A., *Φυσιογνωμίες*, Athens, 1960, vol. 2, pp. 30f.

Keeley, E., 'The New Poems of Cavafy', in E. Keeley and P. Bien (eds.), *Modern Greek Writers*, Princeton, 1972, pp. 124f.

Keeley, E., *Cavafy's Alexandria. Study of a Myth in Progress*, London, 1977

Keeley, E. and Sherrard, P., *C. P. Cavafy, Collected Poems*, London, 1975

Kokolis, X. A., *Πίνακας λέξεων τῶν 154 ποιημάτων τοῦ Κ. Π., Καβάφη*, Athens, 1976

Liddell, R., *Cavafis. A Critical Biography*, London, 1974

Malanos, T., *Ὁ ποιητὴς Κ. Π., Καβάφης. Ὁ ἄνθρωπος καὶ τὸ ἔργο του*, 2nd edn., Athens, 1957

Malanos, T., *Καβάφης 2. Φύλλα τετραδίου καὶ ἄλλα*, Athens, 1963

Panagiotopoulos, I. M., *Τά πρόσωπα καὶ τὰ κείμενα*, Athens, 1946, vol. 4

Papanoutsos, E. P., *Παλαμᾶς, Καβάφης, Σικελιανός*, Athens, 1955

Peri, M., *Quattro saggi su Kavafis*, Milan, 1977

Perides, M., *Ὁ Βίος καὶ τὸ ἔργο τοῦ Κ. Καβάφη*, Athens, 1948

Sarejannis, G. A., *Σχόλια στὸν Καβάφη* (preface by G. Seferis, introduction by Z. Lorentzatos), Athens, 1964

Savvidis, G. P., *Οἱ καβαφικὲς ἐκδόσεις (1891–1932). Περιγραφὴ καὶ σχόλιο. Βιβλιογραφικὴ μελέτη*, Athens, 1966

Seferis, G., *Κ. Π. Καβάφης, Θ. Σ. Ἔλιοτ, Παράλληλοι. Ἀκόμα λίγα γιὰ τὸν Ἀλεξανδρινό, Δοκιμές*, 3rd edn., Athens, 1974, vol. 1, pp. 324f.

Themelis, G., *Ἡ ποίηση τοῦ Καβάφη. Διαστάσεις καὶ ὅρια*, Salonica, 1970

Tsirkas, S., *Ὁ Καβάφης καὶ ἡ ἐποχή του*, 2nd edn., Athens, 1971

Tsirkas, S., *Ο πολιτικὸς Καβάφης*, Athens, 1971

University of Padua, Lessico di Kavafis, a cura di Gina Lorando, Lucia Marcheselli, Anna Gentilini, *Studi Byzantini e neogreci*, vol. 2, Padua, 1970

THE POETS OF THE 1930s

Georgos Seferis

Editions by Ikaros: 3rd edn., Athens, 1962; 4th edn., Athens, 1964; *Τρία Κρυφὰ Ποιήματα*, Athens, 1966

Demakis, M., *Ἡ Ποίηση τοῦ Σεφέρη*, Athens, 1974

Durrell, L., *Six poems from the Greek of Sikelianos and Seferis*, Rhodes, 1946

Kaiser, W., *Three Secret Poems*, Cambridge, Mass., 1969

Kapsomenos, E., *Ἡ συντακτικὴ δομὴ τῆς ποιητικῆς γλώσσας τοῦ Σεφέρη*, Salonica, 1975

Karandonis, A., *Ὁ Ποιητὴς Γ. Σεφέρης*, 2nd edn., Athens, 1957

Keeley, E. and Sherrard, P., *George Seferis, Collected Poems 1924–55*, Princeton, 1967

Kokolis, X. A., *Πίνακας λέξεων τῶν ποιημάτων Γ. Σεφέρη*, 2nd edn., Athens, 1975

Levesque, R., *Séféris, choix de poèmes*, Athens, 1945

Levi, P., 'Seferis' Tone of Voice', in *Modern Greek Writers*, Princeton, 1972, pp. 174f.

Mirambel, A., *George Séféris, Prix Nobel*, Paris, 1964

Pontani, F. M. (ed.), *Ommagio a Seferis*, Padua, 1970

Savvidis, G. P. (ed.), *Γιὰ τὸν Σεφέρη, τιμητικὸ ἀφιέρωμα στὰ τριάντα χρόνια τῆς Στροφῆς*, Athens, 1961

Spencer, B., Valaoritis, N., and Durrell, L., *The King of Asine and Other Poems*, translated from the Greek, London, 1948

Tsatsou, J., *Ὁ ἀδερφός μου Γιῶργος Σεφέρης*, Athens, 1973

Warner, Rex., *Poems*, translated from the Greek, London, 1960

Warner, R. and Frangopoulos, T. D., *On the Greek Style, Select Essays in Poetry and Hellenism*, London, 1967

The post-Seferis generation

Georgios Sarantaris

Karandonis, A., *Φυσιογνωμίες*, Athens, 1960, vol. 2, pp. 197f.

CORRIGENDA

p. 205, line 26 for Phormus read Phormis
p. 208, line 31 for Telecledes read Teleclides
p. 234, line 20 for Cithera read Cythera
p. 278, line 2 for Panyasis read Panyassis
p. 339, line 37 for Phaenos read Phaennos
p. 356, lines 36 and 40 for Maecius read Maccius
p. 357, line 2 after Mundus add Munatius
p. 445, line 5 for Endokimos read Eudokimos
p. 703, line 10 for 1875 read 1873
p. 704, line 29 for *mino* read *mimo*
p. 705, note 8 for Chartraine read Chantraine
p. 706, note 28 for spragis read sphragis; note 30 for Schwabel read Schwabl
pp. 707, note 56 and 744, note 20 for Severyns read Sévéryns
p. 708, note 9 for R. B. Kamerbeek read J. C. Kamerbeek
p. 710, note 50 line 6 for μόοχος read μόλδαχος; line 7 for λάχη read λάβη; line 8 for τὼ . . . μόχδῳ read τῶν . . . μόχδων; note 64 line 6 for σελάναν read σελάνναν; line 7 for ἄψ read ᾆψ. The final syllable of the first three lines can be either long (–) or short (‿)
pp. 716, note 119 and 751, note 43 for *Reiner* read *Rainer*
p. 719, note 26 for Phorius read Phormis; note 33 for Hesichius read Hesychius
p. 720, note 81 for *griechischer* read *der griechischen*
p. 722, note 3 for *Die* read *Der*, and for 1958 read 1938
p. 724, note 21 for *Lanschaft* read *Landschaft*
pp. 733, note 28 and 745, note 46 for Bronner (Bruneer) read Broneer
p. 734, note 11 for *griechische* read *griechischen*
pp. 736, notes 23 and 24 for Mühl read Mühll
p. 741, note 17 for Schwarz read Schwartz; note 20 for *Geographi* read *Geographici* and for 1885–61 read 1855–61; note 28 for A. Ehlers read W. Ehlers
p. 742, note 50 for *Trahaeo* read *Tarrhaeo*; note 65 for *griechische Tragödien* read *griechischen Tragoedien*
p. 743, note 72 for *griechische* read *griechischen*; note 14 for Corippius read Corippus
pp. 744, note 23 and 747, note 12 for H. Cronert read W. Crönert; note 24 for O. Crusius read G. Knaack, and for p. 294 read p. 924
p. 745, note 41 for *griechische Tragödien* read *griechischen Tragoedien*; note 62 for Holbein read Hobein
p. 746, note 74 for Setli read Setti and for vol. 26 read vol. 13; note 84 and p. 760, note 6 for Preis(e)danz read Preisendanz; note 2 for *der* read *das*
p. 747, note 21 for Paina read Piana
p. 749, note 78 for D. Wienreich read O. Weinreich; note 82 for Bergh read Bergk
p. 751, note 41 for Schattemann read Schattenmann; note 43 for *Papyrius* read *Papyrus* and for Bickell read Bickel
p. 752, note 112 for *BZ* pp. 534f. read *BZ* pp. 173f.
p. 754, note 37 for St Winkly read St Winkley
pp. 754, 755, 759 and 773 (var.) for G. Schiro read J. Schiró
p. 757, note 13 for Erhard read Ehrhard and for *homeletischen* read *homiletischen*
p. 758, note 61 for Anastios read Anastasios; note 64 for H. F. Tillyard read H. J. W. Tillyard
p. 759, note 73 for Styriotes read Steiriotes
p. 761, note 55 for *Callicles* read *Calliclis*
p. 762, note 90 for *Griechische* read *Griechischer*
p. 763, note 122 for Marzal read Mazal
p. 764, note 127 for Waltz read Walz
pp. 766, note 188 and 767 note 196 for Goosens read Goossens
p. 767, note 205 for Ἐπετεϱὶς read Ἐπετηϱὶς
p. 768, note 227 for *Receuil de chansons populaires grecques* read *Collection de monuments*
p. 770, note 19 for *Byzantinistischen* read *Byzantinischen*; note 31 for *Aevii* read *Aevi*
p. 771, note 44 for *Scharfsinnsproblem* read *Scharfsinnsprobe*; note 50 for *Byzantinische-neugriechische* read *Byzantinisch-neugriechischen*
p. 772, note 15 for *Jahrbücher Österreichische byzantinische* read *Jahrbuch der Österreichischen byzantinischen*
p. 774, note 9 for *Le* read *La*; note 18 for Alexious read Alexiou
p. 776, note 1 for Mousouros read Moussouros

Index of Poets

Note 1: Up to the eleventh century Latin endings to names have been preferred, thus Theodorus. After that date modern Greek endings are used—Theodoros. Exceptions occur occasionally in the transitional period and where demanded by common English usage.

Note 2: During the Byzantine era some poets wrote in Classical metres, usually as later adapters, others in medieval rhythmic metres, and some in both styles. Poets indexed between pp. 381 and 524 may have used either style, or both.